The way to victory is long

The going will be hard

We will do the best we can

    with what we've got

We must have more planes and

    ships—at once

Then it will be our turn

    to strike

We will win through—

    in time

—ADMIRAL ERNEST J. KING
Chief of Naval Operations
December, 1941

THE UNITED STATES NAVY
IN WORLD WAR II

THE ONE-VOLUME HISTORY, FROM PEARL HARBOR
TO TOKYO BAY—BY MEN WHO FOUGHT IN THE
ATLANTIC AND THE PACIFIC AND BY DISTINGUISHED
NAVAL EXPERTS, AUTHORS AND NEWSPAPERMEN.

THE UNITED STATES NAVY IN WORLD WAR II

THE ONE-VOLUME HISTORY, FROM PEARL HARBOR TO TOKYO BAY—BY MEN WHO FOUGHT IN THE ATLANTIC AND THE PACIFIC AND BY DISTINGUISHED NAVAL EXPERTS, AUTHORS AND NEWSPAPERMEN

Compiled and edited by S.E. Smith

With an Introduction by Rear Admiral
E. M. Eller, Director of Naval History

William Morrow & Company, Inc. New York 1966

Published simultaneously in Canada by George J. McLeod Limited, Toronto.

Printed in the United States of America by The Haddon Craftsmen, Scranton, Pa.
Design by Paula Wiener
Library of Congress Catalog Card Number 66-22113
..

Grateful acknowledgment is made for permission to reprint the following:

"Pearl Harbor Attack," from BUT NOT IN SHAME, by John Toland. © Copyright 1961 by John Toland. Reprinted by permission of Random House, Inc. ". . . And Pass the Ammunition," and "Taking Aboard *Lexington*'s Survivors," from AND PASS THE AMMUNITION, by Howell M. Forgy. Copyright, 1944, by Howell M. Forgy. Reprinted by permission of Appleton-Century. "I Can't Keep Throwing Things At Them," from DAY OF INFAMY by Walter Lord. Copyright © 1957 by Walter Lord. Reprinted by permission of Holt, Rinehart and Winston, Inc. "Wake Island Surrenders," from WAKE ISLAND COMMAND, by W. Scott Cunningham with Lydel Sims. Copyright © 1961 by Lydel Sims and W. Scott Cunningham. Reprinted by permission of Little, Brown & Company. "The Philippine Expendables," from THEY WERE EXPENDABLE, by W.L. White. Copyright, 1942, by W.L. White. Reprinted by permission of Harcourt, Brace & World, Inc. "Scratch One," from *The Blue Beetle,* by L.A. Abercrombie and Fletcher Pratt, reprinted from *Proceedings* by permission. Copyright 1944 by U.S. Naval Institute. "First Blood: A War Correspondent Tells of The Marshalls Raid," from TORPEDO JUNCTION by Robert J. Casey, copyright 1942, 1943, by The Bobbs-Merrill Company, Inc., reprinted by permission of the publishers. "Macassar Merry-Go-Round," by William P. Mack, reprinted from *Proceedings* by permission. Copyright 1943 by U.S. Naval Institute. "The 'Galloping Ghost'," by Walter G. Winslow, reprinted from *Proceedings* by permission. Copyright 1949 by U.S. Naval Institute. "Retreat" and "Return," from REMINISCENCES by Douglas MacArthur. © 1964 Time, Inc. Used by permission of McGraw-Hill Book Company. "All Gone, Now," from AMERICAN GUERILLA IN THE PHILIPPINES by Ira Wolfert. Copyright 1945 by Ira Wolfert. Reprinted by permission of Simon and Schuster, Inc. "Attack," from NORTH ATLANTIC PATROL, *The Log of a Seagoing Artist,* by Griffith Baily Coale. Copyright, 1942, by Griffith Baily Coale. Published by Farrar & Rinehart, Inc., 1943. Reprinted by permission of Mrs. Elizabeth M. Coale. "Atlantic Slaughter," from SEA WAR

J. Bryan III, published by Whittlesey House, McGraw-Hill Book Company, Inc. Copyright, 1947, by William F. Halsey. Copyright, 1947, by The Curtis Publishing Company. Reprinted by permission of Brandt & Brandt. "They Had Us on the Ropes," from *The Japs Had Us on the Ropes,* by Vice Adm. C.A.F. Sprague and Lt. Philip H. Gustafson, first published in *American Magazine,* April, 1945. Copyright 1945 by Crowell-Collier Pub. Co. Reprinted by permission of Mrs. C.A.F. Sprague. "Small Boys—Intercept!" from *The Battle as I Saw It,* by Cdr. Amos T. Hathaway, first published in *American Magazine,* April, 1945. Copyright 1945 by Crowell-Collier Pub. Co. Reprinted by permission of Captain Amos T. Hathaway. "Down Periscope," from SUBMARINE!, by Commander Edward L. Beach, USN. Copyright 1952 by Edward L. Beach. Reprinted by permission of Holt, Rinehart and Winston, Inc. "First Strike on Tokyo," from AIRCRAFT CARRIER, by J. Bryan, III, published by Ballantine Books, Inc. Copyright, 1954, by J. Bryan, III. Reprinted by permission of Brandt & Brandt. "Iwo Jima Before H-Hour," from THIRTY YEARS by John P. Marquand. Copyright 1945 by John P. Marquand. Reprinted by permission of Little, Brown and Company. "Okinawa—Triple Exposure," from Higgins, Edward T., WEB-FOOTED WARRIORS, Copyright, 1955, by Edward T. Higgins, Exposition Press, N.Y., 1955. "The End of the Japanese Fleet," from THE MAGNIFICENT MITSCHER, by Theodore Taylor. Copyright, 1954, by Theodore Taylor. Published by W.W. Norton & Co., Inc. Reprinted by permission of A. Watkins, Inc. "Second Dog Watch," from BRAVE SHIP, BRAVE MEN, Copyright © 1964 by Arnold S. Lott, reprinted by permission of the publishers, The Bobbs-Merrill Company, Inc. "Surrender Diary," from THE FORRESTAL DIARIES, by Secretary of the Navy James Forrestal, Edited by Walter Millis with the collaboration of E.S. Duffield. Copyright, 1951, by the New York Herald Tribune, Inc. Reprinted by permission of Princeton University.

The Official U.S. Navy Emblem is reproduced on the boards of this volume by permission of Director, Navy Publications and Printing Service.

CONTENTS

PART II   THE WAR IN THE ATLANTIC

PART III   DOOLITTLE'S RAID TO THE
BATTLE OF MIDWAY

PART IV   GUADALCANAL AND THE
NORTHWARD DRIVE: THE OFFENSIVE BEGINS

PART V   THE MEDITERRANEAN AND FRANCE,
VICTORY IN EUROPE

PART VI   ALEUTIANS TO THE MARIANAS

PART VII LEYTE GULF TO OKINAWA: END OF AN EMPIRE

xiv   Contents

LIST OF MAPS

LIST OF PHOTOGRAPHS

EDITOR'S NOTE

MORE than twenty years have passed since the conclusion of World War II, and in that time a new generation has grown to manhood—a generation which, there is ample evidence to believe, has little knowledge of those epic events which culminated in the Japanese surrender aboard U.S.S. *Missouri*. One feels concern—and did three years ago when this book was first conceived—that this should be so. Then, as now, it seemed wholly incongruous that a war which produced not only awesome Allied battle casualties but the incineration of six million persons by the Third Reich, should be so little known by men of, or nearing, the age of combat in Vietnam. This history has been assembled, therefore, with the hope that it will serve to enlighten them about one vital aspect of that war—the role of the U.S. Navy during America's four long years of participation.

My guidelines were long and firmly established by the distinguished historian, Rear Admiral Samuel E. Morison, whose multi-volumed *History of the United States Naval Operations in World War II* was written shortly thereafter; by Captain Walter Karig's *Battle Report;* and by the U.S. Naval Institute's volumes, *Destroyer* and *Submarine*.

The substance of the history is largely personal narrative with running commentary and connective. Should the reader detect any flaws—if indeed flaws they are—they are the imperfections of men whose personal involvement took precedence over mere battle technicalities. Although an old Navy hand might take me to task for omitting nostalgic touches, I believe that what happened in the wardroom and living spaces should be relegated to one's memories rather than included in a serious work.

I owe a profound debt of gratitude to several persons for their selfless efforts on my behalf. First, to my good friend Rear Admiral Ernest M. Eller, Director of Naval History, for his enthusiastic cooperation and assistance in rounding up otherwise unobtainable permissions and for spending long weekends studying the material as it was being integrated into a manuscript; without his assistance it would not have been possible to accomplish my mission. My gratitude is also due Mr. Dean Allard of the Naval History Division for liberal use of the Navy Archives; Lieutenant W. F. Rope, USN, who chose the photographs; Lieutenant Commander D. K. Dagle, USN, who served not only as coordinator with the Navy Department and Department of Defense, but in addition found time to serve as cartographer of the volume; and Mr. Walter Greenwood and Mr. Fred Meigs of the Navy Department Library, Washington, D.C. for their always available consultation services; and to Mr. L. Harry Brague, Mr. Robert D. Loomis, Mr. Alfred Rice and Mr. Noah Sarlat for their unstinting efforts in the roundup of permissions; and to Mr. J. C. Willey, Editor-in-Chief of Wm. Morrow & Company for his *esprit* and stout heart in helping make a difficult undertaking a reality.

Finally, my deepest thanks to my own Marianne, for her warmth and equanimity during the long voyage.

S. E. Smith
New York, N.Y.

INTRODUCTION

THIS outstanding and dramatic anthology glows with the spirit of man in search of ideals on the great waters. World War II, which changed history forever, was the largest war that man has brought upon himself. Since the sea inevitably decides world wars, World War II was also the largest naval war, as this stirring anthology serves to point up.

Life originally came to the land from the sea. In the aeons since, man, in his long struggle to be free, has repeatedly sought salvation from the sea. Indeed, freedom seems inseparably united with the sea, and tyranny with giant, land-bound nations. Witness in antiquity Greece against powerful empires from Asia; England against Napoleon in the last century; the United States and its allies fringing the sea against Soviet and Red Chinese empires in Eurasia. No period marks the history of man's struggle for freedom more dramatically than the great war that burst like Apocalypse upon the Navy and America at Pearl Harbor. Coming to a close, appropriately, on the main deck of U.S.S. *Missouri,* this war began and ended with a fleet. It seems most fitting, therefore, that this well-selected anthology should be devoted to those giant events which took place at sea—for had they failed, freedom would have failed.

Reading a host of works on the war, the skilled and prolific writer S. E. Smith has wisely selected, for the most part, first-person accounts. They have the large virtues of authentic experience and instinctive reactions based on knowledge from years at sea that inevitably forge a man's character.

Stan Smith himself had a concentrated portion of such experience, serving in both oceans as a bluejacket. On December 7, 1941, he left college in his junior year to enlist. He became a part of the sea, first as a seaman in a patrol craft in the rough North Atlantic, then in the battleship *Arkansas,* where he went up through the important radioman rates. After the North African invasion, Smith transferred to submarines and, in the newly built *Lionfish,* participated in war patrols under Lieutenant Commander Edward D. Spruance, son of the famous admiral who led the Fifth Fleet to its great victories.

Thus, having served afloat most of the war, Stan Smith has an advantage over most writers who might seek to edit such an anthology. He knows "the real thing" from experience. Hence, these gripping extracts bring the war back with a rush of memories that are filled with the beauty of the sea, mixed with its ruthlessness for him who errs, memories of the brutality and cruelty of war, yet of the nobility of man. War seems to call forth both the best and the worst in the human spirit.

In reading these extracts, I was struck by the limited perspective, usually even of those who had written years after the event. This is human. It is the way men reacted and thought at the time. It is the way man has always lived and reacted; for only the duty at hand is real. As on the sundial, all we have of life is "the hour on which the shadow stands." If we live the hour well, we have best served. We have ensured yesterdays of no regrets, tomorrows of hope.

Hence, few understood the vast scope of the war. Few evaluated how individual events fell into the pattern of the whole. Appropriately and necessarily, most saw the tumultuous events, that broke about them like the fury of a storm-torn sea, in the light of only the immediate need and duty.

Moreover, few had any appreciation of the significance to future generations of this world struggle. They did not consciously perceive that this cataclysm was part of the ancient war of man's soul against tyranny—the yearning to be free that must surely come from the Divine. If enough men afloat and ashore had perceived this truth as well as they fought, we would not have made some of the mistakes that caused us, having won the war, to almost lose the peace.

Those who fought so gallantly also did not usually understand the revolutions in inventions and technology that have brought immense new power to national strength afloat. For the past century, these have steadily increased the ability of the sea to strike against the land. Steam first freed ships from dependence on wind and tide. Now, nuclear energy has solved the problems of frequent fueling. Armor has given ships a resistance equal to forts. Improved engines have given ships increased speed and made them harder to hit. At the same time, stereo range-finders, then radar, combined with electricity operating at the speed of light, and the remarkable "mechanical brains" of fire control computers, have given warships' guns precise accuracy—even when those ships are maneuvering at high speed on the unsteady sea.

The submarine and aircraft, in taking navies into the depths of the ocean and into the heavens, have shaped the true trident of Neptune. First heralded as the end of surface navies, by wise integration they have instead brought the United States Navy incredible new power. Incorporating aircraft as part of total fleet strength, the Navy developed the aircraft carrier, with its embarked dive bombers, torpedo planes, and fighters, into one of the most powerful champions of freedom all history records—powerful in World War II, even more powerful today with supersonic planes and guided missiles. The submarine has also steadily increased in deadliness, and since World War II, with nuclear propulsion and polaris missiles, has brought phenomenal new capabilities to the fleet.

At the same time, the United States Navy has made large strides to counter similar new weapons of an enemy. Consider the airplane: In the years between the world wars, and with increasing acceleration after Pearl Harbor, the Navy developed a defense against the airplane that became almost invulnerable. This included the carrier fighter and attack planes, radar, fighter direction, voice raido, anti-aircraft guns, influence fuze, automatic directors that "lock on" the target and solve the fire control problem instantly.

In the quarter of a century following World War I, the crude, anti-aircraft methods progressed to one of the most complex and efficient systems man has ever evolved. Radar measured the range to an attacking plane accurately and with the speed of light, even when far out of sight. The fire-control computers, parents of today's electronic brains, solved the problem of hitting the swift, invisible target miles away in the sky, and solved it without delay. The influence fuze ensured destruction. With these aids, by the middle of the Pacific war, hard-hitting, rapid-firing guns of every caliber made United States' warships so safe from air attack that the Japanese had to switch to those kamikaze tactics so graphically covered in this volume, in which plane and pilot ended up 100 per cent casualties— no way to win a war.

Since then, advances have accelerated both in the plane and in the missile, homing at supersonic speeds unerringly on its target, to protect against it. The surface Navy has not been destroyed by aviation. Because the United States Navy wisely integrated it into all aspects of offense and defense, the airplane brought the fleet immense new potential.

This same increase in effectiveness of strength based at sea applies to almost every other new development of this century, in which changes seem to accelerate change and to multiply the advantages of sea-based strength. Atomic energy, and the submarine in particular, point up this giant shift in balance of power in favor of national strength afloat. Unlike fixed land defenses, swiftly moving ships at sea are unprofitable targets for atomic explosives, and particularly unprofitable for ballistic missiles that must navigate to a precise, motionless point.

Sea power has decided all world wars since our birth as a nation —and most before. A nation's or a coalition's total power (military strength, industry, transportation, agriculture, will of the people, leadership) wins wars; but in a world war this total power can be projected only by the sea, and strength based in ships has made up an increasing part of the total power. Therefore, infinite new power at sea relative to that based ashore opens infinite possibilities. Although this change had been steadily occurring throughout our lifetimes, as the accounts in this anthology show, most men who fought had no comprehension of its scope or meaning. Their only thought was to do the best they could with what they had—while continually seeking more and better means.

Moreover, as this anthology shows, and as we who were there remember, many did not realize that in World War II the door opened wide to the United States as the world leader of man's dream of freedom. After World War I, we had shared this responsibility with others, and the country as a whole did not comprehend the meaning and needs of this responsibility. At the end of World War II, the mantle of leadership passed fully to the United States. Unhappily, too few Americans knew this, or understood, if they did know, the duties such a position implied. Fewer still comprehended that to assume leadership of the world we required a fleet that could reach all shores as the binding force of free nations, joined or divided by the sea according to their strength on it.

Hopefully, this anthology will help create this awareness. For if enough of us are not well aware of our duties and needs, we shall surely fail in our great mission to guide freedom on course through the typhoons of our time.

Stan Smith has therefore performed a true service in presenting these dramatic accounts, that together tell the story of the great war as men saw it afloat. Though few then understood the meaning and significance of the war, the accounts together show that men instinctively fought nobly and well for the goal of freedom, toward which the United States is privileged to lead the world. If leaders today are inspired to serve as selflessly, as wisely, as courageously, we will not fail in our mission.

E. M. ELLER, REAR ADMIRAL, U.S. NAVY (Ret.)
Director of Naval History

LAST DAYS OF PEACE

WITH THE EARLY MANIFESTATIONS OF THE JAPANESE philosophy, *Hakko Ichiu*—"bringing the eight corners of the world under one roof"—we are not concerned. It is sufficient to note that by September 1940, when Japan became a signatory to the Tripartite Treaty and Hitler began to push his Oriental partner into a war with the United States, Japan had already established herself as a first rate military power. For by having thrown off the yoke of the 5-5-3 naval limitations ratio, she had proceeded to build up her combatant strength, while correspondingly increasing pressure on the future Allies for gains in the Pacific. Yet had our future enemy, by her own peculiar standards, been able to avert a major confrontation, there is every likelihood she would have done so. "If I am told to fight regardless of consequence," Fleet Admiral Yamamoto is reported to have told Prince Kanoye, "I shall run wild considerably for the first six months or a year, but I have utterly no confidence for the second and third years. The Tripartite Treaty has been concluded and we cannot help it. Now that the situation has come to this pass I hope you will endeavor for avoidance of an American-Japanese war."

As of the fall of 1941, there were six essential Japanese demands and concessions under discussion in Washington: (1) no further United States assistance to Chiang Kai Shek, and to permit Japan to settle her own affairs with China; (2) no arms build-up of the United

1

States and Britain in the Far East; (3) no interference with Japanese-French relations as to Indochina; (4) American assistance in obtaining raw materials by the restoration of free trade between the two countries; (5) no utilization of Indonesia as a base of operations against any country except China; and (6) Japan to guarantee the neutrality of the Philippines.

At this time, the United States Pacific Fleet was berthed at Pearl Harbor, and Admiral Husband Kimmel was appointed Commander-in-Chief to succeed Admiral J.O. Richardson, the latter having objected strenuously to Pearl Harbor as a base for logistical reasons. Politically, however, it was felt that the presence of the fleet at Hawaii constituted a "restraining influence on Japan," and there, despite a questionable condition of readiness, it remained. Earlier in the year the "ABC-1 Staff Agreement" was concluded with Britain, an agreement which pledged the United States to defeat Hitler first regardless of whether Japan attacked the United States. In the event of a Pacific war, we would launch a series of tactical offensives, and nothing more. This, too, was the conclusion of the ABD (America, Britain, Dutch) conference, which incidentally placed Admiral Thomas Hart's Asiatic Fleet under British strategic direction upon any outbreak of hostilities in the Pacific.

By January 1941, the situation between Washington and Tokyo had worsened considerably, in spite of the appointment of Admiral Kichisaburo Nomura as Ambassador—a man known to be opposed to an open break with the United States. Nevertheless, as talks continued between the future antagonists, Japan began her build-up of military strength in the Marshalls and Carolines. This also was the month when Ambassador Joseph Grew made a significant entry in his diary: "There is a lot of talk going around town to the effect that the Japanese, in case of a break with the United States, are planning to go all out in a surprise mass attack at Pearl Harbor. Of course I informed our government."

In Grew's memoirs, one sees Japan mediating in an undeclared war between Thailand and French Indochina, and gaining for herself not only a monopoly of Indochina rice but also the airport at Saigon, within striking distance of Singapore. Reaction in the Gallup poll to this latest Japanese coup indicated a bare majority of American voters sanctioned a war with our future antagonist, in order to prevent her from seizing Singapore and the Netherlands East Indies. By chance Congress passed the Lend Lease law the next day.

From this time, the pace of Japan's diplomatic machinations

quickened perceptibly. On February 13, she concluded a nonagression pact with Russia, the latter signing because a German attack was expected, the former because she wanted to solidify her position on the Manchurian border. Two months later, Japanese merchant ships were ordered out of the Atlantic and between one and two million conscripts were called up. Grew was then informed that Vichy had agreed to a joint protectorate over French Indochina, meaning free Japanese rule over the entire colony and a direct threat to the security of the Philippines. President Roosevelt's response was immediate and forceful: Japanese assets in the United States were promptly frozen, including oil. War was inevitable unless the United States reversed her policy, or Japan halted her southward march and evacuated China.

As seen from the vantage point of the White House, Army and Navy Intelligence, and the State Department, the events following July 26 made manifest Japan's aggressive intentions. Because we were in possession of our future enemy's codes for the past several months, we were able to intercept and decipher her consular messages. But what her precise actions were to be we did not know. Hawaii, at any rate, was alerted prior to the Embargo Act. Admiral C. C. Bloch recalled: "Admiral Kimmel had a conference on the subject and I suggested to him the advisability of sending out reconnaissance planes with the median line of the sector pointing to Jaluit. I think the sector was 15 to 20 degrees. And we sent planes out every morning to 500 miles." The die was cast, and both sides during the remaining four months of peace stalled for time.

Despite the earnest efforts of some Japanese officials to prevent a war, Foreign Minister Toyoda spelled out his country's intentions in an intercepted message to his Washington representative. The message was received by Cordell Hull on August 4, and stated that Japan "must take measures to secure the raw materials of the South Sea. Our Empire must immediately take steps to break asunder this ever-strengthening chain of encirclement by England and the United States." By now the Mid-Atlantic Conference between President Roosevelt and Prime Minister Churchill was over, having resolved that "any further encroachment by Japan in the southwestern Pacific would produce a situation" in which the Allies "would be compelled to take countermeasures even though these might lead to war . . ."

Correspondingly, Japan had set herself a deadline to go "against America, England, and Holland" during the first part of October, unless oil inventories were unfrozen. She could not by any estimate afford to wait. In October, because of dissension at her top echelons, Toyoda resigned and General Tojo formed his cabinet. Several weeks later, Japan's Army and Navy concluded a "Central Agreement" in the event of war, which provided this blueprint of initial attack: (1) simultaneous landings of amphibious forces in Luzon, Guam, the Malay Peninsula, Hong Kong, and Miri, British North Borneo. All except the last to be preceded by air attacks; (2) carrier air attack on the United States Pacific Fleet at Pearl Harbor; (3) rapid exploitation of initial successes by the seizure of Manila, Mindanao, Wake Island, the Bismarcks, Bangkok and Singapore; and (4) occupation of the Dutch East Indies and continuation of the war with China.

Renewed "negotiations" (Hull termed the initial meeting an ultimatum) were stalemated, and on November 24 Admiral Harold Stark, Chief of Naval Operations, sent this message to Admiral Kimmel at Pearl Harbor and Admiral Hart at Manila:

"Chances of favorable outcome of negotiations with Japan very doubtful. This situation coupled with statements of Japanese Government and movements of their naval and military forces indicate in our opinion that a surprise aggressive movement in any direction including attack on Philippines or Guam is a possibility . . . Utmost secrecy necessary in order not to complicate an already tense situation or precipitate Japanese action."

Other negotiations followed, with the United States Fleet committed to surveillance in two oceans, simultaneously realizing that Tojo intended to strike somewhere in the Pacific. The "where" of it was the big question. On November 27, the situation was at its gravest when Stark sent Hart and Kimmel his "war warning" message.

This dispatch is to be considered a war warning. Negotiations with Japan looking toward stabilization of conditions in the Pacific have ceased. An aggressive move by Japan is expected within the next few days. The number and equipment of Japanese troops and the organization of naval task forces indicates an amphibious expedition against either the Philippines, Thai, or Kra Peninsula, or possibly Borneo. Execute appropriate defensive deployment preparatory to carrying out the tasks assigned to WPL 46.

Meanwhile, the two-phase Imperial Japanese Navy's attack operation had already been set in motion. The first phase was opened

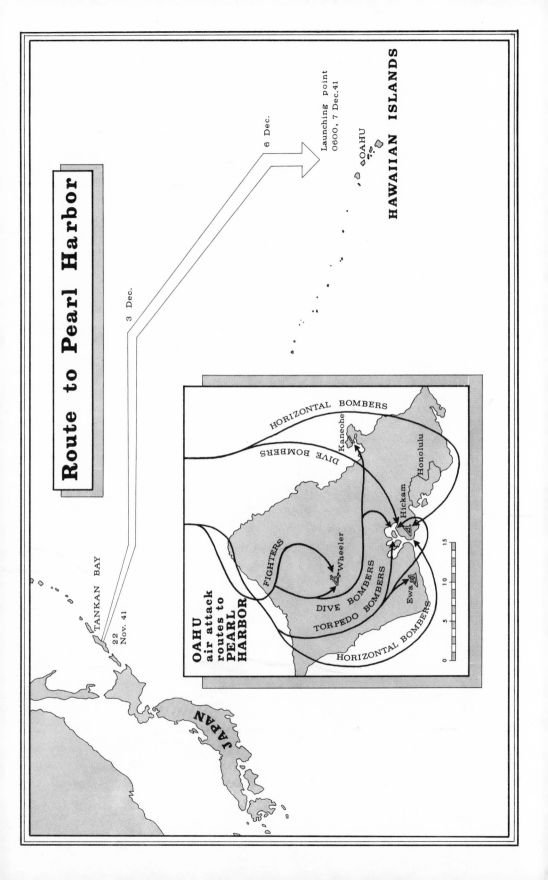

Route to Pearl Harbor

HAWAIIAN ISLANDS

OAHU

Launching point
0600, 7 Dec. 41

6 Dec.

3 Dec.

TANKAN BAY
22 Nov. 41

JAPAN

OAHU
air attack
routes to
PEARL HARBOR

HORIZONTAL BOMBERS

DIVE BOMBERS

Kaneohe

Honolulu

Hickam

FIGHTERS

Wheeler

DIVE BOMBERS

TORPEDO BOMBERS

Ewa

HORIZONTAL BOMBERS

0   5   10   15

PART I

PEARL HARBOR TO THE END IN THE MALAY BARRIER

WITH APPROXIMATELY HALF OF THE UNITED STATES Fleet based in the Atlantic against the possibility of a submarine war with Hitler, Japan's combatant strengh as of mid-1941 was greater than that of the nations she was to make her adversaries. Against one hundred and twenty-seven warships of the United States Pacific Fleet (less the few ships, primarily destroyers and submarines, of the widely dispersed Asiatic Fleet) and fifty belonging to our allies, the British Commonwealth and the Netherlands, Japan was able to muster two hundred and thirty combatant ships of every category. In addition to numerical superiority, Japan possessed two other priceless ingredients for starting a war—tactical position and surprise attack. Thus, by noon of "the day that will live in infamy," the Imperial Japanese Navy held a

9

mastery over the greatest of oceans that would last for the next six months.

There were two United States Navy task forces at sea December 7, 1941. One task force, commanded by Rear Admiral John Henry Newton in the heavy cruiser *Chicago,* was formed around the aircraft carrier *Lexington* and was Midway bound on a search and battle problem; the other, under the redoubtable Vice Admiral William F. Halsey in *Enterprise,* was secretly steaming toward Wake Island to deliver a cargo of Marine fighter-plane reinforcements. At sea, too, were seven heavy and light cruisers patrolling to the south and south-westward, while the main body of the United States Pacific Fleet, less carriers—eighty-four warships—was based at Pearl Harbor.

The first shot of the war was fired at 6:45 A.M., more than an hour and a quarter after the old, four-stack destroyer *Ward* had sighted the periscope of a midget submarine operating in a restricted area just outside Pearl Harbor. *Ward* was under the command of Lieutenant William W. Outerbridge, and she was returning from a night's patrol when contact was made. By the time Outerbridge had called the warship to General Quarters and had gotten up speed, the strange craft had disapppeared. *Ward* remained in the area, searching with her sound gear. Seventy-five minutes later surface contact was regained and Outerbridge passed the word to his No. 1 gun, after radioing Pearl Harbor that he intended to attack. (He quite naturally had qualms about firing on an unidentified vessel although under orders to do so since the submarine was in a restricted area.) The first round drove the submarine down. Simultaneously, *Ward* dropped a string of depth charges over the spot where lookouts had last seen the periscope. Thereafter, Outerbridge informed Pearl Harbor by radio that he had completed his attack.

It was now almost 7 A.M. Japan's first strike, launched by aircraft carriers *Akagi, Hiryu, Kaga, Soryu, Shokaku* and *Zuikaku* in the predawn darkness, was nearing the coast of Oahu.

The story of the epochal attack is here told in three parts, the first by the brilliant journalist, John Toland, whose *But Not In Shame,* a documented assessment of the first six months of the war in the Pacific, stands as a classic of dramatic reportage.

I.

PEARL HARBOR ATTACK

Banks of cumulus clouds collected around the peaks of the mountain ranges east and west of Pearl Harbor on Sunday morning. But over the great naval base, lying in the valley between, were only a few scattered clouds. Visibility was good and a wind of 10 knots blew in from the north.

At 7:45 A.M. several civilian pilots were lazily circling over the area. There wasn't a single military ship visible. Eighteen planes approaching from the carrier *Enterprise* were scheduled to land at Ford Island within the hour.

The only Army Air Corps planes aloft in the vicinity were the 12 Flying Fortresses from California earmarked for MacArthur. They were due to land at Hickham Field, several miles south of Ford Island, in about an hour. But of the Oahu-based Army planes, not one was on patrol. Still on four-hour notice, they were all tightly bunched together wing tip to wing tip for security against saboteurs at Hickham, Bellows and Wheeler Fields. So were the Marine planes at Ewa.

Of all the military planes in Hawaii, only 7 Navy PBY's were on patrol . . .

About 25 miles to the northwest Japanese pilots in the leading attack planes were marvelling at the peaceful green scene below them. The entire island seemed to be lazing luxuriantly in the early sun. Not even a trace of smoke was coming up from the motionless mass of ships in Pearl Harbor.

At 7:49 A.M. Commander Fuchida from his high-level bomber gave the attack signal in Morse code, "TO . . . TO . . . TO." Four minutes later the great naval base was spread out below him like a huge relief map. It looked exactly as he had imagined. Still no fighters were climbing up to challenge; nor was there a single mushroom explosion of anti-aircraft fire. It was unbelievable. They had achieved complete surprise.

Even before a single bomb dropped he now radioed: "TORA . . . TORA . . . TORA" (Tiger). The repeated word was heard by Admiral Nagumo. It was also heard directly on board the *Nagato*, at Combined Fleet Headquarters in Japan. When the message was brought to Yamamoto he said nothing, his face betrayed no emotion. The other officers spontaneously cheered when the laconic message was read aloud. The *Nagato* was engulfed in excitement. The message decoded meant: "We have succeeded in surprise attack."

Still no bomb had fallen. Except for the roar of approaching planes all was quiet in the Honolulu area . . .

At that same moment, near the center of the island of Oahu, Japanese fighters and bombers began to dive on the Army's Wheeler Field, adjacent to Schofield Barracks.

Second Lieutenant Robert Overstreet, of the 696th Aviation Ordnance Company, was sleeping in the two-story wooden BOQ. He was awakened by a terrific noise. At first he thought it was an earthquake. "Looks like Jap planes," he heard someone shout. "Hell, no," said someone else. "It's just a Navy maneuver."

Overstreet's door opened and an old friend, Lieutenant Robert Skawold, looked in. His face was white, his lips trembling. "I think Japs are attacking."

Overstreet looked out the window, saw planes circling overhead. They seemed to be olive drab. One dove on the barracks, coming so close he could see the pilot and a rear gunner. On the fuselage and wing tips were flaming red suns. He finished dressing as he ran out of the barracks and headed for his organization. Soon he came onto a group of fighter pilots.

"We've got to get down to the line and tag some of those bastards," shouted one, Lieutenant Harry Brown. Another pilot pointed to the burning hangars and the ramp. There the closely grouped planes were already ablaze.

"Let's go to Haliewa," said Brown. This was an auxiliary field on the north coast where a few P-40's and P-36's were kept. Brown and several other pilots piled into his new Ford convertible and left. Lieutenants George Welch and Kenneth Taylor followed in the latter's car.

Hundreds were milling around in shocked confusion as bombs fell and buildings erupted. Overstreet weaved his way through the mob toward the permanent quarters area. On the Circle he saw Brigadier General Howard Davidson, the fighter commandant, and Colonel William Flood, the base commander, standing by their front doors in pajamas, staring at the sky, their faces aghast.

"Where's our Navy?" said Flood. "Where're our fighters?"

"General," shouted Overstreet, "we'd better get out of here. Those planes have tail-gunners." He ran toward the ordnance hangar. To his horror it was in flames. Inside were a million rounds of machine-gun ammunition ticketed for Midway Island. Suddenly the hangar began to explode, like an endless row of huge firecrackers . . .

At 7:55 A.M a V-formation of planes suddenly appeared from the west. [Aircraft mechanics Jesse Gaines and Ted Conway were walking toward the flight line at Hickham Field.] As they began to peel off, Conway said, "We're going to have an air show."

Gaines noticed something fall from the first plane. He guessed in alarm that it was a wheel.

"Wheel, hell, they're Japs!" cried Conway.

As Gaines said, "You're crazy," a bomb exploded among the neatly packed planes on the field. The two men began to run toward the big three-storied barracks, "Hickham Hotel." Gaines saw some gas drums and dove behind them for protection. Fighters were now diving in a strafing attack, their machine guns spitting orange flames . . .

The Japanese plan was simple but efficient. First, to prevent an air counterattack, the airfields were being systematically wiped out. In the first few minutes the Navy bases, Kaneohe and Ford Island; the Army bases, Wheeler, Bellows and Hickam; and the lone Marine base, Ewa, were all but crippled.

A moment after the first bomb fell, the Pearl Harbor signal tower alerted Kimmel's headquarters by phone. Three minutes later, at 7:58 A.M., the message heard around the world was broadcast by Rear Admiral Patrick Bellinger from Ford Island:

Air Raid, Pearl Harbor—This is no drill.

Closely on its heels, at 8:00 A.M. Kimmel's headquarters radioed

Washington, Admiral Hart in the Philippines and all forces at sea: *Air raid on Pearl Harbor. This is no drill.* Even as the messages were going out, torpedo planes were diving on the main target, Battleship Row.

Admiral C. C. Bloch was shaving at his quarters in the Navy Yard. He thought workmen were blasting in the nearby stone quarry. When the explosions continued he told his wife, "I'm going outside and see what that noise is." He ran out the front door. Overhead he saw a plane in flames. He went back into the house. "The Japanese are bombing us. I've got to get to the office. Don't stay down here."

At the naval housing unit adjacent to Hickham Field, First Class Metalsmith Lawrence Chappell was in bed. A plane roared over-head.

"What are those planes?" asked his wife, starting toward the window. "It's too late for the Bomber Patrol."

"Probably stragglers."

"The Rising Sun! The Rising Sun! *Japanese!*" cried Mrs. Chappell.

"You're foolish, go back to bed." Another plane roared over and Chappell went to the window. A torpedo plane swept by, so close he could see the pilot turning around, unconcerned. He hurriedly dressed and ran outside. Now he heard anti-aircraft fire and saw flames and billows of black smoke rising from Pearl Harbor.

Kimmel was watching the torpedo attack from the hill at Makalapa near his quarters. Short was standing on the *lanai* of his home near Fort Shafter watching the billows of smoke in the west and wondering what was going on at Pearl Harbor.

The smoke was rising from Battleship Row, on the east side of Ford Island where seven battleships, the heart of the Pacific Fleet, were moored. They were not protected from aerial torpedoes by nets because of Pearl Harbor's 40-foot depth. This matter had been discussed many times by Kimmel and Stark. Even the British had been consulted. Everyone agreed a minimum depth of 75 feet was necessary for torpedoes.

This unanimous conclusion was surprising since the British themselves had made a successful plane attack on the Italian fleet at Taranto the previous year with specially rigged torpedoes. The Japanese bombers diving on Battleship Row were proving as clever as the British. They were dropping torpedoes with ingeniously constructed wooden fins, specially designed for shallow water.

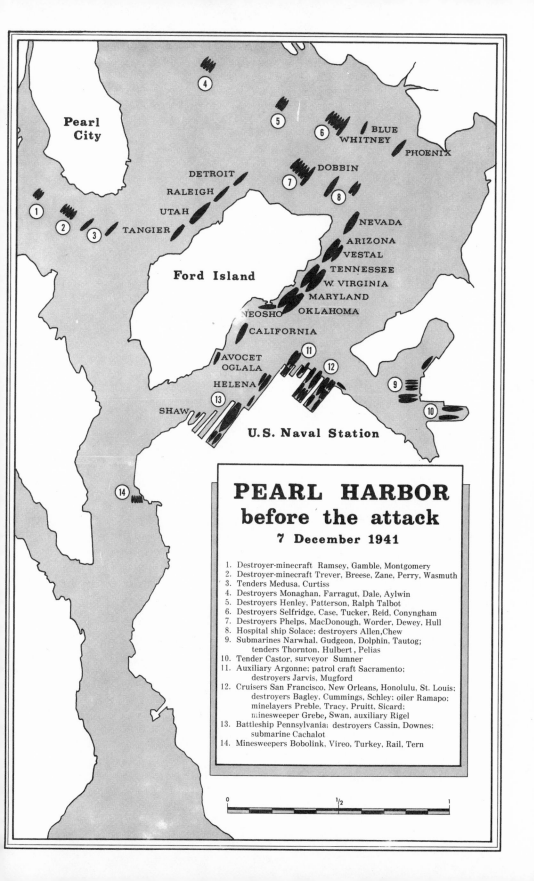

Pearl City

DETROIT
RALEIGH
UTAH
TANGIER

Ford Island

NEOSHO

CALIFORNIA

AVOCET
OGLALA

HELENA

SHAW

BLUE
WHITNEY
PHOENIX

DOBBIN

NEVADA
ARIZONA
VESTAL
TENNESSEE
W. VIRGINIA
MARYLAND
OKLAHOMA

U.S. Naval Station

PEARL HARBOR
before the attack
7 December 1941

1. Destroyer-minecraft Ramsey, Gamble, Montgomery
2. Destroyer-minecraft Trever, Breese, Zane, Perry, Wasmuth
3. Tenders Medusa, Curtiss
4. Destroyers Monaghan, Farragut, Dale, Aylwin
5. Destroyers Henley, Patterson, Ralph Talbot
6. Destroyers Selfridge, Case, Tucker, Reid, Conyngham
7. Destroyers Phelps, MacDonough, Worden, Dewey, Hull
8. Hospital ship Solace; destroyers Allen, Chew
9. Submarines Narwhal, Gudgeon, Dolphin, Tautog;
   tenders Thornton, Hulbert , Pelias
10. Tender Castor, surveyor Sumner
11. Auxiliary Argonne; patrol craft Sacramento;
    destroyers Jarvis, Mugford
12. Cruisers San Francisco, New Orleans, Honolulu, St. Louis;
    destroyers Bagley, Cummings, Schley; oiler Ramapo;
    minelayers Preble, Tracy, Pruitt, Sicard;
    minesweeper Grebe, Swan, auxiliary Rigel
13. Battleship Pennsylvania; destroyers Cassin, Downes;
    submarine Cachalot
14. Minesweepers Bobolink, Vireo, Turkey, Rail, Tern

0   1/2   1

Not far from Battleship Row, Yeoman C. O. Lines of the oil tanker *Ramapo* was in the crew's quarters. Boatswain's Mate Graff rushed down the ladder. "The Japs are bombing Pearl Harbor!" he yelled.

The men in the room looked at him as if he were crazy.

"No fooling," he said.

Someone gave a Bronx cheer.

"No crap. Get your asses up on deck!"

Lines hurried topside to the fantail. He thought Graff was ribbing as usual. Then he heard a dull explosion and saw a plane dive toward the battleship *California*.

She was the last of the seven big vessels in Battleship Row. Two torpedoes hit her almost simultaneously. The ship took an 8-degree list and began to settle. Her fractured fuel tanks began to flood an entire lower deck. Bombs now fell and half a dozen fires flared. In minutes oil gushing from the ruptured ship burst into flame. She was surrounded by a wall of fire. The word was passed: Abandon ship.

Ahead, in tandem formation, were the *Maryland* and *Oklahoma*. A torpedo couldn't hit the *Maryland* because she was berthed inboard, next to Ford Island, and was protected by her mate. But the outboard ship, the *Oklahoma*, was hit by four torpedoes within a minute. As she listed to port, Commander Jesse Kenworthy, senior officer aboard, ordered the ship abandoned over the starboard side. He calmly walked up the ship's side over the blistered ledge and then over the bottom. Soon the ship settled, its starboard propeller out of the water. Below more than 400 men were trapped in the rapidly filling compartments.

Next in Battleship Row came another pair, the *Tennessee* and *West Virginia*. Like the *Maryland,* the *Tennessee* was inboard and safe from torpedo attack . . .

~~~~~~

AT SEA, THE DAY BEGAN ABOARD THE AIRCRAFT CARrier *Enterprise* at first light when she sent off her complement of Marine fighter planes, the new Grumman F4U's. Soon after, at 6:15 A.M., two planes departed for Ford Island in order to land a member of Halsey's staff. Twelve minutes later (the carrier was now heading back to Pearl Harbor), the other aircraft of Scouting Six departed for the naval base. During the next hour, Halsey shaved and put on a fresh uniform in his flag quarters; he was still there at 7:55 A.M.

when Lieutenant H. Douglas Moulton, his flag secretary, answered the phone from the Radio Room: Pearl Harbor was under air attack! Halsey jumped to his feet in dismay.

Meanwhile, the planes of Scouting Six had started to arrive over Pearl Harbor. One of these was Ensign Manuel Gonzales. In the carrier's Radio Room where Commander Charles Fox was on duty, the frantic voice of the pilot was distinctly heard: "Don't shoot! Don't shoot! This is an American plane!" There was no further communication from Gonzales; nor was there any in due course from eleven other planes of the squadron.

A heavy cruiser, *New Orleans,* was moored in the Southeast Loch of the Navy Yard. Her only casualties were sustained when a fragmentation bomb dropped nearby and shrapnel raked her topsides. The story of the cruiser's fight is told by Presbyterian Chaplain, Lieutenant Commander Howell Forgy, whose legendary conduct during the battle inspired the popular war song, *"Praise the Lord and Pass the Ammunition."* When the attack opened, Forgy was in his quarters thinking about the sermon he was scheduled to deliver. He had decided on "We Reach Forward," based on Paul's words, "Forgetting those things which are behind, and reaching unto those things which are before."

2.

"...AND PASS THE AMMUNITION"

... The heavy cruiser moved slightly. A tug was probably shifting us to another berth. There was little noise challenging the tranquillity of the Hawaiian morning, save a muffled tat-tat-tat as though the little Irving boy were running a stick along one of those white picket fences back home.

The silence suddenly exploded into the deafening clang-clang-clang of the general alarm.

I wondered why the officer of the deck could never get into his head the fact that the general alarm was not to be tested on Sundays. I consoled myself with the thought that this "bust," as the Navy calls its blunders, would bring the commander on his neck.

The clang-clang-clang continued stubbornly, and the shrill scream of the bo'sun's pipe beeped through the speaker.

"All hands to battle stations! All hands to battle stations!"

"This is no drill! This is no drill!"

But I wasn't buffaloed. We knew that the army had been on an alert throughout the islands until the previous night. This must be some admiral's clever idea of how to make an off-hour general quarters drill for the fleet realistic.

I bucked a line of Marines hurrying up the ladders through the hatch to their battle stations at the machine-guns and AA batteries topside.

The Leathernecks were pulling on their jackets and panting unprintable things about general quarters as they scampered upward. Every one grumbled about GQ—especially at this hour, when their Sunday-morning-after-Saturday-night liberty was interrupted so abruptly.

Down in the innards of the ship I could hear a rhythmic thudding against the side of the hull. That meant the five-inch anti-aircraft guns of other vessels in the harbor were firing. I thought I could hear that tat-tat-tat again. Maybe it was machine-gun fire.

I sauntered into sick bay, my battle station.

Behind me, cinching up his tie, came Lieutenant Commander Edward Evans, senior medical officer. His face appeared worried as he stepped through the door.

"What's it all about, Doc?" I asked him.

The sound of the guns of the other ships kept beating through the steel sides of the *New Orleans*. It sounded like a Hollywood version of jungle tom-toms.

"I don't know," he said, expressionless. "I just saw a plane falling out of the sky. It was burning."

I told him I thought that was carrying a drill pretty far.

He gave his head a little twist to the side and looked beyond me.

"I don't know, Padre. This might be the real thing."

We stood there a minute, just saying nothing and listening. The noise was increasing, and we knew more ships had begun firing. We heard the fast, dull pumping of the pompom guns as they joined in the racket. They sounded like some one trying to say "pawm-pawm" with his mouth half-closed.

"I think I'll run topside and take a look, if you don't mind," I told him.

I moved quickly this time. Faster than when I came down from my room. Much faster.

I ran to the well deck, where I could get a clear view of the harbor.

Off our starboard quarter, about five hundred yards, the mighty *Arizona* was sending a mass of black, oily smoke thousands of feet into the air. The water around her was dotted with debris and a mass of bobbing, oil-covered heads. I could see hundreds of men splashing and trying to swim. Others were motionless.

Flashes of orange-red flames snapped out of the AA guns, bright against the jet clouds ascending all along Battleship Row.

The cage-like foremast of the *Arizona* poked through the smoke at a crazy, drunken angle.

The *Weavie*—that's what we called the *West Virginia*—looked as though her back had been broken. She was sagging amidships, and her bow and stern angled upward.

Forward of the *Weavie* the *Oklahoma*'s main deck was disappearing beneath the water. She was rolling on her side, and her big bottom was coming up. I could see hundreds of her crew jumping into the water. Dozens of others were crawling along her exposed side and bottom, trying to keep up with the giant treadmill.

Off our starboard beam I heard the drone of airplane motors. I saw a Jap dive-bomber gliding down toward Battleship Row. He seemed to be loafing in, deliberately taking his time to pick out just what he wanted to hit.

I couldn't take my eyes off him. I followed him down until I saw the bombs drop out of his belly. Sticking out of the cockpit was the helmeted head of the Jap pilot. There was something mocking about the big rising-sun balls under the wings of the plane.

Minutes seemed to tick away while the bombs moved downward. I gaped with a sense of fascinated helplessness. I couldn't resist trying to reach out to stop those bombs before they hit.

They were coming down for the big battleship *California*.

The bombs hit her amidships, right by the stacks. A flash, fire and smoke jumped into the air all at once.

The Jap opened his throttle wide and raced away from his victim with a terrific roar. Now our own guns began thundering in my ears. The sky all around the plane was laced with streaming trails of tracers. The Jap couldn't get through that stuff—but he did.

More planes came, one after another. With a sort of abandon, they floated by in slow, aggravating glides, right through the very center of our noisy barrage of AA fire.

I wondered if the devil himself could have immuned these planes against our shells. What was this new, horrible, evil power that turned Pearl Harbor into a bay of terrible explosions, smoking ships, flames, and death?

Coming from the direction of Diamond Head, another Jap bomber sloped into its glide.

It seemed as though every gun of the *New Orleans* and the entire fleet nozzled a cone of fire at it. The wall of exploding steel was in the right place this time. The plane's dive became steeper, and it tumbled out of the sky. A long ribbon of black crepe trailed out behind it as the plane disappeared. It crashed in the backyard of Naval Hospital.

We'd got one! They could be hit!

I felt better. The men around me on the well deck and the sweating gun crews on the quarterdeck above shouted like freshmen at the first touchdown of the day. I guess I shouted and screamed as loudly as any one.

Mike Jacobs, master at arms, was standing near me. He grinned at the string of smoke in the sky and drawled, "I guess chaplains can cuss like bo'sun's mates when they have to."

Maybe he was right.

Lieutenant Francis Lee Hamlin, handsome and wiry main battery officer, moved alongside me. With the ship's big guns useless against the swarms of Jap planes, he stood as helpless as I, watching them drone in, drop their loads, and scream off toward the sea.

"Padre," Lee said, grinning under his long, dark-brown hair, "I figure if the Lord is going to look after any one in this, He's going to look after you. If you don't mind, I'll stick close by."

I knew Lee was only kidding, but as I ran toward sick bay on the double, he was close behind me.

The passageway below was dark, and our heels made weird hollow sounds on the steel deck. No lights were burning, because someone on the dock decided we might want to get under way in a hurry. In a burst of misguided initiative he had cut all lines from the dock to the ship—including the power line.

Far forward we could see sunlight pouring into the wardroom.

"We'd better dog down the ports in there," I heard Lee holler. Open port-holes not only invited the machine-gun bullets of the Jap strafers above, but they would provide an easy entrance for sea water if we took a hit.

The wardroom had a queer, deserted appearance. For the first time since I had been aboard there were no officers sitting in the white, linen-covered chairs. The felt table tops reflected the sunlight in a green flood against the gray walls.

Only "Deacon" Smith, the stocky little Negro mess-boy, was in the room. He was already at work closing the ports and dogging them against the awful panorama outside.

Lee and I slammed others shut, and the room grew darker and darker. It seemed there was no one in the world but the three of us.

Things were running through our heads so rapidly that none seemed to stop long enough for us to find out what they were.

We heard the exploding bombs, the burning ships' magazines letting go, and the never-ending barking of the big AA guns, the pumping pompoms, and the rattle of machine-guns. We wondered how long it could last—and how many seconds or minutes or hours would pass until we and the *New Orleans* would become a part of the terrifying funeral pyre that now was Pearl Harbor.

Smith was working feverishly, and as he moved closer I could hear him singing.

The cacophony of the guns and bombs grew louder and louder, and so did the throaty, rich baritone voice of the young Negro.

"Swing low, sweet char-iot" the "Deacon" sang in defiance of the enemy's chariots swooping down with their deadly loads.

"—A-comin' fo' to car-ree me home."

I turned to Lee and we both grinned. Somehow we found in the little mess attendant's music a beauty and a faith renewed.

"Swing low—" he sang on. His voice boomed out to new heights as his own music reassured him. He had no way to shoot the enemy out of the sky, but he seemed to feel he could sing death away.

I lost Lee in the pitch-darkness and felt my way to sick bay to report to Dr. Evans what I had seen in those few terrible minutes topside.

"You're right, Doc. This is the real thing."

He was pacing back and forth in the room, his face white and grave. The noise from above had told him more than I could.

His instruments were ready, and so was he. He knew the heartbreaking stream of broken human beings that would keep coming into that little sick bay until this war was history. He had seen it before, in the First World War and during China service.

Dr. Evans was a skilled veteran, ready but not eager for the blood-stained months ahead.

Outside sick bay I heard the booming voice of a big gunner's mate named George. His red hair took on an eerie hue under the dim blue battle lights.

"Get those . . . . lines down the hatch to the magazine," he shouted.

Ropes tumbled through the hatches from the deck to the cruiser's bowels far below.

Suddenly the impact of our helpless, hopeless situation hit me. We had been under a temporary overhaul, and the ammunition hoists were without power. The gunners topside were ducking machine-gun bullets and shrapnel, training their guns by sheer guts and sweat, and they had no ammunition other than the few shells in their ready boxes.

The sharp voice of barrel-chested young Lieutenant E. F. Woodhead snapped through the foul clouds of expended powder smoke that were coming below through the ventilators.

He was gathering every man in sight—the shipfitters, the big turret men, the repair parties—every one who had no specific job at the moment.

"Get over by that ammunition hoist," he ordered. "Grab those shells and get them to the guns!"

The big five-inch shells, weighing close to a hundred pounds, were being pulled up the powerless hoist by ropes attached to their long, tube-like metal cases.

A tiny Filipino messboy, who weighed little more than the shell, hoisted it to his shoulder, staggered a few steps, and grunted as he started the long, tortuous trip up two flights of ladders to the quarterdeck, where the guns thirsted for steel and powder.

A dozen eager men lined up at the hoist.

The parade of ammunition was endless, but the cry kept coming from topside for more, more, more.

I saw a Jewish boy from Brooklyn reach for a shell before he had caught his breath from the previous trip. The sweat from his face was no longer coming in big drops. Now it was a steady stream that ran along the ridge of his nose, splashed to his chin, and fell away. His legs tried to buckle under the punishing weight, but he wouldn't let them.

The boys were putting everything they had into the job, and it was beginning to tell on them.

But no one complained.

I wished I could boost one of the shells to my shoulder. The cool metal of the shell casing against my shoulder and neck would feel good. I would be busy, and feel better inside. But a chaplain cannot fire a gun or take material part in a battle.

Yet those devils—coming out of the sky without warning and sending to their death thousands of men of a nation at peace—were violating every rule of God and man.

There was little time for more reflection as I climbed the ladders to the quarterdeck above.

Minutes turned to hours. Physical exhaustion was coming to every man in the human endless-chain of that ammunition line. They struggled on.

They could keep going only by keeping faith in their hearts.

I slapped their wet, sticky backs and shouted, "Praise the Lord and pass the ammunition."

~~~~~~

PAT BELLINGER'S *Air Raid, Pearl Harbor—This is no Drill,* sent at 7:58 A.M., was picked up by a West Coast naval radio station and instantly relayed to Washington. It landed on the desk of Admiral Harold Stark, the Chief of Naval Operations, who immediately burst into the office of Secretary of the Navy Knox. "My God," exclaimed Knox, "this can't be true! This must mean the Philippines!" Stark replied that it was no mistake, and Knox called the White House. President Roosevelt was lunching in the Oval Room with Harry Hopkins. The President's first reaction was shocked disbelief; then he called Secretary of State Cordell Hull and told him the news.

In Honolulu, San Francisco, Washington, and New York, where Japanese diplomats were frantically burning their secret papers, the reaction of the man in the street was one of unanimous rage and incredulity. But most had never heard of Pearl Harbor.

New York's Radio Station WOR interrupted its regularly scheduled broadcast of the Dodger-Giant football game to flash the news to its listeners. In the same city's Carnegie Hall, announcer Warren Sweeney interrupted the Philharmonic, which was playing Shostakovitch's Symphony No.1, to repeat the bulletin. He followed this shortly with a record of "The Star Spangled Banner."

Among the best of the published Pearl Harbor accounts is one by Walter Lord, who recounts in minute detail the catastrophe in Battleship Row.

3.

"I CAN'T KEEP THROWING THINGS AT THEM"

Up in the *Maryland*'s foretop, Seaman Leslie Vernon Short had abandoned his hopes of a quiet morning addressing Christmas cards. After a quick double-take on the planes diving at Ford Island, he loaded the ready machine gun and hammered away at the first torpedo planes gliding in from Southeast Loch.

In the destroyer anchorage to the north, Gunner's Mate Walter Bowe grabbed a .50-caliber machine gun on the afterdeck of the *Tucker* and fired back too. So did Seaman Frank Johnson, who was sweeping near the bridge of the destroyer *Bagley* in the Navy Yard. Seaman George Sallet watched the slugs from Johnson's gun tear into a torpedo plane passing alongside, saw the rear gunner slump in the cockpit, and thought it was just like in the movies.

Others were firing too—the *Helena* at 1010 dock . . . the *Tautog* at the sub base . . . the *Raleigh* on the northwest side of Ford Island. Up in the *Nevada's* "bird bath," a seaman generally regarded as one of the less useful members of the crew seized a .30 caliber machine gun and winged a torpedo plane headed directly for the ship. It was to be an important reprieve . . .

Another plane glided toward the *Nevada*. Again the machine guns in her foretop blazed away. Again the plane wobbled and never pulled out of its turn. The men were wild with excitement as it plowed into the water alongside the dredge pipe just astern. The pilot frantically struggled clear and floated face up past the ship. But this time they got him too late. Marine Private Payton McDaniel watched the torpedo's silver streak as it headed for the port bow. He remembered pictures of torpedoed ships and half expected the *Nevada* to break in two and sink enveloped in flames. It didn't happen that way at all. Just a slight shudder, a brief list to port.

Then she caught a bomb by the starboard anti-aircraft director. Ensign Joe Taussig was at his station there, standing in the doorway, when it hit. Suddenly he found his left leg tucked under his arm. Almost absently he said to himself, "That's a hell of a place for a foot to be," and was amazed to hear Boatswain's Mate Allen Owens, standing beside him, say exactly the same words aloud.

In the plotting room five decks below, Ensign Charles Merdinger at first felt that it was all like the drills he had been through dozens of times. But it began to seem different when he learned through the phone circuit that his roommate Joe Taussig had been hit.

The men on the *Arizona,* forward of the *Nevada,* hardly had time to think. She was inboard of the *Vestal,* but the little repair ship didn't offer much protection—a torpedo struck home almost right away—and nothing could stop the steel that rained down from Fuchida's horizontal bombers now overhead. A big one shattered the boat deck between No. 4 and 6 guns—it came in like a fly ball, and Seaman Russell Lott, standing in the antiaircraft director, had the feeling he could reach out and catch it. Another hit No. 4 turret, scorched and hurled Coxswain James Forbis off a ladder two decks below. The PA system barked, "Fire on the quarter-deck," and then went off the air for good. Radioman Glenn Lane and three of his shipmates rigged a hose and tried to fight the fire. No water pressure. They rigged phones and tried to call for water. No power. All the time explosions somewhere forward were throwing them off their feet.

Alongside, the *Vestal* seemed to be catching everything that missed the *Arizona.* One bomb went through an open hatch, tore right through the ship, exploding as it passed out the bottom. It flooded the No. 3 hold, and the ship began settling at the stern. A prisoner in the brig howled to be let out, and finally someone shot off the lock with a .45.

Forward of the *Arizona* and *Vestal,* the *Tennessee* so far was holding her own; but the *West Virginia* on the outside was taking a terrible beating. A Japanese torpedo plane headed straight for the casemate where Seaman Robert Benton waited for the rest of his gun crew. He stood there transfixed—wanted to move but couldn't. The torpedo hit directly underneath and sent Benton and his headphones flying in opposite directions. He got up . . . ran across the deck . . . slipped down the starboard side of the ship to the armor shelf, a ledge formed by the ship's 15-inch steel plates. As he walked aft along the ledge, he glanced up, saw the bombers this time. Caught in the bright morning sun, the falling bombs looked for a fleeting second like snowflakes.

The men below were spared such sights, but the compensation was questionable. Storekeeper Donald Brown tried to get the phones working in the ammunition supply room, third deck forward. The lines were dead. More torpedoes—sickening fumes—steeper list—no lights. Men began screaming in the dark. Someone shouted, "Abandon ship!" and the crowd stampeded to the compartment ladder. Brown figured he would have no chance in this clawing mob, felt his way to the next compartment forward, and found another ladder with no one near it at all. Now he was on the second deck, but not allowed any higher. Nothing left to do, no place else to go—he and a friend brushed a bunch of dirty breakfast dishes off a mess table and sat down to wait the end.

Down in the plotting room—the gunnery nerve center and well below the water line—conditions looked just as hopeless. Torpedoes were slamming into the ship somewhere above. Through an overhead hatch Ensign Victor Delano could see that the third deck was starting to flood. Heavy yellowish smoke began pouring down through the opening. The list grew steeper; tracking board, plotting board, tables, chairs, cots, everything slid across the room and jumbled against the port bulkhead. In the internal communications room next door, circuit breakers were sparking and electrical units ran wild. The men were pale but calm.

Soon oily water began pouring through the exhaust trunks of the ventilation system. Then more yellow smoke. Nothing further could be done, so Delano led his men forward to central station, the ship's damage control center. Before closing the watertight door behind him, he called back to make sure no one was left. From nowhere six oil-drenched electrician's mates showed up—they had somehow been hurled through the hatch from the deck above. Then Warrant Electrician Charles T. Duvall called to please wait for him. He sounded in trouble and Delano stepped back into the plotting room to lend a hand. But he slipped on some oil and slid across the linoleum floor, bowling over Duvall in the process. The two men ended in a tangled heap among the tables and chairs now packed against the "down" side of the room.

They couldn't get back on their feet; the oil was everywhere. Even crawling didn't work—they still got no traction. Finally they grabbed a row of knobs on the main battery switchboard, which ran all the way across the room. Painfully they pulled themselves uphill, hand over hand along the switchboard. By now it was almost like scaling a cliff.

In central station at last, they found conditions almost as bad. The lights dimmed, went out, came on again for a while as some auxiliary circuit took hold. Outside the watertight door on the lower side, the water began to rise . . . spouting through the cracks around the edges and shooting like a hose through an air-test opening. Delano could hear the pleas and cries of the men trapped on the other side, and he thought with awe of the decision Lieutenant Commander J. S. Harper, the damage control officer, had to make: let the men drown, or open the door and risk the ship as well as the people now in central station. The door stayed closed.

Delano suggested to Harper that he and his men might be more useful topside. For the moment Harper didn't even have time to answer. He was desperately trying to keep in touch with the rest of the ship and direct the counterflooding that might save it, but all the circuits were dead.

The counterflooding was done anyhow. Lieutenant Claude V. Ricketts had once been damage control officer and liked to discuss with other young officers what should be done in just this kind of situation. More or less as skull practice, they had worked out a plan among themselves. Now Ricketts began counterflooding on his own hook, helped along by Boatswain's Mate Billingsley, who knew how to work the knobs and valves. The *West Virgina* slowly swung back to starboard and settled into the harbor mud on an even keel.

There was no time for counterflooding on the *Oklahoma,* lying ahead of the *West Virginia* and outboard of the *Maryland.* Lying directly across from Southeast Loch, she got three torpedoes right away, then another two as she heeled to port.

Curiously, many of the men weren't even aware of the torpedoes. Seaman George Murphy only heard the loud-speaker say something about "air attack" and assumed the explosions were bombs. Along with hundreds of other men who had no air defense stations, he now trooped down to the third deck, where he would be protected by the armor plate that covered the deck above. Seaman Stephen Young never thought of torpedoes either, and he was even relieved when the water surged into the port side of No. 4 turret powder handling room. He assumed that someone was finally counterflooding on that side to offset bomb damage to starboard.

The water rose . . . the emergency lights went out . . . the list increased. Now everything was breaking loose. Big 1000-pound shells rumbled across the handling rooms, sweeping men before them. Eight-foot reels of steel towing cable rolled across the second deck, blocking the ladders topside. The door of the drug room swung open, and Seaman Murphy watched hundreds of bottles cascade over a couple of seamen hurrying down a passageway. The boys slipped and rolled through the broken glass, jumped up, and ran on.

On the few remaining ladders, men battled grimly to get to the main deck. It was a regular log jam on the ladder to S Division compartment, just a few steps from open air. Every time something exploded outside, men would surge down the ladder, meeting head-on another crowd that surged up. Soon it was impossible to move in either direction. Seaman Murphy gave up even trying. He stood off to the one side—one foot on deck, the other on the corridor wall, the only way he could now keep his footing.

Yeoman L. L. Curry had a better way out. He and some mates were still in the machine shop on third deck amidships when the list reached 60 degrees. Someone spied an exhaust ventilator leading all the way to the deck, and one by one the men crawled up. As they reached fresh air, an officer ran over and tried to shoo them back inside, where they would be safe from bomb splinters. That was the big danger, he explained: a battleship couldn't turn over.

Several hundred yards ahead of the *Oklahoma*—and moored alone at the southern end of Battleship Row—the *California* caught her first torpedo at 8:05. Yeoman Durrell Conner watched it come from his station in the flag communications office. He slammed the porthole shut as it struck the ship directly beneath him.

Another crashed home farther aft. There might as well have been more—the *California* was wide open. She was due for inspection Monday, and the covers had been taken off six of the manholes leading to her double bottom. A dozen more of these covers had been loosened. The water poured in and surged freely through the ship.

It swept into the ruptured fuel tanks, contaminating the oil, knocking out the power plant right away. It swirled into the forward air compressor station, where Machinist's Mate Robert Scott was trying to feed air to the five-inch guns. The other men cleared out, calling Scott to come with them. He yelled back, "This is my station—I'll stay here and give them air as long as the guns are going." They closed the watertight door and let him have his way.

With the power gone, men desperately tried to do by hand the tasks that were meant for machines. Yeoman Conner joined a long chain of men passing powder and shells up from an ammunition room far below. Stifling fumes from the ruptured fuel tanks made their work harder, and word spread that the ship was under gas attack. At the wounded collecting station in the crew's reception room Pharmacist's Mate William Lynch smashed open lockers in a vain search for morphine. Near the communications office a man knelt in prayer under a ladder. Numb to the chaos around him, another absently sat at a desk typing, "Now is the time for all good men . . ."

Around the harbor nobody noticed the *California's* troubles—all eyes were glued on the *Oklahoma*. From his bungalow on Ford Island, Chief Albert Molter watched her gradually roll over on her side, "slowly and stately . . . as if she were tired and wanted to rest." She kept rolling until her mast and superstructure jammed in the mud, leaving her bottom-up—a huge dead whale lying in the water. Only eight minutes had passed since the first torpedo hit.

On the *Maryland* Electrician's Mate Harold North recalled how everyone had cursed on Friday when the *Oklahoma* tied up alongside, shutting off what air there was at night.

Inside the *Oklahoma* men were giving it one more try. Storekeeper Terry Armstrong found himself alone in a small compartment on the second deck. As it slowly filled with water, he dived down, groped for the porthole, squirmed through to safety. Seaman Malcolm McCleary escaped through a washroom porthole the same way. Nearby, Lieutenant (j.g.) Aloysius Schmitt, the Catholic chaplain, started out too. But a breviary in his hip pocket caught on the coaming. As he backed into the compartment again to take it out, several men started forward. Chaplain Schmitt had no more time to spend on himself. He pushed three, possibly four, of the others through before the water closed over the compartment.

Some men weren't even close to life as they knew it, but were still alive nevertheless. They found themselves gasping, swimming, trying to orient themselves to an upside-down world in the air pockets that formed as the ship rolled over. Seventeen-year-old Seaman Willard Beal fought back the water that poured into the steering engine room. Seaman George Murphy splashed about the operating room of the ship's dispensary . . . wondering what part of the ship had a tile ceiling . . . never dreaming he was looking up at the floor.

Topside, the men had it easier. As the ship slowly turned turtle, most of the men simply climbed over the starboard side and walked with the roll, finally ending up on the bottom. When and how they got off was pretty much a matter of personal choice. Some started swinging hand over hand along the lines that tied the ship to the *Maryland,* but as she rolled, these snapped, and the men were pitched into the water between the two ships. Seaman Tom Armstrong dived off on this side—his watch stopped at 8:10. Tom's brother Pat jumped off from the outboard side. Their third brother Terry was already in the water after squeezing through the porthole on the second deck. Marine Gunnery Sergeant Leo Wears slid down a line and almost drowned when someone used him as a stepladder to climb into a launch. His friend Sergeant Norman Currier coolly walked along the side of the ship to the bow, hailed a passing boat, and stepped into it without getting a foot wet. Ensign Bill Ingram climbed onto the high side just as the yardarm touched the water. He stripped to his shorts and slid down the bottom of the ship.

As Ingram hit the water, the *Arizona* blew up. Afterward men said a bomb went right down her stack, but later examination showed even the wire screen across the funnel top still intact. It seems more likely the bomb landed alongside the second turret, crashed through the forecastle, and set off the forward magazines.

In any case, a huge ball of fire and smoke mushroomed 500 feet into the air. There wasn't so much noise—most of the men say it was more a "whoom" than a "bang"—but the concussion was terrific. It stalled the motor of Aviation Ordnanceman Harand Quisdorf's pickup truck as he drove along Ford Island. It hurled Chief Albert Molter against the pipe banister of his basement stairs. It knocked everyone flat on Fireman Stanley H. Rabe's water barge. It blew Gunner Carey Garnett and dozens of other men off the *Nevada* . . . Commander Cassin Young off the *Vestal* . . . Ensign Vance Fowler off the *West Virginia.* Far above, Commander Fuchida's bomber trembled like a leaf. On the fleet landing at Merry's Point a Navy captain wrung his hands and sobbed that it just couldn't be true.

On the *Arizona,* hundreds of men were cut down in a single, searing flash. Inside the port anti-aircraft director one fire control man simply vanished—the only place he could have gone was through the narrow range-finder slot. On the bridge Rear Admiral Isaac C. Kidd and Captain Franklin Van Valkenburgh were instantly killed. On the second deck the entire ship's band was wiped out.

Over 1000 men were gone.

Incredibly, some still lived. Major Alan Shapley of the Marine detachment was blown out of the foremast and well clear of the ship. Though partly paralyzed, he swam to Ford Island, detouring to help two shipmates along the way. Radioman Glenn Lane was blown off the quarter-deck and found himself swimming in water thick with oil. He looked back at the *Arizona* and couldn't see a sign of life.

But men were there. On the third deck aft Coxswain James Forbis felt skinned alive, and the No. 4 turret handling room was filling with thick smoke. He and his mates finally moved over to No. 3 turret, where conditions were a little better, but soon smoke began coming in around the guns there too. The men stripped to their skivvie drawers and crammed their clothes around the guns to keep the smoke out. When somebody finally ordered them out, Forbis took off his newly shined shoes and carefully carried them in his hands as he left the turret. The deck was blazing hot and covered with oil. But there was a dry spot father aft near No. 4 turret, and before rejoining the fight, Forbis carefully placed his shoes there. He lined them neatly with the heels against the turret—just as though he planned to wear them up Hotel Street again that night.

In the portside anti-aircraft director, Russell Lott wrapped himself in a blanket and stumbled out the twisted door. The blanket kept him from getting scorched, but the deck was so hot he had to keep hopping from one foot to the other. Five shipmates staggered up through the smoke, so he stretched the blanket as a sort of shield for them all. Then he saw the *Vestal* still alongside. The explosion had left her decks a shambles, but he found someone who tossed over a line, and, one by one, all six men inched over to the little repair ship.

At that particular moment they were lucky to find anyone on the *Vestal*. The blast had blown some of the crew overboard, including skipper Cassin Young, and the executive officer told the rest to abandon ship. Seaman Thomas Garzione climbed down a line over the forecastle, came to the end of it, and found himself standing on the anchor. He just froze there—he was a nonswimmer and too scared to jump the rest of the way. Finally he worked up enough nerve, made the sign of the cross, and plunged down holding his nose. For a nonswimmer, he made remarkable time to a whale boat drifting in the debris.

Signalman Adolph Zlabis dived off the bridge and reached a launch hovering nearby. He and a few others yelled encouragement to a young sailor who had climbed out on the *Vestal's* boat boom and now dangled from a rope ladder five feet above the water. Finally the man let go, landed flat in the water with a resounding whack. The men in the launch couldn't help laughing.

Still on board the *Vestal,* Radioman John Murphy watched a long line of men pass his radio room, on their way to abandon ship. One of the other radiomen saw his brother go by. He cried, "I'm going with him," and ran out the door. For no particular reason Murphy decided to stay, but he began feeling that he would like to get back home just once more before he passed on.

At this point Commander Young climbed back on the *Vestal* from his swim in the harbor. He was by no means ready to call it a day. He stood sopping wet at the top of the gangway, shouting down to the swimmers and the men in the boats, "Come back! We're not giving up this ship yet!"

Most of the crew returned and Young gave orders to cast off. Men hacked at the hawsers tying the *Vestal* to the blazing *Arizona.* Inevitably, there was confusion. One officer on the *Arizona's* quarter-deck yelled, "Don't cut those lines." Others on the battleship pitched in and helped. Aviation Mechanic "Turkey" Graham slashed the last line with an ax, shouting ,"Get away from here while you can!"

Other help came from an unexpected source. A Navy tug happened by, whose skipper and chief engineer had both put in many years on the *Vestal.* They loyally eased alongside, took a line from the bow, and towed their old ship off toward Aiea landing, where she could safely sit out the rest of the attack.

When the *Arizona* blew up, Chief Electrician's Mate Harold North on the *Maryland* thought the end of the world had come. Actually he was lucky. Moored inboard of the *Oklahoma,* the *Maryland* was safe from torpedoes and caught only two bombs. One was a 15-inch armor-piercing shell fitted with fins—it slanted down just off the port bow, smashing into her hull 17 feet below the water line. The other hit the forecastle, setting the awnings on fire. When a strafer swept by, Chief George Haitle watched the firefighters scoot for shelter. One man threw his extinguisher down a hatch, where it exploded at the feet of an old petty officer, who grabbed for a mask, shouting "Gas!"

The *Tennessee,* the other inboard battleship, had more trouble. Seaman J. P. Burkholder looked out a porthole on the bridge just as one of the converted 16-inch shells crashed down on No.2 turret a few feet forward. The porthole cover tore loose, clobbered him on the head, and sent him scurrying through the door. Outside he helped a wounded ensign, but couldn't help one of his closest friends, who was so far gone he only wanted Burkholder to shoot him.

Another armor-piercing bomb burst through No. 3 turret farther aft. Seaman S. F. Bowen, stationed there as a powder carman, was just dogging the hatch when the bomb hit. It wasn't a shattering crash at all. Just a ball of fire, about the size of a basketball, appeared overhead and seemed to melt down on everyone. It seemed to run down on his skin and there was no way to stop it. As he crawled down to the deck below, he noticed that his shoe strings were still on fire.

Splinters flew in all directions from the bombs that hit the *Tennessee.* One hunk ripped the bridge of the *West Virginia* alongside, cut down Captain Mervyn Bennion as he tried to direct his ship's defense. He slumped across the sill of the signal bridge door on the starboard side of the machine-gun platform. Soon after he fell, Ensign Delano arrived on the bridge, having finally been sent up from central station. As Delano stepped out onto the platform, Lieutenant (j.g.) F. H. White rushed by, told him about the captain, and asked him to do what he could.

Delano saw right away it was hopeless. Captain Bennion had been hit in the stomach, and it took no medical training to know the wound was fatal. Yet he was perfectly conscious, and at least he might be made more comfortable. Delano opened a first-aid kit and looked for some morphine. No luck. Then he found a can of ether and tried to make the captain pass out. He sat down beside the dying man, holding his head in one hand and the ether in the other. It made the captain drowsy but never unconscious. Occasionally Delano moved the captain's legs to more comfortable positions, but there was so little he could do.

As they sat there together, Captain Bennion prodded him with questions. He asked how the battle was going, what the *West Virginia* was doing, whether the ship and the men were badly hit. Delano did his best to answer, resorting every now and then to a gentle white lie. Yes, he assured the captain, the ship's guns were still firing.

Lieutenant Rickets now turned up and proved a pillar of strength.

Other men arrived too—Chief Pharmacist's Mate Leah . . . Ensign Jacoby from the flag radio room . . . Lieutenant Commander Doir Johnson from the forecastle. On his way up, Johnson ran across big Doris Miller, thought the powerful mess steward might come in handy, brought him along to the bridge. Together they tenderly lifted Captain Bennion and carried him to a sheltered spot behind the conning tower. He was still quite conscious and well aware of the flames creeping closer. He kept telling the men to leave him and save themselves.

In her house at Makalapa, Mrs. Mayfield still couldn't grasp what had happened. She walked numbly to a window and looked at Admiral Kimmel's house across the street. The Venetian blinds were closed, and there was no sign of activity. Somehow this was reassuring . . . surely there would be some sign of life if it was really true. It didn't occur to her that this might be one morning when the admiral had no time for Venetian blinds.

By now Captain Mayfield was in his uniform. He took a few swallows of coffee, slopping most of it in the saucer, and dashed for the carport. He roared off as the CINCPAC officer car screeched up to the admiral's house across the street. Admiral Kimmel ran down the steps and jumped in, knotting his tie on the way. Captain Freeland Daubin, commanding a squadron of submarines, leaped on the running board as the car moved off, and Captain Earle's station wagon shot down the hill after them.

In five minutes Admiral Kimmel was at CINCPA Headquarters in the sub base. The admiral thought he was there by 8:05; Commander Murphy thought it was more like 8:10. In either case, within a very few minutes of his arrival, the backbone of his fleet was gone or immobile—*Arizona, Oklahoma,* and *West Virginia* sunk . . . *California* sinking . . . *Maryland* and *Tennessee* bottled up by the wrecked battleships alongside . . . *Pennsylvania* squatting in drydock. Only the *Nevada* was left, and she seemed a forlorn hope with one torpedo and two bombs already in her.

Nor was the picture much brighter elsewhere. On the other side of Ford Island the target ship *Utah* took a heavy list to port as her engineering officer, Lieutenant Commander S. S. Isquith, pulled his khakis over his pajamas. The alarm bell clanged a few strokes and stopped; the men trooped below to take shelter from bombing. Isquith sensed the ship couldn't last, and he had the officer of the deck order all hands topside instead.

The men were amazingly cool—perhaps because they were used to being "bombed" by the Army and Navy every day. When Machinist's Mate David Gilmartin reached the main deck, he found the port rail already under water. Twice he crawled up toward the starboard side and slid back. As he did it a third time, he slid by another seaman who suggested he throw away the cigarettes. To Gilmartin's amazement he had been trying to climb up the slanting deck while holding a cartoon of cigarettes in one hand. Relieved of his handicap, he made the starboard rail easily.

As the list increased, the big six-by-twelve-inch timbers that covered the *Utah's* decks began breaking loose. These timbers were used to cushion the decks against practice bombing and undoubtedly helped fool the Japanese into thinking the ship was a carrier unexpectedly in port. Now they played another lethal role, sliding down on the men trying to climb up.

As she rolled still further, Commander Isquith made a last check below to find anyone who might still be trapped—and almost got trapped himself. He managed to reach the captain's cabin where a door led to the forecastle deck. The timbers had jammed the door; so he stumbled into the captain's bedroom where he knew there was a porthole. It was now almost directly overhead, but he managed to reach it by climbing on the captain's bed. As he popped his head through the porthole, the bed broke loose and slid out from under him. He fell back, but the radio officer, Lieutenant Commander L. Winser, grabbed his hand just in time and pulled him through. As Isquith got to his feet, he slipped and bumped down the side of the ship into the water. Half dead with exhaustion, harassed by strafers, he was helped by his crew to Ford Island.

Others never left the ship—Fireman John Vaessen in the dynamo room, who kept the power up to the end; Chief Watertender Peter Tomich in the boiler room, who stayed behind to make sure his men got out; Lieutenant (j.g.) John Black, the assistant engineer, who jammed his foot in his cabin door; Mess Attendant Smith, who was always so afraid of the water.

Of the other ships on this side of Ford Island, the *Tangier* and *Detroit* were still untouched, but the *Raleigh* sagged heavily to port. Water swirled into No. 1 and 2 firerooms, flooded the forward engine room, contaminated the fuel oil, knocked out her power. In the struggle to keep her afloat, no one even had time to dress. As though they went around that way every day, Captain Simons sported his blue pajamas . . . Ensign John Beardall worked the port antiaircraft guns in red pajamas . . . others toiled in a weird assortment of skivvies, *aloha* shirts, and bathing trunks. Somehow they didn't seem even odd: as Signalman Jack Foeppel watched Captain Simons in the admiral's wing on the bridge, he only marveled that any man could be so calm.

Ford Island, where all these ships were moored, was itself in chaos. Japanese strafers were now working the place over, and most of the men were trying to make themselves as small as possible. Storekeeper Jack Rogovsky crouched under a mess hall table nibbling raisins. The men in the air photo laboratory dived under the steel developing tables. Some of the flight crews plunged into an eight-foot ditch that was being dug for gas lines along the edge of the runway. This is where Ordnanceman Quisdorf's unit was hiding when he and another airman arrived in the squadron truck. But they didn't know that— they thought they had been left behind in a general retreat. They decided their only hope was to find a pair of rifles, swim the north channel, and hole up in the hills until liberation.

Nor was there much room for optimism in the Navy Yard. On the ships at the finger piers, the stern gunners had a perfect shot at the torpedo planes gliding down Southeast Loch, but most of them had little to shoot with. The *San Francisco* was being overhauled; all her guns were in the shops; most of her large ammunition was on shore. The repair ship *Rigel* was in the same fix. The *St. Louis* was on "limited availability" while radar was being installed; her topside was littered with scaffolding and cable reels; three of her four five-inch anti-aircraft guns were dismantled.

The little *Sacramento* had just come out of drydock, and in line with drydock regulations most of her ammunition lockers had been emptied. The *Swan* plugged away with her two three-inch guns, but a new gun earmarked for her top deck was still missing. A pharmacist's mate stood on the empty emplacement, cursing helplessly. The other ships were having less trouble . . .

On all these ships the men had more time for reflection than their mates along Battleship Row. On the *New Orleans* the ship's gambler and "big operator" sat at his station, reading the New Testament. (Later he canceled his debts and loans; threw away his dice.) A young engineer on the *San Francisco*—with nothing to do because her boilers were dismantled—appeared topside, wistfully told Ensign John E. Parrott, "Thought I'd come up and die with you." Machinist's Mate Henry Johnson on the *Rigel* remarked that now he knew how a rabbit felt and he'd never hunt one again. A few minutes later he lay mortally wounded on the deck.

Their very helplessness turned many of the men from fear to fury. Commander Duncan Curry, strictly an old Navy type, stood on the bridge of the *Ramapo* firing a .45 pistol as the tears streamed down his face. On the *New Orleans* a veteran master at arms fired away with another .45, daring them to come back and fight. A man stood near the sub base, banging away with a double-barreled shotgun.

A young Marine on 1010 dock used his rifle on the planes, while a Japanese-American boy about seven years old lit a cigarette for him. The butt of his old cigarette was burning his lips, but he never even noticed it. As he fired away, he remarked aloud, "If my mother could see me now."

Ten-ten dock itself was a mess, littered with debris from the *Helena* and *Oglala* alongside. In the after engine room of the torpedoed *Helena,* Chief Machinist's Mate Paul Weisenberger fought to check the water that poured aft through the ship's drain system. The hit had also set off the ship's gas alarm; its steady blast added to the uproar. Marine Second Lieuenant Bernard Kelly struggled to get ammunition to the guns. In keeping a steady supply flowing, it was a tossup whether he had more trouble with the damage or with conscientious damage control men, who kept shutting the doors.

Topside was a shambles. The *Helena's* forecastle, which had been rigged for church, looked as if a cyclone had passed. The *Oglala,* to starboard, listed heavily; her signal flags dropped over the *Helena's* bridge. Across the channel, Battleship Row was a mass of flames and smoke. Above the whole scene, a beautiful rainbow arched over Ford Island.

Just below 1010 dock, the *Pennsylvania* and destroyers *Cassin* and *Downes* sat ominously unmolested in Drydock No. 1. Likewise the destroyer *Shaw* in the floating drydock, which was a few hundred yards to the west. Aboard the *Pennsylvania* the men waited tensely. Lieutenant Commander James Craig, the ship's first lieutenant, checked here and there, making sure they would be ready when the blow came—or at least as ready as a ship out of water could be. He told Boatswain's Mate Robert Jones and his damage control party to lie face down on the deck. He warned them that their work was cut out, and to be prepared for the worst . . .

It was much the same on the ships anchored in the harbor. Radioman Leonard Stagich sat by his set on the destroyer *Montgomery* writing prayers on a little pad. In the transmitter room of the aircraft tender *Curtiss,* Radioman James Raines sat with three other men listening to the steady booming outside. No orders, so they just waited. With the doors and portholes dogged down and the ventilators off, it grew hotter and hotter. They removed their shirts and took turns wearing the heavy headphones. Still no orders. They kept moving about the room, squatting in different places, always wondering what was going on outside. From time to time the PA system squawked meaningless commands to others on the ship, which only made them wonder more. Still no orders.

But the most exasperating thing to those at anchor was just sitting there. It took time to build up enough steam to move—an hour for a destroyer, two hours for a larger ship. Meanwhile, they could only fire their guns manually, dodge the strafers, and watch (to use their favorite phrase) "all hell break loose."

The destroyer *Monaghan* had a slight edge on the others. As the ready-duty destroyer, her fires were already lit; and then of course she had been getting up steam since 7:50 to go out and contact the *Ward*. Commander Bill Burford would be able to take her out in a few minutes now, but at a time like this, that seemed forever.

At the moment the destroyer *Helm* was still the only ship under way. Twenty minutes had passed since Quartermaster Frank Handler genially waved at that aviator flying low up the channel. After the first explosion Commander Carroll quickly sounded general quarters . . . swung her around from West Loch . . . caught Admiral Furlong's sortie signal . . . and was now ready to get up and go. Turning to Handler, he said, "Take her out. I'll direct the battery."

Handler had never taken the ship out alone. The channel was tricky—speed limit 14 knots—and the job was always left to the most experienced hands. He took the wheel and rang the engine room to step her up to 400 rpm. The engine room queried the order and he repeated it. The ship leaped forward and raced down the channel at 27 knots. To complicate matters, there wasn't a single compass on board; everything had to be done by seaman eye. But Handler had one break in his favor—the torpedo net was still wide open. So the *Helm* rushed on, proudly guided by a novice without a compass breaking every speed law in the book.

By this time Handler was game for anything; so he took it in his stride when at 8:17 he came face to face with a Japanese midget sub.

He saw it as the *Helm* burst out of the harbor entrance—first the periscope, then the conning tower. It lay about 1000 yards off the starboard bow, bouncing up and down on the coral near the buoys. The *Helm* guns roared, but somehow they never could hit the sub. Finally it slid off the coral and disappeared. The *Helm* flashed the news to headquarters: "Small Jap sub trying to penetrate channel."

Signal flags fluttered up all over Pearl Harbor, telling the ships of the fleet. From the bridge of the burning *West Virginia,* Ensign Delano read the warning and sighed to himself, "Oh, my God—that too!"

~~~~~~

SIMULTANEOUSLY WITH THE STRIKE ON HAWAII, JAPAN attacked the Philippines, Guam, Wake, Hong Kong, Thailand, ranging as far east as Kota Bharu in British Malaya in a perimeter of seemingly half the world; and in that area her naval might was bolstered by convoys in which tens of thousands of battle-hardened veterans of the China campaigns longed to storm ashore and assert the Emperor's will for a greater "Co-Prosperity Sphere." One objective of these troops was Guam in the Marianas, one of our tiniest advanced bases in the Pacific, which had been principally used by the United States Navy for forty-two years as a communications center. The entire island garrison was composed of 30 naval officers, seven Marine officers, five naval nurses, six warrant officers and 246 members of the Insular police—a less than minuscule force which was promptly overwhelmed in a few hours.

Next on the enemy's timetable for conquest came Wake Island. Strategically important to Japan because it was only 620 miles from Roi and Namur Islands in the Marshalls, and as such could be used as a weapon against them, the capture of Wake Island was undertaken December 8 with a preinvasion air strike by the enemy's Fourth Fleet. While this raid destroyed many of the island's facilities and killed several civilians, it did nothing to dampen the garrison's ardor for a fight. The raid was followed up three nights later by the arrival of three light cruisers and several destroyer transports, lifting 450 special naval landing troops and a small number of regular garrison troops. However, accurate Marine gunfire drove off the flagship, light cruiser *Yubari.* Closing to within 6000 yards of the beach, she twice sustained hits. Other Marine batteries, meanwhile, worked on the destroyer transports with similar results, and the Japanese deferred their landings. The Marine commander, Major Devereux, and his opposite number, Commander Cunningham, were elated.

In Pearl Harbor at this time, a Wake Island relief expedition was formed under the command of Rear Admiral Frank Jack Fletcher—some cruisers and destroyers screening the aircraft carrier *Saratoga*. These departed December 16 and promptly ran into heavy weather; moreover, Fletcher's destroyers were badly in need of fuel; in a ten-hour period only three of his tin cans had fueled, and heavy seas had parted several fueling hoses. Whatever the reason, Fletcher decided to abandon the expedition.

Wake Island was left to fend for itself with a superb Marine fighter squadron and a handful of guns.

On December 23, the Japanese returned, and in force. Rear Admiral Kajioka aboard the flagship, now repaired, came with two other light and four heavy cruisers, plus destroyers, for gunfire support. In the interim, the enemy was sending over devastating bomber strikes from Kwajelein in the Marshalls, and the attrition in men and planes had all but exhausted Wake's capacity to fight on.

By 2:34 A.M., December 23, Kajioka was ready. His force effected four simultaneous landings with more than 1000 troops. The enemy swarmed ashore and fanned out.

Within the hour Japanese troops had captured the hospital and the remains of the airfield; then an air attack began which coincided with a concerted bombardment by the naval units.

The key events of the island's capture are told by Winfield Scott Cunningham and his collaborator, Lydel Sims. Many of the notes which served to refresh Cunningham's memory were jotted down later, while in a Japanese prisoner-of-war camp.

REAR ADM. W. SCOTT CUNNINGHAM

WITH LYDEL SIMS

4.

WAKE ISLAND SURRENDERS

The invaders grounded two destroyer transports off the south shore of Wake and sent troops ashore from both. Two barges unloaded onto the beach at Wilkes. Two other landing craft put men ashore on Wake just east of the channel entrance. Other troops, as best can be determined, landed on Wake's inner shore from rubber boats that entered the shallow lagoon from the northwest.

As these landings began, the bulk of the active defense on Wake fell to mobile forces comprised of Marines, sailors and civilians, for a major portion of the defense battalion's strength was immobilized at the three-inch and five-inch guns. The area from Camp One eastward toward the airstrip was defended by Lieutenant Poindexter and the defense battalion's mobile reserve, augmented by Boatswain's Mate Barnes and fifteen sailors, and a considerable number of civilians. Each end of the airstrip was guarded by machine-gun crews. Near the airstrip's western end, Lieutenant Kliewer of the fighter squadron took a stand with three others at the generator which was wired to set off the mines along the strip. The three-inch gun on the beach south of the airstrip was manned by Lieutenant Hanna and another Marine and three civilians. A defensive line was formed around the gun by Major Putnam, other surviving members of the fighter squadron, and a dozen civilians.

These were the hot spots on Wake as the fighting began.

Hanna and his crew at the three-inch gun poured fifteen rounds into one of the destroyer transports within minutes after it was grounded, and then began firing at the other, but the invasion troops were already swarming ashore. As they advanced on the gun position, Putnam's little defense line fought back, giving ground stubbornly until at last it formed virtually a circle around the gun. Some Japanese remained to contest the position while others proceeded past the pocket and into the brush.

At Camp One, landing craft approaching the channel were fired on by machine guns. When they grounded on the reef offshore, Poindexter, Barnes and others began throwing hand grenades. Barnes scored one direct hit just as the troops began to disembark, but it was not enough to stop them. They began to pour ashore as the Camp One defenders grouped and fought back.

Devereux had done his best to maintain contact with his units, but it was fast becoming impossible. Within half an hour after the first landing, telephone communication had been lost with Camp One, Lieutenant Hanna and the defensive line under Major Putnam, and Battery A to Peacock Point. And reports from Wilkes were becoming more and more fragmentary. We knew only that a considerable force had landed there and was being resisted. Later, contact was lost altogether.

From Peale, the only area where no landings had been made, Lieutenant Kessler reported by telephone that he could use one of his five-inch guns on a destroyer off Wake. I told him to go ahead. I also authorized Captain Godbold to send some of his men down to join the fighting. It could have been a mistake if troops were about to land there too, but we had a real crisis on Wake that took precedence over a possible one on Peale. Accordingly, a truckload of men under Corporal Leon Graves came roaring down the north-south road and were directed to go in support of Major Putnam's group. But in the confusion they never made it; eventually they wound up in a defensive line set up at Major Devereux's command post.

In the midst of everything else, a ludicrous problem arose for me to deal with. A civilian cook came boiling into my command post, drunk as a lord from that evil concoction known as "swipes" about which I had been warned before the war began. He wanted to go out and tackle the Japs single-handed. It was quite a while before we could get him quietly disposed of.

Meanwhile the enemy was moving deeper into the island from its beachheads, and beginning to spread out through the brush. Lewis's

Battery E, inside the head of the wishbone, had been firing in answer to the steady shelling we were receiving from the cruisers offshore; now his position came under fire from invasion troops. And down at the point of the wishbone, motar fire began to fall on the five-inch gun positions of Lieutenant Barninger's Battery A.

At the machine-gun setup on the eastern end of the airstrip, Corporal Winford J. McAnally was in command of a force of six Marines and three civilians. An hour before dawn he reported the enemy was beginning to attack strongly up the north-south road—evidence either that the invasion of our south shore had been successful or that the Japs were landing at yet another spot.

By now I knew beyond doubt that the enemy had landed at three places and perhaps more. As yet no planes had arrived, but we could expect them by dawn. The offshore shelling continued without letup.

Admiral Pye had asked me to keep him informed. I decided it was time to do so. At five o'clock I messaged:

Enemy on island. Issue in doubt.

This message, interpreted as a final gesture of defiance, was to provoke great comment back in America when it appeared in the accounts of Wake's defense, but as a matter of fact no bravado was intended. At the moment I began to write the dispatch, a phrase I had read sixteen years before came into my mind. It was from Anatole France's *Revolt of the Angels*. He was describing the assault made upon the heavenly ramparts by the legions of Satan. "For three days," he wrote, "the issue was in doubt."

Why I should have recalled those words at such a time I do not know, but they seemed appropriate and even hopeful. In France's story, the victory had gone to the side of the angels. And while I knew we were outnumbered and outgunned, I was still unable even to consider the prospect of defeat. It would be more than an hour before the notion actually sank into my mind that we might not, somehow, make out.

In one sector our forces were indeed making out, and would shortly do far better than that. That was on Wilkes.

A force of one hundred Japanese had landed there to wipe out the defenders—Captain Platt, with seventy Marines and a number of sailors and civilians. The enemy had captured Gunner McKinstry's three-inch gun emplacements but had been blocked from expanding their beachhead. Even as I sent my dispatch, Captain Platt was reorganizing his forces for a counterattack that, before seven o'clock, would virtually wipe out the invaders, killing at least 94 and ending all immediate threat to Wilkes.

It was a substantial setback to the enemy, but I did not know of it until after the surrender. Among the various reports I received was one at dawn that Wilkes had fallen.

This word came from observers on Peale, who were about a mile away from Wilkes across the lagoon. When daylight came they could see Japanese flags displayed at many places on Wilkes, and concluded that the islet had capitulated. As I had no reason to question the report, the assumed loss of Wilkes was one of the considerations I had to take into account in sizing up the situation.

But brilliantly as Wesley Platt had conducted his operation, still Wilkes was only a small fraction of the total defense, and even the truth about conditions there could not have altered the final outcome. On the big islet, Wake, were concentrated most of the defenses and the defenders, and on Wake the situation was steadily deteriorating. Each group of defenders was pinned down while the enemy enjoyed wide freedom of movement.

As the build-up of enemy strength increased the pressure northward, chiefly against the machine-gun position held by Corporal Mc-Anally, Devereux ordered Major Potter to set up a final defensive line south of his command post. But the unrelenting pressure continued. And as dawn came, the carrier-based planes swarmed over us like angry hornets.

Devereux and I had been in regular contact throughout the battle, and each time he reported to me he described the situation in darker terms. My own word to him that no relief could be expected made the picture even worse. At 6:30, when it appeared that his was the only position not yet overwhelmed, he reported enemy pressure there was getting heavy and gave the opinion that he would not be able to hold out much longer.

I knew the time had come to consider the question that only a few hours ago had been unthinkable. Accordingly, I asked for his opinion. Would I be justified in surrendering, in order to prevent further and useless loss of life?

Devereux evaded a direct answer. He said he felt the decision was solely up to the commanding officer. I was well aware of that, of course, but I was not willing to act without reviewing the situation as fully as possible.

We talked a while longer. He asked if I knew that Wilkes had fallen. I said that I did. At last I took a deep breath and told him if he felt he could hold out no longer, I authorized him to surrender.

I hung up the phone and sent a final dispatch to the Commander in Chief, reporting two destroyers grounded on the beach and the enemy fleet moving in. Then I had all codes, ciphers and secret orders destroyed, and ordered the communicators to haul down our transmitter antenna. It would be too easy for the Japanese dive bombers to spot. Besides, I had no more messages to send.

Devereux called me again about 7:30 and asked whether I had reached the Japanese commander by radio. I told him I had not. He repeated his statement that he could not hold out much longer, and I repeated mine that he was authorized to surrender. He said he was not sure of his ability to contact the enemy, and asked me to try. I promised to see what I could do.

But before I could do anything, it was all over. Devereux rigged a white flag, left his command post, and moved south down the road toward the enemy, giving our troops the cease-fire order as he reached them. I became aware that the surrender had begun when someone reported that bed sheets could be seen flying above the civilian hospital near Devereux's command post.

I looked around me at the men in my command post and could think of nothing to say. In a sort of daze I walked out of the unfinished magazine, tossed my .45 pistol into a nearby latrine, got into my truck, and drove away.

I went, not south to the enemy, but north to the cottage I had occupied in the early days of the defense. It was battered and badly damaged but, moving mechanically through the debris, I took off the dirty old khakis I had been living in night and day, shaved and washed my face, and put on a clean blue uniform. Then I got back into the truck, drove down the road, and surrendered.

~~~~~~

IN THE PHILIPPINES, AS AT PEARL HARBOR AND WAKE, the enemy's strategy was to destroy United States air power first. To this end, the enemy ignored Cavite Navy Yard upon the opening of hostilities and concentrated instead on General MacArthur's Far Eastern Air Force, while at the same time marshalling his troops for a multi-pronged amphibious invasion whose objective was the capture of Manila. On the first day, a strong force of Japanese fighter planes and medium bombers attacked Clark and the neighboring Army air fields. Forty seven American bombers and fighters were lost as against seven enemy planes. At noon on December 10, the Japanese attacked again in the Manila area, and although a few P-35's and P-40's roared off to engage them, the remnants of MacArthur's Air Force were promptly overwhelmed. The airfields north of Cavite— Iba, Nielson, and Nichols—were reduced to rubble, and almost immediately afterwards, Cavite Navy Yard received the full attention of the Japanese squadrons.

The story of this costly attack (some 1500 Philippine lives were lost in the Navy Yard alone) is recounted by the distinguished author, W. L. White. Uniquely, it is told through the eyes of PT men who fought in the initial Philippine battle. The first to speak is Lieutenant Robert B. Kelly; then Lieutenant John D. Bulkeley, winner of the Congressional Medal of Honor.

5.

THE PHILIPPINE

EXPENDABLES

"The big alarm came at noon on December 10—we'd pulled up along-side a mine sweeper for water when word came that a large flight of Jap planes was headed toward the Manila area, coming from the direction of Formosa. We pulled away from the tender, out into open water, and fifteen minutes later we saw them—several formations —I counted about twenty-seven to twenty-nine planes in each—two-motor bombers—lovely, tight, parade-ground formations, coming over at about 25,000 feet. But, I thought, when our fighters get up there and start rumpling their hair, those formations won't look so pretty. Only where were our fighters?

"The Japs passed on out of sight over the mountains, and then we began hearing the rumble of bombs—only first we felt the vibrations on our feet, even out there in the water, and we knew something was catching hell. But what? Manila? Maybe Nichols Field? Or even Cavite, our own base? We couldn't know."

"I did," said Bulkeley laconically. "I was there, at Cavite. The Admiral sent us a two-hour warning that they were coming—from Formosa, and headed on down in our direction across Northern Luzon.

"So we hauled our boats out into the bay. They kept beautiful formations, all right. The first big V and fifty-four planes in it, and they came in at about 20,000, with their fighters on up above to

49

protect them from ours—only ours didn't show! We couldn't figure it.
First they swung over Manila and began to paste the harbor shipping.
It was a beautiful clear day, and I remember the sun made rainbows
on the waterspouts of their bombs. They were from a hundred and
fifty to two hundred feet high, and it made a mist screen so dense you
could hardly tell what was happening to the ships. It turned out
nothing much was—they only hit a few.

"But then that big beautiful V pivoted slowly and moved over
Cavite—began circling it like a flock of well-disciplined buzzards.

"They were too high to see the bomb bay doors open, but we could
see the stuff drop slowly, picking up speed; only as we watched we
found we had troubles of our own. Because five little dive bombers
peeled off that formation, one by one, and started straight down for
us. When they were down to about fifteen hundred feet, they leveled
off and began unloading. Of course we gave our boats full throttle
and began circling and twisting, both to dodge the bombs and to get a
shot at them. Our gunners loved it—it was their first crack at the
Japs. I remember Chalker's face; he's a machinist's mate from Tex-
arkana—a shootin' Texas boy. He was pouring 50-caliber slugs up at
them, cooler than a pail of cracked ice, but that long, straight,
pointed jaw of his was set. Houlihan, who was firing the other pair of
50's, was the same. They'd picked put one plane and were pouring it
up into the sky, when we saw the plane wobble, and pretty soon she
took off down the bay, weaving unsteadily, smoking, and all at once,
two or three miles away, she just wobbled down into the drink with
a big splash. So we know the 35 boat got one. Meanwhile the 31 boat
had shot down two more. After that the planes didn't bother strafing
the MTB's. Guess the Jap pilots back at their Formosa base passed
the word around.

"It certainly surprised our navy too, which had never guessed a
torpedo boat could bring down an airplane. Later on I got a kidding
message from Captain Ray, chief of staff:

Dear Buck: I really think your gang is getting too tough. The
latest report is that "three dive bombers were seen being chased
over Mariveles Mountain by an MTB." Don't you think this is
carrying the war a bit too far?

"About 3:30 the Japs left, so we went on back in to Cavite to see
what had happened. They'd flattened it—there isn't any other word.
Here was the only American naval base in the Orient beyond Pearl

Harbor pounded into bloody rubbish. We didn't have time then to think about where our American planes could have been, because the place was a shambles, and we began loading in the wounded to take them to Canacao hospital. The first boatload was all white Americans except one Negro—from a merchant marine boat—with a compound fracture—his shoulder bone was sticking out and it looked brick-red against his black skin. We put a tourniquet on him and never once did he whimper—a very brave guy. There was half an inch of blood on the landing platform at Canacao—we could hardly keep on our feet, for blood is as slippery as crude oil—and the aprons of the hospital attendants were so blood-spattered they looked like butchers.

"We went back to Cavite and offered to carry more wounded. The big base was one sheet of flame except for the ammunition depot. Only a piece of the dock was left, and through the shimmering flames you could see only jagged walls. Then we saw Admiral Rockwell—he was directing the fire apparatus which was trying to save the depot. He is a tall man, a fine figure of a sailor, but his head was down that day. In a dead voice he told us we'd better get out—that the magazine was liable to go up any minute. We offered to take him with us to Mariveles, but he said no, his job was here, to do what he could to save the magazines.

"So we picked up from the gutters and streets a lot of cans of food we knew we would need—they were from the bombed warehouses—stacked them in the boat, and set out."

"The weirdest thing I saw there," said Ensign Akers, "was a native woman—every stitch of clothing blown off by a bomb, running around screaming, completely berserk. But you could see she wasn't wounded, and so everybody was too busy to catch her and calm her down. How she got there no one knew or even asked."

"I was back there a couple of days later after the fires were out," said Ensign Cox, a goodlooking yellow-haired youngster from upstate New York. "They were burying the dead—which consisted of collecting heads and arms and legs and putting them into the nearest bomb crater and shoveling debris over it. The smell was terrible. The Filipino yard workers didn't have much stomach for the job, but it had to be done and done quickly because of disease. To make them work, they filled the Filipinos up with grain alcohol. The weirdest thing of all was that the week before I'd bought a bike, and the night before the raid I'd left it locked against a wall. Just for curiosity, I went over to where it had been and there it still was—beside the wall, which was only a jagged ruin, and yet its paint wasn't even scratched. I unlocked it and rode all over the yard, watching those staggering Filipinos, maybe dragging a trunk toward a crater, pulling it by its one remaining leg, or else maybe rolling a head along like over a putting green. The Japs must have killed at least a thousand. Mostly dock workers—they caught them right at dinner hour."

"That raid gave me my first big shock of the war," said Lieutenant Kelly, "but it wasn't the damage they did. From over in Mariveles I couldn't see what was happening after the Jap bombers disappeared over the mountain. I got my shock after they had unloaded and flew over us on their way home—the same beautiful tight formations—not a straggler. Where was our air force? What could it mean? Didn't we have about one hundred and fifty planes—most of them fighters? Were our guys yellow? Or had somebody gone nuts and told them not to take off—let the Japs get away with this? It made you sick to think about it.

"From over towards Cavite we could now see that huge column of smoke rising into the sky as the Japs left the scene.

"But it wasn't until Lieutenant DeLong dropped in at four o'clock in the 41 boat that I knew how bad off we were. He said the Cavite base was a roaring blast furnace—the yard littered with those mangled and scorched bodies—and furthermore that all our spare parts for the MTB's—engines and everything—had been blasted to bits. Machine shops completely gone. Not so much as a gasket left to see us through this war, with the factory halfway around the world.

"Also he said Cavite radio had been hit. That still left the short-wave voice stuff to talk with Manila or Bataan or the Rock, but of course this couldn't be secret from the Japs, so they would be depending on our six boats for courier duty to relay all confidential stuff."

"So I wasn't surprised," said Bulkeley, "when early the next morning I got a hurry call to report to the Admiral in Manila. As our 34 boat cleared the mine fields around Bataan, looking over toward Manila I saw something very queer—shipping of all descriptions was pouring out of that Manila breakwater into the open harbor—destroyers, mine sweepers, Yangtze River gunboats, tramp steamers, all going hell for breakfast. And then I saw them—a big formation of about twenty-seven bombers. By then I was beginning to learn that if we saw planes in the air, they would be Japs, not ours. Then came another formation of twenty-nine, and still another of twenty-six.

"If they were after shipping, we shouldn't get too close to the other boats, so I changed course. They wheeled majestically around the bay's perimeter, and each time they passed Manila a load would go whistling down and presently huge columns of black and white smoke began rising—we could even see some fires, although we were still eleven miles away.

" 'Where in hell is our air force?' our crew kept asking me. 'Why in Christ's name don't they do something?'

"But the thing that really got me was that these big Jap formations, circling the bay like it was a parade maneuver, each time would sail impudently right over Corregidor! Didn't they know we had anti-aircraft guns?

"They knew all right, but it turned out they knew something I didn't. For presently all twenty of Corregidor's 3-inchers opened fire, and it made me sick to see that every one of their shells was bursting from 5,000 to 10,000 feet below that Jap formation. Those pilots were as safe as though they'd been home in bed. Later I found out what the Japs apparently already knew—that the Rock's anti-aircraft guns didn't have the range. And only then did it begin to dawn on me how completely impotent we were.

"When the Japs cleared out," continued Bulkeley, "Kelly and I headed for Manila and docked about three o'clock. When we reported, Commander Slocum told me the Admiral was considering sending our three boats on a raid off Lingayen, and were we ready? We said we were rarin' to go. So he said to stick around a couple of hours, and meanwhile to load the boats with files, records, and so forth, because they were moving headquarters. It had escaped so far, but right here on the water front it was too vulnerable—sure to get smacked. Through the open door we could see the Admiral conferring with his chief of staff and half a dozen other high officers. On the wall was a chart of the waters off Luzon, and on it black pins which represented Jap boats.

"But just then," said Kelly, "Commander Slocum looked down at my arm, which was in a sling, frowned, and said I should get over to see the fleet doctor. The doctor took off the bandage and began to talk tough. Said he couldn't do anything, and that I was to get that arm to a hospital as fast as I could.

"I was dead set on that raid, but I decided it wouldn't be tactful to bring that up, so I said, 'Aye, aye, sir,' and skipped it. We loaded the boat with records, and then went back to headquarters, where we were told that the Jap convoy off Lingayen included eight transports and at least two battleships . . . but that we weren't going to be sent. They were saving us for 'bigger things.'

" 'My God!' my junior officer said later, 'I didn't know they came any bigger! What do they think we are?'

"Anyway the Admiral patted Bulkeley on the shoulder and said, 'We know you boys want to get in there and fight, but there's no sense sending you on suicidal missions—just now.'

"So that was that, and we went on out across the bay, to our thatched village."*

~~~~~~

DISASTER AFTER DISASTER FOLLOWED IN DECEMBER. On the 10th, the eve of the invasion of Singapore, the Allies were dealt a stunning blow when one hundred land-based Japanese aircraft sank the Royal Navy's battleship *Prince of Wales* and the battle cruiser *Repulse,* causing heavy loss of life. Not only did this feat grievously damage Allied morale in the Orient, but also it was accomplished on the open sea in which capital ships had never before been successfully attacked.

However, there was one small exception to the long string of catastrophes that month: *Drayton,* a Mahan-class destroyer of 1450 tons, made history with the first verified sinking of a Japanese warship in the war. Under the command of Lieutenant Commander Laurence A. Abercrombie, the "Blue Beetle"—so named because of her bluish experimental color—was on escort duty with a convoy to Palmyra on the afternoon of December 24 when Fate decreed a meeting with a full-sized submarine. Abercrombie received the Navy Cross, one of three he gathered during the war.

Collaborator Fletcher Pratt, author of many books on naval warfare, was the military expert for the *New York Post.*

---

* Sisiman Bay, a little cove east of Mariveles Harbor

6.

SCRATCH ONE!

. . . It was only a four-ship convoy, a job lot consisting of a couple of the old four-pipers converted to fast supply ships and an ex-surveying ship for Palmyra, with one of those little interisland steamers for Christmas, carrying some army engineers and material for a landing strip. We were all the escort they had, and we had the only sound-gear in the convoy, which threw a good deal of a burden on Ferrell, my first-class soundman.

He was a kid, only nineteen, with a round, boyish face, owing money in quarter and half-dollar bits to everyone aboard, completely irresponsible. Not, as you might think, a lad who made these small touches to beer ashore. He never drank anything, but he liked to have a good time in a shooting gallery or on a roller coaster and forgot to pay up when he got back to the ship, just as he always forgot what time it was and overstayed his liberty. I'd give him extra duty when that happened and didn't feel any compunction about it, because he had one of the keenest pair of ears I ever saw growing out of a human head.

He was on duty at 1440 on the day before Christmas, when our convoy was just a little south of the islands. It was a good thing we had him there too. He came rushing out of his box to the bridge.

"Captain, do you see anything on the port bow, bearing 120 true?" he demanded excitedly.

I picked up my binoculars. "Not a thing."

"Well, sir, it must be a sub then, 'cause I have a good sound contact."

I turned to the officer of the deck, who happened to be Ensign Simmons, a former cadet from the Merchant Marine who was our sound officer. "Send all hands to battle stations."

Dutch Kriner sent an emergency submarine-contact signal to the convoy. They snapped smoke from their funnels and bore out sharp to starboard at their best speed, which was about 10 knots for the interisland steamer, as the sirens shrieked all over the ship. Of course we had to have one of those incidents that showed how much we were still amateurs in war. Just as Bing Mitchell reported all stations manned and ready, someone below got excited and pulled the sound-gear switch. Ferrell's instrument went dead.

"Contact lost!" he shouted through the door.

"Just another big fish," said Mitchell, but before he had finished saying it they got the switch closed again and Ferrell yelled.

"Contact regained, Zero-thirty true, range about 500 yards."

This was close quarters. "She's inside our turning circle," said Bing.

"Full right rudder," I ordered the helmsman; and to Ferrell, "Hold your contact!"

Maybe I did the wrong thing—some of those people who figure things out on the maneuvering board told me afterward that I did—but that sub was so close in on our left that we couldn't turn into its track, so I went around the other way, hoping to pick him up. It was a marvel that we made it, but with the help of Ferrell and some wonderful work by the helmsman we did.

"Contact good, sir," shouted Ferrell as I gave an order to steady her on a course north; then, "Contact closing rapidly."

It was a sub, all right—a fat, happy sub, running submerged merely because it was daylight, heading for Pearl, probably expecting nothing so little as to find American ships on the way.

"Range 400 yards." Simmons had his stop watch out.

"Stand by to attack with depth charges," I ordered. "All engines ahead full."

"Contact lost." Simmons punched his stop watch.

"Stand by to drop!" I said.

"Now," said Simmons, bringing down the arm he had lifted.

"Drop one!" I said, and as Shelly, the torpedo officer, repeated it, the chief torpedoman swung the lever. (We didn't have K-guns in those days, it was all from the racks.) "Drop two! Drop three!"

At that speed the shock of a depth charge makes you feel as though the whole world were being violently shaken from side to side, and down in the engine-room their feet go to sleep. A shout went up from the whole ship as I leaned around the signal rack to look at our wake. In the center of the boiling water where our depth charges had fallen, oil was welling to the surface with fragments of debris in the middle of it.

I shouted for the rudder to be put hard left, and we charged back into the slick, dropping three more depth charges. More oil came up; we swung out the sound gear, ranged again, and Ferrell shouted that he had picked her up, now turned and headed southwestward from the point where we had hit her. He was a wonder to do it with all that racket in the gear and well deserved the special letter of commendation from the Admiral that he got along with his promotion later.

Bing Mitchell said, "She'll probably go deep, Captain. Better give her a deep barrage."

The Commodore had rushed to the wing of the bridge with me, his nose lifted like a bird dog's to catch the odor of the slick as we ran through it. "Get a rag, get a rag," he was shouting. "Get me a line and some rag. We'll bring up a sample of that oil." He was the only one to remember that frequent reports of depth-charging submarines had come in before and that what looked like an oil slick was all too often merely debris from the depth charges themselves.

As we swung toward the slick for the third time, he lowered the rag triumphantly from his nose, not noticing that it was one of his best towels, picked up in the excitement. "Diesel, all right," he said, and we were over the slick again with Ferrell shouting, "Lost sound contact!"

Drop one, drop two, drop three again, and we came full left.

Before we had completed the turn I heard another shout: "Look, a submarine!" It was, too; the bow of an enormous submarine, fully 50 feet of it, pushing up through the water slowly at a steep 70-degree angle, dripping oil, the net cutter at the bow looking like a set of teeth and the diving planes at its side showing the characteristic Jap shape.

"Commence firing!" I yelled.

Nothing happened. Everybody simply stood there pop-eyed with a mouthful of teeth, looking at the monster as though it were a movie.

"Commence firing!" I shouted again, and then ran out into the wing of the bridge to yell at the top of my lungs to Dewey, the gunnery officer, "For God's sake, why don't you commence firing?"

I heard him yell in return to his talker but never heard what he said because at the same moment all the .50's seemed to open up at once. They went right in, stitching a row of holes along that bow, but I don't know whether they had any real share in it. Even as they were hitting her the sub tilted majestically to the vertical, then slid backward and down with gathering speed.

We completed our turn, rushed past the spot, and just for luck I dropped four more charges into it. Oil boiled out of that pit of sea, spreading and spreading till it covered a circle a mile in diameter, and from beneath it came the shock of an explosion, heavier and deeper than our own depth charges. The last barrage must have set off something within the sub itself.

The *Drayton* had sunk an enemy warship, one bigger than she was. That would have got us double prize money in the old days of the Navy when they were still paying prize money . . .

~~~~~~

DURING THE ENSUING TWO MONTHS, THE UNITED States Navy's position in the Pacific was essentially defensive: she reorganized her forces at command level while awaiting an opportunity to strike a blow, while numerous warships from the Atlantic steamed through the Panama Canal to bolster combatant strength. But the most significant changes at this time were the appointments, during the latter part of December, of Admirals Ernest J. King and Chester W. Nimitz as Chief of Naval Operations and Commander in Chief Pacific Fleet, respectively. Frequently described as "so tough he shaves with a blowtorch," King was a firm and uncompromising administrator and leader, whose first statement reflected his personal philosophy in unmistakable terms:

> The way to victory is long
> The going will be hard
> We will do the best we can with what we've got
> We must have more planes and ships—at once
> Then it will be our turn to strike
> We will win through—in time.

By contrast Nimitz, the kindly, soft-spoken Texan who restored confidence to the Pacific Fleet, was beloved by seamen and admirals alike; it was he who implemented King's policy. One of his first bold strokes, which went a long way to restore confidence, was the Marshalls operation of February 1. While it was not calculated to drive the enemy out of the Pacific, Nimitz knew perfectly well the effect such an offensive operation would have on our sagging national morale. The plan, which gave a delighted Halsey (on *Enterprise*) a free hand, was this:

Halsey was to deliver a strike and bombardment on Maloelap and Wotje, enemy seaplane bases in the eastern Marshalls; the big punch was to be a torpedo-bomber strike on the Japanese stronghold of Kwajalein. At the same time, Fletcher (on *Yorktown*) was assigned to carry out raids on Jaluit, Makin, and Mili to the southeast. Two bombardment groups were to work over Maloelap and Wotje from the sea. The raid, while not an unqualified success because of heavy mists which shrouded one objective, resulted in seven small enemy ships sunk and three others, including the light cruiser *Katori*, damaged. For our part (the American forces numbered two hundred warships), damage was sustained aboard the light cruiser *Chester* when the enemy sent over eight twin-engined bombers. A light bomb penetrated the main deck and killed eight men and wounded eleven.

Aboard one of the heavy cruisers, Rear Admiral Raymond A. Spruance's flagship, *Northampton*, was the gifted *Chicago Daily News* war correspondent Robert J. Casey, who chronicled the strike.

7.

FIRST BLOOD: A WAR CORRESPONDENT TELLS OF THE MARSHALLS RAID

February 1, *Sunday*. At sea. Mostly clear with occasional overcast. A beautiful day to die in.

At this writing we don't know where one of our cruisers is. She took a walloping from high-level bombers at Kwajalein atoll and got a direct hit on her well deck. The carrier is slightly damaged. She just threw one of her planes overboard after a strafing that made the afternoon one of anxiety and prayer. We have only one plane left in commission out of four. (We lost one in a landing accident this morning. The other two were shot up on deck by our own ack-ack in action.) We are now theoretically on our way back to Pearl Harbor but I alas have no faith in these offhand pronouncements by our guides and guardians. More than once today we looked at the bottom. We'll get to Pearl Harbor when we get there . . . when and if.

Here is the chronology of a day of battle—as weird a day as I have ever experienced in war.

Commander Chappell woke me at about half-past four. I had slept through the noise of the alarm clock and he said that he didn't want me to sleep through a battle. I went down to the wardroom and ate a hearty breakfast of ham and eggs (simulated). After that in a leisurely fashion I gathered up my life belt, gas mask, field glasses, ear plugs, paper and fountain pen. And I clambered up through the dark to the searchlight platform just above sky control on the foremast.

There with Bob Landry I watched the moon fight it out with a pale sun and eventually lose.

6 A.M. Moon full—yellow. For a moment a band of cloud slips over it like the belt of Saturn. But it remains brilliant, too brilliant. Aft, the planes begin to gurgle and roar.

6:15 A.M. Guns of after turrets are swung skyward. The planes get off one after another in quick and noisy sequence. They are gray blots against a gray sky with a ghastly blue halo of burning gases accompanying them.

6:40. The sun is struggling up through low-lying clouds. Eight seaplanes go off toward the west in ragged formation. Land is taking shape hazily like a narrow streamer of smoke on the starboard horizon.

6:45. Lookout sings out smoke coming from island dead ahead. This blackish cloud, round and rolling, is clearly visible in spite of hue of the dawn's early light.

6:59. We swing farther in toward land and turn loose forward guns in bombardment. We hear no commands. We see no unusual preparations but this is an historic moment. This is the first time in this war (save for some ack-ack at Pearl Harbor) that the Pacific fleet has fired on an enemy. The island is a typical atoll hardly visible save for the breakers along its coral reefs. Planes are on our starboard, low. Some anxiety until they are identified as our own. The carrier planes have gone home and for better or worse this show from now on is ours.

7:05. Lookout: "Ship dead ahead, sir!" And there it is! About halfway between us and the horizon. . . . A little thing like an ocean-going tug, which has come blithely out of the dawn to run squarely across the bows of a destroyer. A bit of irony. We increase speed to eighteen knots and turn slightly to starboard. The destroyer keeps on after the unfortunate tub—and starts firing. The sea around the Jap is tufted with white splashes. There are yellow-white glares from the Jap's deck—several of them—which from where I sit indicate that he has four guns and is using them.

7:10. The Jap turns parallel to our course. So does the destroyer. They exchange shots without result—several salvos knock down, drag out, toe to toe.

7:11. A destroyer is spotted on the horizon. The guns swivel and we lie back to blast. But it's one of our own coming back from a sub-hunt. There is some more to-do about a wandering plane that turns out to be an SBD returning to the carrier somewhere over the horizon.

7:12. A.A. flashed from the island. The _____, our associate cruiser, is throwing out salvos that burst with a green color. The coral beach is festooned with smoke plumes. The destroyer continues to fire. So does the Jap. This is an inspiring duel but it's beginning to look like a bad piece of gunnery.

7:16. Our eight-inch batteries go off and wreathe the ship and surrounding sea with a yellow acrid haze. We keep firing at half-minute intervals—following the lead of the _____. I was thrown flat on my face at the first blast and so far have been unable to get up any farther than my knees.

The light is getting better and we have a chance to view the fantasy of eight-inch guns painstakingly blowing a mangy, palm-dandruffed atoll to pieces. The great battle between the destroyer and the sea-going barge proceeds with noise and smoke and no end of dangerous-looking waterspouts. But the issue remains in doubt. I'm beginning to bet on the little guy.

7:26. The Jap is still up. . . . Seems likely to stay up indefinitely. We shift our fire. . . .

This atoll like so many of its kind in the Pacific is really a string of small islands about a lagoon, remnants possibly of coral erections on the rim of a volcanic crater. The entrance to the lagoon of Wotje is to the left of us as we look at the island but straight ahead of us the land dips abruptly into the sea, presenting an opening about a quarter of a mile wide through which we can see a large part of the lagoon.

And now, like something in a worn and hazy movie, an 8,000-ton freighter has steamed out from behind the island on the north of the opening and into plain view. There will be no better protection for her in back of the south island than she had when she started but in theory a moving target is harder to hit than a stationary one. . . . Our shells are smashing into the lagoon alongside her—two over, two short —a vicious bracket. Ack-ack begins to smash all around us. This is odd inasmuch as no planes are near us but there's no reason to suppose that a five-inch ack-ack shell won't bother us if it crashes into the bridge or sky control or, for that matter, almost anywhere else above the decks.

7:27. Somebody sights a submarine moving out of the lagoon toward the south passage. While we are assimilating that one the warning is passed to be on the alert for bombers inasmuch as near-by bases must now be aware of our attack. Everything seems to be happening at once—or on the verge of it.

7:28. Comes a terrific mixture of splashes about the Jap ship. You might take the bursts for bomb explosions but there are no planes above. Probably the destroyer crews are putting out something special in the way of quick fire. . . . We have completed our first run across the face of the island. We turn about with the other cruiser. The ship in the lagoon is still moving through a mist of spray and smoke. She appears to have been hit. The destroyer goes on with its interesting and interminable work.

7:32. The guns turn loose all at once with a brain-jolting slap and your diaphragm caves in. The yellow smoke bolts out the target for a moment. Then clears. The hiss of compressed air cleaning the gun tubes comes as an obbligato. This is an ideal day for a battle. But it has a stiff wind which we are now heading into. It's enough to blow your eyeballs out.

7:33. The struggle between the destroyer and the Jap spitkit comes to a quick end. The destroyer makes a hit on the starboard and disables two guns. Apparently the Jap commander has one gun left on the port side. He is listing badly but he swings slowly around as more clunks rain on him and churn up the sea. He fires one last erratic shot with his remaining gun. He sinks.

"Well," says the navigator, "if the Japs want to put up a monument to that little guy I'll contribute."

7:40. Firing is fairly regular on the atoll now but doesn't show many results. We can see now—as the day advances—two more ships just over the reef in the lagoon. The one we were shooting at first is behind the south island, up or down I can't say. One of the pair now visible seems to be turning around. The other begins to move southward across the open space. Apparently the crews of both ships were taken by surprise and they've been until now getting the engines started. There is something of Pearl Harbor in this in more ways than one.

7:41. Destroyer milling about scene of kill is far away on our horizon now. It has large bone in its teeth and seems to be on the way to rejoin us.

7:45. The sun hits Wotje's low profile and shows color of its straggly palms and moth-eaten verdure. It is like all other south-sea atolls—a top of delicate green, an outcrop of grayish coral and yellowish beach. Over the front of it spin shreds of black smoke.

7:55. Sky control announces two submarines coming out of the harbor. The ship which first began to move from the trap beyond the open reef now swings south to get protection of the south island. One salvo seems to bracket it—to "straddle" it as they say in the Navy. It leans over to starboard and seems about to capsize. But it recovers and steams on with green and blue plumes of bursting shell in its wake.

8:15. We are beginning to notice artillery resistance other than the five-inch ack-ack that has kept sprinkling us liberally. Perhaps they've been working unobserved in the dim light of the morning but at the moment we are in no doubt about their being here. A couple of them are tossing six-inch shells out here with no hint of economy. The sea between us and the island is tufted with them. And now and then, in the fashion of another and better war, they throw a bit of time-fuse shell at us for adjustment. Some of this probably was mixed up with the ack-ack. If so it wouldn't have been discoverable.

Our five-inch batteries have turned loose to strafe the beach. They are probably the noisiest contrivance ever invented by man. Their effort mixed with the sickening roar of the main battery produces a din that nears the limit of human endurance. Lots of odd things come out of the five-inch tubes along with the shell, including odd bits of ashes, and red fire balls.

8:16. The barrage on the ship remaining in sight in the lagoon has been steady—and terrible. Now comes a bracket so close that most of the superstructure is hidden by an upheaval of water like Old Faithful. The ship starts down by the head, shivers, leans over to starboard. . . . In a matter of seconds she is gone.

8:20. Firing ceases. Brass shell cases of the five-inch batteries are dumped overboard. In the lull you have time to note numerous fires along Wotje beach. We seem to be withdrawing. Our destroyer is far on the western horizon.

8:25. I guessed wrong. The clamor is on again worse than before. Almost immediately we see results. There is a burst of red flame and a tremendous black cloud rolls skyward. Oil, would be my guess, and a big tank of it. Lieutenant Jim Brewer in fire control announces that twelve torpedo planes and seven bombers have taken off from a Jap island—apparently one where our preliminary attack wasn't strong enough to hold them. The fire burns mostly black with darting spears of red in it. Another ship comes across the open space in the lagoon streaking for protection back of the north island.

8:30. Our fire has shifted to the north end of the atoll. It's not so spectacular now as the bursts go over the crest but we've been told that three or four naval auxiliaries are in there. Shells from the shore batteries are falling nearer—the last batch about 200 yards off the port side and square in deflection.

8:35. A group of four shells tosses white water to starboard. We're bracketed.

Our turrets are working faster but not on the land battery. Maybe we don't recognize it socially. Continuous concussion caves in your stomach. Five-inch guns firing into the sunlight throw off large golden rings of burning vapor that chokes you when it comes back. Cotton in your ears is small comfort now.

8:41. Another string of geysers ahead of us. The Jap battery is in no hurry but, boy! it's working well. The range is now perfect. Deflection which has to change as we move is not badly calculated. Over on the island four white plumes are rising—wooden buildings maybe.

8:35. A group of four shells tosses white water to starboard. We're closer to scraping our stern. From our platform we can see a widening circle of green—like an excrescence in a swamp—spreading out over the deep blue water. Our fantail cuts off the view of one side of the patch—which shows how close the shell came. . . . Apparently the bridge is going to do something about this. We can hear the telephone men relaying an order already sent over the engine room telegraph— left rudder. We swing about as on a pivot. The top rolls over until we are looking down into blue water. You'd think the whole thing would keep going right on over into the drink. But we come up with a jerk at right angles to our original course and right side up. Four shells, all in a pattern, fall astern and to port. So we've come out of the bracket.

8:50. Our guns fire from the stern. There is a crash from the flight deck. A muzzle burst in Gun No. 8 of the five-inch battery. The tube miraculously held together although it is bulged to a bottle shape, and nobody was hurt.

Shells begin to pile up on the end of the island where the land battery is flashing at us. We are doing a sort of cumbersome adagio dance, the sort of movement you might expect of an elephant in bayonet drill. . . . Our wake, a broad path of light blue with fringes of white on a stretch of calm cobalt, is a glittering corkscrew. . . . "The rolling English drunkard made the rolling English road. . . ."

8:52. Geysers around the cruiser ahead of us. . . . Apparently a second battery has been working on her. She shifts. A second salvo falls short of her. The Jap firing is accurate enough but the guns seem to be working at the limit of their range—there are few overs.

8:53. We let loose a fine salvo at a ship in the lagoon which seems already headed for the beach. I shall make a note of it, to paste in my hat for study if I ever have to go to a gunnery school again, or to consult when anybody says anything about the law of averages. . . . Five guns fired—the two forward turrets; two shells went over, two were short and very near and the fifth made an error of fifty mills to the right, smashed into the coral right at water level, hit a subterranean oil storage and started the biggest fire ever seen in the south Pacific. I pause for a reply. . . . The ship goes on toward the beach.

8:53. Another black fire starts from the previous column of smoke and north of it. Almost immediately two smaller blazes spring up to the north of that.

The air is filled with beautiful little white birds that come out from the land to look at us and go away again. In the sunlight they look like butterflies or flying fish.

It is a pleasure to report that we are now maneuvering well out of range of the shore batteries whose efforts continue to pockmark the ocean between here and the shore.

8:54. A third fire of first magnitude but with more red in its black plumes has burst out well toward the north end of the north island—far to the right of the other principal blazes. The smoke column is now hundreds of feet high and spreading out in a cloud toward the south over the atoll.

8:55. We plaster the land batteries with everything we've got—a smash that makes the ship lean back and slide sideways in the water—and turn about. The northernmost fire and the one we touched off in error in the middle of the island seem to have combined in one fine blaze. It is now erupting gray and black smoke with high bursts of red in it where hot gases belatedly ignite.

8:57. A lookout announces: "Plane approaching—bearing two-five-oh." Lieutenant Brewer, on the platform below this one, repeats it into the telephone. . . .

"Our plane!" bawls the lookout and Brewer repeats that. Then he puts down the telephone and signals for an orderly to inform the Marine battery—the pompom ack-ack outfit. "Our plane!" he calls. "Tell it to the Marines."

The island fire has all the characteristics of oil except for the gray mixture which may indicate explosives, I hope.

9:00. We draw away. We are now about ten miles off Wotje. Bursts are leaping up on the south end of the island. The destroyer is still in there firing incessantly. It probably went in close to finish off the ships inside the lagoon. We are headed mostly south. . . . A string of signals breaks out on our halyard, another string on the ———. It's my guess that the first phase of the show is over.

9:05. Here's a startling mystery. There was an odd noise—like a burst alongside amidships. A detail went to look into the matter but there's no answer to it unless the five-inch battery has had another muzzle burst.

9:10. The far-away atoll now seems to have no height. It is a long white-green streak on the horizon with flame running over it and smoke plumes like a couple of black waterspouts balanced on it. There are occasionally three distinct columns of smoke two black, one gray—all about three hundred feet high.

9:30. "Periscope dead astern!" Thus the lookout. Speed and twist! Speed and twist! The destroyers leap like flying fish. Thud go the depth charges.

9:35. "Periscope off port beam." Speed and twist! Speed and twist! The periscope couldn't be a half-filled five-inch shell casing, could it? Who can say? Speed and twist!

9:40. All planes returning. You can see the rendezvous far astern. Our destroyer seems to have finished its job and is coming up like a fox terrier with its tail in the air.

10:00. Planes overhead but only seven. Eight took off. We slow down to pick up planes. Four go to the other cruiser. So it's one of ours that's gone. Which?

10:10. The missing plane comes streaking in from the west. Cheers.

10:16. Last of the trio that came back first is taken aboard. So we learn that the late-comer is Davis who apparently is still flirting with a jinx. He circles about, heads down into the slick on the starboard side.

10:20. He's down . . . heads in. The signalman isn't very deft and Davis gets the signal to cut off too late. He slides too far and his engine conks. Before he can start again a wave throws him against the side of the ship. A wing crumples.

10:23. The plane is astern with Davis and his radio-man sitting on the wings of it. The floats are submerged.

10:24. So begins a ponderous maneuver to launch a powerboat. The key to the winch is missing. Find it. There's no plug for the bottom of the boat. Whittle one. Why doesn't someone start the winch? Why not?

10:25. The ship is moving about the plane in a narrowing circle.

The cockpits are under water now. The aviators have inflated their rubber boat and are preparing to get into it.

10:29. A destroyer goes by. The boat crew is still hopelessly fiddling with the gear. The destroyer seems to be awaiting a signal before going in to pick the lads up. In the meantime their situation is getting critical. There goes . . .

10:30. General Quarters with bells and bugle! Eight planes reported about fifteen minutes away and heading toward us. The can is left to do what can be done about picking up Davis.

10:42. Plane off port bow flying erratically.

10:43. Plane identified as a bird. . . . The captain says that the report of the approaching Japanese planes came from the carrier—which we ought to be picking up presently—and that fighter planes are being sent off to deal with the situation. All seems well and yet this would be the time to feel uncomfortable if we intended to.

10:44. Lookout sings out: "Plane approaching bearing two-two-oh!" We zigzag. The plane, if any, takes off somewhere. We see nothing of it.

10:45. The captain has received a report that the cruiser which left to attack another atoll was severely bombed for nearly an hour. She got one hit on the well deck which killed about eight men. She is now steaming back to the rendezvous at a speed which would indicate that she's not seriously damaged. She apparently stepped into something. The island she attacked was supposed to be without air defense. It had plenty.

10:55. "Two planes off port beam!" Invisible to me. After a while I could make one of them out. It seemed to be heading in the direction of Wotje whose smoke plumes are still visible above the horizon.

10:56. Lieutenant Brewer calls into telephone: "Find out how many or how few are going in or coming out."

10:58. He gets his answer—three fighters over the island. Very likely ours. The air of uneasiness is getting noticeable. Obviously we know that the Japs are on the prowl but with our planes up it's difficult to tell where they're prowling.

11:04. Ship on horizon. She's identified as our carrier. All this identification business is done by the lookouts. I can't see anything on the horizon at all except a wisp or two of smoke from Wotje.

11:15. Near-by planes identified as friendly. The carrier now looms up over the rim of the sea as we zigzag toward her. She looks as big as the *Queen Mary*.

11:20. The atoll is now completely out of sight but the smoke of the oil fires is still thickly visible sixty miles above the horizon. Two more warships are coming into sight near the carrier—also quantities of planes.

Report to the bridge from the carrier: Eight Jap planes managed to get off during the attack on Kwajalein—heavy bombers. They followed our bombers back to the carrier. Carrier fighters got four of them.

11:25. The carrier swings northeast. So do we. We are still at general quarters.

11:58. Secure from general quarters. A tired, dirty mob troops down the iron ladders. Details start out to clean up the ship, to put electric-light globes back in their sockets and to take mirrors and other flat glassware off the floor, and to turn on the water. The first lieutenant's detail goes around inspecting damage which is considerable as a result of detonation.

12:20. Buffet luncheon: Beans, cold meat, pickles, stewed peaches. . . . Very acceptable.

1:15. I go to bed feeling as if I could sleep for a week.

1:45. Bugle and bawl of Donald Duck to general quarters. "Planes approaching!"

1:50. This time there's no fooling about it. Five planes—big bombers—come slanting out of the overcast which is thick above 2,000 feet and start in a long glide straight for the carrier. This is the first time I have ever seen dive bombing attempted by two-engine planes the size of a Douglas transport. All the ack-ack in the group lets loose.

At less than 2,000 feet they straighten out and drop their clunks. It's a fine job of bombing. Water rises to a height of 200 feet and covers the carrier for her entire length. It seems impossible that any of her should be left.

But the water comes down and the mist disperses and we see that the carrier has spun about. The bombs fell precisely where she was when the planes came out of the cloud. But by the time they hit she was somewhere else. The planes come back for another glide. Where our fighters are I'll never tell. Maybe I'll never know.

2:00. Four more bombs—half-ton clunks—drop astern and to the starboard of the carrier as we come about parallel. Another plane streaks out of the clouds on a long glide. Our ack-ack blasts. The plane seems almost to stop in midair as it bursts into flames. Then it continues on toward the deck of the carrier.

We'll never know whether the pilot was alive or dead when the plane came to its finish. In either case he probably had no time to know that his attempt failed. The big bomber hit the end of the flight deck, all right, its momentum virtually spent. It crashed one plane and slid over into the sea.

The marine gunner who accomplished most of this miracle looks startled: "He was there and now he's gone," he said. Which is true. There's no trace of him or his crew—not even a spot of oil.

2:10. This is the fastest I've ever traveled except in a speedboat somewhere on a calm lake. We are sticking our nose into it and flinging spray up over the bridge. Our wake looks like a waving green stair carpet with white fringe and no particular pattern on a blue floor.

2:30. The radio continues to report planes—obviously Japanese— in various quarters at no great distance. Obviously this will keep going on all day. The price you pay for raiding bases is that you get strafed by landplanes which are difficult competition.

3:00. The other cruiser lets off a blast—about four salvos of ack-ack for no reason that we can see.

3:10. Now and then the cans on the horizon do some shooting.

3:20. Black bursts low on horizon—a torpedo attack. The trouble is that we don't know what happened or how it came out. Apparently you don't mention battles in this war so long as they don't affect anybody but yourself. Your own worries are particularly your own.

3:30. Radio announces two or three planes fifty miles away and inbound. The sun is getting low, making observation to the west more and more difficult. The sky is covered with spotty clouds.

3:45. The atmosphere aboardship reminds me of the *Valiant* in a similar situation. There is no sound save the throb of the blowers and the vibration of the hard-driven engines. There is little motion as the gun crews man their guns and the fire-control details stand with heads bent and their hands clapped over their headphones. Somewhere out there are the Japs. They have made one attack and have missed and have lost face. They will have to make another attempt.

3:59. And here they come. The lookout sings: "Two planes approaching bearing two-four-oh. They seem to be heavy bombers." There is a clamorous conference among the observers: a moment's excitement and then calm again. . . . After all the air has been pretty well filled with Grummans.

4:00. The first lookout calls: "They're just coming out of a patch of cloud. There they are. Both of them. They certainly are heavy bombers. Most certainly!" Then another lookout and another: "Enemy aircraft approaching bearing two-five-oh." "Enemy aircraft approaching at 6,000 feet."

Then sky control: "Commence firing."

Once more bedlam. I was on my knees under the ship's bell on the searchlight platform when the riot started. I had trouble getting to my feet with the shock and plunge of the ship. I smashed my head against the bell and battered my bones on the rails and skinned my knees.

Two bombers came over at 5,000 feet, sailing as usual toward the carrier. Their shooting was pretty good.

4:02. Four bombs drop near the carrier. One bursts almost dead ahead and no great distance off. The water piles up on the carrier deck but apparently there's no damage.

4:04. It is plain from the position of the bursts that our five-inch ack-ack isn't bothering the raiders much. Their altitude is beyond the range of machine guns and minor ack-acks. But as in other combats of the sort I've seen, they continue to fire anyway.

4:05. Two of our fighters come from somewhere and begin to climb. We cease firing save for a few odd shots from the other cruiser and a destroyer. The fighters get altitude with amazing speed and take off after the bombers to the southwest.

It is difficult to get yourself adjusted to the silence that comes now. It has been a weird afternoon—everything you could ask for except a cavalry charge.

4:10. We sit down again to wait. So long as the Japs have bombers to fly we shan't be safe for the rest of the afternoon—and even sundown won't bring complete respite. We'll have a full moon in a reasonably clear sky. It's obvious, however, that if the Japs are going to attack they'll most likely do it before six o'clock. They were taught the rule that your bombing is better by day.

5:00. The carrier's planes begin to come back and land.

5:10. The bridge has received a message that the carrier planes shot down one of the two bombers.

5:20. I start down the ladders from my perch and run into one of the gunnery officers. He says a message has just been received that a torpedo plane has been intercepted about five miles dead astern and is now in a dogfight with our planes. . . . What a day! . . .

LET US FOR THE MOMENT TURN AGAIN TO THE PHILIP-
pines. Other than the appalling loss of life, the attack on the Cavite
Navy Yard cost the Navy one submarine, two yard tugs, a supply of
motor torpedo boat spare parts, 230 precious torpedoes and a rather
first-class installation. However, the main body of the Asiatic Fleet,
about 40 warships, escaped unscathed. Before telling of the Asiatic
Fleet's subsequent actions, an explanation is necessary: While Admiral Thomas C. Hart's command was technically an arm of the
Pacific Fleet, it was not of it. It was an entity unto itself whose area
of primary responsibility had lain elsewhere—the China Station and,
latterly, the countries of the Malay Barrier. Inasmuch as part of this
minuscule force had been deployed by its astute commander a month
before the war, and part on the night of December 8, there were
practically no prime targets for Japanese bombers.

Hart's strong right arm at sea was Rear Admiral W. W. Glassford,
who arrived on December 8 from the China Station and was
promptly shipped on to the Netherlands East Indies. On January 7,
Glassford, with a small cruiser-destroyer task force in Soerabaja, Java,
was advised that a large Japanese amphibious invasion was making
up in Macassar Strait, the gateway to oil-rich Balikpapan, Borneo, the
enemy's objective. That same day, Hart arrived in the submarine *Shark*
from the Philippines and assumed naval command of the ABDA
(American, British, Dutch, Australian) Command. This organization,
under overall command of Field Marshal Sir Archibald Wavell, had
been designed to protect the interest of the four allies.

Glassford's striking force, consisting of the destroyers *Ford, Pope,
Parrott, Paul Jones* and the light cruiser *Marblehead,* was given the
green light to attack and break up attempted enemy landings at
Balikpapan. But only the four destroyers sortied—at the last minute
Marblehead fouled her bottom and was forced to retire. However, the
resultant battle on January 23—a furious night torpedo slugfest—was
a tactical American victory. The landings were broken up and three
transports, probably more, were sunk.

William P. Mack, at present a Rear Admiral, was a young chief
engineer aboard *Ford* that night when the Asiatic Fleet went into
action for the first time.

A captured Japanese photograph taken during the attack on Pearl Harbor, December 7, 1941. *Navy Department.*

Panoramic view of Pearl Harbor under attack. *Navy Department.*

Burning and damaged ships at Pearl Harbor. From right to left: USS *Arizona*,
USS *Tennessee*, and USS *West Virginia*. *Navy Department.*

The USS *Arizona* (BB-39). *Navy Department.*

A Japanese drawing from a plane shot down at Pearl Harbor. Translation: "Hear! The voice of the moment of death. Wake up, you fools." *Navy Department.*

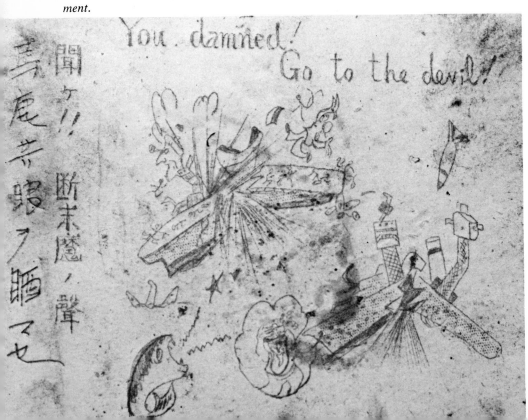

A Japanese two-man submarine beached on the island of Oahu during action with U.S. forces, Sunday, December 7, 1941. *Navy Department.*

The March of Death, Bataan, about May, 1942. These prisoners—from left to right, Samuel Stenzler, Frank Spear, James McD. Gallagher—were photographed along the March from Bataan to Cabanatuan, the prison camp. Their hands are tied behind their backs. *Defense Department Photo.*

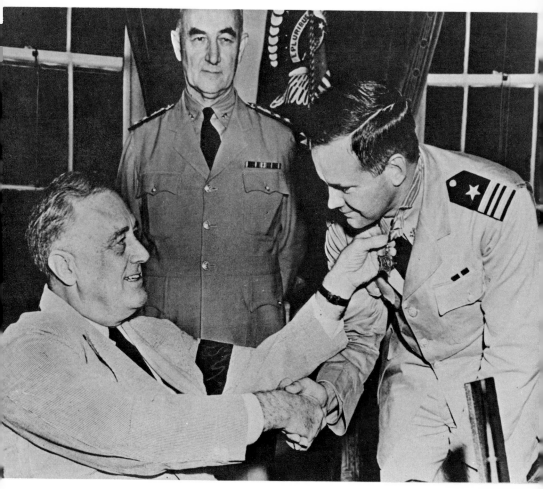

Lt. Cdr. John D. Bulkeley receives the Medal of Honor from President Roosevelt for his leadership of Motor Torpedo Boat Squadron Three during combat operations in Philippine waters. *Navy Department.*

Ships in North Atlantic convoy, 1942. *Navy Department.*

Ships in convoy, 1942, location unknown. *Navy Department.*

A depth charge fired by the USS *Murphy* (DD-603) explodes. Round No. 1, 600-lb. charge, depth 50 feet, speed 20 knots. *Navy Department.*

Plane attack on two German submarines by planes of the USS *Card* (CVE-11). One sub, damaged by Lt. (jg) Sallenger and unable to submerge, was believed sunk after four successive attacks. The larger U-boat, a 1600-ton minelayer supply boat, remained on the surface and soon two TBF's (Lt. C. R. Stapler and Lt. (jg) J. C. Forney) and two F4F's (Lt. N. D. Hudson and Lt. E. E. Jackson) arrived and continued the attack on it. *Navy Department.*

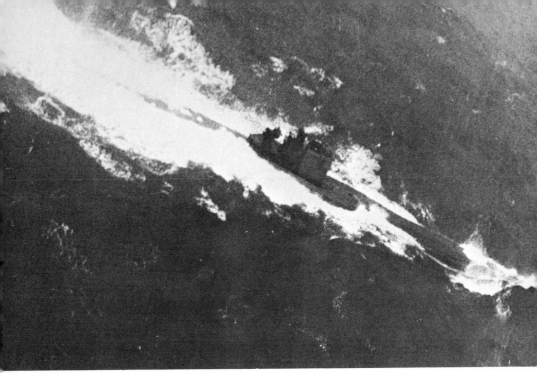

German submarine U-402 sinking after an attack by a patrol team from the USS *Card*—F4F pilot Howard M. Avery and TBF-1 pilot Ensign B. C. Sheela. TBF-1 dropped a 500-lb. bomb. *Navy Department.*

A U.S. Navy blimp over a convoy in the Atlantic, 1943. *Navy Department.*

The USS *Borie* (DD-215) is bombed by TBF's of the USS *Card* (CVE-11) after her skipper, Lt. Charles H. Hutchins, gave the order to abandon ship. The destroyer was damaged beyond possible salvage as a result of ramming a Nazi sub on the morning of 1 November, 1943, at 0153, just after she had encountered and sunk another enemy sub in the vicinity. In the hour's battle which followed this second contact, the *Borie* rode up over the starboard bow of the sub, thus damaging the destroyer's port side forward and flooding her forward engine room. The U-boat's main battery was put out of commission with the *Borie*'s first salvo at a range of 40 feet. The results: the second Nazi sub sunk. The *Borie*'s losses: 27 officers and men. *Navy Department.*

Salvage crew at work aboard captured German submarine U-505. Photo taken by the USS *Guadalcanal* (CVE-60). *Navy Department.*

U-505 lying alongside the USS *Guadalcanal. Navy Department.*

8.

MACASSAR

MERRY-GO-ROUND

Finally it came. The *Ford* had been monotonously patrolling off the Postillion Islands, at the southern entrance to Macassar Straits. We knew the Japs were coming. Borneo was next on their timetable after Manila and Davao. The planes of Patwing Ten had been sending reports of a growing Jap Force at Davao. This Force could have only one objective, Balikpapan, on the eastern cost of Borneo, fronting on Macassar Straits.

Our orders were clear, "Make a night attack on a Japanese Force heading for Balikpapan." Reconnaissance reports began to trickle in. The job was going to be tough. "Twenty transports, twelve destroyers, several cruisers." We figured that the Japs would have so many ships there they'd never notice us. That's exactly what happened.

We started up the straits that evening, timing our approach to arrive off Balikpapan at about 2:00 A.M. The seas were extremely heavy; we had to make 27 knots to get there. The result was something even old William Cramp would have shuddered at. He built well when he put those boats together. They bucked mountainous seas that threatened every minute to strip the bridges right off their hulls. I could only moan every time my guns went under green water. I was sure they'd never fire when the time came.

The long run up the Straits gave us time to organize for battle. We weren't much, but we were full of fight, and what's more, we were the

"Fighting Fifty-ninth." Destroyer Division Fifty-Nine was under the command of Commander P. H. Talbot, U.S. Navy, and was composed of the *John D. Ford,* flagship, the *Pope,* the *Parrott,* and the *Paul Jones* in column in that order. We'd made many a practice night torpedo attack, but never one with the chips down. In fact, we were to make the first one ever made. I remember running over in my mind the lofty War College comments on the expected life of a destroyer in a night action. I couldn't remember whether it was measured in seconds or minutes, but I knew it wasn't much of either. Our crews were well trained, tough, and eager for action. Our officers were the same, and as experienced as any in the peace-time Navy. We were confident, but made all preparations just the same. The charts showed 300 miles of trackless jungle south of Balikpapan. I knew we'd have a long walk south if any of us were fortunate enough to survive and get ashore if we were sunk. I sewed a box full of fish hooks, twine, razor blades, quinine pills, and Dutch money in my life jacket an tied a pocket compass and knife on my pistol belt. After checking over my gun firing circuits as best I could between submergings and giving last-minute instructions to my gun crews, I felt I was ready for anything. My men were spoiling for a fight. I didn't have to tell them *what* to do, just *when.* They were about to take part in the first American naval engagement in the East since Dewey fought at Manila Bay, and they were proud of it.

I've always wondered how a person felt before battle. I still don't know. I fell asleep, or as near to sleep as you can get on a four-stacker that is making 27 knots in a rough sea. When the General Alarm awakened me at 11:00 P.M., the sea had calmed considerably, and as we passed up the straits in the lee of Celebes, the sea was almost calm.

Again I checked my guns, mustered my crews, passed last-minute instructions, and then reported ready to the bridge. I had plenty of time to think now. As my eyes became accustomed to the darkness I was able to make out our division mates astern. Down on deck the repair party was assembling its gear, the cooks were passing out cold rations, and the torpedo tube mount crews and gun crews were making last-minute inspections.

We settled down to that last-minute wait, familiar to any athlete. That's the only way I can describe it, just like that gone feeling just before the kick-off. For more than an hour we plunged on through the night, alert, ready, hopeful. Shortly before midnight the spotter in the foretop sighted an intermittently flashing light on the starboard bow. For a moment I thought it was a searchlight, but soon we made it out as flames from a burning ship. Its position showed it to be near a part of a Jap convoy reportedly bombed by our air force that afternoon. In half an hour we had left it astern, burning as a monument to the accuracy of some bombardier.

At 2:00 A.M. we came abreast of Balikpapan. The loom of gigantic fires became visible. The Dutch, we knew, were busy destroying everything burnable to deny it to the Japs. We could smell burning oil 20 miles at sea. Using these fires as beacons, we turned west and set a course to the area just north of Balikpapan and its mine fields, where we suspected the Japs would attempt to land. At 2:45 A.M. I saw my first Japanese ship. I can't describe the feeling it gave me. I could remember the hours I'd spent studying silhouettes of Japanese warships. Suddenly, here was one, a silhouette all right, but not a picture —a big, black, ugly ship. We passed it so close and so fast that neither of us could take any action. Our plan was to fire our torpedoes as long as they lasted and then, and only then, to open up with our guns. That way we could conceal our presence as long as possible. Consequently, we couldn't fire our guns at this ship, and couldn't train our torpedo tubes fast enough to bring them to bear on him.

We didn't have long to wait for more game. A whole division of Jap destroyers burst out of the gloom and oil smoke on our port bow and steamed rapidly across in front of us and off into the darkness to starboard. Again we kept quiet and attempted to avoid them. Our objective was something far more important, the troop and supply laden transports farther inshore. I don't know why these destroyers didn't see us. Possibly several of their own destroyers were patrolling in the vicinity and they mistook us for their own forces. Maybe that was why the first ship we sighted had not fired on us.

Suddenly we found ourselves right in the midst of the Jap transports. Down on the bridge I could hear Captain Cooper saying "action port, action port," and Lieutenant Slaughter, the torpedo officer, giving quick orders to his torpedo battery. Back aft the tube mounts swung to follow his director. "Fire one," he said. "Fire one," repeated his telephone talker. Then came the peculiar combination of a muffled explosion, a whine, a swish, and a splash, that follows the firing of a torpedo. I watched the torpedo come to the surface once and then dive again as it steadied on its run. Astern, the *Pope, Paul Jones,* and *Parrott* were carefully picking targets and firing. We fired our second torpedo. So did the ships astern. My talker was calmly counting off seconds as our first torpedo ran toward its target. "Mark," he shouted, as the time came for it to hit. Seconds passed. Nothing happened. We knew our first had missed. Then came a blinding, ear-shattering explosion. One of our torpedoes had hit. The explosion of a torpedo at night at close range is an awe-inspiring sight. The blast is terrific, blinding; then comes the concussion wave, which leaves you gasping for breath. It is seconds before your dazed eyes can see anything at all.

Close on the heels of the first close range hit came other hits. The crippled ships began to list and sink. We reversed course and ran through the convoy again, firing torpedoes on both sides as transports loomed out of the dark. By now there were only three of us, the *Paul Jones* having lost us as we came around the last turn. At one time I could count five sinking ships. A third time we reversed course and ran through the demoralized convoy. Once we had to veer to port to avoid a sinking transport. The water was covered with swimming Japs. Our wash overturned several lifeboats loaded with Japs. Other ships looked as if they were covered with flies. Jap soldiers were clambering down their sides in panic. It was becoming difficult to keep from firing at transports that had already been torpedoed. Again we turned for another run through the convoy. So far I believed the Japs had not discovered that we were in their midst, attributing the torpedoes to submarines and believing we were their own destroyers.

Down on the bridge I heard "Fire ten." Just two torpedoes left. Now only the *Pope* was left astern of us. We fired our last two torpedoes at a group of three transports. Now I knew the stage was mine. Many a time I had fired at target rafts, but this was the real thing. "Commence firing" rang in my earphones. I was ready but how different this was from peace-time firings! I could still remember the sonorous arguments of the publications I had studied at the Naval Academy over the relative effectiveness of searchlights and star shells. I didn't use either, nor did we use any of the complicated fire-control apparatus installed. This was draw shooting at its best. As targets loomed out of the dark at ranges of 500 to 1,500 yards we trained on and let go a salvo or two, sights set at their lower limits, using the illumination furnished by burning ships. Finally we sighted a transport far enough away to let us get in three salvos before we had passed it. The projectile explosions were tremendous. Deck plates and debris flew in all directions. When we last saw her she was on end, slipping slowly under. We had sunk the first ship to be sunk by American gunfire since Manila Bay! I only had a minute to reflect on that fact because a transport began firing at us. I turned my guns on her, but before we could silence her a shell had hit us aft. Flames grew and spread around the area. Over the telephones I could hear a torpedoman describing the damage—"four men wounded, the after deckhouse wrecked, ammunition burning." Thirty seconds later the burning ammunition had been thrown over the side, the wounded cared for, and the gun crew was firing again.

By now the *Pope* had also lost us, and we were fighting alone. One more transport we mauled badly, then there was nothing left to shoot at. On the bridge I heard our Division Commander give the order to withdraw. Back aft the blowers began to whine even louder as the Chief Engineer squeezed the last ounce of speed out of the old boat. Later I learned we were making almost 32 knots, faster than the *Ford* had gone since her trials. In the east the sky was growing uncomfortably bright. Astern of us the sky was also bright, but from the fires of burning ships.

For almost 30 minutes we ran south before dawn came. All hands strained their eyes astern for signs of pursuit that we thought inevitable. We could see none. The only ships in sight were three familiar shapes on the port bow that we knew to be the *Parrott, Paul Jones,* and *Pope.* Proudly they fell in astern of us, and we sped south together. Down on the bridge a flag hoist whipped out smartly. "Well done," it said.

All that morning we kept a wary eye cocked astern and overhead, but the Japs must have been licking their wounds, for we never saw a Jap. Our crew ate in shifts, refusing to get more than 10 feet from their guns. Only when we started in the mine fields off Soerabaja next day did they relax and drop off to sleep on deck.

At noon we tied up at Soerabaja with barely enough fuel to make the dock. On the way in we had put a canvas patch over the hole in our after deckhouse and had cleaned up the ship as best we could. The Dutch met us in grand style, and Admiral Hart came aboard to inspect us. The Dutch provided men to help us fuel and provision ship. That done, every man in the crew slept 16 hours . . .

(Editor's Note: Unhappily, when the facts were known six years later, it was ascertained through Japanese records that the three American tin-cans had sunk only 4 transports out of a possible 12, and only one patrol craft.)

BY THE END OF FEBRUARY 1942, WHEN THE LAST great sea battle was fought between the dwindling forces of the ABDA Command and Admiral Kondo's massive Java Invasion Force, a number of óther calamities had befallen the allied nations defending the Malay Barrier. The Japanese were firmly established on both sides of the South China Sea, in Macassar Strait and on the Celebes side of Molucca; moreover, after Singapore's surrender on February 15, the ABDA Command had disintegrated, and both Wavell and Hart were now gone from the scene, the latter having retired. There remained only a handful of United States warships to join the combined American-British-Dutch task force under the petulant Dutchman, Rear Admiral K. W. Doorman, whose main mission was all sacrifice; he was to oppose the most formidable sea force gathered by the enemy since Pearl Harbor.

The sinking of the heavy cruiser *Houston* in the Battle of Java Sea is recalled by one of her survivors, Commander Walter G. Winslow, who spent ten hours in the water until rescued by a Japanese destroyer.

9.

THE GALLOPING GHOST

. . . I stood on the quarterdeck contemplating the restful green of the Java Coast as it fell slowly behind us. Many times before I had found solace in its beauty, but this night it seemed only a mass of coconut and banana palms that had lost all meaning. I was too tired and too preoccupied with pondering the question that raced through the mind of every man aboard, "Would we get through Sunda Strait?"

There were many aboard who felt that, like a cat, the *Houston* had expended eight of its nine lives and that this one last request of fate would be too much. Jap cruiser planes had shadowed us all day and it was certain that our movements were no mystery to the enemy forces closing in on Java. Furthermore, it was most logical to conclude that Jap submarines were stationed throughout the length of Sunda Strait to intercept and destroy ships attempting escape into the Indian Ocean.

Actually there wasn't any breathing space for optimism, we were trapped, but there had been other days when the odds were stacked heavily in the Jap's favor and we had somehow managed to battle through. Maybe it was because I had the Naval Aviator's philosophical outlook and maybe it was because I was just a plain damn fool, but I couldn't quite bring myself to believe that the *Houston* had run her course. It was with this feeling of shaky confidence that I turned and headed for my stateroom. I had just been relieved as

Officer-of-the-Deck and the prospect of a few hours rest was most appealing.

The wardroom and the interior of the ship, through which I walked, was dark, for the heavy metal battle ports were bolted shut and lights were not permitted within the darkened ship. Only the eerie blue beams of a few battle lights close to the deck served to guide my feet. I felt my way through the narrow companionway and snapped on my flashlight briefly to seek out the coaming of my stateroom door. As I stepped into the cubicle that was my room, I took a brief look around and switched off the light. There had been no change, everything lay as it had for the last two and a half months. There had been only one addition in all that time. It was Gus, my silent friend, the beautiful Bali head I had purchased six weeks before in Soerabaja.

Gus sat on the desk top lending his polished wooden expression to the cramped atmosphere of my stateroom. In the darkness I felt his presence as though he were a living thing. "We'll get through, won't we, Gus?" I found myself saying. And although I couldn't see him, I thought he nodded slowly.

I slipped out of my shoes and placed them at the base of the chair by my desk, along with my tin hat and life jacket, where I could reach them quickly in an emergency. Then I rolled into my bunk and let my exhausted body sink into its luxury. The bank was truly a luxury, for the few men who were permitted to relax lay on the steel decks by their battle stations. I, being an aviator with only the battered shell of our last airplane left aboard, was permitted to take what rest I could get in my room.

Although there had been little sleep for any of us during the past four days, I found myself lying there in the sticky tropic heat of my room fretfully tossing and trying for sleep that would not come.

The constant hum of blowers thrusting air into the bowels of the ship, the *Houston's* gentle rolling as she moved through a quartering sea, and the occasional groaning of her steel plates combined to bring into my mind the mad merry-go-round of events that had plagued the ship during the past few weeks.

Twenty-four days had elapsed since that terrifying day in the Flores Sea, yet here it was haunting me again as it would for the rest of my life. My mind pictured the squadrons of Jap bombers as they attacked time and again from every conceivable direction. After the first run they remained at altitudes far beyond range of our anti-aircraft guns, for they had learned respect on that first run when one of their planes was blasted from the sky and several others were obviously hit and badly shaken. But that first salvo almost finished the *Houston*. It was a perfect straddle, and the force of those big bombs seemed as though a giant hand had taken the ship, lifted her bodily from the water, and tossed her yards away from her original course. There had been no personnel casualties that time but our main anti-aircraft director had been wrenched from its track, rendering it useless, and we were taking water aboard from sprung plates in the hull.

That day the crew had only the steady barrage from the anti-aircraft guns and Captain Rooks' clever handling of the ship to thank for keeping them from the realms of Davy Jones. But there was one horrible period during that afternoon when the Nips almost got us for keeps. A five-hundred pound bomb, and a stray at that, hit us squarely amidships aft. Some utterly stupid Jap bombardier failed to release with the rest of his squadron and Captain Rooks could make no allowances for such as him. The salvo fell harmlessly off the port quarter but the stray crashed through two platforms of the main mast before it exploded on the deck just forward of number three turret. Hunks of shrapnel tore through the turret's thin armor as though it were paper, igniting powder bags in the hoists. In one blazing instant all hands in the turret and in the handling rooms below were dead. Where the bomb spent its force, a gaping hole was blown in the deck below which waited the after repair party. They were wiped out almost to a man. It was a hellish battle which ended with forty-eight of our shipmates killed and another fifty seriously burned or wounded.

I strove desperately to rid myself of the picture of that blazing turret—the bodies of the dead sprawled grotesquely in pools of blood and the bewildered wounded staggering forward for medical aid—but I was forced to see it through. Once again I heard the banging of hammers, hammers that pounded throughout the long night as tired men worked steadily building coffins for forty-eight shipmates lying in little groups on the fantail. We put into Chilatjap the followng day, that stinking fever ridden little port on the South Coast of Java. Here we sadly unloaded our wounded and prepared to bury our dead. It seemed that in the hum of the blowers I detected strains of the Death March—the same mournful tune that the band played as we carried our comrades through the heat of those sunburned, dusty streets of Chilatjap. I saw again the brown poker-faced natives dressed in sarongs, quietly watching us as we buried our dead in the little Dutch cemetery that looked out over the sea. I wondered what those slim brown men thought of all this.

The scene shifted. It was only four days ago that we steamed through the mine fields protecting the beautiful port of Soerabaja. Air raid sirens whined throughout the city and our lookouts reported bombers in the distant sky. Large warehouses along the docks were on fire and a burning merchantman lay on its side vomiting dense black smoke and orange flame. The enemy had come and left his calling card. We anchored in the stream not far from the smouldering docks where we watched Netherlands East Indian Soldiers extinguish the fires.

Six times during the next two days we experienced air raids. Anchored there in the stream we were as helpless as ducks in a rain barrel. Why our gun crews didn't collapse is a tribute to their sheer guts and brawn. They stood by their guns unflinchingly in the hot sun, pouring shell after shell into the sky while the rest of us sought what shelter is available in the bulls-eye of a target.

Time and again bombs falling with the deep throated *swoosh* of a giant bullwhip exploded around us, spewing water and shrapnel over our decks. Docks less than a hundred yards away were demolished and a Dutch hospital ship was hit, yet the *Houston,* nicknamed "the Galloping Ghost of the Java Coast" because the Japs had reported her sunk on so many similar occasions, still rode defiantly at anchor.

When the siren's bailful wailing sounded the "all clear," members of the *Houston's* band came from their battle stations to the quarter deck where we squatted to hear them play swing tunes. God bless the American sailor, you can't beat him.

Like Scrooge, the ghosts of the past continued to move into my little room. I saw us in the late afternoon of February 26, standing out of Soerabaja for the last time. Admiral Doorman of the Netherlands Navy was in command of our small striking force. His flagship, the light cruiser *De Ruyter,* was in the lead, followed by another Netherlands light cruiser, the *Java.* Next in line came the British heavy cruiser *Exeter* of *Graf Spee* fame, followed by the crippled *Houston.* Last in the line of cruisers was the Australian light cruiser *Perth.* Ten allied destroyers made up the remainder of our force. Slowly we steamed past the ruined docks where small groups of old men, women, and children had assembled to wave tearful goodbyes to their men who would not return.

Our force was small and hurriedly assembled. We had never worked together before, but now we had one common purpose which every man knew it was his duty to carry through. We were to do our utmost to break up an enemy task force that was bearing down on Java, even though it meant the loss of every ship and man among us. In us lay the last hope of the Netherlands East Indies.

All night long we searched for the enemy convoy but they seemed to have vanished from previously reported positions. We were still at battle stations the next afternoon when at 1415 reports from air reconnaissance indicated that the enemy was south of Bowen Island, and heading south. The two forces were less than fifty miles apart. A hurried but deadly serious conference of officers followed in the wardroom. Commander Maher, our gunnery officer, explained that our mission was to sink or disperse the protecting enemy fleet units and then destroy the convoy. My heart pounded with excitement for the battle later to be known as the Java Sea Battle was only a matter of minutes away. Were the sands of time running out for the *Houston* and all of us who manned her? At that moment I would have given my soul to have known.

In the darkness of my room the Japs came again just as though I were standing on the bridge . . . a forest of masts rapidly developing into ships that climbed in increasing numbers over the horizon . . . those dead ahead, ten destroyers divided into two columns and each led by a four stack light cruiser. Behind them and off our starboard bow came four light cruisers followed by two heavies. The odds weigh heavily against us for we are outnumbered and outgunned.

The Japs open fire first! Sheets of copper colored flame lick out along their battle line and black smoke momentarily masks them from view. My heart pounds violently and cold sweat drenches my body as I realize that the first salvo is on its way. Somehow those big shells all seem aimed at me. I wonder why our guns don't open up, but as the Jap shells fall harmlessly a thousand yards short I realize that the range is yet too great. The battle from which there will be no retreat has begun.

At twenty-eight thousand yards the *Exeter* opens fire, followed by the *Houston*. The sound of our guns bellowing defiance is terrific, the gun blast tears my steel helmet from my head and sends it rolling on the deck.

The range closes rapidly and soon all cruisers are in on the fight. Salvos of shells splash in the water ever closer to us. Now one falls close to starboard followed by another close to port. This is an ominous indicator that the Japs have at last found the range. We stand tensely awaiting the next salvo, and it comes with a wild screaming of shells that fall all around us. It's a straddle, but not a hit is registered. Four more salvos in succession straddle the *Houston,* and the lack of a hit gives us confidence. The *Perth,* 900 yards astern of us, is straddled eight times in a row, yet she too steams on unscathed. Our luck is holding out.

Shells from our guns are observed bursting close to the last Jap heavy cruiser. We have her range and suddenly one of our eight-inch bricks strikes home. There is an explosion aboard her. Black smoke and debris fly into the air and a fire breaks out forward of her bridge. We draw blood first as she turns out of the battle line, making dense smoke. Commander Maher, directing the fire of our guns from his station high in the foretop, reports our success to the Captain over the phone. A lusty cheer goes up from the crew as the word spreads over the ship.

Three enemy cruisers are concentrating their fire on *Exeter*. We shift targets to give her relief, but it is not long after this that *Exeter* shells find their mark and a light cruiser turns out of the Jap line, smoking and on fire. Despite the loss of two cruisers, the intensity of Jap fire does not seem to diminish. The *Houston* is hit twice. One shell rips through the bow just aft of the port anchor windlass, passes down through several decks and out the side just above the water line without exploding. The other shell, hitting aft, barely grazes the side and ruptures a small oil tank. It too fails to explode.

Up to this point the luck of our forces had held up well, but now there is a rapid turn of events as the *Exeter* is hit by a Jap shell which does not explode, but rips into her forward fireroom and severs a main steam line. This reduces her speed to seven knots. In an attempt to save the *Exeter,* whose loss of speed makes her an easy target, we all make smoke to cover her withdrawal. The Japs, aware that something has gone wrong, are quick to press home an advantage, and their destroyers, under heavy support fire from the cruisers, race in to deliver a torpedo attack.

The water seems alive with torpedoes. Lookouts report them approaching and Captain Rooks maneuvers the ship to present as small a target as possible. At this moment a Netherlands East Indies destroyer, the *Koertner,* trying to change stations, is hit amidships by a torpedo intended for the *Houston.* There is a violent explosion and a great fountain of water rises a hundred feet above her, obscuring all but small portions of her bow and stern. When the watery fountain settles back into the sea it becomes apparent that the little green and grey destroyer has broken in half and turned over. Only the bow and stern sections of her jackknifed keel stick above the water. A few men scramble desperately to her barnacled bottom, and her twin screws in their last propulsive effort turn slowly over in the air. In less than two minutes she has disappeared beneath the sea. No one can stand by to give the few survivors a helping hand for her fate can be ours at any instant.

It is nearing sundown. The surface of the sea is covered with clouds of black smoke, which makes it difficult to spot the enemy. It is discovered that Jap cruisers are closing in upon us, and our destroyers are ordered to attack with tropedoes in order to divert them and give us time to reform. Although no hits are reported, the effect of the attack is gratifying for the Japs turn away. At this point the engagement is broken off. The daylight battle has ended with no decisive results; however, there is still the convoy, which we will attempt to surprise under the cover of night.

We check our losses. The *Koertner* and H.M.S. *Electra* have been sunk. The crippled *Exeter* has retired to Soerabaja, escorted by the American destroyers, who have expended their torpedoes and are running low on fuel. The *Houston, Perth, De Ruyter,* and *Java* are still in the fight, but showing the jarring effects of continuous gunfire. Only two destroyers remain with us, H.M.S. *Jupiter* and H.M.S. *Encounter.*

The *Houston* had fired 303 rounds of ammunition per turret, and only fifty rounds per gun remain. The loss of number three turret has been a great handicap, but there are no complaints for the *Houston* has done well. The Chief Engineer reports that his force is on the verge of complete exhaustion and that there have been more than seventy cases of heat exhaustion in the fire rooms during the afternoon's battle. We are in poor fighting condition, but there is plenty more to be done.

During the semi-darkness of twilight we steam on a course away from the enemy in order to lead any of their units which might have us under observation into believing that we are in retreat. When darkness descends we turn and head back.

Shortly after this H.M.S. *Jupiter,* covering our port flank, explodes mysteriously and vanishes in a brief but brilliant burst of flame. We are dumbfounded, for the enemy is not to be seen yet we race on puzzling over her fate and blindly seeking the transports.

An hour passes with nothing intervening to interrupt our search, and then high in the sky above us a flare bursts, shattering the darkness. Night has suddenly become day and we are illuminated like targets in a shooting gallery. We are helpless to defend ourselves, for we have no such thing as radar, and the plane merely circles outside our range of vision to drop another flare after the first one burns itself out, following it with another and still another.

We cannot know for sure, but certainly it is logical to assume that the enemy is closing in for the kill. Blinded by the flares we wait through tense minutes for the blow to come.

On the ship men speak in hushed tones as though their very words will give our position away to the enemy. Only the rush of water as our bow knifes through the sea at thirty knots, and the continuous roaring of blowers from the vicinity of the quarterdeck, are audible. Death stands by, ready to strike. No one talks of it although all thoughts dwell upon it.

The fourth flare bursts, burns, and then slowly falls into the sea. We are enveloped in darkness again. No attack has come and as time passes it becomes evident that the plane has gone away. How wonderful is the darkness, yet how terrifying to realize that the enemy is aware of our every move and merely biding his time like a cat playing with a mouse.

The moon has come up to assist in our search for the convoy. It has been almost an hour since the last flare, and nothing has happened to indicate that the enemy has us under observation. During this period Ensign Stivers has relieved me as officer of the deck. I climb up on the forward anti-aircraft director platform and sprawl out to catch a bit of rest before the inevitable shooting begins. I hardly close my eyes before there comes the sound of whistles and shouting men. I am back on my feet in a hurry and look over the side. The water is dotted with groups of men yelling in some strange tongue which I cannot understand. H.M.S. *Encounter* is ordered to remain behind to rescue them.

Now we are four, three light cruisers and one heavy. We plow on through the eerie darkness. Suddenly out of nowhere six flares appear in the water along our line of ships. They resemble those round smoke pots that burn alongside road constructions with a yellow flame. What exactly are they, and how did they get there? Are they some form of mine, or is their purpose to mark our path for the enemy? No one dares to guess. Either eventuality is bad enough.

As fast as we leave one group astern, another group bobs up alongside. We cannot account for them, and this oriental deviltry is as bewildering as it is confusing. None of us has ever seen such a phenomenon before. We continue to move away from them, but other groups of floating flares appear.

The uncertainty of what is to follow is nerve wracking. We look back and there, marking our track on the oily surface of the sea, are zig-zag lines of flares which rock and burn like goulish jack-o-lanterns. We leave them on the far horizon and no more appear. We are again in welcome darkness.

At approximately 2230, lookouts report two large unidentified ships to port, range 12,000 yards. There are no friendly ships within hundreds of miles of us, therefore these are the enemy. The *Houston* opens up with two main battery salvos, the results of which are not determined, and the Japs reply with two of their own which throw water over the forecastle. With this exchange of fire the Japs disappear in the darkness and we make no effort to chase them, for we need all of our ammunition to sink transports.

There is no relaxing now. We are in the area where anything can happen. Hundreds of eyes peer into the night seeking the convoy, as we realize that the end of our mission is approaching.

During the night the order of ships in column has been shifted. The *De Ruyter* still maintained the lead, but behind her comes the *Houston,* followed by the *Java* and *Perth* in that order.

A half hour passes without incident, and then with the swiftness of a lightning bolt a tremendous explosion rocks the *Java* 900 yards astern of the *Houston.* Mounting flames envelop her amidships and spread rapidly aft. She loses speed and drops out of the column to lie dead in the water, where sheets of uncontrolled flame consume her.

Torpedo wakes are observed in the water, although we can find no enemy to fight back. The *De Ruyter* changes course sharply to the right, and the *Houston* is just about to follow when an explosion similar to the one that doomed the *Java* is heard aboard the *De Ruyter.* Crackling flames shoot high above her bridge, quickly enveloping the entire ship.

Captain Rooks, in a masterpiece of seamanship and quick thinking, maneuvers the *Houston* to avoid torpedoes that slip past us ten feet on either side. Then joined by the *Perth,* we race away from the stricken ships and the insidious enemy that no one can see. How horrible it is to leave our allies, but we are powerless to assist them. Now that Admiral Doorman has gone down with his blazing flagship, the Captain of the *Perth* takes command, for he is senior to Captain Rooks, and we follow the *Perth* as he sets a course for Batavia.

What an infernal night, and how lucky we are to escape. It seems almost miraculous when the sun comes up on the next morning, February 28, for there have been many times during the past fifteen hours when I would have sworn we would never see it.

The *Houston* was a wreck. Concussions from the eight-inch guns had played merry hell with the ship's interior. Every desk on the ship had its drawers torn out and the contents spewn over the deck. In lockers, clothes were torn from their hangers and pitched in muddled heaps. Pictures, radios, books, and everything of a like nature were jolted from their normal places and dashed on the deck.

The Admiral's cabin was a deplorable sight. At one time it had been President Roosevelt's cabin, but no one could have recognized it now as such. Clocks lay broken on the deck, furniture was overturned, mirrors were cracked, charts were ripped from the bulkhead, and large pieces of soundproofing that had come loose from the bulkheads and overhead were thick in the rubble on the deck.

The ship itself had suffered considerably. Plates already weakened by near hits in previous bombing attacks were now badly sprung and leaking. The glass windows on the bridge were shattered. Fire hose strung along the passageways were leaking and minor floods made it sloppy underfoot.

The *Houston* was wounded and practically out of ammunition, but there was still fight left in her, plenty of it.

These events accompanied by many others played upon my mind in the minutest detail, until at last my senses became numb and I relaxed in sleep.

It was nearly 2400 when, *Clang! Clang! Clang! Clang!,* the nerve shattering "General Alarm" burst through my wonderful cocoon of sleep and brought me upright on both feet. Through two and a half months of war that gong, calling all hands to battle stations, had rung in deadly earnest. It meant only one thing, "Danger"—man your battle station and get ready to fight. So thoroughly had the lessons of war been taught as to the sharp, heartless clanging of that gong that I found myself in my shoes before I was even awake.

Clang! Clang! Clang! Clang! The sound echoed along the steel bulkheads of the ship's deserted interior. I wondered what kind of deviltry we were mixed up in now, and somehow I felt depressed. I grabbed my tin hat as I left the room and was putting it on my head when a salvo from the main battery roared out overhead, knocking me against the bulkhead. We were desperately short of those eight-inch bricks and I knew that the boys weren't wasting them on mirages. I flashed my light to assist me in passing through the deserted wardroom and into the passageway at the other end, where a group of stretcher-bearers and corpsmen were assembled. I asked them but they didn't seem to know what we had run into. I left them and climbed the ladder leading to the bridge.

As I climbed there was more firing from the main battery, and now the five-inch guns were taking up the argument. I realized that it was getting to be one hell of a battle and I started running. On the communication deck where the one-point-one's were getting into action, I passed their gun crews working swiftly, mechanically in the darkness without a hitch, as their guns pumped out shell after shell. Momentarily I caught a glimpse of tracers hustling out into the night. They were beautiful.

Before I reached the bridge every gun on the ship was in action. The noise they made was magnificent. The *Houston* was throwing knockout punches. How reassuring it was to hear, at measured intervals, the blinding crash of the main battery, the sharp rapid crack of the five-inch guns, the steady methodic *pom, pom, pom, pom,* of the one-point-one's; and above all that, from their platforms high in the foremast and in the mainmast, came the continuous sweeping volleys of fifty-caliber machine guns which had been put there as anti-aircraft weapons, but which now suddenly found themselves engaging enemy surface targets.

As I stepped on the bridge the *Houston* became enveloped in the blinding glare of searchlights. Behind the lights I could barely discern the outlines of Jap destroyers. They had come in close to illuminate for their heavy units which fired at us from the darkness. Battling desperately for existence the *Houston's* guns trained on the lights, and as fast as they were turned on, just as fast were they blasted out.

Although the bridge was the *Houston's* nerve center, I was unable to find out what we were up against. This was mainly because the tempo of the battle was so great and every man stationed there so vitally concerned with his immediate duty that I was reluctant to butt in at such a time and ask a question that had little relative meaning. What we had actually run into was later estimated to be sixty fully loaded transports, twenty destroyers, and six cruisers. We were in the middle of this mass of ships before either side was aware of the other's presence.

Suddenly surrounded by ships, the *Perth* and *Houston* immediately opened fire and turned sharply to starboard in an effort to break free. However, the fury of the Japs was not to be denied and the *Perth* was mortally wounded by torpedoes. Lying dead in the water she continued to fire with everything she had until Jap shells blasted her to bits and she sank.

When Captain Rooks realized that the *Perth* was finished he turned the *Houston* back into the heart of the Jap convoy, determined in the face of no escape to sell the *Houston* dearly.

At close range the *Houston* pounded the Jap transports with everything she had, and at the same time fought off the destroyers that were attacking with torpedoes and shellfire. Jap cruisers remained in the background, throwing salvo after salvo aboard and around us. The *Houston* was taking terrible punishment. A torpedo penetrated our after engine room, where it exploded, killing every man there and reducing our speed to fifteen knots.

Thick smoke and hot steam venting on the gun deck from the after engine room temporarily drove men from their guns but they came back and stayed there in spite of it. Power went out of the shell hoists which stopped the flow of five-inch shells to the guns, from the almost empty magazines. Men attempted to go below and bring shells up by hand, but debris and fires from numerous hits blocked their way. In spite of this they continued to fire, using star shells which were stowed in the ready ammunition boxes by the guns.

Number Two turret, smashed by a direct hit, blew up, sending wild flames flashing up over the bridge. The heat, so intense that it drove everyone out of the conning tower, temporarily disrupted communications to other parts of the ship. The fire was soon extinguished, but when the sprinklers flooded the magazine our last remaining supply of eight-inch ammunition was ruined, which meant that the *Houston* was now without a main battery.

Numerous fires were breaking out all over the ship and it became increasingly difficult for the men to cope with them. Another torpedo plowed into the *Houston* somewhere forward of the quarterdeck. The force of the explosion made the ship tremble beneath us, and I realized then that we were done for.

Slowly we listed to starboard as the grand old ship gradually lost steerageway and stopped. The few guns still in commission continued to fire, although it was obvious that the end was near. It must have torn at the Captain's heart, but his voice was strong as he summoned the bugler and ordered him to sound "Abandon Ship."

When I heard the words "Abandon Ship" I did not wait to go down the ladder which already had a capacity crowd, with men waiting; instead I jumped over the railing to the deck below. That was probably a fortunate move, for just as I jumped a shell burst on the bridge, killing several men. I trotted out on the port catapult tower where the battered and unflyable hulk of our last airplane spread its useless wings in the darkness. It contained a rubber boat and a bottle of brandy, both of which I figured would come in handy, but I was not alone in this, for five people were there ahead of me.

Despite the fact that we were still the target for continuous shells and the ship was slowly sinking beneath us, there was no confusion. Men went quietly and quickly about the job of abandoning ship. Fear was nowhere apparent, due possibly to the fact that the one thing we feared most throughout the short space of the war had happened.

Captain Rooks had come down off the bridge and was saying goodbye to several of his officers and men outside his cabin, when a Jap shell exploded in a one-point-one gun mount, sending a piece of the breach crashing into his chest. Captain Rooks, beloved by officers and men, died in their arms.

When Buda, the Captain's Chinese cook, learned that the captain had been killed, he refused to leave the ship. He simply sat cross-legged outside the Captain's cabin, rocking back and forth and moaning "Captain dead, *Houston* dead, Buda die too." He went down with the ship.

During this time I made my way to the quarterdeck. Dead men lay sprawled on the deck, but there was no time to find out who they were. Men from my division were busily engaged in the starboard hangar in an effort to bring out a seaplane pontoon and two wing-tip floats that we had filled with food and water in preparation for just such a time. If we could get them into the water and assemble them as we had so designed, they would make a fine floating structure around which we could gather and work from.

I hurried to the base of the catapult tower where I worked rapidly to release the lifelines in order that we could get the floats over the side and into the water. I uncoupled one line and was working on the second when a torpedo struck directly below us. I heard no explosion, but the deck buckled and jumped under me and I found myself suddenly engulfed in a deluge of fuel oil and salt water.

Up until that moment I must have been too fascinated with the unreality of the situation to truly think about it and become frightened, but when this sudden torrent of fuel oil and water poured over me, all I could think of was fire. It was the most helpless sensation I ever had experienced in my life. Somehow I hadn't figured on getting hit or killed, but now I was gripped with the sudden fear of blazing fuel oil on my person and covering the surface of the sea. I was panicked, for I could figure no escape from it. The same thought must have been in the minds of the others, for we all raced from the starboard side to the shelter of the port hangar. No sooner had we cleared the quarterdeck than a salvo of shells plowed through it, exploding deep below decks.

Events were moving fast, and the *Houston* in her death throes was about to go down. There was only one idea left in my mind, and that was to join the others who were going over the side in increasing numbers. Quickly I made my way to the port side and climbed down the cargo nets that were hanging there. When I reached the water's edge I dropped off into the warm Java Sea. When my head came above the surface I was aware that in the darkness I was surrounded by many men, all swimming for their lives. Frantic screams for help from the wounded and drowning mixed with the shouts of others attempting to make contact with shipmates. The sea was an oily battleground of men pitted against the terrors of death. Desperately I swam to get beyond reach of the sinking ship's suction. As much as I loved the *Houston* I had no desire to join her in a watery grave.

A few hundred yards away I turned, gasping for breath, to watch the death of my ship. She lay well over to starboard. Jap destroyers had come in close and illuminated her with searchlights as they raked her decks with machine-gun fire. Many men struggled in the water near the ship, others clung desperately to heavily loaded life rafts, and then to my horror, I realized that the Japs were coldly and deliberately firing on the men in the water. The concussions of shells bursting in the midst of swimming men sent shock waves through the water that slammed against my body with an evil force, making me wince with pain. Men closer to the exploding shells were killed by this concussion alone.

Dazed, unable to believe that all this was real, I floated there, watching as though bewitched. The end had come. By the glare of Japanese searchlights I saw the *Houston* roll slowly over to starboard, and then, with her yardarms almost dipping into the sea, she paused momentarily. Perhaps I only imagined it, but it seemed as though a sudden breeze picked up the Stars and Stripes still firmly two blocked on the mainmast, and waved them in one last defiant gesture. Then with a tired shudder she vanished beneath the Java Sea.

The magnificent *Houston* and most of my shipmates were gone, but in the oily sea around me lay evidence of the carnage wrought by their last battle. Hundreds of Jap soldiers and sailors struggled amidst the flotsam of their sunken ships; and as I watched them drown or swim for their lives, I smiled grimly and repeated over and over, "Well done, *Houston!*"

THE LONG, HEARTBREAKING STRUGGLE IN THE PHILIP-pines rapidly drew to a close: Wainwright's decimated I and II Philippine Corps were hemmed in on both sides of Bataan Peninsula and were steadily being pushed down toward Mariveles Bay, fronting on the beleaguered fortress of Corregidor. The Navy, what was left of it, consisted of a few auxiliaries and motor torpedo boats under Rear Admiral Francis W. Rockwell, Commandant of the purged Cavite Navy Yard. Food and water were in dire supply, so dire that General MacArthur offered bounties to Philippine guerrillas who would brave General Homma's hordes to bring them in. The Japanese promptly countered by threatening to kill any guerrillas caught smuggling. With the situation worsening by the hour, President Roosevelt ordered MacArthur to leave the Philippines and assume command in Australia. With regret the General and his family departed on March 11, 1942.

Certainly little introduction is necessary for MacArthur. As Supreme Commander of the Allied Forces in the South Pacific, he was the architect of the campaign to drive the enemy from his newly-gained strongholds in the Southwest Pacific. He had begun the war as a retired Lieutenant General of the United States Army and, simultaneously, as Field Marshal of the Philippines. He was the recipient, as was his father before him, of the Congressional Medal of Honor. Few Americans in history have garnered more honors during a lifetime of service to their country.

MacArthur's evacuation from "The Rock" is an oft-told story. But until quite recently, when his reminiscences were published, it was never narrated by the controversial MacArthur himself. The "Buck" to whom he refers is of course the ubiquitous torpedo boat officer, Bulkeley, who evacuated the General's entourage.

10.

RETREAT

Darkness had now fallen, and the waters were beginning to ripple from the faint night breeze. The enemy firing had ceased and a muttering silence had fallen. It was as though the dead were passing by the stench of destruction. The smell of filth thickened the night air. I raised my cap in farewell salute, and I could feel my face go white, feel a sudden, convulsive twitch in the muscles of my face. I heard someone ask, "What's his chance, Sarge, of getting through?" and the gruff reply. "Dunno. He's lucky. Maybe one in five."

I stepped aboard *PT-41*. "You may cast off, Buck," I said, "when you are ready."

Although the flotilla consisted of only four battle-scarred PT boats, its size was no gauge of the uniqueness of its mission. This was the desperate attempt by a commander-in-chief and his key staff to move thousands of miles through the enemy's lines to another war theatre, to direct a new and intensified assault. Nor did the Japanese themselves underestimate the significance of such a movement. "Tokyo Rose" had announced gleefully that, if captured, I would be publicly hanged on the Imperial Plaza in Tokyo, where the Imperial towers overlooked the traditional parade ground of the Emperor's Guard divisions. Little did I dream that bleak night that five years later, at the first parade review of Occupation troops, I would take the salute as supreme commander for the Allied Powers on the precise spot so dramatically predicted for my execution.

The tiny convoy rendezvoused at Turning Buoy just outside the minefield at 8 P.M. Then we roared through in single file, Bulkeley leading and Admiral Rockwell in *PT-34* closing the formation.

On the run to Cabra Island, many white lights were sighted—the enemy's signal that a break was being attempted through the blockade. The noise of our engines had been heard, but the sound of a PT engine is hard to differentiate from that of a bomber, and they evidently mistook it. Several boats passed. The sea rose and it began to get rough. Spiteful waves slapped and snapped at the thin skin of the little boats; visibility was becoming poorer.

As we began closing on the Japanese blockading fleet, the suspense grew tense. Suddenly, there they were, sinister outlines against the curiously peaceful formations of lazily drifting cloud. We waited, hardly breathing, for the first burst of shell that would summon us to identify ourselves. Ten seconds. Twenty. A full minute. No gun spoke; the PT's rode so low in the choppy seas that they had not spotted us.

Bulkeley changed at once to a course that brought us to the west and north of the enemy craft, and we slid by in the darkness. Again and again, this was to be repeated during the night, but our luck held.

The weather deteriorated steadily, and towering waves buffeted our tiny, war-weary, blacked-out vessels. The flying spray drove against our skin like stinging pellets of birdshot. We would fall off into a trough, then climb up the near slope of a steep water peak, only to slide down the other side. The boat would toss crazily back and forth, seeming to hang free in space as though about to breach, and then would break away and go forward with a rush. I recall describing the experience afterward as what it must be like to take a trip in a concrete mixer. The four PT's could no longer keep formation, and by 3:30 A.M. the convoy had scattered. Bulkeley tried for several hours to collect the others, but without success. Now each skipper was on his own, his rendezvous just off the uninhabited Cuyo Island.

It was a bad night for everybody. At dawn, Lieutenant (j.g.) V. E. Schumacher, commander of *PT-32*, saw what he took for a Jap destroyer bearing down at 30 knots through the early morning fog. The torpedo tubes were instantly cleared for action, and the 600-gallon gasoline drums jettisoned to lighten the vessel when the time came to make a run for it. Just before the signal to fire, the onrushing "enemy" was seen to be the *PT-41—mine*.

The first boat to arrive at Tagauayan at 9:30 on the morning of March 12 was *PT-34* under the command of Lieutenant R. G. Kelly. *PT-32* and Bulkeley's *PT-41* arrived at approximately 4 P.M. with *PT-32* running out of fuel; those aboard were placed on the two other already crowded craft. A submarine which had been ordered to join us at the Cuyos did not appear. We waited as the day's stifling heat intensified, still spots on the water camouflaged as well as possible from the prying eyes of searching enemy airmen. Hours passed and at last we could wait no longer for Ensign A. B. Akers' *PT-35* (it arrived two hours after we left). I gave the order to move out south-ward into the Mindanao Sea for Cagayan, on the northern coast. This time Rockwell's boat led and *PT-41* followed. The night was clear, the sea rough and high.

Once more, huge and hostile, a Japanese warship loomed dead ahead through the dark. We were too near to run, too late to dodge. Instantly we cut engines, cleared for action—and waited. Seconds ticked into minutes, but no signal flashed from the battleship as she steamed slowly westward across our path. If we had been seen at all, we had been mistaken for part of the native fishing fleet. Our road to safety was open.

We made it into Cagayan at 7 A.M. on Friday, March 13. I called together the officers and men of both PT's. "It was done in true naval style," I told them. "It gives me great pleasure and honor to award the boats' crews the Silver Star for gallantry for fortitude in the face of heavy odds."

THE LAST GASP OF THE PHILIPPINES PT SQUADRON came on April 9 at Cebu. New Jersey-born Lieutenant (j.g.) Ilaf Richardson, executive officer of *PT-34,* now tells of the death of his stout little warship. After working his way into the hills, Richardson ultimately became a Major in the Resistance and there remained until repatriated in 1944. His collaborator, Ira Wolfert, won the Pulitzer Prize for his news dispatches from Guadalcanal.

II.

ALL GONE, NOW

The entrance to Cebu City has Mactan Island on one side and Cebu on the other and is bordered by shoals. Navigation is further complicated by the fact that, particularly at night in wartime when everything is blacked out, there are no distinctive points there that can be used for fixes. When you've seen one part of the coast of Cebu Island, you've pretty much seen it all. It just runs on and on repeating itself . . .

We went into the wrong channel and ran aground on a jut of coral. It worried us. One past time when we had run aground close to shore, the Filipinos had taken us for Japs and shot holes into us. So I went ashore in the *Thirty-Four's* punt to try to dig up a tug and, anyway, if that failed, to block off whatever shooting there might be with the morning sun. But by the time I got a telephone—at Minglanilia, the railroad station there—the tide had started to come in and the *Thirty-Four's* crew had gone over the side and rocked her off the coral and taken off south in the direction where they thought Cebu lay.

It took Kelly time to figure out he was going wrong and backtrack, and he didn't get into the approach to Cebu City until dawn. By then I was standing on Pier One with an ambulance, waiting for the *Thirty-Four* to tie up.

I could see the *Thirty-Four* working busily towards us. Then the air-raid alert sounded. Then I saw four Jap float planes coming in, looking for whatever had pickled their cruiser. I began to jump up and down. "Jesus," I said, "For Christ sake!" I ran back and forth a little way. There was an Army lieutenant standing there, a tall, powerfully built middle-aged man. "What's the matter?" he asked, and I said, "Why, for Christ sake, they're going to get my boat and I'm not on it."

He knew the way I felt. I could tell he knew by the excited way he looked around to see what could be done about it. There wasn't anything to be done. But I liked him right away for the way he knew how I felt—Jim Cushing, a fellow about thirty-five years old who had been a wrestler once and then a chromium miner in the islands before joining the war.

The Japs came on in a "V". They then peeled out of the "V" one by one to dive. They dove strafing and they dove right into the fire of the *Thirty-Four*. But torpedo boats in those days weren't what they are today, and we had only two twin-fifties on board and two lousy Lewis guns. The boys dished out what we had and the streams of tracers crossed each other in mid-air while I ran up and down, tearing at myself and letting little noises run out of my mouth. Then I saw the fat, yellow bomb coming out and saw the boat rigid under it, just held there flat and still-seeming. I groaned at the top of my voice.

Kelly was an iron-minded man, all right. He knew what he was doing. He didn't change course until the last possible splinter of a second so as to give the Jap no time at all to change aim. Then he flipped the boat over. The boat kicked to the right and the bomb hit the water near by on the port side.

I thought it had hit on the rail. That's the way it looked from where I was. The whole world stopped for me. White water stood up and hung there suspended. Smoke curled out of it while it stood there. The smoke curled like spumes of snow blown off a snow-smothered tree. Then the small, dark green *Thirty-Four* weaseled through, all motors roaring, and I shouted, "Missed! Missed! God-damn, if he didn't make them miss," and looked full at Cushing and he grinned back at me with all his strength.

But—as I found out later—Harris (P. W. Harris, Torpedoman 2/c) on the port turret was already dead. He had been putting bullets smack into the Jap. The Jap had started to smoke. It couldn't gain altitude on the pull-out from its dive. (Later verified reports proved that one Jap plane crashed to the south and west of Cebu City.) "I got one," Harris yelled to Martino (J. Martino, CTM) on the starboard turret. "See it! See it! Did you see it?" turning his head as he yelled and following the plane from starboard to port with head high and neck stretched to receive the bomb splinter. The bomb splinter let him finish what he was saying. Then it went in right under his chin and drove up behind his face into the flesh of his brain.

Then there were more bombs and more strafings. One engine went out and then another. The starboard turret stopped working when Martino took a machine-gun bullet in the thigh. The Lewis gun forward stopped when Hunter (C. M. Hunter, CMM) had his upper arm broken by a bullet. One of a stream of bullets ripping open the canopy of the forward compartment like a can opener went into the groin of Reynolds, lying wounded below, and knocked up through his pelvis and bladder and intestines. The last gun on the boat went out of commission when a Jap bullet tore it right out of Ross's hands (W. L. Ross, QM 1/c), the bullet caroming off the gun and opening his thigh. And now Kelly was in trouble up to his neck and over that, up to his ears and the hairline of his forehead, with no guns left with which to fight back and only one engine with which to maneuver. I saw him sputter and wallow out of sight behind Kawit Island. Then he did not reappear.

I jumped into a car. I don't know how I got it. I was too excited. Cushing jumped in after me. He didn't have any reason. He just did, and we tore on down to Tanke, the nearest point to Kawit. We drove with hand on horn and foot pressing the gas pedal through the floorboard, the ambulance piling after us.

The airplanes had gone away. I ran down to the beach and got a baroto—a dugout canoe—there somehow, I don't remember, just took it, I suppose, and paddled with Cushing for the sound of the *Thirty-Four's* engine. We could still hear it going.

Then we saw the *Thirty-Four* aground behind one of those native bamboo fish traps. The flag was still there. It made me feel strange to see it flapping sluggishly in the breeze as if nothing had happened. I suppose your country is always like that. It goes on and on in its own way whatever happens to you, but it made me feel strange to see the flag flapping away in the same old way, and then I scrambled over the stern and I remember the engine blowing fumes in my face and my wrinkling my face up "whew!"—and then there the whole thing was flat before me. A sieve, that's what it looked like, the deck there, a mangled-up sieve of bullet holes with blood dripping through them.

Kelly had got the wounded ashore on Kawit. They had lit out so fast they hadn't had time to shut off the one engine still working. They had left the dead behind. I found Harris lying quietly below, where they had laid him, KIA, certainly that, oh absolutely that—KIA: Harris, Torpedoman 3d Class, United States Navy. I remember running topside after that, thinking who'd ever have thought Harris would be a KIA, and then seeing Kelly come wading back.

"Congratulations, Mr. Kelly," I said, on his being alive.

"Well," he said, "well, . . ." and stumbled around a little bit in his words, and then said, "Hell, I wasn't worried about me. Hell, they can't get me. I'm too tough."

I was so glad to see him I told him that was true, that was the absolute truth, and then we got busy floating the dead and the wounded ashore on the doors to the forward compartment.

Mrs. Charlotte Martin, an American who lived at Cebu with her husband, "Cap," was at the hospital helping. Reynolds became conscious on the operating table. "I'm going to be very sick, ain't I?" he said to her. That was the only thing he said.

"Oh no," she told him, "only for a little while."

Then she leaned forward to stroke his forehead and saw he was dead.

We tried to save the *Thirty-Four*. After all Dad Cleland's boys still had their pair of pliers and ten-pound hammer. Lt. Tom Jurika made the inspection. There were two pilot boats for the party. There were a lot of Filipino soldiers to help and other people—including Jurika and Cushing. Then two Jap planes interrupted them with a sneak attack. They chopped off their engines and came gliding soundlessly out of the sun, then cut their engines back in with a Godawful grind and came on shooting.

They cut the Number Two pilot boat just about in half. Then they came back for the Number One boat. Everybody was trying to wade ashore. They were spread out in a rough line about forty-five feet long, all intent on getting ashore. There were about fifteen inches of water and four inches of slimy mud under it. You couldn't figure out whether it was faster to swim or wade. Then the explosive bullets came into the Number One boat behind. It sounded like two machine guns going at once—one from the plane, and the explosive bullets hitting sounded just like there was a machine gun working on the pilot boat.

Then the planes went for the men. They strafed the center of the line. Some tried to dive under the water. They saw the white-beaded line of bubbles from the bullets, but they couldn't stay under. They couldn't keep the water over them as a cover. There was too much positive buoyancy there because it was so shallow.

Incidentally, those who swam got to the beach faster than those who waded.

When the attack was over, there were two dead and there was a third fellow who had squeezed himself for safety in a small forward compartment in front of the cabin of the Number One boat. He had been clasping his knees and legs to fit himself in there. His back had been to the diving plane. A bullet hit him in the right shoulder, came out through a lower right rib, and then went on through the thigh bone, coming out just above the knee, and after that had gone through the calf of his leg, breaking the shinbone on the way out. He had six holes in him and four major bones broken by the one bullet.

And the *Thirty-Four* was on fire. She was burning like a Christmas tree, hopelessly and beyond redemption.

WITH THE EXCEPTION OF THE DOOLITTLE TOKYO RAID, first of the strikes on the enemy's homeland, the end of April 1942 marked the lowest ebb of America's fortunes in the Pacific; never again would they sink so low.

PART II

THE WAR IN THE ATLANTIC

~~~~~~

WAR CAME AS LESS OF A SHOCK TO THE EAST COAST. IN effect, hostilities between the United States and Germany had begun several months before Pearl Harbor. A *de facto* war had erupted September 4, 1941, when *U-652* fired torpedoes at destroyer *Greer,* which was en route to Iceland. President Roosevelt reacted bitterly, terming the attack "piracy" and declaring that "from now on, if German and Italian vessels of war enter the waters the protection of which is necessary for American defense, they do so at their own risk." Thus ended the "short of war" policy. It had been inaugurated soon after Dunkirk with the controversial exchange of fifty old destroyers for British bases in Newfoundland and the West Indies, and had been continued with little significant change, other than hemispheric defense measures, until the 1st Marine Brigade was lifted to Newfoundland by Task Force 16 in June, 1941. At this time, the United States Navy undertook the escort of convoys to Iceland (by Admiral King's definition within the Western Hemisphere and therefore in our purview) on a regular basis. Now a second destroyer, *Kearney,* was attacked by a U-boat, and on October 31, a third, *Reuben James,* was torpedoed and sunk with a heavy loss of life. The disaster brought home the full impact of the vicious submarine warfare in territorial waters.

Noted illustrator and muralist Griffith Baily Coale, a reserve Lieutenant Commander, was in the next convoy astern of the doomed *Reuben James*. In his memoirs, he speaks of the fateful night.

I.

ATTACK

Half awake because of the unusually easy motion of the ship, in the unaccustomed quiet I am conscious of the monotony of her listening tubes. A sudden loud explosion brings me upright. Know instantly that it is a torpedo and not a depth charge. Spring from my bunk, jump for the bulkhead door, spin the wheel releasing the dogs, and land on the deck in a split second, with General Quarters still rasping. It is not us. A mile ahead a rising cloud of dark smoke hangs over the black loom of a ship. With a terrific roar, a column of orange flame towers high into the night as her magazines go up, subsides, leaving a great black pall of smoke licked by moving tongues of orange. All the ship forward of No. 4 stack has disappeared. We move rapidly down upon her, as her stern rises perpendicularly into the air and slides slowly into the sea. A moment, and two grunting jolts of her depth charges toss debris and men into the air. Suddenly my nostrils are filled with the sickly stench of fuel oil, and the sea is flat and silvery under its thick coating. Before we know it, we hear the cursing, praying, and hoarse shouts for help, and we are all among her men, like black shiny seals in the oily water. The Captain leaps to the engine telegraph and stops her, rushes to the bridge side, sees all at a glance, and gives a sharp order to put her slowly astern, for our way has carried us through them and over the spot where she just has been. In a minute we have backed our way carefully among them and stopped again. Orders calmly barked, and every man acting with cold precision. Cargo nets rigged over the side, lines made ready for heaving. "We are the *Reuben James'* men!" comes a chorus from one raft, and then we know.

The spirit of these huddled greasy forms, packing the overloaded life rafts, is magnificent and their team work in shouting in unison is a fine example of quick return to initiative and organization in a crisis. But the bobbing blobs of isolated men are more pitiful. Thrice blown up and choking with oil and water, they are like small animals caught in molasses. We are now in a black circle of water, surrounded by a vast silver ring of oil slick. The men to port are drifting toward us and the hove lines are slipping through their greasy, oily hands. Soon many eager hands are grasping our cargo net, but our ship's upward roll breaks their weak and slippery hold. Instantly officers and men are begging permission to go over the side, and in no time three of our officers are ten feet from the ship on a reeling raft, and several chief petty officers are clinging to the net, trying to make lines fast around the slimy bodies of the survivors so that dozens of strong arms above on the deck can heave them aboard. The first man is hauled over the amidship rail vomiting oil. Forward from the lofty bridge I see an isolated man below me and hear his choking curses. Half blind, he sees the bridge above him. His cursing ceases—"A *line,* please, Sir!" I cup my hands and shout. A line is hove and he is towed amidships to the nets. Crossing to the starboard side, I see the obscure mass of another loaded raft. One man ignites a cigarette lighter and waves it in the darkness. They shout in chorus, but our lines fall short. They are drifting away to leeward. We shout through megaphones: "Hang on! We'll get you!" One man alone is trying to swim toward us. "Come on buddy!" I bellow, "you can make it!"

But the line hove with great skill falls short—and we chart the course of their drift. It is a lengthy and desperately hard job to get these men aboard. Our men are working feverishly, but less than half have come over the rail and thirty-eight minutes have passed. The horizon is dull red with the coming of the dawn, and the increasing light makes the mass of our inert ship an easy target for the submarine which must be lurking near. One of our destroyers is continually circling us, as the Captain bellows from the bridge: "Get those men aboard!" After sixty-five minutes a few exhausted men still bob along our side. The Captain says to me: "We are in great danger. I cannot risk the ship and her company much longer." Now there are two or three left. . . . A contact directly astern with a submarine! The telephone buzzes in the wheelhouse—the other destroyer gets it too! There is nothing for it. We order the ensigns on the raft aboard with all haste, the engine telegraph is snapped full ahead, and we leap away, leaving two survivors to swirl astern. We roar away and the other destroyer lets go a pattern of depth charges, the white rising columns of water tinged with blood color in the dawning. We search, lose contact, and return, and the other ship picks up eleven men while we circle her. We hope she got the two we had to leave! A third destroyer comes back to relieve us with orders to search the spot until noon, and we with thirty-six survivors, and the other rescue ship, catch up with the fleeing convoy at twenty-five knots.

"Secure from General Quarters!" Ten-thirty and we can go to breakfast! Hot coffee—Lord, it's nectar! We have been on the bridge since five twenty-three! The ship is a mess—her decks, rails and ladders are covered with oil and the smell of it. At lunch I am amazed to see two perfectly naked ensigns walk into the holy precincts of the wardroom, their eyes, hair, and ears still plastered with oil in spite of the scrubbing that they have given themselves! Ropes, life jackets, and the men's clothes are piled along the decks in black and soggy masses. Four men with hemorrhages are put into officers' bunks. We learn that all the officers died with the blowing up of the forward part of the ship, and we had many friends among them.

Two-ten P.M.—the peremptory rasping of General Quarters! The lookouts have sighted five ships. When nearer they turn out to be five British corvettes and they give satisfactory signals. At nine o'clock, with intermittent moonlight, the gunnery officer high above the bridge has picked up what he thinks is a sub on the surface. He asks permission to fire star shells, and with splitting roars our No. 2 turret fires five shots. Hardly has the whine of the last five-inch shell ceased when the whole surface of the distant horizon is lit brightly by their burst, and we make out an English corvette, off her station. In the dark wheelhouse the Captain turns to me: "Is today more than you bargained for?" "No, Sir!" "Well, I hope it's close enough for you," he says with a grin. At that moment two star shells burst high in the air to eastward, followed by heavy firing. Again the dreary rattle of General Quarters! Two corvettes and one of our destroyers dash off to investigate, and report to us by phone that a couple of escort ships had seen two German subs on the surface sneaking in towards us, had opened fire, made them dive, and dropped ash cans where they were. So for the last time that day, General Quarters is over and I turn in at twelve o'clock. I grope my way down from the bridge past the dim battle light in my hall, into my sealed-up cabin, post my log—and an eerie Hallowe'en is ended.

━━━

WITH THE U-BOAT WAR IN SPATE BY DECEMBER 7, 1941, Nazi submarines rampaged along the East Coast with almost total impunity. Torpedo death came without warning and was everywhere; shipping losses mounted precipitously. In January some 270,000 tons of Allied merchant shipping were lost to the U-boats; next month the figure soared to 427,000 tons; and three months later it exceeded 600,000 tons, despite the best efforts of the United States Navy.

The ordeal of our merchant service is ably described in the following excerpt by the prolific Felix Riesenberg, Jr., author of several books about the sea and a reporter for the now defunct San Francisco *News* at the conclusion of the war.

2.

ATLANTIC SLAUGHTER

Winter gales that lashed the North Atlantic in early January had blown themselves out by the eleventh of that month when a group of twenty German U-boats filed down the East Coast to take assigned stations off seaports from Halifax to Miami. The freezing cold did not bother these submariners the way it would their victims: they were all veterans of the northern convoy route or had fought the RAF and Royal Navy in Channel waters. Here were the world's most skillful underseas fighters; no one of them would miss eight shots at a ten-knot tanker or need even a small part of one hour to sink some unarmed World War I freighter. America was about to witness a slaughter that would make Japanese submarine operations seem amateurish for all their deadly toll.

Closing with the shore, the Germans tuned into the six-hundred-meter wave-band and were amazed at the information being given out by the coastal defense stations of a nation at war. Rescue work was in progress as a result of the recent blow and ships at sea were freely announcing their positions. The air patrol was releasing not only the route of its planes but also the time schedule. To make things even easier for the U-Boats the glow of brightly lighted cities showed far off shore. Each German commander waited impatiently for a signal. This was to be the code word *Paukenschlag* (bang on the kettle-drum) which would be flashed by Admiral Karl Doenitz to open the ravage against American merchant shipping.

Doenitz, then forty-nine years of age and a former submarine officer, was in complete control of all U-Boat operations. After the fall of France he had moved his headquarters to a villa at Kernevel overlooking the Bay of Biscay near the concrete sub pens of Lorient.

Here in the big operations room Doneitz and his staff had worked at top speed for a month to organize Operation *Paukenschlag*. The Pearl Harbor attack had come as a surprise to the Germans, so it was necessary to recall U-Boats from the Mediterranean, South Atlantic and Arctic. Details of assigning stations, making refueling arrangements and correlating intelligence were done in record time. The morale of the staff and seagoing personnel had never been higher as the neutrality restriction was lifted. Doenitz expected to show the world a splurge of sinkings that would never be forgotten.

So far in the war German U-Boats had sunk 1,017 ships totalling almost five million tons. Only sixty-six subs had been lost and these were being more than replaced by the twenty new boats delivered each month. In March the effectiveness of the underseas fleet would be greatly enhanced by the addition of the first "milch cows," the one-thousand-ton tanker submarines. It would no longer be necessary for U-Boats to return homeward for fuel and torpedoes; they could remain indefinitely off United States seaports.

On the eve of the American campaign Doenitz had lost a few of his aces. Gunther Prien who made the spectacular raid into Scapa Flow was buried under the Mediterranean along with Karl Endrass who had earned the Oak Leaves to the Iron Cross. But there were many experienced commanders, men like Hardegen, Gengelbach, Reschke and Guggenberger, who sank Britain's new seventy-plane carrier *Ark Royal*. Many of the submariners were former merchant marine officers whose knowledge of commercial shipping was invaluable in hunting and recognizing cargo prey.

While waiting for the chance to attack American ships, the German submarine command had been receiving regular reports from agents. Some of these were sailors who drifted up to an Eighty-sixth Street restaurant with information which was transmitted via short-wave radio by German American Bund members. In New Orleans, the German consul, an ardent yachtsman, forwarded charts of the passes out of the Mississippi to which were added special markings. It did not matter that in January ten seamen found guilty as Nazi spies were given long sentences by a New York court. There were others to carry on the work.

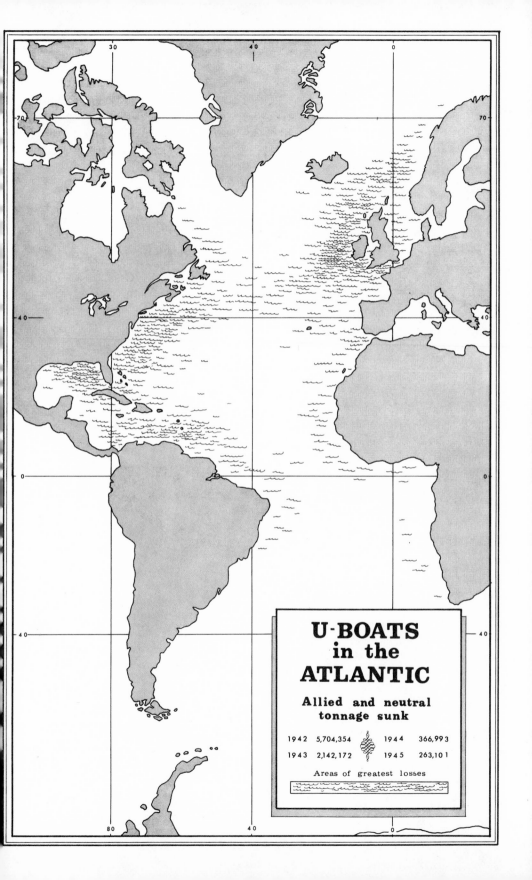

U-BOATS
in the
ATLANTIC

Allied and neutral
tonnage sunk

1942	5,704,354		1944	366,993
1943	2,142,172		1945	263,101

Areas of greatest losses

The U-Boats poised for attack that winter were known as Type VII C. These 770-ton boats were 220-feet over all, twice the length of the wooden Sub Chasers of World War I that were sent out to challenge them; their surface speed was seventeen knots and submerged they could make eight knots. These speeds enabled the subs to catch all but a few American ships of that day; even under water they moved faster than the average convoy.

Between 1940 and 1945 the German yards built 659 of the VII C's which carried a crew of forty-four officers and men on voyages that ranged up to eighty-five hundred miles. Before the end of the war they were equipped with "schnorkels," radar, anti-surface raider-defenses and complicated plotting tables for automatic aiming. At the beginning they were comparatively simple and depended mostly on the skill of personnel.

The early killers were pierced with four bow torpedo tubes and one stern tube. Each carried either twelve or fourteen of the one-ton missiles, and mounted one 20-mm. anti-aircraft cannon and Twin Flak on deck. These were the sea wolves whose commanders received the flash—*Paukenschlag*—on the twelfth of January with commence attack set for the following day.

Admiral Doenitz, a restless man, paced the gleaming floors of his villa, eyes lifting continually to the big wall charts of the world. Gold-headed pins marked the U-Boat kills; soon he expected to see clusters of them between Newfoundland and Florida Straits. In a sense Doenitz was on trial, for Hitler and his closest advisers were as land-minded as the policy-makers of World War I. After a quarter of a century the judgment of Admiral Alfred von Tirpitz on the German high command was again true: "They do not understand the sea." But the Fuehrer would understand figures on destroyed tonnage.

Paukenschlag opened one day early and for Doenitz the smashing start was dramatically apt. In 1914 his first kill as a commander had been a British ship—the *Cyclops*. That was also the name of the ten-thousand-ton freighter blasted without warning on January twelfth south of Halifax. To their death in the frigid waters off Cape Sable went ninety-four men. The same day a Pan American tanker was sunk in the north and the Latvian *Ciltvavia* went under within sight of Cape Hatteras.

Radio broadcasts were interrupted through the next two days and newspaper extras carried banners to announce the arrival of the U-Boats. A big British freighter and a Norwegian tanker were sunk off

Long Island. American seamen ready to sail, or coming on the coast, knew what they could expect.

The first American victim was to be the Esso tanker *Allan Jackson,* bound toward New York from Cartagena, just passing Diamond Shoals off Cape Hatteras at one thirty on the dark morning of January eighteenth. Deep in the water with a 72,870-barrel cargo of Colombian crude oil, the ship was pounding out ten knots over a flat sea. The bridge watch sighted ahead, on lookout for Winter Quarter Lightship.

Captain Felix W. Kretchmer lay on his settee fully dressed with an injured arm propped on a pillow. He heard three bells strike in the wheelhouse and his tired eyes closed as the rhythmic throb of the engines lulled him. He was praying for luck when he dozed off. Then he was hurled from his bank across to the inboard bulkhead.

Shocked awake, the skipper had just gained his feet when a tremendous explosion sounded close below; this time he was catapulted through a doorway into the bathroom. Two torpedoes had ripped into the *Allan Jackson.*

Before he could rise a second time, Captain Kretchmer saw a gust of solid flame sweep his cabin. He was trapped. From out on deck came the hiss of spreading fire and the grind of twisting metal. The deck canted sharply; the skipper grasped a shower stanchion. He could feel the ship sagging and unconsciously moved his feet on the hot deck. Paint began to peel as the flame tongues from the cabin licked toward him. An agonizing, shrill scream from the boat deck caused the skipper to turn his head toward the porthole behind him. Instinctively he headed that way. Hampered by his bad arm he fought desperately to get through the port and finally fell out on deck.

A raging oil fire lit the sea around the foundering ship for three hundred yards. Ladders, decks, the metal boats and even heavy davits had crumbled. Purple water sloshed over the fishplates on the lower bridge deck. Above the noise of the holocaust shrieks pierced the night as men became living torches. No one aboard had ever imagined such a hell.

Still master of his ship, Captain Kretchmer clawed toward the bridge. The vessel's papers—a radio message—distress flares—call the engine room: thoughts raced through the skipper's mind. His hands had just gripped the ladder rail when they were wrenched loose. In the next instant water rose up to his armpits and at first he was surprised at its warmth: the ship was in the Gulf Stream. The water swirled and a great sucking noise drowned out the roar of the inferno; under the sea went the skipper.

With a mighty lung-straining effort Captain Kretchmer struggled to the surface clear of the burning water. By some miracle his hand touched a small length of board. As he clung to it, a large piece of debris bumped him. He did not shout for help because the first object he sighted was the hull of a large U-Boat, metal sides glistening in the flicker of the fire. The skipper, a brave man, kept faith through seven hours and fought off unconsciousness until a destroyer picked him up in the morning.

The first torpedo to strike the *Allan Jackson* had been spotted just after one thirty from the bridge by twenty-five-year-old Melvin A. Rand, Second Mate. He saw the creaming phosphorescent wake 125 feet off and shouted, "Hard left!" to the man at the wheel. Before the ship responded to her helm, she was ripped open amidships. Mr. Rand was knocked off his feet, then lifted on a deck grating and tossed overside. With him went Third Mate Boris A. Vornosoff. They shouted up to the junior officer, Francis M. Bacon who leaped. The three men lashed themselves to planking and tried to lift their arms and legs clear of the water when sharks were attracted to the scene. Drifting off they saw pain-maddened men writhing blindly on deck, their bodies enveloped in flame. Before daylight Mr. Bacon died and drifted off still lashed to his spar.

Back aft, where the crew berths in a tanker, Boatswain Rolf Clausen and his men had been playing cards in the messroom when they felt the forward part of the *Jackson* jerk from the two explosions. By the time they reached the deck, No. 4 lifeboat was afire. Eight men quickly launched the starboard boat; the injured Chief Engineer was lowered into it. No sooner were they water-borne than flames licked at them. They struggled to get clear of the side and were saved from cremation by the discharge of a condenser pump. But the force of the stream pushed them astern into the backwash of the propeller which was still turning over. Oars dug into the oily water, back bent. By great good luck they ratched clear. Fifteen minutes later they picked up Stephen Verbonich, the Radio Operator. In the morning they were picked up by the destroyer which found the two mates and the captain. Cruising in the area, the naval vessel also fished the bodies of four dead from tangles of blackened wreckage. One of these was young Carl Webb, a wiper, after whom a ship would be named two years later.

Ashore that morning, still suffering from extreme shock, the survivors gave newspaper men the "eyewitness" accounts. These were a preview of what lay ahead for unarmed merchant ships, a sample of the experience through which any man might expect to pass if he sailed these hazardous waters. Twenty-two men lost their lives in the torpedoing and burning of the *Allan Jackson*.

The Germans struck again off Hatteras in the pre-dawn darkness of the following day and sent two torpedoes into the thirty-year-old Savannah Line freighter *City of Atlanta*. Ancient plates buckled; the sea poured in so fast that the vessel heeled over on her beam ends before she lost way. The starboard lifeboat hung useless, swaying inboard. Eighteen men who scrambled into the port boat were dumped as it capsized in the falls. Forty-four men were killed. Only three survivors were picked up at daybreak by a Seatrain Texas ship.

The *City of Atlanta* had scarcely settled when a U-Boat slipped up astern of the tanker *Malay* and boldly opened fire with its deck gun. Brave men stood by in the engine room when Captain John Dodge called down that he was going to run. The tanker was bound from Philadelphia toward Port Arthur in ballast; a shot into her gas-filled hods would blow the ship to pieces.

The sixty-nine-year-old skipper bounded in and out of the wheel house yelling course changes to the quartermaster. Men ducked for shelter as the U-Boat raked the decks from two hundred yards astern. Fires started and were put out; the after house and funnel were riddled; cordite fumes choked the men who huddled in the passageways, ready at any instant to leap overboard.

The stern chase continued for two hours and the *Malay* was driven close inshore where the U-Boat turned away. Captain Dodge carefully felt his way off soundings, then shaped a course for Old Point Comfort and radioed the Navy. The danger seemed averted when the *Malay* was suddenly hit amidships by a torpedo.

Unnerved men lowered a boat while the tanker was still plowing through the water and made the mistake of releasing the forward falls; two were thrown overboard as the boat was whipped around. The *Malay* limped into port.

U-Boats sank the *Frances Salman* and the *Norvana* in the next two days along with Allied vessels so that the toll in two weeks off the Atlantic Coast was twenty ships sunk, two hundred merchant sailors dead. In addition there had been a dozen collisions and several groundings when ships and some navigational aids blacked-out. The press, sea unions and steamship companies demanded action from Washington. Why don't we put guns on our merchant ships? Where is the Navy?

Months would pass before the U-Boats were seriously challenged. To the Germans Operation *Paukenschlag* was less demanding, and far more sport, than training exercises in the Baltic. The bright lights of Boston, New York, Atlantic City and Miami Beach were friendly reminders of Berlin. They also served to make excellent silhouettes of ships that were so carefully blacked-out. Night-club, restaurant and theater owners insisted on flashing their neon invitations: in war relaxation was necessary to keep up morale.

To make things even easier for themselves, the U-Boat commanders resorted to guile. In the darkness of January twenty-fourth, off the Virginia Capes, a U-Boat sank a big foreign tanker and from its glow picked up the outline of the ore carrier *Venore*. The submarine raced ahead for an hour then stopped to wait in the path of the oncoming American vessel.

This is the lightship. You are standing into danger.

The bridge watch of the *Venore* snapped to the attention as the blinker message was read. Captain Fritz Duurloo rubbed his chin and scowled.

Direct your course to pass close to me, came the followup from the U-boat whose commander peered into the darkness. He watched the bulk of the ship begin to swing and gave the order to fire One and Two.

Deafening explosions thundered around the *Venore*. Ears ringing, wits dulled by fear, the crew tried to launch boats before the ship lost way. When survivors were rescued next morning twenty men were missing.

As the month of January neared an end two more American ships were bagged. On the twenty-sixth the *Francis E. Powell* was cut in two off Delaware Breakwater with a loss of four lives. Four days later a U-Boat surfaced in the path of the *Rochester* a few hours out of New York. One of the lifeboats ran afoul of the submarine and men fended off, then rowed with all their might in fear of being machine-gunned. Tough young Germans jeered at them and opened fire point-blank at the ship.

Whenever possible U-Boat commanders gave their crews a chance to blow off steam by firing the deck guns. There were many stories during the war of boat crews being machine-gunned, but there is no substantiated record of Americans being so slaughtered by the Germans. It was the Japs who were definitely proved to have committed this atrocity . . .

Public indignation increased as the U-Boat blitz continued unchecked. The Navy established a system of defense based on the 1929 Coastal Frontier Forces and placed in command the best of its antisubmarine officers, Admiral Adolphus Andrews. The new Eastern Sea Frontier, responsible for the safety of merchant ships sailing between Canada and Florida, had only the most antiquated equipment with which to fight a fleet of submarines then estimated at thirty. Ten World War I subchasers joined three seagoing yachts. The surface units were supported by four blimps and six Army bombers. This force did not even sight, let alone engage, the enemy.

Available naval vessels in the opening months of the war had been ordered to transatlantic convoy duty. Guns and armed guards went to ships bound for England and Russia. All aircraft were being directed to higher priority theaters. The Royal Air Force refused to release a number of American-built bombers that were about to be flown to Britain on Lend Lease. Merchant seamen were as expendable as the soldiers fighting against hopeless odds on Corregidor: no other group of the Nation's citizens were left in any such peril.

Hitler reminded the world of this when he came on the air as the month of February opened. He ranted the threat that the U-Boats were only just beginning and that American ships and seamen would soon feel the full might of his submarine blitz. He attempted to frighten sailors off the sea with the warning that any so foolish as to sailors stood scant chance of ever returning.

The Fuehrer's threatening prophecy was almost immediately carried out in a sinking that brought as much suffering and human tragedy as any disaster of World War II.

The Standard Oil Company of New Jersey tanker, *W. L. Steed,* launched in 1918, was logging no better than eight knots on February second as she drew abeam of the Delaware Capes. The ship was low in the water, carrying sixty-five thousand barrels of oil, and seas that broke over the forecastlehead swirled above the well deck to cover the catwalk. A strong northwest wind brought a driving snowstorm; men who had been burned by the Caribbean sun two days before were now bundled up and shivered as they looked out at the white manes of angry seas that broke under the blizzard.

The nerves of all hands were on edge. A submarine had been

sighted two days before and had been seen at intervals up until sunset February first. At seven that night a suspicious light showed astern and the master was called. Captain Harold G. McAvenia, a veteran of World War I, changed course. When the danger seemed past, the ship was brought about to buck the gale again. All boats were swung out; most of the men drank coffee through the night, huddled in the messroom wearing life jackets.

Eight bells struck for midnight and the Third Mate made the last Rough Log entry for the first. The watch was relieved by Sydney Wayland, Second Mate, who later gave an account of the events from twelve forty-five A.M. onward. Here are extracts from that officer's report:

Without warning of any kind the ship was suddenly struck by a torpedo on her starboard side, forward of the bridge, at her No. 3 tank, setting the oil afire.

At that time the vessel was proceeding generally in a northeasterly direction, about 80 miles off the Delaware Capes. The sea was bad, with a strong northeasterly wind. It was snowing hard, making the visibility two miles at best.

The next thing I heard was the engine being stopped by the captain in the pilot house and the general alarm sounded. The master ordered me to get the two amidships boats ready for lowering.

Second Mate Wayland carried out his orders and took No. 2 boat which he successfully launched into the heavy sea with fourteen men. His report told that all boats cleared, leaving no one aboard, but that he never again sighted any of them. From his boat the men were able to see two big U-Boats which shelled the *Steed* until she blew up. His account continued:

Weather conditions were fierce, with the snowstorm and dangerous northwest seas running. Everyone in the boat was suffering from cold, due mostly to lack of clothes.

The men in lifeboat #2 died one after another until February 5, when Chief Mate Einar A. Nilsson and myself were the only ones alive.

On the morning of February 6, Nilsson showed signs of weakness and extreme fatigue. At about 9:30 A.M. I sighted a steamer coming close to us and made every effort, waving and hailing, to get her attention, as she seemed to go past, but finally she hove around, headed for us, and picked us up.

This was the British freighter *Hartlepool* which continued on her voyage and landed the two officers at Halifax on February ninth. They were sent to the hospital and Mr. Wayland concluded his statement:

Mr. Nilsson died the following day. I left the hospital on February 28, after recovering from the pains and suffering experienced.

Another account of the sinking was given by Able Seaman Ralph Mazzucco who was in No. 3 boat with Joaquin Brea, the Boatswain, and Able Seamen Raymond Burkholder and Louis Hartz and Ordinary Seaman Arthur Chandler. As they were swept around the stern of the sinking *Steed,* they had the first sighting of one of Doenitz's newest U-Boats:

Just then a large submarine, estimated at about 2,000 tons, painted a light gray, with guns forward and abaft her conning tower, appeared on the port side. Men immediately manned the guns; the forward one appeared to be a 4-inch and the after one a trifle smaller. They started shelling the ship.

The seamen watched the German lob shells into their ship with astonishing accuracy despite the heavy seas that clawed at the gunners. They then tried to make contact with the other boats but were swept by a walloping cross breaker that carried away all but three of their oars together with the tiller, rudder, sails and boat hooks. Soaked by icy water they bailed frantically to empty the boat. The report from No. 3 continued:

After struggling a couple of hours we had the boat bailed out and then went under the canvas boat cover for protection from the heavy spray and strong wind. Some of us kept joking and talking through the night to keep up our morale. Finally Chandler lay down in a life preserver and fell asleep. The next morning I tried to wake him and realized that he was dead. We carried him to the forward end of the boat.

The same morning Burkholder became delirious. Shortly after noon he died and was also carried forward.

It was so bitterly cold that we decided to start a fire. The lamp in the boat being broken, we poured oil from it on some wood we had chopped up and placed it in the water bucket. The fire burned steadily and helped to dry our wet clothes and thaw us out to some extent. Perhaps it saved our lives. By cutting up the thwarts, stern sheets, forward sheets, bottom board, and one of the oars, we managed to keep the fire going the rest of the day and during the night until we were picked up by a Canadian auxiliary cruiser, HMCS *Alcantara.*

Brea, Hartz and Mazzucco were taken to Halifax and although badly frozen they all recovered.

A final report on the disaster reached Standard Oil from Cape Town, South Africa, following the arrival there of the British vessel *Raby Castle.* She had picked up a boat on February twelfth some four hundred miles to seaward of the position at which the *Steed* was torpedoed. There were four men in that boat but only Elmer E. Maihiot, Jr., was alive. He had been Second Assistant Engineer and died three days after being rescued.

Only four men survived the ordeal while thirty-four perished. To the list of the dead could be added other frightening statistics to show the course of war projected through the loss of a single vessel.

The cargo of the *W. L. Steed,* broken down into a retailing unit, amounted to more than one quarter of a million gallons of oil or one million quarts: close to five hundred thousand dollars. On her wartime voyages the ship had carried *forty-five times* that value of crude oil. Had she continued unmolested through the war, this single vessel would have delivered six million barrels.

While the open boats of the *Steed* battled winter seas, the U-Boats upped their sinking average to two ships a day. Many were attacked so close to shore that Florida and New Jersey residents came down to the beaches to watch the carnage. Travelers in commercial aircraft were witnesses to daylight attacks in the Atlantic and Gulf. Timothy Morgan, a retired watchman of Sarasota, Florida, never forgot the strange experience of seeing a tanker burst into flames five thousand feet below. "The boat looked like a toy," he recalled years later. "We circled while the pilot called shore to get help and we came down low enough to see the submarine dashing off. I never saw so much black smoke. Then tiny white boats—four of them—crawled away from the burning boat like little bugs."

Frantic calls to the Navy by passenger airliners and spectators brought only belated help; Eastern Sea Frontier in late February was still without adequate equipment. The onshore wind carried the menacing boom and crack of gunfire and drove in a pall of oil smoke. White beaches became covered with petroleum scum and littered with dead fish, sodden life jackets and smashed boats, rafts and decking.

Small boys searched the shore and among the things they found were parts of human bodies. This was the unprotected coastline of America in the months of January, February and March of 1942.

Into the seaports came exhausted, unnerved men, oilsmeared and half naked. Many wore dirty bandages over horrible burns. All showed the strain of a wretched experience. But old men with a lifetime of sea service, together with teen age boys on their first trips, showed a common defiance. "Give us guns," they continued to demand. Their answer to the stock reporter's question was, "Hell yes, I'm shipping out again." There was no braggartism and few asked for more than a drink or a cigarette. In ordinary times many of them might be drifters, troublemakers, drunks and brawlers; under stress at sea they showed great courage and later a fierce pride. Without their ship, their clothing or any possessions, they proclaimed the dignity of man.

The waterfront bars and restaurants frequented by sailors were plastered with warnings:

> A SLIP OF THE LIP
>
> MAY SINK A SHIP
>
> DON'T BLAB—THE ENEMY IS LISTENING

Nazi informers were everywhere and U-Boats were being fed information that let them make the best use of their torpedoes. The Germans chided men in lifeboats for being a few minutes late or early at their rendezvous; officers were astonished to hear U-Boat commanders tell them their destination and the cargo they had been carrying.

From the decks of the big gray submarines motion pictures were now being taken of the burning ships under shell fire as crews scrambled into the boats. Machine guns were trained on the survivors to bring out a realistic look of fear while the cameras ground. Later, audiences in Berlin would have no doubt about victory over so spiritless and ragged an enemy.

Navy communiqués were handed out to the newspapers:

Enemy submarine activity continued last week off the East Coast of North America from Cape Hatteras to Newfoundland and southward to the Florida Straits . . .
Strong counter measures are being taken by units of the Navy's East Coastal Command.

In Paul's Bar and the Dutchman's on Eleventh Avenue, New York and in all the bars between there and the Ship's Light on Charles Street, New Orleans, seamen shrugged when they read a Navy release that claimed twenty submarines had been sunk off the coast. Zero was the true count in February. Out in San Pedro a sailor had his AB ticket, lifeboat certificate, identification and social security numbers tattoed on his legs. Men shipping out went "schooner-rigged," taking only bare necessities and checking valuables at the union halls or Seamen's Church Institute. Good-byes to wives and families took on the aspect of finality.

At the height of the sinkings, when some sort of coastal patrol was so badly needed, Captain Arthur O. Brady, USNR, privately voiced a suggestion that had occurred to many who were old enough to remember Prohibition. "Where are the rum runners these days?" he asked, half humorously. "Those fellows knew every inch of water from Florida up to the Bay of Fundy."

Veterans of the Jersey Coast, Long Island and Florida beaches, where they smuggled booze in the 'twenties, had operated fast, armed boats. But in the spring of 1942 those of them not in prison were playing the black market or cargo filching along the waterfronts.

Through the month of February the public because familiar with the pattern of U-Boat attack. Most survivors told of surprise and shock; the tanker disasters brought explosions and burning. Men could not remain on the scorching decks but usually the only place to jump was into a sheet of flame. Here was the paradox of icy water overlaid with searing fire.

To the U-Boats the merchant ships were like game to be bagged in a hunt. Each commander was out to get a tonnage-destruction figure great enough to earn him the Oak Leaves to the Iron Cross. Here is an extract from the log of *U-504* as it swept the waters of Florida commencing on February twenty-first:

> Reached operational area. Fired double salvo at tanker steering south in ballast. Hit fore and aft. Ship sank by stern. Next evening chased a merchant ship but lost her in a rain squall. Half an hour later sank a four-masted ship in night attack. Ship turned turtle. Steered south for Jupiter. Attacked large tanker. Tremendous explosion and ship at once burst into flames. She was carrying 12,000 tons of petrol. Picked up destroyer noises. In the bright moonlight sighted enemy and dived. Was attacked with depth-charges and pursued for three hours, but although enemy passed

overhead several times he did not attack again, and finally cleared off. A little later made submerged daylight attack on a 7,000-ton petrol tanker which blew up. Serious damage sustained on deck from heavy seas which impeded action. Set course for home at slow speed. Sank a ship making for Bombay carrying deck-cargo of motor cars. Ship blown to bits. . . .

This cold account described what by that time was a commonplace slaughtering in the ocean jungle off the sandy coast of Florida. From the Merchant Marine Naval Reserve list of wartime sinkings it is possible to write the obituary of the ships that fell victims to *U-504.*

The first ship caught was the tanker *Republic,* five of whose crew were killed by the explosion. The four-masted ship was a Cuban vessel, and the tanker reported to have burst into flames north of Jupiter was the *Cities Service Empire.* All her lifeboats on the starboard side were smashed; twenty-three of the crew huddled on one raft, and seven men were burned to death.

The merchant ship that escaped in the rain squall on February twenty-second was the *Green Island.* Her SOS was picked up by America's first Pacific-bound convoy out of New York. One of the escorting destroyers raced ahead but was rammed by the *Green Island* which mistook her for a sub in the fading light. A second destroyer made the depth-charge attack on *U-504.*

The petrol-tanker caught just before the sinking of the Bombay-bound vessel was Brazilian. At the time of her torpedoing Sumner Welles was in Rio de Janeiro addressing delegates to a Pan American defense conference.

Operation *Paukenschlag* reached a furious climax midway in March when the U-Boats sank twenty ships in one week. The score for a little more than two months was 145 ships totaling eight hundred thousand tons and six hundred lives. The American Merchant Marine Institute attempted to impress the general public with comparative statistics: the average freighter carried an amount of cargo equal to *four trains* of seventy-five cars each! A standard tanker loaded enough gasoline on one voyage to supply the holder of an "A" ration book with gas for thirty-five thousand *years!* Admiral Doenitz sent more submarines to the American station and was getting ready to commission the first tankers and supply boats. He promised the Fuehrer a total of two hundred ships, one million tons, by April first.

On the last day of March the compilers of ship losses made another record entry: in slightly over twenty-four hours the U-Boats sank six vessels: *City of New York, Tiger, T. C. McCobb, Menominee, Barnegat* and *Allegheny.*

Thirteen days after the *City of New York* went under Robert "Pat" Peck, an ordinary seaman, came into a Delaware port and told how the big American South African Line motor ship was slugged one hundred miles off the coast as she bucked a head gale and waves that ran twenty feet from trough to crest. Only one of the ship's four boats cleared and in it were crowded twenty persons, including a three-year-old girl, her mother and two other women.

Half the men died in the next ten days. The burials were hideous for there were no weights to sink the corpses which would just float away. The child, who had sobbed constantly since the abandoning, gave way to hysterics when her mother died. "Please don't throw my Mummy in the water. Please don't."

U-Boats, lurking between the Down East coast and Florida Straits, had so increased in number that it was necessary for them to burn navigation lights to avoid collisions when they surfaced at night. They refueled or took on ammunition and supplies without fear; commanders even exchanged visits. In Southern waters the Germans stretched out on deck to acquire sun tans.

In Miami there were rumors that U-Boats were receiving regular milk deliveries from a local dairy. It was said that ticket stubs from a Flagler Street movies had been found in the pockets of submariners captured offshore. The FBI investigated five hundred reports of small boats refueling the enemy, all of them false alarms. J. Edgar Hoover's men did capture saboteurs near Ponte Verde, just south of Jacksonville, and twenty-seven aliens were rounded up in the lee of the Miami Naval Air Station at Opa-Locka. These German, Italian and Japanese aliens were operating with radios, cameras and binoculars.

The United States Navy was being sharply criticized, even by its Commander-in-Chief who was then carrying on a confidential correspondence with Prime Minister Winston Churchill . . . Roosevelt wrote:

. . . My Navy has been definitely slack in preparing for this submarine war off our coast. As I need not tell you, most naval officers have declined in the past to think in terms of any vessel of less than two thousand tons. You learned the lesson two years ago. We still have to learn it. By May 1 I expect to get a pretty good coastal patrol working from Newfoundland to Florida and through the West Indies. I have begged, borrowed, and stolen every vessel of every description over eighty feet long—and I have made this a separate command with the responsibility in Admiral Andrews.

"Roosevelt's Navy" was under attack by many amateurs, some of them politicians who had screamed against prewar appropriations. Enemies of the Administration pointed accusingly to the string of islands leased from Britain and longed for the fifty exchanged destroyers.

While pundits of the shore offered caustic and lubberly advice, the Eastern Sea Frontier battled delays, red tape and selfishness. Luxury lighting at Miami and West Palm Beach did not go out until the end of the winter tourist season; sufficient ships for convoy escort were not delivered until April, and the first protected movement of merchant ships—from Hampton Roads to Key West—started in mid-May.

After hundreds of merchant seamen had died, most of them in night attacks, daylight coastal navigation was put into force. Ships sailing between Maine and Delaware Bay anchored overnight in Boston and New York. Because there were no such convenient stopping places south of Hatteras, artificial ports were constructed. These were pens built out of huge booms and submarine nets, spaced 125 miles apart. Freighters and tankers were herded in at sunset through mine fields; during the day they were escorted by 1918 destroyers released from Iceland convoy duty.

The "leap-frog" convoys at the start were far from effective and the U-Boat sinking average remained at better than two per day. But Admiral Doenitz did not like even the mildest opposition and in the spring directed his U-Boats to the Caribbean and Gulf of Mexico. In these unprotected waters the Germans promptly established a new slaughter record.

The problem America faced, and needed to solve with the greatest speed, was one of how to replace merchant ships and crews . . .

~~~~~~

LEAVING THE NAVY AS IT SHAPED UP FOR THE monumental struggle ahead, let us turn to the events aboard an Esso tanker at sea during the U-boat invasion. Able Seaman John J. Forsdal of *R. P. Resor* was aboard the 12,875 ton merchantman when she fell prey to an enemy submarine. It was during her fifty-sixth voyage to the United Kingdom, and Forsdal was one of her few survivors.

3.

"WIPE THE OIL

OUT OF MY EYES!"

On February 19, 1942, the *R. P. Resor,* commanded by Fred Marcus and with Chief Engineer Travis L. Lumpkin in charge of her engine-room, left Houston, Texas, with a cargo of 78,729 barrels of fuel oil, bound, via Baytown, for Fall River, Massachusetts.

She carried a merchant crew of 41 officers and men. With the ensign and 8 Navy gunners of her armed guard, she had a total complement of 50. Sailing without escort, she followed Navy routing instructions and maintained a total blackout at night . . .

About two days out of Baytown, Captain Marcus began steering zigzag courses—long courses on each leg in the Gulf of Mexico and shorter courses, of 15 minutes each, north of Miami. In addition to the crew's lookout watches, the armed guard maintained lookouts day and night, posting one man on the monkey bridge and another at the gun aft.

On the night of the 26th, Captain Marcus was in the wheelhouse when Third Mate Graham P. Covert took over the 8 to 12 watch . . . Ordinary Seaman Orville R. Hogard was stationed as lookout on the wing of the bridge.

The evening was fine and clear. There was a light northwesterly breeze, small ripples on the water, and a long, moderate, lazy easterly swell. It was a brilliantly lighted moonlight night, there being a little better than half a moon showing. The sky was cloudless and the night was so clear I could distinguish the individual lights on the New Jersey shore. The evening was cold and it was necessary to wear heavy clothing and ear muffs.

From 8 to 10 p.m. Able Seaman Forsdal was taking his trick at the wheel. The *Resor* was then steering a base course of 30 degrees by gyro-compass and zigzagging at full speed 15 degrees to the left and right of that course at intervals of 15 minutes. A Navy gunner was on lookout duty atop the pilot house and a seaman stood watch on the foc'sle head. The wheelhouse was blacked out and the vessel was not showing navigation lights. When Forsdal left the bridge at 10 p.m. the ship was steering the zigzag course heretofore explained.

From 10 p.m. to 11 p.m. I was on standby duty. At the latter hour I proceeded to the foc'sle head and relieved Ordinary Seaman Hogard. The *Resor* would soon be about 20 miles east of Manasquan Inlet, N. J.

Just before 7 bells, I was standing slightly to port of the stem. Suddenly I sighted a dark object lying low in the water about two points on the port bow. Although not far distant from the vessel, it was indistinct. I did not hear any engine or a motor exhaust, possibly due to the sound of the *Resor's* bow waves. I immediately turned and walked aft along the port side toward the bell, to report the craft. A few seconds after I sighted the vessel, which I thought might be a small fishing boat, she turned on her navigating lights. I could see that her white light was about 5 feet above her green and red side lights. The lights were then about 200 to 300 yards away and were heading for a point midway between the stem of the *Resor* and the break of the foc'sle head.

A second or so after the strange vessel showed her navigating lights, I rang two strokes on the bell and then reported by voice to the bridge: "Small vessel about two points on your port bow, sir!" The bridge answered: "Aye! Aye!" From the time I first observed the craft until I reported it, only 10 to 15 seconds had elapsed.

As I turned to walk forward, I saw that the lights were about three points on the port bow. They were too dim to show any part of her hull and after a few seconds she switched them off. Thinking that she was a fishing boat because of her small outline and not realizing that a submarine would venture so close to shore, I resumed my lookout without giving further thought to the vessel, which had disappeared in the darkness. At this time, as I recall, the moon was either aft or on our starboard quarter.

I had continued my lookout for a minute or two, when all of a sudden I felt and heard a violent explosion on our port side. Within what seemed a fraction of a second the *Resor* was aflame from her bridge aft and debris was hurled high into the air. I was thrown to the deck and lay there momentarily in a dazed condition. Then to protect myself from falling fragments I crawled under a platform on the foc'sle head which had been constructed for a gun.

When it seemed safe, I got up and went down to the fore deck. In the light of the flames, the submarine was now clearly visible, about four points on our port bow and 400 to 500 yards distant. The enemy vessel, without lights, appeared to be on her way to the Jersey shore and I could hear the noise of a heavy Diesel exhaust. Then she disappeared from view.

Removing my lifebelt and heavy overcoat, I put the lifebelt on again and proceeded to the foremast rigging on the port side, where I tried to size up the situation to see whether I could go aft. I decided that the fire was too severe. Then I released the portside life raft, found a line hanging over the side and lowered myself into the water, which was icy cold.

When about 50 yards from the ship, as I kept on swimming in heavy oil, I heard a second violent explosion. Looking over my shoulder I saw that the oil floating on the water in the vicinity of the ship was afire. I had to swim out to the sea at least 20 minutes to get away from the burning oil.

About this time I heard a voice and paddled toward it, shouting. A moment later I heard another man calling nearer by. It was Radio Operator Clarence Armstrong and I swam in his direction.

Sparks shouted to me and to the other man in the water, whom I could not identify: 'Come over here so we can be together.' He also told us he had a life raft. The *Resor* was then between us and the Jersey shore and I could see the mass of flames growing steadily worse.

Covered with more and more oil, I struggled hard to reach Armstrong, answering him each time he shouted. In the light of the flaming *Resor,* after a period of time I cannot estimate, I arrived at the raft, which was about half a mile distant from the ship. Hooking my arms around the lifelines I rested for ten minutes or so in a state of exhaustion. Sparks was hanging to a lifeline on the other side of the raft.

I was heavily weighted down with cold and clinging oil; the exertion of climbing up on the raft taxed my strength so seriously that I was unable to do anything but lie down. The cold and the heavy oil seemed to be paralyzing my body.

While lying on the raft I observed what I took to be a Coast Guard patrol boat. I told Sparks to keep his chin up, that help was coming. At the same time I was shouting toward the boat so they could locate us. When she passed us she turned around and put a searchlight on the raft. Then a lifebuoy was thrown, attached to a line. I managed to get my arms through the ring but as the vessel went ahead I was hauled off the raft into the sea. Then the patrol boat's headway pulled the life ring from my grasp. I managed to return slowly to the raft, but as I felt warmer in the water, I did not attempt to climb aboard it. Armstrong was still hanging on, but did not reply when I talked to him. (Forsdal did not know, at that time, that the radio operator had died.)

A small boat came over to me and a rope was put under my arms. Soon afterward a picket boat came along and the line secured to my body was passed to it. I cannot remember what happened after that until I found myself on board the boat, which landed me on the New Jersey coast.

Another man had been hauled out of the water by the picket boat before they rescued me. He was a member of the Navy armed guard named Hey.

According to Chief Boastwain's Mate John W. Daisey, commander of the Coast Guard picket boat that rescued the two survivors, "Forsdal was so coated with thick congealed oil that we had to cut his clothes and his life jacket off with knives. They were so weighted with oil we couldn't get him aboard. Even his mouth was filled with a blob of oil."

THE NORTH ATLANTIC WAS FRAUGHT WITH DISAGREE-able duties and by far the worst was the Murmansk Run. This route, while under the aegis of the Royal Navy, was our primary lifeline with Russia and extended from Iceland and Spitzbergen into the Barents Sea. The United States lost some twenty percent of her war shipments to Russia on the Murmansk Run, because of the combined attack of U-boats and the *Luftwaffe*. The stirring drama of Murmansk is recounted by Captain Walter Karig, Lieutenant Commander Earl Burton, and Lieutenant Stephen L. Freeland.

CAPTAIN WALTER KARIG,

LIEUTENANT EARL BURTON AND

LIEUTENANT STEPHEN L. FREELAND

4.

MURMANSK RUN

At first, armed guard duty was the least coveted assignment in the Navy. A normal greeting extended to a shipmate who received orders to the Armed Guard was "Well, so-long fish-bait. It was nice knowing you." An exclusive society was projected, "The Bitter Enders," whose membership was limited to Armed Guard personnel surviving a torpedoing. Someone originated a paraphrase that the Armed Guard ironically adopted as its war-cry: "Stand by. Prepare to Fire. Abandon ship!"

Or, even more to the point, after "Sighted sub: sank same" became famous, was the Armed Guard version—"Sighted sub. Glub! Glub!"

Men—and boys—who had never seen salt spray in their lives returned from one Armed Guard cruise veterans of both the sea and the war.

There was one run that became wardroom and liberty legend. It was told and retold by those that lived through to tell it. And the men who had been on it were forever considered a little higher in the echelon of Armed Guard veterans. It was the "Murmansk run."

The German armies were at the very gates of Moscow by the end of 1941. Relief, in the form of American war supplies, had to get through to the Soviet forces. The shortest practicable route for this material was over the Arctic Circle and around the North Cape of Norway down to the port of Murmansk or into the White Sea to

131

Archangel. Bitter weather and a ruthless enemy combined to make that the most dangerous of voyages.

Not only was there danger from enemy submarines, based all along the Norwegian coast; German airfields were close at hand, and—a more serious potential menace than either—the heavy units of the German fleet, the *Von Tirpitz,* the *Hipper,* and *Scheer* and *Lutzow* together with squadrons of destroyers lurked in the deep rugged Alten Fjord, a constant murderous threat against anything smaller than a battleship daring to pass near their lair.

To combat these heavy craft, the British Home Fleet had to maintain a constant patrol of the waters with ships of similar armor and armament. More than this, the Home Fleet had to protect each Russia-bound convoy. It was a heavy duty for a navy that had already taken serious losses. Help was needed, and help was forthcoming.

On March 26, 1942, Task Force 99, under the command of Rear Admiral Robert C. Giffen, Jr., USN, sailed from Casco Bay, Maine, for Scapa Flow, to operate with the Home Fleet. The Admiral flew his flag from the battleship *USS Washington* (Captain Howard H. J. Benson, USN, commanding) and his force comprised the carrier *Wasp* (Captain John W. Reeves, Jr., USN), the cruisers *Wichita* (Captain Harry W. Hill, USN) and *Tuscaloosa* (Captain Norman C. Gillette, USN), and the destroyers of Desron 8 (Captain Don P. Moon, USN).

The *Wasp* was detached from the Task Force for a special mission upon her arrival, and the remaining ships took up their share of the burden of keeping the big German vessels bottled up out of harm's way.

Late in June a special job came up, one which promised vital action and, possibly, a chance to end the threat of the German "fleet-in-being." Reconnaissance and intelligence agreed that the *Tirpitz* and the Nazi cruisers were being readied for sea. At the same time one of the largest and most important convoys was heading for Murmansk.

The *Tuscaloosa* and *Wichita* were assigned to the Cruiser Covering Force to escort the convoy from Iceland around the North Cape under the command of Admiral Hamilton, RN. The *Washington* joined the heavy units of the Home Fleet under the command of Admiral Tooey, RN.

The prime mission of the Cruiser Covering Force was to get the convoy through, with the secondary mission of luring or delaying any heavy units of the Nazis into range of the big boys of the Allied fórce. German air and submarine attacks were expected in great strength; a previous Murmansk convoy had got through with little damage, which made Hitler angry. The particular convoy, PQ 17, being covered represented some seven hundred million dollars' worth of arms for hard-pressed Russia, which made the Nazis anxious. An added prize for the Germans was convoy PQ 13, outward bound from Murmansk, scheduled to pass PQ 17 to northward of North Cape.

The *Tirpitz* was lured out together with one or two cruisers (reports do not agree), a large screen of destroyers and a whole fleet of covering aircraft. She eluded the heavy ships of the Home Fleet, and, while she never struck at either convoy, her presence in the area caused the Cruiser Covering Force to be withdrawn. The convoy scattered and found its way to Murmansk as best it could under continued heavy air and undersea attack.

"Heavy air and undersea attack" could well have been a standard daily entry in any log of an Armed Guard officer. It would have fitted naturally and normally after that other standard entry "Steaming as before."

One of the veterans of the Murmansk run is Lieutenant Robert B. Ricks, USNR, of Gainesville, Georgia, now skipper of a destroyer escort, who was awarded the first Silver Star Medal presented to an Armed Guard officer.

Lieutenant Ricks was assigned to *SS Expositor* in February, 1942. Even by this time there were not enough men to give every officer a full gun crew. To man his one 4-inch 50-caliber gun and four 30-caliber machine guns, Ricks had only four seamen and a signalman striker—"striker" in Navy language meaning an enlisted man studying for non-commissioned promotion.

At nine o'clock in the morning of March 4, 1942, the *Expositor* left Pier 98 in Philadelphia and headed for New York. Here, a cargo was taken aboard which caused the Armed Guard crew to feel a few shivers against which their pea jackets were no protection.

The cargo was 5,000 rounds of 75-mm. shells, 5,000 rounds of 37-mm. shells and 5,000 cases of TNT. With this lethal load aboard, the ammunition ship was incorporated in a convoy bound for the Clyde Anchorage in Loch Long off Gourock, Scotland. At 2:30 in the morning of March 27, the ships dropped anchor in that great convoy berthing spot. But the *Expositor* was not unloaded. On April 1, they were on the move again, in company with three other American merchant ships, *SS Lancaster, Alcoa Rambler* and *Paul Luckenbach.* The morning was clear and the weather was fine. The water of Loch Long lapped gently on the gray stone seawalls of Gourock. The gun crew watched the brown hills of Scotland fade in and they swapped wise cracks about April Fools' Day. Their destination was certainly the Soviet Union, and on whom would the joke be if they didn't make it?

At four o'clock that afternoon the lead ship in the convoy began to turn. A message had been received from the British Admiralty ordering the convoy to return to Gourock. Anchored again in Loch Long, the reason for the return was made known. The DEMS Office (Defensive Equipment for Merchant Ships, the counterpart of the Navy's Armed Guard) had decided the ships were insufficiently armed. To the men of the *Expositor,* this was another certain proof that they were embarking on the hazardous Murmansk run.

Next day additional guns arrived on board, two 20-mm. Oerlikon AA machine guns and one twin-mount Hotchkiss machine gun. It was an embarrassment of riches. The battle bill for the gun crew had been complicated before with only five men to man five guns. Now, with additional guns, volunteers from the merchant crew had to be drilled in their use.

On April 7, the quartet, under Admiralty orders, left for the Lynn of Lorn, off Lismore Island, Scotland. Three days later, a convoy which now consisted of twenty-five ships, American, British and Russian, steamed out of the Lynn of Lorn bound for Reykjavik, Iceland, its last stop on the way to North Russia. On the 15th the ships arrived off Reykjavik harbor and were ordered to Iceland's convoy anchorage area, Hvalfjordur Bay. Their only excitement en route had been watching the destroyer-escort explode sixteen floating mines by gunfire.

There the ships remained for ten days, surrounded by grim, brown lava cliffs from whose tops bristled anti-aircraft artillery. It was remote from Reykjavik's few urban attractions, and the crew heard with relief that they were to be on the move again, even though it was now officially announced: "Destination, Murmansk."

Then at 0800, April 26, the convoy began to move. On the second day out of Iceland, lookouts reported what was to be a continuous hazard all the way to Murmansk—floating mines.

The third day was stormy. The sky was low and goose-feather-gray and occasional snow flurries blotted out ships ahead. It was still morning when a plane was heard, flying very high. By the sound, it seemed to be circling.

"One of those God-damned vultures," a veteran merchant seaman growled.

The plane kept circling. "He's radioing our position, speed and course," the seaman added knowingly. "And he's smart. The bastard knows enough to keep out of range. He's just a spotter. We'll be in for it in a little while."

"What do you mean?" a novice asked.

"Bombers, that's what."

The *Expositor* plodded along with the convoy. All hands grew as fond of snow as a small boy with a new sled. Sunshine, alternating with the flurries, was reviled. Thus for four hours, and then—

"I don't remember how many planes there were," Lieutenant Ricks says. "We had just passed through a snow squall and were in the clear when we saw them coming in on our starboard bow."

The signal to commence firing was hoisted. The entire convoy seemed to open fire at the same time. The planes roared over the fire-belching ships, their bombs falling off to the starboard side of the convoy. The bombers climbed higher and disappeared into the clouds.

Nobody had a chance to say "scared 'em off, hey?" before one of the planes screamed down through the clouds on a dive-bombing run aimed at the lead ship in the port column. The anti-aircraft cruiser guarding the convoy opened fire with every gun on her deck. Guns from the merchantmen in the first three columns joined on the instant. It was a blanket of fire such as no German pilot had ever expected to face. The bomber never came out of its dive. It crashed about 150 yards off the port side of the number one column without dropping its bomb load.

That was all.

The *Expositor's* Armed Guard crew had had its indoctrinating baptism of fire. Not very exciting at that. Buzz—whoosh—bang—bang! But the old-timers muttered something about "luck" and wondered aloud what the next time would be like, and how soon.

"We felt pretty good about it," Lieutenant Ricks recalls. "We had shot down one of the planes, there was no damage done to us and we had driven off the others. Spirits were pretty high."

The convoy wallowed along resolutely, and without molestation.

Then at 3:30 the following afternoon, two more "vultures" were sighted. Again the spotters carefully avoided flying over the convoy in gun range. They circled far out of firing range. They were still there five hours later, when the last man came up from evening mess blinking at the bright arctic sun. Then, as if the pilot had spent all that time building up courage, one of the planes suddenly streaked toward the port wing of the convoy. As the anti-aircraft fire began to find the range, the bomber tilted off on a wide track and climbed high into screening clouds. A moment later it flashed over the convoy for a second try and again the anti-aircraft fire forced the plane to seek cloud refuge. The pilot seemed determined to have at least one shot at the ships. The third time he came out of the clouds in a steep dive at the port wing of the convoy. It was his last. Streams of tracers poured into the plane and followed it as it crashed into the ocean. The companion bomber made no attempt to attack. It straightened out and disappeared over the horizon.

Gun crews remained at their stations on watch. It was still snowing in flurries and there was the feeling that something else was going to happen.

It lacked about an hour for sunset, which is to say it was one o'clock in the morning when the Commodore hoisted a signal.

"Expect attack!"

Three planes were slanted in toward the starboard and the ships opened fire.

"This was our first glimpse of torpedo bombers," said Ricks. "The three planes continued their approach in formation toward us. It looked like an attempt to pick off the leading line of ships. They came in low, flying about fifty or seventy-five feet above the water."

Then the torpedoes began to drop. The men at the guns kept their eyes on the planes. Above the ear-splitting chatter of the ordnance they heard the hollow, reverberating explosion that even the novices knew meant torpedoes had found targets against hulls.

The starboard plane of the trio crashed in flames, as its companions sheered off into the clouds. Then the gunners could look around.

They saw the SS Bothaven, the Commodore's ship, plunging bow first into the water while men spilled from the decks and swam toward the three lifeboats that had been launched. Where SS Cape Corso had been was a flame-shot column of smoke.

"The explosion of that ship sent flames five hundred feet in the air," said Lieutenant Ricks. "The entire mid-section seemed to blow up. The ship was a flaming mass. It sank in about thirty seconds, and there were no survivors."

SS Jutland, steam pouring from her vents, was dead in the water and its crew taking to the boats from decks that inched closer and closer to the sea.

"Three ships sunk by two torpedoes?" somebody demanded. "A submarine must have got one of them."

And, as if in confirmation, the *Expositor's* lookout shouted: "Submarine!"

"Where away?" The sea beyond the convoy's perimeter was empty. The lookout was correct—fantastically correct. A conning tower was rising in the very center of the convoy and just a few yards from the *Expositor's* starboard quarter!

"The periscope was only about ten or fifteen feet away from the ship," reminisces Lieutenant Ricks, "and the submarine was surfacing. It was so close aboard that none of our guns could be brought to bear, no machine guns, no broadside guns, no nothing. And nobody else in the convoy could shoot at it without hitting us—loaded with TNT. It was kind of embarrassing to say the least."

One of the cooks aboard the *Expositor* was standing on the fantail by the stern gun when the sub's conning tower bubbled up under his bulging eyes. The man stood there, unable to believe what he saw. Then he turned to the mute gun, which had been depressed to its lowest trajectory. The mess hand rushed over to the piece, grabbed it by the barrel and tried to tug it into position to fire, grunting and groaning as he pulled.

The submarine continued to surface until the conning tower was awash, while the *Expositor* widened the distance from it.

By the time the submarine was 25 yards away, the 4-inch gun could be brought to bear on the German craft. The first shot missed. The gun was still too high. The second was a direct hit on the conning tower, at 30 or 40 yards. It was blown completely off.

After the second shot, the submarine appeared to be sinking. Water boiled up in a great froth of air and bubbles. As the man watched the oil spreading over the submarine's grave the lookout yelled: "Torpedo track off port bow!"

The ship jolted as her screws went into reverse. A few feet in front of her bow the torpedo hissed its way to nowhere.

"I think the submarines and aircraft worked in very close co-operation on a job like this," Lieutenant Ricks calculates. "The reconnaissance planes did nothing but circle the convoy, evidently radioing to the subs, or to where the message could be relayed to them, our position, course and speed. Then the subs would lie ahead of the convoy and as we came by would let us have it. This particular submarine that came up in the center of the convoy was evidently hurt by some of the heavy depth charges that had been dropped by the DEs and corvettes after the *Cape Corso* was hit."

This marked the end of enemy action for that day. But as the ships fell into their convoy position, filling up the gaps left by the torpedoed, a fourth casualty was discovered. A British corvette had disappeared in the melee, wiped out by a torpedo.

The only casualty aboard the *Expositor* was a seaman's dungarees. The deck hand, his arms full of 40-mm. ammunition, was on a ladder in the path of the 4-inch gun's blast.

"The concussion ripped his pants off, and I literally mean off," Lieutenant Ricks recalls. "He didn't have a stitch on him. He stood there in a daze for a moment, and then dropped his shells and tumbled to the deck after them. Somebody ran to pick him up. There wasn't any more of a scratch or bruise on him than there was pants. He was just dazed, and he couldn't quite figure out why he was mother-naked."

May 3 was almost logged as an uneventful day, but a few minutes before midnight the attack signal was again jerked up the halyards. This time the Germans changed tactics. Two torpedo bombers appeared, one on each wing of the convoy. They launched their tin fish simultaneously against both flanks of the flotilla. It was a clean miss all the way around. No torpedo found its mark, nor did a shot from the anti-aircraft guns.

Although evidences of submarine activity continued for the remaining week of the voyage, there were no further engagements with the Germans. The Armed Guard crew could not loaf the time away, however. Watches had to be maintained at any cost and the men worked with little rest and less sleep.

On May 6 the convoy anchored in the harbor of Murmansk. The port could accomodate only about ten ships at the docks, which had been bombed and rebuilt many times with timber.

As the *Expositor* berthed, a sailor standing near Ricks made inquiry about liberty ashore.

"I've dated all kinds of women in the world except Russians," he observed. "I'd like to get me a date with a Russian."

He leaned over the rail to watch a Russian woman stevedore walking along the pier below. She stopped to pick up a length of piling obstructing the path and nonchalantly tossed the 120-pound log out of the way. The sailor spat reflectively into the water.

"On second thought," he said, "I don't believe I care to meet these women."

Now the weather sided against the Germans. It snowed. It snowed so hard for two days that the vessel's stern was invisible from the bridge. The blizzard hampered the unloading considerably but it grounded the Luftwaffe until the third day. Then the sun came out, and with it the bombers, skimming close over the ridge of low hills that curved around the harbor.

Twelve of the big multi-motored aircraft headed for the sitting ducks. The gun crews went into action; everybody else scattered for shelter.

It seemed impossible that the Germans could miss. They did; the gunners didn't. Only nine of the bombers flew back toward Finland, two brought down by gunfire and one by a Russian fighter plane that buzzed up to meet them.

After the *Expositor* unloaded she traded places with an ammunition ship.

"I don't know whether that ammunition ship had been spotted or not," said Lieutenant Ricks, "but that afternoon when we had taken her anchorage out in the stream we were the target for a direct attack by six dive bombers.

"Bombs dropped fore and aft and to both sides of us, but they all missed by about a hundred yards. We were completely circled by bombs, but we weren't hit."

The next day, about the same time in the early afternoon, the bombers came again. This time the misses were nearer.

"In fact," Ricks recalls, "the spray from the first bomb completely obscured the ship. The British destroyer that was sitting on our starboard quarter signaled to ask 'What damage?' Just as our signalman prepared to answer 'No damage' a second flight of dive bombers came heading for us.

"The bombs fell so near that the concussion lifted the ship and shook her like a dog shakes a rat."

The twenty-two ships were unloaded in twenty days, despite bombings, blizzards and inadequate wharfing. The men were anxious to leave. Murmansk was a pile of rubble. New buildings were all made of wood so that they could be reconstructed quickly. There was the International Club, open to everyone, for hot tea, chess and tattered old magazines in six languages, but the ship was the most comfortable place to stay when off duty.

On May 21 the convoy left for Iceland. Twice in the first three days submarine contacts were made.

Late in the afternoon of the third day—late by the clocks, not by the sun—a reconnaissance plane began its vulture-like circling beyond firing range. Presently a torpedo bomber joined in the circular vigil above the ships. For three hours the tantalizing surveillence continued. Then each dropped two green flares. Ten minutes later red flares were dropped, signals to lurking submarines.

But, as if in response to the flares, a Hurricane fighter plane was catapulted from a British ship. It started in pursuit of the torpedo bomber. Both planes disappeared in a cloud bank, where the fighter evidently lost its prey, because ten minutes later the Hurricane returned and started to close in on the second German plane. Seconds later the torpedo bomber popped out of the cloud and turned to join the fight. But it was too late to save the reconnaissance plane. A savage burst of fire from the Hurricane sent the first Nazi crashing into the sea. The bomber fled, and the Hurricane streaked after it. The pursuit vanished over the horizon.

The convoy churned on, the empty ships riding high. Then a shout went up from the decks of the watching ships. The Hurricane was returning—alone. It pancaked on the water near its mother ship and a boat put out to it. The men crowding the rails of the other ships saw the pilot taken aboard, his plane abandoned. A little while later a flutter of flags broke out on the Englishman. The pilot had died of wounds. For the remainder of the day all flags were flown at half mast in honor of the fighter who had given his life to save the ships.

Next day the now familiar shores of Iceland were sighted. The voyage was almost over. There was the sub-infested water between Reykjavik and New York to cover, but after what the men had already been through that seemed almost a humdrum chore. The ships remained in Iceland for two dreary, chafing weeks. Only the master of the ship and the Armed Guard officer were permitted to go ashore, and then for the transaction of official business only.

On June 10 the confinement was broken. The ships left under escort. Eight days later the men were reminded that they still were a long way from home. A steamer on the edge of the convoy was torpedoed. Four men were killed in the explosion, the rest taken aboard other ships. Two days later another was torpedoed and sunk. Both times the attackers escaped, undetected.

At one o'clock on June 28, the *Expositor* dropped anchor just off the Statue of Liberty in New York harbor. One Armed Guard crew had returned with all hands intact from the Murmansk run—12,000 miles, 116 days, the ship safe, and the metaphorical scalp of one submarine nailed to the mainmast. It was—just another voyage; tougher than most, easier than some.

Ricks's adventures were probably duplicated scores of times. They are related here not because they are exceptional, but because they are illustrative. And not all gun crews survived the German-Finnish gantlet to tell their stories.

The route to Archangel was, if anything, worse than the Murmansk run for being longer. Consider the experiences of Lieutenant Albert Maynard, USNR, Armed Guard officer on SS *Schoharie,* which brought a shipload of tanks, ammunition and food to Murmansk in a convoy that numbered forty ships at sailing, and twenty-seven upon arrival at the subarctic port.

The convoy was one of the more important, in the constant line of supply to the Soviet Union. Stalingrad and Leningrad were in what seemed to be the last stages of siege and destruction. To make delivery of the desperately needed supplies as secure as possible, the British provided the convoy with an escort of a converted aircraft carrier, a light cruiser, two antiaircraft cruisers, twenty-one destroyers and a small fleet of corvettes, minesweepers and trawlers—a task force in itself. And yet, a third of the convoy was lost.

It was on Sunday, September 13, 1942, on the seventh day out of Iceland, that Lieutenant Maynard looked over the side in the course of gun inspection to see a British merchantman instantly blotted out in steam and smoke. Before the signal to scatter could be raised, a second ship was torpedoed.

The superstitious in that convoy had reason to confirm their distaste for the number 13. Before that September day was done, a wolfpack of submarines ran riot inside the convoy's columns, a swarm of thirty-seven Heinkel torpedo planes made an attack at 25 feet above the water, and a half dozen Ju-88s subjected the ships to a dive-bombing attack. A total of ten merchantment was sunk, some outright, others left crippled with corvette protection only to be sent down later by the Nazis' aerial rear guard.

Lieutenant Maynard, with desperate sincerity, described the lulls in the battle as the unforgettable parts of the daylong fight with an enemy who alternately dropped from the sky or rose from the ocean depths. The business of fighting off dive bombers above, torpedo planes at deck level, and submarines, is too wholly occupying to permit mental note-taking.

"During the attacks our reaction was not fright," Maynard remembers. "But in the letdown periods of quiet, it would be silly to say one of us was not downright scared."

The view over the side was not cheering. Cargo ships in convoy may not pause or break the established pattern to rescue the shipwrecked. That job is left for the escorting warships. But it does not boost the morale of the Armed Guardsman to see men struggling in the icy brine as their own ship passes through the flotsam of battle; they are humanly prone to wonder when it will be their turn to cling with numbing fingers to a shattered spar and see the ships go by.

"There were men in the water, and men in lifeboats," Maynard recalls. "Some of them swearing, some praying, and some mockingly sticking out their thumbs and calling 'Going my way, mister?' as we slid by not a hundred feet from them."

Monday was inaugurated by the torpedoing of a tanker early in the morning. At noon thirteen torpedo planes came out of the clouds and concentrated on the carrier, whose own fighters shot down six of the enemy without loss. Half an hour later twenty Heinkels swarmed over the horizon. One of them torpedoed an ammunition ship which disintegrated just as the plane skimmed over the stricken vessel's masts; the explosion blasted the Nazi plane and its crew to atoms.

Day in, day out, the Heinkels and Junkers plagued the convoy. The thirteenth ship was lost to Finnish dive bombers just as the battered flotilla stood in for the straits of the White Sea, but the convoy had to fight off attacks every day at sea of the four remaining, and for the four moonlit nights of unloading at Archangel.

"And that," Lieutenant Maynard concludes, "is about all that happened on our trip to Archangel," a trip during which he himself once had to grab a fifty-caliber gun and train it against a Voss-Ha 140 boring in on the *Schoharie*. The plane disappeared in a blur of flame and smoke, and tumbled "just like a ball of fire" into the sea.

"I think that was the most fun I had on the entire voyage," Maynard muses.

THE PROBLEMS POSED BY THE DISASTROUS RUN OF convoy P.Q. 17 to Murmansk are discussed by Sir Winston Churchill, Great Britain's formidable wartime leader and one of the most imposing figures of the Twentieth Century. In recalling the event he reveals his correspondence with Roosevelt and Stalin. The strain of Churchill's grave responsibility is evident in the following excerpt, one which also gives us a penetrating glimpse of Britain's ineluctable strategist at work.

5.

P.Q.17

In view of the disaster to P.Q.17 the Admiralty proposed to suspend the Arctic convoys at least till the Northern ice-packs melted and receded and until perpetual daylight passed. I felt this would be a very grave decision, and was inclined not to lower but on the contrary to raise the stakes, on the principle of 'In defeat defiance.'

Prime Minister to First Lord and First Sea Lord   15 July 42
    Let the following be examined:
    Suspend the sailing of P.Q.18 as now proposed from 18th instant. See what happens to our Malta operation. If all goes well, bring *Indomitable, Victorious, Argus,* and *Eagle* north to Scapa, together with all available 'Didos' and at least twenty-five destroyers. Let the two 16-inch battleships go right through under this air umbrella and destroyer screen, keeping southward, not hugging the ice, but seeking the clearest weather, and thus fight it out with the enemy. If we can move our armada in convoy under an umbrella of at least a hundred fighter aircraft we ought to be able to fight our way through and out again, and if a fleet action results so much the better.

    I could not however persuade my Admiralty friends to take this kind of line, which of course involved engaging a vital force to us out of proportion to the actual military importance of the Arctic convoys. I had therefore to send the following telegram to Stalin, about which I obtained the approval of the President beforehand.

Prime Minister to Premier Stalin   17 July 42

We began running small convoys to North Russia in August 1941, and until December the Germans did not take any steps to interfere with them. From February 1942 the size of the convoys was increased, and the Germans then moved a considerable force of U-boats and a large number of aircraft to North Norway and made determined attacks on the convoys. By giving the convoys the strongest possible escort of destroyers and anti-submarine craft the convoys got through with varying but not prohibitive losses. It is evident that the Germans were dissatisfied with the results which were being achieved by means of aircraft and U-boats alone, because they began to use their surface forces against the convoys. Luckily for us however at the outset they made use of their heavy surface forces to the westward of Bear Island and their submarines to the eastward. The Home Fleet was thus in a position to prevent an attack by enemy surface forces. Before the May convoy was sent off the Admiralty warned us that the losses would be very severe if, as was expected, the Germans employed their surface forces to the eastward of Bear Island. We decided however to sail the convoy. An attack by surface ships did not materialise, and the convoy got through with a loss of one-sixth, chiefly from air attack. In the case of P.Q.17 however the Germans at last used their forces in the manner we had always feared. They concentrated their U-boats to the westward of Bear Island and reserved their surface forces for attack to the eastward of Bear Island. The final story of P.Q.17 convoy is not yet clear. At the moment only four ships have arrived at Archangel, but six others are in Nova Zembla harbours. The latter may however be attacked from the air at any time. At the best therefore only one-third will have survived.

I must explain the dangers and difficulties of these convoy operations when the enemy's battle squadron takes its station in the extreme north. We do not think it right to risk our Home Fleet east of Bear Island or where it can be brought under the attack of the powerful German shore-based aircraft. If one or two of our very few most powerful battleships were to be lost or even seriously damaged while *Tirpitz* and her consorts, soon to be joined by

Scharnhorst, remained in action, the whole command of the Atlantic would be [temporarily] lost. Besides affecting the food supplies by which we live, our war effort would be crippled; and above all the great convoys of American troops across the ocean, rising presently to as many as 80,000 in a month, would be prevented and the building up of a really strong Second Front in 1943 rendered impossible.

My naval advisers tell me that if they had the handling of the German surface, submarine, and air forces, in present circumstances, they would guarantee the complete destruction of any convoy to North Russia. They have not been able so far to hold out any hopes that convoys attempting to make the passage in perpetual daylight would fare better than P.Q.17. It is therefore with the greatest regret that we have reached the conclusion that to attempt to run the next convoy, P.Q.18, would bring no benefit to you and would only involve dead loss to the common cause. At the same time, I give you my assurance that if we can devise arrangements which give a reasonable chance of at least a fair proportion of the contents of the convoys reaching you we will start them again at once. The crux of the problem is to make the Barents Sea as dangerous for German warships as they make it for ours. This is what we should aim at doing with our joint resources. I should like to send a senior officer of the R.A.F. to North Russia to confer with your officers and make a plan.

Meanwhile we are prepared to dispatch immediately to the Persian Gulf some of the ships which were to have sailed in the P.Q. convoy. . . .

You have referred to combined operations in the North. The obstacles to sending further convoys at the present time equally prevent our sending land forces and air forces for operations in Northern Norway. But our officers should forthwith consider together what combined operations may be possible in or after October, when there is a reasonable amount of darkness. It would be better if you could send your officers here, but if this is impossible ours will come to you.

In addition to a combined operation in the North, we are studying how to help on your southern flank. If we can beat back Rommel we might be able to send powerful air forces in the autumn to operate on the left of your line. The difficulties of maintaining these forces over the trans-Persian route without reducing your supplies will clearly be considerable, but I hope to put detailed proposals before you in the near future. We must however first beat Rommel. The battle is now intense. . . .

I am sure it would be in our common interest, Premier Stalin, to have the three divisions of Poles you so kindly offered join their compatriots in Palestine, where we can arm them fully. These would play a most important part in future fighting, as well as keeping the Turks in good heart by the sense of growing numbers to the southward. I hope this project of yours, which we greatly value, will not fall to the ground on account of the Poles wanting to bring with the troops a considerable mass of their women and children, who are largely dependent on the rations of the Polish soldiers. The feeding of these dependents will be a considerable burden to us. We think it well worth while bearing that burden for the sake of forming this Polish army, which will be used faithfully for our common advantage. We are very hard up for food ourselves in the Levant area, but there is enough in India if we can bring it [from] there.

If we do not get the Poles we should have to fill their places by drawing on the preparations now going forward on a vast scale for the Anglo-American mass invasion of the Continent. These preparations have already led the Germans to withdraw two heavy bomber groups from South Russia to France. Believe me, there is nothing that is useful and sensible that we and the Americans will not do to help you in your grand struggle. The President and I are ceaselessly searching for means to overcome the extraordinary difficulties which geography, salt water, and the enemy's air-power interpose. I have shown this telegram to the President.

I need scarcely say I got a rough and surly answer.

Premier Stalin to Premier Churchill   23 July 42

I received your message of July 17. Two conclusions could be drawn from it. First, the British Government refuses to continue the sending of war materials to the Soviet Union via the Northern route. Second, in spite of the agreed communiqué concerning the urgent tasks of creating a Second Front in 1942 the British Government postpones this matter until 1943.

2. Our naval experts consider the reasons put forward by the British naval experts to justify the cessation of convoys to the northern ports of the U.S.S.R. wholly unconvincing. They are of the opinion that with goodwill and readiness to fulfil the con-

tracted obligations these convoys could be regularly undertaken and heavy losses could be inflicted on the enemy. Our experts find it also difficult to understand and to explain the order given by the Admiralty that the escorting vessels of the P.Q.17 should return, whereas the cargo boats should disperse and try to reach the Soviet ports one by one without any protection at all. Of course I do not think that regular convoys to the Soviet northern ports could be effected without risk or losses. But in war-time no important undertaking could be effected without risk or losses. In any case, I never expected that the British Government would stop dispatch of war materials to us just at the very moment when the Soviet Union in view of the serious situation on the Soviet-German front requires these materials more than ever. It is obvious that the transport via Persian Gulf could in no way compensate for the cessation of convoys to the northern ports.

3. With regard to the second question, *i.e.,* the question of creating a Second Front in Europe, I am afraid it is not being treated with the seriousness it deserves. Taking fully into account the present position on the Soviet-German front, I must state in the most emphatic manner that the Soviet Government cannot acquiesce in the postponement of a Second Front in Europe until 1943.

I hope you will not feel offended that I [have] expressed frankly and honestly my own opinion as well as the opinion of my colleagues on the question raised in your message.

These contentions are not well-founded. So far from breaking 'contracted obligations' to deliver the war supplies at Soviet ports, it had been particularly stipulated at the time of making the agreement that the Russians were to be responsible for conveying them to Russia. All that we did beyond this was a good-will effort. As to the allegations of a breach of faith about the Second Front in 1942, our *aide-mémoire* was a solid defence. I did not however think it worth while to argue out all this with the Soviet Government, who had been willing until they were themselves attacked to see us totally destroyed and share the booty with Hitler, and who even in our common struggle could hardly spare a word of sympathy for the heavy British and American losses incurred in trying to send them aid.

The President agreed with this view.

President to Former Naval Person   29 July 42

I agree with you that your reply to Stalin must be handled with great care. We have got always to bear in mind the personality of our Ally and the very difficult and dangerous situation that confronts him. No one can be expected to approach the war from a world point of view whose country has been invaded. I think we should try to put ourselves in his place. I think he should be told in the first place, quite specifically that we have determined upon a course of action in 1942. I think that, without advising him of the precise nature of our proposed operations, the fact that they are going to be made should be told him without any qualifications.

While I think that you should not raise any false hopes in Stalin relative to the Northern convoy, nevertheless I agree with you that we should run one if there is any possibility of success, in spite of the great risk involved.

I am still hopeful that we can put air-power directly on the Russian front, and I am discussing that matter here. I believe it would be unwise to promise this air-power only on condition that the battle in Egypt goes well. Russia's need is urgent and immediate. I have a feeling it would mean a great deal to the Russian Army and the Russian people if they knew some of our Air Force was fighting with them in a very direct manner.

While we may believe that the present and proposed use of our combined Air Forces is strategically the best, nevertheless I feel that Stalin does not agree with this. Stalin, I imagine, is in no mood to engage in a theoretical strategical discussion, and I am sure that other than our major operation the enterprise that would suit him the best is direct air support on the southern end of his front.

I therefore let Stalin's bitter message pass without any specific rejoinder. After all, the Russian armies were suffering fearfully and the campaign was at its crisis.

* * *

At a conference of the German Naval Commander-in-Chief with the Fuehrer on August 26, 1942, Admiral Raeder stated:

Evidently the Ally convoy did not sail. We can thus assume that our submarines and aircraft, which totally destroyed the last convoy, have forced the enemy to give up this route temporarily, or even fundamentally to change his whole system of supply lines. Supplies to northern ports of Russia remain decisive for the whole conduct of the war waged by the Anglo-Saxons. They must preserve Russia's strength in order to keep German forces occupied. The enemy will most probably continue to ship supplies to Northern Russia, and the Naval Staff must therefore maintain submarines along the same routes. The greater part of the Fleet will also be stationed in Northern Norway. The reason for this, besides making attacks on convoys possible, is the constant threat of an enemy invasion. Only by keeping the Fleet in Norwegian waters can we hope to meet this danger successfully. Besides, it is especially important, in view of the whole Axis strategy, that the German 'Fleet in being' tie down the British Home Fleet, especially after the heavy Anglo-American losses in the Mediterranean and the Pacific. The Japanese are likewise aware of the importance of this measure. In addition, the danger of enemy mines in home waters has constantly increased, so that the naval forces should be shifted only for repairs and training purposes.

* * *

It was not until September that another convoy set off for North Russia. By now the scheme of defense had been revised, and the convoy was accompanied by a close escort of sixteen destroyers, as well as the first of the new escort carriers, the *Avenger,* with twelve fighter aircraft. As before, strong support was provided by the fleet. This time however the German surface ships made no attempt to intervene, but left the task of attack to the aircraft and U-boats. The result was a particularly fierce battle in the air, in which twenty-four enemy aircraft were destroyed out of about a hundred which came in to the attack. Ten merchant ships were lost in these actions and two more by U-boats, but twenty-seven ships successfully fought their way through.

* * *

Not only did almost the whole responsibility for the defence of these convoys fall upon us, but up to the end of 1942 . . . we provided from our strained resources by far the greater number of aircraft and more tanks for Russia. The figures are a conclusive answer to those who suggest that our efforts to help Russia in her struggle were lukewarm. We gave our heart's blood resolutely to our valiant, suffering Ally.

* * *

The year 1942 was not to close without its flash of triumph upon the thankless task the Royal Navy had discharged, and we must trench upon the future. After the passage of P.Q.18 in September 1942 convoys to North Russia were again suspended. Later major operations in North Africa were to claim the whole strength of our naval forces in home waters. But supplies accumulated for delivery to Russia, and the means of protecting future convoys were closely studied. It was not until late in December that the next convoy set out on its hazardous voyage. It sailed in two parts, each escorted by six or seven destroyers, and covered by the Home Fleet. The first group arrived safely. The second had a more eventful passage. On the morning of December 31 Captain R. Sherbrooke, in the destroyer *Onslow,* commanding the escort, was about a hundred and fifty miles northeast of the North Cape when he sighted three enemy destroyers. He immediately turned to engage them. As the action began the German heavy cruiser *Hipper* appeared upon the scene. The British destroyers held off this powerful ship for nearly an hour. The gun-flashes of the action drew to the scene Admiral Burnett with two British cruisers, *Sheffield* and *Jamaica,* from twenty-five miles away. This force, racing southwards, ran into the German pocket-battleship *Lützow,* which, after a short engagement, disappeared to the westward in the twilight. The German admiral, thinking that the British cruisers were the vanguard of a battle squadron, retired hastily. During this brief engagement the *Sheffield* sank a German destroyer at close range. A running fight followed. The two German heavy ships and their six escorting destroyers struck at the convoy which Sherbrooke guarded. But this stroke failed.

The convoy arrived safely in Russian waters with the loss of one destroyer and no more than slight damage to one merchant ship. Captain Sherbrooke, who had been severely wounded in the early stages but continued to fight his ship and personally to direct operations, despite the loss of an eye, was awarded the Victoria Cross for his leadership.

Within the German High Command the repercussions of this affair were far-reaching. Owing to delays in the transmission of signals the High Command first learnt of the episode from an English news broadcast. Hitler was enraged. While waiting impatiently for the outcome of the fight his anger was fostered by Goering, who complained bitterly of wasting squadrons of the German Air Force on guarding the capital ships of the Navy, which he suggested should be scrapped. Admiral Raeder was ordered to report immediately. On January 6 a naval conference was held. Hitler launched a tirade upon the past record of the German Navy. 'It should not be considered a degradation if the Fuehrer decides to scrap the larger ships. This would be true only if he were removing a fighting unit which had retained its full usefulness. A parallel to this in the Army would be the removal of all cavalry divisions.' Raeder was ordered to report in writing why he objected to putting the capital ships cut of commission. When Hitler received this memorandum he treated it with derision, and ordered Doenitz, the designated successor to Raeder, to make a plan to meet his demands. A bitter conflict between Goering and Raeder raged round Hitler over the future of the German Navy compared with that of the Luftwaffe. But Raeder stuck grimly to the defence of the service which he had commanded since 1928. Time and again he had demanded the formation of a separate Fleet Air Arm, and had been opposed successfully by Goering's insistence that the Air Force could accomplish more at sea than the Navy. Goering won, and on January 30 Raeder resigned. He was replaced by Doenitz, the ambitious Admiral of the U-boats. All effective new construction was henceforth to be monopolised by them.

Thus this brilliant action fought by the Royal Navy to protect an allied convoy to Russia at the end of the year led directly to a major crisis in the enemy's naval policy, and ended the dream of another German High Seas Fleet.

AT THE HEIGHT OF THE ATLANTIC WAR ADMIRAL King, who was charged with the solemn responsibility of welding together all of our combatant sea forces, filed a progress report with the Secretary of the Navy in which he candidly summarized U-boat activities and countermeasures. A formidable naval officer, Ohio-born King was sixty-three years old at the outbreak of the war. Dour, ramrod straight and a "book" man, one scarcely associates Cominch with lighter moments, and yet there were numerous occasions when this man, who had come up through submarines and naval aviation, could turn outward on a far different level from successful pursuit of the war. One such occurred in the chaotic winter of 1943, when King, beset with problems, was the recipient of a letter from an eighth grade student who was writing a biographical sketch of the Admiral for school. He took time off from the war to reply:

Dear Harriet:
I have your letter of January 6—and am interested to learn that you have to do my biography as part of your English work.

As to your questions:

I drink a little wine, now and then.

I smoke about one pack of cigarettes a day.

I think I like Spencer Tracy as well as any of the
movie stars.

My hobby is cross-word puzzles—when they are different.

My favorite sport is golf—when I can get to play it—
otherwise, I am fond of walking.

Hoping that all will go well with your English work, I am

Very truly yours,

E. J. King

Admiral, U.S. Navy

Let us return to King's report.

6.

COMINCH TAKES

A HARD LOOK AT

THE U-BOAT SITUATION

The submarine war . . . has been a matter of primary concern since the outbreak of hostilities. Maintenance of the flow of ocean traffic has been, and continues to be, a vital element of all war plans.

Operating on exterior lines of communication on almost every front, the United Nations have been dependent largely upon maritime transportation. The success of overseas operations, landing attacks, the maintenance of troops abroad and the delivery of war materials to Russia and other Allies concerned primarily with land operations has depended to a large extent upon the availability of shipping and the ability to keep it moving. Shipping potentialities have been the major factor—often the controlling factor—in most of the problems with which the Allied High Command has had to deal.

The principal menace to shipping has been the large fleet of submarines maintained by Germany. Our enemies have employed the submarine on a world-wide scale, but the area of greatest intensity has always been the Atlantic Ocean where the bulk of German U-boats have operated.

The German U-boat campaign is a logical extension of the submarine strategy of World War I which almost succeeded in starving Great Britain into submission. Unable to build up a powerful surface fleet in preparation for World War II, Germany planned to repeat her submarine campaign on a greater scale and to this end produced a U-boat fleet of huge size. The primary mission of this underwater navy was to cut the sea routes to the British Isles, and the enemy undersea forces went to work on this task promptly and vigorously.

The United States became involved in the matter before we were formally at war, because our vessels were being sunk in the trans-Atlantic traffic routes. Consequently, in 1941, we took measures to assist the Royal Navy to protect our shipping. As stated in more detail elsewhere in this report these measures included the transfer of 50 old destroyers to the British, and—in the latter part of 1941—the assignment of our own naval vessels to escort our merchant shipping on threatened trans-Atlantic routes.

The submarine situation was improving as 1941 drew toward a close. Escort operations on threatened convoy routes were becoming more and more effective. British aviation had become a potent factor, by direction action against the U-boats, and also by bringing under control the German over-water air effort that had augmented the submarine offense. Our resources were stretched, however, and we could not, for a time, deal effectively with the change in the situation brought about by our entry into the war on 7 December 1941. Our whole merchant marine then became a legitimate target, and the U-boats, still remaining full pressure on the trans-Atlantic routes, had sufficient numbers to spread their depredations into wide areas hitherto immune. Our difficulty was that such part of the Atlantic Fleet as was not already engaged in escort duty was called upon to protect the troop movements that began with our entry into the war, leaving no adequate force to cover the many maritime traffic areas newly exposed to possible U-boat activity.

The Germans were none too quick in taking advantage of their opportunity. It was not until more than a month after the declaration of war that U-boats began to expand their areas of operation. The first move took the form of an incursion into our coastal waters in January 1942. We had prepared for this by gathering on our eastern seaboard our scant resources in coastal antisubmarine vessels and aircraft, consisting chiefly of a number of yachts and miscellaneous small craft taken over by the Navy in 1940 and 1941. To reinforce this group the Navy accelerated its program of acquiring such fishing boats and pleasure craft as could be used and supplied them with such armaments as they could carry. For patrol purposes we employed all available aircraft—Army as well as Navy. The help of the Civil Air Patrol was gratefully accepted. This heterogeneous force was useful in keeping lookout and in rescuing survivors of sunken ships. It may have interfered, too, to some extent with the freedom of U-boat movement, but the heavy losses we suffered in coastal waters during the early months of 1942 gave abundant proof of the already well known fact that stout hearts in little boats can not handle an opponent as tough as the submarine.

The Navy was deeply grateful for the assistance so eagerly volunteered by the men who courageously risked their lives in order to make the best of available means, but there had to be better means, and to provide them no effort was spared to build up an antisubmarine force of adequate types. Submarine chasers, construction of which had been initiated before the war, began to come into service early in 1942. The British and Canadian Navies were able to assign some antisubmarine vessels to work with our coastal forces. Ocean escorts were robbed to reinforce coastal areas. These measures made it possible to establish a coastal convoy system in the middle of May 1942. Antisubmarine aviation had concurrently improved in quality and material and training of personnel. The Army Air Force had volunteered the services of the First Bomber Command which was especially trained and outfitted for antisubmarine warfare.

The effect of these measures was quickly felt in the Eastern Sea Frontier (the coastal waters from Canada to Jacksonville) where they were first applied. With the establishment of the initial coastal convoy (under the command of Vice Admiral Adolphus Andrews, Commander of the Eastern Sea Frontier) in the middle of May 1942, sinkings in the vital traffic lanes of the Eastern Sea Frontier dropped off nearly to zero and have so remained. While it has not been possible to clear those routes completely—there is evidence that nearly always one or more U-boats haunt our Atlantic Coast—submarines in that area long ago ceased to be a serious problem.

When the Eastern Sea Frontier became "too hot," the U-boats began to spread farther afield. The coastal convoy system was extended as rapidly as possible to meet them in the Gulf of Mexico (under the command of Rear Admiral J. L. Kauffman, Commander Gulf Sea Frontier), the Caribbean Sea, (under the command of Vice Admiral J. H. Hoover, Commander Caribbean Sea Frontier), and along the Atlantic Coast of South America. The undersea craft made a last bitter stand in the Trinidad area in the fall of 1942. Since then coastal waters have been relatively safe.

The problem was more difficult to meet in the open sea. The

submarine chasers that do well enough in coastal waters are too small for ocean escort duty. Destroyers and other ocean escort types could not be produced as rapidly as the smaller craft. Aircraft capable of long overseas patrol were not plentiful, nor were aircraft carriers. In consequence, potection of ocean shipping lagged to some extent. By the end of 1942, however, this matter began to come under control, as our forces slowly increased, and there has been a steady improvement ever since.

The Atlantic antisubmarine campaign has been a closely integrated international operation. In the early phases of our participation, there was a considerable mixture of forces, as the needs of the situation were met as best they could be. For a time some British and Canadian vessels operated in our coastal escorts, while our destroyers were brigaded with British groups in the Atlantic and even occasionally as far afield as north Russian waters. As Allied strength improved in power and balance, it became possible to establish certain areas of national responsibility wherein the forces are predominantly of one nation. This simplifies the problem of administration and operation, but there still are—and probably always will be—some areas where forces of two or more nations work together in a single command, and always there is close coordination in deploying the forces of the several Allies.

There is a constant interchange of information between the large organizations maintained in the Admiralty and in the United States Fleet Headquarters (in the form of the Tenth Fleet which coordinates United States anti-U-boat activities in the Atlantic) to deal with the problems of control and protection of shipping. These organizations, also, keep in intimate touch with the War Shipping Administration in the United States and with the corresponding agency in Great Britain.

Command of antisubmarine forces—air and surface—that protect shipping in the coastwise sea lanes of the United States and within the Caribbean Sea and Gulf of Mexico is exercised by sea frontier commanders, each assigned to a prescribed area. The command is naval except in the Panama area where the naval sea frontier commander is under the Commanding General at Panama.

Since aircraft and surface combatant ships are most effective when working as a closely knit team, it is the policy—in antisubmarine as well as other naval operations—to weld together air and surface forces in a single command in each area.

In the Atlantic Ocean, beyond the coastal area, anti-submarine forces—air and surface—are part of the Atlantic Fleet under the command of Admiral Ingersoll. One of the units of Admiral Ingersoll's fleet is the South Atlantic Force (Vice Admiral Ingram commanding) which guards shipping in the coastal waters south of the Equator and throughout the United States area of South Atlantic. Vice Admiral Ingram's command includes highly efficient surface and air units of Brazil, which country has wholeheartedly joined our team of submarine hunters. This team, incidentally, turns its guns on surface raiders and other bigger game when the enemy provides the opportunity.

It is appropriate to express her appreciation of the services of Netherlands antisubmarine vessels which have operated with exemplary efficiency as part of the United States Naval Caribbean Force ever since we entered the war.

Antisubmarine warfare is primarily a naval function, but, in accordance with the general policy of working together, Army and Navy forces that are available turn to together on the enemy when need arises. Thus it happens that there are instances in which Army aircraft join in the submarine hunt. The assistance of the Army Air Force has been of great value, particularly in the early phases of the war, when naval resources were inadequate. An example of this is the formation of the Army Air Force Anti-Submarine Command in the spring of 1942, which was given the equipment and training necessary to make its members antisubmarine specialists. It operated, under the command of Brigadier General (now Major General) T. W. Larson, in the United States and abroad until last November (1943), when the Navy obtained enough equipment to take over the tasks so well performed by this command.

It is regretted that it is not possible at this time to go into the details of our antisubmarine operations in this report. It would be a great pleasure to recount the many praise-worthy exploits of our antisubmarine forces, but to do so now would jeopardize the success of future operations. The U-boat war has been a war of wits. The submarine is a weapon of stealth, and naturally enough the German operations have been shrouded in secrecy. It has been of equal importance to keep our counter measures from becoming known to the enemy. There is a constant interplay of new devices and new tactics on the part of forces working against the submarines as well as on the part of the submarines themselves, and an important element of our success has been the ability to keep the enemy from knowing what we are doing and what we are likely to do in the future. It is, also, of the utmost importance to keep our enemies from learning our anti-submarine technique, lest they turn it to their own advantage in operations against our submarines.

ALTHOUGH THE U-BOAT MENACE WAS STILL FAR FROM under control, an American offensive was launched November 8, 1942, which secured for us North Africa—the first step on the long road to the eventual storming of Hitler's Fortress Europa. This was Operation "Torch," undertaken two weeks after the British Army commenced its winning drive from Egypt westward. Aimed at French Morocco, with a secondary invasion in Algeria, "Torch" (embracing both operations under the same high command) opened against a background of political intrigue.

With the fall of France in 1940, control of that nation's government devolved on Vichy. However, Marshal Henri Pétain and his military commander in North Africa, General Maxime Weygand, were erroneously thought to oppose collaboration with Germany. Keenly aware of this, President Roosevelt planned diplomatic moves calculated to prevent the powerful French Toulon fleet (as distinguished from the Casablanca fleet) from falling into Hitler's hands. Admiral William D. Leahy and Ambassador Robert D. Murphy were ordered to work on Weygand's sympathies, while General Charles de Gaulle of the Free French lent additional support. Roosevelt's fervent hope was that the Toulon fleet would remain inactive while the Allied invasions were launched, and with a minimum of bloodshed. It was a tall order.

For even as Murphy strove to form a nucleus of French officers loyal to the cause of freedom, collaborationist Admiral Darlan visited Hitler in Berchtesgaden and signed pro-German treaties regarding Tunisia. When on July 25, 1942, the Darlan-Hitler liaison became known in London, plans were made to go ahead immediately and to secure a foothold in North Africa before anything else developed. In strategic concept the joint plan envisioned the following:

1. "Establishment of firm and mutually supported lodgments" (a) between Oran and Tunisia on the Mediterranean, and (b) in

French Morocco on the Atlantic, in order to secure bases "for continued and intensified air, ground and sea operations."

2. "Vigorous and rapid exploitation of these lodgments" "in order to acquire complete control" of French Morocco, Algeria and Tunisia, and extend offensive operations against the rear of Axis forces to the eastward.

3. "Complete annihilation of Axis forces now opposing the British forces in the Western Desert, and intensification of air and sea operations against the Axis in the European Continent."

On August 14, Lieutenant General Dwight D. Eisenhower was appointed Supreme Commander Allied Expeditionary Force. His headquarters was at Norfolk House, London, where planning for the combined operation was already in progress. One month later "Torch" assumed its final form: Task Force 34, under Rear Admiral H. Kent Hewitt, included a Western Task Force, U.S. Army, in which the redoubtable Major General George S. Patton and 35,000 United States Army troops were embarked from the United States; a Center Task Force under Commodore Thomas Troubridge, RN, with about 39,000 United States Army troops underway from the United Kingdom to Oran; and an Eastern Task Force under Rear Admiral Sir H. M. Burrough, RN, with about 33,000 (British and American) Army troops, bound from the United Kingdom to capture Algiers.

For our purposes it is not necessary to go into the preliminary work done by the Amphibious Force Atlantic Fleet; we need only discuss the invasion, focusing attention on the Western Task Force until the stage is set for the Battle of Casablanca. Aggregating one hundred and two warships, transports and auxiliaries when united at sea, the Western Task Force got underway from Norfolk on October 24, despite a caustic prediction from Patton that the Navy would break down at the last crucial minute. "Never in history," observed "Blood and Guts", "has the Navy landed an army at the planned time and place. If you land us anywhere within fifty miles of Fedahla and within one week of D-Day, I'll go ahead and win . . ."

These chicks came home to roost as the United States Navy, after a circuitous voyage in clear weather with no incidents marring the passage, arrived at its destination at midnight August 7—exactly on deadline—and the Western Naval Task Force broke up into Southern, Northern and Center Attack Groups off assigned targets along the North African coast. The landings at Fedahla, fifteen miles north of Casablanca, were punctuated by misadventures and stiff French resistance. The epochal day dawned fair but hazy, with a moderate ground swell and light offshore winds. The invasion was on.

The gifted Rear Admiral Morison details the explosive D-Day events at sea. Twice winner of the Pulitzer Prize, Morison undertook his formidable naval history as the result of an interview with President Roosevelt and Secretary of the Navy Knox, who commissioned him a Lieutenant Commander with the writing assignment of his choice—documenting and interpreting the story of our Navy at war. He served aboard eleven different ships and covered United States' participation in every theatre of war, and was awarded the Legion of Merit with Combat "V."

The following is the first of three distinguished selections from his work which appear in this volume.

7.

THE NAVAL BATTLE

OF CASABLANCA

From the moment when it was light enough to launch planes, until all enemy resistance ceased, the carrier-based aircraft of the Navy showed the utmost fight and aggressiveness. U.S.S. *Ranger,* the one big carrier in Task Force 34, took station some thirty miles northwest of Casablanca and began shoving 'em off at 0615 when it was still quite dark. Nine Wildcats of her fighter Squadron 9 (Lieutenant Commander John Raby) received their "Batter Up!" from anti-aircraft fire when over the Rabat and Rabat-Sale airdromes, head-quarters of the French air forces in Morocco. Without loss to them-selves, they destroyed seven grounded planes on the one field, and fourteen bombers on the other. Four planes in their second flight, which took off at 0845, shot down an enemy plane. In their third flight that day they destroyed seven enemy Dewoitine 520s fueling on the Port Lyautey field, but lost one plane with Ensign T. M. Wilhoite. The fourth flight, taking off at 1145, found no enemy to the eastward. The fifth, departing at 1300, strafed shore batteries; on the sixth, which began at 1515, four planes strafed four French destroyers while five planes strafed and bombed an anti-aircraft battery near Casablanca.

Fighter Squadron 41, taking off from *Ranger* at 0700, made straight for Les Cazes airfield near Casablanca, which it found to be patrolled by ten Dewoitine 520s and six Curtis 75-As. In the ensuing

162

dogfight three of the former and five of the latter were shot down, and fourteen planes were destroyed on the ground. Four Wildcats failed to return. Later in the day the same squadron made several more flights, destroyed grounded planes on airdromes, and strafed the French destroyers (effectively their officers admitted) when they first sortied from Casablanca.

Ranger's SBD squadron, consisting of eighteen Dauntless dive-bombers, was orbiting 10,000 feet in the air over Casablanca by 0700, waiting for the "Play Ball!" With the *Jean Bart* and anti-aircraft batteries on the harbor jetties throwing up everything they had, these planes bombed the submarine basin in the inner harbor, as well as various installations. They were recovered in time for a brief rest before being sent out again to stop the cruiser *Primauguet* when she sortied at 1000.

Suwannee, in the meantime, commanded by that famous Cherokee Indian Captain "Jock" Clark, maintained combat and anti-submarine air patrol for the Center Group. Her only trouble was the prevalent light wind on D-day. Frequently she had to seek areas where ruffled water indicated a better breeze. Most of her planes were recovered with only a 22-knot wind over the deck, which would have precluded flight operations in time of peace. Her Avengers joined those of *Ranger* in bombing missions.

These are typical examples of the unremitting activity of the Navy carrier-based planes. There were probably 168 French planes available in Morocco on the date of our arrival; 172 of ours were brought in by the four carriers. These shot down about 20 enemy planes in the air, and destroyed a considerable number on the ground. Prompt and effective aggressiveness of the Naval air arm, combined with the fact that a considerable part of the French air force welcomed the landing, made this aspect of the Battle of Casablanca rather one-sided.

Air protection to the landing forces was far from complete; it never can be. At least five times on 8 November French fighter planes flew over the Fedhala beaches and strafed our troops; and, on the ninth, high-level bombers made fruitless passes at ships and beaches. Yet, on the whole, the air opposition was very well taken care of. No enemy aircraft interfered with spotting planes from battleships and cruisers, and no air bombs hit the transports. The value of aircraft to protect amphibious operations was conclusively demonstrated; and it was immensely heartening to the Army to see our own planes overhead instead of those with enemy markings. Moreover, in addition to destroying and driving off enemy planes, the naval aviators delivered effective strafing and bombing attacks on French warships and shore batteries in the naval combats of 8 and 10 November.

The Naval Battle of Casablanca was an old-fashioned fire-away-Flannagan between warships, with a few torpedo attacks by the enemy, and air attacks by us, thrown in. Lasting from dawn almost until late afternoon 8 November, it developed out of an action that commenced before sunrise between French batteries in Casablanca Harbor and airplanes of Rear Admiral "Ike" Giffen's Covering Group.

This group consisted of battleship *Massachusetts* on her shakedown cruise, heavy cruisers *Tuscaloosa* and *Wichita,* screened by destroyers of Captain Don P. Moon's Squadron 8, *Wainwright, Mayrant, Rhind* and *Jenkins.* Their mission, besides covering the entire Task Force against a possible sortie by the formidable French ships in Dakar, was to contain the enemy vessels in Casablanca Harbor, destroy them if and when they showed fight, and neutralize shore batteries in or near Casablanca.

During the approach on 7 November the Covering Group steamed on a course about ten miles southwest of the Center Attack Group, in the general direction of Casablanca. Naval tradition, since time immemorial, requires the "skipper" to make a speech to his men before going into battle; nowadays it is done over the ship's loudspeaker system instead of by straight voice or speaking trumpet. Accordingly at 1415 November 7 this message from Admiral Giffen was repeated by the commanding officer of each ship.—

The time has now come to prove ourselves worthy of the trust placed in us by our Nation. If circumstances force us to fire upon the French, once our victorious ally, let it be done with the firm conviction that we are striking not at the French people, but at the men who prefer Hitler's slavery to freedom. If we fight, hit hard and break clean. There is glory enough for us all. Good luck. Go with God.

To which Captain Whiting of the *Massachusetts* added:—

We commissioned the *Massachusetts* only six months ago; never have I seen a more responsive and hard-working ship's company than this one. You have met every demand I have made. We have the finest ship's spirit possible. We are *ready.* If it becomes our

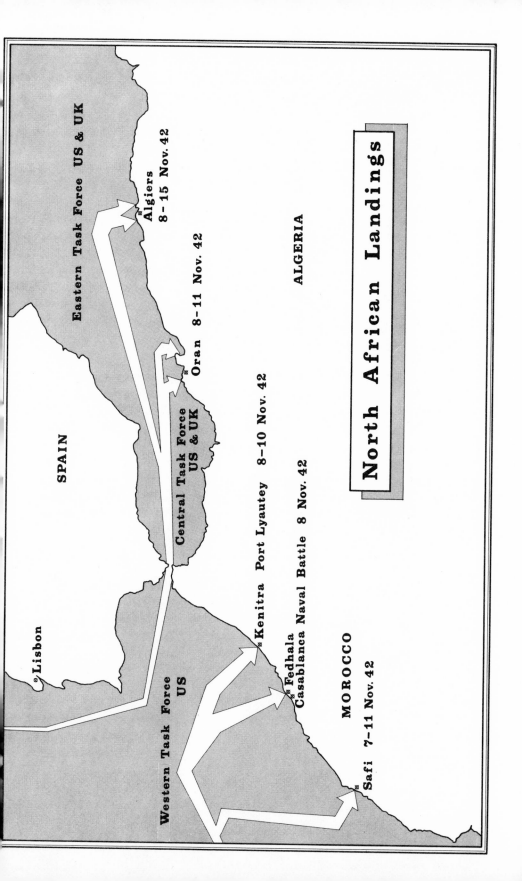

North African Landings

duty to open fire tomorrow, never forget the motto of the Commonwealth of Massachusetts whose name we proudly bear. That motto is: *Ense Petit Placidam Sub Libertate Quietem,* With the Sword She Seeks Peace under Liberty. If we wield the sword, do so with all the strength in this mighty ship to destroy quickly and completely.

At 2215 November 7 Admiral Giffen's group turned away to the Southwestward, and during the night steamed over a trapezoidal course whose base ran parallel to the coastline, about twenty-one miles off shore. After completing the last corner of the trapezoid at 0515 November 8, the big ships continued on a 168° course to the eighteen-fathom shoal bearing 14 miles NW by N from El Hank Light, turned westerly and at 0610 proceeded to catapult nine planes for spotting and anti-submarine patrol. The shore batteries at Fedhala were already opening fire, but Admiral Giffen was too far away to hear the report. He caught Admiral Hewitt's "Play Ball in Center" over the wireless telephone at 0626, but this did not apply to the Covering Group.

Catapulting planes from a cruiser or battleship in early morning twilight is one of the finest sights in the modern Navy. The plane, poised on the catapult, snorts blue fire from its twin exhausts. The ship maneuvers so that the plane will shoot into the wind. Flag signals are made from the bridge and rhythmic arm signals from the plane dispatcher on the fantail. A nod from the pilot, and the plane rushes headlong down the catapult like some hagridden diver going overboard. Just as it leaves the skids, a loud crack of the explosive charge is heard. The plane falls a few yards towards the water, then straightens out and flies off and away.

Immediately after launching their planes the *Massachusetts, Witchita* and *Tuscaloosa* ran up battle ensigns, bent on twenty-five knots, and assumed battle formation. The four destroyers steamed in a half-moon about 3000 yards ahead of the flagship, whch was followed in column by the two cruisers at 1000-yard intervals, their "long, slim 8-inch guns projecting in threes from the turrets, like rigid fingers of death pointing to the object of their wrath with inexorable certainty." At 0640, when the formation had reached a position bearing about west northwest from Casablanca, distant 18,000 yards from Batterie El Hank and 20,000 yards from battleship *Jean Bart's* berth in the harbor, it began an easterly run, holding the same range. Ten minutes later, one of the flagship's spotting planes reported two submarines standing out of Casablanca Harbor, and at 0651 radioed: "There's an anti-aircraft battery opening up on me from beach. One burst came within twelve feet. Batter up!" Another spotting plane encountered "bandits" at 0652 and signaled: "Am coming in on starboard bow with couple hostile aircraft on my tail. Pick 'em off—I am the one in front!" The big ships opened up on these planes with their 5-inch batteries at 0701, and shot one down. The other retired; and almost simultaneously battleship *Jean Bart* and El Hank commenced firing. The coast defense guns straddled *Massachusetts* with their first salvo, and five or six splashes from *Jean Bart* fell about 600 yards ahead of her starboard bow. Admiral Giffen lost no time in giving his group the "Play Ball!" *Massachusetts* let go her first 16-inch salvo at 0704. Actually *Jean Bart* was shooting at the cruisers astern; she never saw, or at least never recognized, *Massachusetts* during the action; so our mighty battlewagon making her fighting debut was reported to the Germans via Vichy as a "pocket battleship."

Jean Bart, the newest battleship of the French Navy, almost 800 feet long and of about the same tonnage as *Massachusetts,* had never been completed. Although unable to move from her birth alongside the Mole du Commerce in Casablanca, her four 15-inch guns in the forward turret and her modern range-finding equipment made her a formidable shore battery. On El Hank promontory, just west of the harbor, was a battery of four 194-mm (approximately 8-inch) coast defense guns and another of four 138-mm guns facing easterly. On the other side of the harbor toward Fedhala, at a place called Table d'Aoukasha, was a somewhat antiquated coast defense battery. We had assumed that the approaches would be mined, but no mines had been laid. The sea approaches to Casablanca were, however, nicely covered by gunfire.

For several minutes *Massachusetts* and *Tuscaloosa* concentrated on *Jean Bart,* commencing fire at a range of 24,000 yards and opening out to 29,000. *Wichita* opened fire on El Hank at 0706 at a range of 21,800 yards, using her own plane spot. *Massachusetts* fired nine 16-inch salvos of six to nine shots each at *Jean Bart,* and made five hits. One penetrated an empty magazine. A second penetrated below the after control station, completely wrecking it, and the nose made a large hole below the waterline. The third and fourth did not meet sufficient resistance to detonate an armor-piercing shell. The fifth, at about 0720, hit the forward turret (then firing at *Massachusetts*), ricocheted against the top of the barbette, and then into the city, where it was recovered and set up as a trophy at the French Admiralty building. The impact of this shell on the barbette jammed the turret in train, silencing *Jean Bart's* entire main battery for about eight hours. Thus, one of the primary defenses of Casablanca, whose guns at extreme elevation might have been able to reach the transport area off Fedhala, was eliminated in sixteen minutes.

Throughout this action, heavy stuff was whizzing over *Massachusetts* and splashing in the water close aboard. Admiral Giffen and Captain Whiting disdained the protection of the armorcased conning tower, and directed battle from the open flying bridge. The Admiral once remarked, as an enemy salvo passed close overhead, "If one lands at my feet, I'll be the first to line up to make a date with Helen of Troy!"

Tuscaloosa concentrated on the submarine berthing area in Casablanca, then shifted to the Table d'Aoukasha shore battery, while *Wichita,* having fired twenty-five 9-gun salvos at El Hank, and silenced it temporarily, took over the submarine area in the harbor at 0727. The range was then 27,000 yards. At 0746 the Covering Group changed course to 270° and commenced a westerly run past the targets, firing on El Hank, Table d'Aoukasha, and ships in the harbor. This action was broken off at 0835 in consequence of a telephone message relayed from the Army ashore, "For Christ's sake quit firing—you are killing our own troops," and "This is from Army—you are killing townspeople, no opposition ashore." Subsequent investigation proved that these casualties were caused by the Batterie du Port, Cape Fedhala, when firing on our troops at the upper edge of Beach Red 2.

Up to that time, the only certain damage inflicted by either side was on the *Jean Bart.* The French scored no hits on the Covering Group, although they made several straddles and near misses, and one shell passed through the flagship's commissioning pennant. Around 0745 bombing planes' and warships' projectiles sank three merchantmen in Casablanca and also three submarines, *Oreade, La Psyche* and *Amphitrite.* Anyway, somebody sank them at anchor. Yet, in spite of all the efforts by Covering Group and carrier planes, eight submarines sortied successfully between 0710 and 0830, and some of them were shortly to be heard from. The shore battery at Table d'Aoukasha—whose guns were described by a French officer as "tout ce qu'il y a du plus vieux"—was silenced only temporarily, and the modern El Hank battery remained completely operational.

The Covering Group had become so interested in pounding *Jean*

Bart and El Hank that its mission of containing the enemy ships in Casablanca Harbor was neglected. At 0833, when they checked fire, *Massachusetts, Tuscaloosa* and *Wichita* had reached a point about sixteen miles northwest of the harbor entrance, and twenty-five miles from our ships engaged in unloading troops at Fedhala. Admiral Michelier, anticipating that this westward run would place the big ships at a safe distance, ordered the destroyer squadrons under his command to sortie from Casablanca and sneak along the coast to break up the landing operations at Fedhala. This was his one desperate chance of defeating the "invasion."

Beginning at 0815, the following French ships sortied from Casablanca:—

Destroyer Leaders of 2500 tons, 423 feet long, five 5½-inch guns, four torpedo tubes, 36 knots

> MILAN   Capitaine de Fregate Costet
> ALBATROS   Capitaine de Fregate Peries

Destroyers of 1400 tons, 331 feet long, four 5.1-inch guns, six torpedo tubes, 36 knots

> L'ALCYON   Capitaine de Corvette de Bragelongue
> BRESTOIS   Capitaine de Fregate Mariani
> BOULONNAIS   Capitaine Corvette de Preneuf
> FOUGUEUX   Capitaine de Fregate Sticca
> FRONDEUR   Capitaine de Corvette Begouen-Demeaux

This force was under the command of Contre-Amiral Gervais de Lafond in Milan. Light cruiser *Primauguet* sortied last, at 0900. Admiral Lafond later informed Admiral Hewitt that when the first sortie commenced he was still ignorant of the nationality of the ships he had been ordered to fight. Other officers later confirmed this surprising fact.

Spotting planes reported the sortie to our Center Attack Group as early as 0818. There then began an anxious twenty minutes for the transports. Wildcats and Dauntless dive-bombers from *Ranger* strafed and bombed the ships, but they continued on their course, and knocked one of the bombers down; its entire crew was lost. Fedhala is only twelve miles by sea from Casablanca, not much to cover for destroyers capable of thirty-six knots; and the transports at that moment were so many sitting ducks for a torpedo attack, or gunfire for that matter. At 0828 the French destroyers began shelling landing boats that were seeking Beach Yellow west of Cape Fedhala, making a direct hit on one, and also firing on *Wilkes* and *Ludlow,* who were patrolling a few miles to the westward of the Cape. *Ludlow* delivered a salvo that started a fire on the *Milan,* then retired at flank speed, and at 0834 was hit by a shell which entered the wardroom country and exploded on the main deck, starting fires which took her out of action for three hours. Splashes and straddles followed her out to 24,000 yards range, and *Wilkes* too fell back on the cruisers. The French sailors must have believed that they had us on the run.

Admiral Hewitt now ordered *Augusta, Brooklyn, Wilkes* and *Swanson* to intercept the French force. Anxiety on board the transports was dispelled by what one of their officers pronounced to be "the most beautiful sight he ever saw." The four ships went tearing into action like a pack of dogs unleashed: *Wilkes* and *Swanson* with their main batteries yap-yapping, dancing ahead like two fox terriers, followed by the queenly *Augusta* with a high white wave-curl against her clipper bow, her 8-inch guns booming a deep "woof-woof"; and finally the stolid, scrappy *Brooklyn,* giving tongue with her six-inchers like ten couple of staghounds, and footing so fast that she had to make a 300-degree turn to take station astern of her senior. At 0848, when the enemy was not more than four miles from our transports, action opened at 18,500 yards, rapidly closing to 17,600; French shells came uncomfortably close but failed to hit; at about 0900 range was opened by the enemy retiring toward Casablanca, to draw us under the coastal batteries.

Admiral Hewitt at nine o'clock ordered Giffen to close and take care of the French ships. The Covering Group came in at 27 knots, and at 0918 opened fire at 19,400 yards, closing to 11,500. *Augusta* and *Brooklyn* broke off and returned to guard the transports, while the fire support destroyers engaged the Batterie du Port on Cape Fedhala, which had reopened fire, and quickly silenced it for the third time. In meantime the French destroyers sent up a heavy smoke screen and followed the excellent defensive tactics of charging out of it to take a crack at their formidable enemy, then in again to throw off the spot planes and range finders. "Our enemy deserves much credit," reported the gunnery officer of *Tuscaloosa,* "for superb seamanship which permitted him to maintain a continuous volume of fire from his light forces while exposing them only momentarily. One well-managed stratagem observed was the laying of smoke by a destroyer on the unengaged bow of the enemy cruiser, which effectively obscured our 'overs' "

These French destroyers did indeed put up a fight that commanded the admiration of all. The Covering Group was unable to polish them off; hurling 8-inch and 16-inch ammunition at these nimble-footed light craft was a bit like trying to hit a grass hopper with a rock. At 0935 Giffen changed course to 280° "because of restricted waters," and began another run to the westward, exchanging shots with the French destroyers and El Hank.

The minutes around 1000 were the hottest part of this action. Several things happened almost simultaneously. The beautiful French light cruiser *Primauguet* (7300 tons, 600 feet long, eight 6-inch guns and twelve torpedo tubes) sortied to assist the destroyers, two of which peeled off from the smoke screen group and headed north to deliver a torpedo attack on the Covering Group. *Massachusetts,* at a range of about 11 miles, and *Tuscaloosa,* at a little less, landed a couple of salvos on the van destroyer *Fougueux.* She blew up and sank in lat. 33°42′ N, long. 7°37′ W, about 6½ miles north of Casablanca breakwater. About the same moment a shell from El Hank hit the flagship's main deck forward and exploded below, injuring nobody. Within three minutes *Massachusetts* sighted four torpedo wakes about 60 degrees on her port bow, distant under one thousand yards. The big battleship was maneuvered between Numbers 3 and 4 of the spread, and just made it; Number 4 passed about fifteen feet away along her starboard side. Four minutes later four torpedoes, from submarine *Meduse,* narrowly missed *Tuscaloosa;* and at 1021 another torpedo wake was sighted, passing 100 yards to port. The French just missed sweet revenge for their too impetuous *Fougueux.*

While the Covering Group was making this run to the westward, sinking ships and dodging torpedoes, three French destroyers began to edge along shore toward the transports. Our big ships were now well below the horizon, as seen from the transport area, so Admiral Hewitt at 0951 ordered his two cruisers and three destroyers to intercept the enemy. When the *Brooklyn* received this order, she was operating to the eastward of the transport area. Captain Denebrink in his eagerness steered a straight course for fifteen minutes, and just managed at 1010, by a timely 90-degree turn, to dodge five torpedoes from the submarine *Amazone,* fired at a range of about three thousand yards. *Augusta,* who was fueling a plane and preparing to set General Patton and staff ashore, catapulted the plane, cut adrift the waiting landing craft and stood over to support *Brooklyn,* handsome as a bridal bouquet with her guns spouting orange bursts of flame.

The second morning engagement, which commenced at 1008 when

one of the French destroyers opened fire on *Brooklyn,* became general when *Augusta* came in at 1020. On the one side were the two cruisers screened by *Wilkes, Swanson* and *Bristol;* on the other, light cruiser *Primauguet,* two destroyer leaders, and four destroyers. *Augusta* and *Brooklyn* steered radically evasive courses: ellipses, snake tracks, and figure eights—dodging shells every few seconds, and footing so fast that their screening destroyers with difficulty kept out of the way. *Brooklyn* was very impressive, reported an observer in *Augusta.* "Her fire consisted of ranging salvos with one or two guns, followed by one or more full salvos, spotted, and then a burst of rapid fire lasting a minute or so." Her adversary was then steering northwesterly to open the range, so as to give her guns the advantage; at seven and a half to nine miles from the enemy one could see little more than black specks of ships constantly emerging from and submerging in the smoke, and gun flashes snapping out of the screen. At 1046 *Brooklyn* received the only hit suffered by either cruiser, a 5-inch dud.

So intent was *Brooklyn* upon the task at hand that she forgot about the Covering Group; and when the superstructures of three ships appeared over the horizon to the westward, firing, and large geysers of green water, far higher than anything she had been dodging, shot up off her starboard bow, officers on the bridge thought for a few seconds that the enemy had led us into a trap—that these ships were the *Richelieu, Gloire* and *Montcalm* from Dakar. It turned out that the green splashes were from El Hank, making a few passes at *Brooklyn,* and that the three ships hull-down were, of course, the Covering Group returning. Great relief on the bridge! At about 1035 *Massachusetts* signaled her re-entry into battle by opening fire on *Boulonnais,* who, hit by a full salvo from *Brooklyn,* rolled over and sank at 1112.

By 1100 *Massachusetts* had expended approximately 60 per cent of her 16-inch ammunition, and decided that she had better save the balance in case that bad dream, the *Richelieu,* came true. Accordingly she pulled out of range with three screening destroyers, while Captain Gillette in *Tuscaloosa* assumed tactical command of the two heavy cruisers and *Rhind,* with orders to polish off the enemy fleet. They closed range to 14,000 yards, closer than our light cruisers were at the time.

At about 1100, just before the reduced Covering Group swung into action, cruiser *Primauguet* took a bad beating from *Augusta* and

Brooklyn. Holed three times below the waterline, and with an 8-inch shell on No. 3 turret, she retired toward the harbor, and anchored off the Roches Noires. *Milan,* with five hits, at least three of them 8-inch, followed suit. Almost at the same moment, destroyer *Brestois* was hit by *Augusta* and a destroyer. She managed to make the harbor jetty. The planes from *Ranger* strafed her near the waterline with .50-caliber bullets, but did not hasten her end. Holed below the waterline, she sank at 2100.

There were now only three French ships in action outside the harbor, destroyers *Frondeur* and *L'Alcyon,* and destroyer leader *Albatros.* They formed up about 1115, apparently with the intention of delivering a torpedo attack on the cruisers, but were soon reduced to ineffectual zigzagging behind a smoke screen by the fire of *Tuscaloosa* and *Wichita.* They had good support, however, from El Hank. After a number of straddles and near misses, this shore battery scored one hit on *Wichita* at 1128, which detonated in a living compartment on the second deck, injuring fourteen men, none of them seriously; the fires were quickly extinguished. Ten minutes later the same cruiser dodged a spread of three torpedoes from one of the French submarines. *Wichita* and *Tuscaloosa,* however, gave back far more than they got. *Frondeur* took a hit aft and limped into port down at the stern; like *Brestois,* she was finished off by aircraft strafing. *Albatros* was hit twice at 1130, once below the waterline forward and once on deck; with only three of her guns functioning she zigzagged behind a smoke screen, shooting at *Augusta.* At that moment *Ranger's* bomber planes flew into action, and laid two eggs amidships. The fireroom and one engine room were flooded, and the second engine room was presently flooded by another hit from *Augusta. Albatros* went dead in the water.

Immediately after, around 1145 or 1150, action was broken off by reason of two rumors, one false and the other misleading. News reached Admiral Hewitt from a plane that an enemy cruiser had been sighted southwest of Casablanca, and he ordered *Wichita* and *Tuscaloosa* to steam down the coast in search of her. From one of our communication teams ashore came word "Army officers conferring with French Army officers at Cape Fedhala. Gunfire must be stopped during this conference." Such a conference was being held, but Admiral Michelier knew nothing about it, and the senior French officer present, a lieutenant colonel, had no authority to decide anything except to surrender Fedhala, where all resistance had already ceased.

Out of the eight French which took part in this morning engagement, only one, *L'Alcyon,* returned to her berth undamaged. But Admiral Michelier had a few cards still up his sleeve, and proceeded to play them well.

The eighth of November had developed into a beautiful blue-and-gold autumn day, with bright sunlight overhead, a smooth sea almost unruffled by light offshore wind, and a haze over the land to which smoke from gunfire and smoke screens contributed. Sea gulls with black-tipped wings were skimming over the water, and so continued throughout the action apparently unconcerned by these strange antics of the human race.

At 1245 *Brooklyn* and *Augusta* were patrolling around the transports; and their crews, who had been at battle stations for twelve hours, were trying to grab a little cold lunch. General Patton at last had managed to get ashore from the flagship. Admiral Michelier chose this opportune moment, when the Covering Group was chasing a ghost cruiser to the westward, to order a third sortie from Casablanca, led by a *aviso-colonial* named *La Grandiere.* At a distance she resembled a light cruiser. She was followed by two small *avisos-draguerurs* (coast-patrol minesweepers) of 630 tons, armed with 3.9 inch anti-aircraft guns, called *La Gracieuse* and *Commandant Delage.* The three vessels steamed along the coast as if headed for the transports. The French, as ascertained later, were simply trying to pick up survivors from the sunken destroyers, but their course then looked aggressive. At the same time two destroyers who had not yet sortied, *Tempete* and *Simoun,* remained near the harbor entrance, milling around temptingly in order to attack some of our vessels under the fire of El Hank. *Albatros* was still outside, but dead in the water.

Again it was *Brooklyn, Augusta,* destroyers and bombing planes to the rescue. Action commenced at 1312, range 17,200 yards, rapidly closing to 14,300. Again the enemy put up a smoke screen, through which the cruisers were unable to find their targets. *La Grandiere* was damaged by one of the bombing planes, but returned to harbor safely, and the two small *avisos* were not touched. During this short action a brazen little tug was observed towing in *Albatros,* who was bombed and strafed on the way, and finally beached at the Roches Noires near the *Primauguet* and *Milan.* This was a bad move on the part of the French, because in that position they were easily attacked from seaward by carrier-based planes who were not bothered to any great extent by the harbor anti-aircraft defenses. *Primauguet* that afternoon suffered several fierce bombings and strafings from *Ranger's* planes, and her whole forward half was completely wrecked. A direct hit on her bridge killed the captain, the executive, and seven other officers; Rear Admiral Gervais de Lafond was seriously wounded, but recovered.

By 1340 the Covering Group was coming up again fast from the westward, and for the third time that day Admiral Hewitt handed over the duty of engaging the enemy to Admiral Giffen, while Captain Emmet's command resumed patrol duties. *Massachusetts* fired one salvo at the small ships, and was promptly engaged by El Hank, but ceased firing after ten minutes in order to conserve ammunition. *Wichita* and *Tuscaloosa* stood in toward the harbor, and engaged *La Grandiere* and *Albatros*.

At the height of this action Colonel Wilbur, accompanied by a French guide and Colonel Gay and driven by Major F. M. Rogers. made a second auto excursion into Casablanca in the hope of dissuading the French from further resistance. The advance post let them pass under flag of truce after disarming the party. They called at army headquarters in Casablanca, and after ascertaining that the Colonel's friend General Bethouart was in jail, and that Michelier was in command, proceeded to the Admiralty on the waterfront. As they passed through the streets of Casablanca, flying the American flag, the population waved and cheered, and a friendly crowd gathered whenever they halted to ask the way. About 1400, word was sent in to Admiral Michelier requesting an interview. An aide came out, saluted, remained at attention, and declared that the Admiral refused to receive them. As Major Rogers was beginning to argue in his best Harvard French, El Hank let fly a salvo at *Wichita*. "Voila votre reponse!" said the Admiral's aide.

The last ruse of Admiral Michelier had succeeded. *Wichita* and *Tuscaloosa,* although not hit, were so frequently straddled by gunfire from El Hank that they broke off action at 1450. Dive-bombers from *Ranger* also engaged this shore battery, but inflicted no lethal damage. At 1530 Admiral Giffen signaled Admiral Hewitt, "Have seven loaded guns and will make one more pass at El Hank." So this day's furious shooting ended in a well-earned tribute to "Old Hank," as the bluejackets named this French shore battery.

The final score of the battle of Casablanca is very one-sided. The United States Navy suffered one hit each on destroyers *Murphy* and *Ludlow,* cruisers *Wichita* and *Brooklyn* and battleship *Massachusetts*.

Three men were killed on board *Murphy* and about 25 wounded, by the Sherki battery. Approximately 40 landing boats were destroyed by enemy action, most of them by airplane strafing when on the beach. The Army casualties ashore that day were very slight. The French Navy lost 4 destroyers and 8 submarines sunk or missing; *Jean Bart, Primauguet, Albatros* and *Milan* disabled. Casualties to all French armed forces were stated by the War Department on 23 November to be 490 killed and 969 wounded. All coast batteries at Fedhala were in our possession at the end of D-day, but those at Casablanca were still in French hands, and operative.

Admiral Michelier still had his two principal assets, the four 15-inch guns of *Jean Bart* and the four 194-mm and four 138-mm coast defense guns of Batterie El Hank. As long as these, and the several mobile and fixed batteries of 75-mm field guns around Casablanca, were undamaged, the Admiral was in a good position to bargain. French naval and air power in Morrocco had been irretrievably damaged, but the main American objective, securing Casablanca, was far from being attained; and until we could get the transports and cargo ships into Casablanca they were highly vulnerable to submarine or air attack and also in danger of foul weather damage.

In general, it may be said that the results were respectable, considering that this was the first major action of the Atlantic Fleet; but no more than might reasonably be expected from American local superiority in gun and air power. Nothing had occurred to upset the principle that coastal batteries have a great advantage over naval gunfire. *Brooklyn* to be sure had done a good job on the Sherki, but even her bombardment technique could not have silenced a determined and well-trained crew of gunners. The value of naval air power was well demonstrated; for the speedy destruction and driving down of French planes left the cruiser-based planes free to spot fall of shot, while carrier-based bombers and fighters delivered attacks on ships and shore batteries.

The French observed their traditional economy in the use of ammunition; but the American ships were lavish, considering that they had no place to replenish their magazines that side of Hampton Roads. If the dreaded Dakar fleet had turned up next day, it is questionable whether the Covering Group would have had enough shells to defeat them.

Of individual ship performances, that of *Brooklyn* was typical for intelligently directed and courageously sustained aggressive action.

Her men remained at battle stations from 2215 November 7 to 1433 November 8, with a single forty-minute interval at noon, and no hot food, without showing signs of discouragement or fatigue. The teamwork and morale of that ship was outstanding. Even the smallest mess attendant, when questioned after the action as to what he had done, since the anti-aircraft gun for which he passed ammunition had never fired, said, "I mostly kept out of people's way, sir—but I did an awful lot of that!"

Equipped with the latest devices to keep main battery trained on a target while steering evasive courses at a speed of thirty-three knots, *Brooklyn* delivered an amazing shower of projectiles, and as she zigzagged and pirouetted, delivering 15-gun salvos and continuous rapid fire from her main battery, her appearance, with great bouquets of flame and smoke blossoming from her 6-inch guns, was a delight to the eye, if not to the ear. *Brooklyn* went far to prove, in this action, that the light cruiser is a most useful all-around fighting ship. She expended almost 1700 rounds of 6-inch common and about 965 rounds of 6-inch high-capacity, on this joyful day of battle, without a single misfire. At the end of the day Admiral Hewitt sent this message to Captain Denebrink: "Congratulations on your gunnery as evidenced by silencing Sherki battery and on your aggressive offensive action shown throughout the day."

Augusta also put in an outstanding performance. Athough much of her space and communication facilities were taken up by the two admirals and two generals on board, and their staffs, Captain Gordon Hutchins fought his ship cleverly and well. Her 8-inch guns could not, of course, shoot as rapidly as the 6-inch of *Brooklyn,* but they probably did more damage.

The Covering Group destroyed the *Jean Bart* as a fighting ship, and probably accounted for the *Fougueux* and *Boulonnais. Massachusetts,* on her shakedown cruise, was full of fight and tip-top in morale; her turret men showed unusual endurance in handling the 16-inch shells for hours on end; out of her 113 officers and 2203 men, only three were in sick bay during the action. If she did little damage to the battery on El Hank, that was because of her ammunition. She carried only armor-piercing (AP) 16-inch shells, with a view to engaging enemy battleships. It was well known that AP projectiles would be of slight use in shore bombardment, for which high-capacity (HC) shells with instantaneously acting fuses are required, and Admiral Hewitt's staff made every effort to procure a supply of these for her; but at that time the Bureau of Ordnance could furnish none. The AP simply drove the gunners of El Hank temporarily to cover; only a direct hit on one of the emplacements could have silenced the battery permanently.

The destroyers too were well handled. They acted as all-around utility ships, shepherding the landing boats to the line of departure in dangerous proximity to the shore batteries, delivering accurate and powerful fire on ship and shore targets, and screening the capital ships and transports from torpedo attack. Many of their officers will appear again and again in this history, especially in Pacific Ocean operations. One of several commended by their skippers was Lieutenant Franklin D. Roosevelt Jr. USNR, gunnery officer of *Mayrant,* "for controlling and spotting main battery with skill and good judgment under highly adverse spotting conditions." These conditions were partly due to the inexperience of plane pilots, partly to the glare of sunlight on the water between our ships and their targets.

Perhaps the best story of the battle comes from destroyer *Wilkes,* when screening *Brooklyn* and *Augusta* in their fight with *Primauguet* and the French destroyers. The officer at the engine-room telephone heard loud reports, and more speed was called for. "What's going on up there?" he inquired. "Enemy cruiser chasing us," was the reply. Before long he was almost thrown off his feet by a sudden change of course, and even more speed was called for. "What's going on now?" he asked. "We're chasing the enemy cruiser!"

WITH THE NORTH AFRICAN INVASION ACCOMPLISHED and the Tunisian campaign begun, the way was clear for expansion of the Allied lodgment. Although heavy fighting was to continue at Casablanca until the 11th, we had nevertheless penetrated the "soft underbelly" of the Axis and were on the long road to victory.

Before turning to another aspect of the North African campaign, let us touch briefly on the international political situation. General Marshall's official comments are pertinent:

> General Eisenhower had announced that General Giraud would be responsible for civil and military affairs in North Africa, but the French military officials on the ground were found to be loyal to Marshal Pétain's government. President Roosevelt's note to

the French Chief of State had assured Marshal Pétain of our desire for a liberated France, but the Vichy answer was disappointing. Our ambassador was handed his passport on 9 November, and orders were dispatched from Vichy to French Africa units to resist our forces, which by then had already accomplished their missions except on the Casablanca front.

Unexpectedly, Admiral Jean Darlan, Pétain's designated successor and commander in chief of all French forces, was found to be in Algiers. . . . He was taken into protective custody, and when it was found that the French leaders stood loyal to the Vichy government, a series of conferences immediately followed with the purpose of calling a halt to the French resistance against General Patton's task force in the vicinity of Casablanca. When, on the morning of 11 November, the Germans invaded unoccupied France, Admiral Darlan rejected the pseudo-independent Vichy government, assumed authority in North Africa in the name of Marshal Pétain, and promulgated an order to all French commanders in North Africa to cease hostilities. This order reached Casablanca a few minutes before the final American assault was to be launched on the early morning of 11 November.

An important sequel to the North African landings is described by Walter Muir Whitehill, King's biographer.

FLEET ADMIRAL ERNEST J. KING

AND CDR. WALTER MUIR WHITEHILL

8.

SUMMIT CONFERENCE

In the days following the North African landings it became clear to the President that a conference to determine strategic plans for 1943 would shortly become necessary. Late in November, Mr. Churchill proposed that Marshall, King and Hopkins repeat their London visit of July, but the President felt the need of sitting down at a table with the Russians either in Cairo or Moscow. As it appeared that free discussion with the Russians could take place only on the highest level, Stalin himself was invited to participate. Mr. Churchill suggested a new Atlantic Conference in Iceland, with the three heads of state housed in ships lying together in Hvalfjordur, but Mr. Roosevelt's comment—"I prefer a comfortable oasis to the raft at Tilsit"— turned plans toward North Africa, which offered a more suitable climate at this season. In the end Casablanca in French Morocco was chosen. Although Stalin never came, the President, the Prime Minister, the Combined Chiefs of Staff, and other governmental representatives assembled there for a ten-day conference, designated by the code word SYMBOL. Tremendous precautions for secrecy were observed during the outward journey, particularly as the President had neither left the country since the United States had declared war nor flown since he became President. Leahy, who accompanied him, was stricken with bronchitis early in the journey, and so, to his keen disappointment, was left behind at Trinidad.

On 9 January, in advance of the President's party, King left Washington by air for Borenquen Field in northwest Puerto Rico. Generals Somervell and Wedemeyer accompanied him while Marshall, Arnold, and Sir John Dill traveled in another plane. During the flight from Borinquen toward Brazil, off the mouth of the Pará River, King crossed the equator for the first time in his sixty-four years. The next night was spent at Belém, before the party continued to Natal, Brazil. The planes then crossed the South Atlantic by night to Bathurst, Gambia, and skirted the coast of Africa as far as Agadir where they flew inland. Landing at Marrakech in French Morocco on the afternoon of 12 January, they spent the night in a handsome villa owned by Mrs. Moses Taylor, and after dinner strolled in the city. King was not in a mood to see sights—not even the bazaars of this ancient city, characterized by Mr. Churchill as "the Paris of the Sahara"—for he felt that in such matters he had done his duty adequately in the course of his European cruises of 1899 and 1903. During the hour's flight to Casablanca the following morning, Sir John Dill accompanied King and reminisced about his duty in India and Palestine.

Casablanca had been chosen for the site of the SYMBOL Conference largely because convenient and secure accommodation was available there. The Combined Chiefs, with their staffs, were lodged in the Anfa Hotel, some four miles south of the city, while the President and the Prime Minister each had an attractive villa near by.

The Joint Chiefs of Staff met on Wednesday afternoon, the thirteenth, and again early the following morning to lay their plans for the conference. King at once suggested that world-wide strategy and basic strategic concepts should be discussed first, and strongly stressed the need of determining the proportions of the total effort that should be delivered against Germany and against Japan. He urged that we resist any effort on the part of the British to deviate from a discussion of world-wide strategy in favor of any *particular* operation until the basic strategic concepts had been settled. He was greatly concerned at this time with preventing the building up of a large excess force of troops in North Africa with no immediate prospect for their useful employment. In this he was in full accord with Mr. Churchill, who several weeks previously had observed: "I never meant the Anglo-American Army to be stuck in North Africa. It is a spring-board and not a sofa."

WHILE DOENITZ EXPANDED HIS U-BOAT OPERATIONS TO
meet the crisis of invasion in the Mediterranean, the Atlantic was
still the principal scene of submarine warfare. Early in 1942
Rear Admiral Jonas H. Ingram's South Atlantic Fleet, built around
four light cruisers operating from Recife, Brazil, beat down stiff
opposition from U-boats which had taken a heavy toll of shipping in
the Trinidad-Recife grid. Another impressive group was Fleet Air
Wing. After mopping up in the Iceland-Greenland-Newfoundland
apex, it shifted operations to the Bay of Biscay and the Azores.
German shipyards, however, turned out U-boats as quickly as they
were sunk (by war's end 810 had been produced) and when one area
got too hot for Doenitz he moved elsewhere. From October to December 1943 U-boats concentrated in the Central Atlantic to feed on
Allied convoys, and the pressure there increased accordingly. At that
juncture the enemy introduced the acoustic torpedo, *Zaukoenig,*
which drew a bead on a ship's propellers. However, the Navy countered with "Foxer," a device of parallel rods which clacked together
when towed and was calculated to lure *Zaukoenig* from effectual
attack.

But the best antisubmarine weapon devised was the Killer-Hunter
Group; a merchantman converted to a baby flattop, or "jeep carrier",
screened by several destroyers. The *raison d'etre* of this outfit was to
kill submarines, and it did. The procedure called for the carrier's
planes to find the U-boat on the surface and either destroy it with
bombs, or if the submarine dove, to coach in a destroyer. This
was the case on the afternoon of October 31 when *U-91* was spotted
and bombed by a *Block Island* Avenger. As the hour was growing
late, Captain A. J. "Buster" Isbell sent destroyer *Borie* surging ahead
to search. An old flush decker, the tin can reached the area after
dark and soon obtained three solid contacts on her sound gear. A
depth charge attack was launched, after which the destroyer's crew
heard and felt heavy explosions below. But the night was not over.

A swashbuckling story which is strongly reminiscent of the War of
1812 is told by the brilliant Pulitzer Prize winning novelist, John
Hersey. Presently Master of Pierson College at Yale University,
Hersey covered the war in the Atlantic and Pacific for *Life* Magazine.

9.

U.S.S. *BORIE'S* LAST BATTLE

In a black, windy night of October 1943, the U.S.S. *Borie,* an old destroyer numbered 215, was making 17½ uncomfortable knots through the Atlantic seas. She had just sunk one submarine and was looking for another. It was 1:53 a.m.

A kind of electric shock hit the *Borie's* blacked-out bridge as a voice announced contact with an unidentified craft bearing 190°, just west of south. That contact was the beginning of one of the strangest ship-to-ship contests in the history of fighting at sea.

The commanding officer of the *Borie* was standing just to the right of the helmsman in the wheelhouse. He was Lieut. Charles H. Hutchins, at 30 one of the youngest destroyer captains in the U. S. Navy and one of the very few in this war to be given charge of a destroyer while only a lieutenant. When he learned of the contact he lowered his head and raised his arm in a characteristic gesture—like a man with a club in his hand about to strike an adversary—and he shouted: "Flank speed!"

As the *Borie* gained speed she began to pitch and pound very hard. Destroyers are wet ships, and they are wettest at high speed. The waves that night ran 15 and 20 feet high, and by the time the *Borie* reached 27 knots, black water was knocking at the highest towers of the ship. So heavy was the sea's impact that four of the portholes on the bridge—30 feet above water level—were smashed. The portholes were of ¾-in. glass, 15 inches in diameter. After that water splashed into the wheelhouse through the broken ports. The temperature of the water was 44°Fahrenheit, 12°above freezing.

In a short time the *Borie* lost surface contact with the target. Lieut. Hutchins at once assumed that the enemy had submerged. He ordered the sound apparatus—the device which hunts for underwater objects by means of echoing sound waves—turned on. Soundman Second Class Lerten V. Kent had only sent out a few impulses when every-one on the bridge, listening to the sound machine's slow *ping-ping-ping,* heard a clear and solid echo. Soundman Kent waited for a second echo before he roared: "Sound contact! Bearing one nine oh."

The *Borie* moved in slowly. Soundman Kent reported every twist in the submarine's bearing. The "talkers" on the bridge—men with power telephones to guns and engine rooms—quietly told the crew what was happening. All through the ship the men were excited. They had gone through dull months. After the first cruise escorting the converted merchantman carrier U.S.S. *Card,* some of the *Borie's* crew had hung a service flag for men transferred to other ships—indicating that they had finally gone to war.

As the old destroyer closed the range on her quarry, Chief Torpe-doman Frank G. Cronin got the "ash cans" of TNT set on their racks aft. When the *Borie* got directly over her target, Lieut. Hutchins gave the order to drop an orthodox deep pattern. Instead of the usual small number for a pattern, depth charges began flying off the stern one after another in an almost endless procession. Something had gone wrong with the depth-charge-releasing mechanism. Soon Sound-man Kent could hear the rumble of many underwater explosions in the sensitive sound stack. To mark the point of attack, Lieut. Hutch-ins ordered a floating flare to be dropped.

The depth-charge attack was not only on a grand scale: it was accurate. It forced the submarine to the surface. Lieut. Hutchins thought the submarine might surface on his right and behind him. Therefore he ordered his 4-inch guns trained on the starboard quar-ter. But the wily German turned around underwater before surfacing. This was the first of a series of tricks on both sides which gave this duel its weird quality.

The first man to see the U-boat on the surface was Fire Control-man First Class Robert Maher. When the submarine popped up to port and astern, Maher forgot his formal naval vocabulary and screamed: "There it is—just to the right of the flare!" It was 400 yards away. It was huge and almost white.

As if by reflex, without a moment's thought, Lieut. Hutchins decided that he could swing his ship around faster than the gun crew could train their 4-inch guns around, so he put his head down, raised his right arm in his clubbing gesture and roared to his helmsman, Seaman Third Class James M. Aikenhead, to put the wheel hard right—away from rather than toward the submarine. Lieut. Hutchins ordered the searchlight turned on. This lit up the sleek gray target, but it also gave the Germans something to shoot at.

The *Borie* got the first shot in, with the No. 4 gun, astern, about halfway through the circling turn. It missed. Then all the *Borie's* guns opened fire. Men on the *Borie* could see Germans scrambling out on the conning tower and manning the machine guns there.

The *Borie* straightened out and went after the submarine, verging to the right so that as she caught up she would be broadside to the enemy. The submarine could make about 12 knots, and the *Borie* was now pounding out 27 again.

The gun duel was one-sided. The Germans never attempted to man their big deck gun, for the U-boat's deck was awash and great waves were breaking over the gun. In any case the second or third salvo from the *Borie* lifted that gun off the deck and threw it in the sea. Men of the *Borie* later said they saw the gun in midair.

Soon the destroyer began to pull up alongside the submarine, and Americans could see Germans clearly and close-to. The U-boat had apparently been surprised, because several Germans were obviously straight out of bed. They came out on the conning tower in nothing but underwear pants. Some were dressed in sweaters and shorts, others in dungarees. Many wore bandanas of green, yellow and red. The long hair of those without bandanas disgusted the Americans.

When the destroyer's machine guns found the conning tower, the German guns fell silent and never fired again. As each German ran to a machine gun he would be horribly killed. There were times when no Germans were visible. Then, in response to long training to pick out some specific target, whether human or not, gun captains began screaming: "Bend up their guns: get those goddam guns bent up."

The U-boat commander, seeing himself out-gunned, tried to out-maneuver Lieut. Hutchins. He swung left and aimed his stern, which carried the sting of torpedo tubes, at the destroyer. Lieut. Hutchins swung left too, at first gently, hoping to stay broadside to the U-boat on the outer of two parallel curves. But the German kept his stern aimed at the *Borie* and fired a torpedo, which missed. Then Lieut. Hutchins tricked the German. He had Aikenhead turn full left rudder. This made the German think the *Borie* was going to cut across the U-boat's stern and come up inside its curve. Therefore the German straightened out. Lieut. Hutchins turned hard right again and the situation was just what it had been a few moments before—the two ships running on roughly parallel straight courses, with the destroyer a little behind the U-boat but catching up.

For the next few minutes the *Borie's* guns drummed the submarine. The electric firing circuit of the forecastle gun stopped working. Gun Captain Kenneth J. Reynolds fired the gun once by pulling the lanyard, but it broke. Rather than take the time to find a piece of string to make new lanyard, he began to trip the firing pin with his hand. He could not get his hand out of the way in time to beat the 25-in. recoil, so that his forearm and wrist were brutally pounded, and later swelled up to three times normal size. All the time the heavy seas were breaking over the forecaste gun and a Negro mess attendant, Steward's Mate Second Class Ernest Gardner, twice grabbed and saved a man just as he was being washed overboard.

The *Borie* caught up with the German and began to pull ahead and it was time to ram. The men of the *Borie* had dreamed, as all destroyermen dream, of ripping into the side of a U-boat and putting it down. Many times, at the wheel, Helmsman Aikenhead had talked of ramming. Just three days before, Lieut. Hutchins had jokingly taken a piece of chalk and drawn on the center porthole, directly in front of the helmsman's eyes, three concentric rings and two lines crossing at their center. He called it the *Borie's* ramming sight.

Now, therefore, Lieut. Hutchins put his head down and lifted his clubbing arm and shouted: "All right, Aikenhead, line her up. Get the sight on."

Aikenhead spun the wheel and in a few minutes said quietly: "All right sir, I got her on."

Lieut. Hutchins shouted an order to be passed on to the crew: "All stations stand by for ram!"

The talkers bent their heads and said into their phones in the parroting, singsong voice of all talkers: "All stations stand by for ram."

The German seemed to be holding his course, as if unaware of his danger. It appeared that there would be a fine collision.

Men on the destroyer braced themselves for the pleasure and the shock. Lieut. Hutchins rushed out into the open on the left wing of the bridge and held tight to the windscreen there. Aikenhead embraced the wheel. Gunnery Officer Lieut. Walter H. Dietz Jr., topside on the director platform, fell in love with the range finder and hugged it tight. Everyone was set.

Then in the last few seconds the German swerved sharply left and a huge wave lifted the *Borie*.

These two things made the moment of impact a disappointment to all hands. There was no shock. No one could hear a crunching noise. The wave lifted the *Borie's* bow high and put it gently on the deck of the submarine, just forward of the conning tower. Momentum and the 30° angle imposed by the German made the *Borie's* bow slide forward on the submarine's. There was scarcely any damage to either craft. In the *Borie's* forward engine room no one even knew the ships had met until the order came down to stop all engines.

And so the two ships came to rest, bow over bow, at an angle, locked in a mortal V.

Disappointment at the collision at once gave way to a crazy elation when the men on the destroyer saw how they had the German pinned down. Lieut. Hutchins worked his clubbing arm as if beating someone's brains out and roared: "Fire! Fire! Open fire!" Then he just yelled: "Yipee!"—over and over. Men on the bridge threw their arms around each other and danced, shouting, "We've got the sonofabitch, we've got the sonofabitch!"

The searchlight bathed the conning tower and all guns which could bear opened up at a 30-foot range. For their part the Germans did not lack a mad courage. They kept coming up out of that conning-tower hatch trying to get to their guns, even in death agonies trying to man their hopeless guns. The sight was a horrible one. One German was hit squarely in the chest by a 20-mm. shell. His head and shoulders flew one way, his trunk another. Some shells took Germans and pitched them bodily overboard. One U-boatman stood there a second without a head.

The situation affected different men variously. Range Finder Operator Seaman First Class Carl Banks, ordinarily a shy, quiet, gentle boy, finding himself now with nothing to do since range had been reduced to zero, marched up and down the director platform shouting: "Kill the bastards! Kill 'em! Kill! Kill! Kill!" Other men were seated and laughed loudly and cracked jokes. Seaman Second Class Edward N. Malaney walked to the left wing of the bridge and, amazed at the size of the submarine, said: "My God, what's that? The *Bremen?*" Other men went quietly about their work. Chief Quartermaster William Shakerly kept taking thorough notes in his log, and in the chartroom Executive Officer Lieut. Philip Brown methodically completed his plot of the course of action.

Then in the middle of the bedlam Lieut. Brown went out on the bridge and reported to the captain. He saluted and said: "I've secured the plot, sir. The hell with charting this battle. All the essential facts are right underneath us." And Lieut. Brown went to the flag bags, where small arms were stowed, and picked himself out a tommy gun. Gunnery Officer Dietz looked down on him from the director platform a few minutes later. He saw his quiet-spoken friend standing there, with his rimless glasses on, waiting cooly until a German torso lifted itself on deck across the way, then raising his tommy gun like a professor raising a pointer at a blackboard, and pulling the trigger and killing another man.

All through the ship, men acted now on their own. The phrase "people's war" came into Lieut. Hutchins' mind as he watched his men. He gave very few orders. The men responded to the months of careful training Executive Officer Brown had given them, and to their own initiatives.

Everyone found something to do.

Standing on the galley deckhouse only about 15 feet away from the conning tower, Fireman First Class David F. Southwick pulled a five-inch knife out of its sheath and threw it at a German who was running for a gun. The knife hit the German in the stomach, and the German went overboard. Chief Boatswain's Mate Walter C. Kurz picked up an empty 4-inch shell case weighing nearly 10 pounds, waited for a German to climb out of the tower hatch, threw the shell case, hit the target squarely and had the satisfaction of seeing him fall into the sea. Chief Gunner's Mate Richard W. Wenz, the strongest man on the ship, who could pick up huge depth charges alone and set them in their racks, now could not be bothered to find the key to the small-arms locker, so he broke the wooden door down with his fist. He distributed .45-caliber pistols, 12-gauge shotguns, rifles and tommy guns to all free hands. Seaman Second Class Edward Malaney, unable to find any other weapon, fired a Very pistol whose signal flares could not kill but could burn nastily.

The gun crews worked as automatically as their weapons and with greater flexibility. Some machine guns should not have fired because they had steel splinter shields between them and the submarine. The crews, at great risk to their lives, fired the guns through the shields, tearing them open, and the guns thereafter had clear fields of fire. Loaders were injured by flying steel from the splinter shields. Negro Officers' Cook Christopher Columbus Shepard, first loader on No. 4 gun decided that ammunition was not coming to him fast enough, ran to the after deckhouse racks, grabbed a heavy shell, thrust it home, climbed into the seat of the firing pointer, who had been blinded, fired, climbed out, ran for another shell—and kept his gun going that way. Among all the 20-mm. machine guns there were only two jams during the whole battle, and each was cleared in a matter of seconds.

Gunnery Officer Dietz—who at the drop of a hat will quote Nelson: "No captain can do very wrong if he lays his ship alongside that of an enemy"—had trained a boarding party, and he was eager to board the submarine. But Lieut. Hutchins passed this word: "We will not board, we will not board."

He had a reason for this order. The fight above decks was going very well. At least 35 Germans had been killed. Nobody had been killed on the *Borie*. But serious reports were coming up to the bridge talkers from the bowels of the ship. The engine rooms were flooding.

The German enemy had not done this to the *Borie:* the weather had. The high seas had twisted the two ships, had reduced the V until the enemies lay nearly parallel, and had banged the two hulls together. The submarine, built to withstand tremendous underwater pressures, was better able to survive the grinding than the destroyer whose skin was only $\frac{3}{16}$ of an inch thick. Water began pouring into both engine rooms. In the after one, a damage control party was able to stuff the leaks enough so that pumps could keep the water down. But the forward engine room became hopelessly flooded.

There the water crept up, first to the men's knees, then to their waists, and finally to their chests. Since the engines were steam-tight from within, they were, of course, watertight from outside, and they kept going even when submerged. As the ship rolled and pitched, the water tore every mobile thing free, and soon the men were being sloshed around the room along with floor plates, gratings, small casks and other debris. Machinist's Mate Second Class Edd M. Shockley and Fireman First Class Mario J. Pagnotta crawled and floated in behind some live steam pipes dragging mattresses behind them, to try to plug the holes; but their efforts washed out. Chief Engineer Lieut.

Morrison R. Brown ordered everyone to leave. He stayed alone to do what he could.

Finally, 10 minutes after the ramming, the two ships worked free of each other. The incredible contest of wit and maneuver began again.

The submarine pulled ahead and out to the left. Lieut. Hutchins could see that the enemy intended to get his tail on the destroyer again, and to fire more torpedoes. That made Lieut. Hutchins decide to fire torpedoes of his own. He ordered the tubes manned. Torpedo Officer Ensign Lawrence S. Quinn made the proper calculations and fired. But a heavy sea threw the aim off. The torpedo missed.

The U-boat went into a tight left circle and the *Borie* did too. But the submarine's turning radius was smaller than the destroyer's and the two ships traveled in concentric circles. Most of the time the U-boat had its threatening tail aimed straight at the destroyer. A good 4-inch hit on the submarine's starboard Diesel exhaust may have penetrated to the torpedo room and prevented the firing of any more torpedoes.

Lieut. Hutchins felt frustrated by his ship's inability to turn shorter than the enemy. He kept having the illusion that his ship was going in a straight line, while the submarine was turning away. He did not want to lose his victim at this late hour. He kept beating the air with his right arm and shouted over and over: "All right, Aikenhead, bring her left, dammit, bring her left."

Helmsman Aikenhead, who weighed only 130 pounds and was very tired from the stiffness of the *Borie's* wheel, kept saying in a pleading voice: "But, Captain, I *am* left, I *am* left."

Lieut. Hutchins would not believe Aikenhead until he looked at the compass which was moving around very fast. Hutchins did not know how many times the two ships made that dizzy circle. All the time he had in the back of his mind his planned rendezvous next morning with the *Card* and her other destroyers, the *Goff* and the *Barry*. He did not want to lose his position, so it was a relief, as the *Borie* turned in those merry-go-round circles, to catch glimpses of his original floating flare. The ships had made many convolutions but had not moved far.

The circling was of no advantage to the *Borie,* so Lieut. Hutchins tricked the submarine again. He turned out his light, hoping that the U-boat would count on shaking the destroyer by sneaking out of that tight circle and away. The submarine did just that. Lieut. Hutchins snapped on the light again and soon found the glistening U-boat streaking off in a northeasterly direction. Range was 400 yards. The *Borie* pursued.

All through the battle so far the *Borie* had been to the right of its adversary. Lieut. Hutchins decided to break through to the other side, so while he chased the enemy he pulled left. And now he gave an order which helped to win the battle. He ordered depth charges set shallow. Aikenhead was about to collapse at the wheel, so the Captain ordered the helmsman relieved.

In spite of the failure of the first ramming, sinking the enemy by crashing into him was still an obsession aboard the *Borie*. The destroyer pulled up to the left of the U-boat. Lieut. Hutchins ordered a collision course. The submarine again held its course until the last moment. This time, instead of turning sharply away as he had the first time, the German turned sharply toward the *Borie*.

This brought up something entirely unexpected: the U-boat captain had decided to pull the temple pillars down and ram the destroyer. With her thin skin the *Borie* stood to lose everything by being rammed.

Lieut. Hutchins had one of his instantaneous flashes of combat genius. To everyone's puzzlement on the bridge, he ordered the new helmsman to turn hard left, and he ordered the starboard engine stopped, the port engine backed full. This had the effect of throwing the ship into a skidding stop, with the stern end swinging to the right toward the oncoming submarine. At precisely the correct moment Lieut. Hutchins lowered his head and raised his non-existent club and shouted to his Depth Charge Officer Ensign Lawrence Quinn: "Okay, Larry, give 'em the starboard battery."

Ensign Quinn flicked three switches. Three round shapes arched in the wind and fell within feet of the submarine—two on one side and one on the other. They went off shallow. The submarine lurched out of the water like a hurt mammal and came to a stop very close to the *Borie's* flank. Men on deck said that if there had been another coat of paint on either ship that would have been a collision.

Somehow the German submarine managed to start up again. It was like a dying animal—like a good Spanish bull that refuses to die and in the very act of dying refuses to admit that he is dying. It slipped around astern of the *Borie* and shot off at an angle.

By this time the Americans, though for the most part unhurt, were dazed by the stubbornness of the enemy. The officers on the bridge have a very hazy memory of what happened next. There were various zigs and zags. Apparently the *Borie* closed in to a convenient range.

Now at last the U-boat captain seemed to realize he was beaten. He sent up distress signals—white, green and red Very flares. A moment later Lieut. Hutchins saw an answering signal from the horizon. He went right to the compass and checked the bearing of this other enemy-220°.

The 4-inch gunners gave the U-boat its final crippling blow. They hit the starboard Diesel exhaust again. The submarine dropped to four knots. The *Borie* got in really close.

The Germans seemed to be trying to abandon ship. They huddled on the conning tower. In a compassion which he later did not quite understand, Lieut. Hutchins ordered all guns to cease firing. But before the order reached all stations Gun Captain Kenneth Reynolds, who was still firing his gun painfully by hand, got off one last round. It blew the bridge structure, with all its occupants, right off the U-boat.

Water from the hole by the exhaust poured into the submarine. Its bow lifted dripping out of the rough sea. The ship slipped under the waves and exploded horribly underwater. After one hour and four minutes of admirably tenacious fighting, the submarine sank.

At once Lieut. Hutchins turned his ship away. He and the *Borie* had had enough fighting for one night.

The *Borie* was in serious trouble. Only one engine would run. Her maximum speed was now 10 knots, which a surfaced submarine could easily exceed. The ship was still taking water forward. The generators were out. The water condensers were impaired so that the turbines were not getting the absolutely pure, saltless steam they needed. Lieut. Hutchins reported by radio to the *Card*: "Just sank number two in combined depth-charge attack, gun battle and ramming. May have to abandon ship."

Lieut. Hutchins tried desperately to get the ship to the rendezvous, which was set for just after dawn. He gave the order to lighten ship. Everything that could be was thrown over the side: both anchors and their chains, ammunition, machine guns, torpedoes and their huge mounts, depth charges, the searchlight, range finder, fire director and hundreds of smaller things. A hole was cut in the lifeboat and it was let over the side to sink—for it had the number 215 on it, and if left afloat it might identify the *Borie* to the enemy. During this process a conscientious storekeeper first class named Joseph San Philip came to the bridge holding the *Title B Book* in his hand. This book contains a list of things aboard ship for which the captain has had to sign his personal responsibility. Storekeeper Philip said: "Sir, who's going to take the responsibility for all this Title B stuff we're throwing away?"

Without saying a word Lieut. Hutchins took the *Title B Book* from the storekeeper's hands and dropped it, too, in the sea.

Dawn broke overcast: the *Card's* planes would have a hard time finding the *Borie*. The emergency gasoline generator for the radio had used up its fuel so that the *Borie* was now silent.

The officers sat around the radio room, wondering what to do. Someone took out a cigaret and lit it with a lighter. Lieut. Robert H. Lord remembered having seen some lighter fluid on another officer's desk. Word was passed through the ship to send all lighter fluid to the radio shack. The generator worked long enough on these contributions for Radio Operator Cameron G. Gresh to send: "Can steam another two hours. Commencing to sink."

At 9 a.m. so much salt had built up in the turbines that the blades locked and the destroyer went dead in the water.

The only hope now was that planes from the *Card* would find the *Borie*. If the *Borie* could send out radio signals the chances of their doing so would be much better. Someone thought of the alcohol in sick bay. After being cut with kerosene it worked the generator all right. Radioman Gresh sent: "Getting bad." Then he sat tapping out three dots and a dash—the letter which in all Allied lands has come to stand for Victory. And a plane rode that letter in and found the *Borie*.

The *Card,* the *Barry* and the *Goff* steamed up at about noon. The *Card* inquired by signal light how things were going. Lieut. Hutchins replied: "I want to save this bucket if I can. Give me a few hours." But things went from bad to worse. Executive Officer Brown inspected the ship. This took as much courage as the battle itself. He forced himself into most of the ship's compartments, never knowing which hatch would be the last he opened. His report indicated that it would be hopeless to try to save the ship.

Toward dusk the *Card* and her escorts returned. It was too rough for a rescue ship to go alongside the *Borie,* and there would not be time for men to be transferred by breeches buoy. There was nothing to do but have them get into the bitterly cold water and cling to rafts.

After his men were off, Lieut. Hutchins went to his room and found a flashlight. And then the young captain went, alone and miserable, through the various deserted compartments of his first ship—into the firerooms and engine rooms, the commissary stores and messing compartments, into officers' country and the wardroom, and finally back to his own domain, the skipper's cabin. The ship was all dark and silent. All hands had abandoned her. So the captain went out on deck and, with the battle flag of the U.S.S. *Borie* under his arm, slipped over the side into water only 12° above freezing.

It was not in the fight but in that water that 27 men were lost. For those who were lost it must have been much as it was for Gunnery Officer Dietz, who was very nearly lost. A slender man, he had never thought himself strong. When he first hit that breath-taking water he thought it would kill him. But he managed to cling to a raft until the *Goff* drifted down on it. He grabbed a life-line and pulled himself up so that his hands held the edge of the deck and of safety. But his hands were so cold that he could not hold on. He fell back into the water. He slipped along the side of the ship, held up by his life belt—a mere rubber tube under his arms. Life lines caught at his throat. The *Goff's* framelike propeller guards hit him in the head and pushed him under. He thought: "I must get away from this and wait." He pushed away from the ship. But when he tried to paddle back his arms would barely move. His mind refused to admit defeat but kept shielding him from fear. "They will come after me," he kept saying to himself. He fainted. Luckily for him his head fell backward instead of forward. A few minutes later hands pulled him aboard the *Barry.*

The margin of luck was not quite so wide for the 27 who were lost. Ensign Richard E. St. John had pulled himself halfway up a life line into the *Goff* when he dropped back into the water to help four men who were too far gone to help themselves. They made it. Ensign St. John was caught under the destroyer and drowned. Engineering Officer Lieut. Brown, who had tried bravely and alone to keep the engines going in water up to his neck, was lost. So was Ensign Lord, who had probably saved the ship by thinking of lighter fluid for the radio. The enlisted men who were lost were: Alford, Blane, Blouch, Bonfiglio, Cituk, Concha, Demaid, Duke, Fields, Francis, Kiszka, Lombardi, Long, McKervey, Medved, Mulligan, Pouzar, Purneda, Shakerly, Swan, Tull, Tyree, Wallace, Winn.

Lieut. Hutchins could not stand up when he was taken onto the *Goff* in the darkening evening. Later he took a hot shower and shook under the steam. Then he had a rubdown, some hot chocolate, a sip of brandy and a little exercise. He spent most of that night on the bridge, waiting for dawn and a glimpse of his ship.

At sunrise the *Goff* made a last sweep for survivors. She found 10 men face down in their preservers. Then she went to the *Borie*. The destroyer had drifted about 20 miles and had settled badly.

Lieut. Hutchins stood on a strange bridge and watched his ship as a Grumman Avenger attacked with a heavy bomb and missed. A second plane hit her amidships. A third holed her again, badly. The *Borie,* her back broken, lifted her protesting bow and then settled fast.

THE COUNTRY'S CALL TO ARMS WAS ANSWERED BY THE flower of our youth, and among the eighteen-year-olds was James Fahey of Waltham, Massachusetts, who enlisted in the Navy in October 1942 and was assigned to the light cruiser *Montpelier*.

Contrary to regulations, Fahey assiduously kept a war diary and was fortunate in that he jotted down his thoughts without official interruption.

10.

ENLISTMENT DAYS

October 3, 1942: I enlisted in the U.S. Navy today. It looks like the Navy got the makings of a very poor sailor when they got me. I still get carsick and cannot ride on a swing for any length of time.

I took my physical examination at the Post Office Building in Boston, Mass., a distance of about ten miles from Waltham, Mass. A fellow next to me was rejected because he was color blind. They told him the Sea Bees would take him. On the way home I relaxed in the old trolly car and felt like the Fleet Admiral himself.

October 7, 1942: I got up early this morning for my trip to Boston, on my way to Great Lakes Naval Training Station in Chicago, Illinois.

Before leaving I shook my father's hand and kissed him goodbye.

It was a clear cool morning as my sister Mary, brother John and I headed for the bus at the corner of Cedar Street. The bus and trolley car were crowded with people going to work. When we reached the Post Office Building in Boston I shook John's hand and kissed Mary goodbye. . . .

After a long tiresome day of hanging around we were finally on our way to the train station. The group was very large and they came from the New England states.

With a big band leading the way we marched through downtown Boston before thousands of people. It took about half an hour to reach the North Station and at 5:30 P.M. we were on our way.

197

When the train passed through my city it was beginning to get dark and I could picture the folks at home having supper. There would be an empty place at the table for some time. It would have been very easy for me to feel sad and lonely with these thoughts in my mind but we should not give in to our feelings. If we always gave in to our feelings instead of our judgment we would fall by the wayside when the going got rough.

It will be a long tiresome trip and our bed will be the seat we sit in, two to a seat.

October 8, 1942: The long troop train stopped in the middle of nowhere today. It looked like a scene from a western movie in the last century. All you could see was wide open spaces with plenty of fields and a small railroad station. It felt good to get some fresh air and stretch our legs for a change after the crowded conditions on the train. Some of the fellows like myself mailed letters and cards home. The postmark on the mail was Strathroy, Ontario, Canada. It was a warm sunny day so we sat on the side of the tracks while waiting for the train to get started again.

At Great Lakes: On the evening of Oct. 9 we pulled into the stockyards at Chicago and stayed there for some time. It gave us another chance to get some fresh air and walk around on solid ground for a change. All the people in the big tenement buildings were at their windows looking at us.

At last the train was on its final leg of the journey. We were a tired dirty lot when the train finally pulled into Great Lakes Naval Training Station in the early morning darkness. The weather was on the chilly side.

They got us up bright and early after a few hours sleep on the floor of a large drill hall. We were far from being in condition for a physical examination but that was the way we started the day and it took a long time. We went from one doctor to another upstairs and downstairs and from one room to another. They checked us from head to toe and even asked us our religion. At last it was over and our first shower in some time. It sure felt good.

We spent four weeks of training and lived in barracks. Our company number was 1291. A Chief Petty Officer was in charge of each company and our chief was liked by all.

Some of the Chiefs are hated because they go out of their way to make it as miserable as possible. They enjoy getting the fellows up at two in the morning and have them stand at attention in the cold for a long time with very little clothing.

The instructor who taught us judo enjoyed taking it out on the new recruits. He sent one of the boys from my company to the hospital in a stretcher. Our chief was boiling mad and if he could have gotten his hands on this punk he would have done a job on him.

You learned that your days of privacy were over while you were in the Navy and they would not return until you were back in civilian life again. When you ate, slept, took a shower, etc., you were always part of the crowd, you were never alone.

No one enjoyed sleeping in the hammocks because they were too tight. It was like sleeping on a tight clothesline. You felt like you were going to fall out if you turned over. You felt safe on your back but you can't sleep on your back all night.

We will never forget our first haircut. When the barber got through there was no hair to cut. It was shorter than short. It was funny to see a nice looking fellow with a beautiful crop of hair get into the barber's chair and leave with no hair at all.

Great Lakes is the largest naval training station in the world and they also have one of the best football teams in the country. I had the pleasure of talking to Bruce Smith the all-American back from Minnesota. He was the number one football player in the country in 1941. You could not help but like him. He slept in our barracks.

We always marched to the mess hall for our meals and kept in step by singing loud and strong.

I had to go to sick call one day because of a bad blow to the ribs I received in a boxing bout but they did not do anything for me even though the pain was killing me. They think everyone is a faker when he goes to sick call, that he just wants time off from work.

We were kept on the go at all times and at last our training was over. It was home sweet home for us. We were very proud of our uniform as we boarded the train for home. After a nine day leave we returned to Great Lakes and stayed here for two days before leaving for Norfolk, Virginia, our next stop.

Late Friday evening Nov. 21, a large group of us boarded a truck for the pier. It was a great feeling as I staggered up the gangway to the ship with my sea bag in one hand and the mattress cover loaded with blankets, mattress, etc., over my shoulder. The name of the ship is the *U.S.S. Montpelier*. It is a light cruiser. At last I have a home and a warship at that.

We slept in our hammocks in the mess hall at first but then we were assigned to divisions. I went to the 5th division. It is a deck division.

It will take some time before we know our way around this large ship. It is over 600 feet long and has many decks and compartments.

Today at eight in the morning we left Norfolk for the Philadelphia Navy Yard . . .

~~~~~~

KILLER-HUNTER GROUPS REMAINED ACTIVE IN THE ATlantic for yet another year, and U-boat sinkings correspondingly declined. On June 4, 1944, a Group built around the jeep carrier *Guadalcanal* found *U-505* about one hundred miles off the coast of Africa and commenced one of the most daring attacks of the war, the only time an enemy submarine was captured intact. The saga of *Guadalcanal's* hunt is recalled by Rear Admiral Daniel V. Gallery, who served as the carrier's commanding officer.

II.

THE CAPTURE OF *U-505*

"Frenchy to Blue Jay! I have a possible sound contact!"

As I reached the bridge the *Chatelain* was wheeling out of our destroyer screen, a long creamy wake boiling up astern, the "submarine" and "emergency" flags whipping from her yardarm. I grabbed the mike and broadcast to the Task Group: *"Pillsbury* and *Jenks* help Frenchy (code name for destroyer *Chatelain*)—others follow me!" We reversed course and got the hell out of there at top speed. A carrier smack on the scene of a sound contact is like an old lady in the middle of a bar room brawl!—she'd better move fast and leave room for the boys who have work to do.

I hollered into the squawk box: "Put those two Wildcats we've got in the air on Frenchy's contact!" Then, with the *Flaherty* and *Pope* scurrying after us, we swung into the wind, sounded general quarters, and scrambled to battle stations to launch more planes.

A salvo of twelve depth charges arched into the air from the *Chatelain* and splashed into the sea. Seconds later the ocean rumbled, quaked and erupted into great white plumes of water. Ordinarily we would have to wait for several anxious minutes while the ocean's reverberations died out, and then have the tin cans begin a wary search of the area—hunting for oil, wreckage, a dead whale, or possibly another sound contact. But this time, almost immediately after the blasts, a Wildcat pilot named John W. Cadle sang out on the

201

radio, "Sighted sub! Reverse course Frenchy and head where I'm shooting."

In the clear Atlantic waters off Cape Blanco, Cadle could see the long dark shape of the sub running completely submerged and maneuvering to go deeper and shake off the destroyers. Cadle pushed over and cut loose with his four .50 caliber guns. These couldn't damage the submerged sub, but the bullet splashes showed us where it was.

Chatelain swung around and dropped another salvo. As the depth-charge plumes were subsiding, Cadle shouted, "You've struck oil, Frenchy! She's coming up!"

Half a minute later the huge black shape of the *U-505* heaved itself up from the depths, white water pouring off her sides. Our quarry was at bay.

When a sub surfaces like this, you never know exactly what it's going to do. She might be coming up to surrender, but she also might be planning to get off one last salvo of torpedoes and take you to the bottom with her. To play it safe, you should clobber her with everything you've got.

This time, however, we were going to try something different. On our last cruise we'd gone after the *U-515* and she'd surfaced right smack in the middle of the Task Group. We'd been forced to throw everything but the kitchen sink at her before she finally up-ended and sank. After we'd fished her skipper out of the water, he told us that his only purpose in surfacing was to get his crew off—the fight had gone out of him. We realized then that if we could get on board the sub quick enough, we might be able to prevent the scuttling and capture ourselves a U-boat. Accordingly, the orders had gone out that nobody was to hit the sub with any heavy stuff, as we'd have a tough enough time keeping her afloat without blowing a hole in her ourselves.

Not since 1815 had an American naval vessel captured and boarded a foreign man-of-war on the high seas, but we were going to try it. The moment the *U-505* broke surface and her hatches popped open, I broadcast to the task group, "I want to take this bastard alive!"

Small black figures scrambled out of the hatches and swarmed onto the decks of the sub. *Pillsbury, Chatelain* and *Jenks* opened up with .50 caliber and 20 millimeter guns, and the men who weren't hit at once dived into the water. Within a few moments her decks were abandoned—nothing was moving. She was running at about 8 knots, fully surfaced, in a tight circle to the right. Unless she was mined, booby-trapped, or loaded with armed men—she was a sitting duck.

"Cease firing!" barked from the squawk boxes on all bridges, followed by an electrifying cry that hadn't been heard on a U.S. Navy ship for 129 years: "Away all boarding parties!"

Whaleboats plopped into the water and took off after the floundering U-boat like harpooners after a wounded whale. As the *Pillsbury's* boat, manned by Lt. Albert David and 11 sailors, overhauled the sub I broadcast over the TBS. "Heigho, Pillsbury! Ride 'em, cowboy!" Not very salty, but it got the message across.

David and his boys had every reason to believe there were still Nazis below decks, setting time bombs and opening the scuttle valves. Even if all the Germans were gone, the U-boat was settling rapidly by the stern and looked as if she was going to up-end and sink any minute. I suppose my men thought about these things as they plunged through the choppy sea toward the dying ship, but the moment their whaleboat touched the U-boat they leaped out on her slippery decks. It was the first time any of these men had ever set foot on a submarine.

"Follow me!" David yelled, scrambling up the superstructure toward the conning-tower hatch—an opening about the size of a sewer top that leads straight down 20 feet into the U-boat. A dead man was lying at the top of the hatch, his glazing eyes staring emptily at the men as they started down. David glanced quickly down into the dark hatch, knowing that almost anything could be waiting for them down in the blackness below. He gestured to two men, A. W. Knispel and S. E. Wdowiak, and they plunged down into the bowels of the ship.

Instead of a burst of gun fire, their only greeting was the eerie hum of engines, still driving the sub in her crazy circle to the right. As soon as he realized the Nazis were gone, David ran for the radio shack. The sub gave a shudder and her stern raised slightly. Any minute she might make her last dive, but he knew the risks were justified if he could find the Nazis code book. It was a 100-1 chance. The primary orders of any Naval skipper are to destroy his code books before abandoning the ship, even if there is no enemy within 1,000 miles, and we had been breathing down the U-boat's throat when she surfaced.

David burst into the radio shack, looked quickly around, and saw that his long shot had paid off. Everything was intact—code book, cipher machines, charts of the English Channel mine fields, recognition signals, and all tactical instructions for submarines. He and his men quickly passed everything up the hatch to the whaleboat. This would turn out to be the greatest intelligence windfall of the U-boat war.

While David and his boys were removing the secret files, the sub, still circling, had settled another ten degrees by the stern. Time was running out, when another lad, Zenon Lukosius, motor machinist mate first class, decided to see what he could do about the water that was pouring in. Surrounded by the bewildering maze of gauges, valves and pipes in the main control room, and feeling the ship settling under him, while water swished past his feet, he carefully looked for the leak. Finally he found it—an 8-inch stream of water spouting through a sea chest with the cover knocked off. The cover was gone. The water was now above the floor plates. Luke bent down, fishing around in the swirling mass of wreckage and sea water, and found the cover. He jammed it back in place, set the butterfly nuts, and checked the inrush of ocean. Had he taken one minute longer, it would have been too late.

By now the *Guadalcanal* had a whaleboat alongside the sub, with a handpicked party that included my Chief Engineer, Earl Trosino, and our only submarine "expert"—a lad who had been a yeoman on one of our own pig boats and could tell us anything we wanted to know about the *U-505's* paper work and filing system. Trosino, even though never aboard a submarine before, was our real expert. Earl is one of those engineers who know machinery like Toscanini knows musical instruments. He can walk into a strange engine room, take a quick look around, and start bringing order out of chaos while the rest of the men are still trying to figure out which way is aft.

As Trosino and his party came alongside, a large swell picked them up and dumped them, whaleboat and all, on the deck of the still-circling sub, smashing the whaleboat and spilling them all out on the deck. They pulled themselves together and scrambled down the conning tower.

Trosino said abruptly to David, "I'm going to stop these engines— you get up on deck and stand by to pick up a towline." David nodded and started above.

But, when Trosino stopped the motors, the sub began settling rapidly by the stern—the only thing that had kept her afloat was the planing effect of the hull. When Trosino felt the floor plates tilting under him, he slammed the switches back and the sub forged ahead and rose again in the water. Earl told me later that as he played with those switches, any one of which might have been booby-trapped, his hair was standing on end as stiff as wire. I had the same feeling myself next day when I went aboard the sub to disarm a suspected booby trap.

While Trosino was stopping the motors, Gunner Burr was doing a job with a very short future. We knew that every Nazi sub had 14 demolition charges scattered throughout the ship and designed where the switch was, so Burr went rooting around uncovering charges and ripping the wires off of them. He found and pulled the fangs on thirteen. We didn't find the fourteenth until two weeks later in Bermuda, but by that time we had located the firing switch—somebody had goofed and left it on safe, so the charges couldn't have exploded, anyway.

The *Pillsbury* now attempted to take the runaway sub in tow. She steamed up alongside on the outboard arc of the circle and put a heaving line aboard like a cowboy roping a runaway steer. But steers have horns and so did this U-boat. The destroyer crowded too close alongside and the sub's bow flipped a long underwater gash in her thin plates. The *Pillsbury* hauled clear and radioed to me, "Sub says they have to be towed to stay afloat, but we don't think a destroyer can do it."

That dumped the job in my lap. I didn't like the idea of taking on a clumsy, water-logged tow when I had planes in the air that would have to land soon, but I didn't have much choice. Trosino pulled the switches again and we all held our breath as the sub slowed down and finally laid dead in the water. She was down by the stern about 20 degrees, her conning tower was almost awash and she seemed to be settling lower every minute. If I took time out now to land planes she might be gone when we got back.

In such a spot you just play it by ear as you go along, crossing each bridge when and if you come to it. I told the planes in the air to be as thrifty as possible with their gas supply, and we steamed over to the spot where the sub was wallowing like a drowning dog trying to keep its nose above water.

We laid our stern within heaving line range of the U-boat's snout, got a messenger line over, and the boys hauled our inch-and-a-quarter wire aboard, working knee-deep in the green seas that broke across the deck. When they reported it secured I kicked the engines ahead. As we picked up speed the sub rose again and took a better trim, but then I noticed that she was still circling. She swung way out on our starboard quarter and hung there with our big wire taut as a fiddle-string. I signaled Trosino to put the rudder amidships, and he answered, "Electric steering gear NG. Can't get at hand steering gear because after torpedo room is flooded and hatch is booby trapped."

I had four planes in the air which would soon be out of gas, so with "Junior" (as we called the *U-505*) reluctantly dragging her heels on our starboard quarter, we swung into the wind, said a short prayer, and brought the planes in. Since there was no strain in doing this I immediately launched a couple of others. We were smack in the middle of the U-boat lanes, had been hanging around this one spot for hours, and we had every reason to suppose that Junior had gotten off a report on our position. There would be a full moon that night—ideal for submarines and very bad for aircraft carriers with subs in tow.

At sunset we brought our boarders back and I got a first-hand report from Trosino. He said he had pumped some of the water out, didn't think any more was coming in, and that unless we hit bad weather he thought we could save our prize.

That night our sonar operators let their imaginations run riot. According to their dope we were surrounded by the whole Nazi U-boat fleet. They had "possible sound contacts" all over the place, and several reported "submarine screw noises." The radar operators caught the fever and spotted disappearing radar blips by the dozen. Some of the lookouts even sighted what I began calling "Porpo-scopes." I guess maybe I got nervous at that, because during the night I steamed too fast and parted the towline. We had to circle the drifting sub until sunrise, keeping track of her by radar. Early next morning we got another towline aboard, and Trosino and a few others and I went over to look into that booby trap. I was an ord-nance post-graduate and felt that I knew quite a bit about fuses and firing circuits.

The booby trap was on the watertight door leading into the after torpedo room. This door had been dogged shut when our first board-ing party went aboard, and in deference to the trap they had left it that way. The Nazis that we'd fished out of the water claimed that the after torpedo room was flooded, and the stern trim seemed to confirm this, but we had to get in there if we were going to straighten out the rudder.

The booby trap was a fuse box with the cover accidentally jarred open in such a way that you couldn't move the main dog on the door without closing the fuse box cover. There were dozens of circuits leading out of that box, and any one of them could have led to an explosion charge. I traced a few of the circuit wires, and found they led to perfectly normal places. I looked at the box for a few minutes, thinking over the possibilities. The men watched me, not speaking.

While it looked like the type of booby trap the Nazis would think of, we knew that they'd gotten off in a hell of a hurry, and that wouldn't have given them much time—considering they would have had only a few seconds to flood the torpedo room and set the trap. And they hadn't put out any other traps. I finally decided that this baby wasn't loaded. I looked at the other boys. "What do you think?"

They shook their heads. "It's up to you, captain."

"Well, we can't stand here all day looking at this damn thing," I said. "Here goes, boys!" I slammed the fusebox cover shut.

Nothing happened.

We carefully eased the door open, ready to jam it shut again if water squirted out, and found the torpedo room was dry. We scrambled in, connected up the hand steering gear, and put the rudder amidships. Trosino pleaded with me to let him start the diesel engines, charge the batteries, and bring the sub in under her own power. I wished later that I'd let him do it, but at the time I was afraid he might open the wrong valve and lose her.

He found a way to recharge the batteries, even though I wouldn't let him run the diesels. He disconnected the clutches on the diesels and persuaded me to tow at 10 knots. This high speed turned over the sub's propellers which spun the armatures of the sub's electric motors. Trosino had set the switches to make the motors act as generators, and they in turn charged the batteries. We were thus able to use the sub's pumps to empty the after ballast tanks and bring her up to full surface trim.

Back on board the *Guadalcanal,* I went down to sick bay to see the Nazi skipper, whose name was Harald Lange. He had shrapnel wounds in both legs and was propped up in a sitting position in his bunk. Lange was a big angular man of about 35, and looked more like a preacher than a U-boat skipper.

I walked in and said, "Captain, my name is Gallery. I'm commanding officer of this ship." He bowed respectfully but said nothing.

"We have your U-boat in tow," I said.

He looked up quickly, his face as shocked as if I had slapped him. "No!" he cried. I pulled out some pictures of his family, taken from his cabin, and he lowered his face into his hands, muttering in perfect English, "I will be punished for this."

I tried to cheer him up. "The Nazis are going to lose the war," I said. "A new government will take over, and this will be forgotten."

"I will be punished," he said. Four years ago I got a letter from him saying he had a good job on the Hamburg docks, so his fears were apparently unfounded.

After getting the sub pumped out and fully surfaced, we squared away on a course to Bermuda, 2,500 miles away. I had just one big worry left now—I had stretched the glide too far on my fuel oil, and didn't have enough left to reach even the nearest port, let alone Bermuda. Nothing in this world can make a skipper look sillier than running out of oil and wallowing around dead in the water waiting for a tow, but CINCLANT (Commander-in-Chief Atlantic) came to my rescue. He split off a tanker and the fleet tug *Abnaki* from an Africa-bound convoy and we rendezvoused with them in mid-Atlantic. The *Abnaki* took over the towing job and, after a long swig of oil from the tanker, we headed for Bermuda.

On June 19 we steamed into the harbor entrance with the traditional broom proudly hoisted at our mast head, and Junior obediently tagging along behind. I turned her over to the commandant, U. S. Naval Operating Base, and got his official receipt for "One Nazi U-boat No. *505*, complete with spare parts."

People often ask me, "Why did the *U-505* give up so easily?" Actually, she didn't give up any easier than most of the other 600 Nazi subs that were sunk at sea. When a skipper thought his boat was fatally wounded, it was standard operating procedure to surface and give his crew a chance to escape and be rescued. No sub ever deliberately surfaced under attack unless her skipper was convinced that she was finished, but I knew dozens of cases in which these abandoned subs remained afloat for hours, under heavy bombardment, before going down. I think the real answer to why we were able to capture the *U-505* with such comparative ease is that we caught her by surprise.

Something like pounding depth charges can be pretty damn unnerving, to put it mildly. From apprentice seaman to skipper, they all know they've only got seconds to decide what to do. If they blow their tanks in time they may make it to the surface and get off before the boat takes her final plunge. If they wait too long, they go down with her. When shock waves are smashing against your hull, you're being slammed crazily about in the water, your lights are out, and your men are screaming that your pressure hull is ruptured, it's hard to think calmly. Lange believed that his men were right about the hull being ripped open, and came to the surface. Scores of other U-boat skippers have made the same decision, and if my men hadn't been able to pull off a crazy stunt never before attempted in submarine warfare, the *U-505* would have gone to the bottom just like the other 600.

For extreme heroism Lieutenant David got the Congressional Medal of Honor, Wdowiak and Burr got Navy Crosses, and the rest of the *Pillsbury's* original boarding party received the Silver Star.

Perhaps the most remarkable part of this fantastic business was the fact that the Germans never found out that we had captured the *U-505*. After the war we learned that she'd been listed as sunk, just like all the others that had failed to return. The Nazis continued to use the codes we'd taken off the *U-505,* and we read every order they sent out to their U-boats. This was the main reason for our high rate of sinkings during that last year. The Nazis changed their codes every few weeks so that we wouldn't get too familiar with their pattern, but the key to all these routine changes was in the *U-505's* code books, and we adjusted to their changes just as easily as we did our own.

The main credit for keeping the Germans in the dark belongs to the 3,000 men in our task group. We got them all together on the way back to Bermuda and explained the vital importance of secrecy. I had a hunch that some of the boarders had picked up souvenirs, so I asked everyone to turn in anything they'd taken off the sub. I pointed out that a souvenir's no good unless you can show it around and brag about it, and any bragging would endanger security. Not only that, but I'd throw the book at any man who disobeyed my order. I announced that Washington had told me that the stuff would all be returned after the war.

Next day we were swamped with the damndest collection of junk I'd ever seen—pistols, cameras, officer's caps, name plates— everything but torpedoes. How they had the time and patience to collect all that stuff from a sub that might sink any minute I'll never know. Anyway, I shipped all the souvenirs off to Washington, and that was the last anybody saw of them. The chairborne commandos in the Pentagon glommed onto them for keeps. Now, whenever I meet one of the lads who was in that boarding party, I know exactly what his first words will be—"Captain, where the hell are those binoculars you made me turn in?"

AT LAST THE U-BOAT MENACE HAD BEEN CONTAINED, and no longer posed a threat to our very survival. Germany had little left to fight with; only new boats and green crews, and few of these with the stomach for aggressive submarine combat. Now attention shifted to the Mediterranean, Mussolini's "Mare Nostrum," and the next phase of the struggle against the Axis. We will return to the Mediterranean theatre after a look at the developing war in the Pacific.

PART III

DOOLITTLE'S RAID
TO THE BATTLE OF
MIDWAY

~~~~~~

ON APRIL 18, 1942, AMERICAN MORALE SOARED WITH
the news that a flight of B-25 Mitchell bombers had attacked
Toyko in a spectacular daylight raid. Considering the staggering succession of catastrophes which had befallen the Allied nations since
the outbreak of the war, the psychological value of the strike was
incalculable. Briefly, this is the story behind the daring mission:
Early in 1942 King and his operations officer, Captain Francis J.
Low, decided upon a blow against Japan designed to uplift the
spirits of the American citizen. With the cooperation of General
H. H. "Hap" Arnold, Commanding General of the Army, their
plan envisioned sixteen B-25 Mitchells embarked in a United States
Navy task force to a point several hundred miles from the enemy's
mainland. From there the bombers were to hit Tokyo. However, as

the planes would not be able to return to the carrier, they were to fly to friendly China and land there. The mission was extremely dangerous for all concerned, but particularly for the Navy, as Japanese search planes and patrol boats were vectored out to seven hundred miles from the mainland.

But accepting the risks (subsequent arrangements were made with General Chiang Kai Shek) sixteen bombers, aggregating two hundred officers and men under the command of Brigadier General James A. Doolittle, were given a month's training at Eglin Field, Florida, where practice takeoffs were conducted from a carrier "flight deck" marked out on the airfield. Then the planes were equipped with special launching gear and flown to San Francisco to await the arrival of the carrier *Hornet*. So secret was the mission that not even Captain Marc A. Mitscher, her commanding officer, knew anything about the precious cargo until a few days before loading. On April 2 Mitscher joined up with Halsey in *Enterprise,* the flagship, and cruisers *Nashville* and *Vincennes,* four destroyers and a fleet oiler, and the task force got underway—*Enterprise* providing the combat air patrol.

"Cheers from every section of the ship greeted the announcement," stated Mitscher's Action Report, "and morale reached a new high, there to remain until after the attack was launched and the ship was well clear of the combat areas."

With the persistent memory of the sunken *Prince of Wales* disturbing his sea voyage, a wary Halsey led his Task Force 16 through rough seas to a launching point considerably farther out than he wished, because of the presence of Japanese patrol boats—six hundred and sixty-eight miles from the heart of Tokyo. On the morning of April 18, a gray and windy day, Halsey launched the planes. The psychological effects of the Doolittle Raid were minimized by the fact that Tokyo was conducting a mock air raid the same day, and when the planes arrived over the city at noon Japanese citizens assumed they were part of the show.

Thirteen bombers singled out the enemy capital and the other three continued on to blast targets in the Osaka-Nagoya area. An account of the extraordinary mission is now told by Lt. Col. Carroll V. Glines, USAF, an aviation writer of note and a highly-rated combat pilot. He presents the tense drama at sea before launching.

I.

LAUNCH PLANES!

Each passing hour was now more fraught with danger. The tenseness was evident everywhere. It could be felt in the wardroom, the crew's mess, on the bridge and in the engine room. How close to Japan could they go without being spotted? No one knew. To add to the uncertainty was an English-speaking radio-news program originating in Toyko: "Reuters, British news agency, has announced that three American bombers have dropped bombs on Tokyo. This is a most laughable story. They know it is absolutely impossible for enemy bombers to get within five hundred miles of Tokyo. Instead of worrying about such foolish things, the Japanese people are enjoying the fine spring sunshine and the fragrance of cherry blossoms."

The log of the *Enterprise* for April 16, shows the increasing tension as Task Force Sixteen plowed into enemy-dominated waters:

"0501—Launched first inner air patrol of 6 fighters, followed throughout the day by patrols of 5, 4 and 6 fighters each. No contacts. Launched first scouting flight of 13 scout bombers to search sector 204-324 to distance of 200 miles, followed in the afternoon by scouting flight of 8 torpedo planes to search sector 204-324 to distance of 150 miles. No contacts.

Activity increased the next day. At 5:37 A.M. the *Enterprise* launched 18 scout bombers for three-hour search missions. During the morning, the *Sabine* pumped aviation gasoline and fuel oil aboard the Big E and then, along with the *Cimarron,* topped off the cruisers and destroyers. At 2:45 P.M., the destroyer *Nonssen* and both tankers left the formation to await the return of the larger ships after the B 25's were launched. A short time later the other destroyers were detached. The two carriers and four cruisers left now increased their speeds to 20 knots. Hardly had the destroyers and tankers receded from view when the wind picked up and increased to gale force.

Meanwhile, the B-25's had been spotted on the deck for takeoff. The lead bomber, Doolittle's, had 467 feet of clear deck; the last one, Lieutenant Bill Farrow's, hung precariously out over the stern ramp of the carrier. Two white lines were painted on the deck—one for the left wheel and one for the nose wheel of the bombers. If the pilots kept their plane on these lines they could be assured of clearing the carrier's "island" with their right wings by about six feet.

The excitement aboard the *Hornet* increased when its refueling was completed and the Mitchells positioned. Up on the bridge of the *Hornet,* Mitscher and Doolittle huddled over a map table.

"Jimmy, we're in the enemy's back yard now," Mitscher said calmly. "Anything could happen from here on in. I think it's time for our little ceremony."

Doolittle agreed . . . When the *Enterprise* had merged with the *Hornet's* force, mail had been exchanged and Mitscher had received some official correspondence from the Secretary of the Navy, Frank Knox. Enclosed were some medals which had been presented to H. Vormstein, John B. Laurey, and Daniel J. Quigley, ex-Navy enlisted men, to commemorate the visit of the U.S. Battle Fleet to Japan in 1908. Vormstein and Laurey, both working in the Brooklyn Navy Yard at the time, had asked in the letter of January 26, that Secretary Knox "attach it to a bomb and return it to Japan in that manner." Quigley, formerly of the U.S.S. *Kearsarge,* wrote from his home in McKees Rocks, Pennsylvania, on March 2:

"Following the lead of my former fleet mates in forwarding thru you, Sir, their Jap commemoration medals via bomb to Tokyo, I herewith enclose the one issued to me and trust that it will eventually find its way back in company with a bomb that will rock the throne of the 'Son of Heaven' in the Kojimachi Ku district of Toyko."

Knox had forwarded the medals to Nimitz at Pearl Harbor, asking that the request be complied with at the appropriate time. "The appropriate time seems to have come sooner than they realized,"

Mitscher said, grinning. "Let's get your boys together and comply with these instructions from on high."

Over the loudspeaker came the announcement, "Army crews, report to the flight deck!" When everyone had gathered around a bomb that had been brought on deck, Mitscher made a short speech about the medals and handed them to Doolittle. Lieutenant Steve Jurika, having heard about the ceremony, added the medal he had received from the Japanese in 1940.

The group posed for pictures and kidded each other goodnaturedly. Several of them wrote slogans on the bomb like "I don't want to set the world on fire, just Tokyo" and "you'll get a BANG out of this!" They knew the time for departure was drawing nigh. Dog tags were checked and last innoculations made. Already their survival equipment had been handed out and the eighty men who were going on the raid had been loaded down like over-eager Boy Scouts. Each crew member had been issued a Navy gas mask, a .45 automatic, clips of ammunition, a hunting knife, flashlight, emergency rations, first aid kit, canteen, compass and life jacket. Besides their clothes, most had added an assortment of extras to their B-4 bags such as cigarettes, candy bars and extra razor blades. "Shorty" Manch, six-foot, six-inch co-pilot on Bob Gray's crew, planned to take along his phonograph and records. "Sally" Crouch, navigator on Dick Joyce's crew, ever mindful of the lectures about the lack of cleanliness in the Orient, jammed rolls of toilet paper into his bags. They were hoping for the best but being prepared for the worst, and their lightheartedness soon became forced as each man wondered about his personal chances for survival.

Mechanical difficulties had been croping up on every plane almost hourly. On the 16th, Lieutenant Don Smith's right engine cracked its blower while he was running it up. Navy carpenters hurriedly rigged up a platform so an engine change crew could remove it. It was taken below decks to the machine shop, quickly repaired and replaced.

Gun turrets did not function correctly, hydraulic lines still leaked, spark plugs fouled and gas tanks dripped. The anxiety of the crews mounted as Doolittle went from plane to plane, questioned the crews, and inspected their planes from the nose wheel tires to the false broomstick guns in the rear. On the afternoon of the 17th, he called the crews together.

"The time's getting short now," he told them. "By now every single one of you knows exactly what to do if the alarm is sounded. We were originally supposed to take off on the 19th but it looks like it'll be tomorrow instead. This will be your last briefing. Be ready to go at any time.

"We should have plenty of warning if we're intercepted. If all goes well, however, I'll take off so as to arrive over Tokyo at dusk. The rest of you will take off two or three hours later and can use my fires as a homing beacon."

Doolittle reiterated the plan in full and, for the last time, gave the men a chance to back out. Again, no one took him up on his offer. He then gave instructions about the 5-gallon gas cans which were to be stowed in the rear compartment. "Don't throw out the empty cans as you use them," he cautioned. "If you do, you'll leave a trail directly back toward the *Hornet*. When the cans are all empty, punch holes in them and throw them overboard all at the same time. Now, any questions?"

There was one question that had bothered many of the men but no one had yet brought it up. One of the pilots, however, decided that he wanted to know what the Boss's answer would be so he asked, "Colonel, what should we do if we lose an engine or something else goes wrong and we have to crash land in Japan?"

Doolittle's answer was quick. "Each pilot is in command of his own plane when we leave the carrier," he answered. "He alone is responsible for the decision he makes for his own plane and crew. Each man must eventually decide for himself what he will do when the chips are down. Personally, I know exactly what I'm going to do."

The wardroom fell silent. Doolittle didn't elaborate so one of the group asked, "Sir, what will you do?"

"I don't intend to be taken prisoner," the scrappy little man answered. "If my plane is crippled beyond any possibility of fighting or escape, I'm going to bail my crew out and then dive it, full throttle, into any target I can find where the crash will do the most damage. I'm 46 years old and have lived a full life. Most of you fellows are in your twenties and if I were you, I'm not sure I would make the same decision. In the final analysis, it's up to each pilot and, in turn, each man to decide what he will do."

He then cautioned them to get rid of any and all identification, letters, orders and diaries that would link them with the *Hornet,* their unit in the States of their training.

The B-25 crews labored all day on the 17th preparing their planes for battle. Ammunition and bombs were loaded aboard. Last minute engine run-ups were made and crew survival equipment placed in each plane. Doc White had thoughtfully climbed on board the *Hornet* in San Francisco with 80 quarts of bourbon—a quart for every man going on the raid. During the voyage, he exchanged it with the Navy medics for pints of medicinal rye. These would be easier to carry in the B-24 bags he reasoned and, if they had to bail out, could be stuffed into their flight jackets. He admonished the group again to take care of cuts they might get. There was now an air of extreme urgency that was felt by all on the *Hornet.*

Earlier that day, Commander Apollo Soucek, the *Hornet's* Air Officer had issued "Air Department Plan for Friday, 17 April 1942":

The Big Bombers on the flight deck will be loaded with bombs during the day. The sequence of events in connection with loading and respotting will be as follows:

(1) Complete fueling ships; tanker shoves off.
(2) Push #02268 and #02267 clear of number 3 elevator.
(3) Bring incendiary bombs to flight deck via number 3 elevator; commence loading on accessible airplanes.
(4) Start bringing heavy bombs to flight decks via regular bomb elevators; commence loading on accessible airplanes.
(5) When all incendiary bombs are on flight deck, secure number 3 elevator and pull #02267 and #02268 forward far enough for loading purposes.
(6) One half hour before sunset, respot the deck for take-off.
Note: All loading will be done under the direct supervision of Captain Greening, U.S.A.

By sunset, loading and positioning were complete. All planes had been fueled; only personal baggage had to be stored aboard. Twenty-four hours later, if all went well, the 16 bombers would be gone. As had been the practice during the voyage, poker games started below decks the instant work was done. The night of April 17 was no exception.

At midnight on the *Hornet,* Ensign Robert R. Boettcher had relieved Ensign J. A. Holmes on watch as officer of the Deck. He noted in the ship's log that the *Hornet,* in company with Task Groups 16.2 and 16.5, was steaming darkened on a course of 267° at 20 knots. The ship's bell chimed off the half hours as the midnight-to-four shift went about its routine chores. Boettcher's task was to stay alert for signs of any enemy sea or air activity and keep the *Hornet* knifing ahead on course.

When the six bells signalling 3 A.M. were chimed, Boettcher

stretched, yawned and asked for a cup of coffee. He had drained the last waning drops when a message was flashed from the *Enterprise* that knotted his stomach: "Two enemy surface craft reported." The Big E's radar had spotted two enemy ships off the port bow at a distance of twenty-one thousand yards. All watch hands stared into the inky blackness; two minutes later a light appeared on the horizon.

The *Enterprise's* short range, high frequency radio crackled out a curt order for all ships to come right to a course of 350° to avoid detection. As the ships obeyed, general quarters was sounded and every man on the six ships fought his way to his assigned battle station. A half hour later, the enemy ships faded from the radar screen and the westerly course was resumed at 4:11 A.M. For the Task Force, the day had begun even though the "all clear" had been sounded at 3:41. The B-25 crews went back to their cabins to resume their interrupted sleep.

At 5:08 the dawn search flight and fighter patrol consisting of eight F4F Grumman fighters and three SBD Douglas scout bombers took to the air from the *Enterprise* to search to a distance of two hundred miles. Three more scout bombers were launched for a combat air patrol above the Task Force.

The weather, which had been moderately rough during the night, was worsening. Low broken clouds hung over the area; frequent rain squalls swept over the ships and the sea began to bellow up in 30 foot crests. Gusty winds tore the tops off the waves and the spray blew across the decks of the ships, drenching the deck crews.

The three SBD pilots climbed to the bottom of the broken clouds in a "single plane relative search." At 5:58, Lieutenant O. B. Wiseman sighted a small patrol craft. He quickly reversed course for the *Enterprise*. Fixing his position as best he could on his small plotting board, he jotted down a message:

Enemy surface ship—latitude 36-04N, Long. 153-10E, bearing 276° true—42 miles. Believed seen by enemy.

Wiseman handed the message back to the gunner in the rear seat and made a throwing motion with his hand.

The gunner knew what to do. He reached in his pocket for a bean bag message container, stuffed the paper inside and peered over the side as Wiseman dived for the Big E's flight deck. Wiseman put flaps down to slow his plane and the gunner opened the canopy. When the SBD was directly overhead, the message plopped down on the deck and was scooped up on the run by a deckhand and delivered to Halsey on the bridge.

Halsey's reaction was immediate. He ordered all ships in the Task Force to swing left to a course of 220° to avoid detection. The question uppermost in everyone's mind was whether or not Wiseman had been seen. About an hour later, at 7:38, another enemy patrol vessel of about 150 tons was sighted from the *Hornet* only twenty thousand yards away. If the *Hornet* could see the small vessel, there was every reason to believe that the Task Force had been sighted and reported. It became a certainty when the *Hornet's* radio operator intercepted a Japanese message which had originated from somewhere close by. Still further confirmation came at 7:45 when Ensign J. Q. Roberts sighted the enemy vessel only twelve thousand yards away.

The moment of decision had come. Halsey ordered the *Nashville* to sink the patrol boat. In the log of the *Enterprise* was noted the following:

By previous agreement with Lt. Col. Doolittle, flight commander of the 16 B-25 planes on the *Hornet,* the plan was to launch one plane from a position approximately 400 miles east of Inuboe Saki at a time to permit arrival over Tokyo at sunset. The other planes were to be launched at local sunset to permit a night attack on Tokyo. However, in case the presence of the force was detected, it was understood the planes were to be launched immediately. If launched from 550 miles from Inuboe Saki, the arrival at arranged destination was remote possibility. If launched from a point in excess of 650 miles, it was calculated impossible to arrive at Hushan, the arranged destination. These factors were all considered and as our position was known to have been reported by the patrol vessel previously contacted, Adm. Halsey ordered the planes launched.

The message Halsey flashed to Mitscher on the *Hornet* was sent at 8:00 A.M.:

LAUNCH PLANES X TO COL. DOOLITTLE AND GALLANT COMMAND GOOD LUCK AND GOD BLESS YOU.

Doolittle, on the *Hornet's* bridge when the message came, hurriedly shook hands with Mitscher and leaped down the ladder to his cabin, shouting to everybody he saw, "O.K. fellas, this is it! Let's go!" At the same time, the blood-chilling klaxon sounded and the announcement came over the loudspeaker: "Army pilots, man your planes!" The B-25 crews had not been fully aware of the drama going on around them up to this point. Some had finished breakfast and were lounging in their cabins; others were shaving and preparing to eat; several were still asleep. A few had packed their B-4 bags but most were caught completely unawares when the call came.

Although their collective goal was the same, the 80 men all reacted differently. "Shorty" Manch had his own ideas about what to take. He grabbed his portable phonograph as well as two .45 caliber pistols and a carbine. He had his records in a cake tin but decided at the last minute to ask his buddy, Lieutenant Bob Clever, navigator on Ted Lawson's "Ruptured Duck," to put the precious platters under his seat. Clever reluctantly agreed.

Doc White hurriedly passed out the two pints of liquor to each man. Lieutenant Dick Knobloch ran from plane to plane handing up bags of sandwiches he had gotten from the galley.

Army and Navy men poured all over the *Hornet's* deck in seemingly wild confusion. Engine and turret covers were ripped off and stuffed up into the rear hatches. Ropes were unfastened and wheel chocks pulled away. A "donkey" pushed and pulled the 25's into position along the back end of the flight deck.

The *Hornet's* speed was increased and her bow plunged viciously into the towering waves. The deck seemed like a crazy seesaw that bit into the water each time the bow dipped.

Once each plane was in position, the job of loading could be completed. The gas tanks were all topped off. Navy crews rocked the bombers back and forth to break up any air bubbles in the tanks so they could pour in a few more quarts of precious gasoline. Sailors quickly filled the ten 5-gallon gas cans allotted each ship and passed them hand-to-hand up into the rear hatches.

The *Hornet's* control tower displayed a huge blackboard which noted the compass heading of the ship and the wind speed. As the crews jammed their personal belongings aboard, Hank Miller climbed up into the forward hatch of each plane, wished the crew good luck and said, sadly, "I sure wish I could go with you guys. I'll be holding up a blackboard to give you any last minute instructions. Give me a glance before you let your brakes off."

On signal, Doolittle in the lead plane started his engines and warmed them up. Near the bow on the left side, Lieutenant Edgar G. Osborne stood with a checkered flag in his hands. He began to swing the flag in a circle as a signal for Doolittle to ease the throttles forward. Osborne swung the flag in faster and faster circles and Doolittle pushed more and more power on. At the precise instant the deck was beginning its upward movement, chocks were pulled from under Doolittle's wheels and Osborne gave him the "go" signal. Doolittle released his brakes and the Mitchell inched forward.

Ted Lawson, waiting his turn in the "Ruptured Duck," described their leader's takeoff:

> With full flaps, motors at full throttle and his left wing far out over the port side of the *Hornet,* Doolittle's plane waddled and then lunged slowly into the teeth of the gale that swept down the deck. His left wheel stuck on the white line as if it were a track. His right wing, which had barely cleared the wall of the island as he taxied and was guided up to the starting line, extended nearly to the edge of the starboard side.
>
> We watched him like hawks, wondering what the wind would do to him, and whether we could get off in that little run toward the bow. If he couldn't, we couldn't.
>
> Doolittle picked up more speed and held to his line, and, just as the *Hornet* lifted up on top of a wave and cut through it at full speed, Doolittle's plane took off. He had yards to spare. He hung his ship almost straight up on its props, until we could see the whole top of his B-25. Then he leveled off and I watched him come around in a tight circle and shoot low over our heads— straight down the line painted on the deck.

The log of the *Hornet* for April 18 records that Colonel Doolittle was airborne at 8:20 A.M. ship time. Instead of following him three hours later, as originally planned, the second plane, piloted by Lieutenant Travis Hoover, had to take off just five minutes later.

"Hoover kept his nose in the up position too long," Lieutenant Hank Miller recalls, "and nearly stalled the plane. After the third plane took off, I put the words "STABILIZER IN NEUTRAL" on the blackboard. I'm pretty sure they saw and took my advice.

"Succeeding take-offs were all good except one—Ted Lawson's—

because he either forgot his flaps or inadvertently put them back into the 'up' position instead of 'neutral.' But he got away with it.

"The flaps on three other planes were up as they maneuvered into position, but the flight deck crew caught them before take-off. The only casualty to the planes themselves was a cracked nose glass on Lt. Don Smith's plane when it was rammed into the tail cone of the one ahead of it. There wasn't enough damage to worry about so he took off in order."

The last plane on the deck, piloted by Lieutenant Bill Farrow, seemed earmarked for disaster from the start. Since its tail was hanging out over the end of the deck, the loading of the plane's rear compartment could not be completed until the 15th plane, Smith's had moved forward. Six deck handlers held down on the nose wheel while Farrow taxied forward. Just as Smith revved up his engines, and the men moved away from Farrow's nose wheel, Seaman Robert W. Wall, one of the six, lost his footing. The sudden gust of air caused him to lose his balance and the combination of air blast and the slippery, pitching deck threw him into Farrow's idling left propeller. There was nothing Farrow could do. The prop chewed into Wall's left arm and threw him aside. His deck mates quickly rushed to him and carried him to sick bay where his arm was amputated a short time later.

Farrow's plane was off at 9:20, exactly one hour after Doolittle's. Doolittle had 620 nautical miles to go to reach Inuboe Saki, the nearest point of land; Farrow's distance was calculated at an even 600 miles with the *Hornet's* position officially fixed at 35°55′N, 153°19′E.

While the Doolittle crews had been getting ready on the *Hornet,* the cruiser *Nashville* began pumping shells at the patrol vessel Ensign Roberts had sighted. Roberts made a glide bombing attack and dropped a 500-pounder but it missed. He strafed with a lone .50 caliber machine gun but could see no damage being done. Other planes joined the attack. The War Diary of the *Nashville* describes the action this way:

0748—Enemy ship bore 201°T at a range of 9,000 yds.
0752—Received order from Adm. Halsey to attack vessel and sink same.
0753—Opened fire with main battery firing salvo fire at range of 9,000 yds.

0754—Shifted to rapid fire.

0755—Checked fire. Target could not be seen.

0756—Resumed firing. Bombing planes made attack on enemy vessel. They returned the fire of the planes with machine guns and a light cannon.

0757—Enemy headed toward the *Nashville.*

0801—Bombing planes made another attack on enemy ship. This fire returned by the enemy.

0804—Opened fire. This fire was returned but enemy shells fell short.

0809—Bombing planes made another attack. Changed course to the left in order to close the enemy.

0814—Increased speed to 25 knots.

0819—Commenced firing salvo fire.

0821—Steadied a course 095T. Enemy vessel on fire.

0823—Enemy vessel sunk.

0827—Commenced maneuvering to pick up survivors. Attempts to rescue one man sighted proved unsuccessful.

0846—Went to 25 knots to rejoin mission.

The skipper of the *Nashville,* Captain S. S. Craven, added an additional note in the log to explain why it had taken so long to sink the small, apparently fragile vessel. He noted that "938 rounds of 6″ ammunition were expended due to the difficulty of hitting the small target with the heavy swells that were running and the long range at which fire was opened. This range was used in order to silence the enemy's radio as soon as possible. The ship sunk was a Japanese patrol boat and was equipped with radio and anti-aircraft machine guns."

As soon as the 16th B-25 had left the deck, the entire task force reversed course to the east and proceeded at full speed in a maneuver the Navy calls simply "getting the hell out." The *Hornet,* now divested of its load of bombers, brought its own planes up on deck and assumed its aerial role of scouting in collaboration with the *Enterprise.* The fact that the enemy patrol vessel had gotten its message off before being sunk probably meant that every enemy plane and vessel within range of the American force would be searching for it. The assumption was well founded for aircraft were spotted on the radar screen of the retreating *Enterprise* but none came closer than 30 miles. The low clouds and poor visibility were proving to be allies.

At 11:30, Ensigns R. M. Elder, R. K. Campbell and J. C. Butler of Bomber Squadron Three were launched from the *Enterprise* on single-plane searches to the southwest. A few minutes later, Lieutenant R. W. Arndt led a three-plane flight off to attack enemy surface vessels reported 58 miles from the task force. Ensign Campbell was the first to make a contact. At 11:50 he sighted a 150-foot patrol boat painted dark gray with a tall radio antenna towering above its deck. Two dive bombing attacks were made but no hits were scored. Campbell pressed the attack firing both the .50 caliber and .30 caliber guns but only minor damage could be seen.

A few minutes after Campbell's attack, Lieutenant Arndt and his two wingmen attacked another vessel. Three 500-pound and five 100-pound bombs were dropped, again without success. As the War Diary of the squadron wryly noted, "there was no apparent damage from bombs except for one 100-lb. bomb near miss which evidently stopped the fire on one small caliber AA gun located aft. The enemy used radical maneuver and returned AA fire with what appeared to be a 1″ gun."

Ensign Butler, searching another sector, sighted still a third patrol boat. It was about 125 feet long and was towing a smaller boat behind. He made three separate bomb runs, dropping one bomb each time. The two 100-pound bombs were duds but the 500-pound bomb landed close aboard on the port side causing fragmentary damage. After the bombing, Butler strafed both boats until his ammunition was gone. He thought he had sunk the smaller boat and damaged the larger one. After landing he reported that "own plane received three hits from enemy fire—not serious."

What Arndt and his squadron mates could not do, the *Nashville* did. As soon as the scout bombers retired, she opened fire on the bobbing patrol boat at forty-five hundred yards. Firing off and on for the next twenty minutes with her 5-inch and 6-inch guns as she closed the distance, she finally obtained results. Overwhelmed by the quantity of lead that filled the air, the Japanese ran up a white flag and the *Nashville* ceased firing. While the *Nashville* circled, the enemy boat slowly sank. Five survivors were spotted and quickly hauled aboard suffering from shock, immersion and fright. Only one, Seaman Second Class Nakamura Suekichi, was injured slightly with a bullet wound in his cheek.

There had been 11 men aboard the patrol boat, the *Nagato Maru,* according to Suekichi. He reported in a letter to the author that ". . .

the waves were high that day and I could not help worrying that our 70-ton *Nagato Maru* would capsize at any moment." He told Navy interrogators that he had spotted some planes while on watch and went below to rouse his skipper, Chief Petty Officer Gisaku Maeda. The skipper assumed they were the usual morning patrol planes from Japan and stayed in his cabin. A short time later Suekichi tried again and said, "Sir, there are two of our beautiful carriers now dead ahead."

This time Maeda was wide awake. No Japanese carriers were supposed to be in his patrol area. He rushed on deck, studied them intently through his binoculars, and said sadly, "Indeed they are beautiful but they are not ours." He went below to his cabin, took a pistol from his sea bag, put it to his temple and pulled the trigger.

"At that time," Suekichi said, "we radioed the *Kiso,* the flagship of the Fifth Fleet, that the enemy had been sighted. When the American cruiser fired on us, I could actually see the approaching shells. The airborne attack by the enemy became more severe, but we really doubted whether they could hit us, so we pointed our small gun at the enemy. Looking back on our actions now, we acted foolishly. But, after all, we thought we were fighting for the great spirit of Nippon. Since we had communicated the discovery of enemy ships and planes, we were positive that no damage would occur in Japan."

While the *Nashville* was completing the action, the planes returned to the *Enterprise* to re-arm. One of them, piloted by Lieutenant L. A. Smith, however, could not make it. Without warning, the SBD's engine began to lose oil pressure and he had to ditch. His plane had been hit by the small caliber fire from the picket ship. He and his gunner, AMM2C H. H. Caruthers, were rescued shortly thereafter by the *Nashville.*

The excitement of the day was not yet over. A small enemy submarine was sighted and attacked before it hurriedly submerged undamaged. Other Japanese patrol vessels and freighters were sighted but not attacked. When the day's activities were studied by Halsey's staff, the number of enemy vessels found was surprising. Halsey reported that "in addition to the radar contact with two craft made at 0310, actual contact showed one submarine, 14 PY's (patrol vessels) and 3 AK's (probably "mother ships" for the patrols) concentrated in an area about 130 miles by 180 miles. A similar concentration was reported by a submarine just returned from patrol in the East China Sea which stated that 65 sampans had been sighted in an area just about the same size as that mentioned above. These are indications of the degree to which the Japanese are using these small craft for patrols and screens around their vital areas." Halsey made no mention of enemy land-based patrol planes which had also been seen. If these planes had found the task force, there is no doubt they would have attacked the carriers offensively, which the patrol vessels could not.

The escaping task force steamed at full speed during the night and at dawn the next day began its patrols again. No more enemy ships were sighted but one scout bomber from the *Hornet,* overdue from the morning patrol, ditched in the water out of gas only seven miles from the *Enterprise.* The plane, piloted by Lieutenant G. D. Randall with radioman T. A. Gallagher aboard, sank in 30 seconds. Neither the plane nor the men were recovered.

It took Task Force Sixteen exactly one week to the hour after launching the B-25's to reach Pearl Harbor. Before docking, Halsey sent a "Well Done" to his skippers and termed the mission a success. "The Japs chased us all the way home, of course," Halsey wrote later. "Whenever we tracked their search planes with our radar, I was tempted to unleash our fighters, but I knew it was more important not to reveal our position than to shoot down a couple of scouts. They sent a task force after us; their submarines tried to intercept us; and . . . even some of their carriers joined the hunt; but with the help of foul weather and a devious course, we eluded them . . ."

(Not one B-25 was lost over Japan; some splashed off the coast and others landed in China; only two pilots were captured by the enemy and subsequently executed.)

INSPIRATIONAL ARTICLES, LIKE SEA VICTORIES, WERE precious few that dismal spring. The best of them appeared in the Naval Institute *Proceedings* and was written by an idealistic young lieutenant commander, Ernest M. Eller, who went on to a distinguished war career after service on Admiral Nimitz' staff in early 1942. A gunnery expert, Eller's primary area of responsibility with Cincpac was the preparation of fleet war reports and training. Later, Eller commanded an attack transport and participated in the landings on Makin and Okinawa, for which he received the Legion of Merit with Combat "V," He is presently the Director of Naval History.

2.

"HOW SHALL WE WIN?"

We shall win the war of idealogies that has brought nations suffering and despair unequalled since the vast upheaval ending the empire of Rome. We shall win and go on to the grand destiny of world leadership that is the opportunity and the duty of the United States. We must win or decline to futility, to the dishonor and death of a nation that is given great strength, great vision, great opportunity to direct earth's fate, but fails to stand up to its part. We shall win but it will not be by material. It will not be by warships and planes, tanks and guns, or soldiers and sailors alone. It will not be by training and morale. All these things we shall have and all are necessary; but all are useless and all will fail without leadership.

It was not from lack of material, however much this was at fault, that France was crushed in the disastrous days of 1940. She was badly led and badly inspired, in war and preparation for war, just as the English had been up to that time, though they have learned much since. The material deficiencies that entered into France's defeat have, however, been played up to such a point that they whitewash and hide a far more serious deficiency. There is danger in both England and this country of placing such reliance on material that we shall forget the soul of war, forget that material is only for men to use, is given life only by men, and even then has little value without wise and courageous direction of men in command.

It is such truths we must hold in our hearts constantly as we go into the unknown future. We must not, in recognizing one cause for defeat, make material our god—the body rather than the life. We must remember constantly that although material, preparation, and all similar things will aid in winning the war, one thing alone can lose it—weak leadership. We can still have all other elements of strength to the highest degree and fail for lack of leaders. The most stupendous factory output may not be utilized, the strongest military might may be allowed to rot away and our proposed colossal material strength be wasted for lack of moral courage in a few men, perhaps in one man, when the day of crisis comes. War is a contest not of machines but of men.

That God is on the side of the strongest battalions, as Napoleon once cynically remarked, may or may not be true; but strength is not merely in numbers, as was his fate to prove in his declining years of leadership when, inspiration and wisdom having failed, he came to rely on mass of numbers. That strength is not merely in material was also Napoleon's destiny to reveal, glowingly, by his early amazing campaigns in Italy and Austria with ragged, ill-fed, and ill-equipped armies that were irrestible when led by him.

Military strength is not a tangible quality that we can weigh and measure as so many tanks, guns, planes, or even men. This is a difficulty of war games and the error of many people in thinking about our nation's future role in the present world upheaval. In every fateful period of history the ultimate balance of strength (and usually the largest component in it) has come from the integrity of purpose, resolution, and energy of men in posts of high responsibility.

Leadership is the soul of all human endeavor. It is the flame that enabled the French under Clemenceau, Joffre, and Foch to stop an unstoppable German Army in 1914, because these men willed to stop it. It is the magic of German success so far in this war, and of the unexpected Russian resistance. It is for lack of this flame, which had burned low and sooty, that France fell in 1940.

It is upon it that we should place our first trust, upon man's moral courage, upon his irresistible determination to win, to drive his purposes to a conclusion, to strike on past all hazard with ceaseless concentration of intent that knows no barrier. It will be the power of leadership that must and will direct us into the great future; and it alone will be the decisive and concluding force in this titanic struggle between the faiths of hope and darkness.

France suffered the crushing defeat of 1940 because she was led by men who believed in the power of the defensive. She placed her faith in walls, in blockade and the Maginot Line, which were supposed to sap German strength until economic and spiritual collapse would strike the killing blow. She was fattening herself on an easy war, remaining strong by sitting. She was as fatefully wrong as were Napoleon's admirals a century and a half earlier in their struggle against English sea power. Mooring their fleets in port, they thought the English Navy would wear out in use while their own gained strength by idling. How false! How patently untrue to any but a timorous mind. The great heart of man grows on privation and danger. Flabbiness comes to muscles not from use but disuse. Weathering the hardships of continuous sea keeping, the British Fleet grew strong and sinewy and proud of its strength to endure. It was the French fleet that declined, deteriorated in material, in discipline, above all in morale and confidence. Under similar conditions the French armies of today weakened sleeping behind the Maginot Line, while the German Army, ceaselessly on the move in drill and attack, gained strength in the school of action. . . .

Man brings his ruin upon himself. Defeat or victory comes out of his own mind. Ruin is always deserved. How fatally a people may in three short generations learn their error, achieve great deeds, and then sink into inaction again! How much the destiny of a whole people, their fortunes, their lives, all their futures hang upon the resolute or indolent souls of a few men . . . !

IN APRIL, WHILE THE UNITED STATES MAINTAINED A defensive posture in the Pacific, Japan, according to a three-fold war plan, prepared to move toward new conquests: to Tulagi in the lower Solomons, and Port Moresby, southernmost Allied outpost in New Guinea, for the purpose of achieving air supremacy in the Coral Sea; to Midway and the Western Aleutians for the purpose of strengthening her defense perimeter and forcing a decisive fleet engagement with the United States Navy; and to the New Caledonia-Samoa chain for the purpose of severing the line of communications between the United States and the Anzac nations. The enemy was soon challenged in the first two areas, and as a result the third operation never came about.

The Imperial Japanese Navy began Operation "Mo," the first offensive, with carriers *Shokaku* and *Zuikaku,* borrowed from Nagumo's Carrier Striking Force based in Ceylon and from Vice Admiral Inouye's Fourth Fleet based at Truk and Rabaul. The rest of the "Mo" force consisted of a Tulagi Invasion Group, a Support Group bound for the Louisades, and a joint Covering Group. Overall command was exercised by Inouye in Rabaul, near the northern extremity of the Solomons.

Fortunately United States Army cryptographers, working closely with Naval Intelligence, had broken Japan's secret code and as a result Nimitz by April 17 knew the enemy's precise intentions. After hastily conferring with MacArthur, who was able to supply about three hundred Allied land-based aircraft, it was decided that this was indeed a major enemy thrust and it was to be met with all available military power.

The Battle of the Coral Sea which followed, the first exclusively carrier-air conflict of the war, is told in four parts: the preliminaries by Nimitz and naval historian E. B. Potter, Chairman of the Naval History Department at the U. S. Naval Academy, and the other parts by men who participated in the battle.

FLEET ADMIRAL CHESTER W. NIMITZ
AND E. B. POTTER

3.

CORAL SEA PRELIMINARIES

The Japanese wanted Port Moresby in order to safeguard Rabaul and their positions in New Guinea, to provide a base for neutralizing airfields in northern Australia, and in order to secure the flank of their projected advance toward New Caledonia, Fiji, and Samoa. They wanted Tulagi, across the sound from Guadalcanal in the lower Solomons, to use as a seaplane base both to cover the flank of the Port Moresby operation and to support the subsequent advance to the southeast. To the Allies the retention of Port Moresby was essential not only for the security of Australia but also as a springboard for future offensives.

In the Japanese plan a Covering Force built around the 12,000-ton carrier *Shoho* was first to cover the landing on Tulagi, then turn back west in time to protect the Port Moresby Invasion Force, which was to come down from Rabaul and around the tail of New Guinea through Jomard Passage. There were close support forces for both landings, and in addition a Striking Force centered on the *Shokaku* and *Zuikaku* was to come down from Truk to deal with any United States forces that might attempt to interfere with the operation. Land-based aircraft were counted on for scouting and support. Altogether there were six separate naval forces engaged in this dual operation. Such complex division of forces was typical of Japanese strategy throughout most of the war. So far, against a weak and disorganized

231

enemy, it had worked well, and it was not inconsistent with concentration so long as the forces were properly coordinated and sufficiently close together to render mutual support. But when the Japanese disregarded these two important conditions they met with disaster.

In the Coral Sea, Japanese coordination was to be provided by a unified command. Vice Admiral Shigeyoshi Inouye, Commander Fourth Fleet, was to direct all forces, including land-based air, from Rabaul. The Allied command was not so well integrated. The battle was to be fought in General MacArthur's Southwest Pacific Theater, but it was understood that any fleet action would remain under Admiral Nimitz' strategic control. The result was that Allied land-based air and naval forces were under separate commands without effective coordination.

Since the Pearl Harbor attack, the United States had broken the Japanese naval code and thus possessed the enormous advantage of accurate and rather detailed intelligence concerning the enemy's plans. Even so, it was no easy matter to gather sufficient forces to meet the threat to Port Moresby. The *Saratoga* was still in Puget Sound undergoing repairs for the torpedo damage sustained in January. The *Enterprise* and *Hornet* did not return to Pearl Harbor from the Tokyo raid till April 25. Although they were hurried on their way as soon as possible, there was little likelihood that they could reach the Coral Sea in time to play a part. The only carriers immediately available were Admiral Fletcher's *Yorktown* force, which had been in the South Pacific for some time, and Rear Admiral Aubrey W. Fitch's *Lexington* group, fresh from Pearl Harbor. From Noumea, New Caledonia came the *Chicago*, while Rear Admiral J. C. Crace RN brought H.M.A. cruisers *Australia* and *Hobart* from Australia. The Japanese, overconfident from their long series of easy successes, assumed that a single carrier division was sufficient to support their new advance.

The two American carrier groups, which had been ordered to join under Fletcher's command, made contact in the southeast Coral Sea on May 1. Two days later Fletcher recieved a report of the Japanese landing on Tulagi. Leaving the *Lexington* group to complete fueling, he headed north with the *Yorktown* group, and during the 4th made a series of air attacks on the Tulagi area that sank a few minor Japanese naval craft. He then turned back south and formally merged his two groups on May 6. The two carriers were to operate within a

Maj. Gen. (then Lt. Col.) James H. (Jimmy) Doolittle wires a Japanese medal to the fin of a 500-lb. bomb. The ceremony took place on the deck of the USS *Hornet* (CV-8), from which the Army bombers took off for the raid on Japan, 18 April, 1942. *Navy Department.*

An Army B-25 takes off from the deck of the USS *Hornet* on its way to take part in the first U.S. air raid on Japan. *Navy Department.*

The Yokosuka, Japan, Naval Base, taken from a B-25 during Doolittle's raid on Tokyo, 18 April, 1942. *Navy Department.*

The Japanese aircraft carrier *Shoho,* after being torpedoed in the Battle of the Coral Sea, 7 May, 1942. *Navy Department.*

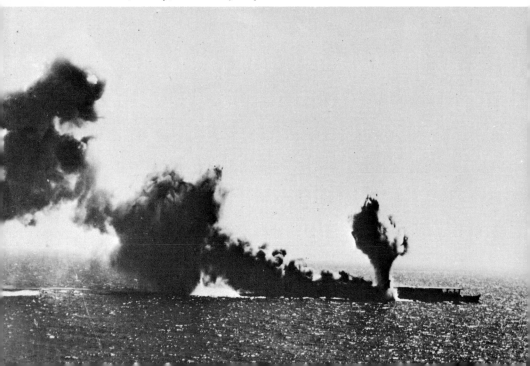

The final stages of the sinking of the *Shoho,* taken by a plane of the USS *Yorktown* (CV-5). *Navy Department.*

The aircraft carrier USS *Lexington* (CV-2) burning following the Battle of the Coral Sea, 8 May, 1942. *Navy Department.*

The USS *Lexington* abandoning ship. *Navy Department.*

The burning *Lexington* after all hands have abandoned ship. *Navy Department.*

Damage on Midway Island before the Japanese raiders were repelled, June 4, 5, 6, 1942. The burning oil tanks were hit by Japanese bombs. Gooney birds in the foreground. *Navy Department.*

During the Battle of Midway, Japanese planes try to escape an A.A. barrage. The carrier at the right is the USS *Yorktown* (CV-5). *Navy Department.*

The *Yorktown* under attack. The first photo shows *Yorktown* just as she sustained a hit in the uptakes during the first attack. Heel is due to turning. *Navy Department.* The second photo was taken just as a second torpedo struck the *Yorktown* during the second attack. Note the Japanese plane which has just crashed into the water. *Navy Department.*

Some of the damage on the USS *Yorktown* during the battle of Midway.
Navy Department.

The sinking of the USS *Yorktown* (CV-5). Navy Department.

An aerial oblique taken during the Battle of Midway showing battle damage sustained by the Japanese heavy cruiser *Mogami* after being attacked by U.S. carrier aircraft. *Navy Department.*

Rear Adm. R. K. Turner, left, and Maj. Gen. A. A. Vandergrift, USMC, commander of landing forces on Guadalcanal, plan the attack on Jap bases in the South Pacific. *Navy Department.*

Guadalcanal, 1942, showing the outlet of the Segilan River. *Navy Department.*

The HMAS *Canberra,* Australian cruiser, afire near Tulagi Island in the Solomons. An unidentified destroyer pulls alongside to remove the crew. Taken from the USS *Chicago* (CA-29). *Navy Department.*

Four Japanese transports beached and burning on the coast of Guadalcanal during the Battle of the Solomon Islands, 1942. *Navy Department.*

Amphibian tractors (amphtracs) come ashore at Guadalcanal Island. *Navy Department.*

Running a gauntlet of anti-aircraft fire, four Japanese bombers come in low at Guadalcanal Island to attack U.S. transports. Black bursts show the intensity of the U.S. A.A. fire. *Navy Department.*

Smoke rises from two enemy planes set on fire by the USS *President Adams* (AP-38) off Guadalcanal, 12 November, 1942. To the right is the USS *Betelgeuse* (AK-28). *Navy Department.*

The sinking of the USS *Wasp* (CV-7) off Guadalcanal. *Navy Department.*

A Japanese bomb splashes astern of a U.S. carrier as the enemy plane pulls out of its dive above the carrier. The Battle of Santa Cruz, 26 October, 1942. *Navy Department.*

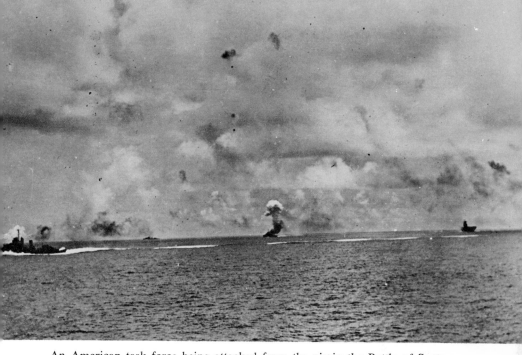

An American task force being attacked from the air in the Battle of Santa Cruz. A carrier on the right is turning sharply. The U.S. destroyer *Smith* (DD-378) has just been struck by a burning, falling Japanese plane. On the left two screening vessels are seen. *Navy Department.*

The USS *Smith* after being struck by a falling Japanese plane. After the plane struck the ship, a torpedo attached to the plane exploded, causing casualties and damage. *Navy Department.*

The USS *Hornet* (CV-8) under attack in the Battle of Santa Cruz. Taken by the USS *Pensacola*. *Navy Department.*

Japanese torpedo bombers attacking the USS *Hornet*. She was sunk in this engagement at Santa Cruz. *Navy Department.*

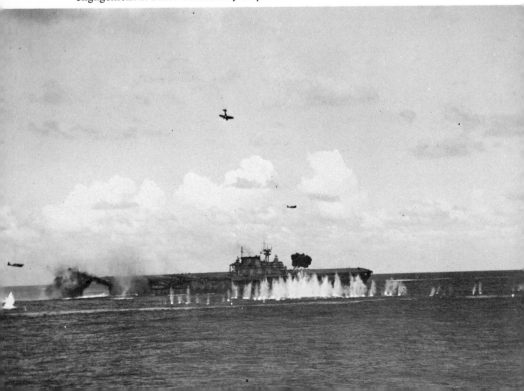

Lt. John F. Kennedy, USNR. *Navy Department.*

Task Force 17 maneuvering to evade attack by Jap planes in the Second Battle of Santa Cruz. Taken by a plane from the USS *Hornet* (CV-8).

A. A. Burke on the bridge of the USS *Charles Ausburne* (DD-570), one of the ships of DESRON 23. Note the Little Beaver Squadron insignia on the side of the bridge. *Official U.S. Navy Photo.*

single circular screen of cruisers and destroyers. Admiral Fitch, because of his long experience with carriers, was to exercise tactical command during air operations.

Fletcher's uniting of his forces was luckily timed, for the *Shokaku* and *Zuikaku* with their escorts, having swung around the southeastern end of the Solomons, had just entered the Coral Sea. The Japanese Striking Force was commanded by Vice Admiral Takeo Takagi, with Rear Admiral Tadaichi Hara commanding the carriers. Takagi, in coming around the Solomons, hoped to catch the American carriers in a sort of pincer movement. He almost succeeded, for on the evening of the 6th he was rapidly overhauling the American force, then refueling, and was actually within 70 miles of the Americans when he turned north.

At dawn on May 7, the American task force was cruising on a northwesterly course south of the Lousiades, which form an extension of the New Guinea tail. A little before 0700, Fletcher detached three cruisers and three destroyers under Admiral Crace and ordered them to push on to the northwest while the carriers turned north. The detached vessels were to prevent the Port Moresby Invasion Force from coming through Jomard Passage, regardless of the fate of the American carriers, which Fletcher expected would come under attack during the day. In sending Crace forward however, Fletcher was depriving a part of his force of carrier air cover and at the same time further weakening his already weak carrier anti-aircraft screen.

Thus far neither Takagi nor Fletcher was sure that the other was in the area, though Fletcher had information that three Japanese carriers were involved in the operation. Takagi was depending on land-based searches which actually sighted the American carrier force but failed to get word through. Fletcher's air searches were defeated by bad weather to the northeast, where the two Japanese heavy carriers were operating.

To the northwest however the weather was clear, and early on the 7th reports began to come in from American scout planes searching in this direction. At 0815 a pilot reported "two carriers and four heavy cruisers" not far north of Misima Island, whereupon Fletcher ordered attack groups launched from both his carriers. The 93 planes were well on their way before the scout returned and it was discovered that the report was an error due to improper coding—that the scout had meant to report two cruisers and two destroyers.

Fletcher made the courageous decision to let the attack proceed, probably thinking that with the Japanese Invasion Force nearby there must be some profitable targets. His boldness was rewarded at 1022 by a report which placed an enemy carrier with several other vessels only 35 miles southeast of the point toward which the strike had been sent. The attack group had to alter course only slightly for the new target.

The Americans came upon the *Shoho* about 1100 and, in the first attack ever made by American pilots on an enemy carrier, smothered her with 13 bomb and seven torpedo hits, which sent her down within a few minutes. Upon their return, Fletcher decided to withhold a second strike until the other two enemy carriers were located. Moreover, he suspected that the enemy knew his position, and it seemed likely that he would soon come under attack.

The Japanese failed to attack Fletcher on the 7th only because of a series of errors which by evening reached the fantastic. Before 0900 on the 7th, Inouye, directing the Japanese operation from Rabaul, had reports of two American carrier forces. One was Fletcher's; the other, some 45 miles to the west, was in fact Crace's cruiser-destroyer force. Then came a report from Takagi of a third American carrier in the eastern Coral Sea. This last was actually the oiler *Neosho,* which had been detached from Fletcher's force the evening before and was proceeding with the destroyer *Sims* toward a rendezvous.

At 0950 Japanese navy planes took off from Rabaul to attack the westernmost of the United States forces. The Japanese pilots returned with reports that they had sunk a battleship and a cruiser. Actually Crace's force survived without damage both this attack and another by B-26's from Australia, which mistook his vessels for Japanese.

The identification of the *Neosho* as a carrier had a serious effect on Japanese operations, for Hara at once launched a full attack upon the hapless oiler and her escort. The *Sims* with three hits went down with most of her crew. The *Neosho* took seven but remained afloat until her crew was taken off four days later.

This erroneous attack left Tagaki and Hara facing a critical situation. As night approached, the weather closed in, but Hara was determined to destroy the American carriers before they could further damage the Invasion Force. Selecting 27 pilots best qualified in night operations, he sent them out at 1615 in the direction in which he estimated the American carriers lay.

It was not a bad gamble, for in the foul weather and poor visibility the Japanese actually passed near Fletcher's force. The American combat air patrol, vectored out by radar, intercepted the Japanese planes and shot down nine. An hour later several of the returning Japanese, mistaking the American carriers for their own, actually attempted to join the *Yorktown's* landing circle until American gunners shot down one and drove off the others. The *Lexington's* radar showed planes circling as if for a landing about 30 miles to the east, which seemed to indicate that the Japanese carriers were very close indeed. Of the Japanese striking group, ten had been shot down, and eleven others went into the water in attempting nightlandings on their carriers. Hara recovered only six of his 27.

The pilots of these planes reported the American carriers only 50 to 60 miles away. Thus each of the opposing commanders was aware of the proximity of the other. Both seriously considered a night surface attack, and both abandoned the idea because they hesitated to weaken their screens with an enemy near. Thus the main action of the Battle of the Coral Sea was postponed another day.

Actually the distance between the two forces was greater than either commander imagined, for postwar plots show that they were nearly a hundred miles apart.

Thus far the antagonists had been together in the Coral Sea for two days, and had twice come within a hundred miles of each other without exchanging blows. On the evening of May 7 each of the opposing commanders felt that the enemy was uncomfortably close. There was every likelihood that a decision would be reached the next day. During the night Fletcher withdrew to the south and west, while Takagi moved north. For both commanders everything depended on locating the enemy as promptly as possible on the morning of the 8th. Both launched searches a little before dawn, and the scouts of each reported the other almost simultaneously a little after 0800.

The contest of May 8 started on curiously even terms. Each force contained two carriers. Fitch had available 121 planes, Hara 122. The Americans were stronger in bombers, while the Japanese enjoyed a preponderance in fighter and torpedo planes. The Japanese pilots had more combat experience, and their torpedoes were better. In another respect the Japanese enjoyed a significant advantage. By moving south through the night Fletcher had run out of the bad weather area in which he had been operating, and on the 8th his force lay exposed under clear skies, while the Japanese remained within the frontal area, under the protection of clouds and rain squalls.

Essentially the battle consisted of a simultaneous exchange of strikes by the two carrier forces. Between 0900 and 0925 both American carriers launched their attack groups. That of the *Yorktown*, consisting of 24 bombers with two fighters, and nine torpedo planes with four fighters, departed first. About 1030 the dive bombers found the Japanese carriers with their escorts in loose formation. While the pilots took cloud cover to await the arrival of the torpedo planes, the *Zuikaku* disappeared into a rain squall. Hence the attack fell only on the *Shokaku*.

When the torpedo planes approached, the SBD's began their dives. Although the attack was well coordinated, it was only moderately successful. The slow American torpedoes were easily avoided, but the dive bombers succeeded in planting two bombs on the *Shokaku*. Of the *Lexington* group, which departed about ten minutes later than the *Yorktown's,* the 22 dive bombers failed to find the target. Only the eleven torpedo planes and the four scout bombers found the enemy. Again American torpedoes were ineffective, but the bombers succeeded in adding another hit to the two already sustained by the *Shokaku*. These three hits put the *Shokaku* out of action for the time being; because the damage to her flight deck prevented her recovering planes, Takagi detached her, ordering her to proceed to Truk.

The Japanese had sent off their group of 70 attack planes and 20 fighters at about the same time as the American launching. Although the American radar picked them up at 70 miles away, only three fighters succeeded in intercepting them before the attack. At a distance of 20 miles, still having met no interference by American fighters, the Japanese planes divided into three groups, two of torpedo planes and one of bombers.

The two American carriers were together in the center of their circle of screening vessels, but evasive maneuvers gradually drew them apart. The screen divided fairly evenly, but this breaking of the circle undoubtedly contributed to the Japanese success . . .

~~~~~~

NOW THE JAPANESE DEVELOPED THEIR ATTACK ON *Yorktown* and *Lexington,* the former combing the wakes of a torpedo spread and instead taking a bomb hit, which did not seriously impair her fighting effectiveness. But the slower "Lady Lex" was in for it. This phase of the battle is vividly recounted by the carrier's skipper, Captain Frederick C. Sherman, one of the most decorated officers in the Navy, who rose to full Admiral and upon retirement wrote feature articles on naval subjects for the *Chicago Tribune*.

True to naval tradition, Sherman was the last man to leave the doomed vessel.

4.

ABANDON SHIP!

At 10:14 a *Yorktown* fighter on combat patrols spotted a Kawanishi four-engine flying boat and promptly shot it down. At 10:55 the radar showed a large group of enemy planes approaching from the northeast.

At 11:13 the *Lexington's* lookout sighted the first of the attackers. The battle was on.

The weather was bright and sunny, with hardly a cloud in the sky. The Japanese had no difficulty in finding us. On the sparkling, tropical sea, we were visible from miles away. Our move to the south the night before had given the enemy this advantage, but it also meant that they had no cloud cover to mask their approach. The clear visibility gave our anti-aircraft guns full play.

Fighter direction was still in its early stage of development. Control was on board the *Lexington* for all the fighters in the air. There were 17 in all, eight from the Yorktown plus the *Lexington's* nine, with Lieutenant "Red" Gill as fighter-direction officer. The single, early model radar we had on board picked up the enemy aircraft at a distance of 68 miles, but gave no indication of their altitude. On those old radars it was also difficult to distinguish friendly from enemy planes. We felt that if our fighters were sent far out on interception, they might miss the contact, owing to differences in altitude and thus be wasted. We were also influenced by the belief that the torpedo planes represented the greater hazard and that they would come in low. Accordingly, we kept our fighters close in overhead, at 10,000 feet, ready to attack when the enemy groups arrived at their "push-over" point. The Dauntless dive bombers on anti-torpedo-plane patrol were stationed at 2,000 feet, 6,000 yards out. We learned in this battle that to break up an air attack it was necessary to intercept it at a much greater distance from the carriers. It must be remembered that this was the first carrier duel in history, and we were learning our tactics by experience. Nevertheless, our defending planes did a magnificent job.

Five *Lexington* fighters were vectored out at 11:02 to intercept the oncoming craft. They made contact 20 miles away and reported one group of 50 to 60 planes stacked in layers from 10,000 to 13,000 feet, with torpedo planes in the lowest level, then fighters, then dive bombers, then more fighters. There were approximately 18 torpedo planes, 18 dive bombers, and 24 fighters in this group.

Two of our five fighters had been sent low to look for torpedo planes. The other three fighters in the intercepting unit climbed madly for altitude and dashed in to attack. Engaged by the Zeros, they shot down several but were unable to stop the bombers before they started their dives. The two low fighters attacked the torpedo planes as they dropped down for their part in the battle, but were unsuccessful in stopping them.

The air fighting now became a melee. Our own planes were mixed in with the enemy and the sky was black with flak bursts. The Japanese spent no time in maneuvering, but dived straight in for the kill. The huge *Lexington* dwarfed the other ships in the formation and bore the brunt of the attack.

It was beautifully coordinated. From my bridge I saw bombers roaring down in steep dives from many points in the sky, and torpedo planes coming in on both bows almost simultaneously. There was nothing I could do about the bombers, but I could do something to avoid the torpedoes.

As I saw a bomb leave one of the planes, it seemed to be coming straight for where I stood on the bridge. Had I better duck behind the thin armored shield? If it had my name on it, I thought, there was no use dodging, and if not, there was no need to worry. At any rate, I had work to do to try to evade the torpedoes.

The ideal way to drop torpedoes was for groups of planes to let go simultaneously on both bows. In this method, if the target ship turned toward one group to parallel its torpedoes, it presented its broadside to the other. The timing was vital. The enormous *Lexington* was very slow in returning. It took 30 to 40 seconds just to put the rudder hard over. When she did start to turn, she moved majestically and ponderously in a large circle. Maneuverability was greatly improved in later carriers.

As I saw the enemy torpedo planes coming in on both bows, it seemed to me that those to port were closer than those to starboard. They were approaching in steep glides, faster than we considered practicable for torpedo dropping. The air was full of anti-aircraft bursts and the din was terrific. When the planes to port were about 1,000 yards away, I motioned to the helmsman, Chief Quartermaster McKenzie, for hard left rudder. It seemed an eternity before the bow started to turn, just as the enemy planes started disgorging their fish.

The water in all directions seemed full of torpedo wakes. Bombs were also dropping all around us. Great geysers of water from near misses were going up higher than our masts, and occasionally the ship shuddered from the explosions of the ones that hit.

In less than a minute, the first torpedoes had passed astern. We quickly shifted rudder to head for the second group of planes. These split up to fire on both bows, the hardest maneuver for us to counter. Then it became a matter of wriggling and twisting as best we could to avoid the deadly weapons heading our way. I remember seeing two wakes coming straight for our port beam, and there was nothing I could do about them. The wakes approached the ship's side, and I braced myself for the explosion. Nothing happened. I rushed to the starboard bridge, and there were the wakes emerging from that side. The torpedoes were running too deep and had passed completely under the ship.

My air officer on the bridge was Commander H. S. Duckworth, "Don't change course, Captain!" he exclaimed. "There's a torpedo on each side of us running parallel!" We held our course with a torpedo 50 yards on either beam and both finally disappeared without hitting.

Enemy planes were being shot down right and left, and the water around us was dotted with the towering flames of their burning carcasses. One plane turned upside down as it hit the water, its torpedo still slung on its belly. Before it sank, we noticed a peculiar wooden framework around the missile's nose and propeller mechanism. This explained why the Japanese were able to drop their torpedoes at such high speeds and altitudes. The cushioning devices permitted them to enter the water without excessive shock to the delicate machinery. It was a scheme still undeveloped by our ordnance experts, and gave the Japanese at least a temporary superiority in torpedo warfare.

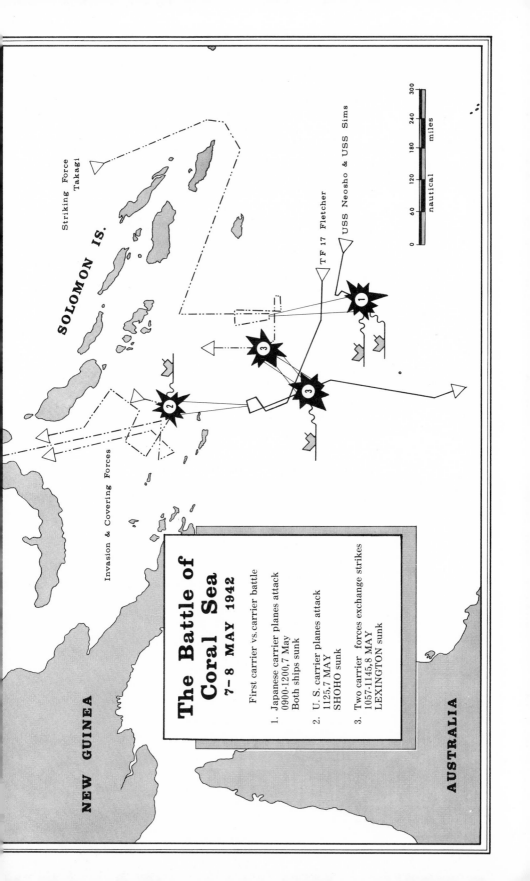

SOLOMON IS.

Striking Force
Takagi

Invasion & Covering Forces

TF 17 Fletcher

USS Neosho & USS Sims

NEW GUINEA

AUSTRALIA

The Battle of Coral Sea
7-8 MAY 1942

First carrier vs. carrier battle

1. Japanese carrier planes attack
   0900-1200, 7 May
   Both ships sunk

2. U. S. carrier planes attack
   1125, 7 MAY
   SHOHO sunk

3. Two carrier forces exchange strikes
   1057-1145, 8 MAY
   LEXINGTON sunk

0   60   120   180   240   300

nautical   miles

Five bombs had landed on the *Lexington.* Two torpedoes exploded against our port side. The water spouts of three near misses which splashed water on the deck were also thought at first to be from torpedoes, but subsequent examination showed only two actual hits by this weapon.

One bomb had hit the port gun gallery just outside the Admiral's cabin. It wiped out most of the gun crews in that vicinity, and started fires. In addition, it killed Commander Gilmore, our paymaster, and Commander Trojalkowski, our dentist, who were in the passageway just inboard, and communications men in an adjacent room.

Bombs started fires in other parts of the ship, but none was especially serious. Fragments killed men in one of the fire-control stations aloft. One bomb passed between the bridge and the funnel and severed the wire pull on the siren, setting it off to add its sorrowful wail to the ear-shattering din.

Suddenly all was quiet again. It was as though some hidden director had signaled for silence. The Japanese planes were no longer in sight, the guns had stopped shooting for lack of targets. The sea was still dotted with burning planes; our own aircraft were seen in the distance, assembling to be ready for further action. But the enemy were through.

I looked at my watch. The entire attack had lasted just nine minutes. It seemed hours since we had first sighted the enemy planes.

Off in the distance to the southeastward, we could see the *Yorktown,* a column of black smoke rising from her flight deck. Evidently she too had been damaged. She had been attacked by both torpedo planes and dive bombers, but with her greater maneuverablilty had managed to evade all torpedoes and was hit only by one large bomb, which had penetrated the flight deck and exploded in a storeroom down below. It had killed 37 men outright and wounded many others. Near misses had caused several fragment holes in the hull along the water line. Otherwise the *Yorktown* was undamaged.

Taking stock on the *Lexington,* we found things not so bad as they might have been. The small fires down below were being fought by the damage-control parties, who reported that they would soon have them under control. No smoke from the flames was showing above decks. The ship had taken only a seven-degree list from the torpedo hits, and this was rapidly being corrected by shifting water ballast. The engine room reported full power and speed available if I wanted it. Our flight deck was intact. We felt like throwing out our chests at our condition after the attack. But our satisfaction was soon to be changed to apprehension.

We proceeded to land our planes which were in the vicinity, and out of ammunition or gas after their air battles. We replenished the ammunition of our guns and refilled the ammunition hoists to be ready for another attack should one come. Lieutenant Commander H. R. ("Pop") Healy, our Damage Control Officer, was down in Central Station, below the armored deck, where directions for all damage control were issued and reports received. He had just phoned the bridge to inform me that all damage was under control. "If we have another attack," he said, "I'd like to take it on the starboard side, since both torpedo hits were to port."

At 12:47, the *Lexington* was suddenly shaken by a terrific internal explosion which seemed to come from the bottom of the ship. It rocked the huge structure more violently than had anything we had received during the battle. Smoke began emerging from around the edges of the elevator on the flight deck.

We called Central Station on the telephone but found the connection broken. The rudder indicator on the bridge was also out. All telephones were dead except a sound-powered one to the engine room. However, reports of huge fires breaking out in the vicinity of Central Station were soon received. The station itself was an inferno. A few men had escaped from it; others were rescued by volunteers who risked their lives in the flames, but the majority, including Healy, had been killed outright by the terrific explosion. Its cause was later established as the insidious accumulation of gasoline vapor, leaking unsuspected from our gasoline storage tanks, which had been weakened by the torpedo hits. It was an unexpected blow, but as yet we had no idea that it was to cost us the ship.

Raging fires, fed by gasoline, broke out from ruptured vents and risers. The water main was broken in the area of the explosion, making the work of combating the flames extremely difficult. Long hoses had to be led from the far after part of the ship, and only very low water pressure could be maintained. It was a losing battle from the beginning, but we did not know it then. We fully expected to save the carrier.

I remained on the bridge to direct the handling of the ship and to receive reports. Commander Mort Seligman, the executive officer, was everywhere, advising and encouraging the fire fighters. Small explosions of ammunition were occurring frequently in the vicinity of the fires, and Seligman was more than once blown like a cork out of a bottle from watertight doors through which he was passing. He brought to the bridge frequent reports of conditions down below. All lights were out and the damage-control men toiled in complete darkness except for hand flashlights. The decks where they were working would grow hot from fires on the decks beneath.

Despite the loss of our rudder indicator on the bridge, we were able to steer from there for a while. It was during this period that we landed the torpedo squadron which returned so late and which we had feared was lost. Then the electric steering gear went completely out and we had to steer by maneuvering the engines, giving orders to the engine room over the one telephone still working. We were unable to use the hand steering in the station below for lack of communications to give the steersman there his course.

The fire continued to spread. More frequent explosions were occurring, and the surface of the elevator in the flight deck was beginning to glow a dull red. A report came from the engine control room that the forward engine-room bulkhead was getting white hot, and that the temperature in that vicinity had risen to 160 degrees. They asked permission, which I promptly granted, to abandon the forward engine room and use only the after engineroom space.

Then the one telephone began to get weaker. It was apparent that it was only a matter of time until it would go out completely. When it did, I realized, there would be no way of getting the men out of the engine rooms. Unless I ordered them to leave, they would stay there, trapped by fire all around them, and hemmed in by red-hot bulkheads, until they perished. Over the weakening phone, I ordered these men to secure the engineering plant and get up on deck. Although we were unable to hear any reply, presently the sound of steam escaping from the safety valves assured me they had received the message. Eventually all of them found their way through the encircling fires to safety on the topside.

We now had no power and the ship lay dead in the water. Without pressure on the main, we were helpless even to fight the fire. I called a destroyer alongside to send over its hoses, but the fire pumps on the small vessels in those early days were of such low capacity that only a trickle of water could be obtained from this source. It seemed outrageous that we could do nothing to put out the fire and save our ship.

At this time, about 5:00 P.M., Admiral Fitch, unperturbed and efficient, leaned over the flag bridge and told me I had better "get the boys off the ship." It was heartbreaking, but it seemed to be the only thing left to do. Reluctantly I gave the order to abandon ship. It was the hardest thing I have ever done. Nevertheless, if we could not prevent the loss of the *Lexington,* saving the lives of her crew was of utmost importance.

The officers and men were as reluctant to leave as I was. We had to order them to go. Most of the wounded were lowered to a destroyer alongside, the remainder going directly into small boats from the other ships. Some of the crew, while waiting to disembark, went below to the service store, which was not in the fire area. They filled their helmets with ice cream and stood around on the flight deck eating it. Knotted ropes were dropped over the side for the men to slide down into the water. Some of them lined up their shoes in orderly fashion on the deck before they left, as if they expected to return. There was not the slightest panic or disorder. I was proud of them.

I noticed one crowd waiting to go over the side at the port after gun gallery. As I approached to see what was delaying them, the men led by Marine Sergeant Peyton, gave "three cheers for the Captain." Their loyalty was inspiring.

Finally, just after sunset, all the crew were off. The water around the ship was black with bobbing heads of swimmers. Small boats from our escorts, cruisers and destroyers were busy picking men out of the water and transferring them to the other ships. After making a last inspection to insure that there were no stragglers, I stood with Commander Seligman at the stern. I directed him to leave, as it was my duty and privilege to be the last one to go. He went down into the water. I stood on the great ship alone.

While I was pausing there, a tremendous explosion took place amidships by the elevator. Planes and debris of all kinds went high into the air. Ducking under the edge of the flight deck to avoid the falling pieces, I decided it was time to go, and slid down the rope to do my stint of swimming until my turn came to be picked up by the rescue boats.

~~~~~~

ABOARD *New Orleans* LIEUTENANT COMMANDER HOWELL Forgy, the cruiser's Presbyterian Chaplain, recounts the drama to rescue oil-covered survivors of *Lexington* and the efforts to assuage the wounded. We have met him before.

5.

TAKING ABOARD

LEXINGTON'S SURVIVORS

"Send up your badly wounded first." Woody clipped the words over the side of the cruiser to the bobbing motor launch rising and falling in the choppy sea.

The coxswain, cautiously inching his craft toward the hull of the big ship, turned his head upward and shouted back.

"They're all badly wounded, sir."

Nearly twenty wire baskets were crowded into the boat. In each basket, helpless under tightly-buckled straps, was a wounded man from the *Lexington*.

A seaman fought against the hull of the *No-Boat* with a boat-hook to break the impact as the waves lifted the launch and its pitiful cargo eight or ten feet into the air, then smashed it downward and against the side of the cruiser.

Sailors in the launch pawed the air to catch the lines tossed over-side from the cruiser. The helpless look in the eyes of a wounded lad on one of the stretchers stabbed through me as the lines were made fast at his head and feet and he began the treacherous transfer to the cruiser.

You knew what he was thinking. If a line should break he would go to the bottom of the sea like a rock. There was no chance to swim—not for these fellows bound hand and foot inside a metal cage.

247

"Easy there!" Woodhead barked. "Ease off on that aft line. Bring his head up a bit . . . that's it. Easy does it."

Dr. Harry Walker reached up to the basket as the seamen eased it to the deck. He spent no more than three seconds looking at the flame-seared man from the carrier. On his forehead a large pink M had been painted in mercurochrome. It told us he had received one injection of merciful morphine before leaving his dying warship.

"Take him to sick bay immediately," Dr. Walker ordered a pair of corpsmen at his side.

Another casualty was on his way up from the undulating launch. You could see he was unconscious. Soggy splotches of red oozed through the white gauze that bandaged his head. Another wide bandage covered a portion of his naked abdomen.

Walker looked calculatingly down at the launch and then toward the other boats pushing toward the cruiser.

"Bring all these men down to sick bay as fast as they come aboard," he ordered. Harry knew what to expect, and he ran to join Dr. Evans in sick bay to begin the dreadful task that was to keep him on his feet for the next thirty-six hours.

The rolling clouds of jet smoke coming from the *Lexington* now just five hundred yards off our port, hid most of her bridge. Her flight deck, leaning in a twenty-degree list, was crowded with more and more men. Some of her crew stood at the edge of the deck, pinched their noses with thumb and forefinger, and leaped feet-first to the sea. They looked like kids at home jumping from a diving-board.

The perilous task of getting the wounded down to the motor whaleboats and launches went on and on. The rows of stretchers on the flight deck grew longer and longer as more casualties were brought topside from the inferno inside the carrier.

I watched the men who leaped into the water. Their arms moved as though they were swimming, but they seemed to struggle, unmoving, in the same spot. Little spots of bright yellow began appearing here and there about the burning carrier as men pulled the rubber life rafts from the *Lex's* planes, threw them into the sea, and jumped in after them.

About fifty of the carrier's proud planes huddled with folded wings like frightened birds at the end of her deck as orange fingers of fire poked through the black smoke and felt about the flat landing area for some place to grab hold.

Between the *No-Boat* and the *Lex* the sea was dotted with little black bumps that were the heads of struggling sailors. Boats from our cruiser and the destroyers moved back and forth, pulling the men from the water. Distance at sea fools a lot of people. The *No-Boat* seemed but a short city block from the stricken flattop, and many of the *Lexington* men thought they could swim it with no trouble. A couple of them came aboard the cruiser hale and hearty; most of them fell to the deck, half-drowned and exhausted, after being pulled from the sea.

Lines dangled from the *No-Boat* deck to the water about every ten feet on the port side. Five or six men crowded about the deck at each line.

Twenty feet off the side of the cruiser a figure splashed almost listlessly in the water. He had swum all the way over from the carrier, but it seemed the energy necessary to propel his tortured body the remaining few feet had been spent. He appeared to be treading water rather than swimming. He pawed at the water intermittently and then just lay there, moving his arms and legs only enough to keep his nose above the surface.

"Keep coming, mate. Just a little bit more and you'll make it," shouted one of the sailors at the top of a line near me.

They hauled the line to the deck and tossed it outward toward the struggling man in the water. The swimmer lifted his arms and grabbed at the air, but the line fell short, hung on the surface a couple of seconds, then sank from sight.

The men on the deck hauled the line back feverishly. One of them raced for a life preserver.

"Keep coming, Mac," the man with the rope encouraged the pitiful figure in the water, "We'll get you this time."

The *No-Boat* men made the life preserver fast to the end of the line and hurled it over the side. It splashed into the water and sent a green-white spray over the bobbing head. I watched the man's hands as they grasped the line. His fists clenched about the rope with the strength of steel vises.

"Hey, Mac! Put your leg through that life preserver and hang on," one of the men called from the deck.

The swimmer obeyed automatically. Eagerly the men pulled him aboard. They grabbed each side of his dripping body as he came over the side and shook the life preserver from his leg.

The lad, a short, two-hundred-pound Filipino cook, collapsed to the deck with a soggy thud. His brown, tropical skin seemed to glow a weird bluish color.

"He couldn't be that fat," observed one of the sailors. "He must be full of water."

There was no time to call for corpsmen. One man rolled the portly islander to his stomach. Another pulled out his tongue and adjusted the man's head on his limp arm.

The water-soaked Filipino was nearly dead. When a husky sailor straddled his back and began artificial respiration, unbelievable volumes of water gushed from his nose and mouth with each stroke.

"Keep pushing," one of the sailors encouraged the man on the Filipino's back. "That guy's got about half the Coral Sea aboard."

The half-drowned figure on the deck grunted and coughed a couple of times. I leaned close to his face and heard him breathe and moan softly.

"He's going to be all right," I said to the sailors working on him. "Good work. Get him in a blanket as soon as you can."

As I walked forward to the well deck the scene was being repeated a dozen times. The sailors lining the side of the ship looked like an excursion of fishermen during the mackerel run. They stood there tossing their lines into the water and hauling their catches back to the deck. Artificial respiration was being applied to prone bodies scattered all along the deck.

A rugged, swarthy master-of-arms from the *Lexington* came up over the side from a rescue boat. His heavy crop of black hair clung wet against the stubble of his square, unshaven face.

As he stepped to the well deck his eyes caught sight of Pope, the *No-Boat's* chief master-of-arms.

"Ye Gods!" the dripping *Lexington* man bellowed. "Hey, Pope! Don't tell me you belong to this ship!"

Pope's face broke into a broad grin when he heard the voice of an old friend and former shipmate. Before he could reply, the newly-arrived survivor turned to the men about him.

"Throw me back into the ocean!" he thundered.

Pope laughed at the affectionate insult, threw his arms about the husky carrier man, and steered him to a bowl of steaming coffee. Cooks and mess attendants were pouring to the deck from the galley with huge kettles of coffee and stacks of soup bowls. The bedraggled survivors clenched their white, water-wrinkled hands tightly about the warm bowls and emptied them rapidly.

Flames, bright orange against the black smoke, were racing aft on the carrier's flight deck now. Only a few men, most of them officers who had been directing the abandonment, remained on the deck. They were clustered in a little group at the bow. They were too far away for me to make out faces or rank insignia, but I knew Captain Sherman of the *Lexington* was among them. He would be the last man to leave the ship.

The flames worked their way back to the half-hundred planes bunched together at the stern. One of the planes caught fire, blazed brightly a few seconds as the flames ran through its wings, then exploded. Plumes of burning gasoline shot like rockets into the air and fell upon the other planes. There was another explosion, and then another, as each plane let go with fiery anger. I could hear the sharp crackling of the dry, tinder-like warbirds as the after portion of the *Lexington* became a huge mass of red and yellow.

The figures at the front of the carrier dived and jumped into the water as fuel tanks from the blazing aircraft sent streams of fire spitting across the deck as though they came from the deadly nozzles of flame-throwers. A boat moved in close to the carrier to pick up the final handful of survivors.

"Sick bay is all full, Chaplain," MacFarland, the chief pharmacist's mate, informed me. "We're setting up a temporary bay in the hangar."

I made my way through the crowded deck. There were hundreds of men from the *Lexington* jammed aboard the *New Orleans* now, and more were coming. A couple of dozen of them, wrapped in blankets, huddled about a steaming coffee pot. They looked like blanketed Indians pow-wowing around a campfire.

I reported to Dr. Farquhar in the hangar. Doc and a corpsman were going down the long rows of the wounded, stretched out on the deck. They were spraying paraffin solution from Flit guns upon the burned hands and legs of the *Lexington* men. The paraffin hardened in a few seconds and protected the horrible wounds from infection. I thanked God for the paraffin we had found in that grocery store.

"What do you need, Doc?" I inquired.

"Blankets, Padre. Lots of blankets for these fellows. We've used up all the medical department's supply."

With a party of men I ran down to the sleeping compartments below. We grabbed every blanket we could find. There was no time for the formality of requisitions or orders. We just ripped blankets off the cots and hurried them up to the hangar.

The long rows of wounded extended from the after part of the hangar forward through the hangar and across the well deck to the crew's galley. There were about one hundred and fifty men lying there on the deck. Many of them were suffering from sheer physical exhaustion and immersion. They were nauseated and shook under terrific chills. They coughed up gallons of sea-water to the deck beside them. There were far too few basins. Others sat upright and held out their hands with palms upraised. They said nothing, but there was a pleading in their eyes as they waited for corpsmen to come along and spray the soothing paraffin on the seared raw meat left by friction burns when they slid down the lines from their mortally-wounded carrier.

Most of the men in this emergency sick bay were so-called mobile cases. Among them, though, were many seriously wounded men who should have been in the main sick bay below. But there was no room down there.

I heard a low, continuous moan and moved down the long row of pain to a young marine gunner. A corpsman working on the boy didn't have to undress him. He merely pulled the shreds of what was left of his uniform away from the lad's charred skin and threw them to the deck.

The Marine had been in an AA gun crew on the *Lex* when a Jap bomb exploded near-by. The six-thousand-degree heat generated by the blast seared nearly half of his body.

The corpsman explored through the charred cloth and burned flesh until he found a space of clear skin where he could inject a dose of morphine to deaden the suffering boy's pain.

Dr. Farquhar knelt alongside the young fellow and examined him.

"Take this man below to sick bay," he ordered.

"There's no more room down there, sir," the corpsman replied.

"Well, make room!" Farquhar snapped back. "This lad needs blood plasma and needs it badly. He's got a 40 per cent body burn and will probably die if you don't get him down there quickly."

Two corpsmen picked up the four corners of the blanket under the marine. He grunted in short, pitiful spasms as they moved him into one of the wire mesh stretchers.

"Easy, fella," one of the corpsmen said in a reassuring hoarse whisper. "You're going to be all right."

The Marine fought back the desire to scream to the full fury of the excruciating pain that ripped through his body.

I followed the corpsmen and their sorry load through the hangar to the well deck. I paused for a moment there and looked at the *Lexington,* still riding high in the water. Her flight deck was a long row of flame, and angry tongues of fire entwined her superstructure.

Suddenly the great flight deck of the carrier opened up amidships in a tremendous explosion. Huge flames squirted into the sky, and enormous chunks of debris went sailing hundreds of feet into the air.

"Take cover!" some one near me shouted just as the noise of the great detonation reached us. I saw several men in a small boat between the *New Orleans* and the exploding *Lex* fall prone and cover their heads with their hands.

Huge pieces of wreckage plummeted into the water from the sky. The lethal hailstorm included big portions of the flight deck and steel bulkheads.

I crawled back to my feet and continued below.

Before we got to sick bay I could smell it. The air was blue with the stench of burned flesh, ether, and vomit. The near-by marine compartment had been commandeered by Dr. Evans, and every cot in there was filled. Temporary cots had been set up in the passageway outside sick bay proper. Corpsmen were busy putting bandages on shrapnel wounds, applying compression pads to stop the dangerous flow of blood, and rigging plasma bottles above the cots. You could see the natural plasma of the men, a watery substance, oozing from their horrible burns. When enough of that leaves their bodies, they die of shock—unless the bottled plasma from the blood of people at home is injected into their veins to replace it.

A corpsman jabbed a long needle into the arm of a lad in front of me. The hollow needle was linked by a long tube to a plasma bottle swinging from the overhead. He secured the needle to the boy's arm with adhesive tape and moved on to repeat the process for the man in the next cot.

Inside sick bay I saw the white figures of Dr. Walker and a couple of corpsmen working on a young seaman. A large piece of shrapnel had entered one side of the boy's neck, severed his windpipe and jugular vein, and come out the other side. Harry was working feverishly about the boy's throat while a corpsman with forceps picked piece after piece of shrapnel out of the patient's chest and abdomen.

A big, husky man cried feebly and reached for some object he could not—and never will—be able to see. The shrapnel that tore into his head ripped through the optic nerve. He bit his white teeth into bleeding lips to keep from screaming as he lived over again those minutes when hell itself broke loose upon him.

I recognized Lieutenant Nixon, an aviator from the *Lexington,* sitting on a cot with his head buried in his hands. I had met Nixon when I shipped from California to Pearl Harbor to begin my duty aboard the *No-Boat.*

"Hello, Nixon," I said. "Do you remember me? I'm Chaplain Forgy."

He looked up at me, puzzled.

"Nixon. Nixon. That's right, isn't it? My name is Nixon. Yes, Nixon. Yes, I remember you, Chaplain."

"How do you feel?"

"How did I get here? Say, where am I?"

"You're aboard the *New . . .*"

He interrupted me with that impatient, pleading voice.

"Pardon me, Chaplain. What did you say my name was? Oh, yes, Nixon."

I told him that he was aboard the *New Orleans,* that everything was all right.

"What's the matter with the *Lex,* Chaplain? She got hit, didn't she? Say, pardon me again. I think you told me before, but I forgot. What did you say my name was? Oh, yes . . . sure . . . thanks."

The thread of memory, blasted thin by extreme shock, dangled the young officer on the brink of amnesia for hours. Over and over again a hundred times he pleaded for answers to the same questions. Who was he? Where was he? What did you say his name was?

Two corpsmen stepped from the operating table with the silent form of the boy with the bad shrapnel wounds. They placed him gently in a cot.

"What chance has he got, Doc?" I asked Walker.

Harry Walker frowned and shook his head negatively.

"I've done everything I can for him, Padre," the doctor said. "It all depends on the Man Upstairs now."

Tirelessly and ceaselessly, hour after hour, the corpsmen moved about the white cots and did their jobs like automatons.

I looked at one of the wounded boys lying motionless in a cot. He beckoned to me with his eyes. I walked to his side, and he slid a hand through the covers and took hold of mine.

"How're you feeling, lad?" I asked him.

"I don't feel so good, Chaplain."

A 30-calliber machine-gun bullet from the Jap strafers had gone through his chest and lodged next to his spine. Quite frankly and simply he looked up, without expression in his face.

"Chaplain," he asked, "would you say a prayer for me?"

I squeezed his hand a bit tighter.

"Let's both say a prayer, fellow," I suggested.

I shut my eyes in silent prayer for a moment. When I looked at him again his eyes were closed. There seemed to be an appearance of relief on his troubled face. I said "Amen" quietly, and the boy opened his eyes and forced a little smile to his thin, blue-gray lips.

I moved on down the bay from bed to bed talking to those of the wounded men who were conscious.

Some time later Dr. Farquhar walked into the room. I asked him how the boys up in the hangar were getting along.

"They'll be all right," Doc said. He paused a moment, looking at me.

"But you'd better go topside, Padre," he added.

I asked if something had gone wrong up there.

"No," he smiled, "but you look a bit green. C'mon."

I followed him, conscious now that I had been nauseated for hours by the sickening stench of sick bay. I was surprised when I stepped out into the well deck to discover it was nearly dark. The cruiser was racing southward through the sea.

"I didn't even realize we were under way," I commented.

Doc said we had been under way for more than an hour. I felt better. None of us dared tempt fate by talking about it at the time, but we all were uncomfortable during those hours when the *No-Boat* sat dead in the water during the rescue operations. A Jap sub, even at distant range, couldn't have missed a big, unmoving target like that.

Miles off in the purple distance I could see the flames of the *Lexington* still burning against the tropical horizon. What a ship, I thought. She's taken all those torpedoes, has been burning for hours and hours, and she's still on top of the water.

I went down to the wardroom for a cup of coffee. Crowded about the tables were several dozen officers from the *Lexington*. Most of them wore clothing borrowed from men of the *No-Boat*. They were clad in everything from dungarees to dress blues.

Suddenly the ship jumped under a violent whip. There was a tremendous report of a great explosion. Coffee spilled, and the cups rattled noisily in their saucers.

"Sounds like one of the cans has been torpedoed," an officer across the table from me exclaimed. We ran to the deck but could see nothing in the darkness.

The bridge reported receiving a message from one of the destroyers that her fantail had been blown off by a torpedo. A few moments later another message came from the same ship. She hadn't been hit at all. It was the *Lexington* blowing up as she sank. The explosion was so great it lifted the stern of the little destroyer—about ten miles away from the *Lex*—clear of the sea. We were fifteen miles from the carrier, and it felt as if the blast came from a depth charge at our side.

The molten steel and her white-hot boilers exploding as the *Lexington* slid beneath the surface detonated hundreds of thousand-pound bombs and torpedoes in one mighty explosion. . . .

We thought that was just like the great carrier. Proud *Lady Lex* was going down to the bottom of the sea, but her final, farewell salute was so tremendous that any Jap subs that might have been within a five-mile radius most certainly went to eternity with her.

Commander Hayter stepped to my side and spoke quietly.

"Padre, you've got a job to do. One of the boys has died down in sick bay. The body's in the way. Can't wait till morning."

He said the sailmaker would have a sack completed in about thirty minutes.

I made my way slowly back to the stench and horror of sick bay. Harry Walker was beginning his twentieth operation of the night. A stretcher party finally arrived with the canvas sack, weighted with lead in the lower end. It was not in keeping with the traditions of the navy to short-cut the full ritual of burial at sea to give this lad a *deep six* in the darkness of midnight, but as I looked around the room I could see that there was no alternative. Life and space were precious. I called for six volunteers from among the *Lexington* survivors to serve as pall-bearers for their shipmate. When I saw the intent, reverent seriousness of their faces I knew the lack of ritual in the lad's burial would be more than compensated for by the true feeling of his surviving fellows.

The stretcher paused a moment as we entered the passageway just outside sick bay. We draped the canvas form with the American flag and continued our long trek to the well deck. *Lexington* and *No-Boat* men stopped whenever we encountered them in the passageways. They stood silent and reverent as all that remained of a fallen comrade passed.

The night was pitch-black as we stepped on to the well deck. The stretcher-bearers made their way to the starboard side where they rested the foot of the stretcher poles on the gunwale. We bumped into one another clumsily as I felt in the darkness for the body.

There was no opportunity to read the burial service in this Stygian cave of the night. I rested my hand on the flag and from memory began to recite the committal service.

"I am the resurrection and the life . . ."

I found the words left my mouth almost mechanically. My own mind was crammed full of thoughts. This was my first burial at sea. How strange, how different from what I had expected. My words seemed to go out into the black emptiness of the universe. Was God, up beyond all this horrifying blackness, looking down upon this lad, or had He turned His back upon this whole day of inhumanity wherein brother rose in deadly battle against brother?

I found myself saying my own prayer within the prayer of the ritual. Mine was a pleading prayer that God would look down, that He would take the spirit of this body to dwell in a heavenly mansion which Christ had gone to prepare. Surely there must be a place up there for this lad who had given his all for those ideals which we believed made our cause just and right.

I couldn't see the other men standing there, but I heard their hushed, subdued, and thoroughly sincere voices as we repeated together the Lord's Prayer.

". . . For Thine is the Kingdom and the Power and the Glory forever. Amen."

"Hold the flag, boys. It doesn't go down."

The men began to lift the poles at the head of the stretcher.

". . . We therefore reverently commit this body to the deep."

The men lifted the stretcher high now until the ends of the poles were above their heads. The canvas sack quietly disappeared in the darkness. There was no splash. The swishing of the sea as the cruiser cut through the waves buried the sound and the body. Miles below the surface of the Coral Sea, we knew, it would come to rest. May his soul rest, too.

One of the boys beside me was folding the flag he had removed from the body.

"Who was he, Padre?" he asked.

I gulped. I wanted to cry like a child, for no one will ever know who was in that sack. There was no means of knowing with a body ripped by shrapnel and scorched like his.

"He was a sailor . . . and some good mother's son," was all I could answer.

Quietly we made our way below.

~~~~~~

SWIMMING IN THE OPALESCENT CORAL SEA, TOO, WAS war correspondent Stanley Johnston, who somehow managed to salvage his notes. Here Johnston, as a survivor in one of the cruiser *New Orleans'* whaleboats, describes the carrier *Lexington's* last moments.

6.

THE GALLANT LADY
SUCCUMBS

It was 6:30 P.M. now and almost dark, as night descends quickly in the tropics. The sun had dropped into the sea and the rescue work was nearly over. Our whaleboat was filled with weary swimmers, some of whom were very ill after having swallowed seawater on top of ice cream, and was disembarking its cargo. All the men except Ensign George Markham and myself had climbed the boarding netting dropped from the cruiser's deck when there was another terrific explosion, one of the heaviest of all, aboard the *Lex*. The 16,000 to 20,000 pounds of torpedo war-head guncotton finally had detonated.

"Everybody take cover," came the shout from the deck officers.

George and I stole one look at the poor old *Lexington* and saw bits and particles, airplanes, plates, planks, pieces large and small all going up into the air in the midst of a blinding white flame and smoke. We pressed lovingly against the heaving steel sides of that cruiser, hugging her for seconds while the debris splashed into the sea for hundreds of feet around.

But even then the apparently indestructible old *Lex* didn't sink. Instead she began to burn harder than ever. The flight deck was now ripped wide open from stem to stern. Apparently this last blast had ruptured great holes in the oil and fuel tanks, for the flames now were shooting hundreds of feet high up into the air where they were crowned by thick black smoke.

In the deepening twilight it was a sight of awful majesty, one that wrung the hearts of all who watched.

After clambering aboard I finally went down to the cruiser's laundry to get myself thoroughly dried. There I met a friendly Marine who was in charge and who loaned me—at his own suggestion—shirt and pants while my own scorched and torn uniform was being washed and dried. My shoes, a favorite pair I had bought in London while covering the Battle of Britain, were put into a hot air drier. I got them back within an hour none the worse for the soaking.

While I was waiting for a dry change of clothing I fished from my pockets sheaves of loose leaf notes and my little black notebook. By drying them in the laundry's steam presser I saved every one and was grateful to find that my hen tracks were still legible though blurred. These were the only items I had salvaged. My watch, money, clothing, typewriter, my valuable toothpaste tube (six weeks later in Washington, D.C., when I tried to buy a tube I was refused because I couldn't produce the old one) and my favorite straight razor had gone down.

I then went back on deck. Night had fallen. It might have been a starry night—but none of us could tell. The leaping, towering flames from the *Lexington* hid all feebler light from the skies. Every bit of flotsam and every outline of the great ship showed up in a blinding glare. Around her the velvety tropic night was the deeper for the contrast. Two destroyers were easing slowly around her burning bulk, nosing in here and there to be sure no one was left in the water.

At 7:15 P.M. Admiral Fletcher aboard Carrier II gave a signal for the fleet to re-form and move away. We had been lying there immobile for at least three hours—the best way of asking for trouble in submarine-infested waters. It was time for us to go but the ships moved off slowly as though reluctant to leave their gallant comrade.

We didn't leave her entirely alone. One destroyer stayed behind, circling around her now cherry-red hull and the maelstrom of fire within her bosom. It was evident that she might burn for hours before sinking. What a signal beacon in the darkness she made! Japanese subs or snooper planes could see her for 100 miles or more and pinprick our position on their charts without any difficulty.

So the Admiral gave orders to sink her.

That lone, remaining destroyer did the job. Standing off 1,500 yards her crew sent four torpedoes coursing—this time into the starboard side. Their explosions were almost lost in the terrific updrafts created by her fires. But their effect was not.

She had been settling slowly through the hours, almost on an even keel. Now she shook herself as the torpedoes pierced her last internal ramparts.

Clouds of steam began to hiss upward with the flames. Her white-hot plates groaned and screamed as the water caused them to shrink and buckle. Inside her there were new blasts, rumblings, concussions —as pressures caved in bulkheads, as gasoline vapors exploded. And now the settling was more rapid.

Still she remained upright, dipping neither bow nor stern. Gradually the waves folded over her. One of her officers standing beside me, watching this final act, murmured: "There she goes. She didn't turn over. She is going down with her head up. Dear old *Lex*. A lady to the last!"

ALTHOUGH SPORADIC ACTION CONTINUED THE NEXT day, the main engagement ended with the sinking of the carrier *Lexington*. Both sides withdrew, licking their wounds. Often called the battle of blunders, Coral Sea was a tactical victory for the Japanese and a strategic victory for the United States. More to the point, the invasion of Port Moresby was decisively turned back—and in that one finds a degree of compensation for the loss of a carrier. On the other side of the coin, the Japanese had lost *Shoho* and the air groups of the damaged *Shokaku* and *Zuikaku* were sorely depleted, thus depriving the enemy of the conceivable "difference" in the upcoming Battle of Midway.

Now let us discuss the second and greater advance building up at this time, the one into the Central Pacific, which quite rightly alarmed Nimitz even more. Japan viewed Midway—the outermost link of the Hawaiian chain, and some 1,135 miles from Pearl Harbor—as "a sentry for Hawaii." It was the king pin in Yamamoto's grand strategy for the conquest of the United States. Less than six miles in diameter, Midway was discovered by an American sailing master in 1859 and shortly thereafter was claimed for this country by U.S.S. *Lackawanna*. The island is guarded by two islets, Sand and Eastern, through which one approaches a deep green lagoon. Over the years until 1942 Midway's principal occupants were "gooney birds" (a variety of albatross), Japanese feather hunters, a Pan-American Airways terminal, and the Navy, including a small contingent of Marine fighter planes. With the island in Japanese hands, Yamamoto's carriers would have a fixed fueling base and a much desired point from which her forces could draw the United States Pacific Fleet into a decisive engagement.

The Japanese formula for victory was as follows: 1) a diversionary raid by her Second Mobile Force in the Western Aleutians to confuse Nimitz; 2) an air raid on Midway by the Carrier Striking Force to soften up the island for a 5000-man invasion; and 3) the Aleutians force to take up a position between Midway and the Aleutians in the event Nimitz came out to fight. These were the essentials. Yamamoto assumed that Nimitz would not let Midway go by default, thus giving him a chance to exploit the superior firepower of the Imperial Japanese Navy.

Correctly anticipating his opposite number's strategy, Nimitz hastily arranged his sea power. Of his carriers, *Yorktown,* having returned May 27 damaged from the Coral Sea, was in drydock and was not available until May 31, after fabulously swift repairs by the yard. *Enterprise,* just returned from the Doolittle Raid, was available with a trained air group. *Hornet's* air group lacked battle experience, while *Saratoga* was still on the West Coast. Moreover Halsey, who missed the battle of his life, was in a Pearl Harbor hospital with a case of hives. (Rear Admiral Raymond A. Spruance took over his post; Fletcher, senior to Spruance, was Officer in Tactical Command. One of the ironies of the battle is that Spruance, a non-aviator, had an air staff, while Fletcher, also a non-aviator, had none. Nimitz therefore let the junior admiral exercise independent command.)

Nimitz formed and positioned a Northern Pacific Force consisting of five heavy and light cruisers and ten destroyers. He then bolstered Midway's meager defenses with as many guns and planes as he could muster and sent the rest of the United States Pacific Fleet in two task forces to sea: three carriers, eight heavy and light cruisers, seventeen destroyers, twenty-five submarines, and two fleet oilers. Along the outer Hawaiian chain Nimitz stationed ten picket ships and a Midway Fueling group of two destroyers and an oiler.

Yamamoto's three forces aggregated five carriers, eleven battleships, including the 18.1 inch *Yamato,* his flagship, fourteen heavy and light cruisers, fifty-eight destroyers, seventeen submarines and more than two score ships of the train. However, a substantial part of this force, including one carrier, was assigned to the Aleutians Diversionary Attack.

The Battle of Midway is recounted in five parts.

7.

MIDWAY PRELIMINARIES

The first surface group to get under way was Rear Admiral Kakuta's Second Mobile Force, assigned to the Aleutians. Of those destined for Midway, with which we are immediately concerned, Nagumo's Carrier Striking Force sortied from the Inland Sea of Japan on the evening of 26 May. Yamamoto, with the Main Body, followed them two days later. The transports of the Midway Occupation Force departed Saipan the evening of 27 May, Kurita's Close Support Group of four powerful heavy cruisers and two destroyers left Guam at the same time and steamed 75 to 100 miles ahead of the transports; the seaplane carriers tagged along behind.

Yamamoto was suffering from stomach trouble and "seemed in unusually low spirits," but the Main Body as a whole was feeling very snug and secure behind the 18.1-inch guns of *Yamato* and the 16-inchers of the other fast battleships. All hands were "singing war songs at the top of their lungs," confident of annihilating the Pacific Fleet. Sailors whose duties did not involve much exercise were put through daily calisthenics and there was much sun-bathing topside until the Main Body entered the weather front on the afternoon of 1 June.

Commander Striking Force was feeling none too easy despite his tactical superiority. His carriers had returned to home waters on 23 April after their Indian Ocean raid and so had had barely a month for upkeep and repair of ships, refresher training for anti-aircraft crews and flight training for aviators. That, to be sure, was three weeks more than Fletcher and Spruance had. "We participated in the operation," wrote Nagumo after the battle, "with meager training and without knowledge of the enemy."

Of course he knew where to find Midway, his first objective. Striking Force orders were to "execute an aerial attack on Midway . . . destroying all enemy air forces stationed there" on 4 June, in preparation for the landing on the 5th. This looked like an easy assignment, and the high command was so confident of success that it provided the Occupation Force with new Japanese names for the two islets and for Midway itself, the last meaning "Glorious Month of June." So it was, but not for them!

Midway was so crowded with Marines, planes, supply and oil dumps and other installations that there was scarcely room for the "gooney birds," whose hoarse dissent from these goings-on could be heard above the humming of plane motors and the booming of the surf. Captain Simard and staff, Colonel Shannon and his staff had their hands full with defensive preparations such as mining all likely approaches and landing beaches. Radio traffic, most of which had to be coded or decoded, air-search operations, unloading ships, and "housekeeping" on an immense scale kept everyone busy. A demolition plan was tested shortly before the battle, and somewhat too realistically; a sailor threw the wrong switch and 400,000 gallons of aviation gasoline went up in flames. The fire was kept under control and over half a million gallons were left; but thereafter all planes, including B-17s, had to be refueled by hand from 55-gallon drums.

The first consideration was air search. It was imperative that the enemy be discovered at the earliest possible moment in order to prevent him from sneaking within plane-launching distance and "pulling a Pearl Harbor" on Midway. Beginning 30 May, 22 Catalinas searched daily the sector SSW to NNE 700 miles out, and another PBY took off during the graveyard watch in order to be at the expected launching position of the enemy carriers at dawn. As Intelligence had reported that two enemy forces would rendezvous 700 miles west of Midway, there was added a daily search-attack mission by Army Flying Fortresses, to arrive at that point around 1500 each day. Nothing was sighted until 3 June. About 300 miles to the northwestward of Midway there was a "weak front," rendered almost stationary by a large high-pressure area centered northeast of the island,

and affording perfect cover for Nagumo's carriers. More than once they could hear the motors of American search planes in the clouds above them; but most of the Midway-based aircraft were not yet equipped with radar and could pick up ships only visually. It was so thick around the Japanese Striking Force at noon 2 June that Admiral Nagumo lost visual contact with his own ships; at 1330, when his staff navigator figured that the designated point for a change of course toward Midway had been reached, the Admiral had to break radio silence to give the order.

Rear Admiral Robert H. English, Commander Submarine Pacific Fleet, had charge of deploying the 25 submarines at his disposal. Twelve boats were collected for a Midway Patrol Group by sending some out from Pearl between 21 and 24 May and pulling in others from the Mandates and elsewhere. These were assigned patrol stations west of Midway. Three more, the "roving short-stops" of the disposition, patrolled a scouting line 200 miles north of the Hawaiian chain and halfway between Midway and Oahu, in case the enemy should attempt a diversionary attack on Pearl Harbor. Four submarines were sent to patrol about 300 miles north of Oahu, and six more supported the Aleutians Force.

Admiral Spruance's Task Force, built around *Enterprise* and *Hornet,* departed Pearl 28 May "to hold Midway and inflict maximum damage to the enemy by strong attrition tactics." Admiral Fletcher's *Yorktown* force sortied at 0900 on the 30th, with orders "to conduct target practice and then support Task Force 16."

Spruance on the last day of May and Fletcher on the first of June met oilers *Cimarron* and *Platte* and had their last fueling until after the battle. Spruance then doubled back to meet Fletcher at 1600 June 2 at lat. 32°N, long. 173°W, about 325 miles northeast of Midway. The carriers were now beyond the scope of land-based air searches and had to protect themselves. *Hornet* flew a search mission 150 miles out on 1 June, with no contacts; *Enterprise* searched the sector west to northwest on the morning of the 2nd, but all planes returned early on account of bad weather. The enemy carriers were still behind their protective weather front.

That day, Admiral Spruance made the following visual signal to the ships of his Task Force:—

An attack for the purpose of capturing Midway is expected. The attacking force may be composed of all combatant types including four or five carriers, transports and train vessels. If presence of Task Forces 16 and 17 remains unknown to enemy we should be able to make surprise flank attacks on enemy carriers from position northeast of Midway. Further operations will be based on result of these attacks, damage inflicted by Midway forces, and information of enemy movements. The successful conclusion of the operation now commencing will be of great value to our country. Should carriers become separated during attacks by enemy aircraft, they will endeavor to remain within visual touch.

First air contacts on the enemy were made by Midway-based planes on the Occupation Force. Ensign Jack Reid was flying a Catalina almost 700 miles from Midway shortly before 0900 June 3. His sector covered the point at which Intelligence expected two Japanese forces to rendezvous; the pilots used to draw straws to see who would fly it at dawn. Reid had run down to the end of his arc, on the westerly bearing from Midway. It was time to turn back, but he decided to go on for a few minutes. Suddenly he sighted 30 miles ahead what appeared to be the main enemy fleet, looking like miniature ships in a backyard pond. "Do you see what I do?" he asked his co-pilot. "You're damned right I do!" was the reply. Popping in and out of clouds, they tracked the force for several hours, and by 1100 were able to report eleven ships making 19 knots to the eastward. This was probably the combined transport and seaplane groups of the Midway Occupation Force, which was then indulging in a final battle drill including the arming of flame throwers. United States Marines will learn with envy that their opposite numbers of the "Kure" Special Naval Landing Force, in one transport, were supplied with ten cases of beer after the drill, and got away with it all.

Captain Simard at Midway reacted immediately to the contact report, sending out nine B-17s. At 1624 the same day, 570 miles out, they found the transports, made three high-level (8,000 to 12,000 feet) bombing attacks and reported having hit "two battleships or heavy cruisers" and two transports; but actually these planes made no hits. Next, four amphibious Catalinas, each armed with one aerial torpedo, were sent to attack this formation. A radar contact at 0115 June 4 led them to where the transports were set forth in bright moonlight. At 0143 three torpedoes were dropped and one hit the oiler *Akebono Maru*. The explosion killed or wounded 23 men and slowed the ship temporarily, but she regained formation.

The battle was on. "The whole course of the war in the Pacific may hinge on the developments of the next two or three days," recorded the Cincpac annalist on receipt of this news. It did. The action about to be joined was one of the most decisive of the war.

At 1800 June 3, after the first air attacks had been made by Midway-based planes on the Japanese transports, *Yorktown, Enterprise* and *Hornet* were a good 300 miles ENE of Midway, 400 miles east (and a little south) of the point where Nagumo's carriers were steaming at 25 knots toward their planned plane-launching point. Admiral Fletcher had received the first reports of contact with the enemy in good season; and although they were reported to him as the Main Body of the Japanese Fleet, he correctly estimated that our planes had seen only a transport group with escort. He trusted his original Intelligence report to the effect that an enemy carrier force would be approaching Midway from the northwest, to launch an air attack on the atoll at dawn June 4. And that is exactly what Nagumo was doing. So Fletcher changed course to the southwestward (210°) at 1950 June 3 with the object of arriving by break of day at a position about 200 miles north of Midway, whence he could fly an attack against Nagumo's carriers, provided their position had been ascertained. He correctly assumed that his presence was still unknown to the enemy, and that he might avoid detection next morning until Nagumo's planes were already winging their way to Midway. Thus, during the night of 3-4 June, the opposing carrier forces were approaching one another on courses which, if maintained, would have crossed a few miles northwest of the atoll.

Thursday, the Fourth of June, a day fatal to Japan's hopes of victory, began to break shortly after four o'clock. By sunrise, at 0457, there was a gentle (force 3) tradewind blowing from the southeast, enough for launching planes against an enemy to the westward without much loss of distance. Everyone hoped it would breeze up, but by 0800 the wind had fallen away to mere light airs (4 to 5 knots) which forced the carriers to steam at 21 knots away from the enemy in order to launch or recover. Visibility—35 to 40 miles—was much too good for the carriers' health; the air temperature throughout the day was pleasantly cool, 68° to 70° Fahrenheit.

As it was *Yorktown's* turn to search, at 0430 she launched ten SBDs to cover the northern semicircle to a radius of 100 miles, a proper precaution against being jumped by the planes of unlocated carriers. At that moment, Nagumo was about 215 miles to the westward, sending off his first strike on Midway. He still had the breaks in the matter of weather; from *Kaga's* log it is evident that the Striking Force was not yet out of the "front." Yet, despite a low (50 per cent) cloud cover and visibility of only 15 miles, American search planes from Midway managed to spot their fast-approaching enemy.

At 0534 June 4, the long awaited word was received on board *Enterprise:* "Enemy carriers." This was an intercepted message from a searching PBY to its base at Midway. Next, at 0545 came a plain English dispatch from the same source: "Many enemy planes heading Midway bearing 320° distant 150." Then, at 0603, "Two carriers and battleships bearing 320° distant 180 (miles from Midway) course 135° speed 25." That position was about 200 miles WSW of Task Force 16. These were the first indications received by any United States command afloat as to where the enemy carriers were. The position given was incorrect by about 40 miles and only two of the four flattops were sighted; but at least Fletcher and Spruance now knew the approximate whereabouts of the Striking Force.

Admiral Fletcher wished to recover *Yorktown's* search mission and await further intelligence before launching a strike, and so passed the ball to Admiral Spruance. At 0607, only four minutes after receiving the last contact report, he ordered Spruance with *Enterprise* and *Hornet* to "proceed southwesterly and attack enemy carriers when definitely located," and promised to "follow as soon as planes recovered."

Thus, only ten minutes before the air battle over Midway commenced, Fletcher sparked off the train of events that resulted in the loss of four Japanese carriers.

~~~~~~

ABOARD *HORNET* WAS TORPEDO SQUADRON 8, REVERED in naval history for its almost total sacrifice. For this phase of the battle we turn to the gifted *Life* war correspondent Sidney L. James, now an executive of Time, Inc. The "Skipper" to whom he frequently refers is of course Lieutenant Commander John C. Waldron, who gave his life in leading the attack on the Japanese carriers; Ensign Gay was the sole survivor of the squadron.

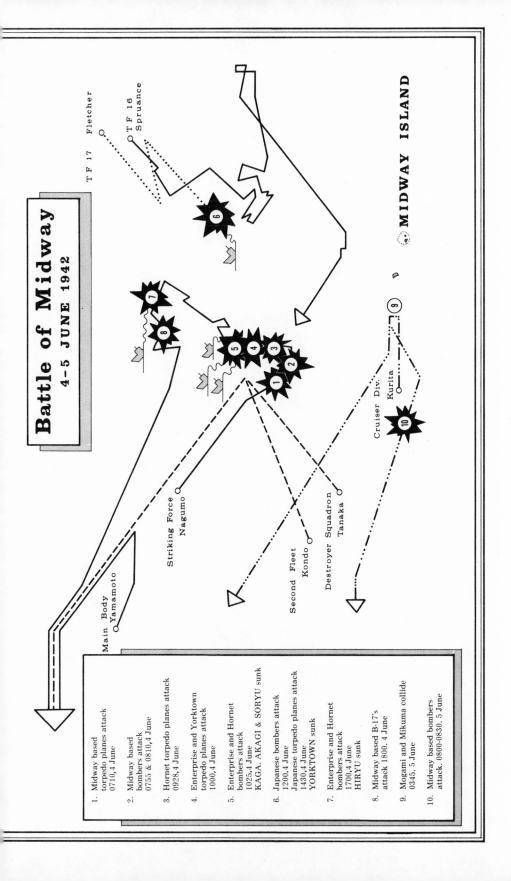

Battle of Midway
4-5 JUNE 1942

TF 17 Fletcher

TF 16 Spruance

MIDWAY ISLAND

Main Body Yamamoto

Striking Force Nagumo

Second Fleet Kondo

Destroyer Squadron Tanaka

Cruiser Div. Kurita

1. Midway based torpedo planes attack 0710, 4 June

2. Midway based bombers attack 0755 & 0810, 4 June

3. Hornet torpedo planes attack 0928, 4 June

4. Enterprise and Yorktown torpedo planes attack 1000, 4 June

5. Enterprise and Hornet bombers attack 1025, 4 June KAGA, AKAGI & SORYU sunk

6. Japanese bombers attack 1200, 4 June Japanese torpedo planes attack 1430, 4 June YORKTOWN sunk

7. Enterprise and Hornet bombers attack 1700, 4 June HIRYU sunk

8. Midway based B-17's attack 1800, 4 June

9. Mogami and Mikuma collide 0345, 5 June

10. Midway based bombers attack. 0800-0830, 5 June

8.

SLAUGHTER OF TORPEDO 8

At 3:30 A.M. the pilots of Torpedo 8 . . . gathered in the ready room, there to sit through a critical dawn. As they entered the low-ceilinged, white-walled steel room, their practiced eyes turned first toward the illuminated 3 ft.-by-3 ft. screen above the teletype machine. Projected from the machine below was the last message that had been received: four PBY patrol planes had made a moonlight torpedo attack on a Japanese occupation force near Midway at 1 A.M. As they settled in their comfortable leather chairs they hauled out their flight charts and copied off the data that had been chalked in the neat columns on the blackboard up front: wind, course, speed, visibility, dew point, nearest land, etc. But the teletype remained silent, and soon most of them had pushed the arm button on their chairs so that they could spend the remainder of their watch in their usual semireclining position. Whatever tension there was relaxed with them.

After daybreak, when it was announced that the ship was secure and they were dismissed by the Skipper, Abbie, as usual, moaned, "I'm hungry," and they went to the ward room for breakfast, where Rusty Kenyon ordered his usual plate of beans, for which he got his usual ribbing from the rest of the boys. By 8, the sun was up in a brilliant sky and most of them were back in their quarters. Scarcely had they got themselves settled for their after-breakfast rest, when the

271

loudspeaker barked for their attention: "All pilots report to ready room." When they got to the ready room they found a new message on the teletype screen: "Midway was attacked this morning by Japanese aircraft and bombers." There was a scraping of wood on wood as each man jerked open the drawer built into the bottom of his chair, and a flurry of commotion as they hauled out helmets, goggles, gloves, and the pistols and hunting knives which the Skipper had made "must" equipment for them against a forced jungle landing. Then they began to copy off the latest flight data from the blackboard.

Presently the teletype began tapping again. The pencils stopped. And all eyes turned up to the screen to read the message, letter by letter, as it was projected: "E-N-E-M-Y N-A-V-A-L U-N-I-T-S S-I-G-H-T-E-D W-I-T-H-I-N S-T-R-I-K-I-N-G D-I-S-T-A-N-C-E. E-X-P-E-C-T-E-D S-T-R-I-K-I-N-G- T-I-M-E 0-9-0-0." Then, after a pause, of almost breathless silence: "L-O-O-K-S L-I-K-E T-H-I-S I-S I-T."

Pencils began to scratch again as the pilots put every last bit of information onto their flight charts. Ellie Ellison leaned over toward Tex Gay with a broad grin. "Good luck," he whispered, as he extended his hand across the aisle to meet Gay's. "Pilots man your planes," ordered the loudspeaker. As the boys rose in silence, the Skipper addressed them: "I think they'll change their course. If you check your navigation, don't think I'm getting lost, just follow me. I'll take you to 'em." As they hurried from the room and climbed up the ladder to the flight deck, not another word was spoken.

Their silence was the grim silence of a football team that has been given the next play by the quarterback and is moving up from the huddle to the line of scrimmage. Before stepping onto the ladder, Tex Gay sidestepped to the sick bay nearby and picked up a tourniquet, which he stuffed into his pocket. When they got on deck, their planes were already there in neat rows. The mechanics were busy and the whine of the inertia starters drowned out the clatter of their trotting feet on the deck. Tucked neatly under the belly of each Douglas Devastator was a white-nosed torpedo—a pickle, as the boys preferred to call them. When they saw the pickles, the boys forgot about the Japs for a split second, for never before had they wheeled their Devastators off the deck with a live pickle in tow. Thus, as they hit the seats of their planes, they were giving more thought to the load they were carrying than to the enemy they were going to carry it to.

When the bull horn blared, "Twelve-minute delay in take-off," Whitey Moore climbed out on the folded wing of his plane and called to Gay who was in front of him and due to be the first of the group to take off: "Tex, if you'll test the wind, I'll test the weight." At 9:12, a stand-by order was shouted and if anything else was said it was lost in the roar of the spinning motors. One after the other the signalman waved off the scouts, the fighters and the dive bombers. Finally, Torpedo 8 was waved up and Tex Gay took his plane off with no difficulty.

After they rendezvoused in the sky, the Skipper took the lead and the 15 planes of Torpedo 8 fell into the prearranged formation in which the Skipper had chosen to take them on their first adventure. Flying in six sections of two and a seventh section of three, with Gay bringing up the rear, the Skipper led them on a course south of west at 300 ft.

After an uneventful hour, the Skipper's voice broke the radio silence: "There's a fighter on our tail." What he saw proved to be a cruiser plane flying at about 1,000 ft. It flew by without paying any apparent attention, but the Skipper and boys knew it had probably radioed an alarm back to the Jap fleet and that they would doubtless be met by a reception committee of fighters.

They kept to their course and the flight continued uneventful until the motor of the plane Plywood Teats was flying, in the last section, began to spurt oil. When the windshield was obscured, Plywood reached outside with a rag to wipe it off. As he did so, he transferred the stick to his left hand. Unwittingly, his thumb pressed the trigger button on the stick and sent eight or ten rounds whizzing past Abercrombie's plane. Quick to understand what had happened, Abbie mopped his brow in mock panic and then grinned broadly at Plywood, who appeared to be roaring with laughter.

Almost another hour had passed since they had seen the Jap plane when two columns of smoke were sighted beyond the horizon. The Skipper dropped down low and the boys followed. Now they roared forward at torpedo-attack level, barely skimming the waves. When they burst over the horizon, it looked as if the entire Jap fleet was before them. They identified the carrier *Soryu* and a cruiser as the burning vessels set afire the day before, and counted in all three carriers, about six cruisers and ten destroyers. The ships were moving away from Midway, as the Skipper had guessed, and the carriers were loaded with planes which apparently were being refueled and rearmed. The Skipper immediately broke radio silence to send his contact report back to the U. S. carrier, giving position and strength.

Then the action the Skipper and the boys had been waiting for began. Anti-aircraft fire went up from the ships and the surface guns began hurling explosive shells. Some 30 Zero fighters that had been circling high above the fleet, awaiting their arrival, began to dive. But the Skipper paid no attention to them. He wiggled his wings, as a signal for the boys to follow, and opened up the throttle.

As the Zeros swooped down on them, the Squadron's rear gunners opened up, making a terrific racket of machine-gun fire, punctuated by the louder, less rapid explosions of the cannon on the Zeros. By the time they were within eight miles of the Jap fleet they were caught in a barrage of fire from the ships.

When the first plane plunged into the water the Skipper, apparently forgetting to press his intercockpit communication button, was heard asking his radioman, Dobbs, in the rear seat: "Was that a Zero?" If Dobbs answered his voice was not heard, but in any case it was not a Zero. It was the first plane of Squadron 8 to go down.

When the second went down, Radioman Bob Huntington spoke from the back of Gay's plane. "Let's go back and help him, sir," he said. "To hell with that," Gay blurted, "we've got a job to do." Then the Skipper got it. His left gas tank hit, his plane literally burst into flame. Tex Gay could see him stand up and try to get out but it was no use. The waves that had been lapping at his undercarriage claimed him and Radioman Dobbs. Dobbs, a veteran enlisted man, had been ordered back to San Diego to become a radio instructor for the duration, after this engagement.

The barrage from the Jap ships grew deadlier. Surface shells, aimed to hit the ocean just ahead of them, were throwing up spouts of water which licked the bellies of the planes. Anti-aircraft filled the air with acrid black smoke. One by one, the planes of Torpedo 8 went down. Flying so close to the water, they might as well have been crashing into a stone wall when they hit it. Tex Gay's mind flashed back to his childhood for a comparison with what was going on around him. There was a far-off day when he had tossed orange peelings in the water from a speedboat. It reminded him of that. The planes hit the water and they were gone, as though they were moving in the opposite direction

There was one plane to Gay's left, close by, and another in front of him and below the nose of his plane. He lowered the nose to see what plane it was and it was gone. When he looked to the left, that plane was gone too. Now there was only Gay's plane left. The Skipper had lost his hope of "a favorable tactical situation." "The worst" had "come to the worst," and there was "only one plane left to make a final run-in." Tex Gay doesn't remember whether at the moment the Skipper's message actually flooded through his mind again, but he had seen the Skipper die and he was determined "to go in and get a hit."

Then the voice of Radioman Bob Huntington came into his ears over the intercom from the rear seat. "They got me," it said. "Are you hurt bad?" asked Gay. "Can you move?" There was no answer. Tex took his eyes off the waves long enough to see that Huntington was lifeless, his head limp against the cockpit. As he turned back, he felt a stab in his upper left arm. The hole in his jacket sleeve told him what had happened. He shifted the stick to his left hand, ripped his sleeve, pressed a machine-gun slug from the wound with his thumb. It seemed like something worth saving, so he sought to put it in the pocket of his jacket. When he found his pocket openings held shut by his safety belt and parachute straps and life jacket, he popped it into his mouth.

He kicked his rudder to make his plane slip and skid so as to avoid the Zeros. He was heading straight for the carrier that the Skipper had picked out. The ship turned hard to starboard, seeking to put its bow forward and avoid his torpedo. He swung to the right and aimed for the port bow, about a quarter length back. When he pushed the button to release his torpedo nothing happened. Apparently the electrical releasing equipment had been knocked out. Since his left arm was practically useless from the bullet and a shrapnel wound in his hand, he held the stick between his knees and released the torpedo with the emergency lever. By now he was only 800 yd., from the ship and close to the water. He managed to execute a flipper, turning past the bridge of the carrier and clearing the bow by about 10 ft. As he passed over the flight deck he saw Jap crewmen running in all directions to avoid his crashing plane. He zoomed up and over but as he sought to turn back, four Zeros dived on him. An explosive bullet knocked out his left rudder pedal and he careened into the sea, a quarter of a mile from the Jap carrier.

The impact slammed his hood shut tightly and the plane began to sink. He opened the hood and rose to the surface. As he reached the surface, he heard the explosion of his torpedo striking home on the

Jap carrier. Floating beside him was a black rubber seat cushion and a deflated rubber boat. Apparently the Jap bullets had broken the straps which held them secure. Afraid that the Zeros would dive again and machine-gun him, Tex held the seat cushion over his head. Two cruisers steamed close by him and a destroyer all but ran him down. The white-clad sailors on the destroyer saw him and ran to the deckside to point him out. However, he was unmolested. In about ten minutes the dive bombers from his carrier, apprised of the Jap fleet's location by the Skipper's contact report, swooped in. As they exhausted their bomb loads, more came in. The Jap fleet was in utter confusion, with most of its air arm trapped on the decks of the carriers where they had been refueling. For two hours the bombers dived, sending their destructive loads into ship after ship.

Thus, with all of its 15 planes destroyed and all but one of its pilots killed in its first engagement, Torpedo Squadron 8 had done its part to rout, for the first time in the war, a Japanese fleet. It had also kept the planes which were refueling on the carrier's deck from taking off in time to meet the attack. Had the Skipper not played his hunch with his faithful boys following his wake, the planes that were caught refueling on the decks of the Jap carriers might have had time to take the air again to reverse the tide of battle . . .

OF FORTY-ONE TORPEDO PLANES LAUNCHED ALMOST simultaneously by the three American carriers, only six returned. However, their sacrificial effort was not in vain, for the Japanese carriers, maneuvering desperately, had to concentrate their fighter and firepower on the torpedo planes—with the result that the Zero fighters were at low altitude when the incoming Dauntless dive-bombers from *Hornet* screamed down to the attack virtually unopposed; also the Japanese carrier decks were loaded with refueling planes which proved a boon to Lieutenant Commander Clarence McCluskey's thirty-six *Enterprise* dive-bombers, next over the targets.

This phase of the battle is told by Lieutenant Clarence E. Dickinson, by the war's end a three-time Navy Cross winner. His collaborator, Boyden Sparkes, was a free-lance magazine writer.

LIEUTENANT CLARENCE E. DICKINSON
AND BOYDEN SPARKES

9.

"THE TARGET WAS
UTTERLY SATISFYING"

Our squadron flew in six wedge-shaped sections, inverted V's, three planes in a section, two sections in a division. We were in step-down formation, both as to sections and divisions; and the second and third divisions were kept closed up just as tight as we could manage. The skipper, Gallaher, was leading the first division. As executive officer I had the second and Charley Ware, as flight officer, was leading the third. Our eighteen gunners, as they sat in their cockpits, facing to the rear, were spaced as men would be sitting on a flight of steps. Any enemy fighters making runs down on us from the rear would thus confront the muzzles of thirty-six .30-calibre machine guns . . .

About a quarter past twelve Lieutenant Commander McCluskey at the front and top of the formation picked up the enemy some forty or forty-five miles ahead and to the left. We headed for them as fast as we could go. What McCluskey had distinguished first, almost halfway to the far horizon, on that dense ocean blue were thin, white lines; mere threads, chalk-white. He knew those must be the wakes of the Japanese ships . . . Because I was less high, it was not until about five minutes after McCluskey saw them that I could see them, too . . .

This was the Japanese striking force. I could see a huge fleet, so many ships that I knew it was their main body. I wanted to keep looking at it but I was obliged to make sure we kept close formation on the skipper's division ahead of me, watch out for my own pilots

277

and also keep an eye out for enemy planes. The enemy combat patrol should have been up at the altitude where we were flying, around 20,000 feet. I expected them and kept looking around . . . We made a slight change to the left to get on a course that would bring us ahead of the enemy. Consequently, within a few minutes, off to my right I had an intoxicating view of the whole Japanese fleet. This was the culmination of our hopes and dreams. Among those ships, I could see two long, narrow, yellow rectangles, the flight decks of carriers. Apparently they leave the decks either the natural wood color or possibly they paint them a light yellow. But that yellow stood out on the dark blue sea like nothing you have ever seen. Then farther off I saw a third carrier. I had expected to see only two and when I saw the third my heart went lower. The southwest corner of the fleet's position was obscured by a storm area. Suddenly another long yellow rectangle came sliding out of that obscurity. A fourth carrier!

I could not understand why we had come this far without having fighters swarming over and around us like hornets. But we hadn't seen a single fighter in the air and not a shot had been fired at us.

Every ship in that fleet bore a distinguishing mark . . . each battleship, cruiser and destroyer advertised itself as Japanese with this marking painted on the forward turret. The turret top appeared as a square of white with a round, blood-red center. But on the deck of each carrier, bow or stern, the marking was exactly like that which appears on their planes . . . On the nearest carrier I could see that this symbol probably would measure sixty feet across; a five-foot band of white, enclosing a fifty-foot disk of red. An enticing target!

There were planes massed on the deck of each carrier and I could clearly see that the flight decks were undamaged, in perfect condition to launch.

"DeLuca, stand by for anything. There ought to be fighters coming."

"I've got everything under control back here, Mr. Dickinson." The calmness with which he spoke pleased me.

"Okay, DeLuca. We'll be going down in a few seconds."

The fleet was passing under us now; we were almost at the middle of its position. Some of the craft below us were recognizable because on our own ships we had collections of scale models of many Japanese ships; our own kind of voodoo. I had studied them thoroughly. Sometimes, to get a dive bomber's view I had placed a model on the deck and then, standing on a chair, looked down on it. So I was confident I could recognize at least some Japanese ships of war that I never before had seen. Certain characteristics of her silhouette made me feel sure that the most distant, that fourth carrier I had first seen coming out of the storm area, was the *Hiryu* and I guessed one of the nearer ones to be her sister ship, the *Soryu*. Now we were at an altitude between 15,000 and 16,000 feet. The next thing I heard through my headphones was the voice of McCluskey.

"Earl Gallaher, you take the carrier on the left and Best, you take the carrier on the right. Earl, you follow me down."

Lieutenant Best, assigned to the other target was the skipper of Bombing Six. I had been unaware of it but Bombing Three, from a third carrier in our force, had been launched after we left. They had arrived at the same time and fortunately their commander had picked the one uncovered carrier in the group of three below us. I continued to be amazed by our luck. We had dreamed of catching Jap carriers but none of us had ever imagined a situation like this where we could prepare for our dive without a trace of fighter opposition; we had supposed the Jap fighters would be coming at us from all angles. I did not understand why they were not, because those bright yellow decks below were absolutely unblemished. Then I saw some of their fighters milling about, close to the water . . . they were finishing a job . . . our torpedo squadrons, one from each of the American carriers, had made an attack at noon . . .

I saw McCluskey's plane and those of his two wing men, nose up and we passed under.

Right after the skipper and his division had started I kicked my rudders back and forth to cause a ducklike twitching of my tail. This was the signal for my division to attack. In my turn I pulled up my nose and in a stalled position opened my flaps. We always do this, throw the plane up and to the side on which we are going to dive, put out the flaps as brakes and then peel-off. I was the ninth man of our squadron to dive.

By the grace of God, as I put my nose down I picked up our carrier target below in front of me. I was making the best dive I had ever made. The people who came back said it was the best dive they had ever made. We were coming from all directions on the port side of the carrier, beautifully spaced. Going down I was watching over the nose of my plane to see the first bombs land on that yellow deck. At last her fighters were taking off and that was when I felt sure I recognized her as the *Kaga;* and she was enormous. The *Kaga* and the

Akagi were the big names in the Japanese fleet. Very likely one, or more, of their newer carriers was better, but to us those two symbolized that which we had trained ourselves to destroy.

The carrier was racing along at thirty knots, right into the wind. She made no attempt to change course. I was coming at her a little bit astern, on the left-hand side. By the time I was at 12,000 feet I could see all the planes ahead of me in the dive. We were close together but no one plane was coming down in back of another as may easily happen.

The target was utterly satisfying. The squadron's dive was perfect. This was the absolute. After this, I felt, anything would be just anticlimax.

I saw the bombs from the group commander's section drop. They struck the water on either side of the carrier. The explosions probably grabbed at her like an ice man's tongs. Earl Gallaher was the next man to drop. I learned later that his big bomb struck the after part of the flight deck, among the parked planes and made a tremendous explosion which fed on gasoline. I had picked as my point of aim the big red disk with its band of white up on the bow. Near the dropping point I began to watch through my sight . . .

As I was almost at the dropping point I saw a bomb hit just behind where I was aiming, that white circle with its blood red center . . . I saw the deck rippling, and curling back in all directions exposing a great section of the hanger below. That bomb had a fuse set to make it explode about four feet below the deck. I knew the last plane had taken off or landed on that carrier for a long time to come. I was coming a little abaft the beam on the port side on a course that would take me diagonally across her deck to a point ahead of her island.

I dropped a few seconds after the previous bomb explosion. After the drop you must wait a fraction of a second before pulling out of the dive to make sure you do not "throw" the bomb, spoil your aim as certainly as when you jerk, instead of squeeze, the trigger of a rifle.

I had determined during that dive that since I was dropping on a Japanese carrier I was going to see my bombs hit. After dropping I kicked my rudder to get my tail out of the way and put my plane in a stall. So I was simply standing there to watch it. I saw the 500-pound bomb hit right abreast of the island. The two 100-pound bombs struck in the forward area of the parked planes on that yellow flight deck. Then I began thinking it was time to get myself away from there and try to get back alive.

I realized that I had seen three Zero fighters taking off the *Kaga* during my dive. As I pulled out over the carrier I saw them again some three or four hundred feet below me and to the right. You do not see Zeros unmoved . . .

So far DeLuca had seen nothing coming from behind or above but any one of those three below was in a position in which, simply by pulling up his nose he could kill me very easily. However, two had passed underneath me, going to the left. When the third passed underneath and went to the left I took a deep breath. The other two had gone after a group of our planes already retiring from the action. The group might well deal with them but I felt quite naked. This third Zero climbed. And how they climb! He went rapidly astern and started a run on us from the rear and above. He started firing when he was 800 yards away, which is much too far. When he was closer, six or seven hundred yards away, DeLuca threw a burst at him. The Jap quit at once and went off to play with something else.

Over on my right a destroyer was shooting at me. He had my range all right but his bursts were popping about a thousand yards ahead of me. He could correct that easily. So each time he would shoot I would pull up, then duck right down to the water.

For some reason I was outguessing him even more easily than I had believed possible at the speed of my plane. Then I looked at the instrument panel. Instead of making between 220 and 250 knots I was crawling. I was only doing about ninety-five! I looked around and discovered with a shock that my landing flaps were down.

Undoubtedly I had grabbed the wrong handle after my dive but at this time I really did some grabbing. Some of our people who were still around told me later on that to them it seemed as if I were demonstrating my Douglas dive bomber. Landing flaps were opening; diving flaps were opening; my wheels were up and down and my activity was like a three-ring circus. Finally everything was closed and, happily for me, somebody put a couple of small bombs on the destroyer that was shooting at me. But I did not know that right then.

Another fighter had passed to the right of me and had slowly drawn ahead. He was stalking a group of our planes that were crossing my course, and his. When this fighter was only a short distance ahead of my fixed guns, I must admit I caught myself thinking, "If I miss him he'll be alive and awfully mad at me." But he was too good an opportunity to let go. I took a good bead on him and began shooting. I fired ten or twenty rounds from each of the guns, two armor piercing bullets for each visible tracer. The Jap pilot must have been hit because suddenly his plane fell off on the left wing and went down, spun into the water, and disappeared.

DeLuca had seen that plane go by us and had heard my guns firing. He yelled over the radio: "Do you think you got him, Mr. Dickinson? Did you get him?"

"Yes, DeLuca, I think I did."

"That's good, Mr. Dickinson."

"Can you see any more back there? I'll take care of the front. You take care of the rear. For Christ's sake keep a good look out."

"Sure, Mr. Dickinson. I'm looking out mighty good . . ."

As we went away from the *Kaga* I could see five big fires in the middle of the Japanese fleet. One was either a battle ship or a big cruiser. The destroyer that had been shooting at me was lying still and smoking heavily amidships where her boilers are. But the three biggest fires were the carriers. They were burning fiercely and exploding. I looked back when I was a couple of miles away. In spite of the succession of incidents this was no more than a few minutes after my bombs had landed on the *Kaga*. She was on fire from end to end and I saw her blow up at the middle. From right abreast the island a ball of solid fire shot straight up. It passed through the fleecy lower clouds which we estimated to be 1200 feet above the water. Some of our flyers who were up higher saw this solid mass of fire as it burst up through the clouds, and they said the fire rose three or four hundred feet still higher. Probably that was gasoline but many of the explosions I was seeing in those three carriers were, I think, from their own bombs parked below on the hangar decks in readiness for planes to be rearmed.

I could not afford to wait another second. My gasoline gauges had suddenly assumed an importance greater than the blazing, ruined carriers. I was dubious about our chances from here on. There was no plane for me to join on the flight back towards our carrier. Those who had been behind me in the dive had passed me during that interval when my flaps were down. I could see some of our planes ahead of me streaking for the carrier but I couldn't afford the gasoline to go wide open trying to catch up with them. When I left the enemy my inboard tanks registered, each one, thirty gallons. If we had to go more than 150 or 175 miles on the return flight sixty gallons ought to be enough, if I was careful. It might not get me aboard but it would get me back . . .

Trying to bring myself home I kept watching my gas gauges. But the right-hand tank, which I was using, suddenly quit. Yet the gauge registered seventeen gallons. Seventeen from thirty—there must have been only thirteen gallons in that tank as we started away from the enemy. I felt as if the devil had just stolen seventeen gallons from me. I switched to the left-hand inboard tank and then immediately began to worry over how much there really was in that one.

AMONG THE FINER ACCOUNTS OF MIDWAY IS THADDEUS V. Tuleja's minute-by-minute narrative of the death of the Japanese carriers. His account of the closing phases of the decisive battle starts at the point when Lieutenant Commander Maxwell F. Leslie and his squadron took off from *Yorktown*.

IO.

TURNING OF THE TIDE

. . . (Leslie), leading his squadron of seventeen dive bombers, had been flying on a course of 225°to 230°, driving hard for the expected point of interception with Nagumo's carriers. If the Japanese were not sighted at this hypothetical position of contact, he was instructed to turn to the right and fly up the last bearing of the enemy reported earlier by search planes from Midway.

Leslie's flight had begun with mishap. His aircraft recently had been equipped with new electrical bomb-release mechanisms. It was the practice for each pilot to arm his bomb after the squadron cleared the carrier and moved into formation. This action would cock the trigger device in the bomb's nose fuse so that it would detonate upon striking its target. When Leslie reached an altitude of 10,000 feet he signalled his squadron to arm bombs, and then leaned over to throw his own electrical arming switch. Either because of faulty wiring or perhaps because of mechanical failure, Leslie's 1000-pound bomb, instead of arming, fell away and dropped harmlessly into the sea.

Feeling his craft suddenly become lighter, Leslie turned in dismay to Lieutenant (j.g.) Paul "Lefty" Holmberg, who was riding in the squadron's Number Two position, just to Leslie's left. Holmberg made signs with his hands to tell Leslie what had happened, and then ordered his gunner to signal the mishap to Leslie's rear-seatman. For a few moments Leslie either could not understand or would not

284

accept the meaning of Holmberg's gestures. Then Ensign Paul Schlegel, flying on Leslie's right side, began to wave his hands frantically, making it painfully clear to the squadron commander that he had lost his bomb.

For Maxwell Leslie this was a bitter twist of fate. He had been in the naval service for twenty years, twelve of which were spent in the air arm of the fleet. He had flown fighters, bombers and scout planes, and at different times during his career had been attached to the carriers *Lexington, Ranger, Enterprise, Saratoga* and *Yorktown*. Since Pearl Harbor he had trained for this moment and had whipped his squadron into a state of splendid war readiness. Now with the supreme test awaiting him, he was entering the battle without a bomb. "When this bad news was confirmed," Holmberg was later to write, "the skipper made many frustrating motions with his hands and lips, as if to say his luck was damnable." Within a few minutes Leslie found out that three other aircraft of his squadron had suffered arming accidents, which meant that he had only thirteen planes with bombs. But at all cost he had to maintain the discipline of the squadron, and he decided to lead the dive anyway and assist in whatever way he could with his fixed machine guns.

He continued to climb until the squadron reached an altitude of 20,000 feet, and it was from this height that he eventually sighted smoke smudges on the horizon to the right of him and correctly assumed that they were from Nagumo's fleet speeding northward toward the American carriers. Immediately he signalled his squadron to wing over to the right to a northwesterly course, and by 10:20 the Japanese ships were only a few miles ahead of him. The mass of clouds which had previously concealed Naguma were all to the left of Leslie now and he could see a number of large enemy ships starting what appeared to be full-speed evasive turns. Since the Japanese fighters had been busy at low altitudes for almost an hour butchering the torpedo planes, there were none at the upper level where Leslie was. He therefore had plenty of time to pick out his target—a fat carrier almost dead ahead of him.

In the meantime McClusky, having missed the Japanese force at the point of interception because of Nagumo's change of course, continued southward for a little while. Finding nothing in sight, he had decided at about 9:30 to turn to the northward, hoping that Nagumo was to the right of him. His eventual turn *away* from Midway proved to be a masterful stroke of judgement, for it closed the range between himself and the Japanese carriers. However, he was not able to see the smoke which had alerted Leslie because, being to the southwest of *Yorktown's* dive bombers, the cloud cover blocked his view. He might have flown over an empty ocean until his fuel gave out and then, after jettisoning his bombs, made the long glide downward to crash land on the sea. Had this happened, Leslie, with only thirteen effective dive bombers, would have had to face the full power of Nagumo's fleet alone. The planes that rode with Leslie and McClusky represented all that was left of the American air strike.

It had been more than an hour earlier, while Nagumo was driving off the last of Midway's air attacks, that the submarine *Nautilus,* having tried unsuccessfully to torpedo a Japanese battleship, came under a ferocious depth-charge attack by enemy destroyers. While the attack was going on, Nagumo turned his Striking Force away from the area, leaving one destroyer behind to hunt down the American submarine. This lone warship was the *Arashi,* skippered by Commander Yasumasa Watanabe. When after an intensive search Watanabe's sonar operator failed to regain sound contact with the *Nautilus,* he decided to give up the hunt and set course to overtake the rest of the fleet. He was now many miles behind Nagumo and he rang up for FULL SPEED AHEAD. The *Arishi's* bow plowed into the waves.

Watanabe was driving hard on a northeasterly course; McClusky was heading to the northwest. Their course converged and at 9:55, when McClusky glanced down through a break in the clouds, he saw the *Arishi's* white trail. He could tell that she was making high speed and guessed that her captain was doing exactly what, at that crucial moment, he was doing—catching up with the rest of the Japanese force. Quickly he estimated the destroyer's course and put his thirty-seven dive bombers on it. So at 10 o'clock that morning, while Leslie was closing in on the Japanese carriers from one direction, McClusky was closing in from another.

Admiral Yamamoto, mastermind of the whole operation, had stationed himself to the northwest of Midway with a force including three battle ships, one light cruiser, a light carrier and nine destroyers. This fleet, had it been in a position to help Nagumo, could have brought an assortment of well over two hundred anti-aircraft guns to battle with the American dive bombers. But Yamamoto, acting upon instincts which will forever confound naval analysts, positioned his fleet hundreds of miles to the west of Nagumo and therefore could bring no support to his carrier commander when he needed it most.

Leslie came upon the Japanese carriers just at the moment they were breaking formation to avoid Massey's torpedo planes. The *Akagi,* carrying her bridge island on the port side, had been steaming westward for several minutes at full speed and was now astern of the *Soryu,* whose sister ship *Hiryu* was far to the north and barely visible. The *Kaga,* with her bridge structure on the conventional starboard side, rolled northward and was almost abreast of the *Soryu's* starboard beam. When the dive bombers appeared, *Akagi* made a dash to the south. In the meantime, *Kaga* and *Soryu* put their rudders over hard and spun around in a tight clockwise turn.

Leslie had already descended to 14,500 feet and was preparing to attack with the bright morning sun at his back. The *Akagi* was to his distant left, so he studied the two carriers ahead of him, both of which were turning to the south. These radical course changes, besides being evasive, indicated that the enemy carriers were getting ready to launch an air strike, since their bows were now faced into the wind.

The 26,900-ton *Kaga,* even from Leslie's great height, looked huge to him when contrasted with the 10,000-ton *Soryu.* "Our target was one of the biggest damn things that I had ever seen," one of Leslie's officers said later. Using only a slight change of course to the left or right, Leslie could have attacked either carrier, but the *Kaga,* because of her great size, was marked for destruction.

Leslie patted his head, a signal which told his wingmen that he was putting his bombless plane into a dive. From level flight he dove down at a 70° angle, with the wind rushing past his wings at 280 knots. Within seconds Holmberg arched over, a 1000-pound bomb beneath his fuselage. Then came the others. The large carrier was squarely in Leslie's sights. He saw dozens of planes spotted for take-off, and forward there was a large red sun painted on the carrier's flight deck on which he took careful aim. At 10,000 feet he opened fire with his machine guns, peppering the deck and bridge with 50-caliber bullets. At 4000 feet his guns jammed; he pulled out and began to climb. Behind him came Holmberg, who could now see the first flashes of gunfire from the fringe of the *Kaga's* flight deck. His dive was perfect as the red disk on the flight deck loomed in his sights. Shrapnel tore at his plane. At an altitude of 2,500 feet, he pushed the electric bomb-release button and immediately jerked at the manual release lever to make sure that his bomb got away.

There was a tremendous burst of fire near the superstructure. Pieces of the *Kaga's* flight deck whirled in the air; a Zero taking off into the wind was blown into the sea; the bridge was a shambles of twisted metal, shattered glass and bodies. Captain Okada, his uniform torn and burned, lay dead amidst the smoking wreckage of his command post. Then came three more vicious explosions, hurling planes over the side, tearing huge holes in the flight deck and starting fires which spread to the hangar deck below. Screaming sailors ran around aimlessly, trailing flames. Officers shouted orders against the deafening blasts. Gasoline poured from the planes' ruptured fuel tanks, and some of the pilots who had not been lucky enough to escape the first bomb blast were cremated at their controls.

The fire raced along rivulets of gasoline, spreading disaster below decks. Men trapped behind blistering bulkheads were roasted alive. Hoses rolled out in a frantic effort to hold back the flames caught fire. Some officers and men, their uniforms smoldering and their faces blackened by smoke, were driven back to the edge of the flight deck and from there they leaped into the sea. Then the fire traveled to the bomb storage lockers. Suddenly there was a thunderous detonation, and sheets of glowing steel were ripped like so much tin foil from the bowels of the ship. The hangar deck was a purgatory within a few minutes, and great clouds of black smoke rose from the *Kaga,* carrying with them the smell of burning gasoline, paint, wood, rubber and human flesh.

Less than two minutes after Leslie's bombers transformed the *Kaga* into a flaming cauldron, McClusky's squadron was ready to pounce on the *Akagi* and *Soryu*. The destroyer *Arashi* had led the *Enterprise's* dive bombers directly to the Japanese Striking Force. Even before Leslie had winged over into his dive, McClusky was picking out his victims. He saw two carriers just ahead turning into the wind to launch aircraft. Dividing his flight into two sections, he called out targets and then signalled his descent. One flight pushed over toward the *Akagi,* the other toward the *Soryu*. It was 10:26.

The first of McClusky's 1000- and 500-pound bombs whistled toward their targets. One bomb crashed near *Akagi's* after elevator and detonated with a hellish blast in the hangar, where a number of planes were waiting to be lifted to the flight deck. The shock wave exploded torpedo warheads, tearing men to bits and starting dozens

of gasoline fires. Damage control parties struggled heroically to iso-
late the flames, but clouds of hot black smoke enveloped them and
one by one the men collapsed from the fumes. Another bomb struck
the flight deck, scattering planes and pilots into the sea. Within a few
minutes the flagship was a floating pyre.

Because of the inferno, damage reports were slow in coming to the
bridge, but the *Akagi's* skipper, Captain Taijiro Aoki, hearing the
dull thunder below decks, had no illusions about the fate of his ship;
nor did Rear Admiral Ryunosuke Kusaka, Nagumo's Chief of Staff.
Both men understood that the bomb hits were fatal and that the
Akagi was doomed.

Nagumo, however, was unwilling to accept the fact that the tide of
battle was shifting with such appalling speed in his disfavor. Aoki
politely told him that the ship was finished and would have to be
abandoned. Nagumo's anger flared up. The situation *had* to be
brought under control; he would not leave the ship. Kusaka, who was
well acquainted with Nagumo's fiery temper, tried to intervene as
diplomatically as possible.

"Sir, our radio is smashed and we cannot communicate with the
other ships. Should you not transfer your command to another vessel
so that you can continue to direct the battle?"

Nagumo still refused to abandon ship. Finally Kusaka directed
several officers to take the Admiral by the hand and pull him away.
By now the fires were swirling around the bridge, blocking their
descent by ladder, and they had to make their escape by a line hanging from the bridge structure.

The scene on the flight deck was grotesque: craters belching
smoke, twisted wreckage, and the bodies of officers and men scattered
everywhere. The unmanned machine guns, heated by the fires, began
to spray bullets in all directions. Now and then a dull explosion came
from deep inside the ship.

A destroyer came alongside the *Akagi* and took the Admiral and
his staff to the cruiser *Nagara,* from whose mast Nagumo broke his
flag. From her bridge he watched his splendid command disintegrate.

The *Soryu* had been bombed too. Her engines were stopped, water
poured into the bilges, the pumps failed to work, and hundreds of
scorched sailors, fleeing before the flames, threw themselves into the
sea. *Soryu's* commanding officer, Captain Ryusaku Yanigimoto,
stood resolutely on his blackened bridge. A destroyer pulled alongside and an attempt was made to persuade him to leave the doomed

ship. He refused to be rescued and was last heard calmly singing the Japanese national anthem, while clouds of smoke closed about him.

All three carriers were fiery derelicts now, and fire fighting parties left on board fought a losing battle against the flames. Many sailors from the *Kaga* were swimming in the oily water when a torpedo from an American submarine streaked toward their burning ship. Instead of exploding it struck the *Kaga's* side at an angle and then came apart, the warhead sinking and the buoyant after section floating free. Immediately several Japanese sailors swam over to the floating part and hung on.

The *Kaga* burned fiercely throughout the entire afternoon and by twilight was a gigantic torch lighting up the evening sky. At 7:25 she was shaken by heavy explosions, and slipped beneath the waves with hundreds of her crew.

Akagi's fire fighters were able to do no better against the searing flames which gutted their ship. At 5:15 that evening Captain Aoki ordered the Emperor's portrait removed. With a solemn ceremony, the picture was unhooked from the bulkhead, carried through an honor guard, and then placed on board a destroyer which carried it away. Two hours later the raging fires had reached the engine rooms, and Aoki ordered his crew to abandon ship. All through the long night she drifted, throwing her flickering light against the black sky. She was still drifting the next day when dawn broke, and she was finally sent to the bottom by a torpedo from a Japanese destroyer, in order to prevent her from being boarded and salvaged by the enemy. She went down about twenty miles to the westnorthwest of *Kaga,* but many of her crew were saved.

The *Soryu,* last to be hit during the morning dive bombing attack, was the first to go. Flames engulfed her, and at 7:13 that evening she rolled under, carrying her captain and over 700 of her crew with her. She went down only twenty-five miles to the northwest of *Kaga.*

Although the three carriers managed to stay afloat for hours the battle had early been decided by Leslie and McClusky. The dive bombing attack had taken place between 10:24 and 10:26, and in those two crucial minutes Nagumo lost seventy-five percent of his carrier force—marking the beginning of the end of Japan's imperial ambitions in the Pacific.

However, even while the three carriers were burning, the Japanese tried to wrest an ultimate victory from defeat. While Nagumo shifted his flag to the *Nagara,* tactical command was assumed temporarily by Rear Admiral Hiroaki Abe, who rode in the cruiser *Tone.* At 10:50 he informed Yamamoto and Kondo, commander of the Midway invasion fleet, that fires were raging aboard the *Akagi, Kaga* and *Soryu,* but that he planned to attack the enemy carriers with the surviving *Hiryu.* This Japanese carrier, because she had been so far north when the American dive bombers arrived, was not immediately sighted and therefore enjoyed immunity for another six and a half hours. From her masthead flew the flag of Rear Admiral Tamon Yamaguchi. While several destroyers circled about the three burning carriers, Abe signalled Yamaguchi to launch an air attack against the American ships; Yamaguchi, a forceful and farsighted individual, had already given the command. At 10:40, just sixteen minutes after Leslie had led his own attack against the *Kaga,* eighteen Japanese dive bombers, under Lieutenant Michio Kobayashi, with a light fighter escort, were taking off from the *Hiryu's* flight deck, and by 11:00 they were speeding northeastward. The bombers climbed to 13,000 feet and took their heading from several American planes which were returning from their recent attack, unwittingly leading the enemy to their carrier.

The American carrier which Admiral Abe decided to attack was the *Yorktown,* for the Japanese scout planes which sighted Task Force Seventeen did not discover Spruance's two carriers. At 11 o'clock that morning, the *Yorktown,* hull down to the northwest, was spotting ten planes for a reconnaissance flight which was to fan out from 280° to 020° (for Fletcher was still convinced that there was a fourth enemy carrier somewhere to the northwest). Following the launching of the search group, the *Yorktown's* hangar deck was spotted with seven aircraft fully gassed and loaded with 1000-pound bombs. Thirteen more were readied on the flight deck for immediate launching, while a dozen fighters rose into the wind to orbit above the *Yorktown's* wake on combat air patrol. These planes had just been launched when two bombers from the *Enterprise* attack group, with tanks almost dry, touched down on the *Yorktown's* flight deck. They had been badly shot up in the action and were immediately struck below. Then four of *Yorktown's* own fighters landed with sputtering engines and wobbly wings. Some exhausted pilots landed on the wrong carriers; but they were the lucky ones. Many never got back.

While these aircraft were winging homeward, Lieutenant Michio Kobayashi's eighteen dive bombers and six Zeros were dropping down to lower altitudes to avoid detection by enemy lookouts. Precisely at 11:59 the *Yorktown's* radar officer, Vance M. Bennett, watched a group of phosphorescent "pips" moving in from the left on the scope. Their speed told him that they were returning echoes from approaching planes. For a few seconds he tracked them. They were forty-six miles away, coming in on a course of 250°, which would bring them directly to the *Yorktown*. Immediately he called to the bridge, warning both Admiral Fletcher and Captain Buckmaster of the impending attack. At that moment there were several fighters being gassed. Refueling was stopped instantly. On the *Yorktown's* stern there was an auxiliary fuel tank holding 800 gallons of aviation gasoline. Buckmaster ordered it dumped over the side. Fuel lines were drained and then refilled with carbon dioxide gas under twenty pounds of pressure. Watertight doors were slammed shut and dogged down, and the fighters which had been circling over the *Yorktown* were vectored out to meet the incoming Japanese.

Lieutenant Commander Leslie, who had already led his dive bombers triumphantly into the carrier's landing circle, was ordered to form a combat air patrol and to stay clear of the *Yorktown's* anti-aircraft fire. Doctors and pharmacists mates rushed to the wardroom, where they waited for wounded shipmates to be carried in; gunners cocked their weapons; and damage control parties, stationed throughout the ship, were poised for the first explosion. On the flag bridge Admiral Fletcher, helmet pushed down over his head, pored over a large chart and plotted his next move, while the officers and men about him buttoned up their shirts to the neck, rolled down their sleeves, and tucked trouser legs into their socks as a precaution against flash burns.

In a few minutes the *Yorktown* was ready for action. Her cruisers and destroyers were maneuvering at 25 knots into an anti-aircraft screening formation, 2000 yards away from her. Every gun that could be trained toward the western sky was fixed on the tiny cluster of Kobayashi's planes rising from the distant sea. American fighter pilots, with guns blazing, intercepted the Japanese squadron when it was still twenty miles to the west of the *Yorktown*. Captain Buckmaster, through his binoculars, could see a long trail of black smoke with a bright spot of flame leading it downward to the sea. Then came others as his fighter planes lashed furiously at Kobayashi's bombers.

Marc Mitscher, staring northward from the *Hornet's* bridge, could also see the falling planes. Suddenly he sighted several aircraft heading for his ship and braced himself for an attack; but after a few tense moments they were identified as American dive bombers. They were, in fact, planes from Leslie's flight which, having been waved off from the *Yorktown* because of the Japanese attack, were trying to land on the *Hornet* before all their fuel was gone. Mitscher cleared the deck for them, but one aircraft, flown by a wounded pilot, crashlanded with such force that all its machine guns began firing, spattering the bridge and deck with .50 caliber bullets which killed an admiral's son and four enlisted men and knocked down twenty others to the deck.

Far away on the horizon *Yorktown's* fighters took a heavy toll of Kobayashi's bombers. Eleven plummeted into the sea, and only seven of the original eighteen were able to break through the combat air patrol and the anti-aircraft fire from the carrier's screening cruisers and destroyers. As the Japanese planes approached their diving position, Captain Buckmaster had his 5-inch guns firing, his engines turning for their maximum speed of 30.5 knots, and his helmsman shifting the rudder from left to right to throw off the enemy's aim. Then the lead plane arched over to begin its dive.

Everyone dropped instinctively as the first bomb came down, but it missed the *Yorktown,* throwing up a geyser of gray water on the carrier's starboard side. The pilot never pulled out of his dive. After leveling off, he flew close aboard the port side of the ship, thumbing his nose at the *Yorktown's* bridge. A bullet ripped into his tail and he plunged into the sea off the carrier's bow. The second Japanese pilot released his bomb just before his plane drove through a withering anti-aircraft cross-fire and disintegrated in its flight, part of its wing falling on the *Yorktown's* deck. The bomb crashed on the starboard side of the ship near the Number Two elevator and tore a huge hole in the flight deck. Many of the men who were manning the guns in this area of the ship were killed, and bomb fragments, spattering the deck below, started fires in three stored aircraft. Lieutenant A. C. Emerson, the hangar deck officer, made a desperate lunge for the sprinkler system, releasing a curtain of water which doused the flames.

The next bomb came down in a perfect trajectory, ripped through the flight deck and detonated with a hollow roar deep inside the smoke stack. The sudden flash of heat was intense. Shards of burning paint flaked off the stack; photographic film in the ship's dark room caught fire; flames spread into the Executive Officer's compartment, and the uptakes were ruptured. Clutching the weather screen of the flag bridge, Commander Walter G. Schindler, Fletcher's Gunnery Officer, watched the attack with a British naval observer, Commander Michael B. Laing, who, between bomb drops, jotted down hasty notes.

The third and last bomb to hit the *Yorktown* speared through the starboard side and exploded below decks. The terrific heat generated by the detonation started wild fires in a rag stowage compartment which was alarmingly close to the forward magazines and gasoline tanks. The fuel storage compartment was quickly bathed in carbon dioxide and the magazines flooded. Meanwhile damage control parties tried to smother the burning rags.

This was the extent of Kobayashi's spirited attack. His decimated flight returned to the *Hiryu,* while smoke billowed from the *Yorktown.* The retreating Japanese air strike consisted of only five dive bombers and three fighters, and it was not Kobayashi who led them away, for he had fallen in flames.

The second bomb had stabbed its way into the very bowels of the *Yorktown.* Three uptakes, which carried combustion gases away from the fire rooms, were severely shattered; two boilers were completely disabled, and the fires under three others were snuffed out; and choking, acrid smoke in several of the fire rooms drove personnel up the ladders. The ship's speed dropped abruptly: twenty knots, fifteen, ten, then six.

The officers and men in the Number One boiler room sweated behind their gasmasks. With two burners working, they managed to keep a head of steam in the boiler, restoring to the battered ship a limited amount of her former strength. At 12:20, however, all engines stopped and the *Yorktown* came to a halt.

Admiral Fletcher now faced the same unpleasant necessity which Nagumo had faced less than two hours before when the *Akagi* was hit. The *Yorktown's* radar was crippled, leaving her blind; planes in the air, in need of refueling, were directed to land on the *Enterprise* and *Hornet;* and *Yorktown's* immobility, which transformed her into a sitting duck, rendered her useless as a flagship. It became imperative for Fletcher to transfer his flag to another ship so that he could direct the battle and maintain communications with Admiral Spruance. Reluctantly he signalled Rear Admiral William W. Smith, Cruiser Group Commander riding in the *Astoria,* to take him off the burning carrier, and then he ordered Spruance to send air cover to the *Yorktown.*

While Fletcher rounded up several key people of his staff, the *Astoria's* motor launch was lowered to the water's edge, then bucked through the slight swells, finally positioning itself below the massive gray wall of the carrier's side. Manila lines dangled from the flag bridge to the launch and officers and men began the long seventy-five-foot descent, hand over hand. Admiral Fletcher put a leg over the weather screen, got a grip on the line and then thought better of it. "I'm too damn old for this sort of thing," he said. "Better lower me." A bowline was tied in another line, looped around his waist, and he made the descent to the launch with several sailors paying out the line from the smoking flag bridge. Once on board the *Astoria,* Fletcher said, "Tell the *Portland* to take the *Yorktown* in tow." The *Portland* was another cruiser attached to Task Force Seventeen.

Admiral Spruance, whose *Enterprise* was hull down on the horizon, had sighted the smoke pouring from Fletcher's flagship, and at 12:35 he signalled the cruisers *Pensacola* and *Vincennes,* both of his own screen, plus two of his destroyers to strengthen the *Yorktown's* anti-aircraft barrage in case another Japanese air attack developed. And one did.

Before Leslie's and McClusky's bombs fell, Nagumo had ordered a new, fast scout plane to take off from the *Soryu* and shadow the American force. This pilot managed to see thing which the pilots of the *Hiryu* attack group had missed. *Kobayashi's* fliers, after bombing the *Yorktown,* reported enthusiastically by radio that the enemy carrier—the only one the Japanese knew anything about at the time—was smoking and dead in the water. This news, of course, cheered the Japanese admirals, but only temporarily. When the pilot of the *Soryu* scout plane returned from his search mission and found his carrier in flames, he immediately landed on the undamaged *Hiryu,* rushed to the bridge and informed Admiral Yamaguchi that his radio had not been working and he could only now report that the American force was composed not of one carrier but three!

Yamaguchi immediately decided to launch another attack, but there were only ten torpedo planes and six fighters ready for immediate take-off. Feeble as the strike was, Yamaguchi could not waste a moment, for he had to cripple the other two American carriers before they crippled him. He ordered the flight launched without delay.

The strike was put under the command of Lieutenant Tomonaga, who had led the attack on Midway earlier that morning. He climbed into his cockpit with Oriental calm, although he must have known that for him this flight had no return. His left wing tank had been shot full of holes over Midway and he roared off the *Hiryu's* flight deck with only his right tank topped off.

At 12:45 Tomonaga's flight was heading eastward while the *Yorktown's* repair parties, with feverish speed, put out the fires, cleared away the charred wreckage and patched up the holes in the flight deck. By 1:40 that afternoon the jagged holes in the exhaust uptakes were closed off and repairs deep inside the ship were well enough along to allow the engineers to cut in four boilers. A coppery haze drifted from the lip of the *Yorktown's* stack. Slowly she began to move; men cheered; the blue and yellow breakdown flag, flying from the foretruck since the attack, was hauled down with a jerk, and then the engine room reported: "We're ready to make twenty knots or better."

Fighters on combat air patrol were called down for refueling, and the ship turned majestically into the wind. Leslie and Holmberg, who had been waved off during the first attack were now signalled to land. Only moments before, their fuel tanks had run dry and they were forced to glide down near the *Astoria,* crashing into the sea. Leslie and his gunner climbed into their rubber raft and were soon picked up by the cruiser's launch. Holmberg, who made a fine water landing despite the fact that one wheel would not retract, stepped out on the wing of his plane with his chartboard and parachute. His gunner dragged out the rubber raft, inflated it, and they both stepped inside just as the plane sank. The raft had been punctured by a piece of shrapnel and within a few minutes both men were treading water. However, the launch arrived quickly, hauled them in and brought them to the *Astoria*.

Fighters had already landed on the *Yorktown* and were being refueled when the ship's radar operator picked up another flight of planes on a bearing of 340°, thirty-three miles away. The alarm clanged throughout the ship, fueling was stopped, guns were manned, and Buckmaster braced himself for another attack. Gasoline lines were again drained and refilled with carbon dioxide; six fighters orbiting overhead were vectored out to meet the incoming attack, and eight of the ten fighters on board, each with a little more than twenty gallons of gasoline in their tanks, began rolling off the flight deck and climbing into the bright northwestern sky.

Tomonaga's air strike was intercepted when it was about ten miles from the *Yorktown*. While the American fighters engaged the Zeros, Tomonaga ordered his torpedo planes to break formation and attack the carrier from different angles. Two or three, spattered with machine-gun bullets, crashed before they could launch their torpedoes; Tomonaga was able to drop his only an instant before his plane took a direct hit and exploded, scattering pieces of wing and fuselage over the sea. The encircling cruisers and destroyers looked like a mass of flame as every gun fired at the attackers.

The last *Yorktown* fighter to take off was in the battle before its wheels were cranked up. The pilot banked to the right, opened fire on a torpedo plane, climbed and was hit in turn by a diving Zero. With his aircraft out of control he looped over, bailed out, floated down to the water and was rescued by a destroyer after he had been in the air only about sixty seconds.

Of the five enemy planes which survived the attack, four made fairly accurate torpedo drops. The *Yorktown* twisted violently and avoided two torpedoes, but the other two crashed into her port side. There were muffled explosions, like rolling thunder, and it seemed to those on deck that the *Yorktown* had been lifted a foot or two out of the water. Paint flew off the bulkheads, books toppled from their racks, and electrical power failed, plunging the lower decks into darkness. The whine of the generators petered out; the rudder, turned to the left at the time of the explosions, was jammed tight, and the steam pressure which had given the *Yorktown* a momentary reprieve vanished.

Men stared at each other; a few looked over the side, dumbfounded, and saw beneath the yellowish haze of the explosion a pool of black oil which was pouring from the *Yorktown's* ravaged side. The deck was no longer even. Shortly after the torpedo attack the clinometer showed a list of seventeen degrees, and this continued to increase until it reached an alarming twenty-six degrees. Chairs in the officers' wardroom glided along the deck and tumbled in disorder against the port bulkhead, and the pots and pans in the galley hung at a rakish angle. It was difficult to walk and many sailors could not get their bearings in the darkness below and bumped into one another as they tried to find a way out of their listing compartments. Up on the flight deck hoses were being run out, and a mess attendant, member of a gun crew, was running around with a 5-inch projectile cradled in his arms.

Commander C. E. Aldrich, the ship's damage control officer, informed Captain Buckmaster that without power for counterflooding he could do nothing to correct the list. Lieutenant Commander J. F. Delaney, the engineering officer, had already reported that all the fire rooms were dead and all power lost. The list had diminished the *Yorktown's* righting moment and the flooding reduced her stability.

The torpedo had plowed into *Yorktown's* side fifteen feet below the waterline, and the concussion wave warped the quick-acting doors on the third deck. Many of the living compartments on the fourth deck were flooded, and gurgling sea water had already reached the first platform level in the forward and after engine rooms. She was heeled over so far to port now that Buckmaster felt she might turn turtle in a few minutes. Wearily he turned to an officer nearby. "Pass the word to abandon ship," he said.

WITH THE IMMEDIATE SINKING OF THREE OF YAMA-moto's carriers—the fourth lingered a bit before going down—the Midway operation was cancelled. In addition to these losses, 350 Japanese planes were destroyed and the best of her naval aviators were dead. The next day, June 5, dive-bombers and torpedo planes from *Hornet* and *Enterprise* found heavy cruiser *Mogami* and sank her. As the battered armada steamed to sanctuary, an air officer described Fleet Admiral Yamamoto: Dazed, glassy-eyed, "he sat sipping rice gruel helplessly on the forward bridge."

The United States victory had turned the tide of war. Yamamoto now realized that Japan had lost the initiative in the Pacific. He had hoped to win the war within one year, or before American industry could attain peak war production, and the conquest of Midway had been the key factor in his overall plans. Its loss, but particularly the loss of his first-line carriers and trained pilots, which required more than two years to replace, was the essence of Yamamoto's setback. Midway clearly presaged Japan's ultimate defeat; her hitherto unbeaten Combined Fleet was never again to sortie for such grandiose purposes.

Rear Armiral Ernest M. Eller analyzes the great victory. We have met him before.

II.

THE BATTLE ANALYZED

. . . Japan still had overwhelming numerical superiority; she still could have succeeded in her first need of destroying the aircraft carrier heart of the Pacific Fleet and winning the Pacific. That she failed can be laid to crucial errors by the Japanese admirals as much as to the genius of leadership of Admirals Nimitz and Spruance and the sacrificial heroism of the resolute air groups of our three lonely available carriers: *Enterprise, Hornet,* and *Yorktown.*

Some of the gross Japanese errors were:

Failure to allow for the unforeseen, the likeliest event of war. They fatuously depended on surprise and lack of fleet opposition as at Pearl Harbor. They did not allow for the possibility of codes being read or submarine reports of fleet sorties. They had no submarines reporting U. S. carrier movements at Pearl Harbor. They stationed submarines south of Midway too late to warn of the passage of Fletcher and Spruance's carrier task forces. Even after being sighted approaching Midway, they did not send out a vigorous search on the fateful morning of June 4, 1942.

Division of force. Despite every other error, Admiral Yamamoto might still have retrieved the day and won Midway had he kept his force concentrated. His main goal was "decisive fleet action" yet he split his strength into many fragments from the Aleutians to Midway in a complex plan. Thus dispersed were four smaller carriers with

299

combined air strength equivalent to two heavies. What a difference they would have made had they been near by on June 4th!

His main force of seven battleships and seven cruisers cruised hundreds of miles from the fast carriers. That deprived him of night engagement chances and deprived the carriers of added sorely needed anti-aircraft protection, for the Japanese were inferior to the U. S. Navy in adequacy of anti-aircraft armament.

Overconfidence. This entered into the foregoing errors. It also caused the Japanese to omit the fine carrier *Zuikaku* from the Midway operation. On May 20th she reached Japan undamaged from the Coral Sea, except for a depleted air group, but was not used since it was "impossible to give the replacement personnel enough shipboard training" to make her effective.

On the other hand, *Yorktown,* with bomb damage estimated to take 90 days to repair, reached Pearl Harbor the afternoon of May 27th, was repaired by 1,400 yard workmen feverishly working day and night, took on a new air group drawn from three other groups, and sailed just in time for Midway on May 31st!

Overconfidence led to the final nail in the Japanese coffin of errors. After launching the Midway strike early on June 4th, Admiral Nagumo had ninety-three planes standing by armed for possible ship targets. He had started to rearm them for shore attack when a search plane reported our ships. Although involved in repelling shore-based air attack and recovering his first strike, he could have launched a partial strike against our carriers at any time in the hour between the last attack by Midway shore-based aircraft (fifty-two airplanes, no hits) and that of the first carrier torpedo airplanes . . .

Regardless of their numerous disastrous errors, the Japanese might still have won except for the timely, aggressive, and resolute action of the U. S. Navy. Commentators on the Battle of Midway have ascribed the United States success against much larger forces to breaking and reading the Japanese code. This far oversimplifies. Reading the code was undoubtedly a key; but the Japanese might have been transmitting false information as a ruse.

It took great courage for Admiral Nimitz to pull his first team from the South Pacific where Japanese success ran at flood tide. It took courage to send his ships against numerically overwhelming odds. It took the utmost vigor and audacity in action of the crews that faced the odds. The issue long hung in the balance and was finally tipped to our side by the heroism and skill of a handful of carrier pilots.

A large reason for our victory was the cool, resolute, and unerring leadership on the scene by Admiral Spruance. He has been criticized for retiring to the east during the night of June 4th and for not pushing to the west after June 6th. Those then on Admiral Nimitz' staff know that the "fog of war" hung heavy and dark. For long we were not sure of victory or its extent. An even thicker haze shrouded those in the middle of the mêlée.

But in his calm, accurate, daring mind Admiral Spruance weighed all factors and played his strength to the utmost. Twice Admiral Yamamoto tried to trap him. Twice Admiral Spruance outwitted him: "Toward sundown on June 4th," he says, "I decided to retire to the eastward so as to avoid the possibility of night action with superior forces. . . . The Japanese did order a night attack. "When the day's action on June 6th was over . . . we were short of fuel, and I had a feeling, an intuition perhaps, that we had pushed our luck as far to the westward as it was good for us . . ."

PART IV

GUADALCANAL AND THE NORTHWARD DRIVE: THE OFFENSIVE BEGINS

THE UNITED STATES TOOK THE OFFENSIVE FOR THE first time when on August 7, 1942 the Marines stepped ashore on Guadalcanal and Tulagi in the remote Solomon Islands. The violent campaign in the South Pacific which followed lasted more than a year and cost the lives of thousands of Allied seamen; dozens of warships were sunk in the black, shark-infested waters, where six major naval engagements were fought. Even today, with a perspective of thirty-odd years, the names "Watchtower" and "Ironbottom Sound" retain a grim, trenchant clarity synonymous with death. Guadalcanal, dis-

303

covered by the Spanish explorer Don Alverado Medana in 1568, lies at the lower end of a double-stranded island chain extending five hundred and sixty miles on a northwest-southeast track, through which flows the narrow, deep-water New Georgia Sound, aptly nick-named The Slot by American sailors.

Almost nothing was known of the Solomons when Admiral King and Vice Admiral Robert L. Ghormley initially discussed the offensive, which was designed, among other things, to protect our lines of communication with Australia. Informed that he was to be Commander South Pacific Force and Area—"an important and difficult task"—Ghormley was ordered to establish headquarters in Auckland, New Zealand, and an advance base in the Fijis; and he was to prepare to mount an amphibious invasion in early autumn, using the 1st Marine Division. Subsequently Ghormley called on the Bureau of Personnel for fifty officers to form a staff, headed by Rear Admiral Daniel J. Callaghan and Marine Brigadier Dewitt Peck, and on May 1 he departed for the South Pacific.

From the start colossal problems plagued "Operation Watchtower," and one of the worst perhaps was securing current maps of the target area—the only maps available were German, dating back to the turn of the century. This ludicrous situation was eased in due course by a great number of interviews with Anzacs who had lived in the islands. Persistent intelligence officers and cartographers began to arrive at a picture of the Solomons, and the picture was far from sanguine. Guadalcanal, ninety miles long and twenty-five wide, was muddy and malaria-infested, and it rained more often than not; forbidding mountain ranges rose eight thousand feet above the sweltering floor of the jungle; vast fields of shoulder high kunai stretched out for miles on the plains. A few prospectors lived in the ridges and scratched the alluvial sands for grains of gold, while below there was an occasional copra planter.

By contrast, Tulagi was almost pleasant. A community formerly under British rule, with an Australian Air Force base, copra plantations, a Lever Brothers trading post and even tennis courts, this island was the seat of civilization in the Solomons. Its shopkeepers were predominantly Chinese, descendants of the four hundred who had swum across Savo Sound when the schooner *St. Paul* fought it out with King Solomon's shoals in 1865, and lost. Because of its good harbor, the Royal Navy established a coaling station here twenty years later, and soon a few missionaries came out.

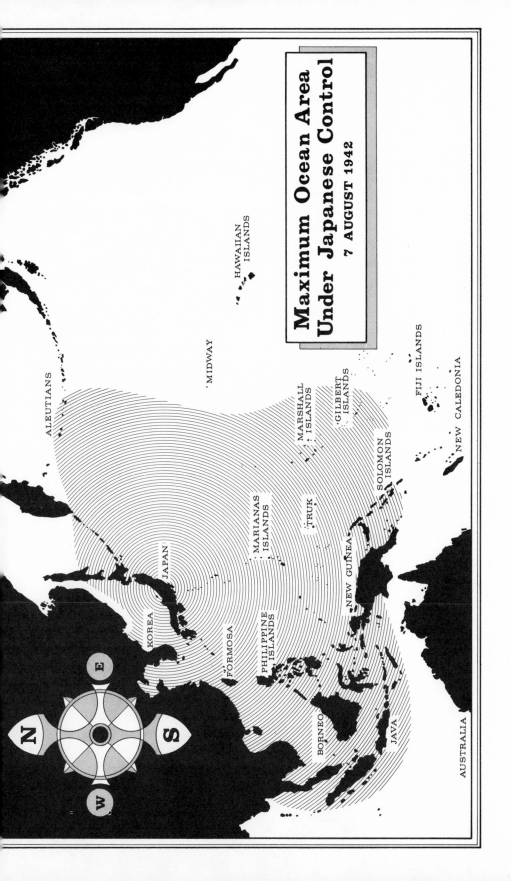

Maximum Ocean Area
Under Japanese Control
7 AUGUST 1942

Up to this stage of the conflict, the principal opponents of Japanese rule had been Australian coastwatchers—those extraordinary and intrepid souls who risked instant death spying out enemy movements. They reported by tele-radio to their headquarters in Sydney via an inter-island network which the Imperial forces were unable to silence at any time during the war. They were aided by woolly-headed Melanesians, the local defense force and one of the better reasons for our success in that otherwise soporific emerald inferno.

The many-faceted story of Guadalcanal is presented by a number of distinguished authors. We have first Nimitz and Potter, who tell us something of the problems of strategic decision which preceded the invasion, and of the mounting of "Operation Watchtower" on a crash basis.

FLEET ADMIRAL CHESTER W. NIMITZ AND E. B. POTTER

I.

THE INVASION IS MOUNTED

After Midway, both Admiral Nimitz and General MacArthur were of the opinion that the counteroffensive should be launched . . . There were difficulties. Nimitz, as Commander in Chief Pacific Fleet and Pacific Ocean Areas, controlled the marines, the transports to carry them to the beachhead, and the carriers and gunnery vessels needed to support them. The Solomons however were all within MacArthur's Southwest Pacific Area. Accordingly, Nimitz and MacArthur each, with some reason, insisted that the entire campaign should be under his command. The latter moreover had his own idea about how to attain the objective. Give him the fleet and its carriers and the 1st Marine Division, said MacArthur, and he would go in and recapture Rabaul in a single uninterrupted operation.

There is much to be said for MacArthur's bold strategy. Rabaul was growing steadily more formidable. With each month of delay it would be harder to capture. Once it was in Allied hands, the Japanese in the Solomons and on Papua would be hopelessly cut off, the threat to Australia and United States-Australia sea communications would be entirely removed, and the way would be open for an Allied advance on the Philippines. But the Navy was unalterably opposed to sending scarce carriers and its single division of amphibious troops across the reef-strewn, virtually uncharted Solomon Sea into the teeth of a complex of enemy air bases. Later on, with more carriers and more amphibious troops at their disposal—and more experience in using them—naval strategists could afford to be more daring. They would in fact stage amphibious assaults on the most strongly defended enemy positions using air support from carriers only. But in the present circumstances they favored the step-by-step approach as the more likely to achieve success and avoid disaster. They insisted moreover that Pacific Fleet forces should remain under naval control.

Here was an impasse that could be settled only in Washington, for Nimitz and MacArthur was each supreme in his own area. Here also was another of the many difficulties resulting from divided command within a single theater. Should the entire Pacific have been put under a single officer? There were convincing arguments for such a move. There were equally strong arguments that with a military front extending from the Aleutians to Australia, the strategic problems of the various areas were on too large a scale for one officer to grasp. Proponents of the latter view decried uncritical adherence to the principle of unified command. These advocated unified command only within a geographic entity that gives coherence to operations. Their opinion prevailed, and for better or worse, MacArthur's Southwest Pacific Area and Nimitz' Pacific Ocean Areas remained separate and independent commands, responsible only to the Joint Chiefs of Staff.

It was within the Joint Chiefs that the differences were resolved. In a series of conferences, General Marshall and Admiral King reached agreement and on July 2, 1942 issued a directive that substantially followed the Navy's proposals. The opening operations, seizure and occupation of the Santa Cruz Islands, Tulagi, and adjacent positions, would be under the strategic control of Admiral Nimitz. To facilitate command problems in this first step, the boundary between the South Pacific and the Southwest Pacific Areas was shifted westward to 159° East Longitude, just west of Guadalcanal. As soon as a suitable base had been secured in the Tulagi area, the strategic command would pass to General MacArthur, who would coordinate a move up the Solomons with a second thrust—up the Papuan Peninsula to Salamaua and Lae. The two Allied advances would then converge on Rabaul. Target date for the initial invasions, called Operation WATCH-TOWER, was set for August 1.

Admiral Nimitz, anticipating the Joint Chiefs' directive, had almost completed basic planning for Operation WATCHTOWER by the first week in July. Vice Admiral Ghormley, as Nimitz' deputy in the South Pacific Area, would exercise strategic control, with Vice Admiral Frank Jack Fletcher, of Coral Sea and Midway fame, in tactical command of the Expeditionary Force. From King's staff, where he had headed the War Plans Division, came Rear Admiral Richmond Kelly Turner to command the Amphibious Force. The 1st Marine Division, which would make the assault, was to be commanded by Major General Alexander A. Vandegrift, who had learned the business of fighting in the jungles of Nicaragua and the theory of amphibious warfare on the staff of the Fleet Marine Force.

A month was of course an uncomfortably brief period in which to assemble forces, work out details, and complete training and rehearsals for so complex an operation as an amphibious assault. Moreover, adequate reinforcements and proper air and surface support were hard to come by. The invasion of North Africa, planned for November, had top priority for everything. MacArthur's three divisions, assigned to the protection of Australia, could not be touched. South Pacific bases would have to be stripped of part of their defense forces to provide garrison troops to follow up the marines. Little wonder the somewhat baffled participants in Operation WATCH-TOWER soon began calling it "Operation Shoestring."

While Fletcher and Turner were conferring with Nimitz at Pearl Harbor, there came the startling news that an American patrol plane had sighted an airstrip under construction on Guadalcanal. This information put a more urgent complexion on the WATCHTOWER project. Obviously Guadalcanal would have to be included in the Tulagi-Santa Cruz plan, but King and Nimitz would allow no more than one additional week to prepare for the expanded operation. D-day was set definitely for August 7. The airfield had to be captured before the Japanese could complete it. Whoever first put it into operation might well be the victor.

In the latter part of July the situation took another turn when a Japanese convoy landed 1,800 troops near Buna, on the Papuan Peninsula directly opposite Port Moresby. This invasion was a source of grave concern to MacArthur, particularly as the Southwest Pacific Forces had been on the point of occupying the Buna area themselves. But in the South Pacific the news was received with a certain measure of relief. Japanese attention was focused on the old target of Port Moresby, not upon the end of the Solomons chain. Rabaul was looking southwest instead of southeast. Surprise was possible.

Steaming from points as widely separated as Wellington, Sydney, Noumea, San Diego, and Pearl Harbor, the various components of the Watchtower Expeditionary Force, some 80 vessels in all, met at sea on July 26 south of the Fijis. Here Admiral Fletcher held council aboard his flagship, the carrier *Saratoga*. Admiral Ghormley, then shifting his headquarters to Noumea, could not be present. He at no time saw the fleet over which he exercised a distant control or met all his top commanders to discuss operation plans. After a less than satisfactory landing rehearsal in the Fijis, the fleet steamed westward. In the Coral Sea it shaped course due north and headed for Guadalcanal through rain squalls that grounded all aircraft, including Japanese search patrols.

Guadalcanal, part of the drowned volcanic mountain range forming the Solomons, rises steeply in the south from a narrow coastal flat. Only on the north side of the island are there plains broad enough to provide level ground for airfields. Here on Lunga Plain, mostly rain forest traversed by numerous creeks and small rivers and broken here and there by coconut plantations and grassy fields, the Japanese had landed and begun their airdrome. This was the main Allied objective. The secondary objective was the Japanese seaplane base in the Tulagi area, 20 miles to the north . . .

~~~~~~

RICHARD TREGASKIS, WHOSE *GUADALCANAL DIARY* was published while its author was an International News Service correspondent, was aboard one of the transports standing in to Guadalcanal. He reconstructs D-Day.

2.

THE LANDINGS

Friday, August 7

It was no trouble to get up at four o'clock this morning, without benefit of alarm clock, for my mind had been trained for this day for a long time.

Everyone was calm at breakfast. We knew we must be very near our objective by this time, probably at the moment passing directly under the Jap shore guns. And the fact that we had got this far without any action made us feel strangely secure, as if getting up at four o'clock in the morning and preparing to force a landing on the enemy shore were the perfectly normal things to do of an August morning in the South Seas. We had a heavy breakfast and passed a normally humorous conversation.

Up on the deck the situation was the same. Everyone seemed ready to jump at the first boom of a gun, but there was little excitement. The thing that was happening was so unbelievable that it seemed like a dream. We were slipping through the narrow neck of water between Guadalcanal and Savo Islands; we were practically inside Tulagi Bay, almost past the Jap shore batteries, and not a shot had been fired.

On the deck marines lined the starboard rail, and strained their eyes and pointed their field glasses toward the high, irregular dark mass that lay beyond the sheen of the water, beyond the silently moving shapes that were our accompanying ships. The land mass was Guadalcanal Island. The sky was still dark; there was yet no predawn glow, but the rugged black mountains were quite distinct against the lighter sky.

There was not much talking among the usually vivacious marines. The only sounds were the swish of water around our ship, the slight noises of men moving about on the forward deck.

Up on the bridge I found the ship's officers less calm than the marines. Theirs was the worry of getting the ship to anchorage without her being sunk, and they seemed high-strung and incredulous.

"I can't believe it," one lieutenant said to me. "I wonder if the Japs can be that dumb. Either they're very dumb, or it's a trick."

But there was no sign of any tricks as we plowed on into the bay, and the sky began to throw light ahead of us, and we could see even the misty outline of Tulagi and the Florida group of islands squatting to the east and north.

Now the rugged mass of Guadalcanal Island, on our right (to the south), was growing more distinct, and the sharp shoulders of the high mountains could be seen. But there was no sign of any firing from shore, nor were any enemy planes spotted.

Suddenly, from the bridge, I saw a brilliant yellow-green flash of light coming from the gray shape of a cruiser on our starboard bow. I saw the red pencil-lines of the shells arching through the sky, saw flashes on the dark shore of Guadalcanal where they struck. A second later I heard the b-rroom-boom of the cannonading. I should have been ready for that, but was nervous enough, so that I jumped at the sound.

Our naval barrage, which was to pave the way for our landing, had begun. I looked at my watch. The time was 6:14.

Two minutes later, a cruiser astern and to our starboard side began firing. There were the same greenish-yellow flashes as the salvo went off, the same red rockets arching across the sky, geysers of red fires where the shells struck shore, a terrifying rumble and boom of the explosion.

Now, fore and aft, the two cruisers were hurling salvo after salvo into the Guadalcanal shore. It was fascinating to watch the apparent slowness with which the shells, their paths marked out against the sky in red fire, curved through the air. Distance, of course, caused that apparent slowness. But the concussion of the firing shook the deck of our ship and stirred our trousers legs with sudden gusts of wind, despite the distance.

At 6:17, straight, slim lines of tracer bullets, a sheaf of them, showered from the bay in toward the shore, and simultaneously we heard the sound of plane motors. Our planes were strafing, we knew, though in the half-light we could not make out the shapes of the aircraft.

Then there were more showers and sheafs of tracers needling into the dark land-mass, and we could see the red lines forming into shallow V's, as after they struck into their targets, they ricocheted off into the hills.

A moment later my heart skipped a beat as I saw red showers of machine-gun tracers coming from low on the shore and apparently shooting seaward at an angle toward our ships. Was this the answering fire of the Japs? Was heavier firing going to follow? Was this the beginning of the fireworks?

The answer was not clear. When the firing was repeated a few seconds later, it looked more like ricochet than it had before.

Whatever the firing was, it stopped shortly after that, and from then on, there was no visible Jap resistance.

At 6:19 another cruiser, dead ahead of us, began firing. A moment later other warships joined, and the flash of their firing, and the arcs of their flying shells, illumined the sky over a wide span ahead.

Other ships of our force—the group under Gen. Rupertus—had turned to the left toward Tulagi, and there were the heavy reports of cannonading coming from them now.

At 6:28, I noticed a brilliant white spot of fire on the water ahead, and watched fascinated, wondering what it was, while it burgeoned into a spreading sheet of red flame. Planes were moving back and forth like flies over the spot.

"It's a Jap ship," said the ship's officer standing next to me. His field glasses were leveled on the flames. "Planes did it," he said. "They were strafing."

Now the sheet of red flame was creeping out into a long, thin line, and then it was mounting higher and higher into a sort of low-slung, fiery pyramid. For long minutes we watched the flames while the din of our thundering naval guns increased and reached a climax around us.

Ahead of us, to the left of the still brightly burning Jap ship, I saw a bright, white pinpoint of light blink into existence. It was a masthead light riding atop the Australian cruiser which had led our procession into the bay. (The *Canberra*, sunk in subsequent naval action in the Solomon Islands area.)

Our ship was still moving forward, however, and the flaming ship ahead was growing nearer. In the light of the red-orange flames we could see that it was not a large ship, and that it was low in the water. Possibly it was 120 feet long. "What kind of ship is it?" I asked a deck officer.

"They say it's a torpedo boat," he said. But it was in fact a schooner which had been carrying a load of oil and gasoline—whence the flames.

Our dive-bombers were swooping low over the beach. In the growing daylight you could see the color of the explosions where bombs were landing. Some, which struck at the edge of the water, had a bluish tinge. Others, hitting farther back in the sand and earth, were darker.

As the planes dived, they were strafing. The incandescent lines of their tracers struck into the ground, then bent back ricocheting toward the sky to form the now-familiar shallow V.

Our ship and one other, the vanguard of the transport fleet, slowed and stopped. Immediately, the davits began to clank as the boats were lowered away. There were a hubbub of shouts and the sound of many men moving about the ship. On the forward deck, a donkey engine began to chuff and puff. It was time for the beginning of our landing adventure.

It was daylight, but ahead the mass of flames that was the burning Jap boat glowed as brightly as in the dark of night. There were new explosions, as we watched, within the fire—probably gasoline tanks. A burning oil slick spread across the water astern of the boat. And the thought crossed my mind that if there had been anyone alive aboard that ship, he certainly was not alive now.

Our ship and the other transports had swung bow-in toward Guadalcanal, and landing boats were in the water. More were on the way down to the tune of clinking davits. All around us, we could hear the muffled thrumming of engines; boats were cutting in and out at every angle, circling, sliding close alongside. It was cheering to see that each boat carried a small American flag at the stern.

Troops, a mass of moving green uniforms, jammed the forward deck. A sailor leaned over the rail with a signal flag, beckoning landing boats to come up beside the rope nets that served as dismounting ladders. There was something peaceful about the bustle of activity. For a moment one almost forgot about the Japs who might be waiting on shore with machine guns and artillery to blast us out of the water as we came in for a landing.

Our accompanying cruisers, which had stopped firing for a few moments, were opening up again. One, lying astern and to our starboard side, was sending salvo after salvo into a dark point of land. A column of dense black smoke was rising from the spot where the shells were landing. And as we watched, the base of the column glowed red and orange, and the boom of a distant explosion came to us.

We knew a gasoline or oil dump had been hit, because the red flames continued to soar at the base of the smoke column, and from time to time there were new explosions, so that the flames leaped momentarily higher into the sooty black smoke.

I walked among the troops gathered on the forward deck, and found them silent and nervous—a contrast to the gaiety and song which had filled the few preceding days. There did not seem to be much to say, although a few lads came up with the inevitable, "Well, this is it."

The first of our marines clambered over the rail and swung down the rope nets into the boats. The boats pulled away and more came up, and the seeping waterfall of marines continued to slide over the side.

I got word that it was time for me to debark. I took one last look around the ship. Toward Guadalcanal shore, I could see the cruisers still pasting shells into the landscape. On the point of land (Kukum) where the bombardment had set afire a fuel dump, there was a new fire now: two columns of smoke instead of one. From Tulagi-way, across the bay, one could hear the sounds of heavy cannonading. The landing must be going ahead there.

THE FIRST OF THE BLOODY SEA BATTLES OCCURRED ON the night of August 9 in Savo Sound—the narrow body of water between Guadalcanal and Tulagi—and was the worst defeat ever inflicted upon the United States Navy. Determined to oust the invaders, Rear Admiral Gunichi Mikawa, Commander Outer South Seas Force, brought down a task force of five heavy cruisers, two light cruisers and a destroyer from Rabaul, his mighty base near the headwaters of the Solomons. Simultaneously, all available aircraft of the 25th Air Flotilla were sent off for repeated air strikes.

Mikawa took two days to make the voyage, emerging from The Slot into Savo Sound shortly before midnight of the 9th. The American transport *George F. Elliot,* which had been struck by bombs and

Solomon Islands and "The Slot"

RABAUL

Buka

Bougainville

Choiseul

Santa Isabel

Malaita

THE SLOT

New Georgia group

Guadalcanal

San Cristobal

Rennell

0   50   100   150   200

nautical miles

prematurely abandoned by her merchant crew, provided an excellent beacon for the enemy task force. Aided by its glow and by countless American communication failures, Mikawa's expert gunners turned-to with a vengeance. The Allied warships were at Condition II (generally, half the crews at Battle Stations), patrolling in a boxlike formation at the approaches to the Sound. Undetected, Mikawa alternately took on our Southern and Northern Forces, shattering our cruisers with torpedoes and simultaneously with a terrific volume of fire that sank heavy cruisers HMAS *Canberra,* as well as *Astoria, Quincy* and *Vincennes.* More than one thousand seamen went to their deaths. Caught by surprise, the ships never had a chance. After opening fire on the Southern Group, during which he torpedoed *Chicago* and turned HMAS *Canberra* (this warship and *Astoria* lingered a few hours) into a floating pyre, Mikawa engaged the unsuspecting Northern Force and his gunnery was equally effective.

We have two narratives of the savage battle; by United Press war correspondent Joe James Custer, who was aboard the ill-fated *Astoria,* and by newspaperman Richard Newcomb, who gives a dramatic account of the events aboard *Vincennes* and *Astoria.*

3.

ASTORIA'S ORDEAL

I was awakened by the strident, rapid notes of the bugle blaring out of the loud-speaker in my cabin, and I thought: "G.Q. already? Why, I just went to bed!"

I was warm and relaxed and comfortable under the sheets, and I hesitated to get up; I never did for the routine pre-dawn General Quarters, anyway.

The bugle ran on—it sounded perhaps a dozen notes, then *smash!* The ship lurched violently under a crushing impact.

TORPEDO!

My head jerked off the pillow, with that thought.

A vivid, yellow flare flashed through the openings of the green curtain over the door; almost simultaneously, the yellow flash lit the slats of the porthole.

We're in action! The Japs!

Even as my bare feet hit the deck, I concentrated on the most rapid way to dress. Pants first: I pulled them off the chair, wiggled into them. I reached for the flame-proof jacket, and as I pulled it over my head I suddenly "knew" something: I "knew" that I would get hurt. I "knew" something else, too: I "knew" that I would *not* get killed. It was there, as vivid and clear as though someone had told me; it was so clear I grasped frantically at the thought: *Where?* But it was gone. I had a vague hope, perhaps a prayer, that it might be around

320

my hips, somewhere; that would be less likely to be a permanent injury.

The premonition accomplished something: I was suddenly cool and calm: What is to be, is to be.

I fumbled in the dark for my shoes—no time for socks. As I pushed my feet into them, the ship lurched again.

I stepped quickly out onto the deck and into the blinding glare of a searchlight. Vaguely, I was conscious of bodies huddled on the deck, of an overtone of muffled sounds, like mumbled prayers.

There was the crash of an exploding shell right around my ears, and the sudden *rat-tat-tat* of unseen fragments ricochetting all about me, like steel popcorn sprayed up against the inside walls of a cage. I couldn't see them, but I could hear them whistling by and spattering off the overhead.

I ducked instinctively, and realized how futile the gesture was.

I must get my life jacket, and my steel helmet—but quickly. I took the half-dozen steps to make the turn around the cabin and came to a dead stop—the *Astoria* was on fire, amidships! Less than fifty feet away, the flames were leaping high; there was a fierce crackling; the outlines of the planes on the catapults, shrouded in flame.

McKnight! Where's Mac? He'll know what to do . . .

There were life jackets near by, I remembered, so I turned back. The Jap ship had shifted her searchlight a few feet; its bright white flood of light was now slightly forward of the superstructure, playing on the No. 2 turret. The searchlight was powerful, appeared to be perhaps a thirty-six-incher; behind it, I made out the dim lines of the enemy. Her silhouette suggested a cruiser. She was slightly forward of our starboard beam, at a distance about 5,000 yards, I judged.

She fired again, just then, and the flames belched out of her guns; I wondered if my eyes were playing tricks: I thought I could actually see the shells in mid-air, red blocks wrapped in an aura of burning smoke, floating toward us.

Our forward guns roared, and there was the earsplitting crash of the massive eight-inchers.

The flames appeared bright yellow in the glare of the white searchlight; I realized that was what I saw in my cabin, our guns going off.

The deck heaved from the concussion, and the acrid smoke of gunpowder filled my nostrils. Behind me, I sensed, rather than heard, someone falling; I turned around to make out the shadowy form of a man on his knees, struggling to regain his feet on the heaving deck.

Mac!

I stepped over and grabbed his arm: "Mac, that you?"

"No, it's me, Ray. Ray Woods."

"You hurt, kid?"

"No, I'm all right."

He was up on his feet now, and steady. I shouted in his ear: "Where's Mac?"

"I don't know, I haven't seen him."

"I'm going in to get a life jacket. Better come along."

I walked quickly into the radio shack, caught a glimpse of a towering mass of flame just ahead of the *Astoria;* it seemed as though a gigantic matchbox had been ignited, and mushroomed into one vast ball of crimson flame. I learned afterward that this was the *Quincy,* as a torpedo crashed into her ammunition hold.

There were a half-dozen men where I was, and a young junior officer. Johnny Datko was there, and I was glad. The life jackets were strung up on the bulkhead, I noted with relief. "Better get them down?" I suggested to the officer. "We might be needing them."

He pulled out a jackknife and climbed up on the settee to reach the bundle. We huddled in a group below, waiting for them.

"Anybody hurt?" Johnny asked.

"Yeah, I think I got a scratch," one striker said quietly.

Apparently Johnny didn't hear him, for he asked again: "Anybody hurt?"

I nudged Johnny and pointed to the youngster. The j.g. was still fumbling with the cords binding the life jackets. Would he *never* get them down?

Johnny pulled the striker's shirt down off his right arm, and pointed his flashlight. A shiny bit of shrapnel reflected an angry little gleam of light, then the blood covered it up from sight.

"Just a scratch, you'll be O.K."

We jostled against each other, and I had the feeling the ship was wheeling to port; an explosion near by shook us up. The j.g. was jarred off the settee, and the life jackets cascaded after him.

Simultaneously our lights went out, and Johnny switched on his flashlight, gave cool, calm orders. In a few minutes the lights went on again. By that time we noticed that the Jap searchlight had penetrated into the room: the starboard porthole had been sprung by the concussion.

As we struggled into the kapok jackets, the power failed again; once more the room was plunged into darkness.

"Secure the watch on the equipment," Johnny ordered. "It's failed."

We were wedged in tightly, shoulder to shoulder, Datko on my left, Tommy on my right; I was struggling into my life jacket when there was an earsplitting crash and the room filled with flying shrapnel.

Tommy moaned. I felt his hands jerking up to clutch at his back. Johnny pointed his flashlight at the sound, and we caught the sailor as he started slipping to the deck, laid him out on the settee. His eyes were glassy; through pain-tightened lips he gasped: "Kidneys—kidneys . . ."

Pulling his shirt up out of his dungarees, we turned him on his stomach. There was no blood, but his extreme pain told its own story.

Six inches to the left, I thought, and it would have been me.

Just then as I bent over Tommy, I felt some hot, flaky substance on the back of my neck; for a second or two it burned, then stopped abruptly. Apprehensively, my hands went around my neck; I couldn't feel anything: "Flying bits of shattered tubes, probably."

Johnny was busy with his flashlight: he found a cast-metal cover from a switch had blown off its mounting on the bulkhead when the shell exploded. That undoubtedly was what had penetrated the sailor's back; its round, smooth contour explained why no blood had shown.

"His ribs may be broken, though," Johnny whispered.

"Lungs?"

"Guess they're O.K. He's quieted down considerably. Let's try to get him to his feet."

Tommy made it, wobbly, but indicating he could travel under his own power. There was another casualty, but a minor one: a bit of shrapnel in a striker's arm, just above his shoulder. The kid shrugged off attention: "I'll be O.K."

A rapid glance told us what had happened: a shell had penetrated the steel bulkhead on the starboard side, completely wrecked the large chart desk, then continued on through the portside bulkhead. It crossed my mind that some of us, in this group, might die; it was only by a miracle that we had survived, for the shell might have exploded in the room and wiped us all out. The Japs were using hard-steel, high-penetration shells which ripped through steel plates like cheese before exploding. There was a gaping hole, large and terrible, where the shell had entered; through it, we saw the darting flames of the fire raging on the gun deck below.

"We'd better get out of here," I suggested to the j.g.

"Where'll we go?" he retorted, his tone indicating that one place was just as good, or as bad, as another, considering the circumstances.

I persisted: "Apparently they've got the range on the superstructure, so any other place can't be worse. And it'll be easier to go over the side from the main deck, if we have to."

We started moving in an orderly group, inching forward to the hole in the bulkhead, wary of possible explosions. I wondered if we were trapped. But nothing happened, so we squeezed through the hole left by the shell, the jagged opening still warm to the touch. For some reason unknown even to himself, Datko crawled through the wreckage of the door, which was crumpled by the blast.

Out on the deck again, we saw fires raging all about us, on the decks below. Amidships, the *Astoria* was one mass of flame.

A congestion developed on the ladder, and there were warnings: "Take it easy, now; take your time—no crowding."

In the dark, we felt our way from one step down to the next; Johnny turned on his flashlight.

"Turn out that light!" a voice yelled from below. "Want to give the Japs a target?"

"With the whole ship on fire," Johnny muttered, flicking his light out.

There was little conversation, and that was carried on in low, disconnected whispers, as though even voices might attract Jap shells. There was a little swearing, too. I could make out Curley's low muttering over and over: "The Goddam Japs, the bastards! The dirty bastards . . ."

On the communications deck, at the foot of the ladder, a bottleneck developed as the sailors huddled close together in the shelter of the superstructure. There was no place to go.

Off our port quarter, a Jap warship had her searchlight playing on us, and her guns were flashing. Geysers of water spouted where the shells fell short. One of them was a vivid blue; somebody was using illumination charges. Our heavy· guns were answering, again and again, and the *Astoria* shook with the concussions. The acrid smell of gunpowder was heavy; at times, I could hear the crackling of the flames amidships.

A crimson string of tracers reached out from somewhere aft of our ship, and arched over to the Japs—and another. Then an answering rosary of death spurted from the enemy's decks.

The Jap's heavy guns continued firing—red flashes, followed, seconds later, by detonations, like the clap of thunder through closed walls. Then the massive, shapeless blotches of crimson floating in mid-air, and again I wondered: was I actually seeing shells in mid-air?

Directly in front of us, some men were on the move, to the forward part of the ship. Davidson, the communications officer, came by, and paused directly in front of me, his eyes searching the superstructure. I called to him, but he didn't hear me in the din, so I moved forward: "How's it look?"

He answered something I couldn't hear, and moved off, forward. I started back for the shelter of the superstructure, when I noticed a sailor on the edge of the communications deck kneeling: he was playing a hose on the gun deck below. I moved forward and looked over his shoulder.

A "ready box" was afire. About the size of a steamer trunk, built of steel, and containing shells for the five-inch guns, it was covered with a rubber mat which was smoldering. The sailor played the hose on the mat, but in a few minutes the stream grew feeble, stopped altogether; the power was off. The sailor moved away with the hose, and I edged forward for a better view of the flaming gun deck below . . .

There was a tremendous white flash—a huge sheet of flame—then crimson spurts flaring in all directions. I heard the whir-whir of shrapnel on all sides . . . and suddenly I felt a hot, piercing stab of pain in my left eye . . . shooting stars sprayed in violent streaks.

Perhaps I cried out, I don't know. But in that instant I knew what had happened. I was hurt—my eye.

I stood there stolidly for a long moment, then I felt my hands slowly moving up to my face, hesitantly, for I was afraid to find out.

My fingers felt the warm, sticky blood, and I wiped them down my cheek. "I'll never see Hawaii again . . ."

In that instant, I remembered the flying shrapnel, so I turned my back on it and walked unseeing ahead, reaching out with my arms towards the group I had just left.

I felt my hands contacting the human wall, and fingers on my arms: "Are you hurt? Who is it?"

It was Datko's voice, and I was glad of that; we had been good friends.

"It's me, Johnny. Custer."

I realized my voice was a low whisper, for he bent his head down so that his ear brushed my lips; I repeated, more loudly: "Custer, Johnny. Think it's my eye."

"Here, put your arms around me and hold on. You'll be all right."

It felt good to hold onto something firm, and I stood there inhaling deeply; I was still aware there might be another explosion, and kept my back toward the gun deck. If it came, it would be easier to catch it in the back. I was glad I'd picked up the kapok life jacket; that might stop some shrapnel. But no helmet . . . I berated myself: "Serves you right, not having a helmet." And I realized almost at once that a helmet would have done me no good, for the protection comes only part way down the forehead, does not cover the eyes.

I stood there, and lost all track of time, with my arms on Datko's shoulders, apprehensively wondering if the shrapnel would strike again. My thoughts began to wander: "So this is how it feels to die . . ." Angrily, I rebuked myself for being a sentimentalist: I *knew* that I wasn't going to get killed, I remembered; and as I recalled the premonition I grew calm again, steadied down.

And I suddenly became angry and bitter: "That sonofabitch Hitler!" Instinctively, my resentment was against him: "That madman—paperhanger—murderer! The dead, the suffering all over the world—the sonofabitch!"

There was a movement as the group surged forward a bit; Johnny hissed over his shoulder: "Easy, take it easy; there's a man hurt here." Immersed in my thoughts, I was only vaguely conscious of the undertone of queries, and the answers: "The reporter . . . eyes . . ."

I began to wonder, then, about what lay ahead: how would I get around, when it came to going over the side? Johnny seemed to read my thoughts: "How do your legs feel?" They felt strong, firm. Physically, I felt all right; no dizziness, no nausea. There was a rim of pain around my forehead, but it wasn't severe. We continued to stand there in silence, waiting. Then Datko spoke to the group: "We'd better figure on moving out of here pretty soon, fellows; the fires are dying down a little."

His voice was steady and reassuring; he took pains to tell me of every move in advance: "Think you can walk all right? Fine. We'll move forward, around the deck house, and try to get somewhere near the fo'c'sle. Hold on to me, and take it easy. Here, put your arms on my shoulders and move with me."

Carefully, he shuffled backward, and I moved ahead, trying to from a mental picture of our position; behind me, I heard the scraping of feet as the seamen followed us.

A few minutes later, Johnny halted: "Right before us is a big crack in the deck, about a foot wide. Be careful to step clear over it, you could twist an ankle."

I had an idea: "Wait a minute." While he held me, I put my head down and with both hands tried opening the eyelids of my right eye: briefly, I caught a glimpse of a jagged tear in the deck. I shut my eyes again, and with Johnny holding me by the elbow, cleared the crack with one long step. We moved on, a few more feet, then Johnny stopped again and backed me around: "Sit down here. You're directly behind the No. 2 turret, almost under it." It felt good to rest my back against the heavy steel. I was conscious of a vast relief, too: I had seen with my right eye . . . perhaps everything was all right . . . everything would be all right.

I was conscious, too, that the ship had not stopped shuddering; explosion after explosion rocked the *Astoria*, there was a constant shock of concussion. I couldn't tell if our guns were firing, or if we were being still pummeled by Jap shells. The air was heavy with gunpowder fumes, and it became increasingly more difficult to breathe. In the background, I could hear the roar and crackling of fires on the ship.

"I'm going to leave you for a few minutes," Johnny said. "They're trying to cut down some life rafts, and I'll give them a hand. Be right back."

I felt he came close to adding, "Don't go away," but checked himself.

He wasn't away very long, and he brought news: "There's a lot of activity on the main deck below, around the No. 1 turret. They're bringing the wounded down around there, and I think it'll be better for you. Here, let me help you up. We'll try it."

A moment later, he told me we were going down the side. "There's

a boom right here, under your feet. Feel it? We'll climb down on it."
He placed my feet on the bar. "Now, take it easy, I'll hold on to
you." The boom slanted at a steep angle, but by carefully sliding one
foot after the other, I made it without difficulty. We stood still a
moment to get our bearings; I felt movement around me, of men
brushing by. "Look out for my leg," a voice said, near by; the words
were tense, filled with pain. Johnny whispered to me to be careful
going past the sailor sitting immediately before us; I pried my eyelids
open again to gauge the steps, and saw a tubby, round-faced sailor in
dungarees sitting on the deck, his bare legs stretched out before him
—the right leg hung by shreds, below the knee; his dungarees were
blood-soaked.

My stomach turned within me; I shut my eyes, and Johnny steered
me carefully, shuffling along. We made a turn to the left—and there
was a sudden crushing explosion right over us. We held on to each
other tightly, as the deck heaved and shuddered under our feet. I
thought we were going down, but Johnny tightened his grip on me,
and we remained upright, swaying. There was a ringing in my ears, a
vibration that pulsated in painful waves. We waited fearfully for another blast.

None came, and we resumed our slow shuffling. Johnny backed me
into a sitting position, and I felt my back resting against a heavy
chain; a few minutes later, he prodded me forward and slipped something that felt like a pillow between my backbone and the anchor
chain.

"I thought we were goners, that time," he said. "Guess the No. 2
turret fired, just as we were right under the barrel. Boy, I couldn't see
a thing, and I couldn't hear a thing. My ears are still ringing."

As I opened my eyes the panorama before me appeared in
pantomime, soundless at first with the ringing in my ears, but gradually the *boom! boom!* of gunfire began to penetrate again. The Japs
were still firing, and I wondered if the shells would come our way.
Tracers hung from our fantail to the Jap, and back again; star shells
exploded spasmodically—the big guns belched flames, again and
again.

I wondered if the Japs would rake our fo'c'sle, and I wondered
how it would feel to have my head torn off, sitting there and not
seeing Death come roaring through the darkness. If I have to go, I
thought, let it be like that—quickly. . . . Feeling that this might be the
end, I recalled that that was the time your life was supposed to pass

before you in swift retrospect, and so I prompted my imagination; but all I could grasp was a vague mental picture of the palm trees and the beach at Waikiki—nothing else seemed to register, nothing more clear-cut—and I abandoned the attempt. More strongly than ever, I had the feeling that everything was going to be all right. I felt that it had to end sometime, and that was a comforting thought: "That's right—it has to end sometime, it can't go on forever."

There was constant movement about me, and occasionally I pried my eyelids open for brief glimpses. The fo'c'sle was jammed with men, many of them lying on their backs. Occasionally, someone moaned, but more often there was a quiet reminder: "Look out, take it easy—this man's hurt."

A gun roared somewhere. Suddenly, the Jap searchlight went out and sea was black again where it had been bright in the spotlight and the lightning of gunfire. In the new darkness, the flames from amidships leaped high, and I caught glimpses of them licking the superstructure.

I wondered if the after part of the *Astoria* had been shot away, and that reminded me of the superstructure and the bridge: could there be anyone alive up there? It was silent and ominous; what about the skipper?

Voice near by: "There's no water pressure, sir; we've tried all the valves. Fire mains must be out."

Then the Captain's voice, out of the darkness of the bridge: "Will you officers down below get some rescue crews organized at once! Go down to the Captain's cabin and remove the wounded! Remove them before the fire spreads down there!"

His voice was shrill, anxious; but it was comforting to hear him, to know the skipper was alive!

There were hurried orders about us, and the shuffling of feet. Johnny whispered: "I'm going down to help; be back as soon as I can."

The Captain's voice again: "Some of you officers organize fire brigades, and help check these fires! The water mains are out!"

Again hurried orders, the clattering of feet. I sat back, and the absence of gunfire somehow made everything seem more cheerful, the bustling of men, more hopeful. I wondered how long the battle had raged. A half-hour? An hour? I had no idea; I was just thankful it was over.

I had the uneasy thought that perhaps the Japs were even then maneuvering to close in on us, to come alongside and shell at point-blank range.

Then I began to realize that I was aching all over; I felt hot and cold in turn. The acrid smell was deep in my nostrils, I began to feel nauseated. As Johnny returned, I grabbed his arm. "I'm gonna get sick to my stomach. Get me over to the rail, quick!"

"You can't move," Johnny said. "There isn't a square foot of space anywhere around here—all jammed with wounded. Here, get to your feet. Open your mouth. Take a deep breath. Another one. Again . . ."

I stood gulping and gasping, and the choking in my throat subsided although the air was foul and heavy with gunpowder and burning paint.

"The flames are under control around the fo'c'sle," Johnny said. "We used buckets and helmets and everything else we could lay hands on. And you should have seen the helmets! I saw three that were so badly smashed up they had no shape at all. One guy told me he was knocked cold, and his helmet twisted all out of shape, by a chunk of shrapnel or something—but it saved his life. All the rafts are shot away. Every gun I saw is a shambles, the five-inchers, too."

On his way below to help with the wounded, the decks were so hot he could barely stand it, and he wondered how the injured could hold up. In the Captain's cabin the smoke was thick, and he had to stick his head out the door and gulp in fresh air before he could duck inside; some of the men were wearing gas masks.

"I stumbled onto a cot with a wounded man on it; he seemed to be unconscious. Somebody said he had a badly injured back. Both his hands were badly burned, the top layers of skin peeled off . . ."

Johnny motioned to a couple of sailors for help, and they picked up the cot and headed for the door; but it was too narrow: "We had to stop and take out the end sticks; the man came to, and the pain must have been terrific—he kept waving his arms as though he wanted us to hurry, hurry! Or maybe he wanted to help get the cot through, but of course he couldn't. God, he must have been in awful pain!"

After what seemed like ages, they made it up the narrow iron passageway, out to the fo'c'sle, and deposited the cot there.

"There's a destroyer coming up alongside," Johnny interrupted his story. "Probably to take the wounded off. Here, let's get going. I'll get you aboard."

He moved me cautiously backward, step by step, and I felt the railing against my back. But the destroyer had left: "Came alongside, and started to tie up, then suddenly went off. Maybe they think we'll blow up and take 'em with us."

That was something else to think about: the ammunition depot for the No. 1 turret was almost directly beneath us. So was the paint locker; a fire there could blow off the whole bow. The word was passed: "The smoking lamp is out." It meant nothing to me—I had no desire for a cigarette.

"We may have to swim for it," Johnny observed. "Think you could make it?"

"Where's the nearest land?"

He turned me about-face, and I opened my eyes for a moment: perhaps three miles away, the outline of land was dimly discernible. Guadalcanal? Johnny thought it might be, although he wasn't certain. I thought I could make it; my legs felt strong, my head clear.

But it was a dismal prospect: sharks—perhaps Japs mopping up. Whose ships were those vague forms moving about in the darkness? No telling friend from foe. And yet we couldn't stay on the burning ship . . .

"Don't you worry about anything," Johnny advised. "I'll stick right with you in the water. Here, let's see if your life jacket is on tight."

His investigation revealed that I had put my jacket on backward: the "horse-collar" was inside. Patiently, he untied the strings, and I put it on correctly.

By this time it was raining, a cold, driving rain. I opened my mouth and let the water run down my face and on my tongue, cool and refreshing. I recalled the saying that it generally rains after a battle: the concussions of the big guns disturb elements in the atmosphere much as thunder and lightning. Whatever the cause, the downpour was welcome, for it provided hope that the fires might be quenched aboard the *Astoria*. For about an hour, it rained, and it did help controlling the fires topside. It grew steadily colder, too, and I found myself shivering and chilled.

Johnny had left to help with the bucket brigade and first-aid groups, and returned with a corps man who was treating the wounded on the fo'c'sle, with the aid of a flashlight. The corps man swabbed my eye with a wet cloth, then painted carefully with iodine; it stung briefly.

"The *Bagley* will come alongside pretty soon," he said. "Get them to put a bandage on when you go aboard. You're all right for now."

I leaned back against the railing and relaxed. The *Bagley:* it was a grand and glorious thought, comforting. I had been apprehensive about going over the side, into the shark-infested waters.

Johnny was off again. I wondered what time it was, and someone near by asked: "How long before daylight?" And I recognized the voice of Lieutenant Bates. "Oh, three-four hours, maybe." There was a calmness in his voice, a cheerfulness that instilled confidence. Things could be much worse.

Johnny returned in a little while: "The *Bagley's* coming alongside. Get ready."

The destroyer pulled up on our starboard bow, almost directly beneath us. Sailors began helping the wounded to their feet, or carrying them in their cots.

There were several dozen before me, and I told Johnny to help with them; I was O.K. on my feet. The destroyer was completely blacked out, men on her deck flashing a light briefly to get bearings on each patient, then working swiftly by touch to complete the transfer. Johnny came back, panting: "Damn near fell in the drink; lost my footing. Well, let's get going."

We went over the side, and he handed me down to waiting hands below. A Marine held me as I stumbled onto the *Bagley's* deck: "Here, this notebook fell out of your pocket." That was a surprise; it was the first I knew that I had a notebook in my flame jacket. He crammed it into his pocket.

I wanted a drink of water. The Marine pulled my arm around his waist, and we started moving down the deck. I heard Greenman's voice again, from the *Astoria's* bridge, far above: "Able-bodied men stay aboard—not abandoning ship!" A spontaneous cheer went up.

The Marine and I made our way back towards the *Bagley's* fantail, and then into the seamen's mess hall, converted into a first aid station. The corps man examined me, applied more iodine, tied a bandage around my forehead, over my left eye.

"Here, drink this," he said, mixing something into a thick coffee cup. "This'll settle your stomach."

It had an evil smell and taste, but I downed it in a gulp. My guide put his arm around my waist, and we started forward; but as we hit the fresh air the concoction came up in my throat; I leaned over the rail . . . I felt much better, after that.

We stopped to see the doctor, in the officers' wardroom, converted into a sick bay. Charley Gorman, the Marine, opened the door, and I took one look inside: it was like a butcher shop: naked and partially naked bodies, the red flesh and bone showing where the blood had been washed away. The doctor was bending over a man on the table. One look was enough: an emergency operation, no time to be bothering the doctor. We backed out quietly.

"I'll get you a bunk in the CPO quarters," my guide said. As we went below, Gorman said that the *Bagley* had thrown four torpedoes at the Japs.

Below, the bunks were filled with wounded; red splotches seeped through some of the sheets. I went into the CPO wardroom and sat on a bench, while Gorman disappeared to search for an empty bunk.

Some burn cases were sitting around, their flesh black and lumpy with the thick applications of jelly patted there by corps men. They sat silently, smoking cigarettes, and I realized that I had yet to hear anyone complain, or so much as moan. Some of the more able-bodied managed to smile occasionally. Two buddies, reunited, one as patient and the other as nurse, kidded: "What the hell, you're not hurt! Have you good as new in no time, you old so-an'-so."

Datko came in, tired and pale.

"You look pretty good," he said. "How about some chow? I'm starved. All right if I raid your icebox?" he asked aloud.

The *Bagley* men waved their invitations. Datko poked around, came to the long table with a bowl of canned tomatoes, crackers, butter, and coffee, and ate ravenously: "I don't know when I've tasted anything more delicious."

Gorman returned: "Found a bunk for you." It was an upper; I kicked off my shoes, and discovered I hadn't tied my shoelaces, those eons ago when I put them on aboard the *Astoria*. I fell into a sound, dreamless sleep before my head touched the pillow.

4.

DEATH BOARDS *VINCENNES*

AND *ASTORIA*

The *Vincennes,* pounded by shells as few other ships in history, lasted about eighteen minutes. The first salvo whistled in about 1:51 A.M. and each shell, it seemed, had been intelligently aimed at a vital spot. One clipped the bridge and killed Commander Miller, others hit the carpenter shop (aways a fine spot for fires), the hangar (best fire spot of all), Batt II, directing guns, and the antenna trunks, severing all communications. Short of an open magazine hit no attacker could ask more. Out went radio and searchlights, battle phones, and power on the turrets; the fire mains ruptured and the planes went up in a bright blaze amidships. In one salvo the Japanese had set a fire to aim by and the ship was slashed to less than 50 per cent efficiency.

She still had steam and Captain Riefkohl ordered 20 knots and a course change to the left, turning down to help his friends in the Southern Force, should they ask him. They never did, and further-more they never told him anything. How could he know he was now heading down between 2 enemy columns just waiting to smash him? But they were, and they did.

While she lasted, the *Vincennes* got off a second main salvo and Lieutenant Commander Robert R. Craighill thought he saw the target turn and disappear out of control. It was the *Kinugasa* and she was hit all right, but not that badly. The Japanese searchlights snapped off, but not for the reason the Americans thought. They thought

334

they had shot them out, but the truth was the Japanese were now on range and needed no more light.

Salvo after salvo slammed into the *Vincennes,* 8-inch, 5.5-inch, 4.7-inch, and even machine-gun fire from somewhere. Fire broke out in the movie locker, the cane fender storage, and the searchlight platform.

In forward battle station Commander James D. Blackwood had a Negro mess attendant on the table, sewing up his jaw, when a 5.5-inch shell exploded in the room. Dr. Blackwood, twenty-two years in the Navy and a fine old gentleman in his sixties, was killed instantly along with every member of the medical team around him. The mess attendant bounded from the table holding his jaw together with his hand and ran from the room with only a leg scratch.

Captain Riefkohl, frantic now with fire raining in from both sides, turned hard right again. Trying to escape, he rang for 25 knots, but the speed never exceeded 19.5 and in the turn 2, perhaps 3, torpedoes slashed through the port side. A hit in main battery control aft killed Lieutenant (j.g.) Victor J. Fama, the control officer there, hits were scored on Turrets I and II, and it was not yet two o'clock, the battle less than nine minutes old.

Steering power failed in the pilothouse and control was shifted to steering aft. A forward steam line burst with a terrible hiss and Boatswain C. F. Baker flooded down the forward magazines. Captain Riefkohl tried a frantic left turn by stopping the port engine, but there was no response. He sent a messenger, who never returned.

Shortly after 2:00 A.M., by some miracle the main battery got off two more 6-gun salvos, their last, firing at a searchlight which did not, however, go out. Two more searchlights picked out the burning *Vincennes* and the shells fell without mercy. The forward director jammed in train, and shells hit the machine shop, forward mess hall, starboard catapult tower, well deck, and radar room. The *Vincennes'* colors were carried away by shot, and Captain Riefkohl, unaware that the age of gallantry had ended, ordered another set hoisted. Chief Signalman George J. Moore and a chief quartermaster, risking life in that hail of steel, raised a new set on the starboard yardarm, using the last remaining halyard.

The Japanese gunners were delighted. They thought it signified an admiral's flagship, and they redoubled their fire. In one last great blast shells smashed Turret II, top and side, and silenced every last gun in service. Lieutenant Commander Robert Lee Adams, the gunnery officer, was forced to report, "Captain, we have absolutely no guns to fire with. Everything is out."

"All right," the captain replied, "you tell the men to get down below from exposed positions and see if they can seek cover." Captain Riefkohl never forgot his men, and he ordered messengers sent along decks and below to order the men out—those who were left.

The slaughter finally ceased and the *Vincennes* was left alone to die. The list increased steadily between 2:15 and 2:30, and the captain ordered all life rafts put over the side. The wounded were helped into life jackets. Lieutenant Commander Samuel A. Isquith and Lieutenant W. A. Newman, medical officers, stayed on duty at aft and amidships dressing stations until the end. It was not long in coming. Captain Riefkohl gave the order to abandon ship about 2:30 A.M., and was washed off an upper deck about 2:40. Ten minutes later the *Vincennes* sank, only a mile or two from her sister, the *Quincy*. When they drew up the *Vincennes'* List of Known Hits later, it showed at least 56 large-caliber hits and many more probables, not to mention at least a half-dozen torpedoes.

The *Astoria* died a stubborn death, in two distinct phases. Early in the battle the ship had been cut in half by fires amidships and by the severance of communications. As far as Captain Greenman knew there was no one alive aft, and he feared the worst. But many other things demanded his attention.

While the fiasco of "Commence firing," "Cease firing," "Commence firing," was being enacted on the bridge, there was no lack of action elsewhere. In Turret II, Ensign Raymond C. McGrath, just out of the Academy, got the word on his phones, "Flares on the port quarter. The *Australia* is firing." (The *Australia* did not fire a shot that night). Turret II got off three salvos and then heard a terrific jolt (Turret I was finished, temporarily). Turret II fired again, despite failures in the powder and shell hoists, but then came to the limit of train to port and had to swing around to starboard. On the fifth salvo only the left and center guns fired, but then she got off 3 barrels, 2 again, 3, and another 2. She was done, as main battery control and Director I were out, due to smoke and shell. McGrath ordered the trainer to bear on what he thought was an enemy to port—it was the *Quincy*—and fortunately all power failed in the turret. Men were fainting now from smoke and fumes, and McGrath led them out. Ordered back to flood the magazines, he led his turret captain and gunner's mate to the control panel and pressed the buttons. Nothing happened, and finally they went below and opened the valves by hand.

On Spot II, Fire Controlman First Class W. W. Johns somehow missed the word to evacuate. He picked up a target at 4,000 yards—a searchlight—and turned to find himself alone. A sight setter and trainer appeared from somewhere, the ready lights went on for Turrets II and III, and Johns fired—a 6-gun salvo. A second salvo was fired, but the third time only Turret III light came on and that was fired. A Japanese cruiser appeared, but at that moment the Director jammed, Turret III reported no power, and Plot said it was abandoning due to smoke. Johns quit then and took his men out.

The record of the *Astoria's* 5-inch guns told her story. No 1 got off twelve rounds, No. 2 one round before the barrel was hit, No. 3 six rounds, No. 4 ten rounds before the ready service ammunition blew up, No. 5 six rounds, No. 6 seven rounds before its ready service exploded; No. 7 after seven rounds was hit by a shell, and No. 8's ready service went up on the tenth round. Altogether, 8 guns and only 59 rounds, a tribute to the power and accuracy of Japanese gunnery.

Lieutenant Donald E. Willman, putting on his phones in Sky Forward, heard the bridge say, "Don't fire, they may be our own ships." It was too bad, because there was very little time this night and such confusion cut it even shorter. When he received the order, "Commence firing," he was able to get off only 2 to 4 rounds before his Director was smashed and he had to abandon it. He started down among his 5-inchers to tell them to go to local control, but an explosion broke his arm and cut his leg and he fainted. Lieutenant R. G. McCloy was there, bloody and dazed, and finally a 5-inch battery officer, Lieutenant (j.g.) Vincent P. Healey saved the gunners, Willman rousing long enough to give permission to abandon the gun deck.

In Sky Control, Seaman First Class Lynn F. Hager had the bridge phones on his head and the first words he heard after the erroneous "cease fire," were "Fire every damn thing you've got." The last order he heard was, "Get those damn searchlights." Between those two orders, seemingly only minutes apart, lay the whole battle.

Lieutenant George M. K. Baker, Jr., the radio officer, reached Main Radio just as the lights went out. He snapped on the battle lanterns and in their light read a contact report that had just been decoded. It placed the Japanese force of 3 cruisers and 3 destroyers, previously reported earlier in the evening, slightly farther south of Bougainville. He had no time to reflect on this, or even to remember the contents exactly, for the force had now arrived, and to verify this sent two 8-inch shells into the *Astoria's* radio room. One pierced the bulkhead near the door to the communications office, the other passed through an armored door into the coding room, exploding in a blinding orange flash. The rooms were instantly a shambles of blood and bodies, smashed desks and chairs. Of those not yet dead, Radio-man Third Class Joseph T. Muskus lost a leg, Chief Radioman Samuel R. Gladden was terribly wounded, and Electrician C. F. O'Neill was hit. Chief Pay Clerk B. Q. Swinson put a tourniquet on Muskus' leg and gave him a hypo. There was nothing to be done for Gladden, but he wanted a cigarette, so Swinson lit one and put it in his mouth.

Two more shells hit Radio I, followed by another pair, and then a final one. The room was shot to pieces now, and all the able-bodied could do was move the (hopeful) wounded out to the deck, where they might have a chance.

It was much the same everywhere topside, the shells boring in relentlessly with a roar like an express train. The highest intensity came between 2:01 and 2:06 A.M., and thereafter the shelling tapered off until 2:15, when it stopped as suddenly as it had begun.

Lieutenant Commander Truesdell, coming out of Director I, saw nothing but fire topside. Appalled, he worked his way through fire and bodies to the bridge and told Captain Greenman he should leave, the ammunition room directly over his head was afire. Very well, said Captain Greenman, he would take station forward of Turret II on the communications deck, and he wished all wounded men to be brought down to the forecastle. Truesdell offered to search all topside stations and assure that all men still alive were brought out. Lieutenant Commander Topper reported there seemed to be no fires below the *Astoria's* second deck, and Lieutenant Commander Hayes said the engineering spaces were watertight. There was just a chance the ship might be saved. As to what was happening aft, Lieutenant Com-mander Hayes said he had no idea, but he assumed the ship was afire to the stern.

It was not quite as bad as that. Commander Frank E. Shoup, Jr., the executive officer, leaped from his bed at general quarters and ran aft, putting on his pants and shirt over his pajamas. At his battle station, Batt II, he found only his talker, Quartermaster Second Class

J. U. Walker, and no one else ever arrived. Shoup saw nothing to starboard, but stepped out on the port-gun platform in time to greet an arriving shell, which blinded him temporarily and burned his hands and face. Almost immediately the boat deck, well deck, and gun deck were hit and broke out in flames. The ship's boats began to burn, and Walker reported he had no contact with the bridge. The announcer system went dead and suddenly Batt II was on fire, with flames blocking both ladders down to the fantail.

Fire was driving all men from the mainmast section and they scrambled down as best they could. Monkey lines had been rigged aft of the machine-gun platform and finally Shoup and Walker went down that way, satisfied that all living and wounded who could be moved had escaped the caldron.

Machinist's Mate First Class O. S. Sells was saved only by the intrepidity of his shipmates. They saw him pinned under the whale-boat davit, surrounded by fire and apparently dead. Then his hand moved. Shipfitter First Class C. C. Watkins raced in, followed by Shipfitter Third Class Wyatt J. Louttrell and Water Tender Second Class Norman R. Touve. Standing in flames they forced the davit up and pulled Sells free. On the way out of the flames they picked up Fireman Second Class J. R. Bene and dragged him to the fantail too. Those who saw it were awed by the courage of these men.

Forward, Captain Greenman was under increasing strain. He had noted that the *Astoria* now had a list of some 3 degrees. It might mean only that the after magazines had been flooded, but more likely that some part of the hull was open to the sea. Fires were raging unchecked, with every fire main ruptured. By 3:00 A.M. some 400 men were gathered on the forecastle, about 70 of them wounded and many dead.

A bucket brigade was organized, with the faint hope that the fire might be forced back amidships, but flames belched from every passageway and ventilation duct. The main fear was the 5-inch magazines. Captain Greenman was satisfied that the 8-inch magazines had been flooded, but if the 5-inch went up every man on the forecastle might be blown to bits.

The bucket brigade, dipping water from the sea, worked slowly aft on the starboard side of the gun deck, and a gasoline handy-billy pump was rigged, but its puny stream seemed ludicrous against the wall of flame. Fire had now reached the lower ammunition hoists, and 1.1 and 5-inch shells could be heard exploding below. Any moment might bring real disaster.

Captain Greenman dared not delay longer, and ordered the *Bagley* to be brought alongside. The destroyer, reached by blinker earlier, had been ordered to stand by. Eerie lights blinking from the forepeak of the burning cruiser signalled the *Bagley* to approach and Commander Sinclair brought his vessel into a very smart Chinese landing (bow to bow, like mare and foal nuzzling). The ships were lashed together and the transfer began, the wounded being lifted across first. Able-bodied men followed, and finally Captain Greenman and his officers jumped into the destroyer, leaving the *Astoria,* they thought, for the last time. It was 4:45 A.M.

As the *Bagley* cast off, flashing lights winked out from the stern and for the first time Captain Greenman learned that men were alive back there. The *Bagley* signaled them that they had been seen and would be picked up later. The destroyer, jammed with wounded and shipwrecked sailors, backed off slowly, and began pulling from the sea dozens of men who had been forced off the 3 cruisers. A soft rain began to fall and it seemed to Captain Greenman, as he looked at his ship, that the fires amidships might be dying. Thus ended Phase I of the *Astoria's* ordeal.

~~~~~~

MIKAWA BROKE OFF THE MAIN ACTION AND TURNED north, completely disregarding a precious opportunity to get at the American transports. But Japan had gained a great sea victory and Yamamoto was properly grateful. He messaged: "Appreciate the courageous and hard fighting of every man of your organization. I will expect you to expand your activities . . ." Mikawa did not escape altogether unscathed, however. Submarine *S-44* was on war patrol off the coast of New Ireland the following morning and as the homeward bound task force passed close aboard, Lieutenant Commander John R. "Dinty" Moore fired a spread of torpedoes at cruiser *Kako* and down she went within five minutes.

Meanwhile, Fletcher with his three carriers began a retirement toward Noumea and Turner followed a few hours later with the other ships at Guadalcanal. Vandegrift was furious. He had been left with barely enough supplies for thirty-seven days; had been left in his own picturesque language, "bare ass." The only thing he did have was the

Navy's solemn promise to bring reinforcements and supplies as soon as possible. But now the unpalatable prospect facing the Marines was apparent: Japanese air, surface and submarine forces would shortly manifest themselves in great numbers, and the Marine general braced himself. On August 15 Ghormley's promised reinforcements arrived in part. The Marines were cheered by the sight of destroyer-transports *Calhoun, Gregory, Little,* and *McKean* closing the beach through Ironbottom Sound (the dolorous nickname for Savo Sound.) Aboard were bombs, aviation gasoline and approximately one hundred and fifty men of Cub One, a Navy construction battalion, who were to help build the airstrip which the Marines subsequently named Henderson Field, in memory of a pilot lost at Midway. Much of the Corps' bitterness since Turner's pullout evanesced in a welter of full stomachs and feverish unloading of cargoes. Again, on the 20th, three APDs steamed into Guadalcanal waters to bring the Marines one hundred tons of supplies.

In Rabaul, meanwhile, Lieutenant General Haroushi Hyakutate had arrived fresh from Tokyo's tea houses to command the Nineteenth Imperial Army. Unlike Vandegrift, Hyakutate was a book soldier who lived by the Imperial manual. The manual told him that "the character of the American is simple and lacking in tenacity and battle leadership . . ." and "if they have a setback, they have a tendency to abandon one plan for another . . ." The Japanese general was then gathering his army. It was to be composed of crack combat units stationed in China, the Philippines, Singapore and Borneo, and on paper it numbered some 50,000 troops. Already on hand was Colonel Kyono Ichiki's detachment of nine hundred and sixteen men. By the process of simple deduction, this appeared enough to begin chewing up the estimated 10,000 Marines.

On August 21 Marine patrols found thirty-one soldiers of Ichiki's force along the sandy banks of the Tenaru River; thirty-one were killed. This was only the beginning of the first of many great Marine battles fought on Guadalcanal. It opened at 1:30 A.M. Along a narrow sandbar barely fifty yards long, two hundred bayonet-fixed Japanese raged across toward Marine positions, screaming and shouting in a typical *banzai* charge. They were led by saber-waving officers who charged imperviously across the shallows into the teeth of rifle, machine gun and grenade fire—withering fire which cut down a number of the officers and men but did not stop the charge from crossing the river. Marines fought bayonet to bayonet, knife to knife, smashing and hurling back the insanely shrieking enemy. By daylight every enemy soldier who attained the Marine position was dead, and those who managed to crawl away into a nearby coconut grove were later killed by a Marine charge late in the afternoon. Ichiki, found dead with a bullet in his brain, had burned his colors at the end of the battle. Fletcher Pratt, biographer of the Marine Corps, remarks that in the colonel's diary a precise schedule was found: "August 17. The landing. August 20. The march by night and the battle. August 21. Enjoyment of the fruits of victory . . ." The Tenaru River battle was written into Corps history as a model of coordination, firepower and Marine fortitude . . .

On August 20 the converted merchantman *Mormacmail,* now the jeep carrier *Long Island,* steamed in with two Marine squadrons of Wildcats and Dauntless dive-bombers. On August 24 carrier *Enterprise* contributed her entire complement of dive-bombers. And by the end of the month still another air group of the Combat Air Transport flew in. The pitched and often-lopsided battles of these few against countless Zeros and Bettys were many. Yet the Marine and Navy pilots somehow held their own, for everything depended on keeping Henderson Field operational. On August 24 another sea battle, which had been threatening since Mikawa's victory, took place in the Eastern Solomons. It was an unqualified American victory, which not only consolidated our position on Guadalcanal but saw the end of Japanese carrier *Ryujo* and a 10,000 ton transport brimming with troops.

But the very next day the destroyer-transports *Calhoun* and *Little* were sunk by Japan's 25th Air Flotilla from Rabaul, while it was covering a run, down through The Slot, of the so-called Tokyo Express—the enemy's destroyer-transport ferrying service to Guadalcanal. The *raison d'etre* of the Express was to bring in troops—despite American efforts to the contrary, a never ending supply. Usually coming down on the dark of the moon (nights were normally of twelve hours' duration), the Express became the nemesis of our destroyers and PT boats patrolling in The Slot.

For the Navy this was a period of parry and thrust, with a third major naval engagement looming on the horizon. For the Marines it was a time of waiting, for Vandegrift fully anticipated a large scale attack from the 4,000 enemy troops estimated to be on the island. The general's list of grievances was growing in inverse proportion to his dwindling aircraft and human casualties, and he was not only angered but alarmed. So was the naval high command under whom he operated. We had started this desperate campaign on a shoestring, with less strength than the Japanese, and our losses had made the unfavorable margin even greater. Everything possible was being done and would be as the Navy took blow after blow, punching hard in return. The bitterly fought campaign of knock-down, drag-out battles on the sea, ashore and in the air, has no parallel in the war. No more gallant epic can be found in the Navy's long role of heroic service to the country.

Although Vandegrift strengthened his eastern flank, a major enemy attack developed on the night of September 12 along the Lunga River, which pushed back Captain John B. Sweeney's company to within 1,500 yards of Henderson Field. The screaming charges were punctuated with cries of "Roosevelt die! Marine pigs!" The demoniacal fury of the attacks against a curtain of Marine fire ended in death for most, while survivors were hauled off into the jungles before daylight. (Coincidental with *banzai* charges, Japanese warships roamed the waters off Guadalcanal with impunity, lobbing in shells and dropping green flares for the troops.)

At sea, September 15 was a bad day. Carrier *Wasp* was torpedoed by an enemy submarine and was given a *coup de grace* by a destroyer when all attempts to save the ship failed.

Reinforcements for both sides steadily poured into Guadalcanal: Hyakutate with the first of 25,000 men, and the United States Army's 164th Infantry Regiment of the American Division, which had been stationed in New Caledonia. To cover the arrival of the 164th, Ghormley scraped together everything he could find to provide an escort of three task groups; one of these was the cruisers and destroyers under Rear Admiral Norman Scott. Simultaneously, the enemy stepped up his air raids on Henderson Field. On the afternoon of October 11 Scott's Task Force 64 received intelligence indicating that a large cruiser-destroyer force was moving down The Slot at high speed. WE WILL INTERCEPT. ALL SHIPS PREPARE FOR ACTION, signaled the admiral.

The enemy force coming down was Rear Admiral Arimoto Goto's Bombardment and Guadalcanal reinforcement groups aggregating three heavy cruisers, eight destroyers and two seaplane carriers, packed with reinforcements and supplies for the Imperial Army.

At 10 P.M. Scott's force was patrolling in the waters off Cape Esperance, the northernmost tip of Guadalcanal. The flagship, *San*

Francisco, was at the head of the cruiser column, followed by *Boise, Salt Lake City* and *Helena;* in the van were destroyers *Duncan, Laffey* and *Fahrenholt;* and *Buchanan* and *McCalla* brought up the rear. At 10:28 P.M., Scott ordered a course change which put Task Force 64 on a line with Savo Island, where he hoped to intercept. At 10:52 P.M., the first of a series of sighting reports from Scott's float planes reached the flagship's bridge: ONE LARGE AND TWO SMALL VESSELS X WILL INVESTIGATE X

Scott closed steadily, confident in his battle plan. At 11:52 P.M., during a night described in dispatches as "black as spades, punctuated by occasional flashes of heat lightning," *Helena's* new radar reported a contact twenty-seven thousand yards distant. This was swiftly followed by *Boise's* report of five "pips." *Helena's* Captain Gilbert C. Hoover requested permission to fire, and a moment later Captain Edward C. "Iron Mike" Moran of *Boise* asked the same. Permission was granted instantly, and the battle broke out.

Helena's first salvo drew blood, her 8-inch shells raining down in profusion on the unsuspecting Japanese force; *Salt Lake City* took on a cruiser four thousand yards off her starboard bow and had the satisfaction of seeing her shells rip into Goto's flagship at almost point-blank range, while the destroyers flailed away at anything they could find, big or small. The story of *Boise's* battle is told by Frank D. Morris, the biographer of the celebrated warship.

5.

"PICK OUT THE BIGGEST!"

. . . The night was moonless and the solid blackness offered the Japs a perfect opportunity for sneaking in their ships and troop reinforcements. The same black cloak covered the movements of the *Boise's* task group and, as the men topside stood at their battle stations, they could barely make out the silhouettes of the other ships. Men coming on deck from below stepped into what at first seemed an impenetrable pool of darkness, bumping blindly into shipmates, but as eyes became adjusted, details began to emerge from the soft, warm gloom. First the familiar outlines of the deck; gradually, the masts ahead of and behind the *Boise;* and finally, after long minutes, the blurred and deceptive shapes of the other ships of the task force. There was no sound in all the blackness except for the sharp hiss and wash of the water spilt by the *Boise's* sharp prow, and the hum of her powerful machinery far below.

Earlier in the evening, that blackness had been sundered by an accident that, for a time, threatened to spoil the whole surprise party. An observation plane, on being catapulted from one of the other cruisers, had crashed into the sea and caught fire. The plane didn't sink immediately, but stayed afloat for what seemed like hours. A tall column of flame, fed by high-octane gas, lit up the sky for miles around. For a while it seemed almost certain that this fiery, revealing beacon would be detected by the enemy ships the *Boise* group were hoping to intercept, giving them a chance to get away. But nothing happened.

Seven bells. Eleven-thirty. The *Boise* men had been at General Quarters for hours now. Captain Moran stood in the center of the flying bridge, looking straight ahead. Behind him, wearing a phone headset under his dishpan-shaped steel helmet, stood Mr. Laffan, the gunnery officer. At Mike's right was Bill Butler, the anti-aircraft boss, also wired for sound. On the Skipper's other side, Ensign Davis, the *Boise's* signal officer, waited for orders.

In a lofty perch just abaft the bridge, Sam Forter, a young lieutenant just two years out of Annapolis, presided over the forward director of the main battery. His director crew was crowded around him in the tiny space allotted them. Most of the room was taken up by the range-finder and other instruments and their accessories, with occasional niches just big enough for the men themselves.

Lieutenant Forter was a kid with dark hair, brushed straight back, and narrow, piercing eyes. As director officer he held a strategic job—to locate enemy targets and set in motion the wheels that would establish almost instantly the direction and distance of those targets. In a recent night battle practice, Sam had distinguished himself by his remarkable proficiency in locating targets with a minimum of error. And aboard the *Boise* he had another distinction—his home town was Boise, Idaho.

In a director station just below and forward of the forward director were the 'eyes' of the five-inch guns of the *Boise's* secondary battery. An assistant gunnery officer, Lieutenant Dave Edwards, of Piedmont, California, was in charge here. These directors, plus two similar directors aft, did the actual 'seeing' for the *Boise's* gunners. The subsequent brainwork, after the target had been sighted, was done in the plotting room below decks. Here mammoth, intricate calculators waited with gaping maws for a lot of figures to be thrown in—estimated range, direction of target, speed of both ships, windage, etc. With Buck Rogers efficiency and speed this jumble of figures was mechanically translated into a precise solution to be punctuated a few seconds later by the roar of the *Boise's* guns. The whole system of directors, 'plot' and spotting (checking up on hits or misses after the first rounds are fired), is called fire control.

The *Boise's* fire-control men were on edge tonight. They instinctively sensed that another night battle practice was imminent, only this time it wouldn't be practice. The men in the turrets and at the broadside batteries also had a hunch. They were responsible for keep-ing in shape the steel muscles that did the actual punching. Now, in the dim light of the turrets, standing by the deck mounts, they waited impatiently for the punching to begin.

William Garfield Thomas, turret officer of Turret One, sat up in his tiny cubical waiting for a phone call. The words he wanted to hear were "Commence firing." Bill had been in the service a little more than two years and was now a junior-grade lieutenant. He was one of the most popular J. L.'s aboard ship. His disposition was famous in the wardroom; no one could ever ruffle him. The boys called him 'Beaverhead' because he wore his hair close-cropped.

'Beaverhead' was proud of his turret and of the crew that he had trained to man it so well that it had become one of the *Boise's* E turrets. Tonight he wanted to add a couple of J's—for Japs—to that honor. Hours before, he had reported, 'Turret One manned and ready.' Now he was waiting for further orders.

The men stationed at the five-inch guns on the open deck were all in the same expectant mood. At Gun One on the starboard side forward, Gun Captain King tested his primer for the fifteenth time and the resulting 'ping' was satisfactory. Over his phone, King heard a soft chant, repeated several times: "Pass the word from gun to gun. This won't be a dummy run." Around him the first and second load-ers and ammunition-passers shifted their weight from one foot to the other as they talked in low tones. "Boy, this looks like our chance to get in some real licks. Come on, Yamamoto, bring on those ships!" The invitation, directed to Admiralty Headquarters, was sincere.

About twenty minutes before midnight that invitation was an-swered. The task force had scouted the waters in the vicinity of Cape Esperance, where enemy ships would be most likely to be encoun-tered, and had approached to within a couple of miles of Savo Island before puttting about on a west-northwest bearing to intercept any Jap ships that might be coming down from their bases to the northeast. Lieutenant Forter, up in his director, was still staring into black space when suddenly he blinked at a distant group of objects barely visible on the *Boise's* starboard bow.

"On the target!" Sam spoke into his headset phone.

"How many ships?" Iron Mike's question was relayed through the gunnery officer, now standing beside him.

"Seem to be five, sir."

"Pick out the biggest and commence firing!"

Down in the turrets there was an instant tautening of nerves and muscle as Mike Moran's order was relayed to the pointers and trainers seated beside their guns. The turrets shook as fifteen guns fired in a single tremendous blast, lunging backward in swift recoil before sliding forward again. Breeches flew open, the next shells were out of the hoists and rammed home with beautiful precision, and again the turrets shook: this was the rhythm of fire for which these men had trained so long.

Other cruisers in the *Boise's* column had opened their searchlight shutters. The beams, clear and pulsating, sliced through the darkness and found their targets. Then the five-inch guns crackled and star shells shot out into the sky, to burst and hang like fiery flowers behind the Jap ships, silhouetting them clearly.

The first salvo was a direct hit. Iron Mike knew that the follow-up salvos were just as well aimed when he saw the target start blazing amidships and, in the brilliant light of that blaze, young Sam Forter's choice was justified. The victim was a Japanese cruiser of either the Nachi or Kako class, mounting eight-inch guns against the *Boise's* six-inchers. The middle-weight *Boise* had climbed into the ring with a light-heavy and had scored a knockout in the first round.

For four solid minutes the *Boise's* main battery poured hot steel into the blazing Jap. The pointers and trainers saw their shells go out in flat arcs, their ends reddened from the heat of the explosion that had started them on their way, seemingly moving slowly across the night through the searchlight beams before dropping on the target. Other ships in the task group were also pounding away at the Jap. Most of the hits were amidships and the explosions and resultant damage gradually cut her in two like a blow-torch slicing an iron bar. A series of fires was blazing away on the heavy cruiser now, her guns were silenced, and her internal explosions were popping like firecrackers in a tin can. She broke in two. Her bow slid under the waves, and the screws were still turning on her up-ended stern as it sank separately. As she went under, the *Boise* men saw the smoke of her destruction form a wreath over her grave.

"Cease firing!" Mike rang the bell ending Round One.

The *Boise*—the erstwhile Reluctant Dragon—had drawn first blood—Jap blood. The men on deck were jubilant. Below, an announcement over the ship's loudspeaker system broke the news to those who couldn't see the show. There were cheers and yells of glee. The Hollywood sailors pounded each other on the back and shouted for more.

"Shift target and resume firing!" Again Iron Mike barked an order to his gunnery officer. That order, passed on to Lieutenant Forter, was hardly necessary, for that gentleman instantly had his director trained on a second target, a Jap destroyer, and the *Boise's* starboard secondary battery of five-inch guns was starting to work it over. Other ships in the *Boise's* task group had been concentrating their fire on a cruiser, which now was ablaze and was exposing the destroyer target beautifully. The range was closing rapidly now as the two opposing columns of ships approached each other and started swapping short jabs.

Again the first shells fired by the *Boise's* guns hit true and hard. There were occasional splashes in the water on either side of the Jap can, but in between these splashes were direct hits as the four secondary-battery guns on the *Boise's* starboard side spat out their five-inch parcels of destruction. Ammunition was coming up from below in a steady stream, and neither Gun Captain King nor the other gun captains were wasting it. They ended that round very quickly. The deluge of fire was too much for the Jap and in less than a minute she broke in two and disappeared. It probably had taken the Japs well over a year to build this ship. The *Boise* had disposed of her in less than sixty seconds.

Iron Mike and the other officers on the bridge were fascinated. Signal Officer Davis had never seen a more thrilling sight in his twenty-three years in the Navy. "She looked just like an automobile going over the brow of a hill," he said happily. "She just slid under and went out of sight."

To the gun crews and the men on the directors this was getting pleasantly monotonous. "Sighted Jap. Sank Jap." They were in the groove. The months of daily gun drills under Mike Moran's relentless rule were understandable now. As soon as one target became a shattered clay pigeon, another loomed up in their sights waiting to be hit.

The *Boise* was no longer feeling her way along in the dark. Blazes on other ships in the Jap force had been started by the accurate shelling of the cruisers and destroyers of the task group. There were several inviting targets displayed in this glare and now, between rounds, Mike crouched down in a huddle on the flying bridge with Gunnery Officer Laffan and Bill Butler.

"Which one shall we get next?" The grin on Mike's face didn't conceal his excitement.

"How about that destroyer over there—she's nearest." Laffan

pointed at another Jap destroyer. The can was silhouetted against the blazing ships around her.

"Let's get her!" Mike reached for his binoculars and trained them on the *Boise's* next victim. "Shift target and resume firing."

Both main and secondary batteries opened up on the Jap destroyer and both were on the beam. Before many rounds had been fired, a chain of explosions and fires aboard her vividly showed the *Boise* gunners where their shells had landed. The heavy blast of gunfire from Mike Moran's men was too much for her thin sides. The destroyer slid behind a curtain of smoke pouring from other destroyers in her force and she never came out of it. When the smoke had lifted, she was no more.

There was plenty of illumination over the Japs then. Three of their ships were ablaze, one of them with two fires burning brightly. These were all that was left of the original force of six. Lieutenant Forter had missed one in his initial report. The remaining ships had been hit, but some of their guns were still firing and inflicting damage.

The *Boise* herself wasn't shellproof. About this time the signal bridge reported splashes on both port and starboard sides, close aboard. These were salvos from an enemy heavy cruiser some distance ahead on the *Boise's* starboard bow. And as Mike Moran's men fired on her, the Jap cruiser returned the fire with gusto. Splashes from her salvos came nearer and nearer, throwing salt water over the *Boise's* decks, superstructure, and anti-aircraft guns.

Finally one of these shells, an eight-incher, smacked into the *Boise's* starboard side, forward, just above the waterline. It exploded in the crew's mess hall. Two lighter shells, probably five-inch, hit the starboard side of the superstructure, and another pair pierced the side of the ship and let go in the Captain's cabin, wrecking the interior and setting it afire. "Tell the gentlemen I'm sorry I wasn't at home," Iron Mike murmured when news of what had happened to his cabin was relayed to him.

Topside, the *Boise's* deck gunners were bearing the brunt of the enemy's return fire. Gun Captain King and his entire crew were hurled to the deck when Gun One, the first five-inch gun on the starboard side, was struck by a Jap shell and put out of action. Shell fragments and hot empty shell cases from their own expended ammunition showered around them as they struggled to their feet. Joe Vignali, a "hot-case" man, had just yanked one of these empty powder cartridges from the gun when the explosion knocked the case out of his hand. It bounced up, struck the overhead, and started to fall back.

Vignali was an agile cuss—although he had been knocked down by the same hit, he was up on his knees in an instant and actually caught the hot case in his arms as it descended. "Never dropped one yet," he yelled above the din. "Ain't goin' to start now!"

Another member of the gun crew, First Class Seaman Pitzer, wasn't so lucky. A large shell fragment struck his knee, mangling it badly. When he tried to get up, he found he couldn't, and he subsequently was carried off to a battle dressing station.

Sightsetter Lowry, on Gun Three near-by, felt a sharp spray against his leg, but he stuck to his post during the remainder of the action. After he finally collapsed and was carried off, one of the *Boise's* doctors dug thirty-two pieces of shell out of this leg and showed him the tin hat he had been wearing. In it was a jagged hole two inches across—a souvenir of that shell blast.

Mike Moran's men had been so occupied in their job of knocking off the three Jap ships that it hadn't occurred to them that the *Boise* herself might be hit. One of them, a chief named Schermerhorn who acted as trainer on Sam Forter's director, was surprised and indignant when that barrage of Jap shells found their mark. "What the hell!" he bellowed. "The sons of bitches are shooting back at us!"

Below decks, the results of that shooting were keeping many people busy. Where the *Boise* had been hit, solid bulkheads split wide open, paint was burning, and gas from the exploding shells swept aft, choking everyone it encountered.

From Central Station, Tom Wolverton was dispatching fire-fighting and repair parties to damaged areas of the ship. Telephone circuits connected him with his 'branch offices'—separate repair parties stationed forward, aft, and amidships. His job now was comparable to that of a prize-fighter's second. His men did their work between rounds, moving quickly and surely to get the champ ready for the next bell.

Commander Wolverton had also taken upon himself another job. Most of the ship's personnel were closed off below decks in sealed compartments behind dogged hatches and, naturally, were missing most of the real excitement. They could hear the muffled roar of the *Boise's* guns and the occasional sound of enemy shells bursting ominously close, and that didn't help much. So the Damage Control Officer volunteered to man a microphone on the ship's loudspeaker system and broadcast a running account of the battle from reports relayed to him by phone from observers on deck.

When Mr. Wolverton had first passed the word that the enemy had been engaged, he noticed that most of the men around him in the Central Station had suddenly gone tense. Grim expressions were frozen on their faces and hardly a word had been said.

He recognized the symptoms immediately. These men, as brave as any aboard, were facing an enemy they couldn't see and their nervousness was natural. Their reaction reminded him of a remark his four-year-old son had made, the first time Wolverton had taken him for a ride on a roller-coaster, when the car was approaching the top of the first steep dip. The men with set faces stationed around him had heard this story and had chuckled over it. Now, Wolverton decided, was a good time to remind them of it. In the stillness of that crowded Central Station, deep in the *Boise's* interior, a voice boomed out ridiculously in baby talk: "Daddy—I want to go home now!"

The effect was magical. Grins spread over a dozen faces as men settled back and relaxed. Psychology Professor Wolverton then resumed his other jobs as Damage Control Officer and radio announcer.

There were no sealed envelopes this time, no prearranged plot. This damage control problem was real.

"Carpenter Thomas—Carpenter Thomas. Fire in the Captain's cabin. Lay aft with your repair party and report!"

When Thomas and his men reached Iron Mike's living quarters, they found a flaming shambles. Apparently the shells had landed squarely in the center of the room before they exploded. As they dragged their fire hoses through the five-by-three foot hole the explosion had made, the repair-party men saw a twisted mass of metal furniture on the deck. Everything inflammable in there was ablaze. The deck and bulkhead had been punctured and gouged as the shells burst into a thousand flying fragments. Over in one corner, Mike's bunk was going up in smoke, and the place was a mess. A ship's clock had been knocked from its position on top of Mike's desk and now was lying broken on the deck, face up. The blast had stopped it at five minutes before midnight.

Trying to put out a raging fire in a ship still being rocked by enemy shells is no choice assignment, but within five minutes Carpenter Thomas reported to Mr. Wolverton that the blaze was under control. Meanwhile, a second fire farther aft in the mess hall had been doused even more quickly by another repair party.

The Jap cruiser responsible for all this damage was now paying the price. Her heavier eight-inch guns were still throwing steel haymakers at the light cruiser, but most of the *Boise's* guns—plus those of the other ships in her group—were answering in kind. As he watched them hammer this fourth target, Iron Mike had reason to be proud of the marksmanship of his gun crews. First he saw a series of fires spring up on the Jap's deck, then there were several violent explosions. That was the beginning of a very quick end for Target Number Four.

The crews of the starboard deck guns had borne the brunt of the hits in the Captain's cabin. They had carried away the electrical leads on Gun One, putting it temporarily out of action, but the crews of the other three five-inch guns, although tossed around by the blast, were back on the job almost immediately. At the most, they missed only one salvo. A stand-by man jumped into Pitzer's place at Gun Three, and everything continued to function as smoothly as though there had been no interruption.

Dan Brand, a young reserve lieutenant—Brown, '40—who was a secondary battery officer, had been standing twenty feet away from the spot where that shell had landed. As he was getting to his feet, he saw Frank Hurst, a chief boatswain's mate and battery officer of Gun One, trying to unscramble himself from a pile of empty shell cases. The hit that had disabled his gun had thrown him against a bulkhead, and the empty cases showered around him as they hit the overhead and bounced back to the deck.

Chief Hurst, a plank-owner, had been in gunnery for thirteen years. He sized up the situation immediately. A fire had started on the splintered deck, so the first thing he did was to empty the ammunition hoist of all live shells while two other men in his crew played a hose on the blaze. Luckily the ammunition-passers had just completed a round trip from hoist to gun, so there was no live ammunition exposed at the time of the hit.

Gun Captain King checked his mount. The damage to the electrical leads meant there would be no more director control. King spent all of two minutes testing and inspecting the rest of the mount and went into a quick huddle with Brand and Hurst.

"I think we can fire it manually. I'm going to try kicking them out," he told them.

Lieutenant Brand watched anxiously as the first shell was loaded and rammed by hand. He knew what can happen to a gun when you try to fire it after it has been disabled. Injury to the barrel or breech mechanism might cause the gun to blow up and kill everyone in the vicinity. But he and Chief Hurst also had complete confidence in King's gunnery ability, which was backed by five years of experience. He, too, had been aboard the *Boise* since her commissioning and he was as familiar with each of her guns as a mother hen with her chicks. He gave the order to fire.

The five-inch gun spoke sharply and the message it carried was a direct hit on the enemy heavy cruiser—not bad for a cripple. And as round after round was "kicked out" by King, Brand and Hurst had the satisfaction of seeing the manually operated weapon score a total of three punishing hits on the Jap before the "Cease firing" order came. King himself didn't see these hits. He was too busy trying to get more.

It was now almost midnight. The not so Reluctant Dragon had been in action less than a quarter of an hour and, with the other ships in her task group, had disposed of four enemy ships. Two of these had had guns heavier than the *Boise's*. Iron Mike stood on the flying bridge and watched tracer shells from his main battery crisscross tracers from the secondary as they plowed their way toward the Jap ships. The range was almost point-blank now. Both forces were now steaming on 'collision' courses that ultimately would bring them together at the apex of a huge V.

Signal Officer Davis realized then it was for this moment he had joined the Navy twenty-three years before. To him it was just like a skeet shoot. Fix your sights on the 'pigeon' just released and—bang! —it disappeared, shattered. Turn half-around and there was another pigeon. Bang!—no more pigeon. Turn and shoot! Turn and shoot!

One of Lieutenant Forter's assistants in the main battery director had quit his job as butcher in an A. & P. store to join the Navy. Ronald Eagle was now a fire-control man, third class, and tonight's fireworks display reminded him suddenly of the mine feuds and accompanying gunplay he'd seen down in his home town in 'Bloody Harlan' County in Kentucky. Now Ronald was complaining to his boss.

"Gee, Mr. Forter, they keep yelling for ranges. How the hell can we give 'em ranges when the damned targets disappear so fast?"

"That's easy, Eagle. Just find another target."

Eagle was watching the second Jap heavy cruiser disintegrate under the shell-fire the *Boise* and her accompanying ships were pouring on its decks and sides. Most of the Jap ship's length looked like a mass of white-hot steel and, in sharp contrast, the bow, still untouched by the bombardment, was a dark gray. Eagle could even see her two anchors jutting from their hawsepipes. Amidships, her twin stacks and two plane catapults were outlined against a flaming background.

The fourth round was ended in as many minutes. When Iron Mike saw several explosions break the Jap cruiser into pieces, he gave the order to cease firing. Then he went into another arms-around-the-shoulder huddle with his gunnery officers, Laffan and Butler. The *Boise* still had tons of ammunition left. She had been lugging it around with her all these months for just such a party. There were more Jap ships out there, Mike reasoned: let's send them a few shipments of steel.

For two full minutes the *Boise* had immediately available targets. The deck gun crews spent the time cleaning up around their mounts. Dozens of empty cartridge cases, cluttering the deck around each gun were heaved over the ship's side and the debris caused by the hits on the cruiser's starboard side was cleared away. The gunners would need plenty of operating room when they resumed firing. A heavy, sweetish odor blanketed the ship—cordite fumes from the hundreds of rounds of ammunition fired.

"Well, what'll we get next?" Iron Mike put it up to his assistant coaches huddled with him on the flying bridge.

"There's one burning over there. How about him?" Gunnery Officer Laffan pointed toward a Jap destroyer that had just burst into flames, evidently the result of a hit by one of the *Boise's* companions.

"Okay," Mike replied. "Let's get him. Shift target and resume firing."

Mr. Laffan had Sam Forter, high in the forward director, on the wire and was indicating the ship on which the *Boise* was now to train her main battery. Forter had also seen her blaze up and in no time at all he had the range. A very few seconds later, the *Boise's* six- and five-inch guns were whamming away at the Jap destroyer, and very few whams were wasted. Two minutes after Mike Moran's men had opened fire on their latest target, there was one less Japanese destroyer for the editors of *Jane's Fighting Ships,* the Bible of the world's navies, to record.

Even Gun One was still in there punching. She was operating on local control with Gun Captain King kicking them out.

"Gun One. Sky Forward testing. Gun One. Sky Forward testing." It was Lieutenant Edwards calling from his director.

"King speaking."

"How are you making out?"

"We're doing all right, sir. The gun's a little wobbly, but she's still firing."

"Nice work . . . but be careful."

Carpenter Thomas and his repair party were still mopping up the fire in Iron Mike's cabin. Some of his men had been sent to douse the deck of the radio shack, directly above, when it threatened to catch fire. Others were busy stopping up the hole in the *Boise's* side just above the waterline. Mattresses backed by bedsprings were jammed into the opening as a temporary patch to prevent flooding of the compartment by the bow wave the galloping *Boise* was kicking up. The shell that made this hole had completely demolished the quarters of a half-dozen of the cruiser's junior officers, and the repair party men working in that section had to fight their way through the wreckage.

"Enemy destroyer contacted . . . The *Boise* has opened fire on the destroyer . . . She is blazing in several places . . . Enemy destroyer sunk by gunfire." Tom Wolverton's blow-by-blow narrative over the loudspeaker system was getting hotter than a Joe Louis fight broadcast. It was a godsend to the men cooped up below. Down in the engine and fire rooms there was comparative quiet and calm. The men stationed there were interested primarily in keeping up the steam pressure so that the *Boise* could maintain her speed. Extra boilers had been lit off to provide for power for possible emergency speed increases. There was little excitement here. One man walked around the steel catwalks, taking bearing temperatures and reporting them to the officer on watch. All through the action he continued this prosaic assignment as placidly as though he were making a regular run on the Staten Island ferry.

Midnight had passed and Mike Moran, with Laffan and Butler, was looking about for another Japanese target. For the moment there was none handy, and Sam Forter was training his director on a 'searching' course, trying to make it six in a row for the *Boise*. Down in the magazines and handling rooms the men who had been shipping ammunition topside in wholesale quantites were having a much-needed rest. Gunner's Mate Paul Kunkel had been feeding an ammunition hoist in the forward handling room and was still standing by, but the hoist had been shut down. His powder-handling crew consisted of a half-dozen Guamanians and several colored mess attendants. They stood there now, immobile, their bodies glistening with sweat from their recent exertion and the heat of the below-decks space that by now reeked with powder fumes.

At five minutes after midnight, Iron Mike was startled by a cry from the signal bridge: "Torpedo approaching ship on starboard bow!"

A signalman with eagle eyes had sighted the white foam of the torpedo track.

ALTHOUGH JAPANESE TORPEDOES SLASHED IN AROUND their flaming target, all of them missed. However, Moran's doughty command was now definitely out of action.

Now let us look back at the other American warships. When the battle opened, Task Force 64's favorite target was Goto's unsuspecting flagship, *Aoba,* which was promptly inundated with forty large-caliber shells. The Japanese admiral was mortally wounded and Captain Kijuma, the flagship's commanding officer, took over. Meanwhile, destroyers *Furutaka* and *Fubuki* were holed and sunk, while *Duncan* (soon to be abandoned) was caught in a crossfire: shells ripped into the chart house, bridge and gun director, killing everyone there, while others battered her communications center and radar plotting rooms; the forward third of the ship became a glut of flames. More shells landed below in her forward engine room, and all power was lost. At the same time American destroyer *Fahrenholt,* victim of a communications failure, was caught in a crossfire. Shells ripped through her thin-skinned hull, flooded her gun plot, and wrecked her fire control wiring; others struck below, causing a loss of power and releasing a murderous jet of steam. *Salt Lake City* absorbed a few hits while engaging an enemy cruiser, and *San Francisco,* leader of the group which had pumped heavy fire into *Kinugasa* and *Aoba,* came away relatively unscathed.

While the battle was a clear-cut American victory, removing some of the sting of Savo, the Japanese reinforcement groups did manage to land their troops and supplies on the island. Nevertheless, the Navy's fortunes were in the ascendancy.

Only two nights after Scott's victory, Japan sent down a mighty bombardment group formed around the battleships *Haruna* and *Kongo* to maul the defenders of Henderson Field. While the Marines cowered in their foxholes, some nine hundred 14-inch shells pummeled the airstrip in the worst assault of the campaign. For eighty uninterrupted minutes the Japanese ranged with impunity along the coast hurling their explosives, until a squadron of newly-arrived PT boats sneaked out of Tulagi to give battle, much as a mosquito tangling with a whale. However, Admiral Takeo Kurita was so annoyed that he broke off his bombardment. In his wake he left a burning, chewed-up airstrip and a good number of thoroughly shaken Marines.

So desperate was the situation that Nimitz in Pearl Harbor observed: "It now appears that we are unable to control the area in the sea around the Guadalcanal area. Thus our control of the positions will only be done at great expense to us. The situation is not hopeless, but it is certainly critical."

Scarcely a fortnight after Cape Esperance another major confrontation appeared imminent as Yamamoto's forces, numbering four carriers, five battleships, fourteen cruisers and forty-four destroyers, were poised for the capture of Henderson Field. Opposing the Japanese armada were two carriers, two battleships, nine cruisers and twenty-four destroyers divided into three groups. On October 23 United States forces were off the Santa Cruz Islands, east of the Solomons, when a PBY flying boat "snooped" an enemy carrier and reported her position. Task Force 16, under Rear Admiral Thomas C. Kinkaid in battle-scarred *Enterprise,* launched a combined search and strike. Heavy weather, however, prevented accurate reconnaissance and the battle did not break out until the morning of October 26. Although in the ensuing engagement the United States lost carrier *Hornet* and suffered damage to several other warships, enemy carriers *Shokaku* and *Zuikaku* were so heavily damaged that they were out of the war for months. But, most important, the battle was a tactical American victory, for the thrust on Guadalcanal was decisively turned back and we gained precious time to reinforce and prepare.

Commander Edward P. Stafford, biographer of *Enterprise,* narrates the events of Santa Cruz.

6.

ACTION OFF SANTA CRUZ

At 3:00 P.M. on the twenty-third, the combined task force began a sweep to the northwest to interpose between Guadalcanal and the threatening enemy fleet to the northward.

By destroyers and barges at night and an occasional daylight landing, the Japanese had slowly built up their forces on Guadalcanal. Their strongest naval forces since Midway were at sea; four carriers —*Shokaku, Zuikaku, Zuiho, Junyo*—eight heavy cruisers, two light cruisers and twenty-eight destroyers. The goal of the Japanese Army on Guadalcanal and the Navy a few hundred miles to the north was Henderson Field. The Army was to capture the field. Carrier planes would fly in at once. Caught between the carriers and Henderson, U. S. naval forces would be sunk or forced away and the U. S. Marines, cut off, could be mopped up. The evil-smelling, worthless, priceless island would be back in Japanese hands, the threat of an American counter-attack up the Solomon chain ended, and the march to cut the U.S.-Australian life line could be resumed. But first it was necessary to capture Henderson Field.

October 22 was selected as the date on which the all-important airport would change hands. The Marines upset the schedule by driving back tank and infantry attacks. They upset it again around midnight of the twenty-third. By this time the Big E had arrived from Pearl to double U. S. naval strength in the Solomons.

By the twenty-fourth the big enemy sea forces had been circling between Truk and Guadalcanal for nearly two weeks. Oil and patience were running low. Admiral Yamamoto in Truk radioed the Army commander on Guadal that unless Henderson Field could be delivered quickly, naval forces could be counted out. Fuel would be too low to risk battle.

In the small hours of the twenty-fifth, the Army announced Henderson in Japanese hands and Yamamoto's fleet turned southeast. At daylight the enemy soldiers were no longer so sure about Henderson, and Kinkaid was approaching head-on at 20 knots with *Enterprise* and *Hornet* SBDs fanning out ahead. Unless the Japanese retreated hurriedly, they were committed to action, Henderson or no Henderson.

At ten minutes of one on the afternoon of the twenty-fifth Admiral Kinkaid, then some 250 miles east and a little north of the Santa Cruz Islands, learned the whereabouts of his enemy. A PBY out of Espiritu had found two carriers 360 miles ahead steaming southeast at 25 knots. With the range closing at nearly fifty miles each hour, 12 armed SBDs left *Enterprise* at 2.30 P.M. covering from west through north out to 200 miles. An hour later the air group commander led off an attack group of 12 more Dauntlesses and 7 Avengers escorted by 16 fighters. The search extended beyond the Santa Cruz Islands and well to the northward over the darkening Pacific. It found nothing. It was an hour after sunset when the planes got back over the carrier. Many of the younger pilots had never made a night carrier landing. Lieutenant Frank Miller flew his Wildcat into the sea forty miles from the ship and was killed, probably as a result of insufficient oxygen during the long, high-altitude flight. Three TBFs and three SBDs used the last of their fuel in the landing pattern and ditched. Destroyers picked up all the crews. The moon was just clearing the horizon as the last plane caught a wire and was snubbed to a stop on the Big E's blacked-out deck.

All night Admiral Kinkaid's ships zigzagged northwest toward the enemy at 20 knots.

Every man in *Enterprise* knew the next day would bring action with the enemy. The brand-new, eager air group was just ten days away from the classrooms and training flights of Kaneohe. Throughout the ship new men wondered how they would act under the bombs or guns of the Japanese and the old hands went carefully about their duties assuring themselves that their particular equipments were ready for the morning and, to the best of their ability, closing their minds to the coming battle.

Commander John Crommelin called his pilots together in the wardroom. While they sat in their open-collared khaki along the green-covered tables with coffee cups before them and the smoke flattening out among the trunks and cables on the overhead, he gave them the straight, true, vigorous words they needed to hear. They had all been carefully and thoroughly trained, he told them; they knew how to drop a bomb and have it hit. And he damned well expected them to do just that. The safety and success of the Marines in their long, miserable struggle for Guadalcanal now depended 100 per cent on how well the Big E's pilots did their duty. There was no room for waste, no excuse for misses. If they were going to get out there and miss, it would have been better if they had stayed back in the States and given *good* pilots their bunks and a crack at the enemy. Crommelin's Alabama accent thickened as he made his last point and the lights on the low wardroom overhead glittered on his sandy, graying hair. He hoped no one had any illusions about being overworked. The men in that room were a major part of all that stood between the Japanese and Guadalcanal. And on Guadalcanal depended the war in the South Pacific. He would use them however and whenever necessary and the better they were the better their chances. He would use them over and over and over again. Now they were to rest and knock those sons-of-bitches off the face of the earth in the morning.

All the *Enterprise* pilots knew Crommelin's combat record, had seen him slow roll across Kaneohe at a hundred feet to give them confidence in their planes, knew he was requiring nothing of them he was not well able to perform himself and they went to their bunks and fell asleep with his words stringing across behind their eyes—". . . over and over and over and over again."

Before daylight on the twenty-sixth—while early breakfast was being served to sailors with faces still creased from their bedding, while aircraft were being armed and rechecked and pilots briefed—a message was received from the headquarters of the commander, South Pacific Force, at Noumea. It was in a familiar style. Three words:

ATTACK. REPEAT, ATTACK

Only one man could have sent it and the Big E's men knew him well. Bill Halsey was back in the war.

Halsey had taken over as commander, South Pacific Area and South Pacific Force, on the eighteenth and it was by his order that Kinkaid's task force was engaged in the northwestward sweep which had found the enemy. A new confidence stirred through the *Enterprise*.

At 6:00 A.M., twenty-three minutes before sunrise, sixteen Dauntlesses left the Big E's deck and fanned out in pairs to search the morning sea from southwest through north to a distance of 200 miles. A few moments later eight Wildcats clawed steeply up to establish a Combat Air Patrol and six more SBDs circled out on the watch for subs.

The battlefield had been chosen. It was a thousand square miles of the South Pacific lying just to the northward of the fiercely malarial Santa Cruz islands. The sea was calm except for the long ground swell that is never still and the friendly ripples of a six- to ten-knot breeze. From 1,500 to 2,000 feet drifted white and gold cumulus clouds covering nearly half the dawn sky. Above them there was no ceiling and below visibility was unlimited.

Like exploring fingers the Big E's scouting sections probed westward across the sea that had to hold the enemy. Eighty-five miles out, Welch and McGraw of Bombing Ten passed a single-float enemy scout on the opposite course, and twenty minutes later they made the first contact, the strange pagoda-like superstructure of a *Kongo*-class battleship breaking the clean line of the horizon ahead. The two SBDs pulled up into the bases of the low clouds and circled the enemy force at ten miles, alternately in the bright sunlight and the gray turbulent insides of the cumulus. At 7:30 A.M. the "dits" and "dahs" of Welch's contact report beeped loudly into the Big E's code room with the unhurried clarity of a communications drill:

TWO BATTLESHIPS, ONE HEAVY CRUISER, SEVEN DESTROYERS. LATITUDE 8 DEGREES 10 MINUTES SOUTH, LONGITUDE 163 DEGREES, 55 MINUTES EAST. COURSE NORTH. SPEED TWENTY KNOTS

Bareheaded and short-sleeved among the Big E's helmeted and lifejacketed bridge crew, Admiral Kinkaid paced and fretted. The admiral stopped for a minute to watch the big bedspring antenna of the air-search radar slowly sweeping the sky, then walked to the rail and looked for the twentieth time at the loaded SBDs and TBFs crowded together on the flight deck. Ducking through the crowded pilothouse to the starboard wing of the bridge, he lifted the binoculars hanging around his neck and saw a bigger deck load of planes ready on the

Hornet ten miles away. This was the Big E's day to search and follow with a small strike. The real punch was on the *Hornet*.

At ten minutes of eight Kinkaid heard what he had been waiting to hear. The radios in the coding room came alive again and the watch could recognize the firm clear hand of Chief I. A. Sanders, flying with Lieutenant Commander J. R. "Bucky" Lee, skipper of Scouting Ten:

TWO CARRIERS AND ACCOMPANYING VESSELS, LATITUDE 7 DEGREES 5 MINUTES SOUTH, 163 DEGREES 38 MINUTES EAST

The admiral stepped into Flag Plot and looked closely at the chart. Two hundred miles to the northwest. The bright flags soared out of their bags to the yard arms and the shutter clattered on the 36-inch signal searchlight trained on the *Hornet*. Force speed went up to 27 knots and the bows swung into the northwest.

Fifteen miles east of the Japanese carriers, Lee and his wingman, W. E. Johnson, noses up and throttles forward, struggled for attack altitude. In Lee's rear seat Chief Sanders hammered out his contact report three more times to be sure it was received and then dropped his key and swung his guns up to the ready. Below them the enemy ships, as though in terror of the two thintailed SBDs, turned westward at high speed and fouled themselves with thick clouds of black smoke. From high overhead two four-plane sections of the Zero CAP spiraled down to attack. Lee and Johnson turned their Dauntlesses into fighters with guns at both ends, and in a wrapped up, heavy gutted, low-altitude swirl of wings and props and stringing tracers, with the horizon usually vertical and the ocean frequently overhead, shot down three of the overconfident Zeros before ducking into the friendly cumulus. In the desperate aerial game of hide and seek that followed, Lee and Johnson became separated. There was no chance of approaching the enemy ships again, alone, and, their mission completed, they returned singly to the ship.

Lieutenant Birney Strong, with Ensign Charles Irvine on his wing, were at the tip of the third of the Big E's probing fingers to the northward, a hundred miles from the two carriers reported by Chief Sanders. They had believed John Crommelin's words and absorbed the aggressive, determined spirit in which they were spoken. Garlow and Williams in their two rear seats had copied Welch's contact report on the battlewagons. Obviously the action was all to the south. Here the 500-pound bomb they each carried was wasted, the two loads of fuel and ammunition lugged around the sky for nothing.

Strong could hear John Crommelin's confident voice loud in the wardroom: "There is no room for waste, no excuse for misses!" Working fast, he plotted the Japanese battleship position on his board, drew the course line, figured briefly in pencil off to the side, glanced at his fuel gauges and motioned to Irvine, close on his wing. The right wings of the two Dauntlesses tipped up sharply as they turned south. Both pilots as they started climbing on the new course, eased back their mixture controls, watching the RPM and listening intently to the engines. They would need every yard they could get out of the gas left in their tanks now that they had added to their long search a climb to attack altitude, an extra hundred miles, and a fight if they could find it.

When Lee's report on the carriers came in a few minutes later they had to alter heading only a few degrees.

Lieutenant Stockton Birney Strong had no illusions about the two-plane attack on a task force that he was planning. He had been on carriers since the war began. The Gilbert Island strikes, Coral Sea and the August battle off the Eastern Solomons were all behind him, plus raids on Tulagi and the Lae Salamaua area off New Guinea. At Eastern Solomons he and Ensign Richey had located the *Ryujo*, carefully and accurately reported her position, course, speed and the composition of her force but had not attacked through the fighters and the flak. Strong had been thinking about that since the twenty-fourth of August and every time he thought about it, he thought it had been a mistake. He would not repeat it.

In the bright sunlight at 14,000 feet the four men in the two slim Dauntlesses stalked the heart of the enemy's naval strength.

The carriers that Lee and Johnson had found were *Shokaku* and *Zuikaku*. Their CAP was up, their guns loaded and trained out. A heavy cruiser and seven destroyers surrounded them.

Although they had been navigating only between careful visual searches and checks of engine instruments and fuel gauges, guessing at wind drift, Lee's contact report and Strong's interception were exactly accurate. At 8:30 A.M. Strong picked up two narrow yellow decks sliding toward him far below. They were *Shokaku* and the light carrier *Zuiho*. *Zuikaku*, a few miles away, was out of sight under a cloud.

Chuck Irvine saw them at the same time and moved in close. Both pilots charged their guns. Garlow and Williams clicked the safeties off their twin 30s. Strong led the section in a left turn, heading for an up-sun attack position. Below, the small yellow rectangles disappeared occasionally under puffs of cloud. The Zeros and the AA were overdue. Strong knew that luck alone was providing him with these moments and he was not a man to question the gift. Directly up-sun from *Zuiho,* the nearest carrier, he patted his head to Irvine, pulled up, split his flaps and rolled into the long dive that since December had become the purpose of his life. A thousand feet behind, Irvine followed down. Still there were no Zeros. Unruffled by any flak the dive was as smooth as a training exercise. The gunners lay on their backs wondering at the empty sky, waiting for the bouncing of the AA while the two pilots leaned forward, sweating with pure concentration, an eye pressed to the tubular scope where every pressure of right hands and toes moved the crosshairs on the expanding deck. There was time to notice that both decks were empty, that the enemy air groups had been launched. In succession at 1,500 feet their left hands went down and forward, found the release handles and pulled. It was done. And as the bombs fell away the AA came up and the Zeros closed from all directions. But it was too late. Both bombs plunged into the enemy flight deck near the stern and opened it wide with two splintering blasts rapidly followed by a pouring of black smoke.

Then the SBDs were flat down on the white caps, slipping, jerking, twisting under the lash of AA fire from the ships and repeated runs by the Zeros. With mixtures, throttles and prop controls all pushed forward over the end of the control quadrant, bombs gone, the pilots dodged and weaved and tried to cover each other. But Garlow and Williams, with their swinging, hammering .30-calibers, held the only real hope of getting the section back to base. Occasionally a Zero got careless. One of the first to attack ceased firing too soon and banked away, showing the plane's defenseless belly. Garlow stitched it thoroughly with lead during the instant it was exposed, and the fighter exploded into flame and rolled inverted into the sea. A few moments later Williams got one too and after that the attacks were not pressed home so closely. But the Zeros still came on, banking in from astern, all prop disk and wings with the guns blinking along the leading edges. And they could not all miss. Holes appeared in Irvine's right wing and tail, slowing him. Strong, seeing the holes and remembering his depleted fuel supply, doubted that they would make it home. But it was important that Admiral Kinkaid (and Commander Crommelin) know of the damage to the carrier. So with the Zeros still attacking, and Garlow doggedly giving them burst for burst, he opened up on his radio and announced the two hits, giving position, course and speed of the enemy force. Then he repeated it. The task force commander had to have the tactical information and John Crommelin had to know that with two SBDs they had put two 500-pound bombs on the target—two out of two. No waste of bombs or planes or gas or training. You couldn't do any better—unless you could get home too.

The two Dauntlesses took to the scattering clouds and at nine o'clock after a forty-five-mile chase, the last of the Zeros turned back. Now it was only a problem of flying home. But home was a hunted carrier, maneuvering on unknown courses at unknown speeds and maintaining radio silence some 150 salt-water miles away. With nearly empty tanks and shot-up airplanes only a direct and perfect course would provide a chance of success. At 10:26 A.M., Robin Lindsey's paddles waved Strong and Irvine aboard the *Enterprise* on the first pass, and with insufficient fuel for another had it been necessary.

Every SBD of the sixteen-plane dawn search returned safely to the ship. Half had made contact with the enemy. They had shot down seven Zeros attempting interception and left a carrier and a cruiser burning.

Now it was time for Thomas Kinkaid to strike his enemy. It was, in fact, past time.

A *Hornet* strike of 29 planes went off first. *Enterprise* followed with every flyable plane aboard except for 20 fighters of the CAP, and another *Hornet* group of 25 fell in behind. Loaded with bombs and torpedoes and with the target 200 miles away, the various formations could not wait to join up, but departed immediately and separately in the direction of the enemy.

The *Enterprise* strike consisted of eight Avengers, heavy with the long torpedoes in their bomb bays, three SBDs with 1,000-pound bombs and an escort of eight Wildcats. Behind and above, Commander Gaines, the air group commander, controlled the flight from a ninth TBF. With six Dauntlesses at the bottom of the sea after last evening's long search, six more on antisub patrol for the task force and sixteen straggling back from the morning scouting flight, the Big E was desperately short of dive bombers.

The attack group, conserving fuel, climbed slowly out on course. To the right and left, ahead and a thousand feet above, the two four-plane divisions of Wildcats weaved gently back and forth, throttled back to avoid outdistancing the slower Dauntlesses and Avengers. Navy Cross winner Lieutenant Commander James Flatley, the skipper of the "Grim Reapers" of Fighting Ten, led the right-hand division, Lieutenant John Leppla the left. Lep had been hand-picked by Flatley out of a Dauntless squadron on the old *Lexington* where he and his gunner John Liska had also won a Navy Cross at Coral Sea.

Twenty minutes after take-off and about forty-five miles from the ship, the fighter pilots at 6,000 feet were getting around to charging their guns, wondering what lay ahead of them and how they would conduct themselves. Below and behind them, at 4,000, some of the Avengers had not yet turned on their radio transmitters. The earphones of all the pilots crackled gently. Nothing was on the air. Jim Flatley led his division in another shallow turn to starboard and held it for about a minute. Then slowly he turned back and glanced over his left shoulder at the formation. The TBF piloted by Lieutenant Commander John A. Collet, the CO of Torpedo Ten, was spinning, with flame and smoke pouring from the engine and back over the cockpit. A second Avenger was slanting toward the sea, the canopy shattered and the pilot slumped in his seat. Behind and below, the four Wildcats of the other division were locked in a series of tight turns and climbs with a dozen Zeros. Two Zeros were falling away from the action in black ribbons of smoke. Ahead another was turning toward the TBFs for a second run. Flatley attacked in a diving left turn; the Zero turned right and pulled up but Flatley recovered above him and attacked again with a long burst at maximum range. The Zero began to smoke but continued straight ahead; on his next attack the fighter skipper hammered it into the sea.

When the seemingly endless string of Zeros flashed down out of the sun and through the torpedo plane formation, Ensign Dusty Rhodes reacted like the others in his Wildcat division, with shocked disbelief for about two seconds and then with a hard right turn toward what was left of the other group, shucking his drop tank, charging guns, jamming throttle, RPM and mixture into the stops in an attempt to close the dangerous speed advantage the diving Zeros held and to keep them off the remaining bombers.

The heavy, rugged F4F required an altitude advantage, which its weight could quickly convert to speed, in order to match the maneuverability of the Zero. Here the Zeros had caught the Wildcats slow and committed to the altitude of the bombers they were escorting, so they could not even dive away to gain speed and fight it out at low altitude. While Leppla's division closed up under full power and turned in to the enemy, the Japanese fighters literally looped around and through their formation, making run after run until the blue wings were pocked with holes from the 20-millimeters and 7.7s, canopies were smashed, pilots wounded.

Rhodes and Reding had opposite kinds of trouble, both bad. Rhodes' drop tank would not release and enemy tracers set it flaming like a huge blow torch under his wing. Reding's tank released and fell away but when it did his engine stopped, leaving him helplessly spiraling down trying to restart while Rhodes circled over him with his built-in fire, covering and receiving repeated runs by the Zeros.

In this sudden nightmare of looping, swirling fighters, of flame and tracers and engines screaming under wide-open throttle, with the G forces of wrapped-up turns tugging at his abdomen and the horizon everywhere except horizontal, Dusty Rhodes had his canopy riddled, his pushed-up goggles shot off the top of his head and his instrument panel so completely shattered by gunfire that his electric gunsight swung by its wiring before the empty space where it had been. And somehow in the midst of the holocaust his mind had time to remember how impressed he had been with the bullet hole in Machinist Runyan's instrument panel which he had seen on first reporting to the Big E, and to hope he could get this one back to show the guys.

Dusty did not see Al Mead after leaving the formation to cover Reding, and the last he saw of John Leppla was Lep in a head-on run against one Zero and with another on his tail. Later he caught a glimpse of a half-opened, streaming chute dropping seaward and thought it must be Lep. Then Chip Reding got his engine going on the internal tanks, and Dusty's fire burned itself out with the last of the fuel in his drop tank, and the two F4Fs joined up against the cloud of Zeros.

Rhodes' radio was shot to pieces along with his instrument panel and Reding's whole electrical system was out, including radio, but, by hand signal and an understanding developed out of long hours of flying together, they joined to execute a defensive, scissoring maneuver worked out by Jimmy Flatley and his friend Jimmy Thach which was beginning to be known as the Thach weave. Neither pilot could see his own tail but each could see the other's. Rhodes started out to Reding's left. Reding saw a Zero begin a run on Rhodes' tail and at once turned left toward Dusty to bring his guns onto the enemy. Rhodes, seeing Chip's turn and knowing its meaning, turned right toward Chip to draw the Zero into Chip's line of fire. The Zero turned away and the two F4Fs leveled out again, having reversed position, with Rhodes now on the right, ready to execute the same maneuver again. They worked the weave together for minutes that passed like hours and the Zeros usually turned off when the Wildcat noses began to bear on them. But there were too many. While Dusty and Chip were weaving against a couple behind, several more were making runs from ahead or the flanks. Then, at about 2,500 feet, Rhodes' engine stopped, its bearings burned out and fused together, the prop not even windmilling—just stationary before him. He nosed over to keep his speed and started a turn upwind to ditch, but the Zeros were not finished. Another one came in from behind and Dusty felt both his rudder pedals go slack as the control cables parted. He thought he might be able to set it down on ailerons and elevator and he remembered an old chief in flight training who had said never bail out below a thousand feet, but well below five hundred. Dusty Rhodes, in nearly a single explosive motion, hurled back the shattered canopy, stood up in the cockpit, booted the stick full forward into where the instrument panel had once been and pulled the ripcord of his chute. The riddled Wildcat with its dead engine shot under him, the parachute opened and snatched him erect, and as he swung down under it he hit the water.

He hit hard and went deep but going down he released the snap hooks that held his chute and when he broke the surface again he was clear of it. Overhead, he could see Chip Reding's F4F headed south with three Zeros behind it and in the sudden watery silence he could hear the whine of the four engines under full power. He noticed that one of the Zeros was smoking.

When he rejoined the Big E's strike group, Flatley found it halved. The enemy ambush, driving straight out of the sun so close to friendly forces, had destroyed outright two Avengers, including the squadron commander's, forced a third to ditch and sent a fourth back to *Enterprise* with a damaged engine. Three of Leppla's four fighters had gone down, and the survivor, Chip Reding, dazed and shaken at the sudden overwhelming attack and heavy losses, outran three Zeros and gentled his riddled Wildcat back toward the Big E.

The Big E's best punch was now reduced to four Avengers and three Dauntlesses with a four-Wildcat escort. Commander Gaines, unnoticed or disregarded by the enemy, made a radio report of the action and continued with the reduced attack group.

At 10:30 A.M. the enemy battleships and cruisers came in sight, ploughing northward between the spreading shadows of the cumulus. For ten minutes the planes circled, searching behind the building clouds for the carriers. Then Lieutenant Thompson, leading the Avengers after the loss of his skipper, asked Flatley if he had enough fuel to go another ninety miles in search of the carriers. Flatley's fighters decidedly did not. Having shucked off their wing tanks to counter the Zero ambush, they had barely enough to return. Accordingly, the Big E's strike took on the enemy battleship force instead.

The three SBDs (Bombing Ten planes flown by Scouting Ten crews) lined up on a *Kongo*-class battleship. Richey put his big bomb in the water close aboard the starboard bow, Henry Ervin got a hit flush on the top of number two turret and Estes planted his amidships on the starboard side. The big battlewagon shook and smoked but plowed ahead on her mission.

While Jim Flatley's fighters kept the gunners busy with repeated strafing runs, the Avengers circled in low to attack a heavy cruiser. They bored in close and dropped the big fish straight but the enemy skipper was able to evade them all.

On the way home a single Zero pilot made the last attack of his life into the combined fire of the three SBD gunners, and two-thirds of the way back, the Big E's eleven planes passed directly over shouting, whistling, waving Dusty Rhodes, seated uneasily in a half-inflated, half-swamped one-man raft some 165 miles north of Santa Cruz and east of the Stewart Islands, nursing a bullet nick in his left leg, and full of salt water and a feeling of amazed gratitude that he was still alive. They did not see him.

The dive bombers of *Hornet's* first strike did much better. They avoided contact with the enemy air until nine Zeros tangled with the escort Wildcats over the battleships. None got through to the SBDs, and at 10:30 they found *Shokaku* and *Zuiho*. Even from 12,000 feet they could see smoke coming from two holes in light carrier *Zuiho's* flight deck. With *Zuikaku* under a cloud at the moment of attack, it was *Zuiho* that Strong and Irvine had hit. The *Hornet's* bombers fought through the enemy CAP and put several 1,000-pounders into *Shokaku*. They left her burning from stem to stern and barely making steerage way.

The torpedo planes of that first strike, and her entire second wave, like the Big E's battered attack force, never found the carriers but made some hits on a cruiser.

Admiral Kinkaid's morning attack was over. *Shokaku* and *Zuiho* were out of the battle, a battleship and a cruiser badly battered. But *Zuikaku* and *Junyo* were untouched and, worse, unlocated and now launching strikes.

The Zeros that surprised and shot up the Big E's strike only forty-five miles from her deck were part of a sixty-five-plane attack group from *Shokaku, Zuikaku* and *Zuiho,* which fifteen minutes later had the United States task force in sight. The fighting ships of Kinkaid's Task Force 16 were formed into two tight, gray circles ten miles apart. Each circle, with the flat rectangle of a carrier at the center, raked the morning sea with parallel white lines at 27 knots. High overhead and westward in the enemy direction thirty-eight Wildcats circled, controlled through the eye of radar and the voice of radio by the *Enterprise* fighter director officer.

As close around the Big E's priceless deck as high speed and full rudder would allow were a new battleship, and an anti-aircraft light cruiser. Eight destroyers formed an outer ring around the heavy ships. One of them was the *Shaw,* a ship that had had experience with Vals flown from *Shokaku* and *Zuikaku.* They had caught her helpless in dry dock and blown off her bow in Pearl Harbor on the seventh of December. The same skipper and some sixty of the same men were aboard.

Hornet, flying the two-star flag of Rear Admiral George Murray, the Big E's old skipper, was protected by two anti-aircraft cruisers, two heavy cruisers and six destroyers.

Shortly after ten o'clock, her deck empty and every flyable plane in the air, *Enterprise,* at the center of her armored circle, was passing under the base of one of the big cumuli that covered more than half the sky. Warm rain rattled in her gun tubs and on the helmets of her sailors. Radar had enemy aircraft on the scope close in and several divisions of Wildcats were ordered to intercept.

It was too late and most of the fighters out of position.

The enemy strike group missed *Enterprise* in the shadow of her rain squall and spread out, diving, to attack the *Hornet. Enterprise* and *Hornet* Wildcats scrambled desperately after the enemy planes, following them down through the thickening five-inch bursts and the shifting tracer streams. Lieutenant Stanley W. Vejtasa, climbing steeply, was able to slow one down with a long burst from his six guns just before the enemy pilot reached his push-over point. Lieutenant Albert D. Pollock, carefully conserving his ammunition and firing only two of his outboard guns, silenced the gunner of an enemy dive bomber with his first burst, then, with the Japanese well into his dive on the *Hornet,* he turned on all six guns and burned the belly out of the enemy plane. He had to pull up hard to avoid the wreckage. Ensign Steve Kona of Pollock's flight got one in the same dive. Ensign Donald Gordon on his second attack blew up a torpedo plane ten feet off the crests of the swells and just a few hundred yards from the force. "Flash" Gordon was ten days out of Kaneohe and this was his first action.

But most of the bombers got through. Over George Murray's task group the automatic weapons of the new anti-aircraft cruisers and the five-inch guns of those and the other ships poured tons of hot steel and high explosive into the sky. Many of the Japanese planes, still unmistakable with their obsolete fixed landing gear, suddenly caught fire in their dives and twisted out of control. Others, hit by the five-inch, disintegrated in a flash and a ball of yellow flame and black smoke from which large and small pieces fell. But there were too many, and they dived in close and made their drops courageously and well. The commanding officer of an enemy bombing squadron, already badly hit, drove through the *Hornet's* flight deck with two big bombs. Four more bombs and two torpedoes stopped her and set her afire and a torpedo plane flew into her port bow.

At 10:25, when *Enterprise* turned eastward into the wind to recover her search planes, the men topside could see *Hornet* off to the southwest dead in the water at the base of a slanting column of black smoke. *Hornet's* four big bronze screws had made their last revolution, and the deck from which Colonel Doolittle's B-25s had flown to Tokyo would rest that night on the dark mud of the abyss three miles below the Big E's keel.

Enterprise was now the only effective United States aircraft carrier west of Oahu.

The Japanese may not have known that, but they knew very well she was the only one left to cover Guadalcanal. And Nagumo still had two untouched carriers, with their strikes on the way.

At eleven o'clock *Enterprise* radar reported large groups of hostile planes at twenty-three miles, closing. Again the Wildcats flew to intercept, and again they were mostly below and behind when they finally saw the bombers. Frequently the leader of a four-plane division of F4Fs would be told to "look on the port quarter" or "look on the starboard bow." To a pilot miles away and frequently out of sight of his task force, such directions based on the ships' heading at the moment meant nothing, and the division leaders would have done better had they simply been stationed high above the force and out in the enemy direction, provided with radar data on enemy aircraft and permitted to act according to their own judgment. The radar performed well, but poor use was made of the information it supplied.

Some two minutes after radar's warning, Dave Pollock, orbiting over the task force with three F4Fs of his CAP division, noticed one of the destroyers dead in the water beside the bright yellow oval of a rubber life raft. A pilot was being rescued and Dave hoped he was one of the Big E's fliers, missing on the morning strike. As he watched there was some sort of activity in the bright blue sea a few hundreds yards off the destroyer's beam. Something was circling erratically just under the surface and leaving a wake. A torpedo. From a mile up Dave could make it out well enough, but he knew that from the low deck of the destroyer, or even from her thirty-five-foot bridge it would be hard to see. He had to warn the ship but he had radio contact only with the FDO and there was no time on the already too-busy circuit to relay. He decided to go down and explode the tin fish with his guns. He knew the jittery shipboard gunners would fire on him but at least he could call attention to the torpedo. He turned over the lead and dived his Wildcat for the water. As expected, the destroyer opened fire at once, and her sisters joined in viciously. Pollock, cursing, tried to ignore the tracers and made repeated strafing runs on the circling torpedo, his bullets churning the sea around it. After the second run, the surface gunners saw his friendly markings and ceased fire. The destroyer simultaneously recognized his warning, and her screws began to churn just as the torpedo exploded amidships in a towering burst of white water and tumbling debris. Pollock sadly pulled up and rejoined his division.

The destroyer was the *Porter*. She completed the rescue of Lieutenant R. K. Batten and his gunner R. S. Holgrim. Batten had ditched his Avenger after the morning ambush of the Big E's strike. The *Porter* could not be salvaged with the enemy so close. Batten and Holgrim jumped across to the *Shaw* when she came alongside to take off survivors, and watched from her deck as she sunk the wounded *Porter* with her five-inch guns.

While the badly positioned, poorly directed Wildcats were struggling for a shot and Pollock was trying in vain to save the *Porter,* the Big E's fire controlmen were working hard to bring the new fire-control radar onto the approaching enemy. Theoretically and in controlled tests, the five-inch guns firing under the direction of this equipment could knock down targets at long ranges and invisible from the ship in clouds or darkness. Now its scopes would not pick up the incoming planes. At 11:15, as at Eastern Solomons, the men of *Enterprise* could see the shining dive bombers of the Imperial Navy plunging out of the clear sky directly overhead. They were flashes of silver that made small popping noises. At first they seemed ridiculously small and unmoving, but they looked unmoving only because they were moving straight toward the eye of the looker. Then swiftly they began to grow, and on all the waiting ships the gunners opened fire. One of Flatley's Reapers, glancing down at that moment, thought the *San Juan* had been hit and exploded, but she had simply commenced firing with all her guns. On *South Dakota* a hundred muzzles flamed in steady mechanical unison and the dark brown powder smoke sprang from her decks and superstructure and drifted out astern. The *Portland* and every destroyer in the screen hammered steel into the sky. But in *Enterprise* Orlin Livdahl's gunners had the easiest shooting. For them there was no deflection. Each plane was pointed down the barrels of her guns. She was the bull's-eye of the task force target.

On the bridge Captain Osborne B. Hardison held his helmet on with his left hand as he looked straight up at the chain of dive bombers twisting down on his ship, and maneuvered with full rudder to spoil their aim. A scant thousand yards away 45,000 tons of battleship matched his every turn, remaining at the Big E's side like the wingman in a flight section.

Enterprise staggered through a storm of bombs and falling planes. The sea spouted into columns around her and her hull jarred and rang with the water hammers of submerged explosions. For four minutes she fought it out with the seasoned, determined Japanese airmen who were less than two hours off the decks of her old enemies, *Shokaku* and *Zuikaku.* Half of them were caught and dismembered in the shifting web of tracers and became momentary flares of gasoline on the broad surface of the Pacific. Others were harrassed by the rising metal into dropping early and turning away, often into the guns of Flatley's frustrated Wildcats. Through the measured booming of the five-inch and the steady hammering of the smaller guns the men topside could hear the mounting roar of enemy engines which faded suddenly as they pulled out across the deck. Below, men braced their feet wide on the oily gratings of the engine and fire-rooms as the Big E heeled to full rudder, first one way, then back. The men of the repair parties had checked and rechecked that the 662 water-tight compartments were buttoned up tight, with every hatch and door and scuttle not used to fight dogged down solidly. Now they sat on the steel decks of passageways and small compartments with their tools and apparatus around them in the dim red battle light, and waited for the clank and the blast that would give them something to do.

It came at 11:17. John Crommelin, standing life-jacketed and helmeted on the open bridge and watching the incoming dive bombers with professional detachment, suddenly announced, "I think that son-of-a-bitch is going to get us." The 550-pound bomb ripped through the forward overhang of the flight deck just to port of the center line, was in the clear again for some fifteen feet, went through the fo'c'sle deck and then left the ship again through her portside. Its delayed-action fuse, intended to fire in the vitals of the ship, detonated it in the open air just above the ocean surface and close to the port bow. Fragments sprayed the side of the ship, leaving jagged holes of all sizes from a quarter of an inch to a foot. A Dauntless parked on the starboard bow was blown overboard. With it to his death went Sam Davis Presley, a first class aviation machinist's mate, manning the twin 30s in the rear seat.

Another man was killed and several wounded in the Radio Direction Finder Room. A tank was flooded with salt water. A small fire licked the edges of the hole in the flight deck and others burned below in the holds. Another SBD caught fire and gasoline ran from its pierced wing tanks to feed the flames. Machinist Bill Fluitt, the gasoline officer, charged forward on the flight deck, yelling and getting help as he ran. He took down the guard rails and, as the attack went on and enemy gunners swept the deck with machine-gun fire, pushed the burning plane and its rapidly baking 500-pound bomb overboard.

Ralph Baker, a first class photographer's mate, calmly taking pictures of the action on the forward edge of the flight deck, had his left index finger severed and his camera deeply dented by a bomb fragment as he held it a few inches from his head.

In the same minute, another bomb hit just aft of the forward elevator in the middle of the flight deck and broke in half. Part exploded in the hangar deck, destroying two spare planes lashed to the overhead and five more below them. The nose half went through two more decks and detonated in the officers' quarters where Repair Party Number Two was stationed. Repair Two was wiped out. So was the medical party which had been manning the battle dressing station there. Forty men were blown apart or fatally seared by the blast. Stubborn fires flared up in bedding, clothing and the personal effects of the officers whose quarters had been demolished. Light, power and communication lines were cut. The fire mains were damaged. Salt water from the ruptured mains mixed with blood and oil. Pieces of men, internal and external, slid back and forth as the ship heeled, and the choking smoke poured into the hanger deck and out through the small neat hole above. From forward and aft Herschel Smith's damage control parties closed in on the flaming shambles.

Of the six men in the handling room crew adjacent to Repair Two, four were killed. The other two were knocked out by the blast and came to in the dark, smoke-filled wreckage littered with the torn bodies of their shipmates. Jim Bagwell, a third class gunner's mate, groped his way, only half alive, through the flames to where a shattered hatch let in light from the hangar deck above. As he started painfully up the short vertical ladder, William Pinckney, a third class officers' cook and the only other survivor, found the same hatch. In the first seconds after the bomb, the burnt area was worse than any imaginable inferno. Flames towered out of the smoke that burned the eyes and lungs. There were dark holes where the steel deck had been. Even a half-conscious man could smell gasoline enough to blow the whole deck again any second.

Carefully, little colored Bill Pinckney helped Bagwell up the ladder, but when the gunner's mate got his hands on the hatch combing at the top he yelled sharply with pain and fell back to the deck unconscious. With fires above and below, the hangar deck hatch was hot enough to sear the flesh. Nearly blind with smoke and barely able to breathe, still in shock and his ears ringing from the bomb blast a few feet away a few seconds ago, Pinckney picked Bagwell up and lifted him through the hatch to safety before he climbed the ladder himself.

The battle did not stop to let *Enterprise* dress her wounds. The chain of Vals still unwound down the sky, each link lashing viciously as it flashed overhead. *Sho* and *Zui's* pilots could see the holes and the smoke and they were eager to complete the kill. Their bombs threw tons of water on the Big E's deck, knocking her men from their feet, throwing the guns out of position. The bullets of their gunners searched her decks and gun positions. On their five-inch, 40s, 1.1s and 20s the Big E's men steadily and angrily returned the fire. And *South Dakota* supported them with a beautiful seamanship which kept her close, and a constant, effective fire from a hundred guns.

Japanese aircraft fell out of the sky at the rate of one to every two bombs dropped. At a single instant three were visible from the Big E's bridge, bright flares streaking black smoke down toward the sea. The cost was high, but just one bomb might finish the only carrier the Americans had left and give Guadalcanal back to the Emperor.

At nineteen minutes after eleven there was a muffled explosion aft of the island on the starboard side and almost every man standing on his feet aboard the *Enterprise* was knocked to her deck. The wounded, driven ship shook the full length of her eight hundred feet so violently that any given point whipped up and down through a foot and a half, every second for several seconds. Machinery and equipment were flicked from their foundations. With the carrier turning hard to port, the flight deck slanted to starboard, and each time it whipped, the parked planes rose in the air and banged down nearer the starboard side. The farthest SBD forward and to starboard went overboard; a little farther aft another landed in the gun gallery. Tools and equipment secured to the overhead crashed down onto the hangar deck. Mercury spilled from the big master gyros. The entire foremast rotated one-half inch in its socket, throwing out of alignment all the complex antennas mounted on it. The after-bearing pedestal on one of the high-pressure steam turbines which drive the ship was cracked. A fuel tank was opened to the sea and *Enterprise* began to leave a broad trail of oil for the enemy to follow. Two empty fuel tanks were flooded and she listed a little to starboard. At 11:20 the attack appeared to be over.

Loading crews cleared the hot piles of empty casings from around the guns. Some of the 40-millimeter crews, working fast, changed barrels; the used barrels hissed briefly in the cooling tanks.

On the bridge Captain Hardison stood close to his talker, receiving reports of damage and corrective action being taken from Herschel Smith and George Over in Central Station. He quickly granted permission to counter-flood as necessary to take the list off the ship and frowned at news of the heavy casualties in Repair Two.

Admiral Kinkaid hunched over his chart in Flag Plot with his staff and listened to radio reports of the attempts being made to save the *Hornet*. Admiral George Murray was shifting his flag to the cruiser *Pensacola* since radio communications no longer existed in *Hornet*. *Northampton* was attempting to take her in tow.

Enterprise was showing less smoke as the fire-fighting crews from forward and aft converged on the fires around Number One elevator. Her propulsion machinery, except for the cracked bearing pedestal, was undamaged and she maintained a steady 27 knots. But in the battle dressing stations, Commander John Owsley, the senior medical officer, Chief Pharmacist's Mate Adair and other medical personnel worked steadily against pain and loss of blood and death, injecting drugs, applying tourniquets and splints, dressing burns, suturing wounds, amputating shredded limbs.

And down on the first platform deck ten men were trapped in the five-inch ammunition handling rooms for the forward guns. The only way out was through the access trunk directly above which now was eight feet deep with salt water from the hoses which battled the fires overhead. One of the men trapped was little twenty-year-old Vicente Sablan of Guam, who at Pearl Harbor had known the Japanese to be "very bad and tricky. But we Americans too smart. We catch him and give him hell." Sablan had grown much older in the ten months since those words were spoken and most of his aging had been to the sound of the remote hammering of the guns on deck and the huge booming of near misses in the deep handling room where he was now sealed with nine other men, three Caucasian, four Negro and two Filipino.

At 11:27 a lookout reported a periscope off the starboard beam, and the Big E leaned hard to put her stern to it before it was identified as a porpoise.

At 11:44 another periscope was reported in the same position but there was no time to maneuver. Fifteen torpedo planes were boring in from both bows to catch the *Enterprise* as they had done the *Hornet,* whichever way she turned.

Admiral Nagumo had launched these torpedo planes with his dive bombers from *Sho* and *Zui*. They were to attack at the same time, dividing the fire of defending guns and complicating almost hopelessly the problem of evasion. But they had arrived half an hour after the bombers, and now it was the guns of the task force against the shining Kates, flat on the water, holding their torpedoes for close-in drops.

The regularly spaced black five-inch bursts building neat rows close to the surface flamed one plane five miles out. Briefly the spray rose above the greasy smoke where he went in. Captain Hardison held his ship on course, waiting for the AA to take effect, waiting to see which group of planes dropped their torpedoes first. On either bow the destroyers increased speed with chuffs of smoke to take position between the carrier and her enemy and take the torpedoes themselves if necessary. The guns were trained horizontally and there was no problem of loading at high-elevation angles or squinting into the bright sky. The tracers skimmed straight and flat to meet the planes. Three miles out a Kate on the port bow pulled up suddenly, rolled inverted and crashed. Two more came apart and skidded in as the 20-millimeters opened up at two miles. Then, in quick succession the five remaining Kates on the starboard bow made their drops and turned away. Captain Hardison looked quickly to port; four more were coming in but had not yet released. To starboard and a little ahead now he could see the parallel wakes of three torpedoes close together and moving fast, the middle one slightly ahead. It was a beautiful drop and if the Big E continued on course they would hit her amidships and rip out her insides. For a second the bridge watch was silent, poised. The quartermaster at the helm, the seaman at the engine order telegraph, the officer of the deck, waited for the skipper's command. At the end of that long second it came.

"Right full rudder."

"Right full rudder, sir!"

The helmsman spun his wheel, pulling over the top and down hard with his right hand, letting it carry around to the bottom, then reaching up for another hold, getting his back into it, bending his knees a little with each downward pull. The gray pointer slid down the right side of the rudder angle indicator mounted by the wheel until it stopped at 35 degrees right. Back in the steering engine room the starboard ram was all the way aft, the full gleaming length of the port ram exposed. The three-story rudder with its top ten feet below the hull was angled far out to starboard and the wash of the starboard screws poured onto it, increasing its effect. The Big E's stern began to slide across the sea to the left, and slowly the bow came right toward the bubbling echelon of the torpedo tracks, as though to meet them. The flight deck with its smoldering holes leaned down to port and, having done all that could be done, Captain Hardison stood on the port wing of the bridge to witness its success or failure. Admiral Kinkaid came silently to stand beside him.

Now there were only a few hundred yards separating *Enterprise* and the three bubbling lines on the sea's surface. They seemed to increase speed as the bow swung onto them and then from the bridge they were out of sight under the port overhang of the turning deck as the captain ordered: "Rudder amidships" and the quartermaster spun the wheel down to port. The Big E straightened up from her turn and the three torpedoes, running straight and true, passed ten yards down her portside, parallel, at 40 knots.

Enterprise, safe for the moment from the most threatening of the torpedoes launched against her, was now headed straight for the destroyer *Smith,* which already had enough trouble without being run down by a carrier. An enemy torpedo plane, smoking and barely under control after tangling with a pair of Wildcats, had flown straight into her forward gun mount. Flames shot up higher than her mast, engulfing her bridge and superstructure, and as they were beginning to recede the Kate's torpedo had baked off with a roar, making everything forward of the stack untenable. Somehow, the destroyer had stayed on course and at fleet speed, and her after guns continued to hammer away protectingly at the planes attacking *Enterprise.*

Captain Hardison came left again and cleared the *Smith,* which dropped back and then moved up astern of *South Dakota* and buried her burning bow in the high wake of the battlewagon. In another few minutes her fires were out and her skipper returned to the bridge and resumed his duties in the screen.

But *Enterprise* was still in trouble. Another torpedo was sighted on the starboard bow. There was no room this time to turn inside it. It was too close and too fast. The bow was already across the torpedo course. Once again Captain Hardison came hard right, and the Big E's stern skidded clear to port as the "fish" passed thirty yards to starboard. A half-mile farther up the fading torpedo wake, *Enterprise* plunged past the wreckage of the Kate that had dropped it. From the debris two half-drowned oriental faces looked up in hatred.

From dead astern now five more Kates, fast and low on the water, maneuvered for attack position. Like Gene Lindsey attacking the *Kaga* at Midway, but with far faster aircraft, the Japanese pilots swung wide for a shot at the Big E's port beam. Like the *Kaga's* late commanding officer, Osborne Hardison kept swinging to starboard, presenting only his narrow stern as a target while the task force guns blasted steadily at the circling torpedo planes. And, as it had been at Midway, the tactic was successful. Within a mile of *Enterprise,* three were shot down in rapid succession by the storm of 20-millimeter fire from every gun in the force that would bear. The fourth, nearly at dropping point, pulled up sharply, releasing his torpedo in a climbing turn, then continued in a diving left bank to the sea. The fifth made a good drop from nearly dead astern and Captain Hardison paralleled the torpedo attack and watched it pass his ship to port.

There would have been eleven more to deal with if it had not been for Lieutenant Vejtasa.

Swede Vejtasa was the leader of a division of four F4Fs launched at 9:00 A.M. to augment the twelve Wildcats already on Combat Air Patrol and to intercept the enemy dive bombers. With him were Lieutenants Harris and Ruehlow and Ensign Leder. Although caught underneath the incoming raid, Vejtasa, by climbing hard and shooting well, was able to knock down a Val before it could begin its dive on the *Hornet.* Since he was too late and too low to intercept the other bombers, he led his division in an attack on two which had completed their drops and were retiring. Both flamed and fell off into the sea. For a long time, under orders from the FDO, Vejtasa's flight circled at 10,000 feet searching the sea for torpedo planes, while more dive bombers came in overhead to attack *Enterprise.*

Shortly before noon, Swede heard the FDO order another flight of fighters out to the northwest and led his own in the same direction. Just as the FDO warned that the incoming aircraft might be friendly search planes returning, he made out eleven dark-green, shiny Kates below in a stepped-up column of three-plane Vs with a two-plane section at the rear. Ruehlow and Leder, after a brush with a pair of Zeros, had spotted the Kates and were already attacking. With Harris close on his wing, Vejtasa pushed over in a steep, fast, high side attack. The enemy torpedo planes were already close and slanting in at 250 knots to make their runs on *Enterprise.* On their first pass Vejtasa and Harris each set a Kate explosively afire, then used their speed to overtake one of the three-plane Vs just as it entered a large cumulus. In the turbulent gray belly of the cloud Harris and Vejtasa became separated but Swede did not lose the enemy. He was angry at the misdirection of the FDO and the chances lost all morning but he was clear and cold in his head. The Wildcat in his hands felt like the smooth stock and grip and trigger of a familiar rifle. And he was careful and absolutely accurate. He began with the left-hand plane of the V. He flew in close, directly astern and blew him up with two short bursts of his six guns. Methodically, Vejtasa kicked rudder and slid his Wildcat to the right in behind the leader. His first burst brought the Kate's rudder soaring up and over his head, his second as the enemy began to yaw set him on fire and he fell away in a spiral to the left. In the cloud the tracers glowed like accelerated Roman candles. Still in the gray damp of the cloud, Vejtasa eased over behind the remaining enemy who began a shallow right turn. Swede's six guns raked it from engine back to tail in a single long rattle of bullets and it flamed violently and nosed abruptly downward.

In the shredding fog above him and to the left, Vejtasa saw the shadow of another Kate and he pulled up hard in a low side run but failed to knock him down. He followed him out of the cloud where the task force AA at once took over. Swede could see the enemy was too high and too fast for an effective drop and let the AA have him. It was this plane that crashed the *Smith*.

Vejtasa circled at 3,000 feet outside the ring of destroyers and with the last of his ammunition shot down a fifth torpedo plane as it was attempting to retire low on the water after its run.

Thus did Swede Vejtasa, on a single-combat flight, shoot down two enemy dive bombers and five torpedo planes with one more probable. Out of the eleven Kates which he discovered deploying for an attack on his ship, he personally destroyed five and led his wingman on a run that accounted for a sixth. Three others jettisoned their torpedoes and fled and it was the opinion of Vejtasa's commanding officer, Jim Flatley, that "the other two were so demoralized that they were ineffective."

Captain Hardison, by clear, fast thinking and flawless timing, had evaded nine torpedoes dropped with the same determined skill as those which had just reduced *Hornet* to a drifting hulk. It is improbable that without Swede Vejtasa's help he could have evaded eleven more.

At noon, under the low broken clouds, *Enterprise* was making 27 knots at the center of her bristling task group. *South Dakota,* still on her starboard quarter, could see she was down by the bow. Black smoke streamed aft from the holes in her flight deck. Within a radius of twenty miles, almost her entire air group circled in small formations or singly, low on fuel and ammunition, waiting to come aboard. *Hornet's* successful strike, having laid *Shokaku* open like a sardine can, had only the Big E's damaged deck on which to land. But *Enterprise* could receive no planes on her holed and smoldering deck, with the raw ulcer of bomb damage below and bogies still showing on her scopes. With her guns trained out and ready, her radars and binoculars searching the sea and the sky, she concentrated on repairing her damage and saving the lives of her men.

The second bomb had ruptured three decks just aft of Number One elevator on the Big E's center line. A tangle of broken planes was burning in the hangar deck and flaming gasoline had run down into the forward elevator pit. On two decks staterooms, washrooms, dressing stations, gear lockers and ammunition handling-rooms were demolished. Flames licked at severed electrical cables, wrecked equipment and steel rubble in the smoking darkness. Doors and hatches were blown open, decks and bulkheads blasted out of shape, piping slashed, machinery scored and riddled. And below the worst of the damage, in the ammunition handling-room for the forward five-inch runs, were Sablan and his nine mates. Aft of them were the five-inch powder magazines, on both sides narrow void spaces separating them from fuel tanks and, on the other side of a solid watertight bulkhead forward of them, workshops and elevator machinery. Below them was aviation gasoline and above were smoldering storerooms directly under the bomb explosion point. There was only one access to them, a vertical trunk leading up through the storerooms to the wrecked living quarters. There was a firmly closed watertight hatch in the trunk on the overhead of their compartment. A similar hatch directly above in the deck of the demolished living space had been blown off by the bomb. The trunk was eight feet deep in salt water and chemical foam from the fire fighting above and clogged with wreckage and parts of bodies. There was no light and dangerously little air. The battle telephone was dead. Paul Petersen, electrician's mate second class, was senior petty officer in charge. With him were Carl Johnson (another electrician's mate), five officers' cooks—Bagsby, Richardson, Cordon, Taijeron and Sablan—two mess attendants—Ramentas and Howard—and Schwarb, a seaman. There was no panic, or hysteria. Petersen conserved the batteries in his battle lanterns and told his men to remain quiet in order to use a minimum of the valuable air. One man kept on the headset of the silent phones, hoping that they would come alive again. Overhead they could hear the encouraging sounds of the fire fighting. The two electricians knew how the ship was organized for damage control and that if she survived the action they would be rescued. The ten men waited in the dark.

In Central Station, Herschel Smith and George Over marked the damaged area on their big schematics and received reports from fire-fighting and repair parties. A few minutes after the explosion scores of men were at work to minimize its effect.

The combined labor of the repair parties began to show below decks. The fires went out under salt water and foamite, and blowers were rigged to suck out the smoke and provide fresh air. The wounded were taken out and emergency lighting strung. The battle telephone connections were repaired and Chief Forrest got in touch with Petersen below.

"For Christ's sake," he told him, "don't open that hatch. There's eight feet of water on top of it. Just relax and we'll get you out, but it's going to take a little while."

At a quarter past twelve John Crommelin began to take aboard his planes, holes or no holes, damaged or not. Back on the port corner of the deck Robin Lindsey signaled them in with his eloquent paddles. No LSO ever had more difficult conditions. Many planes were damaged and not under full control. Number Two elevator was temporarily stuck in the down position, leaving a huge square hole in the deck less than three hundred feet from the stern. With continuous reports of bogies and periscopes coming in, *Enterprise* twisted under the low clouds, her deck heeling each time the rudder was put over. To the incoming pilots the narrow, smoking, shifting deck with a yawning pit in the landing area looked impossible. But they remembered Lindsey's competence and their empty tanks and grimly came on in. One after another, answering Lindsey's signals, they snarled in over the wake and dropped onto the extreme stern. The arresting cables pulled out reluctantly and stopped each plane aft of the stuck elevator. Then with a roar of throttle they taxied around the hole and forward out of the way.

Only a few pilots got aboard before a third attack came in. The others rolled up their wheels and banked away as the task force guns opened up at 12:21.

Twenty more of Nagumo's dive bombers slashed at the Big E, dropping suddenly out of the cloud bases in 45-degree dives. The fat clouds sheltered them at first from the searching gunfire but, when they broke out, their shallow dives were terribly vulnerable. The Big E's seasoned, angry gunners chopped down eight and riddled others so that they dropped short and turned away. Robin Lindsey threw down his paddles and jumped into the rear seat of an SBD he had just landed to empty its remaining ammunition into the attackers. Near misses threw up their familiar water spouts around the ship. With *Enterprise* leaning hard to port in a tight starboard turn, one bomb glanced off her exposed starboard side below the water line and detonated eight feet away and fifteen feet below the surface, dishing in her side and flooding two void spaces through breaks in the skin. The ship lashed throughout her length, her decks again whipping a full foot for several seconds. Number One elevator jammed in the up position. The damage controlmen sweating under jury lights on the third deck were knocked sprawling into the blood and oil and torn metal underfoot. Petersen, Sablan and the others tensed in their dark hole where water, leaking down through broken vent trunks, was by now nearly up to their waists.

Some two hundred feet above the sealed-off, slowly flooding handling room, the whiplashing near misses and enemy strafing had so damaged the Big E's main antenna that her search radar was blinded. Without her radar, *Enterprise* could see only as far as the eyes of her lookouts, which were thwarted by clouds, haze, dazzling sunlight and shadow. She was helpless to control her fighters. Lieutenant Brad Williams was the radar officer, in fact the first, in the U.S. Navy, to be so designated. More even than his admiral or his skipper, Williams knew the capabilities of his equipment and the odds against the survival of a radar-blinded ship under those enemy infested skies. He climbed the mast with a loaded tool box and went to work at the highest and most exposed point on the ship while Captain Hardison and his gunners fought off the enemy planes. The painted metal under his hands was granular with salt and sooty with stack gas and he had to hold strongly to it with one hand while trying to repair the antenna and its drive motor with the other. It was not a single-handed job and Williams finally had to lash himself to the antenna and work with both. If he noticed the continued strafing or the near misses or the violent swinging of the radar platform as the Big E leaned into her turns, no one below could tell it. He could almost look down into the five-inch muzzles that were answering the strafing of the Vals and feel the heat when they fired. The 40s and 20s along the deck edge barked steadily and their tracers soared past him to meet the enemy. The bomb that glanced off the Big E's starboard side missed him so closely that for a moment, as he looked up, its blunt torpedo shape was foreshortened to a ball. The bomb's blast destroyed his hearing for weeks and would have knocked him off the mast but for his lashings. Working hard and fast, hampered by bolts jammed with paint and salt corrosion, Williams finished the job. In the radar room below it was evident that *Enterprise* would see again. Eager to get back into operation, a technician switched on the antenna training motor and Brad Williams revolved a dozen times at the masthead, his angry shouts swamped by the voices of the guns, until an officer on the bridge noticed that his majestic sweeps around the horizon were apparently unintentional.

There were perhaps three minutes of tense and busy silence for the men topside and of relative relief for the sailors trapped in the darkness below before the repaired radar picked up another strike inbound. Coached on by radar, the high-power telescopes of the forward range-finder found it seventeen and a half miles away at 17,000 feet. There were fifteen Vals in two groups with an escort of nine Zeros above. After nearly two and a half hours of attack and the threat of attack, the defending Wildcats were out of ammunition and low on fuel. Now it was up to Orlin Livdahl's gunners and their determined supporters on *South Dakota* and the other ships of the force.

At eleven miles, still only high flecks of sunlight in the sky, the enemy raid disappeared behind a rain cloud. For two minutes the many barrels swung silently and the thousands of young eyes stared upward, trying to penetrate the clouds and outstare the glaring sun. Then the Vals were overhead, steep in their dives, and the guns blasted into action again. By this hour of the early afternoon, the kids who gripped the wide handle bars of the 20-milimeters and peered through cartwheel sights to follow the tracer flight, and the ones who sat in the farm-tractor seats of the 40s rotating with their humming mounts, were true veterans. They had seen that their weapons could kill the enemy before he could kill them, and seen too the bloody damage of the bombs. Now they were cool and steady and Orlin Livdahl's careful training was paying off. Glancing up, most of them could see him high in the island at Sky Control—exposed, calm, deliberate, completely competent. As the Vals strung down for the third time that day, Livdahl's tracers rose to meet them, shifting and converging steadily with no breaks as the loading crews worked smoothly and the well-kept guns had few jams or failures. Battery officers shifted targets to take the most threatening enemy under the heaviest fire. Chief Turret Captain Willson alone probably saved the Big E from serious damage when he directed his five-inch mount against a dive bomber which had already missed but was turning back to crash on board.

In *South Dakota* a bomb detonated on top of the forward turret, which was so well armored that most of the gun crew didn't know of the hit, but a fragment seriously wounded the battlewagon's skipper and steering control was shifted to the executive officer aft, who for a moment had no communication with the helm. Big, fast, heavy *South Dakota*, so magnificently handled throughout the battle, headed straight for *Enterprise,* and Captain Hardison turned away just in time.

San Juan took a heavy bomb that went through all her light decking and out through her bottom before it exploded. The blast shook the fast but fragile cruiser so fiercely that circuit breakers protecting her steering mechanism popped and she too lost control of her rudder in a high-speed starboard turn. The ships of the task group saved themselves by scattering until she regained control.

At 12:45 P.M. radar finally showed a sky clear of the enemy and *Enterprise* began again to take aboard her planes. Fighters and dive bombers were given precedence over the longer-legged Avengers but even so there were many ditchings. The pilots who survived the skips and dragging splashes had plenty of time to get out their rafts while the planes floated nose down, held up for a while by the empty fuel cells in the wings. The destroyers were kept busy with rescue work.

Number One elevator, the farthest forward, seemed permanently jammed. With planes landing over the other two, it was impossible to strike any below, and by four o'clock the Big E's long deck was so jammed with *Enterprise* and *Hornet* aircraft that Robin Lindsey could bring no more aboard. Slim Townsend's flight-deck crew, after the long morning of work and action, fell to again. By lowering planes on the after elevators, and launching thirteen Dauntlesses for Espiritu, they made enough room to get the last air-borne Avenger aboard.

It seemed that the enemy had made his last attack. Probably he had little left to launch. He had lost 100 planes in the attacks on *Enterprise* and *Hornet* and in the defense of his own ships. Two of his carriers were out of action. More planes must have gone down from fuel exhaustion and accidents.

Admiral Yamamoto ordered his carriers to retire to the northwest and sent fast surface forces in for a night attack. But Kinkaid, with ten months of experience with the Japanese, outguessed him and pulled off to the south. The enemy destroyers found only the burning, listing derelict that had been the *Hornet* and quickly sent her on her long tumble to the bottom . . .

THE STRUGGLE FOR GUADALCANAL DRAGGED ON. BUT by November, with reinforcements pouring onto the island and with the Navy punching back at Japanese positions at Point Cruz and the Umasani River, the key naval engagement loomed on the horizon.

One of the best versions of the somewhat confused but decisive Naval Battle for Guadalcanal was written during the war by Captain Walter Karig and Commander Eric Purdon. We have met the gifted Karig before; collaborator Purdon was a former Midwestern newspaperman.

CAPTAIN WALTER KARIG

AND COMMANDER ERIC PURDON

7.

THE NAVAL BATTLE

OF GUADALCANAL

. . . There was no respite for either side.

The Japanese intensified their efforts to cut the American supply line and step up the capacity of their own. With the former they achieved considerable success, but with the latter they were not so fortunate. Their only means of reinforcement was by the Tokyo Express, and twenty-four of our submarines made its periodic journeys through the Slot hazardous. During the first half of November the submarines sank at least six ships, and damaged seven more of assorted classes.

On land, Navy and Marines were co-operating to push the Japanese back. On October 30 the light cruiser *Atlanta* and four destroyers bombarded enemy positions back of Point Cruz for eight hours. The next morning the 5th Marines struck across the Matanikau River, and on November 3 our troops had advanced beyond Point Cruz. Our offensive had to be checked here, because the previous night Japanese cruisers and destroyers had managed to land 1,500 men and artillery east of Koli Point. On November 4 the *San Francisco, Helena* and *Sterett* bombarded this new force, and destroyed stockpiles of newly delivered stores and ammunition. Only about 700 Japanese were left alive. They escaped to the jungle, where the 2nd Marine Raider Battalion met them, and so there were none.

By November, United States air defenses on the island had been greatly improved. The development of landing strips around Lunga proceeded rapidly, and both Marine and Army aircraft were adding to the enemy's discomfort.

On the 7th, Guadalcanal planes attacked an enemy light cruiser and ten destroyers. They scored one bomb and two torpedo hits on the cruiser, damaged two destroyers and shot down sixteen planes.

The Japanese continued to try to lighten the pressure on the defending forces. The darker the night the more certain the Marines could be that enemy units by squads and platoons were being sneaked ashore. In counteraction, PT boats from Tulagi attacked repeatedly. On the night of November 6-7 they sank a destroyer. Two more were damaged on other nights.

Such reinforcements dribbling in to the beleaguered Japanese were far from adequate and the cost in transportation was profligate. The Japanese realized that they would have to make another major strike. Again they gathered and concentrated a fleet in the Rabaul-Buin area.

This time, the Japanese said in effect, we won't be stopped. Nothing the Americans can bring together will be strong enough. And the roving, watchful reconnaissance planes, emblazoned with the star of the United States, counted sixty enemy ships in anchorages of Buin, Faisi and Tonolei.

They included four battleships, six cruisers, two carriers, and thirty-three destroyers besides more than a score of transports and cargo ships.

Vice Admiral William F. Halsey, Jr., Commander South Pacific Force and South Pacific Area, had no force like this. Only one carrier, the *Enterprise,* was near-by, and she was in Noumea being repaired. The Big E could not possibly be ready to fight again until the third week in November, the wounded ship's bedside report had it. But news of impending battle hastened recovery.

The Allied forces on Guadalcanal had received some reinforcements from Efate on November 6. Now seven more United States transports were scheduled to sail from other ports with much-needed supplies and men. These would have to be protected and, probably, a major enemy offensive simultaneously would have to be beaten back. If we couldn't accomplish that, the Solomons campaign would be finished—and with it our position in the entire South Pacific would be dangerously compromised.

In all, about 6,000 men were to be put ashore from the seven transports. For their protection Admiral Richmond Kelly Turner had a force of only twenty combatant ships: three heavy cruisers, one light cruiser, two anti-aircraft light cruisers, and fourteen destroyers. These were based at Noumea, New Caledonia, and Espiritu Santo, New Hebrides.

Task Force TARE's Noumea section sailed first on the afternoon of Sunday, November 8. Espiritu Santo Section 2 followed next morning, with the first section leaving early Tuesday. All were to rendezvous on Wednesday morning, the 11th, southeast of San Cristobal.

By the afternoon of Monday, November 9, there was no longer any doubt that the Japanese had started a vast amphibious offensive. Reconnaissance and intelligence reports led Admiral Turner to estimate that the enemy planned to use two to four carriers, possibly two to four fast battleships, as well as cruisers and destroyers, to the northward of Guadalcanal. As protection for at least one division of troops in eight to twelve transports, the Admiral reasoned, two heavy cruisers, two to four light cruisers, twelve to sixteen destroyers, and several light minelayers would probably operate eastward from Buin. He anticipated that land-based planes would start bombing Guadalcanal on Tuesday, and that the airfield would probably be bombarded by surface craft Wednesday night. A continuous and concentrated carrier air attack on Henderson Field would probably take place on Thursday, with further naval bombardment and landings, perhaps after midnight, on Thursday night near Cape Esperance or Koli Point.

Although no carriers were directly involved, many of these hypotheses were accurate.

Since the enemy invasion force was expected in the Guadalcanal area by Friday, November 13, it was very important that our transports should have finished unloading by that time and be well out of danger. Therefore they would have to finish by Thursday. The combatant ships, no longer charged with the protection of the transports, would then be able to carry the fight to the Japanese.

According to the original plan, Admiral Scott's cargo vessels from Espiritu Santo were due off Lunga Point, Guadacanal, at 5:30 A.M. on Wednesday, November 11. The forces under Admirals Turner and Callaghan were to reach Indispensable Strait that night, after which the Noumea transports would pass through Lengo Channel and reach the unloading point Thursday morning. Admiral Callaghan was to precede the transport group with his three cruisers and six destroyers and arrive at the end of Sealark Channel two hours before midnight. There he was to be joined by Admiral Scott's fighting ships, except for three destroyers detached as anti-aircraft and antisubmarine protection for the three Espiritu Santo transports. During the night he was to pass through Sealark Channel to Savo Sound and strike any enemy forces he might find, with attention to any possible transports in their rear. If none were found he was to return and cover the unloading during the day. As far as the landing itself was concerned, all the troops were to be put ashore first, carrying two days' rations and ammunition. Those who were on the beach were to work continuously at unloading the boats. As Admiral Turner said, the safety of the position of the troops ashore on the island depended entirely on the rapidity with which the ships were emptied.

Admiral Scott's ships were right on schedule, reaching Guadalcanal at 5:30 on Wednesday morning. And four hours after their arrival they had their first air attack. Nine Aichi type 99 bombers escorted by fifteen Zeros chose the transports as they peeled off from 10,000 feet.

Rocked by heavy anti-aircraft fire, and pounced upon by our Marine land-based fighters, the bombers dropped three bombs near the *Zeilin,* flooding her No. 1 hold. The *Libra* and *Betelgeuse* were slightly damaged by other near hits. Then the half of the bombers that had survived the anti-aircraft fire roared away with our fighters close on their tails, falling one by one as they tried to escape.

Unloading operations were promptly resumed. At 11:27 a flight of twenty-five medium and heavy level bombers, protected by five Zeros, caused another alert. These planes, however, occupied themselves with the ground installations on the island. Ten more bombers fell to the combined fury of ack-ack, and the Marine fighters lost one Grumman.

At twilight Admiral Scott's ships retired to Indispensable Strait for the night. The *Zeilin's* damage required that she return to Espiritu Santo, so the *Lardner* was detached to escort her.

Meanwhile, Admiral Turner and Admiral Callaghan's combined forces were approaching on schedule. On the morning of the 11th the *Portland's* four seaplanes had been sent back to Espiritu Santo, because the battle of Savo had shown that cruiser planes on board during action are a serious fire hazard. Although air search from Guadalcanal had detected no enemy surface vessels in the vicinity,

Admiral Callaghan wanted to be sure, so he sped ahead of the transports, and made two thorough sweeps through the waters to the east and west of Savo Island. He rejoined Admiral Turner's transports at dawn on Thursday.

Admiral Turner's four transports anchored off Kukum Point at half past five Thursday morning and the *Libra* and *Betelgeuse* anchored two miles east of Lunga Point. Combatant vessels were formed in two protective semicircles about them.

At 7:18 a Japanese 6-inch shore battery opened up on *Betelgeuse* and *Libra*. The *Helena, Barton,* and *Shaw* turned their guns against it and blasted that menace. Neither of the cargo ships was hit, and debarkation was not interrupted. What was one shore battery compared with the fifty bombers expected to arrive at any minute?

The alert didn't come until afternoon, a good three-quarters of an hour warning enabling our ships to up anchors and get into previously designated formation to repel attack.

Just after two o'clock two dozen Mitsubishi type-1 torpedo bombers and eight Zeros roared in low over Florida Island. Over the beach they dipped down close to the water's surface, skimming toward the transports at 200 miles an hour, in a long line abreast. It was a terrifying charge of aerial cavalry, but it ran headlong into point-blank fire of the screening ships so devastating that four or five enemy planes were immediately blasted from the air and as many others set ablaze. It was holocaust. In a desperate attempt to avoid destruction the formation split into two groups, one swerving across the bows of our ships and the other swinging around astern. So violent was the maneuver that their torpedoes were jerked haphazardly into the sea.

But the attempt to escape was fruitless. The land-based Marine and Army fighters, five of the Zeros already bagged on the approach, now eliminated every remaining bomber but one. But the attack had drawn blood.

A Mitsubishi which dropped its torpedo on the starboard side of the *McCawley* was set afire by that ship's guns. The pilot swerved his blazing plane in a suicide course for the *San Francisco*. Although he was practically parallel to her and disintegrating under her guns, he managed to strike Battle II and the after control structure with one wing, and sideswipe the ship like a scythe of flame before diving into the water. Several fires broke out, all soon extinguished, but thirty lives had been mowed down and three after 20-mm. guns on the after superstructure demolished. Their crews were killed to a man as they steadfastly stood to their guns, firing until the plane hit them.

The transports anchored again at about 3:25, two hours' unloading time lost.

By late afternoon it was calculated that the transports could be 90 per cent unloaded before nightfall. Then scouting aircraft sent in reports of three strong enemy forces steaming toward Guadalcanal, close enough to arrive during the night if they kept to their course. They were not accompanied by transports. Obviously their mission was to attack our transports and bombard our positions ashore.

Admiral Turner did some quick calculations. He decided to withdraw his transports to safer waters and to send Admiral Callaghan to meet the Japanese.

Leaving only one damaged destroyer, two low-fuel destroyers, and two minesweepers to cover the transports, he assigned to Admiral Callaghan five cruisers and eight destroyers, as a welcoming committee for at least two battleships, three cruisers, eleven destroyers and two seaplane tenders, with more perhaps in the offing. Well, so had we something in the offing too. To the southwest, Admiral Kinkaid's task force was steaming toward the area, and the invincible *Enterprise,* her wounds patched, was with him. They wouldn't be near enough for action this night, but the following morning, Friday the 13th, would be in fly-off position at Guadalcanal.

There was no moon when the ships' clocks showed it was Friday the 13th, November, 1942. Nor were there any stars, for the sky was overcast with ink-black clouds. In a single column, Admiral Callaghan's thirteen ships entered Lengo Channel for a search of the Savo Island area. They were in Battle Disposition "Baker One": the *Cushing* leading, followed in order by the destroyers *Laffey, Sterett* and *O'Bannon,* the cruisers *Atlanta, San Francisco, Portland, Helena, Juneau,* and destroyers *Aaron Ward, Barton, Monssen* and *Fletcher.*

Only five of these ships were equipped with search radar: *Portland, Helena, Juneau, O'Bannon* and *Fletcher.* Their antennas revolved, sending out probing beams of microwaves through the inky dark.

The *Helena's* clocks said 1:24 when blots appeared on her scopes. The report was flashed to Admiral Callaghan on the flagship *San Francisco:* Three groups of ships off the port bow, at distances ranging from thirteen to fifteen miles!

Course was changed to head directly for the enemy. The two fleets closed rapidly and the warning eye of radar showed that now the

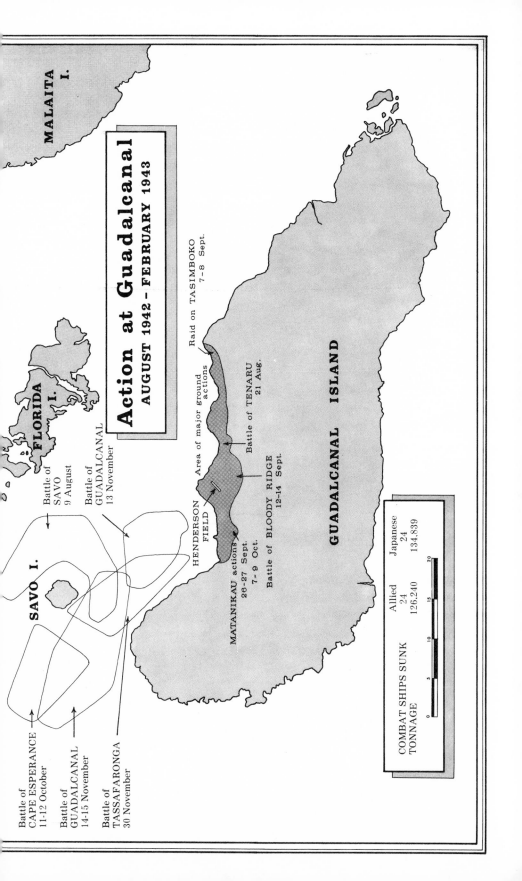

Action at Guadalcanal
AUGUST 1942 – FEBRUARY 1943

MALAITA I.

FLORIDA I.

SAVO I.

GUADALCANAL ISLAND

HENDERSON FIELD

Area of major ground actions

Raid on TASIMBOKO
7–8 Sept.

Battle of TENARU
21 Aug.

Battle of BLOODY RIDGE
12–14 Sept.

MATANIKAU actions
26–27 Sept.
7–9 Oct.

Battle of
SAVO
9 August

Battle of
GUADALCANAL
13 November

Battle of
CAPE ESPERANCE
11-12 October

Battle of
GUADALCANAL
14-15 November

Battle of
TASSAFARONGA
30 November

COMBAT SHIPS SUNK	Allied	Japanese
	24	24
TONNAGE	126,240	134,839

0 5 10 15 20

enemy was split into four groups—*on either side of our ships*. All told there were between eighteen and twenty Japanese ships. To the right were two light cruisers and several destroyers; to the left were two heavy cruisers and two or three destroyers to be met first, then a battleship, *Hiyei,* and three or four destroyers. To the north and somewhat to right was another battleship, *Kirishima,* and escorting destroyers.

At 1:45 Admiral Callaghan ordered the task force to stand by to open fire at a range of 3,000 yards. At this point, the cat's eye of radar showed enemy ships on both sides of our column, but the opposing forces were invisible to each other. The seconds ticked by as the yardage decreased. Suddenly the Americans tense on deck saw the Japanese flash recognition signals—red over white over green, and then at once realizing their mistake, they flared their searchlights, port and starboard, illuminating the United States force as if it were on holiday display. Then, down the track of light screamed the first enemy salvos.

The time was 1:48.

Coolly, Admiral Callaghan sent the order. "Odd ships fire to starboard, even to port!" The guns of the task force opened up, and so began a free-for-all fight with little semblance of co-ordination on either side, a fantastic battle, the likes of which had not been fought since navies abandoned sail, in which ships fought independently and both sides had to exert care not to hit their own ships.

At a conservative estimate, the Japanese could throw three times as much steel per broadside as the Americans. They could also pound our ships from both sides and from ahead. The American fleet was in a box. But the Japs had not expected to fight a surface engagement. They had been ordered to bombard our positions on Guadalcanal, especially the airfields and supplies, to clear the way for another landing, and so their guns and ammunition hoists were loaded with bombardment ammunition. Despite the initial Japanese accuracy of fire, the amount of damage caused the American ships by the lighter shells was low.

Immediately as the enemy illuminated, what was believed to be a light cruiser two miles to starboard came under fire from the *San Francisco* and *Sterett.* Seven main battery salvos from the *San Francisco,* and the Japanese ship—a large destroyer—blew up in a gaudy display of firewords. The job was accomplished in one minute flat.

Now, a searchlight is a two-way affair, and if our ships were lit up, the beams led back to their source. On the port side, the *Atlanta, Juneau, Helena, Aaron Ward, Barton, Fletcher, Laffey* and *O'Bannon* opened up on illuminating vessels, concentrating on two in line. The *Atlanta* and *Juneau* blasted a light cruiser, while the *Helena, Barton* and *Fletcher* attacked a heavy cruiser. Both enemy ships burst into flame and retired. Seeing her target out of action *Fletcher* shifted fire to the next ship in line which she reported as either "a *Natori*- or *Tenryu*-class cruiser." She was joined by the *Sterett,* which fired thirteen salvos. Both Japanese ships were thought to have sunk almost immediately. In the same area "an enemy destroyer exploded" and two others were seen to be on fire.

The *Atlanta,* an odd-numbered ship, had been unable to open fire to starboard as ordered because our destroyers were in the way. While she was shooting at a cruiser to port, a division of Japanese destroyers crossed half a mile ahead of her. Concentrating her forward guns on the last in line, the *Atlanta* put twenty shells into her and she "erupted into flame and disappeared." The after group of guns continued to fire at the cruiser until she, too, vanished.

The *Atlanta* herself was not unscathed. By now she had sustained thirteen 5-inch hits and some 3-inch from the light cruiser, mostly around the bridge, and twelve 5-inch hits from the destroyers, and she was fighting fires forward. Then, as the enemy ceased fire, the cruiser was struck by one or two torpedoes forward from a destroyer to port. All power was lost, except the auxiliary diesel, and the rudder was jammed left. The *Atlanta* began to circle back toward the south.

The *San Francisco* saw a "small cruiser or large destroyer farther ahead on the starboard bow," and shifted her fire to the vessel which "was hit with two full main battery salvos and set afire throughout her length." The range was 3,300 yards. At about the same time, as nearly as can be judged, "a heavy cruiser" came up in the dark on *Atlanta's* port quarter and opened fire against her at a range of about 3,500 yards, bearing 240° relative. The *Atlanta* reported that nineteen hits were scored on her with 8-inch armor-piercing ammunition. Although many of the projectiles failed to explode, her hull was holed several times, and her damaged bridge was shattered. The shells were loaded with green dye, the *San Francisco's* color. As the first shot struck, Captain Samuel P. Jenkins of the *Atlanta* rushed to the port side to get off torpedoes. When he returned to starboard, Admiral Scott and three officers of his staff had been killed, as well as a large number of others. The foremast collapsed, fires were blazing everywhere, and the *Atlanta* was dead in the water.

The remodernized Japanese battleship *Hiyei* was being engaged by the destroyers *O'Bannon* and *Aaron Ward*. The *O'Bannon's* guns shot out the battleship's searchlight and started several blazes. Then the *San Francisco* took the *Hiyei* under fire and scored at the waterline with two salvos.

The engagement had now become a battle royal, in which the temptation was to shoot first and identify afterward. The sea was crosshatched with torpedo tracks and plumed with geysers of shell splashes. When the *San Francisco* shifted her fire to the *Hiyei*, that vessel did not shoot back. Instead, mistaking foe for friend, the battleship frantically blinker-signaled the code for "error."

Admiral Callaghan had to get his ships in some semblance of order. Over the short-range voice radio, TBS, he broadcast: "Cease firing!" The order did not get through to the other vessels, but the *San Francisco* stopped firing at the *Hiyei*.

The enemy battleship, probably thinking her signal obeyed, bore down on the destroyer *Laffey*, which put on a burst of steam and managed to cross the enemy's bows with a few feet to spare. As the destroyer slid by she swung out her tubes and fired two torpedoes, but the range was too short and the missiles bounced, unarmed. Simultaneously the destroyer blasted the battleship's bridge with all guns she could get to bear, before a salvo from the Japanese smashed her own bridge as well as her No. 2 turret.

Meanwhile, at 1:52, the *Portland's* second salvo to starboard ripped into one of the enemy destroyers making a torpedo attack on the American column, but it was a poor exchange because the *Portland* herself had a screw sheared off by a torpedo, and the cruiser *Juneau* and the destroyer *Laffey* were mortally wounded.

Lieutenant Roger W. O'Neill, a doctor aboard the *Juneau*, felt the jolt of the torpedo's hit. "I can assure you it was terrific," he said. "It had sufficient concussion to cause the deck to buckle. . . . From what I could gather, the torpedo hit somewhere between frames 42 and 45 and entered the forward fireroom on the port side. The hit was below the armor belt. . . . All hands, approximately seventeen, inside this forward fireroom were killed immediately. . . . The chief engineer was quoted as having said, in his opinion, the keel of the ship had been broken by that initial torpedo hit. Immediately following the hit, the ship seemed to rise and settle deeper and listed somewhat to the port side. All lighting forward of the after mess hall was lost. We had also lost all our engine room generators for power and we couldn't fire our guns. . . . We immediately left the scene of action because we were injured to the extent that we could not fire and there was nothing left for us to do."

At 1:54, with the battle only six minutes old, Admiral Callaghan again gave the order to cease fire, but few heard it because of damage to their TBS, and the melee continued. The *Cushing* firing six torpedoes at the *Hiyei* and was immediately blasted by destroyer and cruiser salvos that put all her guns, except her 20-mm., out of commission. One minute later the *Barton* stopped to avoid colliding with a friendly ship and was struck with one, and then two torpedoes. She broke in half and sank in ten seconds, the loss of life tragically increased when a destroyer astern, and herself under attack, tore through the *Barton's* swimming survivors at high speed.

At 1:56—eight minutes of the battle gone—the *O'Bannon* closed to within half a mile of the burning battleship *Hiyei,* readied her torpedoes, and fired a spread of three at the colossus. There was a tremendous explosion on the enemy ship, and a sheet of fire completely covered her. Burning particles fell on the destroyer, which was swung north to avoid colliding. From her decks five burning ships could be counted astern, whether friend or enemy none could tell.

Now, the *San Francisco* again had the blazing but still firing *Hiyei* on her starboard bow, with the battleship heading parallel on the same course. On the flagship's starboard quarter an enemy cruiser was groping for her range, and a Japanese destroyer cut across her bow, turned hard left and raked her port side, all guns blazing.

The *San Francisco's* predicament was called out to the fleet over voice radio, and the *Portland* responded, asking for directions. Admiral Callaghan, broadcasting the appeal to get "the big ones," told the *Portland* to concentrate on the *Hiyei,* a shining mark. The American cruiser fired four main battery salvos at a range of two miles and made fourteen hits on the enemy battleship. The *San Francisco* also gave the *Hiyei* everything she had in one grand broadside just as the enemy cruiser found her range and the *Hiyei's* third salvo smashed her bridge, killing Admiral Callaghan and mortally wounding Captain Young.

The *San Francisco* kept firing at the *Hiyei* as long as the main battery would bear, and the Japanese battleship threw two or three more salvos before the duel was broken off. The *San Francisco* had received fifteen major-caliber hits and uncounted lesser ones. Twenty-five separate fires were aggravating that damage. The officer of the deck, Lieutenant Commander Bruce McCandless, was conning the damaged ship, while Lieutenant Commander Herbert Schonland, who had succeeded to command, continued to fight the fires below.

After just fifteen minutes of battle, most of our ships were seriously shot up. Target for twenty direct hits, the destroyer *Cushing* was lying helpless. The *Laffey* and *Barton* had sunk; the *Sterett* had lost her foremast; the *O'Bannon* was slightly damaged. The cruiser *Atlanta* was burning, and the *San Francisco* and *Portland* were badly holed. The *Helena* had received minor injury. The *Juneau* had crawled from the scene of action, her back broken. Only the *Aaron Ward, Monssen* and *Fletcher* were untouched.

The *Aaron Ward's* immunity was short-lived. In pursuit of a cruiser she received three 14-inch, two 8-inch, and five smaller hits, and was put out of action. Then the *Sterett* was caught in a cross fire while pumping torpedoes at the *Hiyei* and sustained several 5-inch hits on her bridge.

At twelve past two, twenty-four minutes after the opening gun, the *Helena* tried to reassemble the scattered American units. Most of the Japanese ships had turned in headlong retirement, firing haphazardly at each other as they withdrew. The *Sterett,* despite her serious damage, closed with a limping enemy destroyer and set her afire with two torpedoes and two 5-inch salvos, before the Jap was able to return a single shell. When the Japansee destroyer blazed up, the light from the explosion revealed the *Sterett* to other enemy stragglers who immediately took her under fire, and the courageous destroyer absorbed eleven more direct hits, setting ready-service powder afire. Now the destroyer had only two guns still serviceable; her remaining two torpedoes were jammed in their tubes. But the engines were all right and the *Sterett* managed to get away at flank speed, just as the near-by *Monssen,* one of the two ships left unscathed, was illuminated by star shells. Believing them to have come from a friendly vessel trying to make formation, the destroyer flashed recognition lights. Immediately searchlights lit her up and a salvo of medium-caliber shells hurtled down, putting her out of action. Steering was lost, and her upper works became a mass of flames. Without guns, torpedoes or power, the ship was ordered abandoned. The commanding officer and several others were trapped on the bridge, but managed to jump into the water from the rail, all suffering serious injury.

At last, though, the *Helena* instructed all the ships to form on her and head eastward. The only means of communication left to the *San Francisco* was a flashlight, and by it she signaled the news of Admiral Callaghan's death. The *Cushing* was sinking, and her crew abandoning ship. The *Fletcher* formed up, and shepherded the *Helena* and *San Francisco* out of Sealark Channel, meeting up with the damaged *Juneau* in Indispensable Strait. The *O'Bannon* and *Sterett* retired through Lengo Channel and joined the four others in a limping procession toward Espiritu Santo, none knowing that the *Juneau* would never get there.

Daybreak found the battle area still smoking. The *Portland* was circling, her steering out of control. Dead men, and some still living, dotted a sea foul with oil and wreckage.

Two miles to the south lay the *Atlanta,* her fires out. The *Cushing* and the *Monssen* were burning to the northwest and north, and presently the latter blew up and sank. The *Aaron Ward* was dead in the water seven and a half miles to the north. Northwest of Savo Island the battered *Hiyei* was slowly steaming, circling, her steering also shot away; a destroyer was standing by the stricken giant. Six and a half miles from the *Portland,* south of Savo, lay a Japanese destroyer with two small boats alongside.

The crippled ships glowered at each other. Then, suddenly, angrily, the cruiser *Portland* pumped six 6-gun salvos at the Jap destroyer. The last one exploded the after magazine and the destroyer sank. According to Admiral Nimitz, this destruction of an enemy vessel while steering was still out of control was "one of the highlights of the action."

Half an hour later the Japanese battleship, like a dying rattlesnake striking in final fury, hurled eight 2-gun salvos at the *Aaron Ward,* which was about to be taken under tow by Lieutenant James L. Foley's tug *Bobolink* from Tulagi. Then the Japanese firing stopped, for out of the sky was descending a formidable antagonist—planes from Guadalcanal to give her the coup de grace.

At ten o'clock the *Atlanta* and *Portland* were still helpless off the enemy-held shore. The *Bobolink* returned from taking the *Aaron Ward* to Tulagi, and took the worse-hurt *Atlanta* to Lunga Point, a fruitless labor because salvage operations proved to be of no avail, and a demolition party led by Captain Jenkins himself sank the cruiser that night.

In the afternoon the sturdy, homely, tireless *Bobolink* came back for the *Portland*. Towing was slow and difficult and it took until the following morning, almost exactly twenty-four hours after the battle, to berth the *Portland* in Tulagi.

During all that salvage and sporadic shooting during the daylight following the engagement, survivors were being picked up by small craft and taken to Guadalcanal.

So ended the first phase of what naval history will record as the Battle of Guadalcanal.

In thirty-four minutes of slam-bang furious action a vastly inferior American force had, at great cost, stopped Japan's South Pacific fleet and turned it back in staggering retreat. That fleet's mission had been to blast a hole in the Americans' grip on the Solomons through which would be poured the army of veteran troops even then bearing down on Guadalcanal.

The battle cost us five ships—the new anti-aircraft light cruiser *Atlanta* and the new destroyers *Barton, Laffey,* and *Monssen,* the older but modern *Cushing*. The heavy cruisers *San Francisco* and *Portland* were severely damaged, the light cruiser *Juneau* more so, her sister ship *Atlanta* less. Three destroyers had been hurt in varying degrees of severity—*Aaron Ward, Sterett* and *O'Bannon*. Only the *Fletcher* came through relatively unmarked by the most savage fleet action of modern times.

The Japanese, fully aware of the presence of the American cruisers and destroyers in Guadalcanal waters, admittedly did not believe that the light force would challenge Nippon's superiority in ships and fire power. The enemy once more suffered much less material damage than did the victors—one battleship and two destroyers sunk, two cruisers and three destroyers damaged. But he had lost the field again. The object of the Japanese fleet was to flatten the American positions on Guadalcanal. The mission of the handful of American ships was to prevent that accomplishment, no matter the cost, and— they succeeded . . .

FOLLOWING HIS MID-NOVEMBER VICTORY AT SEA, HAL- sey was quickly to consolidate his gains. In aid of Vandegrift's seri- ously depleted 1st Marine Division, his transports brought up the 164th Infantry Division and the 8th Marine Regiment, and plans were made to bring up the 6th Marine Division and the 182nd

Infantry from New Caledonia. Meanwhile, Vandegrift followed up the victory by pushing to the westward and engaging the land forces of the enemy at Point Cruz. By the 30th PT tender *Jamestown* and fifteen replacement motor torpedo boats had arrived to bolster Guadalcanal's defense force. At this time the Japanese High Command, desperate to supply more reinforcements for the land fighting, formed a task force of eight destroyers and six transports. Opposing this were five cruisers and four destroyers under command of Rear Admiral Carlton H. Wright, newly arrived in the South Pacific. The two forces clashed at Tassafaronga, where American sailors met Rear Admiral Raizo Tanaka for the first time. Although the United States Navy was superior in ships and firepower, Tanaka displayed his brilliance in night torpedo attack by inflicting far heavier damage than he sustained: he sank a heavy cruiser, *Northhampton,* and put three others out of action for nearly a year as against the loss of one destroyer.

As the year ended Japan seemed more than ever resolved to recapture Guadalcanal. In Rabaul, ready to launch an all-out attack, was General Hitoshi Immamura with 50,000 troops. At this time nightly PT battles with Tanaka's destroyers were becoming commonplace. The Japanese began to move their troops by barge from Munda, a new staging area in southern New Georgia. Meanwhile, American submarines were taking a heavy toll of Japanese shipping within striking distance of the Solomons, with destroyers as the prime target. One such "hot" war patrol was conducted by *Wahoo,* with big, affable Lieutenant Commander Dudley W. "Mush" Morton—a legend among submariners—in command. (Executive Officer, Lieutenant Commander Richard O'Kane later won the Congressional Medal of Honor aboard the submarine *Tang.*)

Captain George Grider and collaborator Lydel Sims describe a typical Morton patrol.

CAPTAIN GEORGE GRIDER

AND LYDEL SIMS

8.

MUSH THE MAGNIFICENT

Everybody liked Mush. He had done a thorough job of getting acquainted with the *Wahoo* and its crew during the second patrol. He was always roaming the narrow quarters, his big hands reaching out to examine equipment, his wide-set eyes missing nothing. He was largely without responsibility on that patrol, and he had been one of the boys. The tiny wardroom always brightened when Mush squeezed his massive shoulders through one of the narrow doorways and found a place to sit. He was built like a bear, and as playful as a cub. Once he and I got into an impromptu wrestling match after our coffee, and he put a half nelson on me and bore down just a little. Something in the back of my neck popped, and my head listed to port for weeks afterward. Even today it comes back occasionally, and I always think of Mush.

The crew loved him. Submarines are perhaps the most democratic of all military units, because within their cramped confines there simply isn't room for echelons of rank and dignity. Even so, for many officers the transition from camaraderie to authority is a jerky and awkward one, so that their men are never completely at ease. It was not this way with Mush. His authority was built-in and never depended on sudden stiffening of tone or attitude. Whether he was in the control room, swapping tall tales with Rau, the chief of the boat, or wandering restlessly about in his skivvies, talking to the men in the torpedo and engine rooms, he was as relaxed as a baby. The men were not merely ready to follow him, they were eager to.

But there had been times on the second patrol when his casually expressed opinions suggested the absence of any reasonable degree of caution. It is one thing to be aggressive, and another to be foolhardy, and it would be a mistake to think that the average man in submarines was a fire-breathing buccaneer who never thought of his own hide. Most of us, in calculating the risk, threw in a mental note that we were worth more to the Navy alive than dead—and to our wives and children as well. But when Mush expressed himself on tactics, the only risk he recognized was the risk of not sinking enemy tonnage. Talking it over at Paradise Beach, Roger and I were mildly concerned.

Another thing that worried us was that Dick O'Kane, the exec, clearly had no reservations about Mush. The two were in agreement on everything. And we still weren't too sure about Dick. He talked a great deal—reckless, aggressive talk—and it was natural to wonder how much of it was no more than talk. During the second patrol Dick had grown harder to live with, friendly one minute and pulling his rank on his junior officers the next. One day he would be a martinet, and the next he would display an overlenient, what-the-hell attitude that was far from reassuring. With Mush and Dick in the saddle, how would the *Wahoo* fare? Nevertheless, we looked forward almost eagerly to the prospect . . .

Even before we left the harbor at Brisbane, the impact of our new skipper was felt. Meals in the wardroom took on the nature of parties; instead of staring at our plates and fretting over our responsibilities, as we had grown accustomed to doing, we found ourselves led along by a captain who was constantly joking, laughing, or planning outrageous exploits against the enemy. Overnight, it seemed, the photographs of Japanese ships that had been pasted all over the *Wahoo* even in the head, came down—not by order, but through some unspoken understanding that Mush would approve—and in their places went some of the finest pin-up pictures in the U. S. Navy. Identification of silhouettes is a useful occupation, but some silhouettes are more rewarding than others.

Our instructions were to proceed to the Carolines. To this day I don't remember exactly where we were supposed to go, because we never got there. But there was one sentence, almost incidental, in our orders that was to have considerable significance. En route, we were to reconnoiter Wewak harbor.

To reach the Carolines we would sail north from Brisbane and follow the northeast coast of New Guinea upward, past Buna, where General MacArthur's troops were even then driving back the Japanese, and on up along the enemy-held shore. And somewhere along there, reports indicated, was a harbor called Wewak that might hold enemy ships. We were to see what we could find.

If we hurried, Mush decided, we could spend more time there than our operation order had allowed. So as we moved along the New Guinea coast, we stayed on the surface for greater speed. It was a strange and unfamiliar experience to see enemy land lying black and sinister on the port hand, to feel the enemy planes always near us, and yet it was invigorating. Contrary to all tradition on the *Wahoo,* we kept to the surface during daylight hours for six days, submerging only for one quick trim dive each morning, though we were almost never out of sight of land and often within close range of enemy airports.

The *Wahoo*'s combat attitude had changed in other ways. Now, instead of two officers, four lookouts, and the quartermaster on the bridge when we were on the surface, we cruised with only one officer and three lookouts, but somehow we felt we had never been so well guarded. And Mush had removed the bunk previously installed for the skipper in the conning tower. When he was ready for sleep, he went down to his stateroom and slept like a baby, leaving no doubt that the officer of the deck was on his own, that he was trusted, and that he was thoroughly in command unless or until he asked for help.

Only occasionally did Mush intervene. One day he wandered up for a bit of conversation when I was on the bridge, and suddenly as we talked we sighted a plane about eight miles away. About the same time, the radar picked it up and confirmed the range. We had always dived when we sighted a plane in the past, so I turned for the hatch. Mush's big hand landed on the back of my collar just as I reached the ladder.

"Let's wait till he gets in to six miles," he said softly.

I turned and went back. Great Lord, I thought, we're under the command of a madman.

We stood and watched as the plane closed the range. At six and a half miles his course began to take him away from us, and in a few minutes he had faded from sight. By gambling that he hadn't seen us, Mush had saved us hours of submerged travel, but even though it had worked, I wasn't sure I was in favor of it.

Meanwhile, as we neared the area where Wewak should be, the chart problem became acute. Our orders gave no hint of its position and none of our charts of the New Guinea coast showed it by name; it could have been any one of a dozen unnamed spots. How could we reconnoiter a harbor whose location we didn't know?

At first, most of us had considered this only a minor problem. If we didn't know where Wewak was, we didn't know. We could take a look at some of the more promising spots, and make our reports, and be on our way. Then one night in the wardroom a different light was put on the matter. Mush, Dick, Roger, Hank Henderson, and I were looking at the charts, speculating on which tiny dent in the coast might be Wewak, when Mush asked innocently what we understood to be the meaning of the word "reconnoiter."

I may have hammed up the answer a little, but not much.

"Why," I said, "it means we take a cautious look at the area, from far out at sea, through the periscope, submerged."

Mush grinned. "Hell, no," he said. "The only way you can reconnoiter a harbor is to go right into it and see what's there."

Roger and Hank and I looked at each other in sheer consternation. Now it was clear that our captain had advanced from mere rashness to outright foolhardiness. For a submarine, as anybody knew in those days, was a deep-water ship that needed broad oceans and plenty of water under its keel to operate. And harbors are often treacherous at best, even when you enter them in surface ships handled by experienced pilots equipped with the very latest charts. It would be madness for the *Wahoo* to submerge and enter an enemy harbor whose very location on the map we didn't know.

Later, submarines penetrated other harbors, but if any had done so at that time, none of us knew about it, and it was against every tradition that had been built up on the *Wahoo*. Yet here was this skipper of ours, grinning at us under his jutting nose as if he had just told a funny story, assuring us we were going to do it and we'd damned well better find out which harbor was Wewak or he'd just pick the most likely one and go in.

After word of this attitude of Mush's got out, the search for a chart of Wewak harbor increased markedly. And in the end it was Bird-Dog Keeter, the motor machinist's mate who had sighted the *Wahoo*'s first victim, who came to the rescue. I was making a tour through the engine room one night when I found Keeter poring over a book. He looked up, grabbed my arm, and yelled over the roar of the engines:

"Hey, Mr. Grider, is this the Wewak we're going to?"

I grabbed the book out of his hand. It was an Australian high-school geography book he had bought while we were on leave, and he opened it to a page that showed a map of New Guinea. Sure enough, there on the northeast coast was a tiny spot marked WEWAK.

A couple of months before, the idea of entering an enemy harbor with the help of a high-school geography would have struck me as too ridiculous even to be funny. Now I almost hugged the book and charged forward to the wardroom with it as if it were the key to the destruction of the entire Japanese Navy.

Mush took one look at it and reached for our charts. The wardroom began to hum with activity.

One of our charts did have a spot that seemed to correspond with the latitude and longitude of Wewak as shown in the book, but even then we weren't much better off. On our big chart, the Wewak area covered a space about the size of a calling card—hardly the detail you need for entering a harbor. We were on the track now, though, and Mush's determination to enter Wewak, regardless, made what we had seem a lot better than nothing.

Dick O'Kane and his quartermaster, a man named Krause, took over. First, Krause made a tracing of the area from our chart onto a piece of toilet paper. Next, we took my old Graflex camera and rigged it as an enlarger, using the ship's signal lamp as the projector light. We clamped this rig to the wardroom table and projected the enlarged image onto a large sheet of paper spread on the wardroom deck. Then, with all lights turned out, Dick and Krause traced the projected lines on the new sheet, and we had a chart. It might have made a cartographer shudder, but it was a long way ahead of no chart at all.

What we saw was a rough drawing, not of a harbor, but of a protected roadstead with islands on all four sides. And there was a name for one of the islands: Mushu. In the general triumph, this was taken as a positive omen of good hunting. And as I reassembled my Graflex, I could not help reflecting that it, too, was an omen. It was a camera that had been used in World War I by my father and his friend and fellow flier Elliott Springs. My father had been killed in action, and Elliott had saved the camera and given it to me as a memento. I had always treasured it as something special and had got myself named ship's photographer in order to bring it along on the *Wahoo*. When I thought that a chart fashioned with the help of an ancient camera used by my father more than a quarter of a century before on another side of the world in another war would lead us into Wewak harbor, I too began to believe there was some kind of guiding destiny behind the *Wahoo*'s third patrol.

So, in the limited time remaining, we planned and discussed and prepared. Every scrap of information we had been able to get about Wewak was transferred to our chart. From what we assembled, it appeared that it might be plausible after all to penetrate the harbor. There was plenty of room; the harbor was about two miles across in most places, and we believed the depth might be as much as two hundred feet in most areas. Mush was delighted. He ignored the uncertainties and concentrated on the fact that we would have deep water, if we stayed where it was, and unmistakable landmarks, if we could spot them in time to use them.

It was summer in that hemisphere, and the sun rose early. We adjusted our speed to arrive at Wewak just before dawn on January 24. At three-thirty in the morning, just as the eastern horizon was beginning to gray, we dived, two and a half miles off the entrance, and proceeded submerged toward Wewak harbor.

Actually, there were several entrances, but we were sure of only one. The harbor extended about nine miles in from this point, making a dogleg that obstructed the view. We approached around the western end of one of the islands to investigate the bay beyond, but before Dick could see anything else, he spotted two torpedo boats in the periscope, headed in our direction. This was no time to be seen by small boats, so we ducked down, waited awhile, and tried again.

This time the torpedo boats were gone. There was a small tug in the distance with a barge alongside, but no other shipping in sight. We poked around into another area, a strait between two of the islands, and Dick saw something that may have been radio masts on the far side of a third island. Mush suggested we go around for a better look, but this time a reef showed up to block our way.

We spent the entire morning nosing around that harbor, trying to find out what was in it and where the safe water was. As Dick spotted light patches of water in the scope, he called off their locations and we noted them on our chart as shallows. From time to time we could pencil in landmarks. One of these we called Coast Watcher Point.

A strong southward current had been complicating our problems ever since we entered the harbor, and it was this current that was responsible for the naming of Coast Watcher Point. It swept us so close to the point that all of us in the conning tower, taking turns at the periscope, could see a Japanese lookout, wearing a white shirt, sitting under a coconut tree right on the point. We saw him so clearly, in fact, that I am sure I would recognize him if I passed him on the street tomorrow.

Except for this chance the rest of us had to look, Dick O'Kane had made all the periscope observations. Mush had a unique theory: he believed the executive officer, not the captain, should handle the periscope throughout an approach and attack. This, he explained, left the skipper in a better position to interpret all factors involved, do a better conning job, and make decisions more dispassionately. There is no doubt it is an excellent theory, and it worked beautifully for him, but few captains other than Mush ever had such serene faith in a subordinate that they could resist grabbing the scope in moments of crisis.

Right now, Mush was in his element. He was in danger, and he was hot on the trail of the enemy, so he was happy. For all the tension within us, we managed to reflect his mood. The atmosphere in the conning tower would have been more appropriate to a fraternity raiding party than so deadly a reconnaissance. Mush even kept up his joking when we almost ran aground.

This happened because of the dual nature of a periscope. It is a very precise instrument with two powers of magnification: a low power that magnifies objects one and a half times, to give you about the same impression you would get with the naked eye, and a six-power magnification to bring things in very close. So everyone was concerned when, on one of his looks, Dick called from the periscope:

"Captain, I believe we're getting too close to land. I have the periscope in high power, and all I can see is one coconut tree." If only one coconut tree, even magnified six times, filled his scope, then we were dangerously close.

"Dick," said the captain in a tone of mild reproof, "you're in *low* power."

In the electric silence that followed, Dick flipped the handle to high power and took an incredulous look.

"Down periscope!" he yelped. "All back emergency! My God, all I can see is one *coconut!*" We backed away from there in record time.

By early afternoon, Mush was beginning to lose his good humor.

We had spent half a day looking for a target worth shooting at, and none had showed up. But we had got a good idea of the harbor, and now we went in farther, to where we could get a good look around the dogleg and down the bight, and there at the very end of the dogleg Dick saw what appeared to be the superstructure of a ship. At first sight, he reported it looked like a freighter or a tender of some sort, at anchor.

"Well, Captain," somebody in the conning tower said, "we've reconnoitered Wewak harbor now. Let's get the hell out of here and report there's a ship in there." We all knew it was a joke, however much we wished it weren't.

"Good God, no," said Mush, coming to life, "we're going to go in and torpedo him."

Dick asked him to come over and help identify the potential target, and the two of them stood there like a couple of schoolboys, peering through the scope each time it was raised, trying to decide what kind of vessel lay ahead. At last they agreed, and Mush looked happily around the conning tower.

"It's a destroyer," he said.

Much has been written about the changes great fighters undergo in battle. It has been said that when General Nathan Bedford Forrest, the great Confederate cavalry officer, went into battle, his face became a deep, mottled red, his voice altered, becoming shrill and high-pitched, and his whole countenance took on a look of indescribable fierceness. Mush Morton changed, too, but in a wholly different way. Joy welled out of him. His voice remained the same, but his eyes lit up with a delight that in its own way was as fearful as Forrest's countenance must have been. Here, we were to realize before the *Wahoo*'s third patrol ended, was a man whose supreme joy was literally to seek out and destroy the enemy. It was to drive him to terrifying magnificence as a submarine commander, to make him a legend within a year, and to lead eventually to his death.

Now, as the rest of us worried about the depth of the water, the pull of the unknown currents, the possibility of reefs between us and our target, he smiled at us again.

"We'll take him by complete surprise," he assured us. "He won't be expecting an enemy submarine in here."

Mush was right about that. Nobody in his right mind would have expected us.

We went to battle stations. The conning tower, already crowded,

became even more so. Roger Paine took his post at the Torpedo Data
Computor, the mechanical brain mounted in the after corner. Jack
Jackson, the communications officer, supervised the two sound operators. As assistant approach officer, I turned over my diving duties to
Hank Henderson and crouched near the top of the control-room
ladder, manipulating a small device known as an "is-was"—a sort
of attack slide rule used in working out distances and directions.
There were also two quartermasters, a fire controlman, the helmsman, and a couple of others in the tiny compartment.

Dick made his sightings cautiously, easing the periscope up only
far enough to see the tops of the masts of the destroyer. We moved at
a speed of only three knots. The sea above us was as calm as glass, a
condition that makes periscopes very easy to see. All unnecessary
auxiliary motors, including the air conditioning, were shut off now;
we were rigged for silent running. Voices dropped to whispers, and
perspiration began to drip from our faces as the temperature rose
toward the 100-degree mark. We had the element of surprise on our
side, and nothing else. We were now six miles inside an uncharted
harbor, with land on three sides of us, and in a minute or so the
whole harbor would know we were there.

The outer doors on our six forward torpedo tubes were quietly
opened. We were approaching the range Mush had decided on, three
thousand yards. It was a little long, but it should keep us in deep
water.

"Stand by to fire One."

Dick O'Kane, crouched around the periscope barrel, flipped his
thumbs up to indicate he wanted the scope raised one last time. The
long cylinder snaked up. Dick rode the handles, clapping his eye to
the eyepiece as soon as it was clear of the floorboards. He let the
scope get about two inches out of water and took a quick look
around.

"Down scope." There was an urgency in his whisper that brought
tension to the breaking point. "Captain, she's gotten under way,
headed out of the harbor. Angle on the bow ten port."

Now our plan to catch this sitting duck was gone a-glimmering.
She was not only under way, she was headed almost directly at us.
The only reasonable thing to do was to get out. Later, perhaps, we
could get a shot at her in deep water. But Mush was in no mood to be
reasonable.

"Right full rudder!"

Without a moment's pause, he was shifting to a new plan of attack. Now we would run at right angles to the destroyer's course and fire our stern tubes at her as she passed astern.

The conning tower burst into action. Periscope down . . . Roger twirling knobs on the TDC . . . Mush crouched in the middle of the conning tower, breathing heavily, spinning the disks on the is-was . . . orders being shouted now rather than whispered. The destroyer's speed, increasing as she got under way, could only be guessed at. Roger cranked a reading on the TDC, which would automatically generate the correct angles for the gyros. The ship swung hard to the right. Within one minute we were ready to fire.

"Up periscope . . . Mark! . . . Target has zigged . . . Angle on the bow forty starboard." Now the destroyer was heading across our bow. More frantic grinding of knobs, another quick guess at his speed—fifteen knots this time.

"Ready . . . Stand by to fire. . . . Fire One. . . . Fire Two. . . . Fire Three."

The boat shuddered as the three torpedoes left the forward tubes.

"All ahead standard." The bow had begun to rise under the loss of weight forward.

Steam torpedoes leave a wake as wide as a two-lane highway and a lot whiter. There was no point now in lowering the periscope, for at that range the enemy could simply look down the wakes to where x marked the spot. Dick brought the periscope up to full height and watched. After a couple of centuries, he spoke.

"They're headed for him."

Torpedoes run at about fifty knots, but the interval between firing and hitting seems endless.

"The first one missed astern. . . . The second one missed astern. . . . The third one missed astern."

Groans sounded in the conning tower. We had guessed too low on his speed.

"Get another setup!" There was a fierce urgency in Mush's voice. "Use twenty knots."

"Ready."

"Fire Four!"

Again the boat shuddered, and Dick's eyes remained glued to the scope. And again the news, given to us piecemeal between long pauses, was bad.

"Target turning away."

"Damn!"

"The fourth missed. . . . She's swinging on around. . . . Now she's headed right at us."

The situation had changed drastically. Warned by the wakes of the first three torpedoes, the destroyer had begun a fast, determined turn away from us, continuing it for 270 degrees until now she was headed toward us, ready for revenge. A destroyer is named for its ability to destroy submarines, and this one was coming at us now with a deck full of depth charges. We had fired four of our six forward fish. We had four more in our stern tubes, but it would take too long to swing to fire them, and even longer to reload our forward tubes.

"All right," said Mush. "Get set for a down-the-throat shot."

We had talked about down-the-throats in wardroom bull sessions, but I doubt if any of us had ever seriously expected to be involved in such a shot. It is what the name implies, a shot fired at the target while he is coming directly toward you. No one knew for sure how effective it would be, because as far as I know there was then no case in our submarine records of anyone's having tried it. But it had one obvious virtue, and two staggering disadvantages. On the one hand, you didn't have to know the target's speed if the angle was zero; on the other hand, the target would be at its narrowest, and if you missed, it would be too late to plan anything else. In this particular case, we would be shooting a two-ton torpedo at a craft no more than twenty feet wide, coming toward us at a speed of about thirty knots.

A few minutes before, I had been thinking fatuously what a fine story I would have to tell Ann and Billy on my leave. Now I remembered with relief that I had left my will ashore at the beginning of the patrol.

"Ready." From Roger, at the TDC.

"Stand by to fire."

"Range eighteen hundred."

"Fire five!"

"Periscope is under water. Bring me up."

Hank had momentarily lost control, under the impact of the firing, and we had dropped below periscope depth with that destroyer boiling down on us. "Bring her up, Hank, boy, bring her up," the skipper called down the hatch. An agonizing wait, then, with Dick clinging to the periscope.

"Captain, we missed him. He's still coming. Getting close."

It is strange how, in such situations, some portion of your mind can occupy itself with coolly impersonal analyses of factors not directly connected with your own hide. I found part of myself marveling at the change that had come over Dick O'Kane since the attack had begun. It was as if, during all the talkative, boastful months before, he had been lost, seeking his true element, and now it was found. He was calm, terse, and utterly cool. My opinion of him underwent a permanent change. It was not the first time I had observed that the conduct of men under fire cannot be predicted accurately from their everyday actions, but it was the most dramatic example I was ever to see of a man transformed under pressure from what seemed most adolescent petulance to a prime fighting machine.

"Stand by to fire Six."

"When shall I fire, Captain?"

"Wait till she fills four divisions in low power."

"Captain, she already fills eight."

Even Mush was jarred. "Well, for Christ's sake," he yelled, *"fire!"*

"Fire Six!" From Dick. Mush echoed him with, "Take her deep!"

We flooded negative and started down, and I went down the ladder and took over from Hank. I couldn't take her really deep, because we had no idea what the depth of the water there was, and it wouldn't help to strike an uncharted reef. But I took her as far down as I dared, to ninety feet, and we rigged for depth-charge attack.

We were no longer the aggressor. Now our time as well as our torpedoes had run out, and we were helpless to fight back. All we could do was grab on to something and stand by for the final depth-charging of the U.S.S. *Wahoo.* Our time had come, and we waited for the end almost calmly.

The first explosion was loud and close. A couple of light bulbs broke, as they always do on a close explosion, and I remember watching in a detached way as the cork that lined the inside of the *Wahoo's* hull began to flake off in little pieces.

We waited for the second blast, each man lost within himself, looking at objects rather than at other men, no eyes meeting, as is appropriate for the final moments of life.

And the silence continued. Ten, twenty, thirty seconds, until I looked up and saw other eyes coming into focus, faces taking on expressions of wonderment. It was a voice from the pump room that broke the spell.

"Jeez," it said, "Maybe *we* hit him!"

There was something ridiculous, almost hilariously so, about the voice. Up in the conning tower Mush heard it, and laughed.

"Well, by God, maybe we did," he responded, his voice now a roar. "Bring her back up to periscope depth, George."

Almost frantically, we wrestled her back up.

Again, Mush left the scope to Dick. He took a long look.

"There she is. Broken in two."

Bedlam broke loose on the *Wahoo*.

I waved to Hank to take over in the control room, grabbed my Graflex, and shot up the ladder. Mush had named me ship's photographer, and I was going to get a shot of that target one way or another.

It wasn't easy. Even Mush wanted to take a look at this, and every man in the crowded conning tower was fighting for a turn by the time the skipper turned aside. But at last my chance came.

The destroyer was almost beam to, broken in two like a matchstick, her bow already settling. Apparently, her skipper had lost his nerve when he saw our last torpedo heading toward him and put the rudder over to try to miss it, and by swinging himself broadside to it he had signed the destroyer's death warrant. Now, as she began to sink, her crew swarmed over her, hundreds of men, in the rigging, in the superstructure, all over her decks. As we struggled for positions at the periscope, some of the destroyer's crew returned to their places at the forward deck gun and began firing at our periscope. They continued it as she sank slowly beneath the waves.

Somehow I got a few pictures and moved out of the way. And now Mush, who was almost a tyrant when it came to imposing his will on us in emergencies, returned to the democratic spirit he always showed when something good happened. "Let everybody come up and take a look," he called.

The whole crew came up by turns, overflowing every inch of the control room and the conning tower, each man shoving his way to the scope and bracing himself there for a long, unbelieving look before turning away with whatever word represented the extreme limit of his vocabulary. I heard some remarkable expletives that day.

We were still celebrating when a bomb went off close aboard, and it dawned on us that there was a long way to go before we were out of the woods. Down we went again to ninety feet, realizing there was an airplane up there on lookout for us, and started to pick our way out.

In a moment we began to hear the propellers of small boats, buzzing around the water above us like waterbugs as they searched for us, and we realized the only way to get out of Wewak harbor safely was to keep our periscope down. In addition to the unknowns of current and depth, we had another unknown. Now we must run silent, which meant even the gyrocompass had to be turned off. The only compass we could use was the magnetic compass, never too reliable inside all that steel. We had to make four miles, take a turn to the right, and go about two more miles before we got to the open sea, and if we turned too soon, we were going to run into the island where we had seen the coast watcher sitting under the coconut tree. If we didn't turn soon enough, we were going to hit the reef ahead.

On the way down the dogleg before the attack, I had noticed a young sailor on the sound equipment, listening with great intensity, though he wasn't particularly needed at the time. Now he spoke to Mush.

"Captain," he said, "as we were coming in, I could hear beach noises on that island. I think I can tell from them when it's abeam."

None of us in the conning tower knew exactly what beach noises were. Since then, I have read that oceanographers say all sorts of things, particularly shrimp, make noises in the ocean, and shrimp in large beds are common in shallow water in that area. Whatever it was, if the man on the sound gear thought he could help, we were ready to listen.

So, relying on him, we prepared for our turn. We waited until he reported the sounds were abaft the beam, then we made our turn, holding our breaths and hoping, and it worked.

We surfaced after dark, about two miles outside the harbor, and looked back. The Japanese had built bonfires on almost every point, on the shore and on the islands, all along the roadstead. They must have been sure we were still in there, and waiting for us to surface. I have always been grateful, mistakenly or otherwise, to the shrimp along Mushu Island and Coast Watcher Point for getting safely out after our reconnoitering of Wewak harbor.

~~~~~~

PT BOATS FOUGHT A PITCHED BATTLE WITH TANAKA'S Tokyo express on the night of December 11, and again on the night of January 2. We have the word of Captain Yasumi Toyama,

Tanaka's Chief of Staff, that enemy destroyermen evinced no special fondness for their nightly sortie down The Slot. "We are more a freighter convoy than a fighting squadron these days," Toyama recorded. "The damn Yankees have dubbed us the Tokyo Express. We transport cargo to that cursed island . . . What a stupid thing! . . . Our decks are stacked high with supplies and our ammunition supply must be cut in half. Our cargo is loaded in drums which are roped together. We approach the island, throw them overboard and run away. The idea is that the strings of barrels will float until our troops on the island can tow them ashore. It is a strenuous and unsatisfying routine."

But the Japanese destroyers fought well, even with deckloads of cargo, and January 2 is a fine case in point. It was a donnybrook, with ten destroyers taking on eighteen PTs off Cape Esperance. One of the motor torpedo boat skippers was Lieutenant (jg) John Clagett, who brings us PT warfare at its grimmest.

9.

"FIRE TORPEDOES WHEN YOU'RE ON, WHITEY!"

It was black dark. Guadalcanal faded from view, except for the eerie illumination of the lightning. Savo was a shadow. The wake rolled back, glowing green.

"Lots of phosphorescence tonight," muttered Whitey.

"Yes."

A faint hum to the north grew into a roar, and the two planes skimmed again low across the dark bowl of the sky. We knew we were the objects of this search, and almost ceased to breathe as the planes circled twice, then vanished.

Up on the mountain over Esperance the three lights winked out.

The quartermaster touched my shoulder.

"There they are, sir."

And they were. A number of dark shadows moving over the dim line between sky and sea, on the starboard bow.

"Come right. Whitey, you fire 'em."

The bow swung to the right. I gave the alarm over the radio. Hardly had I finished the terse phrases when another voice joined: "Josephine. Off Aruligo! They're close!"

And another: "They're coming around the north side of Savo. Two destroyers."

The gunner's voice came, with a strained accent: "Skipper! Behind us, this side of Savo! Some more of 'em!"

420

"Jesus Christ!" whispered Whitey. It wasn't profanity; it was a prayer. We were completely surrounded.

The *One Eleven* moved steadily toward the middle column. They would be the troop carriers. They were heading for Esperance. Action and the world seemed suspended in an eternity as the range closed. My knees were weak, and my stomach was heavy and cold. My hands were wet, and the heavy glasses nearly slipped from them. I fought to keep my voice steady.

"Speed up a little, Kinlaw. We want a good shot at 'em. We got to make 'em good."

The pulse of the engines stepped up slightly. The range narrowed. Seven hundred yards. Silence, and the soft beating of great black wings. Six hundred yards. The green white wake at the bow of the landing ship was plainly seen now. Thunder muttered louder. I sat back on my little seat high on the cockpit. My legs shook a little. Five hundred yards. The gunner in the forward turret sighed. It could be heard in the quiet.

"Fire torpedoes when you're on, Whitey."

"Three and four, fire." The boat lurched. Two torpedoes threw up spray and vanished, trailing green wakes. "One and two, fire." The other two fish hit the water. A bit of excess oil in one of the tubes flared up. I groaned. The boat turned abruptly about, the engines moved up the scale, and the wake rose and spread. Red flares mushroomed out from the leading ships. Shells rumbled overhead. Searchlights came on. Tracers streaked. The engineers opened the mufflers, Kinlaw shoved the throttles, and the *One Eleven* tore through the exploding water at full speed. Her bow climbed, and the wet spray shot back. I noticed oddly that my sleeves were still rolled up, and thought of the hell Westy would raise over that. As in a dream I saw the leading Jap explode in a tower of fire.

Shells landed near the bow. The boat pitched. I whipped out my forty-five and fired two shots, the emergency smoke-signal. Mike had been waiting. The smoke rose in a billowing cloud. The boat turned and leaped. Shells burst on the starboard now, cracking shrapnel through the air, and dazzling us.

"Hard left! Left!" I shouted. And the world turned to glaring flame! It was hot, and sulphur was thick. The bow dropped, flame and fragments flew, and I heard myself crying, "Oh, Jesus Christ! We're hit!" and thinking simultaneously, "That's a trite thing to say!" It was searing hot; and then it was black fog, and piercing the black came a terrible scream. "Oh, my God! The pain! The pain! I can't stand it—"

The black fog lifted. It was oddly quiet, except for the crackling of greedy flames. I was alone in the cockpit, and the flames leaped about me. I was standing. I tried to walk, my one thought to escape this terrible hotness that was devouring. I couldn't walk, my knees buckled, and I crawled on hands and knees through a wall of flame, over a deck where fire oozed through the cracks. It was like a nightmare, when you're in some invisible morass, with death at your heels. I thought of the thousand gallons of hundred-octane gas beneath me. It might go at any second. At last I was at the edge of the deck. Without hesitation, and with my last strength, I heaved down into the welcome blackness.

The cool, cool water, delicious and unbelievable in its coolness, closed over me. I sank into the coolness. I thought crazily: *That's my last ride in a PT boat."*

My life-jacket dragged me to the surface. Face and hands felt numb but there was no pain. The *One Eleven* swung around, broadside presented, and I saw the length of the deck covered with flames, and the shattered side.

The steel helmet was heavy on my head. I reached up my hands to unbuckle the strap, but to my amazement they wouldn't work; and agony shot through the fingers when they touched the rough canvas of the strap. I tried to take the heavy seven-fifty binoculars from around my neck, but failed. I tried to unbuckle the pistol belt, but the fingers wouldn't function, and pain forced me to stop. Light from the burning boat was all about me. I held my hands up in it. They were swollen and dark, and long strips, white in the firelight, hung from them and floated in the water. The air started to burn, and I slid my hands beneath the water.

"I'm burned!" I said to myself. "I'm burned bad as hell!"

My face too was burning. I dipped it into the water. The burning stopped. Nature brings an anesthetic with severe injuries. I felt no great pain, and somehow fear seemed a muffled and useless thing. I felt like a spectator.

A shape drew near to the edge of the light. Red flashes burst from it, and I heard a faint rattling. A flurry of splashes rose from the water a few feet away. More flashes, and more little spouts. I was mildly interested. I heard a familiar voice from a hundred yards away. It was Whitey.

"Get the hell out o' here! They're shooting at us!"

A dull panic filled me. I rolled to my side and tried to swim. No use. The resignation overtook me again. The firing continued spasmodically for a while, and then the Jap, forsaking pleasure for business, fled into night. The flames from the boat died, but as I looked about the bay I could see five other separate fires, glowing where ships and PTs were burning fiercely.

The helmet was growing heavier. With an effort I could stay on my back for a while, and then I'd roll over on my face. The helmet's two pounds would slowly force my face under water. I would gather strength and thrust my head back. Then again the unceasing weight would push it slowly beneath the surface. This seemed to go on forever.

I heard Whitey shouting the names of the crew, and listened to the answers. When Whitey called, "Skipper! Skipper! Are you O.K.?" I summoned enough strength to answer: "I'm all right. A little scorched but still kicking. Everybody accounted for?"

The answer came back: "Everybody here except Phil. Nobody's seen him. I'm afraid he never got into the water. Sparks is hurt awful bad. I've got some morphine in him, and he's out now. Some of the other guys are hurt. Nobody else seems bad."

More ages passed. The little wavelets slapped my face. I pushed it from the water. The helmet pushed it back. Someone in a great black cloak drew the rim of it across my eyes, and the fierce scene of burning ships faded away.

I came to again, choking. I was very low in my lifejacket. It wasn't tight enough, and I was slowly slipping out of it. It was hard to open my eyes. They were swelling shut. I saw a gleam of phosphorescence in the water beneath me. It described a circle. A shark! I choked back a panic that tried to rise at the thought of the depths beneath me and the thousands of dead men there. Was I to join them?

I raised my voice. It sounded almost normal, and I was surprised at its strength.

"Oh, boys! Boys! Where are you?"

A hail came back: "Over here, Skipper. Are you all right?"

"I'm afraid not, fellows. My hands are burned and I can't get my helmet off, and my eyes are swelling shut, and I'll be out of this life-jacket pretty quick. Can a couple of you swim over here and give me a hand?"

The voice came back: "Hang on, Skipper. We'll be with you in a jiffy. Keep yelling so we'll be able to find you."

I continued to yell, and the friendly anxious voices came closer.

Just when I thought I couldn't hold my head up another minute, Long and Elsass swam out of the darkness and grabbed my life-jacket with strong hands. They tore off the helmet, let the glasses sink into the water, and took off my forty-five. They retied the life-jacket, turned me on my back, and started towing toward Savo, two miles away.

"That was just in time, boys. Thanks a lot. I'll never forget it."

"You should' a' yelled sooner, Skipper. How are you?"

"Not so hot, boys. You haven't got something you can hit me over the head with, have you?"

"Nothing lighter than a forty-five, Skipper. We've got a little water, though. Have a drink."

I hadn't realized how thirsty I was until I discovered I had emptied the light canteen. It brought new life. My eyes became even harder to open. The night stretched on for eternity on eternity. The black robe covered me again with its soft folds. I awakened to concussions in my ear. Long was firing his forty-five in the water to scare off the sharks, which were closing in. I was burning up. Thirst grew to an unbearable thing. But there was no water. That was a mockery. No water, but cool water lapped my chin. It was all I could do to refrain from opening my burning lips, and letting the coolness run down my throat. Something restrained me.

I heard Whitey dimly.

"Sparks is dead. We've got to leave him. Damn those Japs! Why doesn't someone come?"

More black ages, scarlet-lined with thirst. Then Walter Long shook me gently.

"Skipper, we've found a floating coconut, and I've got it open. We're not hurt, and we don't need it. Here, open your mouth."

Almost gasping in eagerness, I threw back my head, felt the rough bark of the nut on my lips, and drank deep of a nectar that dashed through my veins, drove madness from my blood, and gave the power to open my eyes and murmur broken thanks.

The minutes crawled by. There was no light. Once a PT boat searching untiringly for survivors passed close enough for us to hear the engines. We fired and screamed, but weren't heard, and the boat passed us by. It left hope in its wake though. Each man knew his friends would keep at it all night, and all the next day if necessary.

The cold of the water seemed to creep all through my body. Sharks came again, to be frightened off by the concussion of forty-fives fired close to the surface. They weren't really hungry. Luckily none of us three were bleeding. I could feel the dead of Iron Bottom Bay calling me, and dragging at my feet dangling helplessly in the water. Just in time the dark Someone came to my rescue again, and I drifted off into unconsciousness.

When I forced my eyes open, it was dawn. A clear light covered the bay. It was like waking from a nightmare—and finding the nightmare still with you. It was wonderful to be able to see again, and I seemed dully numb. Nothing hurt much, and nothing seemed worth worrying about. The clinging dead men seemed to have sunk again to the dark bottom. I tried to realize that Phil and Sparks were now among them. I couldn't keep my eyes open for more than a minute. I sank into a half stupor. The water now felt cold, but it soothed the burns and made them bearable. I longed for water to drink. Even more I longed for something solid beneath my feet, something dry to lie down on, to go to sleep on, something between me and the sharks and waiting monsters of the black depths. And faintly over the water floated the sweet smell of the islands, of flowers and black earth.

"Where are we, boys?"

"Just about where we were, Skipper. The tide's pretty strong, and we haven't made much headway."

Even in the deep lassitude that was on me I could realize something of the devotion and unselfishness these two men had displayed. They could have let me go, and been safe on good dry land hours ago, but they had fought on, through the long night, to give me a chance for life. Walter Long, ship's cook. . . . Mike Elsass, torpedoman: If you read these words some day, just this: Thank you, friends.

The sun climbed above the horizon. It turned the water to gold, and new hope warmed us with its rays.

Long said, with a gulp of thanksgiving:

"Here comes a PT. She's heading for us. Get out your forty-five, Mike. Everybody splash and yell."

Two forty-fives cracked in unison. Mike and Walter yelled. I threshed my feet in the water and was surprised at the strength that hope brought with it. There were a few minutes of unbearable suspense, and then Mike announced quietly, but in a happy voice:

"They see us, Skipper! They're coming for us! We'll be out of this in a few minutes!"

It was too much for me. Everything went dark. When I opened my eyes again, the side of a PT towered high above us. Its apparent height from the surface was surprising. I felt as if I would kiss the boards if I could move. Then I felt lines beneath my shoulders and knees. I was lifted slowly into the air, out of the water that seemed to hold on with clutching fingers to the prey that was escaping it. And then the blessed dryness, and the solidness of the warm deck that was so protectingly beneath me. I sighed and relaxed my mental grip on the valve in my brain to which I had held all through the dark hours lest I scream, and cry, and grow mad from fear. I opened my eyes. A ring of familiar, anxious faces bent over me. . . . I managed a smile, even though my lips felt huge and stiff.

"Good morning, fellows. Thanks a lot. Got any water?"

A canteen was held gently at my lips, and I forgot everything as the sweet water poured down my parched throat. . . .

"How are you, Johnny? Want some morphine? Gee, we're sorry this happened to you."

I thought with longing of the morphine and sleep. But I remembered the two boys who had been killed. I didn't know whether any one else had seen that Jap explode, and I wanted Phil and Sparks to have at least the credit of having taken some Japs with them.

"Not till I can make my report. I don't feel so bad. It just feels like something awful heavy on top of me."

"Here's Mr. Westholm's boat coming over. Doc Lastreto's aboard, and he'll fix you up. They're coming alongside now."

Things went black again. The next impression was the kind face of the Doc bending over me, lips grim beneath the Groucho Marx mustache, of gentle hands, and the Doc saying:

"Hello, Clag, old boy. How're you feeling?"

I answered something, then drifted off again. Next I remembered giving my report to someone, slowly and painfully, but with the feeling that when it was finished, I could sleep. The words seemed to form of themselves. I was conscious of someone working over me as I talked, of cooling things on my arms and hands. I finished, paused, and then whispered:

"Thank Long and Elsass for me. Say hello to Whitey and the boys." I didn't feel it when the morphine needle pierced my arm, but I drifted gratefully away into wonderful sleep, in utter comfort, upheld by the warm, soothing clouds of the merciful drug. My dark night was over.

I had faint memories of being carried in a stretcher along a surface that resounded hollowly, like a wooden dock, and of being transported in some sort of open vehicle. Then came an interval of fiery discomfort as someone with a soothing voice hacked and sawed away at my Naval Academy class ring. The ring came away after a long time, and I mustered the energy to ask that the ring be kept with me. It was in pieces now, but it could be fixed. Familiar life was vanishing away, and I felt a strong desire to hang onto something that was a material link with my past. The blackness drifted down again.

There followed a long and hazy time, in which nothing seemed completely real. I was kept filled with dope, which kept me comfortable, but it did queer things to my mind. Mostly, though, it was dark. I felt myself being carried, and then lifted at a sharp angle. Then I felt something rising and falling beneath me, and there was a roar in my ears. . . .

A long time later I awoke again, and was in a hospital ward on a cot. My eyes didn't open, but I heard someone mention Espiritu Santu, and *Solace.* I was very confused. More time passed, lots of it. My mind seemed to be getting hazier and to be splitting in two. Several times I met myself walking down a gray street.

Then somehow the dull heat that seemed to surround me constantly, melted away. I felt the bed heaving and there was no mistaking the cradle of the sea. My mind became clearer, and I could smell salt air. Then one day I opened my eyes to see a brown-haired girl bending over me with a glass of water. . . .

She lifted my head. It frightened me to feel that I couldn't do it myself. I took the glass tube between the center of my lips and drank thirstily. It felt cold and good.

"Thanks. Where am I?"

"You're on the hospital ship *Solace,* and we're halfway to New Zealand. They'll fix you up as good as new in the big hospital there."

"When will I get back to the Solomons?"

"It'll be a long time, Lieutenant. You're slated for transfer to the U.S."

Home. It hadn't been so long, but it seemed like centuries. I sank again into darkness, but it seemed reassuring now. . . .

IN JANUARY JAPAN DECIDED TO ABANDON GUADAL-canal, despite her substantial troops at Rabaul. It was in January, too, that Rear Admiral Waldron L. "Pug" Ainsworth and a cruiser-destroyer force bombarded the enemy's staging area of New Georgia, pouring some 3,000 rounds of 6-inch and fifteen rounds of 5-inch into the Munda sector. This was the first offensive action of the Guadalcanal campaign, and it did much to elevate morale. Meanwhile, General Alexander M. Patch, USA, who had relieved Vandegrift, prepared to mount an offensive calculated to push the enemy off the island. Using the 2nd and 8th Marines to clean up the Matanikau, he launched his other troops at Mount Asten, three miles from Henderson Field, where there were strong pockets of enemy resistance. The drive began on the 2nd, and did not stop until all resistance ended; this meant a total mop-up, including the 25,000 troops of the Japanese Seventeenth Army. The interim period was marked by other furious battles with Tanaka and another bombardment on January 22/23 of the enemy's positions at Vila. Then, a few days later, the Battle of Rennell Island developed when it appeared to Halsey's staff that another reinforcement of Guadalcanal was in the wind. As a result of the ensuing engagement the Navy lost the heavy cruiser *Chicago*, plus two destroyers severely damaged.

Despite efforts to the contrary, the enemy's evacuation continued. Some 12,000 men were pulled out by the indomitable Tanaka, leaving 14,800 killed and 1,000 prisoners. However, the enemy was still full of fight, as is evidenced in the following excerpt by Foster Hailey, *New York Times* war correspondent.

10.

DIVE-BOMBING ATTACK

By February 1 the ground forces on Guadalcanal had driven the enemy out of his former headquarters at Kokumbona Village, ten miles west of Henderson Field, and across the Poha River, the last natural defense line for several miles. The decision was made to land a force to the south of Cape Esperance and start a drive from both directions.

To Captain Briscoe's destroyer squadron was given the task of safely escorting the LCT's and the small destroyer-transport around the cape to a landing near Nugu Point. We had gone out west the night before to sweep the area for hostile submarines or surface vessels, as the operation was scheduled to begin at 2 A.M. There was a delay, and it was after dawn before we picked up the small transport train and started past Savo.

It was a hot morning, with high, broken clouds, and we cursed the slowness of the LCT's as they waddled along deep in the water, their sunken decks chock-a-block with trucks and supplies and men. As we cleared the passage with the destroyers patrolling on either side of the line of LCT's one of the LCT captains must have decided he knew more about the course than the leader, because he took off in a direction that eventually would have landed him on the Russell Islands. The squadron leader had to steam ahead and shoo him back.

The lateness of the start forfeited any element of surprise for the

429

expedition, as we were clearly visible from the enemy-held beach of Guadalcanal. They were undoubtedly in touch by radio with their air bases on up the Solomons and the fleet units that had been reported maneuvering south of Truk.

"We'll probably get the hell bombed out of us," one of the telephone talkers said as we stood on the shaded wing of the bridge watching the slow progress of the train. There were several of our own planes around, however, and we thought we would have plenty of protection.

The first troops were just going ashore at 11:30, several hours behind schedule but apparently without opposition, when headquarters announced an air raid coming in.

"Oh, oh. What did I tell you," the talker said as he dug out his tin hat from its storage place in the flag locker.

For some reason, the planes did not attempt to interfere with the landing operations but centered their attack on Henderson Field. From twenty miles away we could see the black anti-aircraft bursts against the white clouds over the island.

The first few LCT's and the destroyer-transport were in nuzzling the beach by then, and the *Nicholas* and the *Radford* turned back to sweep astern of the stragglers. Some three miles astern of us were the squadron leader and the *DeHaven*.

We were steaming along on a northerly course when two miles ahead and at about five thousand feet altitude a large two-motored bomber burst out of a cloud bank.

There was a moment's hesitation, as one of the officers yelled he thought it was one of our own PBY's. Finally, the skipper identified it to his own satisfaction and ordered fire control to open up on him.

"Wham, wham," "wham, wham," the two forward guns began to bark.

Before the shells had reached the plane's position, Lieutenant Johnny Everett, who originally had identified it as a PBY, again was shouting that it was one of our own planes at which the guns were shooting. The captain ordered fire control to check fire.

The *Radford* meanwhile also had opened fire and was pouring out her 5-inch projectiles at a fast rate.

We waited anxiously for the shellbursts. Directly ahead of the plane one blossomed, then a second. Both had exploded within what looked to be ten yards of the plane. If it was one of our own planes it was just too bad.

"My God, we've shot down one of our own planes," Johnny moaned as the big airship, looming black against the white cloud nosed over and plummeted straight for the water.

As it fell directly on our course, we got a good look and dissolved any doubts as to its identity. It was a Mitsubishi '01. Just before it hit the water we saw a door open and someone plunge out, then a spurt of flame, but there was no explosion.

As the plane fell, other shellbursts from the *Radford* blossomed in the area where our own two had exploded, and over the short-wave radio circuit someone on the *Radford* yelled, "We got him. We got him."

Immediately there was an indignant howl from our bridge, and Skipper Hill strode purposefully to the microphone.

"We got that plane," he said. "We were the first to open fire, and we claim him as ours."

"We opened first," the *Radford* retorted.

"Knock off the chatter," ordered the commodore.

The *Nicholas* by that time was passing the spot where the plane had fallen. There was little wreckage. Only a gasoline tank, its aluminum bright and shining, a few scraps of wing and what looked like two or three bodies in life jackets.

We did not stop to investigate, as we knew there must be other enemy planes in the area. Sure enough, in a moment, another Mitsubishi '01 popped out of a cloud. Again the *Nicholas* and the *Radford* both opened up. Black bursts were all around the Japanese pilot, and he was smoking and wabbling as he ducked into another cloud, but still flying. It seemed doubtful, however, that he ever would get home.

A whole flock of Zero fighters also passed astern of the force soon after, but they were flying high and fast, made no passes at us, and no one opened on them.

A soon as the raid was over, we turned back to the scene of the crash of the first plane. As we had countermarched, the *Radford* was now ahead of us instead of trailing, and Captain Briscoe ordered her to investigate the wreckage.

We took the commodore's command as tacit acceptance of the *Radford's* claim that her guns had shot down the Japanese bomber. The whole *Nicholas* crew was in a fret. As a wholly unbiased observer, I offered to make an affidavit to the effect that the good *St.*

Nicholas had first opened fire on the enemy and it was her guns that had shot him down.

"You know what I think?" said a young lookout, grinning down from the fire-control platform just above the bridge. "I think we ought to anchor alongside the *Radford* tonight and go over and talk this over with them, say about three hundred of us."

For two-and-a-half more hours anger bubbled among the *Nicholas's* crew. Then there came more important things to think about.

The first LCT's to land had completed their unloading at 1 P.M. and headed back for Tulagi. The *Nicholas* and the *DeHaven* were assigned to escort them. The squadron leader and the *Radford* were to bring the others.

We headed north toward Cape Esperance and then turned east through the passage between the cape and Savo Island. The skies were beginning to clear, and there were only a few fleecy white clouds. There was much plane activity. Two Airacobras swept past on a reconnaissance of the enemy-held beaches. High over Henderson Field we could see four or five planes circling, apparently on routine high patrol.

The LCT's, rid of their load, were chugging along at a better pace than they had taken going out; but it still was slow, uninteresting work. The two destroyers were maneuvering on either side.

Shortly after 1430 (2:30 P.M.), headquarters again warned of an approaching air attack, but canceled it five minutes later. The destroyers, which had rung for flank speed when the alarm was given, dropped to a slower pace.

At 1443 headquarters again came back on. His voice sounded more urgent this time as he announced that "the condition is red," and Captain Hill ordered enough turns put on to take the *Nicholas* up to a faster speed. As all hands scanned the skies for the enemy planes, we noticed that the *DeHaven* still was meandering along at slow speed. Apparently Captain Toland thought this too was a false alarm.

There was no sign of unusual activity over Henderson Field. We could see the planes still circling over it, some twenty thousand feet up. There was another large group of planes somewhat to the north of the island, headed our way, but they were too far away to be identified. The planes circling the field seemed to be paying them no attention, so we thought they must be friendly.

We were almost through the south passage, with Savo on the port quarter, when out of a small cloud just ahead of the force and at about six thousand feet altitude we saw a plane diving at the *De-Haven*. Lieutenant Commander Lou Snider, spending his last day in fire control before turning over the job to Lieutenant Mitchell ordered our guns to open fire.

The enemy plane must have been sighted at about the same time from the *DeHaven* because we saw a bubble of white froth at her stern, as her propellers began to thrash a faster beat. Then her automatic weapons opened fire on the diving bomber.

Straight and true the enemy flier dove, at a steep angle, to within less than one thousand feet of the little can, then dropped his bomb and straightened out. There was the flash of an explosion between the *DeHaven's* stacks, followed by a billowing cloud of black-and-brown smoke.

Other enemy planes were diving and all our guns were yammering.

Then there was a shout from one of our signalmen:

"Plane diving on us, starboard quarter."

Out of the corner of my eye I saw another explosion on the stern of the *DeHaven,* and then my whole attention was centered on the plane diving at the *Nicholas.*

The *Nicholas* was turning flank speed, the wake boiling high above her fantail as she squatted like a running horse and tore along through the glassy water.

The enemy bomber came over the edge of the cloud and started down. His front view silhouette was as distinct as in a drawing. There was the round cowling of the motor, the two wings like pencil marks protruding on either side and, sticking out below, the two wheels with their wind pants.

"An Aichi," I said to Ensign LaSalle, who was standing beside me.

"Looks like it," he agreed.

Captain Hill had swung the ship hard right when the first report of the bomber diving was received, and the destroyer was heeled far over as she made the turn. Every gun on the ship was firing, the red tracers of the 20-millimeters arching up to a converging cone at the nose of the enemy bomber. LaSalle grabbed up a Tommy gun from the bridge wing and started firing that.

The Japanese pilot was aiming straight for the bridge where we were standing. There was a flicker of fire from his wings as he came within range and opened up with his machine guns and then, out of the belly of his plane, from behind the wheels, we saw his bomb release and start to fall.

I had a feeling of detachment, which is not uncommon, others have told me, as I watched it come down. I was sure it was going to hit. I was standing near the pilot-house door under what protection the apron of the fire-control platform gave, and the flag box cut off my view aft so that I lost the bomb just before it hit. By that time, however, I saw it was going to miss, but by a very narrow margin.

The first bomber had not yet released his bomb when the report came that another was coming in on the port quarter. In not more than three or four minutes eight of them dove at our destroyer, which was twisting and turning at flank speed six thousand feet below them. Big John Stone, the lieutenant in charge of the 1.1 battery just aft of number two stack, said none of the eight bombs missed the ship by more than twenty or thirty feet.

"It was almost miraculous to see our stern swinging just far enough to get out of the way," John said.

Suddenly the guns stopped yammering and the usual sounds of the ship, that had been obscured by the cacophony of war, were heard again, the blowers sucking the air to the boilers, voices on the bridge. Somewhere a man was crying like a heartbroken child.

From the bridge we could see one man lying on the small platform just under the 1.1 battery. It really was only a piece of a man. One arm and half the trunk seemed to be gone. A gunner's mate was standing by one of the 20-millimeters nearby looking in puzzlement at his right hand, from which blood was streaming to the deck. Two men were helping a third into the after dressing station, where young Dr. W. J. Doyle was taking care of the wounded. Several men were lying on the deck.

The ship was steaming steadily at high speed, apparently little damaged. The engine room had reported water coming in through a hole in the side, but they soon had it plugged. Steering control had been lost for a few seconds on the bridge, but it had been quickly restored. The shock of one of the near misses had broken a connection.

Before going aft to check on the dead and wounded, and the damage, I swept the immediate vicinity with my glasses to check on the *DeHaven* and the LCT's. The little fellows were all right, circling near where a great cloud of black smoke rose up from the sea to a height of hundreds of feet. I could see no ship at the base of the smoke.

"Gone," said Captain Hill, who saw me looking. "I saw a bomb hit her just forward of the bridge. It must have penetrated to the magazine, for there was a terrific explosion and she broke right in two. I doubt if anyone came off the bridge. The explosion just blew it to pieces."

The attack obviously being over, Captain Hill had turned back toward the smoke that was the *DeHaven's* funeral pyre. As it began to thin we saw the sea covered with debris, and a great circle of oil that glinted like a rainbow in the afternoon sunlight.

In evading the attack at high speed we had traveled several miles away from where the other destroyer had gone down, and the LCT's, their forward ramps in the water, already were nosing through the wreckage pulling oil-covered survivors aboard when the *Nicholas* arrived and put over her whaleboat.

In half an hour it was certain all the living had been found, and some of the dead, floating in their life jackets, so Captain Hill ordered the LCT's to come alongside and transfer the wounded to us.

There were surprisingly few. It was live or die on the *DeHaven* that day. Many of the one hundred and ten survivors did not have a mark on them. Almost two hundred men had died.

One of the most stoical of the survivors was Chief Machinist's Mate R. C. Andrews. He was a big man in his late forties, with a thick black moustache. As he clambered aboard the *Nicholas* he used only one hand. The other was badly torn. One finger was hanging only by a piece of skin. He examined his injured hand critically— Doctor Doyle was caring for the worst cases first—then reached in his pocket for his knife.

"Here, son, cut this off," he said to a young seaman standing by him.

"Aw, I can't, Pop," said the youngster. "Let it alone. Maybe the doc can save it."

"Nope, she's too far gone," the Chief said; and as casually as if he were cutting off a chew of tobacco he severed the piece of skin and tossed the finger over the side.

One of our own men, Gunner's Mate 3/cl. Lewis Samuels, was almost as casual about his shattered hand. He reported to Doctor Doyle, who cleaned and bandaged his hand, gave him a tetanus shot, and told him to lie down.

"I can't Doc, I got to get back to my gun," Samuels answered.

"You sit down there; never mind your gun. You've lost a lot of blood."

"I had to take care of another patient then," Doctor Doyle said later. "The next time I looked around Samuels was gone."

Samuels helped get the *DeHaven* wounded aboard and was busy, with his one good hand, tidying up around his 20-millimeter mount when the doctor found him an hour later and ordered him into one of the Higgins boats that had come to take the wounded to the navy hospital.

Just as we were getting the last of the wounded aboard, the squadron leader and the *Radford* came boiling up. The squadron leader took aboard the uninjured survivors, and then the three destroyers headed for Lunga Point at high speed to put them ashore. A Japanese task force, first reported as consisting of two heavy cruisers, two lights, and sixteen destroyers had been sighted coming down "the slot." There was no time to mourn the dead or comfort the living. The squadron and half a dozen PT boats were the only force available to stop them. We had to be about it.

"Are you all right?" the commodore asked Captain Hill.

"Two dead, one dying, sixteen injured, and one gun out," was the answer. "Otherwise, O.K."

"Disembark survivors and wounded men and join," the commodore signaled.

As we hurriedly put the *DeHaven* survivors into the Higgins boats and turned away to follow the squadron leader back out past Savo, the *DeHaven's* men gave a cheer for the *Nicholas*. Leading it was Samuels, his hand now in a sling.

"Keep her floating, you guys," he yelled at his shipmates lining the rail.

We saw him waving with his good hand as long as we were in sight.

At dinner that night, a subdued meal in contrast to the usual uproar, we put all the stories together and decided that six planes had dived on the *DeHaven*. Three of them hit her. Eight had dived at us. Although some observers reported seeing as high as seven enemy planes go into the water, it was finally decided that not more than four or five had been shot down. We thought the group probably was from a carrier. They had an escort of Zeros. Two-thirds of the *De-Haven's* crew had been lost, including Captain Toland, who a few days before, when I was preparing to shift from the *O'Bannon,* had asked me to come aboard his ship. Only three of her eighteen officers had survived.

Lieutenant Mitchell resolved the question of the man I had heard crying. It was Hector Constantino, Chief Radio Electrician.

Hector was a chunky little man who still spoke with an accent. He had come to the United States from Greece just before the last world war. Two days after he arrived he was robbed of his savings by two fellow countrymen. Hector enlisted in the army. After serving through the war he left the service for a few months, but then enlisted in the navy. He had been in the navy since that time. He was one of the most deeply patriotic men I ever knew. To him the United States meant everything he cherished.

"It's no pose with Hector," Mitch explained. "He cries whenever he hears of one of our ships being lost. He did the other night when the message came through about the *Chicago*. He just happens to be built that way."

It was an emotionally and physically exhausted crew that took the *Nicholas* out west of Savo that night. Few of them had had any sleep for forty-eight hours, since we had been out on patrol all the previous night. They had seen their shipmates killed and wounded and a sister ship destroyed in exactly six minutes. The deck was still slippery with blood in places. There had been no time to clean up. Now they were going out to intercept the Tokyo Express. Three ships against twenty. All other American ships in the area—freighters, tenders, corvettes, and the escorts—had been ordered to leave.

Months later, in my notebook, I found this: "The mighty Davids go out to tackle Goliath. What a story if it comes off!"

The sun set early behind a bank of clouds, and the dark came down. Heat lightning was playing along the horizon. Far to the left, as we cleared Savo, were visible the hilltops of the Russell Islands. Thirty miles to the northwest loomed the bulk of Santa Isabel. Between the two lay "the slot," empty, quiet, ominous. Back up its 250-mile length, somewhere on the way down, was the enemy force.

Captain Briscoe, the commodore, led us out the north passage and then southwest toward the Russells. We were in column, the squadron leader, in advance, then the *Nicholas,* and behind us the *Radford.*

If there were 8-inch-gun and 6-inch-gun cruisers in the enemy force, as was the first report, the only chance for the three outgunned, outnumbered American cans was to surprise the enemy and be within torpedo-launching range, inside ten thousand yards, before we were discovered. It would be suicide to go in against the fire of the heavy guns.

Before leaving the vicinity of Tulagi, Captain Briscoe and the PT squadron commander had agreed on search areas. The destroyers were to cover the approach from the south, and the PT's the approach from the north. Search planes were up "the slot" to watch.

As the early hours passed with no further report on the enemy, it appeared possible they had turned back. They were almost past Savo at midnight before we saw them. At almost the same time the PT boats, sweeping the north channel, ran smack into them.

"My God, it's the whole Japanese navy," we heard one of the young PT skippers exclaim.

The Japanese ships opened fire as the PT's attacked, sinking two of them and so damaging a third that it had to be beached. But not before they had scored a hit on one destroyer, which caught fire and burned for some time before it sank. Dive bombers from Guadalcanal also joined the fight, and the clouds above Savo were lighted for half an hour with the flash of guns and bombs and the flares dropped by the planes.

When Captain Briscoe made contact with the enemy force, now identified as twenty destroyers, he turned the squadron north and headed for the Japanese ships. They were about twenty thousand yards away at this time.

Planes had been around all the evening, but none had attacked, and we did not know whether they were enemy or friendly. As the squadron turned toward the Japanese ships, however, the planes turned toward the three destroyers and started dropping flares to mark our course. The commodore turned away.

For two hours the Japanese force stayed inside Savo, losing two more ships either to our planes or to mines, which had been sown off Tassaforanga Beach in anticipation of just such a visit, and then they pulled out at high speed.

When the commodore saw them coming out he again attempted to close, but again the enemy planes probably warned their ships of our approach, and again we turned away.

Circling, we followed them up "the slot" for several miles, but we never got close enough for a torpedo attack. Planes from Guadalcanal still were harrassing them as they retired. At daylight other planes took up the chase. They found sixteen destroyers, and scored a hit on one and a near hit on another.

At the time it was thought the enemy force was bringing reinforcements in to the dwindling Japanese garrison on Guadalcanal. Instead they were evacuating the officers. The men were left to die.

As we steamed past Savo the next morning en route to Tulagi we saw many abandoned Japanese small boats in the water and debris from damaged or sunken Japanese ships.

That afternoon the commodore, whose original squadron of five destroyers now had dwindled to three, and one of those damaged, recommended that the squadron be withdrawn. The commodore's logical evaluation of the situation was that his ships were too valuable to use on suicide missions and the force wasn't big enough to really slug it out with anything the Japanese would send down. Admiral Halsey must have agreed with him, for orders came for the *Nicholas* to return for repairs and for the others to join up with a force of cruisers maneuvering south of the Solomons. Late that afternoon we said goodbye to Tulagi with no regrets.

THE ADVANCE FROM GUADALCANAL BEGAN FEBRUARY 21, in the Russells, sixty miles to the northwest. "Extensive preparations were now being made for the invasion of New Georgia," wrote Admiral King, "and although there were no noteworthy naval engagements for some time, aerial operations were intensified in the South Pacific area. Japanese raids were frequent and heavy even though carried out at severe cost to the enemy. During this period of stepped up air operations, our advance base in the Russell Islands was in constant use by our planes." By April Guadalcanal, although still constantly under air attack, was considered little more than a rear guard base where tired destroyer officers and PT skippers could drink their beer in relative comfort at the *Club de Slot,* a thatched roof hut overlooking Savo Sound. Guadalcanal, too, was the haven of harried *Comairsols*—wizened, taciturn Rear Admiral Marc A. "Pete" Mitscher, one of the most formidable flag officers of the later war— who commanded all Navy, Army, Marine Corps and New Zealand aircraft and pilots in the area.

Notwithstanding Mitscher's endeavors to build up his air defenses, attacks on Guadalcanal continued through May and June. On the

16th the island was subjected to one of the most devastating air strikes of the campaign. A force of enemy aircraft estimated at one hundred and sixty fighters and bombers was engaged by more than one hundred American fighters from the Army, Navy and Marine Corps. One hundred and seven enemy aircraft were destroyed at a cost of six fighter planes, one lighter and one cargo ship. On the night of June 29 Rear Admiral A. Stanton Merrill bombarded Vila-Stanmore and the Buin Shortlands near the southeast end of Bougainville, preparatory to the invasion of New Georgia the following day.

The landings at Rendova and the struggle to capture the Japanese air base of Munda on New Georgia are reported by war correspondent-novelist William Bradford Huie.

II.

MEN AND MUD

It was a wet dawn in the Solomons, July 1, 1943. D-Day, H-Hour at Rendova. Through murky half-light, tropical rain fell in sheets. Heavy, flat-bellied tank lighters battered down the waves—*krrump, krrump*—as they pushed from the transports toward East Beach. In the boats tight-lipped Seabees, Marines and soldiers (Amphibian Task Force 31, composed of the 24th Naval Construction Battalion, the Ninth Defense Marines and the 172nd Infantry Combat Team) crouched by the wet flanks of bulldozers and watched the palm-fringed beach edge closer. After eleven months of conquest and consolidation at Guadalcanal, our forces were at last reaching up the "slot" of the Solomons for the big Jap air base at Munda on New Georgia Island. From Rendova, Munda would be within reach of our heavy howitzers.

The high whine of Jap .25-calibers cut across the water as the bandy-legged rats in the palms began sniping at our coxswains. The men cursed, crouched lower, gripped gunbutts harder. As though the rain weren't enough, salt water drenched the men as the boats churned through heavy surf. The boats skidded in soft sand; ramps dropped; there was a brief, fierce skirmish; and the Japs who were left alive faded back into the coconut groves. Automatic-weapons troops pushed in two hundred yards to form a defense arc, while the Seabees began furiously unloading trucks, tractors, heavy guns, ammunition and supplies.

441

The Jap ground forces had been dispersed easily. Now the real battle was joined; the battle against nature and time and the inevitable Jap bombers. Men and supplies are vulnerable while they are in landing craft; they are even more vulnerable during the period they are on the open beach. So in every beach operation the Seabees must drive hard to get ashore; drive even harder to unload; then exert the last drop of energy to get the supplies off the beach, dispersed and hidden.

Leading the Seabees was 48-year-old Commander H. Roy Whittaker (Civil Engineer Corps, USNR, Philadelphia, Pa.), a pint-sized construction veteran with the energy of a jackhammer. He described the action.

"Where we landed the soil was unbelievably marshy," he said. "The mud was deep and getting deeper. A swampy coconut grove lay just back of the beach, and we had to cut a road through there. Guns had to be transported from our beach over to West Beach so that shells could be hurled across the narrow strip of water onto the Jap positions at Munda. And still that rain poured.

"All day long we sweated and swore and worked to bring the heavy stuff ashore and hide it from the Jap bombers. Our mesh, designed to 'snowshoe' vehicles over soft mud, failed miserably. Even our biggest tractors bogged down in the muck. The men ceased to look like men; they looked like slimy frogs working in some prehistoric ooze. As they sank to their knees they discarded their clothes. They slung water out of their eyes, cussed their mud-slickened hands, and somehow kept the stuff rolling ashore.

"A detachment under Irv Lee (Lieutenant Irwin W. Lee, CEC, USNR, Monmouth, Ill.) fought to clear the road to West Beach. The ground was so soft that only our biggest cats could get through. The Japs were still sniping, but in spite of this the men began felling the coconut palms, cutting them into twelve-foot lengths and corrugating the road. Our traction-treaded vehicles could go over these logs, but the spinning wheels of a truck would send the logs flying, and the truck would bury itself. To pull the trucks out we lashed a bulldozer to a tree, then dragged the trucks clear with the 'dozer's winch.

"When night came we had unloaded six ships, but the scene on the beach was dismal. More troops, Marines and Seabees had come in, but the mud was about to lick us. Foxholes filled with water as rapidly as they could be dug. There was almost no place near the beach to set up a shelter tent, so the men rolled their exhausted, mud-covered bodies in tents and slept in the mud. As the Japs would infiltrate during the night, the Army boys holding our line in the grove would kill them with trench knives.

"Next day, at 1330, without warning, the Jap planes came in with bomb bays open. All of us began firing with what guns had been set up, but most of the Seabees had to lie in the open on the beach and take it. We tried to dig trenches with our hands and noses while the Japs poured it on us.

"The first bombs out two main fuel dumps, and we had to lie there in the mud and watch our supplies burn while the Japs strafed us. One bomb landed almost under our largest bulldozer, and that big machine just reared up like a stallion and disintegrated. Then every man among us thought that his time had come. A five-ton cache of our dynamite went off, exploding the eardrums of the men nearest it. That soggy earth just quivered like jelly under us.

"When the Japs had exhausted their ammunition they flew off, leaving us to put out the fires and treat our wounded. I'll never forget the scene on that beach. In our outfit two of our best officers (Lieutenant Lee and Lieutenant George W. Stephenson, CEC, USNR, Klamath Falls, Ore.) and twenty-one men were dead. Many more were wounded, others were missing, and a number were out of their heads. Our galley equipment, most of our supplies, and all the men's seabags and personal belongings were destroyed.

" 'Okay, men,' I yelled, 'we got nothing left but what we got on, so let's get back to work.'

"All that night Doctor Duryea (Lieutenant-Commander Garrett Duryea, Medical Corps, USNR, Glen Cove, N.Y.) worked with our wounded. The biggest job was to get them clean. That's one thing about being a Seabee. Aboard ship you bathe, wash down with antiseptic, and put on clean clothing before an action. In the Air Force you can take a bath before you take off. But when a Seabee gets hit, he's usually on a beach in the mud. Mud seems to be our element. When we die we die in the mud.

"Next day, while we worked in relays, chaplains from the Army and Marines helped us bury our dead. Three more had died during the night. Not one of those boys would have ever thought of himself as a hero, but I felt proud to have been their commanding officer. They were construction men, most of them from the oil fields of Oklahoma and Texas, and, with never a complaint, they had died in the mud trying their damnedest to get a job done.

"By the morning of the fourth day we had opened the road to West Beach, but what a road it was! We had literally snaked those big 155's through two miles of mud, and the Marines began setting them up. We were also developing a storage area some distance from the beach and were trying desperately to reduce our hazards on the beach. It takes men with real guts to unload on an open beach without air cover. Our men had been under constant strain for ninety hours; at least fifty of them were running high temperatures from constant exposure to mud and water; they could only jump between gasoline drums and powder barrels when the Japs came over; and the beach, as always, was a potential torch with ammunition, Diesel oil and gasoline everywhere. The mud was too deep for trucks. To move the inflammable stuff back into the storage areas, the men had to emplace themselves in the mud in bucket-brigade fashion. For hours they'd work that way, passing the heavy packages back into the camouflage area and sinking deeper into the mud each time they handled a package. And still the rain poured.

"Late that afternoon we got our first big thrill. From over on West Beach the Marines opened up on Munda with the 155's. Our men stopped work and cheered almost insanely. The others stationed with bulldozers and winches along the road to West Beach joined in the cheer. No group of men had ever endured more in order for guns to begin firing. It hurts American construction men down deep to have to lie in mud and be strafed by Japs; and now those 155's were giving it back to the Japs with interest. The firing was a tonic to us. The men went back to unloading furiously.

"We had received some additional equipment, but that night we still had only enough tents and cots for our expanding sick quarters. The men had tried to pitch a few shelter tents, but the tents would sink in the mud. There was still nothing else to do but wrap yourself in whatever you could find and sleep in the mud. When you are sufficiently exhausted you can do that, but after you pass forty you have one helluva time getting up in the morning.

"On the fifth day we continued to unload troops, supplies and equipment. Our storage areas became more congested, due to our distribution difficulties and also due to delays in transhipments over to our positions on New Georgia Island, from which we were also attacking Munda. The Seabees sent many small working parties to help the Army and Marines, yet our beach condition grew worse under the continuing heavy rains. At 1400 the Japs bombed us heavily, but this time the damage was much lighter because of the furious anti-aircraft fire. The Army and Marines had many guns set up by this time, and the Seabees helped man the guns on twenty LSI's and two LST's at the beach. We were able to prevent the Japs from strafing us, and seven Jap planes crashed in our immediate area.

"Seabee casualties were only one man missing and one wounded in this raid, but our number of psychopathic cases had begun to mount. We had to evacuate ten men who had become hysterical. As men grow physically exhausted, they become more and more susceptible to nervous collapse under bombing.

"By the sixth day the 155's were pouring shells onto Munda almost incessantly, and we still had the supply road open, but our position seemed more impossible than ever. None of us could remember anything except mud and bombs. The rains seemed to get heavier. But somehow the men kept working. Word came that 5000 troops had been landed on New Georgia near Munda. Munda was doomed if we could just hold out and keep those 155's firing. The Japs knew this as well as we did, so at 1315 they came at us again. But this time it was a different story. Our own air forces were ready to take up the fight now, and our planes came in and tangled with the Japs right over our heads.

"We lay in those muddy foxholes for an hour and watched the air battle. Since we couldn't fire the AA guns without endangering our own planes, there was nothing else for us to do but lie in our grandstand seats and count the falling Japs. Each time a Zero would burst into flames our exhausted, mud-covered men would leap up and cheer wildly.

"Knowledge that we now had air cover improved our morale on the seventh day. Also we had managed to borrow three stoves from the Army and Marines and were providing the first hot food for the men. Three air battles were fought over us during the day, but our planes didn't allow the Japs to get close enough either to bomb or strafe us. That night the Japs came over three times, forcing us to hit the water in the foxholes, but most of us had given up hope of ever being dry again.

"On the eighth day we continued to unload supplies, repair landing boats and haul the ammunition through the mud to the 155's. The Marines kept up the shelling of Munda almost continuously. One enemy air attack in the afternoon lasted for fifty minutes, but our planes were opposing the Japs constantly, and we suffered little damage. During the day we evacuated seven additional cases of war hysteria. That night we had to hit the foxholes twice.

"On the ninth day the Japs attempted four large-scale raids, but our damage was slight. Our air cover was now functioning perfectly except at night. We evacuated three more cases of war hysteria, and that night we had to hit the water three times as the Japs bombed us rather heavily. But our bombardment continued, and our roads were still open in spite of the continuing rain.

"On the tenth day we had five light enemy raids, and evacuated additional cases of war hysteria, but morale continued high."

While the 24th Battalion was suffering its long ordeal at Rendova, helping to make possible the shelling of Munda, across forty miles of water, at Segi Point, New Georgia, the 47th Seabee Battalion was just as furiously playing its role in the Munda drama. The 47th, led by Commander J. S. Lyles (CEC, USNR, Wagoner, Okla.), had been assigned the task of ripping an airstrip out of the jungle so that our bombers coming up from Guadalcanal to bomb Munda could have fighter protection over the target. Success of the whole operation depended on the speed with which this airstrip could be built. The first wave of the 47th began landing at Segi at 1010 on June 30, just twenty hours before the 24th began landing at Rendova.

The landing at Segi had been planned as a sneak operation. It was hoped that the battalion could get ashore unobserved by the Japs and could get a head start on the airstrip before the Japs attacked. To facilitate this strategy, a Seabee scouting party led by Commander Wilfred L. Painter (CEC, USNR, Seattle, Wash.) had slipped ashore from native fishing boats on the night of June 22. The following day Commander Painter selected an abandoned coconut plantation now overgrown with jungle as the site for the airstrip, and the party began laying out the field.

Lieutenant Garland S. Tinsley (CEC, USNR, North Charleston, S.C.) was acting as lookout for the scouting party, and on the second day he saw Japs approaching the shore from two directions. One bargeload of Japs landed a mile west of the proposed airfield and two bargeloads landed a mile and a half east of the field.

Tinsley reported Condition Black, and the party got set for a fight. However, by lying doggo for forty-eight hours, the group eluded the Japs, who took to their barges and disappeared. On D-Day the scouts had the field laid out, ready for work to begin, and they were standing on the beach to direct the landing.

Thanks to this advance survey, when the 47th's big HD-12 bulldozers and power shovels rolled off the boats, they at once began pushing down the coconut palms, clearing the strip. From that moment the 47th battled time and the jungle around the clock. Equipment "unraveled" off the boats as needed. Supplies were unloaded and dispersed. Floodlights were ready before darkness on the first night. A bivouac area was cleared. AA guns were manned; exterior guard posted. And, above all, work proceeded on the airstrip with all possible speed.

Construction of the strip involved the clearing of an initial area of 250 by 3500 feet; grading and draining the area; covering a minimum area of 100 by 2500 feet with twelve to eighteen inches of coral; and then laying the steel pierced plank, or Marston mat, on a minumum surface of 75 by 2500 feet. This 75 by 2500 feet is regarded as the minimum safe surface from which our fighter craft can operate. Our airstrips are thus built in sections, with the aim of producing a minimum "fighter strip" in the shortest possible time; and then lengthening and widening the strip gradually up to the 300 by 5000 feet necessary for heavily loaded four-motored bombers.

At 0822 on July 11 the pilot of a Navy Corsair fighter brought his plane down on the strip in an emergency landing which saved both himself and his ship. He pronounced the field ready for use, and the exact time was recorded: 10 days, 22 hours, 12 minutes after the first landing boat had ground ashore! While the Seabees have restored captured Jap fields in much less time, this then stood as a world's record for converting jungle into a landing area.

Amazingly, the Japs did not discover the activity at Segi until the seventh day. This was due both to their preoccupation with our forces at Rendova and to a clever arrangement for handling the lights at Segi. Whenever Jap planes would take off from the Munda field at night, our forces at Rendova would flash the warning to Segi. The 47th would then douse its lights and continue limited construction activities in the dark until Rendova reported that the Japs had returned to Munda.

Here's what the speed record at Segi meant to the Munda operation: It was fighter planes from Segi which helped relieve the Jap aerial pressure on the men-in-the-mud at Rendova. The Segi fighters stood at Ready Alert, and when our bombers came up from Guadalcanal to bomb Munda, the Segi fighters roared into the air to escort the bombers over the target. Conversely, it was the Seabees, Marines and soldiers on Rendova who, with their shelling, so monopolized the attention of the Japs that the 47th had their field virtually completed before the Japs got on to the fact that it was there.

"When the Japs did discover us," Commander Lyles reported, "we got a severe pounding. They hit a dynamite dump, one of our fuel dumps, and peppered our bulldozers and trucks with shrapnel. But they arrived too late with too little.

"In at least one way the Japs helped us set our record. On our fifth day we got the news that twenty-three Seabees had been killed over at Rendova. Our men redoubled their efforts. Many of them insisted on working eighteen-hour stretches in order to rush the air cover."

During the eleven days in which the 47th was setting its record, fourteen inches of rain fell at Segi Point!

Three weeks after the opening of the airstrip at Segi, the last Jap had been killed at Munda. On August 9, 1943, advanced platoons of the 73rd Seabee Battalion began work on the blasted Jap air base. The Japs had been unable to operate the field for eight weeks, but Commander Kendrick P. Doane (CEC, USNR, Forest Hills, N. Y.), leader of the 73rd, was ordered to have the field in operation by August 18.

On August 11 additional units of the 73rd arrived, and Commander Doane ordered round-the-clock operations. The weather gods smiled at last, and a full moon came out to make artificial lighting unnecessary. In just two more days the men had repaired the north and south runways, and American planes began landing at Munda on the afternoon of August 13. During that night the battalion completed additional hardstands off the runways, and on the 14th the field received forty-eight additional planes.

On August 15 the 24th Battalion, which had fought the mud battle at Rendova, arrived at Munda; and the two battalions set to work to make Munda a major base. The Japs had dug an elaborate tunnel system in the coral, and many of them had died in the tunnels from our flame-throwers. The Seabees cleaned out the Japs and converted the tunnels into de luxe living quarters.

In November, 1943, Admiral Bill Halsey declared that Munda was the finest air base in the South Pacific. A citation for Commander Doane read, in part:

"Prior to his commencing work at Munda there were no roads, and the airfield and taxiways were unusable due to the bombardment and shelling of the area by our forces prior to its capture. In spite of shortage of personnel and equipment, and faced with a task of great magnitude, Commander Doane was able, nevertheless, by virtue of his planning, leadership, industry, and working 'round the clock' to make serviceable the Munda airfield on August 14, 1943, a good four days ahead of the original schedule. Though subjected to shelling and bombing, both in the camp area and on the airfield, Commander Doane and his men have expanded the size and facilities of the airfield at a phenomenal rate."

On receipt of his citation Commander Doane commented: "It's easy to perform construction miracles with men like the Seabees. They are the world's finest construction men. Courage is innate with them. They volunteered to do a job, and all they want is a chance to finish that job as soon as possible. When we took men like this and put them into one organization, we loaded the dice against the Japs."

To support their claim to being the toughest, don't-give-a-damnedest outfit in the service, the Seabees have accumulated many stories, both factual and apocryphal.

On a certain Pacific island, it is said, natives were mopping up the remaining Japs. One day a group of natives wiped out a party of Japs, but the natives hesitated to kill a strange animal which the Japs had brought to the island. The animal was a goat, and after observing the goat curiously, the natives returned to their chief for instructions as to whether or not they should kill the strange beast.

"What manner of beast is it?" the chief asked.

"Oh, he's very strange, majesty," the natives replied. "He has fierce eyes, long horns, a shaggy beard, will eat anything, and stinks like hell."

"Spare him," the chief ruled at once. "Don't kill him. He's what the Americans call a Seabee."

While this story may be apocryphal, it is a fact that several Seabee battalions have billy goats as mascots.

DURING THE AMERICAN ADVANCE UP THE SLOT, THE Tokyo Express made nightly runs through Blackett Strait and Kula Gulf to supply and reinforce the Japanese troops at Vila. Early on the morning of July 5 Ainsworth, embarked in a task force of cruisers and destroyers, intercepted the enemy in Kula Gulf. In the subsequent action Japan lost two destroyers sunk; the Navy lost light cruiser

Helena. It was a battle of American gunfire versus Japanese torpedoes, two of which struck *Helena* almost simultaneously. One who survived the night was Lieutenant C. G. Morris, the warship's radio officer, who tells of the vessel's last engagement. His collaborator is Hugh B. Cave, *Saturday Evening Post* war correspondent.

12.

KULA GULF

As radio officer, I went over the ship, rounding up the department heads and reading them the dispatch. They were relaxed, some of them sleeping, all of them tired from our job at Kolombangara and New Georgia. Now the ship came awake with almost comical quickness. There were quick conferences. The sleepy, satisfied *Helena* became magically a beehive of fighting men. She was tense again, on tiptoe. You felt it on foc'sle and quarterdeck, throughout the ship. A giant fist was doubling up, knuckles whitening for combat. Turbines and men vibrated together.

I wondered, as we passed Guadalcanal with the sun setting redly into her 9000-foot peaks, how many more times, if ever, we should see that familiar shoreline again. We had hated the island once. For months it had been a background for violent actions in which the *Helena* had played a major role. No man had ever expressed a yearning to see Guadalcanal again. Now the hated island was a symbol of security, the most familiar and therefore the most profound symbol we possessed. We watched in silence as the *Helena* steamed westward, past Savo, past the Russell Islands.

The weather had roughened; the sky was overcast and dark. We wanted that. Darkness was a thing we prayed for. And with all information now in hand and the entire ship informed that we were moving up The Slot to intercept the Tokyo Express in Kula Gulf, there was time for praying.

451

It was seven P.M. Relieved of further duties, I went to my room and hit the sack for three hours, and read my Bible. I read the Twenty-third and Ninety-first Psalms over and over. . . . "Thou shalt not be afraid for the terror by night. . . . A thousand shall fall at thy side, and ten thousand at thy right hand, but it shall not come nigh thee. . . ."

Those are comforting words. When I went on deck, I saw men thumbing worn pages of the little Bibles that many of them carry. Toughened old seadogs, veterans of many a battle and many a crap game, were unashamedly praying. Some listened with solemn concentration while others read aloud. Afraid? Not if you strip the word of its too glib definition and search it for the courage and nobility that so often give it a fuller meaning. The *Helena* was not afraid.

By ten P.M. the order had been given to dog all doors and stand by at battle stations. In a total blackout now, the ship rushed through the night, following the broad boiling wake of a ship ahead. In Radio I, my battle station, all equipment was manned, all frequencies covered. An incredible amount of stuff poured in—information, battle plans, instructions. I fed it to Captain Cecil on the fighting bridge as we neared our destination.

That night could not last forever, even with each of its hours drawn endlessly through the teeth of tension and the *Helena* racing at full power through the dark. The Japs were due in. We had passed the tip of New Georgia some time ago, and now from the navigating bridge came the telephoned report that we were entering Kula Gulf.

The ship held its breath. Kula Gulf was Jap; it was a tricky, treacherous area, night-shrouded now, in which anything might happen. The men were quiet. Silence moved on cat's feet over the entire ship, thickening, solidifying, until its effect was uncanny.

The next hour was the longest. We were inside Kula Gulf and still no contact. For hours there had been no talk on the TBS—talk-between-ships. Now, over Radio I's communication circuit, came the voice of Lt. Russell Gash, of the *Helena*. He was calm and almost matter-of-fact as, on TBS, he called the flagship. His message was for Admiral Ainsworth—Rear Adm. Walden L. Ainsworth, USN of Wonalancet, New Hampshire, who was awarded the Distinguished Service Medal for his Kula Gulf defeat of the Japs.

"Enemy sighted" . . .

The palms of my hands itched and I stood up. No one spoke. Men who had held their breath let it out in unison, and the sound was a vast sigh of relief.

Quiet orders were issued over TBS as the formation changed course and closed range. The admiral asked each ship if she was ready, and the replies were prompt. A few minutes later, at 1:55 A.M., the order was given to open fire. The *Helena* let go her Sunday punch.

She had plenty. She had always had plenty. This 10,000-ton "fightingest ship in the Navy" was armed with fifteen 6-inch guns, and they spoke with a thunder that shook the night apart. The *Helena* shuddered, rearing on her haunches to spit out steel. She had never fired like that before. She seemed to know that the show tonight was of special importance. A ship can know such a thing.

In the radio shack there was a steeling of minds against the thought that some Jap shell might come screaming through the steel plates by which we were hemmed in. But you know what such thoughts can do to you, how quickly they can shake a man, crack him, and you have shut them out so often that it now becomes automatic—muscular, not mental—and the men are outwardly quite calm. There is a continuous deafening thunder from the guns, while the ship leaps like a shingle in heavy seas.

Just thirty seconds after the first defiant bellow, a report reached us from the bridge, "One down!" The speaker might have been watching workmen fell trees in a forest. "Two down! . . . There goes another!"

Later, we learned how those Japanese ships had gone down. How they were enveloped in a literal hurricane of continuous fire and were torn apart in a matter of seconds. Other ships in the American task force loosed their thunder in salvos, but the *Helena's* fire was continuous and for nine minutes not a heartbeat of silence interrupted the bellowing of her guns.

An enemy destroyer, smothered under that avalanche of 6-inch shells, came apart as though made of paper and burst into raging flames. She sank in a matter of minutes. A Jap destroyer sped from the destructive fire of the *Helena's* secondary batteries, was ranged as she fled, and blew up. . . .

Then the *Helena's* batteries, both main and secondary, concentrated on two more of the Emperor's ships, mauling them severely while Jap destroyers darted through the inferno to launch torpedoes. In nine minutes the *Helena's* veteran gun crews fired more than 1000 rounds, an all-time record, and the devastation to the Japanese fleet was unbelievable.

Suddenly, in the radio room, I was flung into the air by a louder roar. At 2:09 the *Helena* had caught a Jap torpedo. In a heap on the deck of the shack I looked about in total bewilderment, unable to believe we had been hit. I reached for my radiophone; it was sprawled on the deck. The ship was trembling—a curious, fluttering tremble, almost dainty, like that of a young girl frightened in the dark.

I picked myself up slowly, and so did the others, piled atop of one another in a fantastic heap. The *Helena's* guns had ceased firing. The silence was a smothering thing that made breathing difficult. In that whole room there was but one sound—the soft and stealthy settling of dust disturbed by the torpedo's impact.

I had located the earphone and put it back on, and now returned to my post, stiff-legged and strange, as a man learning to walk again after a shock. The others went back to their posts too. No one had spoken. The radio was silent. TBS had nothing for us. There was only the terrible trembling of the ship, and now for the first time a sensation of being afraid. Not of the Japs, but of the unknown.

We were getting over that, becoming calm—waiting, I think, for someone to speak and break the spell—when the second torpedo hit. The explosion slammed us to the deck again in the same grotesque heap. But no one cried out. The lights died and for a moment we struggled in darkness to extricate ourselves. Then the battle lights came on, a dim, weird glow through which the shaken dust swam redly in space.

The *Helena* was done for. I knew it. We all knew it. The second explosion had cleared my mind and I saw things very clearly. But it had to be official before orders could be issued, and so I went out to be sure. She was listing badly, her back broken. There was water over the quarter-deck, midships. Men stood at their stations, restlessly at attention, awaiting the command to abandon ship. The ship herself, trembling in torment, struggled to warn us time was short.

Returning to the radio room, I found the men there on their feet, strapping on money belts and fastening life jackets. They were bruised, shaken, their eyes glazed, but none needed assistance. We went about destroying important papers and publications. When I ordered the bulkheads undogged, officers and men filed out as they had a thousand times before when going off watch. It was then 2:20, just eleven minutes after the first torpedo hit.

The abandon-ship order had been given when I stepped on deck, but there was no panic, almost no noise. And now, strangely, there seemed less need for haste. That warning tremble in the ship had ceased. Men picked their way carefully through the piles of ammunition cans strewn over the deck. Others were lined on the rail, watching the battle in the distance. Some had gone overside and I saw hundreds of heads in the sea—small white blurs bobbing about in the black night, seemingly suspended in space. It was hard to think of them as men. It was harder to realize that the *Helena* was no longer in action. Beyond us the battle of Kula Gulf raged to its climax, and the horizon was garlanded with looping streamers of fire. *Like Brooklyn Bridge,* I thought.

The ship was sinking midships, her bow and stern high, belly sagging, but there was no hurry. I stood at the rail, gazing at the eerie display of fireworks over there across the gulf, and the echoing thunder of the guns made me feel better about the *Helena*. We were giving the Japs a beating.

There's time enough, I thought, *to go to your room for the papers you want.* The ship herself had said so. She was not trembling. "Go ahead," she said. But the way was cluttered. I had to go slowly, with a hand half lifted in front of me. On the starboard side of the foc'sle I came upon a man sitting cross-legged on the deck, and I said, "Well, it's all over." He didn't know it was all over. He was dead.

My room was at the bottom of the ladder, forward of No. 2 turret. I reached for the ladder and caught myself just in time, lurched backward and stood shaking, cold and scared again. Another step and I should have fallen into the sea, headlong. Because nothing was there now. The *Helena's* bow had been blown off just where my room had been. The torpedo had gone through my room. *This is how you feel,* I thought, *when you come home one night and find only a heap of ashes where the house had stood.* And the fear took away that foolish feeling of security. *Get off the ship,* I thought frantically. *Get off now.*

She was really going down fast. On the foc'sle, some of the men were trying to cut away the big life rafts, and I ran to them and tried to help. We got the rafts into the water while the sea swirled in an ugly, oily whirlpool over the quarter-deck.

It was time to go. Before leaving the radio room I had snatched up my life jacket and officer's cap, and now, automatically, I jerked the cap hard on my head and leaped. It was not a tremendous jump. The water was but five feet or so below the deck. And it was warm, almost pleasant. But my weight carried me deep into it, and when my mouth filled with the warm water, it was not clean and salt, but foul with oil. A man jumped on top of me with heavy shoes, and his heels bit deep below the edge of my cap. The pain was unbearable. For a moment I blacked out.

Around the bow, where I had jumped, the suction of the sinking ship was greatest. It gripped and clung, exerting a steady downward pull. With every gasping breath you drew the sickening oil into your stomach, and up it came with a rush. As we struck out to one of the life rafts, some of the men were terribly sick. We helped as many as we could. Others, exhausted by the agony of vomiting, went under. Not many, but a few.

On the raft we had more trouble. The suction pulled us, raft and all, toward the *Helena*'s sinking hull. We found a line holding us fast to the ship, and cut it, but still the suction held us. When thrown from the deck, the raft had turned in mid-air and was now upside down, the paddles lashed beneath it. In that sea of oil no man could stay under long enough to release them.

And so, as senior officer, I organized a hand-paddling detail— "Push, paddle, kick! Push, paddle, kick!"—which took us away from the danger.

We saw the *Helena* go. It was a sad, an unbelievably sad moment. What does one say? Not what you might expect. Nothing smart or slick. Just the so-called corny phrases you have heard time and again in the movies or read in fiction: "She was a grand ship." "She sure was swell."

She went down gracefully and quickly, like the queen that she was.

There were hundreds of us somewhere in that crowded, night-black sea, clinging to rafts or bits of debris, floating in life belts or swimming aimlessly in the dark. Our little group clung to the overturned raft and looked at the place where the *Helena* had vanished, and felt alone, deserted, and it was the end of all the world.

And then the sea began bubbling, boiling, above the grave of our ship. We watched it, wide-eyed and alarmed. Up from the depths lurched a strange, awesome shape, a metal island, all wet and gleaming, the sea pouring from its sides as it emerged.

Fifteen feet high, this gleaming thing loomed above the sea in the dark, while the sea rocked it and the waves from its resurrection rolled out to bring us its message.

It was the *Helena's* bow, her white "50" proudly standing out against the wet gray steel. Down there on the floor of Kula Gulf, under forty or more fathoms, our ship had broken in two. The strakes or keel holding her together midships had let go. This much of her—a ship's spirit proudly encased in steel and bravely holding aloft her identifying numerals—had returned to comfort us. We were not alone.

Those of us who still clung to the raft gazed at her in silence. Here was something no man could fail to feel, whatever his faith. It was not a question of religion. I have talked to some of those men since, to be sure of that. By recalling lessons in ship design and compartmentation, one can explain readily why she came up. But there in the darkness of Kula Gulf, surrounded by death and loneliness and fear, such material explanations were inadequate . . .

It was with a sense of gratitude and humiliation that we pushed and paddled our raft toward the risen remains of the ship. Other rafts, too, sought security in the *Helena's* presence. When the battle ended, the *Helena* would be missed. Our destroyers would surely come seeking her.

Ringed about her, we made ourselves as comfortable as possible, some in the water, some on the rafts. Lt. Comdr. James Baird, the senior officer present, took charge, but there was little to do but wait. It was 2:30 A.M. the sea calm, the water warm, the oil thick and slippery and strangling. But we did not curse the oil too bitterly. Without it, there might have been sharks.

The battle continued. American and Jap ships hurled shells across the darkness, and Jap batteries on Kolombangara thundered intermittently as the hours passed. I was not conscious of fear. For about four hours I clung to a short piece of rope which hung over the side of the raft, and was not aware of exhaustion or even of any great expenditure of effort. But when at last I tried to let go the rope, my fingers had stiffened so rigidly about it that they had to be pried loose.

The battle ended. Admiral Ainsworth's force had wiped out all but two of the Japs, and those two had stealthily slipped away into some dark part of the gulf. Our ships retired. There was silence and a strange peace. The flagship asked for a roll call.

We learned later the story of that roll call. One by one, the ships' names were read over TBS and checked off. But there was silence when the *Helena's* radio name in that engagement was spoken. Again and again the call went out. Then at last the truth had to be faced. In a heavy voice, the TBS officer said, "I'm sorry to report, sir, ———— doesn't answer."

"———— doesn't answer." Twelve times in the triumphant aftermath of major engagements the *Helena* had promptly answered the roll. This time—silence.

On orders from the admiral, a pair of destroyers slipped back into the gulf, feeling their way through the dark. On the alert for the two Jap ships thought to have escaped destruction, they circled the area on a sweep. Before long, one of them sighted the bow of the *Helena*.

What happened then was not the fault of the destroyer men. It was no one's fault. The object which had been sighted could not be the *Helena;* it was too small. Since nothing else American was in the gulf, it had to be Jap.

One destroyer opened fire. Huddled about the *Helena's* bow, crowded on the lashed rafts or hanging wearily in the water, we had been unaware of any movement in the darkness until the destroyer's guns opened up on us. Then the night was ripped by flame. Shells screamed into the sea all about us.

Some of us groaned. Others swore. No man's eyes were sharp enough to identify the ship, and most of us thought she was Jap. We knew what that meant, if she steamed up to us. After what our Navy had done to the Emperor's fleet, there would be no prisoners taken tonight. Machine guns on that swift black shadow would be trained on us.

A little while ago, despite weariness and the fatalistic feeling that perhaps, after all, we were not going to be rescued, the men had been amazingly cheerful. They had swapped names, told where they came from, helped one another to fight off the increasing weariness. There had been the sharp, witty exchange of gags and double-talk.

Now the night was a thundering hell and the sea all about us was tortured with explosions. Shells crashed into the steel monument about which we were clustered. Our little world was being hammered apart. There was no panic, even then. One or two men let go and struck out into the darkness, the rest stared steadily at the black hulk of the destroyer. Was she a Jap? Or was she one of ours, confused by the floating remains of the *Helena?*

What took place then was a kind of town meeting of the sea—a polling of opinions, orderly and without undue haste, despite the destruction that felt for us from the ship's batteries. There was calm discussion of the several possibilities. If we signaled, and she was American, would she believe us? If Jap, would she strafe us?

Commander Baird called for a vote. Should we signal or not? The "ayes" won it. One man—one only—had a flashlight and, miraculously, it was in working order. From hand to hand it went until it reached the fingers of Lt. Comdr. V. W. Post, Communications Officer. On a lurching raft Commander Post was raised to the shoulders of two sturdy men, and the light blinked its message, Five Zero. Help!" And then we waited.

There are no new ways of saying how long a minute can be. It was a long time, a very long time, because we didn't know. If our luck had run out, the answer to our signal would be not the small red flashes for which we prayed, but almost certain death in the roar of the destroyer's guns—men against a wall of sea, facing a firing squad of Jap 4.7's.

We waited, and the answer was a series of quick red blinks in the dark. And then we cheered. But there was still danger. In the darkness of the gulf, the two escaped Jap ships had laid in hiding, awaiting an opportune time to slip out and run for safety. These two ships, giving up the fight, had undoubtedly crept close to shore and sought security in silence. Our task force knew of their existence, but not where they were. Kula Gulf is big. The night was dark.

No doubt there were some Jap chuckles when American shells menaced the lives of the *Helena*'s survivors. No doubt. Jap heads came together, scheming. Now, as our two destroyers steamed up and stopped dead in the water to take us aboard, the sea about the *Helena*'s bow was suddenly alive with torpedoes. Those Jap ships— and probably some lurking enemy submarines also—were seeking revenge.

It was a ticklish business. The Japs had only to point their tubes at stationary targets. Our destroyers could not linger long in such a perilous area; they could but rush in, snatch a few of us from the sea and speed out again, with all hands alert for those telltale white feathers of phosphorus in the wake of enemy fish. Time and again, they raced in and out again, while the *Helena*'s men scrambled up ladders or clung to trailing lines and were pulled aboard.

Then the Japs, recklessly bold, showed themselves in a dash for freedom. It happened as my turn came, and I was dangling on a line midway between the sea and the deck of the destroyer, which had slowed in passing to take me aboard. Suddenly, the gunners on the

American's deck found an enemy cruiser in range and hurled a blistering challenge at her.

The little destroyer reared in the water like a kicking mule, and I swung there against her throbbing plates, helpless, battered, hanging on with God knows what. But that, too, passed. As the ship leaped forward at top speed to pursue the fleeing Japs, I was hauled aboard and assisted to the wardroom, where others from the *Helena* had found haven before me. There we sat, aware now of what we had gone through. Aware, too, of the awful noise of the destroyer's guns, as she and her sister ship engaged not one but both of the enemy. It was almost more than we could endure.

But it ended, as everything else had. There was a brief, violent skirmish in the dark—our two American cans slugging it out in a running battle with the Jap cruiser and destroyer. The torpedoes that streaked through Kula Gulf were American now, and our destroyers' gun crews were superb in their marksmanship. The Japs were sunk as they fled.

When these two Japs settled to the floor of Kula Gulf, the battle was over. There were no more of the enemy . . .

A SECOND BATTLE FOR KULA GULF FOLLOWED SWIFTLY as the enemy attempted another reinforcement run to Munda. On July 12 the Tokyo Express met Ainsworth's cruisers and destroyers. Because of a TBS failure at a critical juncture, and accurate Japanese torpedoes, cruisers *St. Louis* and *Honolulu* and New Zealand's *Leander* sustained severe damage, while destroyer *Gwin* was set afire and had to be abandoned. Against this the Imperial Navy lost the cruiser *Jintsu* and four destroyers. But the Tokyo Express kept coming. On the night of August 2 the Japanese supply train made a high speed run through Blackett Strait. American torpedo boats were stationed in the area, and one of them was Lieutenant (jg) John F. Kennedy's 109 . . . later immortalized by Robert J. Donovan.

13.

PT 109

When the "Express" reached Vila around 12:30 A.M. the *Hagikaze,*
Arashi and *Shigure* lay to in lower Blackett Strait a thousand yards
from shore to unload. The *Amagiri,* which in Japanese means "Heavenly Mist," dropped off behind them to guard against any attack
through the narrow neck of the strait between Kolombangara and
Arundel Island.

From Kolombangara dozens of barges and landing craft swarmed
out around the three drifting destroyers like junks around freighters
in Hong Kong harbor. Sailors heaved cases of food and ammunition
overboard onto their decks. Soldiers swung down landing nets.

The whole operation took place under the most intense pressure
for haste. With their engines dead the destroyers would be easy targets for enemy ships, planes or submarines. Also, the sailors, looking
ahead, wanted to get away as quickly as possible so as to be out of
range of American fighter planes when daylight came.

"Hurry, hurry!" they kept exhorting the debarking troops. The
soldiers, stumbling about on dark stairs and decks, resented the
abrupt treatment they were getting. Why should they be in a vast
hurry? *They* weren't going back to Rabaul.

In spite of the grumbling and confusion the unloading was carried
off with dispatch in darkness broken only here and there by down-
ward-pointed masked flashlights in the hands of petty officers. On

each of the three destroyers four parties of twenty-five sailors went to work on the stores of cargo. These crews were stationed fore and aft on each side of the ships. Barges lined up at these stations. The sailors would toss along boxes and crates until a barge was full. Then the loaded barge would pull out and another would move up in its place.

On the bridges of the destroyers were hooded signal lamps, with each ship's lamp masked in a different, identifying color. Less than an hour after their arrival the dim red lamp on the *Hagikaze* signaled: "Let's go home." Nine hundred soldiers and more than seventy tons of supplies were already ashore or on their way to the shore in barges.

The destroyers' engines were started. After allowing five minutes for warming them up, Captain Kaju Sugiure in the flagship *Hagikaze* gave the signal to get under way. Although there was every reason to suppose that PT boats would still be lurking up in Blackett Strait, the Japanese nevertheless preferred this route around the southern shore of Kolombangara to the risk of going out through Kula Gulf and meeting destroyers or cruisers. They did not know that Captain Burke was waiting north of Kolombangara with six destroyers, but experience suggested as much. To whatever extent Japanese sailors were harassed by PT boats, they preferred to deal with them than with the heavy guns of cruisers and destroyers.

The forty-five minutes or so that the other destroyers had spent at Vila were anxious ones for Commander Hanami on the covered bridge of the *Amagiri*. Cruising back and forth across lower Blackett Strait, he was constantly worried that a PT boat, a destroyer or even a PBY would discover him.

While the islands around him were held by his own troops, these narrow waters were treacherous for Japanese ships. Anywhere he turned Commander Hanami knew that an American man-of-war might be waiting. Navigating in the dark was dangerous because of the reefs. There were no adequate charts for this area of the Solomons. Furthermore, the *Amagiri* carried no radar. To a degree this disadvantage was offset by a group of trained lookouts who searched the darkness through ten affixed, wide-angle night binoculars.

It was with great relief that Commander Hanami finally received a signal from Captain Sugiure that the *Hagikaze, Arashi* and *Shigure* were starting back up the Kolombangara coast. He immediately ordered the coxswain to head northwestward at increasing speed to rejoin them.

Approximately in his path several miles distant was *PT 109,* with Kennedy steering away from Kolombangara in a westerly direction toward Gizo, following *PT 162* and *PT 169.* Kennedy had no orders other than to patrol off Vanga Vanga and to look for whatever he could find. His mission boiled down to a matter of guessing where in the impenetrable blackness he might find a target.

Encountering no sign of enemy ships in the middle of Blackett Strait, Kennedy made a fateful decision. He overtook Potter and Lowrey and suggested that the three boats reverse their direction. He believed they would have a better chance of rejoining the missing boats if they returned to the vicinity in which they had all been scattered in the first place. The other two skippers agreed. The three boats turned about and with Kennedy now in the lead headed toward the southeast, the direction from which the Heavenly Mist was blowing at a speed of thirty knots.

Commander Hanami strained forward from the starboard side of the *Amagiri's* bridge, impatient for the broader passage of Vella Gulf. Captain Yamashiro paced the port side. Between them stood Lt. (jg) Hiroshi Hosaka, the torpedo officer, constantly checking the readiness of his own crews. The wheel was in the hands of Coxswain Kazuto Doi.

The ship was still on general quarters. Lookouts hunched against the binoculars. Lt. Nakajima, the medical officer, waited in his quarters behind the bridge. Petty Officer 2/c Mitsuaki Sawada gazed out an open window in the forward gun turret, wondering whether they would make it back to Rabaul without trouble. Lt. (jg) Shigeo Kanazawa, a gunnery officer, was poised on the cover of the bridge.

Aboard *PT 109* Ensign Ross was standing on the foredeck by the 37-millimeter gun. Behind him was Kennedy at the wheel. At the skipper's right was Maguire and just beyond and above Maguire was Marney in the forward gun turret. On the skipper's left, outside the cockpit, was Ensign Thom, lying on the deck. Standing behind the cockpit was Mauer. Aware that Kennedy still hoped to meet some of the other dispersed PT boats that must be wandering about the strait, Mauer was peering through the night for a familiar form.

Albert was on watch amidships. Harris, off duty, was sleeping on the deck between the day-room canopy and a starboard torpedo tube.

He had removed his kapok jacket and was using it as a pillow. McMahon was on watch in the engine room. Johnston was dozing on the starboard side of the deck near the engine-room hatch. Zinser was standing close by. Starkey was the lookout in the after gun turret. Kirksey, off duty, was lying aft on the starboard side.

The boat was moving so quietly that Ross, scanning the dark, could barely hear the idling engine above the soft sound of the breeze and the splash of water against the bow. He had the sensation of gliding in a sailboat, and he was gratified that they were in deep enough water that we would not have to worry about reefs for a while.

"Ship ahead!" a lookout shouted to Commander Hanami.

"Look again," Hanami ordered.

"Ship at two o'clock!" Marney shouted to Kennedy from the gun turret.

Kennedy glanced obliquely off his starboard bow. Ross was already pointing to a shape suddenly sculptured out of the darkness behind a phosphorescent bow wave. For a few unregainable moments Kennedy thought it was one of the scattered PT boats. So did Mauer. So also did some of the crews of *PT 162* and *PT 169,* who sighted the *Amagiri* at about the same time or perhaps seconds earlier. As the shape grew, Kennedy and Mauer quickly recognized that it was not a PT boat. On *PT 169* Potter called a warning on the radio, but it either was not received aboard *109* or else arrived too late.

"Lenny," Kennedy said in a matter-of-fact voice, "look at this.

Ensign Thom stood up.

What followed took place within the span of perhaps forty seconds or less.

In the *Amagiri*'s forward gun turret Petty Officer Sawada received an order: "Fire!" The destroyer was already so close to the smaller boat, however, that he could not depress the guns in time to aim.

On the foredeck of *PT 109* Ross frantically grabbed a shell and rammed it at the 37-millimeter. It slammed against a closed breech. He knew he would never have time to load.

Commander Hanami, now recognizing the American vessel as a PT boat, decided that his best protection would be to ram.

"Hard a-starboard," he called.

Coxswain Doi, informed that the object ahead was a PT, expected just such an order on the strength of what he had heard discussed about the best tactics in such a situation. He turned the wheel about 10 degrees to starboard.

To Ross the destroyer originally appeared to be traveling on a parallel course. Now he distinctly saw the slender mast heel toward *PT 109,* indicating that the destroyer was turning in his direction.

"Sound general quarters," Kennedy told Maguire.

Maguire turned around, took a couple of steps out of the cockpit and yelled, "General quarters!"

"We're on general quarters," Albert said to Starkey. Starkey's battle station was the after starboard torpedo, so he climbed down from the port gun turret and started across the deck.

Back in the cockpit, Maguire fingered a Miraculous Medal suspended from a chain around his neck. Ross crouched under the bow gun.

On the bridge of the *Amagiri* Lt. Hosaka considered ordering his torpedo crews to fire, then decided it would be useless. *PT 109* was too close. Torpedoes would pass under her.

Kennedy spun his wheel in an instinctive attempt to make a torpedo attack on the *Amagiri.* The torpedoes, however, would not have exploded even if they had struck the destroyer, because they were not set to fire at such a short distance. Moreover, *PT 109,* idling on a single engine, was moving so sluggishly that there was no chance to maneuver against the swiftness of the destroyer.

Seeing what was coming, Maguire grasped his Miraculous Medal and had begun to say, "Mary, conceived without sin, pray for us . . ." when the steel prow of the *Amagiri* crashed at a sharp angle into the starboard side of *PT 109* beside the cockpit.

Harold Marney, the newcomer, the youth who was taking the wounded Kowal's place in the forward turret, was crushed to death, probably at the moment of impact, and his body never found.

The wheel was torn out of Kennedy's grasp as he was hurled against the rear wall of the cockpit, his once-sprained back slamming against a steel reinforcing brace. It was the angle of the collision alone that saved him from being crushed to death with Marney. The destroyer, smashing through the gun turret, sliced diagonally behind the cockpit only several feet from the prostrate skipper. Helplessly looking up, Kennedy could see the monstrous hull sweeping past him through his boat, splintering her and cleaving the forepart away from the starboard side of the stern.

In the engine room McMahon had had no warning of danger. He was standing among the engines, casually touching the manifolds to make sure they were not getting too hot and regulating the scoop controls, which fed sea water through the cooling system. From time to time, as a means of getting optimum functioning, he would alternate the engine on which the boat was running.

Something on one of the guages caught his attention, and he was climbing over machinery to look at it when a tremendous jolt flung him sideways against the starboard bulkhead and toppled him into a sitting position alongside an auxiliary generator. In disbelief he saw a river of red fire cascading into the engine room from the day room. His reason told him that this was impossible because a hatch separated the two rooms, and he himself had dogged it down before leaving Rendova. It did not occur to him that the hatch and most of the bulkhead had been sheared away and the gasoline tanks over the day room had been ignited by friction sparks or a broken electrical cable.

The river of fire rose about him. It seared his hands and face and scorched his shins, exposed by his rolled-up dungarees. He held his breath to keep the flames from his lungs. He was fairly engulfed in a world of blinding light and roasting heat and then without any transition he was immersed in a watery darkness, his lungs almost bursting. Sheared away by the destroyer, the flaming stern was pulled down by the weight of the engines. Without the sensation of descent, McMahon found himself under water fighting to get to the surface, which appeared from below as a wavering orange glare. Bobbing to the top at last in his kapok, he emerged in a sea of fire. The burning gasoline was spreading across the water in a garish patch of light that could be seen by Lt. Evans on his hilltop a few miles away. He knew that a ship must be on fire, and he supposed he might hear more about it in time.

Johnston's plight was scarcely less desperate than McMahon's. In his sleep he was knocked into the sea in his heavy Army shoes, steel helmet, blue shirt, socks, dungarees and kapok. He opened his eyes to see the sliding hull of the destroyer. Looking up in shock he saw Japanese sailors running on the deck. As the *Amagiri*'s stern swept by him the suction of the screws yanked him under the surface. The downward churn of the water spun him head over heels into the depth like a piece of clothing in a washing machine.

Johnston wondered if he was doomed. He did not pray, but he thought of his wife, Nathalie. As the descending currents released him, he pulled his way upward. The struggle seemed hopeless. He did not know how far under he was. He decided to give up and die. Then he thought that his wife would consider him a coward, and he resumed his toil. The pain in his lungs was excruciating. Seeing no light, he feared he was still near the bottom. Giving up would be easy now, even desirable. Again, however, the thought crossed his mind, "Nat will think I'm yellow." He resumed the climb on his watery ladder. Faintly the orange glow flickered above his straining face. Now determined to survive, he thrashed his way to the top, gasping for breath and beating the flames away with his hands.

As the *Amagiri* ripped through *PT 109* Captain Yamashiro smelled something that reminded him of smoldering cotton. Lt. Hosaka could feel heat on the bridge. Petty Officer Yoshitaka Yamazaki, a medical corpsman, had been crossing the deck to the sick bay when he heard someone shout that a PT boat lay ahead. He felt a thud, saw a burst of flame and was stabbed with the thought that the Americans had fired a torpedo into the *Amagiri*.

"What's happened?" Petty Officer Masayoshi Takashima called from his torpedo station.

"The port side's afire," Shigeo Takemura shouted up to the bridge. Takemura, a communications man with a torpedo crew, thought that the enemy's torpedomen had succeeded in doing what the *Amagiri*'s had failed to try. He supposed the flames were pouring out of the destroyer.

In the starboard engine room Petty Officer Shigeo Yoshikawa felt a shock. Lt. Shigeru Nishinosome noticed that the ship's engines were starting to shake. In the port engine room Petty Officer Yoshiji Hiramatsu heard a scraping noise against the hull and feared the *Amagiri* had hit a reef. He observed that the starboard propeller shaft was vibrating. In the auxiliary engine room Petty Officer Takao Tan heard a thud and hastened up to the deck, thinking they had been hit by a torpedo.

As the *Amagiri* swept on she fired two shots back at *PT 109,* but both missed. By now the vibration was so severe that Hanami had to reduce his speed to investigate the trouble. Part of a blade of the starboard propeller had been sheared off, causing the shaft to shake. Also, the bow was dented. This was the extent of the damage, however, and no one was hurt.

Hanami found that by lowering his speed to twenty-eight knots he could sail without excessive vibration. In answer to an inquiry from the *Hagikaze* about the fire he radioed to the other three ships that he had sunk a PT boat. Wild cheers swept through the *Shigure.* Their mission a complete success, the four destroyers returned to Rabaul.

Though hurled about by the crash, Kennedy, Ross, Mauer and Maguire were still on the bow, which was kept afloat by its watertight compartments. Mauer was thrown to the deck, bruising his right shoulder. Maguire was flung out of the cockpit back against the day-room canopy. His helmet was pushed down on his brow, but he pried it off in time to see the *Amagiri* passing through behind him.

As the impact of the destroyer tilted the deck sharply to port, Ross let go of the loose bow gun for fear it would topple overboard and carry him to the bottom. He mistook the first flare of flames for a bright search light. Thinking the enemy was about to fire down on them, he slipped off the starboard side into the water and hid in the shade of the hull. Gasoline fumes choked him, and he fainted.

Pulling himself up from the corner of the cockpit, Kennedy's first thought was that a gasoline tank might explode from the heat. "Everybody into the water," he yelled.

"Wait for me," Maguire pleaded. His rubber lifebelt had failed to inflate. An extra kapok was in the charthouse, but he was afraid of being left alone aboard. Kennedy waited until he had fetched it, then, putting his hand on some debris, vaulted overboard. Maguire and Mauer went in with him. Kennedy did not feel any pain, and at the point where he entered the water the flames had been washed aside by the *Amagiri's* wake.

As the three swam out a safe distance, the forepart of *PT 109* was left a battered, deserted hulk, drifting in two hundred fathoms through the glare and hiss of flames. The stern had already disappeared.

Andrew Jackson Kirksey, the quiet Georgian with the strong premonition of death, had perished with Marney. Kirksey had been lying on the starboard side from which the destroyer came and toward the stern. He might have been killed on impact and hurled yards into the water or he might have been crushed and gone down with the stern. No one knew. Ensign Thom, McMahon, Johnston, Albert, Harris, Starkey and Zinser were, like Ensign Ross, floating about in fire or fumes, some of them unconscious.

Harris, his head pillowed on his kapok on deck, had been awakened by a shout to worse than a nightmare. He saw what looked to be an enormous prow knifing straight at him only feet away. He sprang up and dived sideways over the torpedo tube, and while he was still in the air the *Amagiri* crunched into *PT 109*. Some part of the boat, perhaps the tube, snapped up and struck him in the left thigh, painfully knocking him several yards beyond where a dive would have carried him. Somersaulting through the dark, he could see fire break out. Then he landed in the water in a sitting position, astonished and thankful to find that he had his kapok on, untied.

A moment before it had been his pillow. Now it was wrapped around his chest, keeping him afloat. In the instant between jumping up and diving he must have pulled it on, but he had no recollection of doing so. Shaking the salt water out of his eyes he saw the stern of the destroyer vanishing into the dark and heard two shots.

Neither Zinser nor Starkey ever saw the *Amagiri*. On deck Zinser heard the cry of "General quarters" and the next thing he knew he was flying through space. For a moment he could see flames. Then he fainted. While walking toward his battle station at the after starboard torpedo tube, Starkey was sent reeling. He thought they had been hit by a shell. His helmet knocked off, he toppled into one of the smashed quarters, which was lighted up by flames. He thought that this was what hell must be like, and then he lapsed into unconsciousness.

As the fire on the water around the boat subsided, Kennedy concluded that there would be no explosion. He and Maguire and Mauer swam back to the bow of the boat and climbed up on the deck. At Kennedy's direction Mauer got out the blinker, a two-foot-long tube with a light inside, and started walking around the hulk, flashing the light periodically as a beacon to any members of the crew who might still be alive in the water.

Apart from Maguire and Mauer, Kennedy did not know what had become of his crew. He was impatient for the other boats to come to his aid, but they never appeared. Just before the collision *PT 162* had attempted an attack on the *Amagiri,* but Lowrey's torpedoes did not fire, and he turned away to the southwest. Just after the collision, *PT 169* fired two torpedoes to no effect, whereupon Potter moved out of the vicinity. Presumably skippers of other boats thought that the crew of *PT 109* had perished in the flames and that Blackett Estrait was no place for loitering with Japanese destroyers steaming through. As the hours—and years for that matter—passed, the men on *PT 109* were bitter that they were not rescued, yet their bitterness never focused on any one man or any one boat.

As soon as Mauer was ready with the blinker, Kennedy removed his shoes, shirt and sidearms and dived overboard in a rubber lifebelt to search for the others. He was to be in the water approximately thirty of the next thirty-six hours. Fortunately, it was warm and calm.

On the hulk Maguire and Mauer received the first inkling that others were alive when they heard Zinser's voice in the darkness calling, "Mr. Thom is drowning. Bring the boat!" Dreading to swim back into the fumes, Maguire nevertheless got a line from the rope locker on the bow. He tied one end to a broken torpedo tube and the other end around his waist. With a prayer he stepped into the water and swam toward the sound of Zinser's voice, leaving Mauer, shipwrecked for the second time in three months, a solitary figure afloat on what was left of *PT 109*.

Ross, having fainted in the bright light of the flames, awoke in darkness, wondering where he was and what he was doing. As his head cleared, he saw two men not far from him. Swimming over to them, he found that one was Zinser, whom he did not know by name, and the other was Thom. Zinser was moaning. Thom was gibbering. When Ross shook him, Thom reached out his huge arm and tried to climb up on him as if he were a log. Fending him off, Ross cried, "Lenny, Lenny, it's me!" After some sparring in the water Thom came to and appeared to be in good condition. Zinser was all right too, and they started to shout for the others.

Maguire was swimming toward them. The gasoline fumes nearly suffocated him, and he prayed that he would not faint. He had no difficulty finding the men because of their voices.

"Are you all right, Mr. Thom?" he asked.

"I'm all right," Thom said.

"Can you keep going?"

"I can make it."

Maguire could see that Zinser did not need any help beyond an occasional tug he was getting from Ross. Guided by the blinking of Mauer's light, Maguire, Ross, Zinser and Thom swam slowly back to the boat, where Albert presently splashed out of the night to join them.

After leaping into the water just in time to escape being crushed by the *Amagiri*, Harris drifted off alone. At first he felt severe pain in his left leg from the blow he had received while diving, but in time his leg grew numb and he could not use it. Bobbing about in his kapok, Harris supposed that he was the sole survivor. This thought haunted him until he saw someone drifting out of the flames sixty feet away. With his own left leg dragging, Harris swam laboriously toward the man, whom he could not recognize because he was floating with his helmet partially covering his face. The man evidently was in such a state of shock that Harris could not even recognize his voice, although he could make out that the man was saying that he could not use his hands and was appealing for help to get his helmet off. It was only when Harris pried the helmet loose that he recognized Pat McMahon. The night was too dark for Harris to see well, but he could tell that McMahon was in serious condition.

Not knowing what to do or where to go, Harris treaded water by McMahon's side. Once the fire had burned out, the night was blacker than ever. Harris believed that he and McMahon were the only two alive, and he could not imagine what would become of them. The thought that the others were dead had taken such a hold on him that he was startled when he heard voices somewhere.

"Mr. Kennedy!" he yelled. "Mr. Kennedy!"

"Over here," he heard Kennedy call back.

"McMahon is badly hurt," Harris told him.

"I'm over here," Kennedy shouted. "Where are you?"

"This way," Harris called. He could hear the splashing of Kennedy's arms and legs. It sounded far off. Periodically, Kennedy would pause and call "Where are you?" and Harris would answer "Over here." Harris heard the splashing grow louder, and then he saw Kennedy's head coming out of the dark. McMahon lay helpless in his kapok. Despite the cooling effect of the water his whole body felt warm.

"McMahon is too hurt to swim," Harris told Kennedy.

"All right, I'll take him back," Kennedy said. "Part of the boat is still floating."

Kennedy did not mention any other names, but the sound of voices in the distance lifted Harris's spirits. McMahon, however, was without hope. He could not use his arms at all.

"Go on, skipper," the crew's "old man" mumbled to Kennedy. "You go on. I've had it."

Kennedy clutched McMahon's kapok and began towing him toward the boat, which by this time had drifted a considerable distance from the swimmers. The men aboard kept calling to give their position, and Kennedy followed the sound. At first Harris stayed abreast of Kennedy and McMahon despite his numb leg. Then, his strength on the wane, he dropped behind. "Come on," Kennedy urged him. Harris resumed swimming, but the burden seemed unendurable.

His left leg dragged. He was drowsy. It felt luxurious just to slump back in his kapok and drift. Drawing farther and farther away, Kennedy would call back to him, and he would respond by lifting his heavy arms to swim awhile. Then, tiring, he would drift again. It had been cool on deck and before taking a nap he had pulled a sweater on above his jacket and his shirt. The weight of his clothes and his shoes anchored him. "The hell with it," he would say to himself. He no longer could hear Kennedy, but this did not seem to make any difference to him any more. When he had the strength he would swim; when he did not, he would go limp and say "The hell with it."

It seemed as though he was alone for a half-hour or longer before he again heard Kennedy splashing toward him, calling, "Where are you, Harris?" As Kennedy reappeared, Harris wearily told him, "I can't go any further."

"For a guy from Boston, you're certainly putting up a great exhibition out here, Harris," Kennedy snapped.

Harris cursed and swore at Kennedy. He was aggrieved that Kennedy did not realize how much his leg troubled him. "Well, come on," Kennedy persisted. Harris asked the skipper to hold him up while he took off his kapok to shed his sweater and jacket. Kennedy gripped his arm and held him precariously on the surface. Had the exhausted and dispirited Harris slipped from Kennedy's grasp he might have gone down like a stone. But with his heavy clothes and his shoes off and his kapok back on, Harris found he could move through the water, and he and Kennedy swam slowly back to the boat.

Thom, meanwhile, was having even greater difficulty rescuing Johnston. When Johnston had come gasping to the surface after escaping from the churning propellers, he swallowed gasoline and inhaled fumes. Retching forced more fumes into his lungs. His brain became clouded. He was confused, violently sick and semiconscious. His neck was burned. He saw the floating bow and men on it. When he called out, Thom heard him and swam to his side. By this time, however, Johnston was almost helpless. At Thom's urging he would kick a few times or try the dog-paddle, but it was so much easier to sleep.

"Come on, Bill, let's go," Thom would say, shaking him. Johnston would kick for a while and then fall back to sleep, not caring whether he ever reached the boat.

"Let's keep paddling," Thom pleaded. He himself was only a fair swimmer, and it took him a long time to drag Johnston to the floating bow.

Starkey was among the last to make it. The part of the boat into which he had been flung by the crash quickly filled with water and he floated free. The thought that he was all alone surrounded by Japanese frightened him. So did the danger of sharks. "Oh my God. Oh my God," he kept saying. He floated without being able to make up his mind what he should do until he saw some debris near him. He climbed up on a mattress. His face and hands were burned, though not severely. As he lay on the mattress, he thought of his wife, Camille, and four-year-old daughter, Shirley, and he remembered the day he had enlisted after Pearl Harbor. Then he saw the dark outlines of the boat. It looked a couple of hundred yards away at least, but the sight gave him courage. He took off his shoes and swam to rejoin the others, who were either lying on deck or drifting in the water, hanging on to the hull.

Kennedy called the names of the crew. Everyone answered but Marney and Kirksey. He inquired whether anyone had seen them or had any idea what had happened to them. No one had. Kennedy called, "Kirksey . . . Marney . . ." From time to time during the night others kept repeating the call, but there was never any answer.

All the survivors seemed to be in fair condition except McMahon and Johnston. Both of McMahon's hands were covered with third-degree burns, and his face, arms, legs and feet were burned. In the water the burns had glowed warmly, but when the men lifted him up on deck he felt as if his whole body were on fire. He took off some of his clothes to relieve the friction on his burned skin. Despite the terrible surface heat, however, he became so cold that he had to put the wet clothing back on.

Johnston was alternately unconscious and wracked by spells of vomiting. He did not speak, and the others were at loss to know what was the matter with him. Maguire thought Johnston was dying. It was a problem to keep him from rolling down the slanting deck into the water. Someone suggested lashing him to the boat, which provoked a long discussion in the dark, because others felt that there would be no way to prevent Johnston from being carried to the bottom if the boat should suddenly sink. In the end some of the men held lines around him for a time, but did not tie them down.

During the long hours of darkness most of the men had climbed up on the hulk and reclined with their feet braced against some fixture to keep them from sliding off the deck. They spoke in low voices about the prospects of rescue after daylight. Some thought PTs would return for them; others guessed that a PBY would pick them up.

When dawn broke over Wana Wana they could see Rendova Peak thirty-eight miles to the south. They knew almost exactly where they were. They knew that the other boats would be back at the base now, that Lumberi would be stirring with the morning's activity and that their absence would set in motion a search that should lead speedily to their rescue. There was already some cause for this optimism.

~~~~~~

CONSOLIDATION OF UNITED STATES CONTROL OVER the sea lanes and Japanese losses made it necessary for the enemy to support its forces at Kolombangara by barge traffic at night, running along the shores of Vella Lavella. But Japanese impatience with these token measures brought a cruiser and three destroyers, escorting transports, into Vella Gulf on the night of August 6. This led to still another surface action in this area, for a task group under Commander Frederick Moosbrugger interposed itself and took the Japanese by surprise. The resulting engagement, lasting about forty-five minutes, cost the enemy three destroyers severely damaged against none for the Navy—a resounding victory which paved the way for the invasion of Vella Lavella on August 15, and New Georgia on the 25th.

September was spent in the consolidating of our position. No major surface action took place until October 6 when a task group of three destroyers under Captain F. R. Walker sighted a superior force of enemy ships south of Choiseul. The enemy was disposed in two groups, outnumbering us about three to one. At 10:30 P.M., when the enemy was almost dead ahead, Walker engaged. *Selfridge, O'Bannon* and *Chevalier* fired torpedoes. *O'Bannon's* target, destroyer *Yagumo,* quickly burst into flames. Scratch one. However, this was offset when an enemy torpedo hit in under the No. 2 gun aboard *Chevalier,* blowing the bow forward of the bridge cleanly off. Out of control, the destroyer plunged into the next ship ahead, *O'Bannon.* Then *Selfridge* caught a torpedo. Thus abruptly the battle ended—the Japanese racing for sanctuary, while a destroyer put a torpedo into the floating hulk of the doomed *Chevalier.* More than one hundred lives were lost this night.

Meanwhile, our advance toward fiddle-shaped Bougainville had already begun. Daily air strikes by Mitscher's forces since October 26 had softened up Kahili, Ballale and Karu. The amphibious forces were ready to disembark on November 1 when another task force under Merrill bombarded enemy positions on Bougainville preparatory to the landings. Following the bombardment Merrill was ordered to patrol north of Vella Lavella, and to intercept enemy warships en route to disrupt landings. This was the background of The Battle of Empress Augusta Bay, detailed by Theodore Roscoe.

14.

EMPRESS AUGUSTA BAY

When word reached Admiral Koga at Truk that the Americans had dared to put foot on Bougainville, he radioed instructions to strike the interloper and strike hard. Rabaul's air strength was mustered, and with air power to back him up, Rear Admiral Sentaro Omori set out from Rabaul late in the afternoon of November 1 with a blood-thirsty surface force. Mission: to blast the Americans at Cape Torokina.

In Omori's force were heavy cruisers *Myoko* and *Haguro,* light cruisers *Sendai* and *Agano,* and six destroyers. Five troop-carrying assault transports sortied with the force, intending to land a thousand soldiers on the Torokina beaches to give battle to the U.S. Marines. But these APD's were late for the rendezvous, and after an American sub was sighted near St. George Channel, Omori was glad to send them home. He wanted freedom for fast maneuver.

He needed it. Halsey had the word on his sortie, and ComSoPac had lost no time in dispatching Rear Admiral Merrill's task force to intercept the southbound Jap's. When Merrill received this flash assignment his cruisers were off Vella Lavella, enjoying a breather after the strenuous bombardment work of the previous day. Commander B. L. ("Count") Austin was on hand with DesDiv 46. Captain Arleigh Burke's DesDiv 45 was refueling in Hathorn Sound at the entrance of Kula Gulf, but these destroyers topped off with dizzy speed, and by 2315 in the evening of November 1, Merrill's force was racing headlong to meet the warships of Admiral Omori.

Omori did not expect to encounter a cruiser-destroyer force. He expected, perhaps wishfully, to encounter a transport group. Bearing down on Empress Augusta Bay, he had his Imperial naval vessels disposed in a simple formation with heavy cruisers *Myoko* (flagship) and *Haguro* in the center; light cruiser *Sendai* and destroyers *Shigure, Samidare,* and *Shiratsuyu* to port; light cruiser *Agano* and destroyers *Naganami, Hatsukaze,* and *Wakatsuki* to starboard.

Merrill's force was disposed in line-of-bearing of unit guides. In column to starboard were Burke's van destroyers: *Charles Ausburne* (Commander L. K. Reynolds); *Dyson* (Commander R. A. Gano); *Stanly* (Commander R. W. Cavenagh); and *Claxton* (Commander H. F. Stout). In center column steamed cruisers *Montpelier* (flagship), *Cleveland, Columbia,* and *Denver.* To port steamed Austin's rear destroyers: *Spence* (Commander H. J. Armstrong); *Thatcher* (Commander L. R. Lampman); *Converse* (Commander D. C. E. Hamberger); and *Foote* (Commander Alston Ramsay).

Omori's force suffered the first blow when an American plane, detecting the Jap approach, planted a bomb in the superstructure of heavy cruiser *Haguro.* That was at 0130 in the morning of November 2. Lamed by the hit, *Haguro* reduced the formation's speed to 30 knots. Then one of that cruiser's planes reported Merrill's task force coming up. The airmen erroneously notified Omori that one cruiser and three destroyers were in the offing. When, a few minutes later, he was informed by another air scout that a fleet of transports was unloading in Empress Augusta Bay, he sent his formation racing southeastward, hot for a massacre. Apparently the "transports" sighted were destroyer minelayers *Breese, Gamble,* and *Sicard,* at that time working along the coast under escort of destroyer *Renshaw.*

The night was black as carbon. Several of Omori's warships carried radar apparatus, but he put more reliance on binoculars. American "Sugar George" radar was to out-see Japanese vision on this occasion.

Merrill's cruisers made the initial radar contact at 0227. He had already decided to maintain his ships in a position that would block the entrance to Empress Augusta Bay. Once action was joined, he intended to elbow the enemy westward, thereby gaining sea room which would enable him to fight a long-range gun battle with least chance of danger from Jap torpedoes. But his destroyers were to open proceedings with a torpedo attack, and the cruisers were to hold their fire until the "fish" had opportunity to strike the foe.

These plans were carefully laid, and they were known, chapter and verse, by Captain Arleigh Burke, leader of DesDiv 45. Commander Austin and DesDiv 46 were not so well versed in the detail. They were new to Task Force 39, and Austin was not thoroughly acquainted with Merrill's battle techniques.

As soon as radar contact was established, Merrill headed his formation due north. After a brief run, Burke's van destroyers sliced away northwestward to deliver a torpedo strike as planned. Merrill then ordered a simultaneous turn to reverse course. Austin's destroyers were instructed to countermarch, and then hit the enemy's southern flank with torpedoes as soon as they could reach firing position.

While Merrill's cruisers were swinging around the hairpin turn, Burke's destroyers were tacking in on Omori's portside column. At 0246 Burke shouted the word over TBS, "My *guppies are swimming!*" But the Japs had sighted Merrill's cruisers, and Omori was turning his formation southwestward. Because of this sudden turn, the barrage of 25 "guppies" sailed on into silence and oblivion, and Burke's briskly executed attack failed to score.

Meanwhile, the *Sendai* column launched torpedoes at the American cruisers. But Merrill had not waited for this counterfire. When C.I.C. informed him of Omori's southwestward turn, he ordered his cruisers to let go with gunnery. I.J.N. *Sendai* was chief target for this booming fusillade. She caught a cataract of shells just as she was swinging to starboard, and the explosions blew her innards right out through the overhead.

Sendai's abrupt come-uppance threw her column into a jumble. In the ensuing confusion, destroyers *Samidare* and *Shiratsuyu* collided full tilt, and went reeling off in precipitous retirement. That left the *Shigure* all by herself, and she chased southward to join the Jap cruiser column.

Myoko and *Haguro* made a blind loop that tangled them up with the *Agano* column. Although Jap starshells had turned the night into a dazzle, the heavy cruisers failed to sight Merrill's ships, and they maneuvered right into a tempest of American shellfire. Steaming in a daze, *Myoko* slammed into destroyer *Hatsukaze* and ripped off a section of that DD's bow.

Meantime, Burke's "Little Beavers," having launched torpedoes, became separated. And they did not get back into battle until 0349, when *Ausburne* spotted *Sendai* and hurried the vessel under with a

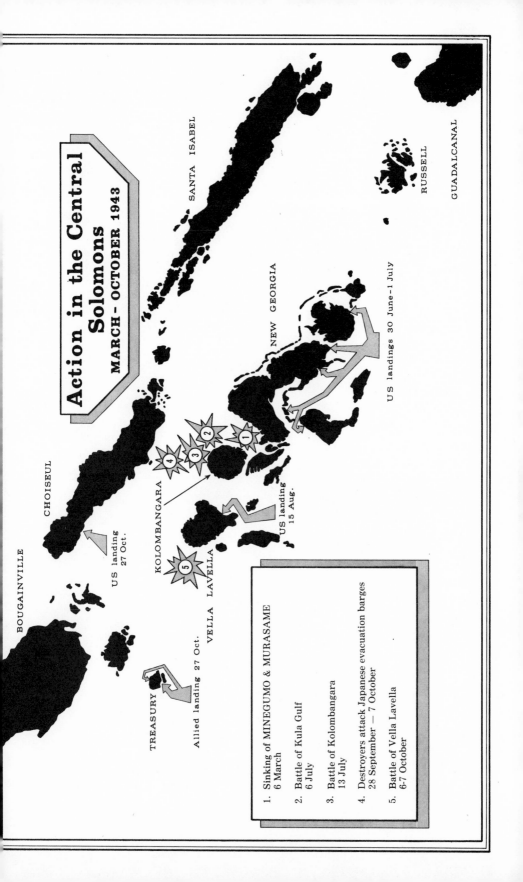

Action in the Central Solomons
MARCH – OCTOBER 1943

BOUGAINVILLE

CHOISEUL

US landing
27 Oct.

KOLOMBANGARA

TREASURY

Allied landing 27 Oct.

VELLA LAVELLA

US landing
15 Aug.

NEW GEORGIA

US landings 30 June–1 July

SANTA ISABEL

RUSSELL

GUADALCANAL

1. Sinking of MINEGUMO & MURASAME
   6 March

2. Battle of Kula Gulf
   6 July

3. Battle of Kolombangara
   13 July

4. Destroyers attack Japanese evacuation barges
   28 September – 7 October

5. Battle of Vella Lavella
   6-7 October

volley of shots. Then *Samidare* and *Shiratsuyu,* the two DD's which had collided, showed up on the radar screen. Burke took off after these departing enemies at top speed.

Commander Austin's DesDiv 46 destroyers had run into hard luck. Destroyer *Foote* misread Merrill's signal to turn, and fell out of formation. While racing to rejoin Austin's column, she was hit in the stern by a Jap torpedo which had been aimed at the American cruisers. Cruiser *Cleveland* swerved just in time to miss the disabled DD by 100 yards. But destroyer *Spence,* farther down the line, was not so lucky. Swinging hard right to give the cruiser column a clear line of fire, she sideswiped destroyer *Thatcher.* The 30-knot brush sent sparks and sweat-beads flying, and removed a wide swath of paint, but both DD's kept on traveling at high speed. Then at 0320 a Jap shell punctured *Spence's* hull at the waterline. Salt water got into a fuel tank, contaminating the oil, and this slow poison soon reduced the destroyer's speed. As if this was not enough misfortune for one division, Austin's DD's lost a fine chance to strike at *Myoko* and *Haguro* with torpedoes. When his flagship sideswiped *Thatcher,* Commander Austin dashed out on the bridge to see what was what. Some bright "pips" blossomed on the radar screen; Austin would have fired torpedoes at 4,000 yards or so, but the C.I.C. officer reported the targets were American. So the little scrape with *Thatcher* cost something more than a paint job.

A moment later *Spence* made contact with cruiser *Sendai.* At that time the Jap vessel was a staggering merry-go-round, but her guns were still firing, and she was as dangerous as a wounded leopard. Austin maneuvered for torpedo fire, and *Spence* and *Converse* flung eight "fish" at the cripple. They did not sink her—Burke's destroyers would presently perform that chore. Austin's three DD's raced on northwestward in an effort to catch *Samidare* and *Shiratsuyu.*

By 0352 *Spence, Thatcher,* and *Converse* had overhauled the two Jap DD's, and 19 American torpedoes were fanning out to catch each by the fantail. The 19 torpedoes scored a perfect zero. Some may have been improperly adjusted, but the zero probably had its source in improper fabrication.

In counterattack, *Samidare* and *Shiratsuyu* flung shells and "fish" at Austin's three destroyers. If the Jap "fish" missed, the marksmen at least had an excuse for poor torpedo work—the two Jap DD's were dodging to escape a tempest of shell fire, and both ships had been badly damaged by collision.

Now *Spence* was running low on fuel, and what little she had was contaminated by salt water. Autstin relinquished his tactical command to *Thatcher's* skipper, Commander Lampman, and veered away with *Spence* to disengage. The maneuver brought his flag destroyer into line for a salvo from Arleigh Burke's fast-shooting division. At 0425 a pack of projectiles slammed into the sea around *Spence*

Over the TBS Commander Austin shouted a plea to Burke. WE'VE JUST HAD ANOTHER CLOSE MISS HOPE YOU ARE NOT SHOOTING AT US

Captain Burke's answer was a classic of Navy humor. SORRY BUT YOU'LL HAVE TO EXCUSE THE NEXT FOUR SALVOS THEY'RE ALREADY ON THEIR WAY

Austin made haste to get *Spence* out of the vicinity. In dodging Burke's ebullient fire, *Spence* picked up a good target in Jap destroyer *Hatsukaze*.

Hatsukaze was the DD which *Myoko* had rammed, and she was in no condition to dodge well-aimed salvos. *Spence* closed the range to 4,000 yards while her gunners pumped shells into the disabled Jap. *Hatsukaze* was soon flaming and wallowing, her engines dead. Austin yearned to finish off this foe, but *Spence's* ammunition was running low, so he put in a call for Burke's destroyers to complete the execution. Thereupon an avalanche of 5-inchers from DesDiv 45 buried *Hatsukaze*. About 0539 the ship rolled over and descended into the grave.

Spence joined up with DesDiv 45 as Burke ordered a retirement. Unable to catch *Samidare* and *Shiratsuyu,* destroyers *Thatcher* and *Converse* were also retiring. As day was making, Admiral Merrill had already headed his cruiser column eastward. While his DD's were trying to tag fleeing Japs, Merrill's cruisers had been maneuvering across the seascape in a duel with the Jap heavies. For over an hour the opposing formations had dodged about like gamecocks in a pit, neither side able to score a death dealing blow. Convinced that he had tangled with no less than seven heavy cruisers, Omori pulled out at 0337 and fled northwest up the coast of Bougainville. The American cruisers chased until daybreak, then Merrill turned back, anticipating aircraft from Rabaul.

Around 0500 Burke's voice came cheerfully over the TBS. His destroyers were still to the west of Merrill's cruisers, and he requested permission to pursue the fleeing Japs. According to Captain Briscoe, Merrill's answer to this was,

ARLIE THIS IS TIP FOR GODS SAKE COME HOME WE'RE LONESOME

So Burke came steaming south with his seven DD's to keep the cruisers company.

"We were glad when those destroyers showed up," another cruiserman recalled. "As we pulled away from Empress Augusta Bay the radar screens broke out in a rash of aerial pips. It looked like a blizzard coming down from Rabaul."

Destroyer *Foote,* with her stern blown open, constituted a problem at this crisis. *Claxton* was ordered to take the disabled ship in tow, while *Ausburne* and *Thatcher* steamed as escorts. Vectored into position by a fighter-director team, 15 Allied aircraft flew to intercept the Jap planes racing down from the Bismarcks. Some 100 Jap carrier planes were too much for the Allied 15, and bulk of the defense fell upon Merrill's weary gun crews.

About 0800 the Jap aircraft attacked the retiring ships. The formation roared right over damaged *Foote,* some ten miles astern of the cruisers. Lamed though she was, *Foote* put up an umbrella of flak. No bombs were dropped upon her, and she saw a plane plunge into the sea.

Five minutes later, the Jap birds swooped down on Merrill's task force. He had the force disposed in a circular AA formation. As the bombers came over, he maneuvered to bring main batteries to bear, and the destroyers opened up with AA fire at about 14,000 yards.

Merrill described it in his Action Report:

> The scene was of an organized hell in which it was impossible to speak, hear, or even think. As the ships passed the first 90 degrees of their turn in excellent formation, the air seemed completely filled with bursting shrapnel and, to our great glee, enemy planes in a severe state of disrepair. . . . Planes were in flames as they passed over the flagship, exploding outside the destroyer screen. . . . Ten planes were counted in the water at one time, and seven additional were seen to crash well outside the formation.

At the height of the battle, Merrill ordered a 360° turn which kept the warship carousel steaming clockwise. All the gunners seemed to be catching prizes from the air. Three Japs bailed out in parachutes and landed almost in the center of the wheeling formation. "Bettys" blew up in the sky and exploded in the water. Of the 70 or 80 planes which attacked, perhaps two dozen were shot down (Jap figures were never forthcoming). The Japs landed only two hits on cruiser *Montpelier,* damaging a catapult and wounding one man. At 0812 they broke off the attack and ran northward, pursued by Allied fighter planes.

The Battle of Empress Augusta Bay and its aerial epilogue were over. On the sea and in the air the enemy had taken a colossal thrashing. A light cruiser and a destroyer sunk, two destroyers disabled, heavy cruiser *Myoko* dented by collision, heavy cruiser *Haguro* severely damaged—Omori's force slunk home in sorry defeat. In Merrill's force destroyer *Foote* was the one serious casualty, and even she would live to fight again. Cruiser *Denver* and destroyer *Spence,* with minor damage, would lose little time on the binnacle list.

LIGHT CRUISER *MONTPELIER* ARRIVED IN THE PACIFIC at the end of November. We meet again the young diarist, Seaman First Class James J. Fahey.

15.

"THEY CAN FORGET THAT

ISLAND FROM NOW ON."

Friday, November 19, 1943: Things are pretty quiet at Bougainville. I guess the Japs' back is broken. They can forget that island from now on.

They allowed a few men from each division to go on the beach this afternoon, for a few hours of recreation. There is nothing over there but jungle and swamp. There is a native village further inland but only officers are allowed there.

Some of the men who visited the *Denver* while she was in port said that twenty-five men were killed and many were wounded. The wounded consisted of men with broken backs, eyes blown out, bodies crushed, etc. The flooded compartments have sailors floating around in their waters. One of their dead, a chief, still had his pipe in his mouth. The odor from the bodies, still sealed aboard, is overwhelming. They cannot retrieve the bodies until dry dock is reached.

Sunday, November 21, 1943: We are still at Purvis Bay. A great many of the men are washing their blues. We have hopes of being in Australia by January of '44. We had movies on the forecastle for all hands as it was too hot below. Our regular movies were held in the hangar deck but because of the extreme heat, this was impossible.

Today I went to church services on Tulagi. This was the first time on the beach in over a month. We sang hymns. The same ones I used to sing in grammar school. It brought back memories. I could hear

485

the birds singing in the jungle. It's much better here than at Purvis. This time last year, the Marines were fighting the Japs on the same spot. The fighting that took place here was a nightmare. Now peace and quiet has returned. The Japs are buried close by. Many are sealed in caves that are not too far away. They refused to surrender. It was much easier to seal them in their natural graveyard than risk huge losses. All of the huts are made of big leaves cut from the jungle. It doesn't take the natives long to build a hut. The little church is also made of the same substance. Bamboo is also used in these crude living quarters. The floors are generally dirt. As for the natives, they are intelligent in appearance. A large cage is teeming with birds. I never saw such striking colors before. The birds were captured by the natives from the jungle. Some were of enormous size while others had a resemblance to parrots.

I spent quite a bit of time talking to a fellow who was on one of the invasion barges in action at Bougainville. He said that the Japs mowed down over 300 Marines in nothing flat while they were attempting a charge on the beach. That we were only taking a small part of Bougainville, enough for our airfields. The Japs were to be pushed back into the jungle and there they would starve. If an attempt was ever made to clear the island of Japs, the process would take years to accomplish. There are thousands of Japs there and many of them are veterans of the China War. When the airfield is in operation, Rabaul will be rendered useless. The Japs will be forced back to their powerful island of Truk approximately 700 miles away. Truk is the Pearl Harbor of the Japanese Empire. No white man has set foot on this island in over twenty-five years. A formidable fortress, Truk can boast of its thousands of troops stationed there, ready and waiting to defend its shores.

I returned to the ship after church services on Tulagi. The *Denver* left for the States today.

Wednesday, November 24, 1943: Sitting at anchor in Purvis Bay, we took on fuel today. Espiritu Santo in a few days is the word. I hope so. Nothing fit to eat in over a month. A troopship arrived this morning. It left this afternoon for Bougainville. It steamed up from the Fiji Islands. This will be the last ride for many of those troops. Some will come back crippled for life. Going, they are young and in the best of health. Returning, they are old and beaten shells that once were men. Troops are transported there nearly every day. Crowded landing barges are usually their lot. The barges are very small and many of the troops are stricken with seasickness. On rainy days they are herded below where the heat is unbearable and no air reaches them.

Yesterday, the destroyer *Foote* left for the States, half of its bow was blown off. It happened at Bougainville in our sea battle. The patch job was a credit to the Navy. Jap torpedoes were the damaging agent and it was a sight to behold.

A number of the men were diving off the side of the ship having a grand old time until an officer happened by. Result . . . No diving . . .

Twenty new "boots" are on board today. They arrived by transport. No movies last night on account of rain. One of the movies that we have viewed while here was *Edison, The Boy*. Mickey Rooney was the star. It was enjoyable.

About a month from now, summer begins. It's hot enough as it is. I can imagine what we will be in for weather-wise. For now, darkness creeps in at about 7 P.M. Listening to the news report, I learned that the invasion of Tarawa in the Gilberts has begun. It's over 1000 miles to the north of us, north of the equator. It gave no date of the invasion . . .

FIVE CLASSIC LINES SUMMED UP THE FIGHTING PHILOSophy of the extraordinary squadron leader, Arleigh A. Burke, then a Commander, and by war's end Admiral Marc Mitscher's Chief-of-Staff, a much-decorated hero who eventually rose to become the only three-term Chief of Naval Operations.

16.

DESRON 23 DOCTRINE

If it will help kill Japs—it's important
If it does not help kill Japs—it's not important
Keep your ship trained for battle!
Keep your material ready for battle!
Keep your boss informed concerning readiness for battle!

THE CLOSE OF THE YEAR MARKED THE BEGINNING OF
the effort to capture Rabaul, and the climax of the drive up through
the Solomons. The campaign finally ended in victory on February
15, 1944 when American troops landed in the Green Islands, one
hundred and twenty miles from Rabaul.

Behind lay bloody Guadalcanal—an epitaph, an enduring symbol
of American bravery and sacrifice.

488

PART V

THE MEDITERRANEAN AND FRANCE, VICTORY IN EUROPE

~~~~~~

IN JANUARY 1943, TWO MONTHS AFTER THE NORTH African landings and six months before the successful conclusion of the Tunisian campaign, a preliminary plan was drafted for Operation "Husky"—the invasion of Sicily. Predicated on the assumption that such an assault would extend Allied influence in the Mediterranean to the point where Italy would be forced to withdraw from the war, while Germany would undoubtedly have to divert a number of troops from the Russian front, the plan for "Husky" (ultimately set for July 10, 1944) envisioned an American force assembled in North Africa and a British force assembled in the Near East, converging on the mountainous, triangular-shaped island a few statute miles from the Italian mainland.

American naval might was again under Admiral H. Kent Hewitt, now three-stars, who established headquarters in Algiers on March 17 and shared a suite of offices with Commander in Chief Mediterranean, Fleet Admiral Cunningham, RN. While the two worked together on rough plans "like brothers", it was not until May 13 that Supreme Command reached a final decision as to how the ambitious assault was to be effectuated, by eight divisions over a hundred-mile front. On that day Hewitt learned that his Western Naval Task Force was to attack the south coast between Licata and Scoglitti, while the Eastern Force (British, under Vice Admiral Sir Bertram C. Ramsey) was to attack in the Gulf of Noto and along the Pachino Peninsula. Other measures were calculated to provide complete air supremacy, containment of the Italian fleet, and the seizure of Pantelleria in order to provide a base for fighter planes. After establishment of a beachhead, American and British troops were to capture Augusta, Catania and Gerbini Airfields, and thence move across the island and seize Messina, a primary objective of the invasion.

Charged with landing Patton's Seventh Army, the Western Naval Task Force was divided into three Attack groups:

Task Force 81 (DIME Force) was commanded by Rear Admiral John F. Hall, with the 1st Infantry Division embarked (Major General Terry Allen), one combat team of the 2nd Armored Division, and a Ranger battalion. This force was supported by thirteen destroyers and the light cruisers *Savannah* and *Boise,* and was responsible for landings at Gela.

Task Force 85 (CENT Force) under Rear Admiral Alan Kirk, with the 45th Infantry Division embarked (Major General Troy Middleton) was scheduled for landing at Scoglitti. In support were sixteen destroyers and the light cruiser *Philadelphia.*

Task Force 86 (JOSS Force) under Rear Admiral Richard L. Conolly, transported the 3rd Infantry Division (Major General Lucian K. Truscott—"You are about to meet the Boche. Carve your name in his face."), and two Ranger Battalions. Eight destroyers and light cruisers *Birmingham* and *Brooklyn* offered support for the Licata landings.

The British (Eastern Naval Task Force) were positioned on the right flank of Task Force 85, lifting five divisions of Montgomery's Eighth Army for landings between Pozallo and Cape Murro di Porco.

Thus was convened the greatest armada in history—greater even than at Normandy. Excluding landing craft lifted to the invasion aboard ship, there were more than 4000 British and American combat ships and beaching craft.

Practically speaking, Sicily's defense was in the hands of four Italian divisions, two Panzer divisions, and an undetermined number of German E-boats and Italian motor torpedo boats. So far as Mussolini's "fleet-on-paper" was concerned, it fortunately remained committed to the defense of the mainland.

Aboard Conolly's flagship *Biscayne* was the beloved correspondent Ernie Pyle. Esteemed by GI Joe for his warm human-interest stories filed for United Features Syndicate, thin, balding, forty-three-year-old Pyle was famed as a newspaperman who not only told the GI's story but also shared his unhappy lot in foxholes and shell craters. From his war memoirs, written a year before his life was snuffed out by a sniper's bullet on Ie Shima during the Okinawa invasion, we have a rare glimpse of Pyle aboard ship. He recounts the events from D-5, prior to the time that JOSS Force set sail from Bizerte, when that harbor was subjected to a particularly severe German air raid.

I.

INVASION PRELUDE

The sailors went into . . . action just as soldiers go into the first battle—outwardly calm but inside frightened and sick with worry. It's the lull in the last couple of days before starting that hits so hard. In the preparation period fate seems far away, and once in action a man is too busy to be afraid. It's just those last couple of days when there is time to think too much.

One of the nights before we sailed I sat in the darkness on the forward deck helping half a dozen sailors eat a can of stolen pineapple. Some of the men of the group were hardened and mature. Others were almost children. They all talked seriously and their gravity was touching. The older ones tried to rationalize how the law of averages made it unlikely that our ship out of all the hundreds involved would be hit. They spoke of the inferiority of the Italian fleet and argued pro and con over whether Germany had some hidden Luftwaffe up her sleeve that she might whisk out to destroy us. Younger ones spoke but little. They talked to me of their plans and hopes for going to college or getting married after the war, always winding up with the phrase "If I get through this fracas alive."

As we sat there on the hard deck—squatting like Indians in a circle around our pineapple can—it all struck me as somehow pathetic. Even the dizziest of us knew that before long many of us stood an excellent chance of being in this world no more. I don't believe one of us was afraid of the physical part of dying. That isn't the way it is. The emotion is rather one of almost desperate reluctance to give up the future. I suppose that's splitting hairs and that it really all comes under the heading of fear. Yet somehow there is a difference.

These gravely-yearned-for futures of men going into battle include so many things—things such as seeing the "old lady" again, of going to college, of staying in the Navy for a career, of holding on your knee just once your own kid whom you've never seen, of again becoming champion salesman of your territory, of driving a coal truck around the streets of Kansas City once more and, yes, even of just sitting in the sun once more on the south side of a house in New Mexico. When we huddled around together on the dark decks, it was these little hopes and ambitions that made up the sum total of our worry at leaving, rather than any visualization of physical agony to come.

Our deck and the shelf-like deck above us were dotted with small knots of men talking. I deliberately listened around for a while. Each group was talking in some way about their chances of survival. A dozen times I overheard this same remark: "Well, I don't worry about it because I look at it this way. If your number's up then it's up, and if it isn't you'll come through no matter what."

Every single person who expressed himself that way was a liar and knew it, but, hell, a guy has to say something. I heard oldsters offering to make bets at even money that we wouldn't get hit at all—two to one we wouldn't get hit seriously. Those were the offers but I don't think any bets actually were made. Somehow it seemed sacrilegious to bet on our own lives.

Once I heard somebody in the darkness start cussing and give this answer to some sailor critic who was proclaiming how he'd run things: "Well, I figure that captain up there in the cabin has got a little more in his noggin than you have or he wouldn't be captain, so I'll put my money on him."

And another sailor voice chimed in with "Hell, yes, that captain has slept through more watches than you and I have spent time in the Navy."

And so it went on one of the last nights of safety. I never heard anybody say anything patriotic, the way the storybooks have people talking. There was philosophizing but it was simple and undramatic. I'm sure no man would have stayed ashore if he'd been given the chance. There was something bigger in him than the awful dread that would have made him want to stay safe on land. With me that something probably was an irresistible egoism in seeing myself part of an historic naval movement. With others I think it was just the application of plain, unspoken, even unrecognized, patriotism.

For the best part of a week our ship had been lying far out in the harbor, tied to a buoy. Several times a day "General Quarters" would sound and the crew would dash to battle stations, but always it was only an enemy photo plane, or perhaps even one of our own planes. Then we moved in to a pier. That very night the raiders came and our ship got her baptism of fire—she lost her virginity, as the sailors put it. I had got out of bed at 3 A.M. as usual to stumble sleepily up to the radio shack to go over the news reports which the wireless had picked up. There were several radio operators on watch and we were sitting around drinking coffee while we worked. Then all of a sudden around four o'clock General Quarters sounded. It was still pitch-dark. The whole ship came to life with a scurry and rattling, sailors dashing to stations before you'd have thought they could get their shoes on.

Shooting had already started around the harbor, so we knew this time it was real. I kept on working, and the radio operators did too, or rather we tried to work. So many people were going in and out of the radio shack that we were in darkness half the time, since the lights automatically went off when the door opened.

Then the biggest guns on our ship let loose. They made such a horrifying noise that every time they went off we thought we'd been hit by a bomb. Dust and debris came drifting down from the overhead to smear up everything. Nearby bombs shook us up, too.

One by one the electric light bulbs were shattered by the blasts. The thick steel bulkheads of the cabin shook and rattled as though they were tin. The entire vessel shivered under each blast. The harbor was lousy with ships and every one was shooting. The raiders were dropping flares from all over the sky and the searchlights on the warships were fanning the heavens. Shrapnel rained down on the decks, making a terrific clatter.

The fight went on for an hour and a half. When it was over and everything was added up we found four planes had been shot down. Our casualties aboard were negligible—three men had been wounded —and the ship had suffered no damage except small holes from near-misses. Best of all, we were credited with shooting down one of the planes.

This particular raid was only one of scores of thousands that have been conducted in this war. Standing alone it wouldn't even be worth describing. I'm mentioning it to show you what a taste of the genuine thing can do for a bunch of young Americans. As I have remarked, our kids on the ship had never before been in action. The majority of them were strictly wartime sailors, still half civilian in character. They'd never been shot at and had never shot one of their own guns except in practice. Because of this they had been very sober, a little unsure and more than a little worried about the invasion ordeal that lay so near ahead of them. And then, all within an hour and a half, they became veterans. Their zeal went up like one of those sky-rocketing graph-lines when business is good. Boys who had been all butterfingers were loading shells like machinery after fifteen minutes, when it became real. Boys who previously had gone through their routine lifelessly had yelled with bitter seriousness, "Dammit, can't you pass those shells faster?"

The gunnery officer, making his official report to the captain, did it in these gleefully robust words: "Sir, we got the son of a bitch."

One of my friends aboard ship was Norman Somberg, aerographer third class, of 1448 Northwest 62nd Street, Miami. We had been talking together the day before and he told me how he'd studied journalism for two years at the University of Georgia, and how he wanted to get into it after the war. I noticed he always added, "If I live through it."

Just at dawn, as the raid ended, he came running up to me full of steam and yelled, "Did you see that plane go down smoking! Boy, if I could get off the train at Miami right now with the folks and my girl there to meet me I couldn't be any happier than I was when I saw we'd got that guy."

It was worth a month's pay to be on that ship after the raid. All day long the sailors went gabble, gabble, gabble, each telling the other how he did it, what he saw, what he thought. After that shooting, a great part of their reluctance to start for the unknown vanished, their guns had become their pals, the enemy became real and the war came alive for them, and they didn't fear it so much any more. That crew of sailors had just gone through what hundreds of thousands of other soldiers and sailors already had experienced—the conversion from peaceful people into fighters. There's nothing especially remarkable about it but it was a moving experience to see it happen.

When I first went aboard I was struck with the odd bleakness of the bulkheads. All paint had been chipped off. I thought it was a new and very unbecoming type of interior decoration. Shortly, however, I realized that this strange effect was merely part of the Navy procedure of stripping for action. Inside our ship there were many other precautions. All excess rags and blankets had been taken ashore or stowed away and locked up. The bunk mattresses were set on edge against the bulkheads to act as absorbent cushions against torpedo or shell fragments.

The Navy's traditional white hats were to be left below for the duration of the action. The entire crew had to be fully dressed in shoes, shirts, and pants—no working in shorts or undershirts because of the danger of burns. No white clothing was allowed to show on deck. Steel helmets, painted battleship gray, were worn during engagements. Men who stood night watches were awakened forty-five minutes early, instead of the usual few minutes, and ordered to be on deck half an hour before going on watch. It takes that long for the eyes to become accustomed to the darkness.

Before we sailed, all souvenir firearms were turned in and the ammunition thrown overboard. There was one locked room full of German and Italian rifles and revolvers which the sailors had got from front-line soldiers. Failure to throw away ammunition was a court-martial offense. The officers didn't want stray bullets whizzing around in case of fire.

Food supplies were taken from their regular hampers and stored all about the ship so that our entire supply couldn't be destroyed by one hit. All movie film was taken ashore. No flashlights, not even hooded ones, were allowed on deck. Doors opening on deck had switches just the reverse of refrigerators—when the door was opened the lights inside went out. All linoleum had been removed from the decks, all curtains taken down.

Because of weight limitations on the plane which had brought me to the ship, I had left my Army gas mask behind. Before departure, the Navy issued me a Navy mask, along with all the sailors. I was also presented with one of those bright yellow Mae West life preservers like the ones aviators wear.

Throughout the invasion period the entire crew was on one of two statuses—either General Quarters or Condition Two. "General Quarters" is the Navy term for full alert and means that everybody is on full duty until the crisis ends. It may be twenty minutes or it may be forty-eight hours. Condition Two is half alert, four hours on, four hours off, but the off hours are spent right at the battle station. It merely gives the men a little chance to relax.

A mimeographed set of instructions and warnings was distributed about the ship before sailing. It ended as follows: "This operation will be a completely offensive one. The ship will be at General Quarters or Condition Two throughout the operation. It may extend over a long period of time. Opportunities for rest will not come very often. You can be sure that you will have something to talk about when this is over. This ship must do her stuff."

The night before we sailed the crew listened as usual to the German propaganda radio program which featured Midge, the American girl turned Nazi, who was trying to scare them, disillusion them and depress them. As usual they laughed with amusement and scorn at her childishly treasonable talk.

In a vague and indirect way, I suppose, the privilege of listening to your enemy trying to undermine you—the very night before you go out to face him—expresses what we are fighting for.

WITH THE INVASION UNDERWAY, LET US LOOK IN ON Hewitt's flagship. The scene aboard *Monrovia,* in which Patton and his staff are embarked, is one of constant movement from communications office to bridge; of messages being coded and transmitted. The bridge is filled with anxious officers peering at sky and sea, worrying about the air cover. Screwed up in his admiral's seat, Hewitt is a study in concentration. A Vermonter and a recipient of the Distinguished Service Medal, the Admiral remains calm even on D-1 (doing double acrostics!), while the forces are headed northward and the weather begins to make up.

2.

UNDERWAY

By 1630, when Gozo had been sighted from the *Monrovia,* the wind was blowing from the west with a force of about 6/7 . . . It would make the coast on which we were to land, which had a NW-SE trend, a lee shore. We could not, of course, anticipate the sort of surf we might have encountered on the Moroccan coast in TORCH, but the chop might cause considerable difficulty. Subsequently, it was learned that General Eisenhower and Admiral Cunningham, on Malta, were so concerned with the weather as to have been on the point of postponing the operation. Luckily, they held on. At the time, my principal worry was that the landing craft might be so slowed as to delay unduly their arrival at their destination. This was a contingency which was effectively taken care of by Admiral Conolly, who dashed about in the *Biscayne,* shepherding his convoys, and having them cut corners, with the result that they were *exactly on time* in spite of the adverse conditions. When I observed the rolling of some of the British LCI(L)s, as they rounded Gozo, I could not but wonder how effective some of the troops were at first going to be. But perhaps they were all the more willing to get ashore. The Eastern Task Force, fortunately, would have a lee for its landing.

My mind was greatly relieved by the prediction of my efficient aerographer, Lieutenant Commander R. C. Steere (whose forecast of surf conditions off Morocco in TORCH had been so accurate), that the wind would probably subside greatly by 2200. This prediction again proved to be correct. As darkness fell, the shipping around Gozo made quite an inspiring sight. Ahead were our landing craft, inshore of us was British KMF-18, slightly behind schedule, and numerous British landing craft. Astern was Admiral Kirk's second section, which was then detached to proceed to the CENT assault area. Also coming in from the westward were the cruisers of the Covering Group, proceeding to take stations with their assigned assault groups.

. . . Much had already been accomplished by the strategic bombing command in attacking enemy air fields and in softening the beach defenses. To avoid premature disclosure of the point of attack, and consequent concentration of the defense, it had been necessary to follow initially a very general bombing program, with only casual attention to vital objectives, until the last day or so prior to the landing. This was a situation quite different from small island attacks in the Pacific where, with the enemy cut off by sea, the defenses could be bombed and shelled for days on end prior to an actual landing.

As we neared the coast, evidence of our air attacks was clearly visible in the A.A. fire, the flares, and the conflagrations noted at various points along the beach. The British beacon submarines were picked up on schedule, the transports arrived in their areas, and the work of getting out boats and disembarking the troops was commenced. Some of our own vessels were illuminated and silhouetted to us by searchlights played from the beach, but they did not seem to have been sighted by the enemy . . .

LET US PROJECT THE NAVY'S SUCCESSFUL ADVANCE TO the point where *all* forces have arrived at their assigned beaches . . . Off Scoglitti, aboard Kirk's flagship, *Ancon,* one is keenly aware of the presence of Lieutenant John Mason Brown, celebrated newspaperman turned naval officer. In 1942, at the age of forty-two, Brown resigned his post as drama critic of the New York *World-Telegram* and applied for a commission. Urbane, erudite and witty, he was known to the flagship for his unique broadcasts to all hands—informal accounts of what was happening on the Sicilian and, later, Normandy beachheads.

Here, Brown, who continually sought out combat assignments, reviews the approach and bombardment of Kirk's CENT force.

3.

BATTLE STATIONS

11:30 P.M., *July 9*

"H" hour, the hour of hours, is almost here. It is now 11:30 P.M., and the attack is scheduled to begin at 2:45 A.M.

When we passed Malta—unconquerable Malta—toward the middle of the afternoon, and later came to Gozo, we knew our next island was Sicily. We are near Sicily now, still moving towards it in the darkness. It will not be long before we reach our anchorage off Scoglitti on Sicily's southern shore.

Already we have had our hints of "D" day's approach. Throughout the afternoon the gray sky has been filled from time to time by coveys of Spitfires. Several convoys have come within sight on the lunging waters. Six aircraft, said to be hostile, were reported twelve miles away from us in the late twilight. Then, just about an hour ago, fires and flares were seen ahead, and distant guns were heard. It is towards these guns and fires that we are steering. The enemy is there. Even the extra slab of ice cream on the pie after tonight's steak dinner was a pleasant way of our being told that something extra was soon to be expected of us.

Let the cynical laugh, but we have seen something of a miracle tonight. All afternoon our hearts have grown the heavier with the increasing heaviness of the sea. Things have looked bad for us—very bad—these past eight hours or so. By some ugly mischance the first storm we have had in the Atlantic or the Mediterranean overtook us this afternoon when, having traveled so far, we were at last so near.

By 2:30 P.M. the Mediterranean was being swept by a 30-knot wind. As the waves rose under sullen skies, they subjected the little PC boats now with us to a terrible beating. The destroyers were surf-bathing uncomfortably. Even the largest transports were wobbling. One by one, three of their barrage balloons were blown away from them, as easily as a child's balloon slips through his fingers in the park. By 5 o'clock the gale had increased until, as darkness came on, the waves swelled into more and more sizable mountains. The PC boats were by then egg-shelling their way, not so much through as on the heavy seas. The prospect of trying to send landing craft into the beaches against such odds was disturbing, to put it mildly.

Many of us remembered the Spanish Armada's fate. We did not want to remember it, but we did. Nature had undone that formidable Spanish Task Force, dashed its galleons to pieces on the rocks, and scattered them, when in full and proud array it had reached England's shores. We were a far larger armada. Would we be the victim of the same misfortune?

The weather reports were encouraging. "The sea will calm before midnight," Lieutenant Commander John Corry had said from the beginning and kept on saying, even when the seas at hand grew rougher.

Then suddenly, a little while ago, the miracle of which I spoke occurred. No matter where you may be stationed, you must have felt it. The wind died down almost as abruptly as it had started. Look over the sides now in the faint light left by a storm-clouded quarter moon, which is nearing the horizon, and you will find the Mediterranean still choppy, still tossed by a heavy surf, but, compared to what it was only a short time back, as quiet as if God had put his hand on it. This ought to be the best of good omens.

Some transport planes, carrying our paratroops, were reported off to starboard shortly before I stumbled down from the bridge to find a place for this microphone on the floor of a darkened passage off the Chart Room. Although I could not see the planes, I heard the roar of their motors, full of power, full of defiance.

Midnight, July 9

Perhaps you can hear it. The distant gunfire of which I spoke last time has greatly increased. The fires are still burning on the beaches ahead. If anything, they are brighter, because we have been pushing quietly in to our anchorage. They cast a glow in the sky the way a city does at night. They are not easy to make out as yet. One of the fires looks as if it were a bit inland. In shape it is rectangular enough to be the outlines of a lighted airfield, which of course it is *not*.

These fires mean that our planes have been busy. So do the inquisitive enemy searchlights which have been sweeping the sky from the beaches to the west.

Scoglitti, our objective, must be about five miles away from us in the darkness just now. Our convoy is reaching its destination safely and without confusion.

If our first sight of Sicily has consisted of fires burning in the night on a land we cannot see, there is a reason for this. According to plans, the Northwest African Air Force was scheduled to conduct an air offensive throughout the whole Mediterranean area prior to our coming. By these heavy air attacks the Allies have sought to compel Axis air forces to withdraw from fighter range of the desired beaches in Sicily in order to maintain their own cities, industries, armies, and air bases.

Before daylight this morning a heavy bombing attack is scheduled to be made on all Sicilian airfields, and for the balance of the day a fighter group of approximately thirty-six planes is supposed to be maintained over each of Sicily's three main airfield centers. American fighter squadrons will be based on Malta and other near-by islands.

Those paratroopers we heard heading inland will have been dropped with others during the night in the area of the Task Force to our west. The guns we hear at first will not necessarily mean that the Italians and the Germans have spotted us. Most probably they will be anti-aircraft guns, called into action by our paratroopers and our transport planes.

12:45 A.M., July 10

That crunchy, bumpy noise you may have heard five minutes ago was our anchor on the way down. It's blacker than coal up here. Our ships are still slipping into position. They are gathering like conspirators. We can't see them, but we can feel them, the way in a dark room you know someone else has entered, is creeping past you, or is standing next to you.

A searchlight from time to time cuts the sky above the beaches. A few tracer bullets are being batted out, like hot baseballs, by the enemy's shore batteries. The sound of ack-ack can be heard inland.

Don't be alarmed by the submarine just off our port side. It's one of ours. I hear the sight of it cost a soldier his dinner. He had wandered out on deck to get some air and see the show in which he will soon take part. Tonight's second slab of ice cream and the see-sawing of the Mediterranean had not been getting along too well. The soldier was holding his head in his hands when, to his horror, one of his eyes rolled open to discover the periscope, the conning tower, and finally the whale's back of a submarine loom out of the tar-colored waves beside him. "Jesus Christ! he is reported to have said, at the same time that he said good-by to the ice cream and raced below.

Everything else is under control.

1:30 A.M., *July 10*

A great wave of planes—our planes—has swept over us. They were our transports coming out. Although only a few of them could be seen, all of them could be felt and heard. They mean that our 82nd Airborne Division paratroopers have been landed and are already at work.

The darkness up here has grown. It's hard to make out the person next to you on the Admiral's Bridge, unless in passing he just happens to be silhouetted against one of those fires still burning on the beaches.

The small boats should be in the water by now. One of ours has returned with Captain Mitchell, from some errand in the night. From transport after transport these small craft are being lowered. They must be filled with anxious men; the small boat men who are the point and glory of this Force.

Shortly before I came down, another wave of probably fifty of our transport planes has roared above us, heading out from Sicily, their mission completed, their paratroopers landed in the blackness of an unknown land.

Before the thunder of their motors could be heard, a lull appeared to have settled on the shores ahead. Then came the first faint drone of the approach, and some tracer bullets rose skyward, no doubt to greet them.

2:40 A.M., *July 10*

We are within five minutes of what should have been the time for "H" hour. But "H" hour has been delayed until 3:45 at the request of the Commander of Transports. Blame the choppy seas for this, and difficulties they have caused in getting the small boats out. So take time off to get your second wind.

Don't think that things have not been happening above, in spite of this delay. Do you remember those enemy searchlights which I have mentioned several times? Well, they have given us some uneasy moments. There's a hell of a lot of difference between our searchlights when they are looking for the enemy, and enemy searchlights when they are looking for us.

As far as I can make out, there have been three of these searchlights sweeping from the shore. When we were stealing in, and even after we reached our anchorage, they swept only the sky. They kept raking it back and forth, back and forth, sticking up like nervous white fingers in the darkness. They were after our planes then, and didn't seem to know we were here.

Even when they followed the transport planes out, these searchlights swung far above us—which was precisely what we kept hoping they would do. One of these beacons, however, carried its search toward the horizon until its lowered light hovered over our ships to port. Then it blinked and went out, apparently not having spotted anything of interest.

This made us breathe the easier.

But only for a while. Because in a few minutes those searchlights were in motion again. The same one that had blinked before, woke up in alarm. When it came on, it was aiming straight above it at the sky, which was still all right with us. Then it began circling its light out to sea, lower and lower each time, until it started skimming the waves. In its sweep it landed on one of our ships lying at an angle. It paused there for an awful time before starting to move again. Then it swung slowly past the other vessels ahead, seeming to halt for the same awful time on each one of them, icing them with light or showing them up as silhouettes, as neat and black as you will ever find on any Ship Identification cards.

The beacon finally reached us. Our turn came just the way it used to in school. Waiting for it wasn't pleasant. The light cut closer and closer until it was full upon us, blinding us when we looked straight at it. It wasn't hard, then, to make out the faces on the Admiral's

Bridge. It would have been hard *not* to make them out. The faces of the men up there looked the way an actor's face does without make-up under a spotlight. You know that sallow look? Even the ship's gray was lighter than the sun at midday had ever made it.

I thought they had found us. I couldn't see how they had missed us.

"Can they see us?" I asked Captain Wellings, our Gunnery Officer.

"No. We can see them all right," he smiled, "but I don't think they can see us on a night like this. Anyway we are out of their range of vision."

This was good news. It still is.

With such targets as these three enemy beacons screaming for attention, our gunners must be going crazy. But so far they have managed to hold on to their itchy fingers and keep the secret of our being here—if it still is a secret.

Those guns, those deep-throated, distant guns you may hear, don't belong to us. They are British and come from the east coast. From the sound of them the show must be on there. And on in a big way.

3:15 A.M., *July 10*

The searchlights are still at it. When I got back to the bridge, it looked for a moment as if a gunner on a near-by ship had blown one of them out. Since we are said to be outside their seeing range, the moment this gunner let go wasn't an entirely happy one. His wanting to fire was human enough. There was the beacon ahead, begging for attention. And there was the gunner eager to oblige. It would have been as simple as that if, by releasing his tracers, he had not given away the secret of our being here.

As these tracer bullets arched through the sky, some words— almost as hot—shot out on the bridge.

For a few minutes the light went out. Then another of the three beacons came on, sweeping the ships in earnest. It was followed by the third. Before long the first light blazed out, now on again, now off again, like a lightning bug. The gunner had missed his mark. He has been answered by tracer bullets coming out from the shore.

At 3:10 there was a big explosion on the beach ahead. For a fearful moment it blew the darkness away as if it were smoke, putting fire in its place.

Since I made my last report, the huge British guns have continued booming to the east. The sky has become fairly active. Some red and white tracers have been chasing one another inland, following a high, arched course. Three enemy parachute flares, dropped from a plane or planes coming in from west of Scoglitti, have been hung off our starboard bow.

The orchestra is warming up. The stage is set. The curtain is scheduled to go up in a few minutes now.

4:15 A.M., *July 10*

The Fourth of July was never like this! These are the biggest fireworks I've ever seen. Our guns have really been speaking up, and it looks like they are much more than just big talkers. The sky is as bright as a summer parasol with the sunlight streaming through it.

The darkness is fighting a losing battle. Light is everywhere. Never for long. Always changing. Always in the swiftest motion. Then the night seeps back, only to be driven away again. Overhead it's all dots and dashes that you can see, quivering as they race to rise and fall; dots and dashes, and streamers of heat, and rockets overtaking rockets.

Light and noise. The noises are as different as the lights. There's the froglike *glump* of flak as it thuds through the water after a brief splash. There's the staccato stitching of the 20- and 40-millimeters. There's a sigh, a whine, and a whistle coming from something—I don't know what.

There are big guns, little guns, medium-sized guns—all of them fluent, and all of them demanding to be heard from, whether they are on the ships around us, in the Task Force ahead, with the enemy on shore, or the British to the east. The big guns bellow in a full, damp, dull tone. They sound the way a goldfish bowl might sound if—water and all—it exploded in your tummy.

Under this flaming cover the small landing boats have been pushing into shore. Bright as the sky is, the sea is still so dark that I have been able to see the Viking outlines of only a few of our little boats. But once in a while, in the din, the sputter of their motors has been heard.

Our big guns appear to have got two of those prying searchlights. They have been snuffed out for quite a while. It was a cruiser, I think, that scored a bull's-eye on one of them. The beacon scarcely had time to wink. Then it was done for.

Those planes are enemy planes. Although there don't seem to be many of them, there are enough. So far as I can make out, they came toward us in the uppermost darkness, under which all the lights are sandwiched. During the last half hour they have been hurtling back and forth, heard but not seen, and not leaving us unseen.

They headed for our beaches, dropping flares over them. Then they turned wheel for us, particularly for our cruisers, still dropping flares. The flares have been both to port and starboard. One of them has hung right over our Force like an old-fashioned light over a dining room table.

They are strange things, these German flares; disturbing but completely undisturbed. All the other lights are twitchy, nervous, explosive, darting. But these flares have a fearsome serenity. The parachutes supporting them do more than rest on the air. They doze there, as calm and unmoving as if they were beyond the law of gravity.

The other lights are momentary. These appear to be eternal. The others kindle the air around them with sparks, and then dash on or out. These just hang like fixtures. They are bright enough to cast shadows on the bridge, which up until now has been dark, except for that stab by the beacon.

They burn singly, these flares. Without warning a street lamp comes on, far up in the sky, blinding enough to be burning a whole city's current, and the sea below lights up the way Broadway used to look. This street lamp stays on for what seems an eternity, almost without moving. When it at last goes off and you begin to breathe again, another street lamp—the twin of its parent—bursts into light some yards below the first. If anything it is brighter than its predecessor, because it is nearer. Then the same thing happens again and again, and this necklace of light gradually extends itself, showing its stones one by one, until the final pendant dangles just above you.

The Germans can't be accused of leaving us in the dark. But so far they have only shed light. We have done our bit, too. Our tracers are arching on these flares from all sides. And a big fire is burning on a hill to starboard.

Good news. Word has just been received that initial landings have been accomplished on all of our beaches, and that, in general, slight opposition has been met with from the ground forces of the enemy.

This means that the little boats from all our transports have pushed in, wave by wave, to their designated landing places and that our troops have established themselves on shore. For the details we shall have to wait. What matters is that the Sicilian invasion is by now a fact.

The sky is still noon-bright up here in splotches. There have been more flares. More enemy planes, too. One of these has falconed down towards the *Spelvin,* its motors angry, as if to dive-bomb us. It was a rumble, a roar, a rumble again—and a bad moment. As a matter of fact, being anchored here in the light—waiting—has given us a lot of bad moments; though, thank God, so far only to think about.

6 A.M., *July 10*

It's dawnish up here now. Sicily's coast line has begun to take shape. It is still indistinct; still part of the vanishing night. Far inland, to starboard, the kind of mountain Mount Etna might be, if only it were within seeing range, is slowly working its way into the dawn. The pink-blue daylight is creeping down to the beaches. You might expect to hear birds. Instead the sky rattles with anti-aircraft fire and the hurried booming of the big guns on our cruisers and destroyers, and that near-by British monitor. The shore line also rumbles every now and then with battle sounds like a kettledrum.

The Admiral's Bridge was dark the last time I felt my way up to where Lieutenant Burton was standing. But only for a minute. At 5:20, directly ahead of us, a great blob of light bleached and reddened the sky, tearing the night into shreds. It was followed by a blast more sullen and deafening than any we have so far heard. What we saw scattered across the sky was a ship from the Task Force to the west of us.

We had scarcely been able to say, "Look! They got one!" when the German planes which had done the getting could be seen flocking towards us. Again there were not many. Again there were enough. Say, six; flying low, leaving a trail of big splashes behind them in the water where their bombs had fallen. One of them slanted down across our bow, barely missing the cruiser off our port side.

While these planes have swung back and forth, we have been watching the sky for more than them. We have been waiting, waiting, for those promised British Spitfires to come to us from Malta and give us cover.

They must have been a little late. They were due over us at 5.

They would have been welcome then. They were no less welcome only a few minutes ago, when they were sighted off our stern. They are equally welcome now, when, like birds of deliverance, they have flown across us, high, high up in perfect formation, sweeping the copper-colored sky.

As a matter of fact I'm afraid they were too warmly welcomed by some of our gunners, who knew just enough about aircraft identification to be sure that anything with wings must be a target. Fortunately the Spitfires were out of range. No less fortunately they are with us. We can all feel the more comfortable now.

6:30 A.M., July 10

You can see Scoglitti now to port. It's a group of drab white houses clustered around a church tower. The beaches on either side of it could be any beaches seen in the freshness of an early morning, if it were not for the little boats nudging into them and the swarming dots visible through binoculars on the sands. The fields and slight hills backing these beaches could be any peaceful hills and fields, if it were not for the smoke rising here and there from fires burning on them. Even so, they look almost as tranquil as if they were the Contour Maps, increased in scale and come to life.

The sea and the sky are different. They are full of war. The ships in our Task Force are all around us. They look refreshed by the morning sun, and are unhurt. Our gunners continue to pivot, covering whatever passes in the sky.

It's quieter up here, though one of our destroyers has been blazing away at a shore battery that has been firing on her from one of the hills.

The unloading shuttle service has started.

7:15 A.M., July 10

We are weighing anchor now to move closer in to shore.

The Spitfires have been patrolling once more. They have come back again and again, in spite of their warm welcome.

Everyone topside has been nibbling on or at "K" rations and feels the better for coffee, with its illusion of breakfast.

Most of the shore batteries are silenced by now, due to the spectacular accuracy of Naval gunnery. One by one they have been snuffed out like candles.

Some jeeps have been lowered into the landing boats panting

alongside of us. And the LCT's are now going in, rolling quite a bit and crowded with boys in khaki, only a few of whom look seasick and are holding their heads. These LCT's have been escorted and given fire cover by our destroyers. The Army is leaving us in large numbers. As it does so, one of our cruisers is thundering away at an inland target, and a big fire is burning on the beach to port.

8 A.M., July 10

For the moment, all's quiet. We have just dropped anchor. And after shaking hands with the Admiral, General Middleton of the 45th Division has gone ashore. In the same boat with him went Clark Lee, the INS correspondent. Fires are still smoking off the beaches, and guns rumbling intermittently.

The chief news is that there seems to have been no serious opposition. A message from shore says, "Considerable artillery and prisoners taken."

THE GELA LANDINGS COMMENCED FOR REAR ADMIRAL Hall's DIME Force at midnight of the 10th along a 5000-yard stretch of beach. Aboard transport *Barnett* was Col. John W. Bowen's 25th Regimental Combat Team and the gifted novelist Jack Belden. When the first wave of LCVP's struck out for Beach Blue, a long, rough ride from the line of demarcation, Belden was present.

4.

"SHOOT OUT

THAT GODDAMN LIGHT!"

"Go to your debarkation stations."

The voice on the loud-speaker rang with a harsh metallic note through the wardroom.

The men sat up and blinked their eyes, and for a moment all of them stared at each other with expressions that seemed to say: "This is it." Then a few of them broke out in foolish grins and rose slowly from their chairs . . .

It was pitch-dark in the passageways. In the inky blackness men stumbled against each other, but no one uttered a word. In silence we made our way toward the bulkhead door through which a little light from the boat deck outside shone. As we passed through the door, a hand reached out and squeezed each one of us briefly on the arm. "Good luck," said a voice. It was the chaplain.

The moon was still shining dimly on the deck, but though we could now see, we clung close to each other for fear of becoming separated. From every passageway men, shuffling in dreary, silent attitudes, were coming out to swell the tide of those going in on the assault waves. They made a depressing sight—a composite of dead and dull faces and drab bodies loaded down with military gear. As we turned the corner of a bulkhead, the man ahead of me halted hesitantly before a boat which was swinging violently back and forth, first toward the deck and then away from it. Several voices behind us

511

shouted and tried to allay any feelings of doubt we had. As we hesitated, they shouted cheerfully: "Get in. What are you waiting for?"

These words, spoken to show us that we were at the right boat, did not produce the action desired. The man who was leading our group paused on hearing those words, raised his hands in a helpless gesture and called back to the others: "I can't get in." As he said this, the men back of us yelled as if they were going to throw a fit. The leading soldier, however, remained adamant and made no move to get in the boat.

From my vantage point, it was evident that he was quite right in refusing to do so. The boat was rocking to and fro on its davits, coming close against the ship's side at one moment and swinging far away at the next. The only way to enter the boat was to slide down a short knotted line and drop in. But to attempt to drop in that swinging boat would be suicidal. One slight slip would mean a plunge down into the water, which was slapping now with a loud and menacing sound against the ship's side below us. So both the soldier and I remained standing where we were, looking at the dark void between the swinging boat and the ship, making no attempt to get in.

The crowd behind us, growing impatient, again yelled imperatively at us. Goaded by the angry voices, the soldier by me said: "Goddamit, there's no one here. Where the hell's the navy?" At these words, the men behind us transferred their disapproval from us to the whole American Navy.

"Dammit! Get some sailors!" one officer yelled.

As yet the delay had not been serious, but in our overwrought state of mind it assumed exaggerated proportions, increasing our nervousness to a state of shaking, angry doubt.

"God!" said an officer who had come up beside us, "if we can't get our boats launched from the ship, what's it going to be like in the water when they start shooting at us?"

The soldier by my side laughed bitterly. "Snafu! That's us. Always snafued."

At last two or three sailors arrived, the boat was secured firmly, the soldiers slid one by one down the knotted ropes, and the boat descended past the ship's side into the choppy water.

As we drew away from the ship, our moment's irritability dropped away from us as quickly as it had come. There was an immediate sense of gladness at getting started and a heightened awareness. When

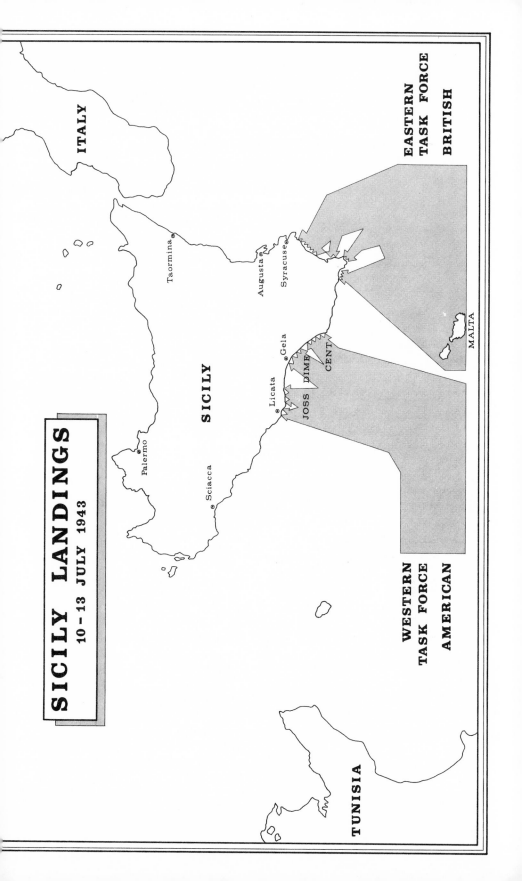

we got away from the shelter of the fleet, this feeling, however, soon gave way to another. We became sick.

The rocking of the small landing craft was totally unlike anything we had experienced on the ship. It pitched, rolled, swayed, bucked, jerked from side to side, spanked up and down, undulated, careened and insanely danced on the throbbing, pulsing, hissing sea. The sea itself flew at us, threw the bow in the air, then, as it came down, swashed over us in great roaring bucketfuls of water.

The ensign standing on the high stern of the boat ordered the sailor by the bow to close the half-open ramp. As he moved to do so, the helmsman in the stern yelled: "I can't see. . . ."

He did not finish his sentence. At that moment there was a loud hissing sound, then a dull squashing crash, and a wave of water cascaded through the ramp, throwing down those who were standing on the deck and overrunning the boat with water.

"Bail with your helmets!" called the ensign in a voice of extreme irritation.

Kneeling now in the puddle which sloshed up and down the length of the boat, the men scooped up the water with their helmets, staggered uncertainly to their feet, threw their load overboard and then went down on their knees again to repeat the process.

Meanwhile, the ensign kept the boat zigzagging over the water searching in the sea for the boats of our assault wave. From time to time he would shout out to another boat: "Are you the second wave?" When he would receive a negative answer, he would curse loudly, turn the boat in another direction and begin searching again.

For a long time we coursed back and forth over the water, picking up one boat here and another there. Then we went into a circle, going round and round in the shadow of our fleet till, certain that every boat was present, we broke out of the circle formation and headed in a line toward a blue light, which, shining to seaward, was bobbing up and down some distance ahead of us.

The uneven motion of the boat was now almost unbearable. Hemmed in between the high steel bulkheads of the boat, the men crouched like beasts, shivering from the cold spray, silent, but uneasy with imminent sickness. One by one they vomited, holding their heads away from their loosely clasped rifles, and moaned softly. One man clambered up the side of the boat and crawled out on the narrow ledge running around the top and clung there like a monkey, with one hand clasping the boat and the other fumbling at his pants. The boat was rocking heavily; the man was swaying with its motion, and it seemed momentarily as if he would fall into the sea or a wave would wash him overboard. The ensign in a sharp voice commanded him to get back inside the boat.

"I have to move my bowels, Sir," the man said in a tone of distressed pain.

Someone tittered.

"Jesus! What's so funny about that?" said a soldier, and he got up and grasped the man, who was now half-hanging over the side by his shoulders. "Here, Joe," he said, "hold on to me."

From that time on, our dash toward the unseen shore became a nightmare of sickness, pain and fear. The boat had gathered speed now and we were beginning to bound from one wave crest to the next with a distinct shock. There were no thwarts, no seats of any kind in the boat; only the deck itself to sit on and the steep, high hull of the boat to lean against. The motion of the boat threw us all against one another. My hand in bracing my rolling body had accidentally come to rest on the shoulder of a young boy. I looked down at him and saw that he was holding his head in both of his hands and quietly vomiting. "It's the motion that gets you," I said.

"The what?" the boy said.

"The motion. It's different from on the ship. You'll get used to it. You'll be all right."

"Oh, sure. The motion. You ain't kiddin'. I'll be all right." He bent his head down, a sudden spasm contracting his shoulders, and he spewed from the mouth. "Oh, sure, I'll be all right."

I stood up and took a quick look over the boat's side. Astern our great fleet fled, diminishing, sinking beneath the waves. The boat had begun to pitch and shudder now, swooping forward and down, jolting almost stationary for a moment, then lifting and swooping again; a shot of spray smashed aboard over the bows like a thrown bucket of water, and I knelt down again.

The boat pounded on. It rolled us against iron pipes, smashed us against coils of wire and jammed us on top of one another, compounding us with metal, water and vomit. There was nothing we could do but wait, herded helplessly between the high, blank walls of the boat, huddled together like blind men not knowing where we were going or what was around, behind or ahead of us, only looking at one another with anxious eyes. That not being able to tell what was ahead of us, to catch even one slight glimpse of the universe outside our tossing, rocking world, was almost unbearable, leaving us, as it did, prey to all manner of nighttime fancies. The unnatural and unwholesome motion of the boat, churning my stomach into an uproar, the bare and opaque walls of the hull, shutting out everything but the vault of the sky overhead, evoked in my mind a picture of the world outside that was fantastic and terrifying. Instead of feeling myself part of a group of American soldiers going ashore on a carefully planned invasion, I saw myself and the men as strange phantoms flung out across the maw of the sea, into the blackness of eternity, fast revolving away from any kind of world we ever knew. I felt as if we had been caught up in some mysterious rocket, and that we were being borne onward in this bouncing projectile of machinery toward a nether-world goal as incapable of taking command over our own destinies as a squirrel in a cage.

In a moment of hollow doubt I stood up, edging my eyes over the gunwale and looking out into the comparative world of light around us. The sea was sparkling with tossed spray. Ahead, and on either side of us, boats were dodging and twisting through the choppy waves, and from their sterns, waving from side to side with the motion of the boats, showers of gleaming water streamed out behind like the plumes of birds. What was causing the water to gleam was a wide streak of light. It sprang like the tail of a stationary comet from a ball of incandescent yellow that was shining on the edge of the blackness off to our left.

Suddenly, the light swung across the water, fastened on our boat and illuminated us like actors on a darkened stage. In the glare, I saw the green, pale faces of the soldiers and their bodies huddling close against the hull. Then the light shot past and over us.

"Why don't they shoot out that goddam searchlight?" growled a voice from the depths of the cavernous boat. "Jesus! We'll be drowned without knowing what hit us!"

"Steady there!" said the voice of Captain Paul Carney. "Take it easy."

Again I craned my neck upward, just getting the top of my helmet above the hull and looking out with fascinated eyes. The light had now swung onto a small group of boats which were thrashing wildly from side to side trying to escape off into the darkness. From somewhere ahead faint red flashes began to flicker like fireflies. Then red balls, describing a high arc like a tennis lob, arched over our heads and fell down toward the illuminated boats which could not seem to shake off the hunting glare of the searchlight. At this I drew in my breath and involuntarily I shouted: "They're shooting at the boats." Below me, from the soldiers crouching with their heads toward the bottom of the boat, floated up an echo: "Shooting at the boats—Jesus!"

Abruptly, our boat slowed down. Above me, and slightly to the right, hung a blue light, seemingly suspended in the air. Dimly I discerned the outlines of a naval patrol vessel. Out of the darkness above mysteriously came a metallic voice: "Straight ahead! Go straight ahead. You'll see a small light on your right. Land there. Look out for mines. Good luck."

It was all very eerie—rocking there on the sea and hearing a voice calling out of the black above us. But I had no time to think of this. Our engine gave a sudden full-throated roar as the ensign cut off the underwater exhaust. The boat leapt forward. The other boats behind us raced around to either side of us, and we sped forward like a charging football line. "Hurry!" I thought. "God! If we can only make it!" The sea cascaded through the ramp and a broadside of water catapulted down on us. The boat shuddered, bucked, then plunged onward in a confident show of power.

All my senses were not alerted to the straining point. A flush of thrill and excitement shot through me like flame. It was wonderful. It was exhilarating.

Smash! Pound! Roar! Rush!—toward the goal. Here we come! Wheee! My mouth was open and I giggled with insane laughter.

The sailor by the bow tapped me on the shoulder. I peered around. The boy was pointing. Ahead—directly ahead—two strings of dotted red lights were crossing each other. They came out from right and left, like two necklaces of strung red and black beads, and crossed each other in the air some distance before us.

"Machine guns!" the sailor shouted. "Theirs." The little fireflies of light were growing very close now. "Going right through them!" the sailor shouted. He made a gesture with his hand across his throat. "Right through them."

Snap! I heard a sharp cracking sound. Snap! Snap! Snap! Jittering, I ducked down below the side of the boat. Then I half slid, half fell to the deck, huddling low with the rest of the soldiers. I was on fire inside, but outside I was cold. I could feel all my flesh jerking. It was not from excitement. No longer did I feel any thrill. The boat was pitching and rocking like a roller coaster. I knelt now and was sick. Gasping for breath I wiped the strings of sputum from my lips, drawing my sleeve across my chin. Dimly I saw the boy beside me on all fours with his mouth wide open and his head bent down. I tried to pull myself together and sidled over and held his head. My gesture was almost automatic. I told myself I had to be of some use. But I no longer cared about anything. The boat seemed to be spinning like a merry-go-round. Dazed, I wished that a shell would come along and end all this horror, wetness and misery. If we could only get out of this insanely rocketing prison. If the boat would only stop for just a moment.

Soon I was almost beyond feeling. All I knew was that we were enclosed in an infernal machine, shuddering through the darkness, toward the edge of the world, toward nowhere. I did not feel the boat slow down. I neither heard nor saw men get to their feet. At first, all I felt was a violent shudder. Then I heard the engine break out into a terrible throbbing roar. At last, there was a jerk and a bump and the boat came to a halt.

"Open ramp!" shouted the ensign at the stern.

Glancing fearfully toward the bow of the boat, I saw it swinging down, like a huge jaw opening. Halfway down it stopped, stuck. We would see nothing. Only a half-open hole.

The soldiers stared at the hole as if fascinated. Grappling at the side of the boat, they pulled themselves to their feet, and peered uncertainly out into the darkness through the ramp. For a brief moment they stared at each other, then bent their heads down, shuffling their feet. No one moved.

The ramp jerked down farther until it was level with the water. Still nothing could be seen. Still no one moved.

"Get off!" Major Grant's voice was imperious.

No one moved.

"Jump off!" he hollered again. "You want to get killed here? Get on that beach!"

With these words he leapt out into the darkness. Another man with a coil of wire followed. The others hesitated as if waiting to see what happened to those who had jumped.

I felt I would go crazy if I stayed in the boat any longer. I advanced to the ramp. "Here it comes," I thought and jumped.

The water struck me like a shock. I kept going down. "It's over my head," I thought. My feet sank down and touched bottom. My chin was just at the water. I started to push forward. A sharp crackle burst the air near by. There was a whine and whizz overhead. Then a metallic, plunking sound as if something was striking the boat.

The water was growing shallower. I bent my knees, keeping only my helmet-covered head above the water. I felt as if I were wearing a shield. Finding I wasn't hit, I realized the machine-gun fire was so far surprisingly light. "Hell!" I said to myself, "this is not as bad as the Mareth Line."

It was dark. The fires that had been visible from the ship could not be seen here. Ahead of me I made out a sandy beach, rising in a slight slope. Figures were crawling on hands and knees up the slope. Every few moments they halted and lay flat on their stomachs. By now the water was really shallow. I straightened up and dashed for the beach. Bullets snapped overhead. I threw myself flat on the sand. At last, I was on dry land.

AXIS REACTION TO THE MULTI-PRONGED INVASION was swift and violent, with shore batteries, Stuka dive-bombers and Hermann Göring tanks effecting the loss of several ships and personnel carriers. Minesweeper *Sentinel* was among the first to be sunk, the victim of an enemy dive-bomber at Licata. In Gela, where Darby's Rangers made a splendid stand with the help of Navy pin-point gunfire, the Nazis hurled shells from 100-mm coastal guns and eased in tanks for support. There at 4:58 A.M. destroyer *Maddox* took a Stuka bomb under her starboard propeller guard which completely demolished her stern. She sank two minutes later with a heavy loss of life. An officer on a nearby ship described the explosion: "A great blob of light bleached and reddened the sky, tearing the night into shreds. It was followed by a blast more sullen and deafening than anything we have heard so far." Fierce land fighting and unique Navy versus tank battles characterized the Scoglitti landings. In the British sector, where essentially the same type of fighting was experienced, air activity was greater, and the toll was heavier. Subsequent events at Sicily were marked by increased Axis air activity and fierce tank engagements, of which we are told by Theodore Roscoe, whom we have met before.

5.

END OF A CAMPAIGN

Had some prewar class in destroyer gunnery been informed that DD's might one day tangle with enemy tanks, skeptics might have answered with an incredulous, "Oh, yeah?" Yet as World War II progressed, destroyer gunners found themselves shooting at practically everything on the sea, under the sea, in the air—and on land. Even tanks.

In the American sector of southwest Sicily the Germans had available some 60 tanks. Around 0830 of D Day morning about 30 of these crawling armored monsters—members of the famous Hermann Göring Panzer Division—were spotted on the upland roads above Gela, lumbering down from the foothills, eager to gore and chew their way across the "Dime" area beachheads.

Spotting planes flashed the alarm. And "alarm" was the word for it. At that hour the assault forces had not yet landed their anti-tank guns or the heavy artillery to cope with such tanks. Nor did the Army at that date possess weapons which could readily demolish these Hermann Göring models. In the path of this rumbling herd, troops of the American 1st Division were directly threatened. Something had to be done to stop the enemy tanks, and stop them soon. The call went out for Navy gunfire.

Cruiser *Boise* and destroyer *Jeffers* took the leading tanks under fire at 0830. The cruiser's salvos ruined at least one tank and perhaps disabled others. However, some of them, scattering, nosed steadily forward until they reached Gela's outskirts, and others debouched across the coastal plain at the mouth of the Acate Valley.

Then destroyer *Shubrick* (Lieutenant Commander L. A. Bryan) hurled shells at a tank column on the Gela-Ponte Olivo road. Other "Dime" destroyers, moving to firing positions some 800 yards off the beach, blazed away at the Hermann Göering specimens. Not long after the destroyers opened fire, the tanks turned tail and returned, leaving several burned out hulks behind them.

They were back again the morning after D-Day. To the destroyers *Boise* relayed the word from her spotter, and the DD's once more squared off for a tank-shot.

This time the anti-tank gunnery featured the marksmanship of destroyers *Laub* (Commander J. F. Gallaher) and *Cowie* (Commander C. J. Whiting). On fire-support mission in the joint "Dime-Cent" fire-support area, the two DD's flung pinpoint salvos at the Göerings as they came snorting across the Gela plain.

Scorched by shellfire, the tank group turned this way and that in a desperate effort to find cover. Several tanks were exploded by hits. Others, disabled, sat down on their haunches and burned. Fourteen demolished tanks were counted on the field by the time the enemy retreated and the cruiser-destroyer barrage was over.

Laub was credited with the destruction of at least four tanks. *Cowie* was also commended as a big-game hunter. And "Nimrod" honors were divided among the other destroyers in on the shooting.

So Gela, in American hands by D-Day afternoon, remained in American hands. Excerpt from the Action Report of Admiral Hewitt:

> The amphibious assaults (at Sicily) were uniformly successful. The only serious threat was an enemy counterattack . . . against the 1st Infantry Division when a German tank force drove across the Gela plain to within one thousand yards of the Dime beaches. The destruction of this armored force by naval gunfire delivered by U.S. cruisers and destroyers, and the recovery of the situation through naval support, was one of the most noteworthy events of the operations.

Tanks were not the only enemy at Gela. In the morning twilight Axis aircraft struck the "Dime" area with cyclone fury. During this raid, the transport *Barnett* was hit, and two other transports were clawed by fragments.

About 1415 the enemy again roared over the coast. And later in the afternoon a flight of Heinkels and Focke-Wulfs attacked. Liberty ship *Robert Rowan,* heavy-laden with ammunition, was hard hit. Destroyer *McLanahan* steamed to the rescue of survivors. About two hours after she was disabled, the *Rowan* blew up like a gargantuan bomb, and part of her wreckage, in shallow water, served as a flaming beacon for enemy bombers that evening.

Between 2150 and 2300, Axis aircraft struck in a series of vicious attacks. The planes dropped magnesium flares to light the targets, and bombs fell on the "Dime" ships in cascades, clumps, and clusters. Cruiser *Boise* and every destroyer in the area, with the exception of *Jeffers,* were shaken by close straddles. Shrapnel of a near miss closely shaved destroyer *Murphy,* and *McLanahan* was shaved by a close one that bounced her stern out of the water.

Mindful of the doom which smote *Maddox,* the destroyer gunners manning the AA batteries put up a sky-searing aerial barrage. *Gherardi* and *Shubrick* scored during this battle.

Another destroyer in the thick of the action was *Benson.* In company with *Plunkett* and *Niblack,* she had that afternoon been screening some minelayers while they buoyed a minefield off Gela. At sunset she joined the destroyer screen around the threatened transport anchorage. At 2155 enemy planes dropped three flares directly astern of the destroyer, brilliantly illuminating the *Benson* and several nearby transports.

At once the ships in the vicinity opened fire on the flares with close-range automatic weapons. In the heat of excitement, elevation safety-angles were disregarded. Hot steel sang, whipped, and ricochetted around the ships in a wild fusillade that endangered all hands. *Benson*'s main battery director-shield was struck by a stray 20mm. projectile, and the blast knocked out her FD radar. Unable to see any planes, *Benson's* gunners restrained their fire, if not their vocabulary.

Benson's Action Report was eventually endorsed with this warm notation:

> The indiscriminate use of 20 mm. guns at unseen targets or targets out of range has resulted in injuries to personnel and material in adjacent ships. . . . Strict fire discipline is necessary and must be continuously stressed.

About 2200 several medium bombs blasted close aboard *Benson,* slashing her starboard side with shrapnel. The destroyer's captain,

Lieutenant Commander R. J. Woodaman, and 18 of the crew were wounded in this and a succession of dive-bomber onslaughts which ensued. *Benson* fought off the planes and was still shooting at 2306 when all destroyers in the area were ordered to lay smoke screen—a measure which brought down the curtain on that night's air battle.

Grimed and sweaty, the Navy gun crews had learned a basic law of gunnery—that friendly projectiles, recklessly fired, can be as dangerous as enemy bombs.

The terrible impartiality of projectiles was demonstrated again in the early hours of the 12th, when 24 Allied planes through error were shot down by American naval batteries and shore guns. By a ghastly blunder the planes had been sent on a course which differed from the one that had been announced—a fatal error which cost the lives of many British paratroopers.

While "Operation Husky" was featured by crack sharpshooting, it also emphasized the drastic need for careful gunhandling, target recognition, and a strict adherence to scheduled moves through zones otherwise subject to friendly fire.

By the evening of July 12 the Americans had a solid foothold on southwest Sicily, the British "Husky" forces were equally well established on the island's eastern coast, and the emptied transports were starting the return run to North Africa. Then, as American and British troops battled their way inland, Allied warships moved around the perimeter of the island to hammer at shore installations and to prevent the Italians from landing any reinforcements.

From captured Pozzallo, Noto, and Syracuse, General Montgomery's British and Canadian divisions hooked northward toward Mount Etna. A wing of Patton's Army drove westward along the coast to Marsala. Another wing pushed directly northward into Sicily's mountainous interior. And a third raced all the way across the island to seize the strategic port of Palermo on the north coast. When the troops reached Palermo on July 22 they slammed shut an Axis escape-hatch, and American destroyers were rushed to the port to keep it locked.

Off Palermo in the afternoon of July 25 arrived Task Group 80.2 under command of Captain C. Wellborn, Jr., ComDesRon 8. The task group contained destroyers *Wainwright* (Commander R. H. Gibbs); *Mayrant* (Commander E. K. Walker); *Rowan* (Lieutenant Commander R. S. Ford); and *Rhind* (Lieutenant Commander O. W. Spahr, Jr.). The group's roster included 12 mine vessels and four patrol craft, the "miners" assigned to the important task of sweeping the approaches to Palermo. Captain Wellborn rode in *Wainwright*.

Upon arriving in the Palermo area, the group immediately took station on a patrol line off the seaport, and the mine group began exploratory sweeping. Evening and night of the 25th proved quiet. But the destroyermen suspected this was the lull before the storm.

In the morning of July 26 the storm broke. *Mayrant* saw it coming at 0931 when her radar picked up aircraft five miles distant. In a few minutes the planes were in view—three Junker 88's.

As the destroyer steamed across the water her gunners opened fire with two ready 5-inch 38's. One of the Junkers broke up into shards. Another flew off at a tangent, dragging a long tail of smoke. The third plane came on.

Mayrant's Action Report vividly describes the destroyer-versus-Junker battle that ensued.

> Speed was changed to flank speed 25 knots, and the rudder was put over to full right. Before the ship had even begun to swing, a stick of 3 or 4 bombs was dropped on the starboard side, distance about 150 yards, by a plane approaching from astern, which had not been previously sighted. This was immediately followed by a plane attacking from the port quarter, which had also not not been previously sighted. This was followed by a stick of one or two bombs dropped approximately 500 yards ahead of the ship by one of the three planes in the initial contact group. At this time it is believed that all guns which were manned were firing on the initial contact on the port bow. However, one of these planes dropped his stick of 4 bombs which straddled the *Mayrant*. One bomb landed approximately 5 feet off the port beam at frame 102½. A second bomb landed off the starboard beam at a distance of about 40 yards. At that instant the ship was accelerating and had swung through approximately 50 degrees of her turn. The ship listed heavily to port and nearly all personnel were thrown to the deck or against bulkheads.

All main and auxiliary steampower lost, *Mayrant* was sorely hurt, dead in the water without steerageway, her forward engine-room and after fireroom completely flooded, and the forward fireroom and after engine-room flooding rapidly. The emergency Diesel generator took over the ship's electrical load for a minute or two, then all electrical power was lost as the generator's cooling system failed.

Helping the wounded, men groped their way out of the black passages and flooded compartments below. Water engulfed the after engine-room at 0945 and simultaneously rose in the forward fireroom to within four feet of the waterline. Commander Walker, at 0953, ordered the whaleboat overside, and directed the jettisoning of all topside guns and gear that could be torn loose.

But the destroyermen did not abandon. Although the ship had no more than 14 inches of freeboard and a 4 degree list, the compartments which were not flooded showed no sign of leakage, and the vessel remained stubbornly afloat.

When *Wainwright* and *Rhind* came up to stand by, *Mayrant's* seriously wounded were transferred by whaleboat to Captain Wellborn's flagship. After the wounded were transferred, the boats fetched pumps and hoses from *Rhind, Wainwright,* and minecraft *Skill* and *Strive* which were on the scene.

At 1046 *Strive* snugged up alongside the disabled destroyer to furnish power for the pumps and for *Mayrant's* 5-inch and 40mm. guns. The *Skill* also came up to give a hand.

With *Strive* alongside and *Skill* tugging on a tow line, the half-sunk destroyer was started for Palermo at 6 knots. But three more enemy bombers came drilling down the sky at just this critical time, and once more *Mayrant's* gunners raced to their mounts.

Roaring over at high noon, the planes picked *Wainwright* and *Rhind* for targets, and bombs fell close aboard the zigzagging DD's. The destroyermen elevated a fiery canopy that burnt the wings of one aircraft and brought it down crashing—a kill credited to *Rhind*.

It would seem the bombers missed an opportunity by failing to attack disabled *Mayrant*. Perhaps not. Although her engines were paralyzed, her AA guns were not, and they were firing all-out when the enemy fled.

Mid-afternoon found *Mayrant* off the entrance to Palermo, after a 15-mile tow. *Strive* and a subchaser jockeyed her into the harbor. Reporting the episode, *Mayrant's* Commanding Officer made special mention of the *"fine seamanship and invaluable assistance"* which *Strive* contributed that day. He concluded that without help from the minecraft, the destroyer might have gone down.

Mayrant's battle casualties were two men lost, 13 wounded. Among the wounded was a young lieutenant, Franklin D. Roosevelt, Jr. A large segment of the American public remained unaware of the fact that the President's son had been injured while serving as a two-striper in a destroyer off Palermo.

Also serving in *Mayrant* were Lieutenant (jg) Donald E. Craggs, U.S.N.R., and Chief Machinist's Mate Harold M. Steeves. When the bombs struck the ship, the blast wrecked the forward engine-room. F. F. Decker, a Machinist's Mate, was hurled across the floor with a violence that broke his legs. Water plunged over him as he lay stunned and helpless. And Decker would have drowned had not Lieutenant Craggs fought his way across the swirling, steam-choked compartment to drag him to safety. At the same time Chief Steeves clawed through the wreckage to rescue R. W. Peterson, a Machinist's Mate who was trapped in a snare of smashed machinery, plunging water, and scalding steam.

Steeves, Craggs, young Roosevelt—these were the men who kept *Mayrant* on the surface. These, and the men who manned her gun-batteries, her pumps, her bridge. And her skipper, Commander Walker.

Then there were the destroyermen who manned the U.S.S. *Shubrick*. She was the second American DD to undergo a severe blasting at Palermo.

During a raid delivered on August 1, enemy bombs set fire to an ammunition ship, blew up a cargo of gasoline drums stored on the wharf, and damaged destroyer *Mayrant* under repair at the dock. Another raid hit the port about 0400 in the morning of August 4th. At that date and time the warships of Task Force 88 were anchored in the outer harbor. Among those present was destroyer *Shubrick* (Lieutenant Commander L. A. Bryan).

When the alert was sounded, Bryan got his ship under way to occupy a screening station on the starboard bow of cruiser *Savannah* as the latter headed for open sea. As related in *Shubrick*'s Action Report, here is the account of her ordeal:

> Various speeds (5 to 10 knots) were used to maintain position while endeavoring to avoid creating a phosphorescent wake. During this period aircraft flares were being dropped on all sides. Occasionally aircraft motors were heard, and numerous bombs dropped near-by, close enough to shake the ship markedly. It was impossible, however, to see the aircraft, and AA fire was directed at the sound.
>
> At 0430 a plane was heard diving from the starboard side, and

was accordingly taken under fire. Immediately after it passed over, a stick of three bombs landed, one short, one hit, one over. The ship shook violently and it was at once apparent that the hit was a serious one. The bomb, estimated to be either 500 pounds or 1,000 pounds struck just aft of the torpedo tube, at frame 101, three feet to port of the centerline, direction of travel to port about 30° from the vertical. It penetrated the main deck just inside the electrical workshop and detonated in the vicinity of the shell plating at the turn of the bilge, about 5 feet forward of the bulkhead between forward engine-room and after fireroom. The explosion ruptured this bulkhead, creating a hole about 15 feet by 10 feet in the shell plating. Both spaces flooded immediately. Steam lines were ruptured in both spaces, severely burning all personnel present.

All light and power was lost immediately. Due to split-plant operations, the flooding of the two engineering spaces and the intense heat of the escaping steam, it was impossible to effect sufficient repairs to use the port engine. The ship was therefore dead in the water although the bulkheads held water out of the forward fireroom and after engine-room and steam was bottled up in boilers one and two. No further air attack on this ship developed.

Medical assistance was rushed to the disabled destroyer from cruiser *Philadelphia* and destroyer *Knight*. Nine of *Shubrick*'s crew had perished in the blasting. Of the 17 men who were injured, 14 were wounded critically; seven would die in the hospital.

But, as in *Mayrant*'s case, the *Shubrick* remained afloat. A mine vessel and a subchaser tugged the disabled destroyer into the inner harbor where she was tied up to the *Mayrant* alongside the salvage vessel *Chamberlin*.

When the blockbuster struck, the *Shubrick*'s after fireroom was transformed into a torture chamber. Live steam, invisible and murderous, spurted from broken pipes. Men slipped, slid, and floundered in blindness . . . sea water rushed in with a roar . . . they were trapped, suffocating, drowning.

Chief Water Tender J. W. Daugherty, US.N.R., went to their assistance. A blackout device blocked his way. He cut down this gear, and forced an entry into the fast-flooding, steam-fogged compartment. Shouting orders and encouragement, he reached the imprisoned men. For this heroic endeavor, Chief Dougherty was awarded the Navy Cross.

He was joined in the rescue effort by Chief Water Tender J. J. Dennison, and Machinist's Mate W. W. Pemberton. Together these men braved scalding and drowning to fight their way into the fireroom and release their shipmates.

This rescue might have been impossible but for the action of Chief Machinist's Mate F. M. Borcykowski, whose quick-thinking and damage-control work met emergency requirements immediately after *Shubrick* was bombed.

And all of the critically wounded might have died but for the skill and professional acumen of Lieutenant G. M. Caldwell, U.S.N.R., ship's Medical Officer. The destroyer's light had been extinguished. Sterile water was lacking. There were no hospital anesthetists . . . no laboratory facilities . . . no operating room. Caldwell improvised. Someone fetched blankets. Someone held lights. Someone scrubbed a shipmate's arm, preparing it for injection. Quickly and expertly he treated the burned, the maimed, those suffering from shock. Seven of the desperately wounded pulled through.

But there were many of that kind of men in the Navy's Destroyer Service. The foregoing episodes were related in some detail to give an inside picture of destroyer damage and ship-saving which was typical rather than exceptional. Typical of both the ships and the men who served in them . . .

THE FIRST AMERICAN NAVAL FORCES TO ENTER PA- lermo, on July 23, were eight boats of Lieutenant Commander Stanley Barnes' MTB Ron 15, which had sailed from Bizerte the previous night with orders to set up an operating base as soon as the port was secured. By that time elements of Patton's Seventh Army were entering the city.

The story of Barnes' PTs is told by the squadron commander himself as seen through the eyes of Captain Robert J. Bulkley, Jr., historian of that service arm.

6.

PTS AT PALERMO

"At dawn . . . we were off Ustica . . . First thing off we saw a fishing boat putt-putting toward Italy. Going over we found a handful of very scared individuals crawling out from under the floor plates hopefully waving white handkerchiefs. This was the staff of the Italian Admiral at Trapani. The only reason we didn't get the Admiral was that he was late getting down to the dock and his staff said to hell with him. In addition to a few souvenir pistols and binoculars we captured a whole fruit crate of thousand-lira notes which we reluctantly turned over to the Army authorities later. While this was going on, one of the other boats spotted a raft with seven Germans on it feebly paddling out to sea. We picked those up too."

The boats put into Palermo at 0800, and that night Lt. Ernest C. Arbuckle, USNR, in PT *209* (Lt. (jg.) W. Knox Eldredge, USNR), led PT's *216* (Lt. (jg.) Cecil Sanders, USNR) and PT *204* (Lt. (jg.) Eugene S. A. Clifford, USNR) eastward to the Italian coast just north of the Strait of Messina, the narrow strip of water separating Sicily from the toe of the Italian boot. On arrival at Palermo the boats had undertaken a new mission—to prevent enemy supply and evacuation of Sicily by patrolling the northern approaches to the Strait of Messina.

Half a mile off the coast near Palmi the boats found a tug towing the 8,800-ton Italian merchant ship *Viminale*. Sanders scored a tor-

pedo hit on the ship, and then under ineffective fire from shore batteries, the boats strafed the tug until it was smoking and dead in the
water. As the boats retired they saw the *Viminale* sink stern first.
Later, the tug also sank.

Two nights later Lieutenant Mutty, in PT *202* (Lt. (jg.) Robert D.
McLeod, USNR), with PT *210* (Lt. (jg.) John L. Davis, Jr., USNR)
and PT *214* (Lt. (jg.) Ernest W. Olson, USNR), had the squadron's
first encounter with F-lighters. The F-lighters, which from this time
on became the principal prey of the Mediterranean PT's, were somewhat similar to, but considerably larger than, our LCT's. They were
170 feet long, with a cargo-carrying capacity of about 120 tons, and
their hulls were so well compartmented that it was impossible for
PT's to sink them with anything less than a torpedo hit. The PT's
learned after their first few engagements with F-lighters that it was
foolish to try to fight them with guns; the F-lighters were far more
heavily armed than the PT's and far less vulnerable to gunfire.

Mutty's division found seven F-lighters in column northeast of
Stromboli and sneaked in to 500 yards. Each boat fired two torpedoes, and at 300 yards started to turn away. During the turn, the
second lighter in column sent up a flare, apparently a signal to open
fire. All of the lighters immediately opened with a great volume of
76mm., 20mm., and machinegun fire, which the PT's returned. Although it was felt that two torpedoes hit home, German records show
that they all missed. A few seconds later it became apparent that the
fire from the PT's, while hitting the F-lighters, was also giving them a
point of aim. The PT's ceased fire and laid smoke, and the enemy fire
became inaccurate. The *202* had a punctured gasoline tank, several
holes in the hull, and one man wounded. The other boats were not
hit.

On the following night, July 28/29, Lieutenant Arbuckle, in PT
218 (Lt. (jg.) Donald W. Henry, USNR), with Olson's *214* and
Reade's *203* made a torpedo attack on three Italian MAS boats. The
torpedoes were well aimed but passed under the enemy without exploding. The PT's idled away and Arbuckle decided to attack again,
making a gunnery run with the *218,* while the other two boats maneuvered for a torpedo attack. He closed to 100 yards and began to
strafe the lighters. "This," said the action report, "was immediately
returned with a heavy volume of fire from all enemy vessels . . .
directed principally at PT *218*. The boat was hit repeatedly with
20mm. and suffered considerable damage which included the holing

of the vessel below the waterline forward, puncturing of both forward gas tanks, and disabling of one engine. The engagement was broken off in confusion."

Arbuckle, Henry, and Ens. Edmund F. Jacobs, USNR, second officer of the *218,* were wounded. Henry and Jacobs were flat on the deck, but Arbuckle, painfully wounded in the heel, propped himself up and organized the crew to save the boat. The crew's quarters were flooding, one engine was knocked out, and several hundreds of gallons of gasoline had drained into the bilges. Under Arbuckle's direction the crew partially bailed out the flooded compartment and plugged the biggest holes. Three hours later Arbuckle brought his boat alongside the destroyer *Wainwright* at Palermo. Then he collapsed.

On the night of July 29/30, PT's again met F-lighters. This time Lt. (jg.) Richard H. O'Brien in Clifford's PT *204,* with Lt. Norman Devol's PT *207,* engaged two F-lighters escorted by four MAS boats, firing six torpedoes and strafing the MAS boats before heavy fire from one of the lighters forced them to retire. The Italian officer commanding the MAS boats in this action was later interviewed in Capri. He said one F-lighter had been sunk and one MAS boat had been so badly damaged that it was abandoned and sunk by the other MAS boats.

"It seemed after that last engagement," Barnes said, "that the enemy finally got the idea that we weren't going to let them make that northern run any more. They confined their future efforts almost exclusively to running back and forth inside the strait below Messina where nobody could get at them except aircraft."

During this period the squadron continued to undertake special missions for the Office of Strategic Services. "A team under Lieutenant John Shaheen, USNR, arrived quietly and mysteriously for a venture called 'Operation MacGregor,'" Barnes said. "Essentially the idea was to get a letter from our Government through to a certain Rear Admiral in the Italian Navy suggesting that the Italian Navy call it quits and offering certain inducements to that end. Our part of the operation was to land and recover an agent with the letter and to bring someone out for a parley. I gave O'Brien the job of putting the thing over. He trained with members of the team while waiting for a suitable dark moon period, teaching them to handle and navigate a rubber boat. The first attempt (August 10, 1943) at landing in the

Gulf of Gaeta failed when the boats ran into numerous fishing or patrol craft which made an unobserved landing impossible but the second attempt (August 12) was successful. The agent never did meet the rendezvous although the boats were there waiting for him. As it turned out the letter reached the proper hands and, although somewhat late, apparently had considerable influence on the subsequent surrender of the Italian Navy."

At the end of July, Rear Adm. Lyal A. Davidson arrived at Palermo with Task Force 88—two cruisers, several destroyers, and an assortment of landing craft—to support the eastward advance of Lt. Gen. George S. Patton's Seventh Army by fire support and a series of leapfrog landings along the northern coast of Sicily. On the night of 15/16 August, six PT's were assigned to screen one of these landings at Spadafora from possible enemy E-boat attacks. Lieutenant DuBose, commanding the northern PT group, PT *205* (Ens. Robert T. Boebel, USNR), PT *215* (Lt. George A. Steele, Jr., USNR), and PT *216* (Lt. (jg.) Cecil C. Sanders, USNR) sighted and gave chase to two German E-boats off the Italian coast.

"The Germans opened a heavy and accurate fire with 40mm., 20mm., and smaller guns and headed south at high speed," Barnes reported. "Fire was returned with all guns that could bear in the overtaking chase and the range closed to 400 yards. The enemy turned away, laid smoke and dropped depth charges, employing every possible evasive maneuver. The PT's were handicapped by their inability to make more than 25 knots, the *216* lagging the other PT's to such an extent that it was unable to take part in the engagement for any length of time. . . . All PT's were hit repeatedly but miraculously no serious damage was incurred. Four men were wounded on the PT 216. Subsequent interview with an Italian E boat flotilla commander after the capitulation of Italy revealed that in the engagement the German E-boats suffered heavy casualties totalling 14. These included the German flotilla commander who was killed."

Lack of speed prevented the Pt's from conclusive action against the E-boats but, in forcing them to retire, the PT's accomplished their primary mission of protecting our assault forces from E-boat attack. None of the squadron's boats could make more than 27 or 28 knots during the summer of 1943. The boats were overloaded, maintenance facilities were limited, and the engines would not give top performance in the heat of the Mediterranean summer.

Two and a half hours after the engagement with the E-boats, PT *205* intercepted a small sailboat and captured a German officer and six Italian merchant sailors who had been enroute to Italy from the island of Lipari, one of the Eolie group to the north of Sicily. Questioning of the sailors indicated that no Germans remained in the islands and that the Italian inhabitants would welcome a chance to surrender to Americans.

Accordingly, under orders from Admiral Davidson to effect surrender of the Eolie Islands, DuBose set out from Palermo on the morning of August 17 in Lieutenant Steele's PT *215,* with Lieutenant (jg.) Sanders' PT *216* and Lieutenant DeVol's PT *217.* The boats carried an American military government representative, 1 other Army officer, 7 Army enlisted men, and 17 extra enlisted men from the squadron. The destroyer *Trippe* was assigned as a supporting force for the PT's.

The boats entered Lipari Harbor without opposition and found the Italian Naval Commandant of the islands waiting for them on the dock. Within 10 minutes he had surrendered unconditionally the islands of Alicudi, Filicudi, Salina, Stromboli, Lipari, and Vulcano. While the military government officer negotiated with the mayor for establishment of a new civil government for the islands, the PT men rounded up 19 prisoners, and after the commandant had sent radio messages demanding concurrence of the other islands in the surrender, put the radio station out of commission. Only the island of Stromboli refused to agree to the surrender.

The PT's occupied Stromboli late in the afternoon. They found that an Italian chief petty officer and his 30 men had destroyed barracks and confidential papers. The PT men took 19 more prisoners, destroyed a radio station, and the military government officer advised the mayor of the agreement reached at Lipari for civil administration. Then the PT's returned to Palermo to find that Messina had fallen that day . . .

ON JULY 27, TWO DAYS AFTER MUSSOLINI HAD BEEN ousted and placed in protective custody by the Italians themselves, Palermo harbor was opened to Allied traffic. It was at this time that Rear Admiral Lyal A. Davidson's Task Force 88 (Support Force) was organized by Hewitt and sent up to render gunfire missions for Patton's Seventh Army. Davidson entered Palermo harbor with flagship *Philadelphia, Savannah* and five destroyers, *Trippe, Knight, Jeffers, Gherardi* and *Nelson,* and a few hours later was subjected to a fierce working over by a strike of Focke-Wulfs. It was a proper welcome to a "hot" zone, a prelude to a strike by forty-eight German bombers which slipped through the radar defenses on August 1 and blasted Palermo harbor, further damaging the already-damaged destroyer *Mayrant* and obliterating an ammunition train. On August 4 the Luftwaffe struck again; destroyer *Shubrick* was the victim. Raids continued during the enemy evacuation of the island, and there was even a brief sortie by two Italian light cruisers, *Raimondo Montecuccoli* and *Eugenio di Savoia,* which were fortunately intercepted thirty miles from Sicily. At Patton's request, *Philadelphia, Bristol* and *Ludlow* performed bombardment missions at Brolo, and shot down a half-dozen Focke-Wulfs. But the Italian evacuation, organized by Admiral Barone, was a complete success—7000 men escaped in all manner of craft, including German ferries and motor launches. Although Davidson covered Patton's last attacks on the enemy's rear at Spadafora, the evacuation was completed by the 16th. The Sicilian campaign—a limited, costly venture—was over, and more than 3000 men of the combined Allied forces were dead.

Soon decision was reached as to the next major objective, Salerno. In the meantime Montgomery's Eighth Army was given the assignment of crossing Messina Strait to the Italian mainland. Only once before in history had an invasion "up the boot" of Italy been accomplished—fourteen centuries earlier when the Emperor Justinian sent his General Belisarius to the shores of Rhegium, and thence to Naples. Under cover of a fierce artillery bombardment, backed by Royal Navy guns, Montgomery's Eighth crossed the Strait on September 3 and swiftly moved inland. On the 8th a Royal Navy force left Bizerte and steamed for Taranto, occupying that port and accepting the surrender of an Italian cruiser force. (Italy was, in effect, out of the war as of September 3; officially on September 8. Subsequently, a large portion of her fleet was attacked and destroyed by the Luftwaffe while attempting to surrender.)

Operation "Avalanche," headed for Salerno, got underway September 8, with assault convoys leaving from Algiers, Bizerte, Oran, Palermo, Termini and Tripoli and approaching the Italian mainland through the Gulf of Salerno. The principal Army contingent in the

United States Navy's Southern Force was the 36th Infantry Division, commanded by General Mark Clark. Avalanche's naval commander was the brilliant, omnipresent Admiral H. K. Hewitt.

Aboard *Ancon* was Quentin Reynolds, roughhewn champion of uninhibited reporting. He takes us aboard Hewitt's flagship and out to sea.

7.

SHE'S A LUCKY SHIP—
YOU HOPE!

It was a nice, large ship, and so full of apparatus for detection and communication that I felt if I sat down in any given chair I'd be electrocuted. It was the headquarters and flagship in the previous two invasions and there was some reason to believe that the Germans had spotted it. However, that was a chance we had to take. We were going to take a lot of chances in this operation right from the beginning but, as the ball players say, "You can't get a base hit if you don't take your bat off your shoulder . . ."

We spent the night tied up to our dock in Algiers, and I didn't like that. The night before I'd had dinner with my pals of the Second Fighter Wing, and they had told me they expected a raid on Algiers the following night. This was the night. When they raid Algiers they ignore the city and concentrate on the harbor. We had a couple of pretty good sluggers alongside of us: *H.M.S. King George V* and *H.M.S. Howe,* Britain's newest fashions in battleships. They could throw up a tremendous amount of flak, but I've never had much confidence in even the excellent Algiers brand of flak. The odd plane or two can always get through. But nothing happened.

We slipped out so quietly at 7 A.M. that I never woke up. I did get up at ten, had a salt then a fresh shower and decided that the U. S. Navy was all right. I went to the wardroom for breakfast and was shocked to find that the navy stopped serving breakfast at 8:30. This was indeed a blow to a person who believes that nothing worth while ever happens before 10 A.M., whether on land or sea. But there was always coffee, the Negro mess attendants told me. There was beautiful, strong American coffee, and I went into the galley and clowned with the mess boys, hoping they wouldn't notice that I was drinking six cups. They didn't know about that coffee made of acorns I'd been living on in Russia, or the miserable chickory coffee we'd had in Sicily or the Godawful imitation French coffee they gave us in Algiers. The longer I stay abroad the more provincial I become. I begin to think that everything American is better than its European counterpart. In some cases I may be wrong—but not about coffee. Any resemblance between French, Russian, or British coffee and our own real coffee is entirely accidental.

After breakfast I investigated the ship's library and, to my delight, found it filled with detective stories. It would, I decided, be a good trip after all. Then we were called to the operations room forward and briefed. Until now we didn't know where we were headed. We thought Italy, but it might be Sardinia or Corsica. If it were Italy it might be Taranto or Naples or most anywhere else. We were told the whole story of the operation by Commander Richard English, one of the naval planners, and a G-2 officer, and an air force colonel. It was to be Salerno, thirty-five miles south of Naples. It was the logical spot. We were told that, undoubtedly, the Germans knew we were on our way. The audacity of the plan subdued us considerably, especially when we realized the problem of air cover. Our fighters would all have to come from Sicily, 180 miles away. That meant about a forty-minute flight for a Spit or a P-38. We realized that the Spitfire, because of its lower fuel capacity, could stay over us for only a short time. The P-38s, with their longer range, could stick around for about an hour. However, we were to have four British converted aircraft carriers carrying Seafires—Spits modified to land on carrier decks. But still our air protection was going to be mighty thin.

Then General Mark Clark called for us. We went to his cabin just off the bridge. Lanky, likable, Mark Clark grinned when he told us to sit down.

"How do you like our plan?" he asked.

"My God, it's daring!" I blurted out.

"My God, it *is* daring," he laughed. "Sure, we're spitting right into the lion's mouth. We know it. But we have to do that. We had several alternate plans and we studied them all carefully. This seemed to be the only real answer."

"Do you expect either strategic or tactical surprise?" I asked him.

"Certainly not strategic surprise." He stretched out his long legs and made himself comfortable in his chair. "And I doubt if we get any tactical surprise. German G-2 is good. They have studied these maps of Italy as we have studied them. They know we want and need a port in Italy. Naples is the obvious port for us to go after. We could go after it from the beaches north of Naples or go into Salerno as we are doing. They know, as we know, that the coastline north of Naples isn't good for landing an assault force. They know that landing there would stretch our air cover to the breaking point. There is no doubt that they figure us to land on the Salerno beaches." He looked serious, and added, "We may get hurt, but you can't play with fire without the risk of burning your fingers.

"By the way," he said, turning to me, "I have a message for you from Butch. I had dinner with him last night."

"Butch" was Commander Harry Butcher, Naval Aide to General Eisenhower.

"The message was," General Clark quoted, " 'Tell Quent not to get my watch wet.' "

I looked guiltily at the wrist watch I was wearing. My own watch had broken the week before and Butch had lent me his. "I don't even want to get my feet wet, much less Butch's watch," I said fervently to Clark. "But I hope Butch isn't sucker enough to think he's ever going to get this watch back?"

"He has vague hopes—that's all," Clark said.

Clark sat there talking easily, and I marveled at his composure. He was leading the first real invasion of the continent. He was, he told us, "Making the longest end run in history." General Montgomery's slash across the Straits of Messina was merely a quick quarterback thrust. Our end run was the play designed to be the pay-off; the touchdown play. Or, in terms of the ring, Montgomery's attack was the left jab; ours was the Sunday punch. We were going to throw everything we had into it.

And if it missed? Clark, as Commanding General of the Fifth Army would be the goat. A general has to win battles—or else. No excuses are accepted. This was Clark's first big chance, and he sat there relaxed, smiling, confident.

"Are you apprehensive about what their air will do?" I asked him.

"Apprehensive?" he exploded. "I'm scared stiff of what their air will do, but we hope to have two of their air fields by D plus 2 and then our fighters won't have that long pull from Sicily."

"When do you expect to establish headquarters ashore?"

He shrugged his shoulders. "Who knows? If everything goes according to plan—and it never does—I may get ashore on D plus 2. We want to get this ship out of the harbor as soon as possible. It is far too vulnerable. Yet I can't establish headquarters ashore until our communications are set up."

When we left General Clark we felt a little better because of his quiet air of confidence. Clark at forty-six looks thirty-six—if that. He had never commanded large units in combat, but Eisenhower had picked him. General Eisenhower didn't make mistakes—and he was sold on Mark Clark . . .

That noon at dinner (the navy has dinner at noon) I sat opposite the Catholic chaplain, Lieutenant Ballinger. He said Mass on the gun deck at four-thirty every afternoon. I suppose one of the last official acts the Pope ever did for America was to give our army and navy chaplains permission to say Mass any time up to 7 P.M. I told Father Ballinger what Jimmy Sheean had said, and I suggested that he incorporate a special prayer for good weather in his Mass that day. Had any one of his Jersey City parishioners ever suggested that to Father Ballinger in pre-war days, he probably would have laughed. But he didn't laugh this time. Gradually, a thin gauze of tension was wrapping itself around the ship and around each one of us. We were creeping up on Salerno, and we all knew that this was a fight for keeps. Father Ballinger nodded and said quietly, "Not a bad idea."

The weather was real Mediterranean weather at its best. The sun tinted the sea with gold and, because of the varying depths of the water, it took on hues of blue, aquamarine and indigo and, where the water was very deep, emerald green. We had kept a rendezvous, and now ships were all around us.

Our convoy moved smoothly in parallel lines, each ship perhaps three hundred yards from the one in front and a little further from those on either side. Most of the ships were large troop ships and some could be identified as former luxury liners. We were hugging the coast, for our next rendezvous was off Bizerte. We had roast turkey for dinner that night and peach pie and all the coffee a man could drink. I figured that no matter what happened from now on I was ahead of the game. It was the best food I'd had in nearly seven months. Our navy is good to travel with, except for the childish rule made by former Secretary of the Navy, Josephus Daniels, the prohibitionist (some twenty-five years ago,) that no alcoholic drinks could be served on any American naval vessel. I think that to be one of the most un-American orders ever enforced on our armed forces. There is absolutely no reason for it, beyond the fanaticism of our former Secretary of the Navy. The navy of every other country in the world serves drinks, and I never recall a battle being lost because the ships' officers happened to be drunk. Drinks are served in the wardrooms of all British warships, from little gunboats up to battle wagons, and in three and a half years of frequent traveling with the Royal Navy I have never seen any officer or man the worse for drink. A drink tastes mighty good when you come off a bitter-cold, eight-hour watch. It would have been pleasant to sit around our wardroom on the *U.S.S. Ancon,* having a cocktail before dinner and a Scotch and soda afterwards.

I resent the implication that it is all right for British officers to drink on board their ships because they handle liquor well, but it isn't all right for our own naval officers to drink on board because they might run their ship on a rock. American naval officers have too much pride in their ships and their uniform ever to disgrace either. Our naval officers feel rather ashamed of the absurd rule, but they obey it implicitly. In many ports our sailors have made bad names for themselves because when they do get ashore they go to town on that grog as though they were never going to get another drink. In British wardrooms (and RAF stations) no money is passed. Men must sign chits for every drink they buy. Each week the commanding officer looks over the chits. If an officer's bill shows that he has been buying too many drinks, he will be hauled up very quickly before the C.O. and measures taken. But this doesn't happen often. However, it gives the commanding officer a perfect check.

We lay about twenty miles off Bizerte that night. During the early evening I was on the bridge talking to Admiral Hewitt, in command of the whole amphibious part of the show. Hewitt told me that Bizerte was having an air raid.

"Twenty plus are reported en route," he said. "I hope they don't spot us on the way home. By the way, have you heard the news from Italy?"

"Not all of it," I said cautiously, just fishing, of course. I hadn't had any news of Italy.

"Well," Hewitt said, smiling, "it's strictly hush-hush, but we may have some good news soon."

"Italy might fold?" I was surprised, because there hadn't even been a rumor in Algiers about any capitulation. Only smart Herbert Matthews had believed that Italy would surrender. I recalled his remark of a few days before. "I have every confidence in the Italians," Herbert had said. "Yes, I am confident that they will double-cross the Germans just as they've double-crossed everyone else."

The night and the next day passed pleasantly. By now I was completely sold on my two cabin mates. Big Van Alystyne, nearing fifty, was one of the friendliest men I've ever met. We sat around and talked of the two previous invasions. The *Ancon* had been the command ship in those operations, too, and had two very narrow escapes. "But she's a lucky ship," Van laughed, "and we have a lucky skipper."

We passed Sicily and then headed north. By now, of course, we had been spotted by reconnaissance planes. You can't hide a fleet of hundreds of ships in the Mediterranean. It was, in the language of invasion, D minus one. The landing would take place at 3:30 A.M. In that other war it was called Zero Hour. Now it is merely H Hour. We had a magnificent meal that night: cream of celery soup, steak, onions, mashed potatoes and apple pie. You couldn't help but think of the old cliché, "The condemned man ate a hearty meal." The men were greatly disappointed, however.

"In the other two invasions," I heard one of them grumble on deck, "we had apple pie and ice cream the night before. Yeah, and on the Sicily show we each had two lumps of ice cream."

Each member of the crew was given a mimeographed sheet during dinner.

U.S.S. ANCON (AGC4)

PLAN OF THE DAY FOR THURSDAY 9 SEPTEMBER 1943

During Thursday, 9 September it is expected that the *Ancon* will be in the transport area, operating its landing boats, as directed, to debark certain army personnel and equipment; the crew will be at General Quarters to repel enemy attack by air and sea. It is expected that the ship will be hove to for a while and then anchored, with the anchor at short stay ready to slip at a moment's notice, with a full steaming watch on and full steam at the throttles. During the time the crew is at General Quarters it is proposed to feed all hands at their stations. To accomplish this, ship's cooks and bakers will be excused from ammunition details and will occupy themselves with the preparation and serving of food under the direct supervision of the Supply Officer. Food will be brought to General Quarters stations in food carriers by men detailed from ammunition parties. Troops going ashore on Thursday will be fed an early breakfast at 0100, in the crew's messing compartment.

In general, boats will be loaded by details from damage control parties under the supervision of the First Lieutenant and Boatswain.

Subsequent employment of the crew will depend upon developments and the local situation. In general, boats' crews from the 2-A Division will man the boats and will lower their boats as directed.

All hands are directed to have with them, throughout the day and night, helmets and gas masks. Boat crews will have with them such uniform and equipment as has been furnished them.

D. H. SWINSON, Comdr., USNR.

Executive Officer

NOTE: When this vessel is in the combat zone and all hands are at General Quarters, it is expected that for several meals mess tables will not be set up for the service of meals. In lieu thereof the Army Field Ration K will be served to both officers and men at their stations. Paper cups will be provided for the hot coffee.

Sufficient cooks and stewards, stewards' mates and commissary personnel will be secured when directed by the Commanding Officer to act as runners for serving the rations. Lt. (jg) Knowles will supervise the service forward of the crews messing compartment and Lt. Comdr. Nicol aft. Runners will wear helmets and dungarees, keeping the body covered at all times.

Gun platform crews will provide three fathoms of manila line for hoisting and lowering 10-gallon Aervoid coffee containers.

After dinner the Captain of our ship asked me to "brief" the whole crew on the ship's public-address system. The crew had no idea where we were going and they were getting slightly jittery.

"Give them the whole works," the Captain said. "Where we're

landing, how many divisions, and so on. And you might stress the fact," he added casually, "that our air cover is going to be excellent."

"I hope you're right, sir," I couldn't help saying.

"So do I," he answered grimly.

I spoke from the bridge and loudspeakers all over the ship carried the story to the crew. I drew slightly on my imagination and dwelt cheerfully on the 200 Beaufighters which would be over us all night and the 500 Spits and Lightnings which would cover us by day. I became so enthusiastic I almost believed it myself . . .

ONE MUST THINK OF THE GULF OF SALERNO AS A twelve-mile arc, divided in half for the purposes of invasion. The Northern half is to be occupied by the British; the Southern half by the Americans. Behind the beaches are the foothills, rolling back to a sweeping mountain range which is dominated by 3556-foot Mount Soprano. The American beach, divided into Green and Red, fronts on the village of Paestum. It is off this sandy shore that a prolonged bombardment begins in the black of D-Day.

Commander W. J. Burke, who led a contingent of Seabees, was aboard one of the landing craft bound for Green Beach; his collaborator in the following account is William Bradford Huie. Let us close the beach in Burke's ill-fated ramp craft.

COMMANDER W. J. BURKE

AND WILLIAM BRADFORD HUIE

8.

"THE PANZERS WERE

WAITING FOR US."

About 0320, in pitch darkness, the rocket craft let go their barrage. As we lay to in the calm water of the bay some four to five miles off the beach, it was a fascinating sight to watch, through field glasses, the terrific discharge of the rocket batteries. They were fired in bunches, enveloping their craft in brilliant sheets of flame, then soaring high up, over and down toward the beach where thunderous explosions took place.

At 0330—'H' Hour—the first waves of the assault (troops) . . . landed in their small craft . . . followed by waves of LCVP, LCI's and LCT's. The theory was that a few hundred assault troops should seize the beachhead and squelch enemy resistance prior to the main assault landing of the LST's which would follow at about sunrise. Sometime around 0430, shortly before dawn, four German artillery shells fell in the water close to the causeway. Shrapnel fragments fell over the causeways and pounded against the sides of the LST. Twenty-two of our men and Warrant Officer Dick Look were on the causeway, fully exposed to fire, but fortunately no one was hit.

At 0525 our ship, with causeways rigged for 'momentum beaching' was ordered into Green Beach. We were following the course of the YM mine sweepers when, about a mile off shore a large size Italian mine which had been swept to the surface, but not exploded, loomed in the path of the ship. The forward lookout saw the ominous round shape and a frantic effort was made to veer the ship to port, but not enough. The curved end of the inboard causeway hit and rode up over the mine which bounced along under the bottom for about 70 feet before going off against the side of the ship. At the time of the explosion I was sitting on some sand buckets in front of the pilot house. My first blinding impression was of a terrific explosion forward. Thinking we had been hit by an aerial bomb, I threw myself to the deck to avoid shrapnel and fragments. There was a blinding flame, water towered up, objects were hurled aloft, then a blast of air and a deluge of water and oil fell on us. Luckily fire did not break out, although how the numerous gasoline tanks of our cargo escaped being ignited will always be a mystery. The explosion ripped into troop quarters killing and seriously injuring a number of British soldiers.

The ship was still under way, but the causeways were gone and rapidly drifting astern. In the dim light it was possible to see a pontoon or two drifting free, but we did not at first realize that those shadows piled up on the forward weather deck were pontoons blown from the sea. Fortunately a couple of small craft were in the vicinity which went to the assistance of the Seabees aboard the wrecked causeways. We found out later that there was sufficient warning of the explosion for the men to run to the extreme aft end of the causeway where, although they were violently stunned by the terrific detonation, only two were killed; a big, strapping farm boy from Iowa named Jim Achterhoff, and a chap named Jones who had married the day he came into the Navy. Dick Look's eardrums were punctured and several others were seriously wounded.

We did not know whether the ship would stay afloat long enough to reach the beach as she was listing badly. We grounded about 0600, without our causeways, some 250 feet off the shore line with about 11 feet of water at the bow ramp. It was immediately apparent that the beach had not yet been taken. Batteries of 88's and mortars had the range of the beach and kept up the shelling all through D Day. When the extent of the mine damage was finally ascertained, and it was found that the ship would remain afloat, it was decided to retract and attempt to put our combat cargo ashore over one of the other sets of causeways or via LCT's.

When we were about a half mile off the beach, a British destroyer laid down a smoke screen which protected us from further fire from the shore and enabled us to anchor in the transport area between the

Biscayne and the Monitor *Abercrombie,* transferring our cargo to LCT's.

The second LST to be readied for the run to North Beach was the one on which Lieutenant Harry Stevens, Jr. (CEC, USNR, Salem, Ill.), was officer-in-charge of causeways. The other Seabee officer was Ensign M. T. Jacobs (CEC, USNR, Hopkinsville, Ky.). Jacobs, modest, ruddy-cheeked, a former engineer for the Tennessee Valley Authority, told the story.

"At H-Hour—0330—our LST had moved in to within three miles of the Red section of North Beach," he explained. "We were carrying men of a Hampshire regiment of the 46th British Division. On the tank deck we had six Shermans, with a lot of half-tracks, Bren gun carriers, and ducks. The weather deck was loaded with half-tracks and supply trucks. It was a clear night with a million stars but no moon.

"The 16th Panzers were ready for us. When the small craft began hitting the beach, the Panzers opened up with everything they had. Big guns, 88's and machine guns. Our warships including the cruisers *Savannah, Boise* and *Philadelphia,* were with the Southern Attack Force off Paestum, and they returned the fire. The *Savannah* had pulled in to within a few hundred feet of our LST, and she was blasting with everything she had. German bombers started coming over, so even the guns on the LST's started firing. God, it was hot! And right at that moment we got the order to prepare to launch causeways.

"The Hampshires were about as interested in watching us launch the causeways as in watching all the gunfire. We have those causeways secured by many cables and turnbuckles; and when we prepare to launch, the first thing we have to do is remove all the cables except three. Chopping blocks are rigged under the three remaining cables, and three men stand by with axes waiting for the signal to launch. Can you cut a steel cable with an axe? Sure, when the cable is as taut as those cables are.

"At 0415 we dropped the first causeway, and fifteen minutes later we dropped the second one. All this time we had to shout like hell to one another. The Germans had set one of our tugs afire, so we had a sort of half-light from it. After we drop the causeways, the senior officer and ten men stay on the weather deck of the LST to handle the lines, while the junior officer and twenty-four men get down on the causeways to rig them for the run to the beach.

"We opened the bow doors and let out our duck. We had asked for an hour to rig the causeways, but we had rush orders. Those 175-foot sections are plenty heavy in the water. As junior officer, I had to direct the rigging and ride the causeways. We hitched the duck to one section and began maneuvering it toward the other side of the ship. Shells were popping all around us, but while you are rigging you are so busy you don't mind it so much. It's when you start in to the beach and have nothing to do but hold on and pray—that's when you really get scared.

"At 0530 we had finished rigging the causeways into the slide-rule formation alongside the port side of the ship. Mine sweepers had been working in front of us, so we started our run for the beach. I was lying up at the forward end of the causeway, and had plenty of time to look around and see what was going on.

"All twenty-five of us who were lying on the causeways were dressed in two-piece coveralls, helmets and life jackets. We had canteens and 45's on our belts; no other arms. You don't need anybody to tell you to lie flat on that causeway, because you feel like the most exposed man in the whole harbor. And that's just what you are. You look at a Stillson wrench lying in front of you, and it looks big enough for you to crawl under it. Honestly, you get the idea that that wrench gives you some protection.

"Off to my left as we were going in, I could see another LST with her set of causeways. That was Lieutenant Commander Burke, our officer-in-charge, with Mitchell and Look. Firing and bombing were going on incessantly. When we were about a mile off the beach, the causeways ridden by Look and his men hit a loose mine, and there was one helluvan explosion. We could see it in the half-light from where we were riding. Their duck, which was running alongside the causeways, was swamped and sunk. The LST, with her bottom stove in, continued but was unable to effect a landing.

"Look and most of his twenty-four men were blown off the causeways by that explosion. It was several days before all of them were located, since they were picked up by various craft. After we saw that explosion, me and my fellows lay on our causeways and prayed for that minesweeper that was going in front of us.

"About 0620—just before sunup—we hit the beach full speed. We cut the causeways loose, but our luck was holding. The beach condition was such that our LST slid right on up to the water's edge, and we didn't need the causeways for her. All we had to do was throw a

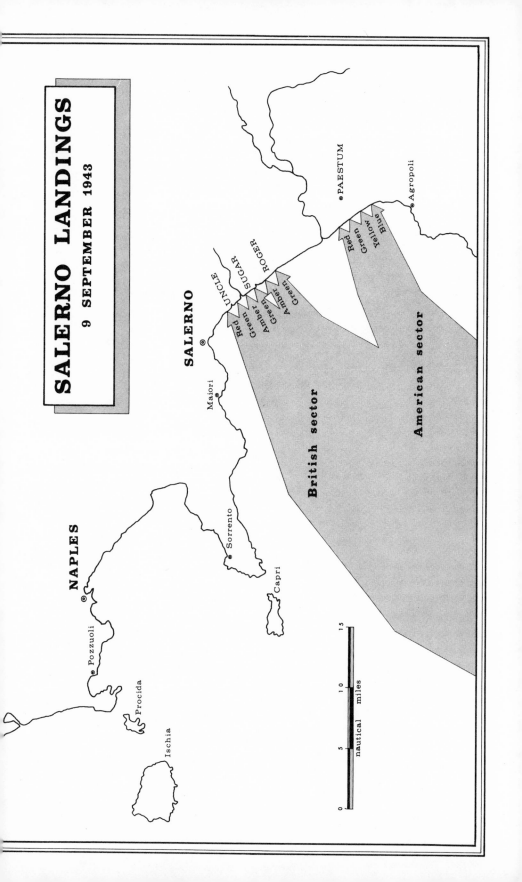

SALERNO LANDINGS
9 SEPTEMBER 1943

NAPLES

Pozzuoli

Procida

Ischia

SALERNO

Maiori

Sorrento

Capri

UNCLE
Red
Green
SUGAR
Amber
Green
ROGER
Amber
Green

PAESTUM

Red
Green
Yellow
Blue

Agropoli

British sector

American sector

nautical miles

0   5   10   15

few sandbags under her ramp and spread the mat. We were held up about ten minutes while the British engineers grappled land mines, but the Seabees used that ten minutes to good advantage. We had long-handled shovels on the causeways with which to fill sandbags, so we grabbed those shovels and dug slit trenches. Shells were bursting all around us.

"The first vehicle to come off, of course, was our bulldozer. *Probably the first American vehicle to land on the continent of Europe was a Seabee bulldozer* driven by Raymond J. Calhoun, Machinist's Mate first, of Troy, N.Y. Calhoun came down that ramp, rolled up the beach about fifty feet through the mine markers, then cut to the left right behind a small tractor which had been landed in a small craft by the Commandos. Just at that second the British tractor hit a mine and was blown to hell, killing the driver. Calhoun was blown straight back, head-over-heels, off his bulldozer, and it was a miracle that he didn't break his neck.

"We began unloading our LST and had her unloaded by 0800. We had the causeways standing by, with the duck hitched to the floating end and the bulldozer hitched to the beach end, ready to hook up to any LST that hung short of the beach. But three more LST's came in, and all of them made it clear to the shore line. That was the best beach we'll ever see for LST operations.

"The Hampshires had pushed on in and were tangling with the 16th Panzers. Shellfire from 88's was still bothering us on the beach. About 1000 I witnessed the goriest sight of the war for me. Seven or eight Hampshires decided that they'd brew up a spot of tea on the beach. They built a fire and had the water boiling when one of them called to me:

" 'Say, chappie, come and have a spot o' tea.'

"I started walking toward them and was within fifty feet of them when a land mine went off right under that fire. The explosion knocked me flat, and when I got up every damn one of those Hampshires was dead and mangled.

"Three of our causeway platoons had reached Red Beach by 0700. Only Mitchell's platoon, which had hit the mine, had been turned back. The LST that McGrath and Butterfield came in with was hit eleven times on the run-in, and one shell hit her elevators so that nothing could be unloaded off of her weather deck. They unloaded her tank deck; then she retracted.

"Late that afternoon our men established a bivouac about 300 yards from where we had landed. We stayed there on the beach for ten days during which the bombing, shelling and fighting continued almost constantly. The crisis was on the fifth and sixth days, when it appeared that perhaps we were going to have to pull a Dunkirk, but those Britishers finally turned the tide. We Seabees had no further casualties on the beach, but we had some close calls.

"Red Woodmancy (Charles W. Woodmancy, Carpenter's Mate second, Mirror Lake, N.H.) who had won the Legion of Merit in Sicily, refused to dig himself a slit trench. He boasted that he could sleep through any barrage the Germans could lay down. He had set up a cot with a mosquito netting over it. One night he slept through an air raid, and next morning he found that a bomb fragment had come inside his mosquito netting and broken the frame of his cot without waking him up . . ."

THEODORE ROSCOE COMPLETES THE STORY OF THE long, tough "road to Rome," which for the Navy led from Salerno through the landings at Anzio in January 1944 (Operation *Shingle*) to the capture of Rome in June 1944 by General Mark Clark's victorious Fifth Army. The destroyers are Roscoe's special interest—the variety of enemy weapons they had to counter, and the many blows they dealt out in return, both on land and sea. We join the destroyer force on the eve of D-Day at Salerno.

Ack-ack fire during a night air raid, Salerno. *Navy Department.*

Allied transports meet rough water in the Mediterranean near Malta enroute to Sicily. View from USS *Ancon* (AGC-4). *Navy Department.*

The USS *Birmingham* (CL-62) firing 6″ guns off Agrigento, Sicily, during the July, 1943 campaign. *Navy Department.*

A U.S. Coast Guard combat photographer caught this American warship giving the Germans defending the shore a jarring blast during the early morning hours of the invasion of Salerno. *U.S. Coast Guard.*

Landing craft streak for the Salerno shore in the prelude to the battle for the mainland. *Navy Department.*

A PT boat with striped camouflage at Salerno Bay, Italy. Other ships of the invasion convoy may be seen in the background. *Navy Department.*

Normandy, June 8, 1944. Watching the invasion operations of Europe from the bridge of the USS *Augusta* are, from left to right: Rear Adm. A.G. Kirk, Commander of Invasion Task Force; Lt. Gen. Omar Bradley, Commander of American Ground Forces; Rear Adm. A. D. Strable (with binoculars); and Maj. Gen. Hugh Keen. *Navy Department.*

Invasion craft heading for the shores of Normandy, France, on D-Day. *Navy Department.*

Landing craft with the French coast in the background, as seen from the USS *Ancon* (AGC-4). *Navy Department.*

With a group of attack transports in the background, two PC's maneuver off the USS *Ancon,* standing by off the coast of France. *Navy Department.*

A rocket ship (LCT-R) releasing rockets in a rehearsal off the English coast in preparation for the invasion of France. The landing craft are in position, ready to speed toward the beach. *Navy Department.*

In the midst of the real thing, helmeted American soldiers crouch, tightly packed, behind the bulwarks of a Coast Guard landing barge off the Normandy shore. Minutes later, they dashed through the surf and up the beach under withering Nazi fire. *U.S. Coast Guard.*

American soldiers wading ashore under heavy machine gun fire. These dramatic photos were taken during the first waves of the invasion. *U.S. Coast Guard.*

Bursting into flame when Nazi machine gun fire exploded a hand grenade, this Coast Guard-manned LCVP, packed with troops, was piloted safely to the Normandy beach on D-Day by a 23-year-old Texan, Coast Guardsman Delba L. Nivens, coxswain, of Amarillo. Nivens unloaded his cargo of invaders and, assisted by his engineman and bowman, put out the fire and made the run back to his assault transport in a hail of German machine gun and mortar fire. *U.S. Coast Guard.*

Heavy seas, threatening to demoralize the Normandy landings soon after D-Day, beat against a barricade of sunken ships a half mile offshore. In a carefully planned operation carried through in the wake of the liberation day landings, 23 freighters, loaded with cement, were "scuttled" to form an improvised breakwater behind which landing craft were unloaded on the French beaches. *U.S. Coast Guard.*

9.

"THANK GOD

FOR THE NAVY!"

Through darkness which was warm and fragrant, the invasion fleet entered a gulf as calm as Peace. The Italian coastline was a silhouette in black velvet. The water inshore lay almost breathless, its gentle swells like the quiet breathing of untroubled sleep.

On schedule the first assault waves moved in. The second waves soon followed, meeting indifferent opposition. Then, as the third waves approached the shore, the Salerno volcano exploded.

From hidden pillboxes, redoubts, and gun emplacements, the Nazis poured shot and shell at the LCI's, the DUKW's, and other landing craft in the shallows. Troops on the beaches were flayed by machine-gun crossfire. Big Krupp guns let out a basso roar and Mark VI tanks charged out of nowhere.

On some of the beaches the American and British troops, enfiladed, were driven back to water's edge. On several, the combat teams were slaughtered to a man. Nazi aircraft swept over to bomb and strafe the reeling landing forces. My midmorning the Salerno shallows were a crimson sludge, and it appeared as though the invaders might be literally blown from the beachhead.

At this point Admiral Davidson's First Support Group stepped in. The bombardment ships had been held at bay by the maze of minefields, and so they were late in taking station in their assigned fire-support areas. But about 1000 of that critical D-Day morning the cruisers and destroyers moved shoreward, and by noon they were all in position. They were just in time.

By that hour the Salerno beaches looked like deathtraps. Nazi artillerymen had rolled forward big batteries which included 88mm. guns, and these rifles, emplaced on ridges, were pounding the sands with a devastating barrage. General Clark described the Germans as *"looking down our throat."* On one beach a herd of Nazi tanks had advanced to within 200 yards of the American foxholes. And at Green Beach counterattacking Nazis broke through and gained foxholes only 80 yards from the water.

Then the fire-support ships opened up. The cruisers and destroyers were unable to repeat their sharpshooting "Husky" performance. Shore fire-control (SFC) parties had become scattered in the bedlam of battle. Some of the SFC men had been killed; some had lost their gear, or been marooned with damaged radio sets. However, two cruisers and one destroyer managed to establish communication with fire-control parties ashore.

And in spite of the fact that most of the bull's-eyes were not spotted with exactitude, cruiser and destroyer salvos began to land on target. Nazi machine-gun emplacements were wiped out. Mobile guns were blown off their wheels, and heavy artillery units were put out of action. A railway battery was either knocked out or silenced. Crashing in from the sea, naval shellfire stopped Nazi tanks in their tracks, blowing a goodly number out of existence.

By D-Day evening the Nazis were falling back. Although the Naval fire support could not be scored in precise statistics, its effectiveness was certified by the following message from General Lange (5th Army) to Admiral Davidson:

THANK GOD FOR THE FIRE OF THE NAVY SHIPS X PROBABLY COULD NOT HAVE STUCK IT OUT AT BLUE AND YELLOW BEACHES X BRAVE FELLOWS X PLEASE TELL THEM SO

Even as the "Avalanche" forces pounded on the doorstep to Naples, a small diversionary force steamed northward to capture a small chain of islands in the Gulf of Naples some 40 miles west of the great seaport.

The diversionary force was led by Captain C. L. Andrews, Jr., in the destroyer *Knight* (Lieutenant Commander J. C. Ford Jr). It included two Dutch gunboats, and enough men to capture the islands of Ventotene, Ponza, Procida, Ischia, and the postcard Isle of Capri.

On Ventotene the Italian garrison cheerfully surrendered. A force of some 90 Germans elected to fight, but were soon either dead or captured. *Knight* and Company quickly scooped up the other islands, and the Navy had a base in hand for the Naples drive.

At Salerno the assault forces gained ground on the morning after D-Day, although the *Luftwaffe* unleashed an almost continuous series of air raids. Allied carrier aircraft and Sicily-based Army fighters dog-fought the German planes. Again the Navy moved in with fire-support for the ground troops.

Admiral Davidson's group had lost the services of H.M.S. *Abercrombie*; the ship had been disabled by a mine on D-Day. During the action on September 10, H.N.M.S. *Flores* was crippled by bomb explosions close aboard. These were the group's only ship casualties. By the evening of the 10th it seemed feasible to assign 11 of the American destroyers in the group to convoy duty. At 2215 they took screening positions around Convoy SNF-1 to escort the formation to Oran—a task which was to prove infinitely more dangerous than the fire-support mission.

The day after Davidson's task group was broken up, Vice Admiral Hewitt's flagship *Ancon* entered Salerno Bay, and General Clark and staff went ashore. The beachhead now seemed well in hand. Unfortunately, the situation was deceiving. During evening twilight of the 13th, Nazi reinforcements stormed into the area. Once more the U.S. VI Corps was fearfully mauled and nearly dislodged from the beachhead.

This time the Navy's cruisers and destroyer *Mayo* moved up to pump salvos at the enemy's tanks, troops, and guns. General Eisenhower now ordered the Strategic Air Force to defer inland railroad bombing and to join the beachhead battle. Air bombings supplementing naval barrages, the Nazi counterattack was battered into a Nazi retreat. Salerno would not be secured for several more days, but Kesselring's forces could no longer hope to reverse the tide of "Avalanche."

Again, the destroyer accomplishment at Salerno remains difficult to assess. As in Operations "Torch" and "Husky," the DD's working in "Avalanche" were members of a great amphibious organization containing all types of ships on all manner of missions. But something of the size and efficacy of their fire-support effort is indicated by the following excerpt from a report by Admiral Hewitt:

The enemy was ready and waiting for the Allied assault when the landings were made at Salerno. Without the support of naval gunfire, the assault of the beaches could not have carried, and the Army could not have remained ashore without the support of naval guns and bombing aircraft. On D-Day alone fire-support ships engaged a minimum of one hundred thirty-two targets. Ammunition expenditure was reported on only seventy, or 53% of the targets, but the weight of explosives hurled at about one-half of the targets more than equaled the weight that twenty-two batteries of 105-mm. howitzer, firing 400 rounds per battery, could have fired had they been ashore and in position. The Army position was precarious on D-Day, and continued so until after the heavy air and naval bombardment on D plus 6 and 7, until the beachhead was secured on D plus 8. Naval gunfire continued on a heavy scale until the 19th of September. By the 28th of September, more than the equivalent of 71,500 150-mm. field artillery project-tiles had been fired at 556 or more targets.

No less an authority than the German military savant, Sertorious, attributed the loss of Salerno to General Von Kesselring's inability to cope with naval bombardments.

By the end of September, Salerno had been won. But the Allies had paid a heavy price for the prize. Some 7,000 British and 5,000 American soldiers had been slain in the fighting. And two United States destroyers had been downed in action. First victim was the U.S.S. *Rowan.*

Late in the evening of September 10, 1943, the destroyer *Rowan* (Lieutenant Commander R. S. Ford) took station in the screen which was forming around the empty transports and cargo vessels of Convoy SNF-1, bound from Salerno to Oran.

Over the inner reaches of Salerno Gulf the night sky was flushed by the crimson breath of angry guns. The distant foreshore resembled a dark grid on which embers smoldered, while smoke coiled and fumed over the glowing coals. The ridges above the shore were charred backlogs festooned with splashes of flame. By contrast the outer reaches of the Gulf seemed cool, the channel there was quiet and shadowy, and a ship, heading seaward, might draw a deep breath of relief.

Rowan had joined the convoy screen at 2240. At midnight she was pacing along—nothing to report. A moment later her startled lookouts glimpsed a phosphorescent streak racing through the water on the ship's bow.

TORPEDO!

The alarm sent all hands to battle stations. The torpedo passed harmlessly ahead. Lieutenant Commander Ford turned the destroyer on the proverbial dime, and drove her down the torpedo's track.

As *Rowan* charged across the water, a flicker of "pips" appeared on her radar screen—E-boats in the offing. Firing by full radar control, the destroyer opened up on the enemy. Guns blazing, she closed the range on one target to 2,000 yards. Then, while swinging in a fast turn, she was apparently struck in the port quarter by a torpedo.

Crash of the explosion was instantly followed by a ship-shattering blast that ripped open the destroyer's stern and blew segments of deck and superstructure skyward. The first detonation had exploded the after magazine.

Men and officers were hurled into the sea. Gunners who had been standing at their mounts found themselves clinging to mats of wreckage. Sailors found themselves swimming desperately through glutinous oil in a fog of steam. *Rowan* was nowhere in sight. The destroyer had vanished. Forty seconds after the explosion, the ship was under the sea.

Loss of life in this sinking was excruciatingly heavy. Rescuers speeding to the scene could find only too few survivors, and many of these were wounded. Heroic lifesaving work by destroyer *Bristol* could not prevent a tragic death toll. She picked up 72 of *Rowan's* complement.

It has never been ascertained that *Rowan* was torpedoed by an E-boat. One of her signalmen declared that he sighted the killers through a spyglass, but no one else saw or heard of them. Although an E-boat torpedoing seemed highly probable, there remained the possibility that the ship had struck a mine.

Among the *Rowan* survivors was her captain, Lieutenant Commander Ford. Reporting the disaster, he praised the initiative of a bluejacket, Torpedoman Second W. F. Garrigus, who had managed to set the depth charges on safe. The man's quick action undoubtedly saved the lives of many swimmers struggling in the swirl where the ship went under.

Rowan was the first American destroyer lost in "Operation Avalanche." In the embattled seas off Salerno she was to have company.

Not far from the spot where *Rowan* went down, destroyer *Buck* was patrolling the approaches to Salerno. This was the night of October 8-9, 1943. The Americans had entered Naples on October 1, only to find the harbor a shambles. Retreating, the Nazis had blown up wharves, demolished docks and marine machinery, and blocked the bay with a sargasso of sunken ships. And while this wreckage was being cleared, invasion shipping continued to make port at Salerno. Hence the patrol in that locality by such destroyers as U.S.S. *Buck*.

Midnight, and all was well. The watch changed with mechanical precision. Down in the after engine-room an ensign listened attentively to the good drone of dependable turbines. Radar and sonar crews concentrated on their instruments.

Then suddenly all was changed. A surface radar contact had been made. *Buck's* captain, Lieutenant Commander M. J. Klein, sounded General Quarters. And whatever the preoccupation of those on or off watch at that hour—coffee, or sleep, or odd job, or reminiscence—all hands sprang as one man to battle stations. These were the same men who had taken the measure of Italian submarine *Argento*.

But while *Buck* was tracking the enemy that morning of October 9, the foe drew a deadly bead on the destroyer. Destroyermen thought they saw a dim silhouette across the water—a ghostly conning tower. Two torpedoes struck the destroyer's bow with killing violence. Smashing explosions burst the ship's hull plates, wrecked her forward compartments, and let in the flood.

In a turmoil of smoke, flame, and steam, the ship sloughed to a halt. Four minutes after she was hit, *Buck* plunged for the bottom. A depth-charge explosion blasted the swirl where the vessel sank. Then thunder and tumult were abruptly swallowed by the sea. Wreckage and oil spread across the surface, and with it drifting rafts, and the gagged shouts of swimming men.

Steaming to the rescue, destroyer *Gleaves* and British LCT *170* picked up 57 survivors. Lieutenant Commander Klein was not among the rescued. In an action that had taken the lives of some 150 of *Buck's* good company, the captain had gone down with his ship.

On the chart *Rowan's* grave is marked at lat. 40-07 N., long. 14-14-18 E. Near-by, within 15 miles, lies *Buck*. Two destroyers lost in the Salerno campaign.

But the invasion of Italy was only getting under way. Within a fortnight the effort would claim still another American DD.

In mid-October, 1943, all roads led to Rome. In particular, all transport highways in the Western Mediterranean were leading to Rome. The Rome haul was a long haul and a tough haul, beset all the way by brigandage and murder and war's legalized high piracy. In early autumn of 1943 the nearest Allied terminal was Salerno. But the Rome haul would eventually get through, largely aided by the work of such stalwarts as the U.S.S. *Bristol*.

On the night of October 12, 1943 *Bristol* (Commander J. A. Glick) was with a destroyer squadron steaming as screen for a transport division. The convoy was on a Mediterranean road which followed the coastline of Algeria. The evening was fine—clement weather and placid seascape under a sky powdered with stars.

At 0400 in the morning the convoy was off Cape Bougaroun, about midway between Algiers and Tunis. The fine night had, if anything, improved. A golden moon, high, full, and bright, laid a luminous path across the water. Visibility was excellent.

Patrolling at 15 knots on the port side of the formation, *Bristol* paced like a restless lion. Topside lookouts scanned sky and water with steady scrutiny. At their sensitive instruments, radar and sonar operators watched and listened. For eternal vigilance was the price of safety on this Mediterranean road.

Yet vigilance and all the detection devices of modern science were sometimes frustrated—and when least expected—by the cunning enemy. Under some conditions of water density and temperature, sonar's "echo-ranging" beams might peter out or be deflected. From undiscovered ambush a submarine might fire with deadly suddenness, its presence first betrayed by a streaking torpedo wake, or—as in *Bristol's* case—a whisper in the sound gear.

At 0423 the destroyer's sonar watch heard the hydrophone effect of a torpedo. The low, rushing whistle of an oncoming 88 mm. shell might have given the ship more warning. Scarcely was the alarm flashed topside when, ten seconds after it first was heard, the torpedo struck *Bristol*.

Smashing in on the ship's port side at the forward engine-room, the blast stopped the destroyer dead with a broken back. Men, guns, fragments of gear and machinery were strewn by the violent explosion. Mortally stricken, *Bristol* sagged in the moon-washed sea, and began to settle under a surge of smoke.

There was time to launch life rafts, to give the wounded a hand, to get overside in "Mae Wests." Not much time. A few minutes after she was struck, *Bristol* broke in two and sank. *Wainwright* and *Trippe* soon arrived to rescue survivors. Dawnlight presently aided the rescue work, and the lifesaving went swiftly forward. All told, 241 men were saved. But in spite of brave work by survivors and rescuers, casualties were heavy. Fifty-two of the crew were lost with the ship.

The submarine responsible for the sinking was never sighted, and so far as is known it eluded the hunt and escaped. It may have fired a long-range shot from periscope depth, and then gone deep into some whale-hole ambush to lie in wait for another convoy.

The road to Rome was a hard and dangerous road for the Destroyer Service, as loss of *Rowan, Buck* and *Bristol* is evidence. And before the autumn was out another American destroyer would go down on that death-stalked "Appian Way." The killers were German aircraft and their victim was U.S.S. *Beatty.*

By November, 1943, engineers and Seabees laboring like giants had cleared some of the Naples wreckage. Booby-traps had been exploded, a few port facilities had been replaced, others were repaired, and channels were open in the bay. Naples was shaping up as a base for the Allied ground forces fighting their way through Italy.

Bound for Naples in the first week of November was a great Allied ship-train, Convoy KME-25A, transporting tons of war supplies and thousands of troop reinforcements for the Army of General Mark Clark. Assembled in the United Kingdom, the convoy contained 15 American and eight British transports. These heavy-laden vessels were screened by a powerful destroyer task group, TG 60.2 under command of Captain C. C. Hartman, ComDesRon 15 . . .

In addition to the seven American DD's, the screen included three British destroyers, two Greek destroyers, and the anti-aircraft vessel H.M.S. *Colombo.* After the convoy entered the Mediterranean and headed eastward for the Tunisian War Channel, the task group was augmented by two American destroyer-escorts from Mers-el-Kebir. The DE's were *Frederick C. Davis* (Lieutenant Commander O. W. Goepner, U.S.N.R.), and *Herbert C. Jones* (Lieutenant Commander A. W. Gardes).

Steaming along the Algerian coast, the convoy followed the sea road which led to the narrow waist of the Mediterranean. Too large to pass through the Tunisian War Channel in columns of three ships each—the favored formation—the convoy was strung out in less maneuverable seven- and nine-ship columns.

The convoy's vulnerability became all too manifest on November 6, as the ships, having left Algiers far astern, were approaching Philippeville. Traveling at 12 knots, they had reached a point on the road not far from Cape Bougaroun, the scene of the *Bristol* ambush, when the enemy struck. Time: 1800. Visibility poor. Diving out of the dark and the daylight, the *Luftwaffe* descended like a flock of vultures on unsuspecting game.

This game, though, could fight back, with sweeping scythes of anti-aircraft fire.

A mixed force of some nine bombers and 16 torpedo planes, the Nazi aircraft attacked at 1804. Speeding in at low altitude, a plane slipped a sharpshooting torpedo into the water, and at 1805 American destroyer *Beatty* was fatally hit.

In the ensuing battle the screen destroyers of Task Group 60.2 put up a worthy defense. The attackers—destroyer-men identified at least one Heinkel 111, a Dornier 217, and three Junker 88's—ran into aerial thickets of ack-ack. *Davison* shot down a plane. *Parker* shot down a plane. *Tillman* shot down a plane. Destroyer-escort *H. C. Jones* shot down a plane. So did British destroyer *Haydon* and one of the transports in the convoy.

Poor visibility favored the aircraft, however, and they had the advantage of high-speed raiders versus large, slower moving targets. They struck at the van destroyers of the screen, at ships on the convoy's port flank and on its quarters. Then they concentrated on the quarters of the formation.

Fire-spitting AA guns broke up the attacks. They brought down a half dozen aircraft. They forced torpedo planes to make long-range drops, and bombers to remain at a high level. But bombs and torpedoes were not the only weapons wielded by the fast-flying enemy. In this onslaught on Convoy KMF-25A the Germans unleashed a new killer.

At first glimpse, destroyer gunners who had never seen it before took the thing for a midget airplane. Then, at close range, it resembled a winged rocket, a streak of red light with a flaring green tail. Released from a high-flying bomber, these phantasmal comets would swoop across the sky, then abruptly plummet down on a target in a screaming dive. Radio-controlled glider bombs!

First employed on Allied invasion shipping at Salerno, the glider bombs had appeared as a lethal menace to anchored vessels. Now they gave Convoy KMF-25A and Captain Hartman's task group some spine-chilling moments. They did not strike any ships, but they came devilishly close.

Dangerous as were the glider bombs in the battle off Cape Bougaroun, aircraft torpedoes were the weapons which wrought the havoc. Before the Nazi planes were finally beaten off, two Allied transports were fatally torpedo-stabbed—the S.S. *Santa Elena* and the S.S. *Aldegonde*. When the aircraft droned away in the dark they left behind them a sea splotched with fire and wreckage—burning ships and demolished planes.

Six planes for three ships . . .

After the battle a call for assistance was flashed to Algiers. From that port on November 7, Destroyer Division 32, under Commander J. C. Sowell, steamed to the scene to conduct rescue and salvage operations. This division contained flagship *Champlin* (Commander C. L. Melson), and destroyers *Boyle* (Lieutenant Commander B. P. Field, Jr.), *Nields* (Commander A. R. Heckey), and *Ordronaux* (Commander R. Brodie, Jr.).

The two transports which had been torpedoed remained afloat until the 7th. But the ships were not to be saved. Nor did the rescuers arrive in time to save destroyer *Beatty*. Long before they reached the battle scene, she had gone beyond all possible salvage.

When *Beatty* was hit, she was maintaining her position in the convoy formation. Stationed on the starboard quarter of the rear ship in the right-hand column, and about 3,000 yards out, the destroyer was target for the first attack which roared in through the twilight.

Lieutenant Commander W. Outerson and others topside scarcely had time to set their teeth before the killing torpedo struck the ship. With a stunning blast the warhead burst against the starboard side at the after engine-room. *Beatty* shuddered to a halt and sagged in the water with a broken keel.

She did not go down off Cape Bourgaroun without a fight. Below decks her damage-controlmen fought fire, steam, and flood with every measure available. Topside, her gunners battled the *Luftwaffe*.

Torpedoes rushed past her, bombs thundered in the water near-by, and glider bombs rocketed overhead. But though *Beatty* could beat off her assailants, she could not win the fight for buoyancy. Steadily the water rose below decks, stifling her power plant, drowning vital machinery.

Her damaged hull could not stand the strain of flooding. With a sudden lurch the ship broke in two. Under a pall of smoke the fore and aft sections sank. The time was about 2305.

Beatty's crew had abandoned smartly, with opportunity to launch rafts and floats, and to make good use of lifesaving gear. Casualties were consequently few. Eleven bluejackets were lost with the ship, and a wounded man died after rescue. The other wounded—an officer and six enlisted men—recovered from their injuries.

Rescuers found the *Beatty* men a tough, enduring lot. Perhaps the pace for endurance and pluck was set by Sam S. Poland, Radarman 3c, U.S.N.R. Manning his battle station at a starboard depth-charge thrower, Poland had been standing practically on top of the spot where the torpedo smote *Beatty*. Hurled overboard by the blast, he was flung into the sea with a double compound fracture of the left leg. All evening and all night he remained afloat, in spite of his broken leg. When his cries were finally heard, and he was sighted by destroyermen of the *U.S.S. Boyle,* Sam Poland was swimming—typical of the never-say-die spirit of the Destroyer Service.

By December 1943 the Mediterranean was no longer a potential Fascist lake. But the Nazis were doing their best to keep the Swastika flying over (and under) its waters. While they concentrated on the Tyrrhenian storm center, they did not neglect Algiers and Gibraltar traffic lanes.

However, the U-boat and *Luftwaffe* menace was gradually being stifled by an unremitting A/S and anti-aircraft campaign. This dual campaign entailed continuous sweeps and round-the-clock patrols which, often unproductive in the Algiers and Gibraltar areas, were particularly tedious for destroyermen on the U-boat hunt.

"You worked your shirt out at the elbows and you seemed to accomplish nothing," a destroyerman said. "Most of those anti-sub patrols off North Africa were as boresome as a cop's beat in Flatbush. But Murder Inc. was out there. You had all the excitement you could use when you ran into those gunmen."

In mid-December destroyer A/S teams killed two U-boats in the Western Mediterranean. The first was downed on the 13th by *U.S.S. Wainwright* and British destroyer *Calpe*.

The two DD's were conducting a sub-hunt in company with destroyers *Niblack* and *Benson*. They were sweeping an area northwest of Algiers and about midway between the North African coast and the coast of Spain when *Wainwright* left the group to investigate a "sub sighted" report. That was at 0120 in the morning of December 13.

Aware that they were "it" in a game of hide-and-seek, the U-boaters promptly ducked. *Wainwright* steamed this way and that, probing with sonar, but her electronic fingers were eluded by the needle in the haystack. At 0229 *H.M.S. Calpe* arrived on the scene to team up on the hunt.

The search continued through daybreak and sunrise—no success. Doggedly the two destroyers kept at it while the clock ticked through the morning, through noon, into afternoon. Persistence paid off. At 1408 *Wainwright's* sonar instruments registered a contact. Her captain, Commander W. W. Strohbehn, directed a booming depth-charge attack. *Calpe* picked up the contact at 1423 and promptly let go with depth charges. *Wainwright* regained sound contact at 1435, and coached her British team-mate up to the target. *Calpe* distributed a pattern of depth charges at 1440, and this blasting rang the bell.

Seven minutes after the last depth charge was dropped, a U-boat came spouting to the surface some 1,800 yards from *Wainwright.* The American destroyer opened fire. Two minutes of that, and the German submariners came out of the conning tower to abandon.

As the Nazi crew sprang overside, Strohbehn ordered the destroyer gunners to cease fire. Then he sent a party across the water to pick up survivors. The destroyermen had time to board the damaged U-boat and bring out men who were calling, "Kamerad!" *Calpe* joined in the rescue of these frantic submariners who preferred a Prisoner-of-War camp to entombment in a sunken U-boat.

At 1530 the two destroyers with their prisoners set a course for Algiers. Behind them on the bottom they left the *U-593.*

On the afternoon of December 16, 1943, a U-boat ambushed a convoy off Cape Falcon, Algeria. Torpedoes smashed into the *S.S. John S. Copley,* and there was death in the afternoon. Then American destroyers steamed out of Mers-el-Kebir to track down the sub.

Under the command of Captain H. Sanders, ComDesDiv 13, the destroyers were *Woolsey, Trippe,* and *Edison.* The last named did not get in on the U-boat kill, but she assisted in screening and in picking up the U-boat survivors. Sanders' flagship, the *Woolsey* (Commander H. R. Wier), and destroyer *Trippe* (Commander R. C. Williamson) did the shooting.

They reached the vicinity of the torpedoing about 1715, and

started the A/S search about 1730. Within 45 minutes of the hunt's beginning *Woolsey's* sonar put the finger on the skulking enemy.

As the destroyer jockeyed in on the attack, the contact evaporated, and the hunters held their depth charges in leash, waiting for a sharper materialization of the target. At 1837 *Woolsey* regained sound contact, and the destroyermen were able to execute a deliberate attack.

Thundering around the submarine, *Woolsey's* depth charges dished in the hull, pulverized light bulbs, and knocked out various electrical fixtures. The blasting also caused leakage, a casualty obviously fatal to a submarine if not soon mended. But persistent leaks may paralyze a submarine long before they flood it. A salty spray shooting in through a damaged gasket may wet the vessel's electrical cables and cause arcing, flashing, and the worst sort of fires and fumes. Sooner or later a leaking submarine must go down permanently or be brought to the surface. The Captain of leaking *U-73* ordered the crew to blow all ballast and take her to the surface.

Whereupon *Woolsey's* SG radar snared a "pip" dead ahead at a range of 1,900 yards—precisely what *Woolsey* and *Trippe* had been waiting for. They shot the ray of a powerful searchlight across the water. As the spotlight fastened on the submarine, the Nazi gunners opened fire. Hot steel whistled across *Woolsey's* deck; two bluejackets were wounded. The submariners were to regret this folly, for both destroyers immediately replied with a hot and accurate fusillade that lashed the U-boat into sinking wreckage. Some 27 Nazis went down with the boat. The destroyermen picked up 34 survivors.

Thus another Mediterranean marauder was eliminated. There were more where that one came from. But the Allies were driving forward, and the calendar was moving into 1944, and the days of Hitler's U-boats were numbered.

Sicily had been tough. Italy was a lot tougher. Nazi General Kesselring pulled his troops out of the southern end of the peninsula and established the rock-ribbed "Gustav" and "Adolph Hitler" lines athwart the peninsula to block the Allied drive for Rome. Fighting northward from Naples, the American Army crashed into the defenses at Monte Cassino, and was brought to a halt. On the Adriatic side of the peninsula the British were stopped at the Sangro River. As the year turned on 1944 the Allied invasion was stalled.

Meantime, German paratroopers had snatched Mussolini from prison, and the Allies had suffered a catastrophic setback at Bari, where the *Luftwaffe* (on December 2, 1943) smashed the Adriatic port with a lightning raid that sent sixteen transports to the bottom of the harbor.

With Naples and the important southern air base at Foggia in possession, American strategists were inclined to favor a holding action, but Churchill argued persuasively for a continued offensive in Italy. Because head-on attacks against the enemy's "mountain line" were proving extravagantly costly, the British Prime Minister promoted an amphibious landing on the Tyrrhenian coast at Anzio. Such a move would outflank the Nazi position at Monte Cassino, and put Allies troops 55 miles behind the "Gustav" line at a point only a few miles south of Rome.

Eisenhower cautioned that the move would be risky, but Churchill's strategy prevailed. Reinforcements were found for the Anzio operation, which was given the code-name "Shingle." As General Eisenhower was leaving for England to become Supreme Commander, Allied Expeditionary Forces, British General Sir Henry Maitland Wilson assumed the over-all Mediterranean command, hence was in charge of the Italian theater. "Operation Shingle" was to go full speed ahead. D-Day was set for January 22, 1944.

The landings were to take place on beaches in a sector which extended from Nettuno, a holiday resort some thirty miles south of Rome, to a point just below the Tiber estuary. Bull's-eye in this target sector was the little port of Anzio.

The invasion shipping assembled in the Naples area, the U. S. Navy and the Royal Navy teaming up with that cooperation which had brought them from the coast of Canada to this Italian littoral. The American naval forces (Amphibious Task Force 81) were commanded by Rear Admiral F. J. Lowry. British naval forces were under Rear Admiral Thomas Troubridge, R.N. The "Shingle" armada contained many of the amphibious vessels and fire-support warships which had carried the Allied invasion to Sicily and Salerno. Newcomers were also in the invasion fleet. A number of French, Dutch, and Greek warships, out to give the gunfire a United Nations tone. And two American destroyer-escorts, soon to show all and sundry that bantam DE's could put up a giant-size battle. . . .

Mission of Task Force 81 was to establish Army Forces ashore on beaches near Cape D'Anzio for an attack on the rear of the enemy's right flank. The warships were to cover the landings, furnish all necessary fire-support, and bolster the attack wherever possible.

Following a misleading course which headed in the general direction of Corsica and then swung back toward Cape D'Anzio, the invasion fleet approached Anzio about midnight of January 21. H-Hour was set for 0200, morning of the 22nd.

Closing the coast, the ships moved in on headlands and foreshore that looked as quiet as scenery in a painting.

The dark foreshore remained fixed and silent as the landing craft started in. Just before the troops reached the shallows, rocket boats sprayed the beaches with a preparatory barrage. By 0400 the vanguard had a solid footing on the beachhead, and scouts were probing inland. Still no reaction from the enemy.

Watching from offshore, sailors who remembered Salerno Gulf were surprised and pleased by this phenomenon. Unfortunately the picture was bound to change. With the morning light, gunfire began to thud and sputter behind the beaches. Presently the *Luftwaffe* put in an appearance. The battle for Anzio was on.

Yanks and Tommies skirmished into Anzio and Nettuno on D-Day afternoon, but the seizure of these little coast towns was only a beginning. Caught off base, the Nazis rushed men, guns, and planes to the area to contain the invaders. German 88mm. shells began to pound the Anzio-Nettuno beaches, and clouds of Swastika aircraft came roaring down the sky over the cape. As Admiral Lowry stated: "Initial bombings during D-Day were light, but increased in intensity from D plus one. The first ten days had approximately seventy red alerts, of which thirty-two resulted in bombing attacks."

An average of three air raids per day for ten straight days. The destroyers screening Task Force 81 had their fill of anti-aircraft work. More than their fill. Morning and night the gunners were kept jumping by dive-bombing and high-level bombing onslaughts. Heaviest raids were at evening twilight, at which time the *Luftwaffe* generally struck with dive-bombers, torpedo-planes, and glider bombs —a vicious combination. They managed, however, to get in only one surprise attack.

Meantime, the Army on D-Day had begun to call for fire-support, and the destroyers had begun to give it. Singly and severally, and sometimes in company with heavier warships, they moved along the coast to shoot at targets designated by shore fire-control parties.

Confusion might have resulted from the fact that American shore fire-control parties were operating with British warships, British shore fire-control parties were working with American warships, and U.S. Army Air Corps fighter pilots, using Army artillery procedure, were spotting for both British and American ships. But communications were exchanged with a glibness that brought results better than satisfactory.

In his report Admiral Lowry stated:

> As revealed by dispatch from VI Corps Commander to Commander Task Force 81, prisoners of war reported that naval gunfire . . . was very effective and demoralizing to German troops. . . . Probably the most important type of fire delivered by naval support units was in the form of interdiction fire on road junctions, highways, crossroads and bridges. By denying the use of certain strategic points to the enemy, our forces were able to organize their position before enemy reserves could be assembled to challenge the beachhead.

One of the first destroyers to give fire-support at Anzio was the *U.S.S. Mayo* (Commander A. D. Kaplan). On D-Day she steamed in to bombard enemy positions on the right flank of the Anzio beachhead. On the following day (January 23) she was still at it. The Germans had moved up heavy guns to lambaste the Anzio beaches, and under this cover a Nazi force was trying to fight its way across the Mussolini Canal. Thanks to *Mayo,* the Nazis were stopped on the towpath of this waterway. "The speed and accuracy of her fire," Admiral Lowry noted, "kept the Germans from counterattacking across Canale Mussolini."

Mayo continued to shell Nazi targets until the evening of January 24, when she was disabled by an underwater explosion of unknown origin. The blast, which occurred at 2001, may have been the work of a mine or an unseen, circling torpedo. The explosion mashed in the starboard side of the vessel, wrecking and flooding the after engine-room and after fire-room, rupturing the bulkhead between the two compartments, bulging the main deck, and breaking the starboard propeller shaft. With six men killed, a man missing, and twenty-five wounded, the *Mayo* crew fought her battle-damage, and kept her above water. She was towed to Naples for temporary repairs, and eventually sent home to the States.

Another destroyer which contributed hot fire-support to "Shingle" was *U.S.S. Ludlow* (Commander L. W. Creighton). At 1019 in the morning of January 26 she answered a call to shoot up a Nazi strongpoint in Littoria. Steaming to the area, she opened fire and lobbed 267 rounds at the target—enough to win her the message: "Nice going. No more Littoria."

Ludlow, too, was struck at Anzio. On February 8, while steaming off the coast, she was hit on the director deck by a 6-inch (or larger) shell. Luckily the projectile was a dud. But before it stopped spinning about the deck, it injured a bluejacket, exploded some ready ammunition, and a fragment of the rotating band slashed Commander Creighton's leg, felling him with a severe wound. The hot projectile, which was spilling its explosive charge, was picked up and heaved overside by Chief Gunner's Mate James D. Johnson—a nervy action which prevented more damage. *Ludlow* went on her way with Lieutenant P. Cutler, U.S.N.R., assuming temporary command of the ship.

Sufficient evidence of the able fire-support loaned the "Shingle" effort by the destroyers may be found in the records of the *U.S.S. Edison* (Commander H. A. Pearce). In action at Anzio this destroyer fired 1,854 rounds of 5-inch 38 ammunition at twenty-one separate targets. With 101 rounds fired on January 29, she turned a parade of Nazi trucks and armored vehicles into a roadside junk pile. From exuberant shore fire-control parties she received one congratulatory message after another. Here are some verbatim extracts.

Fire effective very very good brassed off a bunch of Krauts
Many enemy troops killed by your fire good work
Pilot said your fire was very effective you were hitting right on the artillery pieces you were firing at
Effect of fire machine-gun emplacement in building totally destroyed
Your last target was a tower being used as an observation post you demolished it completely

Bombardment missions were not the only ones deftly accomplished by destroyers at Anzio. As was usual in an amphibious operation, they did all sorts of jobs, some routine, some odd. For instance, some were conducting A/S sweeps around the transport area, and keeping an eye out for possible E-boats. Some destroyers were guiding incoming traffic, and some were escorting empty convoys over the seaward horizon. These latter destroyers in Task Group 81.6, under Captain J. P. Clay, ComDesRon 7, were dealt duties as various as versatility itself. A paramount duty was the covering of invasion shipping with anti-aircraft protection. Most of the destroyers participated in this effort at one time or another.

In fact, this task kept the destroyermen busier than any other detail at Anzio. German artillery and the *Luftwaffe* constituted the chief opposition. The big Krupp guns did not arrive until late in the campaign, but the *Luftwaffe* was already on the job. Enemy air raids averaged three a day for the ten days immediately following D-Day.

Destroyers watched the sky with vigilant radar, hammered the raiders with flak, and rushed about laying smoke screens to cloak threatened shipping. All ships and craft in the area had some sort of smoke-making apparatus. It was used to good effect during twilight and after-dark raids when flashing AA batteries might otherwise silhouette the ships. German aviators, stunting through heavens of fire, were forced to drop their bombs more or less at random on seas of smudge.

But the Heinkels, Junkers, and Dorniers got in a few savage licks. Early in the battle against the *Luftwaffe,* Captain Clay's flagship, destroyer *Plunkett,* was hit. The ship, which was skippered by Commander E. J. Burke, was sorely wounded.

The attack occurred on January 24 in the shadows of evening—the *Luftwaffe's* favorite hour. It was one of those triple-threat onslaughts which featured torpedo-planes, dive-bombers, and glider bombs. Some eight or ten aircraft participated. The planes sighted were identified as Junker 88's. *Plunkett's* Action Report describes the attack's development:

> The action opened when two glider bombs were observed coming in on the port beam. They were identified by a pale green light which marked their trajectory. Almost simultaneously two Junker 88's were observed at a fifty-foot altitude, one to port and one crossing ahead from starboard to port. Fire was opened and speed increased to 27 knots. A turn was made toward the glider bombs. These bombs hit the water about 200 yards astern of the ship.
>
> From this time on the ship was turned so as to keep pointed at the low flying planes. The forward 20mm. gun crews reported seeing a plane at low altitude drop a torpedo at about 800 yards range which paralleled the track of the ship. During the next ten minutes these planes were intermittently sighted trying to obtain favorable positions and at least five bombs fell, missing the ship from 20 to 200 yards. These bombs were believed to have been dropped by dive-bombers although the bombers were not seen.
>
> The silhouette of the ship must have been outlined by the continuous firing at the low level planes. One enemy plane was seen to

crash about 1,000 yards on the port beam and another 1,000 yards on the starboard bow. One was seen heading away trailing smoke. About twelve minutes after the action started this ship was hit on the 1.1-inch gun mount by a bomb. . . .

Estimated to be a 250-kilo job, the bomb detonated with a huge explosion that swept the deck with molten iron and fire. Men perished instantly in the face of this blast; a number were hurled overside or slain by flying debris. The flames touched off ready 1.1-inch and 20mm. ammunition near the gun mount, and the wild fusillade added to the carnage. Her port engine disabled, the destroyer staggered and veered. The starboard engine was stopped to prevent the wind from fanning flames over depth charges aft.

While desperate hands fought fire and explosion, the gunners at the forward 5-inch and 20 mm. mounts blazed away at the attacking aircraft. For five more minutes the ferocious battle continued; then the holocaust aft was brought under control, and simultaneously the planes sped off in the night. Barbarously mutilated, *Plunkett* limped out of the battle area. Some fifty-three destroyermen had lost their lives in the blasting; twenty were wounded. Under escort of destroyer *Niblack* the maimed warship was sent to Palermo. Captain H. Sanders, ComDesRon 13, in *Woolsey,* assumed command of Task Group 81.6.

Plunkett was not the only *Luftwaffe* victim at Anzio. A number of other ships were damaged and several were sunk, including H.M.S. *Spartan.* But losses were relatively light when balanced against the weight of air bombs, torpedoes, and glider bombs which the Nazi aircraft flung at Allied shipping in the first three weeks of "Shingle." And it was at Anzio that a pair of DE's nipped the glider bomb in the bud.

Hatched in dark secrecy in the recesses of Nazi Germany, the glider bomb—it might have been more appropriately called a robot jet—was a dwarf descendant of the murderous "buzz bomb." It did not have the "buzz bomb's" range, nor carry as big an explosive charge, but militarily it was far more dangerous, and its potentialities were appalling.

The big "buzz bomb" was a demolition weapon with enormous destructive power, but it was as senseless as a berserk butcher. The glider bomb, on the other hand, could be aimed. In effect, it operated as a small "buzz bomb" having rocket propulsion and a sentient control-mechanism which answered the directives of a radio signal. Launched by a high-level bomber, it could be guided by remote control, and sent into a meteor-like dive straight for the target. That this weapon possessed great propensities for slaughter was obvious to those who saw its introduction at Salerno and its use against Convoy KMF-25A. Something had to be done to counter it. But what?

Anti-aircraft guns were not the answer. Like comets the robots came rocketing down the sky, too fast for accurate AA fire, too small for snaring in a net of flak. At Salerno the only antidote seemed to be an aircraft counterattack on the high-level bombers which launched the glider bombs. Convoy KMF-25A, without air cover, had been compelled to sweat out the robot onslaught.

It may be remembered there were two DE's in the task group which escorted that embattled convoy—destroyer-escorts *Herbert C. Jones* and *Frederick C. Davis*. In company with the other vessels in the screen, the two little ships did their share of sweating when the glider bombs skimmed into view. Originally constructed as A/S vessels, destroyer-escorts were not as a type dedicated to anti-aircraft, much less anti-glider bomb, warfare. It appeared, however, that this pair was dedicated to that specific endeavor, for the Action Report of *Frederick C. Davis,* contains the following:

On 21 January this vessel departed from Naples. . . . At this time and for three months previously, this vessel together with *H. C. Jones* had comprised Task Group 80.2 whose mission was the investigation and development of countermeasures against radio-controlled bombs. As visualized in advance, therefore, the primary function of these vessels in Operation Shingle was the protection of shipping from this type of missile.

When *Davis* (Lieutenant Commander R. C. Robbins, Jr. U.S.N.R.) first reported for duty with the eighth Fleet, an interceptor unit (Y-team) was placed on board for service in connection with the investigation of glider bombs. This team was composed of three Army men, enlisted men who were technicians in the radio field. Why radio technicians? Because the rocket glider-bomb was radio-controlled. Radio was the key to the robot's performance, the "brain" which worked the steering mechanism and sent the bomb diving down on the target. And someone with quick perception had seen that this "brain" could also be an Achilles' heel.

For that which was guided by radio might also be *misguided* by radio—by jamming the air waves with broadcasts that would throw its radio-directed steering gear out of true.

Hence special intercepting and jamming equipment was rigged on board the *F. C. Davis;* the Y-team was prepared to scotch the robot's signals, if that were possible.

A Y-team with similar gear was placed on board destroyer-escort *H. C. Jones* (Lieutenant Commander R. A. Soule, III, U.S.N.R.). Captain Sanders' flagship, destroyer *Woolsey* (Commander H. R. Wier), also carried this type of apparatus. No one was certain that jamming would do the trick, but all hands involved in the effort were determined to make the try.

So "Shingle" found destroyer-escorts *Frederick C. Davis* and H. C. Jones stationed at the anchorage off Anzio beachhead. Day after day, raid after raid, they were there on duty with their peculiar equipment. Other ships flung up spectacular screens of AA fire. *Davis* and *Jones* were in there firing, too, but their most effective barrages were invisible. Whereas other warships were spraying the sky with TNT, these destroyer-escorts were spraying it with radio transmissions. And while the TNT was bringing down Nazi aircraft, the radio broadcasts were bringing down glider bombs.

Woolsey participated in this special work, but her Y-team equipment was not as effective as that on board the DE's. *Jones* and *Davis* fought the lion's share of the weird battle. They also starred as air raid wardens, detecting the *Luftwaffe's* approach and issuing warnings. Complimenting the *Davis* Y-team on it's performance, Lieutenant Commander Robbins stated, ". . . it should be said that the work of one of these men was truly remarkable, with the result that, prior to the establishment of shore-based radar, *Davis* was much the best and most reliable source for early warnings against enemy aircraft attack."

But the master accomplishment of *Davis* and *Jones* at Anzio was the frustration of the glider bomb—as is indicated by excerpts from the battle reports of Task Group Commander Sanders:

> During the period 22 January-2 February, 1944, there were some 26 bombing attacks by the German Air Force. Radio-controlled bombs were dropped during four of these attacks. . . . The efficiency with which *F. C. Davis* and *H. C. Jones* jammed radio-controlled bombs is an outstanding achievement on the part of these vessels.

During the period of this report (2-7 February, 12-14 February, 1944) there were some thirteen bombing attacks in the Anzio area. . . . Radio-controlled bombs were noted in two of these attacks. No ships were hit. . . . A feature of the glider bomb attacks was the effective deflection of the bombs by jammers in *F. C. Davis* and *H. C. Jones* and to a lesser extent by *Woolsey*. On the last attack two glider bombs were seen to suddenly break off from their flight path and plunge into the sea.

The above are samples. Between the lines one may discern some nerve-wracking drama: the tense moment when the DE's first tried the jamming gear—the cheering when a bomb was deflected—the sober faces of men who realized that a DE with her radio prattling could stand out like a sore thumb. What if those Nazi bombers got the idea these little ships were throwing a wrench in the robot machinery?

One day when the *Luftwaffe* was in the sky, a radioman of the *Davis* Y-team overheard an enemy pilot call to a squadron mate, "Let's all concentrate on Frau Maier." A knowledge of everyday German sent the listener's hair up. "Frau Maier" is slang for "old gossip." The listening radioman had an idea that "old gossip" was the *Frederick C. Davis*.

And no sooner had the intercepted message been reported to the bridge than four enemy planes peeled off and made for the DE. Thirteen bombs fell around her in a tight circle, ringing the ship with geysers. *Davis* rolled and shook. Not a bomb hit her, but flying shrapnel left her with the only casualty she was to suffer during 142 days of "Shingle."

"Frau Maier" continued her gossiping. She was attacked by torpedo planes; she was dive-bombed; she was strafed. She was jolted by near-misses. She was given a close shave by practically every aircraft weapon except one—the glider bomb. *Frederick C.* ("Frau Maier") *Davis* simply talked the robot down.

Excerpt from endorsement on *F. C. Davis* Action Report by Captain J. P. Clay, Commander Destroyers Eighth Fleet:

After Anzio landing, the *F. C. Davis* or *H. C. Jones* remained at the anchorage off the beachhead most of the time. Many enemy aircraft bombing and radio-controlled missile attacks were delivered on the convoys and beachhead anchorage while these destroyer-escorts were present. Their work in investigating frequencies and jamming the radio bombs has been outstanding.

Then the punch line:

As a result of the counteraction against the weapon, the Germans practically ceased using it in this area after February.

Raging at the Anzio beachhead, German General Kesselring managed to pin the Allied forces to the Anzio-Nettuno vicinity. Late in the winter huge 280mm. railroad guns were moved up by the Nazis to hold the line. Abetted by these Big Berthas, the German forces in the area dead-stalled the Anzio invaders.

Finally, when winter melted into spring, the stalemate was broken by mass Allied air raids which smashed up German communications lines as far north as Florence, and virtually obliterated Monte Cassino. Storming forward, the Fifth and Eighth Armies linked up near Anzio on May 25, 1944.

The Allied armies marched into Rome on June 4. Fall of the first Axis capital shook the world. For the Allies, ultimate victory was now within sight. For Nazi Germany and Samurai Japan, defeat loomed on the horizon. As for Italy, Fascism was in its grave.

American destroyers and destroyermen had played no small part in bringing about that dramatic victory.

AT THE ONSET OF JUNE 1944 MORE THAN A MILLION men were assembled in Great Britain for the long-awaited assault on Hitler's *Fortress Europa*. The plan for the invasion of Normandy (Operation "Neptune-Overlord"), originally conceived by Eisenhower two years before, had finally come to fruition. Joint strategy had envisioned an initial landing along a front of from twenty to fifty miles, from the Cotentin Peninsula on the east coast to the River Orne; and this was to incorporate the best features of an airborne assault with an attack by five divisions. Admiral Alan Kirk, long experienced in amphibious warfare and with a background of Embassy service at the outbreak of the war, was given command of the Western Task Force. Later he recalled: "For an invasion of this size we had to have a plan. You have to have a plan, and we had a *beautiful* one!" For more than a year amphibious rehearsals had taken place at Shepton Sands and Torquay, Devonshire, to simulate landings at Omaha Beach even to the point of mock bombardments. The enemy was kept guessing as to exact target date and location; the Army cooperated by collecting a full-scale force on the east coast to give the impression of a *main* Channel assault through the Pas-de-Calais, which resulted in the pinning down of the German Fifteenth Army for a considerable time after D-Day.

German defenses, under the tactical command of Field Marshals Erwin Rommel and Karl von Rundstedt, comprised the Seventh Army, including fourteen divisions behind a defensive Atlantic Wall consisting of a million land mines, beach obstacles, and casemated and mobile guns. There was a strong difference of opinion between Rommel and von Rundstedt, the former relying heavily on his wall and the "fighting to begin at high water mark", the latter trusting in mobile infantry and armored reserves posted to the rear to counterattack where needed.

During the first four days of June there were twice-daily weather conferences. The weather was bad, incessant rain pounding down on the locked-in troops aboard the landing craft. The decision had to be made now, or there would be the risk of a forty-eight-hour delay. Eisenhower listened to the gloomy predictions of his meteorologists. The best of these was "moderating west to northwest winds backing southwesterly; overcast with base at one thousand feet and two-foot waves." At 4:15 A.M. he made his decision:

"O.K. We go."

On the epochal morning Robert J. Casey, Chicago *News* correspondent, was aboard an LST at Southampton. He awoke when the skipper burst into his living space and announced, "We have a date with Hitler. Get cracking!"

10.

MAELSTROM OF SHIPS

Almost immediately the hook was up and we were moving. I went up on deck without knowing why I went and stood in the cold wind looking out over the same scene that I had looked at the day before and the day before that. A lot of queer-looking ships were slowly moving away from their moorings in a series of formations that seemed to have no pattern nor purpose. Now as always, Southampton Water looked like nothing so much as the cradle of chaos.

We slid by an LCT over the rail of which leaned a sergeant, one of those who was presently to toss the dice: his life against the peace and happiness of the world. But there was no look of ecstasy in his eyes. He was raising hell with somebody who had let his blankets get wet. He paused to look at me as we passed almost within touching distance.

"Looks like we're on our way," I said, just to make conversation.

"I'll believe it when I get there," he said. And he returned to the discussion of his blankets and the intimate details of some corporal's ancestry.

This was D-day, and to most of a million men it signified only that there was a new job to be done somewhere. The start of it had somehow all the panoply and thrill that you might associate with the blowing of the eight-o'clock whistle.

577

For a moment it seemed that the sea might be moderating. No fear! The air was clear and crisp at sea level, with scurrying cloud rack above. The wind was roaring. So far as I could see, this day was if anything a little worse than yesterday. But, so help me, as the minutes rolled on and we battered our way through the swells to the Channel it began to look as if this time they actually meant to go through with it.

The timing, I was willing to admit, couldn't have been better, once you granted that we might be able to get across the Channel without floundering. A signalman came up as I clung to a stanchion by the bridge to tell me that Rome had fallen to us that morning.

A destroyer streaked past us. She turned out to be an old Frenchman moving up to a merited place at the head of the column. Some hospital ships broke dimly through the haze over to starboard but even at a considerable distance and in bad light I could recognize them. They were old Channel ships, commanded, I was told later, by the same skippers who had been taking them back and forth through these waters for years. A trip to Cherbourg or Le Havre wasn't going to be any novelty to them.

Once we got under way the captain left the bridge to Lieutenant Davidson and came down to the cabin which, as I had been warned, was the only place on the ship where he could find enough deck space to spread out a map. He and the radio lieutenant and the artillery major lay belly-flat to study the chart. The major wanted to know where his action station might be.

"On any other ship I think I'd like to be in bed," he said. "But I don't like to think of a deck between me and the outside when I'm traveling in this one."

"If you can work an Oerlikon gun you might try that," the captain said. "That ought to keep you out in the open most of the time when the Germans discover us."

"In that case," said the major, "I might as well know where my abandonship station is, too."

"Stand on the deck," the captain suggested, "and when the water gets up to your navel, get off."

There was a lot of conversation during the morning about such things as our prospects. I don't think anybody put much value on them.

At 11:30 we had to slow down because the group supposed to be ahead of us was an hour late.

"The ever-normal foul-up," said the captain resignedly. "We'd better start figuring tide and drift for all hours of the day and for a couple of extra days."

But afterwhile the ships that were supposed to be ahead of us came tearing by into position. I could hardly believe it. We poured on a little more coal and went out past the Needles into a sea that looked like Niagara laid out flat. The boat began to roll from one beam-end to the other and I was glad to see that the ports had steel plates to augment the glass.

In spite of the discomfort, not to mention danger, of our position, I still had plenty of incentive to look at the scene. Behind us, a vague procession in the mist, the destroyers were coming out, an endless line of them, well spaced and stately, like the grand march at a ball. Among them I made out the *Slazak,* the Polish ship in which for a time I sailed the Mediterranean. Another Pole was behind her and farther down the column were a Dane, a Norwegian and a Dutchman. Here at any rate was some of the pageantry I had expected to see.

We couldn't pick a course through the murk. It seemed that the whole Channel was strewn with mines and we were going to have to zigzag all the way over. By noon the roaring sea was worse. The barometer had dropped another couple of points.

About 7:00 P.M. the captain came in from the bridge. He was dog-tired and obviously puzzled.

"They must know what they're doing," he said. "But I certainly don't. This is the worst weather we've had out here for months. Stuff is breaking down all over the place. . . ."

It was breaking down inside, too. The deck was littered with all the detachable junk in the cabin.

"A hell of a night," said the captain. "And it's going to be worse. You wouldn't think it possible, but it's going to be worse." He was right.

Somehow I got to sleep. But not for long. At 1:30 A.M. I was awakened by an infernal row with the engines, which seemed to be starting and stopping every few minutes. There'd be a starter hum and a dimming of lights, a rumble and growl and a phut and then the same thing over again while the ship rode in the trough of the waves and I braced myself to keep from falling out of bed. I got into some more clothes (I was already all dressed except for an overcoat) and went up on deck.

The Channel was covered with a sort of dim twilight—the moon spread out thin by the cloud rack. As my head came up through the hatch I looked off to port. An LCT was bearing down on us. We lurched. I slipped and caught myself and found myself looking off to starboard. Another LCT was bearing down on us. The world seemed filled with ships, ahead of us, behind us, abreast of us, scores of ships all charging without any more purpose or direction than logs suddenly released from a jam.

For our part, we seemed to be running around in circles, backing and filling and scooting forward through holes in the weirdest phalanx of vessels that ever tried to pile up on top of one another. There was virtually no clearance between units now. They were shipping green water over their bows and around them, and around us a frothy sea was boiling with a cold phosphorescence.

On the bridge everybody was calm—outwardly at least—and Lieutenant Davidson volunteered an explanation.

"We are crossing the great mine field," he said. "And these ships have to be made to head into it properly. There's a swept channel, of course, if we can get them to take it."

I looked at him in amazement.

"But what direction is it in?" I bawled into his ear. "No two of these crates are going the same direction."

"They're a little confused," he said, "but I think we can get them straightened out . . . if they don't sink us before we get the job done."

I told him I hoped so. His calm acceptance of the situation made it possible to hope that the miracle might happen and that order might come even out of a mess like this. But it didn't seem likely. The most carefully calculated military operation of all time had begun to show all the prescience and organization of a salmon run.

Davidson had been conservative in saying that the LCT skippers were confused. The odd performance that I had seen when I first came on deck had been bad enough. That was when they were traveling in straight lines. But before I reached the bridge they had begun to twist about and cross one another's bows in a way that made tomorrow's possible interference on the part of the Germans look like a waste of time. Now and then searchlights blinked. Loud hails were bawled from every quarter:

"Keep in the swept channel. . . . Follow the buoys or you'll be sunk. . . ."

I went below wondering how it was all going to come out. I was just too sick to stay on deck and I'd begun to quit caring what happened or when. In an hour or so the captain came down.

"It looks a little better," he said dubiously. "We caught up with a group that was late, and a group that was early caught up with us. But anyway at the moment we're all going the same direction. It's been something to look at . . . a maelstrom of ships."

"So," remarked the senior officer, "This is D-day!"

"Yes," said the captain. "It is. We talk about it for a couple of years and then it gets around to happening."

"It doesn't look like much, does it?" observed the senior officer.

"After last night nothing is ever going to look like much," said the captain. "But I'm glad I'm here. In another few hours we may have some idea about how this war is going to come out."

I looked out through the dim light of breaking day to discover that the impossible had somehow happened . . .

Our own group, a dozen LCTs and some nondescript craft, were stretched out on our port, their bows as perfectly aligned as if they had been breasting a dock.

"D-day!" the captain repeated. "And we're all here. And we're here on time."

The little bridge was packed with men, including the artillery major and a couple of his radio operators, and instruments no end—batteries, transmitters, receivers, antenna rods. Where the captain found space to operate the ship I never could tell.

At 6:00 A.M. flares began to bloom out of the gray ahead of us. They hung motionless in the sky, illuminating nothing, for perhaps five minutes. It seemed likely that Heinie had finally got wind of our presence.

We were headed straight south. Somewhere in the gloom in that direction lay the beach.

The flares were still burning when a squadron of Spitfires came out from shore, flying low over us. And then suddenly, six bursts churned up the water almost immediately ahead. It looked like the short limit of a good bracket. We kept boring steadily in at five knots, our LCTs, still in perfect order, wallowing along beside us.

At 6:05 two bombs smashed in front of the line of LSTs ahead of us and off the port side. The smash of them came back to us eerily distorted by the howling wind. Over on the left of our sector some flak began to shred the clouds.

There was considerable ack-ack directly ahead of us where the beach lay—ack-ack and Very lights and fireworks that looked like starry flowerpots.

Here is the timetable of an amazing morning:

6:12. More Spitfires came over.

6:15. Forty medium bombers came streaking up behind us. The sky was clearing a little but not enough for us to see who they were until they were directly overhead, and we greeted them with our necks pulled well down into our collars. They went on into the gloom shoreward and a few seconds later we saw orange-green flashes. Echoes came back to us presently like coal rolling down an iron chute. I guessed from the timing that we must be a couple of thousand yards off the beach.

The ships were getting closer together now. The forward units were slowing up. Those in the echelons, including our own, were moving up and filtering through. By 6:20 we had daylight—or as much daylight as we were going to get—but we couldn't see anything but ships. There was no sky save the mottled canopy of cloud. The horizons were hidden behind the ever-drifting, ever-changing planes of blue and white. There was no sea save the tossing feathers between your craft and the next.

6:30. We slid up another few hundred yards through what seemed like a moving-picture fade-in and began to leapfrog the infantry landing ships.

They had come into position, well on time, and were putting off their launches. Strings of these little boats, jammed with men, swarmed us in a serpentine course, scraping our sides, dodging under our counter. The men waved cheerily as they passed. Amazingly none of them appeared to be seasick.

They were moving so fast that I thought we must soon lose track of them in the mist. But the dead empty gray of the sea was changing. An oddly diffused light was trickling through it and the launches never got out of sight.

6:35. There is no need for a diary entry to mark this moment in memory forever. Across the thinning gauze of the mist ahead of the charging infantry launches appeared a dim, horizontal streak.

France!

I was seeing it for the first time since we went over the Hendaye bridge in the great retreat four years ago. I tried not to be sentimental about it but right then I was having a lot of difficulty dissociating the historic present from the crowding memories of that desperate past.

"That's Ver-sur-Mer ahead of us." I became aware that the captain had spoken to me twice.

"Oh, yes," I said.

"That's the beach where Admiral Byrd came down at the end of his transatlantic flight."

"He reported that it was a very nice place," I remembered.

"I guess it was," said the captain. "But we won't be able to check. We're going to blow it down."

So we were going to blow it down. I wondered how much more of that there was going to be before we got through with this mess. It was ironic that this green and pleasant land which had suffered so little physical damage in defeat was likely to be obliterated by victory. . . .

Evolved from nowhere by the shifting light, a line of cruisers and destroyers suddenly appeared ahead of us and, as if to give emphasis to what the captain had said, began to fire rapidly and continuously. Flame, sickly-looking orange plumes, began to fringe our advance and spread the dank air with choking brown smoke.

The noise at first was not noticeable in competition with the wind and the rumble of hundreds of marine motors. Then all at once it reached us with a dull wet echo: "Whup! Whup!" I had never known guns to sound like that before.

6:40. We came past a slowly moving cruiser of the *County* class only a couple of hundred feet off our port.

"She's feeling her way," the captain said, "She's not far from scraping the bottom right now."

As we passed she let go both turrets forward. The greenish flame for a moment blotted out everything else in our line of vision and white water boiled around her as she leaned back into the sea. The concussion was enough to upset a stomach even less squeamish than mine. I was conscious of her blasting long after we had gone by.

6:45. Major Loveday took over the microphone from one of his operatives and called to the artillery in the LCTs.

"All ships," he called, giving the code numbers. "Be ready to open fire in three minutes."

6:48. They fired.

6:48¼. "Boy," said the captain, "we made it in time!"

For five minutes the din was indescribable. Nearly a hundred tanks, none of them very far from us, were all blasting at once.

The tanks, mounted six to a landing craft, could shoot over each other but could not traverse their guns. Deflection was taken care of by maneuvering the ships as would be done by submarines firing torpedoes, and it was startling to see how the long line of unmanageable scows responded. They were rolling and flopping up and down in swells at least ten feet high but they never missed an order or failed to make a change in direction in perfect timing.

"It's like a ballet, something. . . ." the captain murmured admiringly. "The dance of the hippopotami out of *Fantasia*."

I started to say that if they were rocket ships you might refer to them as Rockettes, but I thought better of it.

We couldn't, then, see the effect of the barrage that was screaming inland. But puffs of white were spreading over the black zone on the horizon. It looked to me as if we were on the target.

We had slowed down to three knots and were plowing forward, firing as we went. The little infantry launches covered the sea all about us and ahead of us. We couldn't see where they came from. All at once they were just there, passing us like a pack of hounds toward the beach. In the near distance they looked like whitecaps and as numerous.

There was no retaliatory fire. The battery that had got the short end of a bracket on us had either been knocked out or called off. I was surprised to discover that I couldn't remember when it had quit firing.

Out in front of us the beach and cliffs and houses of Ver-sur-Mer were beginning to loom up greenish and wet like something dredged up from the bottom of an aquarium. The shore line was yellow, rising up through green shadow to a ridge. Roofs and angular planes and spires stuck up out of it. One of these, I judged, was a lighthouse that the artillery major had mentioned last night as a particular target.

Our barrage was plainly visible now and it was a good one, marching up the hill in a line of smoke.

7:05. More planes came over and disappeared inland. We couldn't see whether or not they were dropping any bombs. The artillery was raising too much disturbance ashore for a bomb to be noticed. Another group of LCTs came abreast of us and went into action. Apparently they were a little late—as well they might be after so foul a night. We were in the middle of a congestion like Main Street in

Christmas week and guns were popping off on all sides of us. We rode literally through masses of flame.

7:06. A German shell burst ahead of us and to port. It was a small one that raised only a puny jet of water but big enough to finish us off if it had hit.

7:07. Another one hit in the same place. It burst with a sound like tearing canvas.

7:08. A third one. This was almost on top of a destroyer in the screen to the left of the massed LCTs.

7:10. The fourth slug screamed over us and smashed behind the destroyer. Bracket!

7:11. At least one of us on the bridge stopped breathing and waited for the finish. It didn't come. I don't know why. We must have been squarely under the sights of the battery. The shooting was as good as any professional could ask. Another salvo could have finished some of us off with noisy dispatch. But there was no other salvo.

7:15. The rocket ships came up, elbowed their way into spots from which they could fire and turned loose the most amazing display I have ever seen in the artillery business. They let off banks of 200 or 300 at a time and the projectiles shrieked into the murk trailing parallel streamers of fire. They rose with the rush of a hurricane plus a wail right out of the pit—a noise that seemed to shatter until it came back from the end of their flight like the echo of gravel falling on a tin roof.

Off to the left the destroyers were laying down a heavy smoke screen—not that we seemed to need it in weather as soupy as this.

7:17. A shell barely missed the rail of the leading destroyer. The battery commander on the beach apparently was still in business.

7:19. More rocket ships—more fingers of flame clawing the sky off to port. A typhoon of noise went with them and smothering clouds of smoke rolled back to hide the ships.

7:20. Two air bursts spread out black and menacing above the cruiser to port. We waited for the rest of the salvo but it was lost somewhere in the smoke and the noise of our own guns. Red tracers from small guns at the head of the advance began to bead the sky. We never caught a glimpse of the plane they were firing at.

7:21. Six shells burst in the water to port between our LCTs and the destroyer screen. Clean misses, all of them.

7:22. It was light enough now to see villas and summer hotels on the shore immediately ahead. The lighthouse was plainly visible now, a white finger rising from a clump of dark green woods. The rockets were bursting on the crest to the right of it in great splashes of fire that twinkled like spangles. Air bursts were smashing into the top of it.

We fired our last tank salvo . . . squarely on the target.

7:40. An LCT blew up just off the beach with a terrible eruption of colored lights. Our LCTs picked up speed and took position ahead of us on their way in. A shell came over so near that I could have sworn I felt the draft from it.

"I guess," said the captain pleasantly, "that somebody is shooting at us." We had no chance to think about it for just then our LCTs slid up onto the sandy beach. The bows opened and the tanks came roaring out into the front yard of Ver-sur-Mer. We went aground right after them, smashing our asdic dome, and stayed for an uncomfortable hour in a wild storm of machine-gun bullets.

Off on the horizon to starboard a battleship suddenly appeared. I knew her for an American from the moment I noticed the color of the paint on her top rig. Almost before she had come over the rim of the sea she was blasting the distant cliffs with broadsides from her main battery. And I studied her through the glasses unbelievingly and felt an emotional surge that I knew I wasn't going to be able to share with anybody aboard.

So help me! The *Nevada* . . . the last time I had seen that ship was the day she started to come up off the bottom in Pearl Harbor . . .

LET US TURN TO THE INVASION'S HEAVY SHIPS AND transports. Vice Admiral Morton L. Deyo is on cruiser *Tuscaloosa's* bridge, staring out over the awesome scene. In the ensuing excerpt, which opens the previous night the highly-decorated flag officer vividly describes the approach and initial bombardment.

II.

NAVAL GUNS AT NORMANDY

The great spring, wound so tightly, is now released; the vast energy loosed by that fateful signal begins to travel down the length of the coil—slowly, almost imperceptibly, but gaining momentum. Now there is no turning back; the unleashed energy must either turn into an inundating tidal wave to flood the shores of Normandy or shatter itself to pieces at the water's edge.

Our first thought is the weather. It is none too fine a night; murky, fretful, and with an abating wind and sea. The overcast begins to thin as we emerge from the Irish Sea and round the light on Land's End. The Lizard comes abeam and we change course to the northeastward to parallel the coast of Cornwall when, suddenly the morning sun breaks through right in our eyes. Before all our ships have swung to the new course, the clouds have closed in again. But that flood of sunlight works magic against the chilly mist, hanging over everything. I look down from the bridge across the tops of two triple 8″ turrets onto the *Tuscaloosa's* long wet forecastle and see men gathered in small knots or busy with the endless chores of shipboard; they have brightened too and some have begun their customary solemn-faced banter. It seems a good omen, that glimpse of sun.

Meanwhile (Rear Admiral Carlton S.) Bryant's group have forged ahead to join Omaha Force (making a brave show as their signal flags snap in the lessening breeze). We change our formation to a single column of ships. The parade is forming. The leader is HMS *Enterprise,* who will regulate her speed all the way across the Channel to maintain twelve knots advance for our convoy.

Steaming all daylight in so vulnerable a formation and with so few escorting destroyers is possible only if Allied air superiority drives the *Luftwaffe* away. In addition, British anti-submarine patrols in and beyond the Channel must hold the U-boats beyond the armada's long track. Lastly the British Home Fleet far away in the North Sea must discourage any desperate breakout by the German fleet; fortunately by this juncture it is not too possible.

Off Plymouth, at 10:45 A.M. right on schedule, attack transport *Bayfield* slips into her place. She flies the flag of Rear Admiral Moon, who has with him Major Generals Collins and Barton, whose 4th Division will land tomorrow. Still other transports join off Dartmouth, the *Barnett, Dickman* and *Empire.* Also we have eight destroyers in company, the order of ships fixed by the order of entering the assault area. (With such a multitude of ships and craft it would mean hopeless confusion to change the formation of the slower convoys during the crossing, and therefore, all vessels—fast and slow ships—observe similar procedure. The reason for the endless columns, instead of more compact groups, is deference to the enemy's mines . . .)

During the afternoon we begin to pass many of the five knotters, long columns due in the assault area during the later hours of D-Day; a heterogenous assortment of cutters, corvettes, trawlers, sub chasers, large and blunt-nosed LSTs. The faster ones adjust their speed to the slowest . . . The track of our convoy is the westernmost of seven which issue from every opening in England's southern coast . . .

At 6 P.M. off Portland Bill we change course southeasterly for five hours. The weather is improving; sea subsiding; wind fresh and northwesterly; ceiling a little higher but still overcast. As dusk gathers and the tracks begin to converge, more amphibious columns are passed. The numerous LCTs are still rolling and lurching, and their cramped open decks bear uncomfortable soldiers who will rejoice to set foot ashore no matter what awaits them. Yet as we pass these various amphibious ugly ducklings, we are impressed by an air of cheerfulness, even jauntiness in their crowded cargoes. Soldiers wave to us as we pass. One looks us over appraisingly and shouts an offer as he balances precariously on the canting deck. "How'll you trade your tub for this ship—about even?" God preserve America and its humor . . .

As they steam and putt and chug along one feels an inevitability, a sureness of overwhelming strength and unity. Far beyond range of binoculars stretch unending processions moving precisely according to a master plan. Across these treacherous Channel waters which have defied a Napoleon and a Hitler, they proceed, heaving, yawning, gently rolling, or just grandly advancing according to their dimensions. All are parts of an unbelievable mosaic to be spread at the proper moment across the Baie de la Seine and upon the shores of Normandy . . . All day air search radars and lookouts are busy. The few planes we have seen under the overcast are friendly. Where is the *Luftwaffe*? Perhaps the weather has deceived the Nazis into believing we await more favorable conditions. That, in fact, is the case. Of U-boats, heavily relied upon by the enemy, we have heard nothing. The British Coastal Command guards the western approaches with ships and planes . . . So now it is six bells; 11 P.M. Through binoculars we can see the second ship ahead, the old *Nevada* turning to starboard. Next goes *Quincy* and *Tuscaloosa*. Then *Black Prince* in her wake follows us around. The subdued flashing of a marker vessel's light is off the port bow. That is the entrance to swept Channel #2. We are entering #1 and heading almost south. *Enterprise* leading the column, has found the marker buoys. The seven approach lanes of the Invasion have now turned and separated into 10 swept channels through which the columns will now pass to their initial positions. Each of the five forces has two channels, a "fast" and a "slow" one. Channels #1 and 2 are for "Utah"; 3 and 4 for "Omaha", the remainder for the (British) Eastern Task Force. The flagship, *Augusta* (with Admiral Kirk and General Bradley embarked) is with Omaha force. We are about thirty miles north of the Baie de la Seine; two and one-half hours at this speed. The northwest wind is on our starboard beam and subsiding; the sea is flattening through the swell, is still uncomfortable for smaller craft. A high overcast obscures the moon, but its presence begins to be noticed because one can see more ships than before.

Time advances swiftly. There is a sense of listening. Our flag bridge is dead quiet. On the forecastle and upper deck where the crew are now at battle stations, voices are hushed. One seems to feel the presence of millions of men . . . The atmosphere is alive with the spirits of men. One is aware of a sort of quiet exaltation, a more than confidence, as though the Great Leader above is at the helm, reassuring us. We begin ticking off the lighted buoys (so well placed by our sweepers) red to starboard, green to port. One thinks of those mine-sweeping squadrons far ahead, numerous and tough, moving unprotected save for a few destroyers, into the dangerous waters. With exact navigation, working in the darkness and advancing close to the hostile coast these stout sailors have cleared numerous and intricate channels, hundreds of miles of them. Channels, most carefully predetermined, are to be swept so that each of thousands of invasion craft may take its appointed place in the pattern of assault. It is not enough for them to sweep; they must mark as well . . .

Soon we begin to observe over the blackness where land is, golden streaks of light. These are the flak tracers, sketching faint patterns against the sky; searching for allied planes. There! One is hit; a candle of flame up high. Slowly it turns, and slowly falls. And before it reaches earth, the flame is gone. The enemy is obviously alerted; soon we will be detected . . . Another candle is lighted and falls . . . It is nearly 1 A.M. There is a roaring of many planes overhead. All ships have been alerted but at first there are anxious moments lest some trigger-happy ships open up on us. They are the airborne troops, C47s, towing gliders all filled with men of the 101st and 82nd airborne divisions. They are due to drop at H-5 hours, thirty minutes hence. More groups pass over us at intervals—we can see them against the overcast; they are to seize the outlets to the causeways, across which our troops will pass to advance inland.

It is 1:20 A.M. Ahead we can see the lights of the station vessels at "Point Mike" where our channels separate at the boundary of Utah. Already the leading ships have changed course to port, headed for the Transport Area. *Enterprise, Hawkins, Soemba* (the latter to join at daylight) with destroyers *Jeffers, Glennon, Hobson* and *Forrest,* the escorts for the four large transports carrying General Barton's 4th Division troops. Fire Support Unit One—heavy ships *Nevada, Quincy, Tuscaloosa* and *Black Prince* together with Units Three and Four change course to starboard and close the coast. We are thus to be interposed between the transports and shore batteries. Now we enter our channel which is marked by green lights, advancing slowly, hoping not to alert the enemy while giving the minesweepers time to complete the clearing of intricate fire support channels. At slow speeds the current interferes with station keeping so at 2:30 A.M. we make signal to anchor. In this position, we can execute

Bombardment Plan Zebra if the enemy wakes up. If he does not we shall wait here, timing our advance into firing stations to take place about daylight. Our spotting planes are not due to arrive before daylight, so we will postpone action until then, enemy permitting.

We are under the lee of the land now. The wind is westerly about eighteen miles per hour. The slight chop will scarcely interfere even with small craft. Omaha Beach will not have a lee; the weather will be less favorable. All eyes have been drawn in astonishment to the tall lighthouse at Pte. Barfleur. Its light is serenely burning, beckoning to sailors as though no bloody conflict were scheduled for this very day!

We think of the transport area. It is about eleven and one-half miles off shore near the range limit of the medium shore batteries. Converging upon it are numerous convoys of LSTs, LCTs, LCIs, LCMs. Altogether there are nearly 900 craft of various sizes and shapes in the Utah force. The rough seas and the 24-hour postponement have placed a heavy burden upon the leaders of convoys for their schedules call for exact times of arrival. Some are almost sure to be late. This could dislocate the plans . . . Things are now becoming visible around us; dawn comes early. It is time to move in.

No sign from the enemy . . . passing Barfleur light . . . tiny "Dan" buoy lights marking our swept water . . . Some of the minesweepers are now coming out and beginning to widen the channels. Their first work is completed. Well done . . . All ships are ready and gain speed, advancing steadily toward stations. Leading the heavy ships, Old *Nevada* looks majestic and formidable in the early light. Far inshore I see the destroyers, thrusting lean and confident noses toward shore. I expect all Hell to break loose any moment now and am ready for it.

"H Hour" is 6:30 A.M. for Utah beach. (It varies slightly for other beaches due to the difference in tidal conditions.) Our bombardment is scheduled for 5:50 A.M. Our first spotting planes are due over designated enemy batteries at 5:18 A.M.—they should be in radio communication with us a few minutes after the hour. Each of our ships will go to its station, fix its position with greatest accuracy, stream a reference buoy, and remain there. Most Captains will drop an anchor to hold more easily in the strong currents; but this will depend upon the direction of the current and how the ship swings to it. With the eastern light at our backs we shall be silhouetted and plainly visible to those on shore, while they will be indistinct and misty to us. *By this time anyone ashore looking seaward must have observed us.*

At 4:45 A.M. heavy ships are in exact position. Several are talking by voice radio to their spotting planes as they arrive overhead from England. The shore has emerged distinctly. The "question mark" lies before us, somewhat bold in the bulge but low and sandy along the stem. Our radar stands high, looking like a huge bed spring. Smaller ones are also visible, and enemy radar can now be detected by our instruments. They are searching for us. They find us! We have some experimental equipment for causing interference, so we use it and the enemy radar wanders off. That is good fortune of the highest, but not for long. There! The enemy batteries have come to life; it is 5:30 A.M. *Black Prince* is under fire. Tall splashes spring up and subside first short and then beyond her, not very close. Now *Quincy* is getting attention, medium-calibre shells, perhaps 170s. Some ships ask permission to reply. Permission is not granted. I wish to give our planes time to find which enemy batteries are active. Now all our ships are under fire, and enemy shooting improves: the salvos are closer.

At 5:36 A.M., I order the signal "Commence counter battery bombardment" and from *Tuscaloosa's* forecastle inside No. 2 turret comes the shrill, ascending song of the ammunition car speeding upward from the magazines; a metallic thump as the 8″ shell drops into its loading tray. The clatter of shell in the breech reverberates through the gun barrel; a hollow blow as it is rammed hard against its seat. The rest is not heard but already the three turrets, two forward, one aft, have swung to port and are sternly facing their target. Nine long, graceful 8″ rifles rise as one to the correct elevation. Two buzzes, "Stand by", one buzz! Flash; jar; lurch; acrid smoke passes my face. The game has begun, the tension is over. Enemy shooting improves. *Black Prince* is being straddled closely. There are splashes around *Nevada* and *Quincy,* who remain firmly in place and fire deliberately.

Smack! Bang! One short, one over *Tuscaloosa.* Close ones, very noisy, violent. Geysers of water with black, ugly centers lead up as high as our mastheads. There is some trouble communicating with the spotting plane. Flashes and smoke are seen around the point near St. Vaagt. *Tuscaloosa* joins *Black Prince,* using ship spot to silence that one. It is stubborn and quite a battle ensues. Meanwhile destroyers *Hobson, Corry* and *Fitch* have been leading the first waves of landing boats down the boat lane, breaking off in time to be in their stations at 5:40. *Shubrich* and *Herndon* then proceed across to the southern side of the boat lane. Only the heavy ships have planes to spot for them. The destroyers will be close enough to see their targets which consist mostly of strong points just back of the beaches.

Through binoculars the boat lane to the southeastward is alive with craft approaching the line of departure. The first assault wave will be twenty LCVPs, ten for "Red" beach and ten for "Green". Their time of touch down is H Hour. With, or just after them, will be eight LCTs, each carrying four tanks. The second wave following closely, contains thirty-two LCVPs with two more battalions of infantry plus engineers and eight Navy demolition teams to blow up the beach obstacles. The third wave due at H plus 15 includes a dozen tanks and the fourth, two minutes later, consists chiefly of combat engineers to clear the beaches.

What is of vital importance now is whether our engagement with the large shore batteries is preventing them from shooting into the boat lane. A number of large shells landing among tight formations of landing craft could have serious consequences. It could disrupt the order of boats; separate combat teams; throw the timing out of gear and cause great confusion. But so far we can see no shells falling in the boat lane, nor are there any reports of trouble from Moon . . . It appears we are successful and that the large batteries are too busy to think of anything beyond fighting us . . .

To beat down the formidable defenses we have provided a 40-minute "beach drenching" (we wish it were much longer) typical of up-to-date amphibious assaults. This now begins. It is H-40 (5:50 A.M.).

Upon certain designated strong points each of the bombardment ships opens fire. This will give a fairly even distribution of bursting shells all along the landing area and its flanks. The large ships use their secondary batteries (5"), *Nevada* and *Quincy* also employ their big guns briefly to break the seawall in five places. On the open bridge, ears plugged with cotton, helmet straps buckled, we look and listen, bracing our feet as the 10,000 ton cruiser jumps and lurches to the blast of her guns. Everywhere to the west and south and southeast the battle rises to crescendo and reaches its climax. Before our onslaught the enemy batteries falter. Only a few are now reported active by our planes and their shooting is intermittent.

Just before 6 A.M., nearly 300 bombers (B26s) of Brereton's 9th Air Force have roared overhead and dropped many tons of bombs along the beach area. Over in the boat lane the first waves are nearing shore. Preceding them are the Support Craft Group. They are part of our Bombardment Group Organization and operating under our Plan. But we have had no control of their training as they are part of the amphibious team. They number about 35 craft of the LCT type, fitted as gun boats and rocket launchers. Their shallow draft permits them to work in close to the beaches. Just prior to the landing these craft will spray the strong points of Green and Red beaches with rockets while the gun boats engage such active opposition points as they can observe. The cumulative effect of the air bombing and naval shells bursting in the sand virtually blots out the shore to those approaching it. A huge pall hangs in the air; all is now obscured.

The moment of touch down nears. It is almost time to lift our drenching fire from the landing beaches . . .

THE EASIEST OF THE FIVE MAJOR LANDINGS BEGAN, AS scheduled, at Utah Beach, along a nine-mile stretch of the Cotentin Peninsula's east coast. At this time several of Admiral Deyo's support ships commenced a series of gun duels with the Nazi shore batteries. Destroyer *Corry* was taken under intense fire, to which she retaliated in kind—an event brilliantly described by author Cornelius Ryan, who picks up the action aboard the destroyer.

12.

THE FLAG HUNG LIMP

FOR A MOMENT

Off Utah the U.S.S. *Corry's* guns were red-hot. They were firing so fast that sailors stood on the turrets playing hoses on the barrels. Almost from the moment Lieutenant Commander George Hoffman had maneuvered his destroyer into firing position and dropped anchor, the *Corry's* guns had been slamming shells inland at the rate of eight 5-inchers a minute. One German battery would never bother anyone again; the *Corry* had ripped it open with 110 well-placed rounds. The Germans had been firing back—and hard. The *Corry* was the one destroyer the enemy spotters could see. Smoke-laying planes had been assigned to protect the "inshore close support" bombarding group, but the *Corry's* plane had been shot down. One battery in particular, on the bluffs overlooking the coast above Utah—the gun flashes located it near the village of St.-Marcouf—seemed to be concentrating all its fury on the exposed destroyer. Hoffman decided to move back before it was too late. "We swung around," recalls Radioman Third Class Bennie Glisson, "and showed them our fantail like an old maid to a Marine."

But the *Corry* was in shallow water, close to a number of knife-edged reefs. Her skipper could not make the dash for safety until he was clear. For a few minutes he was forced to play a tense cat-and-mouse game with the German gunners. Trying to anticipate their salvos, Hoffman put the *Corry* through a series of jolting maneuvers.

595

He shot forward, went astern, swung to port, then to starboard, stopped dead, went forward again. All the while his guns engaged the battery. Nearby, the destroyer U.S.S. *Fitch* saw his predicament and began firing on the St.-Marcouf guns too. But there was no letup from the sharp-shooting Germans. Almost bracketed by their shells, Hoffman inched the *Corry* out. Finally, satisfied that he was away from the reefs, he ordered, "Hard right rudder! Full speed ahead!" and the *Corry* leaped forward. Hoffman looked behind him. Salvos were smacking into their wake, throwing up great plumes of spray. He breathed easier; he had made it. It was at that instant that his luck ran out. Tearing through the water at more than twenty-eight knots the *Corry* ran headlong onto a submerged mine.

There was a great rending explosion that seemed to throw the destroyer sideways out of the water. The shock was so great that Hoffman was stunned. It seemed to him "that the ship had been lifted by an earthquake." In his radio shack Bennie Glisson, who had been looking out a porthole, suddenly felt that he had been "dropped into a concrete mixer." Jerked off his feet, he was hurled upward against the ceiling, and then he crashed down and smashed his knee.

The mine had cut the *Corry* almost in half. Running across the main deck was a rip more than one foot in width. The bow and the stern pointed crazily upward; about all that held the destroyer together was the deck superstructure. The fireroom and engine room were flooded. There were few survivors in the number two boiler room—the men there were almost instantly scalded to death when the boiler blew up. The rudder was jammed. There was no power, yet somehow in the steam and fire of her death agonies the *Corry* continued to charge crazily through the water. Hoffman became suddenly aware that some of his guns were still firing—his gunners, without power, continued to load and fire manually.

The twisted pile of steel that had once been the *Corry* thrashed through the sea for more than a thousand yards before finally coming to a halt. Then the German batteries zeroed in. "Abandon ship!" Hoffman ordered. Within the next few minutes at least nine shells plowed into the wreck. One blew up the 40-millimeter ammunition. Another set off the smoke generator on the fantail, almost asphyxiating the crew as they struggled into boats and rafts.

The sea was two feet above the main deck when Hoffman, taking one last look around, dived overboard and swam toward a raft. Behind him the *Corry* settled on the bottom, her masts and part of her

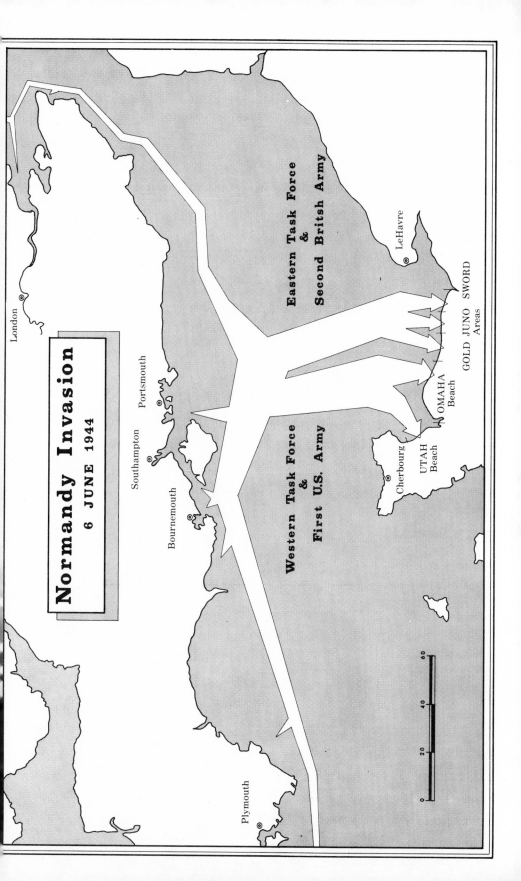

Normandy Invasion
6 JUNE 1944

London

Plymouth

Bournemouth

Southampton   Portsmouth

Eastern Task Force
&
Second Britsh Army

Western Task Force
&
First U.S. Army

LeHavre

Cherbourg

UTAH
Beach

OMAHA
Beach

GOLD JUNO SWORD
Areas

0   20   40   60

superstructure remaining above the waves—the U.S. Navy's only major D-Day loss. Of Hoffman's 294-man crew thirteen were dead or missing and thirty-three injured, more casualties than had been suffered in the Utah Beach landings up to this time.

Hoffman thought he was the last to leave the *Corry*. But he wasn't. Nobody knows now who the last man was, but as the boats and rafts pulled away, men on the other ships saw a sailor climb the *Corry's* stern. He removed the ensign, which had been shot down, and then, swimming and climbing over the wreckage, he reached the main mast. From the U.S.S. *Butler* Coxswain Dick Scrimshaw watched in amazement and admiration as the sailor, shells still falling about him, calmly tied on the flag and ran it up the mast. Then he swam away. Above the wreck of the *Corry* Scrimshaw saw the flag hung limp for a moment. Then it stretched out and fluttered in the breeze.

~~~~~~

DAVID HOWARTH, ANOTHER WHO CHRONICLED D-DAY, sets the scene for the landings. Here, briefly, he gives us a penetrating assessment of the bombardment and the resultant conditions on the beaches.

13.

"THE MORNING WAS

RATHER MISTY."

The conditions of cloud in the early morning varied from place to place, but there is no evidence that they were worse at Omaha than they were at Utah. The difference between the air bombing on the two beaches was a difference in policy and aircraft. At Utah, medium bombers, Marauders, carried out the last-minute bombardment; at Omaha, the job was done by heavy bombers, Liberators. These heavy bombers could either bomb visually or by instruments, which in those days was a much less accurate method. The decision was taken the night before, on the basis of the weather forecast, to use instruments, and this decision was endorsed by the Supreme Command.

The infantrymen, who had hoped and expected to find the defenses in ruins, knew nothing of this decision, or of its implications. Because of the inaccuracy of the instruments, there was thought to be a risk that the bombing would hit the landing craft. The aircrews were therefore ordered to delay their drop after crossing the coast, the length of the delay to vary inversely with the length of the time before H Hour until it reached as long as thirty seconds. This meant inevitably that the center of the weight of bombs fell at first a few hundred yards inland, and crept further away until just before H Hour it was three miles beyond the beach; and none of the bombs, except a few which were badly aimed, fell near enough to the beach defenses to do them the slightest harm.

The results of the naval bombardment were also meager; but this is not so simple to explain. The bombardment looked heavy on paper. There were two American battleships, *Texas* and *Arkansas,* three cruisers of which one was British and two were Free French, and eight destroyers. They were to fire thirty-five hundred rounds of calibers from 5 to 14 inches. Army artillery was mounted on landing craft so that it could fire while it was waiting to go in, and was scheduled to fire nine thousand rounds in the thirty minutes before H Hour. Finally, nine rocket craft were each to fire a thousand high-explosive rockets. What happened to 21,500 projectiles? There are many answers, and none of them conclusive. Only quite a small proportion of the volume of fire was real naval gunnery. The rockets were notoriously inaccurate under the best of conditions. The aiming of army guns in small landing craft could only have been uncertain, because the sea was rough. The morning was rather misty and the beach was soon covered like Utah with smoke and dust, which made spotting difficult for the larger ships. The Germans had taken care to make their emplacements difficult to see and almost impregnable by fire from seaward, and intelligence and reconnaissance had not detected them all. Part of the naval effort, especially of the battleship *Arkansas,* was directed against heavy German batteries far out on the flanks which threatened the sea approaches but did not affect the beach. A naval historian, summing it up, believes the bombardment was simply too light and too short; no more ships could be used, because there was no more room for them in the sea, and the navy needed more time to do the job thoroughly. It was the army, he implies, who restricted the length of the shooting to thirty-five minutes.

Nobody can be certain either exactly how much damage the shelling had done before H Hour, and the guesses vary. The only certain thing is that it did not do nearly enough, and that when the troops started to cross the beach the greater part of the German defenses were still intact and went into action against them.

The weather which had rendered the aerial bombing useless and distracted the gunners' aim caused its greatest havoc among the infantry landing craft and the amphibious tanks. The conditions of cloud at Utah and Omaha were much the same, but the conditions of sea were quite different. The wind was blowing at ten to eighteen knots from the northwest. At Utah, the wind was off-shore, and the closer one went to the beach, the calmer the sea became. At Omaha it was on-shore; and the waves were four feet high, and sometimes six feet. Neither the landing craft nor the amphibious tanks were designed to work in such a rough sea as that . . .

~~~~~~

AT THE 16TH RCT SECTOR OF OMAHA BEACH, WHERE the confusion of war reigned supreme, landing craft were taken under enfilading fire from casemated 75- and 88mm guns on either side of the Colleville exit. On Fox Green beach, a twelve-mile strip, the men who finally reached it lay like a "human carpet", subjected to everything the Germans could throw. Most of the landing craft in this sector were from the transports *British Empire, Anvil* and *Henrico* and were immediately hit, or swamped offshore, or did not even locate the beach.

As a war reporter for *Collier*'s, Ernest Hemingway, winner of the Pulitzer and Nobel Prizes, and considered by many the greatest American novelist, was aboard one of the landing craft in the first wave bound for Fox Green sector of Omaha.

14.

VOYAGE TO VICTORY

. . . The day we took Fox Green beach was the sixth of June, and the wind was blowing hard out of the northwest. As we moved in toward land in the gray early light, the 36-foot coffin-shaped steel boats took solid green sheets of water that fell on the helmeted heads of the troops packed shoulder to shoulder in the stiff, awkward, uncomfortable, lonely companionship of men going to a battle. There were cases of TNT, with rubber-tube life preservers wrapped around them to float them in the surf, stacked forward in the steel well of the LCV(P), and there were piles of bazookas and boxes of bazooka rockets encased in waterproof coverings that reminded you of the transparent raincoats college girls wear.

All this equipment, too, had the rubber-tube life preservers strapped and tied on, and the men wore these same gray rubber tubes strapped under their armpits.

As the boat rose to a sea, the green water turned white and came slamming in over the men, the guns and the cases of explosives. Ahead you could see the coast of France. The gray booms and derrick-forested bulks of the attack transports were behind now, and, over all the sea, boats were crawling forward toward France.

As the LCV(P) rose to the crest of a wave, you saw the line of low, silhouetted cruisers and the two big battlewagons lying broadside to the shore. You saw the heat-bright flashes of their guns and the brown smoke that pushed out against the wind and then blew away.

"What's your course, coxswain?" Lieutenant (jg) Robert Anderson of Roanoke, Virginia, shouted from the stern.

"Two-twenty, sir," the coxswain, Frank Currier of Saugus, Massachusetts, answered. He was a thin-faced, freckled boy with his eyes fixed on the compass.

"Then steer two-twenty, damn it!" Anderson said. "Don't steer all over the whole damn' ocean!"

"I'm steering two-twenty, sir," the coxswain said patiently.

"Well, steer it, then," Andy said. He was nervous, but the boat crew, who were making their first landing under fire, knew this officer had taken LCV(P)s in to the African landing, Sicily and Salerno, and they had confidence in him.

"Don't steer into that LCT," Andy shouted, as we roared by the ugly steel hull of a tank landing craft, her vehicles sealashed, her troops huddling out of the spray.

"I'm steering two-twenty," the coxswain said.

"That doesn't mean you have to run into everything on the ocean," Andy said. He was a handsome, hollow-cheeked boy with a lot of style and a sort of easy petulance. "Mr. Hemingway, will you please see if you can see what that flag is over there, with your glasses?"

I got my old miniature Zeiss glasses out of an inside pocket, where they were wrapped in a woolen sock with some tissue to clean them, and focused them on the flag. I made the flag out just before a wave drenched the glasses.

"It's green."

"Then we are in the mine-swept channel," Andy said. "That's all right. Coxswain, what's the matter with you? Can't you steer two-twenty?"

I was trying to dry my glasses, but it was hopeless the way the spray was coming in, so I wrapped them up for a try later on and watched the battleship *Texas* shelling the shore. She was just off on our right now and firing over us as we moved in toward the French coast, which was showing clearer all the time on what was, or was not, a course of 220 degrees, depending on whether you believed Andy or Currier the coxswain.

The low cliffs were broken by valleys. There was a town with a church spire in one of them. There was a wood that came down to the sea. There was a house on the right of one of the beaches. On all the headlands, the gorse was burning, but the northwest wind held the smoke close to the ground.

Those of our troops who were not wax-gray with sea sickness, fighting it off, trying to hold onto themselves before they had to grab for the steel side of the boat, were watching the *Texas* with looks of surprise and happiness. Under the steel helmets they looked like pikemen of the Middle Ages to whose aid in battle had suddenly come some strange and unbelievable monster.

There would be a flash like a blast furnace from the 14-inch guns of the *Texas,* that would lick far out from the ship. Then the yellow-brown smoke would cloud out and, with the smoke still rolling, the concussion and the report would hit us, jarring the men's helmets. It struck your near ear like a punch with a heavy, dry glove.

Then up on the green rise of a hill that now showed clearly as we moved in would spout two tall black fountains of earth and smoke.

"Look what they're doing to those Germans," I leaned forward to hear a G.I. say above the roar of the motor. "I guess there won't be a man alive there," he said happily.

That is the only thing I remember hearing a G.I. say all that morning. They spoke to one another sometimes, but you could not hear them with the roar the 225-horsepower high-speed gray Diesel made. Mostly, though, they stood silent without speaking. I never saw anyone smile after we left the line of firing ships. They had seen the mysterious monster that was helping them, but now he was gone and they were alone again.

I found if I kept my mouth open from the time I saw the guns flash until after the concussion, it took the shock away.

I was glad when we were inside and out of the line of fire of the *Texas* and the *Arkansas.* Other ships were firing over us all day and you were never away from the sudden, slapping thud of naval gunfire. But the big guns of the *Texas* and *Arkansas* that sounded as though they were throwing whole railway trains across the sky were far away as we moved on in. They were no part of our world as we moved steadily over the gray, white-capped sea toward where, ahead of us, death was being issued in small, intimate, accurately administered packages. They were like the thunder of a storm that is passing in another county whose rain will never reach you. But they were knocking out the shore batteries, so that later the destroyers could move in almost to the shore when they had to come in to save the landing.

Now ahead of us we could see the coast in complete detail. Andy opened the silhouette map with all the beaches and their distinguishing features reproduced on it, and I got my glasses out and commenced drying and wiping them under the shelter of the skirts of my burberry. As far as you could see, there were landing craft moving in over the gray sea. The sun was under at this time, and smoke was blowing all along the coast.

The map that Andy spread on his knees was in ten folded sheets, held together with staples, and marked Appendix One to Annex A. Five different sheets were stapled together and, as I watched Andy open his map, which spread, open, twice as long as a man could reach with outstretched arms, the wind caught it, and the section of the map showing Dog White, Fox Red, Fox Green, Dog Green, Easy Red and part of Sector Charlie snapped twice gaily in the wind and blew overboard.

I had studied this map and memorized most of it, but it is one thing to have it in your memory and another thing to see it actually on paper and be able to check and be sure.

"Have you got a small chart, Andy?" I shouted. "One of those one-sheet ones with just Fox Green and Easy Red?"

"Never had one," said Andy. All this time we were approaching the coast of France, which looked increasingly hostile.

"That the only chart?" I said, close to his ear.

"Only one," said Andy, "and it disintegrated on me. A wave hit it, and it disintegrated. What beach do you think we are opposite?"

"There's the church tower that looks like Colleville," I said. "That ought to be on Fox Green. Then there is a house like the one marked on Fox Green and the timber that runs down to the water in a straight line, like on Easy Red."

"That's right," said Andy. "But I think we're too far to the left."

"Those are the features, all right," I said. "I've got them in my head but there shouldn't be any cliffs. The cliffs start to the left of Fox Green where Fox Red beach starts. If that's true, then Fox Green has to be on our right."

"There's a control boat here somewhere," Andy said. "We'll find out what beach we're opposite."

"She can't be Fox Green if there are cliffs," I said.

"That's right," Andy said. "We'll find out from a control boat. Steer for that PC, coxswain. No, not there! Don't you see him? Get ahead of him. You'll never catch him that way."

We never did catch him, either. We slammed into the seas instead of topping them, and the boat pulled away from us. The LCV(P) was bow-heavy with the load of TNT and the weight of the three-eighth-inch steel armor, and where she should have lifted easily over the seas she banged into them and the water came in solidly.

"The hell with him!" Andy said. "We'll ask this LCI."

Landing Craft Infantry are the only amphibious operations craft that look as though they were made to go to sea. They very nearly have the lines of a ship, while the LCV(P)s look like iron bathtubs, and the LCTs like floating fright gondolas. Everywhere you could see, the ocean was covered with these craft but very few of them were headed toward shore. They would start toward the beach, then sheer off and circle back. On the beach itself, in from where we were, there were lines of what looked like tanks, but my glasses were still too wet to function.

"Where's Fox Green beach?" Andy cupped his hands and shouted up at the LCI that was surging past us, loaded with troops.

"Can't hear," someone shouted. We had no megaphone.

"What beach are we opposite?" Andy yelled.

The officer on the LCI shook his head. The other officers did not even look toward us. They were looking over their shoulders at the beach.

"Get her close alongside, coxswain," Andy said. "Come on, get in there close."

We roared up alongside the LCI, then cut down the motor as she slipped past us.

"Where's Fox Green beach?" Andy yelled, as the wind blew the words away.

"Straight in to your right," an officer shouted.

"Thanks." Andy looked astern at the other two boats and told Ed Banker, the signalman, "Get them to close up. Get them up."

Ed Banker turned around and jerked his forearm, with index finger raised, up and down. "They're closing up, sir," he said.

Looking back you could see the other heavily loaded boats climbing the waves that were green now the sun was out, and pounding down into the troughs.

"You wet all through, sir?" Ed asked me.

"All the way."

"Me, too," Ed said. "Only thing wasn't wet was my belly button. Now it's wet, too."

"This has got to be Fox Green," I said to Andy. "I recognize where the cliff stops. That's all Fox Green to the right. There is the Colleville church. There's the house on the beach. There's the Ruquet Valley on Easy Red to the right. This is Fox Green absolutely."

"We'll check when we get in closer," Andy said. "You really think it's Fox Green?"

"It has to be."

Ahead of us, the various landing craft were all acting in the same confusing manner—heading in, coming out and circling.

"There's something wrong as hell," I said to Andy. "See the tanks? They're all along the edge of the beach. They haven't gone in at all."

Just then one of the tanks flared up and started to burn with thick black smoke and yellow flame. Farther down the beach, another tank started burning. Along the line of the beach, they were crouched like big yellow toads along the high water line. As I stood up, watching, two more started to burn. The first ones were pouring out gray smoke now, and the wind was blowing it flat along the beach. As I stood up, trying to see if there was anyone in beyond the high water line of tanks, one of the burning tanks blew up with a flash in the streaming gray smoke.

"There's a boat we can check with," Andy said. "Coxswain, steer for that LC over there. Yes, that one. Put her hard over. Come on. Get over there!"

This was a black boat, fast-looking, mounting two machine guns and wallowing slowly out away from the beach, her engine almost idling.

"Can you tell us what beach this is?" Andy shouted.

"Dog White," came the answer.

"Are you sure?"

"Dog White beach," they called from the black boat.

"You checked it?" Andy called.

"It's Dog White beach," they called back from the boat, and their screw churned the water white as they slipped into speed and pulled away from us.

I was discouraged now, because ahead of us, inshore, was every landmark I had memorized on Fox Green and Easy Red beaches. The line of the cliffs that marked the left end of Fox Green beach showed clearly. Every house was where it should be. The steeple of the Colleville church showed exactly as it had in the silhouette. I had studied the charts, the silhouettes, the data on the obstacles in the water and the defenses all one morning, and I remember having asked our Captain, Commander W. I. Leahy of the attack transport *Dorothea M. Dix,* if our attack was to be a diversion in force.

"No," he had said. "Absolutely not. What makes you ask that question?"

"Because these beaches are so highly defensible."

"The Army is going to clear the obstacles and the mines out in the first thirty minutes," Captain Leahy had told me. "They're going to cut lanes in through them for the landing craft."

I wish I could write the full story of what it means to take a transport across through a mine-swept channel; the mathematical precision of maneuver; the infinite detail and chronometrical accuracy and split-second timing of everything from the time the anchor comes up until the boats are lowered and away into the roaring, sea-churning assembly circle from which they break off into the attack wave.

The story of all the teamwork behind that has to be written, but to get all that in would take a book, and this is simply the account of how it was in a LCV(P) on the day we stormed Fox Green beach.

Right at this moment, no one seemed to know where Fox Green beach was. I was sure we were opposite it, but the patrol boat had said this was Dog White beach which should be 4,295 yards to our right, if we were where I knew we were.

"It can't be Dog White, Andy," I said. "Those are the cliffs where Fox Red starts on our left."

"The man says it's Dog White," Andy said.

In the solid-packed troops in the boat, a man with a vertical white bar painted on his helmet was looking at us and shaking his head. He had high cheekbones and a rather flat, puzzled face.

"The lieutenant says he knows it, and we're on Fox Green," Ed Banker shouted back at us. He spoke again to the lieutenant but we could not hear what they said.

Andy shouted at the lieutenant, and he nodded his helmeted head up and down.

"He says it's Fox Green," Andy said.

"Ask him where he wants to go in," I said.

Just then another small black patrol boat with several officers in it came toward us from the beach, and an officer stood up in it and megaphoned, "Are there any boats here for the seventh wave on Fox Green beach?"

There was one boat for that wave with us, and the officer shouted to them to follow their boat.

"Is this Fox Green?" Andy called to them.

"Yes. Do you see that ruined house? Fox Green beach runs for eleven hundred and thirty-five yards to the right of that ruined house."

"Can you get into the beach?"

"I can't tell you that. You will have to ask a beach control boat."

"Can't we just run in?"

"I have no authority on that. You must ask the beach control boat."

"Where is it?"

"Way out there somewhere."

"We can go in where an LCV(P) has been in or an LCI," I said. "It's bound to be clear where they run in, and we can go in under the lee of one."

"We'll look for the control boat," Andy said, and we went banging out to sea through the swarming traffic of landing craft and lighters.

"I can't find her," Andy said. "She isn't here. She ought to be in closer. We have to get the hell in. We're late now. Let's go in."

"Ask him where he is supposed to land," I said.

Andy went down and talked to the lieutenant. I could see the lieutenant's lips moving as he spoke, but could hear nothing above the engine noise.

"He wants to run straight in for that ruined house," Andy said, when he came back.

We headed in for the beach. As we came in, running fast, the black patrol boat swung over toward us again.

"Did you find the control boat?" they megaphoned.

"No!"

"What are you going to do?"

"We're going in," Andy yelled.

"Well, good luck to you fellows," the megaphone said. It came over, slow and solemn like a elegy. "Good luck to all of you fellows."

That included Thomas E. Nash, engineer, from Seattle with a good grin and two teeth out of it. It included Edward F. Banker, signalman, of Brooklyn, and Lacey T. Shiflet of Orange, Virginia, who would have been the gunner if we had had room for guns. It included Frank Currier, the coxswain, of Saugus, Massachusetts, and it included Andy and me. When we heard the lugubrious tone of that parting benediction we all knew how bad the beach really was.

As we came roaring in on the beach, I sat high on the stern to see what we were up against. I had the glasses dry now and I took a good look at the shore. The shore was coming toward us awfully fast, and in the glasses it was coming even faster.

On the beach on the left where there was no sheltering overhang of shingled bank, the first, second, third, fourth and fifth waves lay where they had fallen, looking like so many heavily laden bundles on the flat pebbly stretch between the sea and the first cover. To the right, there was an open stretch where the beach exit led up a wooded valley from the sea. It was here that the Germans hoped to get something very good, and later we saw them get it.

To the right of this, two tanks were burning on the crest of the beach, the smoke now gray after the first violent black and yellow billows. Coming in I had spotted two machine-gun nests. One was firing intermittently from the ruins of the smashed house on the right of the small valley. The other was two hundred yards to the right and possibly four hundred yards in front of the beach.

The officer commanding the troops we were carrying had asked us to head directly for the beach opposite the ruined house.

"Right in there," he said. "That's where."

"Andy," I said, "that whole sector is enfiladed by machine-gun fire. I just saw them open twice on that stranded boat."

An LCV(P) was slanted drunkenly in the stakes like a lost gray steel bathtub. They were firing at the water line, and the fire was kicking up sharp spurts of water.

"That's where he says he wants to go," Andy said. "So that's where we'll take him."

"It isn't any good," I said. "I've seen both those guns open up."

"That's where he wants to go," Andy said. "Put her ahead straight in." He turned astern and signaled to the other boats, jerking his arm, with its upraised finger, up and down.

"Come on, you guys," he said, inaudible in the roar of the motor that sounded like a plane taking off. "Close up! Close up! What's the matter with you? Close up, can't you? Take her straight in, cox-swain!"

At this point, we entered the beaten zone from the two machine-gun points, and I ducked my head under the sharp cracking that was going overhead. Then I dropped into the well in the stern sheets where the gunner would have been if we had any guns. The machine-gun fire was throwing water all around the boat, and an anti-tank shell tossed up a jet of water over us.

The lieutenant was talking, but I couldn't hear what he said. Andy could hear him. He had his head down close to his lips.

"Get her the hell around and out of here, coxswain!" Andy called. "Get her out of here!"

As we swung round on our stern in a pivot and pulled out, the machine-gun fire stopped. But individual sniping shots kept cracking over or spitting into the water around us. I'd got my head up again with some difficulty and was watching the shore.

"It wasn't cleared, either," Andy said. "You could see the mines on all those stakes."

"Let's coast along and find a good place to put them ashore," I said. "If we stay outside of the machine-gun fire, I don't think they'll shoot at us with anything big because we're just an LCV(P), and they've got better targets than us."

"We'll look for a place," Andy said.

"What's he want now?" I said to Andy.

The lieutenant's lips were moving again. They moved very slowly and as though they had no connection with him or with his face.

Andy got down to listen to him. He came back into the stern. "He wants to go out to an LCI we passed that has his commanding officer on it."

"We can get him ashore farther up toward Easy Red," I said.

"He wants to see his commanding officer," Andy said. "Those people in that black boat were from his outfit."

Out a way, rolling in the sea, was a Landing Craft Infantry, and as we came alongside of her I saw a ragged shellhole through the steel plates forward of her pilothouse where an 88mm. German shell had punched through. Blood was dripping from the shiny edges of the hole into the sea with each roll of the LCI. Her rails and hull had been befouled by seasick men, and her dead were laid forward of her pilothouse. Our lieutenant had some conversation with another officer while we rose and fell in the surge alongside the black iron hull, and then we pulled away.

Andy went forward and talked to him, then came aft again, and we sat up on the stern and watched two destroyers coming along toward us from the eastern beaches, their guns pounding away at targets on the headlands and sloping fields behind the beaches.

"He says they don't want him to go in yet; to wait," Andy said. "Let's get out of the way of this destroyer."

"How long is he going to wait?"

"He says they have no business in there now. People that should have been ahead of them haven't gone in yet. They told him to wait."

"Let's get in where we can keep track of it," I said. "Take the glasses and look at that beach, but don't tell them forward what you see."

Andy looked. He handed the glasses back to me and shook his head.

"Let's cruise along it to the right and see how it is up at that end," I said. "I'm pretty sure we can get in there when he wants to get in. You're sure they told him he shouldn't go in?"

"That's what he says."

"Talk to him again and get it straight."

Andy came back. "He says they shouldn't go in now. They're supposed to clear the mines away, so the tanks can go, and he says nothing is in there to go yet. He says they told him it is all fouled up and to stay out yet a while."

The destroyer was firing point blank at the concrete pillbox that had fired at us on the first trip into the beach, and as the guns fired you heard the bursts and saw the earth jump almost at the same time as the empty brass cases clanged back onto the steel deck. The five-inch guns of the destroyer were smashing at the ruined house at the edge of the little valley where the other machine gun had fired from.

"Let's move in now that the can has gone by and see if we can't find a good place," Andy said.

"That can punched out what was holding them up there, and you can see some infantry working up that draw now," I said to Andy. "Here, take the glasses."

Slowly, laboriously, as though they were Atlas carrying the world on their shoulders, men were working up the valley on our right. They were not firing. They were just moving slowly up the valley like a tired pack train at the end of the day, going the other way from home.

"The infantry has pushed up to the top of the ridge at the end of that valley," I shouted to the lieutenant.

"They don't want us yet," he said. "They told me clear they didn't want us yet."

"Let me take the glasses—or Hemingway," Andy said. Then he handed them back. "In there, there's somebody signaling with a yellow flag, and there's a boat in there in trouble, it looks like. Coxswain, take her straight in."

We moved in toward the beach at full speed, and Ed Banker looked around and said, "Mr. Anderson, the other boats are coming, too."

"Get them back!" Andy said. "Get them back!"

Banker turned around and waved the boats away. He had difficulty making them understand, but finally the wide waves they were throwing subsided and they dropped astern.

"Did you get them back?" Andy asked, without looking away from the beach where we could see a half-sunken LCV(P) foundered in the mined stakes.

"Yes, sir," Ed Banker said.

An LCI was headed straight toward us, pulling away from the beach after having circled to go in. As it passed, a man shouted with a megaphone, "There are wounded on that boat and she is sinking."

"Can you get in to her?"

The only words we heard clearly from the megaphone as the wind snatched the voice away were "machine-gun nest."

"Did they say there was or there wasn't a machine-gun nest?" Andy said.

"I couldn't hear."

"Run alongside of her again, coxswain," he said. "Run close alongside."

"Did you say there was a machine-gun nest?" he shouted.

An officer leaned over with the megaphone. "A machine-gun nest has been firing on them. They are sinking."

"Take her straight in, coxswain," Andy said.

It was difficult to make our way through the stakes that had been sunk as obstructions, because there were contact mines fastened to them, that looked like large double pie plates fastened face to face. They looked as though they had been spiked to the pilings and then assembled. They were the ugly, neutral gray-yellow color that almost every thing is in war.

We did not know what other stakes with mines were under us, but the ones that we could see we fended off by hand and worked our way to the sinking boat.

It was not easy to bring on board the man who had been shot through the lower abdomen, because there was no room to let the ramp down the way we were jammed in the stakes with the cross sea.

I do not know why the Germans did not fire on us unless the destroyer had knocked the machine-gun pillbox out. Or maybe they were waiting for us to blow up with the mines. Certainly the mines had been a great amount of trouble to lay and the Germans might well have wanted to see them work. We were in the range of the anti-tank gun that had fired on us before, and all the time we were maneuvering and working in the stakes I was waiting for it to fire.

As we lowered the ramp the first time, while we were crowded in against the other LCV(P), but before she sank, I saw three tanks coming along the beach, barely moving, they were advancing so slowly. The Germans let them cross the open space where the valley opened onto the beach, and it was absolutely flat with a perfect field or fire. Then I saw a little fountain of water jut up, just over and beyond the lead tank. Then smoke broke out of the leading tank on the side away from us, and I saw two men dive out of the turret and land on their hands and knees on the stones of the beach. They were close enough so that I could see their faces, but no more men came out as the tank started to blaze up and burn fiercely.

By then, we had the wounded man and the survivors on board, the ramp back up, and were feeling our way out through the stakes. As we cleared the last of the stakes, and Currier opened up the engine wide as we pulled out to sea, another tank was beginning to burn.

We took the wounded boy out to the destroyer. They hoisted him aboard in it one of those metal baskets and took on the survivors. Meantime, the destroyers had run in almost to the beach and were blowing every pillbox out of the ground with their five-inch guns. I saw a piece of German about three feet long with an arm on it sail high up into the air in the fountaining of one shellburst. It reminded me of a scene in Petroushka.

The infantry had now worked up the valley on our left and had gone on over that ridge. There was no reason for anyone to stay out now. We ran in to a good spot we had picked on the beach and put our troops and their TNT and their bazookas and their lieutenant ashore, and that was that.

The Germans were still shooting with their anti-tank guns, shifting them around in the valley, holding their fire until they had a target they wanted. Their mortars were still laying a plunging fire along the beaches. They had left people behind to snipe at the beaches, and when we left, finally, all these people who were firing were evidently going to stay until dark at least.

The heavily loaded ducks that had formerly sunk in the waves on their way in were now making the beach steadily. The famous thirty-minute clearing of the channels through the mined obstacles was still a myth, and now, with the high tide, it was a tough trip in with the stakes submerged.

We had six craft missing, finally, out of the twenty-four LCV(P)s that went in from the *Dix,* but many of the crews could have been picked up and might be on other vessels. It had been a frontal assault in broad daylight, against a mined beach defended by all the obstacles military ingenuity could devise. The beach had been defended as stubbornly and as intelligently as any troops could defend it. But every boat from the *Dix* had landed her troops and cargo. No boat was lost through bad seamanship. All that were lost were lost by enemy action. And we had taken the beach.

There is much that I have not written. You could write for a week and not give everyone credit for what he did on a front of 1,135 yards. Real war is never like paper war, nor do accounts of it read much the way it looks. But if you want to know how it was in an LCV(P) on D-Day when we took Fox Green beach and Easy Red beach on the sixth of June, 1944, then this is as near as I can come to it.

***

ABOARD LIEUTENANT COMMANDER RALPH M. RAM-sey's destroyer *McCook,* as it engaged in a duel with guns emplaced in the vicinity of Vierville, was the late *Saturday Evening Post* foreign editor, Martin Sommers, an early product of the New York *Daily News* copy desk. Sommers covered the war in the Atlantic and Pacific theatres. He was almost always under fire, as we find him now.

15.

THE LONGEST HOUR

IN HISTORY

This was the first hour of D-Day and we were crossing an area where we were under shore guns with a lot more fire power than we possessed. We could see the grim black shore line plainly.

We couldn't fire before H hour minus forty minutes, or 5:50 A.M. unless we were fired upon. During the wait, Lt. Jerry Clancy, an Annapolis man from Jersey City, shook his head and murmured, "What I can't understand is why they don't fire on us." None of us could understand it, and we all wished they would start firing, so we could start firing back. That would be much better than waiting. We were getting mildly edgy because we were also expecting a terrific bombing attack from the air.

A few sweeps detached themselves from their group and loomed directly ahead of our bow; they were our personal own, and they were to lead us to the bombardment area. They would not take us all the way in, but they would take us to 5000 yards offshore. From there we were on our own; and we were to creep in to 3500 yards to take up our firing station. We proceeded to a position directly off Vierville-sur-Mer. To starboard, our particular front ranged to the powerful shore battery at Pointe du Hoe in the direction of Grandcamp. Portside, our assault front extended to Port en Bessin, where the British landings were to begin.

A reverent chorus of Ah's ran through the ship to announce the

617

beginning of the air bombardment. To starboard and to port, thunderous explosions rolled along the shore, followed by high bursts of multicolored flak, and then a geyser of flame here, another there. It was not yet three o'clock; the bombing was on time, after all. The blasts were coming so fast that they merged into one roar. The shore line became a broken necklace of flame.

Now the Krauts are letting go with their rocket guns. They get some planes directly over our beach. That means we are going to have a lot of gun emplacements to work over. Now a bright orange glow spreads over the entire coast line.

"When it's orange-blossom time in Normandy," somebody sings softly on the bridge.

We are now reaching our bombardment station 3500 yards offshore. "It's just four-fifty; we got an hour to wait," Skipper Ramey says. We can see his easy grin through the darkness. He probably is wondering how his officers are going to like it. Although a third of the enlisted men on the McCook are veterans of battles and sinkings in the South Pacific, only one other officer aboard has previously seen full-dress naval action.

As we lay dead in the water, the choppy little waves slapping the thin steel sides of our can seemed to repeat, "Why don't they fire? Why don't they fire? Why don't they fire?"

We try hard to make conversation about the air bombardment, which has grown monotonous and is now waning temporarily. It has been cold on the bridge throughout the night, but now it seems twice as cold as ever before.

"I guess this is about the longest hour in history," one of the lookouts says.

It is, all right. Twenty minutes gone and forty to go. Thirty minutes gone—well, no other half hour can be as long.

Now in the cloudy haze we note that the Glasgow and the Texas are taking their positions behind us. Everything is ready except the ship's clock. The captain is carefully studying the clock.

One tremendous roar shakes the sea for miles around. We blink and steady ourselves—that must be the Glasgow and the Texas. It is.

Now Gunnery Officer Jim Arnold, in his fire-control tower atop the flying bridge, gets the word he's been waiting to hear. Our 5-inch guns speak as one, and to us they sound louder and truer than any we've ever heard.

Our first salvo is low on the first designated target. Arnold quickly works out the problem anew. The guns are corrected and our third salvo sends a pillbox cascading into the air in fragments. "Pillbox" does not convey what some of these things the Germans call *Stutzpunktgruppe* really are. They can be as big as a New England town hall, with walls six feet thick, and most of them are stocked with food, water and ammunition sufficient to support a sizable defense force for months.

Within a few short minutes, on automatic fire, we get our second target and attempt our third. This one is a battery cunningly concealed behind a stone wall down a gulch curving away from the sea. A salvo below, a salvo above, a salvo to the left—this fellow is really stubborn. Jim Arnold's lean, sensitive face now is twisted into something approaching a snarl. His long fingers adjust his instruments— for this moment the scholar has become a killer.

The next salvo smashes the gun and sends it down the gulch, starting a minor avalanche. By 6:15, all our assigned targets that we can reach have been knocked out or previously demolished by air bombing. We have fired 250 rounds in twenty-five minutes of automatic firing.

"Sir, suggest we shift to targets of opportunity," Arnold phones the bridge. "Targets of opportunity" are those enemy surprises that bob up, those strong points we don't know about in advance. There will be plenty of them.

"Permission granted."

Lines of amphibious tanks are churning their way to the beaches, in formation. They skim along so smoothly and gracefully that they appear to be some sort of prehistoric mammals rather than manmade machines. A destroyer to starboard of us has been hit and is pulling out. We take over her targets.

Now we have time to examine the beaches. Our landing at low tide has eliminated automatically the underwater horrors which we'd expected—steel hedgehogs, pyramids of concrete, huge wooden stakes and the dread tetrahedral traps. They are high and dry on the beach, easy marks for the demolition squads now long at work. But the beach is small, very small, a bottleneck between vast stretches of cliff on either side. Everything will have to come across the small beach, a target for the Kraut gunners. We must knock out all their guns, and do it fast.

Between 6:25 and 6:30 the most beautiful and most heartrending spectacle of the day is enacted overhead. Flying Fortresses come over to finish off troublesome spots inland by precision bombing. They risk flying lower than they should, to be sure of sending their solid best on D-Day. Flame and smoke spout from one Fort. It flounders and circles pathetically, losing altitude. We feel acute pain, watching.

One last feeble spiral, and the Fort nose-dives earthward; a burst of flame and a geyser of smoke beyond the cliffs. That is all. Another Fort goes the same way. Now three, now four. During the next two days we are to spend sweating it out with the troops who are taking a shelling on the beach, nothing cuts quite so deeply as the sight of those four beautiful Forts going to glory.

We cruise backward and forward along the shore, searching for targets. There are large splashes off the starboard bow, and a lookout shouts that we are being bracketed by big guns ashore. But the splashes are not repeated, and we never know whether we've been aimed at. We learn that another destroyer has been badly knocked around and is on her way out.

Confusion on the beach has increased. Tanks and infantry seem, to us, to be milling around aimlessly. Tanks should be climbing up the single winding road leading from the beach to the good highway on the cliffs. But some tanks are burning and German fire seems to have increased, though we cannot spot the batteries.

Rear Adm. Carleton F. Bryant, who is spark-plugging the bombardment from the *Texas,* calls all destroyers over the intership radio phone, "Get on them, men! Get on them! We must knock out those guns! They are raising hell with the men on the beach, and we can't have any more of that! We must stop it!"

"Grove, do you see anything?" our watch officer asks plaintively.

Grove is Seaman Second Class Gerald Grove, thirty-eight, of Clarinda, Iowa, who looks old enough to be the father of half the seamen aboard, and also looks as though he would feel much more at home milking cows back on the fárm than spotting enemy guns in battle from the bridge of a pitching can. Grove is married and the father of an eleven-year-old daughter. He never expected to be drafted, but after his induction, he did his best to make himself a seaman, although he did seem a little old for the game. On the *McCook* he became the ship's barber, but Skipper Ramey discovered that the Iowa farmer had the best pair of eyes on the ship, phenomenally keen sight, so Grove is now the star lookout. There are times when a good lookout is worth exactly $8,000,000 worth of destroyer and 300 lives, so when the chips are down on the *McCook,* it is, "Grove, do you see anything?"

Grove sees something this time. He sees a few faint flashes from a stone house tucked away up the gulch within range of the vital road from the beach, and these flashes coincide with the explosion of shells setting our beach-bound tanks ablaze. Range is established and our guns go to work. They blast away pieces of the cliff all around the stone house. Finally, a direct hit—a gun tumbles stern over teakettle from the wreckage.

"Well done, well done," comes the formal commendation from Admiral Bryant.

At least three fourths of the officers aboard and half the men have served on the cooky boat since she was commissioned, and their pride now is boundless.

All afternoon we try to find hidden enemy rocket-gun batteries, which are shellacking our tanks and soldiers as they mill about on the beaches. Naval fire gets some, but the beach is not a pretty picture, with considerable destruction in evidence everywhere and medical corpsmen flashing messages for help in evacuating casualties.

We have knocked out three big pillboxes and six guns, a recapitulation shows as night falls. We now must expect a full night of bombing by the Luftwaffe, and we cannot expect much protection. The skipper isn't worried.

"I spent a whole year ducking the Japs, and I guess I can manage to duck the Luftwaffe for one night," he says.

All night long nobody sleeps. As we maneuver to and fro among the darkest patches of this Channel area, the Luftwaffe is overhead from time to time, but by no means in strength, and only a few ships in the transport area are casualties.

We are very happy to see the second invasion dawn, and again we get to work trying to find those troublesome enemy batteries. By noon, the picture on the beach is changed greatly. Our tanks and troops of "The Big One," the famous 1st Division, have moved up the road and are fighting a few miles inland. Our people have done wonders unloading during the night, and order now emerges from what appeared to be the beginning of chaos on the beach. We close down on every enemy flash until nightfall and, as a finale, after dark we help the boys ashore to knock out the village of Longueville, some miles inland, from where German artillery is shelling our beachhead. The flames from the village light up the sky just at the moment our much-reinforced anti-aircraft opens up on Nazi bombers, which are once more overhead.

Once again, the skipper maneuvers through the night up and down the coast. We are then ordered to return to our home port for reloading and refueling at first light. Our score is three big assigned targets and ten targets of opportunity, and now Jim Arnold can untangle his long legs, climb from his fire-control turret and go below for a couple of hours of shut-eye before he must supervise the loading of ammunition in England.

We boil homeward at thirty knots, leaving a waterfall in reverse six feet high in our wake. We pass miles and miles of France-bound supply ships as we race through the sea highway which is the beginning of our road to Berlin. The sun is climbing in a cloudless sky and the world at six o'clock this morning of June eighth, 1944, seems a very different place from what it did forty-eight hours ago.

THERE WAS CONSIDERABLY LESS GERMAN OPPOSITION on Utah Beach than expected, and the bulk of twenty-six assault waves made it ashore without mishap. This area had received a severe shelling by the heavy ships of Bryant's command, and the results were immediately apparent; but beyond that Utah itself had not been as fiercely defended by the German Seventh as Omaha had been. Here, by the time the second wave landed, Underwater Demolition teams had cleared seven hundred yards of beach and a few land mines, making it possible to avoid congestion at the water's edge. By day's end more than 21,328 troops, 1795 tons of supplies and 1742 vehicles were ashore at a cost of only one hundred and seventy-four casualties.

Such was not the case at Omaha. Instead of a gradually sloping shelf, Omaha's topography was characterized by high, rocky cliffs and a pebbly beach, giving the enemy an almost perfect defense barrier; moreover, German defenses were formidable. In addition to heavily salted rows of iron scullies, or *chevaux de frise,* land mines and anti-tank traps, the topography made for splendid enemy cover. Thus, despite the bombardment by Bryant's force, of the 34,000 troops put ashore on D-Day, more than 2000 were casualties. German shore batteries and machinegun nests made this beach the next thing to pure hell for Rudder's Rangers, for instance, pinned down at Pointe du Hoc.

Nevertheless by nightfall, and despite heavy enemy reinforcements, the Colleville sector—not Caen, the area where a breakthrough was expected—was overrun. We were ashore to stay. The violence, power and speed of the American assault, as Montgomery put it, had carried us right over the beaches and some miles inland. True enough; but the cost was high. Lieutenant W. L. Wade of LCI Group 28 summed up the horror of Omaha: "Enemy fire . . . was terrific—105mm, 88mm, 40mm, mortars, machine guns, mines—everything apparently. And very few shells fell to seaward. The enemy would wait until the craft lowered their ramps and then cut loose with everything they had . . . Rocket boats and gunboats did not faze the enemy in the least; they were too far underground. The soldiers, the battleships, the cruisers and the destroyers did the good work. It seems a miracle this beach was ever taken."

Commander Edward Ellsberg, versatile writer and demolition expert, was a member of the staff of Force Mulberry—the artificial harbors (huge concrete caissons) which were towed to Normandy to facilitate the landing of supplies. In an engineering capacity, Ellsberg reached Omaha with the first wave. He tells the story of Mulberry.

16.

ENTER MULBERRY

Tailing along behind the invasion armada as it sailed away from its ocean rendezvous, Point Yoke south of the Isle of Wight, bound for the Far Shore, came Captain Dayton Clark and his motley flotilla comprising Force Mulberry. They and the Artificial Harbors with them in tow for Normandy were the devices on which rested what chance we had to make the invasion stick.

Clark himself was embarked in a 110 foot subchaser; Stanford, his deputy commander, in another. Both tiny tubs were having a rough time of it in heavy seas. So also were Lieutenant Barton and his squadron of little ST harbor tugs, hardly sea-going vessels either. Then came more queer vessels of all kinds, mostly British, from ships with horns projecting over their bows intended to help in linking up the Whale sections, to shallow-draft ancient excursion side-wheelers pressed into service as tenders, all rolling wildly now they were exposed to the open sea, and a stormy one at that.

Astern came dozens of merchant ships and that dummy battleship, the *Centurion,* going like victims to the sacrifice, all to be sunk to form the Gooseberry breakwaters. For them, the seas on this, their last voyage, were nothing to be concerned about.

And finally, astern of all, came the first flight of Phoenixes, looking like nothing ever seen at sea before, ten massive blocks of concrete towering above the waves, moving majestically along at three knots on long towlines astern the ocean-going tugs. They, of course, could not pretend even to keep up with an armada steaming along at ten. It was obvious to everyone that should the Nazi E-boats sortie out of Cherbourg, the Phoenixes, far astern of all else and their major protective convoys, so slow moving as to be practically stationary, would form ideal targets. Should the E-boats, if able to believe such monstrosities were real and not simply hallucinations brought on by battle psychoses, fire torpedoes at them, they couldn't miss.

And ultimately behind those Phoenixes would come more Phoenixes, mingled with Bombardons, Whales, and the Lobnitz pierheads, all lumbering along behind tugs, all to be assembled finally on the Far Shore in their proper pattern.

It took Captain Clark and his mongrel fleet a long time to cross. Night had fallen on D-Day while still they were at sea—a night for them made tense by complete ignorance of how the assault flung ashore in the storm had gone—whether our G.I.'s were firmly on the beach and they could proceed with their part, or whether Dr. Goebbels had been a good prophet and our assault had been smashed before the Atlantic Wall. The night sky ahead was laced with fiery tracers, vivid flares burst here and there over the dark Channel—very evidently, whatever had happened on the beachhead during the day, Goering and his Luftwaffe had come over Omaha for a night air attack and were then engaged in making it.

Dawn came on D + 1. Captain Clark with his part of Force Mulberry moved into the area off the Omaha Beach, already jammed with thousands of ships; Commander Stanford with his force peeled off to starboard, headed for the Utah Beach.

Clark examined the bluffs and the cluttered area of sea just in front of them. From long before, based on soundings shown on the French charts of that coast, the locations for the Mulberry Harbor and its breakwaters had been laid out. But were those French soundings, made fifty years before, still reasonably accurate on a shoreline notorious for shifting sands? He must find out before he sank his floating breakwater units.

Accompanied by Commander Passmore, Royal Navy, who in a tiny British survey boat only thirty feet long, the *Gulnare,* had made the passage across the storm-beaten Channel with her much bigger sisters, Clark started out to check. He and Passmore with handlines sounded the site for his Gooseberry line first, found it in reasonable agreement with expectations. The *Gulnare* set out the marker buoys for the first six ships to be sunk, and moved on to survey the sites for the Phoenixes.

Clark, grim, tense, and already worn from months of battling on the Near Shore to make a reality of the units needed for Mulberry, as he sounded the depths for his first breakwater also surveyed the scene inshore of him. The Nazi artillery emplacements on the bluffs and cliffs not half a mile off, had, thank God, all been knocked out on D-Day. Some small arms fire, sporadic but annoying, was still coming, oddly enough, from tunnel ends you could see in the cliff faces—Nazis would suddenly pop into view there, fire on the beach below, just as suddenly retreat into the tunnel, safe from reprisal. Till somehow the G.I.'s on the plateau could trace out the intricate tunnel system leading from the bluffs to the villages inland, and flush out the snipers using them as bases, there was no stopping that.

All along the beach, small landing craft and some somewhat larger LCVP's, LCT's, and LCI(L)'s—were busily pouring troops ashore, ferried in from troopships still prudently some miles at sea. And Clark swiftly saw why prudence kept them there. For the beachhead before him, surprisingly enough, was still the target for directed enemy artillery fire—from well inland. Apparently all the mobile field artillery of the 352nd German Division was now massed some miles back in camouflaged positions in the wooded high ground there. And controlled by Nazi observers hidden in the tunnel network piercing the bluff faces, somehow still in direct communication with those guns, all that was necessary to bring down on any spot along the beachhead a galling fall of bursting shrapnel was to provide there a decently attractive target for artillery.

So while the little landing craft, relatively fast on their feet so to speak, and well dispersed along the beach brought in the troops, the really large transports, the oceangoing fleet, stayed far offshore, well out of artillery range. And they were going to remain there too, until Gerow's G.I.'s, pushing inland should, it was hoped, in the next few days overrun those positions and shove the Nazis and their artillery far back into the hinterland, out of range of Omaha.

But that did Clark no good. He was going to have to bring ocean-going freighters close in to shore that very day, within easy range of those unseen batteries, to sink them on his Gooseberry line for his initial breakwater. And that sinking problem, involving all his ST tugs to hold a vessel in position against the tital currents while he blasted out its bottom and set it down, was now going to be complicated by having to be done under enemy artillery fire—something never anticipated.

But there was no way out.

The first Liberty ship destined for the Gooseberry line, the *James Iredell,* started to make its approach. Clark, with Lieutenant Commander Bassett in charge of the ST tugs for the Gooseberries, boarded her, accompanied by Lieutenant Hoague and his specially trained crew of sinking specialists to do the actual blasting.

As the *James Iredell* came inshore, the first vessel of anything like her size to come within range, some shells from inland began to fall in her vicinity—none very close, as she was still a moving target. The bursts were close enough, however, to convince the merchant skipper and his crew that this was nothing they wished any further part in. They refused to go any farther. Fortunately, however, the renovated crews of the ST tugs offered no objections, so with the captain and the crew of that freighter removed, Clark and his tugs took over completely. With a few shells bursting about but none hitting her, under Clark's direction Bassett and the ST tugs brought the *Iredell* in to the marked position about half a mile offshore, and held her there a brief moment while they fired the prepared explosive charges in her holds and blew out her bottom. Down went the *James Iredell.* Enough of her upper hull and her superstructure remained above water, however, to make a fine shelter in her lee.

Captain Clark and his forces in swift succession brought in two more freighters and very neatly put them on the bottom also astern the *James Iredell*—each bow slightly overlapping the stern of the vessel ahead, to leave no gaps in that line of sunken ships as a breakwater.

But by now these activities were awakening great interest in quite diverse spots—the Nazi fire control observers ensconced in their hideouts on the bluffs, and the thousands of G.I.'s still jammed aboard the transports offshore, waiting their turn for disembarkation, all with their eyes glued to the beach, straining to see what awaited them there.

To the Nazi gunnery observers on the bluffs, only one conclusion seemed logical—the Americans were starting to bring in their larger ships to speed up unloading from close inshore. And while, expecting no such thing—they as observers for the batteries inland had not been able to get much fire concentrated on that first ship as it came inshore—still they must have been lucky—a stray shell had evidently touched off some explosives aboard, and they had sunk it!

Should the enemy in spite of this major disaster try such a thing again, they would be more ready the second time.

Their enemy did try it again, and this time, with more shells falling about, once again they must have scored some fortunate hits, for once again, with hatches flying skyward from an internal explosion, down went their second victim!

And a third time, except by then being well alerted, substantial artillery fire was bracketing their target, as under the eyes of the Nazi observers, jubilant at the remarkable results they were getting from their guns inland, it too went to the bottom!

To the startled G.I.'s in the support force watching all this from the packed transports offshore, waiting themselves somehow to be unloaded, there was nothing in what they saw to cause any jubilation whatever. Unaware of what actually was happening (for Operation Mulberry had always been Top Secret) all they could understand was what was plainly going on under their very eyes. There, one by one, moving out of the transport area in which they lay, were big ships just like their own, loaded, so far as they knew, with G.I.'s as was also theirs, heading inshore to unload. And there, before a single G.I. could be seen getting off, under enemy fire the ship was sunk!

To G.I.'s who before D-Day had heard plenty over "Invasion Calling!" as to the white crosses waiting them on the Far Shore, and among whom the wildest stories (unfortunately, most of them true) were already circulating as to what had happened on the beaches to the first waves, what now was visibly going on inshore put morale into the sub-cellar. Was their own troopship the next in line for a similar fate?

And shortly came the pay-off. A huge battleship, British apparently, three times the size of any troopship thereabouts, steamed from the transport area, headed inshore, far closer than any big ship ever before had gone. To the astonished Nazi artillery observers on the bluffs, to the unstrung G.I.'s watching her from offshore, the black muzzles of her menacing 13.5-inch turret guns trained ahead as she steered in meant only one thing—she was going in with her main battery ready to blast those obnoxious inland guns off the face of the earth.

Here was a target worthwhile, though against such heavily armored battleship turrets and protective decks, mobile artillery could not expect to accomplish much. Still every battery the 352nd Division had, directed by those shore observers, concentrated on her.

On came that dreadnaught, disregarding the shells bursting all about, evidently holding her own fire till she had a position that suited her. When close in to the three hulks already protruding from the sea only half a mile offshore, she swung slowly to starboard, obviously to present her whole port broadside to the shore, ready to let go a crashing salvo from all the guns she had.

An even better target for them now, the Nazi batteries inland, firing furiously, bracketed her from bow to stern as she swung parallel to the beach. And then to the horror of the G.I.'s watching and to the delirious joy of the Nazi observers, before she could fire a single broadside, a series of internal explosions shook the ship and down went the *Centurion!*

I listened that night at Selsey Bill to "Invasion Calling." Goebbels had been in a tough spot on D-day evening—with forebodings of disaster on the beachheads pouring in, except for his regular feature, "Lili Marlene," he had dealt only in vague generalities. But by evening of D + 1 he had pulled himself and his propaganda machinery together and was in his usual form. Now, aside from gory prophecies of what should happen to us as soon as Rommel and his Panzers hit our forces behind the beachheads, "Invasion Calling!" had hot news of amazing Nazi successes in the battle still going on for the beaches. German artillery had sunk a number of Allied transports foolishly hazarding themselves trying to discharge close in to the Normandy shore. And to top off all, a British dreadnaught of the *Iron Duke* class, steaming in to strafe the beaches, had also been sunk by the devastating fire of those Nazi gunners! And more! The loss of life on that battleship had been terrific! So swiftly had she gone down, that out of over a thousand men and officers comprising her crew, not more than seventy had been observed able to get on deck to abandon ship! The Allies had suffered a major disaster that insured their swift defeat!

So, Dr. Goebbels? I couldn't keep from smiling as I listened. That harmless old dummy, the *Centurion,* to the very last still pulling the enemy's leg as she had in the Mediterranean, had now done her final bit for her country. She had gone down in a blaze of enemy publicity such as even the actual performance of her real 13.5-inch guns against the German High Seas Fleet at Jutland twenty-eight years before had never centered on her. Quite a finish for an innocuous old hulk.

Tremendous loss of life, eh? My thoughts ran back to the interview I'd had just the week before in Portsmouth with the *Centurion's* new skipper—that Commander in the Royal Navy who was seeking to place her at my service. Hadn't he told me then that his entire crew to steam the *Centurion* across the Channel on her last voyage had been reduced to seventy? He had. And the excited Nazis now were telling the world that only some seventy men out of her entire crew were seen escaping the sinking *Centurion!*

I chuckled. That Royal Navy three-striper had done an excellent job—even by Goebbels' own account, in spite of all the fire Nazi artillery had laid on his ship, while he was sinking her for our Gooseberry breakwater, he'd got his whole crew safely off and away from there. A good show.

WHILE THE NAVY SPENT THE ENSUING TWELVE DAYS reinforcing beachheads and knocking out hidden gun emplacements, the enemy's expected counterattack developed. Over came the first of 1600 air sorties. On the 7th, forty-five torpedo-carrying Junkers, some with glide bombs, began to work over the beaches and transport areas. The following day a Heinkel-111 sank destroyer *Meredith* (the second warship with this name) as she patrolled offshore; destroyer escort *Rich,* transport *Susan B. Anthony* and destroyer *Glennon* were sunk by mines. Off Utah's boat lanes minesweeper *Tide,* LST-*499* and RN netlayer *Minister* also became mine victims. In the next three weeks some two hundred and sixty mines in the American sector and two hundred and ninety in the British were swept. Then the worst storm in forty years struck the Allied invasion area—strong northeast winds with driving rain, gusts to thirty-two knots and steep seas. The mobile breakwaters of Mulberry A began to buckle and drift away.

The harrowing struggle against the weather is reported by Len Guttridge, a free lance writer and former junior grade lieutenant.

17.

ORDEAL ON THE BEACHES

The unforeseen storm hit . . . Normandy . . . head on. Mulberry
B, the still uncompleted British artificial harbor at Arromanches, was
partly protected by offshore reefs; but the American Mulberry A,
newly finished and just open for business at Omaha, found itself in
immediate trouble.

Three pontoon causeways—called Whales—jutting over half a
mile out to sea, began to undulate like roller coasters. At the pierheads, worried officers in charge of unloading ordered their men to
hurry it up.

Farther out, the sea surged angrily against the Phoenix breakwater: a butt-to-butt line of thirty concrete caissons, each the size of
a city block. The surprise blow was striking at the worse possible
time, during the season of high spring tides. Strong winds pushed the
North Sea down through the funnel-shaped Channel, forcing its water
level to climb higher yet.

By mid-morning, waves were breaking against the Phoenix wall
only 15 feet below the Bofor anti-aircraft gun mounted on top of each
unit. By noon, with a full gale blowing, the sea came crashing over
the hand rails around each gun platform. Spume soaked the G.I. gun
crews.

One gunner, clinging to a hand rail as a huge wave swamped him,
shrieked as he felt the rail snap like a twig. Thrashing around in the

631

swirling water, he skittered to the edge of the caisson, was about to topple off, when a sergeant grabbed his leg. The noncom's other arm was hooked about a length of still intact rail.

He spat out a pint of English Channel and grinned. "Going somewhere, soldier?"

"Those goddamn navy screwballs," the gunner spluttered, then recovered his breath. "They'll leave us here to drown."

Another wave struck the caisson. Above its pounding and the whining wind could be heard the more terrifying sound of splintering concrete.

"Cripes," yelled the sergeant, "now they'll *have* to take us off. We're breaking up!"

The crumbling tops of the caissons were almost under water when tugs labored alongside to take the gunners off. Then a new danger threatened. Beyond the Phoenix line lay an outer breakwater consisting of a mile-long barrier of bombardons: two-dozen moored steel lengths sprouting ugly-looking fins scientically designed to diffuse wave action. Each bombardon measured 200 feet. A couple had already snapped their moorings and careened down channel, a terrifying hazard to the Allied shipping which crowded the area.

Now a third broke loose, and waves a hundred feet long bore it like a high-speed battering ram straight for the Phoenix wall. Frantically, a couple of tugs chugged out of its path. One didn't quite make it, had a ten-foot gash ripped in her by the bombardon's wicked fins. She struggled for the beach, her stern flooding rapidly. The runaway bombardon whirled on, to mash its 2,000-ton weight against a Phoenix caisson. Under the impact, the concrete monster broke in half, and the Bofor gun vanished in the sea which came boiling through the breached breakwater.

Mulberry A's third breakwater—code-named Gooseberry—was a two-mile line of blockships, made up of seventy old British, French and Dutch warships, discarded Liberty ships, and the rusting dregs of the Allied merchant shipping pool. They had been sunk near enough to shore for their upper decks and superstructures to show above water, but heavy seas hurled over them now, swamping the landing craft which had scurried close for shelter.

Bracing himself on the spray-soaked open bridge of an LCI hovering near the pierheads, Captain Augustus Clark, USN, Mulberry A Task Force Commander, bellowed over the bullhorn: "Cease unloading operations!"

The last truck rolled out of an LST onto the pier ramp; its driver swallowed apprehensively, and then drove it bucketing down the agitated roller coaster to Omaha Beach. The bow doors of the LSYs closed, diesels began to throb. Still the vessels continued to grind their heavy steel hulls against the pierheads.

Captain Clark's harsh voice sounded again. "Get your damned craft the hell away from here!"

He knew the cumbersome things were difficult to maneuver, especially in such weather, but at the rate reports were reaching him of collapsing pontoons, it wouldn't require much more pressure to crush his Whales completely.

Just then, someone brought Clark word that another breach had been made in his Phoenix breakwater. He cursed into the wind. Already waves in the inner harbor were running five feet high. If all his Phoenixes crumbled, the full force of the enormous water pressure building up in the Channel would sweep across Mulberry A and pulverize it.

And that meant robbing half a million British and American fighting men in Normandy of support troops, food, guns and ammunition. The Germans would swiftly counterattack, and drive the Allied troops back into the sea . . .

Mulberry had been born at the Quebec Conference, in September 1943, when President Roosevelt and Prime Minister Churchill planned the invasion of Europe with their Joint Chiefs of Staff. They knew that following the initial landings, both the Allies and the Germans would concentrate full military strength at the assault points. H-Hour on D-Day would trigger a furious race for buildingup; much of the invasion's success would depend on its outcome.

For Hitler it meant rushing troops and equipment overland, but the Allies would have to ferry theirs across the world's most unpredictable body of water. Vicious cross-currents and sudden storms would make beach unloading risky enough, but what made it even more unsatisfactory were the unusual tidal ranges. At low tide the English Channel recedes as much as half a mile from the high mark. Landing craft could go in only during high tide, and after unloading would have to stay high and dry on the mudflats until the tide came in again to refloat them.

Such waste of time might prove disastrous. The Allies would need a port at the outset. Immediate capture of any was out of the question. A memo from the German General Staff to Hitler, intercepted by Allied Intelligence, ran: *If we hold the Channel ports, we hold Europe.* Obviously, the port cities would be so heavily defended it would take a massive assault to capture any of them—and without possession of a port, such an assault could never be mounted.

To solve the dilemma, the Allies came up with a bold and challenging solution: build their own harbors, take them along on the invasion.

It was a colossal project, requiring months of planning, experiment, and construction. Secrecy had to be as rigidly maintained as for the date of D-Day itself.

Building went on at several British bases simultaneously. The hollowed-out Phoenix caissons alone used up 30,000 tons of steel, over half a million tons of concrete, and a labor force of 20,000 men.

By D-Day, both Mulberries were ready for towing and assembly. A special Task Force 128 was formed to work on the U.S. Mulberry, Captain Clark commanding, and hardly a man connected with the operation escaped the bitter lash of his tongue.

Clark showed no respect for rank or nationality. When the admiral in charge of the British Mulberry doubted whether it could be assembled within the scheduled 12 days, Clark turned on him, snapped, "I'll finish Mulberry A in ten days, not twelve. I'll do it—even if it kills me and every man who works for me."

Only the realization that every officer on the Mulberry teams had been under tremendous pressure and were inclined to be jumpy, prevented the admiral from having Clark court-martialed right then.

The job of riding the Mulberry A units to the Normandy shore went to the 108th Seabees. They moved out on D minus 1.

No crazier-looking Task Force ever flew the American flag. With 40 feet of their bulk rearing above water and their AA guns manned, the Phoenix units resembled gigantic shoe-boxes, dwarfing the tugs that towed them. Each caisson carried a six-man Seabee team. Like some monstrous dead bugs, the pierheads were towed upside-down, 60-foot legs swaying against the sky; ten men riding each pierhead.

Other Seabees were perched on the 480-foot Whale spans, tents sheltering them from the spray. The spans were towed in strings of six; bombardons were also hauled in strings, like huge spiked sausages. All told, 152 straining tugboats lugged the contraptions cross-Channel.

Perhaps the strangest sight of all was the Gooseberry blockships, a fantastic scrap-heap fleet led by HMS *Centurion,* 25,000-ton veteran of the Battle of Jutland. Volunteer merchant crews manned the old freighters, navy men rode the warships. Each vessel carried sand ballast and enough dynamite to blow her bottom out. For its last voyage, the blockship fleet was especially mounted with 20mm AA guns.

Captain Clark supervised the crossing of TF 128 from the bridge of a subchaser. None of the tows could do more than six knots and, as darkness fell, the Channel became rough enough to toss several into near-collision. Jittery gunners on the Gooseberry blockships banged away at non-existent targets, and most of the Seabees riding the sections were violently seasick.

Somewhere in the night a terrific explosion sounded as a Phoenix caisson struck a mine. A Nazi E-boat torpedoed another. The tug hauling Whale tow 528 was sunk by a torpedo; the towline snapped, and the spans drifted blindly. They were sighted next day, but the Seabees had vanished and their deserted shelter tents were spattered with blood.

At dawn on D-Day plus 1, Clark sighted the Normandy shore. A mine sweeper attached to his force struck a mine and disappeared. Off to port, a U.S. destroyer hit another and was blown in half. An ammo coaster hit a third and was blotted out in one flaming blast.

Smoke curled over the beaches ahead. Thunderous gunfire echoed all along the coast. But Clark wasted no time speculating how the men back of that smoke curtain were doing. One thing he knew for certain: they were going to need his Mulberry pretty damn quick . . .

It was Lieutenant-Commander John Bassett's job to sink the blockships. Bassett, USNR, had been a top New York harbor tug-master before the war. First the predetermined sites for sinking were marked with buoys, then each ship was nudged into place by Bassett's handling tugs.

Not only did baffling crosscurrents make it the trickiest task Bassett had ever tackled, but just then German shore batteries began to lob 88mm shells into the operation.

The skipper of the first Liberty ship marked for sinking protested. "I'm turning back," he signaled. To his first mate he grumbled that he hadn't volunteered to get shot at.

Bassett reported to Captain Clark. The Task Force commander didn't hesitate. "Get him off," he rasped. "His crew, too. Take over his ship and sink her yourself."

The merchant skipper put up no resistance as Commander Bassett ushered him off his vessel, took over the bridge, and pressed the detonating button. Deep inside the ship's hold, an explosion rumbled. She started to settle, and Bassett got off.

One after another the beat-up hulks shuddered to internal blasts and sank in the choppy water. The Gooseberry line began to take shape. It was near completion when a German shell crashed on the *Galveston* as her merchant crew were being taken off by a tug. Men screamed and died as shrapnel tore through their bodies. Grimly, Bassett ordered the work continued.

The cost of Mulberry A, already fantastic in terms of dollars, was reaching a sizable figure in human lives. *HMS Minster,* a British tender, had been assigned to Task Force 128. Less than two hours after Captain Clark left her, following a round of talks and some pink gin with the Royal Navy men, the *Minster* struck a mine off nearby Utah Beach, took her complement of eighty to the bottom.

Just after midnight on D plus 1, eight hours ahead of schedule, the first Phoenix caissons loomed off Omaha. Siting them proved the toughest job of all, besides giving Clark an opportunity to heighten his reputation as a pitiless commander.

The lieutenant handling the sinking fumbled the first caisson, lost control completely of the second. As the huge block swung wide— missing tugs and Whale equipment by inches—the lieutenant, perched on it, was mortified to hear Clark's voice scream at him across the water:

"I'll have no more clumsy seamanship from you. *Get off that goddamn Phoenix.*"

White-faced, the lieutenant crawled off the Phoenix and vanished into a tug. Clark gave his job to Lieutenant Commander Bassett, who already had his hands full with the blockships.

Shortly afterwards, a young Seabee officer begged Captain Clark to be allowed a minute's relaxation. The officer seemed on the point of physical collapse; Clark brusquely ordered him back to his station.

The commander of Task Force 128 spared no one, least of all himself. Soon the 108th Seabees were prepared to bet that the man wasn't human, had no need of sleep. He seemed determined to prevent them from getting any too. What they called him behind his back isn't printable, and had they known of his brutal promise to the British admiral, some no doubt would have been close to mutiny.

Deciding on a larger vessel for his headquarters, Clark transferred from the subchaser to *LSI 414,* whose crew grew to regard the haggard, sunken-eyed figure on their bridge with much the same feelings the *Bounty* sailors held for Captain Bligh.

Yet, it was due entirely to Clark's bullying that by D plus 5, twelve Phoenix units were in place, the Gooseberry line was completed, fourteen of the outer bombardons were moored, and the Whale causeways—last to get started because of the clutter on Omaha Beach—were reaching out to sea.

Two days later Mulberry A began to look like a real harbor and increasing numbers of DUKW's, Rhino ferries, LCMs and LCTs engaged in beach unloading lumbered into Mulberry's sheltered water.

Enemy shelling trailed off as Bradley's men fought deeper into Normandy, but Nazi bombers and mine layers came over nightly. Clark seemed deaf to all raid alarms; he kept his Seabees on the job.

On D plus 10, three days ahead of even Clark's own drastically cut schedule, a tug towed the last Whale span into position, telescopic links secured it, and Mulberry A became a reality.

The 108th Seabees had assembled it in record time. None of them had the strength to cheer when the first landing craft unloaded at the pierhead but many of them felt like it. Some stole a glance at Captain Clark. He hadn't relaxed. Bloodshot eyes staring fixedly at the bluffs above Omaha Beach, as if trying to see what was happening beyond them, Clark remained on the bridge of *LSI 414,* his slight body tensed.

There was no telling how long he would have stayed there if his deputy commander, Al Stanford, hadn't physically forced him below for some rest.

During the next two days, tanks, heavy artillery, vehicles, and troops poured into Normandy via Mulberry A. Those of the British and American top brass who had doubted the practical value of prefabricated harbors swallowed their skepticism.

On average, unloading at Mulberry's piers took 64 minutes per ship as against the twelve hours beach unloading required for the vessel to get off again.

The accelerated build-up was bound to increase Allied chances for an early victory. Tonnages unloaded at Omaha hit a satisfying 9,000 tons on June 15th, and again on the 16th, 17th, and 18th.

And then the storm struck . . .

Debris whirling on wave crests bashed repeatedly into the Whale causeways and their pontoons began to crack. Floats broke loose, and tugs dashed from one end of the harbor to the other trying to round them up . . .

LCI 414 was lashed to a rocking pierhead with eight-inch manila hawsers. The vessel was his command post in the fight to save Mulberry A, and he couldn't risk her being swept away by the storm.

All that night Clark hunched over the bullhorn mike in *414*'s conning tower. Hoarse curses and commands streamed from the speaker down on the heads of dazed and soaked Seabee repair crews that slithered up and down the buckling steel surface of the Whales, trying to secure the pontoons.

All down the English Channel, vessels of every type were drifting helplessly through the darkness, dragging their anchors, foundering on the shore or colliding. Some struggled for Mulberry A, not realizing that their presence could only jeopardize the struggle being waged for its survival.

Two British LCTs loomed out of the storm-lashed blackness, headed right for Mulberry's center Whale. Seabees working on it dropped their tools, scrambled for safety along the causeway. On Clark's vessel the signal lamp blinked frantically.

"Stay clear!" he roared. "You'll wreck us all . . ."

Afraid their vessels would sink following the collision, men jumped from the LCTs. Some, falling into the tangle of grinding steel and concrete, were crushed to death. Others, trying to swim for the beach, drowned, or were ploughed under by drifting tugs or battered to death by tossing debris.

So many dead were bobbing about in the sea off Omaha Beach it looked like D-Day all over again.

Mid-morning on June 20th, tugs were still trying to get the British LCTs off the Whale when Clark commandeered a passing LCVP, brought it alongside one LCT and ordered both vessels lashed together.

A Navy lieutenant took over control, gunned the LCVP's high-power motors to a throbbing roar, slowly hauled the LCT clear. It was towed to a safe distance and sunk with a charge of dynamite.

By afternoon other derelicts were removed in similar fashion, but the wind had increased to a howling forty knots and to Clark's fury more vessels came lunging up against his causeways.

Again weary Seabees and civilian tug crews hauled them clear, but by sundown only one tug remained operable. The rest had crippled themselves towing, or been driven ashore by the gale.

The wind blew harder, tearing sheets of spume flat off the wave crests. Another sleepless night for TF 128's commander began with the news that his Whale and pierhead pontoons were now cracking and sinking faster than they could be saved. He was also told that only eight of his Phoenix units were still intact, and learned that all 24 spike-bristling bombardons of his outer breakwater were adrift— chasing each other madly and menacing ships up and down the English Channel.

Each report struck Captain Clark with a hammer-blow realization that his precious Mulberry harbor faced imminent disaster, and there wasn't a damn thing he could do to avert it.

He wondered if he still had a Gooseberry breakwater. Lieutenant Commander Stanford was despatched in a subchaser to find out.

Bucking eight-foot waves, the fast vessel took Stanford out to *HMS Centurion,* the outer blockship. He noticed that the old tubs seemed to hold up well, although the sea thundered across their decks and superstructures, and during a brief lull in the storm's din, he could hear them creak and groan under their terrific punishment.

Stanford boarded *Centurion's* sloping deck, climbed sixty feet to the crow's-nest in her fighting top. As 70 mph gusts tore at him, he gazed down on an awesome scene of destruction.

Dawn was lightening the sky. From horizon to horizon, vessels spun helplessly on a foam-flecked racing sea. All along the Normandy shore, Liberty ships, coastguard 83-footers, tugs, Rhino ferries, and every type of landing craft were piling up, in some places six deep. Waves hurled one LCT halfway up the hundred-foot cliffs of Pointe de la Percée.

As Stanford descended to the *Centurion's* deck, he felt her shudder ominously. He could still hear her plates buckling, rivets popping, after he had regained the subchaser's bridge.

The blockship gave a violent lurch and the subchaser pulled hastily away. Again the seas washed over *Centurion,* but the old battlewagon could take no more. Midway along her 550-foot length she sagged beneath the waves, her back broken.

When Stanford reported back to Captain Clark, he found only the center pierhead intact—*LCT 414* still tied to it by a dozen hawsers— and this pierhead threatened to go the same way as the others.

Throughout that day the storm showed no sign of slackening and

414's skipper, secretly fearful that Captain Clark might be crazy enough to stay till the end and sink with his doomed harbor, made a quick decision.

At nightfall he barked an order, and so quickly was it obeyed that Clark had no chance to countermand. Axes swung and the hawsers parted. *LCI 414* backed off, vanished into the night with the commander of Task Force 128 still on her bridge.

There remained a hundred Seabees on the twisted causeway, but further repair was out of the question. It was now a case of every man for himself.

They crawled to the pierhead and clung there, none of them knowing if it would hold out till the storm died. Every wave crashing into it threatened to plunge all hands to the bottom, and all night long drifting vessels kept banging into the mangled causeway, each impact sending shock tremors out to the shaky pierhead.

Bodies of navy men floated by. Those within reach were hauled in with boathooks. For safety the Seabees had crawled towards the center of the pierhead deck. Sheer fatigue swept them into deep sleep, and in the pale dawn light of D plus 16 it was impossible to tell the living from the dead . . .

THE GREAT STORM TAUGHT A HARD-EARNED LESSON: our invasion forces required a sheltered port; no open channel would do. Hence the move to Cherbourg. By this time the American line extended northwesterly through a point several miles south of Saint-Lô to Saint-Sauveur-le-Vicomte, and from there to the west coast. With General Manuel Quesada's IX Army Air Force providing fighter cover, Bryant and Deyo—behind British and American minesweeping units—eased their warships toward Cherbourg. German coastal batteries opened fire on Deyo's group off Querqueville, and off Fermanville, six miles east of Cherbourg, Bryant's group came under similar attack, from four 280mm (11-inch) guns.

Martin Sommers was aboard *Texas* that day, and details a memorable gun duel.

18.

TEXAS DUELS

NAZI SHORE BATTERIES

"An Allied task force of battleships, cruisers and destroyers carried out the first bombardment of targets in the Cherbourg area this afternoon, Sunday."

— *SHAEF Communique: June 25, 1944*

This pedestrian sentence of twenty-three words will long be remembered by those who read it in the wardroom of the venerable U.S. battleship *Texas* the morning after. It will be rememebred for what it didn't say. The details covered by this pithy statement of fact constitute a unique chapter in naval history.

For the first time, a naval task force made a direct frontal assault on a concentration of heavy shore batteries among the most formidable in the world. The attack was in broad daylight without any possibility of surprise. The casemated enemy batteries for hours bracketed the largest ships of the attacking force. One of the enemy's 11-inch guns saw a coast artilleryman's dream come true when it struck the bridge of the *Texas* with a direct hit.

Another German shore gun put a 9.6 through the side of the *Texas* and deposited it in a warrant officer's cabin. Men were killed in action for the first time in the battleship's thirty years of service. There were two fires spreading on the main deck during the engagement.

There were other hits on the ships of the task force. Yet, from

641

minesweepers to battleships, all vessels in the force carried out their assignments under the continuous fire of the coastal batteries and withdrew safely to their home port in Southern England on the appointed hour. They had fought the shore batteries for a full three hours. The battered *Texas* was firing as she said good-by.

Why was the attack made against such odds? . . .

The Army needed help. Major General Joseph L. (Lightning Joe) Collins, leading his victorious Seventh Corps against the suicidal last stand of the Nazis in Cherbourg, asked for naval assistance in knocking out the great coastal batteries of the fortress. If they were not eliminated when the town was taken, the prize would be valueless; the port the Allies so badly needed could not be used.

The Navy knew what it faced when I came aboard the *Texas* late on the night of Friday, June 23. Rear Admiral Carleton F. Bryant, of Searsport, Maine, and Captain Charles Adams Baker, of Lynchburg, Virginia, had directed the gunners of the *Texas* and accompanying cruisers and destroyers in the victorious bombardment of D-Day. That one was a shooting match, with the big naval guns knocking out battery after battery of the enemy's lighter shore emplacements around Pointe du Hoe and the Vierville-Les Moulins beaches.

But Cherbourg was something else again. Captain Baker, a Virginia gentleman whose soft voice and punctilious décor fool you until you see him in action, remarked in a masterpiece of understatement: "This is considerably more of a hazard."

Strangely, from Admiral Bryant to the youngest seaman, seventeen-year-old Marvin Kornegay, of Mount Olive, North Carolina, all of the 1700 men aboard the *Texas* seemed to welcome the risk.

We who had been on naval vessels on D-Day and the days immediately following could not forget the burning tanks on the beaches and the dreadful punishment we had seen the men of the Fifth Rangers, First Division and Twenty-ninth Division take in that assault. During those days we had dished it out, the Army had taken it from the enemy. Now it was our turn to take it. Something like conscience told us that this was as it should be, no matter how little we relished the thought of what those shore batteries could do to the kind of target we aboard the clumsiest, slowest and oldest battleships in the American Navy would be offering.

The original plan called for the two groups of the task force to attack on Saturday morning. But throughout Friday night, enemy planes were very active in laying new minefields, and the minesweepers—those faithful sloggers of the sea—could not finish their delicate and tedious task in time. Accordingly, it was decided we would cross the Channel during the night hours of Saturday and attack just before the first light on Sunday. But this also was not possible. We finally edged out of the harbor at 3:30 A.M. on what was to be a too eventful Sunday for many of us. One group included Admiral Deyo, flying his flag aboard the U.S. cruiser *Tuscaloosa,* with the battleship *Nevada,* the U.S.S. *Quincy,* the British cruisers *Glasgow* and *Enterprise,* and accompanying destroyers and mine-sweepers.

We on the *Texas,* under the command of salty Admiral Bryant, had with us the U.S.S. *Arkansas,* the destroyers *O'Brien, Plunkett, Barton, Hobson* and *Laffey,* plus minesweepers.

Our destroyers hug us closely as we slip along, expecting a nuisance air raid; the Nazis have been suprisingly active in the air the last few nights. Around 5:20 A.M. comes the alarm: "Enemy glider bombers and torpedo planes in the area." They never appear. We learn why ten minutes later, when our fighter cover, flying in beautiful formation through the soft light of dawn, comes over. Blow by blow, the story is being broadcast to every man on the ship, wherever his duty, by the padre, Lieutenant Le Grand Moody, of Dillon, South Carolina, the handsome and gentle Congregationalist minister who in a few hours is to become one of the heroes of the engagement.

The destroyer *Barton* peels off and leads us into the first-phase assault area, off Barfleur, at 8:30 A.M. The seamen on the bridge buzz around the information that Lieutenant Commander Robert Montgomery, the great movie star of yesteryear, is operations officer on the *Barton.* This somehow adds éclat to our mission. The Navy is very proud of Bob Montgomery because he has made himself a really professional naval officer and because he has successfully avoided becoming a celebrity in uniform.

General Quarters at 9:15 A.M. We all recall the sixty-four hours of general quarters most of us stood over D-Day. The familiar rumble of bombing comes from the point of Barfleur, ten miles away. Our planes are at it again and we hope they are hitting them where they are. The enemy is jamming the radio now. We begin to feel a little cocky, things are so much like D-Day. We're slowing behind our minesweepers. Once again we feel bursting with affection for these ugly little stepchildren of the sea.

Now, at 9:45, we are within range of our first target, a 6-inch gun battery just west of Barfleur and heavily casemated in concrete. But we cannot fire until we are sure it is in enemy hands—there is a chance that Lightning Joe Collins' troops may have taken over. Tensely we wait for a report from our RAF spotter. At 10 A.M. we make contact with him. He reports: "No personnel visible around Targets 1 and 2—believed inactive." Tension mounts—we're likely to be damned if we do, and blasted out of the water if we don't. We ask for a double check on those batteries, but get a report that enemy aircraft is bothering the spotter. The word "bothering" means most anything, as used by the chronic self-belittlers in the RAF.

Now the plane spotter comes through handsomely: "Have gone down to 500 feet and checked both targets. There are bodies around the batteries. No activity."

We relax. We relax all over the place from 11 A.M. to noon. You couldn't imagine a more peaceful Sunday morning, not even in a homeside church. The usually angry Channel is as peaceful as a dairy-farm duck pond, if not quite a mill pond. The waters are washed blue in the bright sunlight and we might be cruising in the Mediterranean. The sailors on the *Arkansas* off our port bow have slipped their dungarees and are lying around their gun stations taking sun baths in their birthday clothes. One of our gun crews is placidly playing pinochle below us.

Peace is wonderful on the bridge, as well. The ship's executive, dark, handsome Commander José M. Cabanillas, one of the few Puerto Rican graduates of the Naval Academy, looks idly over the side of our 30,000-ton battleship and asks: "You like squid, captain? Lot of 'em around here."

Captain Baker says he doesn't much care for squid, except as bait.

"They sure can be good," counters the exec. "My mother used to make them with rice and a sauce of hers. Nothing better."

We all discuss our favorite dishes. It's a good time for it, because a mess boy is handing around our Sunday dinner—mugs of coffee and bologna sandwiches.

Whoom! The *Arkansas,* now astern, ends our mid-Sunday reverie with the crash of her biggest guns. She is on a live, verified target. But we must wait until we get a target verified, not only by our plane spotter but by our shore fire-control party on foot. Nobody at sea, including Lieutenant Colonel Fred P. Campbell, of Catawissa, Pennsylvania, General Collins' liaison with Admiral Deyo on the *Tusca-*

loosa, can tell exactly where the American line ends and the German begins in the scrambled fighting ashore. The Navy is taking no chance on firing on our troops, no matter what risks the extra precautions might involve for us.

There are splashes ahead among the minesweepers and destroyers. We now are as tense as we were relaxed a moment ago. We prepare to fire. Admiral Bryant, from his flag bridge just above our navigation bridge, leans over the rail and shouts: "Let's close in on those sweeps; they're getting it heavy."

"Aye," replies Captain Baker, and we move in to a spot within about 7000 to 8000 yards of the belligerent battery. We are making for it and we know it, but that is what we are here for. A destroyer begins to lay a smoke screen for the sweeps, who churn about like lonny ants, it seems, though no doubt there is professional method in their mad movements. The destroyer just ahead of us gets four near misses. Water spouts high around her.

Lieutenant Weldon James, the U.S. Marine Corps observer, who is standing at my left at the extreme rear of the bridge, grins at me and I grin back, though I don't mean it. Now that bigger game is on its grid, the much too accurate and too active battery ashore turns from the minesweepers to us. An 11-inch shell misses us by 300 yards, but the enemy's shooting improves rapidly. Four near misses, two off the starboard and two to port, bracket us at 12:35 P.M. We're hit below the water line on the port side twice, but the 6-inch shells bounce off the heavy armor of our blisters and explode in the water. They send the ocean geysering as high as the admiral's flag bridge above, a distance of about eighty feet. The enemy is firing 11-inch, 9.6-inch and 6-inch shells. We are bracketed again and again. Eight shells fall around us in a few seconds.

Shifting from foot to foot and trying to laugh at our unsteadiness of hand as we light cigarette after cigarette on the bridge, we suck in our guts by instinct, as though to shrink ourselves into as small a space as possible. Yeoman 1/c William L. Apgar, a cheerful young man from Manhattan, who is taking notes for the captain's report, is concerned because his pencil hasn't been able to catch up. We grin at each other, which seems to be the fashion. Lieutenant James, who was a war correspondent himself when the Japanese bombed him aboard the *Panay* in china, says something about a hit overdue, the way they're falling around. It is no comfort to reflect that he is an expert in these matters.

We are firing salvos from four of our ten 14-inch guns. Lieutenant Commander Richard B. Derickson, of Seattle, Washington, our gunnery officer, steps it up to six-gun salvos—we are not permitted to fire more than three turrets at a time since we are limited to 200 rounds of ammunition for the entire bombardment. The fierce blast of our own guns mingles with the explosion of near misses from the batteries. Even though Commander Derickson signals us just before he fires, it is hard for the novitiate to tell ours from theirs.

By now we all have a single conviction: "It won't be long now." Nobody is scared. The Navy word is "concerned." We are all much concerned.

Captain Baker, preoccupied with his job, and the padre, broadcasting the blow-by-blow throughout the ship, seem to be the coolest parties on the bridge—though this is no time for considered appraisal. The captain darts from the enclosed bridge to the portside wing, then to the starboard wing—wherever the shell falls—to determine the direction of the enemy fire and to give his orders for evading it accordingly. In a matter-of-fact voice the orders come sharply and quickly; the ponderous old *Texas* is no whirling dervish, but we are doing our best to "dazzle them with our footwork."

Another hit or very near miss on the portside, below the water line, more geysers of ocean. A splash to starboard and the captain dashes to the wing to observe. As he re-enters the enclosed bridge, he calls to our helmsman, QM. 3/c Christen N. Christensen, of Brooklyn: "Right hard rudder!"

It is 1:18 P.M.

Crash, shriek, and the sky has fallen, it seems. The enclosed bridge is suddenly dark, as glass, shrapnel and debris of all sorts fly around us. Clouds of yellow-brown smoke obscure everything, and we simply do not know what has happened. Stunned for a fraction of a second, those of us still on our feet mill around aimlessly, trampling one another's feet.

"All hands below!"

It's the captain's voice. Sweeter words were never spoken, no order ever more promptly obeyed. Those of us still able to stand race down the starboard ladders, one deck, two decks. I find myself directly behind Captain Baker, and that is somehow reassuring. Two decks below, the captain climbs over sailors who have taken cover in a hatch, finds another ladder in the darkened enclosure, and climbs up the narrow frame into the conning tower. There he calls for control to be shifted to the conning tower.

The "Right hard rudder" order already had been put into execution by Helmsman Christensen before we were hit. Now there is danger of a collision with the near-by *Arkansas* if we remain too long out of control. But Captain Baker establishes control when the *Texas* is headed 90 degrees north—precisely the desired position for evasive action. In the eerie shadows of the conning tower the captain begins to give his orders.

I go below, where everybody wants to know what happened. All seamen and officers who have no other duties are belowdecks. The loudspeaker system calls for a damage-control party.

"Fire on the fantail. . . . Fire on the fantail."

Somebody comes running from the stern to say it's a big fire on the fantail. Actually there are two fires on the fantail, and spreading. Flame from the 14-inch guns firing directly over the stern has set ablaze gun covers of the smaller guns beneath them. Lockers where gun gear is stored have been overturned by the concussion, and this gear is afire. Ammunition boxes also have been broken open by the blast, and 40mm. shells are rolling about the hot deck.

United States Marine Captain A. A. Bernard, of Norwich, Connecticut, in charge of the Marine crews manning the smaller guns, directs his men in tossing the hot, dangerous ammunition overboard. It is a delicate task, since the Marines must guard against more blast from the 14-inchers overhead. It can be fatal. Finally all the ammunition is overboard, and sailors succeed in extinguishing the fires.

Corpsmen, carrying stretchers as gently as the shells bursting in the water around us and the vibration of our own fire permit, are bringing the wounded from the bridge to the sick bay below-decks aft. There are more of them than we had thought. We still don't know exactly what happened. Staring blankly ahead with unseeing eyes, his shirt covered with blood, Commander Derickson is led by us on his way to the sick bay. How could he have been hurt? As gunnery officer, he was *inside* the fire-control tower, which in turn is *inside* the conning tower. The conning tower is a solid cheese box of fourteen inches of the strongest-known steel armor, with only narrow slits for vision. It is notoriously the safest place on the ship.

Lieutenant James and I circulate around to piece together the story. This is what happened: An eleven-inch high-capacity shell scored a direct hit on the conning tower, about five feet forward and eight feet underneath where we were standing on the captain's bridge. Great jagged hunks of shrapnel tore through the deck of the enclosed bridge and its wings. The forward half of the enclosed bridge deck beneath our feet was blown out and rolled back, so that it cut up and pinned down some of those who were forward near the wheel and other instruments. They were mowed down by shrapnel in addition to being mangled by the edge of the rolled-back deck.

Only those of us aft on the enclosed bridge escaped injury. Of the fourteen men within the eighteen-by-eighteen enclosure of the bridge at the time we were hit, eight were killed or wounded and six escaped.

The captain owed his life to his cool zeal. Had he not darted to the wings of the bridge to locate splashes so tirelessly he would have been trapped near the wheel, his customary place forward on the bridge. As it was, when he gave his "Right hard rudder" order, he was aft on the enclosed bridge, entering from the starboard wing.

Helmsman Christensen, whose last act was to execute the order which may have enabled us to evade a follow-up hit, had his legs torn off as he stood at the wheel and died of his wounds. He was a blond lad of twenty, with a twinkling eye and a peaches-and-cream complexion, one of the most popular men on the ship.

The captain's bridge, we knew, had been hit. But the admiral's bridge, just above us, had not been hit. Wilmott Ragsdale, war correspondent for *Time Magazine,* who had been on the admiral's bridge, reported that while they had felt a definite explosion, they had not thought the hit so close.

That Commander Derickson, in his double tower, had been injured was a near miracle, that he had escaped death was a full-blown miracle. Curiously, although the captain's bridge above was damaged by shrapnel, when the shell hit the thick steel of the conning tower, the main force of the blast was downward.

The conning tower was cast solid, except for a circular plug of steel which had been welded into the top of it. From this plug, a massive instrument called the fire director was suspended inside the fire-control tower, where Derickson sat within the conning tower. This 1120-pound instrument hung directly over Derickson's head. At exactly the split second of the blast, Derickson had leaned to his left to talk to an enlisted-man assistant. When the huge instrument fell, only a prong of it struck Derickson a glancing blow on the head. He suffered a long cut, a severe concussion and shock, but no more.

The action produced another miracle. A 9.6-inch armor-piercing shell (240 millimeters) tore a hole through the portside above the water line, passed cleanly into the cabin of Warrent Officer M. A. Clark of Larchmont, New York, the ship's clerk, where it came to rest. It never exploded, even during the last hour of action while our fourteen-inch guns were shaking the ship with their fire and the enemy was placing more of his shells near us. But this whimsical dud—had Clark been asleep in his cabin it would have done no more than wake him up—did not contribute to our peace of mind as long as it remained aboard.

From the time of the hit on the conning tower, we maintained fire on the enemy, at ranges varying from 10,000 to 20,000 yards. Twice more the durable old *Texas* passed across the grid where enemy fire was so accurately triangulated. The gallant destroyers, still weaving and racing hither and yon while they laid smoke screens and gave support to the sweeps, remained with us until we received orders to cease fire and return to port, at 3 P.M.

We had plastered the enemy batteries with 206 shells from our fourteen-inch guns, a total of 144 tons of sudden death.

Captain Baker returned to the wreckage of his bridge to direct an immediate check of damage. Admiral Bryant called down from above: "I've had enough for one day, haven't you?" Captain Baker concurred, along with everybody else.

As soon as our mission was completed on schedule, at three o'clock in the afternoon, Admiral Bryant received a message which made it all worthwhile. It came from the commanding officers of those faithful little minesweepers, and it said: "Thank you for supporting us excellently and taking all the slugging today. Had we been alone, some of our vessels would have been sunk. Hope your casualties were light."

Meanwhile, down in the ship's hospital the chief medical officer, Commander H. K. Sessions, a lean Navy veteran from Georgia, and his surgeon assistants from civilian life, Lieutenant Charles J. Scala, of New York's Bronx, and Lieutenant (j.g.) J. J. McArdle, of Lawrence, Massachusetts, fought to save lives. Before the *Texas* had sailed for battle, 250 members of her crew had given live pints of their blood to prepare for casualties. Now this blood, along with plasma from donors at home, was administered pint after pint without stint, rapid fire. Those seriously injured had broken and torn legs and arms, causing great loss of blood. All were suffering from intense shock. Without transfusions they would not have had a chance to survive.

The most seriously wounded were prepared for transfer to a shore hospital immediately on our arrival in port. They were Yeoman 1/c Apgar, who had been so worried about the notes he was taking for the captain; Yeoman 1/c Robert L. Umholtz, of Baltimore, Maryland, who also acted as one of the captain's recorders; Seaman 1/c Andrew N. Foyle, of Providence, Rhode Island, with whom I had shared cigarettes on the bridge during those hours of waiting to get it; Seaman 2/c Emil F. Saul, of Baltimore, Maryland, and Seaman 2/c Henry J. Quigley, Jr., of Manchester New Hampshire.

Quigley, who lost his left hand and whose right arm was torn, probably owed his life to the heroism of Padre Moody and Master Bugler 2/c Willy Eddleman, who had brought the fighting spirit of the typical Oklahoman to sea with him from Durant. When the hit threw the bridge into chaos, Quigley fell into the arms of the padre. Quigley, out of his head, fought to get to his feet. The padre held him down, since loss of blood from movement would have been fatal. Eddleman assisted the padre, who gave Quigley first aid and a shot of morphine from the hypodermic needle which all officers had carried into battle. Lieutenant Commander Louis P. Spear, of Berkeley, California, assisted in aiding the other wounded immediately after the hit.

Later I asked the padre, a modernist in theology and a graduate of Furman, Duke and the Yale Divinity School, what he was thinking during those moments when the wounded lay strewn around him, the ship was still under fire, and another hit seemed a certainty. He told me that, again and again, the seventh verse of the 91st Psalm ran through his head: "A thousand shall fall at thy side, and ten thousand at thy right hand; but it shall not come nigh thee." A believer, the padre; a believer with conviction in his heart.

Now reports were coming to us from other ships of our force. The destroyer O'Brien, in the thick of it all the time, had caught a direct hit, ten killed and twelve wounded. The destroyer Barton, a hit or near miss, but not much damage, just a shaking up. The battleships Arkansas and Nevada escaped unscathed, with many near misses. No damage to other ships, except some shaking up from near misses. It looked as though the Texas and the O'Brien had taken the slugging that day.

Lieutenant James, Ragsdale and I talked to some of the Texas gunnery crews. Their spirit was unimpaired. They left the assault area still full of fight. Typical was C.P.O. Henry Lee (Peewee) Myers, of Leechburg, Pennsylvania, who has served twenty-seven of his forty-four years in the Navy. Peewee, whose girth is a testimonial to the way the Navy feeds, still wore his "Shootin' pajamas" when he talked to us—the costume he wears whenever it's time to make noise with the guns, the brightest scarlet woolen underwear I've ever seen.

"I been pointin' for this for twenty-seven years and I wouldn't have missed it for anything," said Peewee Myers, who is chief fire-control man of the *Texas*.

"I figure we knocked out at least four of their big guns in that battery that had us bracketed. They had three guns at the top of the battery, then four in a line, then two below. We got the four in a line, we were on the target. If we'd had more time, I figure we'd got 'em all.

"I think we did our best shooting in this operation between 13,000 and 14,000 yards. But they sure had us bracketed—two under, two over; two under, two over. Some of the boys on the fantail tell us shrapnel sprinkled all around there from near misses astern."

Lieutenant James and I had a cup of tea with Captain Baker in his cabin. His tired eyes, diplomat's mustache, and general suave graciousness gave him an air of an attaché. I reflected that if I had seen him in the cocktail lounge of the Mayflower in Washington, I would never have suspected the salt and iron in him, the bravery and qualities of cool seamanship he had just exhibited in battle. I resolved to have no more snap judgments about people I may see in the cocktail lounge of the Mayflower.

Tactfully, the captain parried all attempts to get "personal stuff." He was appointed to the Naval Academy through a Lynchburg family friend, Carter Glass. There really wasn't much to it, you know. Whenever I tried for more detail he side-slipped into conversation about his twenty-year-old daughter in Washington, Pat, who works for the British air mission, the nurses' aid, shoots golf in the low 80's and is a wonderful girl. And so is her mother, Lee Rochester Baker, of Long Island. But no more about Baker.

Now comes the chief engineer, Commander Kener E. Bond, to have a cup of tea and tell us about a hazard we hadn't suspected. Bond, class of '22 at the Academy, went into business, became a department-store manager in Hamilton, Ontario, and returned to sea when war threatened. "They gave me this job because there wasn't anybody else in the Navy old enough to get along with the crotchety engines on this relic," Bond likes to explain. To understand that, you ought to understand that Bond, who likes to kid everybody and Bond most of all, is, at forty-four, about the youngest and gayest spirit on the *Texas*.

"She sure was saltin' up this time," Bond told us. "For a while there I didn't know whether we were going to make it."

It seems that the old reciprocating steam engines of the *Texas* always salt up. This time the condensers were particularly balky in doing their job of eliminating salt from the sea water used in the cooling system.

Admiral Bryant, son of a Bangor jeweler and descendant of Maine men who made their living from the sea, gave me a retake on the engagement from the maps in his quarters.

"I've decided I'm not very well equipped for this kind of work," I remarked when he had concluded.

He smiled and replied: "None of us is." He thought for a moment, and went on: "The time I was really concerned was the last five minutes, between 2:55 and 3 P.M. We were to stay within range and fire until three, and we'd been getting it heavy. I couldn't help thinking what a bad break it would be if we really got a packet during those five minutes. I was happy to see three o'clock come up, I must say."

DUELS BETWEEN NAVAL GUNS AND NAZI SHORE BATteries were a feature, too, of the Allied invasion of Southern France, which was launched on August 15. The thirty-two-year-old battlewagon *Arkansas* was among the fifty-three ships which softened up the coast east of Toulon in preparation for the landings. One of her turret captains was Chief Gunner's Mate Harold Clements, who in a letter speaks with pride of the part played by the battleship during the bombardment.

19.

THE BIG STUFF

August 22, 1944
U.S.S. *Arkansas*

Dear Mom and Dad:

The Allies struck a heavy blow in the invasion of Southern France several days ago and the American warship, as in the Normandy invasion, was present at the initial assault helping to blast a path for the first landings. Not long after we left port the captain spoke to us describing the task which lay ahead. Meanwhile, we were joined by men-of-war of both our own and other nations. As we plowed onward I wondered if the enemy realized when or where we were about to strike and would he be ready to "take it" and "dish it out."

During the night many shapeless, obscure forms of transports and landing craft were overtaken and left behind in the darkness as we moved into our forward and final position. Angry rumblings of bomb bursts and flashes of fire came from the distant area as bombers unloaded their deadly cargo. Swarms of bombers, fighters and troop transport planes droned overhead passing to and from the engaged area.

When the skies began to glow just before dawn, we found ourselves surrounded with ships and landing craft of all descriptions while the shores of France loomed surprisingly near, shrouded with a haze of

653

dust and smoke from the night bombing attack. We were then well within range of enemy coastal batteries and I for one hoped we would not long delay our opening fire. We had not long to wait, however, as the main battery was trained on an enemy installation of casemated guns and the sounding of the firing buzzer announced "standby for opening salvo." With a deafening roar we sent our salutation to Hitler's crowd on the beach. All around us ships of all nations were blasting away as we fired salvo after salvo while hundreds of landing craft moved shorewards.

As you know, the Army took the beach in stride and moved inland in high gear. We had a number of German prisoners aboard for a while. They didn't have the tough superman appearance the German propaganda experts would have us believe. A couple of nights we were sighted by JU-88 snoopers but a lusty barrage of A.A. fire drove them off.

The gun crews really enjoy throwing the big stuff over here at the Germans and are getting worried for fear the war will be over for the Navy and we will be left out at the finish. Anticipating this possible situation, the gunners are trying to have the engineers install wheels on our ships so we can catch up with the Army and help chase Heinies through the streets of Berlin. . . .

Yours,

Harold

CHERBOURG WAS PENETRATED ON JUNE 26 AFTER INtense fighting by elements of the 9th and 79th Divisions; but fierce yard-by-yard combat continued until the 1st of July, when the cape and the whole of the Cotentin Peninsula was secured. Fifteen days later the first Liberty ships began to discharge their cargoes, the prelude to formal liberation of the port city.

Operation "Dragoon", the final assault on Hitler's *Fortress Europa,* was launched against the coast of Southern France on August 15. The naval attack, once again under the command of Admiral Sir John Cunningham, was carried out by Admiral Hewitt, commanding three American Attack forces: Alpha, under Rear Admiral Frank J. Lowery, Delta, under Rear Admiral Bertram J. Rodgers, and Camel, under Rear Admiral Don Moon. Gunfire support was provided by battleships *Nevada, Texas, Arkansas,* H.M.S. *Ramillies* and the

French *Lorraine;* also heavy cruisers *Quincy, Tuscaloosa* and *Augusta,* light cruisers *Philadelphia* and *Brooklyn,* and a number of destroyers. After diversionary raids and paratroop drops, the main landings began at 8 A.M. on the 15th, and the beachhead was secured the following day, paving the way for the drive to Toulon, Port de Bouc and Marseilles by U.S. forces.

During the next two weeks 190,000 men, 41,000 vehicles and 219,200 tons of supplies were landed, and the Allied advance into Germany began. Once it had crossed the Rhine, there was no stopping Eisenhower's Expeditionary Force, which promptly gobbled up Hitler's Army Group B. Paris was liberated on August 25 but the titanic European struggle, which claimed the lives of hundreds of thousands of Allied fighting men, was to last yet another nine bitter months, until May 6, 1945, when Germany finally surrendered.

PART VI

ALEUTIANS

TO THE MARIANAS

~~~~~~

BY THE SUMMER OF 1943 THE UNITED STATES—AFTER
the capture of Attu and the bloodless occupation of Kiska—had regained possession of the barren, fog-ridden Aleutian Islands which
neither she nor Japan really wanted. Japan had initially seized Kiska
during the diversionary phase of her abortive Midway operation and
thereafter her troops occupied Attu. But Japan evinced no special interest in the 1000-mile Aleutian chain; she merely intended to hold the
islands, not to use them as a staging area for an invasion of the United
States. (Dutch Harbor, which was the only American naval base in
the islands at this juncture, lay some six hundred air miles from
Alaska and 1760 air miles from Seattle). Nevertheless, our reaction
to enemy troops in the Western Hemisphere was an immediate and
devastating blockade, coupled with sporadic raids by the XI Air Force
and an almost daily bombardment by naval forces. When the beleaguered enemy requested reinforcements, Tokyo responded by
ordering Rear Admiral Hosoyaga out from the Kuriles with a force
of two heavy cruisers, two light cruisers, four destroyers and three

transports to run the blockade. But anticipating such a move the United States stationed Rear Admiral Charles H. "Soc" McMorris offshore with a scouting force of one light cruiser, one heavy cruiser and four destroyers. The opposing warships met on the morning of March 23, 1943 off Komandorski.

When the battle opened war correspondent John Bishop was abroad heavy cruiser *Salt Lake City*. Because of wartime security, he was unable to reveal the identity of the other American warships, which were the light cruiser *Richmond* (flagship) and destroyers *Bagley, Dale, Coughlin* and *Monahan*. His account of this classic retiring action opens a few moments after Hosoyaga had been detected.

I.

ACTION OFF

KOMANDORSKI

0837. The first exchange . . . was brief and sharp. The Japs were closing the range rapidly, and as the flagship, now heading the American column, swung left into her westward turn to begin the retirement, the Jap heavies opened fire on her from a distance of twelve miles. Four times at least, without registering a hit, the shell splashes straddled her or leaped close—short, vicious spurts made by armorpiercing shells with delayed-action fuses. As the Jap heavies closed within range of her own 6-inch batteries, she returned the fire with salvo after salvo. Then she checked fire as her turn put the Japs beyond range of her guns. And the Japs were training their turrets around. They had recognized their Target No. 1, the lone American heavy. The first Jap salvo, fired hastily, fell short.

0842. The American heavy cruiser's decks leaped with the enormous concussion of her reply. Sixteen times in the course of her turn away from the Japs she fired full salvos.

Her fourth salvo scored a hit on the leading heavy, the Jap flagship, and touched off an explosion of some kind. At the base of the Jap's bridge a light flared, as no shellburst would flare, to envelop the whole tall bridge and fire-control superstructure in a sheet of flame. The sixteenth salvo hit again. From the vicinity of the Jap's forward stack, smoke billowed suddenly, the thick, black, sluggish smoke of an oil fire.

0848. Following in the wake of the flagship, our heavy cruiser swung around to a heading a little south of west, and steadied on the new course while the four destroyers maneuvered to their stations in line astern on the left flank of the two cruisers. From the American ships, men looked astern to assess the damage done to the Jap flagship. But there were good damage-control parties aboard that Jap. The black pillar of smoke thinned and disappeared, and he came on without losing a knot of his speed or missing a beat of the slow, regular rhythm of his salvos.

The two Jap heavies lay over the American heavy's quarter now, so that her forward turrets, blocked off by her bridge superstructure, could not bear. Only five guns of the after turrets stood against the twenty of the Japs.

The Jap ships showed in dark silhouette against the gray horizon, cardboard cutouts from which clusters of orange flame bloomed and vanished deliberately at thirty-second intervals. The range held fairly constant at about ten miles. The Japs shot skillfully. Time after time, the splashes of a salvo seemed to walk up from astern and on past only a few yards away from the foam which roared sibilantly along the hard-driven sides.

On the open bridge, Captain Rodgers watched the fall of a Jap salvo close aboard and spoke to the officer of the deck, Lieutenant (jg) R. B. Hale, "Fifteen degrees right rudder, Mr. Hale." The helmsman moved the wheel, and the ship, traveling at full speed heeled hard to port, laboring under the pull of centrifugal force, then righted herself slowly as she straightened out of the turn. Another Jap salvo fell. Captain Rodgers judged angle and distance, and said, "Ten degrees left rudder, Mr. Hale." He was calling on all his seamanship and knowledge of gunnery to outguess the Jap gunners. He watched the salvos, estimated how the Jap spotters would correct the errors, and conned his ship with a sure timing and skill which nullified every Jap correction. Comdr. Worthington S. Bitler, the executive officer, described it:

"The skipper zigzagged the ship. . . . We talked normally in between times. . . . The skipper would ask, 'Well, Worthy, which way shall we turn next?' I'd answer, 'Your guesses have been perfect so far, captain. Guess again.' He'd swing right or left, and the spot we would have been in had we gone the other way would be plowed up with ten or fifteen eight-inch shells. The skipper would then look at me with a grin on his face a yard wide and say, just like a schoolboy that's got away with something in school, 'Fooled them again, Worthy.' He did too. It was uncanny."

0856. One of the Jap light cruisers was seen to launch a plane. All but invisible against the gray overcast, it began to work up to a good spotting position on the American ship's beam.

0910. Our heavy suffered her first hit. She leaped and shuddered and seemed almost to stand still in the water, paralyzed by her pain. But then she was racing smoothly on again. A Jap shell, falling steeply, had glanced off her hull near the water line and exploded within a few feet of her bottom. It had bruised her and shaken her cruelly, without breaking her steel skin.

0913. Sky Control reported the Jap spotting plane within range abeam, and Comdr. James T. Brewer, the gunnery officer, prowling restlessly around the bridge with a long tangle of phone wires trailing behind him, ordered the 5-inch batteries to open fire. Less than a minute of ack-ack discouraged the pilot. He pulled up to safety, and uselessness, in the clouds.

0920. The Jap flagship took another certain hit. Smoke rose above his after superstructure, and this time it persisted, drifting away astern without any sign that the Jap damage-control parties were able to smother the fire.

0931. The spotting plane reappeared on the starboard beam. The anti-aircraft batteries of our light cruiser joined with the heavy's to fill the air around the plane with a maelstrom of shellbursts and drive it away, floundering, to the northward with smoke streaming from its fuselage. The next day a Navy PBY sighted the wreck of a plane still afloat bottom up in the sea not many miles from the battleground.

0942. The leading Jap heavy, still smoking, lost speed and dropped astern to bring under control the fire which burned somewhere near his stern. His guns were silenced, and Admiral McMorris took advantage of the easing of the pressure on our heavy cruiser by a move to bring his flagship into the fight once again. He led his force in a swift circle to the northward against the two Jap light cruisers, which, until now, had been steaming along nearly abeam of the American heavy to the north, safely out of reach of her guns. The range to the leading light cruiser closed with a rush, and within a few minutes of making the turn, the heavy, with her forward turrets, and the flagship, with her full main battery, were firing salvos which painted the fleeting white stripes of shell splashes along the leading

Jap's gray hull. He returned the fire, but sheered away in haste to open the range.

0955. The damaged Jap heavy, no longer smoking, cut across the arc of the Americans' turn to the north and re-entered the fight, but he found himself opposed by ten guns instead of five, for now his position relative to the big American ship enabled her forward guns to bear.

The battle track led to the northwest now. Minute after minute the guns of the American heavy thundered their salvos, and minute after minute the plunge of Jap shells all but grazed her as Captain Rodgers conned her along her elusive zigzag. Ahead, the flagship carried on her own duel with the leading Jap light cruiser, a duel for which the Jap seemed to have little stomach, since again and again he sheered nervously out of range after the exchange of a few quick salvos.

To a turret officer watching from his little steel booth, his men might have seemed to be going through a jerky mechanical dance timed by the rhythm of outlandish instruments. Backs heaved with the clack and hiss of breechblocks opening, bowed with the roar of compressed air rushing into the gun barrels, straightened with upflung arms to the shout, "Bores clear!" At the hoot of a whistle, men lifted and lunged, and the loading trays crashed in the open breeches; arms like pistons threw rammer levers, jerked them back with the navy thud of the shells driven home in the rifling. Shoulders swung to the pianissimo slither of powder bags shoved after the shells, and backs bowed and heaved again with the hissing, clashing impact of breechblocks swung closed and locked. Men stepped backward to the whir of gears as the big silver breeches sank into their pits to elevate the muzzles.

All men froze at the sound of the firing buzzer warning with dot-dot-dash. And then the deep concussion, the rearward leap and return of the guns, jarred them to a slavish repetition of their strange dance figure. They knew nothing of what went on outside their turrets, nothing of the calm sea and the bleak gray sky and the faraway silhouettes which flashed the orange flames. All they knew was the insatiable hunger of those silver breeches for powder and more powder, shells and more shells.

1010. Our heavy took her second hit. With the clang of an enormous metal-punching machine, the Jap shell punctured her hull above the water line.

1018. After the American heavy had been cruelly shaken by a

series of very close near-misses, the decision was made to shield her behind a smoke screen. On her fantail, men worked at the valves of the smoke tanks until the chemical smoke was rolling away astern in a sluggish, snow-white cloud. At the same time Commodore Riggs' destroyer flagship led the destroyers in a dash to begin a wild snake dance back and forth across the heavy's stern. Smoke boiled like black oil from their stacks to diffuse and hang in billowing clouds streaked by the white of the chemical smoke, and presently the big ship was hidden to her foremast head from the enemy.

In their fighting tops, Americans and Japs kept an unrelenting watch on the smoke screen, and whenever the fire-control crews sighted the enemy over a depression in the screen or through a gap, the guns blasted a salvo. The battle went on at a slower, irregular tempo. The strain had been intensified, sharpened by those minutes of waiting for the next crash of a salvo.

1058. The Americans looked off to the Jap heavies with a shadow lifted from their minds. Admiral McMorris had led the way through a series of radical course changes aimed at baiting the Japs into damaging countermoves. And he had succeeded. The American force was steaming due south with the Jap heavies dead astern. The road of escape had been opened.

For two hours and sixteen minutes the big American ship had fought off the two Jap heavies and had dealt out in the fighting far more punishment than she had received. She had steamed among hundreds of falling Jap shells, yet had suffered only two hits. A great, an incredible good fortune had guarded her all the way. But fortune now abandoned her.

1059. A shell struck and exploded abovedecks.

1103. A shell struck below the water line.

The first killed two men and wounded several more. The second pierced oil tanks, bulged and wrenched an engine room bulkhead, and loosed a flood of water and fuel oil into several compartments adjoining the engine room.

Down among the white serpents' nests of steam lines, the fantastic shadows and shapes of machinery, in the dimly lit engine-room bilges a struggle began which was no less grim than the gunnery battle above. From the scores of leaks where pipes and steam lines passed through the wrenched bulkhead, the mixture of water and fuel oil from the flooded compartments gushed in a splashing cascade. It gathered and rose in the bilges, water whose temperature was the deadly thirty-two degrees Fahrenheit of the Bering Sea in winter; oil which coagulated in the cold to form heavy shreds and sheets of tarry stuff which clung like black glue. Inch by inch, it rose. If it should rise too far the engines would have to be stopped.

Pumps labored to suck away the flood, and damage-control parties attacked the leaking bulkhead. The men stood thigh deep in the freezing water while they pounded calking into the leaks. Any kind of calking—rags, wiping waste, their shirts, their jackets—anything which could be wadded into the spurting crevices and pounded tight. Still, the level inched higher, to their waists, to their chests, to their shoulders.

Almost they lost their battle. There came a moment at 1125, when the engines in that one engine room had to be stopped. But it was only for a moment. The flood began to recede at last. The men stood exhausted and oil-streaked while the level dropped as inexorably as it had risen, until it was little more than knee deep. They had won. But ill fortune was to strike again.

1140. Word came to the bridge that in the magazines and shell decks which fed the after guns, little powder and not many shells remained. A few salvos more and the guns would be silenced. Those guns had to be fed; they alone were able now to fight off the Jap heavies dead astern. And there was only one way to feed them.

The forward shell decks were opened. Men muscled the heavy shells out to the wind-swept main deck, cradled them in wheeled dollies, trundled them aft. The forward magazines, with all their intricate safeguards against fire and explosion, were thrown open. From the powder-handling rooms deep down in the ship men started chains of powder bags passing from man to man up to the deck below the main deck, and on from man to man along passages, past galleys, through messing compartments and berthing compartments, past workshops and machine shops and offices, on to the powder circles beneath the after turrets, and up to the powder ready boxes.

It was a powder train needing only a spark to blow the ship and her men into nothingness. But the shells flowed steadily, the powder bags slithered to the loading trays. The ship fought on.

Then misfortune struck, its third, its finishing, blow. Its weapon was the water still lying in the engine-room bilges. Through the punctured fuel tanks, the water was creeping secretly into the complex system of pipes and valves, many of them racked by the shellburst, which controlled the distribution of oil from the dozens of tanks to the burners under the boilers. Abovedecks, the terrible warning signal was a burst of white smoke from the two stacks—white smoke which was more steam than smoke. Down in the shimmering heat and the tornado roar under the boilers, burners were snuffing out one by one, two by two, extinguished by that treacherous seepage of water. The white smoke continued to pour from the stacks. And then the sick moment came when the vibrations of the engines, the pulses of the four propellers, died. Their absence was the sudden terrible silence when a dying man stops breathing.

Her momentum carried her on, but she was lifeless.

1150. Speed thirteen knots. No foam raced along her sides. Under her fantail, the sea swirled and eddied lazily.

1153. Speed eight knots. A Jap salvo landed so close aboard that she seemed to lift in the water with the force of the blow.

1154. Her momentum was running out. She barely had steerage way. Another very near miss shook her brutally and she staggered.

1155. She lay dead in the water. Captain Rodgers ordered the flag signal hoisted, "My speed zero."

She lay motionless on the almost glassy sea, 600 feet of her looming dark and massive against the bleak gray sky. She would fight, of course, while a gun could be fired, when the Japs closed for the kill. But she was little more than a helpless hulk. There was not a man aboard who did not expect to die within the next few minutes.

On the bridge Captain Rodgers, still smiling, shook hands with Commander Bitler. All through the ship, officers quietly were inspecting the men under their command, seeing that they had their life belts, their knives, the proper amount of clothing to survive as long as possible in the water—if they should live to go overside. There was one man who got himself ready very methodically for abandoning ship. He took off his jacket and his bulky, windproof overalls. He kicked out of his shoes. He checked his life belt and adjusted it to be ready for inflating as soon as he hit the water. But then, as he stood looking at the murderously cold sea, "To hell with it!" he exploded. And he put on everything that he had taken off. He knew that he had to die, but he preferred a quick death with the ship to the long-drawn twenty minutes of dying which would be his in the grip of that icy cold. There were many more like him.

When, at about 1150, Admiral McMorris received the message that the heavy cruiser's engines were stopped, he took the only course which might save her. He ordered three of the destroyers to go in against the Jap force to launch a torpedo attack and press it home so long as they could manage to remain afloat. It was a tragic decision, forced upon him. At best, a torpedo attack would be little more than a bid for time, a great sacrifice play by the destroyers to draw the gunfire of the Jap force away from the heavy upon themselves, and so to gain time enough for her men to clear her fuel lines of water and get her under way again.

In the roar of wind on the bridge of the destroyer flagship where she steered her wild, smoke-laying snake dance astern of the stricken ship, Commodore Riggs received the orders and acknowledged with the terse yet eloquent compliance of battle communications. He designated the fourth destroyer to stay behind to screen the heavy cruiser with smoke. Then he signaled, "The targets are the heavies," ordered his flagship into a hard, rail-under turn back toward the enemy, and squared away with two others swinging after him. At their magnificent full speed which sent the spray arching from their stems, they steamed off into the guns of the enemy, three little ships against ten, 5000 tons against 50,000.

On the big cruiser, the men who were preparing for death saw nothing of what went on beyond the smoke screen. But they could hear the deep, faraway thunder of Jap 8-inch salvos swelled by a flatter rumble as the destroyers came within range of the Jap light-cruiser batteries.

Time was swift with the certainty that these were their last moments in the living light and air of this earth. Time was interminable with the horror of imminent death. Off in the distance, the thunder of gunfire swelled again with a hard, irregular staccato as the three destroyers opened fire on the Jap heavies. On the clock, the minute hand crept forward. Far away beyond the smoke screen the sound of gunfire slackened to desultory bursts, thudded into silence. The destroyers' attack had run its course.

Later, when the heavy cruiser's men told of those next few minutes, their story lay less in their words than in their faces and their voices when the memory came back to them. Words were not big enough. What happened, they said, they could not believe at first. Their minds were so profoundly fixed in the certainty of death that the truth was beyond believing.

Chronologically, this happened:

1158. The heavy cruiser stirred with a slow pulse of life. Her port engines were turning over, inching her ahead.

1159. A torrent of foam erased the hazy eddies under her fantail. She trembled with a mighty surge of horsepower to her propellers. Her decks leaped to a giant thunderclap as her after turrets resumed firing.

Men were looking at one another with unbelieving eyes. Men were laughing weakly. Men were going through all the complex and indescribable reactions of returning from the thin edge of death back to life and hope again.

Speed had protected the three destroyers at first. They raced on through white thickets of 8-inch shell splashes until they came within range of the Jap light cruisers, and the sea close around them was torn by the storm of shells into a wild white riot of leaping spray. Still they held on until their own guns opened an earsplitting barrage on the leading heavy, while the range closed to 9000 yards, point-blank range for cruiser guns.

Then two 8-inch shells of a salvo struck the leader. They killed five of her men and robbed her of all but fifteen knots of her speed. While she was slowing she launched her torpedoes; a last, despairing gesture of defiance, it was, for at 9000 yards she had little hope of scoring a hit. With a metallic shock and a fierce hiss of air into the torpedo tubes, the beautiful steel shapes made their racing dives into the swells, plunged, rose, steadied and headed away, leaving ruler-straight lines of bubbles behind them. The leader held sluggishly on, awaiting her end, while the rain of steel lashed the surface of the sea around her into white shreds. In the minds of her men now lay the numbing certainty of death.

Six miles astern, where our heavy cruiser had begun to inch ahead and our light cruiser circled near her, waiting for the Japs to close, men heard the thunder of the destroyer attack falter and stop. To them, the silence meant that the three destroyers had finished their journey to oblivion, but—as the big cruiser drove on and up toward her full speed—that their objective had been brilliantly gained.

But then an incident took place whose impact left men standing frozen, as men stand in the presence of the supernatural.

1200. The dead spoke, and with words proclaiming a miracle. A message came from Commodore Riggs: "The enemy are retiring to the westward. Shall I follow them?"

Off there beyond the smoke screen, the two Jap heavies had turned frantically to present the narrow targets of their sterns to the torpedoes, and the two light cruisers and the six destroyers had followed.

Before three American destroyers, one of them a cripple, and before torpedoes launched four and a half sea miles away, the ten Jap ships were fleeing in ignominious confusion. And they held on in their headlong flight. They had had their bellyful of fighting.

1202. The American heavy blasted out a final gust of flame and smoke and titanic sound. The Battle of the Komandorskie Islands was over.

Admiral McMorris and his task group had discharged their mission; they had turned back a Jap attempt in strength to supply and reinforce Attu and Kiska. They had won.

And yet it was a strange, illogical victory; a victory won by three hours and a half of bitter defensive retirement before nearly two-to-one odds; a victory won in the moment of despair when six ships and many hundreds of men reeled helplessly on the crumbling verge of defeat and death.

Later, the heavy cruiser's men were almost casual in their mention of victory, of the significance of the battle in the Aleutian campaign, or of the fact that theirs had been the longest continuous gunnery duel in the whole history of the modern Navy. Their enthusiasms were for the destroyers.

They spoke with profound gratitude of Commodore Riggs and his men. "They're the lads that deserve all the credit," they said. "Perhaps we did slap the Jap flagship around a bit. The destroyers reported that he was smoking badly, and that all but one of his five turrets were trained all haywire, and out of action. But it was the destroyers who turned the trick. They saved our lives. We'll never forget it."

Nor would they ever forget, they said, the sight of those three little ships returning over the calm gray sea from their journey to oblivion. That was like seeing ghosts, at first.

A reverent amazement still moved in their voices when they told about their part in the battle, about the long hours when Jap salvo after Jap salvo plunged close aboard, yet scored only four hits and killed two men. "It wasn't that their gunnery was bad," they explained repeatedly. "The Japs' shooting was really beautiful. There were times toward the end, with the two heavies dead astern, when a few feet of deflection one way or the other would have planted a whole salvo along our center line fore and aft, and we'd have opened up like a split melon. But they just didn't get the hits that their shooting deserved. The way Captain Rodgers handled the ship had a lot to do with it, of course, but there was more to it than that."

In the wardroom one evening, when several officers smoked and drank coffee and talked, still searching many months later for words to describe the ever-mounting tension of those long hours of battle, one man found the right words.

"It was like flipping a coin," he said. "Over and over again for three hours and a quarter, doubles or quits. And every single time it came up heads."

~~~~~~

McMORRIS' BRILLIANT SURFACE ENGAGEMENT MARKED the Navy's only major confrontation of the enemy in Aleutian waters. For the Army, however, there was still one bloody assault to be made: Attu. After a pre-invasion bombardment, the troops landed at Holtz bay on May 11 and the campaign ended two weeks later with the annihilation of the defenders: 2351 Japanese dead as compared with six hundred Americans, out of a landing force of 11,000 troops. Kiska, assaulted on July 28, was found abandoned, after the forces under Admiral Kawase had been successfully evacuated from the Kuriles. The fog-shrouded Aleutians struggle was over.

Now let us consider another phase of the Pacific conflict, the relentless battle of American submarines against the Japanese Empire, which saw almost four million tons of enemy shipping succumb to American torpedoes. We have seen—and will see again—what was termed a successful patrol; but what of an unsuccessful patrol?

Fifty-two American submarines were lost during the war, and one of the earliest reported "missing and presumed lost" was the U.S.S. *Grenadier,* which was the victim, on April 21, 1943, of a lethal depth-charging in Lem Velon Strait of the Malay Barrier. Her skipper was Lieutenant Commander John A. Fitzgerald, holder of a Navy Cross for previous patrols. Forced to scuttle, Fitzgerald and his crew were rescued by a Japanese warship and brought to Penang for preliminary interrogation, later to a P.O.W. camp on the Japanese mainland. Thus began a torturous twenty-eight months' internment which ended only when Japan surrendered.

We present an excerpt from Fitzgerald's fascinating diary, detailing some of the events which occurred during his ordeal as a Japanese prisoner.

2.

LIFE IN A JAPANESE
P.O.W. CAMP

Breakfast was promised to be served later when we arrived at the place of confinement. Everyone was of course in need of food; hardly anyone had eaten since the morning of the 21st. Sandwiches had been put out on board, but because of the nervous tension and excitement nothing had been eaten. The 23rd wasn't too bad because the nervous tension was still so prevalent that I didn't feel the need too much, and am sure the other seventy-five felt the same way. However, came dawn of the 24th and that old gnawing pain in the midriff began to tell. It was maddening to go to that questioning room and see the Japs eating bananas and sandwiches in front of us and drinking cool limeade and milk. No doubt it was one of their aims to get us to break down. The American spirit and manhood was made of sterner stuff; it hurt, yes, but no one indicated it. Upon getting back to my room on the second floor I recall so vividly how I used to look out the window, day after day, and see those coconuts lying about on the ground. Would make gestures of all kinds to the guard regarding getting one of them. All I'd receive would be a shake of the head and a sadistic grin showing all his buck teeth.

One day I encountered a guard of my room who spoke Spanish. We became involved in a conversation in Spanish. He had lived in

670

Brazil for a number of years, but had returned to Japan just prior to the war in the Pacific. All I could get from him was one cigarette. As to the coconuts in the yard "No puede senor."

The three pieces of chewing gum I happened to have in my pocket went a long way to stave off the hunger which was becoming more acute day by day. It was getting to the point where we on the second floor would have to pull ourselves up the stairs by means of the railing on the steps. Anything in the way of food was not forthcoming and all of us were steadily growing weaker, weaker and still weaker. Still no food was forthcoming until the evening of the 27th. My previous efforts to obtain any were with negative results until a Jap commander came to my room that morning. He promised some food by 1300, it finally arrived about 1700, a small teacup of rice broth, and some weak tea, period. In the meantime the men were divided half and half between two school rooms on the ground floor, stone decks; the officers in single rooms on the second floor, wooden decks. The rough treatment started the first afternoon, particularly with the men. They were forced to sit or stand in silence in an attention attitude. Any divergence resulted in a gun butt, kick, slug in the face or bayonet prick. In the questioning room persuasive measures such as clubs, about the size of indoor ball bats, pencils between the fingers and pushing the blade of a pen knife under the finger nails trying to get us to talk. Considering all this, I believe we held up remarkably well. To the best of my knowledge, Knutson, J.S. Radioman 1/c and I were the only ones to receive the water treatment, and I the only one who lost a fingernail . . . The pain caused by the pencils between the fingers of the right hand was so great that I did not realize my left hand was being stabbed with a knife; only when I saw the blood gushing out did I realize what had happened. Of what did the water treatment consist in this case?

Visualize the old circus tent stake driver pounding the peg into the ground. Simultaneously two Japs would arrange themselves one on each side of the victim, taking turns as to see who could drive the hardest. Usually one would soon be knocked down in short order, twenty to thirty or so blows doing the trick. I was then tied to a bench with my head hanging over the edge. The Japs would then elevate the bench to such an angle that my feet were on a plane of about 30 degrees above the head. They would then start pouring tea kettle after tea kettle of water down my nose, holding a hand over my mouth in the meantime; everytime I'd move my head to try for some air a heavy fist would bounce off my chin. Maybe I'd pass out and maybe not. Following this I would receive another club beating until I passed out. Upon coming to they would try to get me to talk; if no go on that, more beatings—finally I would be carried to my room and dumped on the floor waiting for awhile until they decided to try again. It got so that everytime I'd hear that Jap warrant officer coming into the building I'd think it was for me again, or some other poor devil. We all had the same feeling for everyone received beating after beating. However, the beatings, slugs, etc., were quite common for all hands. One became so stiff and sore it was almost impossible to move, let alone change position from standing or sitting or reclining even if able to get away with it.

Whiting, Harty and I were given a bath and ordered to wash our clothes the afternoon of the 28th. Regret to state that because of a paralyzed right arm, Whiting washed my clothes and assisted me in my bath.

The three of us, blindfolded and handcuffed were flown to Tokyo 29 April to 1 May 1943. Stopping, I think at Saigon and either Shanghai or Formosa. We were not informed as to our location. In the plane, during flight, the blindfold was removed, but being desperate characters the handcuffs were left on except when caged up at night and well guarded. The first night we received some hardtack biscuits, one small can of condensed milk and some tea. The cockroaches were quite prevalent among the biscuits. The next night we received a small handful of rice and a few vegetables on a green leaf. Two meals in the plane were Jap commercial airline food and the other Jap field rations. Probably the best quality and quantity we received until late August 1945.

We arrived in the Tokyo Area the evening of 1 May 1943. After a cold ride of about an hour and a half in a truck fitted with a tent covering, blindfolded and handcuffed we arrived at Ofuna. Reminded us of a seascout camp in the hills with little monkeys running hither and yon. Individual rooms were provided, two and a half small steps wide and about five of the same in length, each fitted with two grass mats or "tatamies" as the Japs call them. A cold meal of rice and soup was provided. We were given plenty of blankets, a G-string, some tooth powder, tooth brush, and small hand towel made of raw silk. We were still strictly supervised and not allowed conversation, a condition which had prevailed since the morning of 22 April, and one that was to continue for many months.

The following will give an idea of a portion of some typical days spent as a POW at Ofuna.

At five minutes before reveille a guard would go down the corridors calling out "Soin Ococke, go fun Mae" and at reveille merely "Soin Ococke." After our blankets were folded and placed in a corner of our cell there would be a counting of noses and morning setting-up exercises, which were from time to time carried to extremes in that we would be directed to run around and around the compound, usually until one or more could no longer stand. During the interim, the guards would be ever present with a club which they would lay on with considerable force across the back and legs of anyone falling behind.

After the morning wash up, everyone using the same open air water spigot, fine in summer, but hellish in winter, we would be directed to our individual rooms. A pail of rice and a pail of thin soup would be brought to the building where it was measured out practically grain by grain and drop by drop. This resulted in each individual receiving approximately one tea cup of rice and a cup of soup. With but slight variations once in a while, this constituted our diet three times a day.

The passageways then had to be swept and scrubbed. Prior to the first of May 1943, scrubbing of the passageways occurred but about once a week. However, when Whiting, Harty and I arrived something new was added—we scrubbed them daily. The mop consisted of a heavy piece of rope about three feet long which had been untwisted, no handle being provided other than the pushers' two arms. After wetting the mop in a bucket of water, two or more of these mops would be laid out in line across the hallway. They were then pushed up and down the corridor, bear walk style, until the supervising guard was satisfied that the deck was relatively clean. This never happened until the individuals pushing the mop were thoroughly exhausted and had been belted with a stick or club several times. Later, when B-29 personnel were being captured and placed in Ofuna, it was a daily occurrence to hear from across the compound the beatings being administered during morning clean up.

The "benjos" or toilets were emptied almost daily. This meant the transferring of the contents of the collecting basins by means of a small bucket to larger buckets, then carrying them to and placing them upon a farmer's cart to be hauled away and used by him as fertilizer in his fields. On occasion a bucket rope would break, as a result there was quite a mess to clean up; needless to say, some of the fertilizer to be found its way to those of us doing the carrying.

Quizzing by the Japanese intelligence staff usually occupied a considerable portion of our time, then again nothing would be going on. Conversation was prohibited and books were negligible. As a result we were forced to stand around like a bunch of animals—and in our captors' minds we were probably no more than that. Everyone was always glad when night time came along for in that way we could forget the days past and obtain ever needed rest.

We subsequently learned that during the afternoon of 1 May, all inmates except an Australian flying officer had been transferred to the other wing of the building, nineteen of then occupying about a dozen rooms, necessitating of course, some doubling up in rather cramped style.

Breakfast on May 2nd brought us our regular meal, soup and rice, which is the standard Nip procedure. About a teaspoonful of soya bean paste—"Miso"—and a small bowl of rice, constituted the size of it. Commander A. L. Maher, Naval Academy '22, Gunnery officer of the Houston, came rushing down the passage well ahead of the guard and said "Maher, Gunnery officer Houston, get data to you as soon as possible," and went about his business. He was acting as interpreter in the camp, there being no Jap interpreter in Ofuna. The guard was right on his heels in no time and gave Maher a rather questioning look. It was reassuring for us to see another white man again, and to be braced with this small bit of information. Later in the morning I saw LCDR Dave Hurt across the compound; of course communication of any kind was practically out of the question, being so closely watched. We were later able to get a little information back and forth by means of notes scribbled on scrap paper and left in the toilet (referred to as "benjo" by the Nips). Hurt gave me a line on what he had been feeding the questioning officers, whom we learned to call QK's (Quiz Kids).

Questioning began May 3rd. On from where we operated, how we went to Australia and a thousand and one other things. The *Grenadier* was out of Sydney, so I told them and had arrived direct from Pearl traveling east of the Marshals, past the Fijis, etc. The three of us would try getting our data to each other in one manner or another, so that our stories would not be conflicting. Our chief Q.K. was named Sanimatsu, a commander. He was, prior to the war, in the Naval Attache Office in Washington and had been touring the U. S. getting all the data he could obtain, even had spent a year or so at

Princeton. His English was fair. The interpreter who worked with him had been in the Embassy at Washington, and had attended U.S.C. during his numerous years here in the States. This man's name was J. Sasaki, a Lieutenant Commander Naval reserve . . . Questioning continued practically daily for some time, areas, numbers of boats operating and where, number of subs sunk or badly damaged. Finally I said that some fifty subs had failed to return and that forty some odd were seriously damaged. This statement was made in May or June of 1943. It seemed to satisfy them and they shut up on that score. You can well imagine the questions asked, but I don't think their tactics and methods were as effective as they believe them to be. We became terrific liars and usually got away with it. On matters of commercial design used on merchantman or universally known, and data which could be obtained from "Janes Fighting Ships" we told the truth, which I believed helped us when we were lying about matters which they had no business to know as far as we were concerned.

Knutson, Radioman 1/c arrived June 29, 1943. By the grapevine I gave him all the data I could. He was taken from Penang about 3 May and flown to Surabaya via Singapore. His treatment at Singapore, while there for a couple of days, was fairly decent, except that one time he had to use his hat for a toilet. In Surabaya he was questioned by Jap and German radio and radar experts. When he wouldn't "give" he was starved and hung by his thumbs for ten days. If I am not mistaken our intelligence intercepted some of the Jap reports emitting from Surabaya regarding the interview with Knutson. Some of the reports arriving at Ofuna about this time caused us a bad time but all in all we evaded and denied lots of it, or confirmed other data if it didn't amount to much. Mr. J. Curtin's broadcasts from Australia regarding the base in Exmouth Gulf also caused us a bad time. However, we swore up and down that we knew of no such base on the west coast of Australia. Then they started in on the Brisbane and Perth bases saying that they had D. Fied (D/F'd; traced by direction finder) our coded dispatches from there. We were able to deny any knowledge of these two bases for a long time, however, they never, to my knowledge, got the straight set-up on either base. About fourteen "S" and 7-8 Fleet boats operated from Sydney. Later they didn't know for sure whether a half dozen or two dozen boats operated from Fremantle. That question was bandied back and forth for some time, then was finally dropped as apparently a bad deal . . .

AS WAS EVIDENCED IN THE ALEUTIANS, THE FUNDA-
mental American strategy of bypassing Japanese-held islands, severing their lines of communications and isolating them, was paying off.
Another theatre where this technique was successfully employed was
in the shallow, coral-pitted waters of New Guinea, the sprawling sub-
continent north of Australia, where motor torpedo boats did the
Navy's heavy work of containing the enemy, and did it well.

Before citing typical PT patrols, let us move back in time to 1942,
when the Japanese were making a concerted drive on Port Moresby.
Because of conflicting and overoptimistic reports which had been
reaching President Roosevelt from this theatre, newly commissioned
Lieutenant Commander Lyndon B. Johnson was ordered to investigate the situation, acting as Roosevelt's representative. On June 9,
Johnson went aboard the B-26 "Heckling Hare" as an observer during a flight over the jungles of Lae. The plane left Seven Mile Field in
the beleaguered Allied outpost, and shortly afterwards was taken
under fire by eight Zero fighters.

The following excerpt by aviation writers Martin Caidin and
Edward Hymoff, who interviewed the plane's crew, describes the
future President at the height of the attack.

MARTIN CAIDIN

AND EDWARD HYMOFF

3.

LIEUTENANT COMMANDER LYNDON B. JOHNSON UNDER FIRE

During take-off, Lyndon Johnson remained seated in the radio compartment. But once they became airborne, he moved around the main part of the airplane where he was able to look out through the small window on the left side of the fuselage. He also stood on a small stool in the center of the fuselage so that he could bring his head up into the clear Plexiglas bubble atop the airplane, from where he could survey the entire scene and watch the other Marauders. On the way to Lae, he was able several times to squeeze his head and shoulders between Greer and McMullin and look forward through the cockpit windshield.

When the Japanese attacked, there was no opportunity to spend time up forward, but by looking through the bubble, Johnson had a spectacular view of the attack. The plane rolled and twisted as Greer dove for the clouds, sawing the rudder back and forth. The airplane was filled with sounds; the thunder of the engine, the shrieking wind, the impact of the Japanese bullets and exploding cannon shells, and the stuttering bark of the machine guns firing in bursts at the Zeros.

Several times during the air fight Johnson worked his way back to the waist guns where Lillis Walker was on his knees, moving back and forth from the left waist gun to the one on the right as the best targets presented themselves.

The gunners, hammering away at the Zeros, flinching by instinct when cannon shells went off near them, were amazed with the cool reaction of Lyndon Johnson under fire. This was his first exposure to the enemy; it was the kind of situation in which many a man might be expected to yield to great fright, for it is clear that the "Heckling Hare" was virtually being shot to ribbons in the air. The men stated later that they felt their odds of survival were, at the time, "no better than stinking."

The faulty generator did more than cut power to the right engine. Bob Marshall in the top turret had his hands full because of the snarl in the electrical system. With its twin .50-caliber machine guns and excellent field of fire, the turret provided the most important defense of the airplane. Normally, Marshal could swing his guns rapidly from any one point to another to track and to lead an attacking fighter. But when the generator went out, he could move his guns easily up and down, but he had lost all power to swing them in azimuth—around the line of the horizon.

There was an emergency manual system, but it was strictly emergency and not very good at its job. Marshall had to force the gun barrels against a wind of from three hundred to four hundred miles per hour, and this takes brute strength. There was some help through the gear system, but it was not enough. Moving the guns was a tedious and slow task, and the lack of full power for the turret was a calamitous loss in terms of survival.

At the waist guns, Lillis Walker did not even have time to gripe about the hot shell casings that were slamming against his back and neck. As the turret guns fired, the hot casings splashed down against Walker; they had burned him more than once on missions. But on this flight, as Walker recalled, things were so hot he was not that much bothered by a few burns across the back of his neck.

The running fight lasted, according to the best estimates of both the crew in the bomber and the Japanese pilots as reported after their return to Lae, somewhere between ten and thirteen minutes—which is an eternity when a single bomber is being chewed up by a swarm of wild-flying Zeros. And in the nose of the "Heckling Hare," Claude McCredie cursed angrily when the single machine gun at his disposal jammed. He fought to free the .50-caliber gun, but to no avail.

"Greer yelled at me to get out of the nose," said McCredie. "He ordered me to get back in the fuselage right away and to man one of the waist guns with Walker; that way we would have both waist guns going for us.

"The passageway out of the nose is along a real narrow catwalk. You come up from the nose, through the bomb bay, into the radio compartment. The radio and navigator's table are on one side, and there's a little seat on the left. There's just enough room to squeeze by when someone is in that area.

"When Greer yelled for me to get back to the waist gun, McMullin had to push back out of the way to let me out of the nose. I got to the door ledge and came down the two steps into the navigator's compartment. Commander Johnson was there, looking out the window. He could see right out over the wing; there's a pretty good view out there—although at this moment it was the kind of sight that scared you right out of your wits. That's how I felt when I saw a bunch of Zeros pounding in against us.

"When I left the nose, there were a bunch of Zeros, three or four of them, laying out there on the left side. One would fake a pass at us and when we tracked him with the guns, why, the others would come roaring in to rake us good. They would try to drop down and come up real fast to get us in the belly.

"And Johnson was watching this real close. You can't see too well through that side window if you're sitting down. He was stooped over in a standing position as I came into the radio compartment. He was looking out the window where the Zeros were starting their pass at us.

"He turned to me when I came in the compartment. He lifted his hand and held up three fingers. Then he pointed out the window and smiled. 'There're three out there on the left,' he said.

"I looked out the window, figuring they were still laying off. But they were coming straight at us and firing! And this man was as cool as a cucumber. I took one look at those Zeros . . . the guns and cannon were all firing at us. I just blurted out, 'Excuse me,' and started past him.

"He grinned at me as I went by him as fast as I could, getting back to the waist-gun position."

Harry Baren commented on this: "If we had had another machine gun lying around, this man would have grabbed it and whaled away at the Zeros. It's a helpless feeling just to be in the airplane when the fighters are coming in; you want to do something, to hit back. Ray Flanagan, who used to fly copilot most of the time with us, used to go nuts up in that cockpit. He wanted a gun, or even some rocks to throw at the Zeros—*anything*. He wanted to fight, not just sit there and take it. That's the roughest of all. Johnson had the same feeling all right. He said something to me about wanting to do something, to get a gun in his hands to fire . . ."

McCredie worked his way back to the waist position. Several minutes later, Lillis Walker had to leave the waist gun he was firing to get to the radio compartment. Each time the Marauders flew a mission, they returned with great caution to Moresby; the Japanese had a cute trick of blowing hell out of Seven-Mile Drome even while the Marauders were blasting the Japanese runways. And they had caught some of the American bombers at the worst possible moment. Walker now had to monitor the radio to be sure that Seven-Mile was clear for them to land.

"It sure was rough up there," Lillis Walker said. "We were really getting shot up pretty bad. The Zeros stayed with us, working us over, like they were having a field day with target practice, a long running fight while they kept whacking away at us.

"When I went forward I had to crawl through the bomb bay to get to the radio. And there was this passenger of ours, just as calm as if we were on a sight-seeing tour. I mean that; he was really taking the whole thing as though nothing was wrong. Bullets were singing through the plane all about us and we were being hit by those cannon shells, and he was—well, just calm, and watching everything.

"He was standing on the stool in the compartment; from up there that's a sight to scare the living daylights out of you. A couple of the Zeros were in front of us and coming in, firing everything they had, and you're looking straight into the face of death when *that* happens.

"He had to get off the stool so I could get to the radio. He stepped down and turned to me and said, 'Boy! It's rough up here, isn't it!'

"I just nodded at him.

"Then he asked me, 'You get kind of scared, don't you?'

"Now, that's one question I can answer very easily. I looked him right in the eyes and I said, 'Yeah; I'm *always* scared up here.'

"He burst out laughing at me—I'm sure he felt exactly the way I did, but he just didn't show it. He didn't show it a bit."

THE SEA FIGHT AROUND NEW GUINEA DEVOLVED ON motor torpedo boats, the only craft sufficiently shallow in draft to negotiate its hazardous waters. The first PTs arrived in April 1942 with their tender, *Hilo,* and within the week PT-*122* celebrated the squadron's first victory by sinking a large cargo submarine and two barges. Submarines, however, were not the usual target in New Guinea. Troop-laden barges—*dihatsus*—were the nightly opponents, and by and large they constituted the combat fare for the ensuing two years.

Lieutenant Basil Heatter was among the first arrivals at Milne Bay. He describes fighting Japanese barges—the type of action in which he was eventually wounded.

4.

ATTACK BY NIGHT

Torpedo boat fighting has a style all its own. The PT's become a sort of naval guerrilla force operating hundreds of miles behind the enemy lines in strange waters that have in many instances never been charted, subject to attack from planes, surface units and shore fire, and with the added hazard of patrolling through the long, black nights in waters where the slightest wrong move means a boat with its bottom sliced out on the razor edged coral neggerheads. It is no wonder that after an all night patrol, the boat crews are haggard and unshaven, with red rimmed eyes and weary, aching bodies.

By daybreak the patrols are over. PT frequencies resound to: "Let's head for the barn." It almost seems as though the boats themselves sense that home is ahead. They leap forward in great sheets of sparkling spray. Engines hit wonderful speeds they could never touch on the way out. From off shore you can see the boats whipping back down along the coast like dragon flies skimming the edge of the jungle. And sometimes you can see the quick, orange flash of a Nip shore battery, and then you have the tense few seconds of waiting for the shell, and when it finally lands far astern the boys turn and give him a few bursts just for the hell of it and then the boats flirt their tails at the beach and speed on towards home.

They come in before noon, skirting the reefs that mark the entrance to the little harbor. They come slowly past in column and if the night has been productive they wave their clenched fists overhead in a fighter's salute, proudly semaphoring their score ahead to the men on the beach. And there are times too when they come limping in with a hull riddled with shell holes and men to be lifted over the side and carried to sick bay. It's quite a while before anybody does much talking about those patrols.

When the patrols come in the skippers go ashore to write out their reports. At the same time the execs take the boats over to the fuel dock to gas up. Even though all hands have been at battle stations throughout the night there is still no sleep for anyone until the boats are again in fighting shape. That means refueled, radios and engines checked, and all guns completely stripped down and cleaned. After a night spent plowing through heavy seas a .50 calibre machine gun is a mass of rusty junk, an unholy mess that has to be sweated over for hours. The boys work in the blistering, noonday sun, bearded, stripped to the waist, their tired fingers doing mechanically the job they have done so many countless times before.

When the work is done the boats move over to their nests along the edge of the jungle. These dispersal points are carefully chosen with an eye to protection from air reconnaissance and attack. Each boat crew puts down palm log pilings and builds a rickety dock fondly festooned with signs such as Stork Club, Jack & Charlie's, Cocoanut Grove, etc. Here you find such luxuries as reclining chairs made from ammunition crates, cooking stoves fashioned from oil drums, and hammocks slung in choice, shady spots.

The boats are pulled into their nests and made fast under the creepers and leaves. All hands prepare for extensive sack drill. Afternoon quiet settles down over the harbor. In the shade a bearded gunner wearing ragged shorts puffs on a cherished cigar and rereads last month's letters. He is waiting for the hot, still night to come creeping down the mountains into the jungle.

If the crews are lucky they'll have no patrol that night, and if they're doubly lucky there will be a movie at the base. Soon after darkness they arrive paddling outrigger canoes, dinghies, and even the sawed-in-half shells of belly tanks dropped by P-47's. In spite of projector breakdowns, alerts, and rain squalls the boys sit patiently for hours in the black, jungle night, battling clouds of mosquitos, waiting for the flickering screen that speaks to them of home half a world away.

Next day the boats are ready to fight again. The skippers go ashore for their briefing, chow is taken aboard, ammunition belts fed into the guns, frequencies adjusted, and by mid-afternoon the patrols are again moving out through the reefs toward the open sea. They ease slowly and carefully out between the swirling masses of foam that break over the coral. Far overhead a P-38 gleams for a silver instant in the sun. Off on the horizon a PBY circles lazily over a convoy of LST's bound through the straits for New Britain.

Our boats begin to bite into the heavy seas. Sheets of spray rain over the cockpit, turrets, and after lookout who huddles unhappily behind the engine room hatch. At a signal from the skipper all guns fire a few warm up bursts. Tracers whip out and ricochet off to seaward. Throttles are moved up and the boats pound and thunder as they smash into the crests. The exec wipes the salt out of his eyes and bites grimly on a sodden pipe. Another patrol is under way.

By nightfall the boats are again in enemy waters. They prowl like huge, silent sharks through the shallow bays and lagoons. On each boat a dozen eyes sweep the sea and shore through night glasses. In the blacked out chartroom the quartermaster half naked in the heat, plots his D R Track by the dim, reddish glow of the battle lights.

In a little while the moon comes up. The sea gleams like mercury; the jungle is a black ribbon along its edge. Occasionally you get the faint scent of the land, the sweet, heady aroma of jungle flowers, and sometimes there is another odor on the soft, night breeze, the never to be forgotten smell of rotting flesh. In that country dead men are very dead.

At mid-night the radio hums:

"Dog Fox to Easy Oboe—Over."

"This is Easy Oboe—Over."

"I think we've got something, Bill. Bearing zero four five, range about ten miles, moving fast. Probably a float Zero. Better get set for him—Over."

"Roger. We'll give the bastard a warm welcome. Over and out."

The broad, phosphorescent wake of the boats points like a silver arrow in the moonlight. The Nip has sighted them. He turns and comes in fast and low. The boats wheel hard over and a thousand orange tracers split the night searching for him. The Jap doesn't like tracers. He shys away and hurriedly drops his two small bombs astern of the second boat. Now he's coming in for a strafing run but it's a half hearted attempt. He has no belly for lead. He turns, climbs into the night, and is gone.

The patrol goes on. At three in the morning the lookout picks up four low, black objects creeping into the beach. Barges! Again the radio hums: "Close up. Close up. Port run." The gunners wait hunched in their turrets. The gun muzzles swing in hungry, tentative arcs. Suddenly a Jap twenty millimetre licks out into the night. To hell with silence now. Our boats go roaring in for the kill.

Nip small calibre rifle and machine gun fire whines over the cockpit like a swarm of bees. Our boats are alongside, in position now. They pound and shake under the impact of the guns. The night is lit by hundreds of lines of criss cross tracer. The lagoon shimmers in the red flashes. Billows of gun smoke float through the nightmare scene. Somewhere in the darkness there is the deep pounding of shore batteries. Heavy shells whoosh by like express trains. Scarlet balls of fire come arching up out of the night at us.

But now the barges have almost stopped firing. This is the crucial moment. Our boys keep pouring it in. The four dark shapes are lower now, going down. And suddenly they're gone. The surface of the lagoon is smooth. Somewhere in the darkness Japs are in the water. They're screaming, high, thin screams. The batteries are still firing. Crashing explosions boom over and around us. We turn and run out at high speed.

Once outside we lie to in order to count noses. The lead boat has taken hits along the water line but no one is hurt. Far behind us the Jap tracers are still looping out into the night. Ahead the sky shows the faintest, rosy tinge. Dawn is coming. Another patrol is over. Our boats turn and head for home.

THE JAPANESE WERE DRIVEN FROM HUON GULF ON New Guinea's southeast coast in October 1943, and PT squadrons set up an advance base at Dregger Harbor—a shift of scene which eliminated many hours of "dead time" in getting to and from station, and enabled them to penetrate deeper into enemy territory. By year's end, Army engineers and Seabees were constructing bases, docks and airstrips for operations against a solidly entrenched enemy only a few miles away.

Among the motor torpedo boat officers who fought in the Dregger Harbor campaigns was Lieutenant (jg) Edward I. Farley, here describing one of the more memorable PT actions.

5.

"WE BETTER GET AIR SUPPORT PRETTY SOON!"

December 24, 1943 had mostly been spent cleaning guns, overhauling engines, making routine maintenance checks, and painting. After lunch the boat crews sought cool spots in which to sleep or relax. One crew rigged a diving board under a mangrove, and an acrobatic member tied a rope to a high branch so that he could swing forty feet through the air and into the water. Christmas Eve was warm, too warm to do much more than sit, maybe write letters or daydream, and watch the multicolored tropical fish—some bright purple, others pale blue—feed along the coral reefs.

Christmas Day was still and cloudless, a typical New Guinea day. Everyone looked forward to the big dinner "like at home." Turkeys from the base kitchen were distributed to each boat. Ours was half raw, but Yiengst and Shorty saved the day by recooking the bird until it was just right. Yiengst called on me to say grace. Then we sat down to a feast with all the trimmings—plus atabrine tablets. I provided Romeo and Juliet cigars for all hands, courtesy of my good friend Tom Prindeville in New York.

Christmas packages containing sweets and tinned stuff were opened. Bill Bannard had received a large box of delicacies, which included a tin of kippered herring. Bill didn't like kippers, so he gave them to me, and Yiengst promised to cook them for breakfast.

Breakfast was always a pleasant prospect; and as our uneventful Christmas night patrol approached its close, I looked forward to my kippers. It was about 0600 on patrol station off the south New Britain coast. In company with *Bambi,* the *Jack* had left Dregger and gone to Arawe on the evening of December 25 with mail and passengers. Lieutenant H. M. S. Steele ("Swifty") Swift was Officer in Tactical Command aboard the *Jack.* From 2200 until dawn we cruised back and forth off Cape Peiho, heeding carefully Eric Howitt's piloting instructions, because the waters were particularly treacherous.

Reluctant to return empty-handed, we snooped into Marije Bay about 0730. Sighting nothing, we decided to secure, having already tarried too long. I laid out the return course, turned the boat over to Bill, and then went below to clean up for those kippers.

No sooner had I gotten comfortably seated in the charthouse before a steaming plateful than there was a loud swoooooosh! followed by a muffled explosion off the starboard bow. The *Jack* lifted in the water. Through the charthouse port I saw a twenty-foot column of water cascade onto the foc'sle.

"Oh-oh!" exclaimed Bannard. "That was close!" And a moment later: "Here come more of them. General Quarters!"

I swung topside. Down from the north they swept—four Vals followed by four Zekes—then more Vals and more Zekes, until about thirty planes were upon us.

Ensign Lovorron, Third Officer, took the helm; Bill took charge of the four .50's, leaving me free to coordinate our over-all defense. *Bambi* had immediately broken formation to avoid enfilade and to divide the enemy's fire. About thirty miles ahead, directly on our course for base, there were low storm clouds, good for cover—if we could reach them.

Bill's gunners and the gun crew on the stern 20-millimeter blazed away at each attacking plane. Following the trajectory of each bomb, I kept calling out the amount and direction of rudder. Lovorron executed the directions with understanding alacrity.

Our bow 37-millimeter sent a Vail into a steep glide. Black smoke pouring from its tail, it splashed into the sea. The port turret hit another, which caught fire and dived into the water about three miles to the north. *Bambi*'s machine guns were also spitting furiously. A Zeke climbed steeply, then went into a 180-degree dive and plunged into the sea to the northwest. More planes continued to pour in, in waves of three or four at a time. Barsh, our radio operator, had called Finsch for air support.

"Circuits busy!" he reported.

"Keep trying!" I encouraged him as I yanked back the throttles, narrowly avoiding a nasty-looking bomb that almost had our name on it. It hit the water directly ahead, throwing skyward a column of water which drenched the foc'sle and cockpit.

Although the *Jack* took the brunt of the bombing, *Bambi* received most of the strafing and damage. Her port- and starboard-engine water jackets had been hit and were spurting hot water. One of her fuel tanks had also been hit and was leaking badly. But Motormac Victor Bloom kept his head. Working against time, he taped and stuffed the leaks. With admirable presence, he closed off the tank compartment and smothered the space with CO^2.

After twenty minutes, the planes milled around overhead as if wondering what to try next. Possibly we had knocked down their squadron leader. *Bambi* radioed that "Rum" Ewing had been hit in the stomach and Fred Calhoun, his exec, had taken over. I checked again on air support.

"Circuits still busy!" reported Barsh grimly.

Upstairs, the Vals and Zekes regrouped. Down they came again: More bombs, more strafing. *Bambi* nailed another Zeke, which crashed barely a mile away. The score was now 4-0. I had noticed several cripples limping away at low altitude and guessed they were out of the fight—but there were still twenty or so planes left.

"We'd better get air support pretty soon," I told myself. Suddenly Barsh got the word: "Hold on. We will be with you in five minutes."

And they were. P-40's, 47's and 48's—perhaps forty altogether— came streaking in and lit into the Zekes and the Vals. The heat was off. The Nips tangled only briefly with our planes, then fled west, ours swarming after them. Our pilots told us later that the Japanese hit the water in twos and threes. Only one Val escaped.

A damaged P-47 made a belly landing near us. The pilot had just freed himself from the cockpit when we reached him. Swifty and Seaman First Class Joe H. Cope dived into the sea and between them managed to keep the pilot's head above water until a ladder and line were rigged and we got him aboard. Badly injured about the head, he eventually recovered fully.

Bambi was in fairly bad shape. Calhoun had a bullet in the thigh. Two of the crew were wounded seriously. Three others had minor injuries. We took *Bambi*'s casualties aboard the *Jack* and resumed course to base.

With two engines out, a ruptured gas tank, an eighteen-inch hole in her port side and extensive shrapnel damage, *Bambi* nevertheless made Dregger. There we made our action report and refueled.

Suddenly I was very hungry. It seemed as if days had passed since that moment when I had sat down to breakfast. Yiengst and Shorty and I searched, but we couldn't find the kippers anywhere . . .

NOW THE LONG AWAITED PACIFIC ADVANCE GOT underway. Operation "Galvanic"—the two-phase capture of the Gilbert Islands—was scheduled for November 20, 1943. The plan called for 35,000 Marines to be put ashore on Makin, Tarawa and Apamama within five days, a tall order for Vice Admiral Raymond A. Spruance, Commander Fifth Fleet.

Let us look at the target area of Micronesia which became a gleam in Nimitz' eye even as Halsey attacked in the Central Solomons. The idea was to seize the Gilberts first, the Marshalls next, and from there to continue across to the Marianas. These coral islands were strategically located in the sea lanes between the Philippines and the United States; they also constituted the nerve center of Japan's defense system and were therefore heavily fortified. The Gilberts and Marshalls, with which we are first concerned, are composed of twenty to fifty reefs and islands each, strung out at varying lengths. Kwajalein, largest of the Marshall Islands, is thirty miles wide and sixty miles long. Its highest point of land is twenty-one feet above sea level. But while these islands possessed no intrinsic value other than strategic, their very substance—rock and coral—made them highly-sought and highly-defended prizes, for they were easily adapted to bomber and fighter plane operations.

Shortly before the invasion, the targets were subjected to a considerable "softening up" by one hundred Liberator bombers under Rear Admiral John H. Hoover, commanding all land-based aircraft from his flagship, aircraft tender *Curtis,* stationed in Funafati Lagoon in the Ellices.

Spruance's forces consisted of:

1. Northern Attack Force (TF 52) under the command of Rear Admiral Richmond Kelly Turner, embarked in flagship *Pennsylvania* and bound for Makin from Pearl Harbor, with three additional battleships, four cruisers, three escort carriers and six transports; also one LSD and three LSTs with tanks and amphtracks. General Hol-

land M. "Howlin' Mad" Smith, exercising command of the Marines in both operations (Makin and Tarawa), was aboard the flagship.

2. Southern Attack Force (TF 53) under the command of Rear Admiral Harry W. Hill, embarked in flagship *Maryland* and bound for Tarawa from New Zealand and the New Hebrides (Efate), with two additional battleships, five cruisers, five escort carriers, twenty-one destroyers, sixteen transports and one LSD carrying tanks. Aboard the flagship was General Julian C. Smith of the 2nd Marine Division.

3. Fast Carrier Forces Pacific Fleet (TF 50) under the command of Rear Admiral Charles A. Pownall, embarked in flagship *Yorktown,* with three additional *Essex*-class carriers and five light carriers, six battleships, three heavy cruisers, three anti-aircraft cruisers and twenty-one destroyers.

D-Day dawned clear and fair; the sea was calm. After a last pounding of Makin, Marines stormed ashore and captured the island with relative ease. However, the Navy suffered heavily in this phase of "Galvanic." A torpedo from submarine *I-175* struck the amidships section of carrier *Liscomb Bay,* and the ship exploded, bursting into flame her entire length and heaving planes and men and steel frames hundreds of feet into the air. Twenty-three minutes later she dipped under in 2000 fathoms of water. Fifty-one officers and five hundred and ninety-one enlisted men were killed. Of the other enemy attacks after D-Day, only one was of consequence. Torpedo planes from Roi, in the Marshalls, stuck a fish into *Indianapolis,* which killed or wounded sixty men.

Conversely, as we well know, Tarawa was not costly to the Navy (only destroyer *Ringgold* was hit, and by a dud shell), but it was sheer hell for the Marines. Japanese troops were strongly entrenched at Betio, at the southeast corner of the atoll, behind coral cairns, boat obstacles, and coconut log barricades, with guns ranging from 5- to 8-inch, and concrete bunkers reinforced with sand, iron and corrugated roof plate which could be penetrated only by heavy-caliber shells. Although considerably softened by air strikes and 2000 tons of naval shells, Betio held fast.

Time correspondent Robert Sherrod was assigned to cover the landings. His brilliant dispatches on the murderous battle at Betio are a classic of reportage. His account begins a few hours before D-Day opened, aboard the transport *Zeilin.*

6.

FIRST DAY ON TARAWA

We jumped out of bed at midnight, swimming in sweat. We donned our dungarees and headed for the wardroom. Nobody took more than fifteen minutes to eat his steak, eggs, and fried potatoes and drink his two cups of coffee, but everybody was soaking before he had finished. This was the hottest night of all. Before we filed out, gasping, there was an oversupply of the rumors that attend every battle: one of our cruisers had sunk a Jap surface craft (though not until seventy-seven six-inch shells had been fired, and an accompanying destroyer had let go two torpedoes); one of our ships had been attacked by a Japanese bomber during the night; a searchlight off Betio had already tried to spot our force.

After making last-minute adjustments of my gear, I went up on the flying bridge when General Quarters was buzzed at 0215. There was a half-moon dodging in and out of the clouds forty-five degrees to portside. It was cool up there, with a brisk breeze on the rise. It was possible to make notes when the moon was out. A calm voice came over the loudspeaker: "Target at 112 true, 26,800 yards ahead." "*Blackfish* 870 yards." "*Blackfish* 1000 yards." "*Blackfish* 900 yards." The *Blackfish* was the lead transport, and the *Blue Fox* was next. The faint red signal light of the lead ship slowly flashed on and off as we followed her to Tarawa.

Lieutenant Vanderpoel, the ship's gunnery officer, was talking to

691

me and Lieutenant Commander Fabian, who was to be beachmaster on Tarawa. Vanderpoel was indignant. He had seen a lot of this war, at Guadalcanal, Tulagi, Attu, Kiska. And they had never allowed him to fire his guns on the transport. True, they were not heavy guns such as battleships carry, but they might help. If he could just turn them on the shore, as the warships would turn theirs. "Just once I want to shoot," he said, "but this time they said again 'Transports will not fire.' We sit on these damn transports and we don't get to see anything of the war, and the Marines have to go in and do it all. Damn."

By 0330 the Marines had begun loading the outboard boats for the first wave. The sergeants were calling the roll: "Vernon, Simms, Gresholm. . . ." They needed no light to call the well-remembered roll, and they didn't have to send a runner to find any absentees. The Marines were all there. One of the sergeants was giving his men last-minute instructions: "Be sure to correct your elevation and windage. Adjust your sights."

At 0400 I went below. I stood outside the wardroom as the first and second waves walked through and out to their boats. Most of the men were soaked; their green-and-brown-spotted jungle dungarees had turned a darker green when the sweat from their bodies soaked through. They jested with one another. Only a few even whistled to keep up their courage.

"How many you going to kill, Bunky?" one of them shouted at a bespectacled Marine. "All I can get," said Bunky, without smiling, as he wiped his beloved rifle barrel.

"Oh, boy," said a kid well under twenty, "I just want to spit in a dead Jap's face. Just open his mouth and let him have it."

Said another, "I should have joined the Boy Scouts. I knew it."

They were a grimy, unshaven lot. The order had gone out: they must put on clean clothing just before going ashore, in order to diminish the chances of infection from wounds, but now they looked dirty. Under the weight, light though it was, of their combat packs, lifebelts, guns, ammunition, helmets, canvas leggings, bayonets, they were sweating in great profusion. Nobody had shaved for two or three days.

Outside I saw Dr. Edwin J. Welte, a crop-haired, young Minnesotan who had finished medical school only about five years ago. "Well," he said, "nobody is trying to get out of fighting this battle. Out of the whole battalion only eleven are being left in the ship's sick bay. Five are recurring malaria cases, one busted his knee on maneuvers, one is a post-operative appendectomy, one is a chronic knee that somebody palmed off on the regiment, and the rest are minor shipboard accidents. All the malaria cases will be able to go ashore in two days."

Who else was being left behind? "Nobody that I know of except one pfc. who got obstreperous and they had to throw him in the brig. Only one man in the brig the whole trip, and he's always been a bad character."

We walked back to the junior staff officers' bunkroom, which was full of young Marines indulging in what might have been a college bull session. Outside we could hear the dynamo-hum of the cables letting the boats down into the water. Everybody had on his pack and his helmet, for all these men were going on the assault waves which would start leaving for Betio in ten or fifteen minutes. Young, mustachioed Captain Ben Owens, the Oklahoma boy who was battalion operations officer, looked up as we entered, and said, "Doc, I'm going to get shot in the tail today."

Dr. Welte: "Oh, you want a Purple Heart, huh?"

Owens: "Hell, no, I want a stateside ticket."

Colonel Amey, the battalion boss, came in, stretched mightily, and ho-hummed. I asked him how many Japs we were going to find on Betio. "Not many, apparently," he said. "They've got five-inch guns. They'd have been shooting at us by now."

Owens looked at the deck a minute and said, "That's right. We're only eleven thousand yards offshore now. They've got some eight-inch guns, too. But just wait. You'll hear one whistle over in a minute. When he does those battlewagons will open up on that son-of-a-bitch and rock that island—"

Owens continued, "Maybe the battlewagons and the bombs will knock out the big guns, but I'm not saying they'll kill all the Japs. I still think we'll get shot at when we go in, and I'm still looking for that stateside ticket, Doc."

Jay Odell, a slender young junior-grade lieutenant who learned how to be a naval air-liaison officer after leaving his Philadelphia newspaper job, had been standing in a corner without saying anything. Now he spoke up, "Everybody is putting too much faith in the statistics about the number of tons that's going to be dropped."

Now, at 0505, we heard a great thud in the southwest. We knew what that meant. The first battleship had fired the first shot. We all rushed out on deck. The show had begun. The show for which thousands of men had spent months of training, scores of ships had sailed thousands of miles, for which Chaplains Kelly and MacQueen had offered their prayers. The curtain was up in the theatre of death.

We were watching when the battleship's second shell left the muzzle of its great gun, headed for Betio. There was a brilliant flash in the darkness of the half-moonlit night. Then a flaming torch arched high into the air and sailed far away, slowly, very slowly, like an easily lobbed tennis ball. The red cinder was nearly halfway to its mark before we heard the thud, a dull roar as if some mythological giant had struck a drum as big as Mount Olympus. There was no sign of an explosion on the unseen island—the second shot had apparently fallen into the water, like the first.

Within three minutes the sky was filled again with the orange-red flash of the big gun, and Olympus boomed again. The red ball of fire that was the high-explosive shell was again dropping toward the horizon. But this time there was a tremendous burst on the land that was Betio. A wall of flame shot five hundred feet into the air, and there was another terrifying explosion as the shell found its mark. Hundreds of the awestruck Marines on the deck of the *Blue Fox* cheered in uncontrollable joy. Our guns had found the enemy. Probably the enemy's big eight-inch guns and their powder magazine on the southwest corner of the island.

Now that we had the range the battleship sought no longer. The next flash was four times as great, and the sky turned a brighter, redder orange, greater than any flash of lightning the Marines had ever seen. Now four shells, weighing more than a ton each, peppered the island. Now Betio began to glow brightly from the fires the bombardment pattern had started.

That was only the beginning. Another battleship took up the firing —four mighty shells poured from its big guns onto another part of the island. Then another battleship breathed its brilliant breath of death. Now a heavy cruiser let go with its eight-inch guns, and several light criusers opened with their fast-firing six inch guns. They were followed by the destroyers, many destroyers with many five-inch guns on each, firing almost as fast as machine guns. The sky at times was brighter than noontime on the equator. The arching, glowing cinders that were high-explosive shells sailed through the air as though buckshot were being fired out of many shotguns from all sides of the island. The Marines aboard the *Blue Fox* exulted with each blast on the island. Fire and smoke and sand obscured the island of Betio.

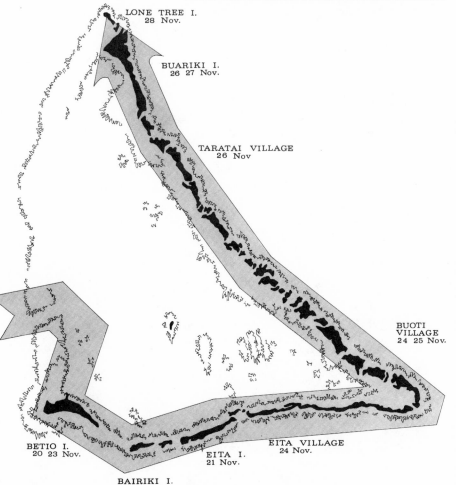

U.S. Marine Path

TARAWA ATOLL

Action 20-28 November 1943

LONE TREE I.
28 Nov.

BUARIKI I.
26 27 Nov.

TARATAI VILLAGE
26 Nov

BUOTI
VILLAGE
24 25 Nov.

BETIO I.
20 23 Nov.

EITA I.
21 Nov.

EITA VILLAGE
24 Nov.

BAIRIKI I.
21 Nov.

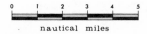

0 1 2 3 4 5

nautical miles

Now the Jap, the miserable, little brown man who had started this horrible war against a peace-loving people, was beginning to suffer the consequences. He had asked for this, and he should have known it before he flew into Pearl Harbor that placid Sunday morning. As the warships edged in closer, coming into shore from many thousands of yards until they were only a few thousand yards away from their target, the whole island of Betio seemed to erupt with bright fires that were burning everywhere. They blazed even through the thick wall of smoke that curtained the island.

The first streaks of dawn crept through the sky. The warships continued to fire. All of a sudden they stopped. But here came the planes—not just a few planes: a dozen, a score, a hundred. The first torpedo bombers raced across the smoking conflagration and loosed their big bombs on an island that must have been dead a half hour ago! They were followed by the dive bombers, the old workhorse SBD's and the new Helldivers, the fast SB2C's that had been more than two years a-borning. The dive bombers lined up, many thousands of feet over Betio, then they pointed their noses down and dived singly, or in pairs or in threes. Near the end of their dives they hatched the bombs from beneath their bellies; they pulled out gracefully and sailed back to their carriers to get more bombs. Now came the fighter planes, the fast, new Grumman Hellcats, the best planes ever to squat on a carrier. They made their runs just above the awful, gushing pall of smoke, their machine guns spitting hundreds of fifty-caliber bullets a minute.

Surely, we all thought, no mortal men could live through such destroying power.

Surely, I thought, if there were actually any Japs left on the island (which I doubted strongly), they would all be dead by now.

It was half hour after dawn that I got a first rude shock. A shell splashed into the water not thirty feet from an LST which waited near the *Blue Fox*. Our destroyers, which by this time were firing again as the planes finished their bombing and strafing runs, were firing very wide, I surmised. A shell hit not more than fifty yards from our stern, sending a vertical stream of water high into the air, like a picture of a geyser erupting.

I turned to Major Howard Rice and said, "My God, what wide shooting! Those boys need some practice."

Major Rice looked at me quizzically. Said he, "You don't think that's our own guns doing *that* shooting, do you?"

Then, for the first time, I realized that there were some Japs on Betio. Like a man who has swallowed a piece of steak without chewing it, I said, "Oh."

By this time our first three waves of boats were already in the water, and the fourth and fifth were getting ready to load. But the sudden appearance of the enemy upset our plans. These valuable transports, with their thousands of troops, could not stand idly by and take a chance on being sunk. By now we were within four or five miles of the target. We had no definite knowledge that all the Japs' big guns on Betio were not still working. Captain John McGovern, commodore of the assault transport division, gave the order. The transports heeled around quickly and set out to sea, whence we had come only two hours ago.

The transports streaked out of the danger zone, with the Japs firing vainly at them as they went. The first three waves, including hundreds of boats from many transports, had no choice but to turn around and streak after the mother ships. As they turned and ran our warships opened up again. By firing his gun the Jap had given away its location. Now the fury of the warships, big and small, mounted into a crescendo of unprecedented fire and thunder. They pounded the Jap with everything in the gunnery officer's book. If there had been an unearthly flash of lightning before daylight, now, at close range, there was a nether world of pandemonium. Hundreds of shells crashed with hundreds of ear-rocking thuds as they poured toward the Jap big-gun position. Soon there was no more firing. The last Jap big gun had been silenced. Now the transports could finish loading their assault waves into the boats, and Betio would soon feel the tread of the U. S. Marines' boondockers.

The fifth wave climbed down the rope nets at 0635, into the landing boats which bobbed drunkenly on the rough sea and smacked into the transport. Within five minutes after we pushed off, a half barrel of water was splashing over the high bow of the Higgins boat every minute. Every one of the thirty-odd men was soaked before we had chugged a half mile. While a Marine held his poncho over our heads I tried to put my fine watch into a small, heavy waterproof envelope. It seemed a pity to lose such a watch, especially since Sergeant Neil Shober, a craftsman with a jeep or with a strip of metal, had made a handsome wrist-band for the watch out of a piece of Jap Zero wing he had brought from Guadalcanal. Into another envelope I dropped my newly filled cigarette lighter and some valuable pictures; into another a pack of cigarettes.

The sun had hardly leaped above the horizon and we shivered as the cool seawater drenched us, it seemed, beyond the saturation point. I remembered the nip of brandy the doctor had given me. I pulled the little bottle out of my pocket and shared it with the Marine standing next to me. If there was ever an occasion for taking a drink at seven o'clock in the morning this was it.

Later that day I was to tremble all over from fear alone, but not yet. We shook and shivered because we were cold. My only memory of the first hour and a half of the ride toward the beachhead is sheer discomfort, alternating with exaltation. Our warships and planes were now pounding the little island of Betio as no other island had been pounded in thei history of warfare. By standing on the gunwale of the boat I could crane my neck around the ramp-bow and see the smoke and dust and flames of Betio. When the attack paused a moment I could see the palm trees outlined against the sea and sky on the other side.

Once I tried to count the number of salvos—not shells, salvos— the battleships, cruisers, and destroyers were pouring on the island. A Marine who had a waterproof watch offered to count off the seconds up to one minute. Long before the minute had ended I had counted over one hundred, but then a dozen more ships opened up and I abandoned the project. I did count the number of planes in sight at one time. It was ninety-two. These ships and these planes were dealing out an unmerciful beating on the Japs, and it was good, good to watch. As we came within two miles of the island we could get a better view of what was happening. There were fires up and down the length of the island. Most of them would be the barracks, the power plant, the kitchens, and other above-ground installations we had studied time and again in the photographs. Once in a while a solid mass of flame would reach for the sky and the roar of an explosion could be heard easily from our position in the water. That would be an oil tank or an ammunition dump. The feeling was good.

It was nearly nine o'clock when the fifth wave arrived at the boat rendezvous and began circling to wait for our turn to go in. I looked around the ramp to see what was on the beach. For the first time I felt that something was wrong. The first waves were not hitting the beach as they should. There were very few boats on the beach, and these were all amphibious tractors which the first wave used. There were no Higgins boats on the beach, as there should have been by now.

Almost before we could guess at what bad news was being foretold the command boat came alongside. The naval officer shouted, "You'll have to go in right away, as soon as I can get an amphtrack for you. The shelf around the island is too shallow to take the Higgins boats." This was indeed chilling news. It meant something that had been dimly foreseen but hardly expected: the only way the Marines were going to land was in the amphtracks ("alligators") which could crawl over the shallow reef that surrounds Betio. It meant that the landings would be slow, because there were not enough amphtracks for everybody, and we would have to use the emergency shuttle system that had been worked out as a last resort. And suppose the amphtracks were knocked out before they could get enough men ashore to hold what the first wave had taken? And suppose the Marines already ashore were killed faster than they could be replaced under this slow shuttle system?

I felt very dull—a brain fed on the almost positive belief that the Japs had fled Betio would naturally be slower than a six-year-old writing a letter. I could not quite comprehend what was happening.

An amphtrack bobbed alongside our Higgins boat. Said the Marine amphtrack boss, "Quick! Half you men get in here. They need help bad on the beach. A lot of Marines have already been killed and wounded." While the amphtrack was alongside, Jap shells from an automatic weapon began peppering the water around us. "Probably a 40mm.," said one of the calmer Marine officers.

But the Marines did not hesitate. Hadn't they been told that other Marines "needed help bad"? Major Rice and seventeen others scampered into the amphtrack and headed for the beach. I did not see them again until three days later, when the battle was over.

The half-empty Higgins boat milled around for another ten minutes, getting its share of near misses and air bursts. One Marine picked a half dozen pieces of shrapnel off his lap and swallowed hard. Two amphtracks came by. One of our Marines stood up and waved at them, told them that we were ready and waiting to go to the beach. But both had already been disabled by direct hits. Both had wounded and dead men in them, the drivers said. We milled around another couple of minutes, looking for a chance at what appeared to be a one-way ride, but always remembering that "they need help bad" on the beach.

The next amphtrack crew said they would take us in part of the way, to where we could wade the rest of the way, but amphtracks were getting so scarce he couldn't take us all the way. We jumped into the little tractor boat and quickly settled on the deck. "Oh, God, I'm scared," said the little Marine, a telephone operator, who sat next to me forward in the boat. I gritted my teeth and tried to force a smile that would not come and tried to stop quivering all over (now I was shaking from fear). I said, in an effort to be reassuring, "I'm scared, too." I never made a more truthful statement in all my life. I was not petrified yet, but my joints seemed to be stiffening.

Now, I realized, this is the payoff. Now I knew, positively, that there were Japs, and evidently plenty of them, on the island. They were not dead. The bursts of shellfire all around us evidenced the fact that there was plenty of life in them. "This is not going to be a new kind of beachhead landing," I said to myself. "This is going to be traditional—what you have always been told is the toughest of all military operations: a landing, if possible, in the face of enemy machine guns that can mow men down by the hundreds." This was not even going to be the fifth wave. After the first wave there apparently had not been any organized waves, those organized waves which hit the beach so beautifully in the last rehearsal. There had been only an occasional amphtrack which hit the beach, then turned around (if it wasn't knocked out) and went back for more men. There we were: a single boat, a little wavelet of our own, and we were already getting the hell shot out of us, with a thousand yards to go. I peered over the side of the amphtrack and saw another amphtrack three hundred yards to the left get a direct hit from what looked like a mortar shell.

"It's hell in there," said the amphtrack boss, who was pretty wild-eyed himself. "They've already knocked out a lot of amphtracks and there are a lot of wounded men lying on the beach. See that old hulk of a Jap freighter over there? I'll let you out about there, then go back to get some more men. You can wade in from there." I looked. The rusty old ship was about two hundred yards beyond the pier. That meant some seven hundred yards of wading through the fire of machine guns whose bullets already were whistling over our heads.

The fifteen of us—I think it was fifteen—scurried over the side of the amphtrack into the water that was neck-deep. We started wading.

No sooner had we hit the water than the Jap machine guns really opened up on us. There must have been five or six of these machine guns concentrating their fire on us—there was no nearer target in the water at the time—which meant several hundred bullets per man. I don't believe there was one of the fifteen who wouldn't have sold his chances for an additional twenty-five dollars added to his life-insurance policy. It was painfully slow, wading in such deep water. And we had seven hundred yards to walk slowly into that machine-gun fire, looming into larger targets as we rose onto higher ground. I was scared, as I had never been scared before. But my head was clear. I was extremely alert, as though my brain were dictating that I live these last minutes for all they were worth. I recalled that psychologists say fear in battle is a good thing; it stimulates the adrenalin glands and heavily loads the blood supply with oxygen.

I do not know when it was that I realized I wasn't frightened any longer. I suppose it was when I looked around and saw the amphtrack scooting back for more Marines. Perhaps it was when I noticed that bullets were hitting six inches to the left or six inches to the right. I could have sworn that I could have reached out and touched a hundred bullets. I remember chuckling inside and saying aloud, "You bastards, you certainly are lousy shots." That, as I told Colonel Carlson next day, was what I later described as my hysteria period. Colonel Carlson, who has been shot at in a number of wars, said he understood.

After wading through several centuries and some two hundred yards of shallowing water and deepening machine-gun fire, I looked to the left and saw that we had passed the end of the pier. I didn't know whether any Jap snipers were still under the pier or not, but I knew we couldn't do any worse. I waved to the Marines on my immediate right and shouted, "Let's head for the pier!" Seven of them came. The other seven Marines were far to the right. They followed a naval ensign straight into the beach—there was no Marine officer in our amphtrack. The ensign said later that he thought three of the seven had been killed in the water.

The first three of us lay on the rocks panting, waiting for the other five to join us. They were laboring heavily to make it, and bullets from the machine guns on the beach were still splashing around them like raindrops in a water barrel. By this time we three were safely hidden from the beach by the thick, upright, coconut-log stanchions of the pier. I watched these five men and wondered how on heaven or earth they managed to come so close to death, yet live. Once I thought the last man, a short Marine, would not get under the pier. Twenty yards away, he fell and went under. But he was not hit. In a moment he was up again, struggling through the water, almost exhausted beyond further movement, but still carrying his heavy roll of telephone wire. When he had gone under I had asked myself whether I had the breath or the courage to go after him. I was relieved when the necessity of answering the question was obviated by his arrival.

We were still four hundred yards from the beach. But now we could crawl in most of the way under the protection of the pier, where we made difficult, if not altogether invisible, targets. After a few minutes of breath-catching we started crawling. A hundred yards from the beach, the pier rested on big coral rocks on the ground, so we had to take to the water again. It was only a little more than knee-deep now.

I looked on both sides of the pier. Our battalion had been supposed to land on the right side, but there was no sign of life anywhere on the right. But on the left there seemed to be three or four hundred people milling around the beach and they were wearing, not Jap uniforms, but the spotted brown-and-green jungle dungarees of the United States Marines. The eight of us decided to go to the left.

We ducked low, creeping along the edge of the pier. We were not even shot at. We came upon a stalled bulldozer. This, I reflected, was the American way to fight a war—to try to get a bulldozer ashore, even before many men had preceded it. Later I learned that a bulldozer is a fine weapon; it can shovel up sand over a low slit in a pillbox, causing the enemy inside to smother. Two Marines tinkered with the bulldozer, but it had sunk too deep in the water that covered an unseen shellhole. A third Marine lay behind the bulldozer seat. He already had a bullet through his thigh. Then the Jap machine gun chattered, rattling its fire against the frontal blade of the bulldozer. We ducked low behind the machine.

"How goes it?" I asked the Marines.

"Pretty tough," one of them said, matter-of-factly. "It's hell if you climb over that seawall. Those bastards have got a lot of machine guns and snipers back there."

After a few minutes the Jap gave up trying to shoot at the four of us behind the bulldozer. I dashed back to the pier, which was only fifteen feet to the left. During the dash I stepped into a shellhole seven feet deep. Then I swam the rest of the way to the pier.

With each movement of the surf a thousand fish washed against the pier—fish six inches to three feet long. Regardless of their effectiveness against Jap emplacements, shellfire and bombing misses could kill a lot of fish by concussion.

I passed a stalled medium tank, which had floundered when it sank into one of the shellholes. A hundred yards farther to the left there was a stalled light tank. To my surprise I saw a nearly naked figure appear from under the water, swim the last few feet to this tank, then jump in through the top of it. At first I thought it was a Marine who had gone to repair the tank. But why would he take all his clothes off, and why swim under water? Perhaps it was a Jap, but why? I reported the incident when I got ashore, but the officer, with his hands already full, paid little attention to the report. We were to hear later from this stalled tank and from many another disabled tank and amphtrack and boat.

Upon reaching the end of the pier I ducked into a foxhole in the sand which was already crowded with three Marines. I took my first close look at bird-shaped Betio. At this point on the bird's belly, behind the pier that stuck out like a leg, there was a gap. This gap was heaped three or four feet high with sand, but the rest of the island's north rim seemed to be a four-foot seawall built of coconut logs which had been driven into the ground. From the water's edge to the seawall there was twenty feet of sand and brown and green coral. These twenty feet were our beachhead. The Japs controlled the rest of the island, excepting this pocket—twenty feet deep and perhaps a hundred yards wide—which had been established by the Second Battalion of the Eighth Marine Regiment, the farthest left of our three assault battalions, plus two other pockets which had been established as fragilely by the other two battalions. The beginning at Betio did not look bright. But several hundred Marines had gone over that seawall to try to kill the Japs who were killing our men as they waded ashore. They went over—though they knew very well that their chances of becoming a casualty within an hour were something like fifty percent.

I stooped low and ran the hundred feet from the end of the pier to a stalled amphtrack which was jammed against the seawall. Beside the amphtrack a dead Marine lay on the sand. He was the first of many dead Americans I saw on Betio. There was a wide streak of blood on the amphtrack, indicating that the dying man had bled a lot.

A big, red-mustached Marine walked over. "Who is he?" he asked.

"An assistant amphtrack driver, sir," another Marine said. "Name was Cowart. He was twenty years old. He married a girl in Wellington."

"Well, cover him up. Will the amphtrack run?"

"No, sir. We've tried to start it, but I guess the starter was knocked out when this man was killed."

I walked over and introduced myself to the red-mustached Marine. His name was Henry Pierson ("Jim") Crowe and he had been an old-time enlisted man. Now he was a major, commanding the assault battalion that had landed at this point.

"Have you seen any other war correspondents, Major?" I asked. The major said he had not. Poor Frank Filan and Dick Johnston, I thought. They were the A.P. photographer and U.P. reporter who were supposed to land with Crowe's battalion.

The major had other business. Many of his Marines had already gone over the seawall to kill Japs. Now telephone wires were being strung between their forward shellhole posts and his command post behind the stalled amphtrack. I saw a chaplain nearby. I asked him if many men from his battalion had been killed. "I just got there," he said. "I haven't seen but two dead except this man by the amphtrack."

I sat down and leaned against the amphtrack, next to the seawall. Now and then bullets would rattle against the amphtrack, but the seawall made a fairly safe place to sit. With several Marines who were there, wiremen, corpsmen, and battalion staff headquarters men, I felt quite luxurious. If I stayed there, in the dip under the wall, I would be quite safe from any of the Japanese bullets which sang overhead in their high soprano. The Jap mortars, like their guns, were being concentrated on our boats as they approached the shore.

Six hundred yards out, near the end of the pier, I watched a Jap shell hit directly on an LCV that was bringing many Marines ashore. The explosion was terrific and parts of the boat flew in all directions. Then there were many Marines swimming in the water.

Two pairs of corpsmen brought two more dead men and placed them beside the dead boy who had been married to the girl from Wellington. Even now the men had been ashore less than an hour. Yet already the smell of death under the equator's sun could be detected faintly.

Our destroyers were only a thousand yards or so offshore by now and they had begun firing on the tail end of the island, where there were no Americans. The battleships opened up from the other side of the island. Their shells made a great roaring sound when they smacked the land behind where we were sitting. Then we could hear the whish of the shells through the air, then the report from the muzzles of the guns. It seemed odd. It was as though the shells were giving an answer before the question were asked.

I took out my soaked notebooks and opened them up to dry on the hub of the amphtrack. Then I fished the waterproof envelopes out of my wet dungarees. My fine watch was ruined—there was an accumulation of green scum under the crystal. The cigarette lighter in another envelope was also soaked and ruined and already rusted, but the pack of cigarettes was still dry, and they seemed more valuable at the time than either of the other items.

A young Marine walked in front of us, about fifteen feet from where we were sitting, and about five feet from the water's edge. A rifle cracked loudly from behind us. The Marine flinched, grabbed at his head, then ducked to the sand. I thought he had been hit, but, miraculously, he had escaped. He picked up his helmet. There were two inch-wide holes in the top of it, one on each side. The Jap bullet which tore through his helmet had missed his head, but not by more than an eighth of an inch. The Marine's only wound was a scratch on his face, where the helmet had scraped as it was torn savagely off his head.

"All right, god damn it," shouted Major Crowe, "you walk along out there standing up and you're sure as hell going to get shot. Those bastards have got snipers every ten feet back there."

Not fifteen minutes later, in the same spot, I saw the most gruesome sight I had seen in this war. Another young Marine walked briskly along the beach. He grinned at a pal who was sitting next to me. Again there was a shot. The Marine spun all the way around and fell to the ground, dead. From where he lay, a few feet away, he looked up at us. Because he had been shot squarely through the temple his eyes bulged out wide, as in horrific surprise at what had happened to him, though it was impossible that he could ever have known what hit him.

"Somebody go get the son-of-a-bitch," yelled Major Crowe. "He's right back of us here, just waiting for somebody to pass by." That Jap sniper, we knew from the crack of his rifle, was very close.

A Marine jumped over the seawall and began throwing blocks of fused TNT into a coconut-log pillbox about fifteen feet back of the seawall against which we sat. Two more Marines scaled the seawall, one of them carrying a twin-cylindered tank strapped to his shoulders, the other holding the nozzle of the flamethrower. As another charge of TNT boomed inside the pillbox, causing smoke and dust to billow out, a khaki-clad figure ran out the side entrance. The flame-thrower, waiting for him, caught him in its withering stream of intense fire. As soon as it touched him, the Jap flared up like a piece of celluloid. He was dead instantly but the bullets in his cartridge belt exploded for a full sixty seconds after he had been charred almost to nothingness. It was the first Jap I saw killed on Betio—the first of four thousand. Zing, zing, zing, the cartridge-belt bullets sang. We all ducked low. Nobody wanted to be killed by a dead Jap . . .

IN THE AFTERNOON OF THE FOURTH DAY OF BLOODY fighting, November 23, the American flag was planted on Tarawa. Our dead numbered nine hundred and eighty Marines and twenty-nine sailors. Considering the valuable lessons learned, however, which were to be applied in the march across the Pacific, the cost was not excessive. For the Corps, covered with glory and high honor, Tarawa constituted its toughest fight to date—tougher by far than Guadalcanal.

The next phase of the Micronesian campaign began to shape up. Among the preliminary steps was the hacking out of airfields on Apamama, the small atoll seventy-five miles from Tarawa, captured November 29 in a bloodless assault. Seabees and Bobcats did their usual incredible job of making the island habitable within a few days.

One who was present was Chief Carpenter's Mate Dee Hardin, who wrote the following letter to his wife on Christmas Day.

7.

"I GOT THE PIPE

YOU SENT ME"

December 25, 1943

Hello, Darling:

Well, here is another Christmas . . . my third away from home and you. Remember how I enlisted so quickly after Pearl Harbor? And then I didn't get to come home before we shoved off. I got the pipe you sent me. This morning I got up early, put on my clean suit and went to church. Now I am smoking my new pipe and trying not to think too much. You just can't think about the nice things at home and the things you are missing and still be in the right frame of mind to fight the Japs. I just put all those thoughts in the corner of my mind and close the door on it. If I'm lucky and come out of this alive, then when it's all over I'll just open the door on my thoughts— but not before. Sounds simple, doesn't it, but it's a lot harder to put into practice. There are plenty of things that I never mention that are enough to drive anyone crazy if he doesn't manage to look at it right. Believe me, we Bobcats are the greatest morale busters in the entire Pacific. Every place we go we run up against Seabees and others who have been in the islands anywhere from six months to a year, and they all have bright visions of going home "by Christmas" or at least in the next sixty or ninety days . . .

When we come around they all shut up like clams now. One of

the chiefs was telling me that his gang was always raising hell and talking of all the celebrating they would be doing back in the States in a few short weeks. But now that they have seen us they are as meek as lambs and ready to break down and cry. Well, I guess if our gang can't take it, no one can. I've always had a high regard for the Marines, but our boys will match them man for man.

Perhaps it's our ability to get things done when the chips are down that has got us where we are now. I don't know if you'd consider that good or bad. We have our own opinion. I thought I'd be able to send you a surprise wire for Christmas, but they wouldn't let me do it. Well, I'll have to be getting on with the war. This can't last forever— or can it?

~~~~~~

STATIONED AT APAMAMA WAS COMMANDER NORMAN Miller, skipper of Bombing Squadron 109, which began softening up the Marshalls as early as January 3, 1944. With collaborator Hugh B. Cave, whom we have met before, Miller (six Air Medals and a Navy Cross) recounts a usual day in the life of a bomber pilot. The name of his PB4Y was *Thunder Mug,* named for Thelma Miller, his wife.

8.

THUNDER MUG

AT APAMAMA

I learned that the squadron bulletin board, for instance, was not getting the attention it deserved. Like most such boards, it had accumulated a mess of routine papers which the men simply ignored. So the name of it was changed to the "Red Hot Dope Board," and a rule was inaugurated that nothing, no matter what, was to remain on it for more than three days. To stir up interest, I posted jokes, cartoons, anything that came along. (This continued throughout our tour of duty, and before long we were getting all sorts of lively items from the folks back home. Thelma, for instance, used to include jokes and newspaper clippings in almost every letter.)

Of course, it worked. A new joke, a new cartoon, becomes an item of major importance in a small community of men who have heard one another's stories over and over and are desperate for something fresh. The board was no longer ignored, and I never again allowed it to become cluttered with needless orders. Only the essential ones were posted. Other information was passed out verbally, when we got together to discuss the "dope."

These discussions, held in the skipper's tent, the mess hall, or the ACI office, often lasted for hours. Pilots, co-pilots and navigators, drifting in and out, would gather around to examine maps of the islands which were likely to be our targets. Ed Lloyd, our ACIO—before the war he had been a Pasadena lawyer—would give us all the information he had been able to pick up concerning these islands, telling us what the enemy had on them, which were strong, which were weak. Then, quite informally, the boys would go on to discuss ways and means of getting in to make trouble for the enemy.

My own particular pet was the Jap stronghold at Truk, and I carried with me a little yellow-covered booklet of Truk target maps. Long before I ever ventured into the place, I did my best to know the names of the Truk islands by heart, what they would look like from the air, where the enemy had set up his major defenses, and where his anchorages were. On Apamama we were a very long way from this Jap bastion, of course, but eventually we would be moving our base into the Marshalls, and then Truk would be within reach. Some day I was going to find out what Truk really looked like—not on maps or in photographs, but the real thing . . .

A strike, let's say, has been scheduled for dawn tomorrow at Island "X"—a tiny place with an unpronounceable name well up in the Marshalls, where reconnaissance planes have reported some important enemy shipping. *Thunder Mug* is handed the assignment. Shafe—Lieutenant (jg) Robert K. Schaffer, my navigator—fusses with his charts and tables for a while, and together we figure out the take-off time. Shafe, a tall, extremely good-looking boy with jet black hair—until it turned gray—used to worry a lot when we were scheming up these missions, but he would go anywhere and the crew worshipped him. In fact, I twice had to remind them gently that we were still in the Navy where it was considered not quite proper for enlisted men to address an officer as "Hey, Shafe!" *"Mister* Schaffer," I used to say, wagging my head. And "Mr. Schaffer" it would be, but I suspect that it became "Hey, Shafe" again more often than not when my ears were turned. Shafe or Mr. Schaffer, he was one of the finest navigators in the Navy, and if Shafe said you would be off the reef at Island "X" at 0502, you'd be there at 0502. Nor did I ever have to vary our course on the way back, to pick up the home island. Nine times out of ten, even after fourteen or more hours in the air, Shafe would bring us home with such accuracy that with only a wiggle of the wings, and sometimes not that, we could sit right down on the runway. Whereupon I usually turned to him and said, "Shafe, you're the lousiest navigator in the business." And Shafe would say, "Skipper, I can't help it if you don't fly the way I tell you to." And I'd say, "Shafe, you haven't stopped shaking yet." And Shafe would say,

"Skipper. I'll never stop shaking. I'm scared stiff. But I can go anywhere you can, by God, and I'll prove it."

Shafe, then, has figured out our take-off time, and I drop in at the operations office to tell Lieutenant "Buzzy" Robinson, our Operations Officer, where we are going, how much gas we'll need, and what sort of bomb load we plan to tote. Then to Ed Lloyd for the latest intelligence on Island "X." Then, armed with maps and charts and all the available dope, we pick up the crew and go down to the air strip to pre-flight the plane—that is, turn up all the engines to be sure they are sweet, see that the radioman has checked his radio equipment, and give the entire plane a thorough once-over. We are going to be in this plane for fourteen hours or more, much of that time over an empty ocean or enemy-occupied islands. Only a very careless crew would embark on such an undertaking without first making certain that to the best of their knowledge the plane was mechanically perfect.

With all the crew present, we get together under the wing, now, for a briefing. "Boys," I say, unrolling the maps, "we're going in to Island 'X' tonight. Here's how we'll do it." With the maps unrolled on the ground, I give them complete information on how we are to approach the island, the targets we'll aim for, the enemy defenses to look out for, and the route by which we will retire. I tell them, too, the details of the alternate plan which is always held in readiness in case something goes wrong. Everything, after all, depends on the crew. They cannot be at their best unless they know what to expect, and if they aren't good, the pilot is simply flying an airplane . . .

So, then, the plane is ready, the crew has been briefed, and we have nothing much to do until take-off time. If it is to be a difficult mission—if, for instance, Island "X" is known to be strongly defended—there is likely to be a little tension about now, though you must look closely to spot it. One man in whom you won't find it is Paul Ramsey, the plane captain—senior enlisted man of the crew—who has no visible nerves whatever and is concerned only with the plane, which is his responsibility. (Secretly, perhaps, he was concerned also with a Jacksonville WAVE, whom he married soon after our tour of duty ended. A competent, soft-spoken boy from York, Pennsylvania, Ramsey knew all there was to know about his plane and is now an ensign, after working his way up in the regular Navy.)

Some of the boys, however, are clowning about, hiding their tension under good-natured kidding; others are soberly discussing the mission and trying to pick holes in the plan of attack which has been outlined to them. They are smart; you don't fool them. If the plan is not perfect, they will find the flaws.

Meanwhile, I have gone back up to the ACI office to be briefed myself by the ACIO, taking with me the co-pilot and navigator. (If more than one plane is to be in on the mission, other pilots, co-pilots and navigators will have gathered there as well.) From Ed Lloyd we get the latest information on enemy shipping, the location of friendly submarines if any are likely to be encountered along our track, and any other intelligence that may be of use to us. We take notes. We discuss the attack from all angles, make suggestions, finally reach the point where the subject is quite talked out.

It is now late afternoon and we have been working on this mission all day. I hand the co-pilot or navigator the briefcase containing my notebook and the charts. He takes it to the plane. The navigator takes along, too, his octant and gear and his own charts, well worked over by this time. We are then at liberty to go to a movie or turn in for a few hours' sleep until take-off time.

To be sure that I won't oversleep, I set my alarm clock and direct the duty officer when to wake me. But sleep is elusive at such a time. Instead, I lie there thinking. Again and again I go over the plan of the mission, seeking flaws in it, wondering if this time I have overlooked some small but vital item which may mean the difference between success and failure, perhaps even between life and death. We know so little about this Island "X" really. What if the Japs have moved that potent AA battery to a position nearer the lip of the channel, where it will blast us as we come up off the water to clear the cliff? What if they have put a lookout on that little outlying island over which we are planning to fly to reach our target?

It is 12:30 when the alarm goes off. The tent is dark. Sitting up, I reach sleepily for clothes and shoes and become aware of the sound of the surf on the island's reef—funny, but you never notice that sound in the daytime; you hear it only at night, when all else is still. At the mess hall, which is a Quonset hut, the co-pilot and navigator are waiting. They, too, are rubbing sleep from their eyes. The crew, up ahead of us, have gone down to the plane.

It's a fair breakfast: fried eggs, the inevitable spam prepared in some trick manner, and coffee or a glass of water. The co-pilot has picked up the flight rations—sufficient food to keep the entire crew going until we return to base—and carries these in a cardboard box under his arm as we climb sleepily into the jeep that is waiting to take us to the airstrip. Under my arm I carry a wadded-up pair of coveralls, the pockets stuffed with a strange assortment of objects: a steel signaling mirror, morphine syrettes, a small pocket compass, dog tags, a long knife with an 8-inch blade, a canteen of water, a pistol and ammunition, and my rabbit's foot. At the plane I strip off my clothes and don the coveralls; it is easier to leave the clothes behind than to go through all the pockets in search of bits of paper that may contain confidential information. Because, of course, we may not come back. A Liberator is a good airplane, but it is only an airplane, not a magic carpet. And the Jap AA gunners and fighter pilots are sometimes very competent people.

The members of the crew are waiting on the airstrip, all of them sleepy but on edge now, eager to be in action. I give them the last minute dope if there is any. Someone—usually it is Bobby Gariel or Thomas Delahoussaye—has a joke to tell or a crack to make. "Now listen, Captain. If those flying fish get into my turret again and spoil my aim, will you *please* pull up to the curb till I bail them out?"

But Shafe says it is time to go. "Okay, let's crank her up." Ramsey, the plane captain, winds up the engines, listening intently to the song they sing. Bobby Gariel, the San Antonio tail gunner, climbs up through a waist hatch and goes aft to his tiny cubicle in the tail, stepping over the little metal "head" can en route. Bobby is dark and wiry, with broad shoulders but disgracefully narrow hips. He fits nicely into the cramped quarters of his tail turret, and while he sits, waiting for action, he thinks up most of the wisecracks for which the crew of *Thunder Mug* is famous. Such as the day he solemnly explained the enemy's failure to halt one of our more audacious attacks on a Jap stronghold. "Sure they saw us coming. They had lookouts all over the island. Trouble was, those Japs rushed to their phones and babbled the alarm in *Japanese*—and who the hell understands Japanese, anyway?"

Eddie Dorris, the eighteen-year-old from Kansas, tall, thin, always a gentleman, shrugs himself up through the hatch to the flight deck and checks his radio equipment. Or, if it happens to be his turn to take the top turret, where he alternates with Wayne Young, he just continues on up, threading his thin body through the turret hatch into the glass bubble above. Despite his youth, he is a remarkably mature kid, keenly observant. He is a particular favorite of the ACIO, who can rely on him after a mission to report quite detachedly on what happened, even to the extent of criticizing the skipper.

Wayne Young is that way, too. Twenty-five or twenty-six years old, from Seattle, he is the granddaddy of the crew, an accomplished radioman. His clowning is of the quiet kind; his jokes are more subtle. He takes his place now at the radio, in a two-by-four niche just behind the cockpit, where, with the headphones on, he makes a few last-minute checks and adjustments.

Lawrence Johnson, the belly-turret gunner, is a big lad from Grampion, Pennsylvania, where he used to be a lumberman. Lumbering was good for Johnny. He is ruggedly built, strong as a horse. But working in the woods has made him unduly quiet, too, and though he is good-looking, with an affectionate small-boy sweetness when he smiles, his face in repose is often heavy and serious. You have an odd desire to mother him—but how in heaven's name can you mother a husky brute with a physique like that! Johnny has no nerves; he is quiet, thoughtful, and no one ever knows whether he is scared or not. Yet he must be scared at times, for his job in the belly turret is nerve-racking. Hour after hour he must squat there in his glass bubble beneath the plane, watching the ocean skim past below him as we fly at high speed just over the water. If the plane should falter at that speed, or if the pilot should make a mistake, Johnny's little bubble-world would be wiped out in an instant, swept away like a drop of water from the belly of a skimming duck. Many a time he picks up spray from the waves as we go rumbling across the sea.

He stands by, now, waiting for the plane to be airborne before squeezing his big bulk into the blister. Then the blister will be lowered hydraulically and he will be in a world of his own until it is hauled up again—a world connected with the rest of the plane only by interphone. The boys don't envy Johnny.

They don't envy Jack Simmen, the bow-turret man, either. Simmen is a big, quiet boy, an excellent gunner, but when we make our low-level attacks his turret is a natural target for the enemy's AA fire. He has calm nerves, and he needs them.

Delahoussaye and Jaskiewicz, the waist gunners, have more space than anyone else in which to stretch their arms and legs. Both are good boys. Both will probably have burned out their gun barrels by the time we get home again, unless they run out of ammunition before that happens. Delahoussaye, from Lafayette, Louisiana, has some French in him and looks it. He is fountain-pen thin and filled

716 Aleutians to the Marianas

with good humor. Jaskiewicz, who hails from Chicago, is precisely what you'd expect with a name like that: big, brawny, tough, incredibly cool. "Whisky Jazz," the boys call him. His heart is as big as the Pacific sky through which presently we'll be flying to our target.

They are all aboard by now: tail-turret gunner, belly-turret gunner, top-turret gunner, bow-turret gunner, radioman, the two waist gunners, plane captain, navigator, co-pilot and pilot. The engines are turning up. In the cramped, crowded little cockpit the co-pilot (I had no regular co-pilot then, and borrowed men from other crews) occupies the hard, postage-stamp seat on the right, and the pilot has squeezed himself down on the one at the left. Between us stands the plane captain with the check-out list, reading off the items to be checked before we "haul the hook." Nothing is left to memory in handling these big planes. Before every take-off and landing, the list is gone through to be sure that all the complicated flight and control instruments have received the proper attention from pilot and co-pilot. I counted those instruments one day. For your information there are 204 levers, switches, gadgets and push-buttons to handle and 60 indicators and dials to read. And I probably overlooked some of them.

We complete the check-off list, turn up the engines and set the turbo superchargers. I turn to Ramsey, the plane captain, with the routine question, "Everything okay?" He nods, and we taxi out, following a jeep down the runway to the take-off position. There is a big sign on the back of this jeep at Apamama. "FOLLOW ME," it says. And so our huge, lumbering, four-engine bomber meekly trails a toy automobile, while the plane captain holds his head out of the top hatch to be sure the path is clear.

Shafe, worrying as usual, solemnly looks up from his navigator's charts. "Skipper, I hope you're right about those AA guns on the point." I hope so too, and grin at him—the boys have told me that no matter how concerned they are about our chances, everything is all right when the skipper smiles. I sometimes have to dig deep for that smile.

With the engines bellowing, we watch the tower for the green light, and at last we get it. *Thunder Mug* rolls down the runway, straining to be air-borne with a load of gas and bombs that would cause a lifting of eyebrows at the factory where she was built. The island drops away in the darkness beneath us. We come about, straighten away on course, and begin the long, lonely flight through the night to our destination. And because it will be many hours before we are able to get out and walk again, each member of the crew begins then and there to apportion out his stored-up energy in calculated dribbles, to make it last. Few words or motions are wasted.

It is a strange and sometimes awesome experience, this flying over an island-dotted ocean at night. There may be a moon to silver every wave-top and trace patterns of extraordinary beauty as far as one can see. There may be no moon at all, and then the sea and the islands are blacked out except for oddly distorted shadow-shapes that well up in the darkness and are gone again—islands like black bubbles turning up from the depths. But sometimes there are no islands. Sometimes for hundreds of miles, even thousands of miles, there is no land at all, anywhere, and then the Pacific is large and lonely.

We are tense, and the tension grows as the distance to the target decreases. The hours drag interminably. I see the co-pilot rubbing his thighs to increase the circulation, and I rub my own, always watching the sea and waiting for the emergence of the next ghostly cluster of islands—if any—along our track.

Beside me on the deck of the cockpit is the chart I always take along, folded so that the portion covering tonight's flight is uppermost. Shafe, facing forward in his navigator's compartment, holds a flashlight ready, and when I say "Light, Shafe," he directs a beam downward and I check on a passing island. "We're okay. That was Namorik. Wasn't that Namorik, Shafe?" But it has to be done quickly, for as we near our destination we are very low over the water, turning up tremendous speed, and if my attention is diverted from flying for more than a second, we may be in trouble.

Yet these quick glances at the chart, especially at the target chart, are highly important when approaching an enemy atoll, for the islands loom up with bewildering rapidity as the target is approached. Then in a matter of seconds the pilot, to orient himself, must make a lightning transition from lines on a chart, seen vertically, to the islands themselves, seen horizontally. And he hopes to heaven, as he does this, that Island "X" will look enough like the map, despite the darkness, for him to spot his objectives.

Now, with but a few more miles to go and the sky beginning to lighten in the east, we are very tense. Just above the surface of the ocean, old *Thunder Mug* roars along at 200 miles an hour or better, as I reach for the interphone.

"Okay, boys, we're going in just as we doped it." No need to tell the crew to be on their toes. They, too, are tense.

Suddenly the islands are upon us, and if we have come in from the west, to silhouette them against the dawn-light, they loom huge and blurred and black above the plane. We are skimming the water—a few feet lower and Johnson, in his belly turret, would find himself in a diving bell. We rise sharply as the islands thicken up about us. And "thicken" is the word. They seem to rush in from all directions, for these mid-Pacific atolls are usually composed of many little land-masses grouped in helter-skelter fashion around a central lagoon.

We know our target. Our course has been charted so that we will hit the maximum number of enemy installations: airfields, ammunition dumps, grounded airplanes, radio towers, or whatever the Japs have there that we know about. And always, of course, the shipping. For the Japs are short of ships, and these cargo vessels and their escorts are the lifeline by which their outlying island bases draw sustenance from the homeland.

So far we are not seen; the priceless element of surprise is still ours. The gunners hold their fire until the co-pilot, watching out the right-hand window of the greenhouse, begins to warn them of targets coming up. That is part of his job, to keep the crew informed over the interphone. "Ship on our starboard bow!" he warns. "Watch it! Planes parked on the apron to port!" Thus warned, the gunners can be ready. Bobby Gariel in the tail, for instance, can train his turret around so that when we roar over the ship in the lagoon, he need only catch it in his sights and blaze away at it.

But the co-pilot must be very good at this sort of thing. He must be hair-trigger quick as the targets come rushing at him, and he must be calm and sure of himself, especially sure of his voice, lest he rattle the men at the guns. The best of all co-pilots was Lieutenant Kasperson, who used to keep up a quick but quiet flow of talk that went something like this: "Delahoussaye, your side, couple of Bettys on the ramp ahead . . . Watch your fire in the belly turret, don't hit the bombs . . . Whisky, get that so and so in the tower . . ." Old Kas worked the gunners surely and confidently, never confusing them. They were seldom so effective as when he stirred them up with his matter-of-fact little pep talks.

So we go in, and the tension which seemed unbearable up to the moment of attack now becomes sheer excitement. Bombing and strafing, we sweep across the target island, our plane lit up like a

Christmas tree as the gunners "give 'em hell" at my signal. We are spouting fire from ten guns, an awesome spectacle, and can see our own tracers ricocheting from the ground—sometimes they ricochet so viciously that *Thunder Mug's* own belly is scarred as we travel through them. And the Japs, if they are alert, are filling the sky around us with their own tracers, easily distinguished from ours because they are a weird greenish blue. Some of them may hit us. Bigger shells, too, may hit us as they come hurtling up from the stronger gun positions, bursting into gaudy blue, red and green flares. But a Liberator can take a lot of punishment.

Often the damage we do is not fully determined, for at treetop height we must use delayed-action bombs to avoid blowing ourselves up with the Japs, and in the four or five seconds before a bomb explodes, the plane has traveled almost a quarter of a mile. The pilot sees almost nothing; he is usually jinking to avoid enemy counter-fire. The waist gunners and the tail gunner may observe the results of our attack if they are not too busy blasting other targets, but their reports are usually brief. The irrepressible Gariel, in the tail, may shout over the interphone, "Beautiful, Cap'n!" or someone else may groan, "Dammit, we missed!" but most of the talking is done later. The job now is to do all the damage possible while our bombs and ammunition last—to smash the air strips the Japs have so laboriously built, sink their ships, burn their planes, knock out their radio and radar equipment; in short, to liquidate these island bases which block our sea-roads to the Japanese mainland. To hell with looking back at what you've done! Look ahead and do more!

And then, before the enemy's AA fire becomes too hellaciously hot, and before his fighter planes take off to knock you down, "let's get the hell out of here—fast!" That was the phrase we used. That was our sign-off. "Let's get the hell out of here!" Later it became the chorus of the squadron song.

So we get the hell out of there—all in one piece, if we've been lucky, but sometimes limping home on three engines, with old *Thunder Mug* offering a fair imitation of a sieve. Perhaps we are chased by enemy planes, and then, full throttle, we hunt for cover in rain squalls or clouds, playing hide-and-seek until the enemy abandons his pursuit.

At last the crewmen relax. The flight rations are handed out. The radioman sends in a coded flash report of what we discovered this time at Island "X"—a report which passes on through many hands and is studied eventually, if important, by officers of all the air and sea forces operating in the area. The co-pilot takes over. Shafe checks the homeward course, so that in the end, after many more miles over that very big ocean, we will hit Apamama on the nose. (And right here let me salute Schaffer and all his kind, for the whole essence of a mission such as the one just described depends on the navigator's ability to place the plane over the target on the right heading at the right time. To Captain Woodruff and Lieutenant Commander Brownell, who established and conducted the Naval Air Navigational School whence these navigators came, unlimited credit is due. And to the boys themselves, many of whom could have been pilots had they not volunteered to study navigation instead, my hat is off in tribute. I have always felt that Navy navigators should wear some special insignia to distinguish them. It's the navigators, God bless them, who get you there and bring you home.)

It is Shafe who brings us home this time, and as *Thunder Mug* rolls to a stop on the Apamama runway, tired men drop stiffly to the ground to stretch arms and legs which have been aching for hours. Twelve, fourteen, sixteen hours in the air is a long time. We took off at 1 A.M. It is now 3 P.M. All that time in the air for twenty minutes over the target! "If I had to sit that long on a day-coach," says Shafe, "I'd sleep for the next two days." But a Liberator, despite its size, is far more confining than any day-coach. Pilot and co-pilot are so hemmed in by instruments that often they stay glued to their chairs the whole way, rather than go through the calisthenics of extricating themselves. If they do "go for a stroll," they must clamber down from the cluttered cockpit to the catwalk, a strip of metal less than a foot wide, thread their way along this between the bomb bays, and wriggle around the belly turret-well to the waist before there is room for anything more than light breathing.

Strolling under such conditions is not only difficult, it is dangerous. I tried it once when we were limping home with our hydraulic system shot up, and stepped without thinking on a catwalk made slippery by a spray of oily red fluid from the shattered hydraulic pipes. If the bomb bay doors had been open, I would not be here. I tried it again on the way home from a mission during which we had jettisoned the belly turret to lighten our load—and a sudden lurch of the plane sent me stumbling toward the open well. Grabbing at everything within reach, I hung on for dear life, scared stiff, as the dark Pacific rushed past below.

But at any rate, we are home, eager for chow and sleep. We don't sleep, though. Not yet. Ed Lloyd, our ACIO, is hungry for information and pounds us with questions. His job is to find out what happened, all that happened, to check and double-check our stories so that there may be no mistakes in the combat report which he must write.

Then, but not until then, the mission is over.

"A lone Navy Liberator penetrated the defenses of Island 'X' yesterday, dropping bombs on enemy installations and damaging enemy shipping in the harbor."

~~~~~~

THE INVASION OF THE MARSHALLS, BYPASSING MALOE-lap, Mili, Wotje and Jaluit in favor of the less heavily-defended target areas of Kwajalein and Majuro, became a *fait accompli* January 31 after a pre-invasion bombardment by battleships and cruisers of the Fifth Fleet. Operation "Flintlock," similar in organization to "Galvanic," embraced three attack groups aggregating two hundred and ninety-seven ships and 27,800 assault troops striking two target areas simultaneously, backed by heavy air support. As at Tarawa, Conolly and Turner led the sea and amphibious power, and Mitscher and Van H. Ragsdale provided the air support. In the Northern Attack Force was destroyer *Phelps,* which assumed a major role in the neutralization of Roi-Namur in Kwajalein Atoll, and on her bridge was Royal Navy observer Commander Anthony Kimmins, who had last seen action with United States forces at Salerno.

9.

INVASION OF

THE MARSHALLS

In the darkness we had seen lights burning on Roi and Namur, where the Japs were obviously trying to repair the damage from the previous day's bombing. Now—as the small flat islands became visible in the morning light with their clusters of palms sticking out of the vast expanse of water—they looked rather like the sort of mirage one would expect after a long march across the Sahara.

Flying fish kept skimming out of the water, wondering what all the commotion was about.

At exactly the appointed second the Captain (Lieutenant Commander D. L. Martineau) ordered "Open Fire" and with a blinding flash of her broadside *Phelps* had the honor of starting the bombardment.

Almost immediately there were more flashes from further out to sea as the battleships, cruisers, and other destroyers let fly.

It was far and away the most staggering bombardment I have ever seen and I have witnessed a good many in my time. Each ship took on not only her own particular island, but an actual spot on that island. The whole northern tip of the atoll ring was surrounded by ships pounding it from every side—and if you watched carefully— you could see the bursts relentlessly and systematically creeping across each strip of land covering every possible point where there might be Jap emplacements or defenses.

Then suddenly—and as if one master hand was controlling the trigger of every gun—the bombardment ceased, and as the great clouds of yellow cordite smoke drifted away in the breeze, gun crews tumbled out of their turrets and enjoyed a quick smoke while empty shell cases were heaved out of the way leaving everything clear for the next phase.

But that temporary lull in the ships allowed no respite for the defenders in the island. Even as the smoke and dust from the last shells were subsiding, dive bombers were roaring in and carrying on the good work. One after the other they came hurtling down, and from where we were close inshore we could watch every bomb leave the aircraft, see the flash as it exploded and almost determine from the palms, coral or concrete thrown into air exactly what had been hit.

On the tails of the last dive bombers came the fighters, tracers from their cannon shells showing up brilliantly in the half light of early morning, and bouncing up like grotesque illuminated ping-pong balls as the shells exploded.

As the last aircraft zoomed up into the sky and flew off to its carrier to reload, the warships opened up again. It was a triumph of planning and concentrated action.

Phelps, being closest inshore, had in addition to her scheduled bombardment program, the responsibility of dealing with individual targets as and when they presented themselves. Now, as the light improved, emplacements, barges, and observation posts became clearly apparent. All of them were systematically blown sky-high.

It was a gunlayer's paradise, and those gunlayers in the *Phelps* certainly knew their job.

By now the second phase of the operation was taking shape. While the preliminary bombardment had been going on, transports and other parent ships had been disgorging their landing craft and scores of different types of amphibious tanks and assault boats were converging on the *Phelps* who had the additional duty of grouping them in their correct waves and then, at the right moment, launching them for their assault.

The wind at this stage was freshening rapidly and had also backed a number of degrees. This meant that the beaches chosen for the first assault would not have as much lee as originally expected. From where we were it was already plainly obvious that the surf was assuming considerable proportions.

As the assault craft approached the nearest beaches it became plainly apparent from the way they were being tossed about in the rollers that it would be extremely difficult to force a landing at those points. One or two craft—determined no doubt to live up to the spirit of their colonel's final message "Good luck to the first Marine to land on Jap soil"—attempted to break through, were swung beam on, and capsized.

The remainder—benefiting by their example—concentrated on those points where there was a better lee and before long the first Marines were safely ashore—almost immediately there was the "Rat-tat-tat" of small arms fire but soon these became more sporadic until about an hour later they finally died away, and it became obvious that the first objectives were secure in our hands.

Meanwhile there had been no let-up from the bombarding ships and aircraft. As the last Fighters had strafed the beaches immediately prior to the assault craft touching down on the first objectives, so the whole bombardment had lifted and moved to the next island to be taken.

Having safely despatched the landing craft for the assault of the first islands, the *Phelps'* next duty was to force an entrance into the lagoon and take up a prearranged position where the next groups of landing craft would rendezvous.

As we steamed slowly through now accompanied by minesweepers everyone was keeping an almost sharper lookout than ever. This was the point, we had decided, where the enemy would have placed every trap in the way of mines and underwater obstructions to halt us and leave us a sitting target for his shore batteries. But almost before we had had time to realize our good fortune we were safely through the narrow channel and inside the roomy waters of the lagoon itself.

From there on it was a comparatively simple task to arrive at the exact point from which to launch the next attack and as we were receiving no interference from shore batteries, the anchor was let go. The first U. S. ship to anchor in a Jap harbor in this war.

It was a strange and unforgettable sight inside that lagoon. There sat the *Phelps* looking rather like a dignified old duck with all her tiny ducklings fussing and spluttering around her. I couldn't help thinking what a wonderful cartoon Walt Disney could have made of it all. From the entrance, we'd just come through, more and more ducklings were streaming towards us, freed at last from their long captivity in their parent ship. There they came in hundreds, splashing along, darting this way and that, and—as you'll always find in even the best organized circles—the occasional "Donald's either late or spluttering around just avoiding collisions with someone else."

On three sides we were surrounded by coral reefs and palm tree islands. Some of these islands—particularly Roi and Namur—were belching black smoke from oil tanks which had been hit. All—with the exception of the two we'd already captured—were being systematically pounded with shells and bombs.

Outside beyond the atoll ring we could still see the transports, and steaming to and fro the battleships and cruisers. Occasionally they would be hidden by an island and the flash of their guns would give an impression of having been fired from the island itself. Then a moment later they would appear from behind and be clearly visible above the white breakers in the coral reefs with the great flashes and clouds of yellow cordite smoke issuing from their guns.

And again from beyond them—from carriers way over the horizon —dive bombers and fighters were continually streaming in to drop their loads and return for more.

The noise was terrific and even our own broadsides—firing point blank at clearly defined targets on the islands about to be attacked— were almost lost in the general uproar.

Then suddenly a terrific explosion—the largest I have ever heard in my life—shook and rocked the lagoon. As an enormous volume of white and black smoke shot upwards from Namur and belched outwards into a colossal mushroom, debris and bodies could be seen spinning round like straws in a gale. Some of the debris looked suspiciously like aircraft wings and we hoped and prayed that they didn't belong to our own spotting aircraft who had been above Namur and were now completely hidden by the billow of smoke.

Obviously a large ammunition dump had been hit.

By now all the landing craft were in position, and at a signal from *Phelps,* they steamed off in perfect formation towards the next islands to be captured.

Just as in the morning attacks, covering fire from larger craft and fighters cleared the way before them, and by dusk all the scheduled objectives for "D" day were in our hands.

And so as night closed down, *Phelps,* a few minesweepers, and some of the larger support landing craft remained inside the lagoon while the large ships watched from outside and the small amphibious assault craft lay high and dry on the beaches of the islands they had captured.

But there was little sleep during the night. The Japs, it was reckoned, would take every advantage of the cover of darkness to sneak out in small boats.

But as the night wore on there was little sign of enemy movement. Obviously the shells still dropping on the main islands, the tremendous weight of explosive which had been poured on them during the previous day, had more than done the trick.

Daylight revealed a grim and murky day with low clouds and rain squalls, but it was soon difficult to discriminate between cloud, rain squall, smoke, and shell-burst as the final bombardment of Roi and Namur started in earnest. I had thought that yesterday's bombardment and bombing could never be surpassed, but now it was intensified to a pitch which almost took one's breath away.

It was so staggering that one just couldn't take one's eyes off it, and when eventually I glanced over my shoulder, the assault craft which I had last noticed outside the lagoon, had by now effected a complete transformation.

The whole northern end of the lagoon seemed to be packed with "ducklings." Yesterday there had been scores of them. Now there were literally hundreds and hundreds.

Soon they were surrounding us, forming up in their proper lines, and waiting impatiently for *Phelps'* signal to attack. Many of their Marines had their faces blackened. Others had favoured a weird khaki background with black streaks. All were gripping their carbines and tommy-guns and obviously itching for action.

The Stars and Stripes were already proudly flying from the islands already captured. These men were determined that it would soon be flying over Roi and Namur.

At first—as the assault craft deployed and touched down along the beaches—they met with little resistance, but as they moved inland across the islands, there were still a number of stubborn Japs offering a last desperate resistance.

The scene ashore was an indescribable shambles. Dead fish of all colors and sizes had been hurled onto the beaches by nearby explosions. Nearly every palm tree had had its top blown off. There was hardly a square foot of ground which had not either been hit or covered with debris.

Dead and mutilated Japs lay about in grotesque attitudes. Pill boxes and air-raid shelters which had received direct hits revealed an awful scene of carnage. The stench was foul and nauseating.

Flies, a few lizards, some birds, a chicken, a pig, a dog, and a few prisoners seemed to be the only living creatures who had survived the Hell of the last few days.

While the prisoners were being led off for investigation the Seabees already were starting to clear the debris, the little dog was being stroked and petted and obviously being groomed for a regimental pet. The pig, on the other hand, was obviously being groomed for the evening meal.

Somehow I felt sorry about that social distinction. I had watched that pig at various moments during the bombardment. I had seen him scamper away as a shell exploded nearby, and then go on sniffing as if nothing had happened. After all he'd been through, I felt he deserved to live to a ripe old age. But I'm probably unduly sentimental, and anyhow the smell of dead Japs had definitely affected my appetite.

And as through all that day, that night, and the following day and night, the grim business went on of exterminating Japs wherever they might be hiding in drains, foxholes, or whatever cover was left, until the last one had been dealt with.

The whole operation had cost us amazingly few lives, thanks to perfect organization, a bold stroke of planning, and brilliant execution.

FOR A MORE PANORAMIC VIEW OF OPERATION "Flintlock", we turn to this account by Captain Walter Karig, Lieutenant Commander Russell L. Harris and Lieutenant Commander Frank A. Manson who open with the contribution of the battlewagons.

CAPTAIN WALTER KARIG,

LIEUTENANT COMMANDER RUSSELL L. HARRIS

AND LIEUTENANT COMMANDER FRANK A. MANSON

10.

MARSHALLS MOP-UP

Much of the destruction this D-Day was caused by the heavy infighting of a pair of rejuvenated battleships—*Mississippi* (Captain Lunsford L. Hunter), repaired after her Makin Island turret explosion, and *Pennsylvania* (Captain William A. Corn), flagship of the Pacific Fleet at the time of Pearl Harbor.

Their major mission was the quick destruction of the coast and anti-aircraft defense guns on the west side of Kwajalein, to prevent shelling of the clustered transports unloading for the assault on Enubuj. Later *Mississippi* moved in to cover a beach reconnaissance party.

Through the gray predawn, *Pennsylvania's* first salvo shrieked toward the target and erupted a black pall of debris-hailing smoke. Aboard ship there was a moment of silence, suddenly broken by one clear, loud exulting yell:

"Reveille, you slant-eyed sons of bitches!"

Nothing was spared. First the gun emplacements were smashed. Then the pillboxes, ammunition dumps, gasoline stowage areas, the sea wall that was supposed to serve as a tank barricade. The small spotter plane circling slowly over the target brought the salvos down to sniper accuracy.

Minesweeps nosed into the lagoon. An anchorage was needed for the transports lying exposed to submarine attack beyond the reefs.

Admiral Turner wanted no repetition of the *Liscome Bay* calamity. Nor did he want little matchbox ships cluttering the anchorage area.

Troops transferred from the large transports (APAs) to the LSTs whose long corridorlike holds were lined with amphibious vehicles (LVTs or Amtracs). They rocked in the water while reconnaissance units paddled ashore for a preliminary look-see at Enubuj, having in mind the mines found on the beaches at Tarawa. The *Mississippi* closed in to cover the joint reconnaissance units as they paddled their rubber boats close to the teeth-sharp reefs. Although not an enemy shot had been fired from the crushed defenses, *Pennsylvania* swung around to guard *Mississippi,* few of whose guns could be brought to bear on the beach while heading directly for the target.

"0904—Resumed fire all batteries. Range 2,500 yards."

"Ole Mis' " was making dead sure that the men in the rubber boats would not be bothered even by a stray sniper bullet.

"0925—Troops land on Enubuj Island," she signaled.

The men went ashore dry. Opposition was negligible. Enubuj Island was secured before noon, and by six that evening the Army's 105mm and 155mm howitzers had been landed and were adding to the uproar on Kwajalein. Ennylabegan also fell like a ripe coconut. These islands, plus Gea and Ninni, were the total D-Day objectives. Gehh had unwittingly been thrown in for good measure.

Meanwhile, from an average range of 3,000 yards, the battleships were methodically destroying Kwajalein Island's blockhouses, pillboxes, barricades, and trench systems. Naval reconnaissance units probed the reefs for mines, Lieutenant William K. Rummel leading his men in two surveys, one at morning high tide and another at low tide. Many landing craft had hung on the reefs at Tarawa. Here LVTs would crawl the reefs, but first they must be made safe by eliminating all mines.

The *Mississippi* had done her job well. The men wading and probing on the reefs were not molested by Jap fire. No mines or other obstructions were found. The investigators worked behind a screen of gunfire from the sea that rocked the beach defenses with 14-inch main batteries and 5-inch secondary batteries, and raked the jumping ruins with 40mm and 20mm.

Half an hour before noon:

"Main battery ceased firing. Morning fire support mission completed. All firing apparently entirely effective. No casualties."

After a morning of sweat and smoke the battleship men left their stations. Five hours of steady fire had left most of them temporarily deaf, but a greater physical discomfort was hunger. When "chow down" sounded from the mess hall, no one was too deafened to hear it.

Late that afternoon the transports eased through narrow Gea Pass into the lagoon. Troops of Regimental Combat Team 184 (Colonel Curtis D. O'Sullivan, USA) and Regimental Combat Team 32 (Colonel Marc J. Logie, USA), who were to assault Kwajalein Island the next morning, were transferred to the LSTs and smaller vessels. During the night the troop-laden craft were harassed by an inaccurate bombardment from light field artillery that had managed to survive the day's terrific bombardment.

Next morning the science of co-ordinated destruction reached new heights.

The *Mississippi* carefully maneuvering through uncharted waters close to the reef drew up at a point 1,500 yards off the landing beaches, Red Beaches 1 and 2. At 0615 she cut loose with her 14-inch broadside.

Promptly at 0800 the 7th Division artillery, massed across the coral-studded water on Enubuj Island, started laying down its barrage.

From 0830 to 0839 nine bombers of Admiral Hoover's land-based air op from the Gilberts saturated the area with 2,000-pound bombs.

From 0845 to 0900 all artillery fire was stopped while Navy dive bombers and torpedo bombers came in low, followed by strafing fighters.

At 0900 the maximum possible gunfire from battleships, cruisers, and destroyers was poured into the beach area. By this time the first waves of LVTs had crossed the line of departure and were churning toward the beach. Leading them in were rocket-launching LCIs, fitted to carry rockets instead of infantry, but now pouring a steady hail of machine-gun fire. Then, like a fighter taking the measure of his opponent before the knock-out blow, the LCI rocket boats fired a few ranging shots from their racks. Two minutes later, at 0920, with a hissing rush of flame and smoke the whole cargo of rockets was let loose in an arc of death.

Eight minutes later artillery fire was lifted 200 yards inland. At 0930 the first waves hit the beach standing up. What they saw was well described in the report of a naval gunfire officer: "The effect of naval gunfire on the island of Kwajalein was devastating. The entire

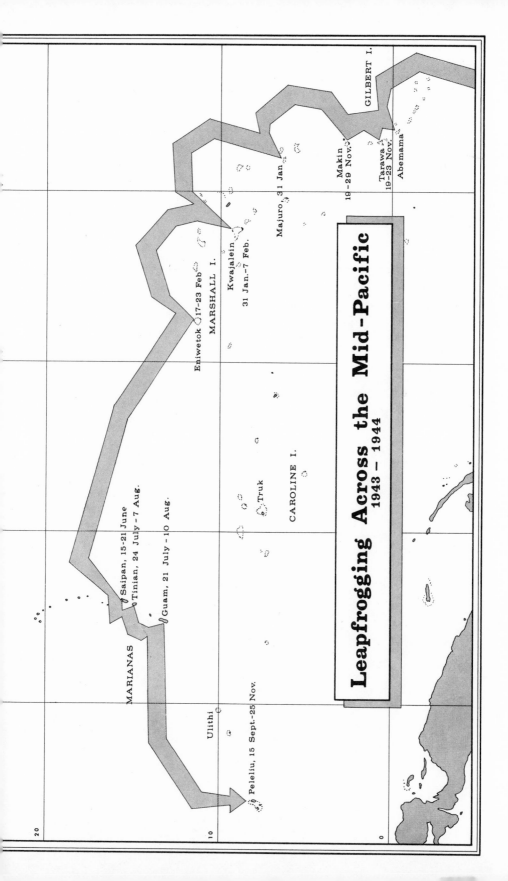

Leapfrogging Across the Mid-Pacific
1943 – 1944

MARIANAS

Saipan, 15-21 June
Tinian, 24 July - 7 Aug.
Guam, 21 July - 10 Aug.

Ulithi

Peleliu, 15 Sept.-25 Nov.

Eniwetok 17-23 Feb.
MARSHALL I.
Kwajalein
31 Jan.-7 Feb.

Majuro, 31 Jan

Truk

CAROLINE I.

GILBERT I.

Makin
18-29 Nov.
Tarawa
19-23 Nov.
Abemama

20

10

0

island looked as if it had been picked up to 20,000 feet and then dropped. The ground was so torn up that it made even movement by foot difficult. It was impossible to tell where the sea wall had stood. All beach defenses were completely destroyed. Practically every defense installation above ground had been hit by gunfire, due to the ships closing the range to where they could see the target and use direct fire. Prisoners of war testified that the terrific blasting effect of the heavy and continuous bombardment terrorized the defending forces. . . ."

The bombardment had made it tough even for our own tanks, which landed with the initial waves; they could not maneuver on the rubble-strewn shell-pocked beaches. As the troops advanced, the terrain inland proved less churned but at no time could the tanks move freely.

With the pedestrian advance sniper resistance increased. Occasional mortar and howitzer fire came from the twisted steel and concrete remains of half-destroyed emplacements. When a particularly strong position was encountered, ships were called on to eliminate it. Specially trained naval officers, ashore with the troops, directed such fire from grid-maps, duplicates of which were aboard the ships, with portable voice radios.

Here is an example of how shore-directed naval bombardment is managed, as logged by the destroyer *Haggard* (Commander David A. Harris).

The *Haggard,* anchored in Kwajalein lagoon, is leisurely lobbing 5-inch shells into ammunition dumps and pillbox areas within view when her radio crackles and the voice of the Shore Fire Control Officer comes through:

Shore: "Come in, please."

Ship: "Go ahead."

Shore: "At present time I cannot give you the front lines but will do so as soon as possible. I have no targets for you but you may fire at targets of opportunity that you can see in Zone T."

Ship: "Roger. We have a possible blockhouse in Zone T and will fire a few salvos at it."

Shore: "Are you firing now?"

Ship: "Affirmative. We are firing at a possible blockhouse in Zone T."

Shore: "I would now like to fire on a real blockhouse in Square 105. I will give you co-ordinates of this point. Fire at Emplacement 486474 in Square 105. I will adjust fire."

Ship: "Firing ship ready."
Shore: "Commence firing."
Ship: "Wilco."
                (Salvo, Salvo!)
Shore: "No change in elevation. Left 200."
                (Salvo, Salvo!)
Shore: "No change. No change. Rapid fire. Three salvos."
                (Salvo, Salvo, Salvo!)
Shore: "Up 50. No change. Rapid fire. Three salvos."
                (Salvo, Salvo, Salvo!)
Shore: "Down 25. No change. Three salvos."
                (Salvo, Salvo, SALVO!)
Shore: "Cease firing. Target neutralized. Good shooting."
Ship: "Wilco."

It was like ordering six cans of soup from the grocery.

Four days later, at 1530 on February 4, when all organized resistance had ceased, the only usable Japanese articles left on the island were a few anchors and some large buoys.

Machine-age war, indeed. It wasn't all going to be like that, though, from here on in.

To the north, at the other end of Kwajalein Atoll, the pattern of destruction was simultaneously being repeated against Roi and Namur. The instruments used were the ships of the Northern Attack Force and the Marines of the 4th Division.

The pulverization with shell and bomb had been every bit as intense as on Kwajalein Island. The plan of attack was the same: on D-Day to capture flanking islands, set up artillery, and bring the transports into the lagoon; on D-plus-1-day to land on the main objectives, Roi and Namur.

H-hour was set at 0900 on January 31. First stop on the schedule were Ennuebing and Mellu islands (Anglicized in the operation orders to Jacob and Ivan) flanking North Pass to the lagoon. A 19-knot wind scattered the slow LVTs at the line of departure. Short choppy seas smacked the treaded vehicles, sending salt spray down the backs of the huddled Marines. But soon they were steamed dry by the hot sun. The control officers aboard the destroyer *Phelps* (Lieutenant Commander David L. Martineau) saw that a concession would have to be made to the elements. H-hour was pushed back about 30 minutes.

In the whole Marshall campaign this was the only change in the planned schedule.

When the much-pounded LVTs waddled ashore through the heavy surf, only light opposition was encountered. Marines sitting on top of their vehicles waved to the pilots, affectionately known as the Rover Boys, zooming low over them. Over the TBS came the report: "Everything looks Jake on Jacob." By noon the two islands were reported secured, and the minesweeps moved in.

Scene II of Act One came that afternoon when the landing craft crossed the lagoon and went ashore on three islands with mouth-filling names: Ennubirr, Ennumennet, and Ennugarret. Again opposition was negligible. Before dark all the Northern Attack Force was anchored in the lagoon as protection against possible submarine attack.

Next morning, in the deep darkness before dawn, the upper decks of USS *Appalachian* (Captain James M. Fernald), Admiral Conolly's flagship, were a grandstand from which to watch battleships, cruisers, and destroyers work on Roi-Namur. Orange-yellow flame from the muzzles of the guns glowed against the low clouds like sheet lightning. The first faint dawn revealed the island as a seaborne fragment of the Inferno. Leaping up to low-rolling masses of black smoke gushed fountains of earth, sand, and water, all spouting flame. Even five miles from the target, the spectators' eyes ached with each flash, and the concussions sucked at eardrums and lungs.

Then came the planes, swarm after swarm—from an infinite hive, it seemed—scattering their hundreds of bombs until the island was eclipsed by one huge pall of smoke. The ships took no recess. Salvo continued to follow salvo relentlessly, doggedly, mercilessly, until noon . . .

From the bridge of the old battleship *Tennessee* (Captain Robert S. Haggart) a slim, alert little man in unadorned khakis watched the entire spectacle. He was James V. Forrestal, Under-secretary of the Navy.

The landings came from the south, from the lagoon. The Japanese had not expected an attack through the back door. Like the British defenses at Singapore, all their guns and fortifications pointed seaward. They had laughed at the British for that—laughed and did likewise. And, to add to the irony, the guns on Roi and Namur had been loot from Singapore.

At high noon Regimental Combat Team 23 (Colonel Louis R. Jones) attacked Roi. Regimental Combat Team 24 (Colonel Franklin A. Hart) attacked Namur, which was connected by an umbilical causeway to its sister island. In a huge arc outlined against the clouded horizon the landing craft moved in slowly, determinedly toward the beaches. Then the scene was blotted out by one of those huge tropical cloudbursts that leave a man wetter than if he had fallen overboard. A half hour later the curtain of rain was blown aside for the last act.

Lieutenant (jg) Sheldon Briggs described his feelings: "I was very much impressed as we went into Roi Island with the apparently carefree attitude with which we practically walked up to the Japanese back yard and with impudence sat there and got our troops and ships ready just to walk right in and take their island. I was also very much impressed with what seemed to me was a stopping of time, time just seemed to stand perfectly still as we all formed up and prepared to go into the beach. I have noticed this on other occasions afterwards, the fact that time just seems to stand absolutely still for just a few seconds before men actually go in to do or die, and many die, you know. . . ."

The Marines quickly pushed across treeless Roi, capturing the excellent airfield and seventy skeletons of Jap planes. By the middle of the afternoon the island was secured except for some isolated groups of die-hards holed up in the drainage system under the airstrip. The next morning these were sprayed out with bullet and flame.

Namur was harder to crack, for the remains of what had been an intricate system of blockhouses had to be overcome. Resistance was isolated, for as Secretary Forrestal's aide, Captain John E. Gingrich, said, "the bombardment and bombing of the island disrupted any possibility of organized resistance. At the time of the landing on D-Day-plus-1 the opposition was scattered with no opportunity for the Japanese to organize. The operation then consisted of destroying the isolated groups of Japanese in their pillboxes and cement blockhouses —which incidentally were two feet thick and reinforced with railroad iron and heavy steel, so that you had to get a direct hit on them with a major caliber shell or bomb to put them out of business. The Marines used flame throwers to dislodge the Japs, who crept all the way back into the underground ammunition stowages. The flame-throwers blew up the ammunition and blew up the Japs inside. But that also blew up a number of our own Marines so the use of flame throwers had to be forbidden in places where ammunition might be stowed, so the Marines just went in with a flashlight and Tommy gun and simply dug the Japs out."

On D-plus-2-Day, February 2, James V. Forrestal explored the islands with Admiral Spruance, General "Howling Mad" Smith, Admiral Conolly, and General Schmidt. Quite an impressive surrender ceremony could have been arranged except for the absence of the party of the second part. Lying with sightless eyes beneath the smoldering rubble was Rear Admiral Yamata, Imperial Japanese Navy, late commander of Namur.

Shortly after noon of D-plus-2-Day the island was declared secured. Garrison troops were landed. The assault troops were withdrawn to rest and be refitted for the capture of Eniwetok to the westward, nearly three months earlier than originally planned.

"Originally the Pacific Fleet forces involved in the capture of Kwajalein were to have gone to the South Pacific for the support of an operation Northwest of the Solomons. This operation was to have been followed by the capture of Eniwetok, the westermost atoll in the Marshalls and the key position in the Japanese air pipe line between Truk and the by-passed atolls in the Marshalls. It was decided to proceed as soon as possible with the capture of Eniwetok. With Eniwetok in our hands we would have complete control of the Marshalls and we would have the base needed for future operations in the Central Pacific, whether these operations were against Truk or the Marianas, which was as yet undecided. The Japanese would be given the minimum of time in which to build up their defenses with the additional troops they had recently put into Eniwetok." (Lecture by Admiral Spruance, October 30, 1946, to the Royal United Service Institution at London.)

The world had never before seen naval power used so devastatingly. Admiral Nimitz in his report said: "It must be appreciated that these assaults and seizures could not possibly have been accomplished so expeditiously with such minor losses without the bombardment preparation exceeding in duration and intensity anything previously known to warfare except possibly that at Verdun in World War I. It had been estimated that 50% of the Japanese were killed by the air, naval, and artillery bombardment prior to the assault, not to mention destruction of defenses and equipment and the stunning effect on the morale and fighting capacity of the survivors. In the Red Beach area at Kwajalein everything was reduced to rubble so that it was impossible to even visualize what 90 per cent of the installation originally consisted of. . . ."

The score in blood was as impressive as the material destruction. The enemy dead totaled 8,122 for Kwajalein and Roi-Namur against

318 Americans killed and missing. Of the 437 prisoners taken, 290 were Korean. Most of our 42,546 troops were unscratched.

MAJURO, LYING AT THE MIDPOINT OF THE JALUIT-Maloelap-Mili triangle in the Marshalls, fell without loss of a man. It had been abandoned as a Japanese base years before. On February 17 United States forces assaulted Eniwetok, defended by 1,000 troops of the 1st Amphibious Brigade of the Imperial Japanese Army; by the time the island was secured the next day none of them was alive.

Closely articulated with the capture of Eniwetok was the first carrier strike on Truk in the Carolines, base of the Combined Fleet and the super-battleship *Mushashi*. Ringed by a reef which made naval gunfire impractical, Japan's "Gibraltar of the Pacific" could only be attacked by air. In a two-day strike on February 17-18, 1944 Mitscher launched seventy-two planes against the island's defenses, while his pilots downed thirty planes, destroyed three hundred and sixty-five on the ground, and sank 200,000 tons of enemy shipping—including two auxiliary cruisers, one destroyer, two submarine tenders, one aircraft ferry and twenty-three merchantmen. It was by far the most severe blow yet suffered by Japan, and it established a pattern of things to come for Mitscher's Fast Carrier Forces.

While the Navy consolidated its gains and girded for the assault on the Marianas six months later, other events took place in the Pacific conflict.

On June 6, 1944 submarine U.S.S. *Harder* was on war patrol in Sibutu Passage, the narrow strait which separated the northeast corner of Borneo from the big Japanese naval base of Tawi Tawi. Her skipper was the legendary Lieutenant Commander Samuel D. Dealey of Dallas, Texas, a Congressional Medal of Honor winner, who subsequently lost his life in an ill-fated attack on an enemy convoy. He is the subject here of an excerpt by Vice Admiral Charles A. Lockwood, Commander Submarines Pacific, and his collaborator, Colonel Hans Christian Adamson.

We join Dealey a few moments after a convoy has been sighted.

VICE ADMIRAL CHARLES A. LOCKWOOD

AND COLONEL HANS CHRISTIAN ADAMSON

II.

MEN AT WORK

The moon was full, brilliant, and climbing higher toward the zenith as the approach proceeded. True, there were intermittent, low cumulus clouds but this attack would have to be run very, very carefully to avoid detection. Radar depth at first (submerged to about 42 feet where the radar antenna would still be above water) and then full periscope depth might do the trick.

Sam Dealey planned to dive ahead of the target group and bore in to a position halfway between the port flank escort and the column of tankers. The enemy's base course, at first, plotted as 180 true with 30 degree zigs right and left at a speed of 14-15 knots, but as soon as he cleared Sibutu Passage the base course was changed to 240 true—straight for the entrance of Tarakan harbor, some 130 nautical miles ahead.

Dealey worked his speed up to 19 knots in a desperate attempt to pull ahead and still keep out of the range of observation of enemy lookouts.

Alas, for the best laid plans, at 2125 the moon broke through and flood-lighted the submarine. The nearest escort destroyer, some 12,000 yards away, sighted the *Harder*.

"It was immediately apparent," reads Dealey's log, "that he was headed hell-bent for the *Harder,* smoking heavily and showing a prominent bow wave. We turned tail toward the destroyer, made flank speed, and hoped that the Jap would get discouraged and return to his convoy, but he had other intentions (none of the friendly variety). His speed increased to 24 knots and the range was gradually whittled down to 9000 yards as he followed down our wake. (At 19 knots we left a wake that looked like a broad avenue for five miles astern.)

"It was painfully evident that our business with the convoy would have to wait until the destroyer was taken care of."

As the range to the pursuing destroyer shortened, Sam, expecting every moment to see the deadly orange flashes of gunfire erupt from her forward guns, quietly said to the O.O.D., (Officer of the Deck), "Sound battle stations. Stand by to dive. Lookouts below."

Hardly had the musical, blood stirring bong, bong, bong of the general alarm died away when he gave the order: "Clear the bridge. Sound the diving alarm. Take her to periscope depth."

As the bridge personnel scrambled below, the O.O.D. jammed the handle of the diving alarm twice against its stop and shouted, "Dive, dive. Take her to periscope depth," into the 1 MC—the bridge microphone.

The raucous, demanding "Ahgoowa, ahgoowa" of the diving klaxon rasped through the compartments; ship control men, already at their stations, deftly opened flood and vent valves; set the bow and stern planes to take her down fast. Vents spouted like a school of whales, the ship pointed sharply downward and the rushing seas rose over the hull. Meanwhile, with swift practiced movements, the engine and maneuvering room crews secured the diesel engines and shifted propulsion to full speed on the electric motors.

Comdr. Dealey, the last man to leave the bridge, yanked down on the wire lanyard to latch the conning tower hatch. As it slammed shut on its seat, the quartermaster was instantly beside him and spun the hand wheel which dogged it shut.

"Hatch secured," he reported.

The entire operation, which required perhaps one minute, had been without hitch or confusion. Whatever may have been the thoughts or blood pressure of these eight or ten men in the conning tower, no sign, except perhaps brightened eyes and a touch of excitement in whispered words, indicated any difference between this and a hundred other dives they had made in months gone by.

"Left full rudder," ordered the Skipper. "Course zero nine zero. All ahead one third. Make ready all tubes."

"Make ready all tubes," repeated the ship's Talker into his microphone. Tall, stalwart Pharmacist's Mate Angelo Locoscio, in undershirt and dungaree trousers, had been chosen for the job of Talker because of his good speaking voice and quick-thinking ability. Too, the demands for his medical services during combat were not likely to be heavy. In submarine warfare, all hands usually come back with whole skins—or they don't come back at all. Tonight, it could be the latter. Destroyers are not recommended targets for submarines. Their high speed and maneuverability make them difficult to hit and, in the event of a miss, vengeance from their 600-pound depth charges could be swift and final. Despite this dread possibility, officers and men went about their duties without fumbling or nervousness. Skill and assurance marked every action. Here and there possibly a wide-eyed newcomer gazed at the faces of the old-timers as though searching for a panacea to quiet the butterflies in his stomach. But, all in all, the atmosphere of the ship was one of confidence—confidence radiating from the Skipper. All hands knew they were watching an expert at work. This was a situation made to order for Sam Dealey and his crew.

"All tubes are ready, sir, reported the TDC (Torpedo Data Computer) officer, Lieut. Tom Buckner.

"Up periscope," ordered Sam; "stand by after tubes."

For the first time that night a look of grim determination came into his face. He had slowed the submarine's speed to 3 knots in order to allow the pursuer to catch up and also to reduce the telltale periscope "feather" to a minimum. Now, as he watched through the periscope with cautious 5- or 6-second exposures, he saw his enemy coming right down the *Harder's* old course at 23 knots, presenting a very easy fire control problem.

At 2159, with a range of 1050 yards, torpedoes set to run at 6-foot depth and with gyros on zero, the skipper gave the order: "Fire!"

The quartermaster at the firing panel slammed the silver-dollar-sized firing button for Tube Number 7; waited 8 seconds by the stop watch held in the palm of his left hand; slammed Tube Number 8; waited 8 seconds more; slammed Tube Number 9. Then he checked fire. Dealey figured three would be enough.

Meanwhile the Talker repeated back the reports from the after torpedo room: "Number Seven fired; Number Eight fired," and so on.

The sonarman, ear phones clamped to his head, also had reports to make as he crouched before his 'scope: "Seven running, sir; Eight running; Nine running. Hot, straight, and normal!"—music to any torpedoman's ears.

The torpedoes, each with a 750-pound load of Torpex, our latest high explosive, in its warhead, sped on with their freight of death and destruction.

Sam, eye glued to the periscope, saw the first torpedo hit just forward of the MOT (middle of the target). The second hit farther aft, and the run of the third was not observed. The target was immediately enveloped in flames and smoke, the tail rose straight in the air and half a dozen of his depth charges started going off.

"2203—Surfaced 1000 yards away," records the *Harder's* patrol log, "watched the destroyer go under, and headed back toward the spot where it had been. A lone life buoy burned over a large oil slick—but there was no ship and there were no survivors to be seen."

The last moments of the Jap DD were observed through the periscope or from the bridge by the Skipper, most of the fire control party, the bridge lookouts, and Capt. Murray J. "Tich" Tichenor. The last named was operations Officer for Comsub's Seventh Fleet, commanded by Rear Admiral Ralph W. Christie, and was aboard the *Harder* just for the ride.

There could be no doubt about it, one enemy destroyer and her crew of perhaps 150 souls had gone to Davy Jones' Locker. As Sam and Murray Tichenor stood at the bridge rail watching the lonesome buoy light, Dealey said very little save to give orders to resume the chase. He was not exultant about his victory. Evidently the thought of having destroyed fellow human beings saddened him even though it was his life against theirs. Or was he thinking of Tex Edwards, his ideal throughout his early years, who had gone down in the same way in the Atlantic with his ship, the four-stack destroyer *Reuben James*.

But there was little time for introspection. Those three tankers were still on their way to the oil docks. All four of the *Harder's* main engines were put on the line at full speed. Because of the loss of time incident to sinking the Jap DD, it was now an even more desperate race to see who would reach Tarakan first.

As the diesels roared into action, Sam turned to Frank Lynch. "Secure from battle stations, Frank," he drawled. "Let the off duty hands get some sleep."

Fate and the Imperial Japanese Navy, however, decreed otherwise. Just two minutes later, at 2217, the radar operator picked up another ship contact at 14,000 yards, evidently a destroyer moving at high speed and headed directly for the *Harder.*

Again the bong, bong, bong of "Battle Stations" was followed by "Dive, dive," and the submarine slid down to radar depth so as to track her opponent more accurately. If this DD was looking for trouble, Dealey was in the mood to give it and, instead of turning away, he headed for the destroyer.

When the range had closed to 8000 yards, Sam increased submergence to periscope depth. However, he had difficulty in obtaining good periscope ranges because the intermittent moonlight did not illuminate the target well enough.

"At 2242," reads the *Harder's* log, "with an estimated range of 1250 yards, with 80 degrees port track angle and target speed of 12 knots, fired 6 bow tube shots with torpedoes set at 6 feet and diverging spread.

"Both range and estimated target speed are believed to have been in error, though 'sound' reported the first two shots running erratic. All torpedoes missed as target made a figure S while combing their tracks. The destroyer turned and headed for the *Harder.* Rigged for silent running, depth charging, and went to 300 feet. Five depth charges exploded as we reached depth."

The enemy's counterattack was not too severe, but a personnel casualty—one caused by an error of a new stern planesman—nearly brought a tragic ending to the *Harder's* triumph. This youngster, whom Dealey with characteristic consideration does not name, observing the plane indicator inoperative—the interior communication (I.C.) circuit had been cut out for silent running—thought he had lost power on the planes and made a quick shift to hand operation. Then he wrongly put the planes on dive instead of rise as the submarine passed 300 feet. Controlling the planes by hand is slow and before the Diving Officer realized the lad's mistake, the ship took a 15-degree down angle and went to a dangerous depth, well beyond that for which she was designed. All available men were rushed from forward to aft to right the ship. The pandemonium which resulted can well be imagined. The rushing of alarmed men through the control room, the crashing of loose gear, and the noise of hardsoled shoes clattering on the steel decks might have shaken the nerve and stampeded the thinking of the most rugged submariners—but not Sam Dealey and the Diving Officer, Sam Logan. They did not stampede easily and their quick thinking and quick orders undoubtedly saved the *Harder* from sharing the watery grave of the Japanese destroyer she had just sunk.

Before the men could be gotten forward again, the *Harder* took a 15-degree up angle and shot up to 250 feet.

Suddenly, over the ship's intercom came a frightened voice: "Hot run in Number 9 Tube."

Frank Lynch and Tom Buckner took off like broken field runners for the after torpedo room. A hot run in a tube can be extremely dangerous.

When the *Harder* took this sudden rise angle, her tail was flung sharply down and the stop bolt in Number 9 tube had carried away. This permitted its torpedo to slide downward past the tripping latch, thus starting the electric propelling motor. Fortunately, this was a Mark 18 electric "fish," a missile that runs at a lower rate of speed than the so-called steam torpedo. The latter high-speed type creates terrific heat which might fuse the steel shell of the torpedo to the inside of the tubes. The truly terrifying thing about such a casualty is the haunting fear that the warhead might be detonated. So far as is known, that tragedy has never happened.

The *Harder's* torpedo eventually ran its batteries down, but the piercing scream of its racing propellers sent plenty of chills up and down the spines of the after torpedo room personnel.

"This whole incident," wrote Sam in his log, "was a personnel casualty which never should have occurred but, considering the noise and concussion of the depth charging at the moment, the Commanding Officer considers that the officers and crew—consisting in part of 20 men on their first cruise—acted with admirable courage and calmness. It is described in detail in the hope that it may help some other sub to avoid a similar experience."

Depth charging continued until midnight and evasive maneuvers opened the submarine out from her attacker. Welcome negative gradients were found on the bathythermograph at 150 feet and 280 feet and these were utilized to lose the destroyer.

Negative gradients are layers of colder water which give good protection to a submarine because they deflect the echo-ranging pings of the pursuing destroyers. Dealey's standard procedure for shaking off a DD was to "keep the guy astern, go deep, and be patient," as he expressed it. This plan had much to recommend it, for, by keeping the stern of the *Harder* toward her pursuer, the smallest target was presented and the "pings" of the searching vessel might be rendered inaccurate by the disturbed water of the submarine's wake current.

When the *Harder* finally surfaced at 0036 of 7 June there was no hope of beating the tankers to Tarakan, so Sam again set a course for Sibutu Passage and his secret mission.

At 0528, with day breaking and enemy airfields too close for comfort, the *Harder* submerged but had a slight misadventure with a reef and was forced to blow ballast tanks, surface, and back clear. Miraculously, none of her delicate sound heads and depth-finding gear were damaged. Fortunately, too, no planes were about, and Navigator Frank Lynch was able to obtain a navigational fix which showed the sub to be far to southwestward of its dead-reckoning position. The 2- to 4-knot current—its direction governed by the flood and ebb tides—which sweeps through Sibutu probably accounted for that.

The *Harder's* adventures for the day were only just beginning, however. She attempted to make use of a rain squall to cover her surface run northward in order to gain more distance toward her objective. This attempt was thwarted in mid-morning by a plane which chased her down but dropped no bombs.

After that she remained submerged and bucked the heavy current with a paltry 5 knots.

"At 1134," continues the log, "the periscope watch sighted a Fubuki type destroyer at a range of 4000 yards, angle on the bow 20 port. (It might have been summoned by the plane or it might have been sent out to avenge the loss of a sister ship the night before.) Sounded battle stations and headed for target."

There was nothing hesitant about the way Sam Dealey handled the situation. Only two months before, in April, Cominch (Commander-in-Chief U.S. Fleet) Fleet Adm. E. J. King had raised the priority of destroyers as torpedo targets to a position above cargo ships. Prior to that time, because of the scarcity of torpedoes, the doctrine had been to avoid enemy destroyers. Now that torpedoes were more plentiful and fleet engagements imminent—Cominch was eager to cripple the enemy fleet. The torpedoes of Japanese destroyers were very formidable, long-range weapons which had wrought havoc among our ships in the Solomons Campaign. Adm. King wanted that menace removed.

To Sam Dealey this expressed desire was an order—one which he was glad to obey. He remembered the *Reuben James*.

"At 3000 yards," wrote Dealey, "the destroyer headed directly at us. (He may have sighted our periscope.) Stood by with four tubes ready forward, to fire down his throat. Angle on bow changed from zero to 10 degrees starboard, then quickly back to 15 degrees port. He was using a fast constant helm (a type of zigzag). At 650 yards, with 20 degrees port track, gyros on zero and a torpedo spread of ¼ a degree, commenced firing just as target started swinging back. Fired one- two- three in rapid succession (about 5 seconds interval). Number Four wasn't necessary! Fifteen seconds after the first shot was fired, it struck the destroyer squarely amidships. Number Two hit just aft. Number Three missed ahead. Ordered right full rudder and ahead full to get clear of the destroyer. At range of 300 yards we were rocked by a terrific explosion believed to have been the destroyer's magazine. Less than one minute after the first hit, and nine minutes after it was sighted, the destroyer sank tail first, observed by the Commanding Officer, the Executive Officer, and Captain Tichenor."

As Murray Tichenor, eye glued to the periscope was saying, "Scratch destroyer number two," the sonar man sang out: "Contact, Captain. Fast screws. Bearing zero nine zero."

Tichenor jumped back from the periscope. Dealey seized the training handles and swung it to starboard, took a quick look and then: "Down 'scope. All ahead full. Take her down fast. Three hundred feet. Rig for depth charge. Rig for silent running."

The Talker relayed the orders via the squawk boxes and the sound of closing watertight doors and ventilation flappers could be heard throughout the ship. Ventilation motors and all others not vitally needed were stopped. Some men wearing hardsoled shoes removed them. Some shifted into sneakers. Unconsciously the pitch of voices dropped.

The *Harder*, slanting sharply downward, had almost reached her depth. Dealey turned to the Exec. "Frank," he said, "slow to creeping speed and bring that destroyer astern. Secure from battle stations. I'm going to catch forty winks."

"Aye, aye, sir," said Lynch, but before Dealey could reach his cabin, a pattern of five depth charges landed above them. The noise and concussion were terrific. The submarine was thrown about like a toy boat on the waves. Cork rained from the overhead; locker doors flew open; light bulbs popped; loose gear was flung everywhere.

There would be no "forty winks" for Dealey.

"All compartments report damage," called Lynch into the mike.

And to Sam Logan, the Diving Officer: "Bring her back to 300 feet."

The terrific pressure had driven the ship down about 100 feet.

One by one, from forward to aft, the compartments reported no serious damage. The damage control detail was called to effect various repairs while the spare hands were attempting to bring order out of the shambles of the control room, when its forward watertight door opened and in stepped a tall Australian officer in short-sleeved shirt and khaki shorts. His uniform was immaculate, his high peaked cap sat his head at a jaunty angle; from mustache to shiny boots he might have stepped right out of Sandhurst. In him you saw the pukka British officer who led his troops across No Man's Land in World War I, swinging his walking stick and looking bored at Death.

"I say, Captain," said he in a perfect Piccadilly accent, "what's all the shooting about?"

"Oh," drawled Sam, "it's just some of your Jap friends, Major, having a bit of sport. They evidently don't want us to pick up your gang of saboteurs in North Borneo."

"Damned rude of them," muttered the Aussie, tugging at his mustache.

Thus did Major William L. "Bill" Jinkins, Australian Imperial Forces, cloak and dagger man par excellence, get his first real baptism of depth charges.

"Well, don't be discouraged," said Sam, "with luck we should get through this damned strait tonight."

The enemy counterattack lasted for two hours, during which seventeen depth charges and a number of lesser charges—probably ahead-thrown projectiles similar to our "mouse traps"—were dropped. Only superficial damage was done and nerves a bit jangled.

The *Harder* slipped away southward under a protective "layer" at 300 feet and at 1550 was able to return to periscope depth. Immediately two Fubuki-type destroyers were sighted and warhorse Dealey promptly sounded battle stations, submerged, and commenced an approach on them. However, at a range of 4000 yards the destroyers reversed course and disappeared.

Things were looking more and more ominous for the *Harder*. Echo-ranging was heard from several different bearings. The destroyers were obviously looking for her. First, two were sighted, then three. One of the latter detachment was equipped with a "bedspring"-type radar on her foremast, so that even night surface running was going to be hazardous. And maybe they had radar-equipped night flying planes.

Two medium bombers had been sighted during the afternoon and one of them had dropped two bombs, although not very close. Despite all her crawling to northward, the *Harder* was still about where she had started some twelve hours before.

And the plight of Major Jinkins' coast-watcher saboteurs was desperate.

At 1725 Dealey again sounded battle stations as he began an approach upon the group of three destroyers which were apparently patrolling in the area of his last attack. However, these too reversed course and the opportunity was lost.

Nevertheless, in spite of all these signs of a concentration designed to end the *Harder's* career, when, at 1840 six DD's in line of bearing were sighted heading for her position, it required all of the persuasive powers of Frank Lynch to convince Sam that discretion would be the better part of valor. Dealey evidently depended upon the judgment of his man-mountain Exec. to restrain the vein of recklessness which he undoubtedly knew ran through his body.

Of this incident Sam wrote in his patrol log: "Looks as though the *Harder* has worn out its welcome here. We felt as if we had a monopoly on the whole Pacific War this date. (Such popularity must be preserved.)

"Made a quick review of the whole picture and decided that discretion here was definitely the better part of valor. The battery was low, air in the boat was none too good, the crew was fatigued, and our navigational position in a narrow strait, with strong and variable currents, was not well known. I really believe that we might have gotten one or two more of the enemy ships, but under the above listed conditions, a persistent and already humiliated enemy (after two sinkings within 24 hours and just off a fleet base) would probably have developed an attack from which the *Harder* might not have pulled through. No apologies are made for my withdrawal. The gamble would have been made at too great a risk.

"Commenced evading to the northward in an effort to lose the destroyers and get on with our assigned task."

Well after the tropic night had fallen, the *Harder* surfaced with the destroyer patrol some ten miles to southward of her, and headed north with two of her four diesels on propulsion and the other two "jamming juice" into the depleted storage battery, or "can," as it was generally called.

The ship's radar screen was purposely kept trained away from the destroyers lest they have the recently developed German radar detector which would warn them of the submarine's position. All lookouts were utilized to watch for night fliers. The moon was full and brilliant.

Suddenly at 2206, radar contact was made on a small object dead ahead at 1500 yards. "It was immediately sighted from the bridge," records the *Harder's* log, "and at first believed to be a small boat. At 1200 yards it was discovered to be a low pinnacle sticking straight up out of the sea, with white foam breaking around it. Ordered full right rudder and came within 400 yards of grounding on this pinnacle as we reversed course. Special credit is due to Wilbur Lee Clark, RT2c, USNR, for his alert watchstanding which undoubtedly prevented a grounding which might well have been disastrous. Headed to the eastward while navigator again took star sights and checked our position.

"Radar now made contact on Sibutu Island light and correct position was established."

Captain Murray Tichenor also was credited with an assist in picking up this pinnacle that was part of the same reef on which the *Harder* had grounded at 0730 this same day. In fourteen and a half hours she had advanced exactly zero miles toward her rendezvous with Major Jinkins' cloak and dagger boys.

However, the thought of two enemy destroyers in their bag—two Rising Sun flags to be added to the rainbow they would fly on returning to port—served as some compensation for loss of sleep and wear and tear on nerves to which those aboard the *Harder* had been subjected for the last twenty-four hours.

The next morning, through the periscope, they sighted the northeast tip of Borneo slowly slipping by. They had won the Battle of Sibutu Passage. The rendezvous could be reached by nightfall.

BY FAR THE MOST AMBITIOUS OF THE PACIFIC AMPHIBIous invasions, Operation "Forager"—the assault on the Mariana Islands—was set for June 15. Although there are fifteen of these islands strung out along the 145th meridian east longitude, the main attack was to be upon Saipan, Tinian and Guam, all of which had been less heavily fortified than Tarawa and Kwajalein because until 1944 Japan did not believe they could be attacked. Nimitz's blueprint called for five hundred and thirty-five combat ships and auxiliaries, lifting 127,521 troops to targets which were as much as 1000 miles away from Eniwetok in the Marshalls. Moreover, the topography of the Marianas differed to a marked degree from that encountered in previous invasions. Mountainous and dotted with caves, the islands offered their defenders a substantial degree of comfort and protection, and the native populations of Saipan and of Tinian, three miles to the south, were fiercely loyal to Hirohito. Guam, on the other hand, had been a United States Protectorate for three generations and its Chamorros remained pro-American to the end. Lieutenant General Yoshitsugu Saito's combined forces in the islands numbered 31,629 troops, including Navy and Special Marines, two operational airfields, and the customary beach defenses and coastal guns.

Against this background Nimitz organized a Joint Expeditionary Force under Spruance, which was composed as follows:

Northern Attack Force (TF 52) commanded by Turner, and with Holland M. Smith embarked, lifting the 2nd and 4th Marine Divisions in thirty-seven transports, auxiliaries and LSDs. This force was formed in the Hawaiian Islands.

Southern Attack Force (TF 35) commanded by Conolly, with Major General Roy Geiger and the III Amphibious Corps (with its support and bombardment groups), all of which were to hit Guam on D-Plus One.

Floating Reserve (TG 51.1) commanded by Rear Admiral W. H. P. Blandy, embarking the 27th Infantry Division under Major General Ralph C. Smith.

The task forces put to sea on June 6, in clear weather and calm seas. It was D-Day in Normandy, and the news was greeted with wild enthusiasm. Rear Admiral Waldron L. "Pug" Ainsworth, commanding the bombardment group, sent this message to his heavy ships:

> "Today a large United States Naval Force of which your ship is a part is on its way to take the Islands of Saipan and Tinian away from the Japs, and make them give up Guam to its rightful owners . . . I promise you days and nights of hard fighting, as we must make the sea safe for our transports and pave the way for our Marines with plenty of shells and bombs. We are trained; we are ready; and we are going into close action. I have the utmost confidence in your ability to put the Japs where all good ones are . . ."

Air power for Saipan was provided by Mitscher's Fast Carrier Forces, which were divided into four groups as follows: under Rear

Admiral Joseph J. "Jocko" Clark (TG 58.1) were carriers *Bataan, Belleau Wood, Hornet* and *Yorktown;* under Rear Admiral A. E. Montgomery (TG 58.2) carriers *Bunker Hill, Cabot, Montgomery* and *Wasp;* under Rear Admiral Joseph W. Reeves (TG 58.3) were *Enterprise, Lexington, Princeton and San Jacinto;* and under Rear Admiral W. K. Harrill (TG 58.4) *Cowpens, Essex* and *Langley.* Two hundred miles east of Guam, on June 11, Mitscher ordered off the first substantial strike on Tinian and Saipan, and thereafter maintained the offensive despite ineffectual counterattacks by enemy land-based aircraft.

The pre-landing naval bombardment was initially provided by seven new battleships under the command of the man who had won for us the decisive Naval Battle of Guadalcanal, Willis Augustus Lee. On D-Minus-Two Lee's command let fly broadsides at Saipan and Tinian but with less than the desired results, because these battle-wagons were accustomed to high-speed rather than stationary targets, having previously operated only with carriers. On D-Minus-One, Rear Admiral Jesse B. Oldendorf took over with five old battleships, and for hours pumped high-calibre shells into the Saipan-Tinian targets. The results were a good deal better, because these ships had practiced their riflery at the Koolau Range in Hawaii. However, battleship *California,* while dueling with a shore battery near Tinian, suffered a hit which killed one man and wounded nine others. Destroyer *Braine* was also hit, with three dead and fifteen wounded. An enemy battery on Tinian's north coast scored another hit on battleship *Tennessee* the next day, June 14, D-Minus-One, and the casualties were eight dead and twenty-six wounded.

During the June 14 bombardment ninety-six frogmen, under Lieutenant Commander Draper L. Kauffman, hit the beaches at Saipan and blew up underwater obstacles there while charting the reef. Taken under heavy fire from all manner of shore emplacements, the Underwater Demolition Teams nevertheless accomplished the first daylight reconnaissance of the war. Their casualties were moderate.

For the story of D-Day, we turn again to Walter Karig, with Russell Harris and Frank Manson.

CAPTAIN WALTER KARIG,

LIEUTENANT COMMANDER RUSSELL L. HARRIS

AND LIEUTENANT COMMANDER FRANK A. MANSON

12.

MARIANAS COMPLETED

Ashore on Saipan—and offshore and over it, too—that part of the United States forces engaged in the primary objective of the Marianas operation was having less easy going than Mitscher's twice-triumphant fleet.

Although tactical surprise had been achieved on June 15, the Japanese had rallied quickly and used their massed mortars and light field artillery with vicious effect. By the end of the third day, the Marines and infantrymen lost very close to 5,000 men in killed and disabling wounded.

Saipan was no coral atoll such as the Marshalls and Carolines. It was no trackless jungle, like Guadalcanal. It was a heavily populated, intensively cultivated island of 81 square miles, containing three well-developed communities of which Garapan on the west coast was not only the largest but the capital of the whole Marianas group. From almost the mathematical center of the island volcanic action had thrust Mt. Tapotchau's peak 1,554 feet high, with lesser mountains, hills, and ridges radiating from in, merging into a high plateau on the north and melting away into the broad, richly arable lowlands in the south. Thus, in a space 12 miles by 5 or 7, every kind of fighting terrain was concentrated.

The Japs knew the island from more than twenty-five years of ownership and development. The American forces knew it only from aerial reconnaissance, and the information was very inadequate. It especially fouled up the landing and penetration of elements of the 4th Marine Division, with the result that a strong enemy force remained established—although surrounded—in the center of the American lines and four bloody days were spent in eliminating it.

The plan of invasion called for the 2nd Marine Division under Major General T. E. Watson to land on the left and to drive north against Garapan along the west coast. On its right, Major General Harry Schmidt's 4th Division was to cut east across the island to Magicienne Bay and then parallel the 2nd's advance on the east coast. The Army's 27th Infantry Division, under Major General Ralph C. Smith, had the job of cleaning up the southern fringe of Saipan and capturing Aslito airfield.

It took three days of bitter fighting for the Marine divisions to win the positions for their parallel march northward along the opposite coasts. By the end of the third day the 165th Infantry of the Army division had captured Aslito airfield, and with the 105th Regiment began the slow yard-by-yard task of herding the retreating Japanese into Nafutan Point the small southernmost peninsula of Saipan.

Four times were the United States ground forces subjected to mass Japanese counterattacks, and thrice in spectacularly unorthodox fashion. The first came on the night of D-Day. Puzzled Marine scouts reported something like an old-fashioned political rally taking place near Garapan that evening. There was much flag-waving, endless stump speeches from Tank-tops, with the enemy troops cheering and milling about in a sort of emotional debauch.

What was happening, as events soon proved, was that the Japanese in reserve were whipping themselves up to fighting pitch. At eight o'clock that night the enemy troops started down the shore road in columns of platoons behind their tanks, still waving flags and whooping it up for the Empire.

The Marines' 6th Regiment braced itself. Tanks and half-tracks began to converge to break up the parade, and word was flashed to the bombardment ships.

Closer and closer came the Japanese, stealthy as the Third Ward Chowder Club marching to its annual picnic. And then some officer either detected signs of diminishing ardor, which is doubtful, or was overwhelmed by the urge to deliver himself of some patriotic epigrams conceived after the march began.

Anyhow, a halt was called and the 2,000 troops clustered for a final harangue. It was almost too good to be true, thought the Navy's spotters ashore. The range was flashed to sea, and a few broadsides from the fire support wound up the jamboree as effectively as a thunderstorm at a strawberry festival.

The 25th Marine Regiment lost 400 yards of hard-won territory to a determined Japanese counterassault carried out in strictly military fashion, ground that was rewon with interest the next day. But the two other grand assaults, while not accompanied by the grotesqueries of the first, ended just as disastrously. In one the Japanese massed their tanks for what appeared to be the makings of a German-style Panzer attack, but sent their armored vehicles against the waiting Marines two or three at a time, without infantry support. One Marine company, "B" of the 6th Regiment, took care of the slow-motion piecemeal drive without trouble. The enemy lost 31 tanks to the unscathed boys of Company B.

Third of the extraordinary Japanese counterattacks was directed against the Army elements which had penned the Japanese into narrow Nafutan Point. Some 600 of the enemy burst out the woods on the night of June 26 yelling "seven lives to repay our country" and fell upon a battalion of the 105th Infantry. They did not stop to fight the surprised soldiers, but raced through their lines toward Aslito airfield, now in full operation thanks to the quick repair job done by the Seabees.

The infantrymen shot the berserk Japanese like shooting rabbits from a blind. Many of the enemy reached the airfield and began smashing up three airplanes before the startled Seabees piled out of their beds and put an end to that—and an end to several score Japanese. The survivors then went whooping off to the northward, where they ran into a small reserve group of the 25th Marines, who were thoroughly irritated at having their rest disturbed.

No doubt some percentage of the Japanese escaped into the hills and woods to join up with the main enemy forces, but more than five hundred dead ones were found scattered along the route of the lunatic lunge. As for their slogan, instead of each Banzai-charger taking seven American lives, the five hundred who were killed were accompanied in death by a bare half dozen infantrymen.

In the first three or four days of fighting, a dead Japanese was a rare sight for the advancing invaders. A dead enemy is almost as valuable as a living prisoner to the intelligence officers, and sometimes more valuable, for he cannot tell lies or destroy important papers on his person.

Yet for all the desperate fighting and vigorous shelling with everything from mortars to the ships' big guns, apparently few Japanese were wounded and almost none killed. It was not for days that the enemy's secret was discovered. They carried all their dead with them in retreating, and buried them secretly . . .

~~~~~~

EVEN BEFORE SAIPAN WAS SECURED INTELLIGENCE reached Spruance aboard *Indianapolis* of a developing Japanese counterattack by the First Mobile Fleet under Vice Admiral Jisaburo Ozawa. The enemy's A-Go plan for decisive action was predicated on the assumption that the United States Navy could be tempted into waters south of the Wolai-Yap-Palau line, where it would fall prey to Ozawa's fuel-conscious carriers and land-based aircraft. However, in due course this plan was amended so that the First Mobile Fleet was permitted to extend its operating range to include the Marianas. Fuel being a critical factor for the Imperial Japanese Navy, the decision had been made on the highest echelons and over the strong objections of certain members of the Imperial General Staff.

When Saipan began to receive the violent ministrations of the Fifth Fleet, A-Go received a green light. With five carriers, four light carriers, five battleships, eleven heavy cruisers, two light cruisers and twenty-eight destroyers, Ozawa departed Tawi Tawi for battle. Opposing him were seven carriers, eight light carriers, five battleships, eight heavy cruisers, thirteen light cruisers and sixty-nine destroyers of Task Force 58. After submarines *Redfin, Seahorse* and *Flying Fish* had made successive contact with Ozawa's forces, Spruance on June 14 ordered air searches to commence. By the night of June 18/19 both Ozawa and Mitscher were ready. The Japanese forces were lined up so that Ozawa's main body was about four hundred miles—and his carriers about three hundred miles—distant from Task Force 58. Mitscher, ordered to rendezvous with Lee while covering Saipan, received from Spruance a wrong estimate of the enemy's position and intentions. Had this not happened, Mitscher might have discovered the enemy sooner and opened the battle on his own terms. Nevertheless, first blood was drawn at 5:30 A.M., June 19 when a *Monterey* Hellcat sighted two Judys and shot down one; thirty minutes later destroyers downed a second carrier-based aircraft. Phase one of the battle of the Philippine Sea, "The Turkey Shoot," was underway.

This unique and stunning American victory is described by Lt. (jg) Stanley Vraciu, one of the great heroes of the battle, with his collaborator, Edward H. Sims.

LIEUTENANT (JG) STANLEY VRACIU

WITH EDWARD H. SIMS

13.

HELLCAT AT THE

TURKEY SHOOT

Pilots aboard *Lexington* had been aware of the impending battle for days. They had been disappointed when *Lexington* and other Task Force carriers did not steam west during the night of the 18th, toward the approaching enemy fleet, in order to launch a dawn strike. No strike went off next morning. And search planes had found nothing. It was nine o'clock.

Vraciu was one of twelve VF 16 fighter pilots on the alert. The squadron commander, Lieutenant Commander Paul Buie, would lead any scramble, Vraciu leading the second division (the second four-plane unit). But there had already been an aerial battle that morning. Japanese fighters based on Guam swarmed into the air at approximately 7:15. They were met by fighters from *Belleau Wood,* orbiting above Guam for that very purpose, and by fighters scrambled by other carriers. The score had been impressive: thirty-five enemy aircraft had been destroyed for the loss of one Hellcat! It was an omen of bigger things to come.

Though search planes had not located the Imperial fleet, it was nevertheless within range and had already launched an all-out strike at the U.S. fleet. At approximately 9:50 radar screens on various ships began to reflect the images of a large raid. At four minutes past ten, general quarters was sounded aboard *Lexington,* and as the warning bell sounded throughout the ship, Vraciu and the other pilots on alert dashed for their fighters. There was no question about it. This was it.

On the flight deck the scene was action in color. Engines were beginning to roar as plane handlers in blue hurried chores. Plane directors were dressed in yellow, hookmen in green, chockmen in purple, fire fighters in red, and there were two monsters in asbestos suits. It was, as Theodore Taylor so ably described it in *The Magnificent Mitscher,* "controlled frenzy."

In a few minutes Buie was roaring off the end of *Lexington,* now plowing through the sea at close to 30 knots, into the wind. After Buie had cleared, and three others, Vraciu, making an "end" speed of 90 knots, pulled back on the stick and dragged the F6F off the end of the flight deck.

Soon the twelve F6F's from *Lexington* were climbing into the west, Buie far out front and the others strung out behind. Vraciu had difficulty keeping up; his engine was throwing oil and Buie had a new engine, which could outperform his own. The skipper was going hell-for-leather for the enemy, as he should have been, but he was pulling away from Vraciu in the process.

Apparently some of the other Hellcats couldn't keep pace either. Vraciu noticed the skipper had lost his wingman, and several others were dropping back. He found himself with several additional fighters, which gave him six in all. Buie pulled away steadily, out front, as the fighters of many carriers streaked into the west, the morning sun at their backs.

The sky was full of contrails. It was a clear day, with a westerly wind and a bright sun as the blue-gray F6F's bit their way up into the higher altitudes. Radar scanners had indicated the enemy's altitude at 24,000 feet, and the defending fighters were straining to reach that height. First reports had indicated the enemy was 100 miles west, bearing 260 degrees.

At this moment the first interception of the enemy was made, not by *Lexington* fighters, but by those of Commander David Mc-Campbell's VF 15, from *Essex.* (During the day this squadron destroyed over sixty enemy aircraft.) After the first interceptions there was a lull in the battle.

Vraciu, meanwhile, had seen no enemy planes and no action. He now experienced trouble with his supercharger. As he reached 20,000 feet and attempted to put the engine in high blower, it cut out every time he pushed the throttle handle forward.

Dismayed, and disappointed because he had been unable to intercept the enemy, Vraciu reported to the fighter director aboard *Lexington*. He was ordered to orbit near the carrier with his six fighters. The F6F's circled their floating base in a wide arc, and waited. Vraciu had time to check his instruments, guns and gunsight. The engine gauges were normal. The engine was smooth and running cool, though it wouldn't shift into high blower. Vraciu could see other fighters orbiting above other ships in the distance. He continued circling . . . for ten, twenty, twenty-five minutes.

Another large enemy air armada is now on the way, unknown to Vraciu at the moment. Aboard *Lexington,* below, the radar screen detects the ominous spots. Suddenly, as the F6F's orbit above *Lexington*, the fighter director breaks in over the radio: "Vector 265!" Vraciu knows by the tone of voice that this is something big.

He banks into a 265-degree heading and quickly pushes the handles which charge his six 50-caliber guns. He checks the gunsight, which is operating properly, and glances behind to see if his comrades are in proper formation. To the side he can see other Hellcats pointed in the direction he is flying, obviously vectored by other carriers to the bogeys approaching from the west.

For ten minutes the Hellcats streak westward . . . down below fighter directors warn the enemy gaggle is very close. Vraciu estimates he is twenty-five miles west of *Lexington*. At that instant he sees them! Three unidentified specks in the sky ahead! "Tally-ho!" he yells into the mike. He is not sure of the identity of the three strangers. They're slightly below the Hellcats ahead. And this can't be the enemy armada.

Vraciu, known for keen eyesight, scans the sky, up and down. The three specks are ten miles in the distance. He looks all around them, then he takes a long look at the air space beneath them. Faintly . . . specks . . . dots . . . a mass of dots! It must be fifty. Vraciu again calls in over the mike: "Tallyho, eleven o'clock low!"

Now the tempo of events picks up. Other carrier interceptors spot the Japanese and rush to meet them. The enemy planes are dangerously close to the U.S. carriers. There is not a minute to lose.

Nerves tingle as the Hellcat pilots watch the silhouettes of the oncoming enemy planes grow larger and larger. They come closer and closer and still the two opposing forces continue on converging courses; the Americans want to intercept as far away from ships of the fleet as possible. Vraciu is so close he can see that the enemy planes are painted a light color, not the usual dirty greenish-brown.

There are Judys, Jills and Zeroes in the enemy gaggle . . . dive bombers, torpedo bombers and fighters! He reports this to *Lexington*.

Now the distance between the several groups of Hellcats and the big enemy formation closes and the Hellcats begin to rack into tight turns as they arrive overhead and prepare to make deflection or six-o'clock passes on the enemy planes, which are at about 17,000 feet.

Vraciu spots one of the enemy planes off to the side. He stands on his left wing and carves an arc, reversing his course, and rolls out on an approach from the rear port quart of the enemy. He checks the sky above for the three enemy fighters; they're nowhere in sight.

The big gaggle is so close to the fleet every Hellcat races to a target and the sky is soon filled with individual actions. Now the enemy aircraft ahead is almost in range of Varaciu's guns. But . . . off to the right, another Hellcat, moving up on the enemy's tail! Vraciu has spotted him just in time. The two pursuers are on converging courses! Vraciu slaps his stick right and down. The Hellcat sticks its nose down and with added speed roars beneath most of the enemy aircraft. Vraciu pulls clear, and turns back toward the melee.

He sees a Judy to the left of the enemy gaggle and slices in behind, pouring on throttle and closing the gap fast. This time he is determined to get the job done; the Judy widens in his gunsight glass and the victim ahead comes within range. Vraciu's finger is on the trigger. His canopy is smeared with oil, his vision obstructed, and he wants to make sure of this one. He is on him. . . . 300 feet, 200!

Now! He squeezes the trigger. The shock and thunder of the Hellcat's six guns silence the engine. Shells converge into such a close pattern that the Judy immediately begins to fly to pieces. Vraciu has only a second or two left, being so close. The F6F's guns throw a murderous stream of shells into the Judy's fuselage.

It's too much. The dive bomber in the sight circle erupts in a fiery explosion. Vraciu manages to steer clear of the smoke and bits of wreckage. In the excitement he shouts into the mike, triumphantly: "Splash one Judy!"

But the enemy is close to the fleet. No time is to be lost. Vraciu pulls the stick into his belly and back out and then back in. He clears his tail and then picks out two more Judys flying side by side. He will make another dead-astern approach. And this time he will try to knock down two on one pass. Checking the sky behind, and finding his tail clear, he dips the stick and starts down on the enemy gaggle, now so low that some of the dive and torpedo bombers are letting down in preparation for the attack on the fleet.

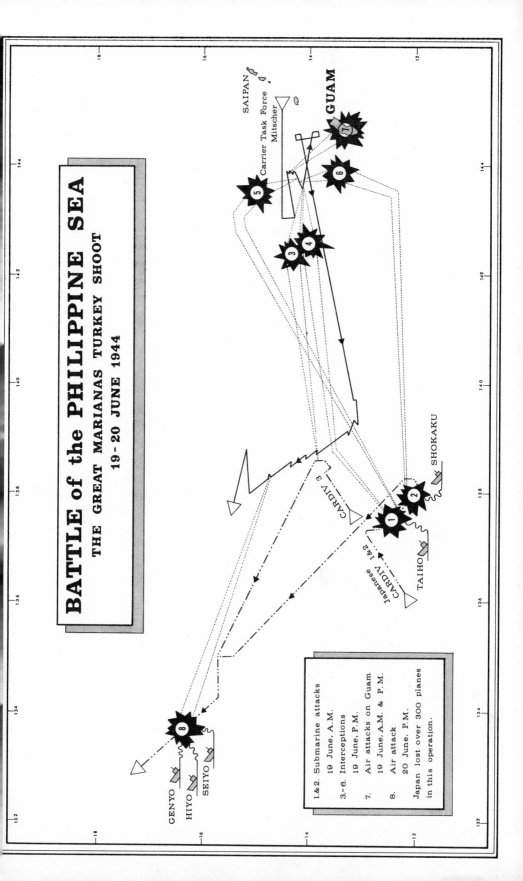

BATTLE of the PHILIPPINE SEA

THE GREAT MARIANAS TURKEY SHOOT
19 - 20 JUNE 1944

SAIPAN

Carrier Task Force
Mitscher

GUAM

SHOKAKU

Japanese 1 & 2

CARDIV 3

CARDIV 3

CARDIV 1 & 2

TAIHO

GENYO
HIYO
SEIYO

1.&2.   Submarine attacks
        19 June, A.M.

3.-6.   Interceptions
        19 June, P.M.

7.   Air attacks on Guam
        19 June, A.M. & P.M.

8.   Air attack
        20 June, P.M.

Japan lost over 300 planes
in this operation.

The air is full of calls and shouts, as other F6F's maneuver desperately to knock the enemy planes out of the sky before they can deliver their bomb loads on the U.S. carriers. The Judys and Jills, meanwhile, seek to avoid the U.S. fighters so they can carry out their attack.

The two Judys ahead fly on. Vraciu will first close the one on the right. He rams the throttle all the way forward. The big Hellcat roars and steps up on the Judys from behind. The rear gunner this time sees the F6F approach, however, and twinkles from his 7.7 machine gun catch Vraciu's eye. Responding, Vraciu opens with his six guns. The rear gunner continues his fire but the accuracy and volume of Vraciu's shooting immediately dooms the Judy, which staggers and begins to fall off on the right wing.

Vraciu keeps up the fire. A long trail of black smoke stretches backward. As the second victim wings over, the Jap gunner in the rear cockpit is still firing away. He goes down still firing; the burning Judy plunges to the sea at the bottom of a vertical column of smoke. Without a moment's hesitation, Vraciu slips left, with left rudder and stick, and is on the other.

The battle everywhere is fast and furious. Two enemy torpedo bombers reach *Lexington* at this time, drop torpedoes intended for Mitscher's flagship. *Lexington* nimbly dodges them. But *South Dakota and Indiana,* in the battleship force farther west, are not so lucky. *South Dakota* takes a bomb and *Indiana* receives a suicider.

But most of the Japanese planes have failed to penetrate the fighter defense. Vraciu is working on victim No. 3 as the battle reaches a climax. Following up his second kill, he is now within firing range of the third Judy, to the left. A short burst produces quick results; the Judy instantly catches fire. Flames and smoke streak backward.

Vraciu follows with another short burst at point-blank range, and watches the burning enemy bomber wobble out of formation and take the fatal dive. Three victories in a matter of minutes! But the attackers continue on course. Vraciu takes time to radio *Lexington:* "Don't see how we can possibly shoot 'em all down. Too many!"

With that sentiment he plunges back into the fray. He had pulled up to radio *Lexington;* now he leans forward in a dive at a fourth Judy!

The Judy ahead is breaking away from the formation. Vraciu curves in behind him, once again closing from the rear. Neither the enemy pilot nor the tail gunner seems to have caught sight of the F6F swooping down from the rear. In seconds, Vraciu is only several hundred feet behind his fourth victim. Carefully lining him up in the gunsight circle, Vraciu again squeezes the trigger.

The effect of his fire is even more devastating than before. The Judy immediately bursts into flame and wobbles wildly to the right. Victory No. 4! It is deadly accurate gunnery. Out the side of his eye Vraciu sees most of the Judys pulling to one side or the other, preparing for runs on the ships of the fleet, now clearly visible ahead and below. The Jills, down low, begin shallow glides, preparing to drop torpedoes at selected targets. Vraciu immediately turns away from his fourth burning victim, now out of control. With full throttle he points his nose at three Judys about to wing over into dive-bombing runs on a ship below.

Vraciu wonders if he can reach the three in time. The distance is short, but the first of the three Judys is almost over the ship target ahead. The Pratt and Whitney strains, and the F6F steadily closes. The blue-gray Hellcat is on the last of the Judys, but the first is over the target. Five-inch flack begins to dot the sky as Vraciu readies his aim to open fire on the third plane. He squeezes the trigger. Aim is accurate. Shells instantly strike the Judy and, as he closes the distance, pieces of the dive bomber's engine fly backward. As the fifth victim disintegrates, he can see the first of the three Judys diving on a big ship below.

Still at full throttle, he banks away from the fiercely burning Judy and aims at the second in the three-bomber formation. Down below, Vraciu sees the first Judy still diving. The Judy ahead now wings over into his dive-bombing run on a destroyer. Vraciu stands on a wing and starts down after him. He'll risk anti-aircraft fire, in an effort to bring down the dive bomber in a vertical dive. It's a dangerous feat.

The wind screams as the big F6F plunges straight down at ever-increasing speed. Ahead, the diving Judy is zeroing in on the U.S. destroyer. Vraciu sees five-inch bursts all around him, and as the altitude decreases the flak gets thicker. He will have to finish the job in seconds. The heavy fighter rockets straight down. He is rapidly overtaking the Judy. At terrific speed, he glances through the gunsight glass and waits . . . seconds. Now! The F6F's guns thunder and tracers streak straight down into the enemy dive bomber. Vraciu hangs on for a few seconds, wondering how long he can fire. At that instant he blinks at a bright explosion—where the Judy had been. The enemy's bomb must have detonated. Vraciu yanks back on the stick, blood draining from his head, and pulls out of the screaming dive.

As he levels out, and draws away from the destroyer, he glances behind to see what's happening below. The first Judy in the formation is now directly over a U.S. battleship, farther away. Vraciu watches, frozen, to see if the enemy pilot will succeed in crashing into the battle wagon. He picks up the mike and radios *Lexington:* "Splash No. Six! One more dive bomber ahead—diving on a battleship." However, the curtain of iron thrown up by the battleship's anti-aircraft guns explodes the dive bomber. A bright flash at a thousand feet! Vraciu breathes a sigh of relief.

Climbing for altitude again, he scans the sky for other enemy planes. Almost miraculously, the sky seems completely cleared of the enemy. In every direction he sees only Hellcats. The enemy formation has been received by the fighters of many carriers.

Still, there must be some of the enemy left; Vraciu looks down on the surface below to see if any Jills are closing the ships just above the water. He can find no enemy planes, either directly on the water or in the sky in any direction. The big enemy gaggle has been wiped out, probably to the last plane. Vraciu himself hasn't done badly; six dive bombers and twelve enemy airmen sent to a watery grave. This was a day Butch O'Hare would appreciate!

On board the carriers below, radar screens show the sky cleared of enemy aircraft. Judys attacked *Lexington, Enterprise* and *Princeton,* but all escaped injury. The fleet is in good condition. Losses suffered by the enemy are staggering. The air battle had raged up and down the line of ships, and the attackers were slaughtered as in no other interception of the war.

Jubilation reigns aboard many of the ships as Vraciu turns toward *Lexington,* the sky now clear, and prepares to land. Some pilots are already putting down on their carriers. Many have great tales to tell. Air Group 15, aboard *Essex,* destroyed more than sixty aircraft. VF 16, from *Lexington,* accounted for forty-four, for a loss of four. Vraciu's total of six is high for the squadron.

Now Vraciu is approaching from his assigned sector, and as he reaches the outer screen of ships around *Lexington,* American anti-aircraft gunners open fire on him.

Startled, Vraciu jinxes immediately, turns away from the fire. His "IFF" is operating normally. Why have the ships fired on him? IFF is a radar device designed to identify him as a friendly aircraft. Rather than take further chances,Vraciu detours around the fire, and heads straight for *Lexington.* Over the radio he offers some philosophy to the anti-aircraft gunners—too strong for print.

Soon he is approaching *Lexington,* which plows through the seas

into the wind, undamaged, taking aboard Hellcats. Vraciu prepares to
come down, circling to the left, banking into the landing approach,
tail hook extended. He is now to be the center of one of the great
human-interest moments of the war. Ahead, the landing signal officer
gives him the "cut," and Vraciu pulls throttle back all the way, feels
himself settling toward the deck. The oil-spattered fighter bangs the
deck, bounces, and then the tail hook engages. Vraciu is snapped to a
stop. The cable is disengaged. He taxies to the parking area, canopy
back, looking up toward the bridge, a grin on his wind-blown face.
Mitscher looks down from the bridge. Vraciu holds up six fingers.
Mitscher gets the message.

Vraciu cuts the engine, unbuckles belt and harness, and climbs out
on the wing. His crew chief and other deck personnel rush to his side.
They beam when he relates how the six enemy aircraft had fallen
before his guns. Another well-wisher hurries up to the twenty-five-
year-old ace. It is the small, tanned face of Marc Mitscher that
catches Vraciu's eye.

By now, photographers and other pilots are crowding around.
Mitscher comes right up to Vraciu and congratulates him personally
for flaming six Japs. He shakes the smiling pilot's hand feelingly, then
steps to one side. Vraciu answers questions for the others.

The photographers go to work, and Vraciu's "flight of six" becomes history. Comparatively unnoticed, to the side, Mitscher enjoys
the scene. Then, embarrassed, he asks to pose with the young flier,
with a qualification:

"Not for publication. To keep for myself."

THE FIRST DAY'S ACTION IN THE BATTLE OF THE
Philippine sea had cost Ozawa dearly: in addition to *Hitaka,* carriers
Taiho and *Shokaku* had fallen to submarines *Albacore* and *Cavalla,*
and he had lost 315 carrier and land-based aircraft. But the commander of the First Mobile Fleet was not quite ready to lay down his
arms. Parenthetically, when Ozawa was interrogated after the war he
was asked if the Turkey Shoot and the submarines' score had made
any appreciable difference in his plans. He replied: "No . . . but a
necessitated change in Japanese movements."

For the conclusion of A-Go, we present Rear Admiral Samuel
Eliot Morison.

14.

PHILIPPINE SEA:

ACTION AND CONCLUSION

June 20 dawned clear and fair, with a golden sunrise. In the course of the day, weak remnants of a cold front brought increased cloudiness and showers. Across Task Force 58 the wind blew due east most of the day, dropping to 10–12 knots' velocity at 0900 and to very light variables at night. In this American sector of the Philippine Sea, as we might call it, the sea remained calm with a gentle ground swell; temperature of both air and water was about 85° Fahrenheit. The glass held so steady, at around 29.85, that altimeter settings for the planes could be forecast with accuracy. Over on the Japanese side of the sea the wind was more often southeasterly than easterly.

Admiral Ozawa did not neglect search. At 0530 nine float planes went out from the van cruisers over a wide sector. They found nothing, and three failed to return. At 0645 Obayashi sent six planes to search the sector from 50° to 10°. One of these, at 0713, reported two American carrier planes. Admiral Kurita, in communicating this to Ozawa after a good lapse of time and receiving some land-based plane contacts via Tokyo, advised a quick retirement to Japan; but Ozawa evaluated the contacts as false (which some of them were) and persisted in his plan to refuel that day and attack the next. Subsequently he admitted that he should have delegated tactical command to Kurita until he could move to a suitably equipped flagship; if he had done so, Kurita would have hightailed out promptly and there would have been no battle on 20 June. Finally, at 1300, *Chitose* and *Zuiho* sent three torpedo planes searching the sector between 100°

and 130°. One of these at 1715 sighted a portion of Task Force 58 and so reported. But that was too late to help Ozawa.

With Commander Mobile Fleet and his staff practically incommunicado, there was great confusion about making rendezvous with the two oiler groups at lat. 15°20'N, long. 134°40'E, as had previously been ordered. The tankers were there and ready to deliver fuel by 0920, but many of the combatant ships were not, because (as Ozawa's staff navigator explained) *Taiho* had been used as a sort of focal point for navigation and *Taiho* had gone down. For hours ships milled around the rendezvous point, flag hoists being made and lowered frequently, light signals blinking, and officers coming as near to making nasty remarks over voice radio as Japanese decorum permitted. Many officers were exceedingly nervous lest enemy planes attack while the disposition was in confusion or fueling. Ozawa did not feel ready to give the fueling order until 1230, and, before it could be carried out, more rumors came in that enemy forces were closing, and the order was canceled. Not a single ship in the Mobile Fleet took in fuel that day.

In the meantime, Task Force 58 was closing distance; and if Mitscher had sent out a fair-sized search during the forenoon watch it would almost certainly have caught Ozawa in this confused situation.

At 1300 Admiral Ozawa's flag was transferred to *Zuikaku*. With improved communications the Admiral learned the bitter truth: that the day before his carriers had lost some 330 planes, leaving but an even hundred operational. Yet the only change that the tough old sailor made in his plan was to postpone his next strike until the 21st. Word came from Vice Admiral Kakuta, the land-based air commander at Tinian, that a good number of Japanese carrier planes had landed on Rota and Guam; true enough, but they were all shot up. And Ozawa assumed that Kakuta's air strength by this time had been augmented by planes staged in from Iwo, Yap and Truk, all ready to help him tear and rend Mitscher. No word had came from Toyoda to deny him a second attempt, so the plan held—strike tomorrow with everything he had.

As hour after hour passed without any sign of their enemy, the Japanese began to hope that he had had enough. First evidence that a stern chase was on came at 1615 when cruiser *Atago* reported she had intercepted American plane radio messages indicating that the Japanese had been sighted. Ozawa at 1645 ordered fueling attempts to be called off, altered the disposition's course from W to NW, and bent on 24 knots.

Atago was right. Task Force 58 had finally pulled up sufficiently so that its afternoon 325-mile search, launched at 1330, reached the enemy. The contact was made at 1540 by an *Enterprise* Avenger piloted by Lieutenant R. S. Nelson USNR, first carrier pilot in all these days of searching and fighting to sight a Japanese combatant ship.

Admiral Mitscher received the intimation that Lieutenant Nelson had seen something, somewhere—nobody could make out what, the message was so garbled—at 1542. A quick decision was wanted, for time was running out; the sun would set by 1900.

He alerted the task force promptly, and at 1553 informed Spruance that he expected to make an all-out strike, even though recovery must take place after dark. At 1557 Mitscher received Nelson's definite contact report, that the Japanese Fleet, spread out in three groups, was heading west at slow speed, apparently fueling. Eight minutes later, at 1605, Nelson corrected his first report and gave the Japanese position as lat. 14°30′N, long. 134°30′E. This placed the nearest enemy group over 275 miles from Task Force 58, which had now reached lat. 14°N, long. 139°E, about 370 miles west of Rota. It was the corrected report that *Atago* overheard.

The danger inherent in this decision, and the reasons why it was made, cannot be better stated than in Admiral Mitscher's own words:—

Taking advantage of this opportunity to destroy the Japanese fleet was going to cost us a great deal in planes and pilots because we were launching at the maximum range of our aircraft at such a time that it would be necessary to recover them after dark. This meant that all carriers would be recovering daylight-trained air groups at night, with consequent loss of some pilots who were not familiar with night landings and who would be fatigued at the end of an extremely hazardous and long mission. Night landings after an attack are slow at best. There are always stragglers who have had to fight their way out of the enemy disposition, whose planes are damaged, or who get lost. It was estimated that it would require about four hours to recover planes, during which time the Carrier Task Groups would have to steam upwind or on an easterly course. This course would take us away from the position of the enemy at a high rate. It was realized also that this was a single-shot venture, for planes which were sent out on this late afternoon strike would probably not all be operational for a morning strike. Consequently, Commander Fifth Fleet was informed that the carriers were firing their bolt.

A little pep talk from Mitscher ending, "Give 'em hell, boys; wish I were with you," the word "Man Aircraft!" at 1610, and the pilots ran across the deck as they never had before; chart boards under their arms, pistols at their hips, oxygen masks dangling from their helmets. At 1621 Task Force 58 turned into the wind, completed launching in the phenomenal time of ten minutes, and was back on its course at 1636. A full deckload was in the air—85 fighters, 77 dive-bombers, 54 torpedo-bombers—from the six big carriers present (*Hornet, Yorktown, Bunker Hill, Wasp, Enterprise, Lexington* and five of the six light carriers (*Belleau Wood, Bataan, Monterey, Cabot, San Jacinto.*) All Hellcats and Helldivers carried belly tanks for extra gasoline. A second deckload was alerted, but Mitscher decided to save that for next day.

At 1825, Japanese pilots sighted Mitscher's fliers; and they first sighted the enemy at 1840 after flying 275 to 300 miles at 130 to 140 knots. Nature had provided a romantic setting which, in other circumstances, would have made the Japanese sailors feel very sentimental. The lower limb of the setting sun was just touching the horizon; the thinnest golden silver of a new moon was setting, and about half the sky was covered with brilliantly colored clouds at altitudes between 3000 and 10,000 feet, which favored the attackers. Surface visibility remained excellent during the gathering dusk. The American planes were so near the end of their tether that there was no time to organize coordinated attacks. Fortunately for them, Ozawa had not yet reformed his battle disposition to receive air attack; the van no longer interposed between the larger carriers and the American line of approach.

Six oilers protected by as many destroyers made up the first group of enemy ships encountered; these had been left astern when Ozawa turned up speed. The seven Japanese carriers were disposed as before in three main groups, the approximate position of flagships *Zuikaku* being lat. 16°26′N, long. 133°30′E. Kurita's van, including *Chitose, Zuiho* and *Chiyoda,* and most of the battleships and heavy cruisers, were on a north-south line of bearing about 38 miles W by N of the oilers. Cardiv 2 (*Junyo, Hiyo, Ryuho*), screened by *Nagato, Mogami* and eight destroyers, was in a single disposition about 8 miles north of the van; both groups were making best speed on course 300° (NW by W). Flagship *Zuikaku,* screened by two heavy cruisers, a light cruiser and seven destroyers, was steaming on course 320° about 18 miles NE of Cardiv 2 and 40 miles NNW of the oilers. The screen was still unequally distributed, all the most powerful gunfire ships being with the van; and it was a very close screen—capital ships only 1.5 kilometers and destroyers only 2 kilometers from the center. Ozawa evidently hoped to compensate with intense anti-aircraft fire for his lack of planes. At about 1600 Cardiv 3 (*Chitose, Zuiho* and *Chiyoda*) had launched 16 planes to attack the Americans at a falsely reported advanced position, and this group was just being recovered when the battle broke. Including these and all other would-be strikes, search missions, near and distant combat air patrol, and a pathetic "interception force" of fifteen, Ozawa managed to get about 75 planes airborne to meet the onslaught of 216 from TF 58. The American pilots believed that not over 35 aircraft participated in the interceptions, which were made very close to the ships; but these few Zekes and Hamps did so well, in view of their meager strength, as to create the impression that only experienced pilots had survived the Turkey Shoot.

During the air-surface battle, which lasted about 20 minutes, every Japanese ship maneuvered independently, turning in tight circles and figure S's, and throwing up intense anti-aircraft fire in a spectrum of colors—"blue, yellow, lavender, pink, red, white, and black. Some bursts threw out sparkling incendiary particles; some dropped phosphorous-appearing streamers." Some of the American dive-bombers, including those from *Wasp,* concentrated on the oilers which they encountered first, and managed to disable two, *Genyo* and *Seiyo Maru,* which were abandoned and scuttled that evening.

Dauntless planes, Helldivers, and Avengers from the Clark and Reeves task groups concentrated on the carriers of Admiral Joshima's division. *Lexington's* pilots claimed to have sunk both *Hiyo* and *Junyo* and to have damaged *Ryuho,* making altogether 16 hits. But *Ryuho* was not hit, and *Junyo* not sunk. *Hiyo* was sunk by torpedoes, one of which the Japanese imputed to a submarine; but no submarine was about. Here is the story of what seems to have happened.

Four Avengers from *Belleau Wood* led by Lieutenant (jg) George

B. Brown USNR in company with four more from *Yorktown,* all armed with torpedoes, sighted Joshima's division on their port hand and *Zuikaku* to starboard, from 12,000 feet. After circling Cardiv 2 to size it up, the *Yorktown* planes sped over to *Zuikaku* as the biggest target. Lieutenant Brown, thinking that *Hiyo* was good enough game and noting a friendly cloud to dive through, led his four planes to attack her. A 180-degree turn was made in the 50-degree dive to place the setting sun behind the planes. As they broke through the cloud and began leveling off, they turned toward the carrier, spreading out so as to approach from different quarters. *Hiyo* looked, and acted, completely undamaged.

The last thing Lieutenant Brown said before he took off was that he would torpedo a carrier at any cost. He did, and the cost was heavy. His plane was hit several times by anti-aircraft fire as he was lowering for a final run; part of the port wing was shot off; fire burst out, filling the center section of the plane with flames which forced the radioman to bail out; and the radioman "booted" the gunner out. As the carrier made a sharp turn to port, Lieutenant Brown, now alone in the Avenger, pressed home his attack. And on the way down the fire burned itself out. His torpedo probably hit; that of his wingman, Lieutenant (jg) Benjamin C. Tate USNR, probably missed; but the third torpedo, dropped by Lieutenant (jg) Warren R. Omark USNR from an altitude of 400 feet, certainly found its mark and exploded.

On the retirement Lieutenant Tate's plane, which had been hit several times by anti-aircraft and had lost the use of its wing gun, was chased by two Zekes, but Tate worked his way into a cloud and eluded them. He then joined wing on Lieutenant Brown, flying very low. Brown's Avenger was badly shot up, and the pilot, severely wounded and bleeding profusely, could no longer steer a straight course. Tate finally lost contact with him. Lieutenant Omark, after fighting off two Vals and a Zeke, overtook Brown and led him toward "home" until long after dark; but Brown's plane, steering erratic courses, disappeared when passing through a cloud and was lost, with its intrepid pilot.

The two crewmen of this plane who bailed out during the attack made parachute landings safely, inflated their life jackets and became interested spectators of *Hiyo's* last moments. Battleship *Nagato,* cruiser *Mogami* and several destroyers steamed around her in circles, almost running down the men in the water, and then retired, leaving one destroyer to stand by. Fires spready rapidly over the carrier until she was burning from stem to stern. Three violent explosions were sharply felt by the swimmers, and several smaller explosions followed. As darkness descended, *Hijo,* down by the bow so that her propellers were out of water, cast a brilliant light on the surrounding waters. About two hours after the hit she disappeared, and the stand-by destroyer swept the area with her searchlight, looking for survivors. Both American crewmen were picked up next day when a part of TF 58 passed through the scene of the battle.

If the five *Enterprise* Avengers led by Lieutenant Van V. Eason that also took part in this attack had been armed with torpedoes, as Lieutenant Brown's had been, they might have sunk *Ryuho;* but they carried only bombs. Approaching in line, they were so tossed about by the anti-aircraft bursts—some from *Nagato's* main battery—as to be compared by the "tail-end Charley" of the pilots to a dancing blacksnake. Fighter planes led by Commander "Killer" Kane of *Enterprise* went ahead, strafing. *Nagato* and *Mogami* gave the "Big E" boys so much attention as to suggest they were seeking revenge for Midway. The large quantities of tracers that their anti-aircraft gunners shot upward, and the 5-inch bursts that showered out bouquets of fiery red confetti with white streamers, made beautiful twilight pyrotechnics but fortunately did no damage. Lieutenant Eason claimed eight hits and observed a tremendous explosion on the carrier, with flames 200 feet high. But whatever damage he did inflict was superficial, for it is not mentioned in the Japanese damage report of the battle, and *Ryuho* did not have to go home for repairs.

As the *Enterprise* Avengers pulled out of their dives, four Zekes got after them, but two broke away "to match two Hellcats that came screaming down out of a melee higher up." The ships continued to fire 5-inch shells at us all the way out to the rendezvous area; looking back, the sky was a mass of bursting shells, flaming planes, and the Hellcats and Zekes still fighting it out above.

Commander J. D. Arnold of Air Group 2 from *Hornet* was deeply concerned lest the biggest carrier escape, as she had at Coral Sea (in which he had fought), through pilots' concentrating on the smaller flattops. He therefore scouted ahead of a group that included *Yorktown's* torpedo-bombers as well as his own, selected *Zuikaku,* and ordered an attack on her. The "Happy Crane" had no Zekes to defend her, but she had not yet run out her luck. All but four of Arnold's Avengers had been armed with 500-pound G.P. bombs instead of "fish," and *Zuikaku* dodged the two torpedoes that were dropped. Dive-bombers from *Enterprise* and *San Jacinto* joined the fray. *"Zuikaku* was also strafed," said Captain Ohmae, "as I well know, since I was on the bridge with Admiral Ozawa when Commander Ishigura, standing by his side, was struck by a machine-gun bullet splinter. The three or four strafing planes were very brave and came in low." In this onslaught the big carrier received several bomb hits and five near-misses. The explosions started several fires on the hangar deck which quickly became unmanageable, and the order Abandon Ship was actually given; but before it could be completely executed the damage control party reported progress, the order was rescinded, and all fires were brought under control. *Zuikaku* returned to Kure under her own power and was repaired in time to get sunk in the 25 October battle off Cape Engano.

Four Avengers from *Monterey,* accompanied by eight from *Bunker Hill* and four from *Cabot* and eight *Bunker Hill* Hellcats, sighted the oiler group first; but the group leader, Lieutenant R. P. ("Rip") Gift of *Monterey,* radioed to his fellows, "To hell with the merchant fleet, let's go get the fighting Navy!" So they continued westward to attack Kurita's van—the *Chiyoda* group—at the southwest angle of the Japanese trapezoid. These Avengers, too, were armed only with 500-pound G.P. bombs. They made one hit on *Chiyoda* aft, which set her afire and wrecked her flight deck; one hit on battleship *Haruna* of the charmed life, which flooded a magazine; and a near-miss on cruiser *Maya* that caused fires to break out. Encountering only two Zekes over the target, they splashed one and made a fairly peaceful retirement. It was perhaps just as well that nearby *Zuiho* and *Chitose,* who counted battleships *Yamato* and *Musashi* in their screens, were neglected by Lieutenant Gift's formation.

Considering the lack of time to coordinate attacks, the pressure that American pilots were under to hit and run while darkness descended over the sea, they were successful. They had sunk another carrier and downed two thirds of Ozawa's remaining aircraft. Only 20 of the 216 attacking American planes were lost in action, and a number of their pilots and crewmen were later recovered. Undoubtedly the attack would have done even better if more of the Avengers had been armed with torpedoes instead of bombs. But air torpedoing in the United States Navy had never entirely recovered from the beating it had taken at Midway, in spite of the substitution of Avengers for the obsolete Devastators, and of better aerial torpedoes fitted with "pickle-barrel" false heads, enabling them to be dropped from higher altitudes and at greater speeds. Dive-bombing had established itself at Midway as the best method to sink carriers. Moreover, few big ships suitable as torpedo targets had been encountered by the carrier planes for a year. All this added up to neglect of air torpedoing in the United States Navy; but the results of this battle reversed the trend.

As the Americans retired, there was no pursuit, and the only attacks were delivered within sight of the Japanese Fleet. Eight torpedobombers from *Cabot* and *Monterey,* and dive-bombers from *Enterprise* and other carriers which were retiring after attacks on *Chiyoda, Hiyo* and *Zuikaku,* were jumped by six or seven Hamps from high altitude. Commander Ralph L. Shifley and his wingman, Lieutenant (jg) Gerald R. Rian USNR, both flying Hellcats from *Bunker Hill,* saw that the Avengers were likely to get into trouble and went after the Hamps with great skill and energy. They saw one splash and another depart from the scene, smoking; actually only one pilot of this Japanese group returned safely to *Zuikaku,* claiming a bag of 19 American planes for himself and his fellows. They did shoot down two Helldivers before encountering Shifley and Rian, but none of the Avengers were even damaged.

Seven torpedo-bombers, which Ozawa had caused to be launched from *Zuikaku* half an hour before the Americans struck, turned back without finding anything. On their way home they crossed the returning American planes but avoided conflict. The story of a Japanese Val's following our planes and making three attempts to light on *San Jacinto,* though firmly believed on board that "flagship of the Texas Navy," is probably apocryphal, as is the tale of a second enemy plane being waved off from *Wasp.* As far as I can determine, not a single Japanese plane came within sight of Task Force 58 on 20 June.

Ozawa would not yet accept defeat. At 1900, just as the air battle ended, he actually ordered a surface counterattack. Admiral Kurita and the entire van, together with heavy cruisers *Myoko* and *Haguro* and a destroyer squadron, were ordered to head east and seek night action. At the end of two hours, since the position of Task Force 58 was still unknown to him, Ozawa reluctantly cancelled the order, and at 2205 Kurita reversed course to rejoin the main body. He never could have reached Mitscher, who at that moment lay about 230 miles to the southeast, recovering planes.

At noon of 20 June, Ozawa had about 100 carrier planes operational in the Mobile Fleet. By nightfall he had lost 65 more, and, of the 27 float planes remaining at noon, 15 were destroyed. His own flag log of Operation A-Go ends this day with the significant entry:—

Surviving carrier air power: 35 aircraft operational.

Thirty-five planes out of the 430 which he had had in his hangars and on his flight decks the morning of 19 June!

Complete darkness fell by 1945. The weather front had moved south during the day, the sky was overcast and the night very dark, and planes returning from the battle were a long way from "home." The pilots knew it was nip-and-tuck whether their fuel would hold out; one, Lieutenant (jg) Milton F. Browne USNR of *Wasp*, had to ditch halfway home, as his gas tank had been punctured. Although TF 58 had slightly closed Ozawa's fleet during the hours subsequent to launching, the carriers had to turn to windward to recover planes. Their distance from the Japanese targets now varied from 240 to 298 miles, depending on the time the planes started to return, and the distance they had to consume while orbiting before having a chance to land. This, and flying at high speed in the hope of beating nightfall, caused many to run out of gas.

Admiral Mitscher opened out his three task groups so that 15 miles lay between them, to give maneuvering room for night recovery. At 1912, for the second time in this operation, he proposed that Admiral Lee's battle line be released from protecting the carriers while they were steaming to windward for plane recovery, and that they push northwesterly at top speed, to be in a position to engage Ozawa's Fleet at daylight. Admiral Lee, apparently, was not consulted, and Spruance a second time refused to allow the battle line to separate. "Consider Task Force 58 should be kept tactically concentrated tonight," he replied, "and make best practicable speed toward the enemy so as to keep them in air striking distance." He figured out that Lee had no chance of overtaking Ozawa, and wished to keep his battle line within signaling distance in order to dispose of any damaged ships that the aviators might encounter next day.

At 2045 the returning planes began to circle over the American carriers. Task Force 58 turned into the light east wind and bent on 22 knots. Admiral Mitscher then made a decision that endeared him to the hearts of all naval aviators; he gave orders to light up the carriers in bold disregard of enemy submarine or plane menace.

That night recovery, lasting two hours, was the most spectacular event of these two crowded days. Lieutenant Commander Evan P.

Lt. Cdr. Lyndon B. Johnson, USN. *Navy Department*.

The leaders of the attack on Tarawa, in the Gilbert Islands, tensely watch the action ashore from the bridge of the USS *Maryland* (BB-46) in November, 1943. Maj. Gen. Julian C. Smith, USMC, is seated in the foreground; Rear Adm. Harry W. Hill, USN, is facing the camera in the background. *Navy Department.*

Marines charging ashore on Tarawa. *Defense Department Photo.*

One Marine, armed with a carbine and a bandolier of bullets, stands ready to go over the top as he waits for his buddy to toss a hand grenade into the Japanese on Tarawa. *Defense Department Photo.*

Marines storming Tarawa get a brief rest while one of their party (right, foreground) relays messages and receives instructions by field telephone. The heavy black smoke (background) is from a burning fuel dump. *Defense Department Photo.*

Only the log gateway *(torii)* of a Japanese Shinto shrine remains after the withering fire of the American invasion of Bititu Island, Tarawa. The arch in the background is believed to have been a Japanese gallows. *U.S. Coast Guard.*

A 5″ anti-aircraft battery aboard the USS *Maryland* (BB-46) shelling a beach in the Marshall Islands on D-2 Day, in November, 1943. *Navy Department.*

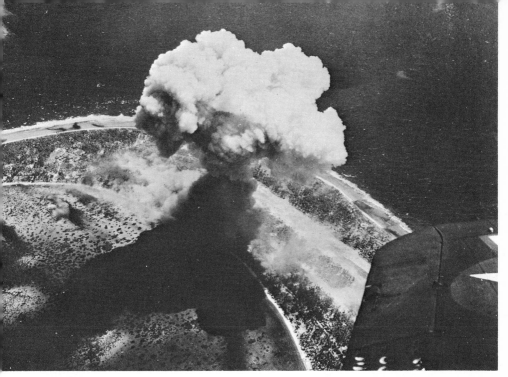

Kwajalein Island in the Marshalls. An ammunition dump explodes as a result of a direct hit from the naval bombardment the day before the land attack. The photograph was taken by a plane from the USS *Enterprise* (CV-6). *Navy Department.*

Fires burning furiously and a bomb exploding on Kwajalein Island on **D-Day**. Allied warships are lying off the atoll and shelling shore installations, while troops from the transports in the upper left come in to make beach landings. *Navy Department.*

Amphibious landing force preparing to land on Kwajalein. Two waves of small landing craft are seen making for shore. Photo taken by a plane from the USS *Coral Sea* (CVE-57). *Navy Department.*

A bomb crater on Kwajalein. *Navy Department.*

Invasion barges and amphibious tanks assembling for the first landing on Roi and Namur islands in the Marshall Islands on D-Day + 1. Taken by a plane from the USS *Chenango* (CVE-28). *Navy Department.*

Sailors receive mail on board the USS *Archerfish* (SS-311), just returned from war patrol. *Navy Department.*

A periscope view of a Japanese merchant ship, torpedoed by a U.S. submarine in the Pacific, settling by the bow. *Navy Department.*

Lt. (jg) Stanley Vraciu (VF-6), ace aboard the USS *Intrepid* (CV-11). *Navy Department.*

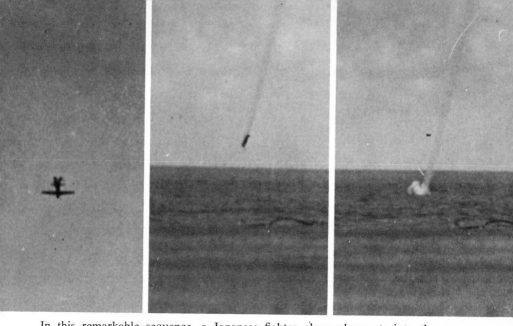

In this remarkable sequence, a Japanese fighter plane plummets into the Pacific off Saipan after being shot down during the U.S. raid on Jap bases in the Marianas, February 22, 1944. In the first picture a black spurt of smoke jets from the tail of the plane; in the second the plane is snapped a few feet above the water, leaving a black trail to mark its plunge; in the final photo a splash of foam marks its last resting place. *Navy Department.*

While a heavy cruiser fires a broadside, loaded landing craft move toward shore on D-Day at Saipan in the Marianas. *Navy Department.*

Naval guns, silhouetted in the sunrise over Saipan on D-Day, point toward Mt. Tapotchau, the highest mountain on the island. Smoke billows from shelled shore installations and landing craft, in the distant background, carry assault troops to the beaches. *Navy Department.*

Below left:
Vice Adm. M. A. Mitscher, USN, CTF 58.3, aboard the USS *Lexington* (CV-16) in the battle of Saipan in the Marianas. *Navy Department.*

Below right:
An underwater demolition team (UDT) in action during the Saipan landing. *Navy Department.*

This is the disconcerting sight which met the eyes of the Japanese defenders of Saipan when they looked seaward on that D-Day morning. *U.S. Coast Guard*.

Aboard the USS *Indianapolis* (CA-35) are, left to right, Adm. C. W. Nimitz, Adm. Ernest King, and Adm. R. A. Spruance. *Navy Department*.

Fleet Admiral Nimitz (CINCPAC), Secretary of the Navy James V. Forrestal and Rear Admiral Sherman (Deputy C-OF-S, CINCPAC) are shown in the admiral's barge at Guam in 1945. (FADM Nimitz photo collection.) *Official U.S. Navy Photo.*

Below left: The U.S. submarine *Wahoo* (SS-238), standing in to Pearl Harbor after a patrol in which she sank one Japanese destroyer and an entire convoy of four ships. Flying from her periscope is a broom indicating she made a "clean sweep" of the enemy. Attached to her mast is a pennant with the ship's slogan, "Shoot the Sunza Bitches," and eight Japanese flags. The upper two indicate the *Wahoo* has sunk two Japanese men-o-war; the other flags indicate she has sunk six enemy merchant ships. The *Wahoo* was commanded by Lt. Cdr. Dudley W. Morton, USN. *Navy Department.*

Below right: A later photograph taken by Lt. Cdr. D. W. Morton, commander of the USS *Wahoo,* during a war patrol in which the *Wahoo* sunk eight Japanese ships. In this photo, a medium-sized Japanese cargo ship goes down just after being struck by a torpedo. *Navy Department.*

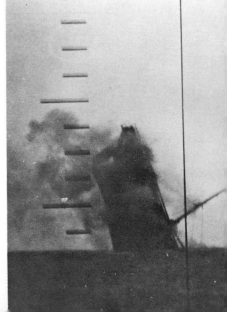

Aurand, who was sent aloft in a night-fighting Hellcat to help shepherd the flock home, had the best view. The scene made him think of a Hollywood premiere, Chinese New Year's and Fourth of July rolled into one. The carriers turned on truck lights, glow lights to outline flight decks, and red and green running lights, and flashed signal lights to identify themselves; all vessels of the screen showed red truck lights and their 5-inch guns threw up a liberal supply of star shell. Each group flagship pointed a searchlight vertically as a homing beacon. The night was pitch black with no visible horizon, and about sixty miles to the south a thunderstorm was making up, whose lightning flashes were mistaken by a number of homing pilots for star shell. Aurand made several trips over to the storm, turning on his running lights and rounding up lost fliers.

One of the best accounts of the night landings is by Lieutenant (j.g.) E. J. Lawton USNR of *Enterprise:*—

> We had almost reached the force when we saw the lights come on. It is clear that the task force did all in its power to make it easier for us to get home. Lieutenant Eason led us in over the *Enterprise* but her deck was fouled for some time. We circled for a few minutes, watching the lights of the planes below fan out in the pattern of the landing circle. But there had been too much strain in the last five hours to reduce things to patterns now; and inevitably, landing circles became crowded, intervals were lost and deck crashes occurred. Many planes—too many—announced that their gas was gone and they were going in the water. Others were caught short in the groove. Seen from above, it was a weird kaleidoscope of fast moving lights forming intricate trails in the darkness, punctuated now and then by tracers shooting through the night as someone landed with his gun switches on, and again by suddenly brilliant exhaust flames as each plane took a cut, or someone's turtleback light getting lower and lower until blacked out by the waves closing over it. A Mardi Gras setting fantastically out of place here, midway between the Marianas and the Philippines.

Lieutenant Eason's tank went dry just as he was approaching the ramp of *Lexington*. He quickly pulled his wheels up, made an S-turn to port, landing in the water alongside, and was rescued by a destroyer within ten minutes. A Helldiver from *Hornet* crash-landed on *Bunker Hill,* although waved off and given Very signals indicating foul deck. The plane up-ended with its propeller fast-lodged in the flight deck; then along came an Avenger from *Cabot* which, although violently warned to keep off, tried to land, knocked a wing off on a gun mount, and crashed the immobilized Helldiver, killing two and injuring four men who were working on the wreckage. Almost half the aircraft landed on the wrong carriers, and when noses were counted there were often found planes belonging to eight or nine different ships on one flight deck. Desperate pilots made passes at everything afloat. Ensign R. W. Burnett USNR of *Monterey,* waved off from his own carrier, mistook the red truck lights on a destroyer for those of a landing signal officer on a flattop, made a pass at the destroyer and splashed alongside. A boat from the destroyer rescued him and his crewmen before they were fairly wet. Another pilot, from a light carrier, said to himself that he wasn't going to land on her short flight deck; he would pick out the biggest damn carrier there was. He did, and found that it was his own!

By 2252 when it was clear that every plane had either landed, splashed, or been shot down, and as the carriers were formed up again into cruising disposition, the sea suddenly took on the appearance of a meadow full of fireflies in June. Pilots and crewmen, swimming or in rubber rafts, were blinking their little waterproof flashlights; and the trilling of the boatswain's whistles that aviators carried to attract attention added hyla-like music to this midsummer scene. Fortunately there was now a flat calm. The destroyers, using their 18-inch searchlights to spot rafts and swimmers, did wonderful rescue work, and all but one were so employed by Admiral Mitscher's orders; anti-submarine screening was completely neglected in favor of saving lives. The great laugh of the evening came at the expense of Lieutenant Commander K. F. Musick, torpedo squadron commander of *Bunker Hill.* He had splashed on an earlier operational flight and had been pulled out by destroyer *Hickox.* This time he ditched again for want of gas and was picked up by the same destroyer, on whose stack, next the painted miniatures of planes shot down, he found a caricature of himself to which a sailor was adding a "hash mark" to celebrate the second rescue!

Because of this hectic night recovery, plane losses on 20 June were much heavier than those of the previous day, but the casualties among aviators were almost the same. According to Admiral Mitscher's report, 6 Hellcats, 10 Helldivers and 4 Avengers were missing, and presumably shot down in combat; 17 Hellcats, 35 Helldivers and 28 Avengers were destroyed by deck crashes or ditching near the task force. The total complement in the lost planes was 100 pilots and 109 aircrewmen, but 51 and 50 were pulled out of the water that night, leaving 49 and 59 unaccounted for by daylight 21 June. An additional 33 pilots and 26 aircrewmen were saved on that and subsequent days. This left the net aviator losses 16 pilots and 33 crewmen. *Hornet,* the lucky carrier, lost 21 aircraft on 20 June but only one pilot and two crewmen, one of whom was killed in a deck crash.

Admiral Ozawa's problem of plane recovery differed only in degree from that of Admiral Mitscher. As soon as the last American plane departed, around 1930 June 20, the few surviving Japanese aircraft came home. Even less prepared for night landings than the Americans, the enemy aviators had worse luck, and the few of them that were left could ill be spared. What with splashes and crashes on damaged carrier decks, less than half of the 100 carrier planes that Ozawa had left early that afternoon were recovered; and only 35 of these were in a condition to fly again. But the engineering plant of every ship afloat was intact. So when Ozawa received Admiral Toyoda's order to retire at 2046 June 20, his 6 remaining carriers, 5 battleships, 13 cruisers and 28 destroyers were able to maintain a speed of 20 knots, ample for escape.

Spruance's stern chase had already begun, but it was not a relentless pursuit. As we have seen, he had rejected Mitscher's suggestion at 1912 June 20, to release Lee's battle line immediately in the hope of catching Ozawa. It was a mathematical certainty that even the faster and best-fueled ships could never overtake able-bodied units of the Japanese Fleet this side of Japan. Even if some of the battle line could have sustained a speed of 30 knots, which is doubtful, they would have closed only 120 miles in 12 hours, a little more than one third of the distance to the enemy. At Mitscher's recommendation, a force speed of 16 knots was maintained "in order to retrieve as many pilots as possible," and that was 4 knots less than Ozawa was doing. By 0130 June 21 the two Fleets were 327 miles apart, the Japanese bearing W by N (285°) from the Americans, and during the first three watches of 21 June TF 58 made good only 150 miles. It was actually losing distance on the enemy.

Spruance's only reason for pursuit under these circumstances was the hope of catching cripples or ships standing by them. For aught anybody on the American side yet knew, *Shokaku* and *Hiyo* were still afloat, and nobody was so optimistic as to assume that one torpedo hit had finished *Taiho*. A report received at 0130 June 21, from a PBM which had been shadowing the enemy force for two and a half hours, to the effect that Ozawas' ships were trailing oil, suggested that some were badly damaged. So, in the hope that either Lee's battle line or Mitscher's carrier planes would catch up with these lame ducks and their consorts at daylight, Spruance steamed westward at economical speed.

Task Force 58 recommenced searching only a few hours after recovery was completed. Several long-range night-flying Avengers were sent out from *Bunker Hill* and *Enterprise* between 0200 and 0300. Next, at 0600, each task group launched a deckload strike of Hellcats carrying 500-pound bombs in the hope of finding cripples. The pilots were instructed to return if they found nothing after flying 300 miles. Nothing did they find; but the Avengers picked up the Mobile Fleet and shadowed it until 0743, reporting the enemy to be on a northwesterly course, 360 miles distant from TF 58. Ozawa had opened the distance. He was already well beyond the effective radius of American carrier bombers.

When this information reached Spruance, it confirmed his belief that the main body of the Mobile Fleet was pressing homeward at a speed greater than Task Force 58 could possibly overcome. But he still cherished the hope of overtaking a few ships that had been slowed down by battle damage. Leaving Mitscher with orders to search for cripples and to seize every opportunity to strike, Spruance at 1050 June 21 directed Admiral Lee, now reinforced by *Bunker Hill* and *Wasp* for air protection, to push ahead at best speed, and himself at 1126 took *Indianapolis* forward to join the battle line. The carriers followed, making good about 15 knots; destroyers of the screen fished out several airmen en route.

By this time some of the destroyers with the battleships were dangerously low on fuel. So there was a further delay, from 1205 to 1454, while battleships fueled destroyers, steaming at 11 to 14 knots. At 1516 a 15-knot speed was resumed, on course 280°.

The Hellcats launched at dawn had now returned, with no information. The next search group, launched at 1500, combed the empty waters of the Philippine Sea for the hypothetical Japanese cripples. Spruance mentally allowed them four hours to make contact. At 1920 June 21, shortly after the sun went down in a big red ball, Commander Fifth Fleet issued orders that, if the late afternoon search sighted no ships, the entire task force would retire. None did they see, since none there were; so at 2030, when *Lexington* was at lat. 16°N, long. 134°40′E, the chase was abandoned and course shaped for Saipan. Lee's ships, having reached long. 133°55′E, right on the edge of the battle area of 20 June, searched carefully for survivors and made a very encouraging haul. Float planes from *Indianapolis, San Francisco* and *New Orleans* picked up nine men. Mitscher, too, sent off an abundance of low-flying searches and a number of destroyers to cover a wide sector from the position where Ozawa's ships had been attacked. Dumbo Catalinas and PBMs from Saipan were enlisted in the search, and these painstaking efforts were rewarded by the rescue of 59 aviators who otherwise must have perished in the Philippine Sea, so far were they from friendly shores.

At the moment Spruance abandoned the chase, the Mobile Fleet was about 300 miles from Okinawa, toward which Ozawa had shaped his course that morning. That evening (21 June) Ozawa called his senior staff officer, Captain Ohmae, into his cabin and dictated a letter to Commander in Chief Combined Fleet, offering his resignation. He expressed the deepest regret that he had lost this opportunity once more to lead Japan on the glorious path of victory. The defeat he ascribed to his own inadequacy, and to the pilots' want of training. Toyoda, after consulting with the navy minister in the Tojo Cabinet, refused to accept Ozawa's resignation. The veteran retained his command, only to be beaten again by Halsey in the Battle of Cape Engano and there to lose most of the carriers that had survived the Philippine Sea action.

In the early afternoon of June 22 a defeated and dispirited Mobile Fleet anchored in Nakagasuku Bay, Okinawa—the great harbor which a year later was to be renamed after General Buckner. Four of the six surviving carriers, together with battleship *Haruna* and heavy cruiser *Maya,* had to proceed to Japan either for repairs or for long-needed upkeep. Worst of all, the Fleet had brought back only 35 serviceable carrier planes.

Task Force 58 made for a prearranged fueling rendezvous with a task group of fleet tankers, about 220 miles east of the point where retirement had commenced. At noon 22 June the oilers were encountered; fueling commenced at once, continued at 10-knot speed, until nightfall, and was completed next day.

While Admiral Reeve's group was still fueling, there took place a remarkable single combat between a *Princeton* plane and a Japanese bomber. An Avenger (TBM-1C) piloted by Ensign Warren C.

Burgess USNR, on anti-submarine patrol at noon 23 June, sighted a Betty flying low over the water and heading away from the carriers. She was probably engaged in a routine search, from Yap or Palau. By making all possible speed—245 to 250 knots—Burgess overtook the enemy, then flying only 10 feet above the ocean. He made two low runs, firing with his twin .50-caliber wing-guns; but both times his guns jammed and he had to drop back. To continue with the account by Burgess's squadron commander, Lieutenant Commander F. A. Bardshar:

> Burgess decided it was time to change his tactics and splash the Betty without the aid of gunfire. He put his plane about two feet above her and sat there in an attempt to force her into the water. He succeeded in forcing the Betty to hit the water with her belly, but she immediately bounced back up to ten feet, her initial altitude, with no damaging results. Abandoning this procedure, Burgess retired to the Betty's starboard side and during retirement the TBM-1C's stinger was able to fire about thirty rounds into the after port side of the Japanese fuselage.
>
> Burgess next decided to adopt the Russian technique of chewing up the enemy plane with his propeller. This was also unsuccessful, although his prop. came within inches of the Betty's starboard wing. Feeling somewhat frustrated, Burgess flew wing on the Betty with about two feet between wing tips. He looked over and waved at the Japanese pilot, who only toothed back at him. At this juncture the turret gunner of the torpedo plane in desperation opened his hatch and emptied all six rounds of his .38-caliber revolver into the Betty, with unobserved results on the enemy but with great elation to the gunner.
>
> Tiring of this, Ensign Burgess crossed over top of the enemy plane and retired to about a quarter of a mile away on the Betty's port side. He managed to get his starboard wing-gun charged, and made a pass at the Betty's port side. This time his tracers went into the starboard engine and it burst into flames. The flames spread to the starboard wing, Betty lost control, her port wing dipped into the water, and she executed a neat cartwheel. Ensign Burgess saw one survivor in the water, who was picked up almost immediately by a friendly destroyer.

Fueling completed, Admiral Spruance in *Indianapolis,* with the fire support ships that he had borrowed from Turner, took station off

Saipan, arriving in the afternoon of 23 June. Three of Mitscher's fast carrier groups were ordered to proceed to Eniwetok for a brief rest; but Admiral Clark had something else in mind.

"Jocko" Clark, who had been O.T.C. at the strikes on Iwo and Chichi Jima the previous week, felt the pressure of unfinished business. Owing to weather and a big battle coming up, he had not had time to give those islands a proper working over. Why not strike them again before retiring to Eniwetok? Accordingly he started north after fueling and at 1400 June 23 "advised CTF 58 by dispatch that unless otherwise directed this Group would strike Iwo Jima . . . morning of 24 June while en route to Eniwetok." Mitscher heartily approved, and thereafter referred to this diversion as "Operation Jocko."

Clark's expectation that there would be plenty of game up north was well founded. The Japanese were trying to reinforce the Tinian and Guam airfields. Owing to foul weather, the squadrons had been so delayed that now there was a backlog of 122 planes on Iwo and Chichi Jima, awaiting word from Admiral Kakuta at Tinian that damaged airfields had been repaired and were ready to receive them.

By 0600 June 24 *Hornet, Yorktown, Bataan* and *Belleau Wood,* with their screen of cruisers and destroyers, had reached a point 235 miles SE by S of Iwo Jima. The weather was rough, but not nearly so bad as on the previous visit. While the three big carriers launched a fighter sweep of 51 Hellcats, each armed with a 500-pound bomb to destroy grounded planes, *Belleau Wood* assumed combat air and anti-submarine patrol for the group.

The 51 Hellcats had an unexpected battle en route. Clark had been snooped by a Japanese patrol plane shortly before reaching his launching position, enabling Admiral Sadaichi Matsunaga, commanding 27th Air Flotilla at Iwo, to fly off all his fighters and a few bombers to intercept. At 0815 they met the Americans about half-way. The Hellcats jettisoned bombs and piled in; then there was a battle royal in the air. At the end of it, 24 Japanese fighters (Zekes and Hamps) and 5 Judys had been shot down, at the cost of 6 Hellcats. Four Hellcats which had clung to their bombs continued to Iwo and dropped them on the airfield; the rest returned to their carriers.

They arrived none too soon. Matsunaga, eager for revenge, had already sent one raid against the carriers, and was about to send a second. The first, consisting of about 20 torpedo-bombers, was completely destroyed—some shot down by C.A.P., others by the task group's anti-aircraft fire. Of the second—9 Jills, 9 Judys and 23 Zekes and Hamps—"The results were vague and the target was not sighted." Intercepted at a good distance from the carrier group by combat air patrol and special scrambles of fighter planes, this raid was turned back after losing 7 Jills and 10 Zekes. Not too vague, after all!

Occasional dogfights continued until 1830. Half an hour later, Clark assumed cruising disposition and proceeded to Eniwetok. A few planes still hovered around, dropping "window" and flares, but no more attacks developed.

This destruction of 66 more planes undoubtedly contributed to the conquest of Saipan. After a third raid on Iwo and Chichi Jima, with which Admiral "Jocko" celebrated the Fourth of July, the Hachiman air group was so weakened by combat and operational losses that on the 7th the remnant of 41 Zekes and 13 bombers was sent back to Japan.

Clark's interest in the "Jimas" had become so marked that the aviators caused to be printed a certificate of membership in the "Jocko Jima Development Corporation," offering "Choice Locations of all Types in Iwo, Chichi, Haha and Muko Jima, Only 500 Miles from Downtown Tokyo." Signed by Admiral Clark as "President of the Corporation," one of these diplomas was awarded to every participant.

A similar interdicting action was performed on the southern flank by the XIII Army Air Force, based at Los Negros. Following strikes on Woleai on 20 and 22 June, B-24s flew an average of 21 daily sorties against Yap for five days, 23-27 June. And for five days slightly earlier, 19-23 June, Kwajalein-based Liberators flew high-altitude bombing missions against Truk. These close to 1000-mile bombing missions were costly—two B-24s shot down and 21 damaged in the attacks on Yap.

The immediate reaction in Task Force 58 to the Battle of the Philippine Sea was one of disappointment and vexation. Admiral Clark, only ten days after, told this writer, "It was the chance of a century missed." Admiral Mitscher thus concluded his action report: "The enemy escaped. He had been badly hurt by one aggressive carrier strike, at the one time he was within range. His fleet was not sunk." Admiral Montgomery wrote:—

Results of the action were extremely disappointing to all hands, in that important units of the enemy fleet, which came out in the open for the first time in over a year and made several air attacks on our superior force, were able to escape without our coming to grips with them. It is true that our troops on Saipan were well screened and protected against the enemy surface force, but it is considered unfortunate that our entire strength was deployed for this purpose and therefore not permitted an opportunity to take the offensive until too late to prevent the enemy's retirement.

At naval air headquarters in Pearl Harbor the line was, "This is what comes of placing a non-aviator in command over carriers." Admiral Spruance had never won wings, but that does not prove that he did not know what to do with naval air power. After all, he more than anyone else had won the Battle of Midway. He was not infallible, of course. In warfare, where decisions have to be made promptly on imperfect intelligence of the enemy, mistakes are inevitable; and in considering a commander's actions we should base judgment on his reaction to factors known or legitimately guessed by him at the time, not on the fuller knowledge that reaches an historian years later.

There was no distinction between Spruance and Mitscher in aggressiveness, fighting spirit or desire to come to grips with the enemy. The difference in their respective attitudes was due to the scope of their respective responsibilites. Mitscher was responsible only for TF 58; hence his absorbing passion was to destroy the Japanese carriers that menaced his carriers. Spruance had the overall responsibility for Operation "Forager"; for the Joint Expeditionary Force as well as the carriers; for the troops ashore on Saipan and the Guam assault force, which was still hanging in the bight. His objective was to secure the Marianas. Inbued with a strong sense of that mission, Spruance refused to be diverted; he was unwilling to accept the risk that the Japanese ships reported up to the early hours of 19 June might be only a detachment of the Mobile Fleet.

On the other side, there are there alleged counts against Spruance. First, Mahan is quoted to the effect that the main object of a fleet is to destroy the enemy's fleet. Second, that a powerful striking force as mobile as the fast carriers should never be tied to the apronstrings of an amphibious operation. Third, that in view of the known strength of Ozawa's Mobile Fleet any possible "end run" could have been dealt with adequately by the ships left to guard Saipan. No danger of a flanking movement actually existed; but, in view of Japanese past performances, the possibility had to be anticipated. Military men never get any credit for guarding against dangers that might occur yet do not; but they are quickly "hanged" if they fail adequately to guard against dangers that do occur—witness Pearl Harbor.

Admiral Spruance, who is able to view his own actions candidly and without emotion, still thought eight years later that he had missed a great opportunity. "As a matter of tactics," he wrote to me in 1952, "I think that going out after the Japanese and knocking their carriers out would have been much better and more satisfactory than waiting for them to attack us; but we were at the start of a very important and large amphibious operation and we could not afford to gamble and place it in jeopardy. The way Togo waited at Tsushima for the Russian fleet has always been in my mind. We had somewhat the same basic situation, only it was modified by the long-range striking power of the carriers."

Yet, would it have been better, as a matter of tactics, to have sought out Ozawa's Fleet on the night of 18-19 June and attacked it next morning? We cannot assume that fortune would have favored the strong—it did not do so at Midway. Our dive- and torpedo-bombers would probably have sunk some of the Japanese carriers; but the Japanese planes might also have sunk some of ours. And the "Turkey Shoot" could never have made such a spectacular score if Mitscher had had to divide his air forces between offense and defense; Ozawa's planes and anti-aircraft would probably have doubled or trebled their small bag of American planes and pilots if he had been on the defensive on the morning of 19 June, and had been able on the 20th to employ his full air strength instead of a poor remnant. Moreover, Japanese land-based air forces at Guam could have got into the fight if the battle had been joined halfway between Ozawa's position and the Marianas. Spruance, by steering east on the night of 18-19 June, against Mitscher's wishes and his own inclination, put Task Force 58 in about the optimum position to inflict the greatest damage on the enemy. His entire fleet was concentrated. All fighter planes were available for interception, and enemy planes that escaped them encountered the anti-aircraft fire of Lee's battle line. And the Japanese planes on Guam were knocked out before they could take the offensive.

We have been discussing the Battle of the Philippine Sea as if it had been simply a carrier-plane battle, but the submarines and the anti-submarine vessels must not be forgotten. By their attrition of the Mobile Fleet even before it departed Tawi Tawi, by sending Spruance the only clear intelligence he had of enemy movements, and by sinking *Taiho* and *Shokaku*, United States submarines contributed heavily to the result. So, too, did the destroyer escorts and destroyers that broke up the Japanese submarine concentration to the south. The I- and RO-boats were then far distant from the Fifth Fleet; but if they had not been smothered by excellent anti-submarine tactics they might well have moved north and done a great deal of damage.

The battle also illustrates the inadequacy of land based bombing, even when Navy-trained, as compared with carrier-based bombing. It may be conceded that Japanese land-based air *might* have given a better account of itself if General MacArthur's timely invasion of Biak had not caused its redeployment at the crucial moment. But the respectable component left on Guam and Yap before Saipan D-Day, instead of wearing down and reducing the strength of the Fifth Fleet according to plan, was annihilated by carrier planes within a space of one week.

One technique in which the Americans fell far short of perfection was air search, on the part of land-based patrol planes as well as carrier planes. Air search should have given the American commanders adequate intelligence of the enemy's force and movements at least 24 hours earlier. If Ozawa's change of course in the early afternoon of 19 June had been reported, or if long-range night searches had been sent out by TF 58 after dark on the same day, they should have made contacts that would have enabled Spruance to get his fleet in position for a "one-two" strike on the 20th. And the PBM and PB4Y searches were ineffective because of communications failures.

In the matter of planes, the F6F Hellcat fully sustained its high reputation, and the two types of Avengers did well when given their proper weapon, the torpedo; but the new Helldiver (SB2C) was outshone by the two remaining squadrons of Dauntless dive bombers (SBD). Unfortunately, nothing could be done about it, since the production lines were rolling with Helldivers; here the Dauntless fought her last battle.

Ozawa may be said to have conducted his fleet well. The Japanese plane searches kept him fairly in touch with the movements of Task Force 58 for 24 hours or more before Spruance knew where he was; and he made good use of the lee gauge. Commander Mobile Fleet avoided the usual (and always disastrous) Japanese strategy of feint and parry; he kept his inferior force together and gave battle at a distance that prevented his enemy from striking back immediately. His handling of the fueling problem, in view of the shortage of oil and scarcity of tankers, was masterly. But all this availed him naught because his air groups were so ill trained. As the Japanese post mortem on the battle said, quoting the modern version of a Japanese classic, the "Combat Sutra," chapter 49: "Good tactics should be applied only by a combat force that is well trained. Hence tactics may be compared to sandals. Good sandals should be worn by a strong-footed man. Then he can walk fast and long. A weak-footed man, even if he wears a pair of good sandals, can never walk as well as a strong-footed man." Ozawa had fine ships and good planes, but his aviators were weak-winged through inexperience, and land-based air failed him completely.

Admiral Mahan never said that destruction of an enemy fleet was an object in itself, but a means to the greater ends of victory and a lasting peace. The Battle of the Philippine Sea contributed as much to victory as if Ozawa's fleet had been destroyed; for without its air arm the fleet was crippled, and the six carriers that survived were useful only as decoys to lure another American admiral to do what Spruance had declined to do. Admiral Toyoda had announced on 15 June, "The fate of the Empire rests on this one battle." He was right. It decided the Marianas campaign by giving the United States Navy command of the surrounding waters and air. Thus, the Japanese land forces in Saipan, Tinian and Guam were doomed, no matter how bravely and doggedly they fought. And victory in the Marianas made an American victory over Japan inevitable.

Admiral Spruance compared his tactics to those of Togo at Tsushima in 1905. An historical parallel more remote in time but closer in fact, because amphibious and land operations were involved, was the Yorktown campaign of 1781. In the naval battle off the Capes of the Chesapeake, on 5 September of that year, Admiral De Grasse defeated an inferior fleet under Admiral Thomas Graves RN that threatened to break into the Chesapeake and raise the siege of Yorktown. The battle itself was not tactically decisive since Graves lost but one of his nineteen capital ships, and De Grasse was criticized for not renewing action. But he covered the British in a week's maneuvering at sea, shouldering them away from the Cape long enough for a second French fleet to enter Hampton Roads with Rochambeau's siege artillery, and later to enter himself. In other words, De Grasse's sense of his mission, to support the Allied land campaign against Cornwallis, prevented him from risking the chance of throwing away his advantage. His cautious tactics rendered Cornwallis's surrender inevitable; and so won the War of Independence, although the British Fleet was not destroyed. Spruance's sense of his mission, to protect the amphibious operation against Saipan, precluded his running undue risks; he failed to annihilate the Japanese Fleet, but he won air and sea command, so that the Japanese forces in those islands were sealed off from any hope of reinforcement.

If General Saito, in command of Japanese forces on Saipan, had been a European, he would have emulated Cornwallis; being Japanese, his forces had to be annihilated. Saipan was Japan's Yorktown; and, although Ozawa's fleet was still formidable in fire power, that did not greatly matter after he had lost his air groups.

In view of the wild statements about Japanese plane losses in accounts of this battle published elsewhere, we have made every effort to arrive at the truth. The fixed points are these:—

Mobile Fleet at dawn 19 June had 430 carrier and 43 float planes operational.

Mobile Fleet at dawn 20 June had 100 carrier and 27 float planes operational.

Mobile Fleet on 21 June had 35 carrier and 12 float planes operational.

In other words, Ozawa lost, in two days' searching and fighting 395 (92 per cent) of his carrier planes and 31 (72 per cent) of his float planes.

How these losses were incurred is more difficult to estimate. According to Japanese records of the successive searches and raids on 19 June:—

	No. Planes	Failed to Return	Returned
Three dawn searches	43	21	22
Raid I	69	42	27
Raid II	130	98	32
Raid III	47	7	40
1000 search	2	2	0
Raid IV	82	73	9
	373	243	130

In addition to those that failed to return, 22 went down with *Taiho* and *Shokaku,* making a total of 265 that were not back on board for the second day's fight, and 130 that were. If 354 carrier planes were launched 19 June (19 of the search planes were Jakes), 76 were left on board for C.A.P. and reserves. Subtracting the 22 that went down with the two carriers, we must add 54 to the 130 that returned from the raids, making 184 that should have been on board the morning of the 20th. But Japanese carrier records state that only 100 were serviceable. How about the other 84? Probably at least 75 carrier planes, plus 6 Jakes, were too damaged, either by fighting or bad landings, to fly again, and the other three were operational losses from the C.A.P.

Thus, Ozawa lost, in all, 330 of his 430 carrier planes together with 16 of his 43 float planes, on 19 June alone. Of the 354 carrier planes in searches and raids, 233 of which failed to return, 19 (of Raid IV) landed on Guam wrecked, and we may guess that at least 20 more, at one time or another, crashed on Guam or Rota. That leaves 194 "failed to return" planes to account for. The great majority of these must have been destroyed by American interceptions, most of the rest by anti-aircraft fire, and a number by operational splashes and crashes. It is impossible from American records to decide exactly how many were accounted for by ships' anti-aircraft fire and interceptors respectively; there are so many duplications. But, to those destroyed by enemy action we must add at least 65 of those that returned to their carriers, which were too damaged to fight again.

In addition the Japanese lost 18 Guam-based planes in air action 19-20 June and "about 62" on the ground. About 30 of these were under repair, so we shall not count them, although they were now completely destroyed. Assuming 32 destroyed on the ground plus 18 in the air, Guam-based losses add 50 to the total score.

In the searches and the twilight battle on 20 June, Mobile Fleet lost an additional 65 carrier planes and 15 float planes. Of these, 19 carrier planes were lost in combat and the rest operationally, according to Japanese sources; but it seems improbable that as many as 46 carrier and 15 float planes could have been lost operationally. I believe that at least 40 were shot down by the American raiders, but the Japanese, not knowing exactly what went on at twilight, listed as "operational" all that were not seen from their ships' decks to be shot down.

The certain final score is this: on 21 June the Mobile Fleet had left only 35 carrier planes (25 of them Zekes) and 12 float planes. In the two days' battle it lost 426 planes. Add an estimated 50 from Ka-kuta's Base Air Force at Guam, and you have 476 total Japanese plane losses in the Battle of the Philippine Sea. The number of aviators lost from the Mobile Fleet was about 445.

WHILE THE FIGHTING WAS STILL GOING ON AT SAIPAN, American warships were bombarding installations along the shores of enemy-held Guam by day and night. Watching them with excitement from his cave overlooking Adelup Point was Radioman 1/c George R. Tweed, an unkempt figure who had been fed, sheltered and clothed by friendly Chamorros at the risk of their lives ever since he had escaped from the advancing Japanese on December 10, 1941. In the late afternoon of July 10 two destroyers, including *McCall,* came in closer to Tweed's cave than ever before. In his dramatic narrative Tweed tells how he frantically tried to attract their attention in order to escape.

15.

"HE *LOOKS* LIKE

A WHITE MAN"

I looked out to sea and saw several ships moving in from the north. I wasn't sure whether they were Americans or Japanese. Five ships cruised into view around the end of the island, six or eight miles out on the horizon. At first I thought they were battleships, but then I saw that they were large, improved heavy cruisers almost as big as the peacetime battleships I had known.

They kept coming. Destroyers and heavy cruisers sailed into view. I hoped they weren't Jap ships bringing support to the island garrison.

As soon as the gray force reached the coast opposite Agana Bay, every ship opened fire. This was no Jap armada! "IT IS OUR NAVY!" I screamed. I was never so thrilled in my life! I wanted to plunge into the sea and swim out to them.

All Jap ships anchored outside the harbor were spotted by planes launched from the cruisers. Light seaplanes continually circled over the island all the time the cruisers were firing.

From then on, twin American destroyers passed my lookout every day as they circled the island. It wasn't until later that I learned they never were the same two.

Those ships gave me an even greater thrill than the airplanes. The planes had given me my first wild hope, but, after all, it was the good old Navy that would actually get me out.

792

But would they? I was afraid to let myself dwell on my escape. If I didn't make it, the disappointment would kill me. But I'd try. By God, I'd try!

I ran down to my cabinet, took out a large oblong of gauze bandage Antonio had got from the dispensary, cut it in two, and nailed each half to a stick to make semaphore flags. Each one was about two feet square, large enough to be seen through binoculars if anyone, please God, on the ship happened to spot me.

As I scrambled back up to my lookout, I tried to recall the semaphore alphabet. I'd known it long before—it's regulation in the Navy. What had I been doing for the past two years? Why hadn't I spent them practicing signaling?

I couldn't figure it out now. The ships were moving. I frantically waved my flags up and down, up and down. Maybe somebody'd look my way.

I waved for fifteen minutes, rested, and waved again. No response. I'd hoped for too much on the first day. The ships were disappearing. They'd be back, though, maybe tomorrow. I had to get that alphabet. When I did catch their eye, I had to be able to tell them something!

I went back to my cave, stood there with a flag in each hand and concentrated. I got the first seven letters without any trouble. They were simple. But what message could I send with them? I figured out five more, twelve in all, that I could be sure of. I knew I'd have to do better than that. The majority of the letters had to be correct to make the message readable. I knew that if I were listening in over the radio and got a somewhat garbled code message I could still make it out if the key letters were right. The signalmen on those ships were experts. They'd fill in for me, if only I gave them enough to go on.

I worked for four days trying to remember that code. By then, I felt pretty certain of nineteen letters, with seven still in doubt. There was a chance that my guesses on some of these seven were right. That was the best I could do. That—and pray for an expert receiver.

For a week, every time an American ship hove in sight I waved those flags. It was back-breaking work, emaciated as I was, but I kept it up for twenty minutes at a time, six or seven times a day. I knew that my only chance was that someone would scrutinize my area with his glasses. Most of the ships didn't stop, but cruised past at a steady pace from the north end of the island, to where I could no longer see them to the south. This took about twenty minutes, all of which I spent anxiously waving the gauze signals.

Trees in the distance cut off part of my view of the sea. I judged as carefully as I could just which ones they were, went down with my machete, and hacked away the tops. Now I had a clear swing of vision for 120 degrees. It gave a few seconds more in which I might be spotted from a ship. I brandished my white flags until my arms were sore, without results. What was the matter with those guys on the bridge?

Antonio came up, and I told him of my efforts. He was very worried. "You had better be careful," he said, "or those Japs over on the next hill might see you waving those white flags."

I knew that he was right. I had been unable to spot their lookout station so could not tell if they could see the cliff on which I was perched. If they ever saw me waving my white flags at the American warships it would not only be my finish but would also cost Antonio his life. He had endangered the lives of his family and himself for so long by helping me that I could not, at this late date, bring almost certain death to these people.

I had to quit signaling. I was bitterly disappointed. Only a few miles stood between me and United States warships and I couldn't bridge that short distance.

But I'd be damned if I'd give up! I'd make a raft and paddle out to them!

I figured out the number of bamboo pieces I'd need to support me and the things I wanted to take. I doubted if I'd have the strength to drag a raft all the way down to the water's edge. I hadn't been as far away as the beach in months. I didn't think I'd have the strength to make more than a few trips loaded with bamboo, but I slipped down to locate a place where I could build the raft in the water and then keep it hidden there. There was no place to hide it. I then decided to hide the bamboo in the bushes near the water until the complete material was assembled and build the raft in the water after dark. I could build it and leave the island by two o'clock in the morning and be six or eight miles offshore by daylight. Surely I would be picked up by an American ship.

I went back home and started working on a paddle. I'd make it kayak style, with a blade on each end. I could make double time with that type, and every second counted for me now.

When July 4 approached, I expected some special fireworks. I wasn't disappointed. Beginning in early morning our planes came over in raid after heavy raid. I shuttled back and forth between my cave and lookout post every few minutes to be sure I didn't miss anything.

On one trip I saw an American fighter plane flying a few thousand feet over Agana. I wished I were in it, headed back for the carrier. At that moment, it was struck squarely amidships by anti-aircraft fire; it smoked up, spluttered, and started down. It struck the water, exploded, and burst into flames. I was cursing the Japs for what they'd done when I saw a white blob mushroom in the sky above the plane and knew it was the pilot floating down in his parachute.

He landed in the bay four or five hundred yards off Agana. The minute he struck, the Japs opened up with machine guns, shooting up white spurts of water all around him. Immediately ten American planes came in low over Agana, bombing and strafing, making the Japs pull in their necks. I was afraid the pilot would be riddled, but then I thought, well, better to go down than have the lousy Japs get you.

The American planes kept up the strafing for half an hour, pulling the fire away from the pilot in the water. It seemed hopeless, though; they couldn't keep it up indefinitely; the Japs would get the pilot when the protecting planes went home. But finally a seaplane came in, dove on the town, strafed the machine gunners, circled back, and landed on the water alongside the pilot. The Jap guns really cut loose. The water was churned white by the bullets.

That little plane must have been perforated like a sieve, but apparently neither it nor its pilot was disabled. The flyer struggling in the water couldn't disentangle himself from his parachute. He wrapped his arms securely around the tail of the plane and it taxied through the water with him hanging on, his heavy parachute streaming out behind him in the water. Five hundred yards away, out from under the guns, they stopped and cut the parachute loose. There was not room for the man in the cockpit. The water-soaked pilot crawled out of the sea, lay down on the wing, and the plane took off. The rescue pilot flew only a few feet above the water, and very slowly, so that his buddy wouldn't roll off. They disappeared over the horizon. It was the best Fourth of July demonstration I'd ever seen.

The Americans developed a system of continual day and night attacks. Twenty or thirty ships, both cruisers and destroyers, would steam in about nine o'clock in the morning, shell the daylights out of a whole section of the beach, then sail out again after putting in a full eight-hour day. Two destroyers would stay on and bombard installations all night. They'd steam around the island, shelling as they went, just to keep the Japs awake and jumping.

The destroyers' firing technique was simple and effective. When they opened up, they'd fire the shells just as fast as they could load and let go. One night about one o'clock they opened up with a fierce bombardment right into our area. One shell dropped about a hundred feet from Antonio's house. It sprayed rocks and dirt into his cistern of drinking water. Several boulders struck the house where he and his frightened family shivered.

Next morning the Japs came to investigate and asked him if he'd drawn this fire by flashing lights out to sea. They warned him that he was under suspicion. When he was sure they weren't watching him, he came up to my cave and asked me to get rid of the semaphore flags entirely. He was afraid that the Japs watching his ranch might catch me trying to signal the American ships.

On July 10, the warships came in as usual, did their day's work, and pulled out. Late in the afternoon I saw that the two destroyers left behind for the night shift were about ten miles south of me. They were closer to shore than they'd ever been. They looked near enough for a man on board to hit the beach with a rock. My heart sank, for they stood almost under the muzzles of a battery of six- or eight-inch Jap guns mounted at Adelup Point.

I'd spotted the battery at target practice shortly before the Americans returned. I could tell that they were large guns from the flash they made, the distance the shells traveled before they splashed at sea, and the spash they made. I knew there were at least three guns in the emplacement, because I'd seen three flashes of fire so close together that they couldn't possibly have belonged to a second salvo. The Japs hadn't used these guns against the Americans so far, undoubtedly because they were saving them for our landing force and they didn't want to reveal their position. I held my breath because I knew they could outshoot the destroyers. A land-based gun is always more accurate than one mounted on a ship at sea. I prayed the Japs wouldn't open up on the destroyers now firing broadsides at the beach as they stood within point-blank range of the Jap battery. Finally they turned, unmolested, and started north in my direction.

I was worn out from the anxiety. It was getting on toward evening, and I had supper ready. I went back to the cave. I'd taken only a few bites when I heard the destroyers' guns firing very near, shooting almost straight in my direction. I'd learned that the sound of a gun firing in my direction is different from the report when it's pointed away. The projectile leaving the muzzle gives an extra, vicious "thug!" in addition to the regular report.

I grabbed my signal flags and pocket mirror. If they were close enough, I'd try a new plan. As I dashed up the cliff to the lookout I heard an anti-aircraft gun and a machine gun nest only two miles below me open fire on the destroyers. The ships' gunners quickly took the range of these Jap shore installations and blasted them to hell.

I had to admire the daring of the ships' commanders in coming so near the coast when they couldn't know what guns might be concealed there. They were hardly two miles from the shore, an easy, murderous range for large enemy guns. As they started right up past me, I scrambled to the very top of the cliff in plain view of the destroyers. With the little three-inch mirror I flashed a beam directly on the bridge of the leading ship. The late afternoon sun was in the sky right behind the warships so that I was sending them a powerful red flash. I danced the reflection all over the bridge. They must have seen it!

I threw down my mirror and grabbed up my signal flags. I waved the flags frantically up and down for possibly half a minute. Then I signaled, "Please answer by searchlight." I cannot read semaphore but am proficient in the reception of Morse code by lights. A signal searchlight winked from the bridge, *"K,"* it said, code for "Go ahead!" I almost blew my top, but I forced myself to start out quite slowly and deliberately with my semaphore. I wanted them to get at least every letter I was sure of. They could figure out the rest. I'll always remember the exact words I sent.

"I have information for you."

Again this beautiful *K* winked across to me.

My head seemed to be going around in circles. I didn't know what I was doing or what I should do next. For a few minutes I manipulated my flags, but I have no idea what I said or whether the message was even intelligible.

I tried to warn them about the large battery that the Japs were holding back to use against our landing force. By now the bombardment of the island was so intense that I knew the landing would be made almost any day. I knew that if the battleships could blast that emplacement out of existence before the landing was attempted, it would save the lives of thousands of American troops.

When I finally calmed down and settled to a deliberate rate of sending, "The Japs have a battery of coast guns mounted at Adelup Point," I signaled.

Then I thought they ought to know that the Japs were killing pilots who made forced landings on the island. "The Japs kill every American who falls into their hands." I wanted the pilots to know what they were up against, so that they could either take a chance on crashing in the sea and being picked up by our ships or hit for the bush and hide out until the island fell if they were shot down inland.

The sun was still shining. The destroyers had slowed down when they spotted me on the cliff. They circled around one spot for probably half an hour while I talked to them. Finally, I'd given them all the information I knew—all I had about the strength and concentration of Jap troops on the island, the nature of off-shore barricades, mine fields, tank traps, and other obstructions, even some data on dummy guns. That was all. I was run down. The strain of trying to get the letters right was terrific.

I'd made no attempt whatever to identify myself. I knew they'd be suspicious. The first thing a spy would try to do would be to identify himself as a bona-fide American. If I told them nothing about myself but just gave them useful information, perhaps that would be in my favor.

I saw they were getting up speed. I was frantic. Through hot tears I slowly and distinctly spelled out, "Can you take me aboard?"

As I half-anticipated, I received no answer. That was all I could expect, I thought, but I still stood there, too exhausted to stumble back to my cave.

Five minutes later, I saw a boat drop into the water. That was answer enough for me! The people on that ship knew I wasn't a Jap! How, I don't know. I didn't care. I was practically delirious as I hoisted my flags for one final message.

"Please wait for me. It will take me half an hour to get down to the water."

I dropped the signal flags where I was, scooped up the mirror, and stuck it in my pocket.

Inside my crevasse, I grabbed my machete, fastened on my holster, opened the cracker can where I kept my pictures and records and stuffed them into my shirt front. I slung the deer light Antonio had given me over my shoulder, and ran for the trail. I half-slid down the three rugged cliffs, using both hands and feet to keep from falling. I cracked my knees against the jagged corners of a shelf of rock and took the hide off. I hardly felt it. I was down by the water's edge in fifteen minutes. Never before had I made it in less than three quarters of an hour.

I couldn't see the motor launch, but judged I was south of it, since I had had to come slantwise down the cliff. I didn't want them to think they were being drawn into a trap. It was getting dark enough to signal with a light. I tapped the end of the wire on the terminal of the battery so that I could send code. First, I just flashed the light rapidly several times.

The ship saw me and swung the signal light toward the beach. "He is half a mile south of you," the signalman said.

Were they talking to me or to the boat? If to the boat, I was turned around, and it was south of me.

"Are you talking to the boat or to me?" I flashed.

"To the boat."

Fine. Everything was as I'd figured it.

"Flash your light so the boat will spot you and know where to pick you up," they signaled to me.

I sent dots of yellow light north, and in a few minutes the launch came in sight.

"Here I am!" I shouted.

Meantime, I plumbed the water for depth. I found a place where it was a good eight feet, plenty deep enough to bring the boat right up to the shore. I didn't want to take any chances on that boat running aground.

I hurriedly snatched up my gear. Where was my pistol? I had forgotten it! I had been so crazy with excitement that I'd gone off and left the one object that had never left my side, day or night, in two whole years. It was too late now. I couldn't go back for it. The boat was within two hundred yards of me.

But it didn't come in. I could see it dimly.

"Come on in! There's plenty of water here!" I shouted to them.

"No, you swim out."

"I can't. I've got too much gear."

"Leave the gear."

There was plenty of water for the boat to come in right to the rock on which I was standing. I didn't want to get my pictures and records wet by swimming.

"You have eight feet of water right here where I'm standing!"

"We are *not* coming in. Swim out and leave your gear there."

"I can't leave it here. The Japs'll find it and kill the man who owns this place." I felt that the Japs must have seen the two destroyers circling in this spot for so long. It was endangering Antonio's life. I could not leave anything behind for that would make his death certain.

"We are not coming in!"

I was worried. I didn't answer. These people were going to get disgusted and return to the ship. Then the Japs, seeing the two destroyers circling this spot, would come out here to look for me. I must get away!

"You swim out. If *you're* all right, then we'll come in and get your things," someone finally shouted.

"Oh, it's *me* you're afraid of!"

"You ain't just a'lying!" I heard one of the fellows in the boat say.

I dropped everything and started tearing off my clothes. Although it was getting dark fast, there was still some light, and when I'd stripped to the hide I heard someone in the boat say, "He *looks* like a white man."

We'd been there so long, making so much noise arguing about the gear, and with the warships circling in that same spot offshore, that I was afraid a Jap patrol might be on its way down there.

"Has anybody there got a gun?" I called out.

No answer.

"I say, has anybody got a gun!" I cried out louder.

No answer. They weren't giving away any information.

"Well, if you have, and you see anybody besides me, let 'em have it. They'll be Japs!"

I swam out to the boat.

When they saw I was really white, two dozen arms reached out for me. They pulled me over the side, and I fell sprawling into the boat. Once aboard, I saw that the thirty men bristled with enough submachine guns to wipe out an entire Jap platoon.

I'll never forget how good it felt to get back with Americans, hear Americans, see Americans, especially Navy men like myself. They were the best looking bunch of men I ever saw in my life. Every one of them had a question.

"Where've you been?"

"Where'd you come from?"

"How long've you been there?"

When I told them I'd been hiding from the Japs on the island for over two years and a half, they didn't believe me. They thought I was a pilot who'd been forced down a week or two previously. One look at me should have convinced them I was telling the truth. I looked like a wild animal. I was naked. My shaggy hair hung amost down to my shoulders. I hadn't shaved for three days.

We went back to shore for my things. On the way the men peeled their own clothes off their backs and threw them over to me. I took a shirt. I put on my own trousers, homemade shoes, and underwear.

I'd never received such a welcome as I got from these Navy men. When we pulled up alongside the ship, they lowered the blocks from the davits, hooked the boat on, and hoisted her up with everybody in it. When we were level with the destroyer's deck, the men in the boat pushed me forward to be the first man out. "Jump on over!" somebody yelled. Half a dozen fellows gave me a helping shove from behind, and half a dozen more caught me as I hit the deck.

One of the six was Commanding Officer, Lt. Comdr. J. B. Carroll. He shook hands, congratulated me, and thanked me for the information I'd sent.

"You got here in the nick of time. We're just sitting down to eat," he said, inviting me to officers' mess.

I sat beside Commander Carroll. There were electric lights, white table linen, china, and silver in an immaculate cabin within a few miles of my hole in the cliff. There was a baked ham, green vegetables, and bread and butter. I hadn't seen bread and butter more than half a dozen times while I was in the bush. Many times in my cave when I was cooking supper I had thought I'd gladly swap everything I had to eat, including all my canned goods, for just one good thick slice of white bread spread with a deep layer of yellow butter.

I was too excited to eat much. I stuffed down some bread and a small helping of green vegetables. That was all.

I made a diagram for Commander Carroll, showing him the exact location of the battery of coast guns.

"You don't know how lucky you are," he said. "After we had blasted that Jap anti-aircraft and machine gun out of existence we came on up the coast, where we spotted the reflection of your mirror. The way you quivered it, it looked exactly like gun flashes. When I saw them I said, 'Aha! Another Jap gun getting smart with us.' We took your range and bearing, trained our guns on you, and were ready to open fire when, at the last second, you dropped the mirror and began waving your flags. Somebody shouted, 'Hold everything! I think someone is trying to signal to us.' If you'd waited another second to start waving your flags, you'd have been blown to hell."

Lieutenant Butler, the medical officer, took me to his office for a once-over. He found nothing wrong; said I'd survived my ordeal pretty well.

"Now," he said significantly. "Is there anything you'd like especially?"

"A shower!" I said fervently.

"Okay. But don't you have a little cough?" he asked in a voice full of meaning. "We're well equipped," he added.

I caught on. I coughed. "Doctor, I've had considerable difficulty with my throat lately," I complained.

"Swell! I've the very thing to fix you up!"

He reached into a cabinet and came out with a pint of bonded rye whiskey.

"Drink this. It'll do you good."

I took one swallow and returned the bottle.

"Go ahead, help yourself," he urged, but I'd not had a drink in so long that I knew it wouldn't take much to set me spinning.

He then led the way into the officers' washroom, and left to get me some clean clothes.

I left my old ones in a filthy heap on the floor and stepped into the luxury of a powerful stream of hot water beating down on my body.

When Lieutenant Butler came back, I was still under the shower. I didn't ever want to get out.

"Take your time," he called in.

As a matter of fact, the actual scrubbing necessary to scrape off the layers and layers of dirt which I imagined were caked on my body in the course of two and a half years in the dusty bush and crude cave, took plenty of time. That soap and shower brush took a helluva beating. I stepped out feeling brand new.

"What's that awful stench?" I asked. Then I saw my dirty clothes piled on the floor at my feet. "My God, if I'd fished up from the ocean anything smelling like that, I'd have thrown it back!"

I put on the clean underwear Lieutenant Butler handed me, grabbed up that pile of dirty clothes and made for the deck to throw them overboard. A dozen men almost knocked me down to keep me from doing it. I was as surprised as hell to see them fight over those smelly clothes for souvenirs. One shoe went one way, its mate, the other.

We went back to Lieutenant Butler's quarters. He gave me the first socks I'd had in over a year, and a fine pair of black shoes that one of the men had sent up as a present to me, without even leaving his name.

The doctor laid out two clean uniforms, one khaki and one gray. I'd never seen the gray before. It'd been adopted by the Navy after Guam was taken by the Japs.

"Who wears that one? I like it," I said, pointing to the gray.

"It's for officers and chiefs."

"Oh, in that case, I'll have to take the khaki. I'm not a chief yet—still first class."

"Well, the khaki's for officers and chiefs, too, so you might as well wear the gray," he laughed.

Once dressed, I looked at myself in the narrow mirror in the door and thought that if I could just get rid of that three days growth of beard and my almost three years' growth of hair down my back, perhaps I could begin to look human again.

"All men who were in the landing party report immediately!" the call came out over the loud-speaker.

The group gathered in the wardroom, and the ship's photographer took pictures.

For the rest of the evening we sat around talking. The fellows gave me cigarettes, matches, chewing gum, in every way showing me that they were glad I'd lived to tell my story and was there with them now. Now it was my time to ask questions.

"Is Germany knocked out yet? Where is General MacArthur now? Why has it taken so long for the Americans to get back to Guam?"

They brought me up to date, telling me about the major war fronts that had developed since early 1942 when I had to abandon my radio, shutting myself off from the outside world. They explained the priorities that the European war front had on men and materials, causing the long delay in the rescue of our far-flung Pacific outpost. They told me proudly about the big task force, of which they were a part, that was now sweeping across the Pacific, giving the Japs hell wherever they had established garrisons. All the men were full of confidence.

When it was time to turn in, Lieutenant Butler showed me to a bunk in the officers' quarters. I undressed and eased into the finest bed I'd felt since the Beauty Rest mattress at Tommy Tanak's in September, 1942.

I heaved a big sigh of relief, closed my eyes, and for the life of me couldn't fall asleep. There were no mosquitoes, no ants, no leaks in the roof, no rain in my face. No wonder I couldn't drop off! Actually, I was just too excited to quiet down and give up.

I put on my clothes and went to the radio room. The chief let me take over for a while and handle some messages. It felt good to know I hadn't lost my know-how at the key. I fanned the breeze with the operators on watch and paced the deck, breathing sea air again and thanking God for my escape . . .

~~~~~~

WITH THE CAPTURE OF SAIPAN, BOMBING SQUADRON 109, under Commander Norman Miller, whom we have met before, moved down from the Marshalls. On July 14 Commander Miller reported to Operations at Isley Field (formerly Aslito Field) for assignment. His was to be a unique mission, approved by Admiral Spruance. *Thunder Mug,* his Liberator bomber, accompanied by another Liberator, was to make the first strike on Iwo Jima, only six hundred and twenty-five miles from Saipan and six hundred and seventy from Tokyo. "See what they've got there. Go after their destroyers especially," Spruance told him.

As we learn from his memoirs, Miller made the most of the opportunity.

16.

FIRST STRIKE ON IWO

We decided to hit Iwo Jima at dusk, and so at two o'clock in the afternoon the planes were taxied to the extreme end of the Isley Field fighter strip and readied for the take-off. Each crew had poured two thousand gallons of gas into the tanks, enough to get us there and back, and hung two thousand pounds of bombs on the racks. We were going to have to take off in the rain, with no wind, from a runway just 3,800 feet long. Skeptical Army pilots lined up along the strip and ground crews stopped work to watch in silence as battered old *Thunder Mug* turned into position. They didn't know our PB4Ys as well as we did.

The crew was ready. Shafe stood between me and my co-pilot, hairy-chested Jim Park—"Alley Oop" we called him. "Let's make it good, Skipper," Shafe begged. "Just to give those Army Joes the laugh." I turned the engines up full, seven inches beyond maximum manifold pressure, and released the brakes. The plane went lunging down the lumpy field like a hound dog off a leash.

With her flaps up, for speed without drag, she roared along until we were doing an uncomfortable 100 miles an hour. Then I lowered the flaps for lift, and *Thunder Mug* tipped her nose up. For a moment her wheels seemed glued to the ground as she strained to free herself. Then we were in the air. Later we learned that a cheer went up behind us, but with the four engines thundering like freight trains in

805

our ears, we didn't hear it. We ourselves cheered, however, when Joe Jobe's plane swept up from the field in our wake.

Keeping close together for added protection, the two Liberators ranged far up to the north, shunning a number of small islands which might have been outposts for the enemy's air-raid warning system. We flew on past Iwo Jima as planned, and arriving too soon at our turning point, had to loaf around over the Pacific for a while, waiting for dusk. When the sky had darkened and the sea had turned gray, we went on in, approaching not from the south but from the direction of the Japs' own homeland.

There was little talk as the two planes skimmed over the water on this last leg of the journey. This was big business; it might even be too big for our pair of unescorted Liberators, and the boys knew that our chances of getting back to Saipan with a whole skin—not to mention a respectable score—would depend largely on our ability to catch the enemy napping. There would be no lingering over this target, no doubling back to deal the foe a second dose. We had been warned soberly that Iwo Jima was bristling with powerful defenses.

So, then, we had to be good—we could make no mistakes—if we were to prove the point I had so strenuously argued in my campaign to get just two of our planes to Saipan. Admiral Spruance and Captain Taff would be keeping an eye on us. We still had to convince them that by using a short, undeveloped advance field and flying far out beyond the radius of single- and twin-engined planes, we could do some important damage to an enemy not yet prepared for attack by heavy aircraft. Of particular importance would be our score against the enemy's lifeline of shipping.

Iwo Jima rises from south to north in a gentle slope which terminates abruptly in a bluff at the northern tip. The bluff towered before us, black against the sky, as we went in just over the sea. We hoped it would hide us. But we could not know whether it would or not until the two planes climbed from the sea, cleared the bluff, and swung down over the air strips beyond.

We were about eight hundred feet apart, Jobe on my port beam, as we cleared the barrier. *Thunder Mug's* gunners anxiously awaited the signal to open fire. "Okay, give 'em hell," I said—and twenty machine guns, ten on each plane, opened up with a spectacular, deafening racket, pinning the Japs to the ground ahead of us as we attacked.

The Japs were surprised, no doubt of that, but they were not panicked. The breed on Iwo Jima didn't scare easily. Our own yellow-red tracers had scarcely begun to ricochet from the ground when the greenish-blue ground fire began to flicker up at us. Only our speed and the surprise of the attack saved us. At two hundred miles an hour, barely 150 feet above the defenders' heads, we were fleeting targets despite our size. These Japs had never before had occasion to fire at anything so low. Their only previous targets had been carrier planes, at higher altitude. Nor had they ever been hit before by multi-engined aircraft. This was the first time Liberators had struck so close to Tokyo.

A few bullets nicked *Thunder Mug's* metal skin as we bore down on the first of the two airfields. Most of the flak, however, exploded in our slipstream, and the fragments that nicked us didn't hurt us.

No one except the Japs will ever know the full amount of damage done to their fields and parked planes that evening. At least thirty, probably forty planes were parked in the revetments and on the taxiways. Some exloded as our streams of machine-gun fire walked up and over them; some burst into flames; others spat out gusts of smoke. Over the interphone came brief reports from our gunners, but they were as busy as drunks in a shooting gallery and had little time or inclination to assess the damage already done. And by now we were really getting a reception. The Jap ground guns all over the island were putting up a barrage so intense that our encounters with enemy ack-ack in the Marshalls and the Carolines seemed tame by comparison. Even the ships off-shore were doing their Sunday best to knock us down. The sky ahead, behind and around us was aflame with gaudy Jap-made lightning.

I was saving the bombs for shipping, and as yet had released none of them. Our machine guns had been able to take care of the jammed planes on the airfields. But now, turning sharply to starboard, I headed for the anchorage on the west side of the island. With fires spreading on the ground behind us, I singled out a destroyer a mile and a half off shore and began a run on her. She was not the only target available but she was the best one, for the Japs were short of destroyers and desperately needed them for escorting their convoys.

This one had been firing at us even before we began our run, and, of course, she had weapons more powerful than anything with which we could answer her. Too smart to waste ammunition, the boys concentrated on the coastal vessels and cargo ships that came in range as we went in. To port, a cargo ship blazed on the water. Close aboard on the starboard side, a wooden coastal spouted flames. It was a good show. But Jim Park and I, in the cockpit, missed most of it. Enemy fire was bursting all around and over us by now, and we could see what most of the crew could not—the destroyer was sweeping the sky in front of us with twin streams of tracers from 20-millimeter deck guns. These twin rivers of fire rose in a rainbow arc between her stacks, so bright they fascinated me, and we were running down them like a train on tracks.

It was the longest, grimmest approach I had ever made, and I almost turned away. We were being hit hard; the Jap had a no-deflection shot and couldn't miss. And for some reason our bow gunner, who should have been doing the talking for our side, had failed to answer back. I didn't know until later that his guns had jammed and he couldn't!

I thought we would never make it, but old *Thunder Mug* drilled on through all the Jap could send, and the ship at last was in the sights.

No one had to guess at the results. *Thunder Mug's* gunners saw what happened, and so did the crew of Joe Jobe's plane, moving along on our left. Two of the bombs were short, but No. 3 hit the Jap at the waterline and No. 4 kicked her forty-five degrees to starboard, blowing most of her stern into the sky behind us. Her gunners were still firing at us as we jinked over to join Jobe, but she was done for.

Joe Jobe, meanwhile, had not been idle. Crossing the air strips with us at 150 feet, he had strafed a number of planes and started three major fires which were still violently blazing, and over the anchorage he had shot up a half-dozen or more coastal vessels while making his run on a cargo ship. At least five of the coastals and two valuable oilers were afire, and the cargo ship was ablaze from machine-gun bullets, when Joe spotted a larger ship farther out and broke his run to go for her. When we joined him a moment after our run on the destroyer, this second cargo vessel, a big one, was exploding all over the water. She kept exploding as we turned for home.

As we headed south toward Saipan, several ships were burning off the island's west shore and five distinct fires blazed on the island itself. We thought we had done a good job. Not a plane had been able to get off the ground to challenge us, and despite the vicious ground fire, neither of our planes was seriously damaged and not a man of either crew was scratched. But as I prepared to send a flash report to Saipan, battered Iwo Jima provided a dramatic postscript. Behind us, three separate and tremendous explosions lit the night, hurling flames and sparks high into the darkness. Only oil or ammunition dumps could have furnished the fuel for such a display. It was the pay-off.

"Skipper," said Shafe, "I can see it in the papers right now. 'Radio Tokyo reports Iwo Jima raided for first time by land-based bombers. Intrepid Japanese fighters turn enemy back with heavy losses. No damage to Japanese island. No comment from U. S. Navy.' "

About eleven o'clock, when our two returning planes were still a good many miles from Saipan, I saw a light winking on the horizon ahead. It shouldn't have been there, and it puzzled me. Saipan has no harbors of any size; our ships were lying in the open roadstead, vulnerable to attack by submarines known to be prowling in the vicinity. This mysterious light could easily be a sub signal of some sort.

It went out as I called Jim Park's attention to it. A moment later there were two of them.

For ten minutes these lights blinked on, went out, came on again. "Jim, we'd better report this by radio," I said. But then, as we neared the island, we saw that the lights slowly *descended* after they had blazed in the sky for a moment. "They aren't signal lights at all," Jim Park said. "They're flares."

He was right. On the northern part of the island, where hundreds of Japs were still hiding in caves and ravines, our Marines were sending up flares at regular intervals during the night to thwart any attempted suicide attack under cover of darkness. For our money, the star shells were excellent long-range lighthouses!

At Saipan we landed on the fighter strip in a drenching rain, and after I had reported to General Hale's Chief of Staff, Captain Davis of the Navy, Joe and I fumbled back through the dark to our camp. We had tents now, set up in the cane field near the air strip. They weren't much—the floors were still mud and the surrounding area was still littered with battle debris—but they were better than sleeping under the wings of the plane. Tired and soaking wet, Joe and I turned in about 3 A.M. and lay there listening to the drumming of the rain on the canvas.

Had we done a good job at Iwo Jima? I thought we had. Together we had seriously damaged and probably sunk a destroyer, a 6,000-ton merchant ship, two small tankers and three coastals, damaged a 3,000-ton merchant ship and set five coastals afire, destroyed at least eight planes on the ground, probably destroyed ten more and damaged many others, started five fires among shore installations and exploded an oil or ammunition dump. Two unescorted Liberators had done that. I hoped Admiral Spruance would be pleased . . .

~~~~~~

NOW THE WAR AGAINST JAPAN MOVED INTO ITS FINAL phase—destruction of the enemy's capability and will to fight on. The tide of battle had inexorably begun to turn at Midway; the approaching last year of the great struggle would find it running full flood.

PART VII

LEYTE GULF

TO OKINAWA:

END OF AN EMPIRE

A WAVE OF UNBRIDLED OPTIMISM SWEPT THE UNITED States during the summer of 1944. The war, an influential section of the press stated categorically, would be over by Christmas; Japan would sue for peace rather than risk invasion of her homeland. These bright and illusory conjectures continued for a while, until it became painfully clear that another year of fighting would be necessary before the enemy could be brought to its knees.

For while MacArthur's forces had battered their way to Vogelkop, New Guinea—virtually assuring total conquest of the sub-continent —and the Navy and Marine Corps had scored a string of notable successes in the Central Pacific, Japan had also been on the move. Shifting her Combined Fleet, in the late spring, from the Inland Sea to Lingga, near Singapore, Japan gave the Allies the distinct impression that she was contemplating a thrust at India, which might deprive the United States Seventh Fleet of the services of an otherwise available force of the Royal Navy. More important, Japanese troops had captured the Chinese railhead city of Henyang on August 8, and by mid-summer were moving on Kweilin and Linchow. The XIV United States Army Air Force had been forced to withdraw from forward airfields in China, necessitating a change of plans for the final assault.

There was much high level debate at this time as to the most feasible approach to the enemy's homeland. Despite the capture of the strategic Chinese shoreline by enemy troops, the Navy favored a plan which would bypass the Philippines in favor of an approach through Formosa. This, King averred, would "put the cork in the bottle" of enemy communications in the China Sea and would permit our air and sea power to blockade Japan into submission. Discussion continued until September 11, four days before the invasion of the Palaus, when a Joint Chiefs of Staff decision was reached: the Philippine island of Mindanao was to be occupied by November 15, and Leyte by December 20.

Fortunately, this timetable was advanced by the appearance of Halsey on the scene with Task Force 38. (It was 38 when Halsey commanded; 58 under Spruance.) On September 9-10 Mindanao airfields near Sarangani Bay were worked over in a series of carrier strikes—some 2400 in two days, with a bag of over two hundred enemy planes as well as a number of ships and installations destroyed. It appeared to Halsey that resistance on Mindanao had been neutralized, and he recommended that both the forces which had been allocated for the invasion of the Palaus and Task Force 38 be turned over to MacArthur for an immediate seizure of Leyte. King and Nimitz endorsed his recommendation and forwarded it to the Joint Chiefs, who required only ninety minutes to approve it: A-Day for Leyte was advanced to October 20. MacArthur was delighted, but had no illusions about the operation:

> "I knew it was to be the crucial battle of the war in the Pacific. On its outcome would depend the fate of the Philippines and the future of the war against Japan. Leyte was to be the anvil against which I hoped to hammer the Japanese into submission in the central Philippines—the springboard from which I could proceed to the conquest of Luzon, for the final assault against Japan itself.

With the initiative in my hands, the war had reached that decisive stage where an important Japanese defeat would seal the fate of the Japanese Empire and a centuries-old tradition of invincibility."

Meanwhile, the invasions in the Palaus and Morotai went along as scheduled. On September 15, D-Day, after a preliminary bombardment by naval forces, Marines stormed ashore on Pelileu to open their campaign. On Morotai, Army forces under MacArthur occupied the island in a virtually bloodless assault. While the two campaigns could not be compared to what was coming up, sporadic Japanese opposition did continue in the Palaus until the following spring.

Let us turn to the Leyte operation. At this time four top commands were designated: 1) MacArthur in command of all ground forces, some air force and the Seventh Fleet; 2) Nimitz in command of the Third Fleet and the VII Army Air Force; 3) General H. H. "Hap" Arnold in command of the XX Air Force; and 4) General Joseph W. Stilwell in command of the China-Burma-India Army Air Force, otherwise known as the XIV AAF. Responsibility for the first phase of the final assault on Japan devolved upon these few, whose sentiments were expressed by MacArthur: ". . . A most ambitious and difficult undertaking . . ."

The island of Leyte, comprising 2,785 square miles, about half of which is mountainous and the rest lush farming land, was first visited by Magellan in 1521. The island lies at the end of an historic channel between Calicoan and Homonhon Islands, the primary waterway in past centuries for other explorers as well as the Moro pirates. In 1944 the population of Leyte numbered about a million people, speaking two Visayan dialects. Warm and hospitable, they were by and large opposed to Japanese rule, and displayed their hostility with a very impressive guerilla movement.

Japan's forces on the island originally numbered six divisions but at the time of the landings—October 20—all but Major General Makino's 16th were elsewhere. The 16th (and all other ground forces in the Philippines) were units of the Japanese Southern Army commanded by Field Marshal Terauchi in Manila. Under him, but exercising independent command, were Japan's Fifth and Sixth Air Forces (Navy) and the Fourth Air Force (Army) with a total of 1,177 aircraft. In principle, the Imperial Japanese Navy under Admiral Soemu Toyoda was prepared for the defense of the Philippines with Operation Sho. But before we examine in detail Japan's plan for the naval defense of the islands—the last and biggest of their "decisive battles"—let us turn to the Third Fleet and its crippling three-day strike on Formosa, which deprived the enemy of a large part of his land-based air strength.

On October 12, from dawn to dusk, Task Force 38 flew 1,378 sorties against Formosan shipping and airfields; next day another nine hundred and seventy-four sorties; the third day just one strike. As a result of this action Vice Admiral Fukudome's Sixth Air Force lost 500 planes, plus two score freighters and small craft and all manner of ground installations destroyed, including ammunition dumps. American losses totalled seventy-one aircraft. However, Japanese aerial torpedoes scored two serious hits on Task Force 38 during this operation—cruisers *Canberra* and *Houston* were badly damaged and put out of action. Three days later Halsey launched his first Philippines' strikes in support of MacArthur, in which carrier *Enterprise,* of Rear Admiral R. E. Davidson's Task Group 38.4, took part.

Commander Edward P. Stafford tells of the pre-invasion aerial activity over Manila. We have met him before.

I.

FORAY TO THE

PHILIPPINES

Shortly before 9:00 A.M., *Enterprise* launched a full deckload against the U. S.-built, Japanese-occupied airfields around the capital of the Philippines. On this first strike, The Big E sent her first team— nine Helldivers under Riera and eight Avengers under Prickett, escorted by four divisions of Hellcats under Bakutis.

The formation crossed the east shore of Luzon with the bombers and torpedo planes at 15,000 feet and the four divisions of fighters stacked above, ahead, and on both sides, with Fred Bakutis' division flying roving high cover at 22,000. With forty miles to go to Manila Bay on the west coast, some three dozen geometrically arranged specks in the sky ahead developed rapidly into as many mottled-brown Oscars, Tonys and Zekes coming in high and fast to intercept.

Fighting 20, outnumbered two to one, closed up, charged guns and waited at 160 knots between the bombers and the enemy. The sleek and agile Japanese planes surrounded the *Enterprise* formation. Dog Smith's men held steadily on course, gunners in the open cockpits of the SB2Cs and the ball turrets of the TBFs cocked and ready, the tight formations of Hellcats waiting for the enemy's first move. Then a single Oscar high on the right flank rolled into a firing run. Bakutis' section of two instantly turned into him and he dived away, recovering far below to begin the climb back. Another on the left

815

did the same thing and also dove away when the escort began to counter. Bakutis' eager young pilots were terribly tempted to follow, knowing their heavy F6s could easily catch and destroy the lighter enemy planes in a dive, but squadron discipline held and they maintained position. The Japanese were apparently trying to draw the Hellcats away in order to get at the bombers. When this tactic failed, they were forced to attack the American fighters which were always between them and their targets. They came in singly and haphazardly, and Bakutis' pilots met them in pairs and fours with the tight teamwork that they had been trained to, and which had worked so well over Formosa two days before.

Planes began to smoke and spiral down the sky on the eastern approaches to Manila—and they were all Japanese. Ensigns Doug Baker and Chuck Haverland, the second section of Bakutis' division, accounted for five between them in a wild, high-altitude scramble which lasted twenty minutes, and during which Baker scattered five attacking Oscars by firing his air-to-ground rockets at their formation and followed up with his guns to shoot down a sixth. Haverland fired at such short range on a diving Tony that oil from its broken engine streaked and clouded his windshield.

Lieutenant Bob Fallgatter's division got three more certainly, and probably five, when six Oscars attempted to attack the bombers as they were beginning their runs on Nielson Field.

En route to the rendezvous point, Lieutenant Leo McCuddin shot down an Oscar from below as it was beginning a run on a TBF. The enemy pilot bailed out and dangled eerily under his chute, dressed from head to toe in solid black.

Ensign Bill Herman, also on his way to the rendezvous, broke up an attack by three Oscars on another F6F, blowing the canopy off one and killing the pilot as he started to climb out.

Ten of the enemy interceptors were seen to crash, and another four probably went down. In the words of Emmett Riera, who had reason to know:

> Escort was superb; not one enemy fighter approached to within gun range of the bombers and torpedo bombers, either during approach or upon retirement; every plane that attempted an attack was either shot down or driven off.

Not a single VF-20 Hellcat was lost.

Clouds covered most of the Manila area, so that the bombers and torpedo planes had to spiral steeply down through a hole to break out underneath and find their targets. Then, with the bottom of the cloud deck at 2,000 feet, they were limited to high-speed, low-level passes across the field. In that shallow layer of clear air between ground and cloud, the AA was the worst the Big E's squadrons had ever seen. The blue planes seemed to be flying through a continuous curtain of smoking tracers. But they unloaded their bombs at foolproof altitudes on ramps crowded with parked planes.

With air opposition temporarily accounted for, the fighters swooped in under the overcast to slam their rockets into the rows of grounded planes, and then all three squadrons headed out across the crowded harbor to rendezvous.

On the way out, Ed Holley, flying an *Enterprise* TBF again as he had done two years before off Guadalcanal, caught a Zeke coming out of a cloud ahead and spun him in with 200 rounds from the wind guns of the big Avenger.

Fred Bakutis, rapidly losing oil from a bullet hole in his engine, went on alone as soon as Luzon was left behind, and arrived aboard to find the task group under attack and the fighters he had left behind as busy here, 200 miles at sea, as his four divisions of escorts had been over the target. Fred landed on the familiar deck, changed planes and got back in the air.

At 10:30 A.M., *Enterprise* CIC had vectored some *San Jacinto* fighters onto a Judy which they shot down twelve miles southwest of the force. At the same time, with more and more bogies showing on the scopes, eleven of the VF-20's fighters, including the air group commander, were scrambled. One division of four, led by Joe Lawler, found five Zekes coming in at 17,000 feet, shot one down, damaged another and drove the others off.

The other four-plane division, led by Mel Prichard, encountered Zekes also and knocked down four.

But three enemy dive bombers and one bomb-carrying Zeke, flying fast and high, eluded the fighters. The first warning was the shouted report of a lookout:

"Enemy dive bombers overhead!"

Task group guns opened with a roar, but three Judys released over *Franklin* and escaped. Two bombs were wide, but one landed close aboard, showering her flight deck and starting a fire on the port quarter.

While the big new carrier spouted black smoke, and repair parties converged on the blaze, a single Zeke, with a bomb under each wing, slanted in toward her starboard bow. All *Franklin's* starboard guns and all those on other ships that would bear turned on the lone Japanese pilot. For a few seconds he flew on into the lead-filled sky, then flipped around in a 90-degree bank and headed home.

Franklin put out her fire in a few minutes and resumed operations, but the enemy attacks continued all day.

At 2:20 P.M., Fred Bakutis was launched with a CAP of twelve Hellcats, and in the next three hours destroyed at least eighteen enemy planes in the vicinity of the task group. The Big E's luck was running strong that fall afternoon. The first bogey to which CIC vectored him was a single, sleek, fast, twin-engine Dinah reconnaissance plane at 23,000 feet, fifty miles out. The F6Fs had to strain to catch it, using full throttle and water injection in a shallow climb from 20,000. But when Bakutis and his wingman, Walter Wood, flamed both its engines and started it on the fiery, four-mile drop to the Pacific, it was more of a victory then they knew. The next two dangerously large formations of dive bombers, torpedo planes and fighters engaged by Bakutis' Hellcats, were circling sixty miles out, apparently awaiting instructions from a coordinator who could now no longer instruct.

Ensign Walt Wood was the hero of the afternoon. Flying on Bakutis' wing as smoothly and reliably as though the two planes were the same weapon, he shared in the destruction of the coordinating Dinah, then made two passes with Bakutis on a formation of Jill torpedo bombers, knocking down one on each pass. Bakutis also got one on each attack. When the division went after a lone Zeke, it was Wood who shot it down and, a moment later, with his division leader out of ammunition, Wood expended his last rounds on still another Zeke which another fighter finally forced into the sea.

Fred Bakutis himself destroyed two, plus the Dinah, and damaged another.

But Fighting 20 had its losses too. Ensign Bruce Hanna pressed an attack so close to a Betty that he sheared off his right wing on the enemy plane and barely managed to escape from his violently spinning F6 before it hit the water. Cut and battered by the high-speed bail-out, he drifted for nearly three days in his rubber raft before an antisub patrol saw him and guided a destroyer in to pick him up.

Ensign Norman Snow became separated in a dogfight with a dozen Oscars, and returned to base in serious trouble with large holes in wings and elevators, his radio transmitter shot up and unable to lower his wheels. Another F6 joined up on him as he circled and, after consulting *Enterprise,* advised him to climb and bail out. But Snow was either wounded and could not get out, or had too little fuel to climb. He landed hard in a tower of spray alongside the destroyer *Mugford,* climbed out and swam toward the ship, which put four swimmers overboard to help him. Hurt and weighted down with his flight gear and parachute, he slipped through the hands of the destroyer sailors and was lost.

On the sixteenth, TG 38.4 fueled and received replacement planes and crews from the escort carrier, *Sitka Bay,* and on the seventeenth closed in to 150 miles to get on with the job of neutralizing the airfields on Luzon.

The early fighter sweep on the seventeenth found the entire Manila area buried under a thick white blanket of clouds, and circled for nearly an hour in the clear sky above, looking in vain for a hole or a way to get through to the enemy.

Strike Able—eight fighters, eight bombers and eight torpedo planes plus a similar group from *Franklin,* all under Dog Smith—had better luck. A hole opened up for them, and they let down below the overcast in the vicinity of Clark Field to find one of the air bases in the Clark complex swarming with planes preparing to take off in the clearing weather. The field was Mabalacat East, ten miles north of Clark. Smith assigned it as the target for his group and dove in to the attack.

Lieutenant Jim Verdin's division went in first with rockets, and Verdin himself smoked four of them into a bunch of eighteen to twenty enemy fighters clustered around the approach end of the runway, their props turning, waiting for take-off. The blast of the rockets engulfed the Japanese planes in a roaring cloud of fire and sailing debris as Verdin's Hellcats swept overhead.

Dog Smith, with Tom Woodruff glued to his wing, followed in a rocket run and then, with rockets away, switched to a pair of Zekes just taking off. Smith put a short burst into the lead Zeke as it was pulling up its wheels and it crashed in a long smear of flame at the edge of the field. Turning hard left and pulling up, he found another Zeke just climbing out and flamed it with another single burst. Dog leveled off and continued straight ahead toward a third Zeke approaching head on. The enemy pilot turned hard right and Smith turned with him, hammering a third burst into the Zeke's upturned belly which set it afire. Three planes in less than a minute with 140 rounds total per gun. Dog Smith did not just happen to be the commander of the most aggressive air group on the most competent carrier in the Navy of the United States.

Other fighters did almost as well, strafing enemy planes still on the ground and blasting those down that were just taking off.

Bombers and torpedo planes followed the fighters in, laying bombs and incendiary clusters on the crowded aprons and hangars at Mabalacat East. The twenty-four planes of Strike Able destroyed twenty-eight enemy aircraft on the ground and in the air, with superficial wounds to one turret gunner of a TBF.

Strike Baker, the same morning, flattened every structure at Legaspi Field in southeastern Luzon, but lost Lieutenant George Wilson and the crew of his Avenger to heavy and accurate medium-caliber AA over the target.

October 18, two days before the Leyte landings, was a busy and a bad day for *Enterprise*. Three strikes and two fighter sweeps went to Manila that Wednesday in increasingly miserable weather associated with the fringes of a typhoon. On every mission but one, pilots and/or crewmen were lost. Flight operations began in the dark at 6:00 A.M. and ended in the dark at 8:00 P.M.

On the morning sweep, Fred Bakutis arrived over Manila Bay with twelve fighters at 25,000 feet, and found the bay and the city cloud-covered as usual. But, to the south, Clark Field was clear, and the Hellcats circled on that direction. Over Clark a flight of seven greenish-brown, snub-nosed Tojos was climbing out, and two of VF-20's division dived to the attack, leaving one up for cover. In the next few moments, other enemy formations joined the fight until the clear sky over the Clark complex was full of mottled-brown and blue aircraft climbing, twisting, diving at full power, their guns clattering, the radio air full of urgent calls and orders in English and Japanese.

In the heavy-gutted, horizon-spinning, cordite-smelling swirl of combat, black-haired, white-toothed Douglas Baker and pint-sized, ex-tumbler Chuck Haverland each shot down three enemy fighters. Bakutis and Foye got two apiece and most of the others one for a total of eighteen.

Bill Foye, flying wing on Lieutenant Jack Laxton, was badly hit, his right wing tip shot off, his elevators shredded and smoke from his damaged engine pouring into the cockpit so that he had to open the canopy to see and breathe. Just before his radio and instruments went

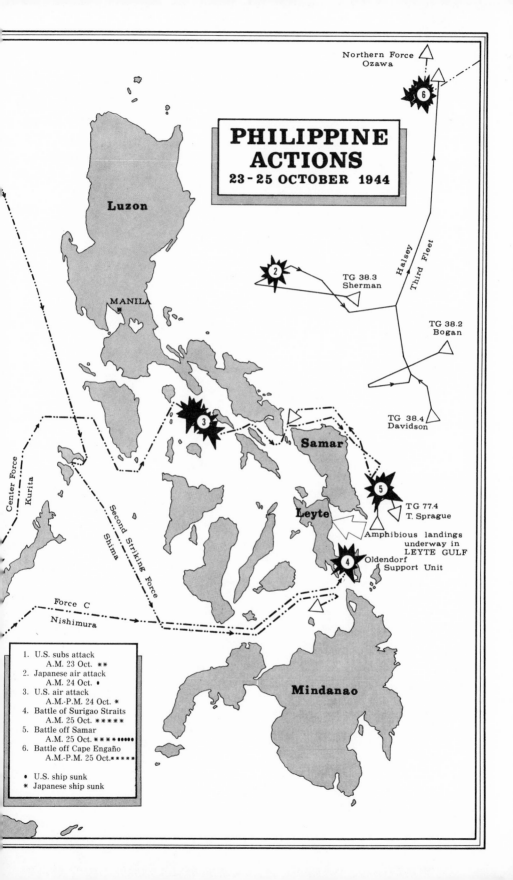

PHILIPPINE ACTIONS
23-25 OCTOBER 1944

Northern Force
Ozawa

6

TG 38.3
Sherman

2

Halsey
Third Fleet

TG 38.2
Bogan

Luzon

MANILA

TG 38.4
Davidson

Samar

3

5

TG 77.4
T. Sprague

Leyte

Amphibious landings
underway in
LEYTE GULF

4

Oldendorf
Support Unit

Center Force
Kurita

Second Striking Force
Shima

Force C
Nishimura

Mindanao

1. U.S. subs attack
   A.M. 23 Oct. ✳✳
2. Japanese air attack
   A.M. 24 Oct. ●
3. U.S. air attack
   A.M.-P.M. 24 Oct. ✳
4. Battle of Surigao Straits
   A.M. 25 Oct. ✳✳✳✳✳
5. Battle off Samar
   A.M. 25 Oct. ✳✳✳✳●●●●●
6. Battle off Cape Engaño
   A.M.-P.M. 25 Oct.✳✳✳✳✳

● U.S. ship sunk
✳ Japanese ship sunk

out, he was able to call to Laxton and Bakutis to say he was hit, losing oil pressure and trying to make Subic Bay for a water landing. A search that afternoon found no trace of Bill Foye or his F6. He was listed as missing.

Had it not been for Fred Bakutis, Ensign John Hoeynck would have been missing too. In a turning contest with three Oscars, one of them clipped about three feet off his left wing and then spun down out of control. The F6 would still fly, but at over 180 knots it began to vibrate as though it would come apart. Hoeyneck climbed out of the fight and called his skipper. Bakutis and Gallagher found him at once, and covered him as he headed east across the mountains to the sea and home. An Oscar also found the cripple, and hung above and astern, making runs but pulling up when the two escorts went into a defensive weave. After four or five cycles, Bakutis had had enough. On the next pass, he reversed his usual turn, jammed on full throttle and water injection, and, with Gallagher on his wing, climbed back after the Oscar. The surprised enemy pilot was caught and slowed by Bakutis' first burst; the second blew off his canopy and killed him as he started out. The two Hellcats dived back to their crippled squadron mate.

Strike Able, nine bombers and eight torpedo planes with eight fighters escorting, in company with a *Franklin* group, hit Clark itself and two outlying fields, strafing, bombing and rocketing Japanese aircraft on the ground and destroying those encountered in the air. The SB2Cs used a new tactic of dropping in their dives at 4,500 feet and then strafing with 20-millimeter cannon during pull-out. The high angle and heavy caliber of this strafing, executed after the bombs were away and pilots could give full attention to gunnery, cost the enemy several planes parked in deep revetments which would have been difficult to hit by usual methods of low-angle strafing and bombing.

On the way to the rendezvous, Ensign John Crittenden intercepted two Tojos attacking one of the torpedo planes. He blew one up in a persistent and stubbornly pressed chase, but found the other on his tail and was unable to shake him with the most violent maneuvering. Dog Smith and his wingman came to the rescue, disintegrating the sticky Tojo with their combined fire.

Strike Baker was launched less than an hour after Able, with 24 more aircraft, to hit Nielson Field and photograph Manila Bay and Harbor. Bombers and torpedo planes destroyed another dozen aircraft on the ground, damaged some twenty others and obtained plenty of excellent photographs of shipping and harbor facilities. But the escorting fighters were kept constantly busy warding off vigorous assaults by enemy interceptors. Twelve Oscars attacked one division of Hellcats from a Luffberry circle above, two or three planes at a time rolling over on their backs, pulling through in split S's for their runs and climbing back to the circle on recovery. The Hellcats climbed, weaving defensively, shot down three and drove the others off. None got through to the bombers below.

The other Hellcat division was jumped by seven Oscars while on a photo run over Manila. Each man in the division killed one enemy, and, in addition, two more were damaged. But in the skirmish, Ensign Walt Wood was hit. He had been Bakutis' wingman three days before in the defense of the task group, with four planes to his credit. Now his blue F6 flipped violently over on its back and dived into the trees below. His body was recovered by friendly Filipino irregulars and buried with full military honors. Handsome, likeable young Wood was serious about flying for his country. In the seconds it took his broken Hellcat to hurtle from the open sky to his death he had scribbled on his knee pad his last words—"hit 3."

Strike Baker flew east through the valleys and under the clouds until they were over the friendly sea, then climbed and headed home.

As a result of Strike Baker's report of a heavy concentration of shipping in Manila Bay, and the fierce fighter opposition they encountered, Strike Charlie was launched at 1:30 P.M. against those ships, preceded by a sweep of thirteen *Enterprise* fighters and twelve more from *Franklin*. In addition to the sweep, Strike Charlie's Helldivers and torpedo-carrying Avengers were escorted by twelve more Hellcats under the air group commander.

As the combined sweep and strike headed slightly south of west toward Luzon and Manila, their little clotted Vs and echelons lost and insignificant in the hugeness of the sky, the pilots could look to their left and see the weather moving northward. Masses of gray and dark gray towering cumulus clouds which the airmen knew from experience held turbulence, hail, heavy rain and violent and unpredictable winds, formed a long line to the south—and the whole front was moving north so fast that the leaders were forced to detour in that direction to stay clear.

Manila Bay was covered by a thick and solid layer of clouds. Fred

Bakutis' fighter sweep continued on to Subic Bay to search for Bill Foye, missing since morning, found nothing, and returned to the Clark area, knocking off two Oscars almost casually on the way.

Strike Charlie circled Manila Bay counterclockwise to the north and west, let down over water, and swept into the crowded harbor between the dark clouds and the dark sea. The bristling, pitted whale's back of Corregidor spat obscenely at them as they passed. Rain squalls streaked their windshields and chopped visibility momentarily to half a mile. But, lying at anchor in the spacious bay and behind the long breakwaters of the south harbor, were scores of cargo ships, about twenty of which were major, ocean-going vessels.

The Hellcats spread out and went in first, as the ships and shore batteries opened up with everything they had, their rockets smoking out ahead in pairs and .50-caliber tracers following as the range closed. With rockets gone, they wheeled and attacked again with guns only, their bullets ripping up the calm harbor water on both sides of their targets, holing and firing ship after ship.

Riera's Helldivers, used to stooping down from 12,000 feet had to settle for high-speed glides through the pouring, crisscrossing flak, releasing their big bombs at 1,000 to 500 feet on the larger ships inside the breakwater and strafing with their 20-millimeter cannon on the way out.

Sam Prickett's Avengers had the most potent weapons and the nastiest job. In order to aim the torpedos that could rip the whole bottom out of a thin-skinned merchantman with a single hit, it was necessary to fly for half a minute straight, steady and not too fast toward the target, presenting, for that time, an easy target for the guns that lined the shore and flashed and clattered on the ships. Like Gene Lindsey's pilots at Midway so long ago, every one of Prickett's TBFs laid its slim "fish" as carefully and close as though the frantic guns were silent and this was a Sunday exercise in Chesapeake Bay. But with their fish away and swimming straight and true toward their targets, the torpedo pilots jerked and skidded, dipped and weaved and fish-tailed with every trick they knew to evade the lead that laced the dusky belt between clouds and sea. There was neither time nor visibility enough to see the results of their attacks, but one of Riera's pilots near by saw two torpedoes fountain against the side of a big tanker.

The bomber crews, who did not have to wait while a torpedo ran some 500 yards to see results, watched their bombs rip into five big ships, some of which were hit by several 1,000-pounders, enough to sink a carrier or a cruiser.

One SB2C caught a steam of explosive tracers and skidded into the Bay. Ensign Les Hornbeak and Fred Swinney, his gunner, were lost.

With the ordeal in the murky bay completed, the planes with the white triangles on their tails had now to get home through the weather which had been steadily moving north across their route.

It was 5:00 P.M. and getting dark when the Big E's squadrons began their climb out of Manila across the spinal mountains of Luzon. The first casualty was handsome, competent Jack Laxton of Fighting 20. In a low-level strafing run over the grass fields south of Clark, an unlucky bullet out of the puny resistance offered by the enemy had entered his engine and severed an oil line. Smoking and losing oil, he climbed out to 9,000 feet with his division and signaled he was OK, but on the other side of the mountains, as the fighters began to let down for the trip home, his engine froze and stopped. Laxton, who had watched the same thing happen to Fred Turnbull off Formosa a few days before, glided down through a hold in the clouds, with Fred Bakutis following, and called repeatedly for Jack to bail out. Laxton vanished momentarily under the clouds and, when he came in sight again, he was at 2,000 feet in an inverted dive. His squadron mates circled the spreading oil slick for several minutes and then headed sadly home through the increasing dusk and the deteriorating weather.

By 5:30, Strike Charlie had been in the air four hours with considerable time spent in climbing to attack altitude, climbing over mountains, and at full power during combat. It was now necessary to swing wide to the northward to avoid the rolling weather front. It was apparent to Dog Smith that all of his planes would be landing after dark and that some of those landings would be well short of the Big E's waiting deck.

The same facts were apparent to Cato Glover and Tom Hamilton in *Enterprise*. They were also evident on the flagship, and Admiral Davison released *Enterprise* with an escort to steam westward to meet the returning strike. But, even at 26 knots, the Big E could only close the range by thirteen miles each half hour and that was not enough.

From some fifty miles out, the bombers and torpedo planes began to ditch. At ten minutes of seven desperately empty aircraft began to appear in the landing circle. It was almost totally dark. Fifteen planes landed before one crashed and closed the deck. Three Helldivers landed in the water close aboard and one Helldiver and four Avengers ditched farther out. One Avenger pilot in the darkness and confusion, and the urgency of his empty tanks, flew into the side of the *Belleau Wood* killing his entire crew. Two TBFs and three fighters landed on *Franklin,* and one of each made the *Wasp.* All the Hellcats landed safely, some with barely enough fuel to taxi out of the arresting gear.

With the strike group down all over the rapidly clouding sea, Admiral Davison released his destroyers from their screening duties for rescue work.

The destroyer sailors put in a long night. They eased out along the track of the returning strike, checking positions where *Enterprise* reported that planes had gone down, straining their eyes through night-tinted binoculars for the tiny point of light in the encompassing blackness of sea and sky that would be the one-cell flashlight screwed to an aviator's Mae West, straining their ears over the hum of machinery and the wash of the waves for the tiny sound of a voice in that waste of water. Sailors in swimming trunks, wearing light canvas harnesses from which long lines were led, stood all night by their rails, ready to dive into the sea to give an "airdale" a hand. Whaleboats were rigged out, ready for lowering, engines checked and crews standing by. Inflated rubber rafts with lines attached were ready to throw overboard, and men stood by to man them. Pharmacist's mates waited on deck with their canvas kits of first-aid materials. Cargo nets lay rolled up in the waterways, outboard of everything, secured at their tops and ready to drop down the side for survivors to scramble up. Clean bunks and blankets and straight shots of medicinal alcohol waited below decks.

By morning, most of Dog Smith's airmen had been rescued. At dawn twenty planes left the Big E's deck to search for the remainder. At 10:40 A.M., twelve more went out, and at 2:15 P.M., eleven more. The search planes swept the sea at low altitude in line abreast and nothing that floated escaped them. Survivors that the destroyers had been unable to locate in the darkness were found, and the "cans" moved in to pick them up. In the course of the searches, Bill Herman and Don Reeder also found a Betty which they promptly destroyed.

On the twentieth the destroyers began returning her pilots and crewmen to *Enterprise.* When it was all over, seven men were missing from Strike Charlie and its fighter sweep—Jack Laxton; Hornbeak and Swinney, shot down over the target; Ensign Don Conaway, Kelimoff and Riggs, the crew of the TBF which flew into the *Belleau Wood;* and Lieutenant Charles Bretland of Torpedo 20, who inexplicably became separated from his crew after ditching and was lost.

And on that busy and dangerous October 18, Wood, Snow and Foye had also been lost. But Bill Foye was not dead. He was lying, with a painfully wrenched neck and back, wrapped in his parachute, in a shelter formed by the roots of a mango tree, while friendly Philippine guerillas fed him and made plans to get him to safety and eventually back to duty. Bill spent the next three and a half months in hiding and running from the Japanese in the towns and jungles of Luzon, in the care of the guerillas and their friends, was finally picked up by a PBY, and when Air Group Twenty pulled into Pearl on the fifteenth of February on their way home, he was standing on the dock, like a ghost, to greet them. On April 26, he reported for duty at Trenton, New Jersey, and mentioned to the medical officer that he still had a stiff neck. X rays showed that his neck was broken, and had been since October 18, when he bailed out low over Luzon. Any bad jolt during that six months could have severed his spinal cord. It took fifteen months of treatment to put him together again.

October 20, 1944, was the day that Douglas MacArthur returned to the Philippines. *Enterprise* played no vital role in bringing the general back, other than to hammer down some airfields which might have provided some resistance. On A-Day, the Big E furnished only two prelanding strikes on the dirt field of San Pablo and the pathetic little town of Dagami near the Leyte beaches. The assigned targets did not seem worth the bombs and rockets used to blow them up, and the pilots were more interested in the incredible array of U.S. shipping which filled Leyte Gulf than in the apparently deserted and undesirable coastline of the island itself. But *Enterprise* was to have a major role in arranging things so that the general could *remain* in the Philippines.

MEANWHILE, THE INVASION OF LEYTE GOT UNDERWAY. The disposition of naval forces was as follows: Minesweeping and Hydrographic Group including Bombardment and Fire Support Units;

Dinagat (Island) Attack Group; Bombardment and Fire Support Group including 12 CVEs; Southern LST Group; Northern Transport Group; Northern LST Group including Covering Group; Southern Transport Group; and Fleet Flagship Group . . . lifting and screening 145,000 Army troops of MacArthur's command.

The first Philippine landings were at Dinagat Island, near Leyte, where the 6th Ranger Infantry Battalion went ashore to dispose of thirty-two Japanese troops; but not before the garrison commander had alerted Toyoda of the invasion. Upon receipt of the message, the Japanese Fleet Admiral issued SHO alert, and Admiral Kurita's First Striking Force steamed out from Lingga Roads, near Singapore.

The enemy's battle plan is recounted by Hanson W. Baldwin, a Naval Academy graduate and the military editor of the New York *Times*.

2.

LEYTE PRELIMINARIES

. . . Admiral Soemu Toyoda, commander-in-chief of the Japanese Combined Fleet and leader of what he knew was a forlorn hope, had his last chance to "destroy the enemy who enjoys the luxury of material resources." From his headquarters at the Naval War College just outside Tokyo, he sent the word "To Conquer" to his widely scattered units.

The Shō plan was daring and desperate—fitted to the last months of an empire strained beyond its capabilities. The Japanese Fleet had not recovered from its cumulative losses, particularly from the heavy blow it had suffered four months earlier in the Battle of the Philippine Sea, when Admiral Raymond W. Spruance, covering our Mariannas landings, had destroyed more than 400 Japanese planes, sunk three Japanese carriers, and broken the back of Japanese naval aviation. In mid-October, when Halsey—in a preliminary to the Leyte Gulf landing—struck heavily at Formosa, Toyoda had utilized his land-based planes and had also thrown his hastily trained carrier replacement pilots into the fight. The gamble failed. But the "pathology of fear" and the curious propensity of the Japanese for transforming defeats into victories in their official reports magnified the normally highly inflated claims of enemy aviators; Toyko declared the Third Fleet had "ceased to be an organized striking force."

An enemy plane dropped leaflets over recently captured Peleliu:

FOR RECKLESS YANKEE DOODLE:

Do you know about the naval battle done by the American 58th
(sic) Fleet at the sea near Taiwan (Formosa) and Philippine?
Japanese powerful Air Force had sunk their 19 aeroplane carriers,
4 battleships, 10 several cruisers and destroyers, along with
sending 1,261 ship aeroplanes into the sea. . . .

Actually only two cruisers—*Canberra* and *Houston*—were damaged; less than 100 U.S. planes lost; the Japanese were to have a rude awakening as the great invasion armada neared Leyte Gulf.

But for Toyoda, the Battle of the Philippine Sea and his futile gamble in defense of Formosa had left the Japanese Fleet naked to air attack. Toyoda had carriers, but with few planes and half-trained pilots. Shō I, therefore, must be dependent upon stealth and cunning, night operations, and what air cover could be provided chiefly by land-based planes operating from Philippine bases and working in close conjunction with the fleet.

Toyoda also confronted another handicap—a fleet widely separated by distance. He exercised command—from his land headquarters—over a theoretically "Combined Fleet," but Vice-Admiral Jisaburo Ozawa, who flew his flag from carrier *Zuikaku,* and who commanded the crippled carriers and some cruisers and destroyers, was still based in the Inland Sea in Japanese home waters. The bulk of the fleet's heavy units—Vice-Admiral Takeo Kurita's First Diversion Attack Force, of battleships, cruisers, and destroyers—was based on Lingga Anchorage near Singapore, close to its fuel sources. The Japanese Fleet was divided in the face of a superior naval force; it could not be concentrated prior to battle.

These deficiencies, plus the geography of the Philippines, dictated the enemy plan, which was hastily modified at the last minute, partially because of the Japanese weaknesses in carrier aviation. Two principal straits—San Bernardino, north of the island of Samar; and Surigao, between Mindanao and Dinagat and Leyte and Panaon— lead from the South China Sea to Leyte Gulf, where the great armada of MacArthur was committed to the invasion. The Japanese ships based near Singapore—the so-called First Diversion Attack Force were to steam north toward Leyte, with a stop at Brunei Bay, Borneo, to refuel. There the force would split; the Central Group, Vice-Admiral Takeo Kurita, flying his flag in the heavy cruiser *Atago,* with a total of five battleships, ten heavy cruisers, two light cruisers, and fifteen destroyers, would transit San Bernardino Strait at night;

the Southern Group, Vice-Admiral Shōji Nishimura, with two battleships, one heavy cruiser, and four destroyers, was to be augmented at
Surigao Strait by a ancillary force of three more cruisers and four
destroyers under Vice-Admiral Kiyohide Shima, which was to steam
through Formosa Strait, with a stop in the Pescadores, all the way
from its bases in the home islands. All these forces were to strike the
great American armada in Leyte Gulf almost simultaneously at dawn
of the 25th of October and wreak havoc among the thin-skinned amphibious ships like a hawk among chickens.

But the key to the operation was the emasculated Japanese carriers, operating under Vice-Admiral Jisaburo Ozawa from their bases
in Japan's Inland Sea. These ships—one heavy carrier and three light
carriers, with less than 100 planes aboard—"all that remained of the
enemy's once-great carrier forces"—were to steam south toward
Luzon and to act as deliberate decoys or "lures" for Admiral
Halsey's great Third Fleet, which was "covering" the amphibious
invasion of Leyte. The northern decoy force was to be accompanied
by two hermaphrodites—battleship-carriers, the *Ise* and *Hyuga,* with
the after-turrets replaced by short flight decks, but with no planes,
and by three cruisers and ten destroyers. Ozawa was to lure Halsey's
Third Fleet to the north, away from Leyte, and open the way for
Kurita and Nishimura to break into Leyte Gulf.

At the same time all three forces were to be aided—not with direct
air cover, but by intensive attacks by Japanese land-based planes
upon American carriers and shipping. As a last-minute "spur-of-the-
moment" decision, the Japanese "Special Attack Groups" were acti-
vated, and the Kamikaze (Divine Wind) fliers commenced their
suicidal attacks upon U.S. ships. As early as October 15, Rear Admiral Masabumi Arima, a subordinate naval air commander, flying
from a Philippine field, had made a suicide dive and had "lit the fuse
of the ardent wishes of his men." All of these far-flung forces were
under the common command of Admiral Toyoda far away in Tokyo.

Such was the desperate Shō I—perhaps the greatest gamble, the
most daring and unorthodox plan in the history of naval war.

It committed to action virtually all that was left of the operational
forces—afloat and in the air—of Japan's Navy—four carriers, two
battleship-carriers, seven battleships, nineteen cruisers, thirty-three
destroyers, and perhaps 500 to 700 Japanese aircraft—mostly land-
based.

But the opposing American forces were far more powerful. Like the Japanese forces which had no common commander closer than Tokyo, the U.S. Fleet operated under divided command. General MacArthur, as theater commander of the Southwest Pacific area, was in over-all charge of the Leyte invasion, and through Admiral Thomas C. Kinkaid, he commanded the Seventh Fleet, which was in direct charge of the amphibious operation. But Admiral Halsey's powerful covering force of the Third Fleet—the strongest fleet in the world—was not under MacArthur's command; it was a part of Admiral Chester W. Nimitz's Pacific Command forces, and Nimitz had his headquarters in Hawaii. And above Nimitz and MacArthur, the only unified command was in Washington.

The gun power of Kinkaid's Seventh Fleet was provided by six old battleships—five of them raised from the mud of Pearl Harbor, but he had sixteen escort carriers—small, slow-speed vessels, converted from merchant hulls—eight cruisers and scores of destroyers and destroyer escorts, frigates, motor torpedo boats, and other types. Kinkaid's job was to provide shore bombardment and close air support for the Army and anti-submarine and air defense for the amphibious forces.

Halsey, with eight large attack carriers, eight light carriers, six fast new battleships, fifteen cruisers, and fifty-eight destroyers, was ordered to "cover and support forces of the Southwest Pacific (MacArthur's command) in order to assist in the seizure and occupation of objectives in the Central Philippines." He was to destroy enemy naval and air forces threatening the invasion. He was to remain responsible to Admiral Nimitz, but "necessary measures for detailed coordination of operations between the . . . (Third Fleet) . . . and . . . the (Seventh Fleet) will be arranged by their . . . commanders."

The combined Third and Seventh Fleets could muster 1,000 to 1,400 ship-based aircraft—thirty-two carriers; twelve battleships; twenty-three cruisers; more than one hundred destroyers and destroyer escorts and numerous smaller types and hundreds of auxiliaries. The Seventh Fleet also had a few tender-based PBY patrol planes (flying boats). But not all of these forces participated in the far-flung air attacks and the three widely separated major engagements which later came to be called the Battle for Leyte Gulf.

Such was the stage, these the actors, and this the plot in the most dramatic and far-flung naval battle in history . . .

ON A-DAY, VICE ADMIRAL WILKINSON'S SOUTHERN AT-
tack Force (TF 79) landed the XXIV Corps (7th and 96th Divisions)
on a 5000-yard stretch of sandy beach at Dulag. From here this outfit
hoped to link up with the X Corps moving down from landings at
Tacloban. While gunfire from bombarding warships smothered the
beaches, Lieutenant Stewart W. Hellman left the transport *Knox* in
an LCVP to go aboard one of the control boats for beach Violet II.

3.

LEYTE LANDING

As we pulled away from the ship the shoreline was still lost in a haze of smoke and morning mist, but as we approached we were able to pick out Catmon Hill off our starboard bow and then the Libarnan Head. These were landmarks which we had studied as we had steamed along in the days which preceded our arrival off Leyte. We hurriedly worked our way in a comparatively calm sea through a maze of landing craft, finally emerging into an open area where all hands immediately cried, "There she is." The PC was on station and waiting for us.

It was nearly 0900. It had taken us over an hour to reach the Control Boat, and as the Captain welcomed us aboard we were conscious for the first time to the terrific din of the prelanding bombardment which was going on. Off our starboard quarter a destroyer was hurling high explosive shells at our particular beach and geysers of water and earth plumed into the sky as the naval gunners raked every inch of the beach from waterline to palm trees. Cruisers and battleships up and down the coast were making the beaches a living hell. Overhead droned our planes, sometimes in pairs, sometimes in groups of 6 or 8, each with its own special mission of destruction to perform before our troops went ashore.

Off our port bow appeared completely bombed out and from several areas fires were burning fiercely and columns of smoke rose straight into the now blue sky. There was no sign of life on the beaches. A line of palm trees 25 to 30 yards back of the water's edge on Violet Two had withstood the naval fire and the grass at their feet was still green. That area, behind the beaches, would require further attention.

A glance behind our Control Boat showed the first waves in Amphibious tanks forming up and advancing to the Line of Departure. Then off to our left a long line of LCI Gunboats, running parallel to the shore line, started their maneuvering for the final 15 minute blast at all the beaches North and South of Dulag. As the LCI's moved shoreward we received the order. "Land the Landing Force," and "Buck" gave the signal which ordered the first wave for Violet Two to go on into the beach: no power on earth could stop us now.

Noisily but methodically the Amphibious tanks went by and from many of them came the friendly hand signal greeting fast being adopted by Yanks everywhere. Making a circle with the thumb and forefinger and the other three fingers outstretched means, in amphib. language, "You're right on the ball—you're doin' OK." We passed back their salute as they went by and turned again to watch the LCI's in their progress.

As the little gunboats reached a position closer in to the shore they opened up with their rapid fire weapons. The din was terrific. The destroyers, too, had increased the tempo of their fire until the sound was deafening and we could only make signs to each other on the bridge. This was American firepower at its peak. This was the ultimate in shore bombardments. The cruisers and battleships were asserting themselves in earnest and we could hear shells whistle overhead that sounded like the Broadway Express as it passes a local.

But the final blast was yet to come. The gunboats were now approaching the beach and with a mighty "swoosh," that defies description, they discharged their rockets. If hell hadn't broken loose before it certainly had now. With a thunderous clap thousands of rockets blanketed practically every square inch on and behind the beaches. Violet Two was for a moment a solid sheet of blinding and exploding flame. This was the force of War operating against the force of nature and there was no doubt of the outcome. What a moment before had been green was now ashen. What a moment before was growing was now scorched. What had been lush jungle and a place of concealment was now a barren, tangled, smoking, dust covered waste. Seeing it was to understand why nothing could live in its path. The "swoosh" of the rockets, their scream in flight and the blaze of fire as they struck with their terrible power will live long in the memory of those who witnessed it.

The LCI's moved quickly out of the way of the advancing waves of LVT's that were approaching Violet Two. They were now less than 500 yards from shore and the Japs back of the beaches were beginning to fire their mortars at the advancing line. A few were overshooting their marks, landing 50 to 75 yards off our bow but for the most part, the geysers of water raised by their fire were closer in to the beach. The boys in the LVT's were now on their own. In all amphibious operations there still remains those last few yards when our troops must go it alone. No matter how intense the barrage on a beach, it must eventually be lifted for fear of hitting our own troops. Such was the case at Leyte and the Japs were desperately using those last few moments to make one last futile effort to resist our invasion of the Philippines.

But it was too late. The first wave of tanks found shallow water, then slowly and lumberingly their hulks emerged dripping from the water and their treads bit solidly into the dark volcanic sand of the beach. Shuffling along steadily to the top of the dune line they passed in their forward progress and fired several bursts from their cannon in an able response to the machine guns we could hear chattering in the tangled undergrowth behind the beach. All up and down the landing beaches of the Southern Attack Force the same scene was being enacted. The first waves had hit. I knew the folks in Ft. Worth, Texas and everywhere were due for a big surprise when they read their morning papers.

The tanks on the beach were now turning slowly, first to the right and then to the left. You could almost hear the boys saying, "Let's take a look around and see what the hell goes on." Then the second waves were climbing out of the water, then the third, and the fourth, and with a certain reluctance mingled with pride we watched our leading waves disappear beneath the palm trees. And this was the way it went all morning long.

On the Control Boat we soon made contact with the beach party on Violet Two and almost the first message concerned casualties. "Send a boat to Red Cross sign on Violet Two," an urgent voice kept repeating. Turning our glasses toward the shore we could make out a knot of men gathered around a disabled tank. Just behind them the beach party had already set up the Red Cross casualty marker. Buck got busy on the radio and before long a voice crackled through my ear-phones, "We have boat for casualties on Violet Two." As the day progressed, wave after wave loaded with troops, tanks, jeeps, trucks, bulldozers, ammunition and supplies passed our Control Boat and moved shoreward on Buck's signal. The sun was now glaring down and we were all wringing wet with perspiration. The galley passed up some cold lemonade that really hit the spot and helped revive Buck's fading voice. He had a fine mechanical bull-horn but during the assault phase it had been held half-forgotten in his hands as he hollered to passing Coxswains.

It was only natural, too, that a few would get lost. "Is this Blue Beach?" came a call from our port side. Looking down we saw an LCM loaded with ammunition. At the helm a short, red-headed, freckled face kid, with anxiety in his voice was cupping his hands to his mouth to shout his question. "Next beach North," Buck called, adding, "Be sure and report to your Control Boat first." With a wide grin the Coxswain gave his craft the gun.

In less than three hours the once deserted beach was a mass of men and materiel and by early afternoon several LST's had their ramps on the beach in front of the town of Dulag and were unloading tons of additional vehicles and supplies. For the balance of the afternoon and all night still more men, more ammunition, more supplies poured shoreward past our Control Boat while navy planes overhead and ships out in the Gulf continued to support our advancing troops . . .

"IN FRESH, SMOOTH-PRESSED SUNTANS, BEBRAIDED HAT, and sunglasses," recalled a *Fortune* correspondent, Douglas MacArthur strode the bridge of the cruiser *Nashville*. This was his day, his personal triumph; and not even the presence of an enemy periscope near the warship disturbed him. While destroyers drove off the submarine, he strode the bridge with Captain C. E. Coney and stared longingly at the beach.

4.

RETURN

. . . There was Tacloban. It had changed little since I had known it forty-one years before on my first assignment after leaving West Point. It was a full moment for me. Shortly after this, we reached our appointed position offshore. The captain carefully hove into line and dropped anchor. Our initial vantage point was 2 miles from the beaches, but I could clearly see the sandstrips with the pounding surf beating down upon the shore, and in the morning sunlight, the jungle-clad hills rising behind the town. Landings are explosive once the shooting begins, and now thousands of guns were throwing their shells with a roar that was incessant and deafening. Rocket vapor trails crisscrossed the sky and black, ugly, ominous pillars of smoke began to rise. High overhead, swarms of airplanes darted into the maelstrom. And across what would ordinarily have been a glinting, untroubled blue sea, the black dots of the landing craft churned toward the beaches.

From my vantage point, I had a clear view of everything that took place. Troops were going ashore at "Red Beach," near Palo, at San Jose on "White Beach" and at the southern tip of Leyte on tiny Panson Island. On the north, under Major General Franklin C. Sibert, the X Corps, made up of the 1st Cavalry and 24th Infantry Divisions; to the south, the XXIV Corps, under Major General John R. Hodge, consisting of the 7th and 96th Infantry Divisions. In over-

839

all command of ground troops was Lieutenant General Walter Kreuger of the Sixth Army.

At "Red Beach" our troops secured a landing and began moving inland. I decided to go in with the third assault wave. President Osmena, accompanied by General Basilio Valdez, the Philippine Army chief of staff, and General Carlos Romulo, my old aide, who had joined me on Bataan in 1942, had sailed with the convoy on one of the nearby transports. I took them into my landing barge and we started for the beach. Romulo, an old stalwart of the Quezon camp, was the resident commissioner for the Philippines in Washington. Noted for his oratorical ability, this popular patriot served on Bataan, and had been the radio "Voice of Freedom" from Corregidor.

As we slowly bucked the waves toward "Red Beach," the sounds of war grew louder. We could now hear the whining roar of airplane engines as they dove over our heads to strafe and bomb enemy positions inland from the beach. Then came the steady crump, crump of exploding naval shells. As we came closer, we could pick up the shouts of our soldiers as they gave and acknowledged orders. Then, unmistakably, in the near distance came the steady rattle of small-arms fire. I could easily pick up the peculiar fuzzy gurgle of a Japanese machine gun seemingly not more than 100 yards from the shoreline. The smoke from the burning palm trees was in our nostrils, and we could hear the continual snapping and crackling of flames. The coxswain dropped the ramp about 50 yards from shore, and we waded in. It took me only 30 or 40 long strides to reach dry land, but that was one of the most meaningful walks I ever took. When it was done, and I stood on the sand, I knew I was back again—against my old enemies of Bataan, for there, shining on the bodies of dead Japanese soldiers, I saw the insignia of the 16th Division, General Homma's ace unit.

Our beachhead troops were only a few yards away, stretched out behind logs and other cover, laying down fire on the area immediately inland. There were still Japanese in the undergrowth not many yards away. A mobile broadcasting unit was set up, and as I got ready to talk into the microphone, the rains came down. This is what I said:

> People of the Philippines: I have returned. By the grace of Almighty God, our forces stand again on Philippine soil—soil consecrated in the blood of our two peoples. We have come, dedicated and committed to the task of destroying every vestige of enemy

The USS *Pennsylvania* (BB-38) and a battleship of the *Colorado* class, followed by three cruisers, move in line into Lingayen Gulf preceding the landing on Luzon in the Philippines. *Navy Department.*

Heavy columns of smoke rise in the sky as Navy carrier-based planes and naval guns hammer the shores of Leyte. *Navy Department.*

The USS *Cony* (DD-508) laying a smoke screen around the USS *West Virginia* (BB-48) during a Jap torpedo plane attack off Leyte in the Philippines. *Navy Department.*

A smoke screen engulfs U.S. warships in Leyte Gulf as Jap planes approach during the invasion of Leyte Island. *Navy Department.*

General Douglas MacArthur and a group of U.S. Army and Philippine officers wade ashore at Leyte Island. *U.S. Army Photograph.*

Japanese from naval craft cling to debris and approach a PT boat for rescue. PT boats were active not only in spotting and attacking Jap naval forces attempting to force the Surigao Strait, but in picking up survivors. Taken from the USS *Hancock* (CV-19). *Navy Department.*

The Allied fleet under attack by the Japanese fleet off Leyte. The DD's and DE's are laying smoke screens while being shelled; CVE's add funnel smoke. Seen from the USS *Kitkun Bay* (CVE-71). *Navy Department.*

An extraordinary photograph of a Japanese battleship of the *Yamato* class receiving a bomb hit forward from an SB2C piloted by Lt. Cdr. Arthur L. Downing. Taken by Downing's rear seat man, L. A. Carver, ARM 1/C. *Navy Department.*

A Japanese carrier hit by bombs dropped from Navy bombers of the U.S. Third Fleet off the Coast of Luzon. *Navy Department.*

Geysers explode in the water around a frantically maneuvering Japanese heavy cruiser as Navy carrier-based bombers plaster Manila Bay. Soon after this photograph was taken, the cruiser was hit and sunk. *Navy Department.*

As the first wave of the Mindoro assault forces nears the shore, a rocket-firing LCI lets go a powerful barrage of deadly projectiles to smother beach defenses. *Navy Department.*

Looking north over Iwo Jima in the Volcano Islands as naval and air bombardments create smoke clouds. Taken by a plane from the USS *Makin Island* (CVE-93). *Navy Department.*

Shelling Mt. Suribachi on D-2 Day, as seen from the USS *Capps* (DD-550). *Navy Department.*

The USS *West Virginia* (BB-48) firing 16"/45 salvos at Iwo Jima. *Navy Department.*

The Fifth Fleet invasion of Iwo Jima, Mt. Suribachi in the background. *Official U.S. Navy Photo.*

An aerial view of the invasion ships at Iwo Jima. *Navy Department.*

Out of the great mouths of LST's, amphtracs crawl through the waters off Futatsune Beach to land Marines on the fire-raked shore of Iwo Jima. These are the early waves, rolling in after a terrific Navy bombardment to dig a foothold on the blackened sands. *U.S. Coast Guard.*

LCI's heading for the beach on Iwo Jima on D-Day, discharging their troops and coming back under fire of our fleet. Taken from the USS *Nevada* (BB-36). *Navy Department.*

Above left:
Establishing a beachhead on Iwo Jima. *Navy Department.*

Above right:
A division of F6F's from carriers of Task Force 58 over Iwo Jima on D-2 Day, with the fleet in the background. *Navy Department.*

A Marine 37mm gun firing on Japanese positions on the slopes of Mt. Suri-bachi, the volcano on the southern tip of Iwo Jima, where the enemy kept up constant fire on the Marines, both on the landing beach and inland. *Defense Department Photo.*

Ie Shima. "I cut across the fields and came across a lot of dead Japs and caves. I was scared as hell and unwrapped my .45 which I had been carrying in some cellophane. As a matter of fact, I walked right across the cave where the Jap machine gun which killed Ernie was hidden, but I didn't even know it at the time . . . All of a sudden I found I was only about 100 yards from the little sign. Then five infantrymen came along the road with a little box camera and asked me if I'd take their picture standing alongside Ernie's sign. I took their camera and made a picture for them, then I made one of them with my own." *Defense Department Photo.*

Okinawa, June, 1945. An F4U Corsair firing a broadside of eight five-inch rockets, comparable to a broadside from a destroyer. This is believed to be the first picture ever made from the tail of a firing fighter. The blast blew the P-38 taking the picture on the right wing, forcing it down and nearly crashing the plane into the target area. The photo plane was only about 40 or 50 feet off the tail of the Corsair, both going around 300 knots. *Navy Department.*

A Japanese plane attempting a suicide dive on the USS *Omman Bay* (CVE-79), 15 December, 1944. *Navy Department.*

The USS *Enterprise* (CVA-6), after an attack by a Jap Kamikaze plane during operations off Okinawa. The *Enterprise* was still afloat at the end of the war, despite the six separate claims of the Japanese to have sunk her. *Navy Department.*

In these remarkable photos, a suicide-bent Japanese "Zeke" (Zero) tries desperately to maneuver onto the deck of the USS *Missouri* (BB-63) somewhere in the Pacific in 1945. It explodes as it hits the starboard side in the second picture. *Navy Department.*

While operating with a fast carrier task force in the "slot" between Okinawa and Kyushu on the morning of May 11, 1945, the USS *Bunker Hill,* her flight deck jammed with planes ready for take-off, was hit twice within thirty seconds by two Jap Kamikazes. These two suicide hits, acting as fuses to the gasoline-filled and bomb-ladened planes, set the stage for one of the most heroic battles of the Pacific War. Fighting suffocating flames and exploding rockets and bombs, the gallant crew sacrificed 392 dead or missing and 264 wounded to save their ship. *Navy Department.*

The USS *Enterprise* (CVA-6) hit in a dive-bombing attack. Taken from the USS *Washington* (BB-56). *Navy Department.*

A.A. fire from the USS *New Mexico* (BB-40) directed at a Japanese suicide plane off Okinawa, Ryuk Islands, as it begins its dive. The plane missed the ship. *Navy Department.*

Blasted from the sky, two Japanese planes give off black smoke in the midst of the American invasion fleet which they attacked off Okinawa. The enemy air attacks, coming with fanatical fury a few days after the Okinawa beachhead was secured, cost the Japanese many planes as U.S. ships filled the sky with bursting metal from anti-aircraft guns. *U.S. Coast Guard.*

VADM Marc A. Mitscher, USN, commander of Task Force 58 operating off the coast of Okinawa, and Commodore A. A. "Thirty Knot" Burke, USN, aboard the USS *Randolph* (CV-15). *Navy Department.*

A landing boat moving toward the beach at Okinawa. Wearing their war paint, Marines present a study in facial expressions just before the firing starts. The inevitable American card game goes on among a group of battle-seasoned amphibious attackers. *U.S. Coast Guard.*

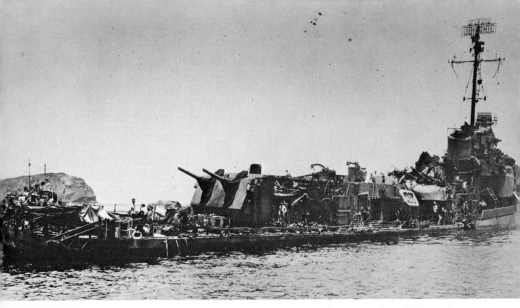

The USS *Aaron Ward* (DM-34), damaged by suicide attacks of 5 Jap planes while operating off Kerama Retto. *Navy Department.*

The *Yamato,* a 40,000-ton Japanese battleship, attacked 50 miles southwest of Kyushu, Japan, by U.S. carrier aircraft. Here she is apparently dead in the water, circled by two DD's. *Navy Department.*

The *Yamato* sinks in the East China Sea. Navy Department.

control over your daily lives, and of restoring upon a foundation of indestructible strength, the liberties of your people.

At my side is your President, Sergio Osmena, a worthy successor of that great patriot, Manuel Quezon, with members of his cabinet. The seat of your government is now, therefore, firmly reestablished on Philippine soil.

The hour of your redemption is here. Your patriots have demonstrated an unswerving and resolute devotion to the principles of freedom that challenge the best that is written on the pages of human history. I now call upon your supreme effort that the enemy may know, from the temper of an aroused people within, that he has a force there to contend with no less violent than is the force committed from without.

Rally to me. Let the indomitable spirit of Bataan and Corregidor lead on. As the lines of battle roll forward to bring you within the zone of operations, rise and strike. Strike at every favorable opportunity. For your homes and hearths, strike! For future generations of your sons and daughters, strike! In the name of your sacred dead, strike! Let no heart be faint. Let every arm be steeled. The guidance of Divine God points the way. Follow in His name to the Holy Grail of righteous victory.

President Osmena and I then walked off the beach, and picked our way into the brush behind the beach until we found a place to sit down. We had made our return and it was time to think of returning the government to constitutional authority. It was while we were finishing our discussion that the beachhead was subjected for the first time to an enemy bombing attack. It shook the log on which we sat, but that was all. As we finally got up to move, I noticed that the rain was no longer falling and that the only soldiers left near the beach were members of sniper patrols.

THE MANY-FACETED SAGA OF THE BATTLE FOR LEYTE Gulf had its real beginnings on October 21. Two of Lockwood's submarines, *Darter* and *Dace,* which were stationed between northeast Borneo and Palawan, picked up a radio broadcast of the landings on Leyte. *Darter's* skipper, Lieutenant Commander David Mc-Clintock, reasoned that the Japanese would take the shortest route to the landing area—Balabac Strait. He was right. This was the track of the Japanese Center Force, which Naval Intelligence had lost sight of after it had weighed anchor at Lingga. The gripping story of the subsequent ordeal of Center Force is recalled by Lieutenant Commander R. C. Benitez, *Dace's* Executive Officer.

5.

DARTER AND *DACE*

October 21 was just another routine day for us in the *Dace*—another day like so many others that we had spent on this and other patrols. The eternal vigilance was maintained, but we were beginning to grow weary and tired of our task. Thoughts turned to the return trip, which according to our orders was to start in two days. Australia was a very popular base of operations, and our thoughts were more on that island, on fresh food, mail from home, and the two weeks of shore leave than on the war. We surfaced at dusk and commenced another surface patrol in the Passage. All was serene until shortly after midnight, at which time the Executive Officer was summoned to the conning tower by the Captain. Without a word of comment he was handed a despatch from the *Darter*. It said, "Fast ships on northeasterly course."

The curtain had risen on the part we were to play in the life and death drama that was to have its finale in the Battle for Leyte Gulf.

The despatch had said *fast* ships so there was no time to lose. At full speed we set a northwesterly course to intercept. Amplifying reports soon came in. They informed us that the contact was a task force; that the *Darter* was trailing but could not overtake; that the enemy base course was 020 T, his speed 20 knots. Those reports represented an excellent solution to a problem in wolf-pack tactics. Our long arduous days of pre-patrol training were paying off. To the south there was the *Darter* in contact, trailing, supplying vital information. To the north there was the *Dace* interpreting that information to gain an attack position. The *Darter's* solution to the problem was more than excellent; it was perfect. Before long we had even been supplied with the Japanese zigzag plan. We could not miss. All we had to do was intercept at dawn.

Intercept at dawn! That was all we had to do, but as the hours passed the navigational problem before us loomed larger and larger. Our calculations gave us an intercept point on the eastern half of an area that up to this time we had gladly avoided. That area was the Dangerous Ground, and our incomplete foreign charts, populated as they were with countless reefs, shoals, and rocks, were mute evidence of the appropriateness of the name which the area bore. Using maximum speed through those treacherous waters we could arrive at the Japanese 0500 position at 0430. The time element was perfect; we could make a dawn attack. But before we could attack we first had to arrive at the proper intercept point. To reach that point we had to travel about four and one-half hours, in waters where we had found the current unpredictable. At the end of that time we had to be at the intercept point; near to it would not do. We had to hit it right on the nose.

The thrill of the chase had gripped the boat. "Hell, man, this is a task force and we got them cold." "Here is where we pick up our citation. . . ." "We will hold reveille on them. . . ." "We will murder those bums. This happens only once in a lifetime." The men were right; it was the chance of a lifetime, and we in the conning tower echoed their thoughts as we kept going forward at full speed while leaving a phosphorescent trail on the black waters of Palawan Passage.

To the Navigator, however, the night seemed interminable. There was no moon so he was denied the consolation of star sights by moonlight. "What if I don't make contact? What if I foul this one up?" he asked himself. For the nth time since midnight he looked at the chart; he checked the courses, the speeds, the times. The Captain came down from the bridge and asked, "How are we doing?"

"Right on schedule. We will hit the intercept point right on the nose—" was the reply. The Captain, busy with his own thoughts, turned away and did not hear the Navigator's low but fervent "—I hope. . . ."

Time, however, was not standing still. It was still dark when at

0430 the *Dace* was slowed and the Captain notified that the ship was in position. At slow speed we began to patrol back and forth along an east-west line. If all went according to plan we would be in contact in less than thirty minutes. Once more we went to battle stations.

Minutes passed—the ship moved back and forth slowly along the scouting line. Minutes passed—the radar operators eagerly scanned the radar scope for signs of the target. Minutes passed—the bridge watch, their eyes glued to their binoculars, tensely strained to make out dim shapes in the half darkness that enveloped us. Minutes passed—and it was suddenly 0500. It was 0500, and we wanted to believe that we were on station. But—where were the Japs? It was all too soon 0505; then 0510; then 0515. Still no contact. The realization that perhaps we had made a fatal error began to grip us. . . .

Our fears, however, had no factual basis. Seconds later we received a message from the *Darter* which said "Enemy changed course to left at dawn."

We had been outmaneuvered: we were hopelessly out of position. The *Darter,* because of her slower speed, had slowly fallen astern during the night. Her fire control party became aware of the unusual change in course at dawn, but they could not immediately assume a change in base course by the enemy. They knew that we were in position and that false information would draw us out; that change in course had to be positively verified. Verification came too late for us to take any action. It had been a gamble and we had lost. With the change in base course the Japs had also increased speed and the *Darter* soon lost contact. The *Dace* immediately started a sweep to the westward in the Dangerous Ground. It was to no avail. The Japs had disappeared as effectively as if they had been swallowed by the sea. Near noon we dismally secured the search. It is true that we had succeeded in sending a warning, and that our high command had become aware that the Japs had begun to move north. But our role had been a negative, unsatisfying one. We had wanted to hit that Jap task force awfully bad.

We began to move south. This was our last day on station and that night we were to start our trip back to the base. Charts for the trip were broken out; the fuel and the lubricating oil were closely checked; another count was made on the provisions. We could have saved ourselves all this trouble, for at noon we received a despatch that a Jap convoy had been sighted heading south in the area. We immediately changed our plans and decided to postpone the return trip until we had worked on this convoy. We arranged a rendezvous with the *Darter* to coordinate a search and attack plan.

At midnight we met as per schedule. Messages were exchanged by line-throwing guns, and both Captains went below to read over the communications. The bridge watches were talking to each other through megaphones when their conversation was cut short by a report from the *Darter* radar operator: "Radar contact—maximum range. It looks like rain," he said.

The information was immediately relayed to us on the *Dace*. "An overeager operator," we said at first. But upon checking ourselves we not only confirmed the contact but identified it as ships. There was no doubt that they *were* ships and that we had made contact at maximum range. Only by the grace of God were we in contact, but this was no time to think of what might have been. Both ships were ordered to close the enemy. Minutes later the radar scope gave us a beautiful picture of many ships, and once again we knew that this was no ordinary convoy. Once again we were in contact with a Japanese task force.

The Captain and the Executive Officer were admiring the radar scope, exclaiming over the beauty of the picture, when with dramatic suddenness the picture disappeared from the screen.

"Now what the hell!" said the Captain. "What is this, a game?"

"Not quite, Captain," answered the unperturbed radar operator. "The radar has conked out!"

This is just fine, we all thought. Here we are in contact with a task force, and our radar decides to take a rest five minutes after we make contact. It just had to be fixed, that is all there was to it. And although it had been a major breakdown, in an hour and a half the radar was back in commission. With a great sigh of relief we saw the Japs appear on the radar scope once more.

We tracked the remainder of the night. The *Darter,* being the senior ship, began making contact reports shortly after the contact was identified. The flow of information was maintained throughout the night, and thus our high command received vital information on the movements of the Japanese fleet. There was no doubt that this was the "A" squad, and it was so reported. The plan had worked. The Japanese had crossed the submarine line; the subs had made contact. From here on it was only a question of maintaining contact as the Japs moved northward, and of eventually bringing to bear our forces at the right time and at the right place. The day had arrived when we could predict the total destruction of Japanese sea power.

We in the *Dace,* although somewhat aware of the tactical situation, were not too concerned with the over-all picture. Our main thought was to hit the task force, and consequently we were very pleased to receive a foolproof plan of attack from the Commanding Officer of the *Darter.* His plan was simple. We had determined the enemy fleet to be in two columns, with the left column slightly ahead of the right column. He proposed to have the *Darter* dive ahead of the left column and the *Dace* dive five miles bearing 045 T from the *Darter.* The attack was to take place at dawn. By this arrangement he placed both submarines in a position of maximum effectiveness. . . . This time a change in the base course at dawn would find us ready. We had profited from our lesson of the day before. This time we knew that one of us was sure to hit at least one ship out of that Japanese fleet that consisted of five battleships, ten heavy cruisers, two light cruisers, and fifteen destroyers.

. . . At 0500 the word was passed to man battle stations. It was a useless command. The men during the night had slowly gravitated towards their stations, and in a matter of seconds each man was reported at his appointed place.

A faint glow to the east heralded the approach of dawn as the radar man at 0510 reported the *Darter* disappearing from the radar scope. She had submerged. We continued northward, feeling alone and naked in the wide expanse of Palawan Passage. Minutes later the diving alarm broke the stillness of the tropical dawn. The *Dace* slid beneath the sea in the most fateful dive of her career.

Neither the *Darter* nor the *Dace* had long to wait. The Japanese, as unwilling and unsuspecting participants, propelled themselves on the stage and were promptly greeted by a salvo of torpedoes from the *Darter.* A series of rapid explosions indicated to all in the *Dace* that the *Darter* had made a successful attack.

"It looks like the Fourth of July out there!" exclaimed the Captain. "One is burning," he continued. "The Japs are milling and firing all over the place. What a show! What a show!"

It must have been a grand show. Those of us unable to see what was happening on the surface hung on to the Captain's words as he continued to describe what he saw. . . .

"Here they come," said the Old Man. "Stand by for a set-up!

Bearing, mark! Range, mark! Down scope! Angle on the bow, ten port. . . ."

. . . With the Captain's words, "Let the first two go by, they are only heavy cruisers," we began to fire. We fired six torpedoes from the forward tubes. Almost immediately they began to strike home— one—two—three—four explosions. Four hits out of six torpedoes fired!

The offensive phase was over. Now it was time to start running, and we wasted no time in doing so. Hardly had the sixth torpedo left its tube when we ordered deep submergence. On our way down, a crackling noise that started very faintly but which rapidly reached staggering proportions soon enveloped us. It was akin to the noise made by cellophane when it is crumpled. Those of us experienced in submarine warfare knew that a ship was breaking up, but the noise was so close, so loud, so gruesome that we came to believe that it was not the Jap but the *Dace* that was doomed.

Anxious, agonizing seconds elapsed as we awaited the reports from the compartments that all was secure. They finally came. We were all right. But then a new, terrifying thought gripped us—could the Jap be breaking up on top of us? We were making full speed in an attempt to clear the vicinity of the attack, but that crackling noise was still all around us; it was perfectly audible to every man on board; we could not escape it. Then relief came with a rush. We were leaving the noise astern. We not only had hit but had sunk a major Japanese warship. The crackling and crumbling noises as she broke up were unmistakable.

Our elation was shortlived, for hardly had we settled down at our running depth when a string of depth charges exploding close aboard announced the arrival of the Jap destroyers. At first we thought they had made a mistake, for this attack was contrary to our expectations. We had fully expected that the destroyers would concentrate on the *Darter* and leave us alone. Another string, just as loud as the first one, exploded close aboard. This time the doubt was dispelled. There was no mistake on their part. We were the target.

"Most inconsiderate of the *Darter,*" said someone.

"The dirty stinkers!" exclaimed another.

"Hold your hats—here we go again!" came from still another.

"Wham!—Wham!—Wham!" said the Japs.

They were going off all around us, and they were close. The boat was being rocked considerably. Light bulbs were being shattered;

locker doors were flying open; wrenches were falling from the manifolds.

The Japs were very mad and we were very scared. . . .

Finally they left us. We stayed deep for a while but later came up to periscope depth. We began to work our way back to the scene of the attack. At the time, of course, we did not know that the *Darter* had sunk an *Atago* class cruiser and damaged a second heavy cruiser, but as we continued northward we sighted masts. It was the Jap cruiser crippled by the *Darter*—lying dead in the water. She was being jealously guarded by two destroyers and two airplanes. We attempted to get in another attack during the day but were unsuccessful because of the effective screen provided by the destroyers and the airplanes. We were not too concerned, however, as we had the cruiser in view at all times and we knew that that night we could team up with the *Darter* to finish her off. We surfaced before the *Darter*. The Navigator got a fair fix. The *Darter* surfaced; we made contact and began to lay plans for finishing the cripple.

The Jap cruiser, however, still had some life in her. Accompanied by the two destroyers she got underway on a southwesterly course at a speed of six knots. We began our attempts to polish her off but soon realized that it was not going to be an easy task. The two destroyers were over officious, perhaps trying to atone for the lack of care they had given the big ships that morning. We went in and out, trying to draw them out, but all to no avail. We were beginning to come to the realization that the only hope of success was in a submerged attack and were discussing the possibility of such an attack when we received a despatch from the *Darter*. There were just three words but they were pregnant with meaning. They were: "We are aground."

The Captain of the *Dace* was faced with a grave decision; either to continue in his attempts to sink the cruiser or to go to the rescue of the *Darter*. His decision was not arrived at hastily, but when announced it had the approbation of every man on board. We were to go to the assistance of the *Darter*. It was hard to give up pursuing a ship that we knew would probably sink with one torpedo hit, and it was hard to give up what we had started so brilliantly the day before; but it would have been doubly hard to abandon our comrades to certain death on the shoals of Palawan Passage.

About an hour and a half later we were within stone's throw of the *Darter*. There was no doubt that she was aground. She was so high that even her screws were out of the water—she seemed like a ship in drydock. We soon realized that getting close to her would not be an easy task. We decided to approach from the stern, that is, to travel over the *Darter's* water. We took position astern and slowly began to close her. The current took charge and we had to make a second approach. The Captain of the *Darter* became quite concerned over the audacity of the Captain of the *Dace.* He kept telling him to stay out a bit; not to come so close; to beware of the reef. We paid no attention and continued to close until we could pass over our bow line. By the use of that line and by the use of the engines we were able to keep away from the reef that, only fifty yards away on our starboard side, exerted its utmost to draw us to it.

The fact that the *Darter* could never get off the reef was obvious from the outset. As soon as the bow line went over, the transfer of personnel began. In the darkness gnome-like figures on the deck of the *Darter* were seen to go down her side into the rubber boats awaiting them below. Minutes later they reappeared at the side of the *Dace* where willing hands hoisted them aboard. There was little conversation. It was a grim and distressing task. There were only two six-man rubber life boats available and it was slow work. We had started about 0200 and it was not until 0439 that the Captain of the *Darter,* the last man to leave the ship, appeared at the side of the *Dace*.

No time was lost in clearing the immediate vicinity, for not only were we in mortal fear of the reef, but upon reporting on board the Captain of the *Darter* informed us that he had set demolition charges on his ship. Upon hearing this report we set the annunciators at *full speed* and never changed them until we considered ourselves a safe distance away.

The allotted time for the charges to go off began to draw near. With bated breath and blinking eyes we saw the second hands of our watches draw nearer and nearer to the zero time. It finally got there. We braced ourselves, expecting the morning stillness to be shattered by a terrific explosion. But only a ridiculously low and inoffensive "pop" came from the *Darter*. . . .

What had happened? Something had obviously gone wrong, and the *Darter,* instead of exploding before our eyes, was very much in evidence on the reef. Some said that the charges were no good. Others that the ship was not ready to die. What difference did it make then? That was no time to philosophize nor to enter into the relative merits of our demolition charges. That was time for action. There was one possible answer—blow her up with our few remaining torpedoes.

We took position on her beam and fired two torpedoes, one at a time. Both torpedoes exploded on the reef without as much as rocking the *Darter*. This confirmed our unexpressed fears that she was too high on the reef.

We had two more torpedoes; we went directly astern of her and fired. The story was repeated. Both torpedoes went off against the reef. It was now 0530. The first streaks of light were beginning to appear in the eastern sky. What to do next? We had to destroy that ship, and there was only one thing to do—hit her with the gun.

"Gun crew, man the gun!" was passed over the General Announcing System. Almost immediately the previously deserted deck became alive with men as our gun crew expertly prepared the gun for action.

We were well aware of the dangerous situation in which we had placed ourselves. We were still in the vicinity of our attack the day before, and we were engaged in a gun action. It was not without some trepidation that we had ordered the gun manned, for now there were about twenty-five men on the topside. A crash dive would be a risky undertaking and might result in some of the men being left topside. It was a chance we had to take. The men had been warned to swim to the reef in case they found themselves in the water. It was a small consolation, but the rapidity of the fire and the percentage of hits scored on the target belied any misgivings that the men might have had.

We were scoring telling hits on the *Darter* and we were beginning to feel a bit easier in our minds about the whole undertaking when a much dreaded cry came from the conning tower, "Plane Contact—Six Miles!"

"Clear the deck—Diving alarm—Take her down!" was the immediate command.

The instinct of self preservation took charge of all of us. Our twenty-five inch conning tower hatch, the only means of ingress into the *Dace,* attracted every one topside as if it had been a magnet. Some walked down; others slid down; still others were pushed down. Some came down feet first; others head first; still others sideways. The Officer of the Deck managed to close the hatch bare seconds before the boat went under.

We all braced ourselves for the bomb explosion that we felt sure would follow. . . . We did not have long to wait, but for the second time that day an awaited loud explosion resolved itself into a distant "pop." We again wondered what had happened. Perhaps if we were to write a book on the subject we could not express it any better than that unknown enlisted man who at the time said, "That dumb ass of a Jap pilot! He made his drop on the *Darter!*"

He was correct. . . .

The Japanese pilot had sighted two submarines on the surface. He could not tell that the *Darter* was aground. He saw one of the submarines diving. Believing that his chance of success was greater with the slower boat, he had decided to bomb the *Darter* instead of the *Dace.* The consensus of opinion was that he had made an excellent choice and we hoped that he had been able to do what we had failed to do earlier that morning with our torpedoes and our gun.

Our troubles, however, were not yet over. There was still one big unanswered question in our minds. Was everyone on board, or was there at this time some poor soul thrashing in the waters above us? We took a quick count. Everyone was accounted for. We checked again and this time there was no doubt about it. We had all made it. . . .

THE JAPANESE COUNTERATTACK DEVELOPED ON THE 24th, and their pincers movement on Leyte Gulf via Surigao Strait manifested itself by nightfall. To cover this dramatic phase of the battle, we turn to Halsey's memoirs. Probably the most colorful flag officer of World War II, Halsey, sixty-three years old when he commanded the Third Fleet and forced the Japanese to their knees, held every decoration awarded by the United States, including the Distinguished Service Medal with four Gold Stars. He was the last flag officer to attain the rank of Fleet Admiral.

Let us join him on flagship *New Jersey* in the forenoon watch of October 23, when *Darter's* contact report was brought to him: MANY SHIPS INCLUDING 3 PROBABLE BBS (battleships) 08-28N 116-30E COURSE 040 SPEED 18 X CHASING.

6.

I TURN NORTH

. . . The tremendous battle . . . now loomed . . . We had two fleets in Philippine waters under separate commands: my Third Fleet was under command of Admiral Nimitz; Tom Kinkaid's Seventh Fleet was under command of General MacArthur. If we had been under the same command, with a single system of operational control and intelligence, the Battle for Leyte Gulf might have been fought differently to a different result. It is folly to cry over spilled milk, but it is wisdom to observe the cause, for future avoidance. When blood has been spilled, the obligation becomes vital. In my opinion, it is vital for the Navy never to expose itself again to the perils of a divided command in the same area.

The Third and Seventh Fleets also differed in functions and weapons. The Seventh Fleet was defensive; having convoyed MacArthur's transports to Leyte, it stood by to protect them with its cruisers, destroyers, old battleships, and little escort carriers. The Third Fleet was offensive; it prowled the ocean, striking at will with its new battleships and fast carriers. These powerful units were concentrated in Pete Mitscher's Task Force 38, which was made up of four task groups, commanded by Vice Adm. Slew McCain and Rear Adms. Gerald F. Bogan, Ted Sherman, and Ralph E. Davison. The task groups were not uniform, but they averaged a total of twenty-three ships, divided approximately as follows—two large carriers, two light carriers, and two new battleships, with a screen of three cruisers and fourteen destroyers. My flagship, the *New Jersey,* was in Bogan's group; Mitscher's flagship, the *Lexington,* was in Sherman's.

The morning of October 23 found McCain's group on its way to Ulithi for rest and replenishment. The other three were standing eastward of the Philippines, awaiting their turn to retire, and meanwhile preparing further strikes in support of MacArthur. On the basis of the *Darter's* report, I ordered them to close the islands and to launch search teams next morning in a fan that would cover the western sea approaches for the entire length of the chain. Experience had taught us that if we interfered with a Jap plan before it matured, we stood a good chance of disrupting it. The Jap mind is inelastic; it cannot adapt itself to an altered situation.

The three task groups reached their stations that night—Sherman, off the Polillo Islands; 140 miles southeast of him, Bogan, off San Bernardino Strait; 120 miles southeast of Bogan, Davison, off Surigao Strait. Their search teams flew out at daybreak on the twenty-fourth. At 0820, one of Bogan's teams reported contact with five battleships, nine cruisers, and thirteen destroyers south of Mindoro Island, course 050, speed 10 to 12 knots. (This force, the Central Force, was the same that had been dimly sighted by the *Darter;* she and a sister sub, the *Dace,* had already sunk two of its heavy cruisers and damaged a third.)

My log summarizes the events of the next few minutes:

At 0822, I rebroadcast Bogan's report at the top of my radio voice.

At 0827, I ordered Sherman and Davison to close on Bogan at their best speed.

At 0837, I ordered all task groups by TBS, "Strike! Repeat: Strike! Good luck!"

And at 0846, I ordered McCain to reverse course and prepare to fuel at sea. If the battle developed as I expected, we would need him.

Our planes hit the Central Force again and again through the day and reported sinking the battleship *Musashi* (Japan's newest and largest), three more cruisers, and a destroyer, and inflicting severe damage on many other units. These seemed to mill around aimlessly, then withdrew to the west, then turned east again, as if they had suddenly received a do-or-die command from Hirohito himself. (A year later I learned that our guess was close. Vice Admiral Kurita, commanding the Central Force, had strongly considered retiring, but had received this dispatch from Admiral Toyoda, Commander in Chief of the Japanese Combined Fleet: WITH CONFIDENCE IN HEAVENLY GUIDANCE, THE ENTIRE FORCE WILL AT-TACK.)

That they might attempt to transit San Bernardino Strait, despite their fearful mauling, was a possibility I had to recognize. Accordingly, at 1512 I sent a preparatory dispatch to all task-force commanders in the Third Fleet and all task-group commanders in TF 38, designating four of their fast battleships (including the *New Jersey*), with two heavy cruisers, three light cruisers, and fourteen destroyers, and stating that these ships WILL BE FORMED AS TF 34 UNDER VADM (Willis A.), LEE, COMMANDER BATTLE LINE X TF 34 WILL ENGAGE DECISIVELY AT LONG RANGES.

This dispatch, which played a critical part in next day's battle, I intended merely as warning to the ships concerned that *if a surface engagement offered,* I would detach them from TF 38, form them into TF 34, and send them ahead as a battle line. It was definitely *not* an executive dispatch, but a battle plan, and was so marked. To make certain that none of my subordinate commanders misconstrued it, I told them later by TBS, "If the enemy sorties (through San Bernardino), TF 34 will be formed *when directed by me.*"

Meanwhile, at 0943, we had intercepted a message from one of Davison's search teams, reporting that it had sighted the enemy's Southern Force—two old battleships, three heavy cruisers, one light cruiser, and eight destroyers, southwest of Negros Island, course 060, speed 15 knots—and had scored several damaging hits with bombs and rockets. We did not send a strike against this comparatively weak force for two reasons: it was headed for Surigao Strait, where Kinkaid was waiting with approximately three times its weight of metal —six old battleships, four heavy cruisers, four light cruisers, and twenty-six destroyers, plus thirty PT's; second, Davison's planes, the only ones able to reach it, were more urgently needed at the Central Force, now that Sherman's group was under violent attack by shore-based planes from Luzon. He shot down 110 of them, but they succeeded in bombing the light carrier *Princeton.* The fires reached her magazines and fuel tanks, and late that afternoon he had to order her abandoned and sunk—the first fast carrier that the Navy had lost since the *Hornet* was torpedoed at the Battle of Santa Cruz two years before, almost to the day.

The captain of the *Princeton* was Capt. William H. Buracker, who had been my Operations officer at the beginning of the war. He would have been detached in a few days, and his relief was already aboard—Capt. John. M. Hoskins. The bomb that gave the *Princeton* her deathblow nearly gave Hoskins his; it mangled one foot so badly that the ship's medical officer, himself wounded, cut it off with a sheath knife. Hoskins was then put into a stretcher and carried through the flames to the fo'c'sle, but before letting himself be lowered to a whaleboat standing by, he smiled, saluted Bill Buracker, and asked, "Have I your permission to leave the ship, sir?"

(Later, fitted with an artificial foot, he requested command of the new *Princeton* and recommended himself as being "one foot ahead of the other applicants"; further, he said, he could beat them all turning out for general quarters, because he was already wearing a sock and a shoe. I am happy to say that Hoskins put the new *Princeton* in commission and is now a rear admiral.)

The discovery of the Southern Force buttressed my conviction that the Japs were committed to a supreme effort, but the final proof was still lacking—their carriers. Neither our sub-marines nor search planes had found them yet, but we were dead certain that they would appear; our only doubt was from what direction. Mitscher thought from the China Sea. My staff thought from Empire waters. I agreed with my staff and ordered a thorough search northward. While we waited for a report, Doug Moulton must have pounded the chart fifty times, demanding, "Where the hell *are* they, those goddam carriers?" At 1730 our guess was proved correct. Sherman informed me, 3 CARRIERS 2 LIGHT CRUISERS 3 DESTROYERS 18-32 N 125-28 E COURSE 270 SPEED 15.

This position, 200 miles east of Cape Engano, the northeastern tip of Luzon, was too far for us to reach, even if dusk had not already fallen. But now we had all the pieces of the puzzle. When we put them together, we noticed that the three forces had a common factor: a speed of advance so leisurely—never more than 15 knots—that it implied a focus of time and place. The crippled Central Force's dogged second approach to San Bernardino, and the weak Southern Force's simultaneous approach to Surigao against overwhelming strength, were comprehensible only if they were under adamant orders to rendezvous with the carriers—the Northern Force—off Samar next day, the twenty-fifth, for a combined attack on the transports at Leyte.

We had no intention of standing by for a test of our theory. Our intention was to join battle as quickly as possible. Three battles offered. The Southern Force I could afford to ignore; it was well within Kinkaid's compass. The Central Force, according to our pilots, had suffered so much topside damage, especially to its guns and fire-control instruments, that it could not win a decision; it, too, could be left to Kinkaid. (The pilots' reports proved dangerously optimistic, but we had no reason to discredit them at the time.) On the other hand, not only was the Northern Force fresh and undamaged, but its carriers gave it a scope several hundred miles wider than the others. Moreover, if we destroyed those carriers, our future operations need fear no threat from the sea.

We had chosen our antagonist. It remained only to choose the best way to meet him. Again I had three alternatives:

1. *I could guard San Bernardino with my whole fleet and wait for the Northern Force to strike me.* Rejected. It yielded to the enemy the double initiative of his carriers and his fields on Luzon and would allow him to use them unmolested.

2. *I could guard San Bernardino with TF 34 while I struck the Northern Force with my carriers.* Rejected. The enemy's potential surface and air strength forbade half-measures; if his shore-based planes joined his carrier planes, together they might inflict far more damage on my half-fleets separately than they could inflict on the fleet intact.

3. *I could leave San Bernardino unguarded and strike the Northern Force with my whole fleet.* Accepted. It preserved my fleet's integrity, it left the initiative with me, and it promised the greatest possibility of surprise. Even if the Central Force meanwhile penetrated San Bernardino and headed for Leyte Gulf, it could hope only to harry the landing operation. It could not consolidate any advantage, because no transports accompanied it and no supply ships. It could merely hit and run.

My decision to strike the Northern Force was a hard one to make, but given the same circumstances and the same information as I had then, I would make it again.

I went into flag plot, put my finger on the Northern Force's charted position, 300 miles away, and said, "Here's where we're going. Mick, start them north."

The time was about 1950. Mick began to scribble a sheaf of dispatches: McCain to close us at his best speed; for Bogan and Davison, COURSE 000 (due north) SPEED 25; Sherman to join us as we dashed by; for Kinkaid, CENTRAL FORCE HEAVILY DAMAGED ACCORDING TO STRIKE REPORTS X AM PROCEEDING NORTH WITH 3 GROUPS TO ATTACK CARRIER FORCE AT DAWN: for the light carrier *Independence,* which was equipped with night fighters, AT 2400 LAUNCH 5 PLANES TO SEARCH SECTORS 320-010 (roughly, from northwest to north-by-east) TO 350 MILES: finally, at 2330, for Mitscher, SLOW DOWN TO 16 KNOTS X HOLD PRESENT COURSE UNTIL 2400, THEN PROCEED TOWARD LAT 16 LONG 127 (northeastward).

The purpose of this was to avoid overrunning the Northern Force's "daylight circle," the limit which it could reach by dawn from its last known position. If the enemy slipped past my left flank, between me and Luzon, he would have a free crack at the transports. If he slipped past my right flank, he would be able to shuttle-bomb me—fly from his carriers, attack me, continue on to his fields on Luzon for more bombs and fuel, and attack me again on the way back. I had to meet him head-on, and I was trusting the *Independence's* snoopers to set my course.

They began to report at 0208: CONTACT POSIT 17-10 N 125-31 E X 5 SHIPS 2 LARGE 2 SMALL 1 SIZE UNREPORTED.

At 0214: CORRECTION X 6 SHIPS 3 LARGE 3 SMALL COURSE 110 SPEED 15.

At 0220: ANOTHER GROUP 40 MILES ASTERN OF FIRST.

At 0235: SECOND GROUP 6 LARGE SHIPS.

We had them!

Later sightings, in daylight, established the composition of the Northern Force as one large carrier, three light carriers, two hermaphrodite battleships with flight decks aft (a typical gimcrack Jap makeshift), three light cruisers, and at least eight destroyers.

I ordered TF 34 to form and take station 10 miles in advance, and my task-group commanders to arm their first deckload strike at once, launch it at earliest dawn, and launch a second strike as soon afterward as possible. Our next few hours were the most anxious of all. The pilots and aircrewmen knew that a terrific carrier duel was facing them, and the ships' companies were sure that a big-gun action would follow.

The first strike took off. at 0630. An hour and a half passed without a word of news. . . . Two hours. . . . Two hours and a quarter. . . . God, what a wait it was! (Mick admitted later, "I chewed my fingernails down to my elbows.") Then, at 0850, a flash report reached me: ONE CARRIER SUNK AFTER TREMENDOUS EXPLOSION X 2 CARRIERS 1 CL (light cruiser) HIT BADLY OTHER CARRIER UNTOUCHED X FORCE COURSE 150 SPEED 17.

We had already increased our speed to 25 knots. If the enemy held his course and speed, he would be under our guns before noon. I rubbed my hands at the prospect of blasting the cripples that our planes were setting up for us.

Now I come to the part of this narrative that I can hardly bring myself to write, so painfully does it rankle still. I can reconstruct it best from a sequence of dispatches in my war dairy:

At 0648, I had received a dispatch from Kinkaid: AM NOW ENGAGING ENEMY SURFACE FORCES SURIGAO STRAIT X QUESTION IS TF 34 GUARDING SAN BERNARDINO STRAIT. To this I replied in some bewilderment, NEGATIVE X IT IS WITH OUR CARRIERS NOW ENGAGING ENEMY CARRIERS. Here was my first intimation that Kinkaid had intercepted and misconstrued the preparatory dispatch I had sent at 1512 the preceding day. I say "intercepted" because it was not addressed to him, which fact alone should have prevented his confusion. I was not alarmed, because at 0802 I learned from him, ENEMY VESSELS RETIRING SURIGAO STRAIT X OUR LIGHT FORCES IN PURSUIT.

When the Southern Force pushed into Surigao soon after midnight of the twenty-fourth, it pushed into one of the prettiest ambushes in naval history. Rear Adm. Jesse B. Oldendorf, Kinkaid's tactical commander, waited until the enemy line was well committed to the narrow waters, then struck from both flanks with his PT's and destroyers, and from dead ahead with his battleships and cruisers. He not only "crossed the T," which is every naval officer's dearest ambition; he dotted several thousand slant eyes. Almost before the Japs could open fire, they lost both their battleships and three destroyers. The rest fled, but Kinkaid's planes caught and sank a heavy cruiser later in the morning, and Army B-24's sank the light cruiser the following noon. One of Oldendorf's PT's was sunk, and one destroyer was damaged.

At 0822, twenty minutes after Kinkaid's second dispatch, I received his third: ENEMY BBS AND CRUISER REPORTED FIRING ON TU 77.4.3 FROM 15 MILES ASTERN. Task unit 77.4.3, commanded by Rear Adm. Clifton A. F. Sprague and comprising six escort carriers, three destroyers, and four destroyer escorts, was the northernmost of three similar task units in the Seventh Fleet's TG 77.4, assigned to guard the eastern approaches to Leyte. The enemy ships were evidently part of the Central Force, which had steamed through San Bernardino during the night. I wondered how Kinkaid had let "Ziggy" Sprague get caught like this, and why Ziggy's search planes had not given him warning, but I still was not alarmed. I figured that the eighteen little carriers had enough planes to protect themselves until Oldendorf could bring up his heavy ships.

Eight minutes later, at 0830, Kinkaid's fourth dispatch reached me: URGENTLY NEED FAST BBS LEYTE GULF AT ONCE. That surprised me. It was not my job to protect the Seventh Fleet. My job was offensive, to strike with the Third Fleet, and we were even then rushing to intercept a force which gravely threatened not only Kinkaid and myself, but the whole Pacific strategy. However, I ordered McCain, who was fueling to the east, STRIKE ENEMY VICINITY 11-20 N 127-00 E AT BEST POSSIBLE SPEED, and so notified Kinkaid.

At 0900 I received his fifth dispatch: OUR CVES (escort carriers) BEING ATTACKED BY 4 BBS 8 CRUISERS PLUS OTHERS X REQUEST LEE (commanding TF 34, the battle line) COVER LEYTE AT TOP SPEED X REQUEST FAST CARRIERS MAKE IMMEDIATE STRIKE. I had already sent McCain. There was nothing else I could do, except become angrier.

Then came the sixth dispatch, at 0922: CTU 77.4.3 UNDER ATTACK BY CRUISERS AND BBS 0700 11-40 N 126-25 E X REQUEST IMMEDIATE AIR STRIKE X ALSO REQUEST SUPPORT BY HEAVY SHIPS X MY OBBS (old battleships) LOW IN AMMUNITION.

Low in ammunition! Here was a new factor, so astonishing that I could hardly accept it. Why hadn't Kinkaid let me know before? I looked at the date-time group of his dispatch, which told when it was filed. It was "242225," or 0725 local time, an hour and fifty-seven minutes ago! And when I compared it with the date-time groups of the others, I realized that this was actually his *third* dispatch, sent eighteen minutes after he had first informed me that TU 77.4.3 was under attack. What had delayed it I have never learned.

My message was on its way to him in five minutes: I AM STILL ENGAGING ENEMY CARRIERS X MCCAIN WITH 5 CARRIERS 4 HEAVY CRUISERS HAS BEEN ORDERED ASSIST

YOU IMMEDIATELY, and I gave my position, to show him the impossibility of the fast battleships reaching him.

The next two dispatches arrived close to 1000, almost simultaneously. The first was from Kindaid again: WHERE IS LEE X SEND LEE. I was impressed less by its desperation than by the fact that it had been put on the air "clear," not in code. I was certain that the enemy had intercepted it, and I was speculating on its effect, when the second dispatch drove all other thoughts out of my mind. I can close my eyes and see it today:

From: CINPAC

To: COM THIRD FLEET

THE WHOLE WORLD WANTS TO KNOW WHERE IS TASK FORCE 34.

I was as stunned as if I had been struck in the face. The paper rattled in my hands. I snatched off my cap, threw it on the deck, and shouted something that I am ashamed to remember. Mick Carney rushed over and grabbed my arm: "Stop it! What the hell's the matter with you? Pull yourself together!"

I gave him the dispatch and turned my back. I was so mad I couldn't talk. It was utterly impossible for me to believe that Chester Nimitz would send me such an insult. He hadn't, of course, but I didn't know the truth for several weeks. It requires an explanation of Navy procedure. To increase the difficulty of breaking our codes, most dispatches are padded with gibberish. The decoding officers almost always recognize it as such and delete it from the transcription, but CINCPAC's encoder was either drowsy or smart-alecky, and his padding—"The whole world wants to know"—sounded so infernally plausible that my decoders read it as a valid part of the message. Chester blew up when I told him about it; he tracked down the little squirt and chewed him to bits, but it was too late then; the damage had been done.

The orders I now gave, I gave in rage, and although Ernie King later assured me that they were the right ones, I am convinced that they were not. My flag log for the forenoon watch that day, October 25, gives the bare bones of the story: "At 0835 c/s (changed speed) to 25k to close enemy. At 0919 c/c (changed course) to 000. At 1115 c/c to 180"—or from due north to due south. At that moment the Northern Force, with its two remaining carriers crippled and dead in the water, was exactly 42 miles from the muzzles of my 16-inch guns, but—I quote from my war diary—

In view of the urgent request for assistance from Commander Seventh Fleet, Commander Third Fleet directed Task Force 34 (Lee) and Task Group 38.2 (Bogan) to proceed south toward San Bernardino Strait, and directed Commander Task Force 38 (Mitscher) with Task Groups 38.3 (Sherman) and 38.4 (Davison), to continue attacks against the enemy carrier force.

(The period between 1000, when I received CINCPAC's dispatch, and 1115, when we changed course, was spent in reshuffling the task force and refueling Bogan's nearly empty destroyers for our high-speed run.)

I turned my back on the opportunity I had dreamed of since my days as a cadet. For me, one of the biggest battles of the war was off, and what has been called "the Battle of Bull's Run" was on. I notified Kinkaid, TG 38.2 PLUS 6 FAST BBS PROCEEDING LEYTE BUT UNABLE ARRIVE BEFORE 0800 TOMORROW.

While I rushed south, Sherman and Davidson struck the Northern Force again and again, and late that afternoon it retired in straggling disorder, with four of our fast light cruisers in pursuit and two wolf packs of our submarines waiting across its course. When the butchery was done, the score for the Northern Force was

Sunk...........4 carriers, 1 light cruiser, 2 destroyers.

Damaged.....2 battleships, 2 light cruisers, 4 destroyers.

A curious feature of this engagement is that the air duel never came off. Our strikes found scarcely a handful of planes on the enemy carriers' decks and only fifteen on the wing. We assume that the rest had ferried into Luzon and that our attack had caught them by surprise, because during the morning our radars picked up large groups of bogeys—unidentified planes—approaching from the westward, but they presently reversed course and disappeared. They must have been unarmed, expecting to arm aboard, and when they saw that their mother ships were afire, they could do nothing but fly back to Luzon again.

Meanwhile, Kinkaid had been sending me another series of dispatches: ENEMY RETIRING TO NORTHEASTWARD. Later, CVES AGAIN THREATENED BY ENEMY SURFACE FORCES. Still later, SITUATION AGAIN VERY SERIOUS X YOUR ASSISTANCE BADLY NEEDED X CVS RETIRING LEYTE GULF. Finally, at 1145, ENEMY FORCE OF 3 BB 2 CA 9 DD 11-43 N 126-12 E COURSE 225 SPEED 20.

This position was 55 miles northeast of Leyte Gulf, but the course was not toward the entrance. Moreover, the dispatch had been filed two hours before I received it, and I had no clue as to what had happened since then. The strongest probability was that the enemy would eventually retrace his course through San Bernardino Strait, and my best hope of intercepting him was to send my fastest ships in advance. The only two battleships I had that could sustain high speeds were the *New Jersey* and *Iowa*. I threw a screen of light cruisers and destroyers around them, as TG 34.5, and told them on TBS, "proceed at 28 knots on course 195. Prepare for 30 knots. Be ready for night action," and I notified Kinkaid that we would arrive off San Bernardino at 0100 next morning, seven hours earlier than my original schedule . . .

WITH HALSEY FRANKLY PUZZLED BY CENTER FORCE'S hit-and-run tactics (Kurita still had four battleships, six heavy cruisers, two light cruisers and eleven destroyers) let us examine the events building up off Leyte, where Rear Admiral T. L. Sprague (TG 77.4) was patrolling with his "jeep carriers". This group of sixteen escort carriers was divided into three subgroups, called Taffeys. Taffey 3 was northwest of Leyte and was commanded by Rear Admiral C. A. F. Sprague. At 6:45 A.M. October 25, Sprague's lookouts blinked incredulously—on the horizon were Japanese cagemasts! This was Kurita's powerful force, and it bore down mightily on Sprague's six carriers, three destroyers and four destroyer escorts. Taffey 3 immediately turned east, launched planes and made smoke. Now the enemy divided: heavy ships to port, light ships to starboard, and began its run in with cruisers in the van.

The Battle of Samar is recounted by two of the men who played out key roles in the drama.

REAR ADMIRAL C. A. F. SPRAGUE

AND LIEUTENANT PHILIP H. GUSTAFSON

7.

"THEY HAD US

ON THE ROPES"

A half-hour after sunrise—0645, to be exact—I received a radio message from one of our planes on local antisubmarine patrol, and I remember that I was very much annoyed. In plain language, the message ran something like this:

"Enemy surface force of 4 battleships, 7 cruisers, and 11 destroyers sighted 20 miles northwest of your task group and closing in on you at 30 knots."

"Now, there's some screwy young aviator reporting part of our own forces," was the disgusted thought that ran through my mind; "undoubtedly he's just spotted some of Admiral Halsey's fast battleships."

"Air Plot, tell him to check his identification," I yelled into the squawk box.

While I waited for a reply, I went back to worrying about the schedule of strikes and patrols we had to send Commander Support Aircraft that day. It would keep my deck crews on the jump until sundown, just fueling, arming, and launching the regular combat air patrols, antisubmarine patrols, and photo, search, and support missions—let alone the special strikes he was sure to ask for. Each day got tougher than the one before, and this was our eighth on Philippine air support for my task group of 6 baby flattops, 4 destroyers, and 3 destroyer escorts operating that morning to the north of the southern tip of Samar Island.

864

About 100 miles to the south and west of us, as a ship would cruise, the shore was black with thousands of men establishing a beach-head on Leyte, and their ships were thick in the harbor. Forty miles to the west of us, where the morning light was just beginning to penetrate, stood the vague, gray outlines of the Samar Mountains, now blacked out all over the northwest by the inky clouds of a heavy squall.

This was the picture . . . at 0648 on October 25 as I got my reply from the pilot who had sent that contact report. "Identification of enemy force confirmed," he radioed. "Ships have pagoda masts."

Pagoda masts! Well, that was the clincher for me, and I knew I was on the spot. But if there still remained the slightest doubt that this was an enemy fleet, it was dissolved a moment later when a thick pattern of anti-aircraft puffs speckled the sky above the squall to the northwest, making it hot for the flier who had smelled them out. And as it turned out, he was giving them hell, too! Pushing over into the flak of the whole Japanese fleet, this plucky lad, Ensign William C. Brooks, USNR, of Pasadena, Calif., dive-bombed a cruiser with his antisubmarine loading—two measly depth charges. I blush to recall any unkind thoughts I ever had about *him*.

The force Brooks had spotted was the middle prong of a three-prong Japanese advance on our Philippines occupation. Lambasted the afternoon before by bombs and torpedoes, this force had been left apparently crippled and in full retreat. During the night the Jap commander had repaired his losses, daringly navigated the perilous San Bernardino Strait at high speed, and slipped down through the mists off the Samar coast toward the docile shipping in Leyte Gulf, a rich prize to be destroyed with frightful leisure.

They'll steam on down close to the Leyte coast, I thought, meanwhile sending out a few cruisers to polish us off. That will be about a 15-minute job. But if we can get this task force to attack us, we can delay its descent on Leyte until help comes, though obviously the end will come sooner for us.

While the ack-ack was still chasing Brooks, we made visual contact with the Jap. Out of the fog loomed his big battlewagons—pagoda masts and all—and opened with their 14- and 16-inch guns at 25,000 yards. He had committed his whole task force to an attack on us! Wicked salvos straddled the USS *White Plains,* and then colored geysers began to sprout among all the other carriers from projectiles loaded with dye to facilitate the spotting of gunfire. In various shades of pink, green, red, yellow, and purple, the splashes had a kind of horrid beauty. No, I wouldn't say it was like a bad dream, for my mind had never experienced anything from which such a nightmare could have been spun. Neither could such dream stuff have been recalled from my reading in some history book, because nothing like this had ever happened in history.

I didn't think we'd last fifteen minutes. What chance could we have—6 slow, thin-skinned escort carriers, each armed with only one 5-inch peashooter, against the 16-, 14-, 8-, and 5-inch broadsides of the 22 warships bearing down on us at twice our top speed? No carrier is built for surface engagements, and these 10,000-ton CVE's were originally intended for convoy escort, airplane transport, and air cover—not even for fleet-to-fleet air strikes. The thought that 6 of us would be fighting 22 Jap warships at gun range had never entered anyone's mind.

Bearing down on us at 30 knots were 4 new Jap super-battleships, in action for the first time: the *Yamato, Nagato, Kongo,* and *Haruna* (32,720 to 45,000 tons), averaging eight 14- and 16-inch guns; sixteen to twenty 5.5-inch and eight 5-inch guns; 7 cruisers of the *Nachi, Mogami,* and *Tone* classes (8,850 to 12,000 tons, speed 35 knots), averaging eight 8-inch and eight 5-inch guns and eight to twelve 24-inch torpedo tubes; 11 destroyers, averaging 1,700 tons, five 4-inch guns, and four torpedo tubes.

Well, anyhow, I thought, we might as well give them all we've got before we go down, so the minute the Japs were sighted I took several defensive and offensive actions in quick succession. At 0650 I shifted from my northerly course and ran directly east, heading at full speed for a friendly little rain squall near by. On the new course, we were bearing almost into the wind, and at 0656 I ordered all carriers to launch aircraft for torpedo and bombing strikes on the Jap fleet. Many of our planes were over the beach on support missions, and I radioed Commander Support Aircraft to send these back on the double. They had bombs which we could use.

At 0657 I instructed my carriers to throw up all possible smoke from their stacks and break out tanks of screening chemical ordinarily used by the planes. Open to the air, these tanks were soon billowing clouds of vapor over the stern. At the same time, I ordered all the escorts to get on the stern of the formation and whip up all smoke they could muster.

From Vice-Admiral Thomas C. Kinkaid, commanding the Seventh Fleet, I requested all available air and surface assistance, particularly from two other groups in our carrier task force. Rear Admiral Felix Stump, commanding the nearest carrier group, 30 miles to the south, responded at once with a series of bombing and torpedo strikes that continued during the next two hours. Planes were also thrown at the Jap fleet by carriers under Rear Admiral Thomas L. Sprague (no relation of mine), operating the third group 70 miles south of us.

Commander Richard L. Fowler, USN, Fargo, N. Dak., leader of the flagship's air group, roared off into the murk with a division of torpedo planes, and himself scored a hit amidships on the battleship *Nagato*. Others of his section hit cruisers. Fowler and the rest of the first attackers flew into a blinding flak thrown up by the whole Japanese force, still in a single group deployment.

Launched hastily—singly or in small units—the Avengers and Wildcats could seldom rendezvous in the smoke and confusion to make co-ordinated attacks; consequently, the torpedo planes often went in without benefit of bombers and strafers to clear the decks ahead of them. Fighters ran impromptu interference whenever they could find a good ball carrier, or, bombs lacking, just flew strafing into clouds of anti-aircraft fire to chase the Jap gun crews and divert the ships from their targets.

Salvos were splashing thickly around all my ships as, at 0713, still heading east, we entered our little rain squall and in its slight shelter finished launching aircraft. This providential rainstorm, plus the funnel and screening smoke laid down by all ships, seemed to bother the enemy fire-control parties to an unusual degree, at times causing lulls in the shelling.

In the squall, I did some thinking. I didn't like my easterly course, because I felt the Japs were not being drawn as far from San Bernardino Strait as I'd like. I wanted to pull the enemy out where somebody could smack him, for if we were going to expend ourselves I wanted to make it count. Furthermore, I felt I should run southwest to meet whatever help might be coming to me out of Leyte Gulf. And still I wanted to keep myself between the enemy fleet and our landing operations to the southwest.

It was a hard decision to make, but at 0730 I changed course to the southeast and then to the south. It was hard, because in so turning we moved in an arc—roughly semicircular—and I feared the Jap commander would cut across the diameter and blast us out of the water as we emerged from our little squall. Racking my brains for some trick to delay the kill, I resolved to throw my destroyers and destroyer escorts at him in a torpedo attack as we emerged from the rainstorm.

As we came out of the squall, I was surprised to find that the Jap commander had not moved to cut us off but had stupidly followed us around the circle. However, going now at almost twice our top speed, he closed in on us with depressing rapidity, slipping up to 25,000, then to 20,000, and soon to 15,000 yards. The volume and accuracy of his fire increased until, at one point, it did not seem that any of our ships could survive for another five minutes.

Some urgent counteraction was demanded at once, and this was the time for my little group of seven escorts to charge our big tormentors. In they went, pressing their attack to close range in the most heroic fashion. And not a single one of these little ships was lost! Results were obscured in the heavy smoke screen, but we know that one destroyer got a direct torpedo hit on a battleship. More important, the escorts turned the battleship fleet away momentarily and created a diversion of immense value.

As the Japs came within range, I ordered the carriers to open up with their peashooters (the single 5-inchers with which each carrier is armed). As he watched the one on the USS *St.-Lo* plug doggedly away over the stern, an old chief was heard to mutter, "They oughta fire that thing under water—we could use a little jet propulsion right now."

At any rate, the *St.-Lo,* singling out a cruiser 1,400 yards astern and closing, scored three hits and started a large fire. His range finder damaged, Chief Gunner S. G. Jenkins, a warrant officer of 16 years in the Navy, did his own spotting for the gun on the USS *Kalinin Bay.* Even so, he made three hits, two on a cruiser and one on a destroyer. As the little 5-incher on the USS *White Plains* banged away, one of the battery officers sang out cheerily, "Just hold on a little longer, boys; we're sucking them into 40-mm. range."

At this point the enemy split his forces, advancing two heavy cruisers on our port quarter which soon moved up abeam of us, closing the range at will and delivering salvos from as close as 10,000 yards. Straddles and hits were being scored all over our force. On the starboard side, the Jap OTC (Officer in Tactical Command) also moved up a group of cruisers and destroyers in a similar tactic, and these also closed the range to 10,000 yards. His battleships he kept in the rear, closing to 10,000 to 15,000 yards. The Japs were now firing at us from three sides.

Within this three-sided "box," my carriers were formed in a large circle, with the destroyers and destroyer escorts in a larger circle around them. I kept this formation on a southwesterly course, squeezing over 10 to 20 degrees to one side and then to the other, according to which side was throwing the hottest fire. Within the rough circular formation, the individual carrier skippers maneuvered violently, chasing salvo splashes on the assumption that the next salvo would land somewhere else. This was the pattern of our movements for most of the two hours and a half we were under attack. During this time I figure they fired about 300 salvos, letting go at 2-second intervals.

Between 0800 and 0900 the whole formation was under continuous fire. My flagship, the *Fanshaw Bay,* was hit 6 times. From the splashes, it appeared that the *Kalinin Bay* was getting the worst working over. She suffered 16 hits. The shells created a shambles belowdecks, her officers told me later, and only the heroic efforts of her crew kept the little ship going. Bos'n's crews wrestled under five feet of water to plug up big holes in the hull; engineers worked knee-deep in oil, choking in the stench of burned rubber; quartermasters steered the ship for hours from the emergency wheel below, as fire scorched the deck on which they stood; and all hands risked their lives to save mates in flooded or burning compartments.

At 0820 the *Gambier Bay* reported being so heavily hit that she lost the use of one engine. Her speed reduced to 14 knots, she dropped back rapidly in the formation and passed through most of the Japanese fleet. As the big enemy warships heaved abeam at 2,000 yards, they pumped twenty 8-inch shells into her unarmored hull until she sank. Swarming down the side on lines, her crew scattered over the water in life jackets and rafts, the hubbub of battle quickly passing them by. Rescue craft came out of Leyte Gulf to pick up some 700 survivors.

The Japs' destroyers and cruisers on our flanks continued firing broadsides at us from 10,000 yards and I never did figure out why they didn't close to 5,000 and polish us off. Around 0840, the Japanese fire from the starboard beam was punishing us so unmercifully that something had to be done. At 0841, I ordered part of our destroyers and destroyer escorts to get between us and the cruisers to throw up a heavier smoke screen. While they were thus protecting the carriers, the destroyers USS *Hoel* and USS *Johnson* and the destroyer escort USS *Roberts* were fatally hit and dropped back out of sight.

All during our flight from the Jap fleet, pilots of all three air groups were hitting the Jap ships with everything in the armory—including the doorknobs. After the first launch from my own task group, the heavy firing, violent maneuvers, and cross wind made it impossible for me to land planes. However, Admiral Stump's group recovered and launched planes without pause. Admiral Thomas Sprague also threw in all the planes he could get off, but unfortunately his carriers were under land-based attack a good share of this time. Deck crews on all these carriers worked at terrific pressure landing planes, refueling, rearming, and launching over and over again at top speed.

Avengers took off with torpedoes as long as they lasted. When the torpedoes gave out, they went in with bombs—sometimes only the little hundred-pounders with which we were supplied to bomb shore objectives. When the bombs gave out, they made dummy runs to divert the Jap ships. For two hours, without so much as a machine-gun bullet to fight with, Lieutenant Commander Edward J. Huxtable, USN., glided his Avenger through the flak to make dry runs on enemy capital ships, once flying down a line of 8 enemy cruisers to divert their course and throw off their firing for a few precious minutes.

The Wildcat pilots were given a free hand to strafe, with the hope that their strafing would kill personnel on the Japanese warships, silence automatic weapons, and, most important, draw attention from the struggling escort carriers. Sometimes two, or four, Wildcats would join up for a strafing run. Again, a Wildcat would join up and run interference for an Avenger. Then, likely as not, it would turn out that the Avenger had no torpedo or bomb and was simply making a dummy run. When their ammunition gave out, the fighters also made dry runs to turn the pursuers. Lieutenent Paul B. Garrison, of Seaside, Ore., made 20 strafing runs, 10 of them dry.

After my task group had been under heavy surface fire for about an hour, I turned to William Morgan, my chief quarter-master, with the remark: "By golly, I think we may have a chance."

To me it was a miracle that under such terrific fire for that length of time only one carrier had suffered a crippling hit. Two others had suffered several hits and three others none at all. And all of my six carriers, except the *Gambier Bay,* were able to make their maximum speed.

But at 0920 the Japs, having given us everything they had in surface fire, opened up with a torpedo attack, launching from 12 to 14 fish on our starboard quarter. Again they showed their timidity by striking from too far away—about 10,000 yards—so that when the torpedoes reached our formation they were near the end of their rope and, fortunately, parallel to our course. Several of our pilots, passing over our carriers between strikes, were quick-witted enough to strafe torpedoes which seemed about to hit ships, and exploded several of them in the water.

At 0925, my mind was occupied with dodging torpedoes, when near the bridge I heard one of the signalmen yell, "God damn it, boys, they're getting away!"

I could not believe my eyes, but it looked as if the whole Japanese fleet was indeed retiring . . .

COMMANDER AMOS T. HATHAWAY, SKIPPER OF THE DE-stroyer *Heermann,* was among the first to engage the Center Force. His account of the destroyer phase typifies the harrowing struggle of the "small boys" against tremendous odds imposed by Kurita. We join the famous tin can skipper a few moments after the battle has opened.

8.

"SMALL BOYS–INTERCEPT!"

In the midst of the battle the *Heermann's* radio barked with a sharp order from the admiral: "Small boys (destroyers) on my starboard quarter, intercept an enemy cruiser coming in on my port quarter." The Destroyer *Johnston* and I turned to obey the order. Forty seconds later it was repeated, with the addition, "Expedite!" The *Johnston* was doing her best, but I realized she was unable to make speed, so I swung past to execute the order independently.

A destroyer can't very well intercept a cruiser without torpedoes, and we had none, since we had used all of ours earlier to smash a Jap battlewagon. I tried to pass this information to the admiral in double-talk. Other ships were doing the same. As I listened, it became evident that there wasn't a torpedo among us. Anything we could do from now on would have to be mostly bluff.

Smoke still hung heavy on the sea as we ripped around the rear of the formation, but as we broke out of the smoke, the first thing I saw was one of our carriers dead ahead, taking a terrific pounding. Directly beyond her, so that only her fantail was visible, was an enemy *Tone* class cruiser. As we tore around to get the cruiser in the clear, I remembered that a *Tone* mounts eight 8-inch guns and a secondary battery of 5-inchers almost as heavy as our entire fire power. This was apt to be interesting.

Just as she switched her fire to us, we saw three more cruisers of the *Atago* or *Maya* class, each mounting ten 8-inch guns, in column astern of her, and behind them two other big ships we had no time to identify. Thus, we were opposed by a total of thirty-eight 8-inch guns and about twenty 5-inch. Our entire strength on the *Heermann* consisted of five 5-inchers.

I had one thing in my favor: a splendid range. Those cruisers made beautiful targets for our little guns at 12,000 yards; we made a difficult target for their big ones. Nevertheless, I must say for them that they tried.

The blast from our number two gun was annoying, so I climbed to the fire-control platform above the pilothouse when the action began. I had a voice tube to the pilothouse, and from this elevation I could conn the ship more readily. My tactics were simple enough and as old as naval warfare. When I saw a splash, I ran straight for it, on the theory that they wouldn't shoot twice in the same place. This worked well enough until the enemy started firing colored salvos to get the range; after than I merely zigged and zagged.

The enemy splashes were consistently close, but not too close. The red splashes were closest. Then all at once a red salvo landed 1,000 yards short. The next red salvo was 100 yards closer. Thus they walked up in steady 100-yard steps until they hit us squarely. Even then, the Nips didn't have sense enough to know they'd found the range. The next salvo landed over us, and we were never hit again.

A good many things happened when the salvo hit. One projectile struck at the water line forward, tearing a jagged hole five-feet wide and flooding the forward magazines. Two others struck forward beneath the water. And another hit the uptake which carries a terrific blast of heat from the forward boiler to the stack.

On its way, this last shell plowed through a big stowage locker packed with dried navy beans. In a split second, it reduced those millions of beans to a gooey paste. The paste was sucked up by the hot blast of the uptake and tossed into the air. Lieutenant Bob Rutter, the paymaster, was standing on the machine-gun control platform on the forward side of the after stack.

The bean paste literally buried him. It was hot and moist, and he thought he had been blinded, until he scrambled out of the mess and wiped it from his eyes. He lost his taste for beans right there.

By all rules of naval warfare, that should have ended the battle. The sea rushed into the forward part of the ship and we began to go down rapidly by the bow. The ship felt as though, racing full speed, she were about to dive headfirst beneath the surface. We were so far down by the head that our anchors were dragging in the bow wave, throwing torrents of water on the deck. Yet, except for our number two gun, which had taken a piece of shrapnel, we were still firing.

The whole ship had shuddered and pitched when the salvo hit. Now, although she was steady except for the forward pitch of the deck, a lot of thoughts raced through my mind.

The one I couldn't forget was that the ships which had slowed down that day had continued to receive more and more damage. So I decided to keep going and take a chance. Thus we raced along, firing rhythmically, wondering how long we could last.

Just twelve minutes later a miracle happened: The Japs turned away. Don't ask me why. They had won the battle. Yet they quit.

In midafternoon we received word they were retreating through San Bernardino Strait.

But not all of them. Just once, as though a curtain were being lifted, the haze rose from the sea. Ten miles away we saw a beautiful sight—a Jap cruiser burning furiously, topped by an enormous mushroom of smoke, dead in the water. While we were admiring her, the curtain closed down, but not before we saw a flight of our planes headed that way to polish her off.

THE FINAL PHASE OF THE BATTLE—PURSUIT OF KURI-ta's Center Force and the slaughter of Ozawa's Northern Force —is summarized by Nimitz, recipient of the electrifying battle dispatches at Pearl Harbor. We pick up the thread after Kurita retires, reassembles his forces and steams around in circles while trying to decide upon his next move.

FLEET ADMIRAL CHESTER W. NIMITZ

AND E. B. POTTER

9.

HIGH HONOR TO ALL

Despite his losses, he (Kurita) thought he had done a good morning's work by sinking, as he supposed, three or four fleet carriers, two heavy cruisers, and several destroyers. Once he shaped course again for Leyte Gulf but presently thought better of it and turned away. By now, he reasoned, the transports and cargo vessels would surely have been unloaded, and with plenty of warning they must have withdrawn from the Gulf. On the other hand, radio intercepts left him with the impression that powerful air forces were assembling on Leyte and that Third Fleet carrier groups were converging on him from all directions. Though the horizon was empty, he felt surrounded. In the circumstances Leyte Gulf might easily prove a trap instead of an opportunity. At any rate, he definitely preferred fighting the next battle in the open sea.

Kurita's orders, like Halsey's, gave him the option of engaging enemy carrier forces if opportunity offered. From Manila that morning had come a radio report of American carriers to the northeast of Samar. After due consideration, Kurita and his staff concluded that these non-existent carriers were their most profitable objective. With the aid of planes from Luzon, the Center Force might yet win a decision—or at least go down gloriously, fighting capital ships. A little after 1300, as the American escort carrier aircraft came in for their final attack, Kurita headed north in search of enemy carriers.

Not long afterward came the first of several attacks by carrier planes coming in from the northeast. These were from McCain's group, which was speeding toward Samar in response to Halsey's summons. McCain's aircraft, because they had to strike from extreme range, were hampered by wing tanks and carried bombs instead of heavier torpedoes. They inflicted no important damage, but they did confirm Kurita in his decision to avoid Leyte Gulf.

At Kurita's request, nearly every operational plane on Luzon made rendezvous with his force in the late afternoon for a coordinated attack on the supposed American carrier group. This was the sort of support Kurita had been trying to get for two days, but now that he had it, no trace of enemy ships was to be found. By this time the Japanese destroyers were low in fuel, and Kurita and his staff were utterly exhausted after three days under attack from surface, sub-surface, and air. In the circumstances Kurita saw retirement from the field of battle as his only alternative. Toward dusk the Center Force headed for San Bernardino Strait, which it entered at 2130. One vessel, the destroyer *Nowake,* having stopped to remove the crew of the doomed *Chikuma,* trailed far behind the others.

By this time the massed power that Halsey had assembled off Luzon the night before was split four ways. Mitscher's forces in the north were divided, with DuBose's cruiser-destroyer group advancing ahead of the carrier groups to pick off cripples and stragglers from Ozawa's Northern Force. In an attempt to beat Kurita to San Bernardino Strait, Halsey had further divided the Third Fleet by detaching from his southbound vessels his two fastest battleships, the *Iowa* and the *New Jersey,* together with three light cruisers and eight destroyers. With this detachment he raced ahead, but the race was futile, for when Halsey arrived off the Strait a little after midnight the only ship of the Center Force that had not already passed through was the *Nowake.* This lone vessel Halsey's cruisers and destroyers quickly sank with gunfire and torpedoes. The fast battleships of the Third Fleet had steamed 300 miles north and then 300 miles back south between the two major enemy forces without quite making contact with either.

Through the night the Japanese Center Force made best possible speed across the Sibuyan Sea. After dawn on the 26th it passed through Tablas Strait on the far side and shaped a southerly course west of Panay. Here it came under attack by planes from Bogan's and McCain's groups, which had made rendezvous off Luzon. The carrier

planes sank the light cruiser *Noshiro* and further damaged the straggling heavy cruiser *Kumano*. That ended four days of attack on the
much-battered Center Force. Kurita escaped with four battleships,
two heavy cruisers, a light cruiser, and seven destroyers—not a powerful force for offensive action but a fleet-in-being-that MacArthur
and Kinkaid would have to take seriously into account in planning
further operations in the Philippines.

The main conditions affecting the Battle for Leyte Gulf were the
greatly superior power of the United States Navy, supplemented by a
few Allied combat vessels; the immense superiority of American air
support; the division of the Japanese fleet, caused by Allied submarine attacks on the Japanese oil supply and augmented by Japanese dispersion tactics; and poor radio communications and generally
inadequate exchange of information among the segments of both
fleets. The America naval forces were undoubtedly hampered by lack
of unified command in the theater of operations; but the Japanese
fleet, despite unified command in the person of Admiral Toyoda, was
even less successful than the Americans in achieving coordination
and mutual support. Out of these conditions developed the most
complex and far-flung naval battle in history, a battle notable on both
sides for remarkable achievements as well as for lost opportunities.

The Japanese, without attaining their main objective of sinking the
amphibious shipping in Leyte Gulf, lost 306,000 tons of combat
ships—three battleships, four carriers, ten cruisers, and nine destroyers. The Americans not only saved their amphibious shipping but also
destroyed the enemy's capacity to fight another fleet battle, at a cost
of 37,000 tons of ships—one light and two escort carriers, two destroyers, and a destroyer escort. The Battle for Leyte Gulf was thus
an overwhelming victory for the United States. Yet the Americans, as
well as the Japanese, failed to employ their naval power with optimum efficiency.

Admiral Kurita, though under the most unremitting attack of any
naval commander in history, fought his way without air support
across the Sibuyan Sea and passed unobserved through San Bernardino Strait into the Pacific. Once there however he failed to recognize or to profit by his opportunities. He made a disorderly attack on
a small American escort carrier unit, became confused, lost touch
with the enemy and with his own ships, took heavier losses than he
inflicted, and retreated back the way he had come. Admiral Nishimura, advancing ahead of schedule via Surigao Strait to cooperate

with Kurita in Leyte Gulf, ran into an ambush and sacrificed his force in vain. Admiral Shima, for reasons he considered sufficient, failed to cooperate with Nishimura, but prudently withdrew from Surigao Strait when he perceived that Nishimura had met with disaster. Admiral Ozawa sacrificed his bait carriers, as he expected, but succeeded in decoying the U.S. Third Fleet away from Leyte Gulf and preserving most of his surface force as well. Though Ozawa saved Kurita from annihilation, he was unable to inform his colleagues of his own success and of Kurita's opportunity. Another Japanese success, limited but ominous for the future, was achieved by the new kamikaze suicide corps which on October 25 made the first of many attacks on Allied ships.

The individual segments of the American naval forces performed brilliantly, but the Third and Seventh fleets, misled by a series of unconfirmed assumptions, also failed to coordinate. Admiral Halsey concentrated upon and battered the Japanese Center Force into temporary retreat in the Sibuyan Sea; he then abandoned that target and uncovered San Bernardino Strait and the American beachhead on the assumption that the Seventh Fleet was prepared to cover the northern approach to Leyte Gulf. Admiral Oldendorf, in possibly the last line battle of naval history, overwhelmed the Japanese in Surigao Strait with a perfect ambush and an almost flawless attack. Oldendorf could hardly have failed to win a victory, for Admiral Kinkaid had given him nearly all the surface combat strength he had, assuming that the Third Fleet was covering the northern approach to Leyte Gulf. Admiral Mitscher, with his usual resolution and effective employment of air forces, worried the Japanese carriers to destruction; yet elements of both the Northern and Center Japanese forces were able to escape because Halsey carried the main American surface strength fruitlessly north and then south through the most crucial hours of the battle, leaving inferior forces to deal with the enemy in two areas. The most memorable achievement of the battle was the combination of American forces off Samar that turned back the Japanese Center Force within a few miles of Leyte Gulf. Here Admiral Clifton Sprague, backed by Admiral Stump and Admiral Thomas Sprague, squeezed every possible advantage from wind, rain, smoke, interior position, and air and surface attack to confuse and repulse an immensely superior enemy. Overhead, the escort carrier planes, untrained for attacking ships, performed like fast carrier aircraft at their best. On the surface, Clifton Sprague's little screening vessels, steaming boldly into battleship and cruiser fire, dodging through smoke and rain, chasing salvos, opposing 14- and 16-inch shells with 5-inch when they had expended their torpedoes, provided the slender margin that enabled the air attack to succeed and most of the escort carriers to escape. The history of the United States Navy records no more glorious two hours of resolution, sacrifice, and success.

~~~~~~

WITH LEYTE SECURED BY MID-NOVEMBER (PTs RE-mained in the area through the following May), the Navy's next stop was Iwo Jima. Before considering this bloody campaign, let us turn to the implacable submarine warfare being conducted in the Pacific—implacable and immensely successful. Japan had started World War II in the Pacific boasting a merchant fleet of some 6,000,000 tons, yet slightly less than four years later all that re-mained in her seagoing caravans was 300,000 tons. Then there were the warship kills by American submarines: another 500,000 tons! What further proof of the aggressiveness and professional skill of the unique service which virtually wiped out the Imperial Japanese Navy?

Captain Edward L. Beach, recipient of a Navy Cross for a patrol during which his skipper received the Medal of Honor, is well known for his submarine writings. In the following excerpt, Beach describes the dramatic encounter between the giant Japanese carrier *Shinano* and the submarine *Archerfish* on November 28, 1944.

10.

"DOWN PERISCOPE"

The story of the *Archerfish* really begins in 1939 in Yokosuka, Japan. The Japanese Naval Ministry was holding secret sessions. The probability of becoming involved in the European war was growing greater and greater; the probability of then finding their nation pitted against the United States was almost a certainty. How, then, to assure Japan of a telling superiority? How to fight that great American sea power in the Pacific? And how to do away with the London Naval Treaty, which limited Japan to an ignominious three fifths of the war vessels allowed the United States?

There was only one answer. The treaty already had been violated —tear it up. Start building in earnest for the war they know is coming.

Secret instructions were sent to the largest shipyard in Japan. Millions of board feet of wood came from the forest reserves, and thousands of carpenters were employed to build a gigantic yard. Houses for 50,000 people were requisitioned and these, too, were fenced in around the fenced Navy Yard. Finally, one day in 1940, an order was issued from the Commandant's office: "From this date henceforth no one leaves the Navy Yard." And so was born the battleship *Shinano*.

By the summer of 1942 she was not quite half finished. This superbattleship with two sisters *Yamato* and *Musashi,* was bigger than any war vessel ever before constructed in the history of the world. Bigger than *Bismarck,* the German behemoth of 50,000 tons. Almost three times as big as *Oklahoma,* lying bottom up in the mud and ooze of Pearl Harbor. Armor plate twenty inches thick. Engines of 200,000 horsepower. Guns throwing projectiles eighteen inches in diameter.

Then at the Battle of Midway, in June, 1942, the flower of the Japanese naval air force met destruction. *Akagi, Kaga, Soryu,* and *Hiryu*—all first-line carriers—were sunk. The attack on Midway was turned back, a complete failure. The Naval Ministry met again in secret session, and decided that completion of new aircraft carriers was paramount. So *Shinano* was redesigned. Some of the tremendous armor plate was removed from her side. Her huge barbettes, turrets, and eighteen-inch guns were never installed, and the weight thus saved was put into an armored flight deck made of hardened steel four inches thick. Under this flight deck were built two hangar decks, and below them another armored deck, eight inches thick. She was capable of storing 100 to 150 planes, and could land them and take them off simultaneously from an airfield nearly one thousand feet in length and 130 feet in width.

But all this took time, and as 1944 drew to a close, the need of the Japanese Navy for its new super carrier became increasingly acute. Finally, in November, 1944, *Shinano* was nearly completed. The commissioning ceremonies were held on November 18; a picture of the Emperor in an ornate gilded frame was ceremoniously delivered to the vessel, and she was turned over to her commanding officer.

Then the bad news arrived. Japanese strategic intelligence reports indicated that air raids on the Tokyo area would become increasingly severe, with a good possibility that the brave new ship would be seriously exposed at her fitting-out dock. There was even a possibility that United States Forces would discover the existence of the huge vessel and make a special effort to destroy her before she could get to sea. This could not be permitted. The Tokyo area was too vulnerable. The ship must be moved to the Inland Sea.

Now the Inland Sea is the body of water formed between the islands of Honshu, Shikoku, and Kyushu. It has three entrances: two, the Bungo and Kii Suidos, into the Pacific, and one, Shimonoseki Strait, into the landlocked Sea of Japan. It is an ideal operating base for an inferior navy which must depend upon being able to hide when it cannot fight.

But *Shinano* is not ready to go to sea. True, she is structurally complete, her engines can operate, and she floats, but she is not quite ready. Her watertight integrity has not been proved. Air tests have been made of only a few of her hundreds of compartments. Many holes through various bulkheads have not yet been plugged. Watertight doors have not been tested, and it is not known whether they can be closed; furthermore, even if they can be closed, no one knows if they are actually watertight. Electrical wiring and piping passing through watertight bulkheads have not had their packing glands set up and tested. Cable and pipe conduits from the main desk into the bowels of the ship have not been sealed. The pumping and drainage system is not complete; piping is not all connected. The fire main cannot be used because the necessary pumps have been delivered.

Most important of all, the crew has been on board for only one month. They number 1,900 souls, but few have been to sea together. Many have never been to sea at all, and *none have had any training whatsoever on board Shinano*. They do not know their ship. *They are not a crew. They are 1,900 people.*

But it is decided, nonetheless, that *Shinano* must sail to safer waters immediately. To do so she must pass out of Tokyo Bay, steer south and west around the southeastern tip of Honshu, and enter the Kii Suido, a trip of only a few hundred miles. But about half the trip will be in waters accessible to United States submarines. That risk she must take. Give her an escort of four destroyers, and send her at high speed so that the submarines cannot catch her. Make the move in absolute secrecy, so that there will be no possibility of an unfortunate leak of information.

The die was cast, and on the afternoon of November 28, 1944, *Shinano* set sail with her four escorting destroyers. Sailors and workmen crowded about her decks, and the gilded frame glittered in the late afternoon sunlight on the flying bridge. From within the frame, the image of the Son of Heaven beamed happily on this mightiest of warships.

Thus was set the stage for the greatest catastrophe yet to befall the hapless Japanese Navy. Work for four years building the biggest ship of its kind that has ever been constructed by man; put 1,900 men on board; install a picture of the Emperor on the bridge, and send her out through a few miles of water exposed to possible operations of American submarines.

There was nothing particularly portentous about the laying of the keel of *Archerfish*. She displaced 1,500 tons, or one-fiftieth the tonnage of the huge vessel fated to be her adversary. She was only one third the length of *Shinano,* and her crew of eighty-two men and officers was about one fortieth of the 3,200 estimated full designed complement of the Japanese ship.

Leaving New London, *Archerfish* zigzags southward through the center of the broad Atlantic, in waters infested by her enemy sisters. Do not think that a submarine is not afraid of other submarines. We are probably more afraid of them and more respectful of them than any other type of vessel would be. A submarine cruising on the surface is a delicious morsel. It almost always travels alone, and its only defense is its own vigilance. Zigzag all day and even at night, if the visibility is fairly good. Keep a sharp lookout and radar watch. Tell yourselves over and over again, "Boys, don't relax. We are playing for keeps now."

The weather becomes perceptibly warmer. Finally, land is sighted, and *Archerfish* slips through the Mona Passage into the Caribbean Sea. Here the waters are even more infested with German submarines than are the wide reaches of the central Atlantic. *Archerfish* puts on full speed and dashes across the Caribbean to Cristobal, at the Atlantic end of the Panama Canal. She arrives early in the morning and proceeds immediately through the great locks, and through Gatun Lake to the submarine base at Balboa on the Pacific end of the Canal.

No danger here from German subs. No time, either, for any rest for the tired crew, for they have lost the edge from their training and must be brought back "on the step" again. One week is all that is available. *Archerfish* is issued nine practice torpedoes, and fires them again and again. Target convoys are provided. Day and night exercises are conducted. Rarely does the crew turn in before midnight, and all hands are always up at 0500. *Archerfish* does not even stop for lunch, but instead distributes sandwiches to all members of the crew, making up for it with a good breakfast and a good dinner.

One week of this; then, her crew once again in fine fettle, *Archerfish* sails across the broad Pacific, on the final and longest leg of her journey to Pearl Harbor. She and her crew have had a pretty steady go of it. They have been training strenuously and incessantly for the past two months with practically no rest, but they cannot be allowed to relax.

They know that the competition in the far western Pacific is mighty tough, so they drill steadily, on every maneuver of which the ship is capable, except the actual firing of torpedoes. *Archerfish* cannot fire torpedoes, because she is transporting a full load of "war shots." One of the most convenient ways of getting torpedoes to Pearl Harbor was to send them by submarine.

Finally land is sighted. A PC boat signals through the early dawn to *Archerfish,* "We are your escort," and swings about to lead the submarine to Pearl Harbor. This is the last stop. Below decks all hands are feverishly cleaning up the ship and themselves. They intend to make a good entrance into Pearl; they are proud of their ship, and will not willingly allow her to suffer by comparison with any other in looks or efficiency.

Finally *Archerfish* gently noses into a dock at the submarine base, Pearl Harbor, where a small group of officers and enlisted men await her. Admiral Lockwood, the Commander Submarines, Pacific Fleet (also known as "Uncle Charlie"), is on hand to greet this newest addition to his forces. With him is an array of talent: the squadron commander, the division commander, the officer in charge of the repair department, the submarine supply officer, a submarine medical officer, an electronics officer, and a commissary officer.

The enlisted men are evidently a working party. As *Archerfish* approaches the dock, they scamper to catch the weighted heaving lines thrown by members of her crew. Pulling in swiftly on the "heevies," they haul heavy hawsers from the deck of the submarine to the dock. Others stand by with a narrow gangway and, when the submarine finally comes to rest alongside the dock, bridge the gap between dock and ship with it.

The moment the gangway has been placed, Admiral Lockwood, followed by his train of experts, walks aboard to greet the skipper, who by this time has jumped down from his station on the bridge. Asking if there are any outstanding emergency repairs or other troubles, Uncle Charlie chats for a few moments. Like a man who has just had a new automobile delivered to him, he is interested in all the new wrinkles and gadgets on board. Then, bidding the skipper good-by until lunch, to which he has been invited at Uncle Charlie's mess, the Admiral leaves the ship.

This is the opportunity the rest of his staff have been waiting for. Each one of them searches out his opposite number on board and makes arrangements for necessary repairs. In addition, there are several last-minute alterations which must be accomplished before the ship can depart. The workmen—all Navy men—who are to perform these operations are to a large extent already en route to the dock with their tools and equipment. By this method of making alterations virtually on the fighting front, so to speak, our submarines always went into battle with the very latest and finest equipment.

Meanwhile, the enlisted men who had come on the dock with the Admiral, and who had handled lines for the ship, have not been idle. Three or four bulging mail sacks, a crate of oranges, a box of nice red apples, and a five-gallon can of ice cream were brought down with them on a handcart. These they now passed over the gangway to the eagerly awaiting crew of *Archerfish*.

On December 23, 1943, while *Shinano* was still building, *Archerfish* departed Pearl Harbor on her first war patrol. Too bad she could not have stayed for Christmas, but orders must be obeyed, and operations seldom take notice of such things. Besides, her crew had been brought up to the fever pitch of enthusiasm. Christmas or no, she was eager to be on her way.

On January 8, 1944, *Archerfish* entered her assigned area, near Formosa. If any of her crew expected even this final lap of her 13,000-mile voyage to war to be a rest cure, they must have been disappointed, for every day of this two-week period was utilized for drill. Practice makes perfect.

To some extent a submarine is a weapon of opportunity. You cannot attack ships which do not arrive. If the seas are too rough, you have the devil's own time keeping an efficient periscope watch, for if you run too close to the surface in order to increase your effective periscope height and see over the wave tops, you stand grave danger of "broaching"; that is, surfacing involuntarily as a result of wave action.

On her first patrol *Archerfish* and her disgusted crew fought heavy weather for two solid weeks, but finally she reported radar contact with four large and five smaller ships heading in the general direction of Formosa. The leading ship was attacked and sunk and *Archerfish's* patrol report stated, "We had celebrated the first anniversary of our keel laying in right smart fashion."

Months passed, and she was a veteran. The vast Pacific was her playground and her no man's land. Then, as Joe Enright, her skipper, recorded in the fifth war patrol report of *Archerfish,* on November 28, 1944, she was patrolling submerged to the south and west of the western entrance to Sagami Nada, or outer Tokyo Bay. No ships had been sighted. No contacts of any kind (except fishing boats) had been made thus far in the patrol, which had begun twenty-nine days before.

At 1718 she surfaced, the visibility having decreased to such an extent that surface patrolling was feasible and desirable. With no premonition of the events which were to give him an enviable place in our naval history, the Commanding Officer ordered the regular routine of nighttime functions. A radar watch had of course been established the instant the ship broke water. Two engines were put on battery charge and one engine on propulsion at leisurely speed. Air compressors were started, and garbage was assembled, ready to be thrown over the side in burlap sacks. The crew settled down to the routine of alert watchfulness which is a concomitant part of night surface submarine operations in enemy waters.

At 2048 Fate finally uncovered her hand and brought together the characters she had been coaching for so long. Four years for *Shinano* and almost two years for *Archerfish*—time means little to the gods. How she must have sat back in her big, soft, easy chair, and chuckled. Having brought the two major characters of her play together, now she would leave it up to them, and see what would happen.

"Radar contact!" These words never fail to bring a shiver of anticipation to the submariner. From the size of the pip, the range, and the speed which the first few hasty moments of plotting show this target to be making, there is no doubt whatever in the minds of any of the crew of *Archerfish* that she is really on to something big. The word passes almost instantaneously throughout the ship, "Something big and fast!"

With the ease and sureness of long practice, tracking stations are manned. On the first word of radar contact, the Officer of the Deck had turned the bow of *Archerfish* directly toward the contact, and had stopped. This gave the plotting party an immediate indication of the direction of target movement. As soon as this had been determined, *Archerfish* roared off in hot pursuit, not directly at the target, but on such a course that she might have an opportunity of getting ahead of him. The main engine still on battery charge was replaced by the auxiliary engine, and all four great nine-cylinder Diesel engines were placed on propulsion. Within minutes after the initial contact, *Archerfish* was pounding along at full speed. 18 knots, throwing a cloud of spray and spume from her sharp knifelike bow as she hurried across the sea.

This is where the long, monotonous labor of patrol starts to bear fruit. Plotting and tracking the target is no simple matter. Every minute a range and bearing; every minute the sing-song "Standby, standby, *mark!*" Every minute plotting parties plot the ship's course and its position at the instant of the "mark"; then, from that point, they draw range and bearing, and thus locate the position of the enemy ship at the same instant. Your own ship twists and turns in the dual effort to gain firing position and to keep range to the target so that he will not sight her or get radar contact on her, but keep close enough so that her radar will have no difficulty in keeping contact on his much larger bulk. After a few minutes of chase, the target's course is determined to be roughly 210. The target's speed is 20 knots; he is zigzagging, and by the size and strength of his radar pip is mighty big and mighty important. Radar also indicates four smaller vessels: one ahead, one on either beam, and one astern.

Joe Enright is climbing all over his ship like a monkey. First up to the bridge to be sure all is under control, then down to Plot to get an idea of what it is doing. Next, a quick look at the radar scope for a personal evaluation of what the operators have on there; then a quick look at the TDC; then back to the bridge. Then the whole thing over again.

The well-drilled crew are responding beautifully and solving the problem like clockwork, but all the information collected by his attack party must be transmitted to the Captain. It must be weighed in his mind; he must collect all the tiny details, any one of which might suddenly assume tremendous proportions. In no type of vessel is the Commanding Officer so personally responsible for the actual handling of his ship as in a submarine.

What is the state of moon and sea? It is better to attack with the moon silhouetting the targets instead of the submarine. But torpedoes run better if fired down the hollow of the waves rather than across them. The two considerations must be evaluated; the best decision reached. Not content with the mere reports of progress from junior officers and crewmen working below, the Captain has to be personally sure that they are not making mistakes. In his climbing up and down from control room to conning tower to bridge, it is necessary that he protect his night vision, as it would not do to have him partially blinded on the bridge when the crucial moment comes. Therefore, all below-deck control compartments are blacked out. No lights are allowed except the dim red glow of plotting party lights and the orange and green lights of the radar. All is silent in the control party, except the hushed reports which are continually going back and forth.

Archerfish is logging only 18 knots. This will not be sufficient. The call goes down from the bridge: "Maneuvering, make all the speed you can! All ahead flank!"

Watching their dials carefully, the electrician's mates in the maneuvering room slowly increase the rheostat settings, and the thrashing propellers increased their speed another 20 r.p.m. The pitometer log registers now a little more than 18½ knots.

Again word from the bridge, "Control, give her a five-minute blow! Blow safety! Blow negative!" The scream and grind of the low-pressure air-blowing pump fill the interior of the ship. This low-pressure pump is used in the latter stages of surfacing when a large volume of air is required to complete emptying the ballast tanks of water. In this case, the intention is to blow out what residual amounts of water might remain or have leaked back in, in order to speed up the ship. Negative tank and safety tank are always kept full of water in order to carry out their designed purposes. Negative tank is so built that when it is full, the submarine properly compensated, and the ballast tanks flooded, the sub has negative buoyancy and will sink. Thus she dives faster. Safety tank, on the other hand, is used to give the ship quick, positive buoyancy, if she should need it. Altogether, these two tanks carry approximately thirty-six tons of sea water. Emptying them, while it decreases the safety factor with which the ship ordinarily operates, also decreases the amount of weight she had to drag around with her and hence increases her speed.

But in spite of these measures, *Archerfish's* speed quivers around 19 knots or possibly a shade more. Still not enough. A third time from the bridge comes the order: "Maneuvering, give her all you've got! To hell with the volts and amps! Watch your motor temperatures, but *give me more speed!*" Shaking their heads—this is foreign to their training and upbringing—the electrician's mates carefully manipulate their rheostats once more. By means of the engine remote-control governor linkage, the r.p.m. of the four huge main diesel engines have already been increased to the maximum, and they are racing just as fast as they possibly can. Doubtfully the generators are loaded a bit more, and the amperes flowing to the four straining motors increase a trifle. The propellers increase their speed by another five or six r.p.m. *Archerfish* has done all she can, and the pitometer log dial now indicates 19½ knots.

At about this point, approximately one hour after the initial contact, the patrol report states, "Saw the target for the first time, an aircraft carrier! From here on it was a mad race to reach a firing position."

It is every submarine skipper's dream to find himself in hot pursuit of such a target. *The jackpot—an aircraft carrier!* The biggest game of all! *Archerfish,* the huntress. Can she bring this monster down in his own environment?

The skipper is all over the ship again, and visits the control stations at frequent intervals. He calls for Lieutenant Rom Cousins, the engineer officer, sends him back into the engineering spaces with instructions to squeeze out every possible extra turn on the laboring screws. He sends Dave Bunting to be sure that all last-minute adjustments are made on his torpedoes. There might even be time to pull and check all fish. When you stick your neck in the mouth of the dragon in hopes of getting a shot at him, you want that shot to be good.

The Communication Officer comes in for his share of attention. Joe Enright jots down a message on a piece of paper and hands it to him. Gordon Crosby disappears into the radio room, codes the message, and then stands watch on the radioman as he transmits: "NPM V W3TU—K . . . NPM V W3TU—K . . . *Radio Pearl from Archerfish, I have an urgent message. . . . Radio Pearl from Archerfish, I have an urgent message.*"

Straining their ears, the radiomen listen to the welter of dots and dashes filling the ether. Radio Pearl is busy; a lot of ships are calling it, and it is receiving a steady stream of messages. *Archerfish* must wait her turn. The answer from NPM says, *Archerfish, from Radio Pearl, Wait.*

But this won't do. "NPM V W3TU 000K. . . . *Radio Pearl from Archerfish, this message is really urgent!*" There must be some means whereby a ship with an excessively important message can demand and receive immediate attention. Only in this way can any semblance of communication and traffic discipline be maintained.

Radio Pearl comes back immediately with a procedure sign to *Archerfish.* "Go ahead, we are ready."

FROM ARCHERFISH TO COMSUBPAC AND ALL SUBMARINES IN EMPIRE AREAS AM PURSUING LARGE AIRCRAFT CARRIER FOUR DESTROYERS POSITION LAT 3230 N LONG 13745 E, BASE COURSE 240, SPEED 20.

NPM answers simply and very specifically, "R," which means,

"Received, I assume responsibility, will forward this message to proper authority."

By this time it is early morning at Pearl Harbor, but Admiral Lockwood has left orders with the duty officer to call him no matter where he may be, upon receipt of such a message. He hurries down to the office with his Operations Officer. It isn't often that one of his submarines latches on to a prize of this kind. Together, with the large wall chart of the Japanese Empire before them, they lay plans to insure the destruction of *Archerfish's* target. In less than an hour messages pour forth from Radio Pearl. The position, course, and speed of *Shinano* are given. All submarines which might be in a position to intercept her are ordered to proceed to various strategic points and there to lie in wait. Then a further message to *Archerfish:* KEEP AFTER HIM JOE YOUR PICTURE IS ON THE PIANO. The levity in this dispatch is not misplaced. Uncle Charlie knows his boys, and his boys know him.

On and on, on and on, straining every nerve, *Archerfish* pursues her quarry. The carrier is tracked at 20 knots. *Archerfish* can do no more than 19 or possibly a shade better. But the carrier is zigzagging. If *Archerfish* can detect his base course and parallel that, disregarding the zigs, she may be able to overtake him in spite of the disparity in speeds. But this is tricky, too, because on a zig toward *Archerfish* the target group might approach close enough for one of the flank escorts to sight the laboring submarine. Conversely, a zig away might lead them out of radar range, where a course change would result in *Archerfish's* pursuing in the wrong direction. So *Archerfish* cannot blindly charge ahead, but must conform to maneuvers of the target; she cannot lose him, nor can she let him get too close. With these considerations, resisting every move which might tend to increase the distance she must run, *Archerfish* doggedly sets about making an end around. Theoretically, it is possible to get around a target going faster than you are. It *is* possible, but mighty damn hard to do!

One hour before midnight the target group zigs toward, not enough to give *Archerfish* an opportunity to dive and attack on this leg, but sufficiently so that one of the flanking escorts approaches perilously near the submarine—6000 yards. Determined to take every conceivable, practicable chance to avoid being forced to submerge prematurely, the skipper orders all bridge personnel below, except for Lieutenant (j.g.) John Andrews, the Officer of the Deck. If *Archer-*

fish receives gunfire on the bridge, there will be only himself and Andrews up there to worry about.

But the escort ignores the submarine, and Joe Enright calls his lookouts back to the bridge.

At midnight the carrier force makes another big zig, to the west. *Archerfish* had expected that he was probably headed for somewhere in the Pacific, and therefore had chosen the left or southern flank of the convoy to trail from. A change of base course in the most probable direction, to the south, she hoped would drop the whole outfit into her hands. But such was not to be. The zig to the west puts the submarine even further out in right field, but doggedly she digs in and continues the chase.

For two and a half hours the pursuit goes on. Racing to crawl up the left flank of the task group, *Archerfish* finds that her top speed is just barely allowing her to pull ahead. But there is obviously no chance of attaining a firing position before dawn. Regretfully, the skipper composes another message.

URGENT—FOR COMSUBPAC AND SUBS IN AREA X TARGET COURSE 275 SPEED 20 X AM TRAILING LEFT FLANK X DO NOT EXPECT TO REACH FIRING POSITION BY DAWN X CONTINUING CHASE.

The answer is prompt. ARCHERFISH FROM COMSUBPAC X KEEP AFTER HIM JOE X ALL SUBMARINES IN THE FORCE ARE PULLING FOR YOU AND ARE BACKING YOU UP.

They are keeping a sleepless vigil at the operations office of ComSubPac, fortified by much coffee and Coca-Cola. But their encouraging message is never received by *Archerfish*.

For at 0300 the sands run out for *Shinano*. Base course is changed again, this time to nearly due south, and incredulously *Archerfish* finds herself almost dead ahead of the target. Fate picks up her dice and stows them away.

"Right full rudder!" The submarine changes course rapidly, heeling to port as she does so. At last *Archerfish* heads for the enemy.

Ah-oooh—gah! Ah—oooh-gah! The diving alarm seems more piercing than usual. *"Dive! Dive!"* *"Flood negative! Flood safety!"* *"Battle stations submerged!"* A few men dash through the ship to their battle stations, but most are already there.

"Hatch secured, sir!"

"Shut the induction!"

"Green board, sir!"

"Bleed air in the boat!" *"Eight degrees down bubble!"* *"Easy on the bow planes!"* *"Blow negative!"* *"All ahead one third!"* *"Fifty-five feet!"* Expertly each man does his job, and *Archerfish* smoothly slips beneath the waves. Radar gets a final range as the antenna goes under water: 11,700 yards, closing fast.

"Up periscope!" The long, shiny tube hums out of the periscope well. Squatting on his haunches before it, hands poised to catch the handles the moment they emerge, Enright resembles an ageless devotee of some obscure occult religion. Perspiration stands out unnoticed on his forehead, his face is immobile, his eyes staring. You would say he is in a trance, and in a trance he is, for his eyes do not see the crowded darkened conning tower around him. His eyes and mind already are on the surface of the ocean, watching the enemy task group as it comes closer—and closer. . . .

Finally the periscope handles appear. Capturing and unfolding them with both hands, the skipper applies his right eye to the eyepiece and swiftly rises with the periscope to a standing position. He has become so accustomed to this procedure that he is entirely unconscious that he has performed quite a neat little stunt—for from the moment the periscope eyepiece appeared out of the periscope well he has been looking through it, has risen to a standing position with it, and has stopped rising smoothly as the eyepiece reached its upper limit. He slowly rotates the periscope from side to side, searching through the faint pre-dawn light.

"Down periscope! Target not yet in sight. What range do you have on the TDC?"

Since it still lacks more than an hour until dawn, the conning tower and control room are still darkened in order to make it possible to see through the periscope. The radar has been secured, and only the faint red glow of the TDC dial lights, the torpedo ready lights, and the sound gear dial lights are permitted. Dave Bunting consults the TDC range dial. "Range, eight oh double oh, Captain. Bearing two nine five."

"Up periscope! Put me on two nine five!" The Captain snaps the command to his exec, "Bobo" Bobczynski, now functioning as Assistant Approach Officer. As the periscope comes up, the latter places his hands beside the Captain's on the handles and swings the 'scope until the etched hairline stands at 295. The skipper looks long and hard, and infinitesimally rotates the periscope from one side to the other.

Throughout the ship the men are waiting for the answer to their unspoken questions: "Have we dived in the right place?" "Have we really outguessed him?" *"Does the Captain see the target?"*

Finally, in a low voice which hardly expresses conviction, and which certainly is far from showing the relief he feels, the Captain speaks. "I see him."

The word flies through the ship. Men look at one another and smile, some a little shakily, but most, a tight-lipped grin of relief and pride. *"We have him in the periscope!"*

The Captain's voice now comes a little stronger. "Bearing—mark! Down 'scope! No range yet!"

"Two nine five," Bobo sings out the bearing. Bunting checks his TDC. Down below in the control room, Plot gets the bearing, plots it. There has been a temporary hiatus, while the ship pulls itself together for the final effort, but it is over now.

"Up periscope! Bearing—mark!"

"Two nine six!"

"Range—mark! Down periscope!"

"Six five double oh!"

"Angle on the bow. Starboard five degrees!"

Things are really clicking now. At 20 knots the target will travel the distance between himself and *Archerfish* in nine minutes and a few seconds. It is time to maneuver to gain a favorable firing position as he goes by.

"What's the distance to the track?" The Captain can't be bothered with doing this calculation himself.

Bobo does it for him by trigonometry, multiplying the sine of the angle on the bow by the range. He has what amounts to a slide rule to make the computation, and the answer is almost instantaneous. "Five five oh yards!"

Much too close! The submarine is also headed toward the target's projected track. At minimum submerged speed of 2 knots, in nine minutes she will have traveled 600 yards, and will be almost directly beneath the target as he goes by. These thoughts and computations flash across Joe Enright's mind in a split second, even as he gives the order to mitigate the situation. "Left full rudder! Left to course zero nine zero!" By turning her bow more toward the target, *Archerfish* will be enabled to fire torpedoes a little sooner, thus catching *Shinano* at a reasonable range; also, she will not close the track so quickly.

All this time *Shinano* is pounding on to his doom. As soon as

Archerfish steadies on the new course, her periscope rises above the waves once more, remains a moment, then disappears. Range, bearing, and angle on the bow are fed into the TDC and plot. Her skipper's mind is functioning like lightning. There are three things which *Shinano* may do: Continue on his present course, which will put *Archerfish* in the least favorable firing position, necessitating a sharp track shot ahead of time. Or, zig to his right, causing the submarine to shoot him with stern tubes. Most favorable would be a zig of about 30 degrees to his left, which would leave him wide open for a square broadside shot from the bow tubes.

"How much time?" rasps the skipper, motioning with his thumbs for the periscope to go up.

"He'll be here in two minutes!"

The periscope rises out of the well. "Zig away, to his own left! Angle on the bow starboard thirty!" The TDC dials whirl as the new information is fed into it.

"Bearing—mark!"

"Three four eight!"

"Range—mark!"

"Two oh double oh!"

Swiftly the Captain spins the periscope, making a quick scan of the situation all around. Suddenly he stops, returns to a bearing broad on the port beam.

"Down 'scope! Escort passing overhead!"

The periscope streaks down. For the first time they are conscious of a new noise, a drumming noise—propeller beats—coming closer. With a roar like that of an express train, the high-speed destroyer screws sweep overhead.

"This is a shooting observation! Are the torpedoes ready?" Unconsciously, the Captain's voice has become clipped and sharp. This is the moment they have worked for all night. He must not fail!

"Shooting observation. All tubes are ready, sir, depth set fifteen feet. Range one five double oh, angle on bow starboard eight five. We are all ready to shoot, sir!"

The cool, self-possessed voice of Sigmund Bobczynski surprises both himself and the Captain. There is no wavering, no lack of confidence here. A quick look of affectionate understanding passes between these two who have traveled so far and worked so long together.

"Up perisocope! Looks perfect! Bearing—mark!"

"Zero zero one!"

"Set!"—from the TDC officer.

And then that final word, the word they have been leading up to, the word they have all studiously avoided pronouncing until now, *"Fire!"*

At eight-second intervals, six torpedoes race toward their huge target. Mesmerized, the skipper of *Archerfish* stands at his periscope watching for the success or failure of his approach. Forty-seven endless seconds after firing, the culmination of *Archerfish's* efforts is achieved.

"Whang!" then eight seconds later, "Whang!" Two hits right before his eyes! But there isn't time to play the spectator. That destroyer who just passed overhead will be coming back, and the trailing escort will surely join the party in short order.

A quick look astern of the carrier. Sure enough, here he comes, and less than five hundred yards away. *"Take her down!"*

Negative tank is flooded and the planes put at full dive. Over the rush of water into and air out of negative tank, four more solid, beautiful hits are heard.

The next thing on the docket after a torpedo attack is usually a depth charge attack, and this case proves no exception. But after their glorious experience, it will take a lot of depth charges to dampen the spirits of these submariners. The patrol report actually indicates surprise that the depth charging was not more severe, and merely states, "Started receiving a total of fourteen depth charges," and a little later, "Last depth charge. The hissing, sputtering, and sinking noises continued."

And what of *Shinano* all this time? *Archerfish* made but one mistake in her report. Her target did not sink immediately, as she believed, and, as a matter of strict truth, it would not have sunk at all had its crew possessed even a fraction of the training and indoctrination of its adversary. After all, *Shinano* was theoretically designed to survive twenty or more torpedoes. If she had been properly handled by her crew, and if she had been properly built, she could have made port in spite of *Archerfish's* six torpedoes.

But water poured from damaged compartments into undamaged ones via watertight doors which had no gaskets; through cable and pipe conduits not properly sealed off and stuffing tubes not packed. The Japanese engineers attempted to start the pumps—and found they had not yet been installed, the piping not even completed. They searched for the hand pumps, but the ship had not yet received her full allowance of gear, and only a few were on board. In desperation, a bucket brigade was started, but the attempt was hopeless. The six huge holes in *Shinano's* side and the innumerable internal leaks defied all efforts to cope with them.

And then her organization and discipline failed. The men drifted away from the bucket brigade by ones and twos. The engineers gave up trying to get part of the drainage system running. The officers rushed about giving furious orders—but no one obeyed them. Instead, fatalistically, most of the crew gathered on the flight deck in hopes of being rescued by one of the four destroyers milling around their stricken charge. Faint, pathetic hope.

Four hours after she had received her mortal wound, *Shinano* had lost all power, and was nothing but a beaten, hopeless, disorganized hulk, listing to starboard more heavily every moment, a plaything of the wind and the sea. There was only one thing left to do.

The Emperor, in his gilded frame, was removed from the bridge and, after being thoroughly wrapped, transferred by line to a destroyer alongside. Then the work of abandoning ship began.

Shortly before 1100 on the morning of November 29 *Shinano* capsized to starboard, rolling her broad flight deck under and exposing her enormous glistening fat belly, with its four bronze propellers at the stern. For several minutes she hung there, lurching unevenly in the moderately rough sea.

Here and there the figures of several men who had not leaped into the sea with the others stood upon the steel plates, silhouetted against sea and sky. Evidently they had climbed around the side and the turn of the bilge as the ship rolled over. Whatever their reasons for not abandoning the ship, they were now doomed, for none of the four destroyers still holding the wake dared approach closely enough to take them off. And the suction of the sinking vessel was certain to take them down with it.

Slowly the massive rudders and propellers started to dip under the seas splashing up toward them. A trembling and a groaning communicated itself to the whole giant fabric, and it began to sway noticeably, swinging the afterparts and the foreparts under alternately. Each time an end dipped, the sea gained a little, and the trembling and groaning increased.

Finally, during one swoop, the stern failed to reappear. Startlingly and suddenly, the bow rose partly out of water, displaying a single eye formed by one gigantic hawsepipe, as if *Shinano* desired a final look at the world she was about to leave. Swiftly then she slid under, stern first, and the last thing seen was the broad bulbous bow, like the forehead of some huge prehistoric Moby Dick, accompanied by the blowing, bubbling, and whistling of air escaping under water.

For several minutes there was considerable turbulence and bubbling to mark her grave, but *Shinano* was gone from the ken of men.

She had known the open sea for less than twenty hours.

FOR MACARTHUR THE NEXT LEG-UP AFTER LEYTE WAS Mindoro, three hundred miles to the north, in preparation for the capture of Luzon. Army forces went ashore there December 15 while the Third Fleet kept the airfields of Luzon smothered under round-the-clock strikes. On December 17, low on fuel, Halsey retired to the east in bad weather. He was still there the following morning when a monstrous typhoon developed and severely battered his fleet. Three destroyers capsized, seven other ships were damaged, and nearly eight hundred men were lost.

The story of this most costly debacle since Savo is eloquently told by Hanson W. Baldwin, whom we have met.

II.

TYPHOON

The destroyers—the little ships that dance in any sea, the ships with empty maws from their days of high-speed steaming—come alongside the tankers and the battleships in the morning. But the ocean will have none of it; this is a job for super-seamen. There's nothing but a mad swatch of white water between oilers and "tin cans" as the hungry little ships try to gulp their food through hoses leading from the oilers' tanks. Some get aboard hundred of gallons before the lines break and the ships swing wildly apart, but most part line after line as boatswains curse and the water boils aboard the well decks and the steel plates run with oil. Destroyer *Hull,* a name soon to be on the lips of all the fleet, from the ASW (anti-submarine warfare) group of a fueling unit, puts forty bags of mail aboard battleship *South Dakota* with "much difficulty," but mail for thirty other ships of the fleet is undelivered; the sea is wild.

"1107. *Spence alongside New Jersey, starboard side, to fuel.*
1128. *Both for'd and after hoses to Spence parted.*"

U.S.S. *Buchanan* tries to transfer pilots by a swaying boatswain's chair to *CVE-18*—escort carrier *Altamaha*—but the sea's too rough. *San Jacinto,* light carrier, gets aboard 172,000 gallons from tanker *Monongahela* before the log noted at 1331 "discontinued fueling because of adverse weather."

Wind—Force 26 knots. Barometer, 29.74. Temperature, 82. Visibility—5 miles. Sea—Force 4.

In early afternoon Com. Third Fleet orders fueling suspended, sets course to northwest, then later to southwest to escape storm center not clearly located. The barometer drops, the winds moan; there's the uneasy leaden feeling of a hand across the heavens, but the Third Fleet steams on in cruising formation—the destroyers screening the "big boys," the AA guns alert, the sonars "pinging," the radars . . . searching, searching. . . .

Monday, December 18 Third Fleet moves through troubled waters, the compulsion of combat dictating its movements. But the storm, with the catholic impartiality of Nature, sweeps across the war, puts in puny framework the efforts of Man. The night is haggard; aboard the destroyers the sideboards are around the wardroom tables, the sleepers are braced in their bunks, but the sharp motion of the aroused ocean shakes and pounds the ships, makes sleep fitful and despairing. Barometers drop steadily, rain squalls and flung spray and spume reduce visibility; station-keeping is difficult—at times almost impossible. The seas make up; the winds beat and buffet; the fleet is battened down.

"But no estimates of the storm center were in agreement"; and not until dawn did Third Fleet realize it lay in the path of the granddaddy of all typhoons. And units of Task Group 30.8—the fleet oilers, and their escorting destroyers and escort carriers—somewhat to the north and east of the main body, are directly athwart the "eye" of the approaching typhoon. Fleet course is ordered changed to 180 degrees—due south—but it is too late; the fury is upon them.

0400 to 0800 The Morning Watch

Nantahala (Oiler)—". . . this ship pitching deeply and heavily."

Altamaha (Escort Carrier)—". . . heavy weather making station-keeping only approximate."

Aboard *Dewey,* DD (destroyer) 349, the officer-of-the-deck reports to the captain that the barometer has dropped seven points between 7 and 8 a.m. Seas are so violent, winds so strong, *Dewey* finds it "impossible," when fleet course is changed, to countermarch to new station.

Morning fuel reports from many of the destroyers are ominous. All were low the day before; some had de-ballasted (pumped salt water out of their tanks) to prepare to refuel. They are riding light and high; stability is reduced. And their crews know that topside weight has been greatly increased since commissioning by more AA guns, fire control gear, and radar. *Yernall* reports 20 per cent of fuel remaining; *Wedderburn,* 15 per cent; *Maddox, Hickox* and *Spence* 10 to 15 per cent.

0800 to 1200 The Forenoon Watch

The forenoon watch opens, in the words of an old seagoing term, "with hell to pay and no pitch hot."

The moaning violence of the wind is terrible; it shrieks and whinnies, roars and shudders, beats and clutches. The sea is convulsed, diabolic; the ships are laboring deeply—laid over by the wind, rolling rigidly through tremendous arcs with sharp violent jerks, pounding and pitching, buried deep beneath tons of water, rising heavily streaming foam and salt from gunnels and hawse pipes. Violent rain gusts, spindrift blown with the sting of hail, a rack of scud blot out visiblity. Third Fleet is scattered; few ships see others; only on the radar scopes do the pips of light loom up to show in wild confusion Man's panoply of power.

The deeply-laden oilers, the heavy battleships, the larger carriers, roll and plunge deeply and work violently but not dangerously through the towering seas, but for the escort carriers, the light carriers and the destroyers, the struggle is to live; the war now is against Nature, not the Japanese; no man in all the fleet had ever felt before the full fury of such a howling, demonic wind. Some of the fleet is in the "dangerous semicircle" of the typhoon where no seaman ought to be; a few ships—through rocked and tossed like chips—are on the fringes of the terrible vortex, but at least one task unit is directly in the center, where the funnel of wind and the boiling ocean leap to climax.

Ship after ship falls away into the terrible troughs and will not answer her helm.

At 0820 the destroyer *Dewey*—DD349—loses bridge steering control; at 0825 the SG radar, short-circuited by the flying scud, is out of operation.

At 0845 escort carrier *Altamaha* records in her deck log: "Mobile crane on hangar deck tore loose from moorings and damaged three aircraft," and, a few minutes later: "Wind and sea approaching hurricane violence. Ship laboring heavily and rolling violently as much as twenty-five to thirty degrees on either side."

The barometer drops as no seaman there had ever seen it fall before; the wind is up.

Aboard U.S.S. *Cowpens,* an F6F5 airplane, triple-lashed on the flight deck, breaks loose on a 45-degree roll, and smashes into the catwalk, starting a fire. Men fight it, as the wind howls and the roll indicator registers 45 degrees with the small bubble of the ship's inclinometer (roll indicator) "two-blocked and off the scale." Men fight it, as a bomb-handling truck breaks free on the hangar deck and smashes the belly tank of a fighter. Men fight it as a wall of solid green water rips open—like a can opener—the steel roller curtains on the port side of the hangar deck. Men fight it as the anenometer, with one of its cups gone, registers a wind velocity of more than one hundred knots. Men fight it as the wind and sea pull out of its steel roots the forward port 20mm. gun sponson and leave it hanging, and tear loose the radar antenna screen from the foremast and fling it into the boiling sea. And men fight it as the motor whaleboat is carried away by a wall of water, as bombs break their battens in the magazine and skitter about the deck, as jeeps and tractors, a kerry crane, and seven planes are flung and blown off the flight deck into the writhing sea. But in the end it is the sea which extinguishes the fire as it was the sea which started it; the F6F5 breaks clear of the catwalk and falls into the tumult of water.

As the day wears on the log books run out of the language of nautical superlatives. Several ships record the barometer at a flat 28 inches, an awesome low; *Dewey* reads hers at 27.30—possibly the world's lowest recorded reading. Oiler *Nantahala,* with other ships of a fueling unit to the northeast of the main body near the storm center, records a wind velocity of 124 knots. The wind shifts rapidly in direction as the typhoon circles, blowing from north and south and east and west—backing and filling as do all circular storms—and increasing in intensity to Force 17, far beyond that ancient nautical measuring-stick of mariners—the Beaufort scale—which defines Force 12, its maximum—"that which no canvas could withstand" —as a "hurricane above 65 knots."

Third Fleet is scattered now, station-keeping impossible, visibility five hundred yards to zero, only the radars—when operative—preventing collisions. Com. Third Fleet in *New Jersey,* his plan to refuel this day long since abandoned, his immediate commitment to MacArthur regretfully canceled, records in his war diary the reports of disaster:

0841. The Wasp reported a life raft to her port, which appeared to have three persons on it.

0907. The Independence reported man overboard.

0911. The Monterey reported that, due to excessive roll, planes on her hangar deck had broken loose and caught fire.
0942. The Kwajalein reported she had lost steering control.
1012. The Wisconsin reported 1 Kingfisher (plane) overboard.
1017. The Rudyerd Bay reported she was dead in the water.
1128. The Cape Esperance reported fire on her flight deck. . . .

The ships—the big and little—are racked and strained, punished and pommeled. The men are dazed; all hands are in lifejackets; none stand topside in exposed positions; muscles are sore and bodies bruised from clinging to stanchions, pounding against bulkheads; a miserable many retch from seasickness, but for hundreds terror calms the queasiness of the stomach. The violent rolls and the terrible mountains of water—seventy feet from trough to crest—are frightening, even to the experienced; some are plain scared, but most have confidence in the stoutness of their vessels.

But this is "one-hand-for-your-ship-and-one-for-yourself" weather; the business is to survive.

The voice of the storm drowns all other voices; the wind has a thousand notes—the bass of growling menace, the soprano of stays so tautly strained they hum like bowstrings. The tops of the wave crests are flattened off by the wind and hurled straight before its violence; rain and spindrift mix in a horizontal sheet of water; one cannot tell where ocean stops and sky begins. . . .

. . . And overall is the cacophony of the ships—the racked and groaning ships, the creaking of the bulkheads, the working of the stanchions, the play of rivets, the hum of blowers, the slide and tear and roar of chairs and books adrift, of wreckage slipping from bulkhead to bulkhead. . . .

Low fuel, attempts to keep station, or to change course to ease pounding spell havoc for some. The seas are so great, the wind so strong, that some of the lighter destroyers are derelicts; all possible combinations of rudders and screws fail to take them out of the troughs; they are sloughed and rolled and roughed far on their sides by wind and water—and drift, out of control, downwind.

The light and escort carriers fare little better; aboard *San Jacinto, Monterey, Altamaha* and others, planes slide and slip; wreckage crashes groaning from bulkhead to bulkhead; the hangar decks are infernos of flame and crashing metal, of fire and wind and sea.

Early in the morning watch *San Jacinto,* Captain Michael H. Kernodle, commanding, tries to "swing to new course to ease her."

The skipper backs the starboard engines, goes ahead twenty knots on the port, but the howling wind will have none of it; *San Jacinto* falls off into the trough, rolls 42 degrees. A plane breaks loose on the hangar deck, skids into other planes—each lashed to steel deck pad eyes with fourteen turns of wire and rope—tears them loose, and the whole deckload crash from side to side with each roll, "rupturing and tearing away all air intakes and vent ducts passing through the hangar decks." Engine spares and other heavy material stowed on the hangar deck break loose and smash and tear into the bulkheads; oily water greases the deck; stream hisses from the ruptured exhausts; the fire sprinkling system, damaged by the wreckage, sprays water indiscriminately over the deck spaces; general flooding results through the broken ventilation vents in fire rooms and engine rooms; the evaporators are out of commission; the galley ovens out; the after gyro compass inoperative; electrical leads severed.

It is Man against the sea, but Man wins; personnel of the damage control and fire-fighting parties lash themselves to lines suspended from the overhead of the hangar deck, and swinging and slithering like pendulums across the slippery deck, risk their lives to secure the mass of sliding, groaning wreckage.

Aboard *Altamaha*—all 14,000 tons of her, planing like a surfboard on the tremendous rollers—the planes she mothers turn against her; fire mains burst; wreckage litters the elevator pit; heavy seas break over the fantail; damage repair parties shore the bulkheads.

In *Monterey,* Nos. 1 and 2 firerooms are abandoned at 0914 because of heavy smoke from a hangar deck fire; ready ammunition is jettisoned; the boilers are manned by skeleton crews using rescue breathing masks; a gasoline vapor explosion kills one seaman; another, trapped by the flames, is burned to death, a third asphyxiated; many injured.

Destroyer *Dewey* labors almost to the death. Throughout the morning watch, with the storm howling like a banshee, the quartermaster on watch scribbles painfully in the deck log, as casualty reports funnel to the bridge:

0950. . . . Dewey reported to CTG 30.8 she was out of control and passed through formation from starboard to port. Heavy rolling caused loss of lube oil suction repeatedly. . . .

1006. Captain ordered all port fuel tanks filled to capacity. 30,000 gallons of oil pumped to port side. Rolling through 40 to 50 degrees.

1020. Lost bridge steering control; steering aft. Telephone circuits began to go. Lost radar and TBS (radio—"Talk Between Ships") contact with rest of formation. . . . Wind and sea rising, barometer falling.

1102. Doctor reported many men had been injured by falling.

1130. Main engines stopped—main switchboard shorted from salt water. Secured main generator. Electrical power and lights all gone. 500 to 1,000 gallons of water entering #2 main forced draft intake on every big roll. Bucket brigade in mess hall and one aft kept water down.

1130. All control and communication lost from bridge. Dead in the water. The air . . . continually filled with salt spray 200 feet in the air or higher. Visibility zero. This blast of salt spray penetrated everything and grounded all electrical connections . . . 8 inches of water in all living spaces produced undesirable "free surface effect." All hands told to remain on port side. Rolling and pounding worse. Inclinometer to 73 degrees to starboard and stopped for a few seconds. Engine room (indicated) 75 degrees. The masts and stacks . . . swinging and expected to carry away at any time. Tops of 3 ready ammo lockers torn off and 80 rounds of 5 inch spilled over the side. . . . All thin shielding of ship stove in—by water on starboard side—by wind on port.

1145. The wind . . . estimated to be more than 110 knots. All hands performed in a commendable manner, especially the engineers . . . no panic.

But *Dewey,* as the morning dies, still lives.

Not so destroyers *Monaghan* and *Spence.*

Monaghan, DD 354, with twelve battle stars on her bridge and a veteran of combat from Pearl Harbor to Leyte, lunges to her doom—the fleet unknowing—late in that wild windswept morning.

She's last heard and dimly seen when the morning is but half spent:

0936. Monaghan to Com. 30.8—"I am unable to come to the base course. Have tried full speed, but it will not work."

1006. Monaghan to unknown ship—"You are 1,200 yards off my port quarter. Am dead in water. Sheer off if possible."

1007. Monaghan to Hobby—"Bearing is 225, 1,400 yards . . ."

Then . . . silence . . .

Monaghan's 1,500 tons of steel are racked and strained; her starboard whaleboat drinks the sea as the davits dip into green water. But there's little intimation of disaster. About eight bells—as the Wagnerian dirge of the typhoon drowns the lesser noises of the laboring ship—the wind pushes *Monaghan* far on her starboard side. She struggles to rise again—and makes it, but sluggishly. In the after deck house forty or fifty men cling to stanchions and pray—silently, or aloud:

"Don't let us down now, Dear Lord. Bring it back, Oh God! bring it back!"

Slowly the ship recovers:

"Thanks, Dear Lord."

But the lights go out; again the deep roll to starboard, again and again she struggles back, shudderingly, from disaster.

Then, about noon, the wind brutalizes her; heavily *Monaghan* rolls to starboard—30, 40, 60, 70 degrees—tiredly she settles down flat on her side to die amid a welter of white waters and the screaming Valkyries of the storm. And there go with her eighteen officers and 238 men. . . .

Spence, DD 512, goes about the same time, but again the fleet unknowing. *Spence* is deballasted, light in fuel; she rides like a cork in the terrible canyon-like troughs. Power fails; the electrical board is shorted from the driven spray; the ship goes over 72 degrees to port—and stays there. The lights are out; the pumps are stopped—the ship's heart dead before the body dies; she drifts derelict. Sometime before noon, the Supply Officer—Lt. Alphonso Stephen Krauchunas, United States Naval Reserve, one-time of Kalamazoo, destined to be *Spence's* only officer survivor—sits on the edge of the bunk in the captain's cabin talking tensely with the ship's doctor. An awful roll throws Krauchunas on his back against the bulkhead "in a shower of books and whatnot." Crawling on hands and knees on the bulkheads (walls) of the passageway, Krauchunas gets topside just before the entering ocean seeks him out. He fights clear along with seventy others—but *Spence,* 2,000 tons of steel with the power of 60,000 horse, is done.

1200 to 1600 The Afternoon Watch

The afternoon watch brings some slight surcease to some ships, climax and desperation to others. The fleet is widely dispersed across a raging ocean; some ships have felt the full fury of the storm; others are still to feel it. Between 1100 and 1400 of that day the peak is reached; "mountainous seas . . . confused by backing winds made the vessels roll to unprecedented angles."

For *Hull*, Destroyer #350, with much of the mail of the fleet still aboard, the afternoon watch of December 18, 1944, is to be her last. The quartermaster has hardly turned the log page before it happens.

Small and old as destroyers go, *Hull* had made heavy weather of it in the morning; the driven spray had shorted everything; in the CIC (Combat Information Center) leaky seams admitted the sea and "sparks were jumping back and forth among the electrical cables."

Hull's tanks are 70 per cent full of fuel oil; she's better off than her lighter sisters, though she has no water ballast. But the storm brooks no objections; gradually *Hull* loses the fight. Her radar is out; her TBS inoperative; the whaleboat smashed and torn loose; depth charges wrenched from the K-guns, and to "every possible combination of rudder and engines" the ship will not respond, and is blown "bodily before wind and sea, yawing between headings of 100 and 080 true."

Shortly after noon, as the seas tower into toppling mountains, the ship lies over on her side in terrible sickening rolls, and the junior officer of the watch is "catapulted completely through the air from the port side of the pilot house to the upper portion of the starboard side."

But still Lieutenant-Commander James Alexander Marks, the young skipper, has hope. . . .

". . . the ship had withstood the worst punishment any storm could offer."

("I had served in destroyers," he later noted, "in some of the worst storms of the North Atlantic and believed that no wind could be worse than that I had just witnessed.")

But the wind increases to an estimated 110 knots; "the force of the wind . . . (lays) the ship steadily over her on starboard side and holds her down in the water until the seas come flowing into the pilot house itself."

Early in the afternoon—probably before 1300—the leaping sea hurtled up into the port wing of the bridge and young Lieutenant Commander James Alexander Marks steps off his capsized ship—his first command—into a sea "whipped to a froth," a sea so wildly angry, so ravening for life that lifejackets are torn from the backs of the few survivors. . . .

Destroyer *Dewey*, battered and racked in the morning watch, makes it—though hurt almost mortally.

At 1230 No. 1 stack carries away and falls over the side in a clutter of wreckage, leaving a gaping wound in the main deck and four hundred pounds of steam escaping from the ruptured whistle line in a shuddering roar that mingles with the berserk voice of the typhoon. The falling funnel carries away the whaleboat davits; this easing of the topside weight—and the skipper's prescience in the morning watch in counter-ballasting the high side—the port side— with most of his fuel, probably save the ship. Nevertheless, green water slops over the starboard wing of the bridge as the ship lies over an estimated 80 degrees to starboard—and lives to tell about it— perhaps the first vessel in the history of the sea to survive such a roll.

At 1300 the barometer drops to an estimated 27.30 inches—the needle off the scale—one of the lowest readings in the long narrative of storms.

But the typhoon has done its worst; at 1340 the barometer registers a slight rise, and at 1439 the wind slackens to about eighty knots.

The storm curves on into the wide open spaces of the Pacific the rest of that day—the eighteenth. The winds still howl; the ships still heave, the ocean is confused, and even on the nineteenth the seas are huge and horrid, but the great typhoon is over. Behind it, it leaves the fleet scattered and broken, with more unrequited damage, as Admiral Halsey later noted, than at any time since the First Battle of Savo Island. Survivors of *Monoghan* and *Hull* and *Spence* are pitifully few; destroyer escort *Tabberer,* herself demasted, picks up the first survivors from *Hull* at ten that night, and others—including Lieutenant Commander Marks—who had lost his first command—the next day. *Tabberer* also rescues ten survivors from *Spence* aboard a life raft on the twentieth; other ships—scouring the ocean now that news of the sinkings is widely disseminated—find a handful of spent and injured sailors, who will forever comprehend, more fully than any living men, the meaning of the fury of the sea.

The great typhoon of December 17 and 18, 1944, cost 790 dead dead or missing—202 from the *Hull,* about 256 from the *Monaghan* (only six were saved), 317 from the *Spence,* three dead in the *Monterey,* others killed or missing from other ships. More than eighty men were injured; 146 planes were blown overboard or damaged beyond repair. The battleships lost planes and gear, but sustained no major damage; the large carriers suffered damage to radars and to the hangar deck roller curtains. But the small ships were battered and spent. Of the light carriers, *San Jacinto, Monterey, Cowpens, Cabot,* and *Langley* suffered badly; the list of the *Monterey's* damages covered nine closely-typed legal pages. The cruisers *Miami* and *Baltimore;* the escort carriers *Cape Esperance, Anzio* and *Altamaha,* and the destroyers and destroyer escorts *Aylwin, Dewey, Buchanan, Hickox, Benham, Donaldson, Melvin R. Nawman,* and *Dyson* required major repair, while nine other vessels sustained more minor damage. The strikes against Luzon were canceled and the Third Fleet straggled —cockbilled and askew—into the atoll of Ulithi.

A Navy Court of Inquiry, summoned to solemn postmortem, found that "large errors (had been) made in predicting the location and path" of the typhoon. Admiral Halsey called the typhoon a "disaster." Admiral Chester W. Nimitz pointed out that the damage done "represented a more crippling blow to the Third Fleet than it might be expected to suffer in anything less than a major action"; and the Commander-in-Chief of the Pacific Fleet noted his determination to inculcate his officers with "the necessity of understanding the Law of Storms. . . ."

The damaged ships were repaired; the typhoon warning service and meteorological forecasts were improved; the war continued toward its triumphant finale . . .

NOW THE FIFTH FLEET BEGAN POUNDING THE JAPANESE homeland with devastating carrier air strikes—not so much a diversion as an effort to reduce enemy air capability. These strikes began on February 10, 1945, and Tokyo received its first lashing five days later. Lieutenant Commander J. Bryan III, one of the air staff officers with Rear Admiral Arthur W. Radford (TG 58.4), took notes during these jubilant days aboard his carrier, which he subsequently entered in his war memoirs. Here Bryan speaks of his shipmates and their epochal mission.

12.

FIRST STRIKE ON TOKYO

February 15th. At sea

Cooper Bright hasn't improved at all in the six months since I last saw him. The fact is, he's worse. In those days, he spent only about half his time devising ribs and insults; now he seems to work three eight-hour shifts a day. If he can make a victim mad, Coop is happy. If he can scare him, he is happier. If he can make him mad and scare him at the same time, he's happiest of all.

This morning Coop slipped a harpoon into the air group. Coop comes from New Jersey, and professes to regard all Southerners with the same contemptuous distaste as Admiral Halsey has for the Japanese. Unfortunately for the South, he has access to air plot's tele-typewriter, which prints its messages in the four ready rooms and the Air Combat Intelligence office, so his slurs automatically get wide publicity. One of our fighter pilots is named Robert E. Lee. Here is what he, and every other southerner in the air group, was slapped in the face with today: "AND SO WE SANG THE CHORUS FROM ATLANTA TO THE SEA, AS WE GO MARCHING THROUGH GEORGIA"—DEDICATED TO ROBERT E. LEE OF VF 3.

Coop may make them mad, but they're grateful to him. His non-sense takes their minds off more lively troubles.

Contact!—trivial, but our first. This morning two Hellcats strafed and sank a small Jap boat. The destroyer *Hailey* was sent over to

909

look for survivors, and the one she found was put aboard us tonight. Prisoners are usually confined in the brig, but this one was taken to sick bay because his leg had been smashed by a bullet during the strafing. The staff Japanese language officer, Bill Kluss, went down to interrogate him and told me about it later.

The Jap was seventeen years old, Bill said, a nice, clean-looking kid. His wound must have been painful, but he never stopped smiling through the whole interview. It began with the stock questions: Name? Sadao Watanabe. Home? Choshi, on Honshu. Officer or enlisted man? The boy said, "I do not understand."

"Aren't you in the Navy? Wasn't that a picket boat you were in?"

"No. I am a fisherman."

"Then what were you doing 400 miles from land?"

The boy said that he and ten other fishermen had put to sea twenty-nine days before. They were only two miles offshore when their engine failed, and they had drifted ever since, living on rain water and fish.

At this point in the story, Bill said, a corpsman put a tray of chow on the boy's knees, and two peas rolled off into the bedclothes. Bill said the boy's ribs looked like a xylophone, but before he took a single mouthful, he hunted for those peas and put them back on his plate—he was *that* hungry. Bill let him finish his meal, then asked, "What happened to the other ten men?"

"They were killed when the Emperor's planes attacked our boat this morning."

"When *whose* planes attacked you?"

"The Emperor's. We didn't understand it, but we had been told that China had no planes."

Bill was puzzled. Presently he asked, "Do you think Japan will win the war?"

"Certainly. China is big, but she is weak."

"Look, Sadao," Bill said. "Where do you think you are now?"

"I don't know. All I know is that I am with friends."

When the real situation was explained to him, he wasn't alarmed or even abashed. On the contrary, he announced that as soon as his leg was healed, he would like to enlist in the United States Navy and spend the rest of his life with his wonderful new friends.

Telling me about it, Bill asked, "How the hell can you dope out people like that?"

February 16th. At sea

All day today Task Force 58 sent its planes against Tokyo. The early morning was still wet and black when the *Yorktown* launched her first strike, and a wet night was falling when she landed her last one. Our pilots flew off and fought, returned for food and fuel, and flew off and fought again. I heard them briefed in their ready rooms, went to flag bridge to watch them take off and land, and returned to the ready rooms to hear them interrogated. I remember very little of what they accomplished, but I remember how they looked and what they said.

The morning began around 0500 in Ready 2, where the fighters were checking over their flight gear and taking down last-minute information from the ticker screen. Considering the nature of their mission, the virtual certainty of heavy interception and thick AA over the target, and the probability of day-long attacks on the ship, everyone was surprisingly cool. I mentioned this to McLeroy: "Not much excitement, is there? It's like any day in any ready room."

Mac said, "Hell, it's too late to get excited now. The time to get excited is just before you join the Navy."

Some of the pilots were discussing the weather, which was foul. One said, "We've only got a 300-foot ceiling outside. It'll be better over Tokyo, though. At least, that's what I keep telling myself. . . ."

Just then the teletype started chattering, and a message tripped across the screen: FLYING CONDITIONS UNDESIRABLE.

A pilot jerked his thumb toward it: "That means the ceiling is below the waterline. I hope they got gills on these airy-o-planes."

Another said, "Ceiling zero, Dodgers five."

The ticker chattered again: FROM CAPTAIN COMBS—THIS IS THE DAY WE HAVE BEEN WAITING FOR. YOU ALL KNOW YOUR JOB AND I KNOW YOU WILL DO IT WITH THE SAME OUTSTANDING RESULTS YOU HAVE OBTAINED IN THE PAST. STICK TOGETHER, TEAM, AND GIVE THEM THE WORKS. WE WILL KEEP THE FIGHTING LADY READY FOR YOUR RETURN. There was a pause, then one line more: THE POOR LITTLE AIR OFFICER SAYS GIVE THEM HELL.

Just before the first strike was called, Fighting 3's skipper, Fritz Wolfe, picked up the microphone. "Another thing. If you have to make a forced landing, I suggest you make it in Lake Kasumigaura. It'll give you time to cool off. If you land on the ground, you may be picked up by civilians. However, it's your plane, so do what you want with it."

The ticker printed, PILOTS MAN YOUR AIR BUGGIES, and they ran up to the dark deck. I was leaving for flag bridge when the air group's Flight Surgeon, Doc Voris, came down the passageway and asked if I'd seen our prisoner.

"Not yet. I'm going down today or tomorrow."

"Be sure to catch him at mealtime. It's a sight for your whiskers. This morning he went through two full trays like a turpentined mare through a five-bar gate."

The first of the F6Fs was taxiing into position as I reached the bridge. Its engine roared louder and louder. Suddenly the plane jumped forward and into the air, and all I could see was its dwindling lights. Another plane followed it, and another and another. Soon the deafening deck was silent again, and there was nothing to do but wait for them to return.

Around 0715, the radio in air plot stated, "We've got plenty of work in the next half-hour." None of us recognized the voice, but we knew it was some pilot on his way to the target. Nick Cline, assistant Operations, said fervently, "Plenty of work, and you ain't kidding, bud!"

A couple of hours later, there was a rumor that the first strike was lost in the weather, but that the second strike was breaking out of the overcast, slapping down the enemy, and ducking back into the overcast. No one on the ship really knew what was happening until 1100, when the first strike landed. The pilots came down to their ready rooms and all of them talked at once, while they shucked off their gear and yelled for sandwiches and coffee.

"Everywhere I looked, there were these goddam biplanes. *Bi-*planes! The wily Jap must be scraping the bottom of his goddam barrel!"

"Konoike had planes all over the field, and not a son of a bitch near 'em. We caught 'em with their pants down!"

"Goddam Phantom planes flew under us and fouled up our run!" ("Phantom" is the call-sign for the air group from another carrier.)

"Japan is nowhere near as pretty as Formosa. Did you see those sand dunes, and the snow on the mountains?"

"Mine didn't flame till the last burst. It hit his port engine, and VOOM!"

"I was chasing this Oscar, and the pilot jumped out with no chute. Son of a bitch hit the ground and *bounced,* so help my Christ! I was so busy watching him, I didn't watch the Oscar, and goddam if it didn't make a shallow turn and pull straight up into me. I fired, and it crashed and burst into pieces."

"Damn Phantom planes dropping their belly-tanks, and coming at you just like Tojos."

"I caught him in a split-S and just sawed him to pieces. The bastard must have been dead already, because he attacked us with his wheels down. I thought it was a Val at first." (A Val is an obsolete Jap dive bomber with fixed landing gear.)

"Who was in 65? He was all the hell over the sky!"

And so on, all day long.

About half the fighters on the second strike had landed when the bull horn warned us, "The next plane coming in is severely damaged. Heads up on the flight deck!"

The F6F came up the groove smoothly and settled down to a perfect landing. As it taxied past flag bridge, I saw that ten or twelve square feet of its port wing, including the whole aileron, had been shot away.

There was a lull at 1400, so I stopped by air plot. Cooper Bright was sitting in a desk drawer, like an oversized Kayo. The Air officer, Comdr. Myron T. Evans, was catching a nap on the transom. The radio was tuned to Tokyo, and Doctor Somebody-or-Other was discussing America's manpower problem.

"The United States has only 1,000,000 men to work its factories," he said. "Every month 100,000 men and women are deserting the war effort. They realize, as does the American Navy, that carrier-based aircraft do not dare come within range of our land-based aircraft, and that—"

Right here the Doctor was cut off the air, and a new voice made this announcement: "An attack by carrier planes is now going on. We have been watching their surface forces for many days, and even now our landbased planes are rising to administer punishment. The purpose of this attack is revenge for our recent destruction of American B-29s. Out of 60 B-29s, we shot down 17. One Japanese fighter plane has not yet returned."

"MT," Evans said, "I wouldn't sit up for it, Mac!"

When the results of the day's strikes were tabulated, it appeared that the four air groups in this task group had destroyed 63 Jap planes in the air and 45 more on the ground. The figures sound big,

but everybody agrees that the interception was far lighter than expected, in view of the fact that we were attacking the area where most
of the planes in the Empire are concentrated.

Jim Smith said, "The explanation is perfectly simple. It means that
the Jap high command is exactly like ours. The closer you get to
headquarters, the harder it is to get anything done. You have to go
through channels, and sweat your way up the chain of command, and
when you've made six copies of everything, some retired admiral
sends them all back because you dropped a comma. If we'd been
attacking an island outpost today, a tough Reserve lieutenant would
have seen us coming and thrown all his planes into the air, and
there'd have been one hell of a fight.

"But headquarters doesn't do things that way. The order to intercept us is probably waiting for some admiral's signature right now,
and the admiral is out playing golf."

February 17th. At sea

The fleet always stands General Quarters for the hour before dawn
and the hour after dusk, since these are the most probable times for
an attack. A gong rings in the dead of night, a bugle blows, and the
bos'n's mate of the watch calls, "General quarters! General quarters!
Man your battle stations!" The sleeping ship springs awake, and men
rush down the passageways and up the ladders, buttoning their
trousers, zipping their jackets, and rubbing drowsiness from their
eyes. A few minutes later the night is silent again, but this is a
different silence. It is a jungle silence, alert and menacing.

A wet wind poured across flag bridge at General Quarters this
morning. Low, scudding clouds screened the whole sky. Once a single
star broke through briefly; the guns of Number 3 mount swung up
and clamped on it while it shone, then swung down, waiting. At first
the planes on the flight deck were dim blurs. Gradually they solidi-
fied, until I could distinguish the F6Fs.

The assistant Air officer, "Pappy" Harshman, picked up his microphone. The bull horn magnified his voice to a bellow: "Prepare to
start engines! . . . Stand clear of propellers! . . . Start engines!"

The starter cartridges hissed and fizzed, but only three engines
exploded into power; the weather had numbed the rest. Crewmen had
to "wind them up," laboriously tugging the heavy propellers around
to build up compression in the cylinders. One engine after another
finally came to life, until all were coughing and backfiring except the

fighter on the port catapult and one in the front rank. These stayed dead. Plane-handling crews shoved them onto Number 1 elevator and sent them below. The gaps they left were filled before the elevator returned.

A flight deck ready for a predawn take-off is like a cross section of the bottommost level of hell: black, cold and roaring. The thunder of the engines shakes the ship. Pale blue flames flicker from their exhausts and are reflected from the wet deck, until the propellers blast the puddles dry. Like pit imps, the taxi crews brandish red and green flashlights as they guide the pilots into take-off position. At such a time, you can almost taste the danger that saturates the deck. Tolerances on a live flight deck are always small, but now they are infinitesimal. An instant's inattention, a slip or even a lurch, an extravagant gesture, a languid response, and a man loses a limb or his life to those murderous propellers. No actuary on earth could list all the ways that you can get killed or maimed on a live flight deck. I once saw a crewman standing just in front of an SBD's port wing, where the Pitot tube sticks out like a lance tip. The pilot of the plane ahead suddenly gunned his engine, the crewman was blown off balance, and the Pitot tube tore his ear and gouged his cheek.

The first strike landed at 1030, and I went down to the ready rooms to hear the pilots' stories. The men trooped in, some of them shouting with excitement, others dumb with exhaustion. Their wet gear dripped pools on the deck while they slanted their hands and made the moaning noises that always go with a description of maneuvers:

"I got some slugs in one, but I blacked out in the middle of it. I don't know what happened to him."

"He must have hit the tail. I wasn't shooting at *him,* I was shooting at the plane. He must have had a spring in his chute, because it popped right open, and he was hanging in it, dead."

"They're crazy! They cluster around a plane on the ground, and you go down and strafe them, and they scatter, and you do a wingover, and they're right back at the plane again."

"Fujiyama was beautiful, but Tokyo looked like Hong-kong, only bigger and browner. It looked like part of the earth—reckon it was camouflaged? Anyhow, it's not like any city at home: no big buildings at all. All the reservoirs were frozen, and there was snow everywhere. I'd hate like hell to go down in that country!"

Pray ye that your flight be not in the winter....

The second strike brought home another cripple today. "Heads up!" the bull horn said. "The next man coming in has no tail hook!"

The plane was F6F Number 2, with a pilot named Reitel. He made a beautiful landing, but his brakes wouldn't hold on the wet surface, and he plowed into the wire barrier at 70 knots. The plane tipped up on its nose, the prop gouged chunks out of the deck, and Reitel pitched forward in his straps, his arms flailing. Then the plane fell back, and he climbed out unhurt. *Yet lives our pilot still....*

The Landing Signals officer, Dick Tripp, invited me aft to his little platform to watch the third strike return, around noon. He brought them in smoothly, plane after plane, with hardly a wave-off. In fact his expert teamwork with the pilots became montonous. But suddenly, as an SB2C's tail hook caught, something fell from its belly and split apart, and the prop-wash blew a white blizzard over the whole after end of the flight deck.

Dick's assistant, Lee Spaulding, said, "Must be shedding their tail feathers."

They turned out to be propaganda leaflets. The pilot had tried to drop them over Japan, but they had hung up until the shock of landing jarred them loose.

Carl Ballinger, the flag Fighter Director officer, bet that the Japs would trail our strikes home to the task force today and work us over with *kamikazes*. When General Quarters blared out at 1600, everybody thought that Carl would collect. False alarm. We secured a few minutes later.

Radiotokyo got on its hip with an opium pipe and dreamed up this one tonight:

"American carrier-borne aircraft under command of Admiral Marc A. Mitscher continued strikes in and around the Tokyo area Saturday, but the attackers failed to cause any serious damage. Preliminary estimates showed that Japanese fliers and anti-aircraft batteries shot down 147 enemy planes and damaged 50 others. In assaults against the large carrier task force, one cruiser was sunk and another large American warship, believed to have been a carrier, was seriously damaged and burned from our attacks. Other damage was done to sundry other American warships."

No, brother! No, no, *no!* It's too soon for us to file an affidavit on exactly how many planes the strikes yesterday and today have cost the task force; all the figures aren't in yet. But taking the *Yorktown's* air group as an average, the total losses won't be more than a dozen, if that many. Air Group 3 has lost one plane—that's all. Frank Onion got hopped yesterday, had a finger shot off, and took some bullets in his engine. His plane ditched and sank, but Frank himself is back aboard the ship already.

And as for a cruiser being sunk and a carrier damaged—apcray!

OUR NEXT OBJECTIVE WAS IWO JIMA, IN THE BONIN IS-lands. Located about halfway between Japan and the Marianas, and only six hundred and sixty miles from Tokyo, the island was of great strategic importance. It contained two airfields and a third which was almost complete, making it a perfect base for B-29 Superforts flying against Japan. Shaped like a porkchop, and only four and a half miles long and two and a half miles wide, the island is dominated by Mount Suribachi, rising five hundred and fifty feet above sea level. The terrain on either side of the mountain is alternately rock and beach-like, and is covered with a brown volcanic ash.

Spruance's invasion forces were as follows: Turner was in com-mand of the Joint Expeditionary Force and Holland M. Smith of the V Amphibious Corps; the Attack Force was commanded by Rear Admiral Harry W. Hill; the Support Force by Rear Admiral W.H.P. Brandy, the Logistic Support by Rear Admiral Donald B. Beary, and Search and Reconnaissance by Commodore Dixwell Ketcham. Vice Admiral Marc A. Mitscher's Fast Carrier Forces were of course in support.

After her defeat in the Marshalls, Japan had fortified the Bonins, with special emphasis upon Iwo Jima, with about 21,000 officers and men and all necessary war equipment. General Kuribayashi, taking advantage of the terrain, had planned his defense so that his main breastwork, a network of closely interwoven caves, lay between the two operational airfields. Here, all too aware of the futility of the delaying action which loomed, he was to make his strongest bid to repulse the invaders.

D-Day for Iwo—where the Marines gathered in twenty-two Medals of Honor in their bloodiest battle of the war—was February 19th. On the 16th of the month Blandy arrived off the island with his task force for strikes and a preliminary bombardment. Aboard the battleship *Tennessee* was the distinguished novelist, John P. Marquand, war correspondent for *Harper's Magazine,* who gives us a vivid picture of the three-day bombardment before the landings.

13.

IWO JIMA BEFORE H-HOUR

Life on a battleship is largely conducted against a background of disregarded words. For example, upon leaving Saipan, the radio loud-speaker on the open bridge produced a continuous program somewhat along the following lines:

"This is Peter Rabbit calling Audacity One—Peter Rabbit calling Audacity One—over . . . Audacity One calling Peter Rabbit . . . Come in, Peter Rabbit—over . . . Peter Rabbit to Audacity One—Shackle. Charley. Abel. Oboe. Noel Coward, Unshackle—over . . . Audacity One to Peter Rabbit—Continue as directed. Over . . . Peter Rabbit to Audacity One—Roger. Over . . ."

Sometimes these guarded code conversations, all conducted with flawless diction in clear unemotional tones, would reach a degree of subtlety that bordered on the obvious.

"Tiger Two is now in a position to give the stepchildren a drink. Will Audacity One please notify the stepchildren? . . . Bulldog calling Turtle. A pilot is in the water, southeast of Hot Rock. Pick him up. I repeat: In the water, southeast of Hot Rock. Pick him up. . . ."

There was never any way of telling whether or not the stepchildren received the drinks which Tiger was kind enough to offer, on whether or not the pilot was rescued from the slightly chilly waters off that unpleasant island of Iwo. Moreover, no one seemed particularly to care. The Admiral and the Captain sat upon the bridge in comforta-

919

ble high-chairs, not unlike those used by patrons in a billiard parlor. Their staff officers stood near them, and behind the staff officers stood the men with earphones and mouthpieces tethered by long insulated cords, and next came the Marine orderlies with their .45 automatics. Occasionally a Filipino mess boy would appear from the small kitchenette below—doubtless called a galley—with sandwiches and coffee for the Admiral and the Captain. He would carry these on a tray, sparkling with bright silver, china, and napery, up two dark companion ladders to the open bridge. Once when the main battery of 14-inch guns was firing, some freak of concussion lifted him a good six inches off the deck. But guns or not, no one appeared to listen to the voices on that radio.

However, as hours merged into days during those vigils on the bridge, that constant flow of words could not help but appeal to the imagination of anyone whose experience on battleships and with naval affairs had been previously limited almost exclusively to an acquaintance with Pinafore and Madame Butterfly. Charley and Abel and Peter Rabbit, who kept shackling and unshackling themselves, gradually became old friends. You began to wonder what was happening now to Audacity and Oboe. It would not have been tactful to ask, since each was a special ship, a unit of the task force, but once one of those characters revealed its identity. This was when Little Abner had words with Audacity off the beach of Iwo Jima on D-day minus two.

"Little Abner calling Audacity," Little Abner said. "We've got three holes and so we're going back to the line."

"What line do you mean?" Audacity asked.

"What the hell line do you think?" Little Abner answered. "The firing line."

Little Abner was an LCI—Landing Craft Infantry, in case you do not understand naval initials. She was one of the LCI's equipped with rockets, assigned to strafe the beach, and the Jap batteries had taken her under fire at eight hundred yards.

In addition to the radio on the bridge, there was also entertainment down below. When the great ship withdrew from the area, and when General Quarters had changed to Condition Two, some unknown hands would place recordings of radio programs from home upon a loudspeaker that reached the crew's mess, the warrant officers' mess, and the wardroom. Thus, above the shufflings on the deck, the clatter of mess tins and dishes, would come blasts of music, roars of laughter and blatant comedy. There was no way of escaping it if you wanted to eat. Though you were seven hundred-odd miles from Tokyo, you were back home again.

"And now Dr. Fisher's tablets for intestinal sluggishness present Willie Jones, and all the little Jones boys, and the Jones boys' orchestra." (Whistles, laughter, and applause from an unknown audience.) "But first a brief, friendly word from our sponsor. Folks, do you feel headachy and pepless in the morning? Just take one with a glass of warm water. But here he is, Willie Jones himself." (Whistles, applause, and cheers from that unknown audience.) "How are you tonight, Willie?"—"Well, frankly, Frank, I'm feeling kind of dumb." —"You mean you're just your old self, then?" (Shrieks, whistles, and applause from the unknown audience.)

There was no way of turning the thing off, but no one seemed to mind. Perhaps after having been at sea almost continuously for thirty months, as had many members of that crew, these sounds gave a sort of reassurance that a past to which everyone was clinging still waited back at home. At the ship's service, days before the ship was cleared for action, you could buy all sorts of reminders of that past. The shaving creams and toothpaste were like old acquaintances. There was even Williams' Aqua Velva, though this line was finally discontinued when it was found that certain members of the crew were taking it internally. There was a selection of homely literature, such as *The Corpse in the Coppice* and *Murder Walks at Midnight* and *The Book of Riddles,* and there were fragile volumes of comics and nationally known brands of gum and candy. When men went to battle stations nearly all of them took a few of these things along. When the ship was closed into hermetically sealed compartments and the ventilating system was cut off you could see them reading by the ammunition hoist. You could see the damage control groups, with their gas masks, their tools and telephones, reclining on the decks slowly devouring those pages and chewing gum. They may not have enjoyed this literature for itself but it must have given them about the only illusion of privacy that there was in a life at sea where privacy does not exist.

"If you write this thing just the way you see it," an officer said, "maybe it might mean something to people back home. They might see what we're going through. They might understand—they never understand back home."

That was what nearly everyone aboard said. They all had a pathetic desire for people at home to know. Of course, if they had thought about it, they would have realized that this was impossible. There was too great a gap between civilian and naval life. There were too few common values. The life aboard a ship in enemy waters was even more complex and difficult of explanation than the life of troops ashore. There was a combination of small personal comforts and of impending danger verging on calamity that was ugly and incongruous. The living quarters of the crew were overcrowded, but they had hot water and soap, hot showers, and all sorts of things you would never get ashore. There were clean clothes, and all the coffee you wanted day and night, and red meat and other hot food, and butter and ice cream. Yet, at the same time, the sense of danger was more intense. You could not run away from it as you could on land. It might come at any minute of the day and night from torpedoes, from the air, from a surface engagement. Almost any sort of blow meant casualties and damage. Even a light shell on the superstructure might cause complications incomparable to the results of a similar blow on land.

There had been some hope that the task force of battleships, cruisers, and destroyers that was scheduled to bombard Iwo Jima for three days before the transports and the amphibious craft appeared, might arrive there undetected, but the force was spotted by an enemy plane on the evening of February 15th. No one aboard saw that speck in the dark sky.

In the junior officers' wardroom there was a complete collection of all the intelligence which had been gathered regarding the island of Iwo. Nothing was a secret any longer. It was possible to scan the latest airplane photographs, which had been taken early in the month. There were maps showing the target areas assigned every unit, with batteries, pillboxes, and antiaircraft installations marked in red. There were reports on the soil of the island. The beach would be coal-black lava sand, and the land rose up from it quite sharply in terraces. Each terrace had been a former beach, since in the past few years the island had been rising from the sea. As one moved in from the water's edge the soil was a soft sand of volcanic ash, almost barren of vegetation and exceedingly difficult for any sort of vehicle to negotiate. Higher on the island were the cliffs of brown volcanic stone, suitable for construction of underground galleries. There were patches of coarse grass full of the mites that cause scrub typhus. There were hot springs, and there was the sulphur mine from which Iwo draws its name (Sulphur Island), and a small sugar plantation to the north near a single town called Motoyama. There were believed to be fifteen hundred troops on the island. The defensive installations were all underground or carefully camouflaged. There was only one practi-

JAPANESE HOME ISLANDS

Plus OKINAWA & IWO JIMA

Hokkaido

Honshu

TOKYO

Shikoku

Kyushu

✳ ⟵ ———— YAMATO sunk 7 April 45, the end of the Japanese fleet

Okinawa action
1 Apr - 2 July 45

Iwo Jima action
19 Feb – 16 Mar 45

cal beach on which to land and there was no chance for tactical subtlety.

The most interesting unit of this informational material was a large relief map made out of soft, pliable rubber that gave a bird's-eye view of the island we were approaching. Every contour of it was there in scale—the cliffs to the northward, the vegetation, the roads, the air strips (two finished and one nearing completion), and Mount Suribachi, the low, brown volcanic cone on the southern tip.

There have already been a good many ingenious descriptions of the shape of Iwo Jima, including comparisons to a mutton chop and a gourd. The whole thing was about five miles long. Mount Suribachi, to the south, was a walled-in crater. Its northern slope was known to be studded with pillboxes and with artillery. Bushes and boulders on this slope ran down to the lowest and narrowest stretch on the island, which had beaches on the east and west. (The west beach, however, would not permit landing operations on account of the prevailing winds.) From here the land gradually rose upward, and the island broadened until it finally reached a width of two and one-half miles. The air strips were on its central spine. The northern shores came down to the sea in cliffs. There were only eight square miles of this bleak, unpromising, and porous dry land.

Anyone could tell that the plans for the seizure of Iwo Jima must have been the main occupation of a large group of specialists for a long, long time. Heaps of secret orders showed the disposition at any given moment of every one of the hundreds of craft that would take part in the invasion. The thousands of pages made a scenario for an operation which might take place in an hour or a minute. Veterans of other invasions were not impressed by the infinite detail. They spoke of the plans for Normandy and the south of France, or they discussed the arrangements for Guam and Saipan.

"If you've seen one of them," they said, "you've seen them all."

No one spoke much on the bridge. It was chilly and rain was falling before daylight. We were a silent, blacked-out ship, moving slowly, and as far as one could tell, alone—except for voices on the bridge radio.

"Battleaxe One," the radio was saying, "Area Zebra. Shackle. Charley. Oswald. Henry. Abel. Unshackle."

"We'll start firing at about ten thousand yards," someone said.

Then the first daylight began to stir across the water and we were among the shadows of other heavy ships, moving very slowly.

"Look," someone said, "there's the mountain."

There was a faint, pinkish glow on the rain clouds above the horizon and the first faint rays of an abortive sunrise struggling against the rain fell on a rocky mass some five miles dead ahead. It was the cone of Suribachi emerging from a misty haze of cloud, and cloud vapor covered the dark mass of the rest of Iwo Jima. After one glance at its first vague outlines, it would have been hard to have mistaken it for anything but a Japanese island, for it had the faint delicate colors of a painting on a scroll of silk.

Our spotting plane was warming up on the catapult aft and you could hear the roar of the motor clearly over the silent ship. Then there was a flat explosion as the plane shot over the water. When it circled for altitude and headed for the island, there was already light enough to see the faces on the bridge.

The Captain dropped his binoculars and lighted a cigarette. The clouds were gradually lifting above the island. It was unexpectedly tedious waiting and wondering when we would begin to fire. The island lay there mute and watchful. A bell was ringing. "Stand by," someone said, and seconds later one of our 14-inch projectiles was on its way to Iwo Jima. The noise was not as bad as the concussion, for your chest seemed to be pushed by invisible hands when the big guns went off. There was a cloud of yellow smoke, not unlike the color of Mount Suribachi. Then everyone crowded forward to gaze at the island. It seemed a very long while before a cloud of smoke and gray sand rose up almost like water from land. Then another ship fired. The bombardment of Iwo Jima had begun and the island lay there in the dingy, choppy sea, taking its punishment stoically without a sound.

Even at a distance of five miles, which somehow does not seem as far at sea as it does on land, one had the inescapable impression that Iwo Jima was ready for it and accustomed to taking a beating. This was not strange, as we had bombed it from the air for successive dozens of days, and fleet units had already shelled it twice. Nevertheless, this lack of reaction was something that you did not expect, even though common sense told you that there would not possibly be any land fire until we closed the range.

Another aspect of that three-day bombardment before D-day was even more unexpected, especially when one retained memories of the heavy and continuous fire by land batteries upon prepared positions in the last World War. The bombardment turned out to be a slow, careful probing for almost invisible targets, with long dull intervals between the firing. Occasionally one could see a cloud of drab smoke arise from another ship, and a long while afterward the sound of the explosion would come almost languidly across the water, and then there would be another plume of dust and rubble on another target area of Iwo Jima. Sometimes, when the breeze was light, the smoke from the big guns of another ship would rise in the air in a huge perfect ring. Of course common sense again gave the reason for this deliberate firing. The fleet had come too long a distance to waste its limited ammunition, and consequently the effect of every shot had to undergo careful professional analysis.

In the lulls between the firing there was always an atmosphere of unremitting watchfulness. While the crews of the anti-aircraft batteries below us sat by their guns, smoking and talking, hundreds of eyes were examining the sky and land. There was air cover far above us. In the distance were underwater listeners on the destroyers and DE's that were screening us. Our own air watch, besides, was covering every sector of the sky—and you also knew that the enemy looked back at us from his hidden observation posts. That consciousness of eye-strain and listening never entirely vanished in those days at Iwo Jima, and, because of it, not a moment on the bridge was restful.

The slow approach on Iwo Jima was somewhat like the weaving and feinting of a fighter watching for an opening early in the first round. To put it another way, our task force was like a group of big-game hunters surrounding a slightly wounded but dangerous animal. They were approaching him slowly and respectfully, endeavoring to gauge his strength and at the same time trying to tempt him into action. We moved all through the day, nearer and nearer to Iwo Jima. Planes from the carrier force came from beyond the horizon, peeling off through the clouds and diving toward the air strip; but except for an occasional burst of automatic fire and a few black dots of flak, the enemy was very listless. Our minesweeps, small, chunky vessels, began operating very close to the island. There were a few splashes near them, but that was all. The Japanese commander was too good a soldier to show his hand.

As the day wore on, we crowded close and objects loomed very large ashore. You could see the coal-black strip of beach where our assault waves would land, and the sea broke on the rusting hulls of a few old wrecks. Above the beach were the gray terraces we had read about, mounting in gradual, uneven steps to the air strip. Beside the air strip there was a tangle of planes, smashed by our bombings and pushed carelessly aside, like rubbish on a city dump. To the north were the quarries which had been mentioned by the Intelligence. You could see caves to the south on Mount Suribachi. We were very close for a battleship and we knew the enemy had 8-inch coast defense guns. We continued firing at pillboxes and at anti-aircraft emplacements, but there was no return fire and no trace of life upon the island. We stayed there until the light grew dim, and then we turned to leave the area until next morning. Twelve hours of standing on the bridge and the concussion of the guns left everyone very tired. We must have done some damage but not enough to hurt.

It was different the next morning—D-day minus two. When we returned to the dull work the island was waiting with the dawn. Today the sky was clearer and the sea was smoother, and the ships closed more confidently with the shore. The schedule showed that there was to be a diversion toward the middle of the morning, and the force was obviously moving into position.

"We're going to reconnoiter the beach with small craft," an officer explained. "And the LCI's will strafe the terraces with rockets."

It was hard to guess where the LCI's had come from, for they had not been with us yesterday—but there they were just behind us, on time and on order, like everything else in amphibious war. The sun had broken through the cloud ceiling and for once the sea was almost blue. The heavy ships had formed a line, firing methodically. Two destroyers edged their way past us and took positions nearer shore.

"Here come the LCI's," someone said. "You can see the small craft with them," and he gave the initials by which the small boats were identified. They were small open launches, manned by crews with kapok life jackets. They were twisting and turning nervously as they came to join the LCI's.

"Where are they going in those things?" I asked.

"They are going to see what there is along the beach," my friend answered. "Someone has to see." He spoke reprovingly, as though I should have known the routine that had been followed again and again in the Pacific.

Eight or ten LCI's—it was difficult to count them—were passing among the battleships, with their crews at their battle stations. They were small vessels that had never been designed for heavy combat. They had been built only to carry infantry ashore, but in the Pacific they were being put to all sorts of other uses—as messenger ships to do odd jobs for the fleet, as gunboats, and as rocket ships. Each had a round tower amidships where the commanding officer stood. Each had open platforms with light automatic guns, and now they were also fitted with brackets for the rockets. They were high and narrow, about a hundred feet overall, dabbed with orange and green paint in jungle camouflage. They were a long way from jungle shores, however, as they moved toward the beach of Iwo Jima.

Suddenly the scene took concrete shape. They would approach within a quarter of a mile of shore under the cover of our guns. Without any further protection their crews stood motionless at their stations.

Afterward a gunner from one of the LCI's spoke about it.

"If we looked so still," he said, "it was because we were scared to death. But then everyone had told us there was nothing to be scared of. They told us the Japs never bothered to fire at LCI's."

They were wrong this time, probably because the small craft that followed gave the maneuver the appearance of a landing. For minutes the LCI's moved in and nothing happened. They had turned broadside to the beach, with small boats circling around them like water beetles, before the enemy tipped his hand and opened up his batteries. Then it became clear that nothing we had done so far had contributed materially to softening Iwo Jima. The LCI's were surrounded with spurts of water, and spray and smoke. They twisted and backed to avoid the fire, but they could not get away. It all seemed only a few yards off, directly beneath our guns. Then splashes appeared off our own bows. The big ships themselves were under fire.

"The so-and-so has taken a hit," someone said. "There are casualties on the such-and-such." He was referring to the big ships, but at the moment it did not seem important. All you thought of were the LCI's just off the beach. We were inching into line with the destroyers.

It appeared later that when we had been ordered to withdraw we had disregarded the order, and thus all at once we were in a war of our own, slugging it out with the shore. There had been a great deal of talk about our gunnery and the training of our crews. There was no doubt that they knew their business when they began firing with everything that could bear. The 14-inch guns and the 5-inch batteries were firing as fast as they could load. The breeze from the shore blew the smoke up to the bridge in bilious clouds. The shore line of Iwo Jima became cloaked in white smoke as we threw in phosphorus. Even our 40-millimeters began to fire. It was hard to judge the lapse of time, but the LCI's must have let off their rockets according to the schedule while the Japanese were blinded by the smoke and counter-fire. When the LCI's began to withdraw, we also moved off slowly. It was the first mistake the enemy had made, if it was a mistake—revealing those batteries, for the next day was mainly occupied in knocking them out.

The LCI's were limping back. One of them was listing and small boats were taking off her crew. Another was asking permission to come alongside. When she reached us the sun was beating on the shambles of her decks. There was blood on the main deck, making widening pools as she rolled on the sluggish sea. A dead man on a gun platform was covered by a blanket. The decks were littered with wounded. They were being strapped on wire stretchers and passed up to us over the side, since nothing as small as an LCI had facilities for wounded. The men who were unhurt were lighting cigarettes and talking quietly, but no one was smiling. The commanding officer was tall, bare-headed, and blond, and he looked very young. Occasionally he gave an order and then he, also, lighted a cigarette. When they began to hose off the blood on the deck, the crew must have asked for fresh water, because our men, gathered by the rail, began tossing down canteens. Then there was a call from our bridge.

"Can you proceed under your own power?"

The blond CO looked up. He evidently had not heard, because the question was repeated.

"Can you proceed under your own power?"

"We can't proceed anywhere for three days," the CO said.

They had passed up the wounded—seventeen of them—and then they passed up five stretchers with the dead—twenty-two out of a crew of about sixty.

"That officer ought to get a medal," I said to someone on the bridge.

"They don't give medals for things like that in the Navy," I was told.

It may be so, but I still hope he gets the medal.

That evening the Japanese reported that they had beaten off two landings on Iwo Jima and that they had sunk numerous craft, including a battleship and a destroyer. There was a certain basis of fact in this, since what had happened must have looked like a landing. One LCI was sinking, waiting for a demolition charge, as disregarded as a floating can.

After the reconnaissance of the beach had been accomplished, the pounding of Iwo Jima continued through the afternoon and through the whole next day. Planes dove in with bomb loads, while the ring of ships kept up their steady fire. At night the "cans," as the destroyers were called, continued a harassing fire. Incendiary bombs were dumped on the slopes of Suribachi. Rockets were thrown at it from the air. Fourteen-inch shells pounded into its batteries. The ship to starboard of us attacked the battery to the north on the lip of the quarry. The earth was blown away, exposing the naked concrete gun emplacements, but now that the novelty had worn off it was all a repetition of previous hours. The scene grew dull and very fatiguing, but the voices on the radio loudspeaker continued tirelessly.

"Dauntless reports a contact. . . . Bulldog is ready to give a drink to any of our pigeons that may need it. Audacity One to Tiger—I repeat: Did you get our message? Over. . . ."

The island lay still, taking it. No visible life appeared until the last day, when an installation was blown up and a few men staggered out from it. Some of us on the bridge saw them and some did not. One Japanese ran a few steps and seemed to stop and stoop to pick up something. Then he was gone. We had probably seen him dying.

The Japanese commander was playing his cards close to his chest, revealing no more targets by opening fire. It was clear that he also had his plan, less complicated than ours, but rational. He might damage our heavy ships, but he could not sink them, or conceivably prevent the inevitable landing. He had clearly concluded to wait and take his punishment, to keep his men and weapons under cover, until our assault waves were on the beach. Then he would do his best to drive them off, and everyone at Iwo knows it was not such a bad plan, either. He did not come so far from doing it when he opened up his crossfire on the beach. Some pessimists even admit that he might have succeeded if it had not been for that coarse, light sand which embedded the mortar shells as they struck, so that they only killed what was very near them.

At the end of D-Day minus one our task force was still there, without many new additions, but it was different the next morning. At dawn on D-Day the waters of Iwo looked like New York harbor on a busy morning. The transports were there with three divisions of Marines—a semicircle of gray shipping seven miles out. Inside that gray arc the sea, turned choppy by the unsettled weather, was dotted by an alphabet soup of ships.

There were fleets of LST's filled with amphibious tanks and alligators; there were LSM's; there were the smaller LCT's, and packs of

LCI's gathering about the kill. The ring of warships was drawing tighter. Small boats were moving out bearing flags to mark the rallying points from which the landing waves would leave. It looked like a Hollywood production, except that it was a three-billion-, not a three-million-dollar extravaganza. There must have been as many as eight hundred ships clustered off Iwo Jima, not counting the small boats being lowered. The officers and crew faced it without surprise. Instead they pointed out small incidents and made critical remarks.

"See the LCVP's," someone said. He was pointing out the tiny dots around the transports where the landing craft were loading. "They'll be moving into position. Here come the planes." It was all working without a hitch, with H-hour not so far away. At nine o'clock exactly the first assault wave was due to hit the beach, but before that Iwo Jima was due to receive its final polishing. Its eight square miles were waiting to take everything we could pour into them, and they must have already received a heavier weight of fire than any navy in the world had previously concentrated upon so small an area.

Anyone who has been there can shut his eyes and see the place again. It never looked more aesthetically ugly than on D-Day morning, or more completely Japanese. Its silhouette was like a sea monster with the little dead volcano for the head, and the beach area for the neck, and all the rest of it with its scrubby, brown cliffs for the body. It also had the minute, fussy compactness of those miniature Japanese gardens. Its stones and rocks were like those contorted, wind-scoured, water-worn boulders which the Japanese love to collect as landscape decorations. "I hope to God," a wounded Marine said later, "that we don't get to go on any more of those screwy islands."

An hour before H-hour it shook and winced as it took what was being dished out to it. In fact, the whole surface of the island was in motion as its soil was churned by our shells and by the bombs from the carrier planes that were swooping down across its back. Every ship was firing with a rising tempo, salvo after salvo, with no more waiting for the shellburst to subside. Finally Iwo Jima was concealing itself in its own debris and dust. The haze of battle had become palpable, and the island was temporarily lost in a gray fog.

"The LST's are letting down their ramps," someone said.

There could not have been a better place to observe the whole spectacle than from the air lookout station above the bridge, but there was too much to see. Only an observer familiar with the art and theory of amphibious warfare could possibly have unraveled all the threads, and an ordinary witness could only give as inaccurate an account as the innocent bystander gives to circumstances surrounding a killing on the street. There was no time any longer to ask questions or to digest kindly professional explanations. All the facts that one had learned from the secret documents were confused by the reality.

The LST's had let down their ramps and the amphibious vehicles which they had carried were splashing through the water, like machines from a production line. Watching them, I found myself speaking to a chief petty officer who was standing next to me.

"It's like all the cats in the world having kittens," I said, and the idea appeared to interest him.

The amphibious vehicles, churning up the sea into foaming circles, organized themselves in lines, each line following its leader. Then the leaders moved out to the floating flags, around which they gathered in circling groups, waiting for their signal to move ashore. The gray landing craft with the Marines had left the transports some time before for their own fixed areas and they also were circling, like runners testing their muscles before the race. The barrage which had been working over the beach area had lifted, and the beach, with the smoldering terraces above it, was visible again. It was time for the first wave to be starting.

It was hard to pick the first wave out in that sea of milling craft, but suddenly a group of the barges broke loose from its circle, following its leader in a dash toward shore. Close to land the leader turned parallel to the beach, and kept on until the whole line was parallel. Then the boats turned individually and made a dash for it. The Navy had landed the first wave on Iwo Jima—at nine o'clock on the dot— or, at least, not more than a few seconds after nine.

~~~~~~

IN A YARD-BY-YARD FIGHT, WITH THE NAVY PROVID-ing air and fire support as needed, the Marines moved in from the beachhead in slow stages, using flamethrowers and grenades. Robert Sherrod, whom we met at Tarawa, briefly described the scene the next morning as seen from his foxhole: "Whether the dead were Japs or Americans, they died with the greatest possible violence. Nowhere in the Pacific war have I seen such badly mangled bodies. Many were cut squarely in half. Legs and arms lay 50 feet from any body. In one spot on the sand, far from the nearest cluster of dead, I saw a string of guts 15 feet long . . . The smell of burning flesh was heavy . . ."

In this manner Iwo Jima was secured one month later, although late in April isolated pockets of resistance were still being encountered.

Operation "Iceberg"—Okinawa—was next. Strategic plans called for a weeklong series of air strikes by Mitscher, as well as by B-29s based in the Marianas, to support the amphibious operations of General Buckner's Tenth Army and General Geiger's III 'Phib Corps. As before, the brilliant tactician Turner commanded the Navy's amphibious forces under Spruance. L-Day (D-Day) was set for April 1, and the pre-invasion bombardment began eight days earlier as the Navy brought up two bombardment groups. Actually there were two invasions—the second at Keramo Retto, a small group of islands off Okinawa.

Okinawa lies in the Nansei Shoto, or Ryukyus, with the Pacific on one side and the East China Sea on the other. Sprawling over some eight hundred and fifty square miles, the Nansei Shoto are a series of drowned volcanic islands numbering about one hundred and forty in all. Of these Okinawa, centrally located in the group, lies about three hundred and fifty miles from China, Japan and Formosa. Its culture is predominantly Japanese and Chinese. The island was annexed by the enemy, and fortified by him.

At the time of the Okinawa invasion Japan launched the second phase of her deadly kamikaze attacks, which had been started on a small scale at Leyte Gulf. While hunting targets in and around Japan, several ships of Mitscher's Task Force 58 were attacked. On March 19 carriers *Wasp* and *Franklin* were hit, the latter seriously. Carrier *Hancock,* maneuvering to escape a kamikaze, crashed into destroyer *Halsey Powell.* Nevertheless tough, taciturn Mitscher continued to send off his air strikes without interruption, and his pilots managed to spot the superbattleship *Yamato* lying alongside a pier at Kobe. At his option he switched targets to Okinawa and adjacent islands during the week preceding L-Day.

Two days before the landings, UDTs went into action. One of the frogmen present was Edward T. Higgins, whose UDT 11 debarked from the destroyer transport *Kline.* His account begins the previous day, while he was still aboard the stripped-down tin can, and continues through to the invasion.

14.

OKINAWA–
TRIPLE EXPOSURE

At 1900 Lieutenant States called a huddle on the fantail of the *Kline* and gave us our orders for the next day, Love Day minus two, March 30. Together with UDT 16 we were to clear the beaches selected for the troop landings, Beaches Red 3 and Blue 1 and 2, with approximately 1,200 obstacles. Roger Hour would be at 0930 in the morning.

We started immediately to prepare our demolition charges. Each charge consisted of one two-and-one-half block of Tetrytol. Around each block we wrapped a piece of prima cord and tied it with a special demolition knot, leaving about two and one-half feet of cord to run from the block up to the master trunk line. Each block was wrapped, in addition to the prima cord, with a length of soft wire with dangling ends to be used to fasten the charge to the obstacle. As each charge was completed it was inserted in a "Schantz pack," a sort of fabric apron with four individual packets to carry the charges. The Schantz pack was then tied to a flotation bladder and set aside ready for use in the morning. In addition to the 1400 charges, dozens of fuses had to be wired, crimped and waterproofed. All the work had to be done in the small space afforded in the ammunition magazine. We took turns, officers and men together, working in the magazine for a while, then going topside for briefing on the demolition operation. These beaches were unfamiliar to us, and we studied the maps and charts like the crew of the *Santa Maria* looking for India.

935

Chart room, powder magazine, smoke, coffee, smoke, coffee, powder magazine, chart room, remember, repeat, check, locate, smoke, coffee, until at 3:00 A.M. we finished and sacked in for the little time we had left. It was already dawn. Across the water we could hear the General Quarters bells of the nearby ships as they heralded the arrival of the day's first Kamikaze planes coming to pay the Emperor's respects to the United States fleet. For the first time we were allowed to sleep through General Quarters on our own ship.

UDT 11 was back on deck at 0600 loading the boats, checking the engines and radios and getting swimming gear in order. Our part of the demolition assignment consisted of the north half of the area covered by the three beaches, comprising about 650 yards of beach and an estimated 600 obstacles. The obstacles were hardwood posts 10 to 12 inches in diameter, pile-driven into the sand and coral and interlaced and reinforced with barbed wire. The area assigned to Team 16, the south half, was substantially the same. As the readying operation progressed, our planes could be heard diving and strafing the shore with machine-gun fire and rockets. Then the fleet moved in and the guns began pounding, harder and harder, faster and faster, until the sound of the planes was lost and the bombardment of the previous day paled by comparison.

As we finished our final briefing on team assignments and boarded the LCP(R)s the record player on the *Kline* was playing a currently popular song, "I'll Be Seeing You." It sent such a wave of nostalgia through the men that for a few minutes they even stopped ribbing me about my swimming costume.

As I had made ready for the approaching swim, I kept remembering the bitter cold water and the leg cramps of the previous day. Casting about for some method of reducing the chill of the water, I had decided to wear the top half of my long woolen underwear. It would add some weight when wet but it would take the edge off the cold. Naturally, I created a sensation when I came up on deck in my chaste garment and climbed into the boat. I could stand the ribbing if the idea worked as I hoped it would. The song, however, brought a welcome respite from the wisecracks, suggestions and invitations coming my way, and I will always remember it with gratitude.

Two boats were going into the beach with demolition swimmers, and one would stand by with a reserve crew in case of trouble. Boats 1 and 2 each carried three seven-man teams, including one officer or chief to a team. No. 4, the reserve boat, carried ten reserve swimmers. Each of the first two boats also carried one UDT observer and one from the Marine Corps, and the third boat carried Lieutenant States, commanding the overall UDT 11 operation.

At Roger Hour, 0930, Boats 1 and 2 went through the destroyer line toward the beach. As we went in, the fire from the fleet increased until it reached a crescendo that threatened to split the very air and water around us. Straight ahead we went until the boats were within 400 yards of the obstacles in the surf. Then the demolition packs went over the side and after them the swimmers, stringing out in groups at 100-yard intervals as the course curved along the beach. As the wake of the boat flattened in the chill water, we picked up our Schantz packs by the web straps trailing from the flotation bladders and kicked our flippers in the direction of the doomed sons of Nippon. Each swimmer except the trunk-line men towed five packs of charges of about 50 pounds of concentrated explosive. The trunk-line men, two crews of three men and one officer each, towed packs loaded with prima cord to be used in stringing the master detonating line along the tops of the obstacles above the water line. Any stray shot hitting one of the charges or one of the prima-cord reels would have effectively blasted the careers of all the swimmers around, a fact of which we became increasingly and acutely aware as we neared our target.

The UDT 16 swimmers reached their unloading zone shortly before us and we could see them enter their demolition area and begin work as we neared our obstacles. For some reason they had started some 200 yards north of the center line marking the division of the beach between Teams 11 and 16. But that was their problem and we concentrated on our own as sniper and machine-gun fire began to reach out from the shore in our direction.

We fanned out in the water to reduce the size of the targets for the Japs. Their fire was getting hotter as we closed upon the beach. The obstacles were only about 50 to 60 yards from some of their pillboxes and machine-gun nests, almost pointblank range for a blind man. Several times I saw bullet splashes in my immediate vicinity, and thinking that I must be in the path of a fixed machine gun or automatic weapon of some sort, I veered to the left. But the splashes followed, coming closer with each burst of fire. Then a small calm voice whispered in my ear, "Higgins, old boy, someone is shooting at *you!*"

Zigzagging frantically, I swam near Norm Elliott, my buddy from

Fort Pierce days, my pal of long standing. He reacted as though I were shoving a floating mine in his direction. Churning furiously away from me, he yelled over his shoulder: "You son of a bitch, get away from here with that Goddam white sweat shirt! Do you want to get us all killed?" That brought the dawn.

My cute idea for keeping warm was working wonderfully well. In fact, it was making things hotter than I had bargained. If my team-mates shunned me, the Japs didn't. They were doing their best to let me know that my long underwear was a howling success in their book. For seconds I debated trying to disrobe in the water, but I knew it was impossible. Even if I could accomplish the feat with all my hardware weighting me down, stopping for even a minute would leave a target even the Japs couldn't miss. The five packs of Tetrytol charges riding just aft of my stern clinched the argument. It was swim and be damned. If I could reach the nearest obstacle and keep hidden I might have a chance. And I made it, ducking and dodging, under and out of water, praying and gasping for breath, jerking the Schantz packs erratically through the water.

The others all made it safely, too, and we all rested for a minute, clinging to the obstacle posts, letting the Schantz packs snag to a halt in the maze of barbed wire. Over our heads the fire support drummed a thunderous tattoo. Our ships and planes seemed determined to keep the Japs in their holes if shells and bombs could do the trick. The little LCI(G)s lay in close behind us, their 20- and 40mm. quads and .50-caliber machine guns pumping in perfect rhythm as they fired scant feet over our heads at the beach. Behind them the destroyers worked back and forth across their grid patterns, slamming three- and five-inch shells in arithmetical pattern into the jungle above the shore line. Beyond the destroyers were the cruisers and battlewagons salvoing their six-, eight- and sixteen-inch guns in great bursts of fire that made their land targets jump and quiver, erupting in clouds of dust and debris. The shells from the sixteen-inch guns sounded above the screaming and whining of the smaller shells, rumbling through the shattered air like runaway freight cars. Over all the F6F fighters and TBM torpedo bombers from the carriers added their own individual tones to the murderous symphony, loosing their bombs, rockets and machine guns barely above the heads of the entrenched enemy. The sound of the Jap small arms and mortar fire was lost in the shuffle. We could spot their positions only by watching the splashes, like handfuls of pebbles tossed in the water around us.

We began our demolition operation with the trunk-line crews starting, one at either end of our beach, to string prima cord along the tops of the posts. Each post had to be attached individually to the trunk-line so that the connecting line from the charge at the base could be tied in. All swimmers except those on the trunk-line detail worked on fixing the charges at the bases of the obstacle posts and running the prima-cord leads up to the trunk line above. To avoid fire from the shore, all crossing from post to post was done underwater. Swimmers came up to breathe only when they were safely behind a post. The pattern had been drilled into us by many months of rehearsal: dive to the bottom of the post, fix the charge with the soft metal wire twisted around the post, surface behind the post with the prima-cord lead, tie the lead into the trunk line, dive underwater to the next post and repeat, repeat until all the posts were tied and all charges connected to the trunk line. Charges properly placed would throw the obstacles into the laps of the Japs on the beach. The one flaw in the schedule was the inability of the trunk-line men to keep ahead of the crews placing charges. This slowed us down but not enough to upset the over-all timing of the team operation.

The center line dividing our stretch of beach from that assigned UDT 16 was marked by the burial vaults of the Okinawa natives in the low cliffs above the shore line. These vaults had been dug into the faces of the cliffs for countless ages and were clearly visible from the beach. In addition to serving us as markers, they were serving the Japs as machine-gun and sniper nests and undoubtedly would have provided excellent box seats for observing our operations, had our protective fire been less efficient. We had noted these markers before, particularly when UDT 16 had started work 200 yards off the center. While watching them for enemy fire during our operations, we noted that Team 16 had pulled out to sea within minutes after we began placing charges. Since we prided ourselves on our own speed in action, we could only conclude that something had gone radically wrong in their area. Speculation ran through our minds as we worked, fixing the charges and tying-in, diving and swimming, fighting the roll of the surf to keep from being smashed against the posts or cut and slashed by the barbed wire. By 1030 we had finished and were swimming back to our boats, Artful Dodger Higgins still trying to keep his white underwear from offering too tempting a target to the Jap snipers. At 1035 we were safely aboard the LCP(R)s, except for one officer and one man from each of the trunk-line crews standing by on the reef as trigger men, awaiting the order from the commander of UDT operations to fire. A check by officers and chiefs in charge of the crews which were laying charges indicated that about 400 charges had been laid along 400 yards of beach. The other 250 yards of beach had been openings left by the Japs to provide channels for their own boats.

When the firing signal was given, Boat No. 1 closed the reef and picked up the firing party. At 1043 the charges detonated. Observers reported that all of the obstacles in the UDT 11 area had been demolished but that few, if any, of the charges in the UDT 16 area had detonated. This confirmed our suspicion that something had gone wrong with Team 16 shortly after they reached their objective.

Boats 1 and 2 returned to the *Kline* immediately, but the reserve boat, No. 4, was dispatched to locate and mark three shoal water areas in the vicinity south of Brown Beach No. 4. Two LCI(G)s were sent along as convoy and, together with a cruiser stationed in the area, gave the men cover fire as they marked the shoals, two of them with buoys and the third with a stranded piece of mine-sweeping gear flying a red flag. They finished by 1400 and shortly thereafter were back aboard the *Kline* with UDT 11 still intact.

As on the day before we reported to Intelligence immediately after boarding the ship. We were dirty and greasy from the debris and slime churned up in the water by the mortar shells, but we stood there and dripped while we gave reports and observations on the shore terrain, the Jap shore pillboxes and fortifications and other items of interest to those who would direct troop landings within the next forty-eight hours.

After the Intelligence reports, we were excused and scrambled for the showers. Under the soothing, relaxing flow of water we talked about the events of the day. The excitement of the previous day was gone; we were veterans now, and we discussed the success of our own operation, the questionable success of my white wool underwear, which I swore under pain of capital punishment never to wear again, and the fact that few of us had suffered muscle cramps from the icy water, a circumstance we credited to the long exposure of the day before and to the shorter length of time in the water on this mission.

Particularly we felt sorry for the men of UDT 16 for the failure of their operation. We heard via scuttlebutt, after boarding the *Kline,* that two of their men had been shot through the head by snipers almost immediately after they entered the obstacle area. While this might have been due to carelessness in exposing themselves to enemy fire, it still should not have caused the team to break and leave their assignment, which it apparently had. Nevertheless, we felt sorry for them and hoped that none of the reports was true, that there was a better, more understandable reason for their failure.

We had noon chow and retired to our bunks, trying to get some rest. We got very little. Our ship was under way, squirming, dodging and turning as the entire bay came under the heaviest Kamikaze attack to date. The Japs knew by now that plans were in motion for an invasion of Okinawa and they were doing their damndest to put as many ships out of commission as possible. The General Quarters bell rang constantly, eliminating any possibility of sleep. So we just smoked and talked.

We knew that our skipper, Lieutenant States, had gone over to the invasion control ship, the *USS Estes,* and we wondered what new assignment was coming up. We wondered until about five o'clock in the afternoon. Lieutenant States didn't return then but we got the word on our next operation: we were to return to Beaches Blue 1 and Blue 2 on the next day to complete the demolition of the obstacles which UDT 16 had failed to remove. Roger Hour was set for 0900.

Our sympathy for UDT 16 hit a zero reading at that point. Going in on the same beaches for the third straight day was asking for it, and we knew it. By now the Nips had had time to familiarize themselves with our style and method of operation and would be ready and waiting, knowing that we would have to make another attempt to clear the obstacles from the remainder of the landing beach. We had expected Team 16 to clear up its own detail, and it was a shock to be told that we had been handed the hot potato.

Before our resentment got too hot, Team 16's officers came aboard to brief us on their beaches. They were such wonderful guys and so obviously sorry and apologetic about the whole thing that we couldn't stay mad. Besides, we had too much work to do. In addition to the long briefing sessions there were a thousand charges to be made up together with the fuses, prima-cord lines and detonators. We ran out of flotation bladders and had to use life belts to carry the Schantz packs. We had to go over our boats and check our operational gear. The pattern followed that of the night before. It was after midnight when we finished, tired, full of strong black coffee and stuffy from too many cigarettes. From midnight until 0200 we went over the entire schedule with the boat and swimming crews who would be in action in the morning. The third platoon had been split in half with Frank Jameson taking half and me, as an acting chief, taking the other half. Our men were all good men, well trained and fire-hardened by now, but so great was our anxiety over the next day's work that we didn't even try to sleep. We drank more coffee and smoked more cigarettes until dawn and then went on deck, watching the fight against the kamikazes overhead and trying to hold down our mounting tension. A few of us did hit the sacks and were excused from General Quarters as the Kamikaze attacks mounted.

Breakfast was oatmeal and it nauseated me to look at it. My stomach was sore from holding in the tension and my nerves were on edge. I didn't think much about it, believing that the coffee and cigarettes were responsible, and went back on deck to see that everything was in order and ready to go.

At 0815 Lieutenant States returned to the *Kline* and gathered the team on the fantail for a last-minute message from the commander of the UDTs. We sat and stood around in our swimming trunks, swim fins and goggles as we heard something we already knew: this job had to be done! Troop landings in force were scheduled for the following morning, April 1, Love Day, Easter Sunday. The beaches had to be open!

Ten minutes after Lieutenant States finished talking, the boats were lowered and we went over the side.

As on the previous day, the barrage from the ships and carrier planes was tremendous. We moved in under what seemed a solid blanket of fire, shells screaming, shrieking and rumbling over our heads toward the beach. The Japs, too, seemed to realize the importance of our final demolition assault. Their fire was heavier than before, and they had added heavier guns to their machine guns and mortars. In the caves above the beach, we could see light artillery mounted on tracks running in and out as they returned the fire from the ships. Their snipers and automatic-weapons men were either more numerous or braver than they had been before. Splashes were kicking up around our boats as we dropped into the ocean 300 to 500 yards offshore. Hastily gathering up our quotas of Schantz packs floating around us, we struck out for the obstacles ahead. Around me heads were bobbing and ducking in the water as the men dived and surfaced in evasive action against the Jap gunners firing from the trees and cliffs on the shore.

Behind us the LCP(R)s stayed in close rather than in their usual place behind the LCI(G) line. The commanding officer of UDT 16 was in the No. 4 Boat with our C.O., and each of the other boats carried an officer observer from UDT 16. We had to admit that the Team 16 officers, having fouled out on their own time at bat, were doing all in their power to help us finish the job. The small LCP(R)s, including Boat No. 5 carrying ten reserve swimmers, stayed out in the open, exposed to enemy guns during the entire time we were mining the obstacles. Just knowing they were backing us up, deliberately exposing themselves, and calling for spot fire against Jap strongholds harrassing us, helped make our job easier.

There were forty men, including six officers, in the water as we closed the obstacles. The assignments duplicated those of yesterday, with the trunk-line crews starting to string prima-cord from opposite ends of the beach toward the center and the rest working with the charges and obstacles. The trunk-line crews ran into trouble right at the start. A few gaps had been blown in the obstacle patterns the day before and the extra swimming required more time than we had anticipated. Otherwise we worked as before, hiding behind the posts when we surfaced, diving between posts, fighting the undertow of the surf that constantly tried to bash our brains out against the posts or to ensnare us in the maze of barbed wire.

Enemy fire diminished as we reached our destination and for some forty-five minutes, our naval and airplane bombardment kept enemy activity to a minimum. From 0930 on, however, Japs began moving about in the area of the burial vaults. Taking advantage of a lull in our own bombardment, they began to pour fire around our heads. Snipers, machine guns, mortars and the small track guns in the caves opened up with a vengeance. Our operation slowed almost to a halt as bullets and shells thudded into the posts over our heads and splashed in the water around our obstacle shields. It was too cold to keep still and too hot to move, so we did both—moved because we had to and held still because moving meant drawing enemy fire.

Behind us Boat No. 4, carrying the skippers of Teams 16 and 11, was having trouble of its own. It had been patrolling the beach as close as water depth would permit and offered a nice, fat, tempting target for the Jap gunners. Lieutenant States immediately radioed for heavier support fire from the fleet to cover an area 100 to 150 yards inland along the entire operational area. For the next twenty minutes all hell broke loose. The whole beach blew sky high. Rocks, trees, sand and earth filled the air and blotted out the sun. One five-inch shell clipped a tree growing near the beach. As the tree separated about half-way up the trunk we could see a body blown from the upper branches describe a crazy cartwheel and fall into the dust and debris below. At least one sniper wouldn't bother us any more.

The increased fire enabled us to resume work on schedule and we wrapped the job up. At Roger plus 87, 1027, the charge tie-ins and the trunk-line connections had been double checked by Allen Hopper and Art Golden of the trunk-line crews, and all swimmers had been picked up by the LCP(R)s except the firing parties standing by for the command to fire. Snipers were still firing and splashes could be seen around the trigger men as they ducked and bobbed in the water.

At Roger plus 100, 1040, the charges were detonated. LCP(R) 4 immediately patrolled the area, reporting to the commander that substantially all obstacles had been demolished, the five or six posts that remained constituting no hazard to landing craft or tanks. In this operation over 1,000 charges were carried to the obstacles and all had been detonated. In addition, 50 or more others salvaged from the previous day's work had been tied-in and used.

In its two days of operations, UDT 11 cleared some 1,300 yards of beach of nearly 1,400 obstacles. The fact that we suffered no casualties seemed almost miraculous. Three factors were credited for this: we had been covered by accurate and intense fire from our ships and planes, we had kept undercover while working on the obstacles, and last, but most appreciated, the Japs were incredibly lousy marksmen.

In spite of the success of our demolition, I was far from happy. During the last several minutes in the water, I had been bothered by nausea and intermittent stomach cramps. Believing that the coffee, cigarettes, tension and lack of sleep of the past few days were responsible I had not worried particularly and had kept working until the job was finished. The swim back to the boats was rough as the cramps increased and I choked to keep from adding the meager contents of my stomach to the already fouled water. As I flipped into the rubber boat and climbed over the side of the LCP(R) I knew I was about finished. The boat crew grabbed me, pulled me in, and shoved the standard two-ounce bottle of brandy into my eager hands. It was no go. The smell of the usually welcome liquid almost turned me inside out.

For the first time it occurred to me that my trouble was serious. Any time I couldn't enjoy a drink of brandy after an hour and a half in ice-cold water, something was wrong. The small calm voice that had whispered in my ear about the shooting during the long underwear episode spoke again, saying, "This is the end, Higgins. Anytime you refuse a drink, old boy, you're finished. Lie down now and lie quietly. The others have work to do." I took the advice and slipped quietly to the deck, where the nausea and cramps took complete control.

I remember being covered with foul-weather gear and held against the roll of the boat as we headed for the *Kline.* The next thing I knew I was being helped over the rail of the ship and a Navy doctor was standing by as they eased me down into sick bay. I lay there with my trunks on, my knife dangling from the cord tied to my wrist, my goggles hanging awry from my neck. My swim fins had been taken off somewhere along the line. Consciousness came and went, and I cared little whether I died or not. I knew that the doc was taking a blood count and I heard him say, "Appendicitis, emergency operation." Then I was going over the side again, this time in a basket stretcher being lowered into one of the small operational boats.

I came to as they were hoisting me over the side of the control ship. The doc was still with me, giving orders to the handling crews as they took me aboard. Added to the continued pain and nausea, I was feeling the shock and letdown from the tension of the hours past. Dimly I realized that the ship's operating room was going full blast with the doctors and hospital corpsmen working at top speed on men from ships hit by Kamikaze planes.

They rolled me out of the basket onto a blanket on the floor. The operating tables were all full. I felt my swimming trunks being stripped off and my knife and goggles being removed. Then a needle punctured my skin for a spinal anesthetic and I blacked out again, wondering hazily if I would ever wake up.

ALTHOUGH LIEUTENANT GENERAL MITSURE USHIJIMA'S 77,000 troops of the Thirty-second Army were in readiness to defend Okinawa, the landings, which began as scheduled on Easter Sunday, April 1, at 8:30 A.M. were virtually unopposed. By nightfall, as the transports debouched troops and cargo off the northern and southern beaches, more than 50,000 men were ashore, and all were frankly wondering what had become of the enemy. Where was his withering fire? What had happened to his usual resolve to die on the beaches? Advancing troops flushed out and captured fifteen Japanese soldiers, and killed another dozen, but the first real opposition was not encountered until the next afternoon, when the 96th Division, at this time south of the Bisha River, met with gradually stiffening resistance. This was Ushijima's rear guard, covering a general withdrawal toward Shuri, and by nightfall his artillery had begun to pound away at the XXIV Corps. There was no doubt now that it had finally gotten into action.

At Okinawa the Navy encountered no such action as at Cherbourg or at Saipan, where its heavy ships had dueled with shore batteries, but it did contribute to the success of the invasion by providing fire support and a fast unloading of cargoes. However, the Navy's main action was in countering the attacks of the Special Attack Corps— the kamikazes—which were mounting in intensity. The first assault developed at 7:10 P.M. on April 1, when a pair of kamikazes crashed into two Northern Force transports. The next day three more transports were "body crashed" with a heavy loss of life. But the Japanese were only warming up. On April 3 destroyer *Mannert L. Abele,* on radar picket duty, was sunk in one minute with many lives lost, and escort carrier *Wake Island* was severely damaged. And now Toyoda loosed the full fury of his Divine Wind.

Some seven hundred planes—three hundred and fifty-five of them kamikazes—were available to the Admiral on fields in Formosa and Kyushu, and on April 6 and 7 he sent them out to attack. The first of a series of ten mass raids opened on the afternoon of the 6th. Although Combat Air Patrol over battleships *New Mexico* and *Idaho* shot down eight planes, other enemy strikes bore fruit. Destroyer *Newcomb,* among others, took a pair of kamikazes down her after stack and amidships, and destroyer *Leutze,* steaming to the rescue, was struck by flaming wreckage and was also bombed. Destroyers *Bush* and *Calhoun,* at other radar picket stations, were also victims of what the Japanese called *kikusui* attacks, and elsewhere over the Third Fleet kamikazes were out in force.

April 6th was also notable for another reason. The superbattleship *Yamato* (72,000 tons laden) was sighted by one of Mitscher's pilots. She was underway with escorts and was obviously headed towards Okinawa on what could be nothing less than a suicide mission. With her 18-inch guns turned loose, she could cause incalculable damage. But Mitscher was a man who played the odds and talking over the report with Captain Arleigh Burke, his Chief of Staff, and Captain James Flatley, his Air Officer, Mitscher decided upon an all-out attempt to destroy the mightiest warship afloat. The subsequent action is described by the Admiral's biographer, Theodore Taylor.

15.

THE END OF

THE JAPANESE FLEET

Mitscher, without awaiting word from Spruance, ordered all task groups to concentrate northeast of Okinawa. Perhaps some of the old battleship-versus-aircraft debates were recalled during the moments he studied the charts with Burke and Flatley. Naval airmen thought they had sunk the *Musashi* in the Battle for Leyte Gulf, but there was also the possibility that submarines had actually put her down. The appearance of the *Yamato* provided a clean-cut chance to prove, if proof was needed, aircraft superiority.

Shortly after midnight on April 6, Spruance directed Mitscher to let the enemy task force come south, leaving it to the guns of Task Force 51, the old battleships, and of Task Force 54, the new ones. Also, Mitscher was to "concentrate the offensive effort of Task Force 58 in combat air patrols to meet enemy air attacks." But Mitscher had already made his plans to sink the enemy fleet with aircraft.

By the time the dispatch was logged in with communications and initialed all the way around, Mitscher was speeding north. Admiral Spruance had not actually countermanded Mitscher's order to the task force to concentrate to the northeast. Unless Spruance explicitly forbade him to make the attack, Mitscher had no intention of letting battleship guns do a job that aircraft could do sooner. Mitscher kept his own counsel. He was doing a bit more than his orders required—perhaps enough more to sink an enemy fleet.

947

A few hours later, Spruance signaled Rear Admiral Morton L. Deyo, who commanded Task Force 51, to form his two battleship divisions, two cruiser divisions, and twenty destroyers for action. Mitscher saw a copy of the dispatch and dismissed it without comment. Throughout the night, ordnance men worked on the fast carriers, readying armor-piercing bombs and torpedoes.

At dawn, Mitscher's search planes fanned out over the sea east of Kyushu. The weather was squally. Meanwhile, both submarines and flying boats had been tracking the oncoming enemy force. Down in the ready rooms, the pilots were impatient. Word of the friendly rivalry with the battleship guns had reached them. The pilots had heard that Admiral Mitscher "planned to ram this one through."

"We knew we'd get it for him if he gave us the chance and we thought he would," said Major Long.

A few minutes after 0800 one of Admiral Clark's *Essex* search planes found the suicide fleet, steaming southward. The report was relayed back to the *Bunker Hill* by a series of communications linking planes, another Mitscher innovation for the task force, introduced because of the relatively short range of aircraft radios. It fanned out to all the task groups and to Admiral Spruance, who ordered Deyo to push his battleship fleet to the attack. At the same time, Mitscher had sent off a force of sixteen planes to cover and track the approaching enemy, but it would be more than an hour before they could make contact. Planes were manned, and as soon as the search aircraft disappeared, Mitscher gave orders to attack the Japanese fleet. It was now 1000. As the planes, from groups 58.1 and 58.2, orbited, joined up, and sped away, the Admiral watched in silence. A few minutes after they were out of sight, he turned to Burke.

"Inform Admiral Spruance that I propose to strike the *Yamato* sortie group at 1200 unless otherwise directed."

"But," said a British observer, "you have launched before you can possibly be sure of their location."

"We are taking a chance," explained Burke, "we are launching against the spot where we would be if we were the *Yamato.*

Actually, with submarines, flying boats, and carrier-based aircraft on the *Yamato's* trail, the chances of finding the enemy were good, even though the weather was thick. But if the planes could not find her, there wouldn't be enough red paint in the fleet to match the color of Mitscher's face. His launch order to destroy the enemy fleet by aircraft ran contrary to Spruance's desire to let the battleships slug it out in what would probably be the last opportunity for a big-ship gunnery fight, then and forever more.

From 1000 until noon, Mitscher's position there on the wing of the *Bunker Hill* bridge was thoroughly uncomfortable. As time stretched by, there was still no signal from Spruance countermanding Mitscher's orders. At last the planes were so close to the *Yamato* that recall would serve no purpose except to save a few dollars' worth of gas. The Avengers carried torpedoes; the dive bombers (Curtiss Helldivers) carried mixed loads of 1,000- and 250-pound bombs; each fighter had a 500-pound bomb as well as a long-range droppable gas tank. Estimated distance to the target was 240 miles.

Shortly after noon, planes from the Clark and Sherman task groups found the Japanese fleet and circled it for the kill. The weather was still bad, with clouds ranging from 1,500 to 3,000 feet, and intermittent rain. The low ceiling and large number of planes—nearly three hundred arrived simultaneously—made co-ordination impossible. Heavy ack-ack began bursting. Even the *Yamato's* eighteen-inch guns were elevated to attempt blasting the Yankees from the sky.

The weather made it impossible to see results, and Japanese jamming made it impossible to hear over the voice radio. In the words of Lieutenant Thaddeus T. Coleman, it was the "most confusing sea-air battle of all time." He said:

Our training instructions, to dive steeply from 10,000 feet or higher, proved useless. Here the ceiling was only 3,000 feet with rain squalls all around. Bomber pilots pushed over in all sorts of crazy dives, fighter pilots used every maneuver in the book, torpedo pilots stuck their necks all the way out, dropped right down on the surface and delivered their parcels so near the ships that many of them missed the ships' superstructures by inches.

However confused the Americans were, the Japanese were worse. A *Yamato* gunnery officer who survived told American interrogators that the combination of dive bombers and torpedo planes made it impossible to take evasive action. The first two waves, he said, left three bomb hits forward of the great turret on her stern, and three torpedo hits in the hull. In later attacks she was hit by at least seven more torpedoes, according to his account.

At any rate, when Admiral Radford's strike group, which was launched late, arrived, the *Yamato* was listing, and his planes struck her on the high side. She finally blew up and sank, joining the cruiser

Yahagi and four destroyers on the bottom. Photographs were handed Mitscher showing the sinking while Admiral Deyo was just getting well into his northward charge with the old battleships. A short while later, after Mitscher had signaled that the enemy had been met and dealt with, Spruance countermanded the previous order sending the ships to destroy the Japanese fleet.

When Admiral Deyo got word of Mitscher's successful attack, he good-naturedly broadcast regrets that his force wouldn't have "Japanese scrambled eggs for breakfast." Mitscher's losses were four bombers, three torpedo planes, and three fighters. Personnel losses were held to four pilots and eight aircrewmen by virtue of quick rescue work.

Mitscher didn't say much, except to congratulate the pilots. But the greatest battleship in the world was marked only by an oil slick, and it was a tremendous personal victory for Mitscher.

THERE WAS NO LETUP FROM THE KIKUSUI ATTACKERS. They came on a round-the-clock basis, and while their favorite targets were the destroyers which circled Okinawa on radar picket stations, they also battered the heavy ships. On April 12 there were raids on *Tennessee, West Virginia* and *Idaho,* with heavy casualties on *Tennessee* caused by a kamikaze which struck an exposed portion of deck. But April 12 was memorable for another reason; at 5:38 P.M., E.S.T. (the 13th at Okinawa) news reached the fleet that President Franklin Roosevelt was dead of a cerebral hemorrhage. Throughout the Navy stunned men with red-rimmed eyes tended their duties in a state of unmitigated shock. We had lost our Supreme Commander, our friend, and many asked, "What will become of us now?" The editor of this work remembers the tomblike silence which pervaded the control room of a submarine in the East China Sea; only the soft drone of the diesels was heard. In a corner a burly machinist's mate sobbed in silence as he watched his manifold. Others prayed for Roosevelt and our new President, Harry Truman.

April 16 was set aside as a day of mourning in the fleets.

At Okinawa, Japan commemorated the occasion in her own way. From the fields of Kyushu, southernmost of the home islands, clouds of kamikazes swarmed down on the radar picket destroyers. The worst attack of the campaign fell upon Commander F. J. Becton's

Laffey at R.P. 1. In the short space of eighty minutes this vessel was struck by six kamikazes and four bombs during twenty-two separate attacks. Thirty-one men were killed and seventy-two wounded and the warship became a floating charnel house. Eight other warships on R.P. duty were battered that afternoon; two were sunk.

As April turned into May the fleet could count nearly 1000 kamikazes shot down, but new attacks developed daily. R.P. 10 became a favorite target. On April 3rd destroyer *Aaron Ward,* under Commander W. H. Sanders, was holding down this post when at 6:22 P.M. "bogies" were reported by radar operators. The ship promptly went to General Quarters.

All the dramatic horror incident to a fatal kamikaze attack is seen in the following account by Lieutenant Commander Arnold Lott, who rose through the enlisted ranks to command a minesweeper.

16.

SECOND DOG WATCH

"Bridge, CIC. Many bogies, many bogies!"

The CIC watch ran a plot—bearing, estimated speed, distance—and called the bridge again.

"Bridge, CIC. Many bogies, moving from south-southwest, will probably pass near next RPS south."

The answer was calm, unhurried. "Bridge, aye."

Throughout the ship the watch still went about its routine duties. In CIC the cryptic symbols on the plotting screen began to take on meaning. "Someone's going to catch hell tonight," said a voice. No one bothered to deny his statement.

Hal Halstead, the CIC officer, watched the plot for a couple of minutes and then called the bridge again.

"Bridge, CIC. Tell the Captain there may be a raid shaping up to the south of us. Suggest routine GQ be moved up a few minutes early tonight."

On the bridge Sanders nodded to Lieutenant Wallace, who spoke to quartermaster Thorpe. "Sound general quarters!" Throughout the ship games, books, letters and coffee cups were dropped as men dashed to their battle stations. By the time Thorpe had scribbled in the rough deck log the entry "1822. Went to GQ." bells and buzzers were sounding all over the ship as phone lines and firing circuits leaped into life.

Within five seconds battle stations began reporting to CIC and the bridge: "MOUNT 51 MANNED AND READY. . . . GUN 44 MANNED AND READY. . . . DIRECTOR MANNED AND READY. . . . SKY CONTROL MANNED AND READY. . . . GUN 42 MANNED AND READY."

In Mount 52 Boles watched Van Paris, the hot shellman, hurriedly cross himself. Van had a big family at home and wanted desperately to go back to them. Well, he'd done everything he could at this point. . . . "MOUNT 52 MANNED AND READY."

The Exec, Karl Neupert, was in CIC now, watching the plot, keeping all the details of the guns, damage control, fire fighting equipment ready in his mind for instant use. CIC was jampacked with men. Bill Sanders would be there too, at first, intently watching the radar screen. Other skippers fought their ships from the bridge, but *Aaron Ward's* captain fought his ship from both bridge and CIC, with radar and radio to give him an instant picture of the situation. It would have been all right with the crew if Sanders and Neupert had decided to do battle from the ship's laundry room for they had seen their Skipper and Exec in action enough by now to know that they were an unbeatable team, no matter where they fought.

All in the few moments since the alarm went, every man on the ship had moved to a battle station. Still the reports came in: "FORWARD ENGINE ROOM MANNED AND READY. . . . AFTER STEERING MANNED AND READY. . . . MIDSHIPS REPAIR PARTY MANNED AND READY. . . . MANNED AND READY. . . . MANNED AND READY. . . . READY. . . . READY. . . . READY. . . ." In the after engine room Pete Peterson checked his phones and then turned to Duriavig. "Bob, help Macukas light off the other feed pump. They've got about twenty-five bogies up there and we'll need all the speed we can get." Then he started making a fresh pot of coffee. Let 'em come. *Aaron Ward* was ready.

Again, for a moment, time seemed to stop as the white wake rolled longer behind the ship and men turned their minds and hearts to the secret thought which always followed the unspoken "This is it!" even as they automatically checked firing circuits, steam pressure, frequency settings, ammunition supply or plasma bottles. Only the shining gun barrels moved, probing and weaving black muzzled patterns against the sky, and the radar antennaes, silently whirling as invisible electronic beams now followed the unseen enemy.

Radarman Hosking, standing near the Captain, watched the blips which showed that "Freddy" was vectoring the fighter planes to meet the enemy. The bogies were still circling, way out. Topside, the fire control director searched the sky and the six 5-inch guns swung with the director as one. *Aaron Ward* had encouraged enemy planes to keep their distance before; the gun crews were confident they could do it again. Then, while Hosking was still panting from his dash to CIC, one of the blips headed in toward the center of the screen. Attack!

"CONTROL, CIC. TARGET BEARING 250 SPEED 180 CLOSING RAPIDLY!"

"CONTROL, AYE. TRACKING, TRACKING!"

On the bridge Thorpe logged the time. 1829. Seven minutes since GQ went. Bright eyed bridge lookout Gerald Simmons spotted the plane first and shouted the alarm. It was away out at 22,000 yards— eleven miles away—but coming in.

"ALL GUNS. AIR ACTION STARBOARD. AIR ACTION STARBOARD." In Control, Rubel and Lavrakas watched the guns slue around in automatic control to follow the director. The main battery guns lifted their muzzles, ready, all pointing at the target the director had picked up for them.

On the guns, men stood with ammo clips in their hands, with tense fingers on firing keys, with quick eyes on target cross wires, with their pulse beating in their ears and with unspoken thoughts now pushed to the back of their minds. *Ready. Be ready.*

Suddenly in the sunset sky a dark pinpoint appeared, took on substance, grew solid, *moved.*

"Oh, boy!" shouted Tom Whelan in Mount 51. "Here he comes!"

"All engines ahead flank!" ordered Wallace, on the bridge. The engineers spun the throttle valves, the turbines howled, and *Aaron Ward* leaped ahead at thirty-two knots.

Ten thousand yards out on the starboard quarter now, the plane, a Val, headed in. The others wheeled in circles, waiting. First it was merely a dot creeping across the back drop of the evening sky, then it was moving, moving fast—3000 feet high and coming in.

"RANGE NINE O DOUBLE O. . . . RANGE EIGHT O DOU- BLE O. . . . RANGE SEVEN O DOUBLE O.

"COMMENCE FIRING, COMMENCE FIRING!"

The main battery guns roared into action at 7,000 yards. Below decks, engineers who fought without ever seeing the enemy judged the course of battle by the sound of the guns. While the 5-inchers slammed out their shells with a dull ba-ROOM ba-ROOM, the enemy was still too far off to worry about. Topside, men watched the fiery tracers streak up and out in red curves, fade to hot points of light and then hover in space until the plane flew into the cone of fire.

Hit! Smoke trickled, then poured from the plane, but it kept coming, and in the director the range dials spun madly down—6,000 yards, 5,500 yards, 5,000 yards, 4,500 yards. *Four thousand yards!*

At 4,000 yards the smoking plane dipped over into its suicide dive, and the 40mm guns opened up with their staccato a-WHOOMP a-WHOOMP a-WHOOMP. Below decks men grew tense; the sound of the forties meant the plane was maybe a couple of miles away, due to arrive in less than a minute, and the next shot had damn' well better be a good one.

"RANGE THREE O DOUBLE O. . . . RANGE TWO FIVE DOUBLE O. . . . RANGE TWO O DOUBLE O!"

Two thousand yards! Now or never! All along the starboard side the little 20mm guns burst into their frantic y-APPITY! y-APPITY! The plane skimmed the water, coming fast.

"RANGE ONE O DOUBLE O. . . . RANGE EIGHT DOUBLE O. . . . RANGE FIVE DOUBLE O."

Get him! In Mount 53 gun captain Dial and his crew pumped out a 5-inch projectile and the plane blew up almost in their faces. SPLASH!

"We got him!" yelled Dave Rubel in Control.

"CEASE FIRE! CEASE FIRE!"

The flaming wreckage tipped into the sea a hundred yards from the ship, and as the plane ended its death dive, startled gunners saw the pilot catapult from the cockpit. With an unopened parachute trailing behind him, he hurtled high across the ship and smashed into the water on the opposite side. To Bill Rader, about to feed a clip of shells into gun 42, it looked like a mess of raw hamburger. One kamikaze pilot had met his ancestors.

Most of the plane disappeared on impact, but the engine, propeller and right wing section skittered the last hundred yards to crash into *Aaron Ward*. The engine slammed into Mount 53, which had shot the plane down, while the propeller twanged into the after deck house like a giant harpoon and pinned shut the door to the after passageway. Later, as men cleaned up the wreckage there, they found a pilot's boot with a foot still in it.

The men in Mount 53 were still bouncing from the sledgehammer blow of the airplane engine crashing into their mount when the thing suddenly crunched to a halt.

"Training gear jammed!"

Shorty Abbott, gun captain on the left hand gun, jerked open the hot shell hatch, peeked under the mount, and saw a smashed airplane engine almost under his feet.

"Get it out of there!" yelled Dial.

Like a pack of frenzied ants, the men swarmed out of the mount and attacked the smoking engine, then jerked back in pain.

"Damned thing's hot!"

"Heave on it. Get it out of there!"

They went after it with bare hands and dragged it out of the way, then piled back into the mount nursing their blisters. But the engine had given them more than blisters. No power!

"CONTROL! MOUNT 53. HYDRAULIC-ELECTRIC SYSTEM OUT. SHIFTING TO MANUAL CONTROL." This meant the pointer and trainer now had to move the 10,000 pound mount themselves by hand gears, blisters or no. This was no time to stop, the fight had just started.

"On target!"

"Load!"

Keep that ammo coming!

The crash set the after battle dressing station on fire and completely destroyed it, but somehow the chief, Tedford, and his helper Fletcher got out. Tedford made it to the main station in the wardroom. Fletcher was killed before he had run a hundred feet. Doctor Barbeiri was already there; he had brought *War and Peace* along with him in case he needed something to help pass the time. Kennedy had borrowed a book from the wardroom library and had a soft chair by the time Doc arrived. Chief Shelley and Gunner Siler hurried in—the early arrivals all got the best chairs—and settled down to wait until the midship repair party had need of them. Not until they heard the phone talker in number two handling room shout "Action starboard!" did they know this was anything more than routine sunset GQ.

Then the guns began. The 5-inchers. The forties. When the twenties opened up they put down their books and waited. This was getting close. Suddenly they felt the ship tremble and shake as the engine from the first Val hit the after mount. The damage control people rushed out on deck. Doc and his helpers put down their books and commenced preparing the wardroom table for surgery. Under their feet the ship twisted and turned and above their heads the guns roared again. The second attack was coming in.

Time 1830. In CIC Glenn Newman on the ground search radar was checking positions of other ships on the station when he heard radarman Beadel, on the air search radar yell, "Here comes another one!" Beadel began calling out the range while topside the director wheeled around to face the attack coming in on the port bow.

"ALL GUNS ACTION PORT, ACTION PORT!"

"RANGE EIGHT O DOUBLE O. . . . RANGE SEVEN O DOUBLE O. . . . RANGE SIX O DOUBLE O."

"COMMENCE FIRING, COMMENCE FIRING!" Again the 5-inchers opened up, followed by the forties and the twenties. When the range closed to 4,000 yards, Beadel jumped off his seat and as the plane moved in to 2,000 yards, he crouched behind the radar, still calling the range. On the bridge, Winston watched the intense cone of fire reaching out to port, and felt that the plane, another Val, was riding directly down the stream toward him.

"RANGE ONE FIVE DOUBLE O. . . . RANGE ONE TWO DOUBLE O!"

Splash! Mount 52 got that one.

"CEASE FIRE, CEASE FIRE."

A few cheered as the flaming wreckage tumbled into the sea. In the gun tubs, gunners kicked empty cartridges aside and checked the ready ammo racks. In CIC men watched the green fingers sweeping the radar scopes; around that sudden battle ground more enemy planes were waiting.

Time 1831. Short seconds after the last plane had disappeared, men on the bridge and in control were startled by a furious burst of fire from gun 42, the port twin 40-millimeter just aft of the bridge. Gun captain Larson had spotted the plane before radar picked it up and opened fire without orders. Frantically the director and the main battery guns swung around to fire on this new attacker, a Zeke, 6,000 yards out and already in its suicide dive. The guns zeroed in, all the 5-inchers, the port side forties and twenties, and the plane started smoking. Hit! Hit!! Hit!!!

Still it came on, growing larger, seeming to increase speed. There was a bomb, a big, mean looking one, hanging under the plane's belly, and in the last hundred yards it dropped loose, curved down and hit the port side of the ship under gun 44 just as the plane flamed into the superstructure.

Willand, the pointer and one lucky man on gun 44, watched the plane coming in, and watched the tracers from his gun slicing into it, right into it, but it kept coming, the prop spinning slower and slower. Although the flash of fire from the twin 5-inch mount on the fantail reached out in front of gun 44, Willand was so busy keeping the gun on the approaching plane he never noticed whether Mount 53 was firing or not. Finally the plane loomed up and Willand yelled "We're not going to get him!" He started to jump out of his seat but it seemed as if a hand touched him on the shoulder and pressed him down again. An instant later the plane hit and a big ball of fire went up in front of him. The explosion blew him out of the seat; he crashed into a ready ammo rack which kept him from going overboard and bounced him back on deck minus both shoes and one sock.

The vast, dull thud shook the entire ship. Lavrakas in the director felt the ship tremble and watched a mass of flame tower above the superstructure deck. Under it was only black smoking wreckage and crumpled bodies. Almost every man around gun 44 had been killed instantly.

On the bridge Winston had spun the wheel for a hard left turn and suddenly felt it go dead. The ship had lost steering control, with her rudder jammed hard left, and commenced chasing her tail in tight port circles like a mad dog.

Except for Rawlins and Willand the gun 44 crew was wiped out—smashed, burned, or blown overboard. The gunners on the four after 20mm mounts had the plane blow up in their faces. Ladon Jones, on gun 28 to starboard, had his gun jam just before the plane struck. He started to dash forward, fell to the deck, looked back, saw Rawlins who had been blown off gun 44 jump up and take over his gun.

"Damn' thing's jammed!" Jones yelled, then grabbed his phone talker, Hendrickson, whose forward dash had suddenly ended when he reached the end of his phone cord, and it jerked him back again, and together they helped Rawlins slam a clip of shells into gun 27 and started firing. The next crash blew Rawlins off that gun too and he was never seen again.

The bomb smashed through the ship's hull below the water line, exploded in the after engine room and ripped a hole fifty feet long through her port side. The ship reeled and shook under the blast. The engine room and fire room flooded, the port engine stopped and the ship soon slowed to fifteen knots. Ruptured oil lines poured more fuel into the fire raging topside, and ammunition commenced exploding in the fierce heat. Telephone and power lines were broken, circuit breakers and fuses went out, and trouble lights began flashing all over the fire control switch boards.

Pete Peterson, in the engine room where the 500 pound bomb exploded, somehow failed to hear it. He was leaning against the cruising throttle waiting for his coffee to perk when he saw a sheet of flame ripple across the forward bulkhead and felt himself sailing through space. He woke up seconds later slumped against a piece of machinery ten feet away. Everything was dark. Instantly he knew that with the emergency lighting system out the after emergency diesel was gone and decided it was time for him to go somewhere else. He scurried for the escape trunk, found it, and clambered up, the last man out of the engine room alive. On the way up Pete passed Ensign Paine who was helping Stole up. Topside, Paine felt that everyone in the black gang had walked up his back bone on the way out. He had lost his right shoe on the way up. On the main deck he met Harry Salisbury, from the damage repair gang, who had lost his left shoe.

"Here, Sal," said Paine, handing over one shoe. "You can wear mine but I can't wear yours." He went barefooted the rest of the night.

The main deck was almost as bad as the engine room. It was sheer catastrophe: wrecked gun mounts tipped at crazy angles, torn steel plates, twisted cables, fire, smoke, exploding ammunition, sprawled dead bodies and men with broken arms or legs trying desperately to crawl out of the way of shipmates battling the roaring flames.

Right in front of Pete lay Moose Antell and Duriavig, who had passed him in the mad scramble to get out of the engine room. Moose had had every bit of his clothing blown off, was wearing only his shoes and a belt with a big sheath knife on it. The next time Pete saw them would be in a hospital. In the same instant he took in the scene around him, he looked outside of it to see a plane crash into the *Little,* a mile or so away, and a big ball of fire unfold above the ship like a deadly blossom.

Pete's shirt and pants were nearly ripped off his body, and as he methodically took his ring, lighter, pen and pencil out of the pockets so he wouldn't lose them, he saw Stefani, who must have made it up from the after fire room, standing beside him.

"Here, Steve," he said, "hold this for me."

Steve put the stuff in his pocket, and just then another explosion lifted him off the deck and he went over the side like a Roman candle.

Steve lost his shoes when he hit the water. The ship was still making plenty of knots and the helmet cut his head. One hand was full of shrapnel, one leg was injured, and his life belt had been torn apart. His biggest worry was the sharks which followed the ship, waiting for the garbage the mess cooks threw overboard every evening just at dusk. He devoutly hoped they had been fed that night. Several hours later Steve was fished out of the water by a rescue ship, but by that time Pete's belongings were at the bottom of the East China Sea.

Just ahead of Pete, Coltra had crawled to the ladder top and "Sparky" St. Clair took his arms to help him on deck but the burned flesh came off in his hands. Silently, Coltra shook his head and painfully made it by himself, then dropped to the deck as wildly exploding ammunition sent everyone diving for shelter. Next, Sparky saw Coltra crawling, inch by inch, toward the sick bay, and with another man he helped carry Coltra there.

When the bomb exploded in the after engine room, electrician's mate Allan Curr was standing by the switchboard there. Chief Mann had just borrowed his flashlight to check the reduction gear—right where the bomb hit—and Jerry Smith in the emergency diesel room had asked for a repeat on a phone message that Mount 53 had been wiped out. Curr had a momentary impression of standing within a gigantic bell while someone slugged it with a mighty hammer, then the lights went out, someone walked over him in the dark, and he heard a voice yelling down the starboard escape hatch to get out. Curr made it. Mann and Smith didn't.

Amid the topside chaos, Curr stood watching more suicide planes diving on destroyer *Little* a mile away. The red hot tracers from *Aaron Ward's* guns zipped into the night like furious bees, slowed, then seemed to hover in space before they floated down past the planes.

In the few seconds after that bomb explosion, many men had fleeting glimpses through fire and smoke of *Little* valiantly fighting off her attackers, but to each of them the immediate danger was so great that *Little's* battle was unreal and of little import, as if it were a movie sequence.

In the forward engine room the whine of the turbines was suddenly interrupted by a thumping noise when the bomb went off and the ship seemed to shudder and jump three feet sideways. A fine sprinkling of dust from overhead beams sifted down on their heads.

Machinist's mate Berry whirled on chief McCaughey, and shouted in fury "Mick, that sonofabitch hit us!"

"Yeah!" Haubrick added "If this keeps up we may have to leave her!"

Mick laughed at him. "Are you crazy? Until the water gets up to our chins we ain't going to leave her. The ship won't sink—the old man wouldn't stand for it."

But she was slowing down. They stood there with the Chief Engineer and watched the revolution indicator for the port engine in the after engine room unwind, all the way down to zero revolutions. Weyrauch, on the phones, automatically checked the circuits.

"AFTER ENGINE ROOM?" *No answer.* "EMERGENCY DIESEL?" *No answer. They were in trouble.*

"AFTER FIRE ROOM?"

"AFTER FIRE ROOM AYE." The voice was gasping, choking. "WE'RE FILLED UP WITH SMOKE BACK HERE. PANERO THINKS THE ENGINE ROOM IS ON FIRE. NO ANSWER IN THERE."

"SKI? THAT YOU? MR. YOUNG SAYS SECURE THE BOILERS, GET OUT OF THERE, HELP TOPSIDE."

Topside could use help. On the bridge, with the view aft blanked out by fire and billowing smoke, no one could see what had happened. There was no communication aft. The phones were knocked out.

"MOUNT 53! CONTROL." *No answer.*

"They got the after mount," Rubel shouted to Lavrakas. Just then they saw a plane start a run on *Little*. "Here we go again!"

"AIR ACTION PORT. ALL GUNS, AIR ACTION PORT."

Again the 5-inchers opened up, the forties joined in. Mount 53, not having heard Dave Rubel announce their destruction, swung around to port, the men cranking frantically by hand, and joined in.

While the guns barked and roared above their heads, the damage control and repair gangs on the main deck rigged fire hoses, ran emergency phone leads where they could, fought fire, and helped wounded men to the battle dressing station.

First to reach the wardroom was Moose Antell, stark naked, skin hanging in shreds from his arms, hair and eyebrows gone. Behind him came a gruesome parade—Coward, Peterson, Parker, all in nearly the same condition. The medics prepared themselves for a long night.

Wounded men seemed to be flooding into the wardroom by that time. Doc sent Kennedy aft to help with minor first aid cases on the fantail and Kennedy worked alone there for part of the night. Ensign Rosengren came down from the sound room to help. Eddie Gaines, who had only been trained to wait on tables and clean staterooms, worked with the doctor the whole night long, a medic like the rest of them. Eddie's big hands were gentle and tender. Men remembered him later as the blackest angel they ever saw.

Soon the wardroom was jammed with wounded. Doc sent Tedford down to set up another emergency station in the mess hall, and as men were treated in the wardroom those who could make it were moved to the mess hall and laid out on deck. Others were dropped into convenient bunks in the officers' rooms. One of these was Paine, who sometime during the night woke up, looked around, and stared in dismay. He was in the Captain's bunk.

"What the hell am I doing in here?" he asked himself, and without waiting for an answer jumped up and got out of there. He spent the rest of the night huddled in a corner on deck, cursing those who stepped on him in the dark, and being greeted in kind.

In the wardroom dressing station, Doc and his helpers worked as hurriedly and efficiently as possible, but certainly not according to the teaching of Lister.

"Plasma!" "Right here." "Sulfa." "Coming." "Penicillin." "I'll get it." "Morphine." "Here 'tis." "Another morphine." "No more needles!" "Use the one you have!" "It's not sterile!" "Sterile hell! Wipe it on your pants."

By that time their pants were not sterile either. By the following morning Doctor Barbeiri, his assistants, their pants and the entire wardroom would have created antiseptic dismay in the Navy's Bureau of Medicine and Surgery. But none of their patients died of infection, that night or later.

Neupert, in CIC, with communications out aft, sent messengers scrambling through the flames and wreckage with word for Biesmeyer and Rainey, and to check on the after engine room. Rubel in Control set up his own emergency system. Brown, on the bridge, could whistle louder than any man in the Pacific Fleet; each time an attack came in

Control passed the word to Brown who whistled at the nearby guns and pointed out the target to them.

Yeoman striker Deacon, phone talker for the Assistant Gunnery Officer, Ensign Ferguson, was still in touch with the radar room and CIC, and over the next several minutes began to gain a fair idea of their plight as messages trickled in. . . . after engine room flooded. . . . after fire room flooded. . . . port engine out. . . . fire out of control aft. . . . fighter director radar out of commission. . . . fire in the after clipping room. . . . steering control lost.

The phones to after steering were also out, and the Exec started another messenger back there, but the sudden eruption of fire on the main deck stopped him. Ten minutes passed before he worked his way aft with the word for Flinn to take over the steering control. During the rest of the battle, locked in their stifling hot steel box, Flinn and his gang steered the ship by hand.

The bomb that wrecked the after engine room knocked out the gas ejection system for the 5-inch mounts and they filled with hot choking fumes. Stacy, hot shellman on Mount 51, passed out and slumped to the deck. Whalen motioned another man into his place, opened the side door and dropped Stacy out on deck. The guns kept on firing. In other mounts men choked, retched, stumbled.

"Open the door. Throw him out!"

"It's against regulations to open the door when firing!"

"Hell with regulations. Open the door." Out they went.

The guns grew hot. With the gas ejection system out, unburned gasses rolled into the mounts when the breech blocks flew open, and erupted into thin wisps of flame. If a powder can split or spilled, a flashback would roast them all crisper than potato chips.

"Flashback!"

"Damn the flashback! Keep on loading!"

With the loss of power, the Mark 14 director was out of action. Mr. Tiwald sent Eves down to the clipping room a deck below to help pass out more 40mm ammunition. By this time the stench of burned flesh and ruptured bodies filled the air, and as he felt his way down the ladder Eves stepped on something horribly soft and yielding. He couldn't see what it was, and he didn't want to see; sheer dread of what it might be filled him with unreasoning terror. Then a roaring fire broke out just aft of the ammo storage. Frantically, he began heaving the cans overboard, as far from the ship as he could. Two men usually handled the heavy cans, but Eves was all alone there; he had to do it by himself. The next morning, he forced himself to go back to the ammo storage to see what he had stepped on. Only a couple of life jackets.

In CIC, Neupert and the "Freddies" watched the green fingers of the search radar. The blips had moved well out of gun range for the moment. The lull was welcome, but suspicious. *Watch them—they're up to something.* The planes circled the formation, like Indians around a wagon train, getting up courage for the next attack. The night was far from over; they were bound to come back. With *Aaron Ward* heeling to port and still steaming in a circle, the Japanese figured she had had it. They would reorganize, bore in for the kill. Quickly, quietly, Sanders and Neupert went over the situation. The Exec had every detail of damage, destruction, and casualty on the tip of his tongue. . . . port engine out, rudder jammed, fire mains out, loss of power, Mount 53 in local, the Mark 14 director out, fire in the after clipping room, the port quad forty wrecked and most of the crew killed, Doc and his gang swamped with wounded men.

Bill Sanders decided that although the ship was still fighting, she had perhaps a little more fight than she could handle, and that some assistance would be more than welcome. He put Woody Woodside on the TBS to call Commander Task Force 51 back in Kerama Retto.

"DELEGATE, THIS IS MONGOOSE. OVER. . . . DELEGATE, DELEGATE, THIS IS MONGOOSE. OVER."

Finally DELEGATE came up on the circuit. "GO AHEAD MONGOOSE."

"DELEGATE, THIS IS MONGOOSE. WE ARE IN TERRIBLE SHAPE AND ARE SINKING. WE HAVE BEEN HIT TWICE AND ARE STILL UNDER ATTACK."

The voice came back in calm, measured tones.

"WE KNOW IT MONGOOSE, WE KNOW IT. . . . BLUENOSE IS ON HER WAY TO HELP YOU."

BLUENOSE! That was *Shannon,* with Commander Edward Foster as skipper. *Shannon* was supposed to be blessed with the luck of the Irish. "Uncle Ed" and the boys were on their way, and *Aaron Ward* needed all the Irish luck the *Shannon* could carry.

Shannon had just put in to Hagushi Roadsted, on the western coast of Okinawa, when she got the word. Snoopers were about, and the familiar old FLASH RED, CONTROL YELLOW had sent all hands to general quarters. Five minutes later, she got the word from DELEGATE. Guns bristling, *Shannon* plowed out and headed for

RPP 10, out beyond Kume Shima. She had a couple of hours to go before she could be of any help to the hard pressed *Aaron Ward;* enroute, *Shannon* sailors prepared for anything—fire fighting, transfer of casualties, rescue of survivors, towing—whatever it was *Shannon* could do it. Whatever it was, *Shannon* had done it. *Shannon* first got into the rescue business on 26 March, when a kamikaze got the destroyer *O'Brien* out near Kume Shima, and she escorted the wrecked ship into Kerama Retto. A week later, *Shannon's* crew watched kamikazes hit three transports—*Henrico, Dickerson,* and *Goodhue,* all at once, and had again helped fight fire, treat wounded, and care for the dead.

As *Shannon* plowed westward, her bridge crew listened to the TBS. Out on the same station with *Aaron Ward,* the *Little* had been hit and had gone down. *Aaron Ward* was damned near to sinking too. . . . no, belay that last word. She was still afloat, and still fighting, too. The Japs were all over the place, holding a field day. *Aaron Ward* had already knocked down five of them. This last news put the *Shannon* definitely in second place, so far as *Aaron Ward* was concerned, for although *Shannon* had fought at lots of enemy planes, so far she had only managed to fight one of them down for a kill. Oh, well, the night wasn't over yet.

"*Shannon's* coming to help. *Shannon's* on her way." The word ran around the ship to a few people who still had phones tied in to CIC. But *Shannon* was a long way off. Time was fast running out on Picket Station 10.

In what time there was, *Aaron Ward's* men fought fire and flood. Doc and his men got the wounded a little better disposed and the repair parties on deck moved some of the dead out of the way of the living. Neupert in CIC, Biesmeyer in damage control, Sanders on the bridge matched information, played what they had against what they could expect. It was going to be close. DELEGATE ordered the small boys to move in and support *Aaron Ward* and *Little* with gun fire as possible. The small boys had anticipated him and were already on the way. The CAP still orbited overhead, but time was running out for them too. "Freddy" sent up the warning about 1855.

"BRIDGE, CIC. SUNSET DUE IN A FEW MINUTES. I CAN-NOT HOLD PLANES ON STATION MUCH LONGER."

"CIC, BRIDGE. ROGER. GIVE US ALL THE HELP YOU CAN."

The sun was nearly down now, but there was plenty of light from fire still leaping up above the wrecked engine room, and in the red glow the damage control and repair gangs worked like demons, dumping hot ammunition, rigging emergency circuits, getting portable fire pumps onto the flames.

Here was a chance, Doc decided, to get back to the mess hall and see how Tedford was making out with the patients there. With Crider, he hurried out, checked over the men, started back to the wardroom. They were just at the galley when the next plane hit and the explosion threw them all the way to the wardroom and through the door. Crider was knocked out. Doc stretched him on the deck and left him there; he was busy. An hour later Crider finally woke up and went on tending the wounded as if nothing had happened.

Time 1859. The lull was finally over. The kamikazes had been milling about, some five miles off the starboard quarter, 10,000 feet high. Now they broke it up and suddenly swooped down in a vicious, well coordinated attack which hit the entire formation. Guns on all the ships roared into action, but the planes plummetted down and nothing could stop them. *Little* got it first. She had taken one hit on her port side, several minutes earlier, with no great damage, and she had knocked one down. But this time they rushed her, one right after another. Nothing could stop them all.

The first plane hit. The second hit. The third flashed down in a vertical dive—hit—and vanished amidships in a tremendous explosion. Lefty thought perhaps *Little's* torpedo warheads had exploded. Actually only their air flasks went up. But the plane's engine or a bomb went into *Little's* after engine room and her boilers blew up. The high pressure steam ripped the ship open like a sardine can. She blazed brilliantly from stem to stern for a few moments, then folded up and disappeared. In less than ten minutes it was all over for *Little* and thirty of her men.

Among the men who watched *Little* go down, none felt quite like Harry Salisbury. He had originally been detailed to the *Little* in Norfolk, but uncompleted dental work made him miss the draft when they left for Bremerton to put the ship in commission and he got the *Aaron Ward* instead. Only the grace of God and a lucky toothache had kept him from going down with *Little*.

"CIC, BRIDGE. LITTLE HAS GONE DOWN" reported Deacon.

"WE'RE NOT INTERESTED IN LITTLE NOW. WE'RE TRY-

ING TO KEEP OURSELVES AFLOAT" Neupert shouted back to him.

As the planes smashed into *Little,* the small boys, *LCSL 25,* and *LLSMR 195,* were racing toward her, steaming side by side. Another plane loomed up out of nowhere, just cleared the 5-inch mount on *195*'s fantail, and then crashed amidships. The "R" in LSMR's designation stood for rockets, and she was loaded with them. They went off in all directions like a Fourth of July celebration. But when the show was over *LSMR 195* was gone.

"There goes the *'95!'*" shouted someone else on the bridge. Lavrakas saw a ball of fire float up from the little ship. He watched for an instant, then turned to look at *Little* but she had nearly disappeared. Only a bit of her bow pointed to the sky and that slipped out of sight as he watched. Next a plane went to work on *LCSL 25,* whose guns killed the pilot, for it zoomed, wobbled, and then overshot the ship but sliced off her mast. *LCSL 25* stayed afloat, but the next time Lavrakas thought to look for the *'95,* she had gone to join the *Little.*

About this time it seemed to Deacon on the bridge that all hell broke loose. A Val, buzzing about the amphibs, suddenly turned on *Aaron Ward* and commenced a suicide dive from about 8,000 yards out. Again the guns ran through their gamut of defiance, the 5-inchers roaring, the forties barking, and twenties yapping. The plane started smoking as the shells smashed in, but it came on until several hits by the 5-inchers blew it to bits and it splashed, 2,000 yards out. Four down!. . . . but more to come.

In Mount 52, the twin breeches were eating up the big 54 pound projectiles when suddenly one of them refused to slide into the firing chamber. The fuse in its nose had jammed, the shell would not go in. Boles and his crew looked at one another in a lightning flash of understanding. The fuse had been set down in the handling room under instruction from Control. No one in the mount knew how many seconds the fuse had been set for, or if it would wait to go off until it was fired, but they all knew if the shell was still in the gun when it went off, Mount 52 would have had it. Together Boles and Van Paris wrestled the shell loose and dragged it out of the gun. Boles undogged the side door. Van stood there, holding the thing in his arms while it counted seconds to itself. The other men just stood there; either Van heaved it out or he didn't. Finally Boles wrenched the door open and Van heaved the shell overboard. *All right, you guys. Don't just stand there. Didn't you ever see a loading casualty before?*

Load! Load! Load!

Boles was glad Van Paris had taken time to cross himself before the action started. There hadn't been any time for it since, and certainly whatever grace Van had won for himself had been spread very thin in Mount 52.

Time 1904. On the air search radar screen in CIC, another blip started for the center. Attack! The ship was still circling and the plane seemed to be maneuvering for a run-in from astern. Finally CIC got the control crew looking in the right direction and they spotted the plane, a twin-engine Betty, 14,000 yards off. The 5-inchers began firing at 10,000 yards, a long five miles, but had difficulty keeping on target, due to the smoke still rolling up amidships and the constant turning of the ship.

The forward mounts continually slammed into the stops which limited their field of fire aft, over the ship, and the gunners had to frantically whip their guns all the way around to the other side to take up fire again. This could be as dangerous for the bridge crew as for the enemy; a couple of weeks earlier, in the same situation, Sanders had been knocked down by the muzzle blast of a gun firing almost directly into his face.

Finally, at 5,000 yards a 5-incher made connection. The plane smoked, flamed, and went into its death spin. "Such a beautiful sight," Rader thought, while around him men who had sweated at their guns for half an hour yelled and cheered. Five down!

Just then a flight of Marine F4Us, sent out to help *Aaron Ward,* came in low over the sea with their running lights on to show they were friendly, but a nervous gunner opened up on them anyway, the other guns joined him, and the Marines fire-walled their throttles getting out of there. *Aaron Ward* was still ready, still fighting. The battle was not yet over. In a few minutes the sun would slip below the horizon. A mile or so away the remaining amphibs huddled together in the dusk, and around the rim of night the kamikazes still droned. *Would the damned things never stop coming?* The fight had gone on just a little more than thirty minutes, yet it seemed like hours—days —an eternity—an eternity filled with the clamor of guns and roar of planes, the stench and reek of burning oil, powder and flesh. For some of the crew eternity had already come; for more of them it was surely to commence in a few short minutes.

More than fifty U.S. Navy carrier-based Curtis Helldivers, General Motors Avengers and Grumman Hellcats flying past Mt. Fujiyama on their way to bomb the Japanese capital. *Navy Department.*

Struck by U.S. carrier-based planes of the Third Fleet, buildings in Kushiro, Japan on Hokkaido are consumed by flames. In the right foreground a locomotive, another target of the attacking planes, has caught fire. The attack on Kushiro occurred during the Third Fleet's daring sweep of the Japanese home islands. *Navy Department.*

Mighty U.S. warships steaming in column off Kamaishi on Honshu, Japan. Among the Third Fleet ships taking part were the USS *Massachusetts* (BB-59), USS *South Dakota* (BB-57) and USS *Indiana* (BB-58). *Navy Department.*

Projectiles from a powerful battleship of the Third Fleet scream their way to targets on the mainland of Japan—the Kamaishi Imperial Iron and Steel Works on northern Honshu. *Navy Department.*

A Japanese suicide dive on the USS *Louisville* (CA-28). *Navy Department.*

This carrier's 40mm guns were blasting as her planes were striking Tokyo. *Navy Department.*

A Japanese battleship of the *Yamato* class and an escorting vessel twist and turn under attack by U.S. Navy carrier planes during a task strike on the Japanese Naval Base at Kure Bay, W. Honshu, Japan. *Navy Department.*

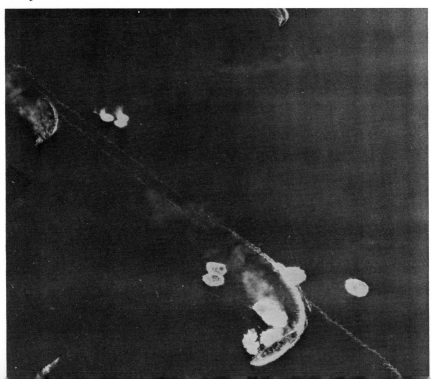

A view of Mt. Fujiyama and Sagami Bay at sunset, with ships of the British and American fleets. In the foreground is HMS *Duke of York*. Taken by the USS *Missouri* (BB-63). *Navy Department.*

Mt. Fujiyama as seen from the USS *South Dakota* (BB-57) in Tokyo Bay. *Navy Department.*

Adm. Chester W. Nimitz, left, Commander-in-Chief, U.S. Pacific Fleet and Pacific Ocean Areas, is welcomed aboard the USS *South Dakota* (BB-57) in Tokyo Bay, August 29, 1945, by Adm. William F. Halsey, Commander Third Fleet. *Navy Department.*

Rear Adm. Robert Bostwick Carney (center with holster), Chief of Staff to Adm. William F. Halsey, is saluted by Vice Adm. Michitaro Tazuka, Commander, First Japanese Naval District, as he turns over the Yokosuka Naval Base to the U.S. Navy. *Navy Department.*

General of the Army Douglas MacArthur, Supreme Commander, and Admiral Chester W. Nimitz, CINCPAC-POA, arrive on board the USS *Missouri* (BB-63) in Tokyo Bay for the Japanese surrender ceremonies. Admiral William F. Halsey, Commander Third Fleet, is a few paces behind them. *Navy Department.*

Japanese envoys aboard the USS *Missouri* in Tokyo Bay after their arrival for the surrender ceremonies. *Official U.S. Navy Photo.*

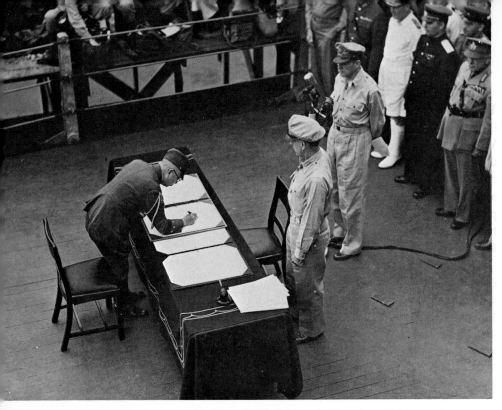

A Japanese respresentative signing the surrender as Gen. MacArthur and representatives of the Allied powers look on. *Official U.S. Navy Photo.*

China signs during the signing by representatives of the Allied powers aboard the *Missouri* in Tokyo Bay. *Official U.S. Navy Photo.*

Time 1908. "AIR ACTION PORT, AIR ACTION PORT!" There they came, two Vals, with a pair of the Marine fighters hot on their tails. The planes mixed up in a brief dog fight out of which one Val plunged in flames, but the other one slanted down in a very steep dive, coming fast. Again the guns took up their chant as the range dials whirled down—the computer said this one was coming in at almost five miles a minute. The guns hammered and roared but the plane jumped and rocked through the storm of fire and kept coming, heading for the bridge and the main battery director, *kept coming, kept coming!*

"Hit the deck!" yelled Sanders, and men piled into corners, behind equipment, anywhere but where they had been. Everyone had the same impression, that the plane was heading right at *him*. Lefty Lavrakas watched the stream of tracers burning into the sky and stood transfixed as the plane seemed to lock onto them and ride them down to the ship. When it was 300 feet away he turned his head from the sight and made his peace with God.

Danny Danford on top of the wheel house knew he was a goner and said his prayers. Ladon Jones, on one of the twenties, knew the plane was going to hit him; in the last fleeting instant he snatched up his shrapnel shield and heaved it at the pilot's face. Brown, on the bridge, knew the plane was going to hit him; it loomed up suddenly as big as a house, right on him, with two exhaust pipes spitting blue fire. He hunched his shoulders and waited for the crash. In CIC the assistant "Freddy" Lieutenant junior grade Fred Koehl, could see nothing but he listened as the roar of the plane drowned out the guns and thought to himself "Why in hell didn't I stay in Ashland, Ohio, where I belonged, instead of volunteering for this mess?"

Then the plane was on them, the roar of its engine filled the night, its wings spread across the sky. *Here he comes!* Suddenly as if a mighty hand had pushed down the right wing, the plane twisted in flight. It banked lightly and roared flat across the bridge. The left wing ripped out the signal halliards, clipped the port forestay, carried away most of the radio antennae, smashed the top of the forward stack in a tremendous metallic scrunch and the whole thing went cartwheeling into the sea to starboard. Larson, on gun 42, almost had his hair parted by the landing gear as it roared past. The broken forestay lashed Rader across the face. He saw it coming, but was too frightened to move—too frightened, in fact, to feel it.

In the plane's wake, bits and pieces of wreckage rained down and men stared at each other, dumbfounded, in a perfect bedlam of noise. The crash had opened steam lines to the whistle and siren and they joined in the tumult to deafen everyone.

Even men floating in the sea where the *Little* had gone down could hear the whistle bellowing, although they could not see what had happened. By that time, what men could see and hear, and what, in the shock of battle, they believed, made for oddly contrasting viewpoints. Weeks later, an *Aaron Ward* sailor who came from the same town as a *Little* sailor received a news clipping from home. The *Little* sailor got home first, and gave the press his account of the battle at Picket Station 10. After his ship sank, he reported, all those *Aaron Ward* sailors did was sail around in a circle, tooting their whistle. Fortunately, for him, the *Aaron Ward* sailors were still in Kerama Retto when he said it.

In the hideous uproar of escaping steam and bellowing whistle, the gunners seemed to be doing a grim pantomime, firing their guns silently. A sheet of flame flashed through the radar room and many of the radarmen, with nothing better to do at the moment, rushed out to help the gunners. They were none too soon.

Time 1913. There came another Val. This one streaked in from ahead and again aimed at the nerve center of the ship, the bridge structure. Despite the steam and smoke swirling around the ship and the fact that they had no warning from director control, the eagle-eyed gunners on the after 5-inch mount picked the plane up visually and opened fire. Larson's gun joined in furiously. The plane streaked in, maybe seventy-five feet off the water, and 2,000 yards out its machine guns commenced spitting death. A strafing run! No one could see the bullets coming, but a man could hear the WHACK PINNING after they went by.

At that instant the pilot raised its nose slightly, aiming right at the upper bridge and director. Dave Rubel, in the director, stood and watched it come—there was nothing else to do and nowhere to go— and shouted to Lefty "This is IT, boy!"

Gun 42, below and in front of Rubel, was pouring out a solid stream of fire—that gun alone fired a thousand shots during the entire battle—with thirty-four-year-old Larson working as calmly as if it was just another drill. Frozen by the thought of what he knew was about to happen, Rubel watched the enemy pilot's goggled head coming nearer and nearer and braced himself for a flaming death. And then he saw Larson do something he would remember all his life.

Larson raised his gun until the stream of fire flowed just above the wing of the onrushing plane. And then coolly, as methodically as if he was back home slicing cheese in the kitchen, he lowered the gun again and the fiery stream of hot bullets literally sawed the wing off.

That man deserves the Congressional Medal of Honor! Rubel said to himself. The crippled plane faltered, swerved, tumbled, just missed the bridge and ended up in a fiery furnace on the main deck near the forward stack, very nearly on top of gun 42.

In the instant before impact, the plane released a bomb which exploded a few feet from the side of the ship, blasted the port side with a hail of shrapnel and blew a hole into the forward fire room. The fire room flooded, the boilers drowned out, the last engine stopped and *Aaron Ward* was without all power, coasting to a dead stop.

Flames from the burning plane leaped as high as the top of the director and the concussion knocked some men off gun 42 and injured others. Out of the fire and smoke a man scurried forward, unharmed, but with the entire seat of his pants missing. Again the switchboards lit up like Christmas trees with circuit overload lights. Men were still picking themselves up from that explosion when another plane, four seconds later, hurtled out of the cloud of smoke and fire and crashed on the main deck. Absolutely not a man on the ship saw that one coming; what with the exploding bomb and raging gasoline fire from the prior crash it made little difference—some of them never knew what hit them.

At that moment, the chaos and destruction topside seemed to have reached an absolute peak. But at least a man could *see it;* he had something to worry about. Things were worse below decks. Down there, all men knew was that terrible things had happened or were undoubtedly about to happen, but no one knew what, when, or where.

In the wardroom, each time the roar of the guns began as another plane came in, a whole mass of humanity—patients, corpsmen, volunteer assistants, the Doctor, everybody able to move—piled under the operating table in one big bloody heap. Men who had been burned left skin and flesh in their tracks, the deck grew sticky and slippery with blood and worse. There were no lights except the small portable electric battle lanterns. In the midst of the noise and confusion, in the fetid air and faltering light, the door opened and Kennedy found himself facing a ghastly apparition, a man with anguished eyes but no face. His mouth and nose were torn away, his jaw hanging loose on one side; he was choking to death.

Again the guns roared, the ship shook. Doc, Kennedy and the bloody man all crouched under the table. Doc could find no surgical scissors in the insane clutter. Kennedy held a bandage over the man's eyes. Doc wiped his shark knife on his pants, and cut away tissue so the man could breath through the gaping hole where his face had been.

As they sought to stop the gush of blood, another sailor burst into the wardroom!

"Hey, Doc! Ballard's up by Mount 52, bleeding like hell!"

"You, Kennedy," said Doc. "Go fix him up."

Kennedy grabbed soap, sulfa powder, gauze and ran up and out into the battle. Wounded men were all over on deck, he jumped over and among them. As he passed underneath the muzzles of Mount 52, the guns opened up on another plane and nearly blew his head off. He grabbed Ballard, dragged him feet first back to the spray shield, bandaged a gash in his upper arm, and then hauled him aft toward the wardroom. At the moment they moved in off deck a plane hit number one stack and fire and wreckage came down all over the spot where they had been.

In the forward magazine, Philip Rapalee and his four man crew were completely isolated from topside and without any knowledge of what was going on. They had been worried enough and the last explosion very nearly spooked them; Rapalee tried again to find out what was happening.

"Hey, you guys in the handling room! What the hell's going on up there?"

"You just keep that ammo coming, Rap! Keep that damn ammo coming!"

"Okay, so they want ammo! We'll give 'em ammo!"

Everywhere below decks, where they could see nothing, hear very little, and only surmise what was happening by distant thumps and a few terse words over a phone now and then, men lived in a dreadful state of suspense, trying not to let their fears overwhelm their hopes. When the plane wrecked the forward fire room, the men working in the magazines and handling room under Mount 52 were as close to it as they could be without actually being in the crash. All they knew was, something terrible had happened. They never stopped passing out ammunition; Marquoitt just had time, between shoving powder cases into the hoist, to say sadly to himself, "You aren't going to see home again."

Wayne Schaefer, who was also handling ammunition for Mount 52, had nearly the same thought. His wife Marjorie was back home in Fort Wayne, Indiana, with their young son Thomas who was just exactly two years old. He had seen the baby only once, Schaefer said to himself, *only once.*

Down in the forward emergency diesel room, Cezus and Lunetta also fought without ever seeing anything. They were sealed up in a steel compartment below the water line with a diesel driven 150 KW emergency generator which automatically cut in if all other power went out, as happened when the forward fire room flooded. When their generator lit off they knew things topside were bad. Laboring to supply power to the guns, the generator was running in overload condition and should have automatically tripped out, but Cezus held the overload trip in by hand—if the gun crews needed juice, he would give them juice until the generator blew itself to bits. He knew that if the ship sank he and Lunetta were going down with it, for they couldn't get out until someone came to let them out.

The shock of the crash rattled things all over the radar room, and Pete Aitchison yelled at Beadel.

"Beadel! You know what? Here we are getting the hell beat out of us and I bet they don't have a dime's worth of insurance on this ship!"

When the radio and radar antennae were wrecked, Reichard, Phillips, and Thibodeau scrambled out of the radar shack and set about trying to rig an emergency antennae. They were working by the forward stack when the second explosion blasted the area with shrapnel. Reichard was pinned to the stack by a splinter of steel through what he thought was his sleeve, until he ripped away and found his arm dangling loosely with blood pouring down over his hand. He watched a gunner, still too young to shave, cruelly burn his hands dragging a wounded shipmate from the flames around a wrecked gun. The boy tried to hold a fire hose but his hands were too raw to manage that, and when a bullet whizzed through the hose and punctured it, he plugged the hole by sitting on it while someone else fought the fire. Rader, blown off his gun and wounded, dashed to the bridge. Then he thought, *no, they'll hit the bridge next,* and ran back to his gun. He was still scared stiff, but he felt safer there.

Seaman Thomas Erin had been in CIC, but with the TBS wrecked he had nothing to do, so went out on deck and took the place of someone on a 40mm gun. Fighting was better than nothing.

The wardroom filled with smoke after the last explosion and the wounded men were near panic. Doc called the bridge for "the word."

"Bridge, battle dressing. Ask the Captain are we going to abandon ship."

"Sir, the Captain says, hell no!"

But somehow, in the chaos and confusion, someone misunderstood someone else and the word did get out.

"Skipper says we're going to abandon ship!"

A couple of men ran from the forward superstructure deck all the way to the fantail and jumped overboard. That they could have jumped from where they were, without scrambling through fire, explosions and torn wreckage, somehow never occurred to them. Before the battle ended a few more went overboard intentionally, some through accident. Later, as the ship floated and refused to sink, some of them gave up waiting to be rescued and climbed aboard unaided.

Mount 42 got the word on abandon ship too. It never occurred to Blunck that he might abandon ship, but he was certain the rest of the crew would go. "Don't leave me," he kept telling Larson. "Don't leave me, I don't want to be left here all alone."

"Who the hell's going anywhere?" said Larson.

Brown, on the bridge, was still hunched over waiting for that first plane to hit him when the second one crashed four seconds later; more 40mm and 20mm ammunition blew up and a rain of fire and hot metal washed over the ship. A red hot jagged piece of the plane, perhaps the size of a silver dollar, pierced the back of his neck and Brown said to himself "I'm dead!" But it went on burning like hell's own ashes, so he decided he was alive after all and tore it off. By then there were so many badly wounded men needing care far worse than he did that Brown refused to bother Doc for treatment, and so he never got the Purple Heart medal he should have had.

Instead, he asked Sanders for permission to disarm the depth charges—if the ship did sink, they might detonate in the water and kill more men. With Hitchcock and Mogensen he hurried aft, pulled out the arming pistols and heaved them overboard; then the depth charges, each loaded with hundreds of pounds of high explosive, followed. There went one hazard for a ship which needed all the luck there was if she was to survive. Suddenly they became aware they were not the only men on the fantail; there were dark shapes, stretchers filled with wounded men, where the medics had placed them to keep clear of the fire and destruction amidships. Brown nearly stumbled over the nearest stretcher.

"Who the hell is this?"

Someone bent down, peered into the face. "Zaloga."

Even in the darkness, they could see he had one arm shattered, one leg hanging by a tendon, a piece of steel speared through the other. But he stirred, recognized Brown's face bent over him.

"Brownie, look at my legs for me," he pleaded. "They hurt. Tell me how badly I'm hurt." Brownie felt sick all over. No wonder the poor devil's legs hurt; both feet were gone, the legs so badly mangled there was no place to put a tourniquet. A great pool of blood glistened under the stretcher.

"You're Okay, Joe," Brownie lied. "You'll be up and around in a month."

Tony would have been okay if he had stayed back on the fantail, but there was nothing to do there, and he had tried to get forward to help, just as a plane hit the port quad 40 and the exploding ammunition cut him down. The campaign was finally over for Zaloga.

The other men held a battle lantern while Brown sprinkled some sulfa powder in Zaloga's wounds. Then someone yelled "Lights out!" and the guns opened up again.

Time 1916. That one was a Zeke, coming in astern at high speed in a steep glide. None of the 5-inch guns could bear on him. Gun 42, with the indomitable Larson still shooting, took him under fire but without result and the plane slammed into the ship near gun 43.

Gasoline from the plane's belly tank sprayed the area and started another raging fire. No man from 43 was ever seen again. Larson on gun 42 was hit in the face by what he thought was a slab of bacon until he remembered that bacon didn't bleed. Many men on nearby guns were killed outright and some of them were blown overboard. Those who did not die in the blast floated around in the dark ocean until the "picker uppers," the small amphibs, fished them out. Lefty Lavrakas looked down at the smashed gun which gunner's mate Long had kept always ready and thought to himself *I've lost a fine shipmate and the best gunner the Navy ever had. If there is a Valhalla, Long has earned it.*

By now the ship was dead in the water, the weather decks and superstructure aft of the bridge were a complete shambles, dead and dying men were tumbled in the wreckage, fire raged uncontrolled and in the inferno exploding ammunition made existence uncertain for those still left.

Through the chaos the repair parties fought fire, rigged pumps, and dragged out the wounded. The repair gang, Lieutenant Biesmeyer, Chiefs Offins and Gains, St. Clair and James and others, were bruised, burned and bleeding; they had already out-labored Hercules but there was still work to do. The ship was low in the water, going over to port, but she was still afloat, still fighting, and they intended to keep her so. The enemy had other plans.

Time 1921. "Here comes another one!" yelled Beadel in CIC.

"God, we can't take another one!" groaned Neupert.

There he came, out of the darkness, low over the water, masked by the smoky haze drifting away from the burning ship.

"AIR ACTION STARBOARD, AIR ACTION STARBOARD."

Guns still on power from the forward emergency diesel trained around but the crew could see nothing. Baffled, they stood waiting. They knew that this time they might have only a few seconds to get the plane before it got them.

"FIRE AFT, FIRE AFT," ordered Control. The forties opened up, shooting blindly.

Suddenly the plane loomed into sight and all the remaining guns trained aft in one supreme effort to knock it down. Relentlessly it bored in, while the gun crews fed shells to the bellowing guns.

For the tenth time in less than an hour they stood at their stations and looked death right in the eyes. "The way to handle enemy planes," Bill Sanders had told them the first time the ship went into combat, "is to shoot them down, one at a time." *Aye, aye, Sir. One at a time it is! Number ten coming down!*

Down it came, down the stream of tracers, down the length of the wrecked ship, and down right into the gunners' faces, with the big bomb under its belly looking bigger every second. The plane crashed amidships, at the base of the after stack, with a blasting, searing flash of exploding gasoline and bomb, and then plane, stack, searchlight tower and guns leaped into the air and smashed back on the shattered deck with a great tumultuous din as if the world had ended. For more of *Aaron Ward's* men, it had.

On the main deck, Tony Macukas, who had escaped fiery death earlier by scrambling out of the blazing engine room, yelled "He's coming in!" and pointed. All around him men dived for shelter, but

Tony was still standing there, pointing, when the plane smashed down on him. Some of the men dived the wrong way and went overboard. The first thing Frank Ceckowski remembered after the crash was Tony pleading for help, and a man kneeling nearby praying. Frank prayed too, but stayed on his feet, just in case.

Jack St. Clair rushed to help Macukas—the plane had pinned him down by his left leg—and yelled at the top of his voice for help but no one heard him. Then Jack realized he couldn't even hear himself, and thought for a second he was dreaming, until he realized that a steam line had broken and the roar of escaping steam was so loud it had absolutely stopped all sensation of sound. Only later did he notice the search light tower had smashed on deck near him without his hearing it.

The tower fell on Jim Berkey; it was on fire and so was he until someone drenched him with a fire hose. When they lifted the tower off, Jim jumped up off deck, ran, and passed out. An hour later, he woke up with someone shooting morphine into him. As he helped lift the burning plane to rescue Macukas, Ceckowski's feet slipped and skidded. He suddenly realized he was standing in the middle of what had been a Japanese pilot a moment before and hurriedly stepped aside. Grim men were frantically pushing and heaving the wreckage overboard and Ski saw a man pick up a leg and toss it into the sea without even noticing what it was.

Gunner's mate Jack Shea, standing with Macukas when the plane hit, could think of nothing better to do than crawl under a portable quarterdeck desk. Burning gasoline ignited his dungarees and he jumped overboard—the ship was so low in the water all he did was walk off to douse the fire. In the water he remembered his flashlight didn't work, but the burning ship made light enough for one of the "picker-upper" boats to find him soon afterward.

The time was now 1922—exactly sixty minutes since the first bogies had been reported. The once trim *Aaron Ward* resembled a floating junk pile from the bridge aft. Stacks, guns, searchlight tower, boat, everything was smashed and battered beyond recognition. Fires raged on deck, in the officer's and chief's quarters, in both clipping rooms, and in the after engine room. The main deck was only inches above water, both fire rooms flooded, after engine room flooded, after diesel engine room, machine shop, shaft alleys, crew's bunkroom, all flooded. Dead and wounded littered the wardroom, mess hall, sick bay, fantail and passageways.

The night was black and deep, except where the *Aaron Ward* burned like a devil's barbecue. There was no electricity, no lights, no power, no pressure on the fire mains. Men fought fire the way they fought fire in Homer's day, with water. There was still plenty of water.

The wrecked decks weren't much of a place to be, but better than where they would be if she went down. . . . "All right, sailors. Over here. Grab a bucket and get in line. Keep them buckets coming. There's lots more water in the ocean. . . ." and plenty already in the ship, too. Back aft another party worked at bailing out a flooded compartment. "But chief, we ain't got no more buckets". . . . "Use empty shell cases, we got plenty of them."

And by that time it certainly looked as if she might go down. Water was lapping across the fantail where some wounded men had been carried out of the way. Sanders had sent messengers scurrying around the ship to find Biesmeyer and Doc, and the three of them met just outside CIC so Neupert could join in the discussion. About the only thing in their favor was that the sea had calmed down until it was like a black mirror. But the stability factor was critical. Biesmeyer ticked off the damage—forward fire room flooded, after fire room, after engine room flooded, after diesel flooded, the big after crew's compartments flooded, machine shop, shaft alleys, all flooded. If a bulkhead gave, she'd be a goner.

"What do you think, Surge?"

"We still have some life rafts. We can load patients onto them. They'll be as comfortable there as anywhere else."

"Good. We stay with her."

Doc and his men bundled some of the badly wounded onto life rafts, and tied them alongside so they wouldn't get lost. They didn't have to reach down to the rafts; the ship was so low in the water they just reached across. The fire fighters, the repair gang, everyone able to help, fought fire, dumped hot ammunition, pushed weights overboard in an effort to help keep the ship afloat. They were going to stay with her.

One of the helpers was Bill McKanna. Bill was a sonarman but his GQ station was in the handling room for a twin forty. When the last plane crashed in, debris put the gun out of commission, so Bill went down to the wardroom to see if he could help with the wounded.

Doc needed no more help then, so he sent Bill up on deck to help Kennedy. The wounded men were all over the place, it seemed. It was dark, except for flickers of light from the fire, and the ship had a sluggish feeling about her. There were some life rafts in the water alongside, looking very small and inadequate.

"Here, Bill," said Kennedy. "We gotta get these men onto the rafts. See if you can get someone to go with them."

Bill yelled for help, but the few men he could see failed to hear him—either they were furiously fighting fire, heaving around on wreckage, or they were just standing there, filled with momentary hysteria.

"I'll go," Bill said, and climbed up on the rail. Just as he tensed himself to jump, someone yelled "Take off your helmet!" That was a good idea. Stefani had been nearly knocked silly earlier when he went overboard with his tin hat on and it konked him a good one. So Bill threw the helmet on deck and jumped.

His feet had no more than left the railing when the voice yelled again: "Look out for sharks!"

It was too late. Bill was on his way down. He hit the water and piled out on the raft so fast his shirt never got wet. Then Wayne Schaeffer jumped down to the raft with him, and between them they got Turner and Viega on board. Viega looked as if a 20mm projectile had gone right through him. It seemed awfully lonesome down there on that raft.

Suddenly there was a hail out of the darkness: "AARON WARD, AHOY THE AARON WARD!" and there came the crummy, dirty, lovely little *LCS 83,* creeping into the circle of fiery light with her fire hoses streaming water and her crew ready to duck in case *Aaron Ward*'s gunners still had itchy fingers. She eased up on the port quarter—the ship was now so low in the water that once her bow slid right up on the deck—and men piled on board the stricken ship to help. Among them were a few *Aaron Ward* sailors who had been blown overboard, had been picked up, and were now coming back for more. There was a fierce fire burning forward, and the *83* boat pushed her nose into the middle of it. Just then ammunition in a 40mm magazine commenced exploding and the men on the *83*'s bow dropped their fire hose and ran. McCaughey wished he could have got hold of that hose, but he didn't need to; the skipper of the *83* boat, Lieutenant Faddin, jumped off the bridge, ran forward, and took the hose himself. Just in case the ship did decide to go down, Doc and his helpers moved a few wounded men from the deck of the *Aaron Ward* to the *83.*

A sailor needed lots of friends on a night like this, and there came some more—the little *LCSL 14* snuggling up to the starboard side of the ship. More fire fighters. More pumps. *Aaron Ward*'s medics hurriedly slung a couple of stretcher patients aboard the *LCSL 14* too. One of these was Turner, gun captain of the starboard quad 40. As Boles helped lift him aboard, Turner whispered "Tell my mother my body wasn't mangled."

"Sure, Jack. Don't worry. You'll be fine."

But Turner wasn't fine. His legs had been nearly torn off in the explosion. No doctor could help him. He died aboard the *LCSL 14* a couple of hours later.

The time was 2000. The second dog watch was over. The battle was finished. The enemy had gone. Yet men still fought, silently, desperately, against man's fiercest enemy, fire; against the sailor's greatest enemy, the sea; against the one who had taken many of them and still might get the others before the night had ended, death.

Black night crowded close around the wounded ship, a backdrop to a Greek tragedy. Leaping red flames painted crazy shadows against the sky and exploding ammunition rocketed toward the stars. But finally the planes were downed and the guns were stilled. The gods of the battle and the breeze marched back to their celestial mountains to consider what they had seen. *Aaron Ward* had met the test and *Aaron Ward* had won.

The sea lay black and flat in the night. The ship hung there, motionless. The routine had run out. The wheels had all stopped. Time had ceased to exist there, long ago; now even the wind had gone. In the stillness, in the silence, men at last had time to think. Radarman Bell had been too busy to know fear for the past hour, but now he knew he was scared as hell. He was not alone.

The time was 2000. No one passed the word to relieve the watch. No one made eight o'clock reports. No one stopped for a cup of coffee or a game of cribbage. There was no coffee and no time for it. No one knew how much time they had left, but in what time there might be they fought to save the ship . . .

AARON WARD'S CASUALTIES NUMBERED FORTY-FIVE killed, missing or dead of wounds; forty-nine others were wounded.

At 7:23 A.M. the following morning Commander Sanders received this message from Nimitz: "We all admire a ship that can't be licked. Congratulations on your magnificent performance." Towed to Kerama Retto, where temporary repairs were effected during the ensuing six weeks, Sanders' doughty tin can was able to steam to New York on one engine where she was decommissioned as being beyond economical repair. She was one of ninety ships either sunk or put out of action since the opening of the Okinawa campaign.

The final push for the island, by elements of the 1st Marine Division, began on June 18. That was the day when five large-calibre shells struck Bolivar's command post, killing the general and several of his staff. Geiger of the Marines assumed temporary command, until relieved by "Vinegar Joe" Stilwell, USA.

Next day, before he committed suicide, Ushijima sent a message to his beleaguered troops to "fight to the last and die." Almost all of them took his advice, and fighting continued to July 2, when the Japanese commander of the islands still in enemy hands tendered his surrender to the Army. The Okinawa campaign was over.

And the end of the war was almost in sight, for as a result of the Potsdam Conference Soviet Russia declared war on Japan on July 18, thus adding to the pressure on the enemy. At this time, however, the Navy suffered one of its worst catastrophes of the war, the loss of the heavy cruiser *Indianapolis,* commanded by Captain Charles B. McVay. The warship was traveling at high speed, unescorted, from San Francisco to Tinian. McVay, under orders to zigzag "at discretion," did so by day but not at night, and it was at night, on July 29, that a Japanese submarine, the *I-58,* picked up the cruiser on her battle periscope, silhouetted in bright moonlight. She fired a spread of six torpedoes at 1500 meters, and a minute and a half later heard two heavy explosions as *Indianapolis* was sundered amidships. Power failed and the warship began to list to starboard. McVay, ordering the radio shack to send a coded SOS, soon passed the word to Abandon Ship, but a large number of officers and bluejackets failed to get the word. Fifteen minutes later, as the cruiser, enveloped in flames, sank in a welter of hissing steam, some four hundred men went down with her. Not until the morning of August 2 did a Pelileu-based Ventura spot the warship's surviving crewmen, for during the intervening days and nights our floating forces were oblivious of their dire predicament. Drifting aimlessly on the sea, many died there, victims of horrible burns and of sharks.

The first rescue ship arrived at the scene the next day, and others soon afterward, but by then there were only three hundred and sixteen of the ship's original 1199-man crew alive. One of the survivors was McVay, who was shortly tried on Guam and found guilty by court-martial of 1) culpable inefficiency in the performance of duty and 2) negligently endangering the lives of others. This marked the close of the only such proceedings in World War II.

On August 6, in an effort to force Japan out of the war, President Truman authorized the atomic bombing of Hiroshima; a second atom bomb was dropped on Nagasaki three days later. Japan had been brought to unconditional surrender through the reluctant use of the most devastating instrument devised by man. Still, until the formal surrender instrument was a *fait accompli,* Nimitz kept up the pressure. On August 9 Task Force 38, with Vice Admiral John S. McCain commanding (Halsey was in conference with the British) struck airfields at Honshu, nipping in the bud a two hundred plane suicide strike planned for Saipan. The following day McCain struck again, completing the job and blasting installations as well.

Then came the Japanese offer of surrender.

Secretary of the Navy James Forrestal, who assumed command of that post upon the death of Frank Knox, noted in his diary the events of the momentous day.

I7.

SURRENDER DIARY

10 August 1945

Captain Smedberg telephoned at seven o'clock that he had a very important message. He came out for breakfast and showed me a copy of a decrypted message from Tokyo to Japanese Ministers at Stockholm and Berne. . . . "Tokyo, August 10—The Japanese government today addressed the following communications to the Swiss and Swedish governments respectively for transmission to the United States, Great Britain, China and the Soviet Union: '. . . . The Japanese government are ready to accept the terms enumerated in the Joint Declaration which was issued at Potsdam on July 26, 1945, . . . with the understanding that the said Declaration does not comprise any demand which prejudices the prerogatives of His Majesty as a sovereign ruler.' "

Major Correa came to breakfast and we both went to the office at 8:15. I telephoned the President congratulations both on the indicated surrender of Japan and on his speech of last evening. I went to the White House at 8:40 to meet the President with the Secretary of State and Secretary of War, Admiral Leahy, John Snyder (then Director of the Office of War Mobilization) and the President's Naval Aide, Captain Vardaman, and Military Aide, General Vaughan. There was general discussion as to the Japanese message. It was agreed that we should await formal receipt of the surrender offer.

Justice Byrnes raised the question of whether the offer accorded with our terms of "unconditional" surrender. Admiral Leahy thought it did but Brynes felt that we might be exposed to the criticism that we had receded from the totality and severity of the Potsdam Declaration. I said that I felt this could be met by an affirmative statement on our part in which we could see to it that the language of surrender accorded fully with our intent and view.

The Secretary of War made the suggestion that we should now cease sending our bombers over Japan; he cited the growing feeling of apprehension and misgiving as to the effect of the atomic bomb even in our own country. I supported his view and said that we must remember that this nation would have to bear the focus of the hatred by the Japanese. . . . It was left that the Secretrry of State would undertake the drafting of a message to be sent when, as and if the formal surrender came in.

10 August 1945

. . . Both the President and the Secretary of State emphasized the fact that they had used the term "Supreme Commander" rather than "Supreme Command" so that it would be quite clear that the United States would run this particular business and avoid a situation of composite responsibility such as had plagued us in Germany.

The President observed that we would keep up the war at its present intensity until the Japanese agreed to these terms, with the limitation, however, that there would be no further dropping of the atomic bombs. He said that he expected it would take about three days before negotiations were completed. He anticipated that we would find that Great Britain and China would acquiesce promptly in our views, but that Russia would not—in fact, he expected that we might not hear from Russia. He said we shall, however, act without them if we fail to hear from them and proceed with the occupation of Japan. . . .

He said he hoped that Mr. Snyder would call promptly a meeting to consider the disposition of surplus, and unless we moved on this promptly we would soon be overwhelmed by a very large volume of surplus products. . . .

10 August 1945

Admiral King dispatched to Admiral Nimitz this morning a message apprising him of the receipt of the Japanese offer of surrender. The message started: "This is a peace warning."

IN THE FORENOON WATCH OF AUGUST 15 HALSEY RE-
ceived word to "cease all offensive operations against Japan," and
he celebrated the good news by breaking his four-starred flag and
ordering *Missouri's* whistle sounded for a full minute! The jubilant
moment was at hand—the incredible moment at the end of the
bloody road!

Seaman First Class James J. Fahey, still aboard the battle-tried
Montpelier at the conclusion of the war, recorded this and the next few
days in his diary.

18.

"IT CAME OVER

THE RADIO . . ."

Wednesday, August 15, 1945: I washed some clothes in a bucket at 1 A.M. while on the midnight to 4 A.M. watch. When I was relieved of watch, I rinsed them out. We are too busy to wash our clothes in the daytime. I caught a few minutes sleep before sunrise General Quarters sounded at 4:45 A.M. I attended Mass in the crew's lounge. We returned this morning at 8:15 to Okinawa. We refueled this morning from a tanker. It came over the radio that President Truman officially declared the war over. All that remains is for the Japs to sign the peace treaty. Some day this week will be set aside as V-J Day. When word was passed the whistles on every ship in the harbor sounded, and everyone on the ship was making plenty of noise. We were alongside the tanker and the light cruiser *Denver* was on the other side of us at the time.

The weather was again hot and sunny. We left the Bay again tonight at 5 P.M. We do not want to take any chances. It was a good night to sleep under the stars. Myers and Renteria enjoyed the candy bars I gave them before we fell asleep. My sister Mary knows every place we go because I have a code name for each spot we are stationed at. It is right under the censor's nose and he does not know what it means.

Thursday, August 16, 1945: We returned to Buckner Bay this morning. Word was sent to Japan for them to send their peace envoys to a small island called Ie Shima. It is not too distant from Okinawa. Ie Shima is where the famous war correspondent, Ernie Pyle, was killed. The password will be Bataan. The Jap officials will leave Ie Shima in one of our bombers for General MacArthur's Headquarters in Manila. The Japs were told to leave Japan in a white bomber with colored stripes on it. The island of Ie Shima is not too far from where we are stationed. We might be able to see the Jap plane as it passes. We left the harbor as usual at 5 P.M. We conducted sunset General Quarters. We are leaving nothing to chance.

Friday, August 17, 1945: We returned to Okinawa at 7 A.M. this morning. Today was the first time we ever had Condition 4 watches. That means we do not have to stand as many watches. It will afford the fellows an opportunity to catch up on some sleep.

I received a letter from my sister Mary. It only took seven days for it to reach here. That's a record. Our band practiced on the fantail today. At last we are going to have a band. All the large ships have their own bands.

The Jap envoys said that they would not arrive today because they were not allowed enough time. They will arrive tomorrow to sign the peace papers. Nearly everyone sleeps under the stars. The climate here is dry, not damp like the South Pacific.

Saturday, August 18, 1945: It came over the radio that the Jap officials will leave Japan Sunday to sign the surrender terms. I saw a dispatch in the Officer of the Deck's shack. It said Jap peace plane will arrive and to hold our fire.

We had mail call today. Ohrt received a package from home with a can of meat and candy in it. We acquired bread from the bakery and made some sandwiches from the meat. We ate the sandwiches this afternoon. It was another hot day. Some of the men were permitted to go over to the beach on Okinawa for recreation. There is not much to do over there but tombs and skeletons are always of interest. It is also very hot there and smells. The fellows are not allowed to enter the tombs but they do. Not too long ago, one of the sailors on recreation stuck his head into one of the tombs to see what it was like inside and at the same time a Jap soldier stuck his head outside. When the Jap saw the sailor, he surrendered to him. There are still plenty of Japs loose around there. One thing about the Navy, they can pick some great places for recreation. Half of the time it would pay to go armed on recreation. The radio announced the Japs in China are surrendering by the thousands. The heavy cruiser *Indianapolis* was sunk,

100% casualties were reported. The *Indianapolis* carries a complement of 1300 men. It was returning from delivering a part for the atomic bomb that was in turn dropped on Hiroshima.

Sunday, August 19, 1945: All the ships here have been refueling for the past few days. We will pull out as soon as Japan signs the surrender. Some of our bombers were attacked over Japan yesterday, while they were taking pictures. The scuttlebutt here is that we will leave for the States September 18 with the cruiser *Denver.* That we will tow the *Pennsylvania* back with us. The other talk is that we will escort a convoy to Japan. Sunday church services were held topside. Protestants and Catholics thanked God that the war is over. At church services I could see the battleship *Pennsylvania,* it must be the last warship to be knocked out of action in World War II. It was not too far away. Water was being pumped from it. The repair crews are working on it. The hole was so big where the torpedo exploded that you could drive a truck into it with plenty of room to spare. The *Pennsylvania* will not be in on the peace celebration. Vice Admiral Oldendorf, commander of battleships in the Pacific, and its Captain, Captain William Moses, were both knocked down when it was hit. At church services I could also see the green hills of Okinawa on this hot, sunny day. Captain Gorry was also at Mass this morning. A large crowd attended church services. We had fellows from about every state in the Union present. There were officers, seamen and Marines. We closed the services by singing "God Bless America." It was very nice.

All the crew talk about now is when we will go back home. The *Montpelier* has fired over 100,000 rounds of five and six inch shells. By the time we reach the States, we will have traveled almost 200,-000 miles. Of that total approximately 95% was spent in enemy-infested waters. The Jap peace delegation arrived today. They landed on Ie Shima. The radio broadcast originated from there for the whole world to listen to. It gave a graphic description of everything that took place. Two twin engine bombers with green crosses and carrying 13 Jap officials landed about 1 P.M. After leaving their planes, they stepped into a C-54 skymaster. At 1:30 P.M. they left for General MacArthur's Headquarters in the Philippines for the signing of the surrender terms. The Japanese pilots were left behind as they did not want to make the trip. Air time will take five or six hours to reach Nichols Field in Manila. Ie Shima was full with military officials who were on hand to witness the history-making event.

The fellows returned from recreation at 5:30 P.M. They said that one sailor was killed and another had his arm blown off when they came across Jap booby traps. This afternoon Joe Renteria dove into the water after a softball that fell from the *Montpelier*. He had quite a rough time swimming back to the ship because of the strong undertow. When he neared the ship Chick Bartholow grabbed him from the Jacob's Ladder. He was exhausted and about ready to go under. It's next to impossible to swim against the strong undertow. It tends to push back anyone that bucks it. The swells look very innocent but are very powerful. It does not take long to be carried out to sea. Sam and Frazer plus Stevo and Olson put on a wrestling bout before they hit the steel for a night's sleep.

Monday, August 20, 1945: Sunrise watch was held at 5 A.M. We secured at 6 A.M. At quarters this morning about 8:15 A.M. We were informed that 10% of the crew will be transferred. A month later another 10% will return to the States. We were paid today. The men can still only draw $10 each.

The radio announced that the peace conference was still going on at 2 A.M. this morning. General MacArthur has not yet appeared at the meeting. American paratroops landed in Manchuria and rescued General Wainwright and other Americans. Another battleship arrived yesterday in the bay.

Tuesday, August 21, 1945: Not much news to report. The radio said that Jap officials left Manila and have returned to Japan. The meeting was held in Manila City Hall. Sixteen Japs participated. General MacArthur did not appear at the conference. He will leave for Tokyo in ten days and sign the peace terms. Everyone was under the impression that the peace terms would be signed in Manila. The Japs relayed all information concerning their airfields and the areas where our troops will land. The Jap government told its people to cooperate with our troops when they land.

Well, it looks like they are going to start transferring the men now. About 20 men were called to the Ex office, they say 10% of the crew will go this month and 20% next month. I will be satisfied if I get home for Christmas.

Friday, August 24, 1945: Hundreds of ships are anchored at Buckner Bay, Okinawa. They consist of all types of warships. Among them are 10 battleships and two hospital ships. Some of the crew of the *Montpelier* were transferred to the States tonight.

Five battleships left for Tokyo Bay and the peace ceremonies. The battleship *Pennsylvania* would have been one of them if it was not hit by a Jap torpedo while they were talking peace. At noon the dope was that our Admiral Riggs would have charge of Task Group 95.02 that will land troops on Japan. I hope this is true. The paratroops are scheduled to land Sunday and the ground troops Tuesday.

Admiral Riggs and Captain Gorry left the ship for the beach this afternoon. The Captains and Admirals from the other ships also went. They had a picnic over there. I guess it is a going away party. They will never have a chance like this to get together again.

Saturday, August 25, 1945: We had Captain's Inspection in blues this morning. Only one division wore blues. It's too warm to wear any clothes at all. Some had heavy blues on, others wore whites and the remainder wore dungarees. The officer asked the crew what uniforms we would like to have our picture taken in. We favored dungarees. This morning at 7 A.M. the temperature was 107 degrees. The bulkheads were so hot that I could not lean my hand against them. This is the hottest time of the year and it seldom rains. The sun beats down all day.

The radio announced the invasion of Japan was called off for 48 hours because of typhoons near Japan. The surrender papers will be signed on the battleship *Missouri* in Tokyo Bay.

Sunday, August 26, 1945: 40 minesweepers arrived at the bay yesterday plus more warships, cargo, supply and one hospital ship. The Captain and a few officers came aboard with huge flowerpots. They acquired them on the beach. Stevenson went over to one of the small islands where the officers had recreation on a clean-up detail. He said that there was a deserted village there. He brought back some things with him that he had found on the island. The island is situated near Okinawa.

The fellows who were transferred a couple of days ago are still on the beach and will not get transportation to the States for at least 6 weeks. They are working pretty hard over there building up the place. I think I will take my chances on going back with the ship.

Tuesday, August 28, 1945: The battleship *Pennsylvania* left Buckner Bay, Okinawa with 5 tugs escorting it, this morning at 7 A.M. It was traveling at approximately five knots. It was sixteen days ago that a Jap torpedo plane put a fish into it. It would have been at Tokyo Bay for the celebration only for this. The crew must be very disappointed.

One of the fellows flooded a big magazine and we were forced to carry all the powder and shells up three decks and dry each one of them. Then they were again stored in the hold. There were thousands of shells and powder cases to be lugged by the crew. It will go tough on the individual who let this occur.

THE MASSIVE THIRD FLEET SET COURSE FOR TOKYO Bay with a reasonable degree of apprehension, for it was not known if any final *kikusui* attacks were contemplated, or if newly-designated Supreme Commander MacArthur's occupation forces would be resisted on land.

Appropriately, Halsey tells us of the period through September 2 when the surrender instrument was signed.

FLEET ADMIRAL WILLIAM F. HALSEY

AND J. BRYAN, III

19.
UNCONDITIONAL
SURRENDER

The Third Fleet's cheers at the news of Japan's surrender had hardly died away when I ordered all ships to turn to and spruce up . . . Aboard the *Missouri,* which had been designated as the scene of the surrender ceremony—she was named for President Truman's native state, of course, and had been christened by his daughter—holystones began to scour through the gray battle paint to the white teak decks beneath; brass also emerged from its dull coat; slipcovers were broken out for our chairs and transoms; and when the fleet entered Sagami Bay, at the mouth of Tokyo Bay, we were smart and shining.

Meanwhile, my staff's preparations went forward. The landing force was put aboard transports. We started a series of reconnaissance flights over Japan to locate the prisoner of war camps and to drop food and medicine. Our task groups massed for an aerial photograph—EXERCISE SNAPSHOT, then our planes had their turn—EXERCISE TINTYPE. We organized a special task force to furnish fire support during the occupation, if needed. Signatories came aboard for conferences: my old friend from the South Pacific, Air Vice Marshall Leonard Isitt, of the Royal New Zealand Air Force, who would sign for New Zealand; and Adm. Sir Bruce Fraser, Commander in Chief of the British Pacific Fleet, who would sign for the United Kingdom.

Every man jack among us was looking toward one moment, the

992

moment we would anchor in Tokyo Bay. Our first anchoring in Japanese waters, at Sagami Bay, would be an appetizer. MacArthur had set this for August 26, but two typhoons formed to the southward, and he postponed it for forty-eight hours on behalf of his air-borne troops. Many of my ships were small—patrol craft, subchasers, and the like; and even if they had not been crowded and short of stores, I would have been reluctant to keep them at sea in typhoon weather, so I requested and received his permission to put in on the twenty-seventh.

We raised the coast at dawn that morning. The Japanese Navy had been ordered to send us an escort through the mine fields, and to deliver officers empowered to arrange the surrender of the Yokosuka Base. When the escort came into view, we identified her as the destroyer *Hatsuzakura*. As stipulated, her guns were depressed, their breeches open, her torpedo tubes empty, and no crew was topside except enough men to handle a small boat. Mick Carney and I watched her from the *Missouri*'s flag bridge. She was so frail, so woebegone, so dirty, that I felt ashamed of our having needed four years to win the war.

Mick pointed toward her. "You wanted the Jap Navy, Admiral. Well, there it is."

The fourteen emissaries were first put aboard the destroyer *Nicholas* for "processing." Not until their side arms had been confiscated and they had been made to bathe and undergo a medical examination, did we distribute them around the Fleet. Two captains and an ensign interpreter were then transferred to the *Missouri*. Here they were searched again, photographed, and marched under guard to Captain Murray's cabin, where the conference was to be held.

Our attitude may sound like a petty attempt to humiliate a beaten enemy, but it was not. It was part of a policy which grim experience had taught us. We would not have omitted our precautions any more than we would have allowed the *Hatsuzakura* to approach us without our crews at quarters, our guns manned, and our planes overhead, ready to go into action at an inkling . . .

By late afternoon the whole fleet was at anchor in Sagami Bay, in full view of beautiful Kamakura, the Japanese Riviera, where the Summer Palace stands. We also had a view of Fujiyama. Its peak is usually cloud-capped, I am told, but that evening was clear, and the sun seemed to sink directly into the crater. Although the symbolism was strongly suggestive, we did not rely on it to the extent of not stationing picket boats and destroyers on the perimeter of our anchorage, nor did we light the ships. We were still being prudent. We had assigned targets to the heavy ships before we stood in, and our guns were not only loaded but trained. Moreover, we had left all but one of our carriers outside, in open water.

My apprehension lessened next day. We lighted ship at dusk and showed movies on the weather decks. The staff officer who had the dogwatch wrote in the flag log, "At sunset, 1815/I (Tokyo time), all ships turned on anchor lights—'The lights came on again in Sagami Wan.'" (*Wan* is Japanese for *bay*.) But we were at general quarters when we steamed into Tokyo Bay on the twenty-ninth—the supreme moment of my career—and it wasn't until September 3 that we began to stand at ease. Even then we still posted lookouts, our radars continued to search, and our ships maintained their high state of watertight integrity . . .

Meanwhile, on the twenty-eighth, elements of the Army's 11th Airborne Division had started landing at Atsugi Airfield, near Tokyo. Navy ships had guarded their line of flight from Okinawa, and as they deplaned, I am told that the first sight to catch their eyes was a large sign, "Welcome to the U.S. Army from the Third Fleet." A brash young pilot from the *Yorktown* had dropped into Atsugi, wholly against orders, and had made the Japs paint it and post it.

MacArthur had directed us not to begin recovering POW's until the Army was ready to do so, but—as with the landings—circumstances forced us to jump the gun. Our first night at anchor in Sagami Wan, a picket boat patrolling close inshore heard a yell from the beach and picked up two British prisoners, whom it delivered to Commo. Rodger W. Simpson, commanding the rescue operation. The Britishers told Rodger a tale of such inhumanity as we found almost impossible to believe, until it was corroborated the following day by a Swiss doctor, representing the International Red Cross. Listening to these men convinced us that now was no time to defer to protocol. I ordered Rodger to take his task group, which included the hospital ship *Benevolence,* up to Tokyo and to stand by for a sudden signal. Chester Nimitz' plane arrived from Guam at 1420 on the twenty-ninth, and he had no sooner broken his flag on the *South Dakota* than I was explaining the urgency of the situation.

"Go ahead," Chester said. "General MacArthur will understand."

Rodger went ashore immediately with his rescue detail, which included Harold Stassen, whom I had lent him as his chief staff officer, and Commo. Joel T. Boone, who had relieved Piggy Weeks as my medical officer. Planes from the fleet guided their small boats up estuaries leading to the prison camps. One was the infamous Omori 8, whose commandant made a show of demanding credentials.

"I have no authority to release these men," he said.

Harold, unarmed as was the rest of the party, told him, "You have no authority, period!" . . .

At 1910 that evening, the first POW's, or RAMP's (Rescued Allied Military Prisoners) as they were now designated, were put aboard the *Benevolence;* by midnight, 794 had been brought out; and within fourteen days, every one of 19,000 Allied prisoners in our area, the eastern two-thirds of Honshu, had been liberated, docketed, bathed, examined, and either hospitalized or sent off for a quiet, comfortable convalescence.

The unspeakable brutality which they had endured at the hands of the Japanese Army—the Navy disclaims any connection with the camps—has been amply described by correspondents; besides, I still can not discuss the subject temperately. But before I leave it, I want to set down the only happy association that it has for me. Rodger Simpson's splendid record in the South Pacific included a daring destroyer raid on Simpson Harbor, at Rabaul; so, in answer to a query of his in Tokyo Bay, we replied, "Roger to Rodger Simpson of Simpson Harbor. If it had not been for that Rodger in Simpson Harbor, we might have been delayed in sending roger to Rodger Simpson in this harbor."

H Hour for our landing forces was 1000 on the thirtieth. Spearheaded by the 4th Marine Regimental Combat Team, British bluejackets occupied Azuma peninsula, U.S. Marines occupied Yokosuka Air Base, and U.S. bluejackets occupied Yokosuka Naval Base. The Japanese seemed anxious to avoid friction, and we met no opposition at any point. Mick Carney, as my representative, accepted custody of Yokosuka from Vice Adm. Michitare Totsuka at 1030; headquarters of the Third Fleet and of the landing force were established there at 1045, and my flag was raised over the station. (Chester Nimitz gave me hell for breaking my flag ashore in the presence of a senior officer and ordered me to haul it down; all the same, it is the first United States admiral's flag to fly over Imperial Japanese territory!)

Another flag incident had occurred earlier that morning, when one of our nucleus crews boarded the battleship *Nagato,* and the American commanding officer directed her captain to haul down his colors.

The captain tried to delegate the job to a bluejacket, but the American told him, "No. Haul them down yourself!"

This flag, along with the Japanese flag that had flown over Yokosuka, I presented to the Naval Academy Museum at Annapolis. A third Jap flag, from the old battleship *Mikasa,* I passed along to Ernie King, with a request that he present it to the Russians, since the *Mikasa* had been Togo's flagship at the Battle of Tsushima Straits.

I visited Yokosuka that afternoon. Despite the Japs' reputation for cleanliness and the fact that one of the surrender terms stipulated that "on delivery to the Allies, all facilities will be cleared of debris, scrupulously clean, and in full operating condition," the filth that I saw was appalling. The officers' club, which had been evacuated only a few hours before, was overrun with rats of an extraordinary size and character. They ignored our presence in some rooms but squeaked angrily when we entered others. They probably had a special membership which reserved certain parts of the club for themselves alone.

The civilians were also dirty. Worse, they were apathetic; I was told that their principal employment was walking up the streets on odd days and down on even. We found occasional evidence of malnutrition in urban areas, but the country folk looked well fed. I had heard from many sources that the average Jap considered me his personal archenemy, so I watched for signs of hatred. There were none. I was never accosted, and I doubt if I was ever recognized.

The only recalcitrance we met was on the part of the civil police. Possibly because we had allowed them to keep their side arms as a badge of authority, they gradually arrogated the additional privilege of not saluting Allied officers. This annoyed me. I directed Scrappy Kessing, whom I had appointed COMNAVBASE Yokosuka, to pass the word to the mayor that his police were to salute all Allied officers without exception, and that this order would be rigidly enforced.

The mayor protested, "How will they know who is an officer and who is not?"

Scrappy told him, "If they don't know, they'd better play safe by saluting every foreign uniform."

Now I come to our focal day, September 2, the day of the formal surrender. Supervised by Captain Murray, Bill Kitchell had worked like a Hong Kong coolie to organize the ceremony. He rehearsed every step of it, provided for every nuance of etiquette, and smoothed away even the possibility of a bobble. The result was the best job of its sort I have ever seen. No court chamberlain could have improved it.

The first guests, correspondents and photographers, arrived at 0710. Next came Navy representatives, then Army and foreign representatives, then Chester Nimitz and his staff, then General Mac-Arthur and his party, and finally the Japanese envoys. Since Chester was SOPA (Senior Officer Present Afloat), I had shifted my personal flag to the *Iowa* near by; Chester's five stars were broken at the *Missouri's* aftermast, and as General MacArthur stepped aboard, his own flag was broken alongside.

The sight they made together was unique, but on the *Missouri* that morning was one flag that outshone them both. Washington had sent it by special messenger—the flag that Commodore Perry had flown in 1854 at almost our identical anchorage.

The destroyer bringing the Army men had not yet moored to us when old friends began calling back and forth. I shouted to Nate Twining, whom I was seeing for the first time since he had been my COMAIRSOLS, but when I spied Skinny Wainwright, whom I hadn't seen since War College in 1933, I could not trust my voice; I just leaned over the rail and grabbed his hand.

Chester and I were at the side to meet General MacArthur. As always, his manner to me and my staff was heart-warming. He greeted us by our nicknames and he remarked to Mick Carney, "It's grand having so many of my side-kicks from the shoestring SOPAC days meeting me here at the end of the road!"

Bill Kitchell escorted him to my cabin, with Chester following and me bringing up the rear. I imagine that history was fairly begging for something quotable from our conversation, or at least something dignified and sonorous, but what we actually said was this:

Halsey: "General, will you and Chester have a cup of coffee?"

MacArthur: "No, thanks, Bill. I'll wait till afterwards."

Nimitz: "So will I, Bill. Thanks all the same."

I had just added, "God, what a great day this is! We've fought a long, long time for it," when Bill Kitchell notified us that the Jap envoys were aboard. I had sent a signal to the destroyer fetching them that she was not to offer coffee, cigarettes, or any other courtesies, but I had been directed to revoke it.

A table with the two sets of surrender documents stood on the starboard veranda deck, almost in the shadow of No. 2 turret. Mac-Arthur and Nimitz took their places behind it, and I joined the line of

Navy officers. The ceremony opened with a short address by Mac-
Arthur, beautifully phrased and forcefully read. His voice was clear
and firm, but his hands shook with emotion. When he had finished, he
pointed to a chair at the opposite side of the table and almost spat
out, "The representatives of the Imperial Japanese Government and
of the Imperial Japanese Staff will now come forward and sign!"

(My flag log records it thus: "0903. Jap envoys were asked to
sign. They did.")

The Foreign Minister, Mamoru Shigemitsu, who was to sign for the
Emperor, limped toward the table, leaning on a cane. He had lost his
left leg to a grenade thrown by a Korean in Shanghai; Nomura, later
Ambassador to Washington, lost an eye at the same time. (I have
been told that Hirohito presented Shigemitsu with an artificial leg
which he has therefore had to wear ever since, although it doesn't
fit.) He took off his gloves and silk hat, sat down, dropped his cane,
picked it up, fiddled with his hat and gloves, and shuffled the papers.
He pretended to be looking for a pen—an underling finally brought
him one—but I felt certain that he was stalling for time, though God
knows what he hoped to accomplish. His performance made me so
mad that when we returned to my cabin after the ceremony, I told
MacArthur, "General, you nearly had a contretemps this morning."

"How's that?" he asked.

"When Shigemitsu was stalling out there, I wanted to slap him and
tell him, 'Sign, damn you! Sign!' "

MacArthur said, "Why didn't you?"

The second Jap, Gen. Yoshijiro Umezu, who was to sign for the
Imperial General Staff, did his job briskly; he didn't even sit down for
it.

MacArthur was next, as Supreme Commander for the Allied Powers, then came their various representatives, led by Chester. His war
plans officer, Rear Adm. Forrest P. Sherman, and I were invited to
stand behind his chair while he signed. Newsreels show MacArthur
putting his arm around my shoulders at this moment and whispering
to me, and many of my friends have asked what he was saying. Again
we fell short of the solemn occasion. MacArthur said, "Start 'em
now!"

I said, "Aye, aye, sir!"

He was referring to a mass flight of 450 planes from TF 38, which
we had ordered to orbit at a distance until we gave the word. We
passed it to them now, and they roared over the *Missouri* mast-

high . . .

~~~~~~

AT THIS TIME NIMITZ RELEASED A STATEMENT WHICH was broadcast throughout the Pacific and the United States:

> On board all naval vessels at sea and in port, and at our many bases in the Pacific, there is rejoicing and thanksgiving. The long and bitter struggle . . . is at an end . . .
>
> Today all freedom-loving peoples of the world rejoice in the victory and feel pride in the accomplishments of our combined forces. We also pay tribute to those who defended our freedom at the cost of their lives.
>
> On Guam is a military cemetery in a green valley not far from my headquarters. The ordered rows of white crosses stand as reminders of the heavy cost we have paid for victory. On these crosses are the names of Sweeney, Bromberg, Depew, Melloy, Ponziani—names that are a cross-section of democracy. They fought together as brothers in arms; they died together and now they sleep side by side. To them we have a solemn obligation—the obligation to insure that their sacrifice will help make this a better and safer world in which to live.
>
> Now we turn to the great tasks of reconstruction and restoration. I am confident that we will be able to apply the same skill, resourcefulness and deep thinking to these problems as were applied to the problems of winning the victory.

~~~~~~

THE PRICE OF VICTORY WAS HIGH. THE UNITED STATES Navy's casualty list—including Marine Corps and Coast Guard— was 56,206 dead, 80,259 wounded, and 8,967 missing.

But now, after three years and eight months of the greatest conflict in the history of mankind, there was peace.

Out of the depths have I cried unto Thee, O Lord.
Lord, hear my voice . . .

PSALM 130

INDEX

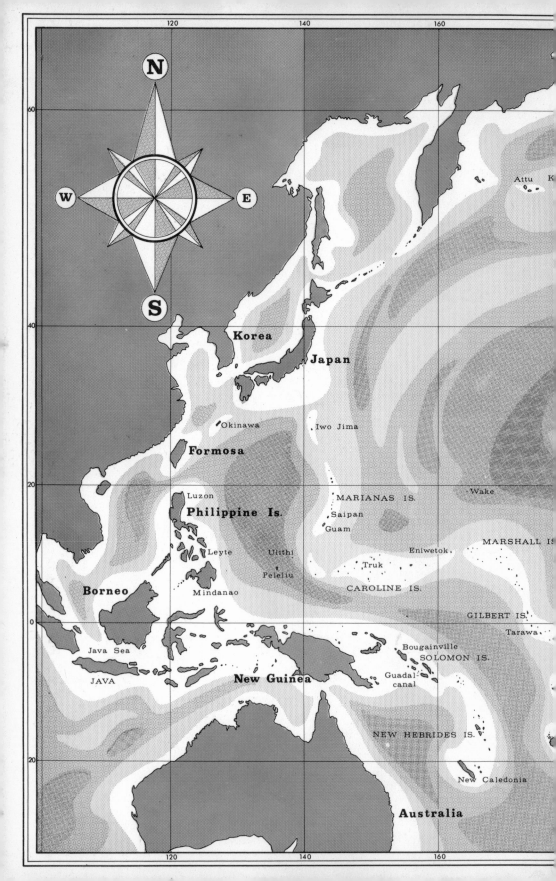